THE ANGKORIAN WORLD

The Angkorian World explores the history of Southeast Asia's largest ancient state from the first to mid-second millennium CE. Chapters by leading scholars combine evidence from archaeology, texts, and the natural sciences to introduce the Angkorian state, describe its structure, and explain its persistence over more than six centuries.

Comprehensive and accessible, this book will be an indispensable resource for anyone studying premodern Asia. The volume's first of six sections provides historical and environmental contexts and discusses data sources and the nature of knowledge production. The next three sections examine the anthropogenic landscapes of Angkor (agrarian, urban, and hydraulic), the state institutions that shaped the Angkorian state, and the economic foundations on which Angkor operated. Part V explores Angkorian ideologies and realities, from religion and nation to identity. The volume's last part reviews political and aesthetic Angkorian legacies in an effort to explain why the idea of Angkor remains central to its Cambodian descendants. Maps, graphics, and photographs guide readers through the content of each chapter. Chapters in this volume synthesise more than a century of work at Angkor and in the regions it influenced.

The Angkorian World will satisfy students, researchers, academics, and the knowledgeable layperson who seeks to understand how this great Angkorian Empire arose and functioned in the premodern world.

Mitch Hendrickson is Associate Professor of Anthropology at the University of Illinois at Chicago, USA. He worked as an archaeologist in northwest Mexico, the Canadian Plains, and High Arctic before shifting his focus to Cambodia in 2001. His initial research on the establishment and role of the Angkorian road system enabled him to develop two ongoing projects in collaboration with the Ministry of Culture and Fine Arts on the technological transformation that enabled expansions of the Khmer Empire and understanding religious transition at the site of Preah Khan of Kompong Svay.

Miriam T. Stark is Professor of Anthropology and Director of the Center for Southeast Asian Studies at the University of Hawai'i at Mānoa, USA. Her 40-year career includes fieldwork in North America, the Near East, and Southeast Asia; she launched her first field project in Cambodia in 1996. Her Cambodian research, through multiple projects in collaboration with Cambodia's Ministry of Culture and Fine Arts, focuses on protohistoric to Angkorian period urbanism, early state formation, and political economy.

Damian Evans is Senior Research Fellow at the École française d'Extrême-Orient in Paris and an Honorary Associate in the Department of History, School of Philosophical and Historical Inquiry at the University of Sydney. He is involved in a diverse array of projects across Southeast Asia encompassing archaeology, heritage, and the earth sciences, and he has initiated and overseen archaeological projects in Cambodia since the late 1990s. His work focuses on using earth observation technologies such as satellite imagery, radar and lidar to understand the relationship between humans and their environments from the deep past to the present day.

ROUTLEDGE WORLDS

The Routledge Worlds are magisterial surveys of key historical epochs, edited and written by world-renowned experts. Giving unprecedented breadth and depth of coverage, they are the works against which all future books on their subjects will be judged and are essential reading for anyone with a serious interest in the subject.

THE ANGKORIAN WORLD
Edited by Mitch Hendrickson, Miriam T. Stark and Damian Evans

THE ANGKORIAN WORLD

*Edited by Mitch Hendrickson, Miriam T. Stark
and Damian Evans*

Routledge
Taylor & Francis Group
LONDON AND NEW YORK

Cover image: Erika Piñeros

First published 2023
by Routledge
4 Park Square, Milton Park, Abingdon, Oxon OX14 4RN

and by Routledge
605 Third Avenue, New York, NY 10158

Routledge is an imprint of the Taylor & Francis Group, an informa business

British Library Cataloguing-in-Publication Data
A catalogue record for this book is available from the British Library

Library of Congress Cataloging-in-Publication Data
Names: Hendrickson, Mitch, editor, author. | Stark, Miriam T., editor, author. | Evans, Damian, editor, author.
Title: The Angkorian World / edited by Mitch Hendrickson, Miriam T. Stark and Damian Evans.
Description: New York : Routledge, 2023. | Series: Routledge Worlds | Includes bibliographical references and index. |
Identifiers: LCCN 2022058733 (print) | LCCN 2022058734 (ebook) | ISBN 9780815355953 (hardback) | ISBN 9781032439266 (paperback) | ISBN 9781351128940 (ebook)
Subjects: LCSH: Angkor (Extinct city)—History. | Angkor (Extinct city)—Civilization. | Cambodia—Antiquities.
Classification: LCC DS554.98.A5 A545 2023 (print) | LCC DS554.98.A5 (ebook) | DDC 959.6/01—dc23/eng/20221214
LC record available at https://lccn.loc.gov/2022058733
LC ebook record available at https://lccn.loc.gov/2022058734

ISBN: 978-0-8153-5595-3 (hbk)
ISBN: 978-1-032-43926-6 (pbk)
ISBN: 978-1-351-12894-0 (ebk)

DOI: 10.4324/9781351128940

The funder for the Introduction, chapters 2, 10, 15, 23, and 30 is École française d'Extrême-Orient (EFEO), Paris.

The funder for the chapter 32 is SOAS University of London.

CONTENTS

List of Figures *ix*
List of Tables *xiv*
List of Contributors *xv*
Acknowledgements *xix*

0 Prologue: An Introduction to the Angkorian World 1
Mitch Hendrickson, Miriam T. Stark, Damian Evans with Roland Fletcher

PART I
Contexts **15**

1 An Environmental History of Angkor: Beginning and End 17
Dan Penny and Tegan Hall

2 Texts and Objects: Exploiting the Literary Sources of Medieval Cambodia 25
Dominique Soutif and Julia Estève

3 'Invisible Cambodians': Knowledge Production in the History of Angkorian Archaeology 42
Heng Piphal, Seng Sonetra and Nhim Sotheavin

4 The Mekong Delta before the Angkorian World 64
Miriam T. Stark and Pierre-Yves Manguin

5 The Early Capitals of Angkor 80
Jean-Baptiste Chevance and Christophe Pottier

6 Angkor's Multiple Southeast Asia Overland Connections 97
Kenneth R. Hall

7 Angkor and China: 9th–15th Centuries 112
Miriam T. Stark and Aedeen Cremin

PART II
Landscapes **133**

8 Forests, Palms, and Paddy Fields: The Plant Ecology of Angkor 135
Tegan Hall and Dan Penny

9 Angkor and the Mekong River: Settlement, Resources, Mobility and Power 154
Heng Piphal

10 Trajectories of Urbanism in the Angkorian World 173
Damian Evans, Roland Fletcher, Sarah Klassen, Christophe Pottier and Pelle Wijker

11 Angkor's Temple Communities and the Logic of its Urban Landscape 195
Scott Hawken and Sarah Klassen

12 Angkor as a 'Cité Hydraulique'? 216
Terry Lustig, Jean-Baptiste Chevance and Wayne Johnson

PART III
State Institutions **235**

13 Angkorian Law and Land 237
Tess Davis and Eileen Lustig

14 Warfare and Defensive Architecture in the Angkorian World 254
David Brotherson

15 Āśramas, Shrines, and Royal Power 272
Chea Socheat, Julia Estève, Dominique Soutif and Edward Swenson

16 Education and Medicine at Angkor 287
Chhem Rethy, Damian Evans, Chhom Kunthea, Phlong Pisith and Peter D. Sharrock

PART IV
Economies 307

17 Angkor's Economy: Implications of the Transfer of Wealth 309
Eileen Lustig, Aedeen Cremin and Terry Lustig

18 The Temple Economy of Angkor 327
Heng Piphal and Sachchidanand Sahai

19 Angkor's Agrarian Economy: A Socio-Ecological Mosaic 338
Scott Hawken and Cristina Cobo Castillo

20 From Quarries to Temples: Stone Procurement, Materiality, and Spirituality in the Angkorian World 360
Christian Fischer, Federico Carò and Martin Polkinghorne

21 Crafting with Fire: Stoneware and Iron Pyrotechnologies in the Angkorian World 385
Mitch Hendrickson, Ea Darith, Chhay Rachna, Yukitsugu Tabata, Phon Kaseka, Stéphanie Leroy, Yuni Sato and Armand Desbat

22 Food, Craft, and Ritual: Plants from the Angkorian World 401
Cristina Cobo Castillo

PART V
Ideologies and Realities 421

23 Gods and Temples: The Nature(s) of Angkorian Religion 423
Julia Estève

24 Bodies of Glory: The Statuary of Angkor 435
Paul A. Lavy and Martin Polkinghorne

25 'Of Cattle and Kings': Bovines in the Angkorian World 459
Mitch Hendrickson, Eileen Lustig and Siyonn Sophearith

26 An Angkor Nation? Identifying the Core of the Khmer Empire 479
Ian Lowman, Chhom Kunthea and Mitch Hendrickson

27 The Angkorian House 494
Alison K. Carter, Miriam T. Stark, Heng Piphal and Chhay Rachna

28 Vogue at Angkor: Dress, Décor, and Narrative Drama 508
Gillian Green

29 Gender, Status, and Hierarchy in the Age of Angkor 525
Trude Jacobsen Gidaszewski

PART VI
After Angkor **539**

30 Perspectives on the 'Collapse' of Angkor and the Khmer Empire 541
Damian Evans, Martin Polkinghorne, Roland Fletcher, David Brotherson, Tegan Hall, Sarah Klassen and Pelle Wijker

31 Uthong and Angkor: Material Legacies in the Chao Phraya Basin, Thailand 554
Pipad Krajaejun

32 Mainland Southeast Asia After Angkor: On the Legacies of Jayavarman VII 574
Ashley Thompson

33 Early Modern Cambodia and Archaeology at Longvek 592
Martin Polkinghorne and Yuni Sato

34 Yama, the God Closest to the Khmers 614
Ang Choulean

35 Inarguably Angkor 629
Penny Edwards

Appendix A 645
Glossary 647
Index 653

FIGURES

0.1 Timeline of the Angkorian World. 7
0.2 South and Southeast Asia, showing key sites. 8
0.3 Southeast Asia, showing key sites. 9
0.4 Heartland of the Khmer Empire, showing key sites and extent of the Angkorian road system. 10
0.5 Greater Angkor, showing major temple sites and the extent of infrastructure. 11
0.6 Capital region of Yaśodharapura, highlighting the urban layout in and around Angkor Thom and Angkor Wat. 12
0.7 Capital region of Hariharālaya (Roluos). 13
2.1 Silver vase with inscription (K. 1294). 28
2.2 Śivakumbha prepared for a dīkṣā (initiation) in Cuddalore, India. 32
2.3 Grinding stone with inscription (K. 1215). 34
2.4 Prasat towers σ, ρ, π, and τ in Preah Khan of Kompong Svay. 36
2.5 K. 1335, detail of the lower part of the southern door jamb. 37
2.6 Detail of vertical 'bayonet-cut' joints in the corbelled vault from prasat tower ρ in Preah Khan of Kompong Svay. 38
3.1 Henri Marchal, a pioneer of the anastylosis method in Angkor, with his Khmer assistant, Chan, and workmen at Banteay Srei temple restoration in 1934. 46
3.2 Henri Marchal and an unnamed Khmer assistant at the restoration of Banteay Srei (Damdek) in 1952. 53
4.1 The Mekong Delta and the Angkorian World before Angkor. 65
5.1 Aerial view of Trapeang Phong. 83
5.2 Archaeological map of the Roluos region. 84
5.3 Rong Chen temple-mountain. 86
5.4 Banteay, the Royal Palace of Mahendraparvata. 87
5.5 Archaeological map of the Kulen plateau highlighting the urban layout of Mahendraparvata. 88
5.6 Newly identified buildings and enclosures within the West Baray. 91
5.7 Archaeological map of the West Baray area. 92
6.1 Potential 12th century communication networks connecting to Angkor. 102

6.2	Pre-1500 Champa coastline ports-of-trade and hypothesised Western overland connections contesting the Malay Peninsula.	105
7.1	Cambodia and China in premodern Southeast Asia.	116
7.2	Cavalry officer leading Cham men into battle.	122
7.3	Musicians in a military procession.	123
7.4	Recent examples of draped images in Angkor Wat.	125
8.1	Land use maps in Southeast Asia and the Greater Angkor region.	136
8.2	Select Angkor monuments and sediment coring sites from which palaeoecological records were obtained.	141
8.3	Summary of palynological records for the four sites across Angkor.	144
8.4	Ecological group data plotted as z-scores and compared across the four sites.	147
9.1	Location of inscriptions used in this chapter.	155
9.2	The Lower Mekong River region.	156
9.3	Angkorian centres along the Mekong and state-sponsored temples.	157
10.1	Archaeological map of the intramural area of Angkor Thom.	177
10.2	Archaeological map of the Greater Angkor region.	178
10.3	Map of Óc Eo.	180
10.4	Archaeological map of Sambor Prei Kuk.	181
10.5	Lidar renderings of gridded urban areas of the Angkor Period.	184
11.1	Comparison of local community temples versus state and other temples within the civic ceremonial centre and suburban centres of Greater Angkor.	196
11.2	Reconstruction of a mediaeval settlement and village shrine in the south of Angkor.	202
11.3	Range of variations in local temple sites and their associated community settlements.	204
11.4	Density of local community temples per square kilometre in Greater Angkor.	206
11.5	Shift in community temple construction within Greater Angkor between the 8th and 13th centuries.	209
12.1	Angkor's complex hydraulic network.	217
12.2	Water flowing out from a reservoir during rainfall, when irrigation not needed.	219
12.3	Water infrastructure associated with Mahendraparvata.	220
12.4	Inferred layout of stoplog sluice gates along the outlet from Thnal Thom reservoir at Mahendraparvata.	221
12.5	West Baray and surrounding water infrastructures and possible proto-baray.	221
12.6	Zig-zag outlet of the Rahal (*baray*) at Koh Ker.	222
12.7	Main reservoir at Koh Ker showing existing and former rivers.	223
12.8	West Mebon inside West Baray.	227
12.9	Two rock carvings of Viṣṇu in Anantaśayin mode, Kbal Spean River, Phnom Kulen.	228
13.1	The statue of Duryodhana now returned to Cambodia, June 3, 2014.	238
14.1	Narrative scenes of warfare from bas-reliefs on Angkor Period temples.	255
14.2	Defensive features of the Angkor Thom gopura.	264
14.3	Lidar elevation model of central Angkor with highlights of landscape features and embankment extensions in the 12th century.	266
14.4	Horizontal and vertical holes in upper masonry blocks of the external enclosure wall of Angkor Wat.	267
14.5	'Gateway gap' masonry fill in the external enclosure wall of Angkor Wat.	268

14.6 Hypothetical reconstruction of defensive structure built along the external enclosure walls of Angkor Wat. 268
15.1 Location of known Yaśodharāśramas, Vīrāśramas, resthouses, and hospitals of Jayavarman VII. 274
15.2 Examples of a typical hospital chapel and fire shrine resthouse. 275
15.3 Lidar image of Prasat Komnap South. 276
15.4 Examples of stela shelters. 277
15.5 Reconstruction of the 'Long Building'. 278
15.6 Plan of Prasat Neak Buos illustrating the location of the potential Yaśodharāśrama and Vīrāśrama. 280
15.7 Plan of Prasat Khna illustrating the location of the potential Yaśodharāśrama and Vīrāśrama. 284
16.1 Distribution of Jayavarman VII hospital chapels. 298
16.2 Organisation of Jayavarman VII hospital chapels. 299
17.1 Distribution of inscriptions and rice land in Cambodia. 311
17.2 Purchase of land by increasingly high-ranking officials. 312
19.1 Agrarian patches identified within Greater Angkor. 346
19.2 The Pre Rup matrix. 347
19.3 The Phnom Bok matrix. 349
19.4 Lidar relief maps of Angkor Wat and Ta Prohm. 352
19.5 Lidar map of Angkor Thom. 353
19.6 Archaeobotanical remains from some of Angkor's major temples. 355
20.1 Range of materials used in Khmer temple construction. 361
20.2 Distribution of sandstone formations and location of major archaeological sites and ancient quarries. 363
20.3 Examples of Terrain Rouge sandstone usage in the Angkor Period. 365
20.4 Examples of 'Grès Supérieurs' series sandstone usage in the Angkor Period. 366
20.5 Examples of Terrain Rouge (a, b, c, e, g, h, i) and Triassic (d, e, f) sandstone usage at Hariharālaya. 368
20.6 Texture and petrography of the Triassic sandstone. 369
20.7 Incomplete sculptures from stone workshops in Greater Angkor. 371
20.8 Evidence of quarries. 373
20.9 Various types of sandstone used in a decorative wall at Banteay Chhmar. 374
20.10 Triassic sandstone quarries. 375
20.11 Triassic sandstone with a characteristic mottled texture. 377
21.1 Angkorian stonewares types and vessel forms. 386
21.2 Iron objects produced during the Angkor Period. 387
21.3 Pryotechnological production sites in Cambodia and northeast Thailand, stoneware (crosses) and iron (circles). 388
21.4 Kiln morphologies in the Angkor Period. 390
21.5 Characteristics of Angkorian iron smelting sites. 391
22.1 Examples of archaeobotanical remains recovered from five Angkor Period sites. 404
22.2 Summary of the archaeobotanical results from five Angkor Period sites. 406
22.3 Proportions of economic crops found in Ta Prohm over time. 407
22.4 Proportion of *indica* and *japonica* rice. 416
22.5 Number of economic taxa identified in each of the sites. 417
24.1 Relief sculptures depicting deity-images in worship. 437

24.2 Brahmanical (Hindu) deities. 441
24.3 Personalisation of images during the reign of Jayavarman VII. 444
24.4 Sculptural innovation, archaism, and transformation. 446
24.5 Types of Buddha images from the late Angkor and Middle Periods. 449
24.6 Angkorian statuary venerated in the present. 450
25.1 Sandstone Nandin statues. 461
25.2 Depiction of cows in Angkorian bas-relief. 464
25.3 Buffalo images from the Pre-Angkor and Angkor Period. 465
25.4 Milk churning imagery. 468
25.5 Scene depicting Brahmins milking a cow and drinking milk from Ta Prohm. 469
25.6 Trapeang in the Angkorian World. 471
25.7 Comparison of modern cattle densities, Angkorian trapeang and temples. 472
26.1 Distribution of Angkor Period temples and inscriptions including the maximum limit of control as defined by B.-P. Groslier. 481
26.2 Proposed extent of the Angkorian heartland. 483
26.3 Communication corridors of the major Angkorian kings. 484
26.4 State-level infrastructures used by Khmer kings to assert influence within the Angkorian heartland. 485
27.1 Everyday life in Cambodia, past and present. 497
27.2 Possible fence posts identified in an excavated wall profile at Angkor Wat. 498
27.3 Overhead view of excavation trenches at Angkor Wat showing flat-lying sandstone pieces. 499
27.4 Possible hearth from excavations within the Angkor Wat enclosure. 500
27.5 Trash pit from excavations within the Ta Prohm enclosure. 501
27.6 Chinese water dropper in the shape of a chicken found in an excavation at Angkor Wat. 502
28.1 Examples of Angkorian individuals wearing sampot. 509
28.2 Śiva wearing a pleated sampot worn high at the waist, Baphuon style, 11th–12th century. 510
28.3 Devatas wearing double-layer sampot ensembles, Angkor Wat, 12th century. 511
28.4 Examples of short sampot chong kben. 512
28.5 Variations in window blind decorations. 516
28.6 Tapestry medallion with paired phoenix, Angkor Wat, 12th century. 518
28.7 Specific motifs found in narrative tapestries. 519
28.8 Clay model of Maitreya from Sum Tsek temple, Alchi, Ladakh, mid-10th to 11th century. 521
29.1 Key sites discussed in the text. 526
29.2 Relationships between Pre-Angkorian and Angkorian elite, 7th–11th centuries. 529
29.3 Mahidharapura-Angkor marriage relationships. 530
31.1 Sequence of Uthong Art style based on classification by Griswold and Buriphan (1952). 558
31.2 Examples of Buddha statues with traits of Style B and C. 561
31.3 Comparison of Style B Uthong and post-Bayon Buddhas. 563
31.4 Post-Bayon Buddha frieze inside Prasat Ta Tuot, Angkor. 564
31.5 Distribution of Uthong Style A, B, and C Buddha statues on the central plain of Thailand. 566
31.6 Four bronze miniature stūpas typical of the Pre-Ayutthaya and Ayutthaya Periods. 568

32.1 12th–18th c. mainland Southeast Asian sites mentioned in the text. 575
32.2 Jayavarman VII period imagery. 582
32.3 Bronze tricephalous elephant statue from the Jayavarman VII period. 587
33.1 Overview map of major Early Modern sites in Cambodia. 594
33.2 Stūpa and sculptures from Wat Sithor. 597
33.3 Archaeological map of Longvek. 598
33.4 Distribution and relative quantities of trade ceramics and types from surface collections (n = 34,385 registered sherds). 602
33.5 Details of infrastructure and excavations at Longvek and the site of Tuol Bay Ka-ek. 603
33.6 Selection of imported ceramic types from Longvek surface collections. 604
33.7 High-value trade ceramics from central occupation mound, Trench 28. 605
33.8 Aerial view from Tonle Sap River looking south. 606
33.9 Selection of brown-glaze storage jars from Longvek ordered by country of manufacture. 607
34.1 Yama judging souls to hell on the bas-reliefs of Angkor Wat. 616
34.2 Statue of Yama, Angkor Period. 617
34.3 Schematic layout of cremation area typical in rural Khmer villages. 620
34.4 Altar dedicated to Yama (far left) placed within the northeast corner of cremation area. 621
34.5 Schematic layout of area for rice cultivation ritual at Thlork village. 623
34.6 Five sand mounds and Yama altar erected for rice cultivation ritual, Thlork village. 624
34.7 Female medium performing dance to Yama before rice cultivation ritual. 625
34.8 Rice stacked between the Yama altar and shelter. 626

TABLES

7.1 Cross-chronology of Chinese dynasties and Cambodian time periods. 114
7.2 Desirable products of Cambodia and China, listed by Zhao Rugua and Zhou Daguan, with botanical names, comments, and variant translations added where appropriate. 115
8.1 Details, including characteristic plant species, relevant to each of the three WWF-recognised ecoregions of the Greater Angkor region. 137
8.2 Vegetation regions surveyed in Ashwell (1993) and the corresponding JICA (2002) land-use type (where possible, based on spatial and/or descriptive correlation). 137
8.3 The array of pollen types identified in the palaeoecological records analysed and the ecological groups to which they were assigned. 142
11.1 Epigraphic territorial terms and their definitions. 202
13.1 Social status and associated fines from K. 323 (889 CE, sts. 78–82). 248
14.1 Epigraphic sources for warfare in the Angkor Period. 256
14.2 Dimensions of temple enclosure walls in the Pre-Angkor and Angkor Periods. 261
19.1 Distribution of recovered plants across the three study sites. 354
20.1 Main characteristics of the different sandstone lithotypes used during the Angkor Period. 364
22.1 Summary statistics of the five sites. 403
22.2 Presence and absence of economic crops in the five study sites. 408
22.3 Charred rice plant parts found in the five sites. 415
24.1 Epigraphic references for the emplacement of pratimā (likenesses) of Hindu deities and Buddha statues. 440
25.1 Pre-Angkorian and Angkorian inscription data on bovines. 466
25.2 Cow products in the Khmer inscriptions. 467
31.1 Thermoluminescence dating results from this study. 560
31.2 Uthong sites identified in each river basin and city in Thailand based on 2018–2019 surveys. 565
33.1 Types of ceramics recovered from surface collection and excavation at Longvek. 601

CONTRIBUTORS

Ang Choulean is Emeritus Professor of Anthropology at the Royal University of Fine Arts (CAM).

David Brotherson is an honorary associate, Department of Archaeology, University of Sydney (AUS).

Federico Carò is Research Scientist in the Department of Scientific Research of the Metropolitan Museum of Art, New York (USA).

Alison K. Carter is Assistant Professor of Anthropology at the University of Oregon (USA).

Cristina Cobo Castillo is Honorary Researcher at UCL Institute of Archaeology (UK).

Chea Socheat is an archeologist of the Authority for the Protection and Safeguarding of Angkor and the Region of Angkor and a research associate of the École française d'Extrême-Orient centre in Siem Reap (CAM).

Jean-Baptiste Chevance is an archaeologist and the Program Director for the Archaeology & Development Foundation—Phnom Kulen Program, Siem Reap (CAM).

Chhay Rachna is Head of the Ceramic Study Office in the Angkor International Centre of Research and Documentation, APSARA National Authority, Siem Reap (CAM).

Chhem Rethy is a distinguished professor of technology and humanities at the Cambodia University of Technology and Science (CamTech) (CAM).

Chhom Kunthea is an epigrapher and researcher in Apsara National Authority (CAM).

Aedeen Cremin is an independent scholar (AUS)

Tess Davis is a lawyer and archaeologist and is currently Executive Director of the Antiquities Coalition and teaches cultural property law at Johns Hopkins University (USA).

Ea Darith is Director of the Department of Conservation and Archaeology for the National Authority for Preah Vihear (CAM).

Armand Desbat is Emeritus research director at CNRS (FRA).

Penny Edwards is Professor of Southeast Asian Studies in the Department of South and Southeast Asian Studies at the University of California, Berkeley (USA).

Julia Estève is Lecturer in Department of Global Buddhism, UTK, Institute of Science Innovation and Culture, Bangkok (THA).

Damian Evans is Senior Research Fellow at the École française d'Extrême-Orient in Paris (FRA) and an Honorary Associate in the Department of History, School of Philosophical and Historical Inquiry, Faculty of Arts and Social Sciences, at the University of Sydney (AUS).

Christian Fischer is an independent scholar and Co-Director of the Molecular and Nano Archaeology Lab & Archaeomaterials Group at UCLA (USA).

Roland Fletcher is Professor of Theoretical and World Archaeology at the University of Sydney (AUS).

Gillian Green is an independent scholar. She is immediate past president of the Asian Arts Society of Australia and formerly Honorary Associate in the Department of Art History (AUS).

Kenneth R. Hall is Professor of History at Ball State University (USA).

Tegan Hall is a landscape architect and Lecturer at the Australian Catholic University and the Queensland University of Technology (AUS).

Scott Hawken is Director of the Landscape Architecture and Urban Design Program at the University of Adelaide (AUS).

Mitch Hendrickson is Associate Professor of Anthropology at the University of Illinois at Chicago (USA).

Heng Piphal is Post-Doctoral Fellow at the Cotsen Institute of Archaeology, UCLA (USA).

Trude Jacobsen Gidaszewski is Professor of South and Southeast Asian History and faculty associate in the Center for Southeast Asian Studies, a Title VI National Resource Center, at Northern Illinois University (USA).

Wayne Johnson is Senior Archaeologist with Place Management NSW (Australia) and Archaeological Field Director for Sydney University's Greater Angkor Project (AUS).

Sarah Klassen is Marie Sklodowska-Curie Fellow in the Digital Archaeology department at Leiden University (NLD).

Pipad Krajaejun is Assistant Professor in the Department of History, Faculty of Liberal Arts, Thammasat University (THA) and a PhD candidate at SOAS, University of London (UK).

Paul A. Lavy is Associate Professor of Art History at the University of Hawai'i at Mānoa (USA).

Stéphanie Leroy is Senior Researcher in archaeometallurgy at the French National Research Center (FRA).

Ian Lowman is an independent scholar based in Aberdeen, North Carolina (USA).

Eileen Lustig is an independent scholar based in Sydney (AUS).

Terry Lustig is an independent scholar based in Sydney (AUS).

Pierre-Yves Manguin is Emeritus Professor at the École française d'Extrême-Orient, Paris (FRA).

Dan Penny is Associate Professor in the School of Geosciences at the University of Sydney and Co-Director of the Angkor Research Program at the University of Sydney (AUS).

Phlong Pisith is Lecturer at the Faculty of Archaeology, Royal University of Fine Arts, Phnom Penh (CAM).

Phon Kaseka is Director General of the Institute of Humanities and Social Sciences, Royal Academy of Cambodia, Phnom Penh (CAM)

Martin Polkinghorne is a Senior Lecturer in archaeology at Flinders University, Adelaide (AUS).

Christophe Pottier is Associate Professor at the École française d'Extrême-Orient, Paris (FRA).

Sachchidanand Sahai is Resident Scholar at the ASPARA National Authority, Siem Reap (CAM).

Yuni Sato is a researcher at the Nara National Research Institute for Cultural Properties (JPN).

Seng Sonetra is a PhD candidate at the Department of History of Art and Archaeology, SOAS-University of London (UK).

Peter D. Sharrock is a Senior Teaching Fellow in the Department of the History of Art and Archaeology, School of Oriental and African Studies, University of London (UK).

Siyonn Sophearith is Lecturer of Cambodian history at the Royal U of Fine Arts and a government official of the Ministry of Culture and Fine Arts, Phnom Penh (CAM).

Nhim Sotheavin is a researcher at the Sophia Asia Center for Research and Human Development, Sophia University, Japan (JPN)

Dominique Soutif is Lecturer of Southeast Asian archeology at the École française d'Extrême-Orient (FRA).

Miriam T. Stark is Professor of Anthropology and Director of the Center for Southeast Asian Studies at the University of Hawai'i at Mānoa (USA).

Edward Swenson is Professor of Anthropology and the Director of the Archaeology Centre at the University of Toronto (CAN).

Yukitsugu Tabata is Professor in the Faculty of Letters, Arts and Sciences at Waseda University, Tokyo (JPN).

Ashley Thompson is Hiram W. Woodward Chair in Southeast Art and Professor in the Department of the History of Art and Archaeology at the School of Oriental and African Studies, University of London (UK).

Pelle Wijker is a doctoral student at Université Paris-1 Panthéon-Sorbonne and the École française d'Extrême-Orient (FRA).

ACKNOWLEDGEMENTS

Chapter 1—Penny & Hall

The authors acknowledge the Cambodian National Authority for the Protection of the Site and the Management of the Region of Angkor (APSARA) for their long-standing support and collaboration. This research is funded by the Australian Research Council and the Australian Nuclear Science and Technology Organisation.

Chapter 2—Soutif & Estève

The research program *Corpus des Inscriptions Khmères* is a collaboration between the École française d'Extrême-Orient (EFEO), the Cambodian National Authority for the Protection of the Site and Management of the Region of Angkor (APSARA), UTK Krungthep, and the Ministry of Culture and Fine Arts of Cambodia. This research has benefited from the financial support of the EFEO and the Dharma project, which has received funding from the European Research Council (ERC) under the European Union's Horizon 2020 research and innovation programme.

Chapter 4—Stark & Manguin

The authors would like to thank their host institutions for supporting their Mekong Delta-based research in Cambodia (Stark) and Vietnam (Manguin). Cambodia's Ministry of Culture and Fine Arts and its Archaeology Faculty of the Royal University of Fine Arts were invaluable throughout the 1996–2009 Lower Mekong Archaeological Project field investigations. Vietnam's Southern Institute of Social Sciences (Ho Chi Minh City) was EFEO's research partner during the work at Óc Eo and surrounding areas. All mistakes remain the authors' responsibility.

Chapter 5—Chevance & Pottier

The authors would like to thank Damian Evans for his careful proofreading; Lionel Courty for the translation; and H.E. Hang Peou, Director-General of the APSARA National Authority, for the unwavering support of APSARA and its departments. The Franco-Khmer Archaeological Mission on the Development of the Angkorian Territory (MAFKATA) is directed by

Christophe Pottier and operates in cooperation with APSARA. MAFKATA takes place under the auspices of the French Ministry of Europe and Foreign Affairs through its *Commission des fouilles* and is co-financed by the French School of Asian Studies (EFEO). The Fondation Simone et Cino Del Duca has also supported MAFKATA. The Archaeology and Development Foundation (ADF) is directed by Jean-Baptiste Chevance in partnership with the APSARA National Authority. This research has been partly supported by the Mohamed S. Farsi Foundation.

Chapter 7—Stark & Cremin

Our thanks go to Cambodia's Ministry of Culture and Fine Arts and to APSARA National Authority for supporting our work in Cambodia since 1996, some of which enabled us to produce the scholarship in the chapter.

Chapter 8—Hall & Penny

The authors acknowledge the Cambodian National Authority for the Protection of the Site and the Management of the Region of Angkor (APSARA) for their long-standing support and collaboration. This research is funded by the Australian Research Council and the Australian Nuclear Science and Technology Organisation.

Chapter 10—Evans *et al.*

The authors gratefully acknowledge the support of the Cambodian Ministry of Culture and Fine Arts and its various agencies, as well as the members of the Khmer Archaeology LiDAR Consortium. The contribution of D.E. and P.W. is funded by the European Research Council (ERC) under the European Union's Horizon 2020 research and innovation programme. The contribution of M.P. is funded by the Australian Research Council.

Chapter 11—Hawken & Klassen

The authors acknowledge the Cambodian National Authority for the Protection of the Site and the Management of the Region of Angkor (APSARA) as well as the EFEO, Paris, and UCL, London, for supporting residencies for Dr. Scott Hawken in June and July of 2019. Thanks also to the School of the Built Environment, UNSW, Sydney, for supporting Dr. Scott Hawken's sabbatical. Additionally, the authors acknowledge the Social Sciences and Humanities Research Council of Canada Postdoctoral Fellowship and for supporting residencies for Dr. Sarah Klassen at the University of British Columbia in 2019 and 2020 Dumbarton Oaks Research Library and the Andrew W. Mellon Foundation (Mellon Initiative in Urban Landscape Studies) for supporting a residency in 2018. The authors are particularly grateful to Dr. Eileen Lustig for her thoughtful feedback on an initial draft of the chapter. The authors would also like to thank the editors for their detailed feedback on the various drafts of the chapter.

Chapter 12—Lustig *et al.*

The authors would like to thank Aedeen Cremin, John Downey, Damian Evans, Marnie Feneley, Nina Hofer, Eileen Lustig, Dan Penny, Sam Player, Martin Polkinghorne, Christophe Pottier, Sakhoeun Sakada, the Royal Angkor Foundation, and Chandana

Withannachchi for their comments, criticisms, and readiness to provide us with the benefits of their specialised knowledge.

Chapter 13—Davis & Lustig

The authors would like to acknowledge the late Philip Jenner for the translations of the Khmer inscriptions that are available online through his Pre-Angkorian and Angkorian dictionaries. In addition, the authors would like to thank the US Department of Homeland Security (ICE) for the ability to reprint the image of the Duryodhana sculpture.

Chapter 14—Brotherson

The author wishes to thank the APSARA National Authority and the Greater Angkor Project. Research was funded by the Australian Research Council, the Australian Postgraduate Award, the Carlyle Greenwell Research Fund, and the Endeavour Fellowship. Thanks also to Michael Charney for comments on an early draft of this chapter.

Chapter 15—Chea *et al.*

The research program Yaśodharāśrama is a collaboration between the École française d'Extrême-Orient (EFEO), the University of Toronto, the Cambodian National Authority for the Protection of the Site and Management of the Region of Angkor (APSARA), UTK Krungthep, and the Ministry of Culture and Fine Arts of Cambodia. This research has benefited from the financial support of the EFEO; the Commission des fouilles of the French Ministry of Foreign and European Affairs; the Dharma project, which has received funding from the European Research Council (ERC) under the European Union's Horizon 2020 research and innovation programme; and the Hal Jackman Foundation.

Chapter 16—Chhem *et al.*

The authors gratefully acknowledge the *Canadian Journal of Buddhist Studies*, who gave us permission to adapt parts of Chhem (2007), from which sections of our text were drawn. Funding for this contribution derives in part from the European Research Council (ERC) under the European Union's Horizon 2020 research and innovation programme.

Chapter 17—Lustig *et al.*

The authors would like to acknowledge the late Philip Jenner for the translations of the Khmer inscriptions that are available online through his Pre-Angkorian and Angkorian dictionaries.

Chapter 19—Hawken & Castillo

The authors would like to thank the Cambodian National Authority for the Protection of the Site and Management of the Region of Angkor (APSARA) and Ministry of Culture and Fine Arts for their support. In addition, we thank Dr Eileen Lustig, Sarah Klassen, and the editors of the book for helpful feedback to improve the chapter. Scott Hawken would like to acknowledge both Damian Evans and Christophe Pottier of the EFEO for hosting his stay in Paris during the writing of the chapter and Dorian Fuller, who hosted him at the Institute of Archaeology at

UCL in London. This chapter was written with the support of the Faculty of the Built Environment, UNSW Sydney.

Chapter 20—Fischer *et al.*

We thank the Ministry of Culture and Fine Arts of Cambodia, the APSARA National Authority, the National Museum of Cambodia, and the École française d'Extrême-Orient. Special thanks go to Dominique Soutif and Bertrand Porte (EFEO) and to the Cambodian team of the stone workshop at the National Museum of Cambodia. Part of this research was supported through grants from the Robert H.N. Ho Family Foundation, the PSL/Scripta and the Corpus des inscriptions khmères projects, the University of California Los Angeles, and by fellowships from the Andrew W. Mellon Foundation at the Metropolitan Museum of Art and the E.W. Forbes Fund at the Freer Gallery of Art.

Chapter 21—Hendrickson *et al.*

The authors wish to thank the Ministry of Culture and Fine Arts and the APSARA Authority for their long-standing support and continued collaborations. Thanks also to Dominique Soutif at the École française d'Extrême-Orient and the University of Sydney Robert Christie Research Centre, particularly So Malay, in Siem Reap. Funding for this work was provided in part by the National Science Foundation, Agence Nationale de la Recherche, and Robert H.N. Ho Family Foundation Program in Buddhist Studies. Finally, thanks to the National Museum of Cambodia for permission to include the effigy vessel image from their collection.

Chapter 22—Castillo

Thanks to the Cambodian National Authority for the Protection of the Site and Management of the Region of Angkor (APSARA) for their continued support. I would like to thank my colleague and friend Mitch Hendrickson, who continued to push me to finish this chapter and had faith in my work through some difficult times. I would also like to thank my many collaborators: Miriam T. Stark, Alison K. Carter, Martin Polkinghorne, Heng Piphal, Rachna Chhay, and the GAP and INDAP teams.

Chapter 23—Estève

This chapter is part of the Corpus des Inscriptions Khmères research program (https://cik.efeo.fr/), in charge of the inventory of 'K. numbers' initiated by George Cœdès (*IC* VIII) and continued by Claude Jacques (1971). It is part of the project Dharma that has received funding from the European Research Council (ERC) under the European Union's Horizon 2020 research and innovation programme.

Chapter 25—Hendrickson *et al.*

The authors would like to acknowledge the late Philip Jenner for the translations of the Khmer inscriptions that are available online through his Pre-Angkorian and Angkorian dictionaries. The authors wish to thank the National Museum of Cambodia in Phnom Penh for permission to publish the image of the buffalo cistern from their collection.

Chapter 27—Carter *et al.*

The authors wish to thank the APSARA Authority for their cooperation and collaboration in undertaking this research. We also thank Dr. Roland Fletcher for his guidance and support of our project. We extend our deepest gratitude to So Malay and Martin King for administrative support and the University of Sydney Robert Christie Research Centre. We also thank the Greater Angkor Project field crews from 2010–2015. This work was supported by the Australian Research Council, National Geographic Society Committee for Research and Exploration, and Dumbarton Oaks.

Chapter 30—Evans *et al.*

The authors gratefully acknowledge the support of the Cambodian Ministry of Culture and Fine Arts and its various agencies. The contribution of D.E. and P.W. is funded by the European Research Council (ERC) under the European Union's Horizon 2020 research and innovation programme. The contribution of M.P. is funded by the Australian Research Council.

Chapter 33—Polkinghorne & Sato

Archaeological data in this chapter were collected with the permission of the Department of Archaeology and Prehistory, Ministry of Culture and Fine Arts, Royal Government of Cambodia. Special thanks to H.E. Minister Dr Phoeurng Sackona, Secretary of State H.E. Chuch Phoeurn, Secretary of State H.E. Prak Sonnara, H.E. Ok Sokha, and Mr Voeun Vuthy. Funding was provided by an Australian Research Council Discovery Early Career Researcher Award and an Australian Research Council Discovery Grant. The authors recognise the contributions of fieldwork teams (2015–2019) and advisors. We acknowledge the community of Ukna Bang Village, Kompong Chhnang Province, for their generosity in the field. Martin Polkinghorne is an honorary research fellow of the University of Sydney.

Chapter 35—Edwards

Thanks to Ben Bartu for his editorial eye, David Chandler for his comments on an earlier draft, and Heng Chhun Oeurn and Chap Prem for research assistance in Phnom Penh on a related project. I would also like to thank Sor Sokny at the Buddhist Institute for permission to reproduce verses from *Niras Nokor Wat*. Draft fragments of this chapter were presented at the Northern Illinois University Graduate Student Colloquium on Southeast Asian Studies, May 2015, and at the Department of South and Southeast Asian Studies, University of California, Berkeley, February 2006. Conversations with Dr. Thibodi Buakamsri and Dr. Trent Walker, during a directed study on Suttantaprija Ind's poem *Niras Nokor Wat* in 2012, deepened my understanding of that poem and the *niras/nirat* genre in general.

0

PROLOGUE

An Introduction to the Angkorian World

Mitch Hendrickson, Miriam T. Stark, Damian Evans
with Roland Fletcher

We have designed this volume as a state-of-the-art summary of research on the Angkorian World for a general readership. Drawing from more than a century of research in several discrete (and only rarely overlapping) disciplines has produced new and exciting views of this important but little-known Asian civilisation. So has inviting this generation of authors from different fields to collaborate in multi-authored chapters. Archaeologists have worked with epigraphers, art historians, and historians to develop innovative and holistic perspectives for this volume that push the boundaries of conventional archaeological research. Angkorian scholarship remains distinct from mainstream archaeological research in its stubbornly interdisciplinary approach and its roots in a particularist French intellectual tradition that emphasised epigraphic and art historical approaches. The fact that most research has also taken place within a heritage context, from the early to mid-20th century EFEO conservation efforts to the post-1992 UNESCO World Heritage era, affects the shape of scholarship. So does the lack of dedicated geographic concessions to different teams (as is sometimes the case in the Near East and Mesoamerica), which has meant that multiple research projects have worked in overlapping areas, with varying degrees of cooperation, to produce competing explanations from the same sites. Such frictions are difficult to navigate but can be intellectually productive; our goal is to highlight the particular kinds of insights that emerge from this context.

Our book comprises 35 original chapters written by leading scholars from Cambodia, the United States, France, Australia, Japan, Canada, the United Kingdom, and Thailand. Despite strenuous efforts at authorial parity and even coverage, we are acutely aware of our volume's shortcomings through its long period of development. Our authorship still skews toward Euroamericans, with fewer Khmer voices than we had hoped. Little room exists in this kind of volume for the conventional culture histories that newcomers to Angkorian studies often seek, which often draw heavily on the Francophone canon that was instrumental to the development of Angkorian research. Limited space has been allocated to some topical debates in Angkorian scholarship, like Groslier's (1979) 'hydraulic city' model and discussions of collapse (e.g. Lucero et al. 2015; Penny et al. 2019). We include a basic timeline of Angkorian history (Figure 0.1) and urge readers to consult previously published overviews, some relatively new (Coe and Evans 2018) and some more established (Briggs 1951; Dagens 2003) for key cultural history, the history of research in the field, and key debates through time. Maps included at the end of this chapter provide the reader with a reference of the spatial extent of the Khmer Empire's

DOI: 10.4324/9781351128940-1

influences (Figure 0.2), its reach, and the location of significant sites mentioned in the text (Figure 0.3). Our editorial mission has been to view the Angkorian World as historical scientists: to inspire new ways of looking at things that acknowledge old paradigms and offer new approaches. The following sections provide rationale for our volume's structure.

Part I: Contexts

This section provides foundational information regarding the study of the Angkorian World, from its heartland (Figure 0.4) to its far reaches. The World's ancient empires all depended on rich local environments, and Angkor is no different. The annual flooding of Cambodia's great lake, the Tonle Sap, fed large populations across the Khmer state, and surrounding regions held myriad forest products that the Chinese sought throughout the polity's lifespan. We have largely limited our focus to the 9th–15th century Angkor Period because of space limitations: our many chapters only graze the surface of scholarship. Some chapters delve into earlier (Pre-Angkorian and prehistoric) developments that were foundational to the Angkorian state. The discussion of early capitals encapsulates the idea of continuity within the larger transformations from small polities to one of the greatest empires in Asian history. Focusing on epigraphic research of minor texts written on objects complements classic research on royal stelae.

We close this section with a discussion of how conventional Angkorian scholarship rendered Cambodian researchers nearly invisible in the study of their own history: despite the fact that French EFEO conservators worked directly with Khmer technical experts (e.g. Falser 2020, 54, 112 for Marchal's conservation work) and despite a florescence in Khmer studies in the mid-20th century (see Dy 2006; Népote 1979; Peycam 2010, 162–64; 2011). This long-standing invisibility was clear even after the Khmer Republic proposed to make Phnom Penh the archaeological centre for a mainland Southeast Asia institute (ARCAFA: Applied Research Centre for Archaeology and Fine Arts or ARCAFA). Only 7 of the 42 individuals listed as specialists in Khmer archaeology for that proposal (SEAMEO 1972, 304–6) were actually Khmer, and of those 7, only 2 were trained as archaeologists (Chea Thay Seng and Roland Mourer). Khmer scholars have gradually become more visible in the last few decades, a development that our chapters seek to illustrate. This transformation includes essential voices that will continue to expand our understanding of Angkor as an empire, a cultural icon, and a heritage site of global significance.

Part II: Landscapes

Here our authors offer broad perspectives on agrarian, hydrological, and demographic contexts of the Angkorian World. Work described in this section's chapters owe much to the extensive archaeological survey programs and remote sensing campaigns that foreign scholars (e.g., those from the EFEO, the Greater Angkor Project, and others) have completed in collaboration with Cambodian institutions, most notably those housed under the Ministry of Culture and Fine Arts (including the APSARA National Authority) and the Royal Academy of Cambodia. The 'lidar revolution' resulting from two separate missions that covered over 2000 km^2 of Greater Angkor (Figure 0.5) and beyond has set the stage for new visions of early urban centres and their associated water management systems. Patterns of occupation around Angkor, and along one of the most important corridors in the Angkorian World, the Mekong, show a degree of consistency and coherence, as well as variability and adaptation to local conditions. Archaeobotanical studies, still in their infancy in Angkorian research, offer new insights into agriculture, subsistence, and land use that are canvassed in our chapters.

Part III: State Institutions

The chapters in this section examine key social traditions that structured ancient Angkorian society by focusing on its capital, which we call Greater Angkor (Figure 0.5). Angkor's success and emergence as Southeast Asia's largest empire were based in large part on the successful operationalisation of a complex and Indic-tinged system of statecraft. Unravelling the intricate genealogies of Khmer kings and locating their religious, art historical, and architectural legacies in time and space have long been mainstays of the literature on the Angkorian World; instead, our volume focuses on selected social processes that force new understandings of Khmer agency and power. How kings became fully legitimate kings rested on systems of bureaucracy and ritual. As the final arbiter and overseer of land ownership, the king sat at the head of Angkorian legal institutions. Physical representations of Brahmanic and Buddhist deities in the state temples of Angkor were central to the reproduction of royal power; we also see that, beyond the capital, local deities became intertwined with Brahmanical practices across the diverse landscapes of the Angkorian World.

Part IV: Economies

In this section, our contributors focus on the myriad activities and structures that facilitated the rise and functioning of the Angkorian state. Greater Angkor's geographic location was instrumental to its deep occupational history and helps to explain its huge population. Temple transactions and donations recorded in the Khmer-language inscriptions attest to the diverse range of products available in this cashless, barter economy and offer insight into the relative value of certain goods. The primacy of rice is attested to both in these records and in the vast landscape of wet-rice agricultural systems that stretch across the lake's northern margins. Tracing the spatial organisation and orientation of these field systems offers insights into the complexity of farming practices and provides another glimpse at the palimpsest history of occupation in Greater Angkor. The Khmer also produced a range of material culture that would come to define their legacy in mainland Southeast Asia, including distinct green and brown glazed ceramics, metal objects, and their iconic masonry temples. The systematic expansion of archaeological field research beyond Angkor has allowed us to pinpoint the sources for some of these products and identify widespread pyrotechnological activity across the Khmer territories, including the region south of Phnom Penh. The discovery of dozens of stoneware ceramic kilns and hundreds of iron smelting mounds illustrates shifting scales of production and how demand for different types of material was linked to major periods of expansion, particularly during the 12th century and the reign of Jayavarman VII. New approaches to the study of sandstone, the building material of choice for the Khmers from the 11th century onwards, also reveal the complex and dynamic interplay between resource availability, architectural transformations, and the historical trajectory of the Khmer Empire.

Part V: Ideologies and Realities

The contributions here survey belief systems that underpinned Angkor's merging of religion and state and examine key structuring principles like gender, ideology, and social organisation. As with other premodern states in mainland Southeast Asia, Angkorian people selectively integrated Indic beliefs and practices into their own specific cultural milieux. Conventional Angkorian scholarship emphasises a syncretic fusion of Hindu/Buddhist and local beliefs as a form of 'Hindicisation' (from Georges Cœdès' classic works [see e.g. Cœdès 1968]). More recent research instead emphasises pluralism, and a kind of 'indigenization' in which Khmer elites selected key foreign elements that supported their political goals and Worldview. The beautiful statues that served as foci for religious veneration in the Pre-Angkor and Angkor Periods are now counted among Southeast Asia's greatest artistic achievements. Our contributors elaborate in detail on their manufacture and elucidate the roles these images played in social and political reproduction across the Angkorian World. One chapter explores roles that key animals like bovids (cattle and water buffalo) played in Angkor's ritual and political economies. Other chapters use material culture and stylistic traditions to map the geographic boundaries of the Khmer polity. Attention then turns to daily life for Angkorian Khmers within and beyond temple walls, from sartorial expressions to gender roles. Image, performance, and agency all shaped daily life in the Angkorian World, and it is this aggregate that our authors study as long-term history.

Part VI After Angkor

This final section challenges the conventional 'collapse' view of Angkor and threads together the centuries-long denouement of the Angkorian period with subsequent developments in Cambodian and Southeast Asian history. Conventional scholarship has long depended on the European 'discovery' of Angkor and on a catastrophic 15th-century 'collapse': two concepts that our authors challenge using environmental and archaeological data from micro to landscape scale. Research on urbanism in Greater Angkor chronicles the decline of this capital, its continued occupation, and a demographic shift south to take advantage of growing maritime networks through capitals at Longvek and ultimately Phnom Penh. Other chapters use art, architecture, epigraphy, and religion to explore Angkorian legacies in the 16th–17th century polities that flourished in the territories of the former Empire. Finally, we underscore that the period 'after Angkor' continues to the present day in Khmer religious practice. This resilience and continuity is illustrated by the enduring presence of Yama, a minor god during the time of the Empire, who now occupies a central role in Khmer Buddhist practice. More than just an immutable assemblage of massive and durable stone monuments, Angkor has always been a canvas upon which to elaborate particular ways of looking at and thinking about the past, and our final contributions trace some of the ways in which ideas about Angkor are expressed in contemporary Cambodian society and culture.

Perspectives

A recurring theme in accounts of Angkor, from the earliest times until the present day, has been amazement and fascination with the prodigious scope of what was achieved, which by certain measures appears to be without parallel in the pre-industrial world. But the sheer scale of Angkor has given rise to its own set of theoretical and methodological problems. Historically, the precious and finite resources that we have available for investigations on the ground have focused on a handful of great temples in the urban centres of places like Angkor, and the artworks and inscriptions they contain, at the expense of the many thousands of smaller Angkorian shrines that sprawl across the Angkorian World. By focusing on the largest of the monuments, researchers have typically ignored the traces of communities and their everyday life that remain inscribed on the surface of the landscape, which are literally and figuratively overshadowed by the stone temples. Because of the unique scale of Angkor, conceptual and definitional problems abound.

As one example, the urban structure of Angkor itself defies easy categorisation: zoomed out to a certain extent, it resembles a sprawling and integrated 'city' of the kind we are now familiar with in the contemporary world: however, it is fully two orders of magnitude more extensive than other 'cities' of the pre-modern world Zooming in for more detail, Angkor Thom (and the Yasodharapura area, Figure 0.6) is a complicated mosaic of urban and rural space, with smaller urban centres that reflect the macro pattern of the settlement complex while also evincing specific local characteristics (Evans et al. 2007). Recent research has underscored the inherent tension in considering Angkor at different scales of time and space: on one level, the layout of Angkor is deliberate and reflects the designs of kings and the religious imperatives of the Angkorian state; on another level, it is the aggregate outcome of countless individual decisions over centuries (Klassen and Evans 2020). The functioning whole has emergent properties—material inertia and systemic vulnerability arising from centuries of reconfiguring the Earth's surface at regional scale (Penny et al. 2018)—that cannot readily or usefully be reduced to the beliefs and designs of individual kings, nor of farmers.

Recognising such differences in analytical scales is critically important to generating robust new insights about Angkor, particularly in identifying correspondences and non-correspondences between different lines of data (Fletcher and Evans 2012). Details matter, from the specific moment when an inscription was completed, associated with the specific intentions of an individual in the larger socio-political context in which they worked; through the schedules of daily routes and walking distances to collect water; the timing of 5–6-km travel distances to and from markets and workplaces; the fortnightly shifts of thousands of people across Angkor with the waxing and waning of the moon; up to the slow incessant movement of water through the canal networks. Angkor's space and time were structured and organised at different magnitudes. So were the products of long-term aggregate labour investment: if Angkor Wat temple was really constructed in three to four decades, as one interpretation of the inscriptions might suggest, labourers must have moved around 200 blocks of two to three tons, every single day, all year round—a feat that few quarry masters can match even today. The masonry of the towers on top of Ta Keo temple alone is estimated to weigh 6000 metric tons. Scaling further out, the West Baray held approximately 55 million cubic metres of water, and its banks extending for about 20 km contained over 12 million cubic metres of deposit. Thousands of human workers, working months and even years, moved these enormous quantities of materials (Pottier 2000, 104,114). Charismatic and effective rulers were necessary for Angkorian society to complete these projects, particularly their association of the Khmer ruler with the *devarāja* (god-king) and view of him as their *cakravartin* (universal ruler). On the other hand, it is likely that the everyday life of ordinary citizens over the centuries unfolded in much the same way regardless of which king sat on the throne or the specific gods to whom he professed devotion.

Temporal scales also vary broadly, from the duration of a single temple's construction to the lifespan of interaction and communication systems. Trade networks that moved textiles from South Asia and China to Angkor lasted for centuries. The Medieval Warm Phase, a period of oscillating higher global temperatures, lasted nearly five centuries. Greater Angkor's water system had a still longer duration, commencing at least with the establishment of Bhavapura with its proto-baray in the 8th century (Fletcher and Pottier 2022, 728–31) and continuing to the eventual abandonment of its last portion in Angkor Thom in the late 16th century (Groslier 1958). Ceramics were traded into Cambodia from China before the 9th century, and the circulation of this material culture continued beyond the demise of Greater Angkor (Brotherson 2019). Underlying all these developments was a rice-based agrarian foundation that reached Southeast Asia no later than the early second millennium BCE (Fuller and Castillo 2022) and created a sophisticated local ecology that facilitated surpluses needed to feed the city. This system was embedded in a much older story of the cropping of floating rice and flood recession rice, which has a long ancestry in the seasonally inundated lowlands of the lower Mekong Basin (Fox and Ledgerwood 1999).

Long-standing approaches to art history, inscriptions, and architecture might seem to offer few insights to many of these questions. Inscriptions, for example, while extraordinarily rich in detail on some aspects of Angkorian society, are frustratingly silent on things like the production of material like iron and ceramics, on water management, on the beliefs and perspectives of non-elites, and on the mechanics of society beyond temples and the royal court. On the other hand, several contributions to this volume underscore the value of using innovative approaches, informed by fields such as digital humanities, anthropology, and the applied sciences, to reap new information from sources that have been intensively studied for a century or more. Quantitative analysis of vocabulary and material culture in inscriptions now allow us to track social and economic changes across time and space (Lustig and Lustig 2019), for example, while studies of the geochemistry of ceramics and iron and petrographic analyses of sandstone allow us to connect artefacts to the specific groups people who produced and used them (Leroy et al. 2018; Polkinghorne et al. 2015).

Archaeology continues to play an outsize role in filling in the gaps in our knowledge that remain, but we must be clear-eyed about its limitations, especially given the ephemeral and non-durable nature of most Khmer material culture. We must also reframe the research questions that we ask, since there are a range of compelling and important questions to which we will almost certainly never know the answers. Scholars working elsewhere in the premodern world have demonstrated the importance of studying slavery, health, and mobility in the maintenance of ancient cities and their states. Yet Angkorian mortuary practices—the systematic cremation of the dead—preclude their study. We have no texts that provide insight into whether, and to what extent, belief systems promoted by kings were accepted by the general population or the degree to which the vast investments of labour in temple construction were motivated by devotion or servitude. Urban anatomy, from neighbourhoods to urban sectors, remains a challenge for Angkorian researchers to parse. Deciphering provincial dynamics, from economic organisation to linkages to the capital, requires more work. So does understanding the structure of the agrarian economy that supported the emergence and functioning of the capital. We hope that these chapters inspire the next generation of researchers to begin their research journeys into the Angkorian World.

Every volume in this Routledge series synthesises vast bodies of scholarship on a given 'World', and most draw from an array of disciplinary approaches that we also tap in this volume. Much of what makes Angkorian research important and difficult is not commonly found across the scholarly communities who crafted previous volumes. These include the impact of Angkor's colonial origins and legacies in current research practice, tensions between particularistic and comparative approaches, and geopolitical dynamics translated into scholarly conflicts. As in so many other archaeological research contexts, we currently lack unified or coherent systems for data collection, data access, and collections management. Yet some challenges seem unique to our field of Angkorian studies, from methodological challenges (and accomplishments) born of work in post-conflict land-mined regions, pressures to pursue less invasive research strategies in World Heritage properties, and an archaeological heritage that its descendant community so values that nearly every national flag since the mid-19th century has included Angkor's silhouette. Archaeology and heritage interdigitate in the Angkorian World to inspire both the kind of pride that encourages Khmers to become archaeologists and nationalism that occasionally also provokes armed conflict.

DATE	PERIOD	MAJOR RULERS	SIGNIFICANT DEVELOPMENTS
1900	Protectorate		
		Norodom Ang Duong	1863 Treaty with French Phnom Penh the capital
1800			
1700			
			Udong the capital
1600	Early Modern/ Middle		
		Ang Chan	Longvek the capital; Rededication of Angkor
1500			
			Khmer court moves south Thai attacks on Angkor
1400			
1300			Zhou Daguan account of Angkor
		Jayavarman VIII	
1200		Jayavarman VII	Angkor Thom Civil war/Cham invasion of Angkor
	Angkor	Sūryavarman II	Angkor Wat
1100			
			Baphuon
1000		Sūryavarman I	
		Rajendravarman II	Yaśodharapura the capital; Pre Rup
		Jayavarman IV	Koh Ker the capital; Prasat Thom
900		Yaśovarman I	Yaśodharapura the capital; Bakheng
		Indravarman I	Hariharālaya the capital; Bakong
800		Jayavarman II	Mahendraparvata the capital; Rong Chen Founding of the Khmer Empire
		Jayadevi	
700		Jayavarman I	
	'Chenla/Zhenla'	Iśanavarman	Iśanapura (Sambor Prei Kuk) a capital
600		Bhavavarman I	
	Pre-Angkor	Rudravarman	
500			
	'Funan/ Fou-nan'		
400			↑
300			Brahmanic and Buddhist evidence in Southeast Asia
200			Angkor Borei/ Óc Eo
100	Protohistoric/ Prehistoric		
0			

Figure 0.1 Timeline of the Angkorian World.

Navigating these challenges takes mindfulness, and we close by offering thoughts about the kind of future research we hope will expand our views of the Angkorian World. At the pragmatic level, more local engagement and less international oversight is needed to decolonise the study of Angkorian heritage field and hear local voices. Standardised researcher protocols, ranging from research ethics to data management systems, would strengthen the field and enhance the research value of more than a century of research collections. As several scholars have argued (see e.g. Heng and Phon 2017; Stark and Piphal 2017), we must eradicate persistent asymmetries between foreign and local researchers in Angkorian studies to move forward. As we commit to doing so, it will not be sufficient to simply dismiss the scholarship that has come before as 'colonial', which is obviously and necessarily true: the hard work that confronts us is to systematically and rigorously reappraise the archaeological record and to critically evaluate what is of enduring value and what is not.

We end with a note on chronological terminology. The timeline (Figure 0.1) is broadly divisible into Prehistoric and Early Historic. Culturally we speak of Pre-Angkor (6th to 8th c. CE) and Angkor Periods (9th to mid-15th c. CE), followed by the Early Modern or Middle Period (16th to 19th c. CE). Historians have also identified different phases within the Early Historic Period that correspond to the rise of state-level political entities, including *Funan* (4th to 5th c. CE) and *Chenla* (6th to 8th c. CE). Different meanings of these terms are described in detail elsewhere (Jacques 1979; Vickery 1986). References to late Angkor typically are associated with the late 13th to 15th century and are typically associated with the decline of the Empire.

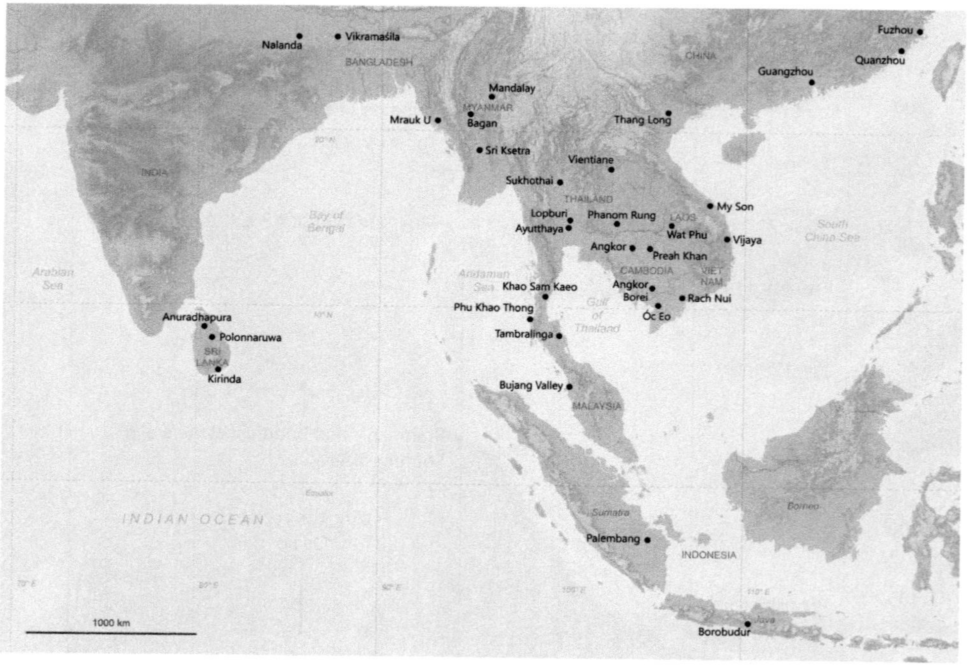

Figure 0.2 South and Southeast Asia, showing key sites.

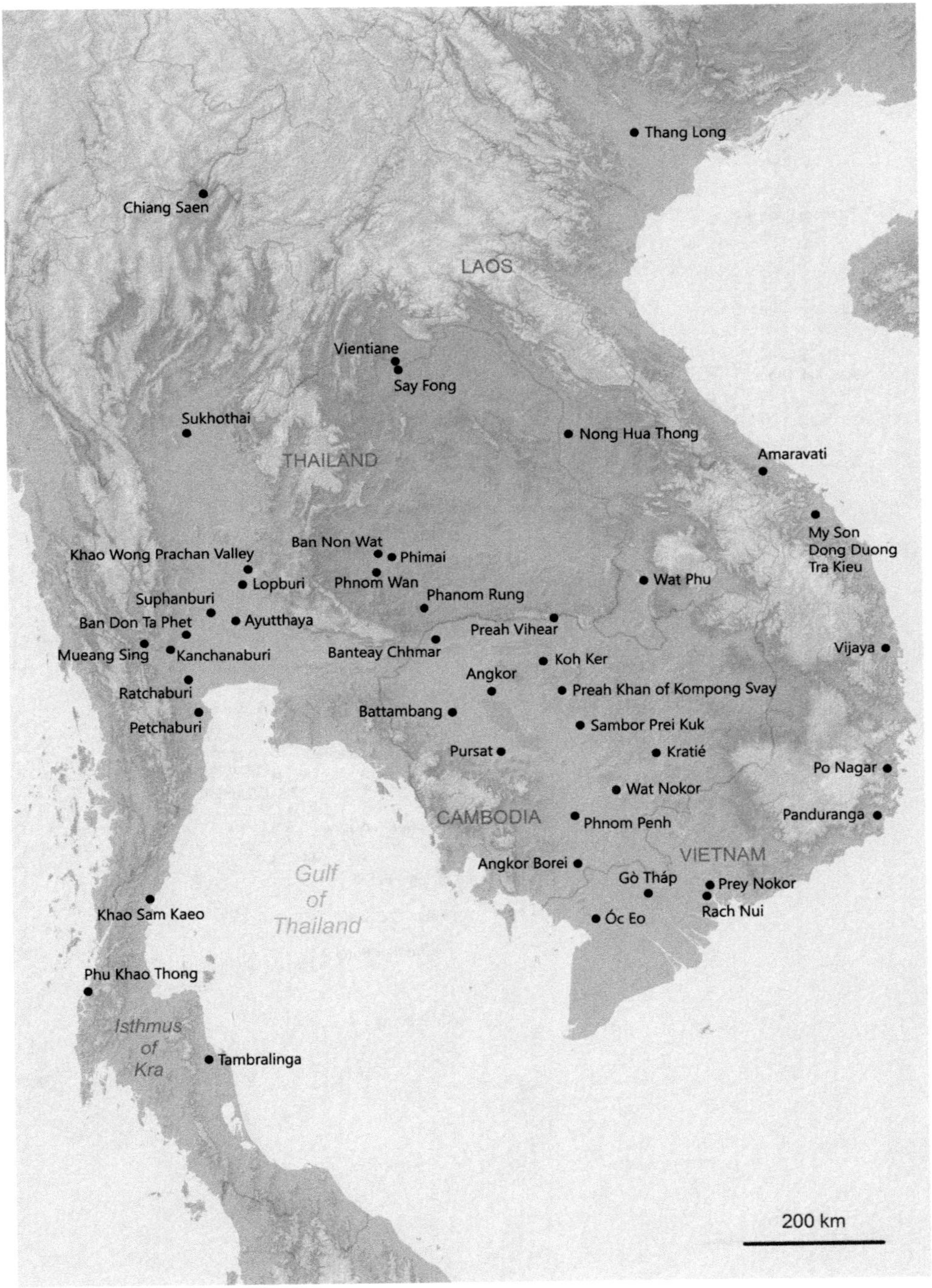

Figure 0.3 Southeast Asia, showing key sites.

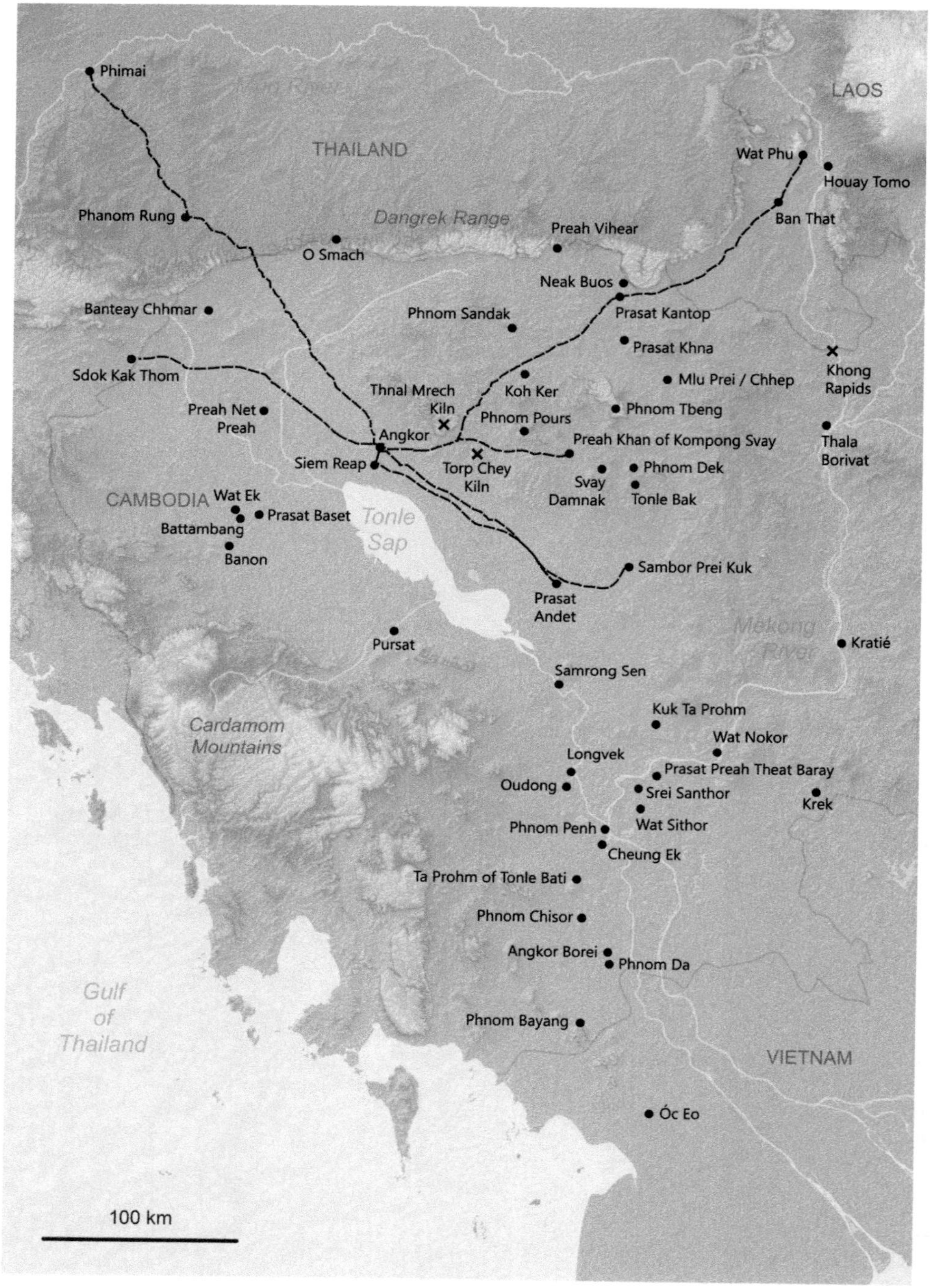

Figure 0.4 Heartland of the Khmer Empire, showing key sites and extent of the Angkorian road system.

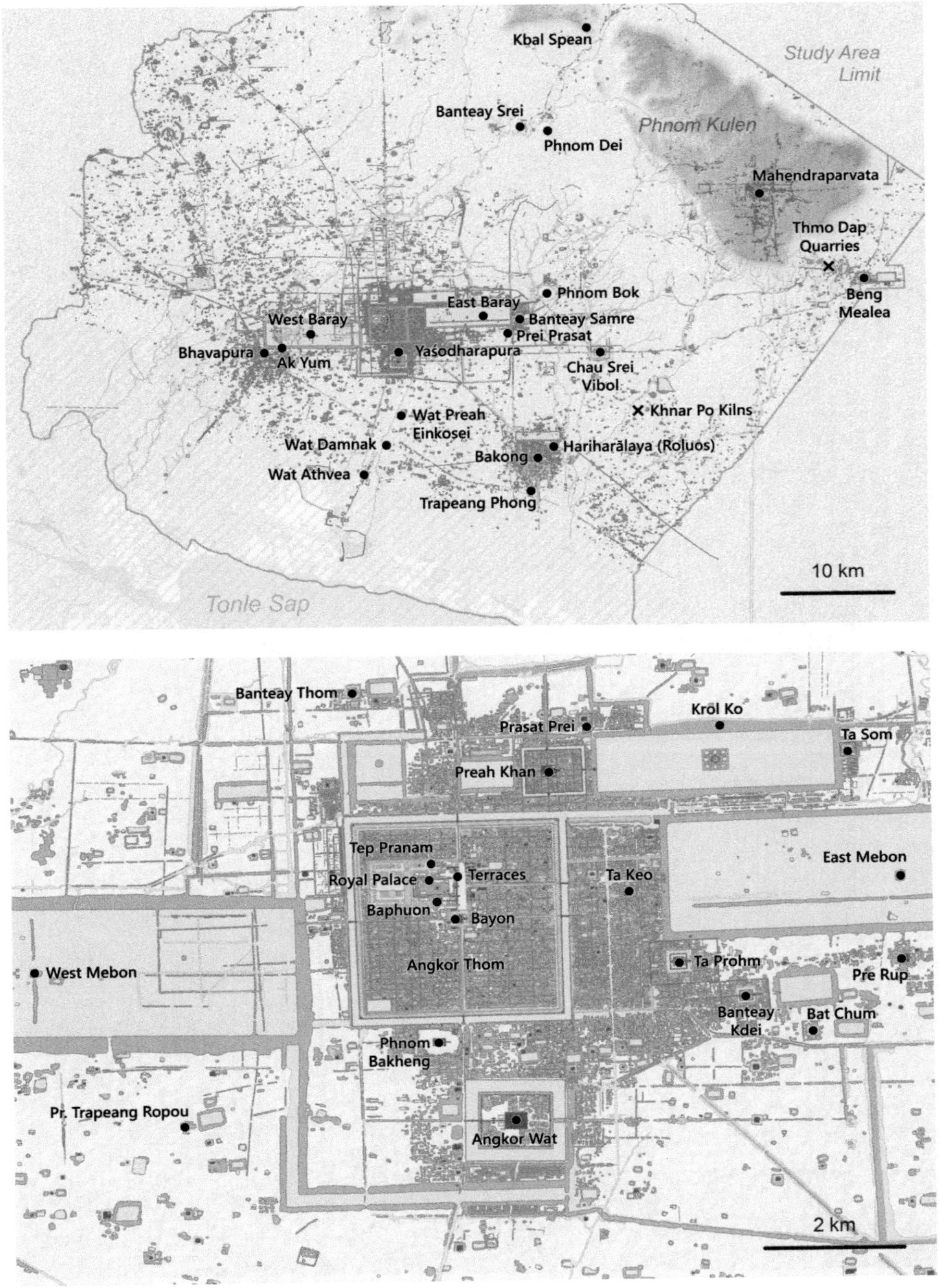

Figure 0.5 Greater Angkor, showing major temple sites and the extent of infrastructure.

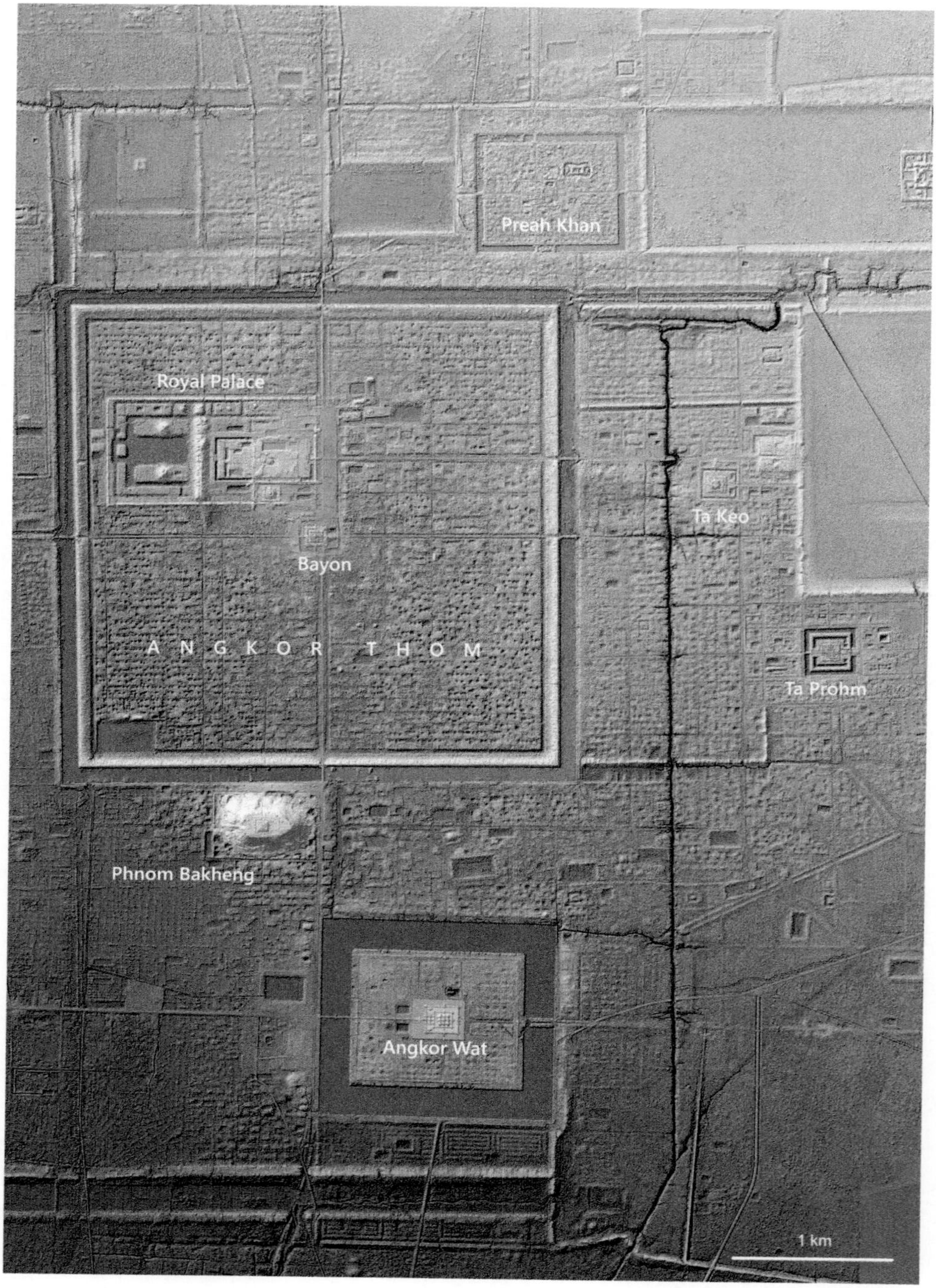

Figure 0.6 Capital region of Yaśodharapura, highlighting the urban layout in and around Angkor Thom and Angkor Wat.

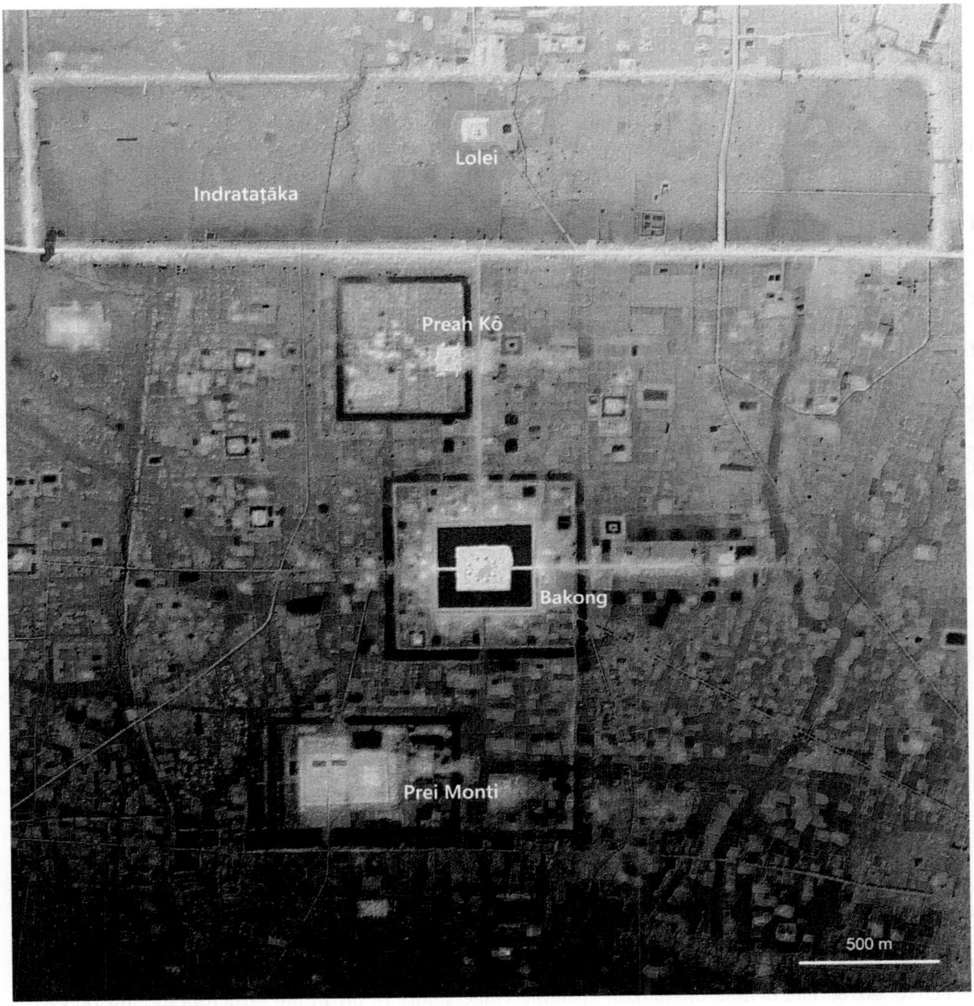

Figure 0.7 Capital region of Hariharālaya (Roluos).

Funding

Funding for this contribution derives in part from the European Research Council (ERC) under the European Union's Horizon 2020 research and innovation programme (grant agreements 639828 and 866454).

References

Briggs, L.P., 1951. *The Ancient Khmer Empire*. Bangkok: White Lotus.

Brotherson, D., 2019. *Commerce, the capital, & community: trade ceramics, settlement patterns & continuity throughout the demise of Angkor*. PhD thesis, Department of Archaeology, University of Sydney.

Coe, M. & D. Evans, 2018. *Angkor and the Khmer Civilization*. London: Thames & Hudson.

Cœdès, G., 1968. *The Indianized States of Southeast Asia*. Honolulu: The University Press of Hawaii.

Dagens, B., 2003. *Les Khmers*. Paris: Les Belles Lettres.

Dy, K.H., 2006. Suzanne Karpelès and the Buddhist institute. *Siksācakr: the Journal of Cambodia Research* 8–9, 55–9.

Evans, D., C. Pottier, R. Fletcher, S. Hensley, I. Tapley, A. Milne & M. Barbetti, 2007. A comprehensive archaeological map of the World's largest preindustrial settlement complex at Angkor, Cambodia. *Proceedings of the National Academy of Sciences* 104(36), 14277–82.

Falser, M., 2020. *Angkor Wat—A Transcultural History of Heritage:* volume 2: *Angkor in Cambodia. From Jungle Find to Global Icon*. Berlin/Boston: Walter de Gruyter GmbH & Co KG.

Fletcher, R.J. & D. Evans, 2012. The dynamics of Angkor and its landscape: issues of scale, non-correspondence and outcome, in *Old Myths and New Approaches: Interpreting Ancient Religious Sites in Southeast Asia*, ed. A. Haendel. Clayton: Monash University Publishing, 42–62.

Fletcher, R. & C. Pottier, 2022. Angkor: a provisional map history of greater Angkor from ancestry to transformation, in *The Oxford Handbook of Early Southeast Asia*, eds. C.F.W. Higham & N.C. Kim. New York: Oxford University Press, 703–31.

Fox, J. & J. Ledgerwood, 1999. Dry-season flood-recession rice in the Mekong Delta: two thousand years of sustainable agriculture? *Asian Perspectives* 38(1), 37–50.

Fuller, D.Q. & C.C. Castillo, 2022. Cereals of Southeast Asia, in *The Oxford Handbook of Early Southeast Asia*, eds. C.F.W. Higham & N.C. Kim. New York: Oxford University Press, 209–320.

Groslier, B.-P., 1958. *Angkor et Le Cambodge au XVIe Siècle d'après Les Sources Portugaises et Espagnoles*. Paris: Presses universitaires de France.

Groslier, B.-P., 1979. La cité hydraulique angkorienne: exploitation ou surexploitation du sol? *Bulletin de l'École française d'Extrême-Orient* 66, 161–202.

Heng, P. & K. Phon, 2017. The position of Cambodian archaeology in current sociopolitical context, in *Handbook of East and Southeast Asian Archaeology*, eds. J. Habu, P.V. Lape & J.W. Olsen. New York: Springer, 83–7.

Jacques, C., 1979. 'Funan', 'Zhenla': the reality concealed by these Chinese views of Indochina, in *Early South East Asia: Essays in Archaeology, History and Historical Geography*, eds. R.B. Smith & W. Watson. Oxford: Oxford University Press, 371–79.

Klassen, S.E. & D.H. Evans, 2020. Top-down and bottom-up water management: a diachronic model of changing water management strategies at Angkor, Cambodia. *Journal of Anthropological Archaeology* 58, June.

Leroy, S., M. Hendrickson, S. Bauvais, E. Vega, T. Blanchet, A. Disser & E. Delque-Kolic, 2018. The ties that bind: archaeometallurgical typology of architectural crampons as a method for reconstructing the iron economy of Angkor, Cambodia (tenth to thirteenth c.). *Archaeological and Anthropological Sciences* 10(8), 2137–57.

Lucero, L.J., R. Fletcher & R. Coningham, 2015. From 'collapse' to urban diaspora: the transformation of low-density, dispersed agrarian urbanism. *Antiquity* 89(347), 1139–54.

Lustig, E. & T. Lustig, 2019. Losing ground: decline of Angkor's middle-level officials. *Journal of Southeast Asian Studies* 50(3), 409–30.

Népote, J., 1979. Education et développement dans le Cambodge moderne. *Mondes En Développement* 28, 767–92.

Penny, D., C. Zachreson, R. Fletcher, D. Lau, J.T. Lizier, N. Fischer, D. Evans, C. Pottier & M. Prokopenko, 2018. The demise of Angkor: systemic vulnerability of urban infrastructure to climatic variations, *Science Advances* 4(10), eaau4029.

Penny, D., T. Hall, D. Evans & M. Polkinghorne, 2019. Geoarchaeological evidence from Angkor, Cambodia, reveals a gradual decline rather than a catastrophic 15th-century collapse. *Proceedings of the National Academy of Sciences* 116(11), 4871–76.

Peycam, P.M.F., 2010. Sketching an institutional history of academic knowledge production in Cambodia (1863–2009)—Part 1. *Sojourn: Journal of Social Issues in Southeast Asia* 25(2), 153–77.

Peycam, P.M.F., 2011. Sketching an institutional history of academic knowledge production in Cambodia (1863–2009)—Part 2. *Sojourn: Journal of Social Issues in Southeast Asia* 26(1), 16–35.

Polkinghorne, M., J.G. Douglas & F. Carò, 2015. Carving at the capital: a stone workshop at Hariharālaya, Angkor. *Bulletin de l'École française d'Extrême-Orient* 101(1), 55–90.

Pottier, C., 2000. Some evidence of an inter-relationship between hydraulic features and rice field patterns at Angkor during ancient times. *Journal of Sophia Asian Studies* 18, 99–120.

SEAMEO, 1972. *Final Report,* volume II. *Preparatory Conference on the Restoration and Animation of Historical Sites* (Phnom Penh, December 4–8, 1972). Phnom Penh: Government of the Khmer Republic and SEAMEO.

Stark, M. & P. Heng, 2017. An archaeological perspective on heritage and capacity-building in Cambodia, in *Post-Conflict Archaeology and Cultural Heritage: Rebuilding Knowledge, Memory and Community from War-Damaged Material Culture*, eds. P. Newson & R. Young. New York: Routledge Press, Taylor & Francis, 195–216.

Vickery, M., 1986. Some remarks on early state formation in Cambodia, in *Southeast Asia in the 9th to 14th Centuries*, eds. D.G. Marr & A.C. Milner. Singapore: Institute of Southeast Asian Studies, 95–115.

PART I

Contexts

1

AN ENVIRONMENTAL HISTORY OF ANGKOR

Beginning and End

Dan Penny and Tegan Hall

The emergence, development, and decline of Angkor were played out, as it were, against a backdrop of changing environmental conditions. These changes occurred over very large areas of the Earth's surface, oftentimes quite removed from Angkor itself, and operated over vast timescales. Whether one views the outcome of these changing conditions through the epistemological lens of determinism or possibilism, it is clear that Angkor's success as a city was built on an ancient geomorphic inheritance and that its scale and organisation were adaptations to inter-hemispheric-scale atmospheric processes.

Here we discuss the beginning and end of Angkor with respect to two large-scale processes: first, the evolution of the lower Mekong River Basin in response to post-glacial sea level rise and the consequent re-organisation of river systems and, second, the influence of synoptic-scale ocean-atmosphere systems on climate over mainland Southeast Asia. In doing so we do not intend to provide an exhaustive environmental history of Cambodia: That is a much larger work and still in its infancy. Rather, we attempt here to introduce the large-scale processes and phenomena that set the boundary conditions within which the emergence and demise of Angkor occurred. We emphasise here that these scaffolding environmental phenomena dictate neither the start nor end of Angkor but merely contextualise the changing landscape of adaptive choices available to the Khmer people.

The Beginning of Angkor: Holocene Evolution of the Lower Mekong River Basin

Angkor is located on the northern shore of the Tonle Sap Lake and owes its florescence during the first millennium CE to lake's remarkable fecundity. The Tonle Sap is a vast freshwater lake, covering an area of approximately 2,400 km^2 in the dry season. The lake is connected to the Mekong River by the Tonle Sap River, with the confluence at Phnom Penh, and the lake thus receives (on average) a staggering 79 cubic kilometres of floodwater as the Mekong River rises during the wet season (Kummu and Sarkkula 2008). As a consequence, the Tonle Sap lake swells in area and inundates the surrounding floodplain, increasing to a maximum area of 10,800 km^2 (Kummu et al. 2014). The majority of this floodwater—nearly 90%—drains from the Tonle Sap as the Mekong River ebbs and the summer monsoon gives way to Cambodia's dry seasons.

DOI: 10.4324/9781351128940-3

As a result of this peculiar natural phenomenon, the Tonle Sap is one of the most productive freshwater fisheries on earth. It supports a range of diverse liminal ecosystems and inundates a prodigious area of floodplain each year during the flood pulse, mantling it with nutrient-laden silt from the Mekong River flood. The natural resources offered by this unique system, particularly its pulsing hydrology, mediate the starkly seasonal climate and provide a foundation to support large populations of human beings. The lake also maintains a point of articulation between the inland agrarian kingdom and riverine and maritime trade routes (see Hall 2023; Stark and Cremin 2023, this volume). Angkor's dependence upon the lake, however, comes as a result of a long geomorphic legacy, or Markovian inheritance (Cowell and Thom 1994), stretching back many thousands of years.

Submerged and infilled valleys, presumably of upper Pleistocene (that is, terminating 11.7 thousand years (ka) Before Present [BP]) or lower Holocene (terminating 8.2 ka BP) age (Haraguchi et al. 2013), have been identified recently within the Tonle Sap basin using sub-bottom profiling, although similar work at a much smaller scale was reported by Carbonnel (1972, 89). The drainage network thus identified represents the glacial-aged surface of central Cambodia, now flooded, and is composed of relatively shallow valleys, up to 15 m deep and up to 1200 m wide (Darby et al. 2020; Best et al. 2017, 2018). During the most recent sea-level minimum (circa 20 ka BP), when global sea levels were approximately 120–130 m below present mean sea level, and during the early stages of the subsequent sea-level transgression across the exposed Sunda shelf, the Tonle Sap basin would have a been a broad floodplain draining to the southeast. Carbonnel (1972) argued that, given an absolute elevation of −12.7 m for the base of an incised channel, relative to mean sea level, that these channels were cut during the most recent glaciation. Comparison with global sea level curves (Lambeck 2014) would suggest, assuming the drainage network of central Cambodia had achieved a graded profile during the late Pleistocene and was thus in equilibrium with base level, that the valley system began to infill from circa 8,000 years BP, when sea levels exceeded −13 m.

The evolution of the Tonle Sap basin during this period is reflected by composition of sediment deposited in the basin in the lower Holocene. Day et al. (2011) describe lower Holocene sediment in the Tonle Sap basin as reflecting alternation between lake and floodplain environments until 8.2 ka, when permanent lake conditions became established. Penny (2006) reports pollen data that date to the period after the basin had begun to flood, from 7980–7790 years BP but observes some slight differences in the flora of the basin, particularly the presence of swamp forest taxa that do not occur commonly in the modern littoral forests (particularly *Ilex*, a Myrtaceae pollen type that probably derives from *Syzigium*, and ferns including *Stenochlaena*) (see Hall and Penny 2023, this volume). Carbonnel described a consolidated clay deposit at the base of the unconsolidated lacustrine muds deposited during the Holocene, which was particularly characterised by iron nodules and mottles. He interpreted this as representative of a formerly exposed surface, presumably the gently dissected flood-plain of the now-submerged river valleys, and inferred there may have been a stratigraphic hiatus, or time gap, between the flood plain and the lake sediments that mantle it. A radiocarbon date taken from 1.8 m below lake floor at the southwest margin of the large lake basin (c. 12°49'32.55"N 104° 4'54.34"E, Core GC11; Carbonnel 1972; Carbonnel and Guiscafré 1965, 194, 199) returned an age of 5,720 + 300 14C years BP (5796–7243 years BP using the SHCal13 calibration curve [Hogg et al. 2013; Hua et al. 2004] in CALIB 7.1.0 [Stuiver and Reimer 1993], with a median probability of 6498 years BP). The wood that yielded this age was interred some 50–60 cm above the floodplain surface, placing the initial post-glacial flooding of that basin at that location in the lower Holocene, as we have inferred. The transition from floodplain to lake is coincident in some of Carbonnel's cores with the deposition of a thin (10–15 cm) bed of relatively coarse sediment that included sand and gravel. Carbonnel and Guiscafré interpreted this as a 'pluvial' episode associated with particularly intense rainfall (1965, 197) but, on the basis of the geomorphic model proposed here, could equally reflect reworking of deposited fluvial sediments during the initial flooding of these incised channels as sea-levels rose and the river systems began to adjust their base levels.

A rapid accumulation of sediment within the Tonle Sap basin once the lake had formed is inferred from numerous radiocarbon-dated cores across the basin. Linear sedimentation rates from these cores all demonstrate relatively high sediment accumulation rates from the Upper/Middle Holocene and a consistent decrease in accumulation rates during the Middle Holocene (Kummu et al. 2008). This includes Day et al.'s (2011) TS-18-XII-03 core—not included in Kummu et al's summary—which reveals a sharp decrease in accumulation rates from about 6000 years BP. This rapid early filling of the glacial-aged drainage network reflects both ample sediment supply and the progressive creation and consumption of accommodation space onshore. More recent work by Steve Darby and colleagues (2020) suggests that sediment deposited within the Tonle Sap basin during the Upper Holocene was subsequently eroded across the entire lake basin as lake levels fell during the Lower Holocene (sometime between 6.2 and 2.0 ky BP) in response to the lowering of sea levels to near their present levels. During that period, wind-generated mixing of the lake water provided sufficient energy to lift and suspend fine particles that had previously settled on the lake bed. As lake levels fell, more turbulent energy became available to do this work and greater volumes of sediment were eroded from the lake bed and transported either elsewhere in the basin or exported from the basin entirely. Darby et al. (2020) estimate that approximately 1.2m of previously accumulated sediment—equivalent to approximately 12 cubic kilometres of mud—were eroded across the entire Tonle Sap basin as a result of that process.

In this way, the geomorphic evolution of the Tonle Sap basin during the Holocene is analogous to that of coastal lagoons globally (Carrasco et al. 2016) and conforms to Adlam's (2014) model of a two-stage process in the development of coastal lagoons: an initial rapid infilling to consume available accommodation space as sea-levels rose and a subsequent reduction in the rate of infilling as the sediment surface began to interact with wind-driven turbulence in the lake. This second phase prevents coastal lagoons from completely infilling (designated as 'maturity' by Roy et al. 2001), despite there being no lack of sediment supply to the basin, until change in the local energy regime can occur, normally through a reduction in surface area through shore-line progradation. In the case of the Tonle Sap, the rapid filling of new accommodation spaces ceased in the Middle to Upper Holocene, and sedimentation in the basin has since been dominated by re-working of previously deposited sediment as lateral growth of the shoreline, particularly along the northern shore of the basin, which is marked by a series of 'ridge-and-swale' structures (Kummu et al. 2008; Penny et al. 2005).

While the glacial and Holocene evolution of the Tonle Sap are comparable with other systems globally and thus easily understood, the evolution of the unique 'pulsing' hydrology of the Tonle Sap is less well resolved. In particular, there remains some uncertainty regarding the timing of the initial connection between the Mekong River and the Tonle Sap lake. Day et al. (2011) claim, on the basis of the isotopic characteristics of lake sediment, that connection to the Mekong River and the subsequent development of a pulsing hydrology occurred between 4,450 and 3,910 years Before Present. This correlates to a change in sediment composition with depth that was observed and radiocarbon-dated at locations across the basin by Carbonnel (1972) and Carbonnel and Guiscafré (1965) to >6547 years BP, by Tsukawaki (1997, fig. 2) to between 5816 and 6421 years BP, and by Penny (2006) to <5717 years BP (all dates calibrated to years Before Present). Darby et al. (2020) suggest the connection to the Mekong River was caused by a rearrangement of river channels on the Mekong Delta in response to changing sea levels, occurring some time after 6.2 ka BP. The variation in age for this common lithological change in the sediment of the Tonle Sap basin—over a period of more than 2500 years—is problematic for a model that emphasises a single 'switch on' of the pulsing connection to the Mekong River. The variation in age across the basin may be better understood as a localised effect of bathymetry on the transition to Adlam's (2014) 'late phase'. This, however, does not adequately account for the changes in sediment character, particularly the shift toward sediment more characteristic of a Mekong River source identified by Day et al. (2011) and others. An additional, unresolved issue for a mid-Holocene 'switch on' lies in accounting for the flooding of the Pleistocene drainage surface and, in particular, the source of water and sediment of sufficient volume to flood the basin and consume the available accommodation space. Currently, only 28% of sediment sequestered to the Tonle Sap basin derives from the Cambodian catchments, with the rest derived from the Mekong catchment through the annual flood pulse (Kummu 2008). Of this suspended sediment, 80% (around 5.7×10^9 kg) is sequestered to the lake and the floodplain. Similarly, 57% of the water supply to the basin annually derives from the Mekong River (Kummu 2008). It might be argued that there cannot have been sufficient water to flood the basin in the lower Holocene without a connection to the Mekong River, nor can there have been sufficient sediment supply from the Cambodian catchments to fill the accommodation space created by rising sea levels.

Whatever the case, the initiation of the flood-pulse during the Holocene was critical to the human history of the basin and created an important boundary condition for the emergence of the Khmer state in the latter half of the first millennium CE.

The End of Angkor: Synoptic-Scale Climatic Drivers

Cambodia's climate is characterised by the seasonal contrasts of the Asian monsoon, the largest and most powerful of the Earth's monsoon circulation systems. The shift from cool and dry winds from north-central Asia during the boreal winter to the rain-bearing winds from the Indian Ocean and the South China Sea during the boreal summer represent a massive interhemispheric exchange of energy and moisture and a dramatically seasonal character to the hydroclimate of mainland Southeast Asia. For Cambodia, the dry season (November to April) is a period of water deficit, where evapotransporative loss is far greater than precipitation, while the wet season (May to October) brings intense rainfall and flooding. Disrupting this seasonal balance are typhoon landings, which bring intense rainfall and significantly alter runoff and suspended sediment loads in the Mekong River and its tributaries (Darby et al. 2016).

These seasonal dynamics of monsoon behaviour over mainland Southeast Asia are particularly complex because the peninsula is influenced by two interrelated but independent components of the Asian monsoon system: the Indian Summer Monsoon (ISM) and East Asian Summer Monsoon (EASM). The interface between the ISM and the EASM is often termed 'IIE' and is identified as an irregular boundary, based on temperature and humidity data, that runs longitudinally between 99 and 103°E longitude (Cao et al. 2012). This irregular boundary will vary its location seasonally as the two components of the monsoon system can be either in-phase or out-of-phase (Wu 2017), creating a spatial and temporal complexity that is described as an intersection zone (Wang and Lin 2002). The confounding effect of overlapping monsoon domains on rainfall in the palaeoenvironmental records is apparent from Cambodia at 13°N latitude (Hamilton et al. 2020) to western-central China (Li et al. 2019) at 32°N latitude.

These seasonal patterns are episodically interrupted by prolonged periods of weak summer monsoon rainfall, which may extend for several years and even into decades. Droughts of this type—sometimes referred to as megadroughts—are invariably associated with variations in sea-surface-temperature (SST) conditions in the Pacific and Indian Oceans (Ummenhofer et al. 2013) which influence moisture availability and alter weather patterns on either side of the Pacific Ocean. In particular, prolonged droughts over Southeast Asia have been associated with El-Niño Southern Oscillation (ENSO) behaviour in the tropical and northern Pacific Ocean (Cook et al. 2010; Fallah and Cubasch 2015). The equivalent quasi-periodic oscillation in sea-surface temperatures in the Indian Ocean—the Indian Ocean Dipole—also influences climate over mainland Southeast Asia by weakening or strengthening the Indian Summer Monsoon that brings precipitation to Cambodia during the wet season (Sinha et al. 2011; Schott et al. 2009). Critically, when sea-surface temperatures become anomalous in both the Indian and Pacific Oceans simultaneously, drought is dramatically intensified over India, Southeast Asia, and Indonesia (Ummenhofer et al. 2013). These prolonged droughts are often associated with the 'canonical' mode of El Niño—that is, relatively warm sea-surface temperatures in the central and eastern Pacific associated with wet conditions over southern North America and relatively cool sea-surface temperatures in the western Pacific associated with dry conditions over Southeast Asia and eastern Australia. The spatial expression of these canonical ENSO droughts is, however, inconsistent with the 14th-century drought over mainland Southeast Asia (Buckley et al. 2010), which created drought on both sides of the Pacific Ocean, implying various 'modes' of ENSO behaviour (Buckley et al. 2019).

Another large-scale driver of climate variability over mainland Southeast Asia is volcanic eruptions. The short-term climatic consequences of volcanic eruptions are related to the injection of sulphate aerosols into the atmosphere during and immediately after the eruption. Sulphate aerosols combine with water in the upper atmosphere to create tiny droplets of sulphuric acid. These droplets are highly reflective of incoming short-wave radiation and thus create a localised fall in the receipt of solar radiation at the earth's surface. The effect is relatively short term, depending on the size and type of the eruption, its location, and its timing relative to seasonal atmospheric circulation systems. In general, however, the climatic effects of even very large eruptions (aerosol injection of 4 Tg or larger) last only 1–2 years (Liu et al. 2016), but, when several major eruptions coincide, the combined forcing can trigger large-scale and sustained climatic change (Miller et al. 2012). Critically for Angkor, volcanic eruptions are known to influence monsoon precipitation (Brönnimann et al. 2019; Liu et al. 2016), and the climatic disruption over mainland Southeast Asia during the 14th and 15th centuries was immediately preceded by a spike in volcanic forcing (Fallah and Cubasch 2015). Cooling triggered by volcanic aerosols alters wind flow patterns and is articulated with SST change in the tropical Pacific (Fallah and Cubasch 2015), which, as we have seen, can force prolonged drought over mainland Southeast Asia.

Climatic conditions during Angkor's tenure as the fulcrum of political and economic power in mainland Southeast Asia varied in response to these forcing processes and their interactions. The corpus of palaeo-climate data becomes vanishingly thin as we move deeper in time, particularly from areas proximal to Angkor. Elsewhere in the region, however, there are indications that the emergence of Angkor's formal urban fabric in the 8th century (see Evans et al. 2023a, this volume) was coincident with relatively weak summer monsoon influence (Sinha et al. 2011; Zhang et al. 2008) and that Angkor's subsequent growth coincided with a long period—roughly 400 years from the 10th century—of relatively strong summer monsoon influence over South and East Asia (Buckley et al. 2014). There was, of course, considerable variability in climate during that period but without any significant trend or particularly extreme variations. Whether this association between a long period of urban growth and relatively propitious climate is coincident or causal has yet to be demonstrated. The demise of Angkor (see Evans et al.

2023b, this volume), however, has been closely linked with climatic instability—specifically, a series of abrupt alterations between prolonged periods of drought and periods of relatively wet conditions that began in the middle of the 14th century and ended in the early decades of the 15th century. This period of climatic instability was first identified in tree-ring records derived from long-lived conifer species in the highlands of central Vietnam, more than 500 km ESE of Angkor. Those data revealed two multi-decadal-scale droughts from 1351–1368 and 1401–1425 CE, which bracketed a period of relatively wet conditions that incorporated some of the wettest years of the past 700 years (Buckley et al. 2010; Cook et al. 2010; Fletcher et al. 2017). The droughts are also apparent in cave speleothem deposits from southern Cambodia, about 300 km south of Angkor (Hua et al. 2017), expressed as a discrete period during which rainfall was insufficient to enable dripwater to accumulate calcite on cave stalagmites. The same droughts are recorded in a range of paleo-climatic archives across South, Southeast, and East Asia (Buckley et al. 2010, 2014).

Concluding Remarks

Angkor's foundation, and its eventual demise as the seat of Khmer power, were social phenomena that were scaffolded by environmental processes of much larger scale and antiquity. The city's prosperity is underwritten by the peculiar pulsing hydrology of the Tonle Sap Lake, whose origin lies in the planet's deglaciation after the last glacial maximum and the starkly seasonal climate that is controlled by the Asian monsoon. Angkor's demise coincided with climatic variability at the outset of the Mediaeval Climate Anomaly and was particularly framed by drought related to variations in sea-surface temperature in distal ocean basins and by the climatic consequences of volcanism.

None of these large and slow processes dictated the social responses that we observe in the archaeological and historical record. In fact, the peculiar scale and form of Angkor's urban fabric—fundamentally a product of sociocultural phenomena—were critical in sensitising the city to the consequences of climatic variability (Penny et al. 2018; see also Evans et al. 2023b and Polkinghorne and Sato 2023, this volume). Equally, political and economic drivers may have encouraged a shift in focus away from Angkor decades before the climatic instability of the 14th century began and a century before the Ayutthayan occupation of the city in the 15th century (see Penny et al. 2019; Lustig et al. 2023, this volume). From beginning to end, the people of Angkor adapted to changing circumstances, and their story should be seen as one of continuity and persistence in the context of a changing planet.

References

Adlam, K., 2014. Coastal lagoons: geologic evolution in two phases. *Marine Geology* 355, 291–96.

Best, J., Darby, S.E., Langdon, P., Hackney, C., Leyland, J., Parsons, D., Aalto, R. & M., Marti, 2018. Holocene evolution of the Tonlé Sap Lake: valley network infill, connection with the Mekong River and rates of sedimentation in Cambodia's Great Lake. *EGU General Assembly Conference Abstracts* 20, 9112.

Best, J., Darby, S.E., Langdon, P.G., Hackney, C.R., Leyland, J., Parsons, D.R., Aalto, R.E. & M. Marti, 2017. Holocene evolution of the Tonle Sap Lake: valley network infill and rates of sedimentation in Cambodia's Great Lake. *American Geophysical Union* 2017, #PP44B-06.

Brönnimann, S., Franke, J., Nussbaumer, S.U., Zumbühl, H.J., Steiner, D., Trachsel, M., Hegerl, G.C., Schurer, A., Worni, M., Malik, A. & J., Flückiger, 2019. Last phase of the Little Ice Age forced by volcanic eruptions. *Nature Geoscience* 12(8), 650–56.

Buckley, B.M., Anchukaitis, K.J., Penny, D., Fletcher, R. Cook, E.R., Sano, M., Wichienkeeo, A., Minh, T.T. & T.M. Hong, 2010. Climate as a contributing factor in the demise of Angkor, Cambodia. *Proceedings of the National Academy of Sciences* 107(15), 6748–52.

Buckley, B.M., Fletcher, R., Wang, S.Y.S., Zottoli, B. & C., Pottier, 2014. Monsoon extremes and society over the past millennium on mainland Southeast Asia. *Quaternary Science Reviews* 95, 1–19.

Buckley, B.M., Ummenhofer, C.C., D'Arrigo, R.D., Hansen, K.G., Truong, L.H., Le, C.N. & D.K., Stahle, 2019. Interdecadal pacific oscillation reconstructed from trans-Pacific tree rings: 1350–2004 CE. *Climate Dynamics*, 1–16.

Cao, J., Hu, J. & Y., Tao, 2012. An index for the interface between the Indian summer monsoon and the East Asian summer monsoon. *Journal of Geophysical Research: Atmospheres* 117(D18).

Carbonnel, J.P., 1972. *Le Quaternaire Cambodgien: Structure et Stratigraphie. Mémoire Office de la Recherche Scientifique et Technique Outre-Mer (ORSTOM) No. 60.* Paris: ORSTOM.

Carbonnel, J.P. & J. Guiscafré, 1965. *Grand lac du Cambodge: sédimentologie et hydrologie, 1962–63: rapport de mission.* Paris: Ministère des Affaires Étrangères.Carrasco, A.R., Ferreira, Ó. & D. Roelvink, 2016. Coastal lagoons and rising sea level: a review. *Earth-science Reviews* 154, 356–68.

Cook, E.R., Anchukaitis, K.J., Buckley, B.M., D'Arrigo, R.D., Jacoby, G.C. & W.E. Wright, 2010. Asian monsoon failure and megadrought during the last millennium. *Science* 328(5977), 486–89.

Cowell, P.J. & B.G. Thom, 1994. Morphodynamics of coastal evolution, in *Coastal Evolution: Late Quaternary Shoreline Morphodynamics*, eds. R.W.G. Carter & C.D. Woodroffe. Cambridge: Cambridge University Press, 33–86.

Darby, S.E., Hackney, C.R., Leyland, J., Kummu, M., Lauri, H., Parsons, D.R., Best, J.L., Nicholas, A.P. & R., Aalto, 2016. Fluvial sediment supply to a mega-delta reduced by shifting tropical-cyclone activity. *Nature* 539(7628), 276–79.

Darby, S.E., Langdon, P.G., Best, J.L., Leyland, J., Hackney, C.R., Marti, M., Morgan, P.R., Aalto, R., Parsons, D.R., Nicholas, A.P. & M.J., Leng., 2020. Drainage and erosion of Cambodia's Great Lake in the middle-late Holocene: the combined role of climatic drying, base-level fall and river capture. *Quaternary Science Reviews* 236, 106265.

Day, M.B., Hodell, D.A., Brenner, M., Curtis, J.H., Kamenov, G.D., Guilderson, T.P., Peterson, L.C., Kenney, W.F. & A.L., Kolata, 2011. Middle to late Holocene initiation of the annual flood pulse in Tonle Sap Lake, Cambodia. *Journal of Paleolimnology* 45(1), 85–99.

Evans, D., R. Fletcher, S. Klassen, C. Pottier & P. Wijker, 2023a. Trajectories of urbanism in the Angkorian World, in *The Angkorian World*, eds. M. Hendrickson, M.T. Stark & D. Evans. New York: Routledge, 173–94.

Evans, D., M. Polkinghorne, R. Fletcher, D. Brotherson, T. Hall, S. Klassen & P. Wijker, 2023b. Perspectives on the 'collapse' of Angkor and the Khmer empire, in *The Angkorian World*, eds. M. Hendrickson, M.T. Stark & D. Evans. New York: Routledge, 541–53.

Fallah, B. & U. Cubasch, 2015. A comparison of model simulations of Asian mega-droughts during the past millennium with proxy reconstructions. *Climate of the Past* 11(2), 253–63.

Fletcher, R.J., Buckley, B.M., Pottier, C. & S.Y.S. Wang, 2017. Fourteenth to sixteenth centuries AD: the case of Angkor and monsoon extremes in Mainland Southeast Asia, in *Megadrought and Collapse: From Early Agriculture to Angkor*, ed. H. Weiss. Oxford: Oxford University Press, 275–314.

Hall, K.R., 2023. Angkor's multiple Southeast Asia overland connections, in *The Angkorian World*, eds. M. Hendrickson, M.T. Stark & D. Evans. New York: Routledge, 97–111.

Hall, T. & D. Penny, 2023. Forests, palms and paddy fields: the plant ecology of Angkor, in *The Angkorian World*, eds. M. Hendrickson, M.T. Stark & D. Evans. New York: Routledge, 135–53.

Hamilton, R., Penny, D. & T.L. Hall, 2020. Forest, fire & monsoon: investigating the long-term threshold dynamics of South-East Asia's seasonally dry tropical forests. *Quaternary Science Reviews* (238), 106334.

Haraguchi, T., Yonenobu, H., Tokunaga, T. & I. Shimoda, 2013. Reconstruction of the past flow channels in the early Holocene at Lake Tonle Sap, Cambodia. American Geophysical Union, Spring Meeting 2013, abstract id. G33A-04.

Hogg, A.G., Hua, Q., Blackwell, P.G., Niu, M., Buck, C.E., Guilderson, T.P., Heaton, T.J., Palmer, J.G., Reimer, P.J., Reimer, R.W. & C.S. Turney, 2013. SHCal13 southern hemisphere calibration, 0–50,000 years cal BP. *Radiocarbon* 55(4), 1889–903.

Hua, Q., Barbetti, M., Zoppi, U., Fink, D., Watanasak, M. & G.E. Jacobsen, 2004. Radiocarbon in tropical tree rings during the Little Ice Age. *Nuclear Instruments and Methods in Physics Research Section B: Beam Interactions with Materials and Atoms* 223, 489–94.

Hua, Q., Cook, D., Fohlmeister, J., Penny, D., Bishop, P. & S. Buckman, 2017. Radiocarbon dating of a speleothem record of paleoclimate for Angkor, Cambodia. *Radiocarbon* 59(6), 1873–90.

Kummu, M. & J. Sarkkula, 2008. Impact of the Mekong River flow alteration on the Tonle Sap flood pulse. *AMBIO: A Journal of the Human Environment* 37(3), 185–93.

Kummu, M., Penny, D., Sarkkula, J. & J. Koponen, 2008. Sediment: curse or blessing for Tonle Sap Lake? *AMBIO: A Journal of the Human Environment* 37(3), 158–63.

Kummu, M., Tes, S., Yin, S., Adamson, P., Józsa, J., Koponen, J., Richey, J. & J. Sarkkula, 2014. Water balance analysis for the Tonle Sap Lake–Floodplain system. *Hydrological Processes* 28(4), 1722–33.

Lambeck, K., Rouby, H., Purcell, A., Sun, Y. & M. Sambridge, 2014. Sea level and global ice volumes from the last glacial maximum to the Holocene. *Proceedings of the National Academy of Sciences* 111(43), 15296–303.

Li, D., Tan, L., Cai, Y., Jiang, X., Ma, L., Cheng, H., Edwards, R.L., Zhang, H., Gao, Y. & Z. An, 2019. Is Chinese stalagmite δ18O solely controlled by the Indian summer monsoon? *Climate Dynamics* 53, 2969–83.

Liu, F., Chai, J., Wang, B., Liu, J., Zhang, X. & Z. Wang, 2016. Global monsoon precipitation responses to large volcanic eruptions. *Scientific Reports* 6, 24331.

Lustig, T., J.-B. Chevance & W. Johnson, 2023. Angkor as a "cité hydraulique"?, in *The Angkorian World*, eds. M. Hendrickson, M.T. Stark & D. Evans. New York: Routledge.

Miller, G.H., Geirsdóttir, Á., Zhong, Y., Larsen, D.J., Otto-Bliesner, B.L., Holland, M.M., Bailey, D.A., Refsnider, K.A., Lehman, S.J., Southon, J.R. & C. Anderson, 2012. Abrupt onset of the Little Ice Age triggered by volcanism and sustained by sea-ice/ocean feedbacks. *Geophysical Research Letters* 39(2), L02708.

Penny, D., 2006. The Holocene history and development of the Tonle Sap, Cambodia. *Quaternary Science Reviews* 25(3–4), 310–22.

Penny, D., Cook, G. & S.S. Im, 2005. Long-term rates of sediment accumulation in the Tonle Sap, Cambodia: a threat to ecosystem health? *Journal of Paleolimnology* 33(1), 95–103.

Penny, D., Hall, T., Evans, D. & M. Polkinghorne, 2019. Geoarchaeological evidence from Angkor, Cambodia, reveals a gradual decline rather than a catastrophic 15th-century collapse. *Proceedings of the National Academy of Sciences* 116(11), 4871–76.

Penny, D., Zachreson, C., Fletcher, R., Lau, D., Lizier, J.T., Fischer, N., Evans, D., Pottier, C. & M. Prokopenko, M., 2018. The demise of Angkor: systemic vulnerability of urban infrastructure to climatic variations. *Science Advances* 4(10), eaau4029.

Polkinghorne, M. & Y. Sato, 2023. Early Modern Cambodia and archaeology at Longvek, in *The Angkorian World*, eds. M. Hendrickson, M.T. Stark & D. Evans. New York: Routledge, 592–613.

Roy, P.S., Williams, R.J., Jones, A.R., Yassini, I., Gibbs, P.J., Coates, B., West, R.J., Scanes, P.R., Hudson, J.P. & S. Nichol, 2001. Structure and function of south-east Australian estuaries. *Estuarine, Coastal and Shelf Science* 53(3), 351–84.

Schott, F.A., Xie, S.P. & J.P. McCreary Jr, 2009. Indian ocean circulation and climate variability. *Reviews of Geophysics* 47(1), 1–46.

Sinha, A., Stott, L., Berkelhammer, M., Cheng, H., Edwards, R.L., Buckley, B., Aldenderfer, M. & M. Mudelsee, 2011. A global context for megadroughts in monsoon Asia during the past millennium. *Quaternary Science Reviews* 30(1–2), 47–62.

Stark, M.T. & A. Cremin, 2023. Angkor and China: 9th–15th centuries, in *The Angkorian World*, eds. M. Hendrickson, M.T. Stark & D. Evans. New York: Routledge, 112–32.

Stuiver, M. & P.J. Reimer, 1993. Extended 14C data base and revised CALIB 3.0 14C age calibration program. *Radiocarbon* 35(1), 215–30.

Tsukawaki, S., 1997. Lithological features of cored sediments from the northern part of Lake Tonle Sap, Cambodia, in*Proceedings of the International Conference on Stratigraphy and Tectonic Evolution of Southeast Asia and the South Pacific*, ed. P. Dheeradilok. Bangkok, Thailand: Department of Mineral Resources, 232–39.

Ummenhofer, C.C., D'Arrigo, R.D., Anchukaitis, K.J., Buckley, B.M. & E.R. Cook, 2013. Links between Indo-Pacific climate variability and drought in the Monsoon Asia Drought Atlas. *Climate Dynamics* 40(5–6), 1319–34.

Wang, B. & H. Lin, 2002. Rainy season of the Asian–Pacific summer monsoon. *Journal of Climate* 15(4), 386–98.

Wu, R., 2017. Relationship between Indian and East Asian summer rainfall variations. *Advances in Atmospheric Sciences* 34(1), 4–15.

Zhang, P., Cheng, H., Edwards, R.L., Chen, F., Wang, Y., Yang, X., Liu, J., Tan, M., Wang, X., Liu, J. & C. An, 2008. A test of climate, sun, and culture relationships from an 1810-year Chinese cave record. *Science* 322(5903), 940–42.

2

TEXTS AND OBJECTS

Exploiting the Literary Sources of Medieval Cambodia

Dominique Soutif and Julia Estève

Introduction

The corpus of inscriptions from Pre-Angkor and Angkor-era Cambodia constitutes the richest written source in Southeast Asia for the period from the 5th to the 14th century, and as the only body of written documents surviving from the Pre-Angkor and Angkor Periods, the Sanskrit and Khmer epigraphy of Cambodia has long provided one of the principal sources for the interpretation of Khmer medieval history.

Although the corpus only contains around 1400 inscriptions, their contents deliver both abundant and varied data. The Indian-language texts are typically devoted to the praise of the gods, to the eulogies and genealogies of kings or high dignitaries, and to the commemoration of their actions, beginning with their religious foundations. The Khmer-language inscriptions usually address more concrete, administrative subjects, such as donation registers or trial records. Thus, epigraphy informs us about many aspects of Khmer civilisation. The study of the varied texts has shed light on the origins, historical evolution, and main events of a civilisation that dominated Southeast Asia for several centuries and has also provided critical understanding of everyday life.

The evolution of archaeological research has naturally made many other methods available to enrich our knowledge, but the study of Khmer inscriptions remains a highly relevant and dynamic tool in the analysis of ancient Southeast Asian civilisations. Indeed, over the past 20 years, the resumption of survey and excavations has led to the discovery of many new inscriptions, while others have been found circulating in art markets, victims of the demand for Khmer art following the end of the war and the reopening of the country. Digital archives and computer search tools have also been employed to reinterpret already well-known inscriptions. In this chapter we present three recent examples to demonstrate how epigraphic works are interpreted to expand our knowledge of Khmer material culture and of the history of the Angkor Period. Our discussion aims to illustrate the reciprocal contributions of philological and archaeological approaches, to show how objects and texts inform each other and how this comparison can document more broadly the material culture of ancient Cambodia.

DOI: 10.4324/9781351128940-4

The Inscriptions

At the beginning of our era, the first phase of Indianisation went hand-in-hand with the introduction of a South India alphabet in Southeast Asia. Initially used for Sanskrit inscriptions, its use very quickly extended to vernacular texts, in our case ancient Khmer. During the last quarter of the 19th c., numerous rubbings of ancient Cambodian inscriptions were made and studied by several researchers, in particular the French Auguste Barth (1885) and Abel Bergaigne (1893) for Sanskrit and Étienne Aymonier for ancient Khmer (1883a, 1883b). Their work, which laid the foundations of our knowledge of ancient Cambodia and notably proposed the first royal genealogies, was followed and refined by that of George Cœdès, who published most of the available texts in the *Inscriptions du Cambodges* (*IC*) (1937–1966) until 1968, then by Claude Jacques (Jacques et al. 2007), Saveros Pou (Pou 1989, 2001, 2011), Philip Jenner (http://sealang.net/oldkhmer/text.htm), and so on. The *Corpus des inscriptions Khmères* research program (*cf.* n. 1) is today striving to continue this process, to coordinate Khmer epigraphic research, and to keep the digital inventory and text corpus up to date.

The corpus of Khmer inscriptions is generally divided into two parts: texts inscribed in Sanskrit verse, often of remarkably high literary quality and devoted essentially to the 'great history', starting with the eulogies of the gods, sovereigns and dignitaries, and texts in ancient Khmer (or 'old Khmer') that provide more administrative data, such as donation lists, trial reports, land transfers, and so on (see Lustig et al. 2023, this volume).

This division of content provides a fairly accurate idea of the core of the Khmer epigraphic corpus, but it remains simplistic and masks its richness, complexity, and diversity. First, this separation is not clear cut. One only needs to acknowledge the corpus of Jayavarman VII (1181–1218) to recognise that some property lists were written in Sanskrit, such as in the inscription of Ta Prohm (K. 273; Cœdès 1906), and an early 10th-century inscription of Īśānavarman II (K. 1320), published recently, includes a long versified list in Sanskrit of annual taxes (Jacques and Goodall 2014). Conversely, inscription K. 227 proves that ancient Khmer was also used to tell the story of the kingdom (Lowman 2012). Khmer texts were obviously only rarely engraved on stone, with the majority of texts—like the later Royal Chronicles—written on long-lost palm-leaf manuscripts.

Our examination of the role of epigraphy in the Angkorian World presents the reader with two important contrasts. First, we have chosen to present two Pre-Angkorian and one Angkorian inscriptions. The first two seem somewhat beyond the temporal scope of this book, but even if the language and certain customs clearly evolved at the turn of the 8th century, these texts address the same themes as the later inscriptions and make it possible to underline the coherence of the entire medieval Khmer epigraphic corpus between the 5th and 14th centuries. Second, while the majority of extant inscriptions are found in stone, we choose to evaluate the importance of lesser-known texts inscribed on portable objects.

When the Text Provides Information About the Object It Is Written On

A significant number of engraved utensils in ceramic have been recovered, but the majority are in bronze, gold, or silver. The inscriptions on their surfaces were made in repoussé or directly in the wax before melting (see Soutif 2009, 594; Estève and Vincent 2010, 147–48; Estève 2011). Until recently, most of the known inscribed objects belonged to the Angkor Period, with a significant quantity attributed to the reign of King Jayavarman VII. These are generally 'commemorative inscriptions', appearing as short texts memorialising the donation of the object bearing it and specifying the date of donation and the name of the divinity to whom it was offered. With few variations, the text always follows a typical formula in Khmer: '[date in *śaka* era], donation (*jaṁnvan*) from [Name of the donor] to [Name of the divinity]' (Gerschheimer and Vincent 2010, 111, n. 13).

The oldest inscription on a metal object published to date—a bronze vase discovered on the art market—is dated to 1007 CE (Soutif 2009, 598). This example proves that this use is not specific to the 12th century and that the rarity of older inscribed objects is probably related to the fact that the materials used for these artefacts were both precious and recyclable. Nevertheless, even this vase is a relatively recent example if we consider that the temporal breadth of the Khmer epigraphic corpus stretches back into the 5th century CE. However, two Pre-Angkorian inscriptions on metal have recently been reported and attest to the age of such objects as media for epigraphy. The first is inscription K. 1264, discovered in Laos (Ban Nong Hua Thong village, Savannakhet province). This bowl formed part of a treasure trove of precious metal objects made of gold, silver, gold-plated silver, bronze, and pearls, including also two silver plates bearing Angkorian inscriptions K. 1262 and K. 1263 (Lorrillard 2010–11, 242–43). The text is engraved on a silver bowl and reports a donation to Śiva. This text differs from later examples. First, the date (7th–8th c.) is not specified, and we can only estimate it on the basis of palaeographical analysis. In addition, it commemorates the donation of the object as well as the donation of livestock, land, slaves, and so on. Moreover, the wording does not correspond to the 'classical' formula that we have mentioned, since the text consists of a Sanskrit stanza (Dominic Goodall, pers. comm. February 2019).

The second inscription, K. 1294, is inscribed on a silver vase with a rounded belly surmounted by a high single-rim neck (Figure 2.1a).[1] An easily decipherable Sanskrit stanza (*indravajrā*) is engraved deeply on the wall of the vase in a flexible, clearly Pre-Angkorian style of writing.

In addition, a word in old Khmer is readable on the neck of the vase just under the rim (Figure 2.1b). It seems that this word was not written by the same hand, or, if it was, it was written with much less care:

K. 1294.1[2]

sarvvakṣitīśārccitaśāsanaśrī-
r vrahmakṣitīśaḥ kṣatadoṣapakṣaḥ
kṣoṇīpatīś śrījayavarmmanāmā
śrīkāmaraṅge dita raupyakumbham | |

The king, by name Jayavarman, the splendour of whose edicts was venerated by all [other] kings, who was both Brahmin and Kṣatriya, who destroyed the enemies that were the problems [in the kingdom][3] gave a silver pot to Śrī Kāmaraṅga.

K. 1294.2

ckāp·

Ckāp is a *hapax legomenon*: it is the first and only occurrence of this word in the Khmer corpus. Its meaning is not understood at this time.[4]

This donative inscription, although brief, provides important data from both a historical and a religious point of view. First, it offers the advantage of naming the donor, a king named

Figure 2.1 Silver vase with inscription (K. 1294): a) entire vessel max. diameter 21 cm; min. diameter 12 cm; height 22 cm (Photo J. Estève & D. Soutif); b) detail of K. 1294 text, (upper) symbol on neck and (lower) complete stanza around vase.

Source: (Photo C. Pottier).

Jayavarman. The question then becomes: to which Jayavarman does it refer? The forms of the letters indicate that this is a Pre-Angkorian text, and this name was coined by early rulers in Cambodia: Jayavarman I (652–end of 7th); Jayavarman I *bis*, whose existence has sometimes been called into question (see Goodall 2015, 75–78, 76, n. 15–18), but whose reign is now attested in at least three inscriptions dating from 763 CE (K. 1236; Goodall 2015) and 770 CE (K. 103 and K. 134; *IC* V, 33 and *IC* II, 92); and Jayavarman II, whose reign (?–ca 839) was marked in 802 by a ceremony intended to maintain Cambodia's independence from Javā—a key historical turning point that conventionally defines the beginning of the Angkor Period (Cœdès and Dupont 1943, 109).

The relatively archaic nature of the characters would rule out Jayavarman II and suggests instead that Jayavarman I *bis* donated the bowl, even if the palaeographical dates are still questionable. However, the distinction is delicate with regard to the first two kings, especially since we have few documents attributed to Jayavarman I *bis*, and both the brevity and the cursive writing of K. 1294 do not facilitate easy comparison. In addition, this inscription is engraved on metal and not on stone like the other texts attributed to Jayavarman I *bis*, which could explain discrepancies in the palaeography.

Returning to the text, two of the expressions used to praise the king provide interesting clues to identify him.

A king 'at the same time Brahmin and Kṣatriya' . . .

We are told that this king was *brāhmakṣitīśa*. There is no other occurrence of this particular compound within the inscriptions, but it is interesting to compare it with similar expressions employed to describe sovereigns. This qualification is indeed far from common, but it is sometimes used to designate certain high dignitaries, starting with Yajñavarāha, the famous founder of Banteay Srei in the 10th c. (*cf.* for example K. 619N, st. X; Finot 1928, 53).[5] The corpus gives only a few examples of comparable titles. The 10th-century inscriptions from the East Mebon (K. 528, st. X; Finot 1925, 312, 332) and Pre Rup (K. 806, st. VIII; *IC* I, 78) describe Rājendravarman's line of descent by the compound *vrahmakṣatra* (← *brahmakṣatra*). However, when considered in the singular, only three occurrences describe monarchs in a comparable manner, and they are all Pre-Angkorian. The first such king is also entitled brahmakṣatra, in the inscription K. 134 (st. I), a text that led Cœdès to suppose the existence of Jayavarman I *bis* (*IC* II, 92). As for the expressions *dvijakṣatra* and *viprakṣatra*, they are both found in the inscription K. 1417 (A, st. VI and B, st. III), still unpublished and which unfortunately provides no date. Dominic Goodall, who has worked on this inscription, attributes it to the same reign, particularly because of its palaeographic parallels with the inscription K. 1236, the best preserved of the three dated inscriptions attributed to this king (pers. comm. January 2019).[6]

. . . and 'whose edicts were revered by all the other kings'.

To our knowledge, the mention that other kings have honoured the edicts of a sovereign is not common in eulogies, and specifically not with the wording in our inscription (*sarvvakṣitīśārccitaśāsana*). Only two formulas are quite similar: in K. 1236, st. VIII we see the use of *rājanyārccitaśāsana*, 'There is a king . . ., with a radiance equal to that of the king of the kings, called Śrī-Jayavarman, whose commands are venerated by princes' Goodall 2015, 76), and in K. 447, st. V *praṇatānekabhūmipārccitaśāsana*: 'whose commands are respected by countless bowing kings'(*IC* II, 193).

As mentioned, these two occurrences are also Pre-Angkorian, but if the first can be attributed to Jayavarman I *bis*, the second, which is dated to 657, belongs to the reign of Jayavarman I.

At best, it may be noted that in the inscription attributable to Jayavarman I bis, this mention of sovereign pre-eminence appears in a set of stanzas playing on an alliteration of *kṣ* (Goodall 2015, 76–77, n. 20), a stylistic trait also used in the stanza from inscription K. 1294. Unfortunately, the evolution of Sanskrit poetic practices in ancient Cambodian texts is still poorly understood and can only provide tenuous support for dating such a text. While the evidence gathered previously does not permit any definitive temporal association, we favour the hypothesis that the bowl was donated during the reign of Jayavarman I bis and therefore to the second half of the 8th century.

Knowledge of the origin of this vase would have greatly assisted in identifying the sovereign, even if the areas of influence of Pre-Angkorian kings remain difficult to define. While the bowl was looted from an unknown site, it bears the name of the beneficiary—a deity named Śrī Kāmaraṅga—that could provide clues, since this god was most likely associated with a specific place. The word *kāmaraṅga* refers to the starfruit tree (*Averrhoa carambola*), a well-documented plant in Southeast Asia and common toponym in the Indianised world, According to Griffiths, *Kāmaraṅga* is a vernacular form of Sanskrit *Karmaraṅga* that also appears as a toponym in inscriptions of Arakan (Griffiths 2015, 301–08).[7] In ancient Cambodia, a city of this name is mentioned in K. 56 of Kdei Ang, a 9–10th century inscription located in the southern Cambodian province of Prei Veng (st. XXVII; *IC* VII, 10). This correlation suggests that it is in fact a theonym, by which the name of a divinity is derived from the name of the place it resides, which in this instance is a particular kind of tree. Such a specific link is not surprising, as the toponyms of ancient Cambodia are, as elsewhere in Southeast Asia, often based on the presence of notable topographical, hydrographic, or botanical elements. What makes this inscription unique is that god names in the Pre-Angkor Period usually do not employ toponyms, and for this period, one would expect a compound ending with *°īśa* or *°īśvara*: 'the Lord of Kāmaraṅga'. This inscription may represent an early example of the common convention in the Angkorian era when toponymic titles increase in frequency, particularly for the gods who receive the title *Kamrateṅ Jagat*, 'lord of the World', which clearly links the god with a locus (a place). An example of this is seen in the Kamrateṅ Jagat Vnaṁ Ruṅ associated with Liṅgapura (Wat Phu) (Estève 2018, 171).

Given that K. 56 is the only Khmer inscription to mention this toponym/theonym, it is tempting to argue that its place of discovery corresponds with its geographic location. This relatively straightforward answer is complicated by the fact that the text mentions many other donations in the cities of Madhavapura, Viṣṇupura, and especially Yaśodharapura, today's Angkor, this latter being located in northern Cambodia (st. XXIV, XXV, XXI, *ibid.*). It is therefore impossible, at this stage, to specify where the Pre-Angkorian city named Kāmaraṅga in K. 1294 was and if it corresponds to the city mentioned in K. 56. It is essential to try to identify the god named Śrī Kāmaraṅga, the recipient of the bowl, but this would require a thorough study of Indian sources that cannot be examined within the scope of this chapter. We can point out that the inscription K. 56 refers to this toponym in the following terms: 'In the city named Kāmaraṅga . . ., he completed [the temple or image] of the enemy of Mura [Kṛṣṇa]'. The inscription thus suggests that the donation was made in favour of a Vaiṣṇava sanctuary, as the Vaiṣṇava theonyms ending in *°raṅga* are attested in the South of India because of the influence of the vast Viṣṇu temple known as Śrīraṅga on an island in the Kāverī River beside Tiruchirappalli.

The Artefact

Although the undated Sanskrit Pre-Angkorian inscription K. 1294 shares similarities with the inscription discovered in Laos mentioned previously (K. 1264), the text contains a significant difference in that it commemorates the donation of the vase itself and not the many items essential to the functioning of a religious foundation. This practice more closely resembles inscriptions found on metal objects of the Angkorian era and requires an examination of what the text actually tells us about the medium on which it was engraved. The inscription describes the vessel as *raupyakumbha*, 'a silver vase', or, more precisely 'a silver' (*raupya*) 'jar, pitcher, water-pot, ewer, small water-jar' (*kumbha*; Monier-Williams 1899, *s.v.*). It may have simply formed part of the treasure of the temple, but it could also designate an object assigned to a specific ritual use, in this case solemn bathing ceremonies.

Hélène Brunner-Lachaux described such jars as playing an important role in the solemn baths of the god:

> The term *śivakumbha*, sometimes reduced to *kumbha* (or *kalaśa*, or *ghaṭa*) when there is no ambiguity possible, is a technical term that refers to a pot full of water representing Śiva during certain ceremonies. Different substances (gold, etc.) are put in water and the vase is prepared in a special way. The *śivakumbha* is accompanied by a smaller vase, usually with a neck, which is prepared in the same way: the *vardhanī*.
>
> (1968, 58, n. 4)

Interestingly, the term *ghaṭa* never appears in the lists of offerings to Khmer gods, and they were apparently rarely if ever employed in the ritual tradition imported into Cambodia. Such vases are indeed offered to Śiva in the foundation stele of Preah Ko (K. 713, st. XXX; 889 CE; *IC* I, 21, 27) and Bakong (K. 826, st. XXXIX; 881 CE; *IC* I, 33), but the text provides no information on their intended uses.

In the inventories of ritual objects in Khmer inscriptions, it is the term *kalaśa* that is most often used to designate the vases intended to pour water daily on the divinities. The bath serves as one of the *upacāra*, 'the acts of civility' making up the suite of daily rituals offered to the deities, a tradition well documented in Cambodia since the Pre-Angkor Period (Soutif 2009, 180–81, 256). On the other hand, we have only found one occurrence of *kumbha*, more precisely of the compound *tāmrakumbha*, or 'a copper jar' (K. 669C, l. 24; 10th c.; *IC* I, 170). Curiously, it appears in an inscription providing a list devoted to cult objects classified by material in the section preceded by the header *nā laṅgau*, 'in copper'. However, the stipulation of the material, *tāmra*, in the compound remains indecipherable.

This 'pleonasm' (*laṅgau/tāmra*) and the fact that we only find one occurrence of *kumbha* lead us to argue that it was not a mere jar but a cult object. We think that the compound *tāmrakumbha* was either used because it was known by this name *and* the exact meaning of the compound did not matter or to accentuate the materiality of the bowl for specific ritual reasons. According to the *Dīptāgama*, there are four graded materials for Śiva's *kumbha*: gold, silver, copper, and earth (Dagens et al. 2007, 584).

Daily ritual during Pre-Angkorian Cambodia adhered faithfully to Indian traditions, a phenomenon enabled by the emergence in India of a strong Tantric tradition that, among other consequences, facilitated the dissemination of Indian normative texts between the beginning of the 5th and the end of the 8th centuries (Soutif 2009, 179, 194). In the inventories, the presence of *vardhanī* (*ibid.* 259) provides a good example of the conformity of Khmer ritual with this standard. Vardhanī refers to the second vase of the solemn bath ritual mentioned by Brunner-Lachaux, but it is mentioned several times alongside ewers and vases linked to the bath in lists where the objects seem to be grouped by ritual and not by material, like the vase of our study. This correlation confirms the identification of our vase as a specific ritual object.

The presence of the Khmer word *ckāp*, which is currently untranslatable, provides an additional clue. We have already noted that the vase had to be 'prepared in a special way' and that different ingredients, precisely listed in the ritual treaties, had to be added to the water. Indeed, as Bhatt explains:

> The pots are covered on all sides except the mouth with a net-like texture made of cotton thread, into which are put fragrant material, gems, grains, etc. Their mouth is covered with tender mango leaves. Coconuts are placed on the top. They are then clad with garments and decorated. A lotus design is made on the altars, plantain leaves are placed over them, in which paddy and other grains are spread. The pots are placed on them and they are filled up with water with proper rituals.
>
> (1993–94, 75; see Figure 2.2)

Figure 2.2 *Śivakumbha* prepared for a *dīkṣā* (initiation) in Cuddalore, India.

Source: (Photo N. Ramaswamy).

It seems that the presence of an isolated and vernacular word (*ckāp*) could express technical information related to the content that this vase was to receive or to the ornamentation described by Bhatt. Thus, this *hapax* further suggests that it was indeed related to the ceremonies of the solemn bathing of the god.

Brunner-Lachaux's description of the vessel could indicate that this object was dedicated solely to a Śaiva foundation, thus settling the identity of Śrī Kāmaraṅga as a manifestation of Śiva. However, it is important to note that both the daily bath and baths of an exceptional nature also characterise Vaiṣṇava traditions (*cf.*, for example, Colas 1997, 316, 340). There is a comparable use in the royal ritual, which is not surprising given that the service of a god in his temple is equivalent to that of the king in his palace. The terms *kumbha* and *kalaśa* are used several times in Sanskrit inscriptions referring to the coronation of the king, which can be understood as the equivalent of the consecration of a religious statue (e.g. K. 989, st. XIV, about Jayavīravarman's in 1002; *IC* VII, 173) or periodic libations, as in the case of Rājendravarman's use of 100 *kalaśa* each month of *Puṣya* (K. 806, st. LXVI; 961 CE; *IC* I, 84).

While there are still uncertainties regarding the name of the city and the meaning of the *hapax*, the inscription already provides us with information about the date and function of this silver vase. Unfortunately, the fact that the context of the vase remains unknown and its lower part is lost prevent a full interpretation of this important artefact.

When the Object Informs the Text

The publication of an inscription engraved on a cult object obviously requires a careful examination of the medium as well as the context of its discovery, which is all too rare since most inscribed objects are found on the art market. To illustrate this issue, we would like to briefly analyse the inscription K. 1215, dating from the 7th–8th century, which is composed of three lines in Pre-Angkorian Khmer. Previous discussions of this text by Saveros Pou (2001, 184; see also Tranet 2000)[8] and Vong Sotheara (2001, 54–56, 67; 2003, 45–46, 190) lacked access to high-quality documents that resulted in interpretations of an incomplete text, in particular Saveros Pou, who considered the text a mere 'inscription fragment'. Our investigation shows that it is actually complete. The new rendition of K. 1215 is as follows:

> (1) *tmo 'aṁnoy· śatagrāmāddhyakṣa*[9] *ta vraḥ ka(2)mratāṅ· 'añ· śrī cakratīrtha*[10] *ge ta (3) sak gi*[11] *lāṅ*[12] *vraḥ ge dau niraya*[13]

A detailed analysis of this text is beyond the scope of this chapter. Although short, this inscription raises several questions that merit thorough interpretation both with regard to the administration of ancient Cambodia (*cf.* n. 30) and with regard to the identity of the beneficiary (*cf.* n. 31). However, it is necessary here to evaluate the translation of Saveros Pou, who interpreted the inscription as follows: 'Offering oxen from Śatṛkramādiyakṣa to V.K.A. Śrī Vakratīmra. People who steal these cows of the god, these will go to hell'. She further noted: 'The word *tmo*, which apparently means "stone", must be an error for *tmur*, a generic term for "*oxen*", because in this brief laconic text, this offering is followed by the sentence *go phoṅ vraḥ*, "the cows of the god"'. Pou's misreading of the imprecation (*go*, 'cow' instead of *gi*: n. 20, 21) explains why she took it as referring to cows as opposed to stones. We argue that knowledge of the medium of the text could have prevented this inaccurate reading.

As a matter of fact, K. 1215 is engraved on the base of a sandstone tray intended to grind spices, aromatic substances, or condiments by means of a roller (Figure 2.3). Cœdès (1920) identified the trays with the Sanskrit *peṣaṇī*, and these objects are often found in excavations of

Figure 2.3 Grinding stone with inscription (K. 1215): a) entire grinding stone; b) detail of K. 1215 text.
Source: (Photos M. Tranet).

Khmer sanctuaries. Cœdès further noted that they are well known in India, both in domestic contexts and in temples, where, in addition to their technical function, they are used in certain ceremonies. A single inscribed example published by Finot (1904) from Campā attests the diffusion within Southeast Asia. These grinding stones were essential for the preparation of meals and offerings of perfumes and fumigations for the god, which, like the ablution, form part of the 'acts of civility' (*upacāra*) that punctuate daily worship.

Epigraphy often bears witness to the activity of crushing ointments, as well as of the presence of grinding stones among the goods of the gods. Grinding practices clearly constituted an activity of sufficient importance that female servants were specifically assigned to it, and, to our knowledge, only women were responsible for this task. Indeed, we regularly find reference in the inscriptions to the *pamas jnau* or *pamas gandha*, 'perfume crushers', or even *pamas vraḥ gandha*, 'holy perfume crushers' (K. 320N2, l. 9, 10; CE 879; Pou 2001, 60). The term *jnau*, defined as 'that which has a good flavour or smell: aromatics, condiments' (Jenner 2009, *s.v.*), is the equivalent of Sanskrit *gandha*, but its use disappeared at the beginning of the Angkor Period in favour of the latter. This phenomenon is probably linked to the transmission of tantric treaties mentioned previously (Soutif 2009, 192). In the inscription K. 832, we can even identify a parallel between the Khmer expression *'nak ta pas gand[ha]*, 'a person who crushes perfumes' and the Sanskrit compound *gandhakārī*, 'a woman making perfumes' (A, st. X and B, col. c, l. 29; 9–10th; *IC* V, 91).

In equipment inventories, there are several occurrences of *tmo/thmo*[14] *pi pas*, 'stone to grind' (see K. 713B, l. 4, 18, CE 893, *IC* I, 22–23; K. 774, l. 4, CE 860, *IC* IV, 64), an object that was clearly dedicated to this use. It should be noted that one of these donations is followed by the mention of 14 pieces of sandalwood (*thmo pi pas 4 candana kaṁnat* 10 4; K. 262N, l. 16; 968 CE, l. 16; *IC* IV, 110), a substance that may be referred to by the Sanskrit *gandha*. However, Cœdès pointed out that to crush sandalwood, a stone 'generally circular, mounted on four feet, is used not as a grinding wheel (since there is no roller), but as a rasp, on which a little sandalwood is rubbed, the powder thus obtained being used to draw certain sectarian marks on the forehead' (1920, 10). It is therefore possible that *thmo pi pas* designates several types of 'crushing stones'.

Although the 'labels' of the inscribed objects rarely specify their names, it seems that this is the case here, as in K. 1294. Although probably more modest than a silver *kumbha*, this '[grinding] stone' nonetheless belonged to the religious equipment of a sanctuary. It is therefore necessary to re-translate K. 1215 as follows:

> Stone; gift of the *adhyakṣa* from Śatagrāma to V.K.'A. (of) Śrī Cakratīrtha[15]. People who steal it will offend the divinity; these people will go to hell.

The Sanskrit compound *adhyakṣa* designates a superintendent, an overseer, an inspector, a ruler, but we know too little about its role and the nature of *Śatagrāma*, 'a hundred villages', to impose a translation for the moment. *Śatagrāma* appears in several inscriptions. It is sometimes a toponym associated with terms designating administrative divisions, a *pramān*, 'province' (?) in K. 989B (l. 8; 1009 CE; *IC* VII, 164) and a *sruk*, 'city, village' in K. 235C (l. 59; 1052 CE; Cœdès and Dupont 1943, 87), but the hypothesis that this term sometimes refers more generally to an administrative division comprising 100 villages cannot be ruled out.

When the Disappearance of a Text Generates a Scholarly Text

The third case study, inscription K. 1335, is not engraved on a portable 'object' but on one of the most common epigraphic mediums of Pre-Angkorian and Angkorian times: a temple tower, or *prasat*. This inscription was discovered at Preah Khan of Kompong Svay by Christophe Pottier in January 2000 on the door jambs of the eastern door of building τ, the easternmost of the four laterite buildings located in the northeastern corner of the second enclosure (Figure 2.4).

The northern door jamb is composed of 24 lines, probably in ancient Khmer, while the southern was engraved with 40 lines, probably in Sanskrit[16]. The uncertainty of the latter is due to the fact that the whole text has been deliberately destroyed and that the few spared letters—particularly in the lower part of the southern doorjamb—do not permit the decipherment of the text (Figure 2.5). On the other hand, they are sufficient to affirm that it is indeed an Angkorian inscription. Moreover, although paleographic dating is tentative, their similarity to the characters of the inscription K. 161 of the 'Monument of the Inscription' located nearby would seem to date these texts to the first half of the 11th century. This inscription praises Sūryavarman I and recalls the date of his coronation in 1002. It is engraved on the doorjamb of the *cella* of a temple located in the third enclosure of the Preah Khan of Kompong Svay (Mauger 1939; *cf. infra*).

The very fact that this inscription was destroyed is particularly interesting. Indeed, the Khmer epigraphic corpus has provided few examples of the purposeful defacement of texts. Cœdès reported only about ten in his inventory (*IC* VIII), to which must be added some recent discoveries. It often proves difficult to specify the reasons for the destruction of a text. However, apart from a few cases of deletion of a divinity's name, most instances of the destructive erasure of a text constituted an act of *damnatio memoriae*.[17] While the practice of erasure seems to be characteristic of Bayon period foundations, including the Bayon (K. 293.28B) and Banteay Thom (K. 1039), there are no clues to determine why the theonyms were removed (*cf.* Cœdès 1951). It is however interesting to mention here Christophe Pottier's discovery that the lower part of the text from K. 774 was completely erased. Initially studied by Cœdès (*IC* 4, 64), he noted that, 'in 911ç. (989 CE), the rights of the temple seem to have been challenged, but the inscription stops there; perhaps it is unfinished'. It can be postulated that in this case

Figure 2.4 Prasat towers σ, ρ, π, and τ in Preah Khan of Kompong Svay. View from the northeast.
Source: (Photo D. Soutif).

the inscription is not 'unfinished' but that the contestation of the rights of the temple was the reason for erasing the lower part of this inscription (Pottier 2000, 23). Once again, it appears necessary for the epigraphist to study the medium before translating the text. Another famous example of this practice are the lists of dignitaries subordinate to Sūryavarman I in which several crossed-out names and passages clearly condemned to oblivion officials who failed to faithfully respect their oath (*cf.* K. 292; 1011 CE; *IC* III, 205).

In light of our proposed palaeographic dating of K. 1335, we argue that the destruction of this text might relate to the conflict between two contenders for the throne of Angkor, Jayavīravarman and Sūryavarman I, sometime at the beginning of the 11th century. Perhaps the effaced texts were commissioned by the loser (Jayavīravarman), or one of his allies who pledged allegiance to him. Scratching out the text literally made him disappear, effectively expunging him from 'history'. According to Vickery, K. 834 also presents the genealogy of a dignitary with erased parts that he explains as follows: 'It is thus possible that the erasures of this inscription were designed to efface the family's previous service at his [Jayavīravarman] court' (1985, 234).

While Sūryavarman I's origins remain difficult to establish with certainty (see Vickery 1985), it is generally believed that he came from eastern Cambodia, where the oldest epigraphic evidence of his reign has been found. If our palaeographic dating is validated, and if the destruction of the inscription was indeed intended to erase the memory of a competitor, then the hypothesis concerning the origin of Sūryavarman I demands revision. Alternatively, this textual

Figure 2.5 K. 1335, detail of the lower part of the southern door jamb.

Source: (Photo D. Soutif).

evidence leads us to assume that Jayavīravarman, or one of his subordinates, dominated the Preah Khan of Kompong Svay area.

Beyond historical considerations, the dating we propose raises questions about architectural history and the evolution of construction techniques. Indeed, the dating of the inscribed door jambs theoretically provides a *terminus ante quem* for the monument. However, the four laterite towers resemble the architecture of Prasat Suor Prat and, according to Mauger, one of its lintels corresponds to a period falling between the Angkor Wat and Bayon styles (1939, 207). Thus, this evidence would date these buildings to the second half of the 12th century.[18] In the same vein, the assembly of the laterite corbelled vault blocks is characterised by the use of vertical 'bayonet-cut' joints (Figure 2.6), a technique that Boisselier has demonstrated first dates to the Bayon period (1966, 129). Although the date of appearance of this technique requires further analysis, it seems difficult to trace it back to the beginning of the 11th century, when stone vaults, even without bayonet joints, were not very widespread.

At this stage, the architectural evidence would support a later date and casts doubt on the early 11th-century erasure of the text we initially proposed for K. 1335. However, the presence of bayonet joints is not sufficient reason to definitively rule out our hypothesis. Indeed, it would seem significant that the same type of joints can be found in the 'Monument of the Inscription' where the inscription K. 161, engraved on the southern doorjamb of the door of the *cella*, has

Figure 2.6 Detail of vertical 'bayonet-cut' joints in the corbelled vault from prasat tower ρ in Preah Khan of Kompong Svay.

Source: (Photo D. Soutif).

been confidently attributed to the reign of Sūryavarman I.[19] However, it seems unlikely that this type of joint was used widely at this early date. Although it is possible the doorjamb of K. 161 was moved from an older temple to the 'Monument of the Inscription', this seems highly doubtful for the two door jambs bearing destroyed inscriptions.

Indeed, we are more inclined to date these sanctuaries to the end of the 12th century. However, if we wish to better understand the first Angkorian installation at Preah Khan Kompong Svay, these deliberately erased inscriptions will require more attention to date both the four laterite towers of the second enclosure and the monument of the inscription.

Conclusion

The corpus of Khmer inscriptions is essentially a 'billboard literature' that delivers only an official version of historical reality, but it is nevertheless a rich body of historical testimony that remains largely untapped. It has been widely translated and interpreted in the past, starting with the works of Auguste Barth, Abel Bergaigne, George Cœdès, Kamaleswar Bhattacharya, Saveros Pou, Claude Jacques, and Michael Vickery. However, over the past 20 years, numerous publications have shown that much of the information has remained insufficiently analysed or at least

List of Inscriptions in the Text

K.	*Reference*	*K.*	*Reference*
56	*IC* VII: 3	713	*IC* I: 18
103	*IC* V: 33	774	*IC* IV: 64
134	Cœdès 1905: 419; *IC* II: 92	806	*IC* I: 73
161	Finot 1904: 672	826	*IC* I: 31
227	Lowman 2012	832	*IC V: 91*
235	Cœdès and Dupont 1943: 56	834	*IC* V: 244
262	*IC* IV: 108	989	*IC* VII: 164
273	Cœdès 1906: 44	1039	Soutif and Estève [to be published]
292	*IC* III: 205	1215	Vong 2001; *NIC* II-III: 184
293	Cœdès 1928: 106	1236	Goodall 2015
320	*NIC* II-III: 55	1262	Soutif [to be published]
447	*IC* II: 193	1263	Soutif [to be published]
528	Finot 1925: 309	1264	Goodall [to be published]
619	Finot 1928: 51	1320	Goodall and Jacques 2014
669	*IC* I: 159	1417	Goodall et al. [to be published]

IC = Inscriptions du Cambodge; Cœdès 1937–66.

NIC = Nouvelles inscriptions du Cambodge; tome I: Pou 1989; tome II-III: Pou 2001.

deserves specialised perspectives such as economic or ritual approaches. The corpus has been examined to explore a diverse range of topics, including religious studies; literature and philosophy (e.g., Bourdonneau, Estève, Gerschheimer, Goodall, Griffiths, Sanderson); astronomy (Billard, Eade, Golzio); ritual practices and mathematics (Soutif); linguistics, especially Khmer linguistics (Jenner, Long Seam, Pou); and economics (Lustig). The inscriptions presented here show new examples of how the combination of archaeological and epigraphic data can generate novel insights and knowledge of the material culture of ancient Cambodia.

Notes

1 This inscribed vase was reported in 2012 by Vittorio Roveda to Christophe Pottier while it was for sale at an antique shop in Bangkok. In February 2016, it was donated by its purchaser, François Mandeville, to the National Museum of Cambodia in Phnom Penh, where it has been accessioned under the number NMC.276.

2 Text based on photos provided to the *Corpus des Inscriptions khmères* research program by Christophe Pottier, Dominique Soutif, Julia Estève, and Bertrand Porte.

3 *Kṣatadoṣapakṣaḥ*: punning second interpretation, to be understood in parallel with the primary, or contextually best-fitting meaning: 'who was a veritable sun/moon in as much as he was one by whom the enemies (*pakṣa*) that are the nights (*doṣa*) are destroyed' (Dominic Goodall).

4 Although this part of the vase is very scratched, the reading seems certain. Nor have we found an equivalent occurrence such as *khcāp* in the Angkorian corpus.

5 We would like to thank Dominic Goodall for drawing our attention to this point and, in general, for the many tips and information he provided us during the preparation of this chapter.

6 This inscription was studied in January 2019 during the Tenth International Intensive Reading Retreat organised at the EFEO Center in Siem Reap by Dominic Goodall (EFEO) and Csaba Dezső (Eötvös Loránd University, Budapest).

7 It seems unlikely to us that it is the same city as the one mentioned in the Khmer inscriptions.

8 Michel Tranet first reported this inscription and gave it the number Ka 24 in his inventory. He provided photographs to the Corpus des Inscriptions Khmères research program. Our edition is based on these documents, and we would like to thank him for allowing us to reproduce them (Figure 2.3).

The inscription was reportedly discovered on a mound with brick remains called Tuol Ku Kam, located about 500 m south-southeast of Wat Komnour, in the municipality of Praek Phtol (Angkor Borei district, Takeo province). It was given to the Royal Palace of Phnom Penh in 2005.

9 S. Pou: *śatṛ°*; Vong Sotheara, S. Pou: *°grāmāddhyakṣa*: *°kramādtyakṣa*.

10 Vong Sotheara, S. Pou: *vakra°*; S. Pou: *°tīmra*.

11 S. Pou: *go*.

12 S. Pou: *phoṅ*.

13 S. Pou: *nairaya*.

14 *Tmo* is the Pre-Angkorian form of *thmo*.

15 This is obviously once again a Pre-Angkorian toponym/theonym association, as in the case of Kāmaraṅga. Associated with a place called Cakratīrtha, ('the holy place of the Disc'), it can be assumed that it was a Vaiṣṇava deity.

16 We base this assumption on the fact that the text of the Northern door jamb is arranged in columns. Although we can find some texts in ancient Khmer arranged in columns, they remain relatively rare, and this arrangement is more common for texts versified in Sanskrit, the space between the columns corresponding to the caesura in the verses.

17 It should be recalled that in ancient Rome, this expression, which can be translated into the 'damnation of memory', consists of a post-mortem sentence to oblivion, which is manifested, *inter alia*, by the erasure of the name of the person in question.

18 These sanctuaries, which face the royal terraces in Angkor Thom, have never been precisely dated, but are generally attributed to the Bayon period, or at least to the second half of the 12th century.

19 We would like to thank Christophe Pottier, who drew our attention to this discrepancy and shared with us his many observations about this technique, starting with its use both in the tower and in the 'monument of the inscription'.

References

Aymonier, É., 1883a. Quelques notions sur les inscriptions en vieux khmêr. *Journal Asiatique* 8(1), 441–505.

Aymonier, É., 1883b. Quelques notions sur les inscriptions en vieux khmêr. *Journal Asiatique* 8(2), 199–228.

Barth, A., 1885. *Inscriptions sanscrites du Cambodge (extraits des notices et extraits des manuscrits de la Bibliothèque nationale 27, 1re partie, 1er fascicule)*. Paris: Imprimerie nationale, 1–180.

Bergaigne, A., 1893. *Inscriptions sanscrites de Campā et du Cambodge (extraits des notices et extraits des manuscrits de la Bibliothèque nationale 27, 2e partie, 2e fascicule)*. Paris: Imprimerie nationale, 181–632.

Bhatt, N.R., 1993–94. Śaiva temple rituals. *Bulletin d'études indiennes* 11–12, 71–84.

Boisselier, J., 1966. *Le Cambodge [Manuel d'Archéologie d'Extrême-Orient, Première Partie: Asie du Sud-Est, Tome I]*. Paris: A. et J. Picard.

Brunner-Lachaux, H., 1968. *Somaśambhupaddhati, texte, traduction et notes, vol. II: Rituels occasionnels (I)*. Pondichéry: Institut Français de Pondichéry/École Française d'Extrême-Orient.

Cœdès, G., 1906. La stèle de Ta Prohm. *Bulletin de l'École française d'Extrême-Orient* 6(1–2), 44–82.

Cœdès, G., 1920. Notes archéologiques: à propos de meules de pierre appelées rasun batau. *Bulletin de l'École française d'Extrême-Orient* 20(4), 8–12.

Cœdès, G., 1928. Études cambodgiennes. *Bulletin de l'École française d'Extrême-Orient* 28(1), 81–146.

Cœdès, G., 1937–66. *Inscriptions du Cambodge*. Vol. I (1937); Vol. II (1942); Vol. III (1951); Vol. IV (1952); Vol. V (1953); Vol. VI (1954); Vol. VII (1964); Vol. VIII (1966). Hanoi and Paris: École française d'Extrême-Orient.

Cœdès, G., 1951. Études Cambodgiennes: 39. L'épigraphie des monuments de Jayavarman VII. *Bulletin de l'École française d'Extrême-Orient* 44, 97.

Cœdès, G. & P. Dupont, 1943. Les inscriptions de Sdok Kak Thom, Phnom Sandak et Prah Vihar. *Bulletin de l'École française d'Extrême-Orient* 43, 56–134.

Colas, G., 1997. *Viṣṇu, ses images et ses feux: les métamorphoses du dieu chez les vaikhānasa*. Paris: École française d'Extrême-Orient.

Dagens, B., Barazer-Billoret, M-L. & V. Lefèvre, 2007 (with the collaboration of S. Sambandha Śivācārya and the participation of Ch. Barois). *Dīptāgama, édition critique, (tome II)*. Pondichéry: Institut français de Pondichéry.

Estève, J., 2011. Dossier objets inscrits du Cambodge ancien. *Arts Asiatiques* 65, 107–58.

Estève, J., 2018. Mapping the sacred: towards a religious geography of ancient Cambodia through a toponymic atlas of Cambodian inscriptions, in *Writing for Eternity: A Survey of Epigraphy in Southeast Asia*, ed. D. Perret. Paris: École française d'Extrême-Orient, 163–74.

Estève, J. & B. Vincent, 2010. L'about inscrit du Musée national du Cambodge (K. 943): nouveaux éléments sur le bouddhisme tantrique à l'époque angkorienne. *Arts Asiatiques* 69, 133–58.

Finot, L., 1904. Notes d'épigraphie: 10. Le rasung batau de Ban Metruot. *Bulletin de l'École française d'Extrême-Orient* 4(3), 678–79.

Finot, L., 1925. Inscriptions d'Angkor. *Bulletin de l'École française d'Extrême-Orient* 25, 289–410.

Finot, L., 1928. Nouvelles inscriptions du Cambodge. *Bulletin de l'École française d'Extrême-Orient* 28, 43–80.

Gerschheimer, G. & B. Vincent, 2010. L'épée inscrite de Boston (K, 1048; 1040–41 de notre ère). *Arts Asiatiques* 69, 109–20.

Goodall, D., 2015. Les influences littéraires indiennes dans les inscriptions du Cambodge: l'exemple d'un chef d'œuvre inédit du viiie siècle (K, 1236), in *Migrations de langues et d'idées en Asie*, eds. J-L. Bacqué-Grammont, P-S. Filliozat & M. Zink. Paris: Académie des Inscriptions et Belles-Lettres, 67–80.

Goodall, D. & Jacques, C., 2014. Stèle inscrite d'Īśānavarman II à Vat Phu: K. 1320. *Aséanie* 33, 395–454.

Griffiths, A., 2015. Three more Sanskrit inscriptions of Arakan: new perspectives on its name, dynastic history and Buddhist culture in the first millenium. *Journal of Burma Studies* 19(2), 281–340.

Jacques, C. & D. Goodall, 2014. Stèle inscrite d'Īśānavarman II à Vat Phu (K, 1320). *2. Texte sanscrit et traduction. Aséanie* 33, 405–54.

Jacques, C., I. Yoshiaki & K. Sok, 2007. *Manuel d'épigraphie du Cambodge, vol. 1, (with the collaboration of Uraisi Varasarin, Michael Vickery, Tatsuro Yamamoto)*. Paris: EFEO UNESCO.

Jenner, Ph. N., 2009. *A Dictionary of Pre-Angkorian Khmer*. Canberra: Pacific Linguistics.

Lorrillard, M., 2010–11. Par-delà Vat Phu. Données nouvelles sur l'expansion des espaces khmer et môn anciens au Laos (I). *Bulletin de l'École française d'Extrême-Orient* 97–98, 205–70.

Lowman, I., 2012. K. 227 and the 'Bharata Rahu' relief: two narratives from Banteay Chmar, in *Connecting Empires and States: Selected Paper from the 13th International Conference of the European Association of Southeast Asian Archaeologists*, vol. 2, eds. M. Lin Tjoa-Bonatz, A. Reinecke & D. Bonatz. Singapore: NUS Press, 241–56.

Lustig, E., A. Cremin & T. Lustig, 2023. Angkor's economy: implications of the transfer of wealth, in *The Angkorian World*, eds. M. Hendrickson, M.T. Stark & D. Evans. New York: Routledge, 309–26.

Mauger, H., 1939. Práh Khẵn de Kŏmpon Svày. *Bulletin de l'École française d'Extrême-Orient* 39, 197–220.

Monier-Williams, M., 1899. *A Sanskrit-English Dictionary*. Oxford: Clarendon Press. [reed, 1990, Delhi, 10th ed.].

Pottier, C., A. Guerin, T. Heng, S. Im, T. Koy & E. Llopis, 2000. *Rapport annuel de la MAFKATA* (Unpublished reports). Siem Reap: APSARA-MEAE-EFEO.

Pou, S., 1989. *Nouvelles inscriptions du Cambodge, Tome I*. Paris: École française d'Extrême-Orient.

Pou, S., 2001. *Nouvelles inscriptions du Cambodge, Tomes II et III*. Paris: École française d'Extrême-Orient.

Soutif, D., 2009. *Organisation rituelle et profane du temple khmer du viie au xiiie siècle*. PhD dissertation. Paris: Université Paris III—Sorbonne nouvelle.

Tranet, M., 2000. Découvertes récentes d'inscriptions khmères, in *Proceedings of the 5th International Conférence of the European Association of Southeast Asian Archaeologists, 24–28 October 1994*, vol. 2, ed. P.-Y. Manguin. Hull: Hull University, Center for Southeast Asian Studies, 103–112.

Vickery, M., 1985. The reign of Sūryavarman I and royal factionalism at Angkor. *Journal of Southeast Asian Studies*, 226–44.

Vong, S., 2001. New Pre-Angkorean inscriptions in Angkor Borei district. *Kambuja Suriyaa* 55(1), 51–68.

Vong, S., 2003. *Silācāṛik nai prades Kambujā samăy mun Aṅgar, 1, Atthapad pak prae, ñep ñeṅ niṅ atthādhippāy [Inscriptions préangkoriennes du Cambodge, 1, textes traduits, compilés et commentés], (in Khmer)*. Phnom Penh: Université Royale de Phnom Penh, Faculté de Sociologie et de Sciences humaines, Département d'Histoire.

3

'INVISIBLE CAMBODIANS'

Knowledge Production in the History of Angkorian Archaeology

Heng Piphal, Seng Sonetra and Nhim Sotheavin

More than a century after the 'collapse' of Angkor and the Khmer Empire, 16th-century King Ang Chan returned to Angkor Wat to restore it as a political and spiritual centre and rededicate other temples to Theravada Buddhism (Groslier 1985, 16–19; Thompson 2004a, 205; 2006, 143–48). Khmers continued to curate and invigorate their Angkorian heritage through ancestral worship and Theravada Buddhist practice through the mid-19th century; for example, King Ang Duong tried to revitalise Cambodia in the face of encroachments by Thailand and Vietnam by restoring (and building new) Buddhist pagodas in Oudong (Edwards 2007, 132). This cyclical Cambodian Worldview, which reinvigorates the past to generate new futures, contrasts markedly with progressive, linear-based approaches to the past that characterise most Western scholarship on the Angkorian World (Thompson 2006, 151–52). Renovating and even transforming 'living' heritage sites continues to be a central concern for Buddhists in both Thailand and Cambodia (e.g., Keyes 1991; Byrne 1995).

Despite repeated calls for diverse perspectives on Cambodia's premodern past and vitality in Khmer-driven scholarship, Cambodian voices remain under-represented in discussions of the Angkorian World. Contemporary heritage management in Cambodia involves multiple museums, World Heritage sites, and heritage units that hundreds of professionals with BAs in Archaeology from the Royal University of Fine Arts (RUFA) manage. Despite this surge in local capacity since the mid-1990s, Cambodian scholarship—like Southeast Asia–based archaeological scholarship more generally (Shoocongdej 2011, 722)—remains nearly invisible in global scholarship. This chapter complements previous work (e.g., Carter et al. 2014; Heng and Phon 2017) and explores why Cambodian scholarship still plays a marginal role in shaping understandings of the Angkorian World by focusing on Cambodia's educational infrastructure and knowledge production during its 20th-century 'modernisation' period.

We argue that four interrelated process explain Cambodians' near-invisibility: (1) frictions caused by competing Western and Khmer perceptions of heritage; (2) intellectual hegemony by the École française d'Extrême-Orient (EFEO) in constructing narratives of Cambodia's aesthetic legacy (Muan 2001) and its Angkorian past; (3) a mid-20th-century desire to 'modernise' Cambodia through Khmer studies that emphasised Buddhism, Khmer language and literature, and folk life; and (4) a lack of colonial commitment to capacity-building in Cambodian heritage

DOI: 10.4324/9781351128940-5

scholarship. Colonial scholarship on Cambodia's premodern past was largely divorced from the consciousness of the Khmer public, who viewed their heritage as a living religious tradition blending Buddhism, chronicular evidence, and folklore. Examining institutional histories and disjuncture between Khmer and foreign approaches to the past highlights complex relationships between archaeology, heritage management and education, colonised knowledge production, and the nation-state.

Heritage and Archaeology in the Context of Khmer Studies

Cambodia entered the 20th century with a cultural renaissance and modernisation that included an expansion of education beyond the traditional pagoda-based structure. New academic institutions that were founded (e.g., Royal Library, Buddhist Institute) became crucibles for the emergence of the *Kambuja Suriya* journal, the first Khmer dictionary, the *Association of Khmer Writers*, and the first Khmer political journal (*Sruk Khmaer* and later *Nagaravatta*) (Clayton 1995; Edwards 2004; Harris 2005, 105–56). Intense cultural and political exchanges between Cambodia and the French Protectorate characterised this period, as the French and the Khmers both positioned themselves as rescuers of the descendants of Angkor to protecting their autonomy from encroaching neighbours of Thailand and Vietnam.

Khmer local responses to geopolitics were more responsible for this renaissance than were western pressures to modernise (e.g., Edwards 2007; Hansen 2007). Khmers increasingly linked Khmer literary traditions, Buddhism, and their Angkorian past to an emerging Khmer national identity, and Angkor Wat became the symbol of the new Cambodia (Thompson 2004b, 2006, 2016). French colonial scholars pushed back against this local narrative, denigrating contemporary Khmer literature and highlighting the rupture between modern Cambodia and Angkor through contrasting the 'degenerate' post-Angkor Period with its Theravada Buddhist literature with Angkor's period of regional dominance (e.g., Cœdès 1931). Some also charged that Khmers lacked self-expression altogether (Pou 1980, 142). These colonial critics misunderstood Khmer literature, which—like Khmer education and knowledge production more broadly—was deeply enmeshed with Buddhism, the monarchy, and a patron-client system (e.g., Ayres 2000; Clayton 1995, 2; Chigas 2000). They also underestimated the local respect for Khmer cultural heritage, which King Norodom explained in 1891 in opposition to a French request to remove statuary from Khmer temples:

> Since antiquity, Cambodian laws and customs under all reigns to this day have never permitted the abduction of pieces of religious sculpture. The Cambodian people set great store by these laws and customs. To allow the removal of statues of monumental stone from the Cambodians would be tantamount to destroying the Khmer religion. . . . [It was impossible] to contravene the laws and customs [of Cambodia], or to attack the Cambodian religion.
>
> (cited in Edwards 2007, 127)

Cultural heritage (and by extension archaeology), literature, social sciences, and religion were interlinked in the 20th-century Khmer Worldview. Khmer-language publications produced from the Royal Library and the Buddhist Institute reflect this holistic view of Khmer studies. Contemporary French colonial scholarship through academic institutions like the École Française d'Extrême-Orient viewed Khmer studies more narrowly: a point explored in the following section.

Institutional Knowledge Production in Khmer Studies

Although Cambodia's educational system began expanding beyond the traditional pagoda primary school system in the late 19th century, it took the country's independence in 1953 to see genuine educational reform. Whether developing a Western educational system was a colonial priority has been debated (Chandler 2008, 190–96; Osborne 2016, 147; cf. Clayton 1995), but French administrators were consistently unsuccessful in implementing an alternative educational system to the traditional pagoda curriculum that most Cambodians preferred, perhaps because French pedagogical goals lay in training future colonial subjects (Népote 1979, 768–76; see Kelly 1977 for Vietnamese parallel). Nonetheless, two academic institutions emerged by the early to mid-20th century and dominated knowledge production in Cambodia: the École Française d'Extrême-Orient and the Buddhist Institute with its associated branches, the Royal Library, and the Mores and Customs Commission (de Bernon 2010). Establishing these institutions both legitimised the French Indochinese colonial administration and its *mission civilisatrice* and it fostered a new generation of pro-French Khmer monks and middle-class students (e.g., Edwards 2007, 19–39; Cherry 2009, 88–90).

The EFEO was launched in 1901 to research, restore, and conserve Cambodian monuments and artefacts through the Angkor Conservation and the National Museum (previously Musée Albert Sarraut). Until WWII, this institution's aim was to study premodern or pre-Theravada Buddhist Cambodia to separate it from Thai influence (Hansen 2007, 109–47), an approach that is characterised as Orientalism (Clémentin-Ojha and Manguin 2007, 18–32). In so doing, the earlier EFEO scholars separated their work from contemporary ethnographers who were not affiliated with the EFEO like Adhémard Leclère and Étienne Aymonier (Peycam 2010, 165–66): although some ethnologists like Gabrielle Martel and Jean Boulbet worked through EFEO in the mid-20th century (Manguin 2010, 26, 28). EFEO and its scholars retained absolute, and later after 1950, preferential rights over archaeological research and publication in Cambodia through 1972.

The French colonial administration founded the Buddhist Institute with the Khmer monarchy in 1930 by re-organising the Royal Library. It remained under the direction of Suzanne Karpelès, an EFEO member, with support from Louis Finot and George Cœdès, through 1941 (Edwards 2004, 80; 2007, 186–90; Khing 2006, 55). Unlike EFEO, which was purely colonial in structure and personnel, Khmers viewed the Buddhist Institute as a fundamentally Khmer institution and centre for Khmer studies: a point made explicitly after Cambodia's independence in 1953 (Buddhist Institute 1963, 69–72). The Buddhist Institute provided a venue for a new stratum of educated Khmer and modernist Buddhist monks and reformers, including the venerables Chuon Nath and Huot Tat, to publish their research and voice opinions that helped shape 20th-century Cambodia's nation, religion, language, and state (e.g., Edwards 2004; Hansen 2007).

Khmer-authored publications from this period drew largely from traditional Khmer genres formed the field of Khmer studies, which encompasses the study of culture and civilisation, literature, folklore, history, and the traditional '*cpāp*' (e.g., Jenner 1976; Pou 1979). Khmer authors published on a range of topics in Khmer studies that drew primarily from folklore and chronicles, such as the background of a place or pagoda (e.g., Pich 1957; Chap 1958a; 1958b; Chuon 1963; Huot 1964), astrology (Um 1934), rituals (e.g., Commission des moeurs et coutumes 1958), and Buddhism in Cambodia (Pang 1960, 1963). Both Cambodian state and French colonial administrators viewed this corpus as potentially subversive. Tight state control over publication attempted to keep rebellions in check and neutralise resistance from traditionalist scholars, who favoured traditional palm leaf manuscripts over the printing press and eschewed vernacular language in Buddhist teaching (Edwards 2004). Few of these publications met Western academic standards but instead were designed as dedicatory pieces during major religious events like commemoration of a new *vihāra* (e.g., Chuon 1963; Pang 1952, 1999; Huot 1993).

Khmer scholars published some literature on the Angkorian World, including guides to the Angkor monuments (Huot 1928; Pang 1941). They referenced Angkor in other genres, including the *niras* (voyage) like 'Voyage to Angkor' (Suttantaprija Ind 1967) and short poems in *Kambuja Suriya* journal. One of the most popular novels, *Phka Srapon* (*Wilted Flower*) by Nou Hach (1989[1949]) depicts an event when the main female character, Vitheavy, visits Angkor on a remorque (bicycle trailer). They also translated some Angkorian scholarship by leading EFEO members (e.g., Cœdès, Finot, Goloubew, Marchal, Pelliot) into Khmer (e.g., Cœdès 1950, 1951; Marchal 1936; Gnok 1944). Khmer writers credited EFEO scholarship but also registered disagreement with French interpretations in a subtle manner. For instance, a translation of Cœdès' article on 'Littérature cambodgienne' (1931) omitted any negative connotations in relation to the Early Modern Period and Theravada Buddhism (Chigas 2000, 140–42).

Mass dissemination of this newly created Khmer scholarship was accomplished in print through the Buddhist Institute's bookstores, a province-focused book bus, and a radio program that Suzanne Karpelès (director, Buddhist Institute) developed (Edwards 2004, 75–78) which solidified a Khmer national identity throughout Cambodia and the Khmer-majority region of Southern Vietnam. Through the post-colonial 1960s, Chuon Nath brought attention to his movement to modernise Buddhism and Khmer literature on a weekly national radio program that he established in 1959 (Kong 1970, 26; D. Ly and Muan 2001, 209; Keo 2011). This program was an extension of the Khmer dictionary project (also under Chuon Nath's leadership) and structured as a dialogue between listeners who mailed in their questions and/or complaints about the 'correct way' to spell and use Khmer terminology. A few of these dialogues were salvaged from the National Radio archives in the 1980s and are available online (e.g., http://5000-years.org, see 5000 Years 2012).

Khmer-created film and music also promoted Angkorian heritage to the descendants of Angkor in post-colonial Cambodia, including Norodom Sihanouk's film projects. *Chhaya Loe Angkor* (*Shadow Over Angkor*, 1967) featured both ancient Angkor and modern Phnom Penh to showcase Sihanouk's Sangkum government, and *Prachea Kumar* (*Le petit prince*, 1968) featured the current monarch, Norodom Sihamoni, inhabiting Angkor as his royal home. These widely shown films provided opportunities for rural Cambodians to see images of Angkor for the first time. At the same time, the *nireas* genre (see Edwards 2023, this volume) published through the Buddhist Institute also influenced the popular music of the 1960s and 1970s, for example, *Romduol Angkor* (*The Romduol Flower of Angkor*), *Bopha Moha Angkor* (*Flower of Angkor*) by Sinn Sisamouth, and *Anussavriy Angkor* (Angkor Souvenir) by Duch Kimhak and Pen Ron. Iconic Angkor was also codified in Sangkum state construction projects in the 1960s, including the Vann Molyvann-designed Independence Monument and Olympic Stadium, both of which drew on the Angkor Period to promote national pride, identity, and continuity (D. Ly and Muan 2001, 1–62; Ross and Collins 2006; Ross 2015). The foregoing examples illustrate how Khmer-produced literature (including folktales and fantasies featuring Angkor), media, and monuments increasingly promoted Angkor as a living ritual space, a place of past greatness, and the source of national identity.

Archaeology as Esoteric Knowledge: EFEO Dominance and Orientalism in Khmer Studies

Most EFEO scholarship on the Angkor Period was imbued with some variant of Orientalism (following Clémentin-Ojha and Manguin 2007, 18–32; Peycam 2010, 158–59), which also guided Angkor conservation and park enhancement projects. Erasing Theravada Buddhism from

Angkor (which involved removing myriad statues and, in some cases, dismantling structures) created a break between the preceding Angkorian Hinduism and Mahāyāna Buddhism, a cause for Angkor's collapse, and the inferior Thai-derived Theravada Buddhism of contemporary Cambodia (Cœdès 1931). EFEO conservators removed the seated Buddha of Phnom Bakheng and the earthen platform extension of Phimeanakas, for example, to show the 'original' Hindu structure (Marchal 1916; Boisselier and Griswold 1972; Chea 2018, 41). Even Henri Marchal strongly advocated this approach during his tenure as conservator of the Angkor monuments, in spite of his pioneering studies of Theravada Buddhism in Angkor (e.g., Marchal 1918, 1922, 1951) (Figure 3.1).

Such intrusive practices, copying contemporary conservation methods in Europe (Warrack 2011, 221–22), created mistrust between EFEO and the local Khmer public. So did the lack of public outreach. Writings by Okñā Suttanta Prījā Ind, who accompanied king Sisowath to Angkor in 1909 (1967, 87; see Edwards 2023, this volume), echoed the public perception that EFEO conservators disliked Buddhism and had looting, rather than preservation, as their ultimate goal. This suspicion was long lived and was occasionally reinforced by subsequent conservators such as Bernard-Philippe Groslier, who observed that the colossal sandstone Buddha of Preah Ngok, which the Khmer Rouge destroyed, was 'artistically not important' because of its Post-Angkorian date (White and Garrett 1982, 584 on the looting perception see Abbe 2021). Ironically, this image is among several works that Groslier (1985) dated to the 16th century but which are now associated with the 13th–15th centuries and the rise of Theravada Buddhism (Leroy et al. 2015; Polkinghorne et al. 2018; Tun 2015).

Figure 3.1 Henri Marchal, a pioneer of the anastylosis method in Angkor, with his Khmer assistant, Chan, and workmen at Banteay Srei temple restoration in 1934.

Source: (EFEO Photo Library MarH0174).

Whether EFEO explicitly sought to emphasise rupture between the Angkor and Modern Khmer Periods, French members focused on Angkor and Khmer scholars were relegated to research on Post-Angkorian and contemporary Cambodia; most of whom worked in the Buddhist Institute. Georges Cœdès assigned the Middle Khmer epigraphic scholarship to Khmer scholar Krassem. Working from the Buddhist Institute in 1935–1936 (Krassem 1984), his work laid the foundation for Pou Saveros' subsequent career of exemplary research (e.g., Lewitz 1972; Pou 1977). The Buddhist Institute also published most Khmer-language scholarship for decades. Its *Kambuja Suriya* journal included articles examining Buddhism, Khmer literature, and the construction of Khmer national identity (Pang 1960; Ly 1960, 1965; Leang 1967). Some Khmer scholars (e.g., Pang 1970; Ly 1973, 1; Tran 1973a, 1a-d) explicitly linked Khmer culture to India's high culture and Buddhist traditions in order to distinguish a pure Khmer race from Thai and Vietnamese neighbours. This overtly nationalist agenda was supported by the (1970–75) Khmer Republic government, particularly through the Khmer-Mon Institute (Peycam 2011, 22).

The Buddhist Institute was also a key player in national shifts toward 'Khmerization'—the use of Khmer, not French, as the medium of instruction (Khin 1999)—during the Sangkum era under Norodom Sihanouk (1953–70). This included mass publication and broad distribution of Khmer studies and language media and their incorporation into the national K–12 curriculum beginning in 1968. The Buddhist Institute's Phnom Penh-based Pali School and its associated Buddhist monk scholars were instrumental. Ly Theam Teng's (1960) volume on Khmer literature (published by Seng Nguon Huot Bookstore), his translation of Zhou Daguan from Chinese sources (Ly 1973), and Tran Ngea's (1973a, 1973b) two-volume Khmer history (published by Moahaleap Printing House) were read widely. Other Institute members, like Gnok Them, Leang Hap An, and Pang Khat, taught courses at the Royal University of Phnom Penh right up until 1975 (Khing 2010). Khmer performing artists also reached ever-expanding audiences through new media, from transistor radios and vinyl records to celluloid film (Fergusson and Masson 1997, 98–105; D. Ly and Muan 2001; Clayton 2005). King Sihanouk's efforts to bring education to the masses consumed up to 20% of the annual GDP and produced a new generation of literate Cambodians by the 1960s (Fergusson and Masson 1997, 99). His program also established the Royal University of Fine Arts in 1965 to provide educational opportunities in Khmer archaeology and art history through its Faculty of Archaeology, a topic to which the next section turns.

Cambodian Archaeologies

Cambodian archaeology was an esoteric discipline closely associated with the EFEO from its founding in 1901 and focused on the ancient Angkor Period. With the Buddhist Institute's 1930 inauguration came an expansion in the range of topics associated with Khmer studies by Khmer scholars, but most French EFEO scholars continued their narrowly archaeological research on Angkor. Cambodian archaeology's origins and development are thus inextricably linked to EFEO's foundation and the EFEO-linked research and conservation institutions that emerged in its wake: Angkor Conservation (1907), the National Museum (previously the Musée Albert Sarraut, 1920), and the École des Beaux Arts (1917): the last two established by Georges Groslier. Motivated like his Orientalist peers to revive the 'classical' Angkorian art, his approach excluded Post-Angkorian and modern art from the school curriculum (Muan 2001). Cambodia's independence in 1953, however, did not shift responsibility for teaching and preserving cultural heritage from the EFEO to a Khmer institution. French EFEO members like Bernard-Philippe Groslier and Madeleine Giteau still oversaw operations, but now Cambodia—not France—paid most of the costs (Clémentin-Ojha and Manguin 2007, 88).

Archaeological instruction for Cambodians began during this post-colonial era of higher educational reform under then-prince/head of state Norodom Sihanouk, using the French system as its model (Fergusson and Masson 1997). In 1965, the prince tasked the creation of the Royal University of Fine Arts (hereafter RUFA), to architect Vann Molyvann, who became its first rector. Drawing inspiration from his alma mater, the prestigious École nationale supérieure des beaux arts in Paris, Vann Molyvann consolidated the École des beaux arts and the National Museum to form RUFA, with its Faculties of Archaeology, Architecture and Urbanism, Choreographic Arts, Music, and Plastic Arts (Ly and Muan 2001, 327–28; Reyum 2001; Vann 2001). Chea Tay Seng, the first Khmer art historian to graduate from the École du Louvre in Paris, was designated as the first dean of archaeology (Peycam 2011, 21–23). RUFA's mission was to train the next generation of Cambodian archaeologists and conservators to assume the roles and responsibilities that EFEO members had fulfilled for more than 50 years at Angkor and elsewhere across the country.

Nationwide educational reform at this time included Khmer as the medium of instruction, but RUFA courses were taught entirely in French by both French and some Khmer instructors, many of whom were conducting field research in Cambodia (e.g., Roland and Cécile Mourer, André Bareau, Jean Éllul, Albert Le Bonheur, Tep Im). Heritage professionals like Bernard-Philippe Groslier, Madeleine Giteau, and Claude Jacques provided occasional lectures and field trips for RUFA students. Like the early colonial insistence on French in the K–12 schools that produced widespread resistance to colonial schools (Clayton 1995), RUFA's requirement that Khmer students pass rigorous French-language examinations as part of their college training hindered success. This five-year program graduated only 25% of its annual cohort because so few students passed the examinations, producing only 50–70 archaeologists by 1975. Many RUFA dropouts joined the military on the cusp of the Third Indochina War (Fergusson and Masson 1997, 102, 107; Chuch 2014; Ang 2000, 1; 2021; Preap 2021, 35).

Yet RUFA's archaeology program produced significant success in its graduates. Graduate Pich Keo was recruited to work at the Angkor Conservation with Groslier and later became the first Khmer director of that institution after Groslier left Angkor in 1972. More than ten graduates from the Faculty of Archaeology at RUFA earned scholarships to study abroad, with some participating in UNESCO-funded training programs in Rome (including Chuch Phoeurn and Son Soubert). Other RUFA graduates pursued MAs and PhDs in archaeology, art history, and anthropology, including Kuoch Haksrea (1976), Ang Choulean (1986), Lan Sunnary, and Sunseng Sunkimmeng. Ponn Chhavann and four other archaeologists participated in an international training program provided by the University of Pennsylvania Museum/Thai Fine Arts Department Ban Chiang project in 1974–1975 (Gorman and Charoenwongsa 1976, 25).

Khmer-led Cambodian archaeology progressed slowly, and its Khmer-led scholarship struggled to make a scholarly impact. As Khmer-language scholarship on Khmer studies increased its readership from the late 1960s to 1975, work published in Khmer and French by RUFA's young archaeologists in the *Annales de l'université royale des beaux arts* and the *Bulletin des étudiants de la faculté d'archéologie* (Ang 2000, 2) never achieved the prestige or readership of work appearing in EFEO publications or the Buddhist Institute's *Kambuja Suriya* journal. The explicitly non-partisan and non-nationalist approach of RUFA scholarship, drawing from academic sources and intended for a specialist audience (Editorial Board 1973, 2; Ang 2021), contrasted sharply with the overtly political work of mainstream scholars at the Buddhist Institute and elsewhere. RUFA's archaeological influence was felt throughout the region. In the early 1970s, RUFA was to house the ASEAN Centre for Applied Research in Archaeology and Fine Arts (ARCAFA), which ultimately was established in Bangkok as the Southeast Asian Regional Centre for Archaeology and Fine Arts (SEAMEO SPAFA) (Pring 2001, 342).

Significant scholarship was produced during the Khmer Republic's 1970–75 period (see review in Peycam 2020, 39–43), but whether nationalist and scientific avenues of knowledge production could have converged in Khmer studies will never be known. Cambodia's Khmer Rouge era effectively put an end to both by 1975 and by 1979 had systematically eliminated all academic institutions and most of their scholars, including Huot Tat and Pang Khat (de Bernon 2010, 32). From 1975 to January 7, 1979, the Khmer Rouge destroyed or drove most of Cambodia's educated population out the country. An estimated 75–80% of higher education teachers and graduates, and 67% of primary and secondary students, vanished or emigrated abroad during the Khmer Rouge Period. By the collapse of the Khmer Rouge regime in 1979, only around 300 qualified professionals in any discipline remained in Cambodia (Duggan 1996, 365).

Post-Khmer Rouge Reincarnation of Khmer Studies

France sheltered the only multidisciplinary Khmer studies program that operated during the 1975–79 period. Centre of Documentation, Research on Khmer Civilization (CEDORECK) was established in 1977 and functioned until 1991 (Peycam 2011, 23–28; 2020, 50–56). Back in their home country, the Pol Pot–era civil war ushered in a protracted hiatus in Khmer studies until Cambodians began to rebuild their country in the 1980s and early 1990s.

Cambodia's post-1979 higher education depended on external funding from Vietnam, the USSR, and other socialist blocs and non-aligned movement countries (Peycam 2020, 66–68). Meeting crucial human resource needs required Cambodia to reopen a series of higher educational institutions in 1979, including the Faculty of Medicine, School of Agronomy, Institute of Technology, and Tuk Thla Vocational School (Kiernan 1982, 180). The Royal University of Phnom Penh (RUPP) opened a few years later and concentrated on teacher training to staff public schools across the country (Duggan 1997, 8). The first Vietnamese teachers recruited to teach at RUPP used French, but the language of instruction shifted to Vietnamese within a few years, and Russian teachers and engineers taught at the Institute of Technology in Russian (Tomasi 2000, 159). Efforts to use Khmer language and textbooks (i.e., Khmerisation) in education finally accelerated in the 1980s (Kiernan 1982, 180), since so few Khmers could use any foreign language, let alone Vietnamese or Russian.

Even as the country's educational infrastructure returned to life, Cambodia's fragmented higher education created a gulf between RUPP and RUFA. RUPP is housed in the Ministry of Education, while RUFA falls within the Ministry of Culture and Fine Arts (MoCFA). Other problems include the lack of coordination between international aid organisations (Duggan 1997) and a tiny national budget for higher education that barely rises above 10% of the total annual government expenditures (http://uis.unesco.org/en/country/kh). In today's market, this current budget is only 50% of the level of funding that the 1953–1970 Sangkum government allocated to education. It is within this national context that the post-Khmer Rouge RUFA, discussed in the next section, evolved from its reopening in 1989.

Archaeological Training: RUFA and Partner Institutions

Only three RUFA archaeology alumni from the 1970s survived the Khmer Rouge Period to participate in post-conflict rebuilding in 1979, when archaeological heritage training began to take various forms (see review in Stark and Heng 2017). Ouk Chea directed the National Museum after its 1979 re-opening, Chuch Phoeurn directed the new Palace Museum, and Pich Keo briefly returned to head Angkor Conservation (where he had worked before 1975) before being transferred to head the National Museum. Both India and the USSR provided short training courses in archaeology and conservation to a few Cambodians (Kiernan 1982, 180; White and Garrett 1982, 585). Ang Choulean returned to Cambodia from France and helped revive the Faculty of Archaeology in 1989 (Ang 2019; Chuch 2021). Whereas the mission of RUFA pre-1975 was explicitly to train the next generation of heritage managers, post-1979 RUFA faculty faced new challenges, including neglected archaeological sites being consumed by vegetation and rampant looting. Compared to the late 19th–early 20th centuries, the situation of heritage in post-conflict Cambodia was dire (see a description of Angkor in 1981 by White and Garrett 1982; compared to early descriptions by Delaporte 1880; Drège Bernon and Josso 2003, 15–16).

RUFA suffered chronic staff and resource shortages (textbooks, laboratories, and field equipment), and most Khmer professors resorted to teaching what they had memorised as students. Similar to the pre-conflict RUFA, the curriculum consisted of a five-year fine arts program focused on Khmer art history which concentrated on the studies of ancient temples, stylistic evolution, Indian and Southeast Asian art history, the history of Cambodia, ethnology, linguistics, and epigraphy. Students were required to complete a thesis based on research (mémoire) to graduate with a degree in archaeology. The faculty was in dire need of international assistance to provide capacity-building for its new students, and this issue was raised at international conferences on Angkor organised by UNESCO in Bangkok in 1990 and in Paris in 1991 (Ishizawa 1992).

International assistance began to arrive in 1990, including a team of French specialists from the Musée Guimet led by Albert Le Bonheur, a Japanese team from the Sophia University Mission led by Yoshiaki Ishizawa, and post-doctoral fellow Judy Ledgerwood (1992, USA). From 1992–2000, UNESCO/TOYOTA launched its training program at RUFA and sought to replicate the pre-Khmer Rouge archaeology curriculum. UNESCO-funded international experts taught courses at RUFA in English, French, or Japanese, with local Khmer teaching assistants serving largely as translators. The Australian Centre for Education and APSO (Ireland) provided English language training, and the Centre Culturel Français provided French language training. The University of Tübingen ran a multi-year training program at RUFA, led by Gerd Albrecht (Chuch 2021).

Field-based archaeological training and short-term training abroad for RUFA students and graduates were supported by multiple institutions, including the EFEO, Sophia University, Japanese Government Team for Safeguarding Angkor, Waseda University, the University of Hawai'i at Mānoa, and the Nara National Research Institute for Cultural Properties (e.g., Endo 1992, 126; JSA 1994, 252–75; Ishizawa 1996, 213–15; Griffin Ledgerwood and Chuch 1999; Ang 2000, 2–3; Stark and Griffin 2004; Nara 2012, 12; Preap 2021). The Center for Khmer Studies (CKS), a non-profit organisation founded in 1999, also provided support for Cambodian participation in foreign archaeological projects and cultural heritage management training at RUFA (Peycam 2020, 91–119).

By the mid-2000s, Cambodia's own trained heritage professionals also began training Khmer students in archaeology and field techniques. Cambodian governmental organisations like APSARA and the Royal Academy of Cambodia (and also the non-governmental Heritage Watch) have provided short-term field training programs at their respective research localities. Since 2012, RUFA has cooperated with Institut National des Langues et Civilizations Orientales (INALCO) to create the Francophone *Manusastra* Project, which provides training in archaeology at the MA and PhD level at RUFA and/or in France (Preap 2021, 37).

From 1989 to 2020, more than 700 students graduated from the Royal University of Fine Arts' Faculty of Archaeology, and many have pursued postgraduate training abroad. These include at least seven MAs and seven PhDs from France (INALCO, Université de Toulouse Jean

Jaurès-Toulouse 2, Université Paris 3-Sorbonne Nouvelle, Université Nanterre), six PhDs and four MAs from Japan (Sophia University, Osaka Ohtani University, Tokyo Fine Arts University, Waseda University), and two PhDs from the United States (University of Hawai'i at Mānoa). Nearly 30 more Khmers have obtained terminal MA degrees in archaeology, art history, or anthropology: two from the United States (Northern Illinois University), two from Germany (University of Tübingen), one from the United Kingdom (University of Surrey; but see subsequently), and one from Canada (University of Western Ontario). Approximately 15 RUFA staff and students received their MAs or PhDs under the 2002 UNESCO institutional capacity-building project in a joint program between RUFA and the Royal Academy of Cambodia (RAC).

Since the inception of its Alphawood funding scheme in 2014, the United Kingdom's School of Oriental and African Studies (SOAS) Southeast Asian Art and Archaeology Program has dominated post-graduate training in Cambodian art and archaeology. By the time of this volume's publication, the SOAS Southeast Asian Art and Archaeology program had graduated 11 Khmers with post-graduate diplomas and 22 Khmers with MA degrees, and two Khmers are PhD candidates. Six Cambodian students are currently enrolled in SOAS postgraduate programs. These programs have produced talented professionals, but lack of adequate funding has constrained RUFA's efforts at sustainable local capacity-building. Until and unless Cambodia invests more resources in supporting its archaeology faculty and heritage managers, talented RUFA archaeology graduates will continue to leave the field—and sometimes the country—to pursue other, more lucrative professions. This 'archaeology brain drain' has affected the nature of contemporary knowledge production and diminished the role of Cambodian scholarship on the Angkorian World.

Post-Khmer Rouge Knowledge Production: Research and Publication

Khmers have long valued and written about their heritage, including the Angkorian World despite structural challenges, the colonial burden, and a more recent history of geopolitical conflict. Most RUFA archaeology graduates who remain in the field, like their peers elsewhere globally, work in heritage management, not academia, and find few opportunities to publish. Archaeology students from RUFA, with support from the non-profit (and now-defunct) Reyum organisation, briefly revived the Archaeology Students' Bulletin in the 2000s. The new non-profit Yosothor for Khmer Culture and its cultural information network, KhmeRenaissance (www.yosothor.org), provide the best outlets for Khmer-language publication online and in print for archaeological research and outreach.

Despite intellectual bridging by Khmer scholars like Pou Saveros and Long Seam (whose students taught epigraphy at both RUFA and RUPP), a deep divide remains between the two universities. RUPP scholars, like their predecessors, publish their work in their internal bulletin, through personally and privately funded print runs, and in *Kambuja Suriya* (e.g., Vong 2010, 2011). The latter was revived in 1994 (Chhon 1994) and, spearheaded by Long Seam, continues its publication in traditional Khmer studies, for example, Buddhism, folklore, culture, translation of old French articles, and epigraphy (e.g., Long Seam 1997; and recently, Chhom 2019; Hun 2019; Vong 2019). Khmer-language publications on archaeology are extremely rare, particularly primary sources like site reports and regional archaeological syntheses (see, for example, Thuy 2020).

Scholarly production of publications on Khmer archaeology remains small relative to the growing number of trained Khmer archaeologists. Nonetheless, the recent advent of online platforms like Wordpress, Facebook, and Khmer newspapers has provided alternative venues for writers from RUFA and RUPP to engage with a public readership. It is fair to say that, despite the continuing low literacy rates and the limited training and resources available for those seeking to publish (Jarvis 2006), online media accommodates a mass public outreach on Khmer studies comparable to that facilitated by radio and movies in the pre-Khmer Rouge Period (Heng et al. 2020).

We would argue, therefore, that despite facing a series of political upheavals and tragedies, Cambodians are actively curating their heritage and contributing to knowledge production in the domain of Khmer studies. Yet their work is rarely known or recognised in international scholarship in Cambodia—and thus we turn our attention to the problem of 'invisible Cambodians'. Institutional weakness in Cambodian higher education is clearly one factor. But given Cambodia's long and intimate relationship with French colonial interventions in Angkorian heritage, we must in turn recognise a longstanding lack of institutional commitment, since the beginning of the Colonial Period in the 19th century, to systematically training Cambodian people in the study of their past. We also acknowledge several key French scholars who were exceptions to this pattern and were instrumental in capacity-building and knowledge production.

Khmer assistants travelled with the renowned colonial scholar Étienne Aymonier across Cambodia, Laos, and Thailand in the 1880s, collecting ethnographic and archaeological data and producing inscription rubbings. Aymonier heartily praised their work and competence in his publications (e.g., Aymonier 1895, 1901); some even recorded their journeys in their own inscriptions in Angkor (Antelme 2014; Guérin and Chhom 2014; Weber 2014). One of the assistants was a prominent figure who held important government offices, owing largely to his noble family and French intervention (Guérin 2017), but little is known about his archaeological work. Many publications by Adhémard Leclère during the late 1800s/early 1900s were also based on contemporary Khmer writers whose works are preserved at the Musée des Beaux-Arts et de la Dentelle in Leclère's hometown of Alançon (France). All these Khmer researchers of the 19th century are largely invisible within the historical record.

The establishment of EFEO in 1901 employed many Khmers in archaeological and conservation work but could have produced more opportunities for meaningful Khmer involvement like Khmer-authored publications. To be clear, the EFEO was a heritage organisation whose primary goal was conservation, not educating local and descendant communities. EFEO helped resuscitate Cambodia's remarkable heritage for more than a century and remains important. Yet the EFEO, despite its 'École' designation, was never a school for Khmer archaeologists and conservators. Before 1975, the EFEO primarily trained Khmers through Angkor Conservation as technical assistants for restoration and excavation/clearance activities. Some of these individuals were exceptionally talented and held the status of 'caporal' (foreman/site manager): They managed field logistics, survey, and mapping and directed excavations (Figure 3.2). For instance, the Caporal Suon oversaw the excavation of Angkor Wat's central tower in 1934–35 under the supervision of Henri Marchal and Georges Trouvé (Conservation d'Angkor and EFEO 1908, 1a, 139–46). Hired from the surrounding communities in Angkor, these invisible workmen provided the foundation for the success of EFEO scholars in research and conservation. Trained Khmers produced sketches and plans of temples and of the broader temple complex to assist with conservation and restoration; one of them, was Mar Bo, who worked with Bernard-Philippe Groslier (1985, 24), published a tourist guide for Angkor (Mar 1969).

The Royal Library/Buddhist Institute under its first director, Suzanne Karpelès, was a rare venue in which Cambodian scholars were visible since its creation in 1925. The library's mission was to support publication by its Cambodian staff and students of the Pali School (Hansen 2007, 144). André Bareau, a renowned Buddhologist, briefly taught at RUFA in the late 1960s

Figure 3.2 Henri Marchal and an unnamed Khmer assistant at the restoration of Banteay Srei (Damdek) in 1952.

Source: (EFEO Photo Library: CAM01679)

and encouraged archaeology students to publish their first articles in the *Bulletin de l'École française d'Extrême-Orient* (BEFEO) (Faculté Royale d'Archéologie de Phnom Penh and Bareau 1969). Two of these students, Lan Sunnary and Sunseng Sunkimeng, continued to publish their research in other journals (e.g., Lan 1972, 2008; Fabricius and Lan 2003; Sunseng 1977). It was not until the 1970s that extensive publication activity by a maverick Khmer female researcher, Pou Saveros, appeared in BEFEO with support from her mentor, Jean Filliozat, who was also the EFEO's director at that time (Pou 1984, 5).

Language challenges continue to hinder the visibility of Khmer scholars today. Publishing through EFEO requires technical competence in French, and publishing for a more global audience requires linguistic competence in English. Khmer-language publications remain largely restricted to the Buddhist Institute and Cambodia's higher educational institutions. Most Khmer scholars do not publish in Western languages, and most Western scholars do not read and speak

Khmer. Limited moral and structural support from both within and outside Cambodia, the fragmented and poorly funded higher education system in-country, and disparate international collaborations often segregated by nationality and institution have all thus contributed to the problem of 'invisible Cambodians'.

The tide has begun to turn in the last two decades as increased numbers of Cambodian scholars have published in international venues on prehistory (e.g., Ly 2001, 2002; Heng 2008; Song 2010; Voeun 2013; Heng et al. 2016), historical archaeology (e.g., Chhan 2000; Ea 2005, 2013; Ea et al. 2008; Heng 2012, 2016; Chhay et al. 2013; Nhim 2019a; Chhay et al. 2020), history (Nhim 2009, 2014), cultural anthropology (e.g., Ang 1986, 1997, 2020; Hang 2004; Phlong 2004; Kim 2011), religion (e.g., Ang 1998, 2007; Siyonn 2005, 2006), or heritage and conservation (e.g., Im 2019; Chan 2011; Chhay 2011; Phon 2011; Song 2011; Seng 2012; Heng and Phon 2017; Nhim 2019b; Heng et al. 2020). These publications are the results of both individual and international collaborative projects that help promote heritage management and integrate Cambodia's research into the regional and global contexts. For example, Voeun Vuthy's work on fish and animal bones from both modern and archaeological contexts remains the standard for zooarchaeology in Cambodia and Southeast Asia (e.g., Voeun and Driesch 2006). Phon Kaseka's long-term research at archaeological sites around Phnom Penh, including Cheung Ek and Sre Ampil, contributes to the documentation of ceramics kilns outside Angkor and Pre-Angkorian and Angkorian archaeological sites located within reach of the rapid urban development that saw many archaeological sites vanished without proper documentation. Heng Sophady's collaborative research with the University of Tübingen in eastern Cambodia and with the French Muséum national d'Histoire naturelle at Laang Spean has continued to shed light on Cambodia's deep history from the Paleolithic to Neolithic Periods. Most of these publications are made possible with assistance from international colleagues and mentors. Nonetheless, there is still a bifurcation with Khmer-language publications that does not materialise in western languages and vice versa because of some structural challenges.

Structural Challenges to Making Khmers Visible in Angkorian Archaeology

Multiple structural challenges facing Cambodian researchers have contributed to the lack of meaningful collaboration in most research on the Angkorian World. The fact that academic and research institutions in Cambodia are government institutions places additional pressure on their employees, who are both teachers or researchers and administrators. Central among these governmental institutions are the APSARA National Authority and MoCFA, which are in dire need of well-trained personnel, both from RUFA and abroad, to rehabilitate their human resources decimated by the Khmer Rouge. To satisfy the state bureaucratic nature, productivity is measured by the time spent doing manual labour like teaching, working in the field, or administrative duties (e.g., meeting, paperwork, etc.). Staff are often assigned to various internal or collaborating research projects. The collective nature of a bureaucratic office, unlike the well-sourced academic institutions abroad that encourage individual publication, produces reports or publications that can be described as 'white papers' or policy documents. This practice pressures writer(s) to label the office as the author, implying that the work belongs to everyone in the office, particularly the high-ranking officers in charge. Individual publication is sometimes discouraged, as writing time for such publication is considered a personal matter. Local researchers often rely on public interviews (newspaper, radio, or TV) to publicise their work rather than publishing in a peer-reviewed academic journal that requires both language proficiency and time commitment.

Differing research agendas between Cambodian and international researchers pose another structural challenge. Unlike the generalising and social science-driven paradigms that shape many Western archaeological research programs, archaeologists in Southeast Asia's post-colonial countries often prioritise nation-building over strictly academic concerns (Trigger and Glover 1981; Shoocondej 2007). In Cambodia, a nationalist agenda of history and culture championed by the Buddhist Institute has penetrated the public education system since the 1960s. Archaeological research in Cambodia, despite being immersed in a comparative and generalising curriculum, still pursues the same agenda to communicate with the general public and to stay relevant. The different agendas between local and international researchers compounded by the language barriers discourage any meaningful collaborative engagement (Glover 2004, 68). Furthermore, underfunded public institutions that lack infrastructural support, like laboratory and equipment for data processing and analysis, as well as the limited language proficiency for local researchers to acquire international grants, also hinder meaningful Khmer-led research projects. The lower wage of c. USD $293–$325 per month (Tith 2022) is barely enough to afford communal meals at home, not to mention paying for food and supplies during fieldwork. Local researchers have relied on collaborative international projects for access to funding, an up-to-date research paradigm, methodology, equipment, and other benefits.

It is ethical that international collaborators be aware of these structural problems facing their Cambodian counterparts and take efforts to create equal opportunities for their local collaborators and the communities with whom they work. These issues are not just Cambodia's problems; international collaborations under these circumstances exacerbate the inequality between rich and poor countries that privilege international collaborators. There is no ready systematic solution to these issues that at the same time avoids repeating the scope of *mission civilisatrice* implemented in the 20th century (Heng et al. 2020). Capacity building for the local collaborators, students, and community members is a remedy to some of these structural issues and should be a required component of international research in Cambodia (Stark and Heng 2017). Another resolution should begin with the involvement of the Cambodian collaborators with the *chaine opératoire* of a research project from conceptualising to securing funding and to fieldwork, data analysis, and publication of the results. Such project would incorporate the local collaborator's or project co-director's research questions into the project agendas and include analysis and writing time built in to the research designs that allow the Cambodian contributor to take leave, work on data analysis, and co-author publications.

Increasing numbers of international collaborative projects including, but not limited to, the Lower Mekong Archaeological Project (LOMAP), Greater Angkor Project (GAP), and Dharma project (EFEO), have begun to implement many of these solutions. Such deep involvement takes a long-term commitment, and provides a hands-on learning experience for Cambodian researchers hoping to garner international funding and collaboration for their projects. Furthermore, the public engagement aspect of such research through capacity building will build a long-lasting relationship and forge shared research interest with the local communities.

Conclusion

The colonial period separation of ancient and modern Khmer studies that gave rise to the Royal Library/Buddhist Institute and EFEO laid an enduring foundation for a divide between Khmer-based research traditions on the one hand and archaeology/antiquity-focused research dominated by non-Cambodians on the other hand. The systematic production of knowledge in the domain of Khmer studies by the Royal Library/Buddhist Institute helped to produce and institutionalise the gap between the Modern and Angkor Periods and—intentionally or unintentionally—reinforced the notion of Khmer identity that underpins nationalism in this domain of research today. The EFEO and its scholars, by contrast, largely monopolised research on Cambodian heritage and archaeology, and few Khmers received comprehensive academic training in these fields even after the Colonial Period ended in 1953.

Despite these obstacles, Cambodians have actively researched and promoted their heritage through a variety of institutions and media. RUFA's development as a modern academic institution was halted by the Third Indochina War and subsequent Khmer Rouge Period, in which most of RUFA's human resources were exterminated. The university's revival after 1989 was hampered by a host of challenges, from neglected temples to rampant vandalism. These challenges, as well as underfunding, prevented RUFA from impacting mainstream education and scholarship until rather recently. Now, however, initiatives such as Yosothor and mass media platforms like Facebook and Wordpress bring locally produced knowledge about Cambodian archaeology and heritage to a much broader audience.

'Invisible Cambodians' in Cambodia's archaeological and heritage management Worlds are a lasting and problematic legacy of French colonial rule. Yet Khmers have actively contributed to heritage management and knowledge production through their service at the Angkor Conservation and their publications in other venues. Today, limited internal and external structural and moral support, lack of training, narrow opportunities to work in the heritage sector, and underdeveloped language skills (on the part of both Cambodian and international scholars) all contribute to the problem of 'invisible Cambodians.' More meaningful, genuine, and cohesive collaborations between international teams and Cambodian counterparts are required to overcome this problem and to narrow the divide between Cambodian and international scholars. Things have begun to turn in the right direction, albeit slowly, over the past decade as an increasing number of Cambodian scholars have published their work in various international venues in English or French. Increasing international collaboration has also involved more Cambodian counterparts in research designs.

In the year 802 CE, the official start date of Angkor, the Khmer king Jayavarman II performed the magic ritual of *kamrateṅ jagat ta rāja/devarāja* to prevent Cambodia from living under the yoke of '*Javā*', a foreign entity, and protect its spiritual power. One might argue that the 16th–19th century Khmer-led restorations of Angkor and the recent post-conflict rebuilding efforts extend and reflect this magic spell. The thin silver lining of foreign-dominated Angkorian studies and conservation is the clear historical value of this work, which contributes to our understanding of the Khmer past. Yet many more Khmers must become visible in this domain, through training and mentorship, to create a future in which Cambodians control their own heritage.

References

5000 Years, 2012. Collection of Samdech Chuon Nath's lectures broadcast on the national radio in the 1960s. June 2012. https://5000-years.org/kh/albums/29 [accessed 25 Jun 2021].

Abbe, G., 2021. The seeing of Khmer artefacts during the colonial era: questioning the perception of Khmer heritage through a study of traded Khmer art pieces (1920s–1940s). In *Returning Southeast Asia's Past: Objects, Museums, and Restitution*, eds. L. Tythacott and P. Ardiyansyah. Singapore: NUS Press, 41–61.

Ang, C., 1986. *Les êtres surnaturels dans la religion populaire Khmère*. Paris: CEDORECK.

Ang, C., 1997. Les manuscrits khmers, survol thématique. *Kambodschanische Kultur* 5, 53–62.

Ang, C., 1998. Collective memory in ancient Cambodia with reference to Jayavarman II, in *Southeast Asian Archaeology 1996. Proceedings of the 6th International Conference of the European Association of Southeast Asian Archaeologists*, eds. M.J. Klokke & T. de Brujin. Leiden: Centre for Southeast Asian Studies, University of Hull, 117–22.

Ang, C., 2000. The Faculty of Archaeology: from the beginning to 1996 https://community.adobe.com/t5/illustrator-discussions/how-to-enable-khmer-font/m-p/12792679. *Bulletin of the Students of the Department of Archaeology* 1, 1–5.

Ang, C., 2007. In the beginning was the Bayon, in *Bayon: New Perspectives*, ed. J. Clark. Bangkok: River Books Press, 362–77.

Ang, C., 2019. An interview with Ang Choulean at Prek Eng, Phnom Penh. Interview by Daravuth Ly.

Ang, C., 2020. *Cuisine Rurale d'Angkor: Essai de Sociologie Culinaire (អាហារនៅជនបទអង្គរ)*. Phnom Penh: Yasothor.

Ang, C., 2021. A short conversation with Professor Ang Choulean on a history of Cambodia's Faculty of Archaeology. Interview by Sotheavin Nhim. Phone interview.

Antelme, M., 2014. Les estampeurs khmers d'Aymonier et leur production épigraphique connue (K, 1089.1, K., 1089.2, K., 1134, K., 1135, K., 1136 et K, 1137). *Bulletin de l'École française d'Extrême-Orient* 100(1), 231–52.

Aymonier, É., 1895a. *Voyage dans le Laos*, vol. 2. Paris: Ernest Leroux.

Aymonier, É., 1901. *Le Cambodge: Les Provinces Siamoises*, vol. 2. Paris: Ernest Leroux.

Ayres, D.M., 2000. Tradition, modernity, and the development of education in Cambodia. *Comparative Education Review* 44(4), 440–63.

de Bernon, O., 2010. Le rôle de l'École française d'Extrême-Orient dans la fondation des institutions savantes du Cambodge, in *Archéologues à Angkor*, ed. B. Dagens. Paris: Musée Editions, 29–32.

Boisselier, J. & A.B. Griswold, 1972. Henri Marchal 1876–1970. *Artibus Asiae* 34(1), 97–101.

Buddhist Institute, 1963. *Centres d'études bouddhiques au Cambodge/Centers of Buddhist Studies in Cambodia.* Phnom Penh: Buddhist Institute.

Byrne, D., 1995. Buddhist Stupa and Thai social practice. *World Archaeology* 27(2), 266–81.

Carter, A.K., P. Heng, S. Heng & K. Phon, 2014. Archaeology in post-Khmer Rouge Cambodia, in *Encyclopedia of Global Archaeology*, ed. C. Smith. New York: Springer, 6059–65.

Chan, S., 2011. Cultural resource management in Phnom Sruk: potential and problems, in *Rethinking Cultural Resource Management in Southeast Asia: Preservation, Development, and Neglect*, eds. J.N. Miksic, G.Y. Goh & S. O'Connor. London and New York: Anthem Press, 117–22.

Chandler, D.P., 2008. *A History of Cambodia*, 4th ed. Boulder, CO: Westview Press.

Chap, P., 1958a. A history of Maha Attharasa (ប្រវត្តិមហាអដ្ឋារស). *Kambuja Suriya* 30(6), 553–59.

Chap, P., 1958b. A history of Oudong (ប្រវត្តិទីក្រុងឧត្តុង្គ). *Kambuja Suriya* 30(5), 467–72.

Chea, S., 2018. Saugatāśrama. un āśrama bouddhique à Angkor (Ong Mong), Thèse de doctorat en théorie et pratique de l'archéologie, Université Paris-Sorbonne.

Cherry, H., 2009. Digging up the past: prehistory and the weight of the present in Vietnam. *Journal of Vietnamese Studies* 4(1), 84–144.

Chhan, C., 2000. The ceramics collection at Preah Khan Temple, Angkor. *Udaya, Journal of Khmer Studies* 1, 295–303.

Chhay, R., P. Heng & V. Chhay, 2013. Khmer ceramic technology: a case study from Thnal Mrech Kiln site, Phnom Kulen, in *Materializing Southeast Asia's Past: Selected Papers from the 12th International Conference of the European Association of Southeast Asian Archaeologists*, eds. M.J. Klokke & V. Degroot. Singapore: NUS Press, 179–95.

Chhay, R., T. Tho & S. Em, 2020. Guide to understanding Khmer stoneware characteristics, Angkor, Cambodia, in EURASEAA14: material culture and heritage, in *Papers from the Fourteenth International Conference of the European Association of Southeast Asian Archaeologists*, ed. ed. H. Lewis. Oxford: Archaeopress, 53–62.

Chhay, V., 2011. Conservation of the Thnal Mrech Kiln site, Anlong Thom, Phnom Kulen, in *Rethinking Cultural Resource Management in Southeast Asia: Preservation, Development, and Neglect*, eds. J.N. Miksic, G.Y. Goh & S. O'Connor. London and New York: Anthem Press, 101–16.

Chhom, K., 2019. The kiri sdach kong inscription K.1419: translation and commentary (សិលាចារឹកវត្តគិរីស្តេចគង់ K, 1419 សេចក្តីប្រែ និងសេចក្តីអត្ថាធិប្បាយ). *Kambuja Suriya* 66(4), 35–54.

Chhon, E., 1994. Announcement on the revival of Kambuja Suriya journal (និវេទនកថាស្តីពីការបោះពុម្ពឡើងវិញទស្សនាវដ្តីកម្ពុជសុរិយា). *Kambuja Suriya* 48(1), 125.

Chigas, G., 2000. The emergence of twentieth century Cambodian literary institutions: The case of Kambujasuriya, in *The Canon in Southeast Asian Literatures: Literatures of Burma, Cambodia, Indonesia, Laos, Malaysia, the Philippines, Thailand and Vietnam*, ed. D. Smyth. Richmond: Curzon Press, 135–46.

Chuch, P., 2014. *Archaeology before & after the War, Unpublished Conference Paper for the Plenary Session at the IPPA's 20th Congress*. Siem Reap, Cambodia.

Chuch, P., 2021. A short conversation with H. E. Chuch Phoeurn on a history of Cambodia's Faculty of Archaeology. Interview by Sotheavin Nhim.

Chuon, N., 1963. *A History of Wat Ounnalom* (ប្រវត្តិវត្តឧណ្ណាលោម) (2nd ed.) Phnom Penh: Wat Ounnalom.

Clayton, T., 1995. Restriction or resistance? French colonial educational development in Cambodia. *Education Policy Analysis Archives* 3(19), 1–14.

Clayton, T., 2005. Re-orientations in moral education in Cambodia since 1975. *Journal of Moral Education* 34(4), 505–17.

Clémentin-Ojha, C. & P.-Y. Manguin, 2007. *A Century in Asia: The History of the École Française D'Extrême-Orient, 1898–2006*. Singapore: Editions Didier Millet.

Cœdès, G., 1931. Les littératures de l'Indochine. Littérature Cambodgienne, in *Indochine (Exposition coloniale internationale de Paris)*, ed. S. Lévi. Paris: Société des éditions géographiques, maritimes et coloniales, 180–92.

Cœdès, G., 1950. Histoire: l'Ancienne Civilisation Khmère (បុរវត្តិសា;;;រនសៃរិឡខែ្មរបុរាណ), *Kambuja Suriya* 22(4), 283–87.

Cœdès, G., 1951. Histoire: l'Ancienne Civilisation Khmère (continued) (បុរវត្តិសា;;;រនសៃរិឡខែ្មរបុរាណ). *Kambuja Suriya* 23(1), 3–9.

Commission des Moeurs et Coutumes, 1958. *Cérémonies des douze mois: fêtes annuelles cambodgiennes (ពិធីទ្វាទសមាស)*. Phnom Penh: Commission des moeurs et coutumes du Cambodge.

Conservation d'Angkor, 1908–1972. *Rapport d'Angkor: Angkor Wat 1908–1950, vol. 1a*. Paris: École Française d'Extrême-Orient.

Delaporte, L., 1880. *Voyage au Cambodge: l'architecture khmer*. Paris: Libraire Ch. Delagrave.

Drège, J.P., O. de Bernon & A. Josso (eds.) 2003. *L'École française d'Extrême-Orient et Le Cambodge, 1898–2003*. Paris: EFEO.

Duggan, S.J., 1996. Education, teacher training and prospects for economic recovery in Cambodia. *Comparative Education* 32(3), 361–76.

Duggan, S.J., 1997. The role of international organisations in the financing of higher education in Cambodia. *Higher Education* 34(1), 1–22.

Ea, D., 2005. The relationship between China and Cambodia: evidence from manuscripts, ceramics and bas-reliefs, in *Proceedings of the International Conference: Chinese Export Ceramics and Maritime Trade 12th–15th Centuries*, eds. C. Pei-Ki, L. Guo & W. Chui Ki. Hong Kong: Chinese Civilization Centre, University of Hong Kong, 267–79.

Ea, D., 2013. Angkorian stoneware ceramics along the east road from Angkor to Bakan at Torp Chey Village. *Udaya, Journal of Khmer Studies* 11, 59–98.

Ea, D., V. Chhay, S. Lam, R. Loeung, S. K. Sok, and S. Em, 2008. New data on Khmer kiln sites. *In Interpreting Southeast Asia's Past: Monument, Image and Text. Selected Papers from the 10th International Conference of the European Association of Southeast Asian Archaeologists*, vol. 2, eds. E. A. Bacus, I. C. Glover and P. D. Sharrock. Singapore: NUS Press, 275–85.

Editorial Board, 1973. Preface (អារម្ភកថា). *Bulletin des étudiants de la Faculté d'Archéologie* 6–7, 2.

Edwards, P., 2004. Making a religion of the nation and its language: the French protectorate (1863–1954) and the Dhammakāy, in *History, Buddhism, and New Religious Movements in Cambodia*, eds. J. Marston & E. Guthrie. Honolulu: University of Hawaii Press, 63–85.

Edwards, P., 2007. *Cambodge: The Cultivation of a Nation, 1860–1945*. Honolulu: University of Hawai'i Press.

Edwards, P., 2023. Inarguably Angkor, in *The Angkorian World*, eds. M. Hendrickson, M.T. Stark & D. Evans. New York: Routledge.

Endo, N., 1992. *Members of the Mission, in Renaissance Culturelle du Cambodge*. Tokyo: Institute of Asian Cultures, Sophia University, 125–26.

Fabricius, P. & S. Lan, 2003. Quelques contes et légendes Khmers. *Péninsule* 46, 25–56.

Faculté Royale d'Archéologie de Phnom Penh & A. Bareau, 1969. IV. Le monastère bouddhique de Tep Pranam à Oudong. *Bulletin de l'École française d'Extrême-Orient* 56(1), 29–56.

Fergusson, L.C. & G.L. Masson, 1997. A culture under siege: post-colonial higher education and teacher education in Cambodia from 1953 to 1979. *History of Education* 26(1), 91–112.

Glover, I., 2004. Writing Southeast Asian prehistoric archaeology: The western contribution-from colonialism to nationalism, in *Southeast Asian Archaeology, WG Solheim II Festschrift*, ed. V. Paz. Quezon City: The University of Philippines Press, 64–80.

Gnok, T., 1944. Angkor in the 13th century according to a Chinese traveler account (រឿងអង្គរ ក្នុងសតវត្សទី ១៣ តាមសេចក្ដីកត់ត្រា របស់អ្នកដំណើរជាតិចិនម្នាក់). *Kambuja Suriya* 16(1), 57–66, 138–44, 189–95.

Gorman, C.F. & P. Charoenwongsa, 1976. Ban chiang: a mosaic of impressions from the first two years. *Expedition* 18(4), 19–26.

Griffin, B.P., J. Ledgerwood & P. Chuch, 1999. The Royal University of Fine Arts, East–West Center, and University of Hawai'i program in the archaeology and anthropology of the Kingdom of Cambodia, 1994–1998. *Asian Perspectives* 38(1), 1–6.

Groslier, B.-P., 1985. L'image d'angkor dans la conscience khmère. *Seksa Khmer* 8–9, 5–30.

Guérin, M. & K. Chhom, 2014. Le périple de Khim et Nov de Stung Treng à Attopeu en 1883, récit d'exploration cambodgien du XIXe siècle. *Péninsule* 69, 103–40.

Guérin, M., 2017. Tup, un lettré aventurier au service de l'orientaliste Étienne Aymonier. *Journal Asiatique* 305(1), 111–18.

Hang, C.S., 2004. Stec Gaṃlaṅ' and Yāy Deb: worshiping kings and queens in Cambodia today, in *History, Buddhism, and New Religious Movements in Cambodia*, eds. J. Marston & E. Guthrie. Honolulu: University of Hawai'i Press, 113–26.

Hansen, A., 2007. *How to Behave: Buddhism and Modernity in Colonial Cambodia, 1860–1930 (Southeast Asia—Politics, Meaning, and Memory)*. Honolulu: University of Hawai'i Press.

Harris, I.C., 2005. *Cambodian Buddhism History and Practice*. Honolulu: University of Hawai'i Press.

Heng, P. & K. Phon, 2017. The position of Cambodian archaeology in current sociopolitical context, in *Handbook of East and Southeast Asian Archaeology*, eds. J. Habu, P.V. Lape & J.W. Olsen. New York: Springer, 83–7.

Heng, P., 2012. Speculation on land use in and around Sambor Prei Kuk, in *Old Myths, New Approaches*, ed. A. Haendel. Monash: Monash University Press, 180–98.

Heng, P., 2016. Transition to the Pre-Angkorian period (300–500 CE): thala borivat and a regional perspective. *Journal of Southeast Asian Studies* 47(3), 484–505.

Heng, P., K. Phon & S. Heng, 2020. De-exoticizing Cambodia's archaeology through community engagement. *Journal of Community Archaeology & Heritage* 7(3), 198–214.

Heng, S., 2008. A study of polished stone tools from Samrong Sen, Cambodia: the French museum collections. *Annali dell'Università degli Studi di Ferrara Museologia Scientifica e Naturalistica* 3, 1–7.

Heng, S., H. Forestier, V. Zeitoun, S. Puaud, S. Frère, V. Celiberti, K. Westaway, R. Mourer, C. Mourer-Chauviré, H. Than, L. Billault & S. Tech, 2016. Laang Spean cave (Battambang province): a tale of occupation in Cambodia from the Late Upper Pleistocene to Holocene. *Quaternary International* 416, 162–76.

Hun, C., 2019. The phum dong inscription K.1259 (សិលាចារឹកភូមិដូង). *Kambuja Suriya* 66(4), 55–81.

Huot, T., 1928. *Some Monuments in Angkor* (អំពីប្រាសាទខ្លះនៅទីអង្គរ). Phnom Penh: Royal Library.

Huot, T., 1964. A history of Wat Prang (ប្រវត្តិនៃវត្តប្រាង្គ). *Kambuja Suriya* 36(2), 215–21.

Huot, T., 1993. *My Dear Friend* (កល្យាណមិត្តរបស់ខ្ញុំ). Phnom Penh: Buddhist Institute.

Im, S., 2019. Angkor and its landscape in the history of Cambodia. *Sophia Journal of Asian, African, and Middle Eastern Studies* 37, 77–89.

Ishizawa, Y., 1992. Policy for the Sophia University survey mission for the study and preservation of the Angkor monuments: principles and proposal, in *Renaissance Culturelle du Cambodge*. Tokyo: Institute of Asian Cultures, Sophia University, 131–37.

Ishizawa, Y., 1996. Training project 1991–1995: a profile, in *Renaissance Culturelle du Cambodge*. Tokyo: Institute of Asian Cultures, Sophia University, 213–15.

Jarvis, H., 2006. *Publishing in Cambodia*. Phnom Penh: Center for Khmer Studies, Publication Department.

Jenner, P.N., 1976. The relative dating of some Khmer CPĀ'PA. *Oceanic Linguistics Special Publications* 13, 693–710.

JSA, 1994. *Annual Report on the Technical Survey of Angkor Monument*. Siem Reap: Japanese Government Team for Safeguarding Angkor (JSA).

Kelly, G.P., 1977. Colonial schools in Vietnam, 1918 to 1938. *Proceedings of the Meeting of the French Colonial Historical Society* 2, 96–106.

Keo, P., 2011. *A Brief Biography of Samdech Supreme Patriarch Chuon Nath* (ព្រះជីវប្រវត្តិសង្ខេបរបស់សម្ដេចព្រះសង្ឃរាជ ជួន ណាត). Washington, DC: Radio Free Asia.

Keyes, C.F., 1991. The case of the purloined lintel the politics of a Khmer shrine as a Thai national treasure, in *Thailand: Aspects of Identity, 1939–1989*, ed. C.J. Reynolds (Monash Papers on Southeast Asia 25). Melbourne: Monash University, Centre for Southeast Asian Studies, 261–92.

Khin, S., 1999. La khmérisation de l'enseignment et l'indépendance culturelle au Cambodge. *Bulletin de l'École Française d'Extrême-Orient* 86, 219–93.

Khing, 2006. Suzanne Karpelès and the Buddhist Institute (Khmer and English). *Siksacakr* 8–9, 55–9; 189–96.

Khing, H.D., 2010. Preah Mohaviriyapandito Pang Khat (1910–1975) [ព្រះមហាវិរិយបណ្ឌិតោ ប៉ាង ខាត់ (១៩១០-១៩៧៥)] (Unpublished Document). http://5000-years.org/kh/play/84036/23

Kiernan, B., 1982. Kampuchea 1979–81: National rehabilitation in the eye of an international storm. *Southeast Asian Affairs* 167–95.

Kim, S., 2011. Reciprocity: informal patterns of social interaction in a Cambodian village, in *Anthropology and Community in Cambodia: Reflections on the Work of May Ebihara* (Monash Papers on Southeast Asia; vol. 70). Melbourne: Monash University Press, 153–70.

Kong, S., 1970. *Perspectives of Samdech Supreme Patriarch Chuon Nath* (ទស្សនៈសម្តេចព្រះសង្ឃរាជ ជួន ណាត). Phnom Penh: Digitized by Tep Sovichet and Pi Bunnin.

Krassem, M.B., 1984. Silā cārik nagaravatt (Inscriptions modernes d'Angkor-Nouvelle préface de Saveros Pou; Bibliothèque khmère Série A, Textes et documents) (2nd éd.) Paris: Centre de Documentation et de Recherche sur la Civilisation Khmère

Kuoch, H., 1976. *Survey of the Southern Provinces of Cambodia in the Pre-Angkor Period*. MPhil dissertation. London: School of Oriental and African Studies, University of London

Lan, S., 1972. Étude iconographique du temple khmer de Thommanon (Dhammānanda). *Arts asiatiques* 25(1), 155–98.

Lan, S., 2008. Le Visnu de Srè Ampil: note documentaire sur l'expression plastique du culte visnuite au Cambodge. *Péninsule* 57(2), 167–81.

Leang, H.A., 1967. *A History of Khmer Literature: From Funan to Oudong (1st century to 1859)* (សិក្សាបុរវត្តិអក្សរសា;;;រខ្មែរ សម័យនគរភ្នំដល់សម័យឧដុង្គ(សតវត្សទី១ដល់១៨៥៩)). Phnom Penh: Kim Eng Bookstore.

Leroy, S., M. Hendrickson, E. Delqué-Kolic, E. Vega & P. Dillmann, 2015. First direct dating for the construction and modification of the Baphuon Temple mountain in Angkor, Cambodia. *PLoS One* 10(11), 1–13.

Lewitz, S., 1972. Les inscriptions modernes d'Angkor Vat. *Journal Asiatique* 260, 107–29.

Long Seam, 1997. *Sthannām vidyā Khmaer (La toponymie khmère)*. Phnom Penh: Buddhist Institute.

Ly, D. & I. Muan, 2001. *Cultures of Independence: An Introduction to Cambodian Arts and Culture in the 1950's and 1960's* (ខ្មែរប្រឈមមុខនឹងវប្បធម៌) (1st ed.) Phnom Penh: Reyum.

Ly, T.T., 1960. *Khmer Literature* (បុរវត្តិអក្សរសា;;;រខ្មែរ) (2nd ed.) Phnom Penh: Seng Nguon Huot Bookstore.

Ly, T.T., 1965. *A Preliminary Study of Khmer Civilization* (សិក្សាសង្ខេបអំពីវប្បធម៌ខ្មែរ) (2nd ed.) Phnom Penh: Seng Huot Bookstore.

Ly, T.T., 1973. *Zhou Daguan's Memoirs on the Traditions of Chenla People* (កំណត់ហេតុរបស់ជីវ តាក្វាន់ អំពីប្រពៃណីយនៃអ្នកស្រុកចេនឡា) (3rd ed.) Phnom Penh: Seng Huot Bookstore.

Ly, V., 2002. Rice remains in the prehistoric pottery tempers of the shell midden site of Samrong Sen: implications for early rice cultivation in Central Cambodia. *Aséanie* 9(1), 13–34.

Manguin, P.-Y., 2010. The EFEO in Cambodia, in *Archaeologists in Angkor: Photographic Archives of the École Française d'Extrême-Orient (French School of Asian Studies). Musée Cernuschi: Musée Des Arts de l'Asie de La Ville de Paris, September 9th 2010-January 3rd 2011*. Paris: EFEO, 25–8.

Mar, B., 1969. *Origins of Angkor Temples* (កំណើតប្រាសាទអង្គរ). Phnom Penh: Pasteur Printing House.

Marchal, H., 1916. Dégagement du Phimànakas. *Bulletin de l'École française d'Extrême-Orient* 16(1), 57–68.

Marchal, H., 1918. Monuments secondaires et terrasses bouddhiques d'Ańkor Thom. *Bulletin de l'École française d'Extrême-Orient* 18(1), 1–40.

Marchal, H., 1922. Le temple de Prah Palilay. *Bulletin de l'École française d'Extrême-Orient* 22(1), 101–34.

Marchal, H., 1936. *Construction Method of Angkor Wat* (វិធីកសាងប្រាសាទនគរវត្ត) (Kambuja Suriya). Phnom Penh: Royal Library.

Marchal, H., 1951. Note sur la forme du stūpa au Cambodge. *Bulletin de l'École française d'Extrême-Orient* 44(2), 581–90.

Muan, I., 2001. *Citing Angkor: The "Cambodian Arts" in the age of restoration, 1918–2000*. PhD dissertation. New York: Columbia University.

Nara, 2012. *Western Prasat Top Site Survey Report on Joint Research for the Protection of the Angkor Historic Site (Monograph 60)*. Phnom Penh, Cambodia: Nara National Research Institute for Cultural Properties.

Népote, J., 1979. Éducation et développement dan le Cambodge Moderne. *Mondes en développement* 28, 767–92.

Nhim, S., 2009. Essay on Cambodian history from the middle of the 14th century to the beginning of the 16th century: According to Cambodian chronicles, in *Investigation of the Angkor Monuments*, ed. S. Reap. Tokyo: Sophia Asia Center for Research and Human Development, 11–25.

Nhim, S., 2014. Factors that led to the change of the Khmer capitals from the 15th to 17th century, in *Renaissance Culturelle Du Cambodge*. Tokyo: Sophia University, 33–107.

Nhim, S., 2019a. Continuity of Angkorian sacred space: an example from Banteay Kdei archaeological excavation. *Renaissance Culturelle du Cambodge* 31, 85–106.

Nhim, S., 2019b. Cultural heritage education in Angkor: from academics in archaeology to the local community. *Sophia Journal of Asian, African, and Middle Eastern Studies* 37, 31–47.

Nou, H., 1989[1949]. *Phka Srapon* [The Faded Flower]. Phnom Penh: Cultural Printing House.

Osborne, M.E., 2016. *Southeast Asia: An Introductory History* (12th ed.) Sydney; Melbourne; Auckland; London: Allen & Unwin.

Pang, K., 1941. *Angkor Guide* (មគ្គុទេសក៍នគរ). Phnom Penh: Buddhist Institute.

Pang, K., 1952. *Human Life* (ជីវិតមនុស្ស). Phnom Penh: Khmer Printing House.

Pang, K., 1960. *History of Buddhism in Cambodia* (in Khmer: ប្រវត្តិពុទ្ធសាសនានៅប្រទេសខ្មែរ) (1st ed.) Phnom Penh: Buddhist Institute.

Pang, K., 1963. *Buddhism in Cambodia,* in *Centres d'études bouddhiques au Cambodge/Centers of Buddhist Studies in Cambodia,* ed. Buddhasāsanapaṇḍity. Phnom Penh: Buddhist Institute, 105–15.

Pang, K., 1970. *Culture and Civilization: Khmer-India* (វប្បធម៌ អរិយធម៌ខ្មែរ-ឥណ្ឌា). Phnom Penh: Buddhist Studies.

Pang, K., 1999. *A Mother's Life* (ជីវិតម៉ែ) (2nd ed.) Phnom Penh: Buddhist Institute.

Peycam, P.M.F., 2010. Sketching an institutional history of academic knowledge production in Cambodia (1863–2009)—Part 1. *Journal of Social Issues in Southeast Asia* 25(2), 153.

Peycam, P.M.F., 2011. Sketching an institutional history of academic knowledge production in Cambodia (1863–2009)—Part 2. *Sojourn: Journal of Social Issues in Southeast Asia* 26(1), 16–35.

Peycam, P.M.F., 2020. *Cultural Renewal in Cambodia: Academic Activism in the Neoliberal Era*. Leiden: BRILL.

Phlong, P., 2004. The impact of tourism on local communities in Beng Mealea, Cambodia. *Historic Environment* 17, 9–11.

Phon, K., 2011. Archaeology and cultural resource management south of Phnom Penh, Cambodia, in *Rethinking Cultural Resource Management in Southeast Asia: Preservation, Development, and Neglect*, eds. J.N. Miksic, G.Y. Goh & S. O'Connor. London; New York: Anthem Press, 123–42.

Pich, S., 1957. Origins of Phnom Penh in the 15th century (ដើមកំណើតទីក្រុងភ្នំពេញក្នុងសតវត្សទី ១៥). *Kambuja Suriya* 29(3), 229–36.

Polkinghorne, M., C. Pottier & C. Fischer, 2018. Evidence for the 15th century Ayutthayan occupation of Angkor, in *The Renaissance Princess Lectures: In Honour of Her Royal Highness Princess Maha Chakri Sirindhorn on Her Fifth Cycle Anniversary*. Bangkok: Siam Society, 98–132.

Pou, S., 1977. *Études sur le Rāmakerti: XVIe–XVIIe siècles (Publications de l'École française d'Extrême-Orient).* Paris: École française d'Extrême-Orient.

Pou, S., 1979. Subhāsit and Cpāp in Khmer literature, in *Ludwik Sternbach Felicitation volume*, ed. Jagdama Prasad Sinha. Lucknow: Akhila Bharatiya Sanskrit Parishad, 331–48.

Pou, S., 1980. Une description de la phrase en vieux-khmer. *Mon-Khmer Studies* 8, 139–69.

Pou, S., 1984. Nouvelle préface par Saveros Pou, in *Silā cārik nagaravatt (Inscriptions modernes d'Angkor-Nouvelle préface de Saveros Pou. Bibliothèque khmère Série A, Textes et documents)* (2nd éd.) Paris: Centre de Documentation et de Recherche sur la Civilisation Khmère, 8.

Preap, C.M., 2021. Faculty of Archaeology (មហាវិទ្យាល័យបុរាណវិទ្យា), in *Royal University of Fine Arts: A Century in Arts and Khmer Culture* (សាកលវិទ្យាល័យភូមិន្ទវិចិត្រសិល្បៈ ដំណើរ១០០;;;ក្នុងវិស័យសិល្បៈនិងវប្បធម៌ខ្មែរ). Phnom Penh: Center for Cultural and Scientific Research, Royal University of Fine Arts, 27–39.

Pring, K., 2001. L'Université des Beaux-Arts (reprinted from *Cambodge Nouveau*, octobre-novembre 1971), in *Cultures of Independence: An Introduction to Cambodian Arts and Culture in the 1950's and 1960's* (ខ្មែរប្រឈមមុខនឹងវប្បធម៌). (1st ed.), eds. D. Ly & I. Muan. Phnom Penh: Reyum, 338–41.

Reyum, 2001. A conversation with Vann Molyvann (October 13, 2001), in *Cultures of Independence: An Introduction to Cambodian Arts and Culture in the 1950's and 1960's* (ខ្មែរប្រឈមមុខនឹងវប្បធម៌). (1st ed.), eds. D. Ly & I. Muan. Phnom Penh: Reyum, 319–23.

Ross, H.G. & D. Collins, 2006. *Building Cambodia: New Khmer Architecture, 1953–1970*. Bangkok: The Key Publisher Unlimited.

Ross, H.G., 2015. The civilizing vision of an enlightened dictator: Norodom Sihanouk and the Cambodian post-independence experiment (1953–1970), in *Cultural Heritage as Civilizing Mission*, ed. M. Falser. Cham: Springer International Publishing, 149–78.

Seng, S., 2012. Restoration and conservation of archaeological objects: from Angkor to Prohear, in *Crossing Borders: Selected Papers from the 13th International Conference of the European Association of Southeast Asian Archaeologists*, eds. M.L. Tjoa-Bonatz, A. Reinecke & D. Bonatz. Singapore: NUS Press, 285–95.

Shoocongdej, R., 2007. The impact of colonialism and nationalism in the archaeology of Thailand, in *Selective Remembrances: Archaeology in the Construction, Commemoration, and Consecration of National Pasts*, eds. P.L. Kohl, M. Kozelsky & N. Ben-Yehuda. Chicago: University of Chicago Press, 379–99.

Shoocongdej, R., 2011. Contemporary archaeology as a global dialogue: reflections from Southeast Asia, in *Comparative Archaeologies: A Sociological View of the Science of the Past*, ed. L.R. Lozny. New York, NY: Springer New York, 707–29.

Siyonn, S., 2005. The life of the Rāmāyaṇa in Ancient Cambodia: a study of the political, religious and ethical roles of an epic tale in real time (I). *Udaya, Journal of Khmer Studies* 6, 93–150.

Siyonn, S., 2006. The life of the Rāmāyana in Ancient Cambodia: a study of the political, religious and ethical roles of an epic tale in real time (II). *Udaya, Journal of Khmer Studies* 7, 45–72.

Song, S., 2010. A study of glass beads from Phum Snay Iron Age archaeological site and settlement, Cambodia: data from excavation in 2001 and 2003. *Annali del l'Università di Ferrara Museologia Scientifica e Naturalistica* 6, 43–52.

Song, S., 2011. Heritage management of wooden prayer halls in Battambang Province, Cambodia, in *Rethinking Cultural Resource Management in Southeast Asia: Preservation, Development, and Neglect*, eds. J.N. Miksic, G.Y. Goh & S. O'Connor. London; New York: Anthem Press, 143–49.

Stark, M.T. & B.P. Griffin, 2004. Archaeological research and cultural heritage management in Cambodia's Mekong Delta: the search for the "Cradle of Khmer civilization", in *Marketing Heritage: Archaeology and Consumption of the Past*, eds. Y. Rowan & U. Baram. Walnut Creek, California: AltaMira Press, 117–42.

Stark, M.T. & P. Heng, 2017. After Angkor: an archaeological perspective on heritage and capacity-building in Cambodia, in *Post-Conflict Archaeology and Cultural Heritage*, eds. P. Newson & R. Young. New York, NY: Routledge, 195–216.

Sunseng, S., 1977. Un manuscrit khmer d'astrologie conservé au Musée Guimet. *Arts Asiatiques* 33(1), 57–131.

Suttantaprija Ind, 1967. *Journey to Angkor Wat* (និរាសនគរវត្ត). Phnom Penh: Buddhist Institute.

Thompson, A., 2004a. The future of Cambodia's Past: a messianic middle-period Cambodian royal cult, in *History, Buddhism, and New Religious Movements in Cambodia*, eds. J.A. Marston & E. Guthrie. Honolulu: University of Hawaii Press, 13–39.

Thompson, A., 2004b. Pilgrims to Angkor: a Buddhist 'cosmopolis' in southeast Asia? in *Indochina: Trends in Development*, eds. B. Nadezhda & D. Valentina. Moscow: Gumanitarii: Moscow State University, Institute of Asian-African Studies, 201–22.

Thompson, A., 2006. Buddhism in Cambodia: rupture and continuity, in *Buddhism in World Cultures: Comparative Perspectives*, ed. S.C. Berkwitz: ABC-CLIO, 129–67.

Thompson, A., 2016. *Engendering the Buddhist State: Territory, Sovereignty and Sexual Difference in the Inventions of Angkor*. New York: Routledge.

Thuy, C., 2020. Results of the first scientific analysis on rice fossil in Cambodia (លទ្ធផលពិសោធន៍វិទ្យាសា;;;រផូសីលអង្ករដំបូងនៅកម្ពុជា). *Kambuja Soriya* 67(1), 33–46.

Tith, K., 2022. Spirits raised: PM announces salary hikes after two-year freeze, 14 June 2022. www.khmertimeskh.com/501093428/spirits-raised-pm-announces-salary-hikes-after-two-year-freeze/ [Accessed on June 15, 2022].

Tomasi, L., 2000. The history of sociology in Cambodia: why sociology was introduced in Pol Pot's former country. *Asian Journal of Social Science* 28(1), 153–69.

Tran, N., 1973a. *Khmer History from the Beginning until the Abandonment of Angkor* (ប្រវត្តិសា;;;ខ្មែរ ពីដើមដល់ការបោះបង់ក្រុងអង្គរ) (1st ed.) Phnom Penh: Mohaleap Printing House.

Tran, N., 1973b. *Khmer History from the Establishment of Chaturmukh until the End of the Reign of HM Sisowath Monivong* (ប្រវត្តិសា;;;ខ្មែរ) (1st ed.) Phnom Penh: Mohaleap Printing House.

Trigger, B. & I. Glover, 1981. Editorial. *World Archaeology* 13(2), 133–37.

Tun, P., 2015. *Bouddhisme Theravāda et production artistique en pays khmer: étude d'un corpus d'images en ronde-bosse du Buddha (XIIIe-XVIe siècles)*. PhD dissertation. Paris: Université Paris-Sorbonne.

Um, P., 1934. *Ephémérides khmères: Revu par L'Oknha Hora Tipachak (Yok)*. Phnom Penh: Editions de la Bibliothèque royale.

Vann, M., 2001. New life infused into the arts in Cambodia (reprinted from Kambuja, May 1965), in *Cultures of Independence: An Introduction to Cambodian Arts and Culture in the 1950's and 1960's* (ខ្មែរ បុរាណមមុខនឹងវប្បធម៌) (1st ed.), eds. D. Ly & I. Muan. Phnom Penh: Reyum, 329–32.

Voeun, V. & A. von den Driesch, 2006. *Osteological Guide of Fishes from the Mekong System in Cambodia*. Phnom Penh: Fishbone Collection.

Voeun, V., 2013. Zooarchaeology at Phum Snay, a prehistoric cemetery in northwestern Cambodia, in *Water Civilization*. New York: Springer, 229–46.

Vong, S., 2010. *Pre-Angkor Inscriptions of Cambodia Vol. 1*. Phnom Penh: Royal University of Phnom Penh.

Vong, S., 2011. Recently discovered new inscriptions from Pre-Angkorian Cambodia in Stung Treng Province. *Saṅgama sāstra Manussa sāstra* 46(76), 26–40.

Vong, S., 2019. The Kiri Sdach Kong Inscription K.1419: background of the inscription and the toponymie 'Suvarṇṇabhūmi' (សិលាចារឹកវត្តគិរីស្តេចគង់ K, 1419 បុរេវត្តិសិលាចារឹក និងស្ថាននាម "សុវណ្ណភូមិ"). *Kambuja Suriya* 66(4), 1–27.

Warrack, S., 2011. Learning from local leaders. *Change over Time* 1(1), 34–51.

Weber, N., 2014. Note sur les inscriptions en cam du pāḷāt' Tut, estampeur d'Étienne Aymonier. *Bulletin de l'École française d'Extrême-Orient* 100(1), 253–58.

White, P.T. & W.E. Garrett, 1982. The temples of Angkor: ancient glory in stone. *National Geographic* 161(5), 552–89.

4
THE MEKONG DELTA BEFORE THE ANGKORIAN WORLD

Miriam T. Stark and Pierre-Yves Manguin

By the mid-first millennium CE or perhaps a bit earlier, Southeast Asia was a crucible of religious and cultural innovation. Stone inscriptions suggest that local Southeast Asian populations used both Pali and Sanskrit as liturgical languages, written in the Brāhmī and Kharosthī scripts, as they adopted Indic religions and practices. Southeast Asia was an integral link in maritime Buddhist networks that connected China with South Asia. These new ideologies assumed the status of 'state' religions that propelled Southeast Asians to build and congregate in their first cosmopolitan urban centres. Brahmins brought rituals, texts, and technical knowledge needed to practise Vaiṣṇavism and Śaivism: Buddhist monastics also brought their literacy and religious accoutrements to the region. Sixth-century CE local artisans were producing materials needed for religious practice, like statuary and buildings to house the images, using a local aesthetic. New religious practices also required the manufacture of portable items crafted in stone, clay, metal, and occasionally other media, from ritual ablution vessels to icons and votive tablets. Such developments took place across the Mekong Delta, creating templates that the Angkorian polity adopted some centuries later.

The early Cambodian state known to the Chinese as *Funan* was one of the better-documented polities that emerged between 500 BCE–500 CE as Mainland Southeast Asians embraced these new cultural and political ideologies and organisational changes. The Lower Mekong Basin (Figure 4.1) was integral to these developments as the location of Funan: entrepôts emerged along its coasts, early cities grew on its alluvial lowlands, and well-established transportation routes crossed its riverine and terrestrial areas. It was also a hearth of the Khmer civilisation, with the region's earliest Khmer-language inscription and ample evidence for Indic-tinged institutions that structured the Angkorian World several hundred years later.

Collapse and regeneration characterised the Cambodian world before the establishment of Angkor (Jacques 1986, 87; Stark 2006b), and conventional histories rely on a historical sequence that begins with the founding of Funan (1st–5th centuries CE) to the rise of *Chenla* (6th–8th centuries CE) and ultimately to the founding of Angkor (9th–15th centuries CE). Early French colonial scholars (e.g., Aymonier 1903; Pelliot 1903a, 1903b) proposed a Cambodian polity called *Founan* or Funan more than a century ago, and George Cœdès (1964, 1968) summarised this elegant history of Cambodia. Recent archaeological, historical, and art historical scholarship (e.g., Vickery 1994, 2003) has challenged the model, yet Funan has emerged intact. It remains a salient first-millennium entity whose rulers begot rulers of subsequent kingdoms

DOI: 10.4324/9781351128940-6

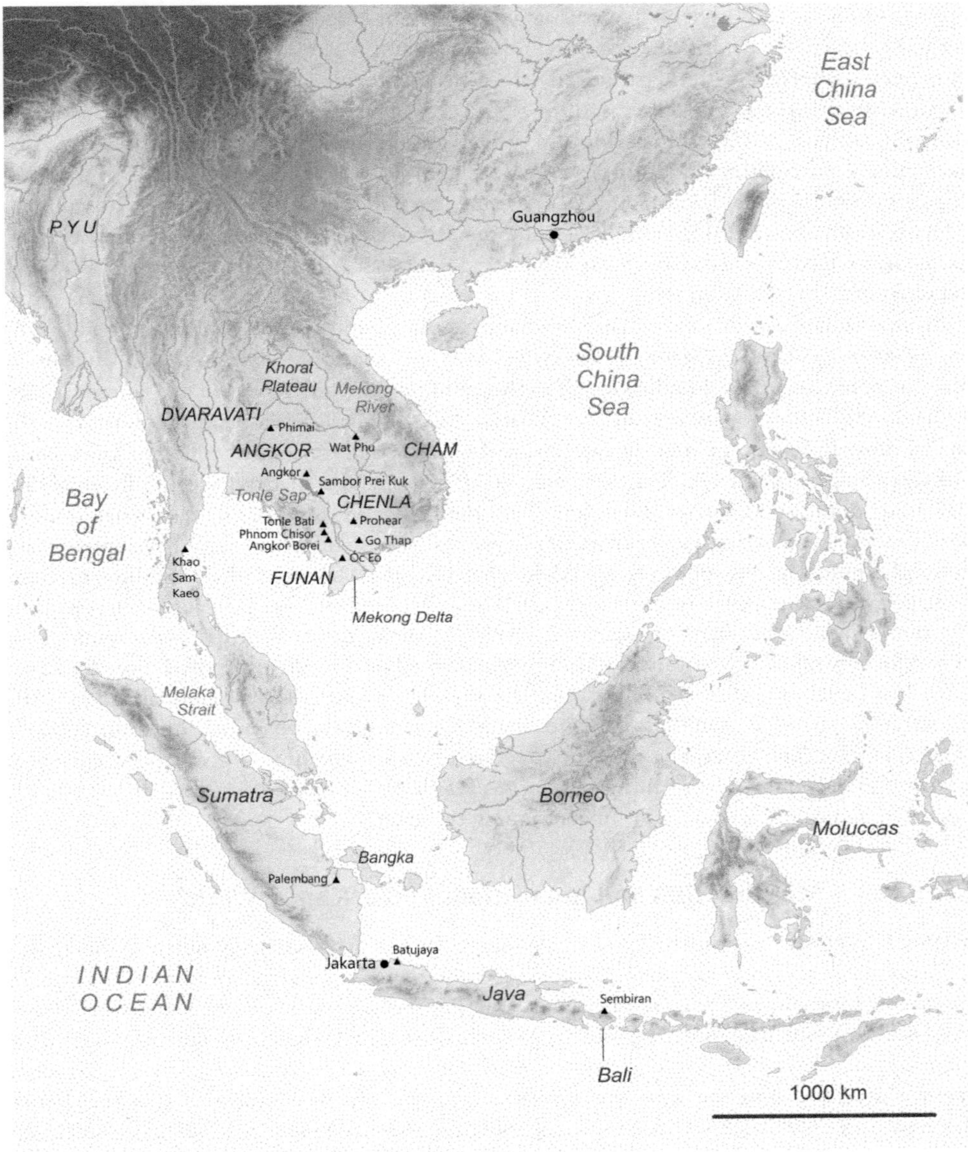

Figure 4.1 The Mekong Delta and the Angkorian World before Angkor.

like Sambhupura, whose capital lay at Sambor Prei Kuk. If we can believe the dynastic history encoded in 11th-century stelae from Sdok Kak Thom, then these progeny included Jayavarman II, the founder of Angkor (Cœdès and Dupont 1943).

Whether the first Khmer-like polities emerged out of Funan and its Mekong Delta epicentre remains a matter of some debate, but by the 7th century CE, Khmer polities arose in multiple localities across the region (Jacques 1986). Boundaries blurred between traditional culture areas as artisans traversed routes from the Dvaravati heartland in central and Northeast Thailand through southern Laos to central Vietnam's coastal Cham kingdoms (e.g., Revire 2016). The fact that the Chinese described kings in regions that South Asian records rarely mentioned has long been a scholarly mystery, particularly since material evidence for South Asian ideas and practices are abundant in this place and time (for recent reviews, see Manguin 2019a, 101–03; Manguin and Stark 2022). Scholarship also suffers from misunderstandings of both South Asia and China as monolithic entities from 200 BCE and 800 CE, a dynamic period of political change in both regions. Some South Asian kingdoms like the Guptas exerted broad cultural influence (e.g., Brown 2011; Stark 2021), and increasing Chinese demand for Southeast Asian goods encouraged interaction between 'China' and Southeast Asia's 'southern barbarians' (Stark and Cremin 2023, this volume).

More than 20 years of archaeological research on this period—a 'millennium-long historiographic no-man's land' (Manguin 2011, xvi)—has forced revisions to the dominant 'Indianisation' (or more technically 'Hindicisation') model most prominently proposed by George Cœdès (1964, 1968). Scholars now agree that Southeast Asia's cultural developments did not exactly parallel those in South Asia but instead followed separate trajectories that reflected knowledge of myriad South Asian technological traditions, art styles, and alphabets. Specifically, how did Maritime Southeast Asia shape developments in the Lower Mekong Basin? Our chapter combines historical and archaeological data to discuss the tempo and structure of developments in the southernmost reaches of the Lower Mekong Basin—the Mekong Delta—and how they set the stage for the emergence of the Angkorian World. Three central issues structure our chapter. The first concerns the shape of Maritime Southeast Asia at the turn of the millennium. The second focuses on how Maritime Southeast Asia affected developments in the Lower Mekong in the first millennium CE. The third concerns how the Mekong Delta's cultural and historical trajectory provided templates for political and social organisation in the 9th–15th century Angkorian state. Understanding these first requires an understanding of geographic and temporal contexts, and the next section characterises Maritime Southeast Asia (SEA) at c. 0 CE: its geography and our data sources for understanding this region.

Maritime SEA and Interactions in the 'Khmer World'

Maritime Southeast Asia (MSEA) had a broad geographic scope, extending north to the Yangtze River, south to Timor and Banda Seas, and west to the Bay of Bengal: or most of the region glossed as Monsoon Asia (e.g., Acri et al. 2017). The earliest historical descriptions of Maritime Southeast Asia date to the turn of the first millennium CE. At this time, settlements that could support relatively large populations were strung along MSEA's coasts and river valleys and served as ports and entrepôts for inland regions, paving the way to urbanisation (Christie 1995; Manguin 2000, 2002a, 2004; Stark 2006a). Southeast Asians living in Mainland and Island Southeast Asia (ISEA) forged different international networks based on the water bodies that surrounded them but were linked by the South China Sea (Gupta 2005; Ray 2014; Manguin 2019a, 114–15). These maritime networks had deep historical roots linking South China Sea communities to China's southern coast and peninsular Thailand (Favereau and Bellina 2016; Bellina 2017), as did communication systems that extended along much of the Mekong River inland to southern Laos (e.g., Carter 2015; Carter et al. 2021).

Institutionalised inequality emerged as locally produced and imported goods circulated within nested levels of economic networks from the local to interregional scales, from the South China Sea to the Bay of Bengal. At its core lay MSEA and the Mekong River, its largest artery. The Mekong and its tributaries linked communities across the Lower Mekong Basin from the Mekong Delta with upstream communities in current-day Lao PDR (Champassak region) and the Khorat Plateau (Northeast Thailand). The Mekong and Tonle Sap converge to geographically demarcate the core of Cambodia, which, from the 9th–14th centuries, formed the Angkorian heartland.

Maritime Routes

Maritime routes were the primary corridors by which South Asian ideas and people reached Southeast Asia. Maritime shipmasters and sea merchants from both South and Southeast Asia plied both coastal routes that flanked the Bay of Bengal and South China Sea along open-sea routes that facilitated access to the East China Sea and the Indian Ocean. These ships ferried commodities and people across this interaction sphere: artisans, priests, proselytes, and likely adventurers (Hoogervorst 2017; Manguin 2019a, 112–15; 2019c; Lavy 2020). Some South Asians may even have lived in Southeast Asia's settlements by the late centuries BCE, particularly along the shores of the Thai-Malay Peninsula (e.g., Wheatley 1961, 179–82). Coastal settlements fringing the South China Sea coasts created a sphere of favoured cultural exchange, functioning within interlocking networks (Favereau and Bellina 2016), and Southeast Asian mariners plied waters as far north as southern China. The straits between the Thai-Malay Peninsula and Sumatra, as well as the Java Sea, were also part of this system (e.g., Leong Sau Heng 1990; Christie 1995, 251, 276; Calò et al. 2015) that linked Southeast Asia to South Asia and its Indian Ocean system.

Political and Religious Impacts

Elite Southeast Asians benefited greatly from this overseas interaction during the first millennium CE, including the acquisition of goods, both utilitarian and exotic. Early trade in raw materials such as gold and tin, aromatic resins or spices—all items very much in demand and produced in Peninsular and ISEA—remain poorly documented in archaeological contexts. Only recently have textiles been brought to light and studied, such as cotton, silk, or asbestos (Cameron 2000; Cameron et al. 2015). High-fired ceramics, mostly Indian-made rouletted wares, and a variety of glass and stone beads (Bellina 2014; Carter 2015, 750) are the most abundant traces of contacts with India. Luxury exotic goods also left a powerful imprint of foreign contact by the 2nd–3rd centuries CE, including gold foil imitations of Roman coins made by embossing or casting and used as pendants, alongside an array of engraved gems and other types of jewellery produced in India and further west (Malleret 1963; Borell 2014; 2017). Documentary, linguistic, and archaeobotanical studies suggest that South Asians also brought with them a wider suite of goods to Southeast Asia beyond just luxury items, like mung beans and sesame, which were both new cultigens (Castillo et al. 2016, 1263; Hoogervorst 2017, 759–61; see also Stark and Cremin 2023, this volume).

Indian-derived religious influence is evident in the material record of the first-millennium Mekong Delta. In the wake of the brilliant Gupta state and as part of the iconic revolution in India in the first centuries CE, we witness the first appearance and sudden multiplication of Buddhist and Vaiṣṇava images in both Mainland and ISEA and perhaps the shrines that housed them (Brown 2011; Manguin 2019b, 63–64; Stark 2015, 2021). Another turning point in South/SEA relations occurred in the waning years of the Gupta Period in the 4th century CE, as the Gupta power base moved south and Tamil Nadu's Pallavas were on the rise. This 'Indic burst' (*sensu* Brown 2017) of accelerated exchanges was felt in both peninsular South Asia and Southeast Asia and must have given newly urbanised Southeast Asians a sense of belonging to a larger community. They found sectarian devotional forms of Brahmanic religion like

Vaiṣṇavism, and later Śaivism, easier to adopt than more orthodox variants of the faith; their embrace of these new ideologies also offered new social paradigms that legitimated institutionalised inequality (Manguin 2019b, 52). These organisational shifts assumed different trajectories across Southeast Asia, reflecting the availability of different raw materials and unfolding across different scales of time (Christie 1995). The pace and intensity of involvement in Maritime Southeast Asian commerce also fluctuated through time for Lower Mekong Basin populations, whose descendants included Angkorian citizens.

Maritime Southeast Asia and the Lower Mekong Basin

At its height, the cultural (if not political) reach of the Angkorian Empire extended west into Thailand, south into the Thai-Malay peninsula, and southeast into the Mekong Delta. But its cultural heartland always lay more narrowly within the Lower Mekong Basin, across which Angkorian monuments, statuary, and artefacts have been documented. Archaeologists have traced the existence of interactional networks across the Lower Mekong Basin back at least 2500 years (e.g., Reinecke 2012). Our earliest clear evidence for these networks lies in technology transfer rather than movement of people, although recent research suggests some mobility by the mid-first millennium CE. A millennium earlier, earthenware ceramic traditions across the region share manufacturing steps (burnishing, reduction firing) that produced dark lustrous ceramics from Phimai (Khorat Plateau) to Angkor Borei and Óc Eo in the Mekong Delta, all the while maintaining distinctive local vessel form traditions (Evans et al. 2016, 463; Stark and Fehrenbach 2019). This inland-oriented Lower Mekong technological tradition would have emerged side by side with the South China Sea (Sa Huynh/Kalanay) ceramic tradition, also known for its nephrite ear ornaments and other artefacts. Both of these networks are reflected in glass bead composition from sites across the Mekong Delta/Funan region (Carter et al. 2021); some regions of the traditions overlapped, with some human mobility that moved goods by the late centuries BCE like stone and glass beads or Dong Son drums (Calò et al. 2015; Carter 2015; Favereau and Bellina 2016; Hung et al. 2013).

What followed in the early centuries CE was the emergence of four cultural regions across the Lower Mekong Basin (following Jacques 1986). The Mekong Delta had its Funan polity, and southern Laos/Champasak also became part of the Pre-Angkorian World by the 6th century (see Heng 2023, this volume). The Mun/Chi River valleys and their Khorat Plateau were slower to embrace Indic traditions, and their Iron Age also extended into the 6th century, when the region became incorporated into the Pre-Angkorian World (Castillo et al. 2018; Evans et al. 2016; King et al. 2017). A fourth area, central (and some of NE) Thailand, had connection to polities along the Thai-Malay Peninsula and may have made the region part of the maritime world as early as Funan (Jacques 1995, 36 et passim). Bioarchaeological patterns suggest a kind of parochialism between 550 BCE and 500 CE, with little inter-regional mobility in and between at least three of these areas: NE Thailand, NW Cambodia, and the Mekong Delta (e.g., Cox et al. 2011; Domett et al. 2011; Shewan et al. 2020).

Despite the emergence of discrete culture areas by the mid-first millennium CE (i.e., Cham, Pre-Angkor, Dvaravati, Pyu), scholars suggest the movement of ideas and technologies across culture areas. Manufacturing techniques used to produce Angkor Borei's and Khao Sam Kaeo's agate/carnelian and garnet beads parallel those in southern India and Sri Lanka (Bellina 2014; Carter et al. 2021). Fine paste ceramics, perhaps kiln fired and wheel made, also appear and included *kendis* of clear Indian inspiration (Coomaraswamy and Kershaw 1928–1929). The region's earliest flat earthenware roof tiles also appear. Roof tiling was an Indian technology used to cover wooden buildings in Óc Eo and Angkor Borei centuries before brick masonry was introduced (Manguin 2002b, 2006; Stark and Fehrenbach 2019). Indic concepts of urban planning also appear to have made their appearance at Óc Eo, and the rectangular moats of the city were first dug during the early centuries CE (Bourdonneau 2007; Manguin 2009). But the next major development occurred in the mid-first millennium CE (see also Stark 2006), when shrines built with brick masonry (Stark 2015, 2006c; Stark et al. 2006; Manguin 2009) emerged in lockstep with the region's earliest Indic statuary. Both were associated with the emergence of Buddhist and Brahmanical cults, which local leaders embraced to consolidate power through interregional linkages that provided elite goods and new ideologies (Stark 2021).

Recent art historical and archaeological research suggests that 'Indianisation' may have been an overstatement in describing the development of first-millennium Southeast Asia. The shared Buddhist artistic idiom across Dvaravati/Pre-Angkor and even Pyu that emerged between the 2nd and 5th centuries CE was distinctly Southeast Asian rather than Indian and Southeast Asian. Brahmanic statuary was also distinctive (Brown 2011; Galloway 2010; Manguin 2010; Revire 2016; Lavy and Polkinghorne 2023, this volume). Few material culture breaks are discernible between the mid-first millennium CE and the early 9th century, when Jayavarman II declared his universal rulership of the polities that would become Angkor.

Prestige goods, rather than simply human mobility, maintained Mainland Southeast Asian networks through the mid-first millennium CE. Archaeological patterns suggest the development of multiple discrete interactional exchange networks for prestige goods like glass and stone beads (e.g., Carter 2015). Southeast Asia's maritime route gained prominence after the 4th century CE. South China lost access to the terrestrial (Central Asian) Silk Road (Sen 2014, 39–41; Wang 1958, 46–47). Hanoi and Canton/Guangzhou emerged as major trading ports as China initiated the Nanhai trade with its southern 'barbarian' neighbours (Wang 1958, 32). It was within this cultural milieu that the Mekong Delta, where Funan emerged as a polity in Early Southeast Asia, became part of first-millennium CE regional interaction.

The Mekong Delta and the Khmer World

The Mekong Delta was the linchpin in this system, linking what is now Cambodia to Maritime Southeast Asia. Asia's third largest river, the Mekong and its tributaries produced one of the World's largest deltas c. 8–9000 years ago as sea levels dropped with the last deglacial meltwater event (Tamura et al. 2009). Today the dynamic Mekong Delta covers much of Cambodia's southeast and southern Vietnam and has continued to expand through the river's heavy sediment load, which has extended the coast southwestward more than 200 km in the last 6–7000 years. This progradation may have accelerated through human activities in the last 600–1000 years and until recently may have grown by 10–20 km/year (Thi Kim Oanh Ta et al. 2002). The Mekong Delta is a mix of seasonally inundated floodplain (northern and central sections), saline peat swamps (interior Ca Mau peninsula), coastal sand ridges, mudflats, and mangrove-fringe areas. Its average elevation is <5 metres above sea level, except in karst limestone formations like those found in the Ca Mau peninsula and in isolated granitic hills that dot the delta's landscape. Today the delta and its farmers are threatened by climate change and upstream dam construction, but until recently its arable northern floodplains were an important rice granary for Southeast Asia, with high biodiversity in bird and aquatic species (Cramb 2020).

Colonial period scholarship on early Indochina continues to influence interpretations of the first-millennium Mekong Delta, with a continued skew toward the 'Indianisation' framework (e.g., Cœdès 1968) and its near-exclusive focus on maritime dynamics at the expense of basin-wide developments. The fact that relatively little archaeological work has been undertaken in this region has further compounded the problem. Economic and political processes have obliterated large sections of the delta's archaeological record through time, ranging from French colonial canalisation projects through war-related damage to more recent processes of urbanisation. Most archaeological knowledge of the area still derives from a handful of field studies (e.g., Malleret 1951, 1959–1963; Paris 1931, 1941) and from interpretations of predominantly Chinese historical sources by Indologists or Sinologists (notably Cœdès 1931, 1937, 1964; Pelliot 1903a, 1903b; see reviews in Manguin and Stark 2022; Vickery 2003). Chinese dynastic histories describe 3rd-century emissaries from the Wu kingdom (229–80 CE) named Kang Tai and Zhu Ying, who arrived in Funan in the 230s in search of forest resources and access to western goods. The rulers of Funan reportedly sent more than 25 missions to China between 226 and 649 CE, bearing gold and other precious gifts like trained elephants, white pheasants, musicians, and at least one rhinoceros, which the Chinese returned to their southern neighbours (Ishizawa 1995). The name Funan does not appear in any of the more than 300 inscriptions from the first millennium CE recovered from the Mekong Delta (from the late 5th to late 6th centuries); named Funan rulers also crafted fewer than six of these inscriptions. Chinese accounts describe a successor Chenla kingdom (both 'Water' and 'Land' Chenla), and the Funan-Chenla scenario dominates most interpretations of Pre-Angkorian Cambodia since Briggs' (1951) and Cœdès' (1964, 1968) magisterial syntheses.

These 'Indological spectacles' (Vickery 2003, 104)—despite almost no documentary data on the region from South Asia—thus offer a rich but decontextualised, understanding of the Mekong Delta's earliest urbanisation and state formation. Limited archaeological research on the Mekong Delta offers needed counterbalance to the largely documentary-based reconstructions of its first millennium CE. Louis Malleret's 1944 fieldwork at the Vietnamese site of Óc Eo (Malleret 1959–63) launched archaeological scholarship on the 'Kingdom of Funan'. However, the archaeology of the Mekong Delta always took a backseat to the archaeology of the Tonle Sap region in Cambodia, which was itself overshadowed by conservation and restoration work at Angkor until the rise of the Khmer Rouge in the early 1970s. Vietnamese archaeologists continued fieldwork activities throughout the Second Indochina war, although they were compelled to work in areas further north for pragmatic reasons (see summary in Nguyễn Phúc Long 1975, 4–7).

Archaeological field investigations, halted during protracted geopolitical conflict, resumed quickly in Vietnam's delta after the end of the Second Indochina War in 1975. Art historical and epigraphic research since then offers new insights on origins and dating of the artistic traditions of the Mekong Delta. Most attention has focused on the dating and artistic influences on Mekong Delta statuary (e.g., Dowling 1999; Kang 2013), but scholars have also used Mekong Delta statuary as proxies for tracking the adoption of Brahmanic cults, and particularly Śaivism and Vaiṣṇavism (Dalsheimer and Manguin 1998; Lavy 2003, 2014; Lê Thị Liên 2011, 2015a; Manguin 2019b). Post-colonial epigraphic work on the latter part of Funan (and subsequent 7th and 8th centuries) provides a much-needed vision of the transition from Funan to Angkor and suggests the Lower Mekong Basin housed multiple polities rather than a single entity that the Chinese glossed as Funan (e.g., Gerschheimer and Goodall 2014; Jacques 1979; 1986, 1995; Vickery 1998; 2003).

This collective archaeological knowledge of the Mekong Delta, conducted primarily within the borders of Vietnam, offers an increasingly nuanced understanding of the first millennium CE in the delta region. The end of fighting and departure of American forces in 1975 opened Vietnam's delta to archaeologists, who have worked regularly on a variety of 'Óc Eo Culture' sites since that time (Lê Xuân Diêm et al. 1995; Lê Xuân Diêm and Đào Linh Côn 1995; Nguyễn Kim Dung 2001; Lê Xuân Diêm 2015b; Võ Sĩ Khải 1998), including the Óc Eo type site (e.g., Trịnh Thị Hòa 1996; Manguin and Võ Sĩ Khải 2000; Manguin 2009) and Gò Tháp/Prasat Pram Loveng (e.g., Đào Linh Côn 1998; Lê Thị Liên Ślączka 2011). Valuable work has also been done on Vietnam's 'pre-Óc Eo' or protohistoric culture sites (e.g., Bui Phat Diem et al. 1997; Nishimura et al. 2008–9; Proske et al. 2009). Archaeologists have only worked at two first-millennium CE sites on Cambodia's side of the delta: Angkor Borei/Phnom Borei (e.g., Bishop et al. 2003; Phon 2004; Pietrusewsky and Ikehara-Quebral 2006; Sanderson et al. 2007; Stark and Bong 2001; Shewan et al. 2020) and the Iron Age site of Prohear (Reinecke et al. 2012). Most archaeological field investigations in the Mekong Delta have focused on monuments, cemeteries, and waterway systems rather than habitation areas (but see Nishimura et al. 2008–9), with a growing number of specialist studies that examine portable goods like beads, ceramics, and precious metals (e.g., Carter 2015; Stark and Fehrenbach 2019), and work on human osteological remains (Francken et al. 2010; Pietrusewsky and Ikehara-Quebral 2006; Ikehara-Quebral et al. 2017; Schlosser et al. 2012; Shewan et al. 2020).

This work, and research by art historians and epigraphers, has inspired scholars to rethink many aspects of the delta's culture history from the protohistoric to historic periods (e.g., Lê Thị Liên 2015b; Reinecke 2012). Our earliest evidence for occupation along the delta's northern fringe dates to c. 2000 BCE, with groups settling inland through the first millennium BCE (Lê Xuân Diêm et al. 1995; Piper and Oxenham 2014; Reinecke 2012). Settlement frequency increases with population infilling that intensified through time (Stark 2006c). Populations from areas around Angkor Borei appear to have settled and transformed landscapes in lowland areas of the basin that were previously unpopulated. Substantial engineering was also necessary to populate areas around Óc Eo and Da Noi, including an extensive, star-shaped canal network (Bourdonneau 2003; Stevens et al. 2004). The K. 5 inscription from Go Thap, which refers to land gained over marshes also points in this direction (Cœdès 1931, 7). The urban site of Óc Eo, settled at the turn of the millennium, may be seen as a pioneering urban and agricultural project, which also provided an easier access to maritime trade. It functioned during six centuries, but failed in the end, when the moated city and surrounding lowland sites were abandoned in Chenla times, leaving only emerged outcrops such as Mound Ba Thê and others in activity into Chenla and Angkorian times, most probably with a much reduced population. Meanwhile, in Angkor Borei and further inland, Chenla (and then Angkor) prospered, based on a more viable agricultural economy (Manguin and Stark 2022). This is also a time when the nexus of maritime trade shifted to the Melaka Strait area, resulting in the foundation of Srivijaya in the 7th century.

Mekong Delta populations looked both inward and to coastal regions throughout the first millennium CE. Shared ceramic technological traditions, like the burnished reduced earthenware tradition, reflect inland relationships with Lower Mekong Basin communities (Stark and Fehrenbach 2019), while glass bead compositional variability reflects discrete distributional networks that linked some delta communities inland and others to the South China Sea (Carter 2015, 751–52). Gradual integration into the South China Sea network brought new ideas and technological traditions in glass and bronze manufacture (Brown 2017, 44–45; Carter 2015). Old networks persisted, but these new ideas did not effectively penetrate areas like the Upper Mun River Valley until the 4th–6th centuries (Evans et al. 2016).

Our understanding of Funan continues to evolve with additional research findings. What seems clear, however, is that Funan was rarely unified into a monolithic political entity and instead comprised multiple, competing population centres joined to each other for economic and perhaps ritual reasons (see also Jacques 1986, 1995; Stark 2003; Wheatley 1983). Abundant arable lands lay inland that could generate surplus needed to support coastal or near-coastal settlements engaged in the South China Sea network. Precise outlines of the delta-wide social and economic webs connecting settlements are difficult to discern for the 500 years leading to the mid-first millennium CE. Yet we know that this interactional system had at least three anchor settlements by the 5th century CE: Angkor Borei, Gò Tháp, and Óc Eo. Chinese accounts describe the cultural and political reach of this polity extending west and south to the Malay Peninsula and up the Mekong River.

Religious pluralism characterised the first-millennium CE Mekong Delta, closely following developments in South Asia (Stark 2021; see Estève 2023, this volume for Angkorian parallel). Vaiṣṇavite, Saivite, and Buddhist iconography is common in statuary, portable objects, and inscriptions (e.g., Lê Thị Liên 2010; 2011; 2015a; Skilling 2011; 2015a; 2015b). Vaiṣṇavism appears, however, to have been the religion favoured by the early royal courts, as attested by both epigraphy and statuary. Traditions of brick ritual architecture and of statuary emerged in the 5th–6th century Mekong Delta (Ray 2014, 136; Manguin 2009; Stark et al. 2006). Although this monumentalism appeared more than 500 years after the earliest adoption of brick architectural technology in South Asia, both South and Southeast Asia experienced an 'Indic surge' (Brown 2017, 46) during the 5th–6th centuries that included the widespread adoption of Sarnath and Gupta styles in Buddhist statuary traditions (Brown 2017, 43–45; Kang 2013). This surge was a landmark event in the history of the Lower Mekong Basin, and in the three centuries that followed, new and enduring templates for urbanism and statecraft were established across the Angkorian World.

We have reason to believe that Funan collapsed in response to internal cultural developments that involved the Mekong River network. What was the shape of settlement in the Mekong Delta and the Lower Mekong Basin after Funan (i.e., 500–800 CE)? Chinese dynastic histories record a 'Zhenla' (Chenla) polity that putatively defeated Funan by the 6th or 7th century, and Pre-Angkorian sites and inscriptions proliferate across the northern Mekong Delta. So do settlements in neighbouring regions, from Cham settlements in coastal Vietnam to Dvaravati sites in central and NE Thailand, and similarities in technology and iconography across MSEA suggest that social and economic webs strengthened during this time. As new coastal settlements emerged in the Isthmus region, Maritime Southeast Asia continued to shape interactions inland from the Mekong delta throughout the Lower Mekong Basin. The Srivijaya sphere also brought portions of ISEA into this broader interactional network (Manguin 2002b; 2004). Local languages proliferated, but populations across the region used elements of a similar Indic-tinged cultural package to build their first maritime and agrarian states. Populations in Cambodia's Lower Mekong Basin established Pre-Angkorian capitals in central and NW Cambodia (Chevance and Pottier 2023, this volume), and the organisation of those settlement complexes offered a template that Khmers would draw from and adapt for the next millennium (see Evans et al. 2023a, this volume).

Conclusions

The ultimate geographic scale of Greater Angkor on the banks of the Tonle Sap Lake and its sheer monumentality make it easy to overlook the importance of the broader geographical context in which Angkor developed. But we must attend to this larger hydrographic region to understand long-term cultural developments in the region, which involved both local innovations and external influences and whose ideas became the key to Angkor's success. Mekong Delta residents during the early to mid-first millennium CE engaged with the South China Sea-based maritime world: opportunities, goods, and even people moved this world inland across the Lower Mekong Basin. By the mid-first millennium CE, peripatetic artisans and ritual specialists likely traversed MSEA, and this exposure created a mosaic of local responses and attracted populations to ever-larger centres that offered public ritual displays and other performances of power. Areas of the Lower Mekong Basin were the crucible for a fundamentally Khmer culture whose language, writing system, urban patterns, and religion anticipated the Angkorian World.

Just when this Mekong Delta became Khmer remains a matter of debate. What language Funan residents spoke is also not clear and has been the subject of sustained and lively debate, with proponents of Khmer, a pre-Khmer Austroasiatic language (e.g., Briggs 1951, 14–15; Cœdès 1968, 36; Nguyễn Phúc Long 1975, 12; Pou 1974, 177; Vickery 2003, 122–25), or even 'Indonesian' (as defended by Malleret 1959–63, vol. 3, 353–60, 417, 450, based on ethnic and cultural grounds). Khmer was certainly one ethnolinguistic group in the lower Mekong at the time when the first dated Khmer inscription was erected at Angkor Borei in 611 CE (Cœdès 1931), and the 7th-century Khmer king Jayavarman left inscriptions from Wat Phu (southern Laos) to the Mekong Delta (Lowman 2016, 107). However, it would take two more centuries before an inscription, from Champa, referred to the 'land of Kambu' (Lowman 2016, 96; Lowman et al. 2023, this volume).

Beyond these academic disagreements over timing and language group, first-millennium-CE cultural developments across the Mekong Delta reflected a distinctly Khmer sensibility in urban form, in brick and stone architectural technologies, and in the written record. This cultural reach, moreover, extended beyond the delta's limits to western Thailand and south-central Vietnam (Heng 2016). Archaeological settlement surveys since the mid-1990s have identified many multi-component sites that contain protohistoric, Pre-Angkor, and Angkor Periods (e.g., Bourdonneau 2007; Evans et al. 2016; Heng 2018; Stark 2006c; Welch 1998). Pre-Angkorian rulers from the 6th to 8th centuries invoked multigenerational roots that hearkened back to an earlier protohistoric era and to rulers of 'Vyadhapura' from whose direct descent they justified their rule (Cœdès 1962, 65; Heng 2016, 500–03). The 11th-to-12th–century Angkorian monuments like Phnom Chisor and Tonle Bati fringe Cambodia's northern delta, underscoring the enduring importance of the region in the Angkorian World whose reach stretched across Vietnam's Mekong Delta as far northeast to Ho Chi Minh city. Scripts, liturgical language, gods, and statecraft all bore the imprint of foreign contact made possible through long distance maritime exchange. Human agents travelled along these networks: mariners, craftsmen, merchants, and missionaries, and shaped changes in settlement and society in the first-millennium Mekong Delta that provided cultural templates for the Angkorian World that followed.

References

Acri, A., R. Blench & A. Landmann, 2017. Introduction: re-connecting histories across the Indo-Pacific, in *Spirits and Ships: Cultural Transfers in Early Monsoon Asia*, eds. A. Acri, R. Blench & A. Landmann. Singapore: ISEAS-Yusof Ishak Institute, 1–37.

Aymonier, E., 1903. Le Fou-Nan. *Journal Asiatique* 10(1), 109–31.

Bellina, B., 2014. Maritime silk roads' ornament industries: socio-political practices and cultural transfers in the South China Sea. *Cambridge Archaeological Journal* 24, 345–37.

Bellina, B. (Ed.)., 2017. *Khao Sam Kaeo: An Early Port-City Between The Indian Ocean And The South China Sea*. Paris: École française d'Extrême-Orient (Mémoires archéologiques #28).

Bishop, P., D. Penny, M.T. Stark & M. Scott., 2003. A 3.5 ka record of paleoenvironments and human occupation at Angkor Borei, Mekong Delta. Southern Cambodia. *Geoarchaeology* 18, 1–35.

Borell, B., 2014. The power of images—coin portraits of Roman emperors on jewellery pendants in early Southeast Asia. *Zeitschrift für Archäologie Außereuropäischer Kulturen* 6, 7–43.

Borell, B., 2017. Gemstones in Southeast Asia and beyond: trade along the maritime networks, in *Gemstones in the First Millennium AD. Mines, Trade, Workshops and Symbolism. International Conference, October 20th–22nd, 2015*, eds. A. Hilgner, S. Greiff & D. Quast. Mainz: Römisch-Germanisches Zentralmuseum, 21–44.

Bourdonneau, E., 2003. The ancient canal system of the Mekong Delta—preliminary report, in *Fishbones and Glittering Emblems. Southeast Asia Archaeology 2002*, eds. A. Karlström & A. Källén. Stockholm: Museum of Far Eastern Antiquities, 257–70.

Bourdonneau, E., 2007. Réhabiliter le Funan. Óc Eo ou la première Angkor. *Bulletin de l'École française d'Extrême-Orient* 94, 111–57.

Briggs, L.P., 1951. The Ancient Khmer Empire. *Transactions of the American Philosophical Society* 41(1), 1–295.

Brown, R.L., 2011. The importance of Gupta-period sculpture in Southeast Asian art history, in *Early Interactions between South and Southeast Asia: Reflections on Cross-Cultural Exchange*, eds. P.-Y. Manguin, A. Mani & G. Wade. Singapore and New Delhi: Institute of Southeast Asian Studies (Nalanda-Sriwijaya Centre), Manohar, 317–31.

Brown, R.L., 2017. The trouble with convergence, in *India and Southeast Asia: Cultural Discourses*, eds. A. L. Dallapiccola & A. Verghese. Mumbai: K R Cama Oriental Institute, 37–50.

Bui Phat Diem, Vuong Thu Hong & M. Nishimura, 1997. Research achievements of the archaeology before "Óc Eo Culture" in the Lower Van Co River Basin, southern part of Vietnam. *Journal of Southeast Asian Archaeology* 17, 72–7.

Calò, A., B. Prasetyo, P. Bellwood, J.W. Lankton, B. Gratuze, T. O. Pryce, A. Reinecke, V. Leusch, H. Schenk, R. Wood, R.A. Bawono, I.D. Kompiang Gede, Ni L. K. Cith Yuliatai, J. Fenner, C. Reepmeyer, C. Castillo & A.K. Carter, 2015. Sembiran and Pacung on the north coast of Bali: a strategic crossroads for early trans-Asiatic exchange. *Antiquity* 89, 378–96.

Cameron, J., 2000. Asbestos cloth and elites in Southeast Asia. *Bulletin of the Indo-Pacific Prehistory Association* 19, 47–51.

Cameron, J., A. Indrajaya & P.-Y. Manguin, 2015. Asbestos textiles from Batujaya (West Java, Indonesia): further evidence for early long-distance interaction between the Roman Orient, Southern Asia and Island Southeast Asia. *Bulletin de l'École française d'Extrême-Orient* 101, 159–76.

Carter, A.K., 2015. Beads, exchange networks and emerging complexity: a case study from Cambodia and Thailand (500 BCE–CE 500). *Cambridge Archaeological Journal* 25, 733–57.

Carter, A. K., L. Dussubieux, M.T. Stark & H.A. Gilg, 2021. Angkor Borei and protohistoric trade networks: a view from the glass and stone bead assemblage. *Asian Perspectives* 60, 32–70.

Castillo, C. Cobo, B. Bellina & D. Q. Fuller, 2016. Rice, beans and trade crops on the early maritime silk route in Southeast Asia. *Antiquity* 90, 1255–69.

Castillo, C. Cobo, C. F. W. Higham, K. Miller, N. Chang, K. Douka, T. F. G. Higham & D. Q Fuller, 2018. Social responses to climate change in Iron Age north-east Thailand: new archaeobotanical evidence. *Antiquity* 92, 1274–91.

Chevance, J-B. & C. Pottier, 2023. The early capitals of Angkor, in *The Angkorian World*, eds. M. Hendrickson, M.T. Stark & D. Evans. New York: Routledge, 80–96.

Christie, J.W., 1995. State formation in early Maritime Southeast Asia: a consideration of the theories and the data. *Bijdragen tot de Taal-, Land- en Volkenkunde* 151, 235–88.

Cœdès, G., 1931. Deux inscriptions sanskrites du Fou-nan. *Bulletin de l'École française d'Extrême-Orient* 31, 1–8.

Cœdès, G., 1937. A new inscription from Fu-Nan. *Journal of the Greater India Society* 4, 117–21.

Cœdès, G., 1962. *Les peoples de la péninsule indochinoise: histoire, civilisations.* Paris: Dunod.

Cœdès, G., 1964. *Les États hindouisés d'Indochine et d'Indonésie.* Paris: de Boccard.

Cœdès, G., 1968. *The Indianized States of Southeast Asia* (ed. W. F. Vella, translated by S. Brown Cowing). Kuala Lumpur/Honolulu: University of Malaya Press/University of Hawai'i Press.

Cœdès, G. & P. Dupont, 1943. L'inscription de Sdok Kak Thom. *Bulletin de l'École française d'Extrême-Orient* 43, 57–134.

Coomaraswarmy, A. K. & F. S. Kershaw, 1928–1929. A Chinese Buddhist water vessel and its Indian prototype. *Artibus Asiae* 3, 122–41.

Cox, K. J., R. A. Bentley, N. Tayles, H. R. Buckley, C. G. Macpherson & M. J. Cooper, 2011, Intrinsic or extrinsic population growth in Iron Age Northeast Thailand? The evidence from isotopic analysis. *Journal of Archaeological Science* 38, 665–71.

Cramb, R., 2020. The evolution of rice farming in the lower Mekong Basin, in *White Gold: The Commercialisation of Rice Farming in the Lower Mekong Basin*, ed. R. Cramb. Singapore: Springer Nature/Palgrave/MacMillan, 3–35.

Dalsheimer, N. & P.-Y. Manguin, 1998. Viṣṇu mitrés et réseaux marchands en Asie du Sud-Est: nouvelles données archéologiques sur le Ier millénaire apr. J.-C. *Bulletin de l'École française d'Extrême-Orient* 85, 87–123.

Dào Linh Con, 1998. The Óc Eo burial group recently excavated at Gò Tháp (Dong Thap Province, Viêt Nam), in *Southeast Asian Archaeology 1994: Proceedings of the 5th International Conference of the European Association of Southeast Asian Archaeologists, vol. 1*, ed. P.-Y. Manguin. Hull: Centre for Southeast Asian Studies, University of Hull, 111–17.

Domett, K. M., J. Newton, D. J. W. O'Reilly, N. Tayles, L. Shewan & N. Beavan, 2011. Cultural modification of the dentition in prehistoric Cambodia. *International Journal of Osteoarchaeology* 23, 274–86.

Dowling, N.H., 1999. A new date for the Phnom Da images and its implications for early Cambodia. *Asian Perspectives* 38, 51–61.

Estève, J., 2023. Gods and temples: the nature(s) of Angkorian religion, in *The Angkorian World*, eds. M. Hendrickson, M.T. Stark & D. Evans. New York: Routledge, 423–34.

Evans, C., N. Chang & N. Shimizu, 2016. Sites, survey & ceramics: settlement patterns in the first to ninth centuries CE in the Upper Mun River Valley, Northeast Thailand. *Journal of Southeast Asian Studies* 47, 438–67.

Evans, D., R. Fletcher, S. Klassen, C. Pottier & P. Wijker, 2023. Trajectories of urbanism in the Angkorian World, in *The Angkorian World*, eds. M. Hendrickson, M.T. Stark & D. Evans. New York: Routledge, 173–94.

Favereau, A. & B. Bellina, 2016. Thai-Malay Peninsula and South China Sea Networks (500 BC–AD 200), based on a reappraisal of "Sa Huynh-Kalanay"-related ceramics. *Quaternary International* 416, 219–27.

Francken, M., J. Wahl & A. Reinecke., 2010. Reflections of a hard life: burials from Gò Ô Chùa, in *Proceedings of the 5th Meeting of Junior Scientists in Anthropology. Freiburg im Breisgau 25. bis 28. März = Beiträge zum 4. Kongress des wissenschaftlichen Nachwuchses der Anthropologie*, ed. C. A. Buhl, F. Engel & L. Hartung. Freiberg: Institut für Humangenetik und Anthropologie, Freiburg University, 16–23.

Galloway, C., 2010. Ways of seeing a Pyu, Mon and Dvaravati artistic continuum. *Bulletin of the Indo-Pacific Prehistory Association* 30, 70–8.

Gerschheimer, G. & D. Goodall, 2014.'Que cette demeure de Śrīpati dure sur terre . . .' L'inscription preangkorienne K.1254 du musée d'Angkor Borei. *Bulletin de l'École française d'Extrême-Orient* 100, 113–46.

Gupta, S., 2005. The Bay of Bengal interaction sphere (1000 BC–AD 500). *Bulletin of the Indo-Pacific Prehistory Association* 25, 21–30.

Heng, P., 2016. Transition to the Pre-Angkorian Period: Thala Borivat and regional perspectives. *Journal of Southeast Asian Studies* 47, 484–505.

Heng, P., 2018. *Political economy and state formation of Pre-Angkorian Cambodia: viewed from Thala Borivat.* PhD dissertation. Honolulu: University of Hawai'i at Mānoa.

Heng, P., 2023. Angkor and the Mekong River: settlement, resources, mobility and power, in *The Angkorian World*, eds. M. Hendrickson, M.T. Stark. & D. Evans. New York: Routledge, 154–72.

Hoogervorst, T., 2017. Tracing maritime connections between Island Southeast Asia and the Indian Ocean World, in *The Routledge Handbook of Archaeology and Globalization*, ed. T. Hodos. London: Routledge Taylor & Francis Group, 751–67.

Hung, H.-C., Nguyên Kim Dung, P. Bellwood & M. T. Carson, 2013. Coastal connectivity: long-term trading networks across the South China Sea. *Journal of Island & Coastal Archaeology* 8, 384–404.

Ikehara-Quebral, R., M. T. Stark, W. Belcher, V. Vuthy, J. Krigbaum, R.A. Bentley, M. Pietrusewsky & M. T. Douglas, 2017. Biocultural practices during the transition to history at Angkor Borei, Cambodia. *Asian Perspectives* 56, 191–236.

Ishizawa, Y., 1995. Chinese chronicles of 1st–5th century AD Funan, southern Cambodia, in *South East Asia & China: Art, Interaction & Commerce* (Colloquies on Art & Archaeology in Asia No. 17), ed. R. Scott & J. Guy. London: Percival D. Foundation of Chinese Art, School of Oriental and African Studies, 11–31.

Jacques, C., 1979. 'Funan', 'Zhenla': The reality concealed by these Chinese views of Indochina, in *Early South East Asia: Essays in Archaeology, History and Historical Geography*, eds. R.B. Smith & W. Watson. New York & Kuala Lumpur: Oxford University Press, 371–79.

Jacques, C., 1986. Le pays Khmer avant Angkor. *Journal des Savants* 1–3, 59–95.

Jacques, C., 1995. China and Ancient Khmer history, in *South East Asia & China: Art, Interaction & Commerce, Colloquies on Art & Archaeology in Asia 17*, ed. R. Scott & J. Guy. London: Percival D. Foundation of Chinese Art, School of Oriental and African Studies, 32–40.

Kang, H., 2013. The spread of Sarnath-style Buddha images in Southeast Asia and Shandong, China by the sea route. *Kemanusiaan* 20, 39–60.

King, C. L., S. Halcrow, N. Tales & S. Shkrum. 2017. Considering the palaeoepidemiological implications of socioeconomic and environmental change in Southeast Asia. *Archaeological Research in Asia* 27–37.

Lavy, P.A., 2003. As in heaven, so on earth: the politics of Viṣṇu, Śiva and Harihara images in Preangkorian Khmer civilisation. *Journal of Southeast Asian Studies* 34, 21–39.

Lavy, P.A., 2014. Conch-on-hip images in Peninsular Thailand and Early Vaiṣṇava sculpture in Southeast Asia, in *Before Siam: Essays in Art and Archaeology*, eds. N. Revire & S.A. Murphy. Bangkok: River Books, 153–73.

Lavy, P.A. & M. Polkinghorne, 2023. Bodies of glory: the statuary of Angkor, in *The Angkorian World*, eds. M. Hendrickson, M.T. Stark & D. Evans. New York: Routledge, 435–58.

Lavy, P.A., 2020. Early Vaiṣṇava sculpture in Southeast Asia and the question of Pallava influence, in *Across the South of Asia: A Volume in Honor* of Professor Robert L. Brown", eds. R. DeCaroli & P.A. Lavy. New Delhi: PrintWorld, 213–50.

Lê Xuân Diêm & Đào Linh Côn, 1995. A propos de la culture Óc Eo: les découvertes après 1975, in *90 ans de recherches sur la culture et l'histoire du Viet Nam,* ed. Nguyễn Đức Diện. Ha Nôi: EFEO-Coéditions, Centre national des sciences sociales et humaines du Vietnam, 302–10.

Lê Xuân Diêm, Đào Linh Côn & Võ Sĩ Khải, 1995. *Văn Óc Eo: những khám phá mới [The Óc Eo Culture: New Discoveries].* Hà Nội: Nhà xuất bản khoa học xã hội.

Lê Thị Liên, 2006. Excavations at Minh Su Mound, Gò Tháp Site, Dong Thap Province, South Vietnam, in *Uncovering Southeast Asia's Past. Selected Papers from the 10th International Conference of the European Association of Southeast Asian Archaeologists*, ed. E. Bacus, I. C. Glover & V. Pigott. Singapore: NUS Press, 232–44.

Lê Thị Liên, 2010. Hindu iconography in early history of southern Vietnam. *Taida Journal of Art History, Taiwan National University* 25, 69–96.

Lê Thị Liên, 2011. Hindu deities in southern Vietnam: images on small archaeological artefacts, in *Early Interactions between South and Southeast Asia: Reflections on Cross-Cultural Exchange*, ed. P.-Y. Manguin, A. Mani & G. Wade. Singapore and New Delhi: Institute of Southeast Asian Studies (Nalanda-Sriwijaya Centre), Manohar, 407–32.

Lê Thị Liên, 2015a. Hindu beliefs and the maritime network in Southern Vietnam during the early common era. *Journal of Indo-Pacific Archaeology* 29, 1–17.

Lê Thị Liên, 2015b. The Óc Eo culture and its cultural interaction with the outside World, in *Perspectives on the Archaeology of Vietnam, International Colloquium, Hanoi, 29th February–2nd March 2012*, ed. A. Reinecke. Berlin/Bonn: German Archaeological Institute, 211–33.

Leong Sau Heng. 1990. Collecting centres, feeder points and entrepôts in the Malay Peninsula, 1000 B.C.–A. D. 1400, in *The Southeast Asian Port and Polity: Rise and Demise*, ed. J. Kathirithamby-Wells & J. Villiers. Singapore: Singapore University Press, National University of Singapore, 17–38.

Lowman, I., 2016. The land of Kambu: Political space and myth in Angkorian Cambodia, in *Le Passé des Khmers: langues, textes, rites*, ed. N. Abdoul-Carime, G. Mikaelian & J. Thach. Bern, Berlin, New York and Oxford: Peter Lang, 95–113.

Lowman, I., K., Chhom. & M. Hendrickson, 2023. An Angkor nation? Identifying the core of the Khmer empire, in *The Angkorian World*, eds. M. Hendrickson, M.T. Stark. & D. Evans. New York: Routledge, 479–93.

Malleret, L., 1951. Les fouilles d'Óc-eo, 1944: rapport préliminaire. *Bulletin de l'École française d'Extrême-Orient* 45, 75–88.

Malleret, L., 1959–63. *L'Archéologie du Delta du Mekong.* Paris: École française d'Extrême-Orient (4 tomes in 7 volumes).

Malleret, L., 1963, Pierres gravées et cachets de divers pays du sud-est de l'Asie. *Bulletin de l'École française d'Extrême-Orient* 51, 99–116.

Manguin, P.-Y., A. Mani & G. Wade (eds.) 2011. *Early Interactions between South and Southeast Asia: Reflections on Cross-Cultural Exchange.* Singapore and New Delhi: Institute of Southeast Asian Studies (Nalanda-Sriwijaya Centre), Manohar.

Manguin, P.-Y., & M.T. Stark, 2022. Mainland Southeast Asia's earliest kingdoms and the case of "Funan." In *Oxford Handbook of Southeast Asian Archaeology*, eds. C. F. W. Higham & N. Kim. Oxford: Oxford University Press, 637–59.

Manguin, P.-Y., 2000. Les cités-États de l'Asie du Sud-Est côtière: de l'ancienneté et de la permanence des formes urbaines. *Bulletin de l'École française d'Extrême-Orient* 87, 151–82.

Manguin, P.-Y., 2002a. The amorphous nature of coastal polities in insular Southeast Asia: restricted centres, expended peripheries. *Moussons* 5, 73–98.

Manguin, P.-Y., 2002b. From Funan to Sriwijaya: cultural continuities and discontinuities in the Early Historical maritime states of Southeast Asia, in *25 tahun kerjasama Pusat Penelitian Arkeologi dan École française d'Extrême-Orient.* Jakarta: Pusat Penelitian Arkeologi/École française d'Extrême-Orient, 59–82.

Manguin, P.-Y., 2004. The archaeology of the early maritime polities of Southeast Asia, in *Southeast Asia: From Prehistory to History*, ed. P. Bellwood & I. C. Glover. London: RoutledgeCurzon, 282–313.

Manguin, P.-Y., 2006. Les tuiles de l'ancienne Asie du Sud-Est: Essai de typologie, in *Anamorphoses. Hommage à Jacques Dumarçay*, ed. H. Chambert-Loir & B. Dagens. Paris: Les Indes savantes, 275–310.

Manguin, P.-Y., 2009. The archaeology of Funan in the Mekong River Delta: the Óc Eo culture of Vietnam, in *Arts of Ancient Vietnam: From River Plain to Open Sea*, ed. N. Tingley. New York and Houston: Asia Society, Museum of Fine Arts, Houston, Yale University Press, 100–18.

Manguin, P.-Y., 2010. Pan-regional responses to South Asian inputs in early Southeast Asia, in *50 Years of Archaeology in Southeast Asia: Essays in Honour of Ian Glover*, ed. B. Bellina, E. A. Bacus & T. O. Pryce. Bangkok: River Books, 170–81.

Manguin, P.-Y., 2019a. Protohistoric and early historic exchange in the Eastern Indian Ocean: a re-evaluation of current paradigms, in *Early Global Interconnectivity across the Indian Ocean World, vol. I: Commercial Structures and Exchanges*, ed. A. Schottenhammer. New-York: Palgrave McMillan, 99–120.

Manguin, P.-Y., 2019b. The transmission of Vaiṣṇavism across the Bay of Bengal: trade networks and state formation in early historic Southeast Asia, in *Early Global Interconnectivity across the Indian Ocean World, vol. II: Exchange of Ideas, Religions & Technologies*, ed. A. Schottenhammer. New-York: Palgrave McMillan, 51–68.

Manguin, P.-Y., 2019c. Sewn boats of Southeast Asia: the stitched-plank and lashed-lug tradition. *The International Journal of Nautical Archaeology* 48, 400–15.

Manguin, P.-Y. & Võ Sĩ Khải, 2000. Excavations at the Ba Thê/Óc Eo complex (Viêt Nam): a preliminary report on the 1998 campaign, in Southeast Asian Archaeology 1998. *Proceedings of the 7th International Conference of the European Association of Southeast Asian Archaeologists, Berlin 1998*, ed. W. Lobo & S. Reimann. Hull/Berlin: Centre for Southeast Asian Studies, University of Hull/Ethnologisches Museum, Staatlich Museen zu Berlin, Veröffentlichungen 70, 107–22.

Nguyễn Kim Dung, 2001. Jewelry from late prehistoric sites recently excavated in South Viet Nam. *Bulletin of the Indo-Pacific Prehistory Association* 21, 107–13.

Nguyễn Phúc Long, 1975. Les nouvelles recherches archéologiques au Việtnam (Complément au Việtnam de Louis Bezacier). *Arts Asiatiques* 31, 3–151.

Nishimura, M., Nguyễn Duy Tỳ & Huỳnh Đình Chung, 2008–9. Excavation of Nhơn Thành at the Hậu Giang River Reach, Southern Vietnam. *Taida Journal of Art History* 25, 1–68.

Paris, P., 1931. Anciens canaux reconnus sur photographies aériennes dans les provinces de Ta Kev et de Châu-Dôc. *Bulletin de l'École française d'Extrême-Orient* 31, 221–23.

Paris, P., 1941. I. Anciens canaux reconnus sur photographies aériennes dans les provinces de Takeo, Châu-Dôc, Long-Xuyên et Rach-Gia. II. Autres canaux reconnus à l'est du Mékong par examen d'autres photographies aériennes (Provinces de Châu-Dôc et de Long-Xuyên). *Bulletin de l'École française d'Extrême-Orient* 41, 365–72.

Pelliot, P., 1903a. Le Fou-nan. *Bulletin de l'École française d'Extrême-Orient* 3, 248–303.

Pelliot, P., 1903b. La dernière ambassade du Fou-nan en Chine sous les Leang (539). *Bulletin de l'École française d'Extrême-Orient* 3, 671–72.

Phon, K., 2004. Phnom Borei and Its Relationship to Angkor Borei. Unpublished report on file with the Ministry of Culture and Fine Arts, Cambodia.

Pietrusewsky, M. & R. Ikehara-Quebral, 2006. The bioarchaeology of the Vat Komnou Cemetery, Angkor Borei, Cambodia. *Bulletin of the Indo-Pacific Prehistory Association* 26, 86–96.

Piper, P.J. & M.F. Oxenham, 2014. Of prehistoric pioneers: the establishment of the first sedentary settlements in the Mekong Delta Region of Southern Vietnam during the period 2000–1500 cal. BC, in *Living in the Landscape: Essays in Honour of Graeme Barker*, eds. K. Boyle, R. Rabett & C. O. Hunt. Cambridge: McDonald Institute for Archaeological Research, University of Cambridge, 209–26.

Pou, S., 1974. The word ĀC in Khmer: a semantic overview, in *South-East Asian Linguistic Studies*, ed. Nguyen Dang Liem. Canberra: Australia National University, 175–91.

Proske, U., D. Heslop & T.J.J. Hanebuth, 2009. Salt production in pre-Funan Vietnam: archaeomagnetic reorientation of briquetage fragments. *Journal of Archaeological Science* 36, 84–9.

Ray, H.P., 2014. Multi-religious maritime linkages across the Bay of Bengal during the first millennium CE, in *Before Siam: Essays in Art and Archaeology*, eds. N. Revire & S.A. Murphy. Bangkok: River Books, 135–51.

Reinecke, A., 2012. The prehistoric occupation and cultural characteristics of the Mekong Delta during the pre-Funan periods. In *Crossing Borders: Selected Papers from the 13th International Conference of the European Association of Southeast Asian Archaeologists*, volume 1, eds. M.-L. Tjoa-Bonatz, A. Reinecke & D. Bonatz. Singapore: NUS Press, 239–56.

Revire, N., 2016. Dvāravatī and Zhenla in the seventh to eighth centuries: a transregional ritual complex. *Journal of Southeast Asian Studies* 47, 393–417.

Sanderson, D.C.W., P. Bishop, M.T. Stark, S. Alexander & D. Penny, 2007. Luminescence dating of canal sediments from Angkor Borei, Mekong Delta, Southern Cambodia. *Quaternary Geochronology* 2, 322–29.

Schlosser, S., A. Reinecke, R. Schwab, E. Pernicka, S. Seng & L. Vin, 2012. Early Cambodian gold and silver from Prohear: composition, trace elements and gilding. *Journal of Archaeological Science* 39, 2877–87.

Sen, T., 2014. Maritime Southeast Asia between South Asia and China to the sixteenth century. *TRaNS: Trans-Regional and -National Studies of Southeast Asia* 2, 31–59.

Shewan, L., R.M. Ikehara-Quebral, M.T. Stark, R. Armstrong, D. O'Reilly, V. Voeun, M.T. Douglas & M. Pietrusewsky, 2020. Resource utilisation and regional interaction in protohistoric Cambodia—the evidence from Angkor Borei. *Journal of Archaeological Science Reports* 31, 102289.

Skilling, P., 2011. Buddhism and the circulation of ritual in early Peninsular Southeast Asia, in *Early Interactions between South and Southeast Asia: Reflections on Cross-Cultural Exchange*, ed. P.-Y. Manguin, A. Mani & G. Wade. Singapore: Institute for Southeast Asian Studies, 371–84.

Skilling, P., 2015a. The circulation of artefacts engraved with 'Apramāda' and other mottos in Southeast Asia and India: a preliminary report. *Annual Report of the International Research Institute for Advanced Buddhology at Soka University for the Academic Year 2014*, 18, 63–77.

Skilling, P., 2015b. An untraced Buddhist verse inscription from (Pen)insular Southeast Asia, in *Buddhist Dynamics in Premodern and Early Modern Southeast Asia*, ed. C. Lammerts. Singapore: Institute of Southeast Asian Studies, 18–79.

Ślączka, A., 2011. The brick structures of Gò Tháp—Tombs or temples? *Bulletin of the Indo-Pacific Prehistory Association* 31, 108–16.

Stark, M.T., 2003. Angkor Borei and the archaeology of Cambodia's Mekong Delta, in *Art & Archaeology of Fu Nan: Pre-Khmer Kingdom of the Lower Mekong Valley*, ed. J. C. M. Khoo. Bangkok: Orchid Press, 87–105.

Stark, M.T., 2006a. Early mainland southeast Asian landscapes in the first millennium AD. *Annual Review of Anthropology* 35, 407–32.

Stark, M.T., 2006b. From Funan to Angkor: collapse and regeneration in ancient Cambodia, in *After Collapse: The Regeneration of Complex Societies*, ed. G. M. Schwartz & J. J. Nichols. Tucson: University of Arizona Press, 144–67.

Stark, M.T., 2006c. Pre-Angkorian settlement trends in Cambodia's Mekong delta and the lower Mekong archaeological project. *Bulletin of the Indo-Pacific Prehistory Association* 26, 98–109.

Stark, M.T., 2015. Inscribing legitimacy and building power in the Mekong delta, in *Counternarratives and Macrohistories: New Agendas in Archaeology and Ancient History*, ed. G. Emberling. Cambridge: Cambridge University Press, 75–105.

Stark, M.T., 2021. Landscapes, linkages and luminescence: first-millennium CE environmental and social change in Mainland Southeast Asia, in *Primary Sources and Asian Pasts: Transdisciplinary Perspectives on Primary Sources in the Premodern World*, eds. P.C. Bischop & E. A. Cecil. De Gruyter: Berlin, 184–219.

Stark, M.T. & S. Fehrenbach, 2019. Earthenware ceramic technologies of Angkor Borei, Cambodia. *Udaya, Journal of Khmer Studies* 14, 109–33.

Stark, M.T., D.C.W. Sanderson & R. G. Bingham, 2006. Monumentality in the Mekong Delta: luminescence dating and implications. *Bulletin of the Indo-Pacific Prehistory Association* 26, 110–20.

Stark, M.T & S. Bong, 2001. Recent research on the emergence of early historic states in Cambodia's lower Mekong Delta. *Bulletin of the Indo-Pacific Prehistory Association* 21, 85–98.

Stark, M.T. & A. Cremin, 2023. Angkor and China: 9th–15th centuries, in *The Angkorian World*, eds. M. Hendrickson, M.T. Stark & D. Evans. New York: Routledge, 112–32.

Stevens, C., P.-Y. Manguin, E. Bourdonneau, Lê Xuân Thuyên & A. Ozer, 2004. Apport de la télédétection à la recherche archéologique: Anciens canaux et structures anciennes du delta du Mékong, in *Géorisques et télédétections. Les Xèmes Journées Scientifiques du Réseau Télédétection de l'Agence Universitaire de la Francophonie*, eds. A. Bannari & F. Blasco. Ottawa, Réseau Télédétection de l'Agence Universitaire de la Francophonie, 52–5.

Ta Thi Kim Oanh, Nguyen Van Lap, M. Tateishi, I. Kobayashi, S. Tanabe & Y. Saito, 2002. Holocene delta evolution and sediment discharge of the Mekong River, Southern Vietnam. *Quaternary Science Reviews* 21, 1807–19.

Tamura, T., Y. Saito, S. Sieng, B. Ben, M. Kong, Im Sim, S. Choup & F. Akiba, 2009. Initiation of the Mekong River Delta at 8ka: evidence from the sedimentary succession in the Cambodian lowland. *Quaternary Science Reviews* 28, 327–44.

Trinh, T.H., 1996. Réflexions sur les vestiges de la culture d'Óc Eo. *Études Vietnamiennes* 2, 60–7.

Vickery, M., 1994. What and where was Chenla? in *Recherche nourvelles sur le Cambodge*, publiées sous la direction de F. Bizot. Paris: École française d'Extrême-Orient.

Vickery, M., 1998. *Society, Economics and Politics in Pre-Angkor Cambodia: The 7th–8th Centuries*. Tokyo: Centre for East Asian Cultural Studies for UNESCO/The Toyo Bunko.

Vickery, M., 2003. Funan reviewed: deconstructing the ancients. *Bulletin de l'École française d'Extrême-Orient* 90–91, 101–43.

Võ Sĩ Khải, 1998. Plans architecturaux des anciens monuments du Delta du Mékong du 1er au 10e siècles AD. Southeast Asian archaeology 1994: *Proceedings of the 5th International Conference of the European Association of Southeast Asian Archaeologists, Paris, October 1994, volume I*, ed. P.-Y. Manguin. Hull: University of Hull, Centre of Southeast Asian Studies, 207–14.

Wang, G., 1958. The Nanhai trade: a study of the early history of Chinese trade in the South China Sea. *Journal of the Malayan Branch of the Royal Asiatic Society* 31(182), 1–135.

Welch, D.J., 1998. Archaeology of Northeast Thailand in relation to the Pre-Khmer and Khmer historical records. *International Journal of Historical Archaeology* 2, 205–33.

Wheatley, P., 1961. *The Golden Khersonese: Studies in the Historical Geography of the Malay Peninsula before A.D, 1500*. Kuala Lumpur: University of Malaya Press.

Wheatley, P., 1983. *Nagara and Commandery: Origins of the Southeast Asian Urban Tradition*. Chicago, IL: Geography Department, University of Chicago.

5
THE EARLY CAPITALS OF ANGKOR

Jean-Baptiste Chevance and Christophe Pottier

Introduction

Our understanding of urbanism in Angkor mirrors the history of the capital of the Khmer Empire. The cross-referencing of the corpus of inscriptions with the remains of religious monuments created by Angkor's elites has given birth to a rather disorderly list of kings, their respective territories, major deeds, rituals, and dates that defined their reigns. In conventional histories of the Angkorian World, Angkor's earliest phases have therefore come to be dominated by the works of Jayavarman II at Mahendraparvata (Phnom Kulen), Indravarman I at Hariharālaya (Roluos), and Yaśovarman I at Yaśodharapura (Angkor) and have overshadowed the reigns of rulers (e.g., Jayavarman III) whose records are less obvious or are too difficult to distinguish within Angkor's complex palimpsest.

According to epigraphy, the origin of Angkor is ultimately attributed to Jayavarman II in 802 CE, a date that corresponds to the declaration of the universality of the king—freed from any foreign dominion—and the new ritual cult of Devaraja (K. 325 inscription, Sdok Kak Thom, 11th century). This ritual, which was occasionally repeated by his successors, was associated by scholars—lacking any particular evidence—with the temple-mountain of Phnom Kulen and more generally with pyramid temples built in subsequent reigns, (Stern 1934). This original 'event' on Phnom Kulen simultaneously froze the official origin story of Angkor, establishing a modern, arbitrary divide between the Pre-Angkor and Angkor Periods at the onset of the 9th century and ultimately deterred subsequent investigations into this part of Khmer history.

A further legacy of early research is that Angkor's capitals have been considered through the lens of their major infrastructural achievements. A foundational article by Stern (1951), still very widely cited today, associates Khmer cities with the sequential construction of three major components: temple-mountain, followed by temples dedicated to ancestors, and finally public works (hydraulic or infrastructural). This analysis was based on the types of remains that were readily apparent on the surface today using imprecisely constructed timelines and without much critical analysis of the ways in which monumental remains were genuinely related to the evolution of the infrastructural remains that lay near or around them. Consequently, the purest version of this canonical urban model is Angkor Thom: the 'Large City', known in inscriptions as Yaśodharapura, that was redeveloped by Jayavarman VII in the late 12th century with

DOI: 10.4324/9781351128940-7

a walled, square 'city' surrounded by a moat and the Bayon temple-mountain positioned at its centre (Goloubew 1935; Groslier 1979; Pottier 2000a).

The authority and predominance of this urban archetype ultimately overshadowed the legacy of earlier capital models such as Roluos, with its monumental core component in an open plan (without boundaries), the 'city of the Baray' (Bhavapura) whose structure was wiped out by later redevelopments, and the monumental complex of Phnom Kulen, which was hidden until recently beneath the dense vegetation canopy. Intensive archaeological research (mapping, excavations, paleo-environmental studies, etc.) at these three sites over the past two decades is finally beginning to shift the narrative about the earliest urban occupation in the Angkor region (Chevance et al. 2019; Pottier 1999, 2017). Furthermore, recent research on the palace precincts of Angkorian kings suggest that these areas were as important as temple-mountain and other kinds of infrastructure in terms of shaping the geometry and urban planning of Angkor's cities over time. This chapter therefore seeks to enrich the temple-mountain centric view of Angkorian urban planning by examining the diachronic development of Khmer urbanism, specifically the duality between the sacred and the secular that linked the space and geometries of its early political capitals (Pottier 2014, 165–68). While these structures are already partially recognisable around the Pre-Angkorian pyramid of Ak Yum, studies of Mahendraparvata and Hariharālaya bring into much sharper focus the modalities, changes, and permanence of these urban forms, which eventually laid the foundations for the development of Yaśodharapura, the last and greatest expression of a 'capital' in the Khmer Empire.

Roluos/Hariharālaya

Our study begins in Hariharālaya (the 'residence of Harihara'), a city identified as early as 1928 as belonging to the Roluos Group and situated today 15 km southwest of Angkor (Cœdès 1928, 121; 1937, 187). This city features prominently within the historiography of Khmer studies as supposedly the 'first' Angkorian capital, the 'first' hydraulic city, and an archetype for Angkorian town planning. According to the Sdok Kak Thom inscription, Jayavarman II stayed twice at Hariharālaya and died there before 839 CE, but no monuments there have definitely been associated with his reign. Most of the major constructions of the capital were dated to a later period associated with Indravarman I based on inscriptions that he commissioned after his coronation in 877 *CE* and include: (1) Lolei Baray, Indratataka, a large 4-km-long water reservoir; (2) Preah Ko often designated as the 'ancestors' temple and perfect example of the eponymous art-historical style, the first style of the so-called Angkor Period (Pottier and Lujàn-Lunsford 2007); and (3) Bakong, a pyramidal monument enclosed by a series of squared moats and concentric enclosures, whose outer enclosure stretched over 1 km^2 and included about 20 regularly spaced satellite shrines. Stern based his perspective in *Diversité et rythme des fondations royales khmères*—the classic work laying out the three 'basic elements' of a royal capital—on these three most visible monumental sites, and this idea is still deeply embedded in the understanding of Angkorian urban planning.

The first inventories of the early 20th century (Aymonier 1900–1904; Lunet de Lajonquière 1902–1911), followed by studies in the 1930s (Stern 1938a), also highlighted the existence at Roluos of a concentration of Pre-Angkorian temple remains. One of them, and the best preserved, is Prasat Trapeang Phong, located south of Roluos right at the edge of land regularly flooded by the annual cycle of the Tonle Sap Lake. Briggs and Groslier suggested that the residence of Jayavarman II and that of his successor Jayavarman III were located there (Briggs 1999[1951], 84; Groslier 1998[1958], 39). Groslier also noted a configuration of 'tiered trapeang' (*trapeang* are ponds in the Khmer language) foreshadowing the great reservoirs or *baray* and considered them a kind of Angkorian hydraulic prototype. He also noted at Roluos the 'cellular' organisation and a '*terramare*' typology typical, in his judgement, of previous Pre-Angkorian settlements. Also at Roluos, Groslier considered Indravarman I's Hariharālaya the first instance of a hydraulic city (Groslier 1979).

Nevertheless, the presentation of this first Angkorian 'city' presented severe shortcomings and some inconsistencies: There were contradictions between epigraphic sources and settlement construction phases, there was the lack of a palatial residence, and the modalities and the duration of the settlements and of occupations were overlooked, among other problems. Once the original arguments of Stern were deconstructed (Pottier 1996), and with the epigraphic dating of architecture offering considerable ambiguity (Pottier and Lujàn-Lunsford 2007), new projects of mapping, high-resolution topographic survey, and archaeological excavation enabled us to arrive at a new understanding of Hariharālaya.

Three excavation seasons, from 2004–06, undertaken in the heart of the city at Bakong temple, including long trenches opened through the enclosures from the temple's pyramid until the outer moat, confirmed the scale and synchronicity of the original general plan and underlined the remarkable scope of the earthworks beyond the temple building (Pottier 2017). Excavations also revealed the scarcity of domestic settlements, which clearly contradicted the mainstream idea, until then only superficially analysed, that there was a high density of habitat in the vicinity of pyramidal temples. What has become clear is that the massive, geometric development of Bakong does not correlate with 'a city', or at least a densely populated urban development project, but rather a religious settlement filled with scattered monastic infrastructure (Pottier et al. 2008).

In terms of chronology, this research has pushed back the foundation date of Bakong and of its large-scale layout of moats and enclosures (Pottier 1996, 2003, 436). In terms of architecture, Indravarman I can now be associated with the sandstone veneer of an earlier laterite pyramid. The foundation of this complex may be dated back to the later part of the 8th century, a century before Indravarman I's reign, and maybe even before that of Jayavarman II (Pottier et al. 2008, 250; Penny et al. 2006), in a site that was occupied at least as early as the 7th century CE (Pottier and Soutif 2016). Moreover, while the central temple of Bakong was still active at least until the 12th century, the limited chronological scope of the occupation identified in the vicinity of the temple nonetheless suggests a major contraction of religious spaces once Hariharālaya was abandoned for Yaśodharapura.

The Royal Palace, previously totally overlooked in any consideration of the urban layout at Hariharālaya (Cœdès 1938; Pottier 1999), has now been located at Prei Monti south of Bakong. Excavations carried out in 2007–2008 in this large 42-ha rectangle, enclosed by one moat, revealed monumental remains—but secular rather than religious—and an unusual quantity and quality of imported ceramic from China and the Middle East. Taken together, this offers evidence of the outstanding status of this area and confirms that Prei Monti was the palatial residence of Hariharālaya in the 9th century (Pottier et al. 2012, 292–294).

Finally, in contrast to the organised and geometric monumental core, Prasat Trapeang Phong probably represents a typology of 'secondary' developments populating Hariharālaya: shrines located on a mound enclosed with a moat, associated with one or several ponds (*trapeang*), and surrounded by detached rectangular platforms grouped in a quasi-organic fashion (Pottier 1999) (Figure 5.1). The 25 test pits dug in 2004 and 2005 at Trapeang Phong over 15 locations showed that the 'tiered trapeangs' resulted from a large-scale redevelopment of the site in the 11th and 12th centuries. Conversely, there were long sequences of domestic occupations from the 7th until the 14th centuries that have been documented in rectangular platforms concentrated to the west of the temple. These occupation layers allowed us to reconstruct the surroundings of

Figure 5.1 Aerial view of Trapeang Phong. View from the southeast. Note the numerous detached rectangular platforms emerging from the flooded landscape at the end of the rainy season.

Source: (Image P. Bâty).

this early temple, which is part of the Hariharālaya complex, and likely the source of its name since two Harihara statues were recovered from Trapeang Phong (Pottier and Bolle 2009). The occupation layers also attested to its gradual evolution and densification. Trapeang Phong may perhaps no longer be considered a possible royal residence or a hydraulic prototype but rather a site typical of the first 'Pre-Angkorian' settlements in the region. It is typical of numerous 'village' settlements using the open and cellular layout of Hariharālaya City, which continued in the early days of the Angkor Period until enclosed grids were favoured (Pottier 1999; Evans et al. 2013; Evans 2016).

Hariharālaya consists of cellular settlements, sometimes very ancient, stretched over 30 km^2, with a core established before the 9th century; it is a monumental, cardinal, and open urban plan based on the duality of the temple-mountain and the Royal Palace, with the temple-mountain sitting at the centre of the composition (Figure 5.2). Until it was abandoned a century later, this planning foreshadowed and generated major developments and diverse infrastructures: monumental causeways (especially that which leads east, extending towards a since-diverted river), roads and canals (leading 14 km towards the Tonle Sap lake to the south and 10 km northeast towards the kilns of Khnar Po), and the development of a 4-km-long baray in the northern part of the city, probably associated with the canalisation of the original Roluos river course. Beyond this centre, the area of extension of the urban development was not delineated or enclosed and is generally characterised by orthogonal and cardinal developments and land parcelling (Pottier 1999; Hawken 2011, 2013). No uniting grid has been identified, although it may now have vanished, covered over by later development.

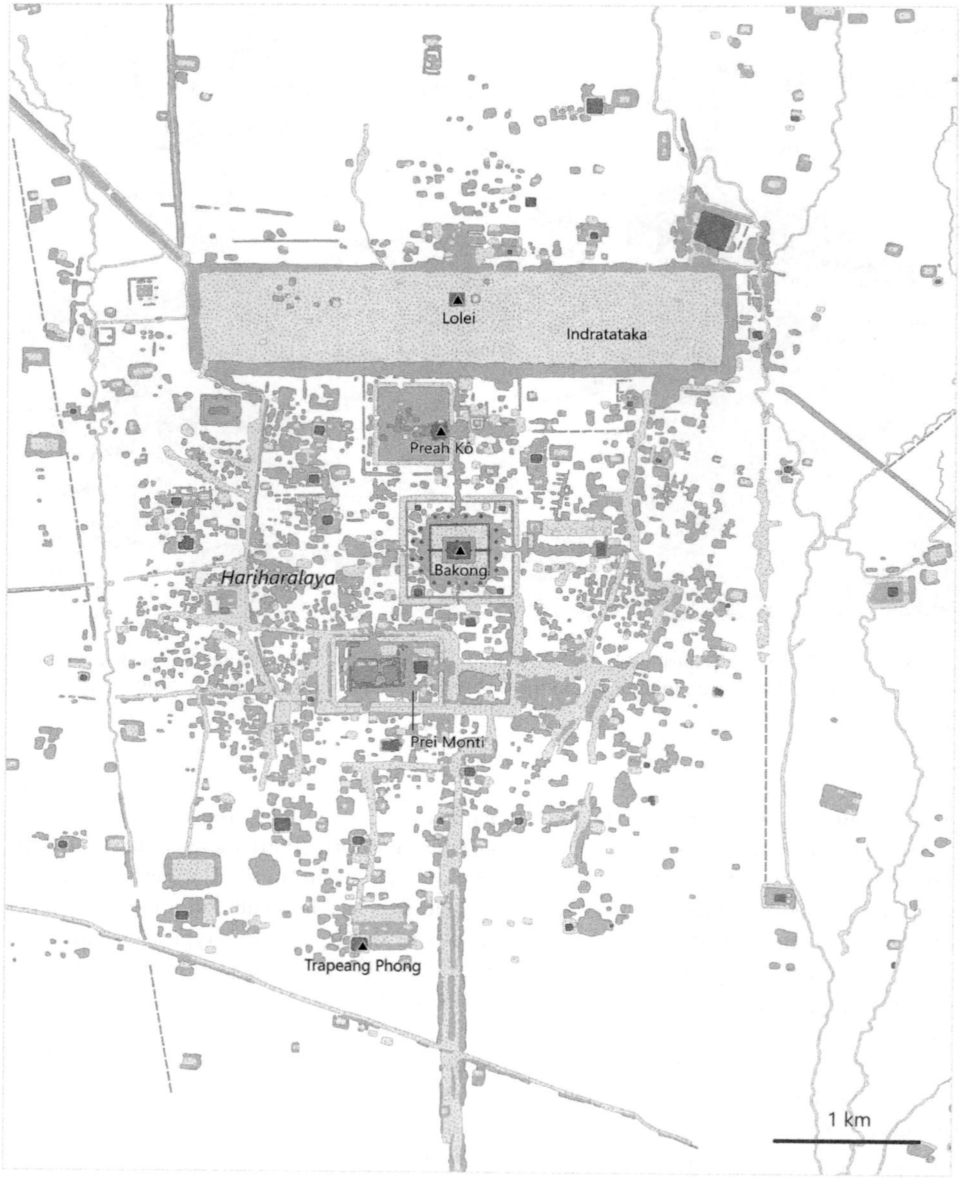

Figure 5.2 Archaeological map of the Roluos region.

Source: (Map by authors with contributions from P. Wijker).

Phnom Kulen/Mahendraparvata

Mahendraparvata is probably the most famous of Jayavarman II's capitals. Its existence on the Phnom Kulen plateau was known from several inscriptions of the 10th and 11th centuries, mentioning both the city and the massif, which were discovered identifying Mahendraparvata and the massif, according to the initial inventories of Phnom Kulen archaeological sites (Aymonier

1900; Finot 1911). Nevertheless, the city was still not associated with the remains of Phnom Kulen with certainty: In the first years of the 20th century, chronologies of Khmer monuments still attributed Bayon-style temples to Jayavarman II. Marchal (1923), Goloubew (1924), and Parmentier (1927, 1935) gradually explored the massif, and Phnom Kulen eventually came to be considered a complex of monuments whose architecture and decor had archaistic features.

The contemporary art historical research of Stern (1927), which was focused on the study of decor and statuary, corrected the chronology of monuments and firmly established the link between the temples of Phnom Kulen and King Jayavarman II. From that point forward, the monuments were understood as remains of a 9th-century city located on top of the massif. In 1932, Stern identified the 'Kulen Style' as the 'missing link in the evolution of Khmer art forming a transition between the 8th- and 9th-century styles'. He later organised an archaeological campaign (1936–1938) revealing many shrines presenting homogeneous architectural and sculptural decorations. This campaign confirmed the style as transitional but also revealed diverging components, as well as influences from the art of the neighbouring Cham civilisation (Stern 1938b). A recent study on the architectural features of Phnom Kulen temples (Chevance 2005) confirms the variety of architectural forms during this period of innovation and experimentation while at the same time suggesting that some shrines date from an earlier period than the rest of the group.

In the 1960s the area was once again under the spotlight (Hansen 1969; Boulbet-Dagens 1973; Boulbet 1979), with a particular focus on dams and other hydraulic structures, although at the time the researchers had not linked them to any kind of urban development. Among the capitals of Jayavarman II, Mahendraparvata was even considered a place of refuge and linked with a hypothetical period of his reign of withdrawal (Jacques 2007, 103).

Since the 2000s, archaeological research conducted by the Archaeology & Development Foundation (ADF) and led by Chevance has uncovered convincing new evidence for the existence of a capital on the plateau. A notable finding is the unexpectedly large size of Rong Chen temple-mountain (Figure 5.3), located on the highest point of the Kulen plateau and apparently the central state temple of a king (Chevance 2011), and the spatial relationship it holds with the nearby site of Banteay. Following surveys and excavation, the layout and architectural organisation of Banteay clearly confirm its status as a royal palace (Figure 5.4) (Chevance 2014). Seasons of excavation since 2009 on both sites have offered evidence that their construction and occupation were contemporary with Jayavarman II's reign. Nevertheless, despite extensive ground survey work that led to significant revisions of the archaeological map of Phnom Kulen (Chevance 2011), this new picture of Phnom Kulen only sketched the urban development: In particular, it underscored our limited understanding of hydraulic structures and did not indicate the existence of domestic settlements.

Campaigns of airborne lidar coverage carried out in the framework of the KALC (2012) and CALI (2015) projects assisted in spectacularly revising the archaeological map of Phnom Kulen (Evans et al. 2013; Evans 2016; Chevance et al. 2019). They revealed a large-scale urban configuration defined by earthen levees. This previously unknown urban infrastructure stretches over a large area of the south of the Kulen plateau and incorporates archaeological sites that had been previously identified, in particular the two major components of the city: the temple-mountain of Rong Chen and the Royal Palace of Banteay. The unfinished five-tiered pyramid of Rong Chen and the Banteay enclosure, stretching across an area of more than 30 ha enclosed by earthen embankments, represent the kind of massive investment in construction that we usually associate with strong and centralised power structures. The lidar campaigns also revealed the existence of another tell-tale marker of a royal city: a large (but unfinished) reservoir, or baray, 1 km in length. Only the southern and eastern banks of that construction had previously been

Figure 5.3 Rong Chen temple-mountain. Three upper terrace levels during excavation, view from the northeast.

Source: (Photo J-B Chevance).

Figure 5.4 Banteay, the Royal Palace of Mahendraparvata. Brick walls and pavements of the southwest main platform.

Source: (Photo J-B Chevance).

identified, and they had not been recognised, until then, as elements of a baray. The reservoir was built at the bottom of the main valley of the plateau, on the eastern axis of the temple-mountain, in order to optimise its position in relation to water catchments: most waterways in the area flowed into it. This reservoir offers evidence that the Khmer had a comprehensive understanding of this undulating topography at a landscape scale—the scale of the entire plateau, essentially—and were sufficiently skilled as engineers to optimise their hydrological network accordingly.

The urban network or frame that was revealed by lidar stretched over most of the southern part of the Kulen plateau, spanning about 40–50 km^2 (Figure 5.5). Organised geometrically and facing the cardinal directions, it formed a grid whose units are squares of 1.5 km^2 per side, made up of four north–south axes and six east–west axes. These axes were excavated in several areas in 2014. They are made up of parallel earthen levees spaced 60 to 80 m apart. The square units were subdivided into smaller plots of land associated with small ponds delineated by modest earthen levees aligned on their axes, which could have formed habitat or farming plots. Previously recorded dams (Hansen 1969) provide evidence for major hydraulic engineering works that formed large retaining reservoirs, key features to settle a large population.

Most of the topographic anomalies revealed by lidar have now been confirmed as either newly discovered archaeological features (traces of land parcels, ponds, platforms) or as elements of previously known sites (dams, temples, temple-mountain, royal palace). Moreover, most of these features are fully connected to, and/or incorporated within, the overall urban

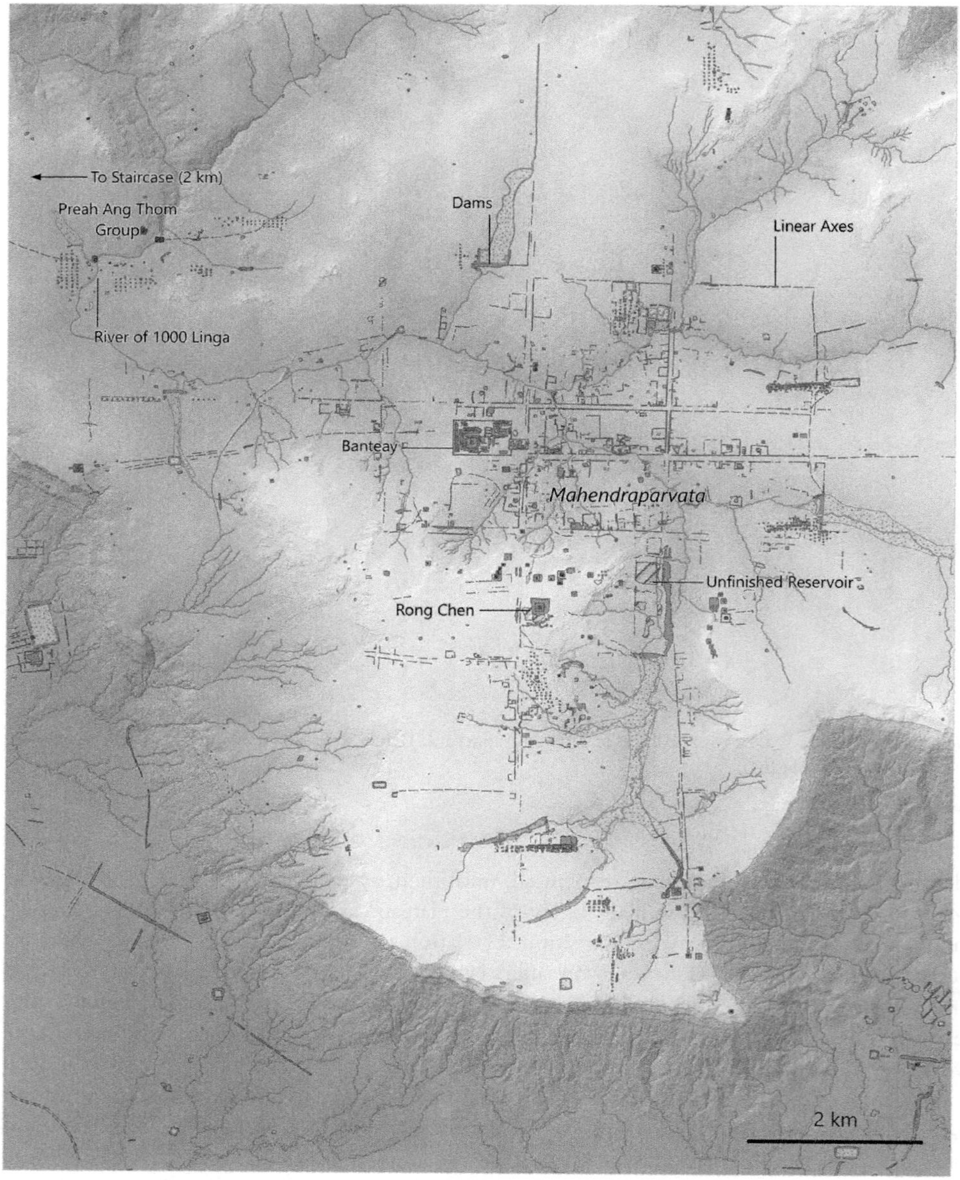

Figure 5.5 Archaeological map of the Kulen plateau highlighting the urban layout of Mahendraparvata.
Source: (Map by authors with contributions by N. Hofer).

framework, thus offering evidence of large-scale urban planning. The only sites that do not fit in the framework are hermitages that appeared later (Chevance 2013) and patterned arrays of mounds—or 'mound fields'—whose distribution and morphology distinguishes them clearly from the overall urban pattern. Excavations confirmed that these mounds were built at a later time, with radiocarbon dating showing the 10th century, although their function is not yet clearly understood (Chevance et al. 2019). The same applies to a laterite staircase, Phleu Cere, sometimes identified as the access from the Angkor plain to Mahendraparvata; in fact, it did not link to the fabric of Jayavarman II's capital but instead leads to sites scattered around Preah Ang Thom, occupied from the 10th century until the 13th century. Recent paleo-environmental studies (Penny et al. 2014) also indicate that the ancient city was occupied after its abandonment as the seat of the royal power (Chevance 2014). Although we can exclude some shrines assumed to date from an earlier period and which are not connected to it, overall, the great majority of features on Phnom Kulen make up one large and coherent urban assemblage.

Today, Mahendraparvata is not considered a group of scattered monuments anymore but rather the opposite: an open urban complex with a regular and extremely well-structured layout connecting with each other major religious, secular, and hydraulic sites despite the constraining environment. It encompasses areas designed to accommodate a significant population during the reign of Jayavarman II in the very early 9th century. This city unified for the first time, within a coherent spatial arrangement, the three main markers of an Angkorian capital: a temple-mountain, a royal palace, and a baray. Archaeological studies show that the temple-mountain was never completed (Chevance 2011), and that the Royal Palace (Chevance 2014) and other parcels of land were only briefly occupied. These clues suggest that Mahendraparvata was an unfinished project at the time that Jayavarman II, according to the Sdok Kak Thom stele (Cœdès-Dupont 1943, 110), moved his capital back to Hariharālaya.

The 'City of the Baray'/Bhavapura

In addition to evidence for early occupation from the Hariharālaya region, the first inventories also recorded some Pre-Angkorian inscriptions and remains to the west of Siem Reap in the Angkor plain, in particular in the vicinity of the southwest corner of the West Baray, at sites such as Wat Khnat and Prasat Prei Khmeng. Research led by Trouvé in the area from 1932, and the discovery of Prasat Ak Yum, a temple-mountain buried under the south dike of the West Baray, initially drew attention to the importance of these Pre-Angkorian settlements. After Trouvé passed away, these remains were incorporated into Stern's (1938a) research into the 'missing link' between the art-historical styles of the Pre-Angkor and Angkor Periods. But field investigations were not continued here, despite Goloubew noting large-scale linear features in the area in the course of aerial surveys (1936, 476).

This concentration of Pre-Angkor Period texts and archaeological remains hinted at the existence of a 'City of the Baray'/Bhavapura in this region. Many scholars suggested that it could have been the location of one of the first capitals of Jayavarman II, either Indrapura (Stern 1938a, 180) or Amarendrapura (Trouvé 1934; Cœdès 1989, 187; Groslier 1998[1958], 19), or that it related to Jayavarman I's capital of Purandarapura (Jacques 1990, 42; Soutif 2009) or Aninditapura/Svargadvārapura (Jacques 1972, 219; Jacques 2012, *pers. comm.*). As the city was not clearly identified, Groslier decided to use the name 'Banteay Chhoeu', which he described as 'an earthen levee bordered by external moat' forming an 'imposing city . . . oriented in a regular manner, almost square, and of at least 3 km per side' (1979, 166 and map 2).

Twenty years later, while accepting the name 'City of the Baray'/Bhavapura, Pottier (1999, 2000b) nonetheless contested the existence and interpretation of this square enclosure. Using an analysis based on remote sensing, he argued that the remains were scattered over a wider area than just the proposed enclosure and that the city was actually overlain by a fabric of canals and land parcels which, although it gave the impression of an enclosed Pre-Angkorian city, was actually developed much later alongside 11th-century West Baray reservoir (Pottier 1999,

119–21, 2000b, 110). Following the lead of Stern, who identified two distinct Pre-Angkor 'Periods', Pottier suggested that this region was the superimposition of 'two Pre-Angkorian settlements' without any boundaries but with distinctive planning. A first phase corresponded to 'isolated shrines, whose position was slightly off [from the typical cardinal orientation], on a northeast axis, isoclinal with surrounding plots of land and topographic environment, probably superimposed onto proto-historical habitats'. The second phase was a watershed moment with the development of 'a planned city', 'geometric' and centred on a new major component that was to be a characteristic of the Angkor Period: 'the temple-mountain', in this case Ak Yum (Pottier 1999, 141, 202–03). Yet the general layout remained unclear: several components had been altered and destroyed, in particular when the Baray and associated developments were built.

The *Mission archéologique franco-khmère sur l'aménagement du territoire angkorien* (MAFKATA), launched in 2000, sought to test these assumptions. The main revelation from the first excavations was that these Pre-Angkorian installations were located in an area already rich with prehistoric remains. In the first year of excavations, the discovery at Prei Khmeng of a necropolis dating from the Iron Age facilitated the study and dating of the critical process of Indianisation in the Angkor region for the first time. Dating from between the second part of the 5th century CE and the end of the 6th century CE, a Brahmanic shrine was built at Prei Khmeng, superimposed upon—and showing no discontinuity from—a succession of domestic and funerary contexts dating back to the beginning of our era (Pottier 2005; Pottier et al. 2009, 62). This area may have been occupied as early as the Bronze Age, since another necropolis dating from this era was unearthed in 2004 and 2005 on the neighbouring site of Koh Ta Meas, in the middle of the West Baray. Settlements from this period remain extremely rare in Cambodia, and Koh Ta Meas provides evidence for human occupation in Angkor stretching back 3000 years while highlighting both permanence and discontinuity in certain kinds of cultural features (Pottier et al. 2004; Pottier 2006).

After the completion of research at Roluos in 2012, the MAFKATA project refocused on the West Baray area with a view to elucidating the scale, morphology, and chronology of the capital associated with Ak Yum. One of the main objectives was to establish its antiquity, and indeed, epigraphic and archaeological studies of the temple, alongside radiometric dates resulting from excavations at Ak Yum, have now dated the city's foundation to the latter part of the 6th century. The research also identifies this area as the location of the Gambhīreshvara shrine which blessed the city of Bhavapura, capital of the Pre-Angkorian king Bhavavarman I (Pottier 2017). The common origins—in Angkor—of urban planning and temple-mountains can now be traced back to one of the first capitals of the *Chenla* polity, two centuries before Jayavarman II.

Nevertheless, the layout of this city remains hard to accurately define, aside at least from its large scale: it stretches over 30 km^2 when associated with the northern site of Phnom Run. For example, investigations have yet to identify the royal residence: surveys attempting to locate it in the areas around Phnom Run and Kôk Ta Pok were unsuccessful; the remaining accessible options are down in the area of Kôk Kpuos (Pottier et al. 2020). Research has identified an initial hydraulic structure, a 'proto-baray' 1300 m to the northwest of Ak Yum. The layout of this U-shaped structure, stretching over 4 km (similar in size to the 9th-century baray at Hariharālaya), is still visible, including even its eastern section that was levelled by the construction of the West Baray. One could suggest that this 'proto-baray' was one of the major components of Bhavapura. Excavations carried out in the area of its main dike close to Prasat Trapeang Sen must be continued to confirm the existence of the 'proto-bray' prior to the 10th century (Pottier et al. 2015, 17).

Surveys carried out from the air and on the ground during the dry season of 2016 focused on a 6-km^2 section of the floor of the West Baray reservoir, which at that time was exceptionally dried out and had never been recorded—even by the lidar campaign in 2012 (Pottier et al. 2017). The resulting mapping work has presented a complicated web of archaeological traces from all periods, within which we can nonetheless clearly identify traces of a series of temple foundations with multiple enclosures in the floor of the West Baray, lying to the north of Ak Yum and south of the proto-baray (Figure 5.6). These findings offer further evidence for the density of occupation and degree of organisation in this area prior to the construction of the Baray and the flooding of the area in the 11th century CE (Pottier et al. 2020).

The mapping also revealed infrastructure pre-dating the Baray, in the form of subtle topographic traces in the floor of the dried-out reservoir, including an ancient river in the northeastern section that was probably canalised, as well as several levels of road and hydraulic networks with cardinal orientations (Figure 5.7). The size, position, and orientation of some of these works are consistent with archaeological features identified to the southern exterior of the Baray, in particular the network of 40-metre-wide canals surveyed 20 years ago within the perimeter of Groslier's 'Banteay Chhoeu'. These findings have led us to revisit and abandon our earlier assumption that this network was developed in the 11th century alongside the West Baray (Pottier 2000b), a hypothesis that had been disputed by other scholars since 2006 (Shimoda and Nakagawa 2009; Bourdonneau 2010). In sum, this new evidence has strengthened the assumption of a geometric city layout associated with the foundation of Ak Yum in the 6th century CE that incorporated previous infrastructural features, with later developments based on an orthogonal grid of 680 m between axes.

Figure 5.6 Newly identified buildings and enclosures within the West Baray. These traces were exposed by an exceptional period of drought.

Source: (Photo C. Pottier).

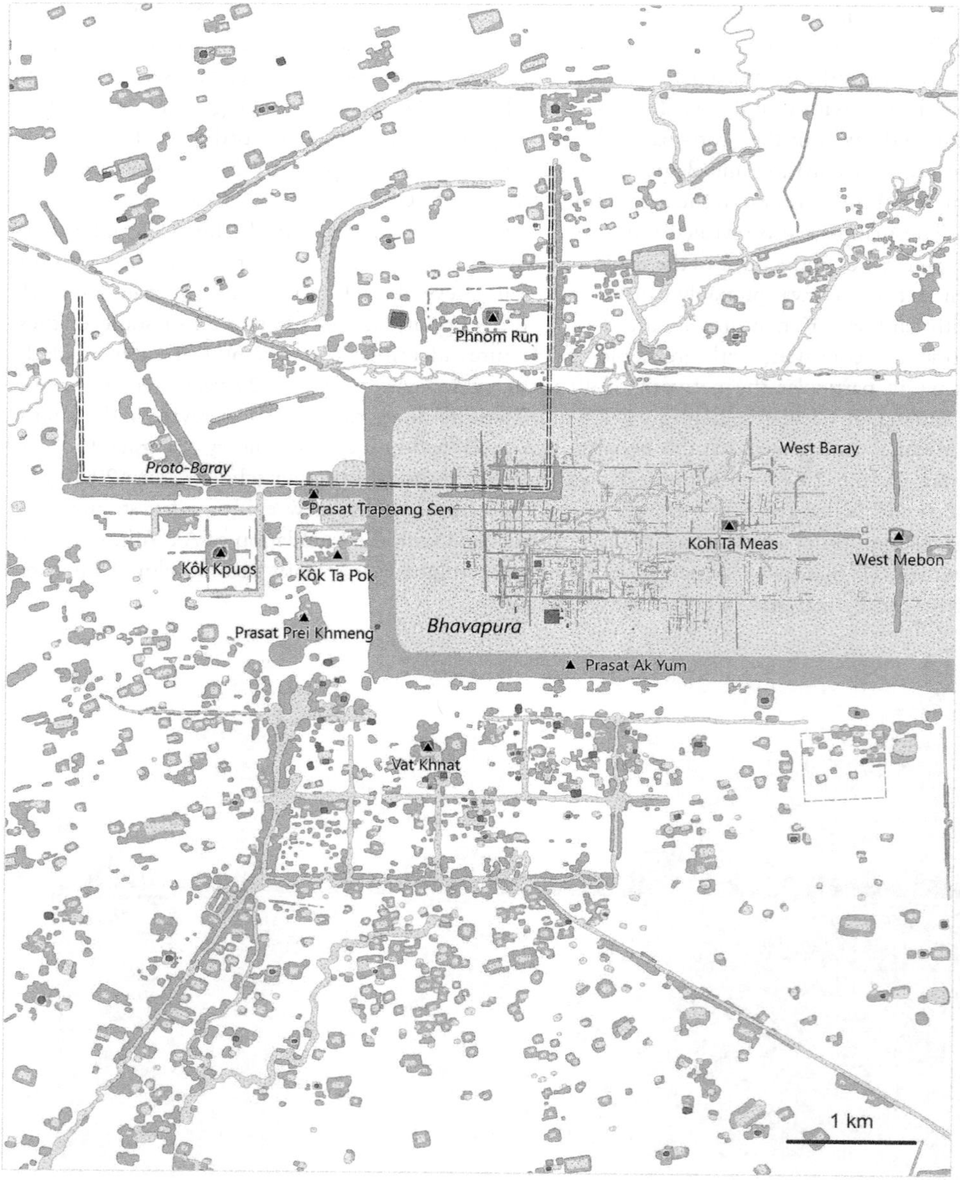

Figure 5.7 Archaeological map of the West Baray area.

Source: (Map by authors with contributions from P. Wijker).

Despite the difference in scale, this gridded structure of the city of Bhavapura relates to what has recently been discovered by Chevance et al. (2019) on Phnom Kulen, although the scale, density, and distribution of the religious constructions instead offer clear similarities with those of the Pre-Angkorian capital of Içanapura, present-day Sambor Prei Kuk, founded by the successor of Bhavavarman I in the 6th century CE.

Angkor, 1000 Years of Urban Tradition

From the founding of Yaśodharapura in the late 9th century until its abandonment in the 15th century, Angkor remained the historical capital of the Khmer Empire and its seat of power for more than 500 years, before it moved to the Phnom Penh region. Throughout the centuries, the monumental components linking the Khmer city superimposed and juxtaposed in the Angkor region to form a large low-density settlement landscape of over 1000 km^2 (Pottier 2005; Evans et al. 2007) whose centre was characterised by an unusual concentration of more than 35 km^2 of infrastructure (Evans et al. 2013). The significance of this monumental cluster and the large scale of the built environment during the Angkor Period has contributed to overshadowing the presence of more discreet remains of previous urban settlements, pigeonholed by a useful but simplistic periodisation. Consequently, the existence of older capitals in the Angkor region has been relegated to a storyline distinct from that of urban planning in the very centre of the Angkor complex.

The past 20 years of archaeological research have revealed that three cities located in the 'outskirts' of Angkor Thom (Bhavapura, Hariharālaya, and Mahendraparvata) were integrated components of the Greater Angkor—historically, physically, functionally, or symbolically. They already included the models and archetypes of Khmer urban planning which continued to structure the landscape throughout the Angkor Period (geometry, temple-mountain, royal palace, reservoir, etc.). Based on these facts, the establishment of a planned city in the Angkor area as early as the later part of the 6th century—Bhavapura—means that the foundation of Yaśodharapura was already part of a centuries-old custom, a milestone in a tradition of urban planning that unfolded over more than 1000 years in the Angkor region.

Our research on the three early cities of the Angkor region has confirmed the fundamental role played by the temple-mountain, which seems to be unique to the Angkor region (until Koh Ker in the 10th century). The close—if not fundamental—relationship between Pre-Angkorian cities and mountains has already been identified for some ancient capitals: Wat Phu (at the foothills of the Lingaparvata massif in present-day Laos), Angkor Borei (north of Phnom Da), Óc Eo (Ba Thê: hill to the northwest), and even Sambor Prei Kuk (Phnom Barieng to the east) (Shimoda 2010, 130–34). This characteristic may also be identified at Angkor, with Bhavapura right opposite Phnom Bakheng, Hariharālaya related to Phnom Bok, and, of course, Mahendraparvata built directly on a massif. But these three early cities in the Angkor region can be distinguished through what seems to be a new and specific component: the existence of a large-scale pyramid temple, a characteristic that was to be continued during the Angkor Period.

These temple-mountain, each built in a prominent place, reached an unprecedented footprint (4.5 ha in Rong Chen), and their influence served to structure their extended environment (over 1 km^2 at Bakong). Although the summit of the city, they were not systematically located at the very centre of urban development. Rather, they were integrated within a geometry that would closely associate them with sites that we know to be palaces: Banteay in Mahendraparvata and Prei Monti in Hariharālaya. These clearly delineated palatial structures, from then on, became a second structuring component of these cities, within a broader, open geometry. Palaces still need to be identified at Bhavapura and to be confirmed in other ancient cities (such as Robang Romeas at Sambor Prei Kuk).

This urban tradition can therefore be characterised by the large scale of these two types of constructions, by its geometry, and also by a kind of diversity that cannot be simply explained by the topography of the area. For example, the early capital on Phnom Kulen featured developments based on precise geometry, despite its location on a plateau where the topography is uneven compared to that of the Angkor plain. Even if their geometries vary alongside the specifics of their urban fabric, size, and organisation, the presence of this genre of geometric patterning undoubtedly links the early capitals of Angkor and preceding polities to a larger phenomenon that associated with Indianisation and that can observed elsewhere in the Lower Mekong basin (Gaucher 2004; Bourdonneau 2010); at the same time, we should underline that geometry alone does not define Angkorian urban planning.

The gigantic scale of these developments is especially striking: 30 km^2 for Hariharālaya and Bhavapura, and 40–50 km^2 for Mahendraparvata, encompassing structures of varying size and concentration. All possessed a geometric urban configuration, either laid out on a structuring framework (Mahendraparvata, Bhavapura) or based on cardinal aspects and major axes (Hariharālaya), and all three cities subsumed and incorporated material legacies of prior occupation.

Each of these three early cities profoundly transformed their immediate landscape, from the location of the hydrological network to the patterns of land-use. The appearance of these urban centres in the Pre-Angkor Period attests to early management of the territorial space on a large scale, implying the existence of socio-political institutions that were already sufficiently centralised and powerful to be able to plan, acquire, develop, and manage these extended spaces. What remains to be studied are the actual or expected demographic consequences of these urban developments (for a recent attempt to tackle that issue: Klassen et al. 2021), the modalities of managing those populations, and what kind of labour input was required to undertake such monumental works. Furthermore, the different occupational spans of these settlements also raise the question of their long-term viability. Once again, Mahendraparvata is somewhat singular, since—in contrast to the two other cities, which were occupied for lengthy periods and located close to soils naturally flooded and replenished by the lake—its location did not offer advantageous access to resources. The ephemeral occupation of Mahendraparvata may attest to the dependence of these early capitals on their farmlands and perhaps underscores the degree to which lived-in spaces across the Angkorian World were usually very effectively enmeshed with agricultural spaces.

References

Aymonier, E., 1900–1904. *Le Cambodge*, 3 tomes. Paris: Ernest Leroux.

Boulbet, J. & B. Dagens, 1973. Les sites archéologiques de la région du Bhnam Gulen (Phnom Kulen). *Arts Asiatiques* 27 (Num. spécial).

Boulbet, J., 1979. *Le Phnom Kulen et sa région, Collection de textes et documents sur l'Indochine XII*. Paris: EFEO.

Bourdonneau, E., 2010. Réhabiliter le Funan. Óc Eo ou la première Angkor. *Bulletin de l'École française d'Extrême-Orient* 94 (2007), 111–58.

Briggs, L.P., 1999[1951]. *The Ancient Khmer Empire*. Bangkok: White Lotus.

Chevance, J.-B., 2005. *L'Architecture et le Décor des Temples du Phnom Kulen, Cambodge*. MA dissertation. Paris: Université de Paris III—Sorbonne Nouvelle.

Chevance, J.-B., 2011. *Le Phnom Kulen à la source d'Angkor, nouvelles données archéologiques*. PhD dissertation. Paris: Université de Paris III—Sorbonne Nouvelle.

Chevance, J.-B., 2013. Pœng Tbal et Pœng Eisei, ermitages angkoriens méconnus du Phnom Kulen. *Aséanie* 32, 11–76.

Chevance, J.-B., 2014. Banteay, Palais Royal de Mahendraparvata. *Aséanie* 33, 279–330.

Chevance, J.-B., D. Evans, N. Hofer, S. Sakhoeun & R. Chhean, 2019. Mahendraparvata: an early Angkor-period capital defined through airborne laser scanning at Phnom Kulen. *Antiquity* 93(371), 1303–21. https://doi.org/10.15184/aqy.2019.133

Cœdès, G., 1928. Études cambodgiennes. *Bulletin de l'École française d'Extrême-Orient* 28(1), 81–146.

Cœdès, G., 1937. *Inscriptions du Cambodge, Collection de textes et documents sur l'Indochine I*. Hanoï: EFEO.

Cœdès, G., 1938. Le fondateur de la royauté angkorienne et les récentes découvertes archéologiques au Phnom Kulen. *CEFEO* 14, 40–48, (Re-published in Articles sur le pays khmer 2, 1992, 277–84).

Cœdès, G., 1989. *Les États hindouisés d'Indochine et d'Indonésie*. Paris: De Boccard.

Cœdès, G. & P. Dupont, 1943. Les stèles de Sdŏk Kăk Thom Phnom Sandak et Práh Vihār. *Bulletin de l'École française d'Extrême-Orient* 43, 56–154.

Evans, D., 2016. Airborne laser scanning as a method for exploring long-term socio-ecological dynamics in Cambodia. *Journal of Archaeological Science* 74, 164–75. https://doi.org/10.1016/j.jas.2016.05.009.

Evans, D., R. Fletcher, C. Pottier, J-B Chevance, D. Soutif, B-S. Tan, S. Im, D. Ea, T. Tin, S. Kim, C. Cromarty, S. De Greef, K. Hanus, P. Bâty, R. Kuszinger, I. Shimoda & G. Boornazian, 2013. Uncovering archaeological landscapes at Angkor using lidar. *Proceedings of the National Academy of Sciences of North America* 110(31), 12595–600. https://doi.org/10.1073/pnas.1306539110

Evans, D., C. Pottier, R. Fletcher, S. Hensley, I. Tapley, A. Milne & M. Barbetti, 2007. A comprehensive archaeological map of the World's largest preindustrial settlement complex at Angkor, Cambodia. *Proceedings of the National Academy of Sciences of North America* 104(36), 14277–82.

Finot, L., 1911. Sur quelques traditions indochinoises. *Bulletin de la Commission Archéologique de l'Indochine* 8, 20–37.

Gaucher, J., 2004. Angkor Thom, une utopie réalisée? Structuration de l'espace et modèle indien d'urbanisme dans le Cambodge ancien. *Arts asiatiques* 59, 58–86.

Goloubew, V., 1924. Le Phnom Kulên. *Cahier de la Société Géographique de Hanoï*, 8, 3–27.

Goloubew, V., 1935. La première ville d'Angkor. *Journal Asiatique 226 (avril-juin 1935)*, 293–9.

Goloubew, V., 1936. Reconnaissances aériennes au Cambodge. *Bulletin de l'École française d'Extrême-Orient* 36(2), 465–77.

Groslier, B.-P., 1979. La cité hydraulique angkorienne: exploitation ou surexploitation du sol? *Bulletin de l'École française d'Extrême-Orient* 66, 161–202.

Groslier, B.-P., 1998[1958]. Travaux dans la région de Rolûos. *Mélanges sur l'archéologie du Cambodge*, ed. J. Dumarçay. Paris: EFEO, 33–49.

Hansen, E., 1969. *Cambodge, Aménagement du Phnom Kulen, septembre 1969. Unpublished report.* Paris: UNESCO.

Hawken, S., 2011. *Metropolis of ricefields: a topographic classification of a dispersed urban complex.* PhD dissertation. Sydney: University of Sydney.

Hawken, S., 2013. Designs of kings and farmers: landscape systems of the greater Angkor Urban Complex. *Asian Perspectives* 52, 347–67.

Jacques, C., 1972. Études d'épigraphie cambodgienne: VII. "Sur l'emplacement du royaume d'Aninditapura. VIII. La carrière de Jayavarman II. *Bulletin de l'École française d'Extrême-Orient* 59, 205–20.

Jacques, C., 1990. *Angkor.* Paris, Bordas.

Jacques, C., 2007. *Khmer Empire.* Bangkok: River Books.

Klassen, S., A.K. Carter, D.H. Evans, S. Ortman, M.T. Stark, A.A. Loyless, M. Polkinghorne, P. Heng, M. Hill, P. Wijker, J. Niles-Weed, G.P. Marriner, C. Pottier & R.J. Fletcher, 2021. Diachronic modeling of the population within the medieval Greater Angkor region settlement. *Science Advances* 7(19), eabf8441. https://doi.org/10.1126/sciadv.abf8441

Lunet de Lajonquière, E., 1902–1911. *Inventaire descriptif des monuments du Cambodge. volume 3. Publication de l'EFEO IV. VIII et IX*, Paris: E. Leroux.

Marchal, H., 1923. *Voyage de Mr Marchal au Phnom Kulen, Mai 1923.* Paris: EFEO Archives.

Parmentier, H., 1927. *L'art khmer primitif*, 2 vol. Paris-Bruxelles: EFEO-Vanoest.

Parmentier, H., 1935. Complément à l'Art Khmer primitive. *Bulletin de l'École française d'Extrême-Orient* 35(1–2), 1–116.

Penny, D., J-B. Chevance, D. Tang & S. De Greef, 2014. The environmental impact of Cambodia's ancient city of Mahendraparvata (Phnom Kulen). *PLoS One* 9(1), e84252. https://doi.org/10.1371/journal.pone.0084252

Penny, D., C. Pottier, R. Fletcher, M. Barbetti, D. Fink & Q. Hua, 2005 (2006). Vegetation and land-use at Angkor, Cambodia: a dated pollen sequence from the Bakong temple moat. *Antiquity* 80(309), 599–614.

Pottier, C., 1996. Notes sur le Bakong et son implantation. *Bulletin de l'École française d'Extrême-Orient* 83, 318–26.

Pottier, C., 1999. *Carte Archéologique de la Région d'Angkor-Zone Sud.* PhD dissertation. Paris: Université Paris III—Sorbonne Nouvelle.

Pottier, C., 2000a. À la recherche de Goloupura. *Bulletin de l'École française d'Extrême-Orient* 87, 79–107.

Pottier, C., 2000b. Some evidence of an inter-relationship between hydraulic features and rice field patterns at Angkor during ancient times. *The Journal of Sophia Asian Studies* 18, 99–119.

Pottier, C., 2003. Nouvelles recherches sur l'aménagement du territoire angkorien à travers l'histoire. *Comptes rendus des séances de l'Académie des Inscriptions et Belles-Lettres* 147(1), 427–49.

Pottier, C., 2005. Travaux de recherche récents dans la région d'Angkor. *Comptes-rendus de l'Académie des Inscriptions et Belles-Lettres* 147(1), 427–49.

Pottier, C., 2006. Under the Western Baray waters, in *Uncovering Southeast Asia's Past, 10th EurASEAA Conference*, eds. E.A. Bacus, J. C. Glover & V.C. Pigott VC. Singapore: NUS Press, 298–309.

Pottier, C., 2014. Présentation. *Aséanie* 33, 147–74.

Pottier, C., 2017. Nouvelles données sur les premières cités angkoriennes, in *Deux décennies de coopération archéologique franco-cambodgienne à Angkor* (Actes de la journée d'études organisée à la mémoire de Pascal Royère par l'Académie des Inscriptions et Belles-Lettres, sous le haut patronage de Sa Majesté Norodom Sihamoni, Roi du Cambodge), eds. A. Beschaouch, F. Verellen & M. Zink. Paris: De Boccard, 43–79.

Pottier, C. & A. Bolle, 2009. Le Prasat Trapeang Phong à Hariharâlaya: histoire d'un temple et archéologie d'un site. *Aséanie* 61–90.

Pottier, C., A. Bolle, A. Desbat, S. Chea, M-F, Dupoizat, A. Vierstraete, A. Beuken, E Bruneau & D. Penny, 2009. Mission archéologique franco-khmère sur l'aménagement du territoire angkorien [MAFKATA]. Rapport de la campagne 2009. EFEO, Unpublished report.

Pottier, C., A. Bolle, E. Llopis, D. Soutif, C. Socheat, S. Sang, H. Komsan & D. Phoeung, 2008. Bakong, soixante ans après, in *From Homo erectus to the living traditions, Choice of papers from the 11th International Conference of the EurASEAA, Bougon, 25–30 September 2006*, eds. J.-P. Pautreau, A.-S. Coupey, V. Zeitoun and E. Rambault. Chiang Mai: Siam Ratana, 244–50.

Pottier, C., A. Desbat, 2020. MAFKATA—CERANGKOR. Rapport de la campagne 2020. Unpublished Report. Siem Reap: EFEO,

Pottier, C., A. Desbat, M-F. Dupoizat & A. Bolle, 2012. Le matériel céramique à Prei Monti (Angkor), in Orientalismes. De l'archéologie au musée. Mélanges offerts à Jean-François Jarrige, ed. V. Lefèvre. Turnhout: Brepols, 291–317.

Pottier, C., A. Desbat, N. Nauleau, K. San, L. Khann, R. Hong, M. Greuin, M-D. Choi, C. Le Meur, S. Biard, M. Auliana, S. Van, S. & S. Uong, 2015. Mission archéologique franco-khmère sur l'aménagement du territoire angkorien [MAFKATA]. Rapport de la campagne 2015. EFEO, Unpublished report.

Pottier, C., A. Desbat, V. Ly, V. Thirion-Merle & G. Thierrin-Michael, 2017. MAFKATA—CERANGKOR. Rapport de la campagne 2017. EFEO, Unpublished report.

Pottier, C. & R. Lujàn-Lunsford, 2007. De brique et de grès. Précisions sur les tours en brique de Preah Kô. *Bulletin de l'École française d'Extrême-Orient* 92 (2005), 457–95.

Pottier, C., V.S. Phin, T. Heng, R. Chhay, F. Demeter, 2004. Koh Ta Méas, un site inédit dans le baray occidental. *Udaya, Journal of Khmer Studies* 5, 167–91.

Pottier, C. & D. Soutif, 2016. De l'ancienneté de Hariharālaya. Une inscription préangkorienne opportune à Bakong. *Bulletin de l'École française d'Extrême-Orient* 100(2014), 147–66.

Shimoda, I., 2010. *Study on the ancient Khmer city Isanapura.* PhD dissertation. Tokyo: Waseda University.

Shimoda, I. & T. Nakagawa, 2009. Ancient roads between new and old city. *Journal of Architecture and Planning* 74(642), 1867–73.

Soutif, D., 2009. Kanloṅ ou mandira, un palais à Purandarapura à la fin du VIIe siècle de notre ère? *Udaya, Journal of Khmer Studies* 10, 239–55.

Stern, P., 1927. *Le Bayon d'Angkor et l'évolution de l'art Khmer, étude et discussion de la chronologie des monuments khmers.* Paris: Annales du musée Guimet, Paul Geuthner.

Stern, P., 1932. *La transition de l'art pré-angkorien à l'art angkorien et Jayavarman II, Études d'orientalisme 1, in Mélanges Linossier,* Paris, Musée Guimet, E. Leroux, 507–23.

Stern, P., 1934. Le temple-montagne khmèr. Le culte du Liṅga et le Devarāja. *Bulletin de l'École française d'Extrême-Orient* 34(2), 611–16.

Stern, P., 1938a. Hariharālaya et Indrapura. *Bulletin de l'École française d'Extrême-Orient* 38, 175–97.

Stern, P., 1938b. Le style du Kulên (décor architectural et statuaire). *Bulletin de l'École française d'Extrême-Orient* 38(1), 111–49.

Stern, P., 1951. Diversité et rythme des fondations royales khmères. *Bulletin de l'École française d'Extrême-Orient* 47(2), 649–87.

Trouvé, G., 1932–1935. *Rapports de la Conservation d'Angkor (RCA).* Paris: EFEO Archives.

6

ANGKOR'S MULTIPLE SOUTHEAST ASIA OVERLAND CONNECTIONS

Kenneth R. Hall

Recent archaeological research, along with epigraphy; temple arts; and surviving Chinese, Vietnamese, Indian, and texts and inscriptions from the 10th-century CE Bay of Bengal region allow a better understanding of Angkor-era networked society and culture. Angkor's overland and maritime networking assumed a vital role in linking evolving regional mainland Southeast Asia societies, cultures, and economic exchanges (Hendrickson 2010, 2011). The Angkorian World's 10th-to-13th-century temple wall carvings and paintings depict military processions, marketplace activities, and imported commodities (notably textiles) at a time when regional roadways connected Angkor to inter-regional maritime networks in the Eastern Indian Ocean, Straits of Melaka, and South China Sea via river arteries and mountain and overland passageways (Green 2000, 2007; also see Hall 2004, 2010, 2011).

By the 12th century, the Angkorian World included a mix of critical roadways, pathways, and riverine transit routes from the capital at Angkor to the Malay Peninsula in the southwest, to northern Vietnam, and to the east where the ports-of-trade of the Cham civilisation opened to the South China Sea (Hendrickson 2010, 2012). The Angkor Period roadways and natural river passages were diverse cumulative thoroughfares that sustained networked commercial, societal, religious, and cultural efforts to expand and thereby become more profitable and politically and religiously inclusive. Societal transitions from the land to the sea supported Angkor's increased participation in that era's lucrative South China Sea trade in the east and the extended Eastern Indian Ocean in the west.

Commodities moved by water and by land. Riverine routes connected Angkor (via the Mekong/Bassac and Tonle Sap Rivers) to the South China Sea and flanked Vietnam's coast northward to Champa; water routes also linked Angkor to points north into Champassak and from there westward into the Khorat Plateau. Extended east-to-west and north-to-south transit routes crossed the Lower Mekong basin and pointed east via mountain crossings to the South China Sea coastline of Vietnam. Some goods moved westward from Cambodia into the Chao Phraya River valley, downstream to the Gulf of Thailand (Murphy 2016, 2018), and into the South China Sea to and through the Straits of Melaka, with alternative overland portages between the Bay of Bengal and the Malay Peninsula to the Gulf of Siam (Thailand). This chapter is ultimately a re-envisioning of Angkor-era networked riverine, overland, and networked maritime trade passageways that conveyed commodities and ideas in multiple directions and sustained Angkor-era mainland Southeast Asia society as documented

DOI: 10.4324/9781351128940-8

in archaeological investigations that align with surviving texts and inscriptions (Murphy 2016, 2019; Groslier 1973).

Angkor Period Khmer Overland Networking

The reign of Sūryavarman I (r. 1002–1050) marked a critical juncture in Cambodian kingship, in which military action was launched to define Angkor's territories, sustaining regional and inter-regional commodity exchange activities and related economic growth. Overall, this period saw a significantly increased population sustained by the expansion of agricultural lands and resulting foodstuffs. Sūryavarman's reign had its base in warfare. He successfully extended and defined Angkor's eastern boundaries against the Cham populations in southern and central Vietnam to the east and against mixed ethnicities in northern and western mainland Southeast Asia, thereby stabilising the Angkor realm's resource base. Sūryavarman I initiated substantial territorial expansion into what is now Thailand and Laos to the north and west of the initial Khmer core. He commissioned a number of societal initiatives, expanded religious networking and commodity transfers, and generally enhanced the economic and societal well-being of his subjects.

Expanding the Khmer agricultural core in this period was the base of the Angkor realm's infrastructure, as the productive agricultural base allowed dramatic addition to the monarchy's sphere of influence. Until the middle of the 10th to the middle of the 11th centuries, the Mon-speaking people populated the upper Malay Peninsula and Chao Phraya River (Thai) regions to the west of the Khmer. Historians view central Thailand as the centre of Dvaravati-civilisation sites until the 11th century, when the Khmer polity expanded into this region (de Mestier du Bourg 1970; see Krajaejun 2023, this volume). In roughly the same period, the Khmer rulers made their first extended military forays into the western area around Lohu (Lopburi/*Lavo*) in the mid-Chao Phraya River plain and to the north in the upper Mun River valley north and west of the Dangrek mountain range.

As documented in that era's inscriptions, Sūryavarman I (1002–1050) consolidated the Khmer realm's administrative control to include the population clusters at western Phimai and Lohu (Lopburi/*Lavo*), and to the north and west of the Greater Angkor core. He followed the former Khmer ruler Rajendravarman II (944–968), who had previously claimed authority over the western Chao Phraya river valley of present-day Thailand and the southern Isthmus of Kra sector of the Malay Peninsula (Vickery 1998). Thus Sūryavarman I significantly enhanced his predecessors' activity zones that bordered Champa and Dai Viet in the east and also extended his realm's territories to the west (Hall 2011, 176–84).

Sūryavarman's extension of Khmer authority into the lower Chao Phraya basin/Lohu (Lopburi/*Lavo*) region had strong economic implications, as Lohu (Lopburi/*Lavo*) became the base for Khmer societal extension into the lower Chao Phraya River and former *Dvaravati* upper Malay Peninsula regions (Glover 2010; Murphy 2013). This southwest presence gave the Khmer access to lucrative international commerce at Tambralinga in the Chaiya-Surat Thani region of modern-day southern Thailand, particularly in the 11th through 13th centuries CE (see also O'Connor 1975). Sūryavarman's territorial annexations provided the Khmers a more direct contact with the international trade routes of that era. The lower Chao Phraya River basin had been a longstanding and productive area for wet rice agriculture, was a riverine transit zone, and was connected to early maritime trade networks of the Eastern Indian Ocean at the Bay of Bengal. Newly established Khmer authority over the Chao Phraya riverine regions at that time provided the Angkor realm with profitable access to maritime trade in the Gulf of Siam, Straits of Melaka, and Bay of Bengal and also to the overland transit routes across the upper Malay Peninsula (Skilling 2003; Revire and Murphy 2014; Revire 2016).

At that time, the networks of the Khmer realm generally followed the river systems of the Lower Mekong basin, using the central riverine artery of the Tonle Sap to reach the Mekong and its tributaries. The Tonle Sap also provided access to an arc of settlements west and southwest of the capital. North of the Dangrek mountains, the notable Ban That Thong inscription was recovered on a tributary linking the Mun River with extended riverine networks to the east; the inscription, dating to the reign of Jayavarman VI (1080–1107), mentions barges that navigated the eastern Mun and Mekong river transit zones (Finot 1912).

A Cham merchant (*Vap Champa*) and Vietnamese traders such as the Yvan of Kamvan Tadin are referenced in a Khmer-language inscription from Phum Mien on the lower Mekong River. They likely sojourned overland across northeastern mountains to connect with the Mekong River eastern Khmer territorial passageway to enter the Cambodian core (see Southworth and Tran 2019 for discussion of potential routes). The traders were said to have arrived from the Nghe An region of Champa, on the coast of present-day Vietnam, by trekking through the connective upland Ha Trai mountain pass and then travelling further downstream via the Mekong River (Cœdès 1954, 183–86; Maspero 1918). As will be discussed later, Nghe An was the terminus of several overland and riverine routes which extended north to connect with commercial developments in the Red River system and ultimately with the northern Vietnamese capital of Thang Long (Hanoi: Whitmore 2019).

One route proceeded southward via the eastern Mekong River to link up with an overland route that connected Ban That to Prasat Kantop and avoided the Khong rapids portage south of Ban That to facilitate a more direct access to the Khmer core. Sambor (Sambhupura), located on the Mekong below the Khong rapids, was connected to an even more easterly route (see Heng 2023, this volume). Sambhupura as a location may have been an upland intermediary centre that linked lowland Khmers with highland populations to their east; slaves, deerskins, and forest products flowed from this region into the Angkorian core. These and other commodities were also marketed beyond the upstream realm to the downstream Chams, whose ports on the South China Sea were a gateway to international oceanic trade (Hall 2017; Osborne 1966, 447). Elsewhere during the reign of Sūryavarman new primary east–west routes north of the Dangrek mountain range followed the Mun River system course through Phnom Wan and continued westward to Phimai in the north and Lohu (Lopburi/*Lavo*) on the southern Chao Phraya River, which linked the interior of Thailand to the Gulf of Siam. These areas were incorporated into the Khmer realm during the reign of Sūryavarman I and flourished commercially. Inscriptions from the Phnom Wan and Phimai regions dating to the last ten years of Sūryavarman I's reign (1040–1050) report that commodities from China, alongside many other items, were available in diverse upstream and downstream markets connected to Angkor (Briggs 1951, 178–82; Cœdès 1964, 63–70).

The late 10th-century temple of Phimai, on the Mun River in present-day Thailand, was of special commercial and administrative importance due to its location. Linked to Angkor by a royal road (Hendrickson 2010, 482, fig. 1), Phimai ranked as highly as Lohu (Lopburi/*Lavo*) in strategic value to the Khmer monarchy and became the centre for regional authority in the northern Mun River valley. With the administrative integration of western Phimai and Lohu (Lopburi/*Lavo*) into the Khmer realm under Sūryavarman, overland networking between these two western centres was beneficial for their marketplace diversity and enhanced their strategic political importance in the multi-ethnic west in relation to the eastern Khmer realm (Phungtian 2000).

These intertwined western communication and exchange networks aided Sūryavarman's efforts to integrate outlying territories into his royal domain (Briggs 1951, 178–79). Another primary east–west overland route extended from the Angkorian core via the modern-day

Battambang region and Svay Chek to Lohu (Lopburi/*Lavo*) and from there further south on the Chao Phraya river to the Bay of Bengal via an overland western trek. Angkor-era epigraphy from these important areas, particularly those recovered at Wat Baset in Battambang and at Bantay Prav in Svay Chek, document commercial exchanges on the western overland passageway to Lohu (Lopburi/*Lavo*) and beyond via overland and southern riverine passages to the Bay of Bengal and the extended Eastern Indian Ocean. These two routes developed into major commercial transfer stations as a result of Sūryavarman I's reign and legacy. Lopburi (or *Lavo*) emerged as a major urban centre on the main route from the Khmer heartland to the west and south (see Krajaejun 2023, this volume).

Western trade routes assumed an especially important economic role in Sūryavarman I's expansive Khmer state in the first half of the 11th century. Although the early inscriptions report the incorporation of strategic intermediary Lohu (Lopburi/*Lavo*) into the administrative structure of the Khmer state during Sūryavarman's reign, there is little detail on economic interchanges between the Lohu (Lopburi/*Lavo*) political and market centre in the west and the eastern Khmer core (Cœdès 1961, 10–15). However control of Lohu (Lopburi/*Lavo*) and the area to its south gave the Khmers direct access to the trade routes of the Isthmus of Kra on the Malay Peninsula that are today located in peninsular (southern) Thailand.

The Chaiya-Surat Thani area, also known as the Tambralinga region, rendered *Tanliumei* in Chinese sources (Wolters 1958), was an important early commercial centre on the Peninsula. Archaeologists have recovered Mahāyāna Buddhist votive tablets at Chaiya dating to the 10th and 11th centuries that are similar in style to those found at Lohu (Lopburi/*Lavo*), suggesting communication between these two early urban centres, though the nature and degree of contact between the two population cores is not clear (Hirth and Rockhill 1911; Lamb 1961). Nevertheless the recovered artefacts and other remains on the upper Malay Peninsula show continued contacts with both Indian and Arab-Persian traders to the west.

Western Oceanic Connectivity With China via Southeast Asia

Mainland Southeast Asia's prominence in the maritime trade networks subsided somewhat by the start of the Angkor Period, when peninsular regions associated with the Srivijaya northeast Sumatra became central for Southeast Asian oceanic trade routes. Where early first-millennium CE commodities travelled via overland Malay Peninsula portages, Angkorian commerce moved instead through the Straits of Melaka maritime passageway. Angkor's westward reach to the southern Chao Phraya delta and upper Malay peninsula was likely stimulated by an interest in securing local footholds there and points further south on the peninsula's coasts to facilitate trade from China into the Indian Ocean networks (Cœdès 1964, 63–70; Jacq-Hergoualc'h 2002; O Connor 1972, 60–62, Figure 34). Goods of foreign origin also entered the Khmer core by land from the east, up the Tonle Sap River, although most contemporary inscriptions focus instead on commercial activities in the early upstream centres rather than listing commodities from the Bay of Bengal and Gulf of Siam (Thailand) western maritime regions (Aymonier 1904, 443; Cœdès 1954, 183–86).

Chinese high-fired ceramics dating to the 9th–10th century have been found at Angkor (see Stark and Cremin 2023, this volume). Chinese diasporic merchants selling Chinese ceramics had ready access to Angkor via the Tonle Sap River and indirect access overland through the eastern Cham coastline and upstream ports. Inscriptions from Sūryavarman I's reign suggest a reversal from previous inscriptions that focused on Khmer ties with the Cham polities to the east; instead we see a focus on points west that were important for trade and resource procurement. *Lavo*, modern-day Lopburi in Thailand, came under Khmer influence by the late 10th century (Baker and Phongpaichit 2017, 23) and welcomed sojourners who arrived overland from south China via eastern mountain passages to Phanom Wan in present-day northern Thailand (Cœdès 1964, 63–70; Sen 2003; Hall 2004, 200). Lohu (Lopburi/*Lavo*) should have been extremely important and exceedingly rich, but few archaeological investigations have explored this possibility. Marketable goods recovered from this era also transited southwards from Lohu (Lopburi/*Lavo*) and Phanom Wan via the Chao Phraya River. This same riverine route was used to transport goods from India, Persia, and Arabia that arrived at the ports of the *Tambralinga* region on the western Malay Peninsula.

International routes that linked Angkor to mainland Southeast Asia's coasts doubtless contributed to the development of the Angkorian civilisation. Maritime routes using the South China Sea moved the bulk of Chinese goods into Southeast Asia (Stark and Cremin 2023, this volume), but some goods also moved overland via northern Vietnam, Laos, and northern Thailand. There were also Chinese and other mixed diaspora stopovers in central and southern Cham/Champa ports-of-trade, with routes heading overland to the west through the mountains and into the Angkorian heartland (Heng 2009). Khmer maritime commercial networks extended to the Chola polity on the Coromandel Coast of India and to the Ly state in the Red River Delta of northeastern Vietnam (Hall 1978, 2020). Khmer sojourners appear to have been especially intent on consolidating trade linkages to productive cotton textile ports of south India, including transit routes across the Isthmus of Kra and the Surat Thani region of the Malay Peninsula. In turn, locals carried goods northward from the Isthmus to Lohu (Lopburi/*Lavo*), upstream on the Chao Phraya River. From there, goods followed one of two exchange networks: the southern overland route to the Khmer dynastic core using royal roads extending to the northern banks of the Tonle Sap or the alternative northern passageway via the Chao Phraya and Mun rivers into northeastern Thailand, and from there south through the O Smach Pass in the Dangrek Mountains to the Tonle Sap plain (Murphy 2019).

Evidence for this latter overland network comes from art history. Murphy (2019) contrasts Dong Duong hairstyles on Buddhist bodhisattva *sema stone* scenes from the Buddhist *Mahanaradakasssapa* Jataka at the My Son and Dong Duong sites (central Vietnam) with those recovered on the Khorat plateau (northeast Thailand) and Laos. He traces stylistic similarities from the western Chao Phraya River south downstream to the Gulf of Thailand and in the Chao Phraya river upstream to the Mun River upstream branches (into northeast Thailand and southern Laos), and southeast down Mekong to central Vietnam (Champa). Access to the Champa coastline from the Angkorian World was also possible using a highland passage extending eastwards from Savannakhet on the Mekong, passing overland via the Lao Bao pass to Tra Lien and Uu Diem on the Cham coastline of present-day Vietnam. Travellers could also take an alternative route moving downstream on the Mekong to Champassak/Bassac/Wat Phu, and from there proceeding overland through the central highlands of Vietnam towards the Cham ritual and political centres of My Son and Dong Duong, both located near the South China Sea coastline (Figure 6.1).

The 11th-century commercial economy of the expansive Khmer polity achieved such importance that the upper Malay Peninsula receded from traditional networks of power and trade in the eastern Indian Ocean and was drawn into that of the Southeast Asian mainland. Thereafter, the primary focus of regional commercial activity shifted away from international trade with India or China and towards evolving regional maritime and overland routes that connected the Bay of Bengal to the west with the coastline of Vietnam to the east. Routes included passages through Myanmar/Burma, the Malay Peninsula, and the Straits of Melaka that had been established centuries earlier but which rose to greater prominence in the 11th century CE (Kulke 1999). Angkor, in contrast, looked eastward at least as much as westward. Commercial

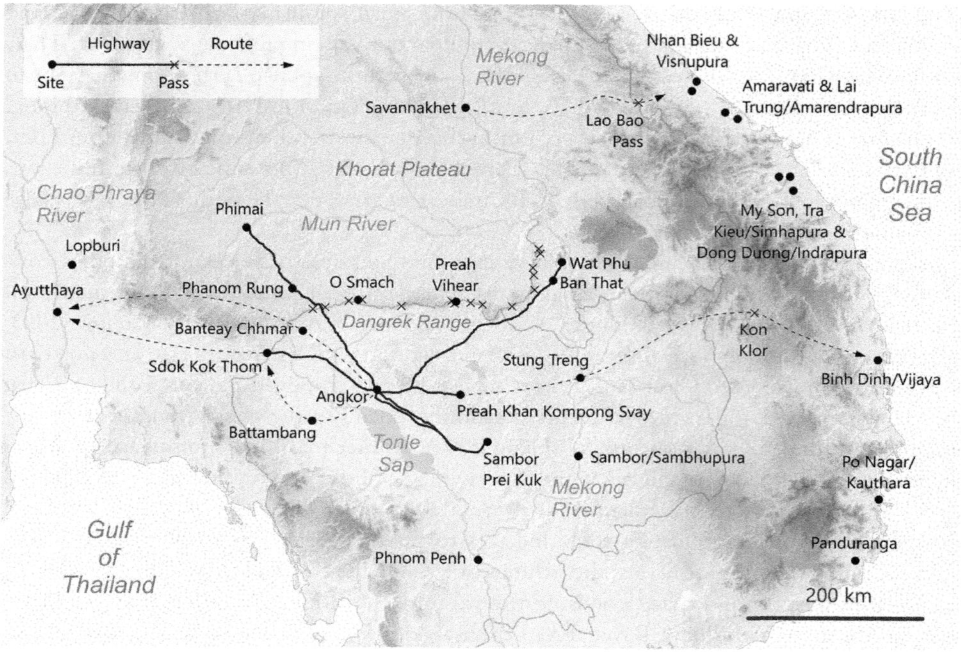

Figure 6.1 Potential 12th century communication networks connecting to Angkor.

and diplomatic links with Vietnamese and Cham neighbours to the north and east, respectively, were the source of a variety of trade goods, as well as intermittent conflict that continued through the remainder of the Angkor era (Whitmore 2017).

By the first half of the 11th century, the Khmers had pushed their control westward into the Chao Phraya Valley of present-day Thailand. From there, they redirected their attention southward toward the Isthmus of Kra. Under Sūryavarman I (1002–1050), Khmer authority had extended into the Lohu (Lopburi/*Lavo*) region, with strong economic implications for the southern regions, but there is no evidence of Khmer direct control over the strategic Thai polity called Tambralinga. Initial Khmer presence in the eastern Tambralinga region of the Malay Peninsula was short lived, as the Burmese extended their authority from the northwest over the southern shoreline of the eastern Bay of Bengal from the 10th century. A variety of evidence documents lower Burma population centres at Thaton and Mergui in 1057 that had taken control over the Bay of Bengal east coast ports-of-trade (e.g., Chutintaround 2002). In the late 1050s the Bagan-based northern Irrawaddy River regime extended their realm into the Malay Peninsula, where they encountered little resistance from the contemporary Khmers, who were at that time defending significant internal regional threats (Luce 1922; Aung-Thwin 2002).

Though the Khmer had withdrawn from the Isthmus post-1050, by the 12th century, Chinese Song-era authors considered the upper east coast of the Peninsula to be within the Cambodian sphere of influence (Wheatley 1961, 65–66, 299–300). The last recorded embassy of Tambralinga to the Song China court (960–1279) took place in 1070, while the Khmer monarchy sent embassies in 1116, 1120, 1128, 1129, and 1131 (Wolters 1958, 605). Some scholars argue that the Khmers came to dominate the upper coast between 1070 and 1130, but others find it more likely, given the Angkor realm's internal political problems in the late 11th and early 12th centuries, that Tambralinga was a neutral polity (although of reduced significance). In this latter scenario, Khmer embassies may have reassured the Chinese that the contemporary disorder in the Khmer realm would not interrupt the flow of maritime commerce with China. The lower Mekong Basin (including the Angkor polity) and what is today peninsular Thailand/ Malaysia were both important at this time as sources of forest products for the Chinese court (e.g., Wang 1958).

In the 12th century, Chinese diaspora merchants were dealing directly with the sources of supply on the Peninsula, Sumatra, and Java rather than with intermediaries in the entrepôts of the Straits of Melaka region; Tambralinga would not have needed to send embassies to China to promote its products. Meanwhile, the Khmer realm was struggling to maintain its control even closer to home. In 1155, for example, the Chinese recorded a gift of elephants from the western Zhenla state (the term Zhenla was used consistently by the Chinese to designate the Khmer realm from earliest times) of *Lohu (Lavo*/Lopburi), an indication that the Chao Phraya valley (*Lohu*) was at that time free of Angkor's control (Wolters 1958, 605).

Despite the loss of their western-most realms by the mid-12th century, the Khmer state maintained ongoing relations with polities in the Isthmus of Kra. The Preah Khan inscription from 1191 CE, during the reign of Jayavarman VII, includes references to localities in a zone offering northern access to the Peninsula, including Ratburi and Phetburi, though there is no record of any specific relationship between the Angkor-based realm and the Isthmus of Kra (Cœdès 1941; Wyatt 2001). A Cham inscription from central Vietnam reportedly refers to a campaign by Jayavarman VII on the Peninsula in 1195, which would indicate an attempt to restore a formal peninsular relationship (Cœdès 1941; Wyatt 1975, 91–102, 1994). A variety of portable clay Buddhist votive tablets dating to the era are found in lower Myanmar, the Bay of Bandon and Nakhon Si Thammarat on the Malay Peninsula, and the Angkor realm and beyond. This distribution offers further evidence of regional interaction between the Isthmus, Angkor, and beyond via the Straits of Melaka and the South China and Java Seas (Hall 2011, 176–84).

These 12th-century tablets link to the multiple focal figures of Angkor Thom (Hall and Whitmore 1976, 197, 318) and are a departure from earlier Mahāyāna style tablets of the 11th century, having more affinity to Theravada Buddhism than to the Mahāyāna tradition favoured by Jayavarman VII. But the tablets are consistent with other evidence that suggests that Jayavarman's Mahāyāna Buddhism was eclectic and highly influenced by the contemporary Tantric traditions that were common to the then Bay of Bengal Buddhist community (Acri 2016; Wyatt 2001). Thus, a networked Theravada Buddhist religious community was spreading along the Bay of Bengal and upper Malay Peninsula by way of maritime and overland communication routes shared by Bagan, Begu, the Thai, and other polities and maritime diaspora communities on the Malay Peninsula, coastal eastern Sumatra, Angkor-era Cambodia, and the political entities in downstream and coastline Vietnam.

As previously noted, by the middle of the 12th century Tambralinga had become a multiethnic centre of Theravada Buddhist scholarship and piety on the Malay Peninsula. The Angkor realm's western contacts with the Peninsula and lower Burma enabled the spread of the Theravada school from this regional base as well. According to Burmese legend, when Bagan's monks were re-ordained in the line of the Singhalese school of Theravada Buddhism at the end of the 12th century, one of the five monks who returned from Sri Lanka was the son of a Khmer king, probably Jayavarman VII (Woodward 1975, 104–07). In addition, art historians believe that the Preah Palilay temple at Angkor Thom, constructed during the reign of Jayavarman VII, exhibits Theravada Buddhist influence introduced by way of Bagan in Burma and riverine Chao Phraya populations on the Thai Peninsula, contrasting with Jayavarman VII's primary patronage of Mahāyāna Buddhism (Boisselier 1966, 94, 275–76; Woodward 1975, 104–07).

These networked cultural exchanges took place at a time when the Khmer were likely losing control over their western-most territories of Lavo—centred at Lohu (Lopburi)—and the wider Chao Phraya river valley (Wyatt 2001, 25–47). These losses corresponded in time to the increasing number of military expeditions that the Khmer monarchs waged against their eastern Vietnamese and Cham neighbours. Such expeditions assume an important role in Khmer history from the late 11th century onwards, when Khmer and Cham inscriptions imply that the Khmer, Cham, and Vietnamese were competing for manpower and resources to finance their courts. Inscriptions from this era memorialise successful expeditions of royal conquest and subsequent redistributions of material and human plunder to Khmer and Cham temples.

Angkor's Linkage With the Cham Coastline

During the expansion of Angkor-era commerce, Sūryavarman I had solicited local and international trade that he might tap through collection of taxes and/or the formalisation of service relationships with merchants, as was done by other contemporary regional rulers. However, his successors did not maintain his commercial initiatives, as they relinquished control of the economically important western sector of the Khmer realm to emerging Thai polities. Trade remained important in the time of Sūryavarman II (1113–1150), the sovereign associated with Angkor Wat, who is thought to have become personally involved in trade with China and to have possessed his own maritime fleet (Wolters 1958: 598–606). During his reign Chinese traders visited Cambodia with cargoes of much-in-demand silk goods and porcelain. In 1147, the Chinese conferred specific favours upon the Khmer polity. Song-era porcelain has been excavated at Angkor, but after Sūryavarman II's reign there is a noticeable gap in epigraphic references to Khmer commercial relations with China until the reign of Jayavarman VII (1181–1218) (Cœdès 1942, 178; also see Stark and Cremin 2023, this volume).

The Legacy of Jayavarman VII (1181–1218)

The 12th-century Angkor realm shifted to the east in pursuit of contact with merchants of the Chinese diaspora associated with ports-of-trade on the Vietnamese coastline. Khmer and Cham political and economic fortunes were thus strongly aligned in the reign of the Khmer monarch Jayavarman VII from 1181, following his long-term youthful residency in the Cham Vijaya coastal region. In Jayavarman's reign the Cham coastline became the focal point of the Khmer South China Sea trade linked to an overland connection via the downstream Thi Nại centre in the Con River valley (Figure 6.2).

Through the 1180s Jayavarman reintegrated the shattered Khmer realm, very rapidly built his famed Bayon Mahāyāna Buddhist temple complex at Angkor Thom, made Mahāyāna alterations to the Angkor Wat temple complex, and promoted a series of Mahāyāna Buddhist pilgrimage stopovers on the strategic roadway between the Angkor core and Phimai to the northwest. From 1012 to 1029 there were seven recorded Khmer eastern missions to the northern coastline of Vietnam at Than Long and another in 1056 to greet a new Vietnamese monarch (Whitmore 2018, 31–36; 2019).

In the initial decade of Jayavarman's reign his realm shifted its maritime trade centring on the Champa capital of Vijaya and its regional port of Thi Nại, where Angkor had direct access to the Cham *Jiaozhi* Ocean coastline circuit and through it to the major South China Song port of Quanzhou (Hall 2011; also see Stark and Cremin 2023, this volume). Until Jayavarman's death in the 1220s and beyond, the Khmer realm retained this link and its control over this central sector of the South China Sea seaboard. This included, for the first time since the 1130s, joint

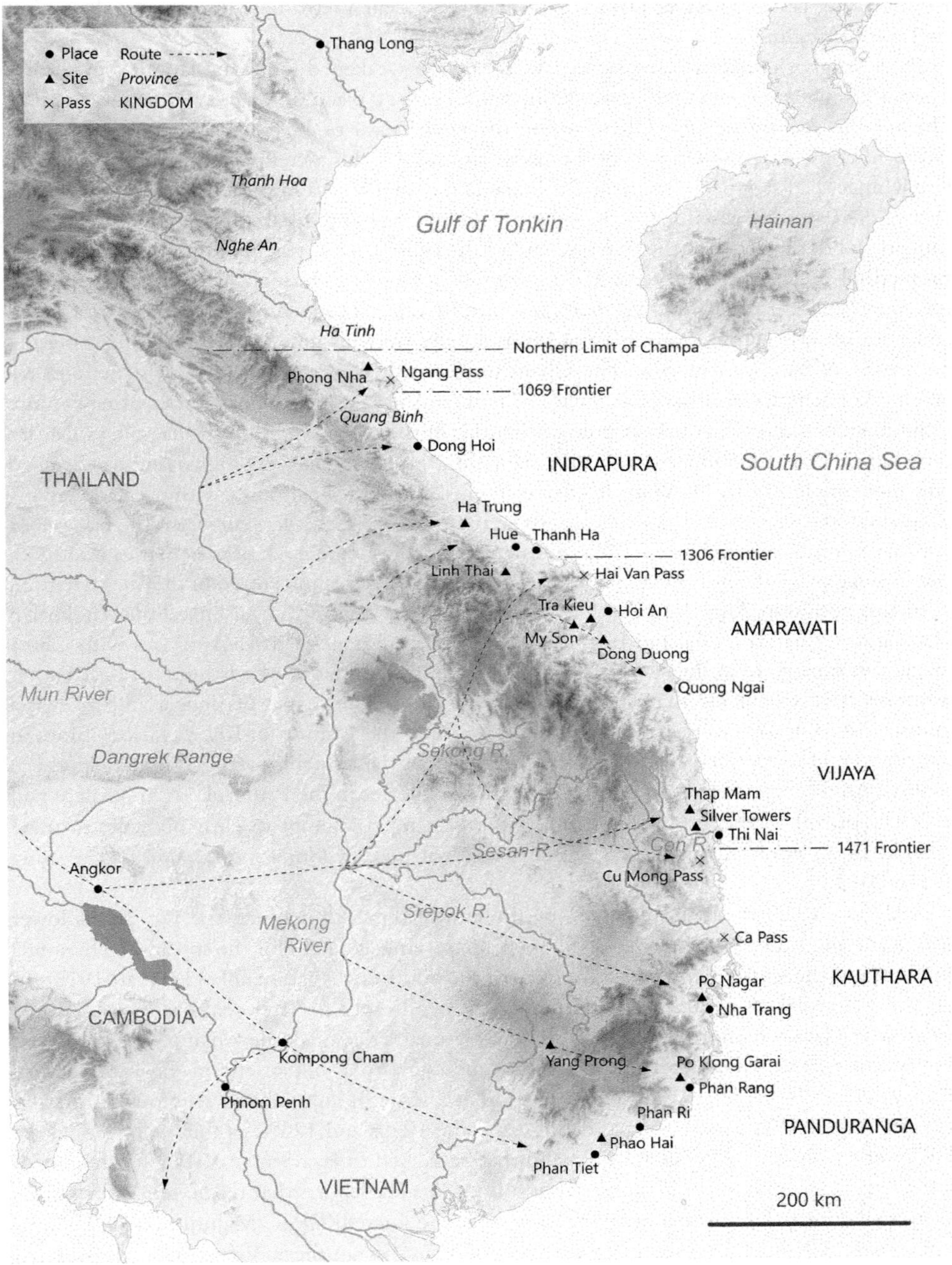

Figure 6.2 Pre-1500 Champa coastline ports-of-trade and hypothesised Western overland connections contesting the Malay Peninsula.

Source: (After Tran et al. 2015).

Khmer/Cham attacks on Đại Việt in 1216 and 1218, coincident with chaos that erupted in the northern Vietnam Red River plain when there were Trần Vietnamese dynasty assaults against the Lý court regime.

Once Angkor's hold over the eastern Vijaya region weakened following Jayavarman's death, a new Cham regime emerged and solidified the primary place of Vijaya within the realm of Champa. To reconstruct this Cham realm, the new Vijaya ruler, Jaya Parameśvaravarman II, had to re-consecrate the temples of the realm and validate his sacral position among localities. The Khmers had stripped Champa of its lingas and drawn Vijaya into their own cosmic sphere (that of the Bayon). Subsequently the ruler of Champa had to re-establish Vijaya within its own domain and dominate the other river valleys of the central coast, placing them under the shade (protection) of his royal umbrella. He accomplished this first through his *Abhiseka* ceremony (see Sahai 1997 for the Khmer parallel), proclaiming himself the new king of his reconstructed land with his official name and placing his 'umbrella' over his new land, thereby marking the emergence of its era of success. The Cham monarch then proceeded to reconstruct and re-sacralise key temples in other river valleys. The new Vijaya regime built a series of new, more monumental temples for the first time on hilltops in their own and other river valleys. Meant to be seen at a distance above the agricultural fields, these temples were higher and less detailed than their predecessors. Showing Khmer elements, the Indic sculptures within Jaya Parames-varavarman II's temples also came to absorb Javanese and Chinese elements from the two major ends of Champa's maritime routes at that time. At the core of these religious activities stood Śiva and his linga, with the new king establishing a thriving Indic realm centred in the Vijaya region.

At this period in Angkor's history its domain over the Bay of Bengal linked the Angkorian World directly to Sri Lanka and Burma. Even more important than Angkor's ties with China during this time were its linkages to Theravada Buddhist polities on the Isthmus of Kra. Earlier historians have speculated that one or another of these eastern Bay of Bengal and mainland Southeast Asia powers must have politically dominated the Isthmus of Kra at various times in that century. However, the cited evidence confirms that the contemporary Myanmar (southern Burma), Angkor, and Sri Lanka polities each had an interest in the Peninsula. A Singhalese raid on lower Burma in the 1160s is best understood to be an attempt to clear obstacles to trade rather than an effort to incorporate distant regional polities (Sumio 2004; Joll 2012; Aung Thwin 2012).

Partly as a result of these initiatives, by the end of the 12th century, the way across lower Burma and the Isthmus of Kra was again open and serving as a path for the spread of Theravada Buddhism to the western and central regions of the Southeast Asian mainland (Wyatt 1975). In this way a networked cultural relationship of great significance for later centuries began. While the Thai and Java regions prospered and southeast Sumatra declined, the Champa realm enjoyed a period of relative strength, albeit one that would come to a sudden end in the 15th century (Andaya 2008: 146–172, 191–201, 222–234). The theme of cultural and religious restoration is centre stage in Cham inscriptions dating from the 1220s and 1230s, as they followed an era of Khmer dominance over the Cham realm that had dated to Jayavarman VII's retaliatory raids in the late 12th century. A Cham inscription from this era reports that restoration efforts were necessary because 'Jayavarman had carried away all the [sacred] *lingas*' (Majumdar 1985[1927]).

The next Cham ruler, based in the region of Vijaya in southern Vietnam, re-consecrated and purified temples, reactivated regional cults, and restored damaged temples. This new construction paralleled the style of Jayavarman VII. As with Jayavarman VII's Khmer predecessors, the earlier temple architecture in the Cham realm had been refined in style, while the new 13th-century construction was more imperial in content, monumental in size, and imposing in scale and subject matter. The new Cham rulers substantiated their legitimacy in a new age in which the Vijaya-centred Cham coastline became the focus of a new Vietnam to south China to the north networked trading community. Common inscriptions dating 1224–1234 proclaim the new Cham ruler Jaya Paramesvaravarman IV (1226–c. 1243) based in Vijaya. He was said to have 'reinstalled all the *lingas* of the south, [viz.] those of Yan Pu nagara [Po Nagar], and the lingas of the north, [viz.], those of Srisanabhadresvara [the focal deity of Mi Son] . . . [following his coronation]'. This is significant since these dates mark the end of Khmer dominance in the Cham realm following Jayavarman VII's reign (Whitmore 2022).

The inclusive Cham realm flourished from the early 13th century while Angkor and Bagan were declining, due in part to their temporary upstream isolation from the higher volume of international maritime trade. Champa, by contrast, prospered in its response to new trade opportunities afforded by the increasing maritime transit between Java and China. At the primary Thi Nai (Qui Nhon) Cham port of that era, Chinese porcelain and silk were exchanged for Champa's highland forest products, especially aloeswood, native cloth, rhinoceros horns, and elephant tusks. Cham (*Zhanzheng*) rice, farmed in intensively cultivated upstream hinterlands, provisioned increasing numbers of maritime sojourners who made stopovers at Cham coastline ports. Regularised contact between the Vijaya lowlands and the central highlands is documented by late 14th-century Hindu icons that have been recovered throughout the highlands, as well as temple towers and stelae with Sanskrit inscriptions. In the early 13th century Cham rulers had begun to formalise their relationship with highland chiefs by ritually bestowing royal titles (Hickey 1982).

In addition to their northern successes during the late 14th century, Cham Vijaya controlled Khmer access to China's marketplace and profited accordingly. By then Angkor was no longer a force on the Peninsula. As the Ming chronicles relate: 'When Zhen La [the Khmer realm] submits tribute, the king of Champa exacts one quarter of it' (Wade 2010). In their 1408 and 1414 tributary missions to China the Khmer delegation complained about Cham expansion, but the Ming court ignored their appeal.

Overland routes from the Vietnam coastline remained a source of upstream and downstream Cham/Khmer highland trade products: gold, silver, aromatics, rhinoceros horn (as an aphrodisiac), and elephant tusks. Several routes served as the remaining Angkor realm's primary access to the South China Sea, whether via Cham ports to the east or Dai Viet in the north. While the southern expansion was primarily agricultural in intent, the shift to the south movement enabled the Vietnamese to assume the commercial role that the Chams had been previously playing among the intensifying networks of international trade most desired by international traders. Victory over Champa put the Vietnamese in a position to monopolise the South China Sea coastal access to the highland products in the Khmer and Vietnamese border zones.

In the south, the remaining Champa polities at Kauthara and Panduranga remained a factor in the coastal trade, as new regional temples represented by Po, the Klong Garai, and Po Rome temple complexes that document the continuing vitality of the Cham. Strategically, from the 16th century, the Mekong Delta became important in allowing Western, Japanese, Chinese, Vietnamese, and Cham maritime diaspora upstream shipping access to the new post-Angkor Cambodian heartland centred at the intersection of the Tonle Sap and Mekong rivers, at what is today Phnom Penh. There Laotian textiles and Cambodian deerskins became major post-1500 international exports, most notably to Japan (Hall 2017, 19–30).

By the 11th century the Việt northern Vietnam polity was experiencing increased overland and South China Sea maritime trade and were doing so in direct competition with the Champa realm to its south. There were two primary avenues for this trade. The first, an interior trade route connecting Đai Việt with the Khmer realm to its west, was an especially serious threat to Cham trading with their Khmer neighbours. In the 10th and 11th centuries the overland trade route from the Champa Nghệ An region ran west through Ha Trai pass and turned south along the upper Mekong River into the Khmer heartland (Maspéro 1918, 29–36). Contemporary Khmer inscriptions describe traders of Việt origin using this route. The development of overland routes from the Khmer core across the eastern mountains was especially threatening to Cham ports, as eastern Angkor realm transporters networked from the eastern Khmer heartlands by riverine links and overland trade across the Vietnam Central Highlands. For example, Vijaya was linked to the Khmer heartland via an overland network and especially the intermediary highland centre of Kon Klor, where there are a Cham temple and epigraphic and archaeological remains from that era that substantiate this overland cultural and trade connection. A Khmer inscription found at Phum Mien on the lower Mekong references Việt use of interior riverine routes and documents a Cham threat (Cœdès 1954, 183–86). A Cham 1050 Pāṇḍuraṅga naval raid up the Mekong River into the Khmer heartland, thereby sacking the Khmer Śambupura urban centre on the Mekong, was either a plunder raid or a reassertion of Cham trade relationship with the Khmer realm (Osborne 1966, 449).

From there trade commodities travelled north on smaller boats or were more often transported overland by foot via the central highlands, connecting to the upper Mekong River and from there north via Khmer and Lao (Land Zhenla) regions into Đại Việt (Jiaozhi). An early terminus of this overland route was via the Ha Trai pass to Nghệ An and from there to the Red River delta. Early merchants, pilgrims, and envoys all made stopovers in the central Cham region prior to making this overland passage to Jiaozhi (the Chinese name for the Red River–centred northern region prior to its independence from Chinese rule as the Đại Việt state in the 10th century). The overland route was also the source of *Jiaozhi*'s most desired highland trade products: gold, silver, aromatics, rhinoceros horn, and elephant tusks. This route, as noted, also served as the Angkor-era realm's primary access to the South China Sea, whether to Cham ports to the east or to Đại Việt ports in the north. Khmer kings thus sent tribute to the Đại Việt court 19 times in the 960–1279 era, in contrast to only 5 to the Song China court (Shorto 1961, 163–71).

Although highland populations in the Angkor-Champa border zone had the option of trading overland with their Khmer neighbours to the west, by the early 16th century, northern upstream territories were loosely incorporated into the Vietnamese state. The northern Vietnamese not only seized Champa's prior profitable maritime trade with China but also imposed a tributary trade system on remaining southern Cham port polities (Shimoki 1998; Whitmore 2019).

In the south the remaining Champa polities at Kauthara and Pāṇḍuraṅga remained a factor in the coastal trade, as new regional temples represented by the Po Klong Garai and Po Rome temple complexes document the continuing vitality of the Cham culture. Post-Angkorian Khmers, whose art and architectural traditions are discussed in this volume for Thailand (Krajaejun 2023, this volume) and Cambodia (Thompson 2023, this volume), continued to use many of these same routes to move their goods into a growing world-system that included the extended Eastern Indian Ocean, South China, Java, and Sulu Seas.

References

Acri, A., (ed.). 2016. *Esoteric Buddhism in Mediaeval Maritime Asia: Networks of Masters, Tests, Icons*. Singapore: ISEAS-Yusof Ishak Institute.

Andaya, L., 2008. *Leaves of the Same Tree: Trade and Ethnicity in the Straits of Melaka*. Honolulu: University of Hawai'i Press.

Aung Thwin, M., 2002. Lower Burma and Bago in the history of Burma, in *The Maritime Frontier of Burma*, eds. J.J. Gommans & J. Leider. Leiden: KITLV, 25–58.

Aung Thwin, M., 2012. *History of Myanmar since Ancient Times: Traditions and Transformations*. London: Reaktion Books.
Aymonier, E., 1904. *Le Cambodge: Les Provinces Siamoises*. Paris: Ernest Leroux.
Baker, C. & P. Phongpaichit, 2017. *A History of Ayutthaya*. Cambridge: Cambridge University Press.
Boisselier, J., 1996. *Le Cambodge, Asie du Sud-Est*, vol. 1. Paris: A & J. Picard & Cie.
Briggs, L.P., 1951. The Ancient Khmer Empire. *Transactions of the American Philosophical Society, New Series*, 41.
Chutintaranond, S. (ed.), 2002. *Recalling Local Pasts: Autonomous Histories in Southeast Asia*. Chiang Mai: Silkworm.
Cœdès, G., 1941. La Stèle du Prah Khan d Angkor. *Bulletin de l' École française d' Extrême-Orient* 41, 255–302.
Cœdès, G., 1942. *Inscriptions du Cambodge*, vol. II. Paris: Bulletin de l' École française d' Extrême-Orient.
Cœdès, G., 1954. *Inscriptions du Cambodge*, vol. VI. Paris: Bulletin de l' École française d' Extrême-Orient.
Cœdès, G., 1961. *Recueil de inscriptions du Siam, Deuxième partie, Inscriptions de Dvaravati, et al.* Bangkok: Vijiranana Library, 10–15.
Cœdès, G., 1964. *Inscriptions du Cambodge*, vol. VII. Paris: Bulletin de l' École française d' Extrême-Orient.
de Mestier du Bourg, H., 1970. La première moitié du XIe siècle au Cambodge: Sūryavarman Ier sa vie et quelques aspects des institutions son époque. *Journal Asiatic* 258(3–4), 281–314.
Finot, L., 1912. L'inscription de Ban That. *Bulletin de l' École française d' Extrême-Orient* 12(2), 1–28.
Glover, I., 2010. The Dvaravati gap—Linking prehistory and history in early Thailand. *Bulletin of the Indo-Pacific Prehistory Association* 30, 79–86.
Green, G., 2000. Indic impetus? Innovations in textile usage in Angkorian period Cambodia. *Journal of the Economic and Social History of the Orient* 43(3), 277–313.
Green, G., 2007. Angkor vogue: sculpted evidence of imported luxury textiles in the courts of kings and temples. *Journal of the Economic and Social History of the Orient* 50(4), 424–51.
Groslier, B.-P., 1973. Pour une Géographie historique du Cambodge. *Les Cahiers D Outre-Mer* 104(26), 337–79.
Hall, K.R. & J.K. Whitmore, 1976. Southeast Asian trade and the Isthmian struggle, 1000–1200 A.D, in *Explorations in Early Southeast Asian History: The Origins of Southeast Asian Statecraft. Michigan Papers on South and Southeast Asia, II.* Ann Arbor: University of Michigan Press, 197, 303–40. DOI 10.3998/mpub.19404
Hall, K.R., 1978. International trade and foreign diplomacy in early Medieval South India. *Journal of the Economic and Social History of the Orient* 21(1), 75–98.
Hall, K.R., 2004. Local and international trade and traders in the Straits of Melaka region: 600–1500. *Journal of the Economic and Social History of the Orient* 47(2), 213–60.
Hall, K.R., 2010. Ports of trade, maritime diasporas, and networks of trade and cultural integration in the Bay of Bengal region of the Indian ocean, c., 1000–1500, in *Empires and Emporia, the Orient in World-Historical Space and Time*, ed. J. Gommans. Leiden: E.J. Brill, 109–45.
Hall, K.R., 2011. *A History of Early Southeast Asia, Maritime Trade and Societal Development*. Lanham: Rowman and Littlefield, 100–50.
Hall, K.R., 2017. The coming of the west: European Cambodian marketplace connectivity, 1500–1800, in *The Coming of the West to Cambodia*, ed. T. Smith. London: Palgrave, 7–36.
Hall, K.R., 2020. Contested histories of the Ming agency in the Java Sea, Straits of Melaka, and Bay of Bengal regions, in *The Ming World*, in ed. K.M. Swope. London: Routledge, 11–42.
Hendrickson, M., 2010. Historic routes to Angkor: development of the Khmer road system (9th to 13th centuries CE) in Mainland Southeast Asia. *Antiquity* 84, 480–96.
Hendrickson, M., 2011. A transport geographic perspective on travel and communication in Angkorian Southeast Asia (ninth to fifteenth centuries AD). *World Archaeology* 43(3), 444–57.
Hendrickson, M., 2012. Connecting the dots: investigating the issue of transportation between the temple complexes of the medieval Khmer (9th to 14th centuries AD), in *Old Myths and New Approaches: Advances in the Interpretation of Religious Sites in Ancient Southeast Asia*, ed. A. Haendel. Melbourne: Centre of Southeast Asian Studies, Monash Asia Institute, 70–88.
Heng, D., 2009. *Sino-Malay Trade and Diplomacy from the Tenth to the Fourteenth Century*. Athens: Ohio University Press.
Heng, P., 2023. Angkor and the Mekong River: settlement, resources, mobility, and power, in *The Angkorian World*, eds. M. Hendrickson, M.T. Stark & D. Evans. New York: Routledge, 154–72.
Hickey, G.C., 1982. *Sons of the Mountains: Ethnohistory of the Vietnamese Central Highlands to 1954*. New Haven, CT: Yale University Press.

Hirth, E. & W.W. Rockhill, 1911. *Chau Ju-kua: His Work on the Chinese and and Arab Trade in the Twelfth and Thirteenth Centuries, Entitled Chu-fan-chi*. St. Petersburg: Imperial Academy of Sciences, 31–3.

Jacq-Hergoualc'h, M., 2002. The Mergui-Tenasserim region in the context of the Maritime Silk Road, in *Maritime Frontier of Burma: Exploring Political, Cultural, and Commercial Interaction in the Indian Ocean World 1200–1800*, eds. J. J. Gommans & J. Leider. Leiden: KITLV Press, 79–92.

Joll, C.M., 2012. Indic, Islamic and Thai influences, in *Muslim Merit-Making in Thailand's Far South*, ed. C.M. Joll. New York: Springer, 25–60.

Krajaejun, P., 2023. Uthong and Angkor: material legacies in the Chao Phraya River Basin, in *The Angkorian World*, eds. M. Hendrickson, M.T. Stark & D. Evans. New York: Routledge, 554–73.

Kulke, H., 1999. Rivalry and competition in the Bay of Bengal in the eleventh century and its bearing on Indian Ocean studies, in *Commerce and Culture in the Bay of Bengal*, eds. O. Prakash & D. Lombard. New Delhi: Manohar, 17–35.

Lamb, A., 1961. Kedah and Takuapa: some tentative historical conclusions. *Federated Museums Journal* 6, 69–81.

Luce, G.H., 1922. A Cambodian (?) invasion of Lower Burma—A comparison of Burmese and Talaing chronicles. *Journal of the Burma Research Society* 12(1), 39–45.

Majumdar, R.C., 1985[1927]. *Champa: History and Culture of an Indian Colonial Kingdom in the Far East*. Delhi: Gian Publishing House.

Maspero, H., 1918. La Frontière de l' Annam et du Cambodge. *Bulletin de l' École française d'Extrême-Orient* 18(3) 29–36.

Murphy, S.A., 2013. Buddhism and its relationship to Dvaravati period settlement patterns and material culture in Northeast Thailand and Central Laos, c. sixth to eleventh centuries AD: a historical ecology approach to the landscape of the Khorat Plateau. *Asian Perspectives* 52(2), 300–26.

Murphy, S.A., 2016. The case for Proto-Dvaravati: a review of the art historical and archaeological evidence. *Journal of Southeast Asian Studies* 47(3), 366–92.

Murphy, S.A., 2018. Revisiting the Bujang Valley: a Southeast Asian entrepôt complex on the maritime trade route. *Journal of the Royal Asiatic Society* 28(2), 355–89.

Murphy, S.A., 2019. Cultural connections and shared origins between Champa and Dvaravati, in *Champa: Territories and Networks of a Southeast Asian Kingdom*, eds. A. Hardy & G. Wade. Paris: École française d'Extrême Orient, 303–21.

O'Connor, S.J.O., 1972. *Hindu Gods of Peninsular Siam: Artibus Asiae Supplementum XXVIII*. Cham: Ascona.

O'Connor, S.J.O., 1975. Tambralinga and the Khmer Empire. *Journal of the Siam Society* 63(1), 161–75.

Osborne, M., 1966. Notes on early Cambodian provincial history: Isanapura and Sambhupura. *France-Asie/Asia* 20(4), 433–49.

Phungtian, C., 2000. *Thai-Cambodia cultural relationships through the arts*. PhD dissertation. Bodhgaya: Magadh University.

Revire, N., 2016. Dvāravatī and Zhenla in the seventh to eighth centuries: a transregional ritual complex. *Journal of Southeast Asian Studies* 47(3), 393–417.

Revire, N. & S.A. Murphy (eds.), 2014. *Before Siam: Essays in Art and Archaeology*. Bangkok: River Books and Siam Society.

Sahai, S., 1997. The royal consecration (*Abhiseka*) in ancient Cambodia. *The South East Asian Review* 22, 1–10.

Sen, T., 2003. *Buddhism, Diplomacy, and Trade: The Realignment of Sino-Indian Relations, 600–1400*. Honolulu: University of Hawai'i Press.

Shimoki, M., 1998. Dai Viet and the South China Sea trade from the tenth to the fifteenth century. *Crossroads* 12(1), 1–34.

Shorto, H.L., 1961. A Mon genealogy of kings: observations on the Nadana Aramabhakantha, in *Historians of South-East Asia*, ed. D.G.E. Hall. Ithaca, NY: Cornell University Press, 163–72.

Skilling, P., 2003. Dvaravati: recent revelations and research, in *Dedications to Her Royal Highness Princess Galyani Vadhana Krom Luang Naradhiwas Rajanagarindra on her 80th Birthday*, Chris Baker, ed., Bangkok: Siam Society, 87–112.

Southworth, W.A. & K.P. Tran, 2019. The discovery of late Angkorian Khmer sculptures at Campā Sites and the overland trade routes between Campā and Cambodia, in *Champa: Territories and Networks of a Southeast Asian Kingdom*, eds. A. Hardy & G. Wade. Paris: École française d'Extrême Orient, 303–21.

Stark, M.T. & A. Cremin, 2023. Angkor and China: 9th–15th centuries, in *The Angkorian World*, eds. M. Hendrickson, M.T. Stark & D. Evans. New York: Routledge, 112–32.

Sumio, F., 2004. The long thirteenth century of Tambralinga: from Javaka to Siam. *Memoirs of the Research Department of the Toyo Bunko* 62, 75–80.

Thompson, A., 2023. Mainland Southeast Asia after Angkor: political and aesthetic legacies, in *The Angkorian World*, eds. M. Hendrickson, M.T. Stark & D. Evans. New York: Routledge, 574–91.

Tran, K.P., T. Luongkhote & K. Phon, 2015. The new archaeological finds in Northeast Cambodia, Southern Laos and Central Highland of Vietnam: considering on the significance of overland trading route and cultural interactions of the ancient kingdoms of Champa and Cambodia, in *Advancing Southeast Asian Archaeology 2013: Selected Papers from the First SEAMEO SPAFA International Conference on Southeast Asian Archaeology, Chonuri, Thailand 2013*, ed. N.H. Tan. Bangkok: SEAMEO SPAFA Regional Center for Archaeology and Fine Arts, 432–43.

Vickery, M., 1998. *Society, Economics, and Politics in Pre-Angkor Cambodia, The Seventh-Eighth Centuries*. Tokyo: The Centre for East Asian Cultural Studies for UNESCO.

Wade, G., 2010. Southeast Asia in the Ming Shi-lu, online internet research site, www.epress, nus.edu.ag/ms (accessed August 8, 2010).

Wang, G, 1958. The Nanhai trade: a study of the early history of Chinese trade in the South China Sea. *Journal of the Malayan Branch of the Royal Asiatic Society* 31, 1–182.

Wheatley, P., 1961. *The Golden Khersonese, Studies in the Historical Geography of the Malay Peninsula before 1500*. Kuala Lumpur: Malaysian Branch of the Royal Asiatic Society.

Whitmore, J.K., 2017. India and China on the eastern seaboard of Mainland Southeast Asia: links and changes, 1100–1600, in *India and Southeast Asia: Cultural Discourses*, eds. A.L. Dallapiccola & A. Verghese. K.R. Cama Oriental Institute: Mumbai, 51–70.

Whitmore, J.K., 2018. Nagara Champa and the Vijaya Turn, in *Vibrancy in Stone. The Masterpieces of the Museum of Cham Sculpture*, eds. V.V. Thang & P.D. Sharrock. Bangkok: River Books, 31–6.

Whitmore, J.K., 2019. Cultural accommodation and competition on the Champa/Việt Coast over two millennia, in *Cross-Cultural Networking in the Eastern Indian Ocean Realm 100–1800*, eds. K.R. Hall, S. Ghosh &. K. Gangopadhyay. Delhi: Primus Press, 224–66.

Whitmore, J.K., 2022. *Haijin*, Melaka, and the Cham/Viet Coast. *Journal of the Economic and Social History of the Orient* 65, 415–45.

Wolters, O.W., 1958. Tambralinga. *Bulletin of the School of Asian and African Studies* 21, 587–607.

Woodward, H.W., 1975. *Studies in the arts of Central Siam, 950–1350*. PhD dissertation. New Haven: Yale University.

Wyatt, D.K., (ed. and tr.). 1975. *The Crystal Sands: The Chronicles of Nagara Śri Dharrmarāja*. Data Paper No. 98. Cornell University, New York: Southeast Asia Program.

Wyatt, D.K., 1994. Mainland powers on the Malay Peninsula. *Studies in Thai History. Chiang Mai: Silkworm*, 22–48.

Wyatt, D.K., 2001. Relics, oaths, and politics in thirteenth century Siam, *Journal of Southeast Asian Studies* 32(1), 3–65.

7

ANGKOR AND CHINA

9th–15th Centuries

Miriam T. Stark and Aedeen Cremin

Linkages with China and South Asia were underway by the first centuries CE (Estève 2023; Hendrickson et al. 2023; Soutif and Estève 2023, this volume), at first overland and later through a maritime network that intensified in the 10th to 12th centuries CE. By the late 12th century, Chinese merchant ships were so familiar to Khmers that one was represented on the walls of the Bayon temple in Jayavarman's Great City. Cambodia was never colonised, yet its millennium-long sporadic diplomacy with China's changing dynasties led to rich economic, cultural, and technological interactions.

When China attempted to bring its southern border provinces and their Yue inhabitants into its sphere of influence, it also pursued diplomatic missions further south with *Nanyang*, the coastal polities around the *Nanhai* (South China Sea) region, to create a ring of 'tributary states' that provided China with increasingly desirable exotica. Although 3rd-century *Funan* populations would not submit to Chinese political control, they seem to have welcomed diplomatic ties that brought them prestige goods. Sixth-century Chinese, in turn, sought products from Southeast Asia's forests, and their embrace of Buddhism also brought needs for *materia medica* from Southeast Asia's subtropical forests.

We divide our discussion into two general periods: the 1st to 10th century Nanhai trade period that Wang Gungwu (1958) first described to the West and the 11th to 14th century Angkor Period, using Chinese dynastic histories and evidence from Cambodia's archaeology, art history, and epigraphy. The chapter concludes by considering how China and Cambodia viewed each other's respective polities through time. From the start of China's Ming dynasty in 1368, interaction with China remained a constant, despite changes within Cambodia indicated by the court's relocation from Angkor closer to the Mekong Delta.

China, Maritime Asia, and Cambodia in the First Millennium CE

Our earliest archaeological evidence for Chinese contact is during the Han dynasty, 206 BCE–20 CE (e.g., Péronnet 2013; Castillo et al. 2016). By then, overland and maritime 'Silk Roads' had been established by Mediterranean and Asian traders (Bellina 2014; Villiers 2001, 25–26). In 111 BCE, Emperor Han Wudi established 'commanderies' on the southern coasts of what is today Vietnam: *Jiaozhi*/Giao Chi (Red River Delta) and *Rinan*/Nhật Nam or Linyi south of the Ngang Pass in Hà Tĩnh or the 'Porte d'Annam' (Allard 2016; Brindley 2015, 4; Carter and Kim 2017, 741–44; Li 2011). Jiaozhi became Han China's largest entrepôt for the Maritime Silk Road

DOI: 10.4324/9781351128940-9

(Cooke et al. 2011). It paid tribute to the Han court, but *Rinan* was largely notional, as the several kingdoms of Linyi/Champa were primarily concerned with their inland Khmer neighbours.

Diplomacy, trade, and religion brought China and Southeast Asia increasingly close through time (Heng 2009, 152–54). The Maritime Silk Route moved people, goods, and ideas (particularly Buddhism) through a complex web of ports and urban centres in Southeast Asia and the Bay of Bengal to both East and South Asia (Christie 1995; Heng 2008b, 33; Ray 1994; Schottenhammer 1999, 17–18). China hosted more than 120 tribute delegations from Southeast Asia between the 3rd to 6th centuries: nearly one every three years (Wang 1958, 119–22).

Additionally, trade missions and non-state commerce provided foreign goods for Chinese ritual and medicine (Gang 1997, 282). By the 3rd century, pilgrims and foreign traders from South and Central Asia (Sen 2017, 542–43) travelled in such volumes that Southeast Asian shipwrights built large cargo and passenger ships, known in China as *kunlun bo* (Pelliot 1925, section VI; Manguin 1993, 261-62). A 5th-century Chinese Buddhist monk, Faxian, sailed from Sumatra to Laoshan (Shandong) on such a ship, fully laden with cargo, that held 200 men, withstood a typhoon, and survived 70 days at sea without making landfall (Legge 1886, ch. 39).

Cambodia was long known for its aromatics (e.g., Hirth and Rockhill 1966[1911], 56, footnote 9), and a 'scent culture' had emerged in China's royal and elite culture by the Han Period (Milburn 2016, 447-59). Cambodia's overland trade went through north-central Vietnam, with goods carried across the Truong Son Cordillera to northern Cambodia and southern Laos (see Hall 2023, this volume). Cambodia also lay on the Western Ship Route (*xi hanglu* 西航路) that flanked mainland Southeast Asia's coastline from Quanzhou in Fujian along Vietnam, Thailand, and the Malay ports to the southwest (Ptak 1998, 2006).

A Chronology of Chinese Documentary Relations with Cambodia

Table 7.1 provides a concordance of Chinese dynasties and Cambodian time periods to guide this chapter, and Figure 7.1 illustrates the premodern Chinese/Cambodian world. Chinese

General time period	*Specific dynasty*	*Date range (CE)*			
China			Cambodia	N Vietnam	S Vietnam
Han		206 BCE–220 CE		Jiaozhi commandery	Linyi
Three Kingdoms	Wu/Wei/Shu Han	220–65 CE	Funan (protohistoric)		
Northern and Southern Dynasties	Jin	265–420 CE			
	Liu-Song	420–79 CE			
	Southern Qi	479–502 CE			
	Liang/Southern Liang/ Western Liang	502–555–557 CE	Chenla		
	Chen	557–589 CE			
	Sui	581–618 CE			
	Tang	618–907 CE	Chenla/Angkor	Annan/Annam prefecture	Champa
	Northern Song	960–1127 CE	Angkor	Dai Viet	
	Southern Song	1127–1279 CE			
	Yuan	1271–1368 CE			
	Ming	1368–1644 CE			

Table 7.1 Cross-chronology of Chinese dynasties and Cambodian time periods.

Products of Cambodia	
Beeswax	Aka Yellow wax (Zhou 2007[1297], 69; Hirth and Rockhill 1966[1911], 53)
Aromatics	Gharuwood aka eaglewood, *Aquilaria malaccensis*, produces a resin called agar, whence the name agarwood.[1]
	Sweet benzoin, *Styrax tonkinensis*, incense and body perfume (Hirth and Rockhill 1966[1911], 198-99)
Decorative elements	Elephant tusks (Hirth and Rockhill 1966[1911], 53; Zhou 2007[1297], 69)
	Kingfisher feathers (Hirth and Rockhill 1966[1911], 53; Zhou 2007[1297], 69)
	Pearls and mother-of-pearl (Hirth and Rockhill 1966[1911], 53)
	Tortoiseshell (Hirth and Rockhill 1966[1911], 53)
Dyes	Gamboge resin, a saffron-coloured pigment. *Garcinia hanburyi* (Hirth and Rockhill 1966[1911], 53; Zhou 2007[1297], 70)
	Sappan-wood, *Caesalpina sappan* (Hirth and Rockhill 1966[1911], 53, 217). Has important medical properties as an antibacterial, and the dried wood gives a crimson red or purple dye; the most important dyestuff exported to China (Lin 1995, 179)
	Sticklac, *Laccifer lacca*, can be used to dye silk, and the residue is a glue (Zhou 2007[1297], 70).[2]
Medicinal	Chaulmoogra oil, *Hydnocarpus anthelminitica* (Zhou 2007[1297], 70)
	Ginger peel, *Zingiber officinale* (Hirth and Rockhill 1966[1911], 53)
	Rhinoceros horn (Hirth and Rockhill 1966[1911], 53; Zhou 2007[1297], 69)
Pitch/gum	Dammar and gourd dammar. Resin, obtained from *Dipterocarpacae* trees. It can be collected in gourds, whence the name (Hirth and Rockhill 1966[1911], 53, 199-200)
Spices	Cardamom, *Elettaria cardamomum*, in great quantity (Hirth and Rockhill 1966[1911], 53, 221-22; Zhou 2007[1297])
	Pepper vine, *Piper nigrum* (Zhou 2007[1297], 70)
Textiles	Raw silk and cotton fabrics (Hirth and Rockhill 1966[1911], 53)
	Cotton is discussed in Hirth and Rockhill 1966[1911], 217-220

[1] Cambodia's is the best (Hirth& Rockhill 1966[1911]:53: 204–5). Shou and chan gharuwoods are the least good (Hirth & Rockhill 1966[1911]: 207). Called 'rosewood' in Zhou 2007[1297], 70.

[2] Called Lac in Zhou 2007[1297], 70.

interest in Cambodia had grown significantly by the 8th century (Lin 1995, 172), and Cambodian/Chinese interaction continued to intensify through the 9th–14th centuries (e.g., Goble 2014). Table 7.2 lists Southeast Asian resources valued by the Chinese that ranged from forest products to spices (see also Heng 2009, 193; Wheatley 1959).

Three Kingdoms, Northern and Southern Dynasty, and Sui Dynasty. By the early centuries CE, the Chinese viewed Southeast Asia's ports as a waypoint for Buddhist pilgrims bound for South Asia but also as source of luxury goods, primarily forest products that moved from interior uplands to the coast for trade (Cœdès 1968, 17-42; Stark and Bong 2001). Who exactly was moving these goods is not known, but Wang Gungwu (1958, 115) has suggested that there were locally based merchants.

The Mekong delta's coastal ports, centres of a polity known as 'Funan', were entrepôts for silk and other goods from southern China (Wang 1958, 53), precious stones (e.g., diamonds, cat's eye gemstones) and cotton from South Asia, borax from Middle Eastern sources, and exports from Island Southeast Asia like asbestos or 'fire-cleansing cloth' (Cameron et al. 2015, 169–70; Sen 2014a, 44; Wheatley 1959, 41). Funan itself was also an important source of benzoin resin from the *Styrax* tree, which had both medicinal and religious uses in China. Burning benzoin produced smoke that was used in Buddhist ceremonies and to expel evil spirits from one's body (Villiers 2001, 34).

Table 7.2 Desirable products of Cambodia and China, listed by Zhao Rugua and Zhou Daguan, with botanical names, comments, and variant translations added where appropriate.

Products of China	
Aromatics, medicine	Lovage, *Levisticum officinale* musk
Medicinal	Angelica, *Angelica acutiloba*, dang-gui or bai zhi
Chemicals	Mercury, cinnabar, sulphur, saltpeter, tung-tree oil, used as a varnish, *Vernicia fordii* (Zhou 2007[1297], 71)
Domestic goods	Paper parasols and kittysols/umbrellas (Hirth and Rockhill 1966[1911], 53), lacquered trays, writing paper, glass balls (or beads, Uk and Uk 2016, 89)
	Fine-toothed combs, wooden combs, needles (Zhou 2007[1297], 77)
Food	Preserves and vinegar, *samshu* (rice or millet liquor), sugar (Hirth and Rockhill 1966[1911], 53)
Metals	Finished gold and silver products, metalwares, including tinware (Hirth and Rockhill 1966[1911], 53)
	Copper dishes, iron pots; pewterware from Zhenzhou (Zhou 2007[1297], 71)
Ceramics	Porcelain (Hirth and Rockhill 1966[1911], 53)
	Celadonware from Quanzhou and Chuzhou (Zhou 2007[1297], 71)
Musical instruments	Skin-covered drums (Hirth and Rockhill 1966[1911], 53)
Textiles	Silk, satin (floating weave on silk) and satinets (satin weave on cotton) (Hirth and Rockhill 1966[1911], 53)
	Fine double-threaded silk in various colours
	Grass mats from Mingzhou
	Yellow grasscloth (or linen, Uk and Uk 2016, 89)
	Hemp, Cannabis sativa ssp. sativa (Zhou 2007[1297], 71)

The Chinese travellers Kangtai and Zhuying described a visit to Funan between 228 and 243 in the *Sanguo zhih*, or 'Records of the Three Kingdoms'. In the early 6th century CE, monks from Funan were employed by the Liang emperors to translate Buddhist scripture in what became known as the Bureau of Funan or 'Funan House' (Ishizawa 1995, 17; Pelliot 1903a, 285), and the Indian sage Paramārtha departed from Funan for China with Mahāyāna Buddhist manuscripts (Pelliot 1903b; Roveda 2012, 56; for review see Wade 2014a, 26–27). The Liang annals describe a spike in the 5th century when Funan and Linyi/Champa dominated Chinese records of tribute missions (Wang 1958, 52). Inland Cambodia, however, seems not to have been involved, as evidence of contact with China is currently limited to one Han Period coin found within a burial at Phum Lovea in the Angkor region (O'Reilly and Shewan 2016, 479).

Tang Period. The Tang dynasty (618–907) bridges the Pre-Angkor to Angkor Periods in Cambodia and encompasses significant geographic shifts in the locus of power from central Cambodia (Sambor Prei Kuk/Isanapura in Kampong Thom) to the Tonle Sap-Greater Angkor region. By the 7th century CE, Southeast Asia's 'holy things' proved as attractive to Chinese consumers as did the region's domestic prestige goods that Chinese consumers had long valued. These included not only incense and perfumes but also specific Buddhist religious icons. Medical compendia appeared at this time, formally encoding knowledge of traditional Chinese medicine, such as the *Materia Medica of Medicinal Properties* (Stanley-Baker and Yan 2017, 455, 474, footnote 29) and Buddhist healing practices, such as *Nāgārjuna's Treatise on the Five Sciences* or 'great medicines' (Steavu 2017, 441). The Chinese used both pharmaceuticals and talismans to treat topical skin injuries, digestive complaints, internal problems, fevers, and traumatic injuries at this time (see Chhem et al. this volume).

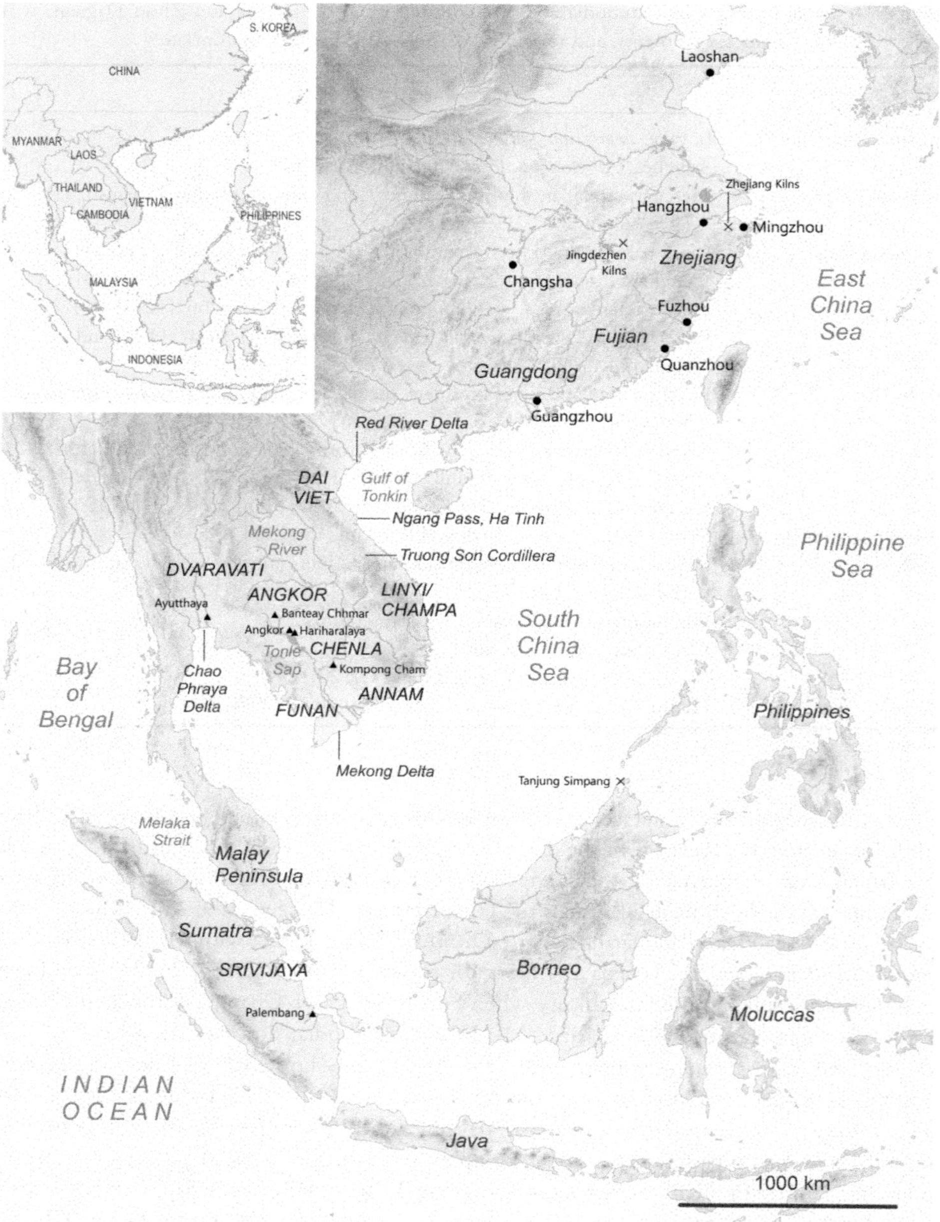

Figure 7.1 Cambodia and China in premodern Southeast Asia. Archaeological sites are filled triangles, and other key localities mentioned in the text are marked with an 'x'.

Arab and Persian traders rarely visited Cambodia, but some Arab accounts mention Cambodia (e.g., Ferrand 1913, 30, 40, 69–71; Tibbetts 1979, 9) as *Qmar* or *Kimari* (Arabic for aloeswood or *Aquilaria*). Cambodia also supplied ginger, cardamom, and other aromatic woods which could be blended with honey and spices to decoct into medicine (including sedatives, laxatives, and digestives) or burnt to drive away evil spirits (Steavu 2017, 449–51). Its rich deciduous forests held sandalwood

Santalum album and gharuwood *Aquilaria malaccensis* that were not only fragrant but were also valued as construction materials by both the Chinese and by the Khmers themselves (Jacob 1993, 292).

Fourteen missions from the Tang court between 710 and 814 brought Chinese envoys to Cambodia bearing gifts for local rulers. Relatively brief Tang Chinese reports on Cambodia (translated in Goble 2014, 7-8, 13-14) describe a *Chenla* polity that bordered both Annam and Linyi/Champa and that was divided into two parts: the mountainous 'Land' Chenla in the north and 'Water' Chenla in the south (Figure 7.1). Both Chenla kingdoms sent envoys to China with goods, including a rhinoceros in 750 and 11 tame elephants in 771. In return, China granted honorary titles to some of the Southeast Asian envoys (Bielenstein 2005, 53).

If Khmers were among the Southeast Asians who lived in Tang-dynasty Chinas Guangzhou as did other Southeast Asians, (e.g., Chiu 1973, 59; Heng 2019, 88), they left no trace. These foreign enclaves or *fanfang* housed non-Sinitic traders: Muslim Persians and Arabs, Parsis (Persians), and Jews. By the 8th century CE there were said to be more than 100,000 foreigners in Guangzhou alone (Sen 2017, 546). Two 9th-century CE Chinese missions to Cambodia were recorded before Guangzhou's 'Canton Massacre' of 838 that ended international relations and sparked more than a century of civil war along China's southern border (Wang 1958, 81-89).

China's political struggles seem to have subsided largely by the 10th century (Heng 2009, 37–58), but there are no Chinese references to Cambodia between 814 and 1117 CE, when the Khmer Empire, centred in the Angkor region, was being created. Both Chinese and Arabic sources from this time suggest the importance of a Sumatra-based polity called Srivijaya, known to the Chinese as *Sanfoqi* and to Arab geographers as *Zābaj* (e.g., Tibbetts 1979; Wolters 1963). Srivijaya's putative capital of Palembang and its satellite entrepôts may have mediated most of Southeast Asia's trade with China during this time (e.g., So 1998), and thus by-passed the growing Khmer polity within the Tonle Sap basin.

China and Cambodia in the Second Millennium

China's interactions with its southern neighbours changed markedly by the early second millennium CE (Wade 2009) when new trade routes, mentioned in the 14th-century CE Ming nautical tracts, were established to avoid the South China Sea's rocky shoals and offered direct Chinese access to points to these regions. The western route, or *xi hanglu* 西航路, involved sailing from Quanzhou in Fujian along the coasts of Vietnam and Cambodia/Zhenla (Ptak 2019, 22–3 et passim). From there ships continued sailing southwest to Malaya, Sumatra, and Java. The eastern route, or *dong hanglu* 東航路, proceeds due south from the trading port of Quanzhou to the Philippines and then to eastern Indonesia. The western route linked Cambodia and coastal Vietnam directly to Chinese maritime traders, supplementing the previously established Champa ports whose linkages to Angkor traversed the Truong Son cordillera (see Hall 2023, this volume). These routes were later codified in Sino-European maps that Ptak (2006, 466–7) has described.

Dynastic Shifts and the Growth of China's Maritime Trade With Southeast Asia

Northern Song (960–1127)

By the dawn of the Song dynasty, elite consumer preferences in China were democratised as a growing upper-middle class sought both Southeast Asian luxury goods and Persian and Arab medicines (Gang 1997, 256). By 1100 China's population was said to number 100 million, and it 'was the most populous, prosperous, and cultured nation on earth' (Hucker 1975, 271–72;

see also Wade 2009, 225–34; Wheatley 1959, 393). Foreign goods became available not simply to the court and its retinue but also in large city markets and at religious festivals. Southeast Asian drugs and incense were even available in the local markets of smaller urban centres (Yoshinobu 1998, 96–109). The Song dynasty eased private trade restrictions, and by the late 10th century, the southern Chinese ports of Guangzhou/Canton, Mingzhou/Ningbo, and Hangzhou/Lin (see Figure 7.1) hosted merchant marine offices. Quanzhou/Zaitun (Fujian) became the most important port in the 11th century (Schottenhammer 1999; Thammapreechakorn 2010, 191).

This stimulation of Chinese trade had a significant impact on the growth of the Southeast Asian maritime system (Heng 2008a, 14–15; Schottenhammer 2017; Wade 2009, 264). By the late 11th century, only 35% of foreign trade was in government hands, and individual traders no longer had restrictions on the length of their trading voyages (Heng 2008b, 31–32, 38; Yoshinobu 1983, 90). Song merchants could now tailor their shipments to consumer preferences, as described in Wang Dayuan's *Daoyi zhi lue* (1349). The Khmers, for example, preferred Chinese satin with dragon motifs, imitation *Jianyang* brocade, and silk umbrellas and parasols (Heng 2008b, 34–35; 2018, 171, 173; Lin 1995, 183).

How Cambodia responded to Song China's economic changes is less clear than the situation in contemporary Java, where studies have focused on records of export goods and the establishment of merchant associations (Christie 1998). Whether Angkorian rulers as early as Sūryavarman I pursued expansionist policies to secure access to international ports via Thailand's Chao Phraya delta remains unclear, but a significant number of 10th- and 11th-century inscriptions make reference to commercial activity (Hall 1975, 320; cf. Vickery 1987, 212–13). Archaeological excavations at the early royal site of Hariharalaya in the Angkor region uncovered 10th-century evidence for Chinese-made glass and Middle Eastern glass and ceramics (Carter et al. 2017, 1025; Pottier et al. 2012, 303–06). These rare objects could have been diplomatic Chinese gifts or, alternately, trade goods, coming through unofficial ports. Chinese sources describe 10th- and 11th-century Hokkien trading expeditions to Champa and Java (Wade 2009, 230) and list Javanese and Champa missions to the Chinese court (Heng 2009, 194), but Chinese attention only returns to Angkorian Cambodia when Sūryavarman II took the throne in the early 12th century CE.

Southern Song Period (1127–1279 CE)

With the establishment of the Song dynasty came an even greater Chinese appetite for foreign goods, but this was also a time of profound military weakness in the Chinese state. Repeated onslaughts by northern foreigners drove the state to move its capital southward to Hangzhou (Zhejiang) by 1127. Only four Angkorian missions are recorded: three during the reign of Sūryavarman II (r. 1113–?1145), who was recognised as king in 1120 and given an honorary title in 1129. The next and last mission was in 1200, from Jayavarman VII, who the Chinese noted 'had been on the throne for 20 years' (Bielenstein 2005, 53). The most information on Cambodia at this time is given in the *Zhufanshi* 诸蕃志 'A Description of Barbarian Nations, Records of Foreign People,' by Zhao Rugua, c. 1225 CE. Zhao was a member of the Song imperial clan and as inspector of maritime trade had the opportunity to talk to many foreign merchants (Hirth and Rockhill 1966[1911], 35). His work is in two parts, the first a set of country descriptions, some taken from earlier texts, and the second a list of commodities (see list in Table 7.2).

Zhao may have met members of Jayavarman VII's embassy to China in 1200 and describes Angkor's Royal Palace and a 'beautiful granite-sided pond filled with lotuses and spanned by a golden bridge, over 300 feet long' within the Royal Palace grounds (Yang 2020, "Zhenla (Chenla)"). This description matches the present Sra Sré (Grand Bassin) in Angkor Thom, which is 125 m long and faced with stone; the construction techniques reflect the style of Jayavarman

VIII (r.?1270 to 1295), but the pool existed well before that time (Glaize 1993[1944], 144–46). Zhao also mentions that 'in the southwest corner of the city is a bronze terrace on which stand 24 bronze towers and eight bronze elephants each weighing 4000 catties (about 25 metric tons)', which could be Jayavarman VII's Bayon (Yang 2020, Zhenla (Chenla)).

Yuan Period (1277–1367)

The Southern Song were conquered in 1279 by the Mongol/Yuan leader Kublai Khan, who also controlled northern China and Korea. The Yuan tried to invade Southeast Asia's northernmost reaches, from Vietnam's Tongking Gulf (e.g., Kimura et al. 2013) to possibly Burma (but see Goh 2009). When that failed, they started to develop maritime trade, intending to take over Southeast Asia's role (Heng 2009, 64). Few tribute missions were recorded, and none list Cambodia among the stopping points (Miksic and Goh 2017, 821; see also Wade 2009, 27; Table 7.2). Shortly after his accession, the second emperor of the Yuan dynasty, Kublai's grandson, Temur Khan (r. 1294–1307), did send an embassy to Cambodia via Champa, presumably to undo Kublai's damage and to impress the new dynasty's power on expatriate Chinese merchants. However, we see no mention of Cambodia in official Yuan histories or tribute missions during this period (Pelliot 1902, 131).

The ports of southern China and Southeast Asia blossomed in the early 13th century with an influx of Muslim traders into the region, particularly into Quanzhou (Ptak 1998; Schottenhammer 1999; Wade 2009, 234). An account from a late 13th-century Chinese emissary to Cambodia offers our most comprehensive glimpse into Angkorian life. In approximately 1296 CE, Zhou Daguan sailed around the coast of Vietnam and up the Mekong to the Angkorian capital of Angkor Thom, where he lived for approximately one year as part of Temur Khan's embassy. A decade or so after his return home to Zhejiang province, he wrote his *Zhēnlà Fēngtǔ Jì* or *Record of Cambodia: The Land and Its People*, which became a popular travel book, most recently republished in Chinese by Xia Nai in 2000 (Zhou 2007[1297], 29-30). Within Zhou's record was some commentary on commodities for which Cambodia was famous: gamboge resin (*Garcinia*), stick lac, and chaulmoogra (*Hydnocarpus wightianus*) oil were important export items (Zhou 2007[1297], 69). As Yuan China's power began to decline by the 14th century, we see a commensurate decline in state-level trade, and smuggling became a major source of Chinese exports (Gang 1997, 267).

Zhou claimed that Chinese sailors often abandoned their ships for the attractions of Ganbozhi (Kambuja/Cambodia) and that one of his informants, Xue, 'a fellow-countryman' from Zhejiang, had lived in Angkor for 35 years (Zhou 2007[1297], 80). Subsequent 14th- and 15th-century Chinese sources also record an expatriate community (Chang 2019, 228, Table 9.3), including, perhaps, members of a Chinese mission who defected to Cambodia in 1404 (Wade 2004, 30). By the dawn of the Ming dynasty, China was connected to Southeast Asia—and specifically to Cambodia—by a dense web of social linkages that included diplomatic, commercial, and personal ties between the regions.

Ming Period (1368–1644)

Angkor's regional pre-eminence had declined when the Ming dynasty re-established Han Chinese rule in China. Perhaps more than any preceding dynasty, the Ming Chinese viewed incorporation of Southeast Asian polities as part of their imperial mandate and wrote extensively about Chinese interactions with specific Southeast Asian 'kingdoms' in their *Ming shi-lu* (明 實 錄) annals, or 'Veritable Records of the Ming Dynasty', and other sources (Wade 2008, 582). Soon after ascending the throne, China's Hongwu Emperor included Korea, Annam, and Champa in his inner circle and also notified Cambodia and Siam of his accession. Yet the Ming policy of blending maritime prohibitions (which suppressed private foreign trade) with tribute missions, particularly within the 14th century, produced a Ming self-image as stewards of Maritime Southeast Asia that may have been little more than an 'illusion of Chinese influence' (Wolters 1963, 545).

Cambodia's relationship with Ming China was never equal but usually conferred benefits to Khmer rulers who were treated like Han kinsfolk: when Cambodian ruler Can-lie Po pi-ya died, the Chinese court offered sacrifices on his behalf and sent paper money to Cambodia (12 August 1405: Wade 2005). Khmer rulers, in turn, expressed gratitude for Chinese Imperial kindness by sending envoys with tribute throughout the Ming dynasty. Taken together, the Ming records indicate that China viewed Cambodia as a stable ally, to be treated with respect.

Not only did the 14th-century Chinese court send tally-slip books to Champa, Cambodia, and Siam to monitor transactions, it also proffered imperial gifts: fine silk textiles, porcelains, ceremonial boots and leggings, the Ming calendar, and paper money. Such gifts were often voluminous, as seen on 21 September 1383, when 32 bolts of silk and 19,000 pieces of porcelain were given to each of the rulers of Champa, Siam, and Cambodia (Wade 2005). Cambodia, in turn, presented trained elephants, aromatics, and beeswax (14 October 1383: Wade 2005). On 10 September 1387, the Khmers sent 59 elephants and 60,000 *jin* (c. 36 tons) of aromatics and on 25 May 1389 gave cloves, sandalwood, gharuwood, rose-water, glass, pepper, and beeswax (Wade 2005). The aromatics were highly valued by the Ming court, which particularly enjoyed burning benzoin in the palace (Wolters 1960, 337).

Angkor's declining status vis-à-vis Ayutthaya (Thailand) evidently did not affect Cambodia's relationship with China during this time, as it was listed first in descriptions of tribute missions and engaged in vigorous trade until the end of the 14th century. Fifteenth-century Ming maritime fleets included Cambodia and Siam on their Southeast Asian routes (Wade 2013, 14–15; *Wubei zhi* map). Cambodia, as Zhenla, remained in the Ming annals until 1452, in part because of China's growing closeness to the country. The collapse of Angkor as a regional power took place as the number of Chinese residents in 15th-century Southeast Asia increased, as did the use of Chinese languages and terms for food items and the emergence of hybrid Sino-Southeast Asian societies (Wade 2008, 619, 628).

China in Angkor

Evidence for Chinese People

The Angkorian perspective on China can be derived from Khmer inscriptions, images, and remains of material culture like ceramics and textiles (see Green 2023, this volume). Only 7 out of more than 1300 inscriptions mention China, and then only in terms of goods in temples or royal storehouses: silver containers, bronze mirrors, and silk fabrics (Lustig 2009, 179, Table 5). Inscriptions from the 12th-century temples of Preah Khan and Ta Prohm mention silk mosquito nets, Chinese boxes, cloth, and grass beds from China, intended as gifts to specific Angkorian divinities (Ea 2005, 271-72). Only one possibly Chinese person is mentioned: 'China' is part of the name of a male slave in a Pre-Angkorian inscription from Kandal Stueng district (K. 877: Cœdès 1954, 67, line 10).

A Chinese community was established in Angkor by the 13th century (e.g., Ea 2005, 275; Groslier 1973, 362; Pottier 1997a, 198). King Jayavarman VII (1181-?1218), a former general of royal descent who expanded and consolidated the Khmer Empire, had Chinese military allies. Bas-reliefs carved onto his Bayon temple show a small platoon of Chinese and Khmer fighting the Cham (eastern gallery, northern wing, relief 70b [Roveda 2007, 312]); elsewhere, Chinese soldiers, led by their general on an elephant and two officers on horseback, walk with musicians through a forest (eastern gallery, southern wing, relief 56c [Roveda 2007, 324]). Chinese civilians appear in some tableaus like the 'Maison du Chinois' (eastern gallery, southern wing, relief 56a [Roveda 2007, 323]), featuring a Chinese man and his Khmer wife and children in their house on one panel and masters seated at Chinese-style table drinking from ovoid Chinese bottles of wine, and attended to by Khmer servants, in another. There is a Chinese junk with passengers (southern gallery, east wing) and a cockfighting scene with Chinese and Khmer competitors (reliefs 58d and 58g [Roveda 2007, 320-22]). At Banteay Chhmar the reliefs include an image of Chinese people meeting the Angkorian king (Ea 2005, 275-76).

Evidence for Chinese Goods

Chinese imports, as listed in Table 7.2, have mostly perished, such as silk and 'satinet' fabrics, skin-covered drums, and paper parasols (see Lin 1995, 175). Objects of precious metal (e.g., gold and silver statuary, ritual objects, and royal trappings) that may have survived are commonly retained in private hands, and archaeologists recover only durable materials such as glass or ceramics. This deficiency can partly be remediated by a study of images.

Horses. War-chariots figure prominently in India's *Mahābhārata* epic and are depicted in many images at Angkor Wat, both pulling chariots and as mounts (Figure 7.2). Actual horses were also highly valued in Cambodia. For example, the 10th/11th-century Prasat Ta Kam inscription (K. 245, 21.3) mentions the gift of a horse as dowry for the grand-daughter of an official and the payment of an elephant and a horse to a *guru* for consecrating images. An elite game of polo is shown in the Royal Palace complex, carved onto the Elephant Terrace (northern section, 13th century). All the horses shown at these and other sites are steppe or mountain ponies of Yunnan type, which would have been brought down the Red River via long-established trade routes (Hirth and Rockhill 1966[1911], 53; Zhou 2007[1297], 69). During the Northern Song Period, when there seems to have been an interest in cavalry, Chinese horses are known to have been purchased through Cham intermediaries from Annam (Cooke et al. 2011, 14, 98–99; Chin 2009, 213–16) or from Hainan, in the late 12th century when the Song refused to supply any more horses to the south into Champa, where Khmers got their horses (Ptak 2009, 221–22). However, even cavalry horses are depicted as steppe ponies (e.g., on the Bayon relief 70b [Roveda 2007, 312]).

Gongs. Angkorian musical traditions incorporated gongs into military ensembles (hanging flat gongs) and royal *pinpeat* orchestras, which might also have come from China, where they had been used for centuries, perhaps as early as 150 BCE (Blench 2006, 240). Angkor Wat's walls contain as many as 23 military ensembles (Knust 2010, 44); one of the clearest is the battle of Kurukshetra in the temple's western gallery. Military bands are also represented on the Bayon (Knust 2013, 131, fig. 5) and at Banteay Chhmar (Jacq-Hergoualc'h 2007, 142-43). Figure 7.3 illustrates musicians in a military procession, following an elephant and followed in turn by standard bearers.

A painted 16th-century *pinpeat* orchestra with a hanging gong was identified recently at Angkor Wat (Tan et al. 2014, 557-61). Whether gongs at Angkor were manufactured in China remains a question, but the recovery of a cargo of Chinese-origin gongs and Song-Period ceramics from the Tanjung Simpang wreck (off the north Borneo coast) suggests China as a possible source area (Nicolas 2009, 64, 66; see Figure 7.1).

Textiles. Silk was China's best-known product. The range of textiles from lightweight gauze to heavy damask was well established by the 10th century, and by the Song Period, the silk industry was highly organised, with production taking place within households and also in official workshops. Silk is often described and shown on Chinese images, and some has been preserved within pagodas or buried in wealthy tombs: a 13th-century tomb at Fuzhou (Fujian) contained

Figure 7.2 Cavalry officer leading Cham men into battle. He is wearing a Chinese-type jacket but has neither stirrups nor a saddle. Behind them is the commander's war elephant. Bayon Temple.

Source: (Photo A. Cremin).

Figure 7.3 Musicians in a military procession. From left to right, a man plays a small percussion instrument; behind him are a drummer and men carrying a large gong, played by a much smaller man in the foreground. Behind him is another drummer. A trumpeter can be seen behind the gong-bearers. Beneath the procession is another one of civilians with elaborate headdresses, wearing jackets and long skirts and holding possibly temple scarves. Bayon, inner gallery.

Source: (Photo A. Cremin).

200 garments and 150 pieces of silk cloth, 'some in the form of bolts' (Vainker 2004, 130). The 'satin' that Zhao Rugua records as particularly desired in Cambodia developed in the Tang Period and is a sumptuous fabric, in which 'the wefts cross several warps or vice versa in one stretch, so that they 'float' and give a smooth lustrous appearance' (Vainker 2004, 85). No Angkor-Period silk survives today, but the Chinese records show that silks of various qualities were sent to Angkor as royal gifts (see Green 2023, this volume). Green (this volume) also describes textiles that were carved into ritual images; draping them in actual fabric has continued to the present day. (Figure 7.4).

Glass Beads. The chemical analysis of glass beads from Angkor sheds some light on trade relationships between Angkor and China (Carter et al. 2017). Survey and excavations by the École française d'Extrême Orient (EFEO) in Hariharālaya produced glass beads from multiple 9th-century localities; coiled beads from this site contained high concentrations of lead, a technological tradition begun in China's Warring States Period (c. 400 BCE). Excavations in areas of 12th-century Angkor Thom also produced glass beads with high lead concentrations and suggest that Angkorian Khmers valued Chinese beads, along with finished gold and silver products, as part of their political and cultural exchanges through time.

Precious Metal Objects. Few of the gold and silver objects (from tableware to jewellery) that were frequent Chinese emissarial gifts to Pre-Angkorian and Angkorian elites have been recovered from archaeological contexts. Frequent epigraphic references to silver—which is not readily available within Southeast Asia—suggests that Angkor had a longer and more fruitful relationship with China than the historical records indicate. Pottier (1997a, 196-200) discusses the possible importation of Chinese silver along with lead. These metals could easily have been purchased with gemstones such as rubies (from Pailin) or sapphires (from Pailin, Attapeu, or Kanchanaburi) that are mentioned frequently in Khmer inscriptions and have been recovered from foundation deposits of major temples at Angkor (Pottier 1997b, 400–01).

High-Fired Ceramics. Chinese porcelains and stoneware arrived in Southeast Asia through both tributary and private commercial distribution routes. Ninth- and 10th-century celadons of Yue type from the Zhejiang kilns (Figure 7.1), and also from Changsha (Hunan), have been excavated from Angkor's comprise royal site of Prei Monti at Hariharālaya. They comprise 45% of the total vessels and were recovered with sherds of Middle Eastern origin (Pottier et al. 2012, 298). Tenth-century finds from various Royal Palace excavations at Angkor Thom represent high-quality ceramics from imperial kilns, which both Bernard Philippe Groslier (1981) and Roxanna Brown (2004, 22) describe as diplomatic gifts, sent from China through formal embassies.

As private commerce increased, the southern Chinese kilns in Fujian and Guangdong provinces mass-produced 'tradewares' for export, responding to local tastes. Jacques Gaucher's excavations at Angkor Thom since the early 2000s have expanded findings from Groslier's earlier work and suggest two phases of importation (Dupoizat 2018, 130-33). Most 10th- to early 13th-century Chinese imports were small circular boxes for personal luxuries (like cosmetics and betel) or mass-produced objects from non-state kilns, traded through private commercial expeditions. Thereafter we see an increase in tablewares, especially bowls, up until the mid-15th century, which probably indicates the greater availability through time of products from the Fujian kilns. In Zhou Daguan's time at Angkor, even ordinary people sometimes used Chinese ceramics for serving rice (Zhou 2007[1297], 76).

Chinese Technologies

Several technological traditions at Angkor, such as high-fired ceramics and mercury gilding of ritual objects, clearly reflect Chinese origins.

Figure 7.4 Recent examples of draped images in Angkor Wat.

Source: (Photo M.-L. A. R. Sioco).

High-Fired Stoneware Technical Developments. Angkorian Khmers selectively adopted ceramic production technologies from East and South Asia to meet the needs of strictly local consumers and likely adopted stoneware ceramic technology no later than the 9th century (e.g., Desbat 2011). Most early Khmer stoneware vessels were covered boxes, modelled after Jingdezhen white-glazed ceramics, but Khmers used the wheel instead of the Chinese potters' mould technology (Thamapreechakorn 2010, 191). Khmer surface kilns also contrasted with the Chinese subterranean kilns that became 12th-century 'dragon kilns', although both traditions share some structural features, like multiple fireholes and fireboxes (Hein 2008, 31). Given the archaic qualities of the Angkorian kiln design, Hein (2008) argues that Khmers adopted their technology from Chinese models introduced into 9th-century northern or central Vietnam rather than directly from China.

Angkorian ceramic roof tile construction technologies reflect both South Asian and Chinese influence and covered Pre-Angkorian temples and, possibly, shrines (Manguin 2006, 276-81; 290; Wong et al. 2021). Zhou Daguan's *Record* indicates that in the 13th century, only elite royal and religious structures had ceramic roof tiles rather than the thatch that commoners employed (Zhou 2007[1297], 49–50). Roof tile manufacture expanded in variety and form through time, and roof tile kilns have been found on Phnom Kulen and in the Angkorian plain (Chhay et al. 2009). Khmer and Chinese artisans used slightly different manufacturing and firing techniques. Khmer roofing methods also contrasted with Chinese methods: Khmers used an interlocking design, while the Chinese employed an 'over-and-under' method (Wong et al. 2021, 149–150).

Mercury Gilding. An unusual but telling indication of Chinese technology transfer is the presence of mercury gilding on several large bronze Angkorian statues, most notably the huge West Mebon Viṣṇu (Gerscheimer and Vincent 2010, 118–19). Mercury gilding had been seen in Cambodia by at least the 7th century: in a cache of seven bronze Buddha figurines found buried in a field in Kampong Cham, two are Chinese and mercury gilded; three are Dvaravati in style; and the remaining two are obviously of Khmer manufacture but made of brass, probably recycled from an Indian import (Jett 2010). This well-known but dangerous method was applied only to items of exceptional value to the Angkorian elite and required specialist artisans, conversant with Chinese methods. Mercury itself would have come from China, in the distinctive ceramic 'mercury bottles', of which a few have been found in excavations at Angkor (Wong 2009, 249–50, 270).

These examples illustrate that China–Cambodia interaction took more forms than simply trade and diplomacy. The two populations lived sided by side and began interweaving through marriage and other information exchange. The growing complexity of these interactions blurs lines of directionality and suggests mutual influence, a point we discuss in the next section.

Discussion and Conclusions

The Angkorian World and its predecessors were never hermit kingdoms. International commerce and political interaction (whether diplomatic or hostile) were intrinsic to the successive polities that rose and fell in prominence. Angkor was built on a deep foundation of intraregional linkages within Southeast Asia and an increasingly complex web of international relationships. The 9th-century establishment of Angkor, then, was neither the start of a completely new state nor of completely new international relationships. Why did China seek this relationship in the first millennium CE and maintain it through the peaks and valleys of its premodern history? It has been suggested that China needed to view these polities as its tributary states, regardless of their behaviour, in order to fulfil China's imperial ideology of 'All under Heaven' (Wade 2008, 581).

The Chinese also fostered relations with Southeast Asians to acquire Southeast Asian goods and to ensure open shipping routes to points further west (Wolters 1963, 543). But why did Cambodia and its neighbouring polities sustain relationships with China? Foreign goods were intrinsic to the construction of patron-client ties that knit together Cambodian rulers and members of their entourages, and the desire for such elite goods seems a constant through time. The intensity of contact varied through time in response to political shifts in both regions that rerouted trade itineraries: sometimes cutting Cambodia out of the networks (for a late 8th-century example, see Rong 2015, 257-58). Eleventh-century Angkorian court elites and middle and merchant Southern Song classes flaunted goods—and scents—from the others' regions that created a kind of legitimacy and 'high culture' that signalled cosmopolitanism. Yet the relation between China and Cambodia was never balanced, and each viewed the other rather differently.

China viewed its southern neighbours like Angkor as protectorates, not peers (Wang 1958, 118). Chinese tributary exchanges gifted goods of higher value to Southeast Asians than they received in return (Gunn 2011, 104). Yet most Chinese-made goods, excepting occasional court gifts, were export-quality goods, not of imperial grade, and produced for a 'middle rank' market (Dupoizat 1999; Heng 2018, 171-74). Angkor, in turn, likely viewed China as a convenient ally. By the 5th century, some Southeast Asian polities submitted voluntarily to vassal status for the goods this relationship offered (Gang 1997, 256). In consequence, many of China's ports were located along its southern border, within independent non-Sinitic polities that were previously known as Yue (not Han), and shared much in common with their Southeast Asian neighbours (Chittick 2015, 140-41).

Buddhism flowed eastward into both regions from South Asia; Cambodian monks helped translate Buddhist texts into Chinese, and 'Funan music' was known to the Chinese for several centuries before it was played in the courts of the early Tang emperors (Wang 1958, 41, footnote 44). Zhou Daguan notes the Khmer usage of a Chinese 12-year calendar, with similar animal symbols, in 1296 CE (Zhou 2007[1297], 63). Craft products like lacquerware required sap from deciduous *Gluta laccifer* trees from mainland Southeast Asia's dry lowland dipterocarp forests but were incorporated into both cultures. By way of the Cham, Khmers may have adopted Chinese military technologies like crossbows and *ballista* catapults, visible in bas-reliefs on the walls of the Bayon and Banteay Chhmar (Jacq-Hergoualc'h 2007, 27-35). The longboat racing that Jayavarman VII promoted may reflect Angkor-Vietnamese diplomacy during the 11th and 12th centuries, when Khmers made 17 missions to Hanoi in the late fall and winter to engage in naval review exercises (Chittick 2015, 151). Whether its origins lay in the Yangtze region (as crossing competitions or *jingdu* exercises, Chittick 2015, 142-46), or in the much older Dong Son tradition, as contemporary Chinese visitors mused (Chittick 2015, 153, footnote 28), remains an unanswered question.

Ideas flowed back and forth between the regions. Khmer artisans made stonewares and earthenwares for a local consumer market and their stoneware ceramics reflect a range of influences—but most are Chinese. The 10th-century *Intan* shipwreck included Chinese porcelain covered boxes with incense residue (Twitchett and Stargardt 2002, 34). A contemporary Khmer elite preference for similar practices with aromatics and cosmetics could explain the high frequency of Chinese covered boxes at Angkor Thom in pre-12th-century deposits (Dupoizat 2018, 132) and the early Khmer stoneware manufacturing focused on covered boxes (e.g., Groslier 1995, 25-26). The 'hybrid South China Sea tradition' of boat-craft that emerged by the 13th century reflected both Southeast Asian and Chinese technologies (Manguin 1993, 270-74). Angkorian Khmers preferred Chinese satin with dragon motifs (Heng 2018, 173) over other Chinese imports. Was this a lateral shift in a culture that previously valued *naga* serpents? Each culture influenced the other, although Southeast Asians did not embrace Chinese notions of social organisation or of statecraft. Wang Gungwu (1958, 113-17) believed that the structure of commodity movement explained this lack of Chinese cultural colonisation of Southeast

Asians. The Chinese sought Southeast Asian goods but did not control the trading networks. Until the Tang dynasty, Southeast Asians likely managed maritime trade between the regions (Sen 2017, 538). South Asians, Persians, and Muslims joined the network by the 8th century (Rong 2015, 251), and Chinese control of this trade system did not develop until the Song Period.

China's relationship with premodern Cambodia thus had exceptionally deep roots and reflects variations on a patron-client theme that buffered political collapse and regeneration by both partners for more than a millennium. Pre-Angkorian Khmers saw advantages to having a powerful northern ally against neighbours like the Cham (Pelliot 1903a, 260-61), and Angkorian Khmer elites benefited from Song court patronage through imperial gifts. Ming emperors during the Hongwu Reign (1368-1398) seem to have favoured Cambodia despite its now-waning political prominence. Not only did Ming rulers admonish Champa for abuses toward Cambodia on 14 May 1388, 15 December 1390, and again on 1 April 1414 (Wade 2005), but the Chinese records further suggest that the state prohibited foreign traders except those from Ryukyu, Cambodia, and Siam (Wade 2004, 6).

Determining whether Angkorian Cambodia was politically dependent on China or practised tightrope diplomacy is indeed a challenge. The precise roles that Chinese people, whether merchants or military or rulers, played in Angkor's history remain somewhat opaque. Yet they helped shape the Angkorian World.

References

Allard, F., 2016. Globalization at the crossroads: the case of Southeast China during the pre- and Early Imperial Period. In *The Routledge Handbook of Archaeology and Globalization*, ed. T. Hodos. New York & London: Routledge, 454–69.

Bellina, B., 2014. Maritime Silk Roads' ornament industries: socio-political practices and cultural transfers in the South China Sea. *Cambridge Archaeological Journal* 24(3), 345–77.

Bielenstein, H., 2005. *Diplomacy and Trade in the Chinese World 589–1276*. Leiden: Brill.

Blench, R., 2006. Musical instruments of South Asian origin depicted on the reliefs at Angkor, Cambodia, in *From Homo Erectus to the Living Traditions: Papers from the 11th International Conference of the European Association of Southeast Asian Archaeologists*, eds. J.-P. Pautreau, A.-S. Coupey, V. Zeitoun & E. Rambault. Bangkok: Siam Ratana Ltd, 239–44.

Brindley, E.F., 2015. *Ancient China and the Yue Perceptions and Identities on the Southern Frontier, c. 400 BCE–50 CE*. Cambridge: Cambridge University Press.

Brown, R., 2004. *The Ming gap and shipwreck: Ceramics in Southeast Asia*. PhD dissertation. Los Angeles: University of California at Los Angeles.

Cameron, J., Agustijanto Indrajaya & P.-Y. Manguin, 2015. Asbestos textiles from Batujaya (West Java, Indonesia): further evidence for early long-distance interaction between the Roman Orient, Southern Asia and Island Southeast Asia. *Bulletin de l'École française d'Extrême Orient* 101, 159–76.

Carter, A.K, L. Dussubieux, M. Polkinghorne & C. Pottier, 2017. Glass artifacts at Angkor: evidence for exchange. *Archaeological & Anthropological Sciences* 11(3), 1013–27.

Carter, A.K. & N.C. Kim, 2017. Globalization at the dawn of history: the emergence of global cultures in the Mekong and Red River deltas, in *The Routledge Handbook of Archaeology and Globalization*, ed. T. Hodos. London: Routledge, 730–50.

Castillo, C., B. Bellina & D.Q. Fuller, 2016. Rice, beans and trade crops on the early maritime silk route in Southeast Asia. *Antiquity*, 90(353), 1255–69.

Chang, Pin-tsun, 2019. The rise of Chinese mercantile power in Maritime Southeast Asia c, 1400-1700, in *China and Southeast Asia: Historical Interactions*, eds. G. Wade & J.K. Chin. London & New York: Routledge Taylor & Francis Group, 221–40.

Chhay, V., R. Chhay, K. San, H.L. Sok & Y. Tabata, 2009. Preliminary results of the Anlong Thom kiln excavation on Phnom Kulen in Angkor: a case study of ALK01, in *Scientific Research on Historic Asian Ceramics: Proceedings of the Fourth Forbes Symposium at the Freer Gallery of Art*, eds. B. McCarthy, E. Salzman Chase, L. Allison Cort, J.G. Douglas & P. Jett. Washington, DC: Archetype Publications, 215–24.

Chhem, R., K. Chhom, P. Phlong, D. Evans & P. Sharrock, 2023. Education and medicine in Angkor, in *The Angkorian World*, eds. M. Hendrickson, M.T. Stark. & D. Evans. New York: Routledge.
Chin, J., 2009. Negotiation and bartering on the frontier: horse trade in Song China, in *Pferde in Asien: Geschichte, Handel und Kultur. Horses in Asia: History, Trade and Culture*, eds. B. G. Fragner, R. Kauz, R. Ptak & A. Schottenhammer. Vienna: Verlag der Österreichischen Akademie der Wissenschaften, 203–18.
Chittick, A., 2015. Dragon boats and serpent prows: naval warfare and the political culture of China's southern borderlands, in *Imperial China and its Southern Neighbours*, eds. V.H. Mair & L. Kelley. Singapore: ISEAS-Yusof Ishak Institute, 140–60.
Chiu, L.-Y., 1973. Persians, Arabs and other nationals in T'ang China: their status, activities and contributions. *Journal of the Hong Kong Branch of the Royal Asiatic Society* 13, 58–72.
Christie, J.W., 1995. State formation in early Maritime Southeast Asia: a consideration of the theories and the data. *Bijdragen tot de Taal-, Land- en Volkenkunde* 151(2), 235–88.
Christie, J.W., 1998. Javanese markets and the Asian sea trade boom of the tenth to thirteenth centuries A.D. *Journal of the Economic and Social History of the Orient* 41(3), 344–81.
Cœdès, G., 1954. *Inscriptions du Cambodge, Tome VI.* Paris: École française d'Extrême-Orient.
Cœdès, G., 1968. *The Indianized States of Southeast Asia.* Translated by Susan Brown Cowing. ed. W.F. Vella. Honolulu: University of Hawai'i Press.
Cooke, N., T. Li & J.A. Anderson (eds), 2011. *The Tongking Gulf through History*. Philadelphia: University of Pennsylvania Press.
Desbat, A., 2011. Pour une révision de la chronologie des grès khmers. *Aséanie*, 27, 11–34.
Dupoizat, M.-F., 1999. La céramique importée à Angkor: étude préliminaire. *Arts Asiatiques* 54, 103–16.
Dupoizat, M.-F., 2018. La céramique importée à Angkor Thom. *Péninsule* 76, 129–86.
Ea, D., 2005. The relationship between China and Cambodia: evidence from manuscripts, ceramics and bas-reliefs, in *Proceedings: Chinese Export Ceramics and Maritime Trade, 12th–15th Centuries*, eds. Pei-Kai, Cheng, Li, Guo & Wan, Chui Ki. Hong Kong: Chinese Civilisation Centre, City University of Hong Kong & City University of Hong Kong Interdisciplinary Research Project, 267–79.
Estève, J., 2023. Gods and temples: the nature(s) of Angkorian religion, in *The Angkorian World*, eds. M. Hendrickson, M.T. Stark & D. Evans. New York: Routledge, 423–34.
Ferrand, G., 1913. *Relations de voyages et textes relatifs à L'Extrême Orient*. Paris. http://archive.org/details/relationsdevoyage (accessed 30 March 2020).
Gang, D., 1997. The foreign staple trade of China in the pre-modern era. *The International History Review* 19(2), 253–85.
Gerscheimer, G. & B. Vincent, 2010. L'épée inscrite de Boston (K. 1048; 1040–41 de notre ère). *Arts asiatiques* 65, 109–20.
Glaize, M., 1993[1944]. *Les monuments du groupe d'Angkor*. Paris: J. Maisonneuve.
Goble, G., 2014. *Maritime Southeast Asia: The View from Tang-Song China. Working Paper Series No. 16.* Singapore: ISEAS/Nalanda-Sriwijaya Centre.
Goh, G.Y., 2009. The question of 'China' in Burmese chronicles. *Journal of Southeast Asian Studies* 41(1), 125–52.
Green, G., 2023. Vogue at Angkor: dress, decor and drama, in *The Angkorian World*, eds. M. Hendrickson, M.T. Stark & D. Evans. New York: Routledge.
Groslier, B.-P., 1973. Pour une géographie historique du Cambodge. *Les Cahiers d'Outre-Mer* 104(26), 337–79.
Groslier, B.-P., 1981. La céramique chinoise en Asie du Sud-Est: quelques points de méthode. *Archipel* 21, 93–121.
Groslier, B.-P., 1995. Introduction à la céramique Angkorienne (fin IXe-XVe s.). *Péninsule* 31(2), 5–60.
Gunn, G., 2011. *History Without Borders: The Making of an Asian World Region* (1000–1800). Hong Kong: Hong Kong University Press.
Hall, K.R., 1975. Khmer commercial development and foreign contacts under Sūryavarman I. *Journal of the Economic and Social History of the Orient* 18(3), 318–36.
Hall, K.R., 2023. Angkor's multiple Southeast Asia overland connections, in *The Angkorian World*, eds. M. Hendrickson, M.T. Stark & D. Evans. New York: Routledge, 97–111.
Hein, D., 2008. Ceramic kiln lineages in Mainland Southeast Asia. *Ceramics in Mainland Southeast Asia: Collections in the Freer Gallery of Art and Arthur M. Sackler Gallery*. http://SEAsianCeramics.asia.si.edu (accessed 9 November 2019).
Hendrickson, M., D. Ea, R. Chhay, Y. Tabata, K. Phon, S. Leroy, Y. Sato & A. Desbat, 2023. Crafting with fire: stoneware and iron pyrotechnologies in the Angkorian World, in *The Angkorian World*, eds. M. Hendrickson, M.T. Stark & D. Evans. New York: Routledge, 385–400.

Heng, D., 2008a. Shipping custom procedures and the foreign community: the 'Pingzhou Ketan' on aspects of Guangzhou's maritime economy in the late eleventh century. *Journal of Song-Yuan Studies* 38, 2–38.

Heng, D., 2008b. Structures, networks and commercial practices of private Chinese maritime traders in Island Southeast Asia in the early second millennium AD. *International Journal of Maritime History* 20(2), 27–54.

Heng, D., 2009. *Sino-Malay trade and diplomacy from the tenth through the fourteenth century. Southeast Asia Series No. 121*. Athens, OH: Ohio University.

Heng, D., 2018. Distributive networks, sub-regional tastes and ethnicity: the trade in Chinese textiles, in *Southeast Asia from the Tenth to Fourteenth Centuries CE. Textile Trades, Consumer Cultures and the Material World of the Indian Ocean. An Ocean of Cloth*, eds. P. Machado, S. Fee & G. Campbell. New York: Palgrave Macmillan, 159–80.

Heng, D., 2019. Southeast Asia-China economic interactions in the late first to mid-second millennium C.E: narrative, sources, and pedagogical objectives. *Journal of Medieval Worlds* 1(2), 83–92.

Hirth, F. & W. W. Rockhill, 1966[1911]. *Chau Ju-Kua: His Work on the Chinese and Arab Trade in the Twelfth and Thirteenth Centuries, Entitled, Chu-fan-chi*. New York, NY: Paragon Book Reprint Corp.

Hucker, C.O., 1975. *China's Imperial Past: An Introduction to Chinese History and Culture*. London: Duckworth.

Ishizawa, Y., 1995. Chinese chronicles of 1st–5th century AD Funan, southern Cambodia, in *Colloquies on Art and Archaeology in Asia, vol. 17: South East Asia and China: Art, Interaction and Commerce*, eds. R. Scott & J. Guy. London: Percival David Foundation of Chinese Art, 11–31.

Jacob, J., 1993. The ecology of Angkor: evidence from the Khmer inscriptions, in *Cambodian Linguistics, Literature and History*, ed. C.A. Smyth. London: School of Oriental & African Studies, University of London, 280–98.

Jacq-Hergoualc'h, M., 2007. *The Armies of Angkor: Military Structure and Weaponry of the Khmers*. Translated by M. Smithies. Bangkok: Orchid Press.

Jett, P., 2010. Buddhist bronzes in Cambodia: a newly discovered cache. *Orientations* 41(5), 48–52.

Kimura, J.M., Staniforth, T.L. Le & R. Sasaki, 2013. Naval battlefield archaeology of the lost Kublai Khan fleets. *The International Journal of Nautical Archaeology* 43(1), 76–86.

Knust, M., 2010. Urged to interdisciplinary approaches: the iconography of music on the reliefs of Angkor Wat. *Music in Art* 35(1/2), 37–52.

Knust, M., 2013. Towards a social history of music in ancient Angkor: the iconography of music on the Bayon temple carvings. *Music in Art*, 38(1/2), 127–43.

Legge, J., 1886. A record of Buddhistic kingdoms being an account by the Chinese monk of his travels in India and Ceylon (A.D. 399–414), in *Search of the Buddhist Books of Discipline. Translated & Annotated with a Corean Recension of the Chinese Text*, ed. J. Legge. Oxford: Clarendon Press.

Li, T., 2011. Jiaozhi (Giao Chi) in the Han period Tongking Gulf, in *The Tongking Gulf through History*, eds. N. Cooke, Tana Li & J.A. Anderson. Philadelphia, PA: University of Pennsylvania Press, 39–52.

Lin, L.C., 1995. Textiles in Sino-Southeast Asian trade: Song, Yuan and Ming dynasties, in *Colloquies on Art and Archaeology in Asia, vol. 17: South East Asia and China: Art, Interaction and Commerce*, eds. R. Scott & J. Guy. London: Percival David Foundation of Chinese Art, 171–86.

Lustig, E., 2009. Money doesn't make the World go round: Angkor's non-monetisation, in *Research in Economic Anthropology*, ed. D. Wood. Bingley: Emerald Group Publishing Ltd, 165–99.

Manguin, P.-Y., 1993. Trading ships of the South China sea: shipbuilding techniques and their role in the development of Asian trade networks. *Journal of the Economic & Social History of the Orient* 36(3), 253–80.

Manguin, P.-Y., 2006. Les tuiles de l'ancienne Asie du Sud-Est: essai de typologie, in *Anamorphoses: Hommage à Jacques Dumarçay*, eds. H. Chambert-Loir & B. Dagens. Paris: Les Indes Savantes, 275–309.

Miksic, J.N. & G.Y. Goh, 2017. *Ancient Southeast Asia*. London: Routledge.

Milburn, O., 2016. Aromas, scents, and spices: olfactory culture in China before the arrival of Buddhism. *Journal of the American Oriental Society* 136(3), 441–64.

Nicolas, A., 2009. Gongs, bells, and cymbals: the archaeological record in Maritime Asia from the ninth to the seventeenth centuries, *2009 Yearbook for Traditional Music* 41, 62–93.

O'Reilly, D. & L. Shewan, 2016. Phum Lovea: a moated precursor to the pura of Cambodia? Sociopolitical transformation from Iron Age settlements to early state society. *Journal of Southeast Asian Studies* 47(3), 468–83.

Pelliot, P., 1902. Mémoire sur les coutumes du Cambodge. *Bulletin de l'École française d'Extrême-Orient* 2, 123–77.

Pelliot, P., 1903a. Le Fou-nan. *Bulletin de l'École française d'Extrême-Orient* 3, 248–303.

Pelliot, P., 1903b. La dernière ambassade du Fou-nan en Chine sous les Leang (539). *Bulletin de l'École française d'Extrême-Orient* 3, 671–72.

Pelliot, P., 1925. Quelques textes chinois concernant l'Indochine hindouisée. *Études Asiatiques publiées à l'occasion du 25ème anniversaire de l'ÉFEO* 2, 243–63.

Péronnet, S., 2013. Overview of Han artefacts in Southeast Asia with special reference to the recently excavated material from Khao Sam Kaeo in southern Thailand, in *Unearthing Southeast Asia's Past: Selected Papers from the 12th International Conference of the European Association of Southeast Asian Archaeologists*, eds. M.J. Klokke & V. Degroot. Singapore: NUS Press, 155–69.

Pottier, C., 1997a. Nouvelles données sur les couvertures en plomb à Angkor. *Bulletin de l'École française d'Extrême-Orient* 84, 183–220.

Pottier, C., 1997b. La restauration du perron nord de la Terrasse des Éléphants à Angkor Thom. Rapport sur la première année de travaux (avril 1996 —avril 1997). *Bulletin de l'École française d'Extrême-Orient* 84, 376–401.

Pottier, C., A. Desbat, M.-F. Dupoizat & A. Bolle, 2012. Le matériel céramique à Prei Monti (Angkor), in *Orientalismes: De l'archéologie au musée. Mélanges offerts à Jean-François Jarrige*, ed. V. Lefèvre. Turnhout: Brepols, 291–317.

Ptak, R., 1998. From Quanzhou to the Sulu Zone and beyond: questions related to the early fourteenth century. *Journal of Southeast Asian Studies* 29(2), 269–94.

Ptak, R., 2006. The Sino-European map (Shanhai yudi quantu) in the Encyclopaedia Sancai tuhui, in *The Perception of Maritime Space in Traditional Chinese Sources*, Vol, 2, eds. A. Schottenhammer & R. Ptak. Wiesbaden: Harrassowitz, 191–207.

Ptak, R., 2009. Hainan and the trade in horses (Song to early Ming), in *Pferde in Asien: Geschichte, Handel und Kultur. Horses in Asia: History, Trade and Culture*, eds. B.G. Fragner, R. Kauz, R. Ptak & A. Schottenhammer. Vienna: Verlag der Österreichischen Akademie der Wissenschaften, 219–25.

Ptak, R., 2019. Hainan and its international trade: ports, merchants, commodities (Song to mid-Ming), in *China and Southeast Asia: Historical Interactions*, eds. G. Wade & J.K. Chinn. London & New York: Routledge Taylor & Francis Group, 21–43.

Ray, H.P., 1994. *The Winds of Change: Buddhism and the Maritime Links of Early South Asia*. New Delhi: Oxford University Press.

Rong, X., 2015. New evidence on the history of Sino-Arabic relations: a study of Yang Liangyao's embassy to the Abbasid Caliphate, in *Imperial China and its Southern Neighbors*, eds. V.H. Mair & L. Kelley, translated by R. Fu & G. Wan. Singapore: Institute of Southeast Asian Studies, 239–67.

Roveda, V., 2007. Reliefs of the Bayon, in *Bayon: New Perspectives*, ed. J. Clark, Bangkok: River Books, 282–361.

Roveda, V., 2012. Buddhist iconography in Brahmanical temples of Angkor, in *Materializing Southeast Asia's Past: Selected Papers from the 12th International Conference of the European Association of Southeast Asian Archaeologists*, eds. M.J. Klokke & V. Degroot. Singapore: NUS Press, 56–81.

Schottenhammer, A., 1999. Local politico-economic particulars of the Quanzhou region during the tenth century. *Journal of Song-Yuan Studies* 29, 1–41.

Schottenhammer, A., 2017. China's rise and retreat as a maritime power, in *Beyond the Silk Roads: New Discourses on China's Role in East Asian Maritime History*, eds. R.J. Antony & A. Schottenhammer. East Asian Maritime History 14. Wiesbaden: Otto Harrassowitz, 189–211.

Sen, T., 2014. Maritime Southeast Asia between South Asia and China to the sixteenth century. *TRaNS: Trans-Regional and -National Studies of Southeast Asia* 2(1), 1–59.

Sen, T., 2017. Early China and the Indian Ocean networks. *The Sea in History: The Ancient World*, eds. P. de Souza, P.L. Arnaud & C. Buchet. Woodbridge: Boydell & Brewer, 536–47.

So, K.-L., 1998. Dissolving hegemony or changing trade pattern? Images of Srivijaya in the Chinese sources of the twelfth and thirteenth centuries. *Journal of Southeast Asian Studies* 29, 295–308.

Soutif, D. & J. Estève, 2023. Texts and objects: exploiting the literary sources in mediaeval Cambodia, in *The Angkorian World*, eds. M. Hendrickson, M.T. Stark & D. Evans. New York: Routledge.

Stanley-Baker, M. & D. Yang, 2017. Dung, hair, and mung beans: household remedies in the Longmen recipes, in *Buddhism and Medicine: An Anthology of Premodern Sources*, ed. C. Pierce Salguero. New York: Columbia University Press, 454–77.

Stark, M.T. & S. Bong, 2001. Recent research on the emergence of early historic states in Cambodia's Lower Mekong. *Bulletin of the Indo-Pacific Prehistory Association* 21(5), 85–98.

Steavu, D., 2017. Apotropaic substances as medicine in Buddhist healing methods: Nāgārjuna's treatise on the Five Sciences, in *Buddhism and Medicine: An Anthology of Premodern Sources*, ed. C. Pierce Salguero. New York: Columbia University Press, 441–53.

Tan, N.H., S. Im, T. Heng & C. Khieu, 2014. The hidden paintings of Angkor Wat. *Antiquity* 8, 549–65.

Thammapreechakorn, P., 2010. The relationship between Chinese Song and Khmer Angkorean ceramics, in *Khmer Ceramics: Beauty and Meaning*, ed. D. Rooney. Bangkok: River Books, 189–209.

Tibbetts, G.R., 1979. *A Study of the Arabic Texts Containing Material on South-East Asia. Oriental Translation Fund, Royal Asiatic Society 44*. Leiden & London: E. J. Brill.

Twitchett, D. & J. Stargardt, 2002. Chinese silver bullion in a tenth-century Indonesian wreck. *Asia Major Third Series* 15(1), 23–72.

Uk, S. & B. Uk, 2016. *Customs of Cambodia by Zhou Daguan [1296–1297]*. Bangkok: DatAsia Press.

Vainker, S., 2004. *Chinese Silk: A Cultural History*. London: British Museum.

Vickery, M., 1987. Review of 'Maritime trade and state development in Early Southeast Asia', by Kenneth R. Hall. *Journal of Asian Studies* 46(1), 211–13.

Villiers, J., 2001. Great plenty of Almug trees: the trade in Southeast Asian aromatic woods in the Indian Ocean and China 500 BC-AD 1500. *The Great Circle* 23(2), 24–43.

Wade, G., 2004. *Ming China and Southeast Asia in the 15th Century: A Reappraisal. Asia Research Institute Working Paper Series No. 28*. Singapore: National University of Singapore.

Wade, G., 2005. *Southeast Asia in the Ming Shi-lu: An Open Access Resource*. Singapore: Asia Research Institute & the Singapore E-Press, National University of Singapore, http://epress.nus.edu.sg/msl/reign (accessed 9 November 2019).

Wade, G., 2008. Engaging the South: Ming China and Southeast Asia in the fifteenth century. *Journal of the Economic and Social History of the Orient* 51, 578–638.

Wade, G., 2009. An early age of commerce in Southeast Asia, 900–1300 CE. *Journal of Southeast Asian Studies* 40(2), 221–65.

Wade, G., 2013. Maritime routes between Indochina and Nusantara to the 18th century. *Archipel* 85, 2–22.

Wade, G., 2014a. Beyond the southern borders: Southeast Asia in Chinese texts to the ninth century, in *Lost Kingdoms: Hindu-Buddhist Sculpture of Early Southeast Asia*, ed. J. Guy. New Haven, CT: Metropolitan Museum of Art/Yale University Press, 25–31.

Wang, G., 1958. The Nanhai trade: a study of the early history of Chinese trade in the South China Sea. *Journal of the Malayan Branch of the Royal Asiatic Society* 31(182):1–135.

Wheatley, P., 1959. Geographical notes on some commodities involved in Sung maritime trade. *Journal of the Malayan Branch of the Royal Asiatic Society* 32(186), 5–41.

Wolters, O.W., 1960. The "Po-ssŭ" pine trees. *Bulletin of the School of Oriental and African Studies* 23(2), 23–350.

Wolters, O.W., 1963. China irredenta: the South. *The World Today* 19(12), 540–52.

Wong, W.Y., D. Ea, R. Chhay & B.S. Tan, 2021. Two traditions: a comparison of roof tile manufacture and usage in Angkor and China. *Asian Perspectives* 60(1), 128–56.

Wong, W.Y., 2009. *A Preliminary study of some economic activities of Khmer Empire: examining the relationship between the Khmer and Guangdong ceramic industries during the 9th to 14th Centuries*. PhD dissertation. Singapore: National University of Singapore.

Yang, S.-Y., 2020. A Chinese gazetteer of foreign lands: a new translation of part of the Zhufan zhi 諸蕃志 (1225). https://storymaps.arcgis.com/stories/39bce63e4e0642d3abce6c24db470760 (accessed 16 June 2020).

Yoshinobu, S., 1983. Sung foreign trade: its scope and organization, in *China Among Equals: The Middle Kingdom and its Neighbors, 10th–14th Centuries*, ed. M. Rossabi. Berkeley and Los Angeles: University of California Press, 89–115.

Zhou, D., 2007[1297]. *A Record of Cambodia: The Land and Its People*, trans. P. Harris. Chiang Mai: Silkworm Books.

PART II

Landscapes

8

FORESTS, PALMS, AND PADDY FIELDS

The Plant Ecology of Angkor

Tegan Hall and Dan Penny

Plants and their ecologies are becoming increasingly recognised for their political and social agency (see Head et al. 2014; Fleming 2017) and as a revealing lens through which cultural history might be analysed (Mercuri 2014; Kull et al. 2018). Exploring the Angkorian World as a region of shifting plant regimes is a particularly relevant approach, given the distinctly agrarian nature of its urban form (Fletcher 2012) and the ubiquity and significance of plants in the lives of the Angkorian Khmer (see Castillo 2023, this volume). The cycles of rice agriculture defined the seasons and work schedules of villagers (Jacob 1978), plants provided currency and the materials for both quotidian and ceremonial activities (Cœdès 1937–1966; Martin 1971), and the clearance of surrounding forests destabilised soils and disrupted the Angkor's hydrological system (Groslier 1979). Overall, the evidence indicates that the evolution and success of Angkor were closely tethered to its ecology.

The Vegetation of Angkor and the Northern Cambodia Plains

Biogeographical mapping suggests that, during the Holocene, the primeval landscape of the central and northern plains of Cambodia comprised extensive mixed deciduous and dry semi-evergreen forests, with flooded forests and grasslands dominating the floodplains of the Tonle Sap (Ashwell and Fitzwilliams 1993; Olson et al. 2001). Examples of these forest types can be seen in the landscape near Siem Reap today. Pockets of dry semi-evergreen forest have returned to the temple enclosures of Angkor Thom and Angkor Wat, and flooded forests persist along the margins of the Great Lake. Vast tracts of these ancient ecosystems have, however, been lost to cultivation—particularly the intensive rice production that sustained the Angkorian kingdom through its dominance of Southeast Asia. Much of this farmland remains in use today or has been left fallow to develop into shrubland and grassland.

The World Wildlife Fund, in their broad-scale classification of Cambodia's forests, places Angkor within the Central Indochina Dry Forests (CIDF) ecoregion (in Cambodia, sometimes referred to as *forêt claire*), bordered to the north and south by the Southeastern Indochina Dry Evergreen Forests (SIDEF) and the Tonle Sap Freshwater Swamp Forests (TSFSF), respectively (Figure 8.1a) (Olson et al. 2001). Characteristics of these ecoregions are outlined in Table 8.1 (from Wikramanayake et al. 2017; Wikramanayake and Rundel 2017). Ecologists working in the area, however, have noted the misleading characterisation of SIDEF as evergreen, given

DOI: 10.4324/9781351128940-11

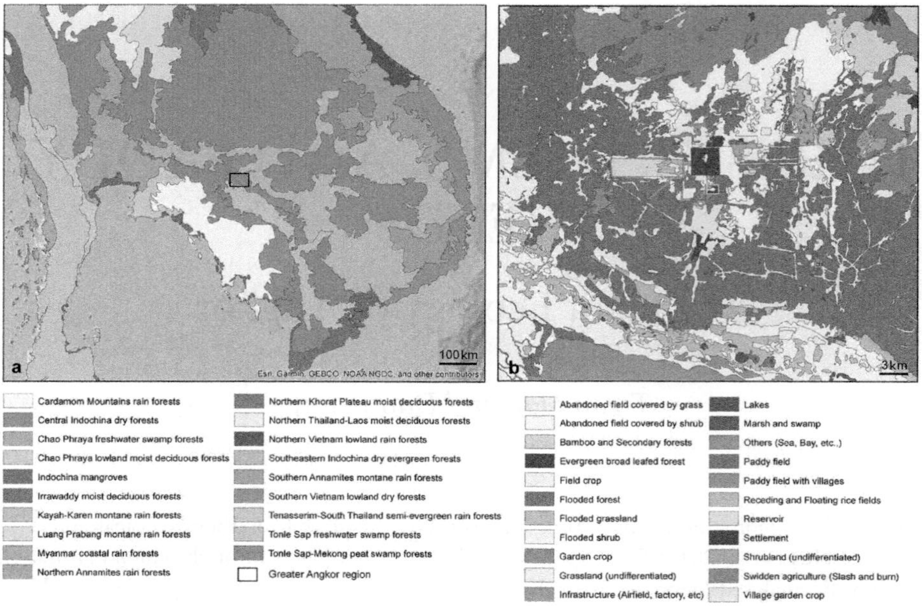

Figure 8.1 Land use maps in Southeast Asia and the Greater Angkor region: a) regional map of the Southeast Asian mainland and the distribution of the World Wildlife Fund (WWF)-recognised terrestrial ecoregions (based on Olson et al. 2001); b) distribution of land use types across the greater Angkor region, based on Japanese International Cooperation Agency.

Source: (JICA 2002).

its inclusion of both deciduous and non-deciduous species. These forests may present as evergreen, with their relatively brief leafless period and a strong presence of evergreen species in the canopy, but would be more appropriately termed semi-evergreen (Rundel 2009).

Smaller-scale vegetation units within these terrestrial ecoregions are variously classified by spatial variations in climate, topography, soil moisture availability, and fire frequency, all of which affect structural and floristic composition (Rundel 1999). In central Cambodia, interactions between these environmental variables create a mosaicked landscape of forest and woodland/grassland types distinctive in their leaf phenology (deciduous/evergreen/semi-evergreen), degree of canopy cover, and dominance of species from the fire-tolerant Dipterocarpaceae family. Ashwell's (1993) surveys document the various vegetation types prevalent today between the Tonle Sap and the northern sandstone outcrops of the Kulen hills. Across the lacustrine soils in and adjacent to the littoral zone of the Tonle Sap lake are flooded forests, shrublands, and grasslands, the distribution and composition of which are dictated by the extent of seasonal inundation. Moving north, the vegetation transitions to a mosaic of remnant forest, secondary regrowth, and farmland, which shroud the older colluvial and alluvial lowlands. Slightly higher elevations along the peneplain feature semi-deciduous and deciduous forests, and swidden agriculture dominates the uplands. Species associated with each of Ashwell's vegetation types are collated in Table 8.2. Current land use, including the distribution of remnant and secondary forest types throughout the Angkor region, mapped by the Japan International Cooperation Agency (2002), are presented in Figure 8.1b and related to Ashwell's vegetation types in Table 8.2.

Table 8.1 Details, including characteristic plant species, relevant to each of the three WWF-recognised ecoregions of the Greater Angkor region.

Ecoregion	*Climate*	*Elevation*	*Characteristic flora*
Central Indochina dry forest	1000–1800 mm rainfall per year (includes a 5–7-month dry season)	Generally < 900 m ASL1	Open forest or woodland dominated by deciduous trees: *Shorea siamensis, Shorea obtusa, Dipterocarpus obtusifolius, Dipterocarpus tuberculatus, Pterocarpus macrocarpus* (Kurz), *Sindora siamensis* (Teijsm. Ex Miq.), *Xylia xylocarpa* (Roxb.), *Terminalia alata* (F. Heyne ex Roth), *Pinus merkusii* (Jungh & de Vries)
Southeastern Indochina dry evergreen forest	1200–2000 mm rainfall per year (includes a 3–6-month dry season)	700–1000 m ASL, but can also be found in moist valleys/ ravines1,2	Evergreen and deciduous trees: *Dipterocarpus alatus* (Roxb. Ex G. Don), *Dipterocarpus costatus* (G. Don), *Dipterocarpus turbinatus, Shorea guiso* (Blume), *Shorea hypochra* (Hance), *Hopea odorata* (Roxb.), *Anisoptera costata* (Korth.), *Ficus* spp., *Tetrameles nudiflora* (R. Br.), *Heritiera javanica* (Kosterm.), bamboos, palms and lianas
Tonle Sap freshwater swamp forest	Seasonally inundated (<6 months of the year)	50–100 m ASL3	Flooded forest: *Euphorbiaceae* spp., *Fabaceae* spp., *Combretaceae* spp., *Barringtonia acutangula, Terminalia cambodiana, Diospyros cambodiana, Mimosa pigra* (invasive)

Table 8.2 Vegetation regions surveyed in Ashwell (1993) and the corresponding JICA (2002) land-use type (where possible, based on spatial and/or descriptive correlation).

Ashwell region/JICA land use type	*Plant components*
Lacustrine plain/flooded forest	Dominated by freshwater mangroves (*Barringtonia acultangula*). From Rundel (2009): Persimmon trees (*Diospyros cambodiana*) and climbing shrubs (*Breynia vitis-idaea, Combretum trifoliatum, Tetracera sarmentosa*, and *Acacia thailandica*) are also common
Lacustrine plain/flooded shrubland	Patches of flooded forest commonly include *Xanthophyllym glaucum* trees. From MacDonald et al. (1997) and Rundel (2009): Common wetland shrubs and small trees include freshwater mangroves (*Barringtonia acultangula*), spurges (*Mallotus plicatus* and other *Euphorbiaceae* species), legumes (Fabaceae), *Elaeocarpus griffithii, E. madropetalus, Hydnocarpus authelminthica*, and *Combretaceae* species
Lacustrine plain/flooded grassland	Rice (*Poaceae*) and lotus gardens (*Nelumbo nucifera*), mung bean (*Vigna radiata*), watermelons (*Citrullus lanatus*)
Ancient alluvial plains, colluvial and associated slopes: dryland rice, other crops and habitations/paddy fields	Rice (*Poaceae*), other cultivated species

(*Continued*)

Table 8.2 (Continued)

Ashwell region/JICA land use type	*Plant components*
Ancient alluvial plains, colluvial and associated slopes: lowland evergreen forests (adjacent plains south of the outcrops and on the slope) —undisturbed and moderately disturbed	Dipterocarps (*Anisoptera scaphula, Dipterocarpus alatus, Shorea thorelii, Shorea cochinchinensis, Vatica odorata*) and other deciduous trees (*Tetrameles nudiflora*), fig trees (*Ficus* spp.), *Garcinia* sp., ironwood (*Mesua ferrea*), lychee (*Nephelium litchi*), Lumbayao (*Heritiera javanica*), crepe myrtle (*Lagerstroemia angustifolia*), wild almond (*Irvingia malayana*), legumes (*Dialium cochinchinense*), rosewood trees (*Dalbergia bariensis*), palms (*Caryota mitis, Licuala* spp., *Plectocomia* sp., *Oncosperma* sp., *Calamus* spp.), tree ferns (*Cyathea* sp.), and other evergreen trees and shrubs (*Diospyros* sp., *Aglaia* sp., *Eugenia* spp., *Amomum elephantorum, Knema corticosa, Altingia gracilipes*). In general, the assemblage of this community depends on elevation and soil moisture levels
Ancient alluvial plains, colluvial and associated slopes —temple forests	Dipterocarps (*Dipterocarpus alatus*) and other deciduous trees (*Tetrameles nudiflora, Afzelia xylocarpa*), wild almond (*Irvingia malayana*), *Diospyros* spp., Thai blackwood (*Dalbergia nigrescens*), crepe myrtle (*Lagerstroemia angustifolia*), paduak tree (*Pterocarpus macrocarpus*), palms (*Caryota* sp.), and the rosewood tree (*Dalbergia bariensis*) From Andre et al. (2012): wild jackfruit (*Artocarpus rigidus*), cassia tree (*Senna siamea*), mampat (*Cratoxylum formosum*), forest ebony (*Diospyros sylvatica*), crepe myrtle (*Lagerstroemia calyculata*), and the *Peltophorum dasyrrhachis* tree
Ancient alluvial plains, colluvial and associated slopes —secondary forests between evergreen forests and paddy fields (often subject to shifting agriculture)/shifting agriculture	Dipterocarps (*Shorea, Dipterocarpus intricatus*), *Memecylon, Peltophorum, Cratoxylum, Parinarium, Diospyros*, and *Eugenia* trees and shrubs, *Calamus* and *Licuala* palms, and Clusiaceae species (varying degrees of openness/shrubland)
Northeastern peneplain —semi-deciduous forests (extending to Prey Sa-ak)	Crepe myrtle (*Lagerstroemia angustifolia*), dipterocarps (*Dipterocarpus alatus, Vatica odorata*), other deciduous trees (*Tetrameles nudiflora, Afzelia xylocarpa, Sterculia foetida*), fig trees (*Ficus* spp.), wild almond (*Irvingia malayana*), mampat (*Cratoxylum formosum*), kapok tree (*Ceiba pentandra*), legumes (*Dalbergia nigrescens*), palms (*Calamus* spp.), climbing shrubs (*Entada phaseoloides*), the large tree *Terminalia nigrovenulosa* and the evergreen *Amomum elephantorum*
Northeastern peneplain —deciduous forests	Dominated by dipterocarps (*Dipterocarpus intricatus, Dipterocarpus obtusifolius, Dipterocarpus tuberculatus, Shorea obtusa, Shorea siamensis*) and other deciduous trees (*Xylia xylocarpa, Terminalia tomentosa*), but bamboo (*Arundinaria* spp.) and cycads (*Cycas siamensis*) also feature

Ashwell region/JICA land use type	*Plant components*
Mountainous uplands —undisturbed forests	Dipterocarps (*Dipterocarpus costatus, Dipterocarpus alatus, Anisoptera scaphula, Shorea vulgaris, Shorea cochinchinensis, Shorea thorellii*) and other deciduous trees (*Tetrameles nudiflora, Afzelia xylocarpa*), *Heritiera javanica*, wild almond (*Irvingia malayana*), fig trees (*Ficus* spp.), ironwood (*Mesua ferrea*), *Garcinia* spp., and evergreen trees and shrubs (*Aglaia* sp. *Cinnamomum* spp., *Aquilaria crassna*), lychee (*Litchi chinensis*), legumes (*Dalbergia nigescens, Sindora cochinchinensis*), velvet tamarind (*Dialium cochinchinense*), *Diospyros* spp., *Eugenia* spp., tembusu (*Fagraea fragrans*), padauk tree (*Pterocarpus macrocarpus*), crepe myrtle (*Lagerstoemia angustifolia*), kapok tree (*Ceiba pentandra*), *Terminalia nigro-venulosa*, also a variety of ferns, lianas, and epiphytes (varies depending on elevation, topography, and soil type)
Mountainous uplands —secondary forests	Swidden forests within a mosaic of evergreen trees (*Trema, Nephelium*), spurges (*Mallotus*), yellow flame trees (*Peltophorum*), palms (*Plectocomia*), herbs (*Eupatorium*), myrtles (*Eugenia* and other *Myrtaceae* species), laurels (*Cinnamomum* and other *Lauraceae* species), oaks (*Lithocarpus* and other *Fagaceae* spp.), *Garcinia, Heritiera*, and *Anisoptera dipterocarps* (composition depends on the age of the forest stand)

The forest mosaic of the central Cambodian plains is also the product of human activity. Land clearance and burning associated with shifting and permanent agriculture have severely reduced forest extent and influenced localised patterns of structural and floristic composition (Baker et al. 2005; McShea and Davies 2011). If burning is frequent and intense, even if land is not clear-felled, semi-evergreen forests can transition to savannah or open-canopy dipterocarp woodland. Forest clearance across the Angkor plain remains prevalent today and has increased in recent decades for charcoal production, tourism purposes, resource extraction, and expanding cultivation (Gaughan et al. 2009).

It is difficult to determine when this forest clearance began across the Cambodian plains north of the Tonle Sap or to what extent vegetation had been altered before the cities of Angkor were established in the 8th and 9th centuries CE. Cultural material and human remains preserved in soils that pre-date Angkor indicate human occupation from at least the beginning of the first millennium BCE (Groslier 1998; Frelat and Souday 2015), which continues (or reappears) through the Iron Age and Pre-Angkor Periods (Groslier 1979, 1998; Zoppi et al. 2004; Pottier 2012). Dispersed settlements throughout prehistory have modified landscapes (see, for example, Chase et al. 2011), but Groslier (1979) implied that only in the Angkor Period did a fundamental shift in the regional ecology occur. His claim that the systematic creation of new hydraulic cities and suburbs from the early Angkor Period onwards converted swathes of pristine forest into monotonous patchworks of agro-urban land uses aligns with the inscriptions, in which mentions of land clearing for settlement increase in frequency from the 10th century CE (Jacob 1978; Hawken and Klassen 2023, this volume). Earlier inscriptions, on the other hand, referred mostly to the gifting of pre-existing villages during efforts to extend territory and/or influence (Lustig 2009). Although Evans has questioned Groslier's view, combining landscape-scale lidar mapping with other lines of evidence to show that many major temple complexes were probably not 'carved *ex nihilo* from the wilderness' (2016, 172), the current evidence nonetheless suggests a marked expansion in the scale of settlement complexes and landscape engineering during the Angkor Period (see Evans et al. 2023, this volume).

The degree of forest clearance and ecological change that had occurred by the Angkor Period, therefore, must have been considerable. The urban landscape of Angkor merged city with country, creating an 'artificial ecology' (Hawken 2011) that spread from the Tonle Sap to the Kulen hills (Gaucher 2002; Fletcher et al. 2003). Over a thousand temple sites were established in a dispersed constellation across Angkor and provided foci for urban settlements that blended residential and agrarian land uses (Pottier 1999; Evans et al. 2007; Fletcher 2012; Pottier 2012). The landscape of Angkor at this time suggests that the Khmer had profoundly reshaped their environment (see also Evans et al. 2013; Evans 2016).

The Khmer Relationship With Plant Life

Plants were central to the urban life of the Khmer. The corpus of inscriptions evokes Angkor as a city replete with forest thickets, gardens, orchards, plantations (of which coconut and areca palms were important), and abundant pasture (Jacob 1978; Hawken and Castillo 2023, this volume). Rice (*Oryza sativa* from the Poaceae family) was the staple crop and commodity. Both wild and domesticated varieties were utilised, using dry, irrigated, bunded, and recession techniques, some of which required the almost total removal of existing vegetation (Delvert 1961). Rice also featured prominently in temple offerings to the gods and religious personnel (Castillo et al. 2018; see also Castillo 2023, this volume). Other important cultivated (or harvested) species included sesame (*Sesamum indicum* L.), mango (*Mangifera* sp.), mung bean (*Vigna radiata*), yardlong bean (*Vigna unguiculata* subsp. *sesquipedalis*), hyacinth bean (*Lablab purpureus*), pigeon pea (*Cajanus cajan*), cotton (*Gossypium* sp.), millet (*Sorghum* sp.), camphor (*Cinnamomum camphora*), sandalwood (*Santalum* sp.), Indian kapok or the silk cotton tree (cf. *Bombax*/cf. *Ceiba*), and the palmyra palm (*Borassus flabellifer*). These plants were used as food sources and medicine and in ritual, textiles, and construction (Phon 2000; Castillo et al. 2018), and any new trees replanted around houses were selected for their economic, resource, or decorative characteristics. The presence of *Borassus flabellifer*, for example, correlates strongly with Khmer urban-agrarian culture since the 'Funan' Period that preceded Angkor (Penny et al. 2006), and the species remains a ubiquitous feature of Cambodian agricultural landscapes today. *Borassus* provides a plethora of useful materials and flourishes only if tended and provided with ample light. The towering, scattered presence of these palms along the horizon of paddy fields has become emblematic of Khmer agriculture.

Given this strong link between landscape ecology and urban life at Angkor, the history of Angkorian settlement and land use should be discernible in records of ecological change through time (see also Evans et al. 2023 and Hawken and Klassen 2023, this volume). These records are reconstructed from long-term, undisturbed sedimentary deposits, retrieved from lakes, bogs, and reservoirs, in which pollen and spores (palynomorphs) released by the surrounding vegetation are preserved. Material within these sedimentary archives can be dated absolutely, using radiometric techniques, providing a temporal context in which to analyse vegetation change. These palynological records are required to either strengthen or re-evaluate the ecological history of Angkor implied by inscriptional and architectural remains, to test assumptions regarding Angkor's landscape modification, and to see what a greater understanding of Angkor's botanical environment can reveal about the city's evolution. Asking ecological questions is especially relevant at Angkor, considering the dependence of the Khmer on maintaining agricultural productivity in a challenging monsoon environment and the supposed role of deforestation, ecological deterioration, and other pathological nature-culture relations in Angkor's decline (Groslier 1979, 1998; Buckley et al. 2010).

Shifting Plant Regimes Through the Angkor Period: Evidence of Land Cover, Land Use, and Occupation Change from Palynological Records

Palynological records retrieved from four sites across greater Angkor (see Figure 8.2) reveal a regional pattern of shifting plant regimes and the response of Khmer society to climatic, economic, and political changes through time. These four records integrate vegetation histories from the inner moat of the Bakong temple-mountain in Roluos (Hariharālaya), the West Mebon temple within the West Baray, the moat of Angkor Thom in the urban core, and the Srah Srang reservoir located just east of Banteay Kdei to present a picture of broadscale landscape change. The depositional records obtained from these artificial water bodies capture a cross-section of construction and occupation phases across the entire Angkor Period.

Pollen and spore taxa collected from these records were identified to varying degrees of specificity, from family to species level, and were collated into ecological groups for this analysis. These ecological groups, and the taxa allocated to each, are presented in Table 8.3. Grouping pollen and spore taxa according to broad vegetation ecologies is useful for two reasons: first as a way to reduce a dataset that is inherently large given the high plant diversity of the dry tropics (without reducing the meaningfulness of the data) and second as a way to rapidly identify

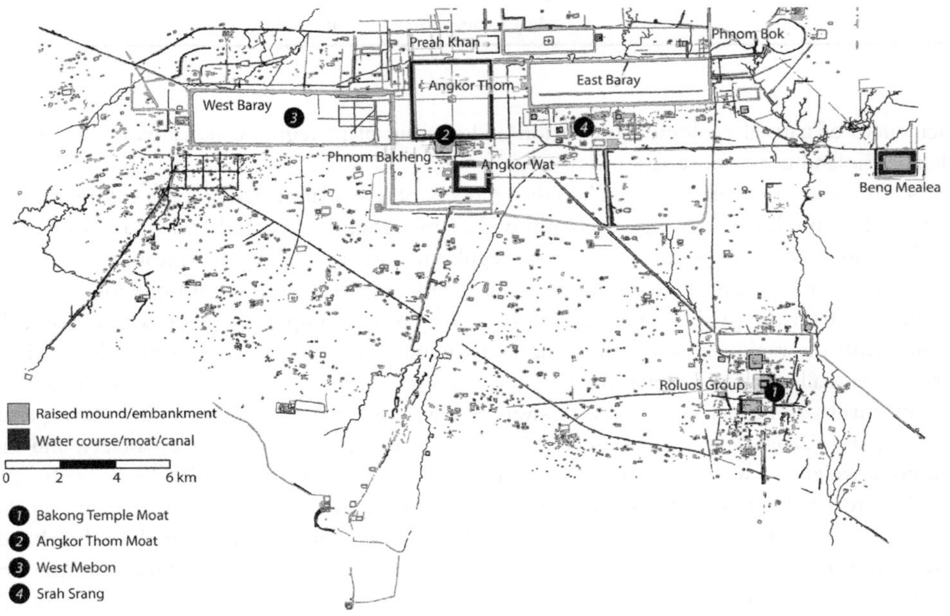

Figure 8.2 Select Angkor monuments and sediment coring sites from which palaeoecological records were obtained.

Source: (Based on Uchida et al. 2005).

Table 8.3 The array of pollen types identified in the palaeoecological records analysed and the ecological groups to which they were assigned.

Ecological group	Taxa
Secondary forest	*Macaranga, Mallotus, Trema, Claoxylon*
Aquatic plants	Cyperaceae, *Drosera, Eriocaulon, Ludwigia, Myriophyllum, Nepenthes, Nymphoides, Persicaria, Nelumbo nucifera, Urticularia, Ceratophyllum, Azolla* (aquatic fern), *Blyxa, Ceratopteris thalictroides* (aquatic fern), *Nymphaea, Rotala*
Dryland herbs	*Alternanthera,* Araceae, *Artemisia,* Asteraceae, Amarantheaceae, *Crotalaria* type, *Liliaceae, Poaceae, Polygalaceae*
Peat swamp (including epiphytes)	*Ilex cymosa, Calophyllum, Eugenia, Barringtonia,* Rubiaceae, *Stenochlaena palustris* (climbing fern)
Ferns	*Lygodium, Monolete* spores, Polypodiaceae, *Pteris, Trilete* spores
Highland/extra-regional forest	*Hernandia, Dacrydium, Dacrycarpus, Gironniera,* Juglandaceae, *Myrica, Pinus, Podocarpus, Quercus, Intsia, Ulmus*
Dryland trees and shrubs	*Antidesma,* Apocynaceae, Arecaceae, *Bombax, Calamus, Caesalpina, Carallia, Cassia, Celastrus* type, *Celtis,* Combretaceae/*Melastomaceae, Dillenia, Diospyros, Dipterocarpus, Elaeocarpus/Tetrameles,* Euphorbiaceae, *Ficus, Garcinia, Grewia, Hopea/Shorea, Lagerstroemia, Lithocarpus/Castanopsis,* Loranthaceae, Lytheraceae, Malphigiaceae, Meliaceae, Menispermaceae, *Mussaenda,* Myrtaceae, *Oncosperma, Pandanus, Phyllanthus, Randia,* Sapindaceae, Urticaceae, Sapotaceae
Agriculture	Poaceae, Arecaceae *Sabal-type,* Anacardiaceae (e.g. *Mangifera), Borassus flabellifer, Citris type,* Cruciferae, Cucurbitaceae (*Luffa* type), *Areca,* Solonaceae, Apiaceae, *Ipomoea,* Labiatae, Malvaceae, *Ocimum, Tamarindus*

incidences of natural ecological succession and shifting plant regimes indicative of significant changes in land use or occupation intensity.

Natural succession processes, such as the recovery of secondary forest and the colonisation of aquatic flora and littoral swamp vegetation within and around water bodies, may indicate waning land use intensities and the cessation of regular maintenance of hydrological infrastructure. Increasing sedimentation within natural or artificial basins (terrestrialisation) provides the ideal environment for the gradual development of mature peat-swamp. Such colonisation generally begins with the rapid invasion of floating and emergent aquatic plants, as well as hydrophilic ferns. Eventually, a thick vegetal mat will develop, providing a substrate for the colonisation of woody shrubs and small trees suited to swampy environs, such as *Ilex cymosa* and *Barringtonia, Eugenia,* and *Calophyllum* species. Given the highly agrarian nature of Khmer society, and the symbolic weight of water infrastructure within Khmer architecture (Groslier 1974; Siribhadra and Moore 1992), these successional shifts in the plant regime strongly imply a decline in the use of a temple district as a focus of residential and ceremonial activity. On the other hand, a reduction in the diversity and/or abundance of species and genera characteristic of the dry tropical forests and a concomitant increase in 'useful' plants and associated agricultural weeds suggests the expansion or intensification of occupation and agriculture.

The Bakong record (Figure 8.3a) begins with the construction of the inner moat between the late 7th and late 8th century, likely prior to the inauguration of the temple by King Indravarman I in 881 CE (Cœdès 1937–66). The initial century-and-a-half of the record maintains high concentrations of taxa from all ecological groups except for ferns and peat swamp. Interestingly, cultivated taxa—in this record dominated by *Borassus flabellifer* and the *Sabal*-type palm—and dryland herbs peak simultaneously with dryland trees and shrubs indicative of open dry forest. Such a coincidence suggests that agriculture was being practised proximal to the moat, within a matrix of sparse, open-canopy forest, for several decades or centuries prior to the dedication of the Bakong temple. The high concentration of *Borassus flabellifer* is especially pertinent, given its very low pollen productivity (Reddi and Reddi 1986). Its sustained and relatively dominant contribution to the pollen assemblage during the first centuries of occupation therefore suggests its strong presence in the surrounding landscape, indicating active cultivation (see Penny et al. 2006).

A clear shift occurs in the early 10th century, when taxa from all ecological groups except aquatic plants, ferns, and the peat swamp community decline sharply. Taxa from regional sources reduce, suggesting a 'drowning-out' of the regional pollen signal by local aquatic and peat-swamp flora. Evidence for the recovery of secondary dry deciduous forest is likely muted by the overwhelming contribution of this local peat-swamp flora to the pollen assemblage. However, the dominance of paddy fields and degraded forest and shrub-land in the local area today (see Figure 8.1b) suggests that regeneration of dry deciduous and evergreen forest has been minimal or was fleeting if it occurred.

Overall, shifting plant regimes surrounding the Bakong temple-mountain indicate a 150-year tenure of occupation at this temple complex, accompanied by moderately intensive agricultural production and the upkeep of open-water moats and reservoirs. From the early to mid-10th century CE, plant taxa associated with agriculture, including grasses (and thus, likely, rice), reduced as land use intensity declined. This shift is coincident with the abandonment of symbolic water infrastructure maintenance, implying an end to the ceremonial use of the temple city, and aligns with the timing of the relocation of the royal court from Hariharālaya in Roluos northwest to Yaśodharapura, in the centre of what was to become Greater Angkor.

Following this shift in the centre of power from Hariharālaya to Yaśodharapura in the early 10th century CE, political and economic life became centred on and around Phnom Bakheng (see Figure 8.2). The extensive citadel of Angkor Thom, immediately to the north of Phnom Bakheng, was constructed over subsequent centuries and reached its pinnacle of development in the 12th century CE (Gaucher 2017; and see Evans et al. 2023, this volume) and provided a hub for an extended city-region that included all of the former political and ceremonial nuclei of Yaśodharapura and integrated urban and agricultural areas that had accumulated over many centuries.

The vegetation record of Angkor Thom (Figure 8.3b) shows a similar pattern of shifting plant regimes to the Bakong, this time between the 12th and 15th centuries. While the record begins prior to the late-12th century excavation of the moat, the pollen here is sparse and represents the poor preservation (i.e. oxidation) of palynomorphs in the dry sediment of the moat's original substrate. However, following the completion of the moat's excavation, and for a period of roughly 200 years, it is clear that within and surrounding Angkor Thom spread a landscape of open dry semi-evergreen forest fragmented by agriculture. The intensity of cultivation reached a height between the early 13th and early 14th centuries, when crop species, including *Borassus flabellifer*, *Tamarindus* and *Solanaceae* (nightshades), and patches of heavily disturbed woodland were abundant. Throughout this time, encroaching vegetation across the moat of Angkor Thom was inhibited.

As with the Bakong vegetation record, the decline in ceremonial use of Angkor Thom manifests as the succession of herbaceous to mature peat-swamp around and across the citadel's moat. In this region of Angkor, the plant regime shift begins in the mid-14th century

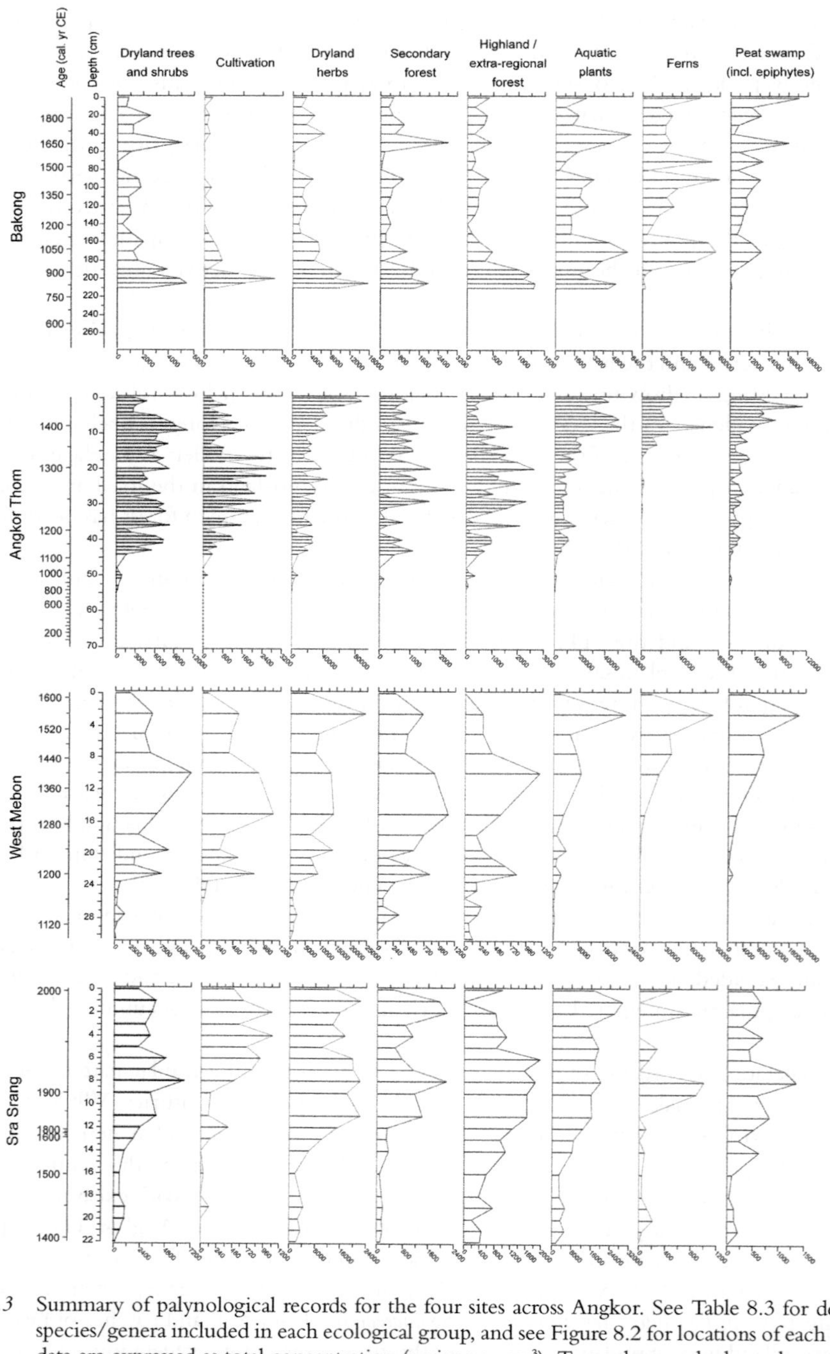

Figure 8.3 Summary of palynological records for the four sites across Angkor. See Table 8.3 for details of species/genera included in each ecological group, and see Figure 8.2 for locations of each site. All data are expressed as total concentration (grains per cm^3). To produce each chronology, selected organic samples were radiocarbon dated and calibrated to the SHCal13 curve (with an offset of -21 ± 6 years) (Hua et al. 2004; Hua and Barbetti 2007; Hua et al. 2012). Age-depth models were produced using Bayesian statistics (Blaauw and Christen 2011). See Penny et al. (2005, 2006, 2007, 2019) for further details regarding sample preparation methodology and analysis.

CE—approximately a half-century later than the initial waning in land use intensity—suggesting a protracted, rather than immediate and wholesale, desertion of this urban centre. By the late 14th and early 15th centuries, dry evergreen forest shows some more sustained recovery; however, by the second half of the 15th century, increases in dryland herbs and weedy taxa species suggest this forest recovery was interrupted by some renewed vegetation clearance in the landscape.

The third vegetation record reconstructs landscape change from the basin of the West Mebon (Figure 8.3c), a water shrine constructed on an artificial island within the vast reservoir, the West Baray. Stylistic dating conventionally places the temple's origin in the mid- to late 11th century (Glaize 1963; Cœdès 1968), in the wake of the baray's completion. However, this masks a more complex construction history: the West Mebon and its various components likely resulted from successive installations and renovations throughout the 11th and 12th centuries (Penny et al. 2005; Leroy et al. 2017; Feneley et al. 2016).

Consequently, the vegetation record captured in the sedimentary basin of the West Mebon begins in the 12th century. In the early part of the record, from the early 12th to the late 14th century, the West Mebon appears to have been bordered by an open waterbody, largely clear of floating vegetation. The surrounding landscape, adjacent to the baray, was likely covered by disturbed semi-evergreen forest, comprising *Celtis*, *Urticaceae/Moraceae*, *Combretaceae/Melastomaceae*, and *Sapindaceae* species, and *Macaranga*, dissected by plots of agriculture. By the late 14th century, however, signs of neglect of the West Mebon appear, in the form of a flourishing aquatic community of *Nymphoides*, *Ludwigia*, ferns, sedges and grasses, and the eventual establishment of woody swamp forest, housing *Barringtonia* and *Ilex cymosa*. Water levels in the West Baray had also possibly decreased enough through the 13th to late 16th centuries (Penny et al. 2005) to allow the expansion of agricultural activity across the reservoir's bed, including the increased cultivation of *Borassus flabellifer* and species of the Anacardiaceae family. This vegetation shift may represent the origin of several communities that were documented within the dry eastern half of the baray in the early 20th century (Pottier and Dumarcay 1993) and/or the intensification of agriculture in the landscape fringing the reservoir (Pottier 2000).

The record from Srah Srang (Figure 8.3d), beginning in the late 14th century, represents the most recent 'time-slice' of vegetation change in Angkor. Srah Srang is located south of the East Baray and to the immediate east of Banteay Kdei, which was built between the late 12th and early 13th century. Sra Srang, however, was likely constructed in the 10th century and renovated in the 12th century. The reason for the lag between the reservoir's construction and the beginning of the vegetation record is unknown. Possibly the reservoir was re-excavated at some point after its construction, which would have removed the earlier sedimentation.

Sra Srang's vegetation record is restricted to the waning phase of Angkor's royal occupation and economic activity. The record begins with a limited pollen and spore assemblage, comprising a mix of dryland forest, grasses, and highland forest taxa, with no clear dominant. Secondary forest species are present but few cultivated plants, other than possible rice species (i.e. *Poaceae*), are apparent in the landscape, reflecting a period of forest recovery and limited occupation and land use.

This growing body of empirical records of vegetation change in Angkor was collected from artificial water-bodies and thus cannot provide evidence of landscape change during the pre-occupation period. As such, the pre-disturbance landscape, and the extent to which it was modified through the prehistoric, Pre-Angkor, and Angkor Periods, remains obscure. Nonetheless, the combined set of vegetation records summarised here reveals a predictable pattern of shifting plant regimes occurring across Angkor in response to the ebb and flow of occupation and dominant land uses, at least through the Angkor Period.

In all four vegetation records, indicative components of primary dry deciduous and semi-evergreen forest, such as *Dipterocarpus* and *Hopea/Shorea*, are only ever rare and/or sporadic. This is partly the result of pollination strategies that lead to the under-representation of these taxa in pollen records but may also suggest that the bulk of remnant forest clearance had occurred in preparation for temple site construction and thus prior to the excavation of its associated water bodies. The strong presence of disturbance species and cultivated taxa further suggests that early use of each site clearly occurred amongst a landscape of highly fragmented dry deciduous and semi-evergreen forest, which was likely degraded by human occupation and cultivation of the land through the Pre-Angkor and early Angkor Periods. An exception may be the Bakong temple, which alone presents a vegetation record beginning with maximum concentrations of both canopy and mid-storey species from dry semi-evergreen and deciduous forests. Given this is one of the earlier sites of royal occupation in the Greater Angkor region, it is possible this site was established among less-disturbed forest. From here, it appears that new temple districts were more often erected upon or proximal to more densely settled sites (see Hawken and Klassen 2023, this volume). Overall, as Khmer urbanism expanded, the domesticated ecology spread and coalesced across the Khmer domain in response to an economy directed by a strongly state-centred political regime. By the 14th century, almost all remnant primary forest in the Greater Angkor region had been replaced by a sweeping, monotonous landscape of paddy fields interspersed with small thickets of economically useful woodlands (Heng 2002; Fletcher et al. 2008; Hawken 2011).

The relocation of the royal court away from the Angkor region in the 15th century presents as another plant regime shift, as the depopulation of central temple districts allowed weedy taxa and secondary forest to spread through temple grounds and swamp vegetation to engulf sacred water infrastructure. Considering the disparity between initial declines in land use intensity and the abandonment of water infrastructure maintenance evident in these vegetation records, this depopulation was gradual and likely partial, perhaps restricted to the elite and industrial/commercial populations. The ecological history of Angkor, therefore, supports Evans' interpretation of a 'gradual demographic decline' (2016, 172; see also Penny et al. 2019) from these urban centres rather than the wholesale 'diaspora' assumed in other research (e.g. Lucero et al. 2015). The lack of a robust signal for the recovery of climax dry deciduous and semi-evergreen forest across the city, even several centuries beyond political abandonment, may also reaffirm arguments by Groslier (1985) and Penny et al. (2019) that the ephemeral political tenure of Angkor's temple-cities occurred against a more enduring back-drop of smaller-scale agricultural land use and settlement.

Tracking the Migration of Angkor's Capitals via Shifting Plant Regimes

Analysing the shifting ecology of Angkor Period temple districts also reveals how peaks in land use, and the focus of ceremonial and political life, shifted across Greater Angkor. Figure 8.4 presents the shifting plant regimes of all four sites through time, comparing the timing of significant transitions (green lines) in the normalised (z-scores) ecological group data. Points of transition in all dryland ecological groups occur asynchronously across space, except for Angkor Thom and the West Mebon sites, which appear to transition in all ecological groups almost simultaneously (at least within the margin of error associated with radiocarbon dating). The coherence in ecological history between these two sites seems unusual given their association with the reigns of different royal houses; however, this likely speaks to the substantial integration of settlement pattern and land use across the central Angkor temple district through the 12th and 13th centuries (Evans et al. 2007; Evans et al. 2013; Evans et al. 2023, this volume).

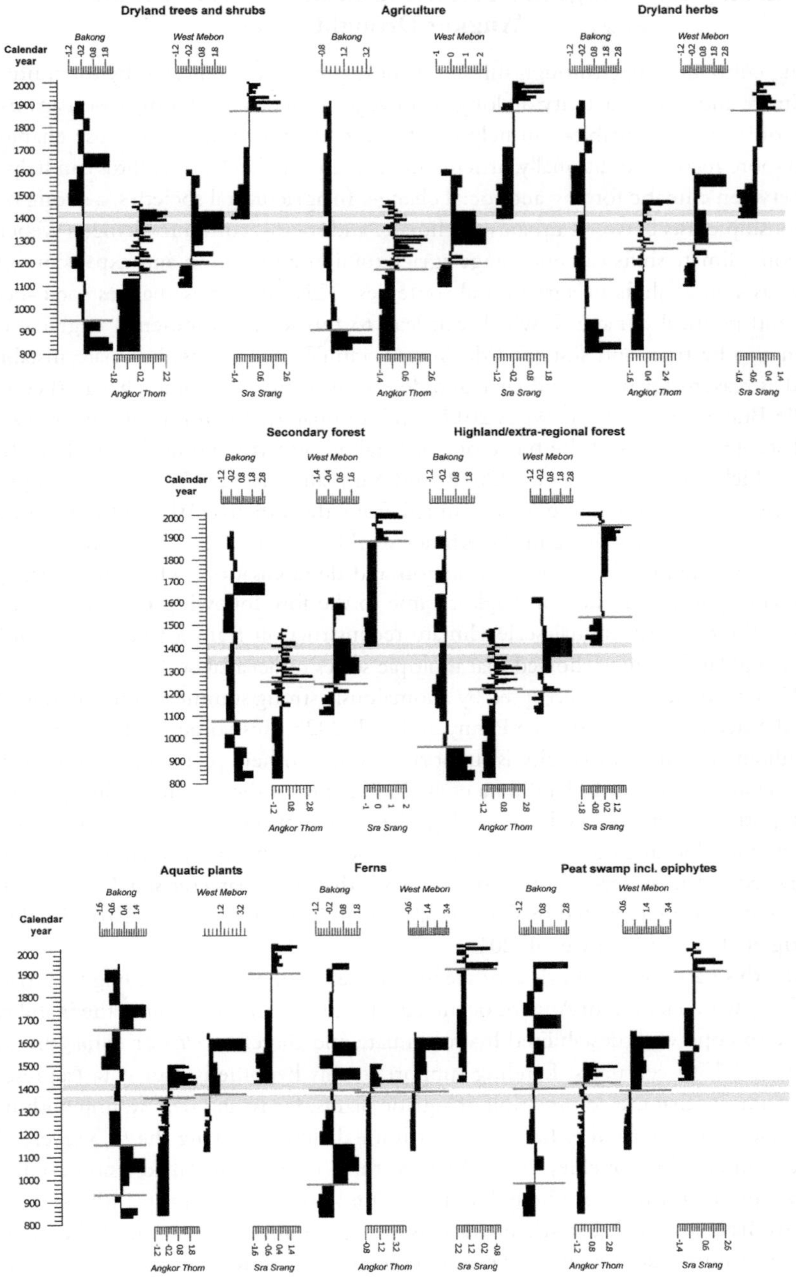

Figure 8.4 Ecological group data plotted as z-scores and compared across the four sites. Z-scores were calculated to normalise the data and allow comparison between sites and to highlight significant shifts in each dataset. Z-scores were calculated using the formula $(x - \bar{x})/\sigma$, where x is the original data value, $\bar{x}$ is the mean of the data set, and σ is the standard deviation. Green lines highlight points of significant transition in the data, and the yellow bars indicate the timing of the Angkor I and Angkor II droughts documented by Buckley et al. (2010).

Ecological Change in Response to Climate Variability and the 'Angkor Droughts'

Interpreting cultural change through shifting plant regimes is complicated by the mutual influence of climate and human activity on long-term vegetation change. Comparison against robust climate records (when available) can help identify the effect of human land use change in the pollen and spore record. Additionally, articulating climate and land-use records can help explore the links between climatic forcing and social change. In agricultural societies, a strong but complex relationship exists between urbanism, climate, and socio-economic change (Weber 1999). Advantageous climate shifts can encourage agricultural intensification and expansion into marginal areas, as well as shifts in agricultural strategies. This, in turn, enhances socio-economic structures and political dynamics, which can lead to further environmental degradation. The inverse can also be true, and sustained declines in rainfall, or increased climate instability, are often cited as reasons for urban and farmland desertion, socio-economic change (Peterson and Haug 2005; Buckley et al. 2014; Weiss 2017), and, ultimately, environmental recovery.

Several studies have linked the trajectory of Angkor's growth and decline to long-term climate cycles. Lieberman and Buckley (2012) and Yamoah et al. (2017) argue that a prolonged period of increasing summer monsoon rainfall from the 8th to 11th centuries fostered the expansion of wet rice agriculture in the Khmer world and that a subsequent return to weaker summer monsoon rainfall led to its contraction and destabilisation. The role of drought and climate instability in the decline of Angkor came to the fore following Buckley et al. (2010)'s publication of a 759-year annual-scale climate reconstruction from a tree-ring record in the Vietnamese highlands, which showed that multiple series of decadal-scale droughts through the 14th and 15th centuries CE, interrupted by anomalously strong summer monsoon rainfall, foreshadowed the decline of Angkor (see Penny and Hall 2023, this volume). The regional impact of this heightened climate variability is supported by speleothem records from southern Cambodia (Hua et al. 2017), east India (Sinha et al. 2007), and southern China (Zhang et al. 2008). A strong hypothesis then emerged, contending that these episodes of extreme variation in rainfall—in particular flooding during the wet periods—overwhelmed the ageing, convoluted, and increasingly redundant water infrastructure network that had characterised Angkor's success as an agrarian state and precipitated its fall (Buckley et al. 2010; Cook et al. 2010; Buckley et al. 2014; Lustig et al. 2018; Penny et al. 2018).

However, this narrative implies a very specific sequence of events, according to a strict timeline: that the elite evacuation of Angkor occurred (at least in part) *as a result* of the inability of the urban fabric to cope with destabilised hydro-climate and therefore *after* or *during* the droughts of the 14th and 15th centuries. Lending support to this hypothesis, our data (represented in Figure 8.4) indicate that the colonisation of aquatic plants, ferns, and peat swamp within temple moats and reservoirs occurred either during or immediately following the two severe 'Angkor droughts' documented by Buckley et al. (2010) at three of the four Angkor sites. Srah Srang is the only exception, as the record here does not begin until the end of the 14th century.

So far, we have assumed that swamp succession represents the cessation of the coordinated maintenance of infrastructure by a governing elite and therefore signals abandonment. However, this interpretation is complicated by the strong correlation between drought and marsh development, because drastically lowered surface and ground-water levels would allow reservoirs to be colonised by herbaceous swamp plants, even as they still functioned to some degree. Fragmentation of supply through the water infrastructure network in the late 14th century (Penny et al. 2018) may have also led to water-level declines and contributed to the scarcity of water—and herbaceous swamp development—in conjunction with drought. The subsequent re-flooding of the basins as droughts receded may have lifted the herbaceous root mat to create the initial substrate for the floating swamp that came to characterise the enclosed reservoirs of Angkor.

Interestingly, mature swamp establishment at the Bakong occurs several centuries after the initial increase in floating aquatic taxa, unlike at the other sites where natural succession is delayed by only decades or less. While the increase in aquatics at the Bakong temple coincides with the 10th-century relocation of the royal seat to Yaśodharapura, suggesting that the moat was no longer being cleared of floating vegetation and maintained for sacred purposes, it seems that the continued development of rooted swamp taxa could not occur until water levels declined sufficiently during the droughts of the 14th and 15th centuries—at roughly the same time that ferns and peat swamp developed across water basins in central Angkor. The delay in mature peat swamp development at Bakong makes sense, however, considering the Bakong moat is deep relative to other temple moats (approximately 5 m below the land surface; Penny et al. 2006), and further highlights the complex interplay that occurs between the influences of climate and water infrastructure maintenance on the growth of swamp communities within water basins across Angkor.

Because of this complexity, it remains uncertain (at least in the ecological record) as to when centralised control of labour shifted away from Angkor. Figure 8.4 shows that herb-swamp taxa respond more consistently and predictably to the weakened monsoon than any other ecological group, implying that droughts had a significant impact on the overall functioning of the water management system. However, despite this collapse of large-scale water infrastructure networks, secondary dry forest recovery and the expansion of dryland herbs and cultivated species continue throughout the 14th and 15th centuries at Angkor Thom and the West Mebon and suggest that some occupation and agricultural land use survived the drought period (see also Castillo et al. 2018). The extent to which state-level authority was co-ordinating this continued occupation at the end of the Angkor Period is difficult to know: At this stage it is impossible to discern whether water infrastructure across the city was no longer being maintained because of its growing operational complexity, intractability, and climate-induced failures or because the power structures required to maintain it no longer remained in place. This ambiguity has implications for determining if continuity or overlap existed between royal houses in Angkor and in the Early Modern capitals in the Mekong riverine region (see Evans 2016).

Conclusion

The suite of palaeoecological records presented here highlights the value in analysing the growth and decline of Angkor as a transitioning ecological landscape. These records reveal the condition of the landscape at the time of temple construction, and during peaks and declines in agricultural land use and occupation across the greater Angkor region and allow us to trace political mobility and drought through swamp invasion in water bodies related to critical infrastructure. With the shortage of reliable written or material cultural records through the end of the Angkor Period, patterns of shifting plant regimes across space and time are an important source of historical data.

In the subtropical monsoon climate of Angkor, urban life succeeded by dominating the environment and in particular by keeping the encroaching forest at bay. Significant anthropogenic transformation of the environment presumably began well before the Angkor Period through patchy forest clearance and crop cultivation. However, throughout the Angkor Period, the combined pressures of an expanding population, the intensification of agriculture, and the establishment of new capitals across the region kept primary forest extent low.

The pollen record shows that there was some attenuation in human land use at the time of the 14th-century CE Angkor droughts, but the limited reappearance of secondary and climax dry forest after this period tends to suggest demographic continuity rather than severe depopulation. An important caveat here is that biases in the pollen record—in particular the low pollen productivity and dispersal of important dry forest species and the overwhelming signal of local swamp taxa in the latter part of these palaeoecological records—may have obscured the signal of forests reclaiming previously occupied spaces and that depopulation in the wake of the 14th-century Angkor droughts may therefore have been more pronounced than our models suggest.

We must also take into account the possibility of very different trajectories in Angkor's densely populated urban core and its low-density hinterland (Klassen et al. 2021). The enduring presence of low-density occupation after Angkor's abandonment as a royal centre would also have substantially inhibited the regrowth of forests in the area. Fundamental changes in ecological community structure, for example, the isolation of remnant forest patches, may also have hindered the regenerative capacity of dry forest communities across the Angkor plains. The invasion of herbaceous and peat-swamp forest communities within several artificial water bodies across Angkor during the 14th-century droughts is nonetheless very clear and indicates the large-scale depletion and disuse of the famous water infrastructure network.

References

Andre, M.F., O. Voldoire, E. Roussel, F. Vautier, B. Phalip & H. Peou, 2012. Contrasting weathering and climate regimes in forested and cleared sandstone temples of the Angkor region. *Earth Surface Processes and Landforms* 37(5), 519–32.

Ashwell, D. & J. Fitzwilliams, 1993. *Zonation and Environmental Management Plan for Angkor: Background Report on the Vegetation Ecology of Angkor and Environs*. Cambodia: IUCN/UNESCO.

Baker, P.J., S. Bunyavejchewin, C.D. Oliver & P.S. Ashton, 2005. Disturbance history and historical stand dynamics of a seasonal tropical forest in western Thailand. *Ecological Monographs* 75, 317–43.

Blaauw, M. & J.A. Christen, 2011. Flexible palaeoclimate age-depth models using an autoregressive gamma process. *Bayesian Analysis* 6, 457–74.

Buckley, B.M., K.J. Anchukaitis, D. Penny, R. Fletcher, E.R. Cook, M. Sano, L.C. Nam, A. Wichienkeeo, T.T. Minh & T.M. Hong, 2010. Climate as a contributing factor in the demise of Angkor, Cambodia. *Proceedings of the National Academy of Science* 107(15), 6748–52.

Buckley, B.M., R. Fletcher, S.Y.S. Wang, B. Zottoli & C. Pottier, 2014. Monsoon extremes and society over the past millennium on mainland Southeast Asia. *Quaternary Science Reviews* 95, 1–19.

Castillo, C.C., 2023. Food, craft and ritual: plants from the Angkorian World, in *The Angkorian World*, eds. M. Hendrickson, M.T. Stark & D. Evans. New York: Routledge, 401–20.

Castillo, C.C., M. Polkinghorne, B. Vincent, B.-S. Tan & D.Q. Fuller, 2018. Life goes on: archaeobotanical investigations of diet and ritual at Angkor Thom (fourteenth to fifteenth centuries CE). *The Holocene* 28(6), 930–44.

Chase, A.F., D.Z. Chase, J.F. Weishampel, J.B. Drake, R.L. Shrestha, K.C. Slatton, J.J. Awe & W.E. Carter, 2011. Airborne LiDAR, archaeology, and the ancient Maya landscape at Caracol, Belize. *Journal of Archaeological Science* 38(2), 387–98.

Cœdès, G., 1937–1966. *Inscriptions du Cambodge. Collection de textes et documents sur l'Indochine*. Paris: École française d'Extrême-Orient.

Cœdès, G., 1968. *The Indianized States of Southeast Asia*. Honolulu: East–West Center Press.

Cook, E.R., K.J. Anchukaitis, B.M. Buckley, R.D. D'Arrigo, G.C. Jacoby & W.E. Wright, 2010. Asian monsoon failure and megadrought during the last millennium. *Science* 328(5977), 486–89.

Delvert, J., 1961. *Le Paysan Cambodgien*. Paris: Mouton et Co.

Evans, D., R. Fletcher, S. Klassen, C. Pottier & P. Wijker, 2023. Trajectories of urbanism in the Angkorian World, in *The Angkorian World*, eds. M. Hendrickson, M.T. Stark & D. Evans. New York: Routledge, 173–94.

Evans, D., 2016. Airborne laser scanning as a method for exploring long-term socio-ecological dynamics in Cambodia. *Journal of Archaeological Science* 74, 164–75.

Evans, D., C. Pottier, R. Fletcher, S. Hensley, I. Tapley, A. Milne & M. Barbetti, 2007. A comprehensive archaeological map of the World's largest preindustrial settlement complex at Angkor, Cambodia. *Proceedings of the National Academy of Science* 104(36), 14277–82.

Evans, D.H., R.J. Fletcher, C. Pottier, J.-B. Chevance, D. Soutif, B.S. Tan, S. Im, D. Ea, T. Tin, S. Kim, C. Cromarty, S. De Greef, K. Hanus, P. Baty, R. Kuszinger, I. Shimoda & G. Boornazian, 2013. Uncovering archaeological landscapes at Angkor using lidar. *Proceedings of the National Academy of Sciences of the United States of America* 110(31), 12595–600.

Feneley, M., D. Penny & R. Fletcher, 2016. Claiming the hydraulic network of Angkor with Visnu: a multidisciplinary approach including the analysis of archaeological remains, digital modelling and radiocarbon dating: with evidence for a 12th century renovation of the West Mebon. *Journal of Archaeological Science-Reports* 9, 275–92.

Fleming, J., 2017. Toward vegetal political ecology: Kyrgyzstan's walnut-fruit forest and the politics of graftability. *Geoforum* 79, 26–35.

Fletcher, R., 2012. Low-density, agrarian-based urbanism: scale, power, and ecology, in *The Comparative Archaeology of Complex Societies*, ed. M.E. Smith. New York: Cambridge University Press, 285–320.

Fletcher, R., D. Penny, D. Evans, C. Pottier, M. Barbetti, M. Kummu, T. Lustig & Authority for the Protection and Management of Angkor and the Region of Siem Reap (APSARA) Departments of Monuments and Archaeology Team, 2008. The water management network of Angkor, Cambodia. *Antiquity* 82, 13.

Fletcher, R., M. Barbetti, D. Evans, H. Than, I. Sokrithy, K. Chan, D. Penny, C. Pottier & T. Somaneath, 2003. Redefining Angkor: structure and environment in the largest, low density urban complex of the pre-industrial World. *Udaya, Journal of Khmer Studies* 4, 107–25.

Frelat, M.A. & C. Souday, 2015. The bronze age necropolis of Koh Ta Meas: insights into the health of the earliest inhabitants of the Angkor region. *Bulletins et mémoires de la Société d'anthropologie de Paris* 27(3), 142–57.

Gaucher, J., 2002. The 'city' of Angkor. What is it? *Museum International* 54(1 and 2), 9.

Gaucher, J., 2017. L'enceinte d'Angkor Thom: Archéologie d'une forme, chronologie d'une ville, in *Deux Décennies de Coopération Archéologique Franco-Cambodgienne à Angkor*, eds. A. Beschaouch, F. Verellen & M. Zink. Paris: Académie des Inscriptions et Belles-Lettres, 27–41.

Gaughan, A.E., M.W. Binford & J. Southworth, 2009. Tourism, forest conversion, and land transformations in the Angkor basin, Cambodia. *Applied Geography* 29(2), 212–23.

Glaize, M., 1963. *Les Monuments du groupe d'Angkor*. Paris: Adrien-Maisonneuve.

Groslier, B.-P., 1974. Agriculture et religion dans l'Empire angkorien. *Etudes Rurales*, 53–6.

Groslier, B.-P., 1979. La cité hydraulique Angkorienne: exploitation ou surexploitation du sol? *Bulletin de l'École française d'Extrême-Orient* 66, 161–202.

Groslier, B.-P., 1985. For a geographic history of Cambodia. *Seksa Khmer* 8, 31–76.

Groslier, B-P., 1998. *Mélanges sur l'archéologie du Cambodge (1949–1986)*. Paris: École française d'Extrême-Orient.

Hawken, S. & C.C. Castillo, 2023. Angkor's agrarian economy: a socio-ecological mosaic, in *The Angkorian World*, eds. M. Hendrickson, M.T. Stark & D. Evans. New York: Routledge, 338–59.

Hawken, S. & S. Klassen, 2023. Angkor's temple communities and the logic of its urban landscape, in *The Angkorian World*, eds. M. Hendrickson, M.T. Stark & D. Evans. New York: Routledge, 195–215.

Hawken, S., 2011. *Metropolis of ricefields: a topographic classification of a dispersed urban complex*. PhD dissertation. Sydney: The University of Sydney.

Head, L., J. Atchison, C. Phillips & K. Buckingham, 2014. Vegetal politics: belonging, practices and places. *Social & Cultural Geography* 15(8), 861–70.

Heng, H.L., 2002. Angkor revisited: lessons to learn. *SPAFA Journal* 12(2), 5–17.

Hua, Q. & M. Barbetti, 2007. Influence of atmospheric circulation on regional $14CO_2$ differences. *Journal of Geophysical Research* 112, D19.

Hua, Q., D. Cook, D. Penny, P. Bishop & J. Fohlmeister, 2017. Radiocarbon dating of a speleothem record of palaeoclimate for Angkor, Cambodia. *Radiocarbon* 59, 1873–90.

Hua, Q., M. Barbetti, U. Zoppi, D. Fink, M. Watanasak & G.E. Jacobsen, 2004. Radiocarbon in tropical tree rings during the Little Ice Age. *Nuclear Instruments & Methods in Physics Research Section B-Beam Interactions with Materials and Atoms* 223–224: 489–94.

Hua, Q., M. Barbetti, V.A. Levchenko, R.D. D'Arrigo, B.M. Buckley & A.M. Smith, 2012. Monsoonal influence on southern hemisphere $14CO_2$. *Geophysical Research Letters* 39(19), L19806.

Jacob, J.M., 1978. The ecology of Angkor, in *Nature and Man in Southeast Asia*, ed. P.A. Stott. London: School of Oriental and African Studies: 109–27.

JICA, 2002. *Land Use Map of Cambodia (50K).* Tokyo: Japan International Cooperation Agency.

Klassen, S., Ortman, S.G., Lobo, J. & D. Evans, 2021. Provisioning an early city: spatial equilibrium in the agricultural economy at Angkor, Cambodia. *Journal of Archaeological Method and Theory*. https://doi.org/10.1007/s10816-021-09535-5

Kull, C.A., C. Kueffer, D.M. Richardson, A.S. Vaz, J.R. Vicente & J.P. Honrado, 2018. Using the "regime shift" concept in addressing social-ecological change. *Geographical Research* 56(1), 26–41.

Leroy, S., M. Hendrickson, S. Bauvais, T. Blanchet, A. Disser, E. Vega. & E. Delqué-Kolic, 2017. The ties that bind: archaeometallurgical typology of architectural crampons as a method for reconstructing the iron economy of Angkor, Cambodia (10th to 13th c.). *Archaeological and Anthropological Science* 10(8), 2137–57.

Lieberman, V. & B. Buckley, 2012. The impact of climate on Southeast Asia, circa 950–1820: new findings. *Modern Asian Studies* 46(5), 48.

Lucero, L.J., R. Fletcher & R. Coningham, 2015. From 'collapse' to urban diaspora: the transformation of low-density, dispersed agrarian urbanism. *Antiquity* 89(347), 1139–54.

Lustig, E., 2009. *Power and pragmatism in the political economy of Angkor.* PhD dissertation. Sydney: The University of Sydney.

Lustig, T., S. Klassen, D. Evans, R. French & I. Moffat, 2018. Evidence for the breakdown of an Angkorian hydraulic system, and its historical implications for understanding the Khmer Empire. *Journal of Archaeological Science-Reports* 17, 195–211.

Martin, M.A., 1971. *Introduction à l'ethnobotanique du Cambodge.* Paris: Centre National de la Recherche Scientifique.

McDonald, A., Pech, B., Phauk, V. & Leeu, B. 1997. Plant communities of the Tonle Sap floodplain. Final report in contribution to the nomination of Tonle Sap as a UNESCO biosphere reserve. UNESCO/IUCN/Wetlands International/SPEC (European Commission), Phnom Penh.

McShea, W.J. & S.J. Davies, 2011. Seasonally dry forests of tropical Asia: an ecosystem adapted to seasonal drought, frequent fire and human activity. In *The Ecology and Conservation of Seasonally Dry Forests in Asia*, ed. W.J. McShea, S.J. Davis & N. Bhumpakphan. Washington, DC: Smithsonian Institution Scholarly Press.

Mercuri, A.M., 2014. Genesis and evolution of the cultural landscape in central Mediterranean: the 'where, when and how' through the palynological approach. *Landscape Ecology* 29(10), 1799–810.

Olson, D.M., E. Dinerstein, E. Wikramanayake, N.D. Burgess, G.V.N. Powell, E.C. Underwood, J.A. D'amico, I. Itoua, H.E. Strand, J.C. Morrison, C.J. Loucks, T.F. Allnutt, T.H. Ricketts, Y. Kura, J.F. Lamoreux, W.W. Wettengal, P. Hedao & K.R. Kassem, 2001. Terrestrial ecoregions of the World: a new map of life on earth. *BioScience* 51, 933–38.

Penny, D. & T. Hall, 2023. An environmental history of Angkor: Beginning to end, in *The Angkorian World*, eds. M. Hendrickson, M.T. Stark & D. Evans. New York: Routledge, 17–24.

Penny, D., T. Hall, D. Evans & M. Polkinghorne, 2019. Geoarchaeological evidence from Angkor, Cambodia, reveals a gradual decline rather than catastrophic 15th century collapse. *Proceedings of the National Academy of Sciences* 16(11), 4871–876.

Penny, D., Q. Hua, C. Pottier, R. Fletcher & M. Barbetti, 2007. The use of AMS 14C dating to explore issues of occupation and demise at the medieval city of Angkor, Cambodia. *Nuclear Instruments and Methods in Physics Research Section B* 259(1), 388–94.

Penny, D., C. Pottier, R. Fletcher, M. Barbetti, D. Fink & Q. Hua, 2006. Vegetation and land-use at Angkor, Cambodia: a dated pollen sequence from the Bakong temple moat. *Antiquity* 80 (309), 599–614.

Penny, D., C. Pottier, M. Kummu, R. Fletcher, U. Zoppi, M. Barbetti & T. Somaneath, 2005. Hydrological history of the West Baray, Angkor, revealed through palynological analysis of sediments from the West Mebon. *Bulletin de l'École française d'Extrême-Orient* 92, 497–521.Penny, D., C. Zacherson, R. Fletcher, D. Lau, J.T. Lizier, N. Fischer, D. Evans, C. Pottier & M. Prokopenko, 2018. The demise of Angkor: systemic vulnerability of urban infrastructure to climatic variations. *Science Advances* 4(10), eaau4029.

Peterson, L.C. & G.H. Haug, 2005. Climate and the collapse of Maya civilization: a series of multi-year droughts helped to doom an ancient culture. *American Scientist* 93(4), 322–29.

Phon, P.D., 2000. *Dictionary of Plants Used in Cambodia.* Phnom Penh: Imprimerie Olympic.

Pottier, C. & J. Dumarçay, 1993. *Documents topographiques de la Conservation des Monuments d'Angkor.* Paris: École française d'Extrême-Orient.

Pottier, C., 1999. *Carte Archéologique de la Région d'Angkor, Zone Sud.* PhD dissertation. Paris: Université Paris III—Sorbonne nouvelle.

Pottier, C., 2000. Some evidence of an inter-relationship between hydraulic features and rice field patterns at Angkor during ancient times. *The Journal of Sophia Asian Studies* 18: 99–120.

Pottier, C., 2012. *Beyond the Temples: Angkor and Its territory. Old Myths and New Approaches: Interpreting Ancient Religious Sites in Southeast Asia. A. Haendel.* Clayton and Melbourne: Monash University Publishing.

Reddi, C.S. & N. S. Reddi, 1986. Pollen production in some anemophilous angiosperms. *Grana* 25(1), 55–61.

Rundel, P.W., 1999. *Forest Habitats and Floristics of Indochina: Lao PDR, Cambodia and Vietnam.* Hanoi: World Wildlife Fund for Nature (WWF).

Rundel, P.W., 2009. Vegetation in the Mekong Basin, in *The Mekong: Biophysical Environment of an International River Basin*, ed. I.C. Campbell. Oxford: Academic Press.

Sinha, A., K.G. Cannariato, L.D. Stott, H. Cheng, R.L. Edwards, M.G. Yadava, R. Ramesh & I.B. Singh, 2007. A 900-year (600 to 1500 AD) record of the Indian summer monsoon precipitation from the core monsoon zone of India. *Geophysical Research Letters* 34(16), L16707.

Siribhadra, S. & E. Moore, 1992. *Palaces of the Gods: Khmer Art and Architecture in Thailand.* Bangkok: River Books.

Uchida, E., C. Suda, A. Ueno, I. Shimoda & T. Nakagawa, 2005. Estimation of the construction period of Prasat Suor Prat in the Angkor monuments, Cambodia, based on the characteristics of its stone materials and the radioactive carbon age of charcoal fragments. *Journal of Archaeological Science* 32(9), 1339–45.

Weber, S., 1999. Seeds of urbanism: palaeoethnobotany and the Indus civilization. *Antiquity* 73(282), 813–26.

Weiss, H., 2017. *Megadrought and Collapse: From Early Agriculture to Angkor.* Oxford: Oxford University Press.

Wikramanayake, E. & P. Rundel, 2017. *Southeastern Asia.* Vietnam and Cambodia: Ecoregions IM0164.

Wikramanayake, E., R. Boonratana, P. Rundel & N. Aggimarangsee, 2017. *Southeastern Asia.* Thailand, Cambodia, Laos, and Vietnam: Ecoregions IM0202.

Yamoah, K.A., C.F. Higham, B. Wohlfarth, A. Chabangborn, S. Chawchai, F. Schenk & R.H. Smittenberg, 2017. Societal response to monsoonal fluctuations in NE Thailand during the demise of Angkor civilisation. *The Holocene* 27(10), 1455–64.

Zhang, P., H. Cheng, R.L. Edwards, F. Chen, Y. Wang, X. Yang, J. Liu, M. Tan, X. Wang, J. Liu & C. An, 2008. A test of climate, sun, and culture relationships from an 1810-year Chinese cave record. *Science* 322(5903), 940–42.

Zoppi, U., M. Barbetti, R. Fletcher, Q. Hua, R.K. Chhem, C. Pottier & M. Watanasak, 2004. The contribution of 14C AMS dating to the Greater Angkor Archaeological Project. *Nuclear Instruments and Methods in Physics Research* 223–224, 681–85.

9

ANGKOR AND THE MEKONG RIVER

Settlement, Resources, Mobility and Power

Heng Piphal

The Mekong, Southeast Asia's longest river, traverses a diverse array of landforms from its origins in the Tibetan Plateau, through the mountainous zones of southern China (the Upper Mekong Basin), and finally into mainland Southeast Asia (the Lower Mekong Basin) where it empties into the South China Sea. The Lower Mekong Basin is characterised by areas of generally low topographic relief, and from Kratie downstream flows mainly through seasonal floodplains (Mekong River Commission 2005, 49). The pulsating flood regimes resulting from annual shifts in the monsoon climate replenish areas along its course with nutrient-rich sediment, particularly in the Delta, and make it ideal for wet rice agriculture. Fisheries and other aquatic resources from the Mekong and its tributaries provide enormous amounts of protein for the surrounding populations.

Known to 17th–19th-century Europeans as the 'Cambodia River' (e.g., Crawfurd 1967, 198; Kersten 2003, 1, 42), the Lower Mekong River, which extends from southern Vietnam, through Cambodia, and into southern Laos, was the cradle of Khmer civilisation. Scholars place the early polities of *Funan* (c. 1st–6th century) in the Delta and *Chenla* (c. 6th–8th century) between Kratie to Champassak (e.g., Heng 2016; Stark 2004; Vickery 1994, 1998). Important Angkorian centres including Bhavapura (Angkor Borei), Vyādhapura (Prei Veng), Indrapura (Kampong Cham), Śambhupura (Kratie), and Liṅgapura (Champassak) flourished along this main artery and its tributaries. The historical origins of Angkor attributed to Jayavarman II (r. c. 790–835) are also indebted to these earlier sites, and subsequent Angkorian rulers often sought to trace their royal genealogies back to these centres along the Mekong (Vickery 1986). On the opposite end of history, the total decline of Cambodia in the 18th and 19th centuries is directly connected to the chokehold on trade flow through the Mekong Delta and its coastal access in Ha Tien (Rach Gia) by competing Thailand and Vietnam (Li 2004a, 131; Rungswasdisab 2004).

Understanding the dynamic of the Mekong region in the Angkorian World entails a diachronic perspective of settlements along both the main river channel and its tributaries from the first millennium CE through the 19th century. For instance, the geographic distribution of Khmer sites through multiple time periods represents a shift in politico-economic interests of the Khmer rulers through time and underscores spatial and cultural limits of Angkor's hegemony across the diverse geographies of mainland Southeast Asia. The epigraphic records of Angkorian rulers also chronicle their efforts to consolidate power in spheres of influence radiating outward from the capital of Angkor, illustrated in Figure 9.1. This chapter

DOI: 10.4324/9781351128940-12

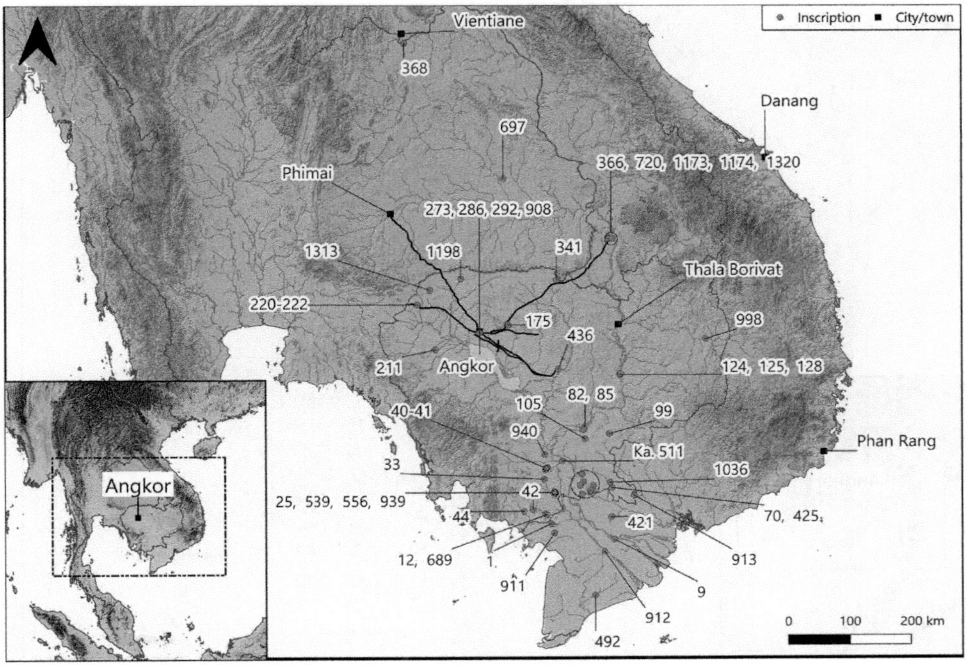

Figure 9.1 Location of inscriptions used in this chapter. Labelled with the inventory K. number, except for Ka 511 from Sre Ampil and a new 11th-century inscription from Thala Borivat.

extrapolates territory locations from the inscriptions and archaeological remains of major Pre-Angkorian and Angkorian centres located along the Mekong River to present their settlement patterns, economic resources, and relationship with Angkor and its rulers through time. To explore the Mekong's integral role in the development of the Angkorian World, we divide the Mekong River between Vientiane and the Delta into three regions: (1) southern region, including the Delta from south Vietnam to the Cambodian plains starting from Kampong Cham; (2) central region from Kampong Cham to Champassak; and (3) northern region from the Champassak region to Vientiane (Figure 9.2). The latter region also includes the Chi-Mun River basin of northeast Thailand, as its historical development from a mixed Mon and Khmer cultural affinities to the later Lao and Thai polities is deeply intertwined (e.g., Lorrillard 2014b, 87).

Occupational History of the Mekong Region

Occupation along the Mekong River is shaped by the natural geographic features within each of the three regions (Groslier 1985; Phann et al. 2007). In the south, sites are distributed across the broad inundated Delta between Saigon and Kampot and progressively converge at Phnom Penh, known also as the Quatre-Bras. North from the Quatre-Bras, the floodplain gradually narrows around the main river channel and the rising topography on either bank serves to constrict occupation toward Champassak. Upstream from Champassak to Vientiane, the settlements are sparsely distributed along the main river channel and major tributaries, including the Chi-Mun, Se Don, Nam Songkhram, and Nam Ngum systems.

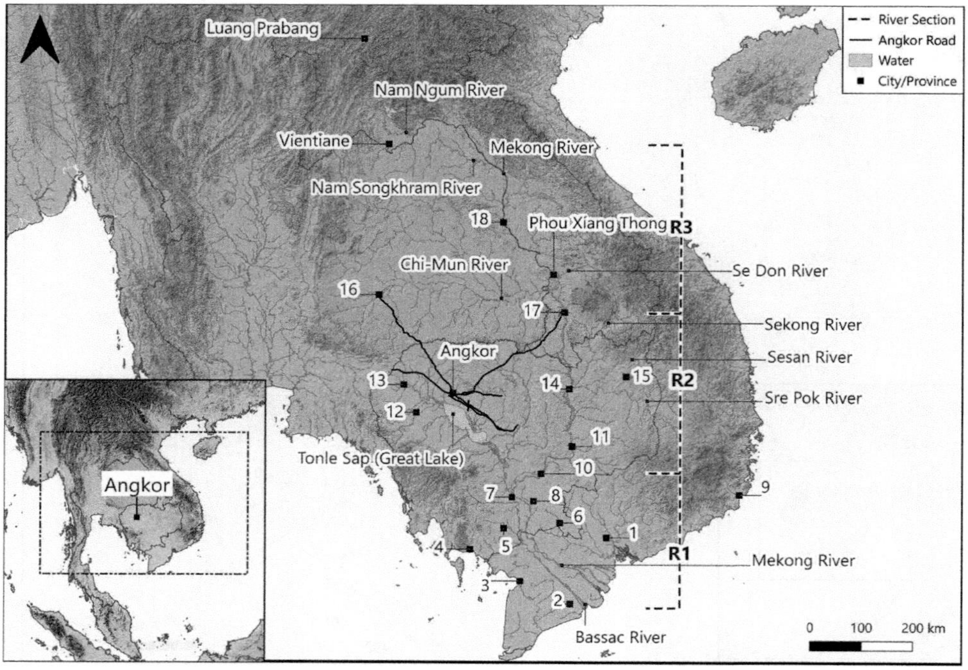

Figure 9.2 The Lower Mekong River region. R1) Southern Region, R2) Central Region, R3) Northern Region. Major cities/towns, tributaries of the Mekong, and river regions discussed in this chapter. 1) Saigon, 2) Soc Trang, 3) Rach Gia, 4) Kampot, 5) Takeo, 6) Svay Rieng, 7) Phnom Penh (Quatre-Bras), 8) Prei Veng, 9) Phan Rang, 10) Kampong Cham, 11) Kratie, 12) Battambang, 13) Banteay Mean Chey, 14) Stung Treng, 15) Ratanakiri, 16) Phimai, 17) Champassak, 18) Savannakhet and Mukdahan.

Source: (GIS data of Angkorian road system; M. Hendrickson).

In contrast to the historic settlement within the Tonle Sap Basin, the evidence along the Mekong River is dominated by remains of Pre-Angkorian brick architecture, a dearth of Angkorian stone monuments, and no evidence of Angkorian roads (e.g., Boisselier 2008; R. L. Brown 1992; Heng 2018; Lavy 2003, 2014; Le 2006; Lorrillard 2013, 2014a, 2014b; Manguin 2009). Only three major Angkorian stone buildings are known across a ca. 600-km stretch of the Mekong River from its Delta to the Laos border below Wat Phu. This scarcity of major Angkorian structures is a product of the geographic interests of Khmer rulers in the Tonle Sap Basin and also because the Pre-Angkorian temple foundations were still functioning during the later period. In some cases, like at Phnom Bayang, we see laterite structures being added to the earlier brick towers (Mauger 1937). A further explanation for the lack of sandstone temples is that the stone sources are exceedingly rare in the Mekong drainage (see Fischer et al. 2023, this volume). Potential support for this geographic scarcity is recorded in the inscription K. 105, 986 CE, from Kampong Cham, which notes an exchange of water buffaloes for laterite to build the temple. Regardless of the infrequent numbers of typical Angkorian temples, areas along Cambodia's Mekong River display evidence for long-term settlement that began at least as early as the late centuries BCE and saw continued use until the present.

Southern Region: The Mekong Delta and Cambodia's Plains

Angkor's interaction to the south extends from the shores of the Delta and follows the Mekong's course northward past Phnom Penh and into the central plain beginning above Kampong Cham town. The Delta was the cradle of the Funan polity (see Figure 9.3) and became the subsequent home for many powerful Angkorian centres/territories, including Vyādhapura, Bhavapura, Aṇinditapura, and Indrapura, the power base of Jayavarman II (r. 790–835?). The Mekong and the smaller Bassac Rivers were the gateway to Cambodia that allowed access to international travellers, from the 3rd-century Chinese emissaries through the 16th–17th-century Portuguese, Japanese, and Dutch traders and missionaries and up to the 19th-century French exploration of the Mekong River (Garnier and Delaporte 1996; Groslier 2006; Ishizawa 2015; Kersten 2003; Pelliot 1903; Zhou 1992[1297]). This section provides evidence of continued occupation within known centres/territories of the Mekong Delta and the continued investment of Khmer rulers from the Pre-Angkor to the Angkor Periods.

Dozens of large and small Angkorian stone and bronze statues (late 9th to 13th c.) found in this region provided the first clues about the region's integration with the Angkorian World (Malleret 1959–1963). Despite the obscurity of settlement data in the Vietnamese Delta caused by agricultural intensification since the 18th century (Li 2004b, 74), colonial reports and recent archaeological work in Cambodia documented numerous Pre-Angkorian and Angkorian sites characterised by mounds, moat-mounds, ponds, temples, and inscriptions across the Delta (e.g., Aymonier 1900; Bruguier and Lacroix 2009; Lajonquière 1902; Malleret 1940, 1959; Manguin

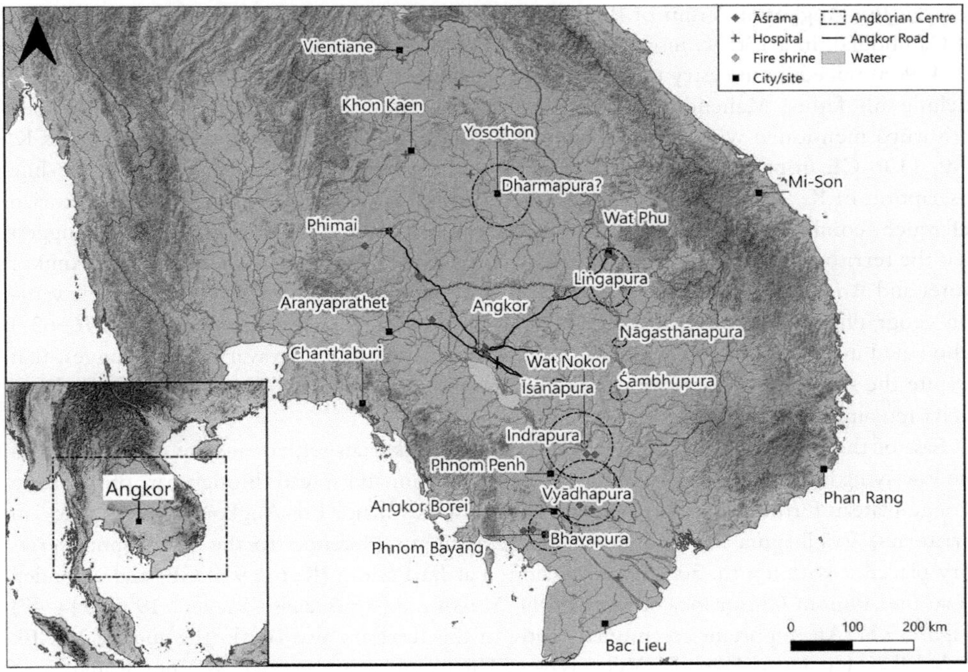

Figure 9.3 Angkorian centres along the Mekong River and state-sponsored temples. The hypothetical location of each centre could fall within each circle, but their exact size is unknown. Known locations of Angkorian Āśrama, fire shrine and selected hospital shrines. Wat Nokor, in Kampong Cham town, is not a fire shrine but housed a Buddhist fire deity.

2009; Parmentier 1916, 1917, 1919, 1920; Phann et al. 2007; Stark 2006; Vo 2003). Settlements in the Delta region are typically concentrated on patches of dry land along small tributaries or canal systems and are rarely located on the banks of the Mekong or Bassac Rivers. Óc Eo and Angkor Borei were the largest centres of the Funan polity but also hosted civic and ceremonial features as early as the 3rd c. BCE (Stark 2006; Stark et al. 2007). This region is also characterised by complex canal systems that radiated out from these centres toward surrounding settlements and were directly connected by a single 80-km-long canal (Groslier 1966; Stark 1998; Bishop et al. 2004; Stark 2006). These canal systems, which predate the Indic-inspired ceremonial structures, provided access from the coast to the Bassac River. This inland system facilitated the interconnection between these settlements and the movement of important items like salt, fish, rice, and other trade goods that persisted through the 19th century (Cooke 2004, 139–46). The discovery of dozens of stoneware kilns at Cheung Ek, c. 5 km south of Phnom Penh, also shows that this was an important area for ceramic production between the 5th to the 13th c. and also had excellent access to trade through the natural and artificial waterways (Phon 2011; Chhay 2008; Grave et al. 2021; Marriner et al. 2018).

The earliest records of the Funan rulers in the Delta are from the Chinese accounts in the 3rd c. CE followed by the local inscriptions of Jayavarman (r. c. 470–514) and Rudravarman (r. 514) (Vickery 2003). These records appeared in the region marked by orange-slipped fineware pottery (c. 200 BCE–200 CE) and suggest the continued importance of this region from the early Historic Period (Heng 2016; Stark and Fehrenbach 2019, 119–24). The inscriptions and temples discovered in the southern zone also provide insights about the locations of early political centres and their respective territories. During the Angkor Period, the colossal Pre-Angkorian Visnu of Phnom Da was called Harikambujendra, 'The Lord Visnu of Cambodia', in a 13th-c. inscription (Bhattacharya 1964; Filliozat 2002). Rājendravarman (944–968) traced his ancestry to the southern centres of Bhavapura and Aṇinditapura. These include his father Mahendravarman from Bhavapura, a fifth-generation ancestor named Viśvarūpa mentioned with a royal shrine (Rājendrāśrama) in the inscriptions K. 556 and K. 830, 1106 CE from Phnom Da, and Bālāditya of Aṇinditapura who appears in a one-line inscription of K. 911 from An Giang (Niu Da) south of Phnom Bayang. These Angkorian references combined with Pre-Angkorian inscriptions (including K. 939 and K. 1) suggest that the territory of Bhavapura and Aṇinditapura may be found in the Delta between Angkor Borei and An Giang (see Vickery 1998, 321–415, 430–432; Pottier 2017, 60 for their varying geographic identification). References to the Pre-Angkorian Īśānavarman (r. 616–637) who ruled from Sambor Prei Kuk and Angkorian rulers through Jayavarman VII suggest that despite the shift of power centre to the Tonle Sap region after the 6th century, the Mekong Delta remained an important area.

East of the Mekong River, Pre-Angkorian and Angkorian settlements are documented in the low-lying area from Saigon through Kampong Cham and spread through part of the Terre Rouge plateau further east. This area hosted at least two major Pre-Angkorian and Angkorian territories, Vyādhapura and Indrapura. The epigraphic references to the Vyādhapura territory placed it within a ca. 50 km radius centred at Ba Phnom (K. 61, 912 CE) and extended to around Phnom Chisor located west of the Mekong River (see also Vickery 1998, 344–47) (Figure 9.3). An important ceremonial centre of this territory was Basak (the ancient Vak Ek or Vakākeśvara) located on the Vaico River. This centre was specified as Vnur Kaṃdvat of Vyādhapura and appeared in Sūryavarman I's oath inscription in Angkor (Cœdès 1942, 142; 1951, 210). Some inscriptions found within this territory suggest that Vyādhapura was a frontier zone with Champa since at least Jayavarman I (r. ca. 657–681). For example, the inscription K. 53 from Prei Veng tells us that a member of the Ādhyapura family was an ambassador to

Champa. Similarly, a 12th-century inscription (K. 1036) from Basak claimed that under Jayavarman I, the author's ancestor went to subdue the Cham (presumably, Phan Rang) and brought 200 war prisoners as an offering to the temple. This information supports Zhou Daguan's observation that the Baria-Saigon (Chen-p'u) area bordered Champa.

Further north of Vyādhapura, another Pre-Angkorian and Angkorian territory of Indrapura incorporated both sides of the Mekong River (Vickery 1998, 414–15) and included the relatively well-preserved and sizable Angkorian structures (11th–13th c.) including the temples of Cheung Ang, Preah Theat Teuk Chha, Kok Yeay Hom, and Wat Nokor. The first is located ca. 35 km east of the Mekong and records Jayavarman IV's endorsement of a joint foundation (K. 99, 932 CE), while the founders of the second and third temples had strong connections with the rulers in Angkor, including Sūryavarman I and Jayavarman VII. The latter temple was another rare example of Jayavarman VII's construction along the Mekong. The locations of these temples and their inscriptions suggest that Pre-Angkorian and Angkorian rulers controlled an area that extended perhaps ca. 35 km or so into the eastern highlands.

The Mekong Delta retained significance to the Angkorian kings who maintained linkages through new endowments to old temples and a few new constructions. Among the known examples are at least seven 9th-century āśramas of Yaśovarman I (889–910) (see Chea et al. 2023, this volume) (Figure 9.3); the temple of Phnom Chisor (Sūryaparvata) built to house one of Sūryavarman I's (1006–1050) four royal *liṅga Suryavarmeśvara*; and the temples of Ta Prohm Bati and Wat Nokor, both rare Jayavarman VII buildings in the Mekong region. Furthermore, Angkorian rulers including Indravarman (878–889), the little-known Tribhūvanādityavarman (r. 1166–1177) (K. 418, 1166 CE from Phnom Svam/Nui Sam in Chau Doc), and Jayavarman VII (r. 1181–1218) made donations to multiple temples across the Mekong Delta. The furthest example, the inscription from Bac Lieu (K. 492, 892 CE), records the endowment by Yaśovarman to a temple near the coast of the Mekong Delta in Vietnam. These acts demonstrate Angkor's continued interest in asserting itself in the south and the trade connections flowing through the South China Sea (see Stark and Cremin 2023, and Stark and Manguin 2023, this volume).

Central Region: A Transitional Ecological System

The central region of the Lower Mekong Basin sees the seasonal floodplain gradually restricted to within approximately 1 km of the river and a landscape transition from young alluvial soils to the upland Terres Rouges (Mekong River Commission 2005). A myriad of small- and medium-sized secondary rivers converge with one another before releasing their water into the Mekong, including the Sekong-Sesan-Sre Pok system of northeast Cambodia, the Se Don and Sekong-Sesu system of southeast Laos, and the Chi-Mun system of the Khorat Plateau of northeast Thailand. The lands beyond the river are historically home to various non-Khmer ethnic groups practising swidden agriculture in the deep forest (Guérin 2001). Discovery of collapsed Pre-Angkorian structures, statuary, and inscriptions deep inland along the Sesan River in Cambodia as well as the Se Don and the Sekong Rivers in Laos indicates that the Khmers did move into these forested areas along the natural waterways (Bruguier and Lacroix 2017; Heng 2016, 2018; Lorrillard 2013, 2014b; Parmentier 1927). However, the majority of Pre-Angkorian and Angkorian communities were located within the narrow river floodplains and formed the heartland for Cambodia's second major Pre-Angkorian polity, known from the Chinese accounts as Chenla (Vickery 1994).

One of the earliest rulers of Chenla, Citrasena-Mahendravarman (r. ca. 598–615), left inscriptions along the Mekong River from Kratie through Wat Phu and into the Khorat plateau along the Chi-Mun system. Historical evidence indicates that the riverine centres of this region were gateways to the eastern highlands, historically inhabited by various non-Khmer ethnic groups, extending into the coastal polities of Champa located in central Vietnam (e.g., Goodall and Jacques 2014; Kersten 2003; Southworth and Tran 2019). The primary occupations in this region are clustered around the prominent sites of Sambor, Thala Borivat, and Wat Phu (Heng 2018). Sambor corresponds to the ancient Śambhupura and became a major centre during the 8th c., when it was ruled by three successive queens (K. 124, 803 CE). Angkor's first king, Jayavarman II, entered into a marriage alliance with one of these queens; later kings, Yaśovarman and Rājendravarman, both claimed that a branch of their ancestors was ruler of Śambhupura, which further reinforces this region's long-held importance as an ancestral homeland for Khmer sovereigns (see discussion in Dupont 1943; Vickery 1994, 208–9). Other forms of political connection to this region took the form of royal edicts governing the management rights of temple properties between the reigns of Jayavarman V (r. 968–1001) and Jayavarman VII (r. 1181–1218) (Osborne 1966).

North of Sambor, the locality of Thala Borivat (Stung Treng), located at the confluence of the Mekong, Sre Pok, and Sesan Rivers, was another major Pre-Angkorian centre ruled by a family member of Bhavavarman I (r. c. 600) and Citrasena-Mahendravarman. Occupation evidence concentrated around this natural transportation nexus corresponds to Nāgasthānapura of a 10th-century inscription K. 436 from Sambor Prei Kuk. A new 11th-century inscription referring to a royal edict granting a rice tax exemption for a local temple also confirms that Thalaborivat was firmly integrated with Angkor (see Heng 2018).

Located above the Mekong's Khone rapids in southern Laos, Wat Phu (Liṅgapura) held a unique status among the Khmer, as its linga-shaped mountain peak housed the Angkorian national god, Śiva Bhadreśvara. By the 7th c. CE the worship of Liṅgapura was so popular that a royal edict by an unnamed ruler directed that its cult be replicated at Prasat Neak Buos (K. 341, 674 CE), a site located ~100 km southwest along one of Angkor's main roads (Hendrickson 2011). This important temple served as a focal point for religious pilgrimage since the 5th c. (see Heng and Sahai 2023, this volume), and inscriptions of Pre-Angkorian ruler Citrasena-Mahendravarman (K. 1173 & K. 1174) record that it was ruled by his father and uncle (Lorrillard 2014b, 206). Unlike other centres along the Mekong, Wat Phu has multiple Angkorian sandstone and laterite structures—including two of Yaśovarman's 9th c. āśramas (see Chea et al. 2023, this volume)—and Angkor's kings repeatedly placed epigraphic dedications here through to the 13th c. (Hawixbrock 2010).

Similar to the Southern Region, the Central Region hosted at least three Pre-Angkorian territories that continued to strive during the Angkor Period. The royal and elite endowments, temple constructions, validations of land rights, and tax incorporate the population of this region to Angkor; so too do the small chapels of the Bayon temple that housed provincial gods, including those from Śambhupura and Nāgasthānapura.

Northern Region: Beyond the Khmer Land

The northern section of the Lower Mekong is characterised by an increasingly rocky riverbed, constriction of lowland areas on both banks, and a steeper rise in overall elevation. This setting, especially through the Phou Xieng Thong (Laos)/Pha Taem (Thailand) mountains to Savannakhet/Mukdahan, limits the amount of cultivable land to narrow pockets of floodplain extending just a few hundred metres from the river and create multiple dangerous rapids that hinder significant commercial river traffic (see Garnier and Delaporte 1996; MCR 2005). These factors may explain the limited evidence of settlements of this main river section and how they only reappear in a relatively large plain from Savannakhet to Vientiane, c. 120 km upstream from Champassak. The archaeological remains of these settlements link them directly to those of the Khorat Plateau on the west side of the Mekong River.

The significant decrease in Angkorian settlement along the Mekong upstream past Champassak and the lack of any major site indicates a decreasing presence of direct Khmer authority in the region. The earliest Khmer evidence in the Mekong and Chi-Mun Rivers is associated with the spatial distribution of Citrasena-Mahendravarman (r. 598–616) inscriptions across these river systems (Heng 2016, fig. 7). Pre-Angkorian and Angkorian art and inscriptions are generally mixed with the more prominent Buddhist sima stones of the Mon civilisation of the Khorat Plateau (Brown 1992; Murphy 2010; Lorrillard 2014a, 2014b). In the northern region, some Angkorian-inspired urbanism, architecture, and statuary has been documented on both sides of the Mekong River and along its major tributaries like Nam Songkhram in northeast Thailand and the Nam Ngum basin in Vientiane (Lorrillard 2014a, 38; Murphy 2013, fig. 1). The number of mid- to late first-millennium CE sites are not only greater than the later Angkorian sites but are also more evenly distributed along the river (Lorrillard 2014b, 191). Traces of Angkorian occupation do appear in the dry plains surrounding the Chi-Mun tributaries of the Khorat Plateau, but the pre-Jayavarman VII Angkorian remains are quite limited (but see Evans et al. 2016; McNeill and Welch 1991; O'Naghten 2014). Angkorian statuary are found as far north as Luang Prabang but may not be indicative of actual Khmer occupation, as they were likely transported from Vientiane or other sites in the Khorat Plateau (Michel Lorrillard, personal communication).

The close cultural affinities between settlements of the northern region with settlements of the Khorat Plateau suggest that connection to the Angkorian World was made primarily through the interconnected settlement system and land route linking Phimai to Angkor (Hendrickson 2011).

Angkor's Mekong: Influence, Political Control, and Resources

Controlling the Mekong River was critical to the functioning of the Angkorian World. The Pre-Angkorian centres along the Mekong were sources of political and ritual prestige and economic resources for the Angkorian rulers and elites. (Goodall 2019; Heng 2016). Kings attempted to establish their ancestry back to Jayavarman II (r. c. 790–835), the founder of Angkor who ruled the southern centres prior to his conquest of Angkor and multiple Mekong centres, including Bhavapura, Aṇinditapura, Vyādhapura, Indrapura, and Śambhupura (see details in Vickery 1998, 321–408). Territorial claims over the Mekong were marked by royal shrines (*āśrama*), inscriptions, and/or images distributed from Angkor (Chea et al. 2023, and Lowman et al. 2023, this volume; Woodward and Douglas 1994). Two royal liṅgas of Sūryavarman I (r. 1002–1049) are also placed at sites near the riverway, one at Phnom Chisor and the other from an unidentified location likely in Kampong Cham along the Mekong River (see Heng and Sahai 2023, this volume). This king also required provincial dignitaries to make an oath of loyalty and included a region in Svay Rieng of the southern Mekong region (Cœdès 1951, 205–19). Three of Jayavarman VII's late 12th-century hospital shrines have been identified in the Mekong region, from as far south as Vinh-Long and Bayang (K. 912 and K. 12) and as far north as Vientiane (K. 368 from Say Fong), over 900 km apart. Two of this king's major temples, Ta Prohm Bati in Takeo and Wat Nokor in Kampong Cham, were also constructed in the southern zone, and gods including those from the Mekong region were housed in small chapels of the Bayon temple.

Angkor's imprint along the Mekong River is also felt through acts of royal largesse and edicts that stipulated land reassignments and tax responsibilities. Inscriptions scattered across the

Angkorian territory, including those from the Mekong region, detail royal involvement in litigation, petitions, and the validation of land rights and of taxation levies. These records not only affirm the political power of rulers in Angkor but also underscore their efforts in controlling the economic resources of distant centres (e.g., Lustig 2009, 2011; Ricklefs 1967). In the other direction, local elites were eager to claim association with the kings of Angkor, and favours made through genealogical links further strengthened their ability to centralise power within local communities (e.g., Lowman 2013). Inscriptions with this type of content occur in the Mekong region as far south as Bac Lieu in the Delta and up to the Khorat Plateau, suggesting a reciprocal political relationship by which the regional elites eagerly accepted Angkor's power.

Communication, Mobility, and Integration

Khmer rulers and elites were attracted to the Mekong for its economic resources, as conduit to strategic locations and a gateway to the outside world. Despite the navigation challenges caused by a series of rapids north of Kratie that required skilled local skippers (see description provided by the 17th-century Dutch traders in Kersten 2003; Garnier and Delaporte 1996), the Mekong River, its tributaries, the Angkorian roads, and the coastal access formed an interdependent system that provided conduits for moving people and resources across its territories. Mekong settlement was also critical to Khmers for the eastward access it provided to the Cham lands of central Vietnam (e.g., Southworth and Tran 2019).

The inscriptions provide considerable evidence for the interconnection with sites along the Mekong. Texts from the 7th century, for example, connect Angkor Borei to Chanthaburi (via the Ha Tien-Kampot coast) and Aranyaprathet in present-day Thailand (Vickery 1998, 284–88). Another inscription (K. 44, 674 CE) and the locations of Angkorian ruler Yaśovarman's *āśramas* connect the coast of Kampot to Phnom Bayang (K. 11, K. 42, and K. 45). Likewise, the inscription K. 940 near Phnom Penh includes a boat travelling from a temple near Phnom Chisor. Angkorian inscriptions document the travels/pilgrimages made by the elites from Angkor to endow temples in the Mekong Delta like Śivapūra (Phnom Bayang) and Vyādhapūra (Basak and Ba Phnom), as well as local elites going from Vyādhapūra to endow temples in Angkor and northwest Cambodia (e.g., K. 175, 878–987 CE; K. 220, 1002 CE; K. 221, 1009 CE, K. 222 and K. 1198; 1014 CE). Angkorian state ritual processions carried gods from the regional centres to the capital, such as Vīraśkti Buddha from Wat Nokor to Preah Khan (K. 908) and Ta Prohm (K. 273) in Angkor, then to Banteay Chhmar (K. 1313) further northwest on a set schedule [Maxwell 2009, 180–85], and the distribution/endowment of state resources to provincial foundations further suggests an importance of the Mekong to Angkor.

The Mekong centres of Sambor (Śambhupura) and Sambok are also recognised in premodern histories as important access points to upland regions in the east (Kersten 2003; Leclère 1903). The discovery of inscription K. 998 (895–96 CE) found deep in the highlands near the Sre Pok River in Ratanakiri (c. 140 km east of Thala Borivat) suggests that Angkorian people had at least some direct interest in these remote areas, even if they did not necessarily hold direct political control over them. The epigraphic records from Angkor and Champa also suggest that sites along the Mekong were campaign bases for Angkorian armies during conflicts between the two neighbouring civilisations. For example, during the reign of Rājendravarman, his general travelled and endowed temples in the Mekong region from Wat Phu, Thala Borivat, and Śambhupura with war booty (K. 436 from Sambor Prei Kuk). This itinerary indicates that one of his targets was the complex of northern Cham centres near Mi-Son, where a Cham inscription (C95, 1056 CE) records a campaign against Śambhupura staged through highlands (Finot 1904, 945; Vickery 2005, 50–51). Another Cham inscription C38D2 (965 CE) from Po Nagar (central Vietnam) also referred to a Khmer attack of this region, possibly through the same highlands (Schweyer 2005, 114).

Resources of the Mekong River

The diversity of landscapes along the Mekong provided an equally rich array of economic resources that were in high demand by the Angkorian state. Flanking settlements benefited from a wide range of readily available local resources, including cultivated crops to forest products as well as manufactured goods like stoneware ceramics (e.g., Brown 1988; Chandavij 1990; Chhay et al. 2012; Grave et al. 2021; Phon et al. 2013). The Mekong and its tributaries also accommodated the upstream flow of other trade goods from China including copper dishes, gold and silver, silk textile, ceramics, and so on, which were exchanged with the resources taken from the banks of the Mekong and adjacent forests (Zhou 1992[1297], 41, 45). The following sections draw on both the local inscriptions and recent external documents to suggest that the Mekong riverine areas offered Angkorian rulers important resources, including cotton, salt, beeswax, honey, forestry products, mineral resources, and their craft products.

Rice, Fish, and Salt

Replenished by seasonal floods, the fertile land of the Mekong Delta produced several different rice varieties, including rainfed, flood-recession, and floating rice agriculture (Van Liere 1980; Fox and Ledgerwood 1999; Biggs 2003, 81; Goodall 2019, 72). Populations along the Mekong transformed the landscapes to build house mounds, elevated shrines (moat-mounds or horseshoe mounds), and water features like house ponds and canals. These construction technologies have enabled population centres to flourish in Cambodia's Mekong Delta since at least the early first millennium BCE. Residential areas and temples, built atop mounds of soil excavated from ponds and/or moats, are common in this area from at least the 6th c. CE (Malleret 1960; Stark 2006). The epigraphic data indicate that rice and rice fields were the main focus of temple endowments in the Mekong Delta since the 7th c., while property boundaries were sometimes delimited by ponds, many of which were associated with the local elites (Vickery 1998, 306–10). Rice was the primary resource in the Angkorian economy. Chinese accounts claim that there were three annual harvests in Funan during the 3rd century and in 'Cambodia' during the 13th century (e.g., Helmer 1997; Groslier 1979; Stark 2006).

Riverine agriculture was extensive within Pre-Angkorian and Angkorian Cambodia across the Mekong Delta and northward past Phnom Penh and along the Mekong's narrow floodplains upstream beyond Kampong Cham. This rice was taxed by provincial governors from the Delta to Wat Phu through the *khloñ srū/vṛhi,* commissioner of rice (e.g., Ricklefs 1967). European accounts of 17th c. Cambodia indicate that rice from the Delta was Cambodia's most important export commodity; indeed, the Mekong Delta has been the documented 'rice bowl' of Vietnam since the 18th century (Bassett 1962, 49; Li 2004b).

The Mekong River's fish populations, which spawned annually in the Tonle Sap Lake, formed the dietary base for the Angkorian Khmers. The complex hydrological systems of the Mekong region are crucial to fish migration into the Tonle Sap and provide the human populations here with rich fishery and waterfowl resources (e.g., ADB 2004; Baird 2009; Hortle 2007; Hortle et al. 2004; Mao 2004). Despite being represented frequently on temple bas-reliefs (e.g., Roberts 2002; Voeun 2004), the scale and practice of Angkorian fish exploitation is unknown. Fish were historically exploited in the Mekong Delta and exported across Southeast Asia (Cooke 2004, 143–145), but only a single damaged Pre-Angkorian inscription from

Angkor Borei (K. 25) mentions fish capture. Perhaps like sugar palm trees, fish and fish products like *prahok* (fish paste) and dried fish were too mundane to be listed in Angkorian inscriptions. The key ingredient for preserving fish was salt, which was produced in both the Mekong Delta's coastal areas and in salt pans of the Khorat plateau (Aymonier 1895; Hendrickson 2011, 450; Guérin 2001, 41; McNeill and Welch 1991, 329; Zhou 1992[1297], 57). The 11th-century inscription K. 206 from Wat Baset records a commissioner of salt, *kaṃsteṅ trvāc aṃpyal*, who was responsible for obtaining taxes for this commodity. Evidence of further historical taxing is seen in a 7th-century inscription from west of Phnom Penh (K. 940), which records a salt tax being levied from boats that belonged to different temples including Piṅgaleśvara of K. 41 located near Ta Prohm Bati, while salt was offered to a temple at Wat Chamnom near Phnom Chisor (Cœdès 1942, 28). This very southern location would tend to imply a trade in evaporated salt from coastal areas. Zhou (1992, 57) reported that salt evaporation was practised along the coast from Chen-p'u (around Saigon) to Pa-chien (unknown). While the salt evaporation fields are historically located in coastal provinces from Soc Trang and Bac Lieu to Kampot and traded upstream to the Tonle Sap Lake in the early 19th century (Nola Cooke 2004, 145), the deeper origins of this industry are unknown (e.g., Proske et al. 2009).

Honey and Beeswax

Honey is a common ingredient in traditional Khmer medicine (Martin 1983, 150) and—like ginger—an ingredient for ritual foods (Jacob 1993, 285). Along with beeswax, these products were important for endowments to Angkorian temples and were included in the list of supplies for Jayavarman VII's hospitals (Chhem et al. 2023, this volume; Cœdès 1906, 80; Jacob 1993; Martin 1983). The late-13th-century Chinese visitor Zhou Daguan (1992, 41) described beeswax collection, which was generally obtained from tree cavities around the villages and boatloads of large and small bee honeycombs that weighed between 18 and 40 pounds. European traders in the 17th century noted that two of Cambodia's major honey-producing regions were found in the Mekong Delta (Bassett 1962, 46–47; Cooke 2004, 143–144) and the northeast highland areas in Ratanakiri (Kersten 2003, 20).

The Mekong Delta, specifically the area known as Vyādhapura, was the most important source for supplying honey and beeswax to the Angkor region and other sites in northwest Cambodia. A 10th-century CE inscription from Sre Ampil (Ka. 511, 925 CE, unpublished) records a royal edict sanctifying a forest being the god's reserve for bees and honey. Quotas of honey and beeswax were also levied from localities bearing names associated with bees in Vyādhapura (K. 654 from Prei Veng; K. 421 and K. 913 from the Plain of Reeds), while another inscription from northwest Cambodia records an annual endowment of rice and beeswax from settlements again in Vyādhapura (Pou 2001, 250 [stanza 53–55]). An official title of 'commissioner of wax' (*khloñ kalmvan* or Pre-Angkorian *kloñ madhu*) and the royal sanction of the distribution of bee products in the epigraphic records from the Delta (Cœdès 1942, 35; 1953, 270) suggest that beeswax and honey were important to Angkorian economy. This is further supported by the fact that the Khmer name for the modern town of Rach Gia, in Vietnam's Mekong Delta, was *Kramuon Sa* or white/pure beeswax (Malleret 1946, 19).

The highland region in north and eastern Cambodia was another important source of bee products that were traded via the Mekong site of Śambhupura (Guérin 2001; Kersten 2003). Gifts from the Jarai minorities who lived across this region to the 17th–19th century Khmer kings included beeswax blessed with magic (Leclère 1903). In a royal inscription of Śambhupura (K. 124, 804 CE), honey/beeswax was used as an article of exchange for oil and other offerings.

Beeswax and honey, however, were absent from the tax items levied from Liṅgapura (Goodall and Jacques 2014), therefore suggesting that the source of beeswax and honey for Angkor was the region from the Mekong Delta to Kratie. The Angkorian royal edicts on bee's products may indicate state control of its collection and distribution, a practice recorded by European traders in 17th-century Cambodia.

Cotton and Textiles

Cotton-based textiles used by the Angkorian Khmer as clothing, wall coverings, and royal accoutrements were obtained from a variety of sources and were also produced in Cambodia (Green 2000; also Green 2023, this volume). The fertile land and vast water supplies along the Mekong from the Delta to Vientiane provide ideal conditions to grow cotton and was historically planted along the river between Phnom Penh and Kratie as well as in Laos (Kersten 2003, 19–20, 36, 45). Vyādhapura was identified in inscriptions as a locus for Angkorian cotton production, following the 11th-century inscription from Banteay Meanchey that records a person with the title *loñ vrai krapās vyādhapūra*, or 'master of the cotton forest at *Vyādhapura*' (Cœdès 1951, 64). Another toponym (*krapās kañcāh*), or 'Old Cotton', appears in an inscription near Ba Phnom (Cœdès 1964, 131 [line 32]), while the present-day town east of Phnom Chisor is also known as Prei Kabas (cotton forest). The repeated use of cotton toponyms in association with Vyādhapūra represents the importance of this resource to the site and contributed to its prestige in the Delta. Further upstream, a line in the royal inscription from Śambhupura (K. 124, 804 CE) indicates that cotton was offered to a temple in exchange for palm syrup, and a large number of unspecified textiles levied from Liṅgapura (Wat Phu) suggest that sources of raw cotton and textiles were being sourced along the Mekong (Goodall and Jacques 2014, 432 [stanza 64–65]; see also Aymonier 1895; Moura 1883; Guérin 2001). This evidence supports the role of cotton production in the Mekong region from the Delta to Vientiane, which provided a backbone of the Angkorian barter economy.

Forest Products and Mineral Resources

Angkorian centres along the Mekong provided the Khmer with access to a range of forest products and mineral resources to the capital. Materials that the 13th-century visitor Zhou Daguan (1992, 27, 59) described in Angkor, from writing materials to animal skin and rattan mats, were made from materials that came from this region. The upland regions that flanked the Mekong have been historically exploited by different Montagnard minorities for commodities such as animal hides, ivory, gum-lac, beeswax, timber, fragrant wood, gold, and so on (Aymonier 1895; Guérin 2001; Kersten 2003) and likely contributed to the rise of early centres in the area (Hendrickson 2011, 450–52; Osborne 1966, 443–49). These spices, fragrant woods, and animal products (e.g., animal hides, bird feathers, tusks, and horns) were eventually used as taxes for state temples in the capital and in distant provinces, including Lingapura in southern Laos (Goodall and Jacques 2014). Raw minerals like gold and silver could have also come from these regions (Champassak/Attapeu, Stung Treng, Kratie) as nuggets and ingots based on the 10th-century inscription K. 1320 from Wat Phu and more recently from the 17th- to 20th-century accounts (Aymonier 1895; Guérin 2001; Kersten 2003, 21–22). Gold and silver were extremely valuable in the Angkorian World and were used for jewellery (for personal use and deities) and to gild statuary, temples, and palaces, as well as being a symbol of hierarchical status (Boisselier, 353–354; Zhou 1992[1297], 2–13).

Other Resources of the Mekong

Angkorian populations across the lower Mekong region donated vast amounts of local resources like coconuts, areca nuts, cows, and buffalo to their Pre-Angkorian and Angkorian temples (Vickery 1998, 272–306). Areca nuts and leaves remained an important form of donation through the Angkor Period and were recorded in the inscriptions of the Mekong region from the Delta to Sambor. Its recent production centres included the 18th/19th-century My Tho area in the Delta (Li 2004b, 80) and modern-day Kampong Cham (NIS-MoP and MoAFF 2015, 196). Cattle and water buffalo continued to be an important trade article of the Mekong Delta through the 18th–19th century. Other resources, like palm syrup, were articles of donation throughout Cambodia's Mekong regions (e.g., K. 689 [Bayang], K. 99 [Cheung Ang], to K. 124 [Sambor]), and the sugar palm tree itself, which is abundantly grown today across Cambodia (NIS-MoP and MoAFF 2015, 208), was only recorded in place names like 'sugar palm grove' (e.g., K. 9 from Sa Dec) or 'sugar palm pond' (e.g., K. 720, 1006 CE from Wat Phu) along the Mekong (Pou 2004, 209).

The evidence of tax levies and palaeobotanical data indicate that resources from the Mekong centres were crucial to the Angkorian economy and that the ruler's engagement in the management and distribution of these resources was a strategy to assert influence as well as to attract and retain allies and followers. This effort is clearly expressed for example in an inscription from Wat Phu (K. 1320) in which the Angkorian king Īśānavarman II, possibly after subduing a local uprising (stanza 60), converted the tax owed by Liṅgapura to a largess for the god Bhadreśvara.

Conclusions

The Mekong and its tributaries were the primary arteries of the Angkorian World, facilitating communication and resources from the coast to the deep hinterlands. The foundation of Cambodia's premodern and early modern polities from Funan in the Mekong Delta and Pre-Angkorian Chenla in the central section to Angkor and Post-Angkorian polities of the Tonle Sap have always been tied to this important river. Epigraphic and archaeological data identified the major Mekong centres, including Vyādhapura, Bhavapura, Aṇinditapura, and Indrapura, in the southern section and Śambhupura, Nāgasthānapura, and Liṅgapura in the central section. These centres provided Angkor with natural resources from agricultural products, fishery, cotton, bee products, and a multitude of forest resources as well as conduits for Angkor to interact with the upland highland groups in the east and the maritime system of the Delta and beyond.

Epigraphic records over time suggest that reciprocal political relationships existed between the rulers in Angkor and the regional elites of the Mekong region. Angkor's kings substantiated their claim to the throne by claiming ancestry to the ancient sites in this area through the renovation, construction, or endowment of temples. The Mekong elites were also eager to acknowledge the superiority of the rulers in Angkor by recording their reigns and tracing their family connections to enhance their prestige and power at home. Royal edicts and petitions by the local elites to the rulers regarding property, resource management, and tax affairs of elite families found in all of the Mekong centres demonstrate that these populations continued to thrive during the time of Angkor. The early modern characterisation of the 'Cambodia River' proposed a symbolic, if not symbiotic, relationship between the Khmer and the Mekong. This river and its resources nurtured premodern polities in Cambodia from the 'domain conquered from the mud' in Funan in the Mekong Delta (Cœdès 1931, 7 [stanza 7]) to the Angkorian World. In a sense of sad irony, Cambodia's modern decline in power during the 18th and 19th centuries was connected to the loss of the Mekong Delta and when the Mekong River became the boundary between competing Thailand and Vietnam. With current threats from hydroelectric dams along the upper and middle Mekong, Cambodia's survival is once again uncertain.

Inscription references

K.	Reference	K.	Reference	K.	Reference
1	Cœdès, IC vol. VI, 28–30	128	Cœdès, IC vol. II, 87	689	Cœdès, IC vol. VI, 47
9	Cœdès, IC vol. V, 35	175	Cœdès, IC vol. VI, 173	697	Cœdès, IC vol. VII, 94
12	Cœdès, IC vol. VIII, 77	211	Cœdès, IC vol. III, 26	720	Cœdès, IC vol. V, 212
25 or 555	Cœdès, IC vol. II, 18; IC vol. VI, 31	220	Cœdès, IC vol. VI, 225	908	Cœdès1941; Maxwell 2009
33	Cœdès, IC vol. III, 148	221	Cœdès, IC vol. II, 54	911	Cœdès, IC vol. V, 85
40	Cœdès 1931, 8	222	Cœdès, IC vol. III, 61	912	Cœdès, IC vol. VIII
41	Cœdès, IC vol. VI, 32	273	Cœdès 1906, 44	913	Cœdès, IC vol. V, 270
42	Bergaigne, ISCC, LII, 387	286	Cœdès 1909, 467; IC vol. IV, 88	939	Cœdès, IC vol. V, 56
44	Cœdès, IC vol. II, 10	292	Cœdès 1913, 11; IC III, 205	940	Cœdès, IC vol. V, 73
47	Bergaigne, ISCC, LIII, 386	341	Cœdès, IC vol. VI, 23	950	Cœdès, IC vol. VI, 115
53	Barth, ISC, XI, 64	366	Cœdès, IC vol. V, 288	998	Cœdès, IC vol. VIII, 225
57	Bergaigne, ISCC, L, 385	368	Finot 1903	1036	Pou, NIC II-III, 149
61	Bergaigne, ISCC, LXIII; Cœdès, IC VII, 20	421	Cœdès, IC vol. V, 272	1173	Lorrillard 2014b, 206
70	Cœdès, IC II, 58	425	Cœdès, IC vol. II, 142	1174	Lorrillard 2014b, 206
82	J. Filliozat 1969; Maxwell 2009, 181	436	Cœdès, IC vol. IV, 20	1198	Pou 2001, 240
85	Cœdès, IC vol. VII, 28	492	Cœdès, IC vol. II, 80	1313	Maxwell 2009, 155
99	Cœdès, IC vol. VI, 107	549	Cœdès, IC vol. II, 155	1320	Goodall and Jacques, 2014
105	Cœdès, IC vol. VI, 183	556	Cœdès, IC vol. II, 19	Ka. 51	Unpublished
124	Cœdès, IC vol. III, 170	653	Cœdès, IC vol. V, 114	Thala Borivat	Heng 2018, 118 (Kantuy Ko 1)
125	Cœdès 1928, 140	654	Cœdès, IC vol. V, 274		

IC = Cœdès, G., 1937–66, Inscriptions du Cambodge.

ISC = Inscriptions sanscrites du Cambodge; cf. Barth 1885.

ISCC = Inscriptions sanscrites de Campã et du Cambodge; cf. Bergaigne 1893.

NIC = Nouvelles inscriptions du Cambodge, tome I: cf. Pou 1989; tome II-III: cf. Pou 2001; tome IV: cf. Pou 2011.

References

ADB, 2004. *Greater Mekong Subregion Atlas of the Environment.* Manila: Asian Development Bank.

Aymonier, E., 1895. *Voyage dans le Laos.* Vol. 1.2 vols. Paris: Ernest Leroux.

Aymonier, E., 1900. *Le Cambodge: Le Royaume Actuel,* Vol 1. Paris: Ernest Leroux.

Baird, I.G., 2009. Spatial (re)organization and places of the brao in Southern Laos and Northeastern Cambodia. *Singapore Journal of Tropical Geography* 30(3), 298–311.

Barth, A.M., 1885. *Inscriptions sanscrites du Cambodge. Extrait des notices et extraits des manuscrits de la bibliothèque nationale*, Tome 27, 1er partie. Paris: Imprimerie nationale.

Bassett, D.K., 1962. The trade of the English East India Company in Cambodia, 1651–1656. *Journal of the Royal Asiatic Society of Great Britain & Ireland* 94(1–2), 35–61.

Bergaigne, A.M., 1893. *Inscriptions sanscrites de Campā et du Cambodge*. Paris: Imprimerie Nationale.

Bhattacharya, K., 1964. Hari Kambujendra. *Artibus Asiae* 27(1/2), 72–8.

Biggs, D. 2003. Problematic progress: Reading environmental and social change in the Mekong Delta. *Journal of Southeast Asian Studies* 34(1), 77–96.

Bishop, P., D.C.W. Sanderson & M.T. Stark, 2004. OSL and radiocarbon dating of a Pre-Angkorian Canal in the Mekong Delta, Southern Cambodia. *Journal of Archaeological Science* 31(3), 319–36.

Boisselier, J., 2008. A Preangkorian wood Buddha and its Indonesian affinities, in *Studies on the Art of Ancient Cambodia: Ten Articles*, ed. J. Boisselier. Phnom Penh: Reyum Publishing, 329–40.

Brown, R.L., 1992. Indian art transformed: the earliest sculptural styles of Southeast Asia, in *Indian Art and Archaeology*, eds. E.M. Raven & K.R. Van Kooij. Leiden: Brill Publishers, 40–53.

Brown, R.M., 1988. *Khmer Wares. In the Ceramics of South-East Asia: Their Dating and Identification* (2nd ed.) Singapore: Oxford University Press, 41–55.

Bruguier, B. & J. Lacroix., 2009. *Guide archéologique du Cambodge: phnom penh et les provinces méridionales*. Vol. 1. Phnom Penh: Édition Reyum.

Bruguier, B. & J. Lacroix., 2017. *De Thala Borivat à Srei Santhor: le bassin du Mekong*. Vol. 4. Guide archéologique du Cambodge. Phnom Penh: JSRC Printing House.

Chandavij, N., 1990. Ancient kiln sites in buriram province, North-Eastern Thailand, in *Ancient Ceramic Kiln Technology in Asia, University of Hong Kong*, eds. C. Ho. University of Hong Kong: Centre of Asian Studies, 233–44.

Chea, S., J. Estève, D. Soutif & E. Swenson, 2023. Āśramas, shrines and royal power, in *The Angkorian World*, eds. M. Hendrickson, M.T. Stark & D. Evans. New York: Routledge.

Chhay, R., 2008. Khmer ceramic technology: a case study from Thnal Mrech Kiln Site (TMK), Phnom Kulen. Presentation presented at the 12th International Conference of European Association of Archaeologists, Leiden, Netherlands.

Chhay, R., T. Tho. & S. Em, 2020. Guide to understanding Khmer stoneware characteristics, Angkor, Cambodia, in EurASEAA 14 volume II material culture and Heritage. *Papers from the Fourteenth International Conference of the European Association of Southeast Asian Archaeologists*, ed. H. Lewis. Oxford: Archaeopress, 53–62.

Chhem, R. D. Evans, K. Chhom, P. Phlong & P.D. Sharrock, 2023. Education and medicine at Angkor, in *The Angkorian World*, eds. M. Hendrickson, M.T. Stark & D. Evans. New York: Routledge.

Cœdès, G., 1906. La stèle de Ta-Prohm. *Bulletin de l'École française d'Extrême-Orient* 6, 44–86.

Cœdès, G., 1909. L'inscription de Baksei Camkron. *Journal Asiatique* 10, 467–510.

Cœdès, G., 1913. Note sur l'iconographie de Běn Mālā. *Bulletin de l'École française d'Extrême-Orient* 13, 23–8.

Cœdès, G., 1928. Etudes cambodgiennes: XXI. La tradition généalogique des premiers rois d'Angkor d'après les inscriptions de Yaçovarman et de Rājendravarman. *Bulletin de l'École française d'Extrême-Orient* 28, 124–46.

Cœdès, G., 1931. Deux inscriptions sanskrites du Fou-Nan. *Bulletin de l'École française d'Extrême-Orient* 31, 1–12.

Cœdès, G., 1941. IV. La stèle du Práh Khằn d'Ankor. *Bulletin de l'École française d'Extrême-Orient* 41, 255–302.

Cœdès, G., 1937–66. *Inscriptions du Cambodge. Collection de Textes et Documents sur l'Indochine*, vol. I (1937); vol. II (1942); vol. III (1951); vol. IV (1952); vol. V (1953); vol. VI (1954); vol. VII (1964); vol. VIII (1966). Paris: École française d'Extrême-Orient.

Cooke, N., 2004. Water World: Chinese and Vietnamese on the riverine water frontier, from Ca Mau to Tonle Sap (c. 1850–1884), in *Water Frontier: Commerce and the Chinese in the Lower Mekong Region, 1750–1880*, eds. N. Cooke & T. Li. Singapore: Rowman & Littlefield, 139–57.

Crawfurd, J., 1967. *Journal of an Embassy to the Courts of Siam and Cochin China* (1st ed.) (Reprinted with an introduction by D.K. Wyatt. Oxford in Asia Historical Reprints). Kuala Lumpur: Oxford University Press.

Dupont, P., 1943. I. La dislocation du Tchen-la et la formation du Cambodge angkorien (VIIe-IXe siècle). *Bulletin de l'École française d'Extrême-Orient* 43, 17–55.

Evans, C., N. Chang & N. Shimizu, 2016. Sites, survey, and ceramics: settlement patterns of the first to ninth centuries CE in the Upper Mun River Valley, Northeast Thailand. *Journal of Southeast Asian Studies* 47, 438–67.

Filliozat, J., 1969. Une inscription cambodgienne en pāli et en khmer de 1566. *Comptes-rendus des séances de l'Académie des Inscriptions et Belles-Lettres* 113, 93–106.

Filliozat, V., 2002. Une statue de Viśvarūpa au musée de Phnom Penh. *Arts asiatiques* 57, 226–28.

Finot, L., 1903. Note d'épigraphie: II L'inscription sanskrite de Say-fong. *Bulletin de l'École française d'Extrême-Orient* 3, 18–33.

Finot, L., 1904. Notes d'épigraphie XI: Les inscriptions de Mi-so'n. *Bulletin de L'École Française d'Extrême-Orient* 4, 897–977.

Fischer, C.F. Carò & M. Polkinghorne, 2023. From quarries to temples: stone procurement, materiality and spirituality in the Angkorian World, in *The Angkorian World*, eds. M. Hendrickson, M.T. Stark & D. Evans. New York: Routledge, 360–84.

Fox, J. & J. Ledgerwood., 1999. Dry-season flood-recession rice in the Mekong Delta: two thousand years of sustainable agriculture? *Asian Perspectives* 38, 37–50.

Garnier, F. & L Delaporte, 1996. *The Mekong Exploration Commission Report, 1866–1868.* Translated by W.E.J. Tips. Bangkok: White Lotus Press.

Goodall, D. & C. Jacques, 2014. Stèle inscrite d'Īśānavarman II à Vat Phu: K. 1320. *Aséanie* 33, 395–454.

Goodall, D., 2019. Nobles, Bureaucrats or strongmen? On the 'vassal kings' or 'hereditary governors' of Pre-Angkorian city-states: two Sanskrit inscriptions of Vidyāviśeṣa, seventh-century governor of Tamandarapura (K, 1235 and K. 604), and an inscription of Śivadatta (K, 1150), previously considered a son of Īśānavarman I. *UDAYA: Journal of Khmer Studies* 14, 63–85.

Grave, P., L. Kealhofer, K. Phon, P. Heng, M.T. Stark, B. Marsh, D. Ea, R. Chhay & G.P. Marriner, 2021. Centralized power/decentralized production? Angkorian stoneware and the southern production complex of Cheung Ek, Cambodia. *Journal of Archaeological Science* 125, 105270.

Green, G., 2000. Indic impetus? Innovations in textile usage in Angkorian Period Cambodia. *Journal of the Economic and Social History of the Orient* 43, 277–313.

Green, G., 2023. Vogue at Angkor: dress, décor and narrative drama, in *The Angkorian World*, eds. M. Hendrickson, M.T. Stark & D. Evans. New York: Routledge, 508–24.

Groslier, B.P., 1966. The Mekong River in history. *Indian Journal of Power and River Valley Development* 16, 20–70.

Groslier, B.P., 1979. La cité hydraulique Angkorienne: exploitation ou surexploitation du sol? *Bulletin de l'École française d'Extrême-Orient* 66, 161–202.

Groslier, B.P., 1985. For a geographic history of Cambodia. *Seksa Khmer* 8–9, 31–76.

Groslier, B.P., 2006. *Angkor and Cambodia in the Sixteenth Century: According to Portuguese and Spanish Sources* (1st English ed.) Bangkok: Orchid Press.

Guérin, M., 2001. Essartage et riziculture humide. Complémentarité des écosystèmes agraires à Stung Treng au début du XXe siècle. *Aséanie* 8, 35–55.

Hawixbrock, C., 2010. Le Musée de Vat Phu et les Collections Archéologiques de Champassak. *Bulletin de l'École Française d'Extrême-Orient* 97–98, 271–314.

Helmer, K., 1997. Rice in the Cambodian economy: past and present, in *Rice Production in Cambodia: Cambodia-IRRI-Australia Project*, eds. H.J. Nesbitt. Manila: International Rice Research Institute, 1–14.

Hendrickson, M., 2011. A transport geographic perspective on travel and communication in Angkorian Southeast Asia (ninth to fifteenth centuries AD). *World Archaeology* 43: 444–57.

Heng, P. & S. Sahai, 2023. The temple economy of Angkor, in *The Angkorian World*, eds. M. Hendrickson, M.T. Stark & D. Evans. New York: Routledge, 327–37.

Heng, P., 2016. Transition to the Pre-Angkorian period (300–500 CE): Thala Borivat and a regional perspective. *Journal of Southeast Asian Studies* 47, 484–505.

Heng, P., 2018. *Organizational change in political economy and ideology: transition from the Early Historic to Pre-Angkorian Period Cambodia, viewed from Thala Borivat.* PhD dissertation. Honolulu: University of Hawai'i at Mānoa.

Hortle, K.G., 2007. Consumption and yield of fish and other aquatic animals from the lower Mekong Basin (MRC Technical Paper 16). Vientiane, Laos: Mekong River Commission.

Hortle, K.G., S. Lieng & J. Valbo-Jorgensen., 2004. *An Introduction to Cambodia's Inland Fisheries (Mekong Development Series no. 4).* Phnom Penh: Mekong River Commission.

Ishizawa, Y., 2015. The World's oldest plan of Angkor Vat: the Japanese so-called Jetavana, an illustrated plan of the seventeenth century. *UDAYA, Journal of Khmer Studies* 13, 41–57.

Jacob, J.M., 1993. The ecology of Angkor: evidence from the Khmer inscriptions, in *Cambodian Linguistics, Literature and History: Collected Articles*, eds. J.M. Jacob & D.A. Smyth. New York: Routledge, 280–98.

Jacques, C. & D. Goodall, 2014. Stèle inscrite d'Īśānavarman II à Vat Phu (K, 1320). *Aséanie* 33, 405–54.

Kersten, C., 2003. *Strange Events in the Kingdoms of Cambodia and Laos, 1635–1644*. Bangkok: White Lotus Press.
Lajonquière, L. de., 1902. *Inventaire descriptif des monuments du Cambodge*, Vol 1. Paris: Ernest Leroux.
Lavy, P.A., 2003. As in Heaven, so on Earth: the politics of Visnu, Siva and Harihara images in Preangkorian Khmer civilisation. *Journal of Southeast Asian Studies* 34, 21–39.
Lavy, P.A., 2014. Conch-on-hip images in Peninsular Thailand and Early Vaiṣṇava sculpture in Southeast Asia, in *Before Siam: Essays in Art and Archaeology*, eds. N. Revire & S.A. Murphy. Bangkok: River Books, 153–73.
Le, T.L., 2006. *Nghệ thuật Phật giáo và Hindu giáo ở Đồng bằng sông Cửu Long trước thế kỷ X (Buddhist and Hindu Art in the Cuu Long river Delta prior to 10th century A.D.)*. Hanoi: Thế Giới Publishers.
Leclère, A., 1903. Mémoire sur une charte de fondation d'un monastère bouddhique où il est question du roi du Feu et du roi de l'Eau. *Comptes rendus des séances de l'Académie des Inscriptions et Belles-Lettres* 47, 369–78.
Li, T., 2004a. Ship and shipbuilding in Mekong Delta, c., 17450–1840, in *Water Frontier: Commerce and the Chinese in the Lower Mekong Region, 1750–1880*, eds. N. Cooke & T. Li. Singapore: Rowman & Littlefield, 119–35.
Li, T., 2004b. The late-eighteenth- and early-nineteenth-century Mekong Delta in the regional trade system, in *Water Frontier: Commerce and the Chinese in the Lower Mekong Region, 1750–1880*, eds. N. Cooke & T. Li. Singapore: Rowman & Littlefield, 71–84.
Lorrillard, M., 2013. Par-delà Vat Phu: Données nouvelles sur l'expansion des espaces khmer et môn anciens au Laos. *Bulletin de l'École française d'Extrême-Orient* 97–98 (for 2010–2011), 205–70.
Lorrillard, M., 2014a. La plaine de Vientiane au tournant du second millénaire. Données nouvelles sur l'expansion des espaces Khmer et môn anciens au Laos (II). *Bulletin de l'École française d'Extrême-Orient* 100, 38–107.
Lorrillard, M., 2014b. Pre-Angkorian communities in the Middle Mekong Valley (Laos and adjacent areas), in *Before Siam: Essays in Art and Archaeology*, eds. N. Revire & S.A. Murphy. Bangkok: River Books, 187–215.
Lowman, I., 2013. The elephant hunt of Jayavarman III: a political myth of Angkorian Cambodia. *UDAYA, Journal of Khmer Studies* 11, 29–57.
Lowman, I., K., Chhom & M. Hendrickson, 2023. An Angkor nation? Identifying the core of the Khmer Empire, in *The Angkorian World*, eds. M. Hendrickson, M.T. Stark & D. Evans. New York: Routledge, 479–93.
Lustig, E., 2009. *Power and pragmatism in the political economy of Angkor*. PhD dissertation. Sydney: The University of Sydney.
Lustig, E., 2011. Using inscription data to investigate power in Angkor's Empire. *Aséanie* 27, 35–66.
Malleret, L., 1940. Chronique. *Bulletin de l'École française d'Extrême-Orient* 40(2), 465–505.
Malleret, L., 1946. La minorité cambodgienne de Cochinchine. *Extrait du bulletin de la société des études indochinoises* 21, 18–34.
Malleret, L., 1959. *L'archéologie du delta du Mékong. Vol. 1. L'exploration archéologique et les fouilles d'Óc-Èo*. Paris: École française d'Extrême-Orient.
Malleret, L., 1960. *L'archéologie du delta du Mékong. Vol. 2. L'exploration archéologique et les fouilles d'Óc-Èo*. Paris: École française d'Extrême-Orient.
Malleret, L., 1963. *L'archéologie du delta du Mékong. Vol. 4. L'exploration archéologique et les fouilles d'Óc-Èo*. Paris: École française d'Extrême-Orient.
Manguin, P., 2009. The archaeology of Fu Nan in the Mekong River Delta: The Óc Eo culture of Viet Nam, in *Arts of Ancient Viet Nam: From River Plain to Open Sea*, ed. N. Tingley. New York: Asia Society, 103–275.
Mao, K., 2004. Biodiversity of Cambodia's Wetlands, in *Wetlands Management in Cambodia: Socioeconomic, Ecological and Policy Perspectives*, eds. M. Torrell, A.M. Salamanca & B.D. Ratner. WorldFish, 14–16.
Marriner, G.P., P. Grave, L. Kealhofer, M.T. Stark, D. Ea, R. Chhay, P. Kaseka & B.S. Tan., 2018. New dates for old kilns: a revised radiocarbon chronology of stoneware production for Angkorian Cambodia. *Radiocarbon* 60, 901–24.
Martin, M.A., 1983. Elements de médecine traditionelle khmer. *Seksa Khmer* 6, 135–70.
Mauger, H., 1937. III. Le Phnom Bàyàn. *Bulletin de l'École française d'Extrême-Orient* 37, 239–62.
Maxwell, T.S., 2009. A new Khmer and Sanskrit inscription at Banteay Chhmar. *UDAYA, Journal of Khmer Studies* 10, 135–201.
McNeill, J.R. & D.J. Welch., 1991. Regional and interregional exchange on the Khorat Plateau. *Bulletin of the Indo-Pacific Prehistory Association* 10, 327–40.

Mekong River Commission, 2005. *Overview of the Hydrology of the Mekong Basin.* Vientiane: Mekong River Commission.

Moura, J., 1883. *Le Royaume du Cambodge.* 2 volumes. Paris: Ernest Leroux.

Murphy, S.A., 2010. *The Buddhist boundary markers of Northeast Thailand and Central Laos, 7th–12th centuries CE.* PhD dissertation. London: School of Oriental and African Studies, University of London.

Murphy, S.A., 2013. Buddhism and its relationship to Dvaravati period settlement patterns and material culture in Northeast Thailand and Central Laos c. sixth–eleventh centuries A.D.: a historical ecology approach to the landscape of the Khorat Plateau. *Asian Perspectives* 52, 300–26.

NIS-MoP & MoAFF, 2015. *Census of Agriculture in Cambodia 2013: National Report on Final Census Results.* Phnom Penh: National Institute of Statistics (NIS), Ministry of Planning (MoP) in collaboration with the Ministry of Agriculture, Forestry and Fisheries (MoAFF).

O'Naghten, H.M., 2014. The organisation of space in Pre-Modern Thailand under Jayavarman VII, in *Before Siam: Essays in Art and Archaeology*, eds. N. Revire & S.A. Murphy. London: River Books, 397–419.

Osborne, M., 1966. Notes on Early Cambodian provincial history: Isanapura & Sambhupura. *France-Asie/Asia* 86, 433–39.

Parmentier, H., 1916. Cartes de l'Empire khmèr d'après la situation des inscriptions datées. *Bulletin de l'École française d'Extrême-Orient* 16, 69–73.

Parmentier, H., 1917. Chronique. *Bulletin de l'École française d'Extrême-Orient* 17(1), 35–57.

Parmentier, H., 1919. Chronique: Indochine française. *Bulletin de l'École française d'Extrême-Orient* 19, 87–127.

Parmentier, H., 1920. Borne inscrite de My-hu'ng. *Bulletin de l'École française d'Extrême-Orient* 20, 1–2.

Parmentier, H., 1927. *L'art khmèr primitif. 2 vols. Publications de l'École française d'Extrême-Orient.* Paris: Librairie nationale d'art et d'histoire.

Pelliot, P., 1903. Le Funan. *Bulletin de l'École française d'Extrême-Orient* 3, 248–327.

Phann, N., N. Chrin, S. Chan, C. Chamroeun & B. Bruguier, 2007. *Carte archéologique du Cambodge.* Phnom Penh: Ministère de la culture et des beaux-arts—École française d'Extrême-orient.

Phon, K., 2011. Archaeology and cultural resource management south of Phnom Penh, Cambodia, in *Rethinking Cultural Resource Management in Southeast Asia: Preservation, Development, and Neglect*, eds. J.N. Miksic, G.Y. Goh & S. O'Connor. London; New York: Anthem Press, 123–42.

Phon, K., R. Chhay, V. Voeun, V. Chhum, S. Khin & M.F. Dega, 2013. *The Ceramic Production Centre of Cheung Ek, Phnom Penh, Kingdom of Cambodia. Internal Report.* Phnom Penh: Royal Academy of Cambodia, Institute of Culture and Fine Arts.

Pottier, C., 2017. Nouvelles données sur les premières cités angkoriennes, in *Deux décennies de coopération archéologique franco-cambodgienne à Angkor*, eds. A. Beschaouch, F. Verellen & M. Zink. Paris: L'Académie des Inscriptions et Belles-Lettres, 43–80.

Pou, S., 2001. *Nouvelles inscriptions du cambodge. Vol. 2 & 3.* Paris: École française d'Extrême-Orient.

Pou, S., 2004. *Dictionnaire Vieux Khmer-Français-Anglais = An Old Khmer-French-English Dictionary = Vacanānukram Khmaer Cās-Pārāṃṅ-Qaṅles.* Paris, France: L'Harmattan.

Proske, U., D. Heslop & T.J.J. Hanebuth, 2009. Salt production in Pre-Funan Vietnam: archaeomagnetic reorientation of briquetage fragments. *Journal of Archaeological Science* 36, 84–9.

Ricklefs, M.C., 1967. Land and the law in the epigraphy of tenth-century Cambodia. *The Journal of Asian Studies* 26, 411.

Roberts, T.R., 2002. Fish scenes, symbolism and kingship in the bas-reliefs of Angkor Wat and the Bayon. *National History Bulletin of the Siam Society* 50, 135–93.

Rungswasdisab, P., 2004. Siam and the contest for control of the trans-Mekong trading networks from the late eighteenth to the mid-nineteenth centuries, in *Water Frontier: Commerce and the Chinese in the Lower Mekong Region, 1750–1880*, eds. N. Cooke & T. Li. Singapore: Rowman & Littlefield, 101–18.

Schweyer, A., 2005. Po Nagar de Nha Trang (seconde partie). Le dossier épigraphique. *Aséanie*, 15, 87–119.

Southworth, W. & K.P. Tran, 2019. The discovery of late Angkorian Khmer sculptures at Campa Sites and the overland trade routes between Campa and Cambodia, in *Champa: Territories and Networks of a Southeast Asian Kingdom*, eds. A. Griffiths, A. Hardy & G. Wade. Paris: École Française d'Extrême-Orient, 323–42.

Stark, M.T. & A. Cremin, 2023. Angkor and China: 9th–15th centuries, in *The Angkorian World*, eds. M. Hendrickson, M.T. Stark & D. Evans. New York: Routledge, 112–32.

Stark, M.T. & P.-Y. Manguin, 2023. The Mekong Delta before the Angkorian World, in *The Angkorian World*, eds. M. Hendrickson, M.T. Stark & D. Evans. New York: Routledge, 64–79.

Stark, M.T. & S. Fehrenbach, 2019. Earthenware ceramic technologies of Angkor Borei, Cambodia. *UDAYA, Journal of Khmer Studies* 14, 109–35.

Stark, M.T., 1998. The transition to history in the Mekong Delta: a view from Cambodia. *International Journal of Historical Archaeology* 2(3), 175–203.

Stark, M.T., 2004. Pre-Angkorian and Angkorian Cambodia, in *Southeast Asia from Prehistory to History*, eds. I. Glover & P. Bellwood. London and New York: RoutledgeCurzon, 89–119.

Stark, M.T., 2006. Pre-Angkorian settlement trends in Cambodia's Mekong Delta and the Lower Mekong Archaeological Project. *Journal of Indo-Pacific Archaeology* 26, 98–109.

Stark, M.T., D. Sanderson & R.G. Bingham, 2007. Monumentality in the Mekong Delta: luminescence dating and implications. *Bulletin of the Indo-Pacific Prehistory Association* 26, 110–20.

Van Liere, W.J., 1980. Traditional water management in the Lower Mekong Basin. *World Archaeology* 11, 265–80.

Vickery, M., 1986. Some remarks on early state formation in Cambodia, in *Southeast Asia in the 9th to 14th Centuries*, eds. D.G. Marr & A.C. Milner. Singapore: Institute of Southeast Asian Studies, 95–116.

Vickery, M., 1994. What and where was Chenla? in *Recherches Nouvelles Sur Le Cambodge*, publié sous la direction de F. Bizot. Paris: École française d'Extrême-Orient, 197–212.

Vickery, M., 1998. *Society, Economics, and Politics in Pre-Angkor Cambodia: The 7th–8th Centuries*. Tokyo: Centre for East Asian Cultural Studies for UNESCO, Toyo Bunko.

Vickery, M., 2003. Funan reviewed: deconstructing the ancients. *Bulletin de l'École Française d'Extrême-Orient* 90–91, 101–43.

Vickery, M., 2005. Champa revised. Asia Research Institute, National University of Singapore. www.ari.nus.edu.sg/docs/wps/wps05_037.pdf.

Vo, S.K., 2003. The Kingdom of Fu Nan and the culture of Óc Eo, in *Art & Archaeology of Fu Nan: Pre-Khmer Kingdom of the Lower Mekong Valley*, eds. J.C.M. Khoo. London: Orchid Press, 35–86.

Vouen, V., 2004. Description of bas-relief carvings of fish at Angkor Wat and Bayon. *Bulletin of the Students of the Department of Archaeology* 3, 39–56.

Woodward, H.W. & J.G. Douglas, 1994. The Jayabuddhamahānātha images of Cambodia. *The Journal of the Walters Art Gallery*, 105–11.

Zhou, D., 1992[1297]. *The Customs of Cambodia*. Trans. P. Pelliot & J. G. D. Paul. Bangkok: Siam Society.

10

TRAJECTORIES OF URBANISM IN THE ANGKORIAN WORLD

Damian Evans, Roland Fletcher, Sarah Klassen, Christophe Pottier and Pelle Wijker

Since the first accounts of 19th-century explorers, structures like Angkor Wat have been considered the focal point of 'temple-cities,' but the size, structure, and population of those cities have, until recently, been topics of debate and disagreement. The core problem is that urban complexes of the Angkorian World were made almost entirely of perishable materials that disappeared centuries ago, leaving behind the religious monuments of stone and brick that have engaged most of the public and scholarly attention.

Nonetheless, archaeologists have been taking to the skies over Angkor for nearly a century to document the traces of urban and agricultural elements that remain inscribed into the surface of the landscape. In the last ten years, lidar technology has helped to fill in the remaining lacunae in our cartography of these landscapes, and after a century and a half of survey and mapping, we have arrived at a series of archaeological maps of Angkorian settlement complexes that are unlikely to change substantially in the future. Very extensive and systematic ground-based surveys have complemented aerial perspectives to document time-diagnostic material such as ceramics, and all of this information has been federated within massive geospatial databases. Our newly comprehensive spatial awareness of places like Angkor has been used to more effectively target excavations and other research initiatives on the ground, adding time depth and granular detail in key locations.

For perhaps the first time, therefore, archaeologists are well positioned to trace the development of Khmer settlement complexes across time and space, from prehistory through the Angkor Period and into the contemporary world. In this chapter, we re-evaluate conventional theories of urban development in the Khmer milieu, which typically define a neat transition between moated prehistoric sites and well-planned, rectilinear, and cardinally oriented settlements and gridded 'hydraulic cities' that define the Angkor Period. Instead, we identify multiple pathways to urban and agricultural complexity that produced a diverse range of settlement patterns across the Khmer Empire. Moated prehistoric sites are, in fact, exceedingly rare in northwest Cambodia; furthermore, the early urban complexes of the Angkor Period are, in many cases, not rigidly planned or enclosed spaces and are better characterised as 'open cities.' At the height of the Angkor Period, it is possible to identify formally planned and gridded urban areas which accord with long-standing views about 'temple-cities'; however, these typically turn out to be the epicentres of extended, lower-density urban landscapes that were patchworks of open spaces, agricultural systems, and residential areas (see Hawken and Klassen 2023, this volume).

DOI: 10.4324/9781351128940-13

In this chapter, we trace the history of archaeological approaches to Khmer urbanism and assess the current state of knowledge about the development of Khmer urbanism over the past two millennia. We then use spatial analytics to offer preliminary assessments of the area, population, and density of settlements and how those changed over time and space. We argue that the new data provide important insights into the historical trajectory of the Khmer Empire and that, more broadly, the scale and structure of Angkorian settlement patterns challenge us to think differently about the nature of early urbanism in tropical environments Worldwide.

Evolving Perspectives From the 19th to 21st Centuries

Epigraphy

As detailed elsewhere in this volume (see e.g. contributions by Soutif, Estève, Goodall, and Lustig), the inscriptional record of the Angkorian World has been the focus of intensive study since the very beginning of scholarship in the 19th century and has long been the cornerstone for our understanding of the Angkorian World. The corpus of inscriptions offers us a wide array of toponyms describing lived-in spaces at various scales (see Table 11.1 in Hawken and Klassen 2023, this volume). However, the nature and size of settlements described by categories in the Sanskrit and Old Khmer languages such as *pura* (typically translated as 'cities') are open to interpretation and debate (Lewitz 1967), with each category likely encompassing habitation areas that varied widely in terms of population, morphology, and spatial extent. It is also likely that these categories had considerable overlap between them and that their meanings were not fixed or standardised but varied significantly over space and time.

It is, therefore, very difficult to infer or reconstruct indigenous conceptions of 'urban' and 'non-urban' space from the inscriptional record, and linguists have tended to rely on apparent links between words in Old Khmer and their present-day equivalents. An example of the ambiguity that arises from this is seen in the Ta Prohm inscription (Cœdès 1906), which refers to donations to the temple from 3140 '*grama*', a word almost universally interpreted in the literature on Angkor as a 'village' (see e.g. Higham 2001, 271), implying some kind of discrete urban settlement which, presumably, ought to be identifiable in the archaeological record.

However, a closer review of the literature reveals that the word *grama* is, in fact, rather ambiguous and has no precise correlate in Khmer (Lewitz 1967, 404). The simple working assumption is that it is equivalent to the Khmer word *sruk*, meaning village, although here, too, there is some uncertainty about the meaning of that word in the ancient context (Lewitz 1967, 404–46). Suppose we adopt Mabbett's (1978, 23) interpretation that *sruk* defines a division of territory where a religious foundation is set up and a community grows. In that case, we may expect—as in present-day Cambodia—an extremely broad spectrum of real-world correlates in the geography of Angkorian urbanism, from multiple overlapping *sruk* in dense urban areas on the one hand to remote and isolated village outposts on the other. Therefore, it is difficult to reliably reconstruct urban geography or demography using inscriptions, and, as Maxwell (2007, 67) has noted in relation to the Preah Khan inscription, attempts to do so can result in confusing, improbable outcomes.

Given the uncertainty and imprecision within the contemporary historical record of the Angkorian World, researchers have relied instead on material remains for evidence of habitation, but this too presents a series of problems, above all the fact that houses of stone were reserved by and large for divinities and that the vast majority of the material used for other kinds of dwellings was non-durable and has not survived to the present day (Coe and Evans 2018). This is true across essentially all of Southeast Asia (Higham 2014), and therefore domestic contexts are very rarely discovered in the region, including in the Angkorian World (see Carter et al. 2023, this volume). Nonetheless, recent work has emphasised that traces of neighbourhoods stretching between and beyond the temples do remain (Fletcher and Pottier 2002). It is worth briefly surveying how urban form at Angkor and beyond has 'emerged' from scholarship over the last 150 years as theoretical perspectives have changed and as innovations in flight and imaging technologies have gradually enabled more detailed views of urban form.

The Earliest Work: Temples and Enclosures

Among the defining features of colonialism was a competition between great powers for possession of exceptional historical monuments, and present-day territorial claims were strengthened through systematic inventorisation and study of heritage sites across the widest possible range of time and space. In Southeast Asia, as elsewhere, an explicitly 'scientific' approach to the study of monuments, artefacts, and inscriptions had emerged and become institutionalised by the beginning of the 20th century (Edwards 2005, 2008; Evans 2007; Falser 2019; Pottier 2006). This work was also essential for establishing the basic framework of Khmer society, including the chronology of its kings and temples, the periodisation of architectural and art historical styles, and the broad contours of its religious and political history within a regional and global context. As Carter et al. (2018) note, there is an assumption throughout this scholarship that the areas within enclosure walls comprise 'temple-cities', despite an absence of compelling evidence.

This focus on the more durable remains of elites continues to predominate in the study of Angkor today, but in early 20th-century scholarship, it was the lens through which almost all new information on Angkor was considered. With the advent of flight, for example, the discipline of aerial archaeology emerged after World War I, and scholars began to trace the subtle traces of human activity inscribed into the surface of the landscape that could only be clearly seen from above (Barber 2017). By the 1930s, scholars associated with the EFEO were regularly flying over Angkor and noting previously undocumented traces of habitation between and beyond the temples, such as depressions and mounds, which were mapped in significant detail (Evans 2007). Ultimately, however, work in this era remained relentlessly focused on defining the footprints of temples and their associated enclosures. The maps that were produced were not published until more than half a century later (Pottier 2006; Pottier and Dumarçay 1993), and an emerging tradition of aerial archaeology in Southeast Asia failed to gain traction or achieve the recognition of kindred traditions in Europe and the Middle East (Evans 2007, 66–67).

The Mid-20th Century: Subsistence, Environment, and Landscape

By the mid-20th century, new perspectives in anthropology—in particular the rise of environmental and landscape archaeology, in which long-term human-environment interactions became a core focus of research—began to impact Angkorian studies with the work of Malleret, Groslier, and others at the EFEO. In addition to ad hoc collections of aerial images collected by Williams-Hunt and others (Moore 2009), researchers for the first time had access to comprehensive and systematic aerial coverage of the landscape thanks to missions undertaken by the French *Institut géographique national* (IGN). Alongside these technical innovations, in the newly emerging discipline of 'settlement archaeology', they had the rudiments of a theoretical agenda in which the study of residential and agricultural activity within and beyond the temples not only made sense but was critically important. On the ground, this work was pioneered by Bernard-Philippe Groslier, who explicitly acknowledged the need to refocus on networks of habitation, assisted by aerial remote sensing (1952).

Groslier set in motion an ambitious program of archaeological research to fulfil this potential but was forced to abandon the project in the early 1970s with the rise of civil war in Cambodia. Although he had very clearly identified what we now recognise as the building blocks of Angkorian urbanism—occupation mounds, communal ponds, linear traces such as roads and canals, community temple foundations—his work on this subject remained mostly unpublished until long after his death (Groslier 1998). Having fled Cambodia for France, he focused his later work on the development of a theoretical approach that continues to resonate in present-day studies of Khmer urbanism and has attracted much controversy: the 'hydraulic city' hypothesis (Groslier 1979).

Urban Infrastructure: Functional or Symbolic?

Although the 'hydraulic city' thesis is most closely associated with a definitive 1979 paper on the subject, its origins can be traced back to work by Goloubew (1941), and Groslier spent nearly three decades elaborating the theory over a series of publications (Evans 2007). Ironically, despite the name, the theory has relatively little to say about the nature of Angkorian urbanism, focusing instead on the role of irrigated rice agriculture and multi-cropping as the source of Angkor's wealth and, thanks to its environmental impacts, a factor in the weakening of the Khmer state and its capitulation to a Siamese invasion in the 15th century. Other chapters deal sufficiently with the 'hydraulic city' thesis and its discontents (see Lustig et al. 2023 and Hawken and Castillo 2023, this volume), but in terms of the development of ideas about urbanism, it embodies two major developments. The first was the idea that Angkor is more than just a ritual-ceremonial landscape consisting of monuments and enclosures—the 'temple-cities' that have remained a staple of the literature on Angkor since the 1800s—but includes an extended network of infrastructure that remained deeply embedded in the urban fabric for many centuries (Groslier 1956, 1958).

The second point that both Goloubew and Groslier were keen to reinforce was that the hydraulic infrastructure had a 'double aspect'. Although it was clearly part of a sacred geography that embodied specific magico-religious ideals, it also served practical and utilitarian purposes, such as providing arteries for movement and communication and ameliorating the sharp seasonality of water supply in the urban context (Evans 2007). This nuance has often been lost in subsequent scholarship, much of which seeks to discredit the 'hydraulic city' hypothesis on the grounds that the water network was ritual and symbolic in nature and therefore not functional (see Evans 2007 for a summary of this debate). Such criticisms present us with a false dichotomy and can be dismissed *a priori* on logical grounds, but it is nonetheless worthwhile considering the ways in which Angkor's urban space may be ordered according to 'ritual' imperatives.

For the last two decades, Gaucher (2002, 2003a, 2004, 2017) has been a leading proponent of the idea that the urban layout of Angkor is structured according to ideals and principles derived from Indian traditions of urban planning, in much the same way as the temples of Angkor themselves represent a specific vision of the Hindu-Buddhist cosmos rendered in earth, water, and stone. Following many years of painstaking ground survey in the central walled enclosure of Angkor Thom beginning in 2000, Gaucher's team was able to identify elements of an urban grid, and cartographic work by his team filled out earlier, schematic maps by Groslier and others (Groslier 1956, 1958) with extraordinary detail.

According to Gaucher (2004, 83), the grid network of the Angkor Thom enclosure (Figure 10.1) conforms sufficiently to ideal models of urban planning laid out in Indian literature such as the *Śāstra* that we may consider it as a 'genuine city', elaborated according to a master plan based on ancient principles. In that respect, Gaucher's approach echoes ideas presented

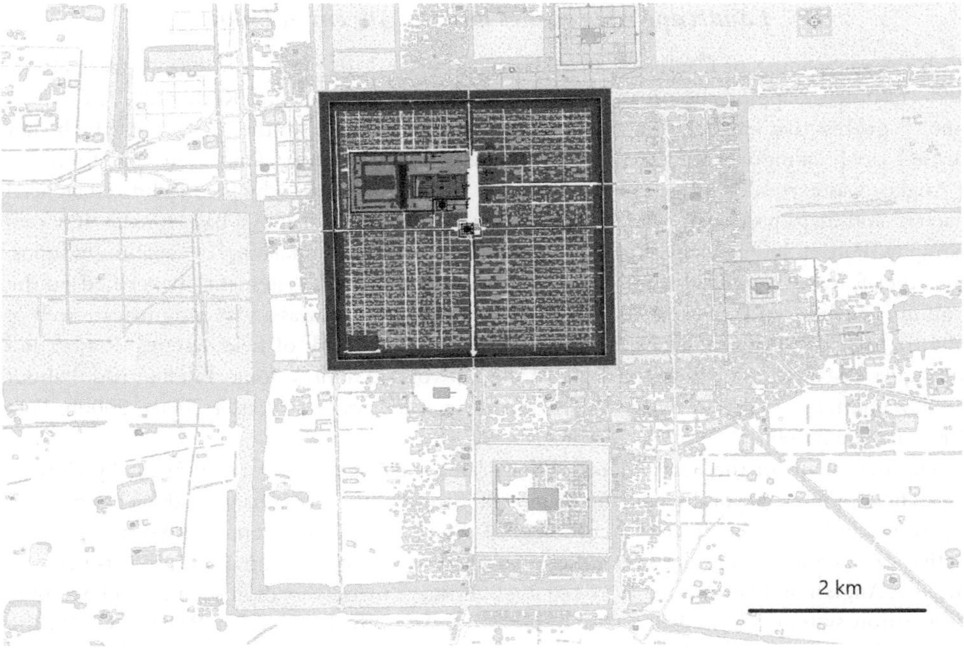

Figure 10.1 Archaeological map of the intramural area of Angkor Thom.
Source: (Based on Gaucher and Husi 2013).

decades earlier by Wheatley (1983), who argued that urban planning in Southeast Asia was based on idealised models described in Indian and Chinese treatises—a theory that, perhaps surprisingly, has not been particularly influential on studies of Khmer urban form. It is also a natural evolution of the original idea of 'temple-cities' since, in this vision of Angkor, the Bayon temple remains the focus of an extended enclosure which neatly delimits and defines the true urban space: Angkor Thom, in this view, is essentially a temple-city writ large.

There are a number of potential problems with this, some of which Gaucher anticipates and deals with in his text (2004). To begin with, models of Indian urban form found in ancient treatises were rarely, if ever, achieved in physical reality; rather, the ideals form an abstract model of urban space in which 'the city is an experiential shape only loosely associated with the physical shape' (Srinivasan 1993). On the other hand, the grid is also highly evocative of the ideal layout of Chinese cities, as Gaucher and others have pointed out (Evans and Fletcher 2015; Gaucher 2004). Historically in China, these geometric plans *were* frequently fully realised in physical space, and more obvious elements of Indian tradition frequently overshadow the influence of Chinese cultural traditions in Angkorian society. There also remains the obvious point that grids are a natural and fundamental layout of urban designs everywhere throughout history and that since the inscriptional corpus of Cambodia is silent on such questions of urban planning, there is no particular way of testing or refuting the theory of Indian inspiration one way or the other. Finally, Gaucher's work excluded the broader grid that had already been identified by Groslier and others (Pottier 2006) and took as its starting point the notion that the walls of Angkor Thom enclosed more or less the totality of the grid pattern of central Angkor—an assumption that was later challenged by the advent of airborne lidar mapping, as we will see.

Landscape Approaches and the Advent of Lidar

With the re-opening of Cambodia to archaeological work in the early 1990s, Pottier (1993, 1999) resumed mapping the urban fabric of Angkor (see Hawken and Klassen 2023, this volume), a process that had been set in motion on a piecemeal basis in the 1930s and which later formed a core component of Groslier's unfinished research agenda. The inventory of temples at Angkor was expanded by several hundred sites in Pottier's work, which consolidated archival material and maps produced over the course of a century and a half as a basis for the new cartography (Pottier 2006). Many thousands of community ponds or *trapeang*, occupation mounds, and other features were identified in the new maps, which were systematically verified on the ground over the course of the 1990s. Connecting these features was a vast and intricate web of infrastructure consisting of embankments, canals, and a network of field systems. Pottier and colleagues began to use the spatial logic of the network to address long-standing issues about the development of Angkor and its urban and agricultural systems (Pottier 2000a, 2000b; Pottier and Bolle 2009).

The new maps of the central and southern areas of Angkor (Figure 10.2) finally allowed researchers to move beyond schematic maps of lines and point locations towards richly detailed depictions and interpretations of archaeological topography. The mapping, survey, and interpretive work completed in the 1990s also established a template for numerous projects that followed at Angkor and beyond. In 1999 and 2000, Pottier's maps were digitised into a geographic information system (GIS). Within the framework of the Greater Angkor Project (GAP), the cartography was then extended into the further northern, eastern, and western reaches of Angkor that were inaccessible to researchers in the 1990s due to conflict (Evans et al. 2007). By

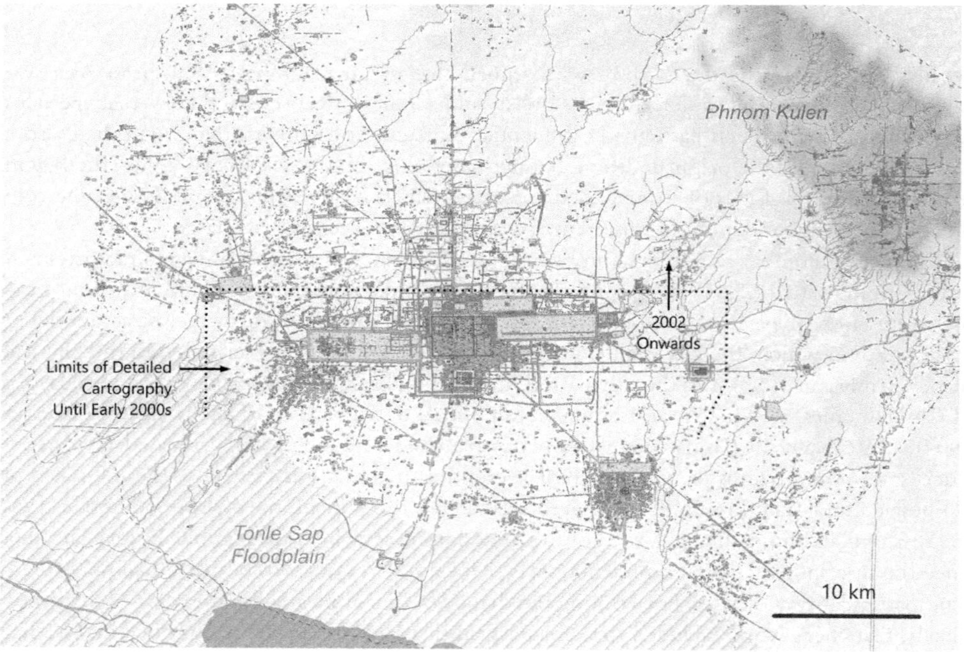

Figure 10.2 Archaeological map of the Greater Angkor region.

Source: (Map by the authors, with contributions from N. Hofer and J.-B. Chevance).

2007, researchers were confident that a more or less comprehensive overview of the Greater Angkor archaeological landscape had been achieved, even if lacunae remained in some areas and ground verification had not yet been completed (Evans et al. 2007).

Elsewhere in Cambodia, other archaeological mapping projects developed in parallel and added similar detail for other urban areas. A project led by Shimoda at the Pre-Angkorian capital of Sambor Prei Kuk used aerial photographs and satellite imagery to document a similar pattern of pond- and mound-based, temple-centric habitation dating from the 5th to the 9th centuries CE (Shimoda 2010), while the LOMAP program led by Stark and colleagues was able to identify even earlier antecedents for this form of settlement organisation dating from the early first millennium CE in the Mekong Delta (Stark 2006; Stark et al. 2015). Other teams across Cambodia were able to replicate these findings and identify patterns of residence and urbanism at places such as Banteay Chhmar and Koh Ker (Evans and Moylan 2013; Evans and Traviglia 2012) and also Preah Khan of Kompong Svay (Hendrickson and Evans 2015), where previously there had existed only schematic maps consisting of points and lines delineating the largest infrastructural elements. Unlike in neighbouring countries, Cambodia had decades of conflict that preserved the heritage landscape from processes of urbanisation and mechanised agriculture. As a result, we can trace the topographic legacy of centuries of urban development in detail on the Earth's surface.

This work, however, suffered from one major shortcoming: in many areas, vegetation cover obscured the subtle topographic traces that researchers were identifying in aerial imagery and using to map elements of Angkorian urban form. A solution to this problem arrived in 2012 with the first deployment of airborne lidar in the Angkor region, and at Koh Ker (Evans et al. 2013), as part of the Khmer Archaeology LiDAR Consortium. Researchers were able to leverage the unique capability to map fine-grained topographic relief even under dense forest canopy to fill in important lacunae in the maps of Angkor and Koh Ker (Evans 2010; Evans et al. 2013; Evans and Fletcher 2015), as well as reproducing and validating the mapping work already completed by Gaucher in Angkor Thom. Within the framework of the Cambodian Archaeological Lidar Initiative in 2015, the 2012 lidar work at Angkor was extended to include most other major temple complexes within the borders of present-day Cambodia, including Banteay Chhmar, Preah Khan of Kompong Svay, the Pre-Angkorian capital of Sambor Prei Kuk, and the Post-Angkorian capital region of Longvek and Oudong (Evans 2016). Since then, these acquisitions of aerial data have been complemented by years-long projects of survey, mapping, and excavation, usually within the framework of broad multi-disciplinary projects involving multiple international teams working in concert with Cambodian researchers. In some areas, ground verification work continues, and analysis of the results will preoccupy researchers for many years to come. Nonetheless, we have recently arrived at what may be considered definitive, final archaeological maps of all of these places, including Angkor, which allows us to make some basic observations about the development of urban form over space and time in the Angkorian World.

Khmer Urban Patterns Over Time

The paradigm of settlement and landscape archaeology continues to inform most of the archaeological work done in Cambodia outside of temple contexts, and this is reflected in many of the contributions to this volume, some of which go into considerable detail on elements of Khmer urbanism in different areas and in different periods (see Heng 2023; Chevance and Pottier 2023; Hawken and Klassen 2023; Hawken and Castillo 2023; Carter et al. 2023; Polkinghorne and Sato 2023). Therefore, the purpose of this section is to offer a broad synthesis of this work to trace the contours of urban development from prehistory to the present day, incorporating the latest results from lidar-derived mapping work.

Early Capitals Beyond Angkor

There are at least four major centres beyond Angkor for which we have sufficient amounts of archaeological data to make assessments of early urbanism.

At Óc Eo, a major trading port of the polity known from Chinese sources as *Funan* (Malleret 1959; Manguin and Khåi 2000; Manguin and Tingley 2009; Manguin and Vallerin 1997), we find perhaps the first example of an urban centre in mainland Southeast Asia organised according to an orthogonal plan, with occupation areas and temple remains organised over an area of more than 400 ha. Located on a floodplain without the presence of large, elevated mounds, Óc Eo was structured along either side of the main axis and was home perhaps to several thousand people. Dating from the first few centuries BCE to the first few centuries CE, it represents a very early integration of monumental architecture and residential occupation within a coherent urban design apparently elaborated according to an overall plan (Bourdonneau 2007) (Figure 10.3).

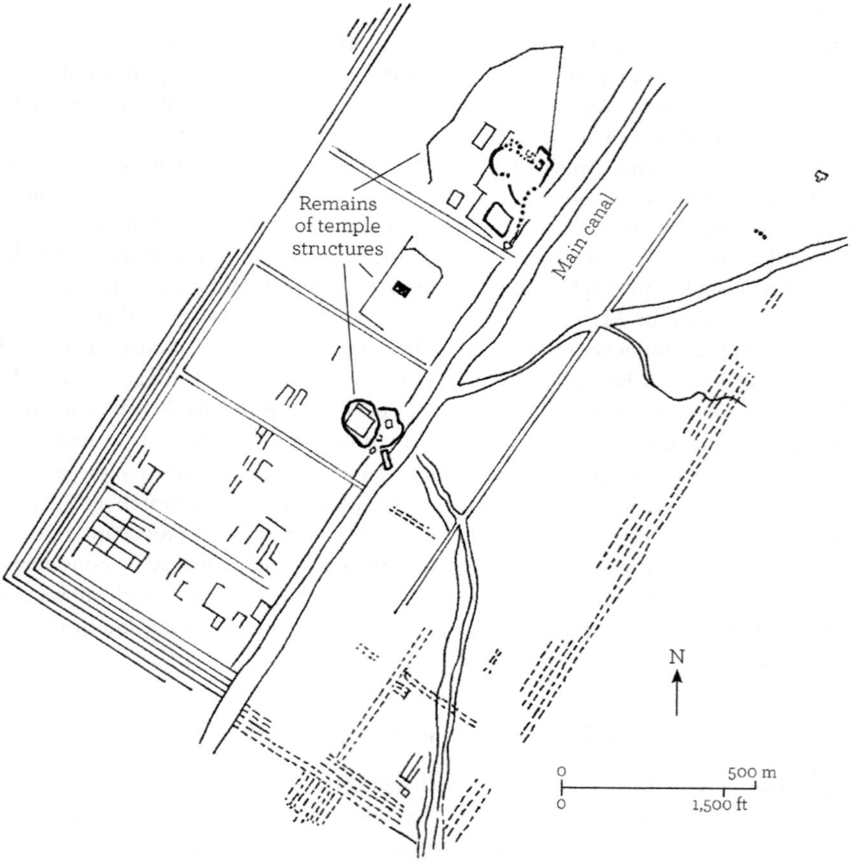

Figure 10.3 Map of Óc Eo.

Source: (Based on Coe and Evans (2018, 91).

Further inland, legacy forms of occupation on large irregular mounds persisted. The site of Angkor Borei in southern Cambodia, perhaps the capital of Funan and linked to Óc Eo by a great canal, has evidence for occupation dating from at least the 4th century CE scattered across 35 km^2 (Stark 2006; Stark et al. 2015). Some of this occupation is located on very large and irregular mounds containing scatters of ponds and temple sites, while other ponds, temples, and smaller occupation mounds are distributed across the surrounding landscape, reflecting a diversity of settlement forms that do not adhere to any obvious grid or plan.

At the site of Sambor Prei Kuk, new maps created from lidar imaging in 2015 (Figure 10.4) add considerable detail to the enclosed Pre-Angkorian city mapped in detail by Shimoda (2010), which includes a vast array of ponds and numerous small shrines in its intramural and extramural spaces, much of it apparently reflecting a rather chaotic and disordered development. Most of the development at Sambor Prei Kuk, including its main group of shrines, appears to coincide with the apparent lifespan of the '*Chenla*' polity from the 6th to 8th centuries, but here, too, there is evidence for occupation dating back to Prehistoric Period (Shimoda et al. 2015).

A defining feature of Sambor Prei Kuk has always been its imposing earthen enclosure, stretching 2 km on three sides, with the other side bordered by the river. In addition to this piece of infrastructure, we can now add an internal system of water management, consisting of a series of canals around the main temple sites. Another network of intramural canals revealed by lidar appears to be the remnants of an interior grid, which seems to conform to the orientation of the exterior wall and is connected to it. Sambor Prei Kuk may therefore represent the earliest evidence of a city grid enclosed within an outer wall.

The nature of occupation at Sambor Prei Kuk partly evokes that of Angkor Borei, with massive mounds dotted with temple sites and ponds but a much greater density of smaller ponds and

Figure 10.4 Archaeological map of Sambor Prei Kuk.

Source: (Map by the authors, with contributions from Kong L. and A. Loyless).

mounds scattered across the landscape, and with a network of large-scale infrastructure imposed upon it. Importantly, the many thousands of occupation mounds and ponds at Sambor Prei Kuk, along with many of its temple sites, stretch far into the extra-mural spaces; the 'enclosure' encloses little aside from the principal shrines.

The fourth Pre-Angkorian urban complex for which we have detailed mapping is the ancient city associated with Wat Phou, in present-day Laos (Santoni et al. 1997; Santoni and Hawixbrock 1998; Santoni and Souksavatdy 1996), dating from around the 5th to 8th centuries. Like Sambor Prei Kuk, it sits on the floodplain astride a major river—the Mekong, in this case—with three walls of approximately 2 km on the other three sides forming an enclosure. Evidence for occupation is relatively sparse with a light scatter of occupation mounds, ponds, and temples, and although there is no evidence of a formally planned grid interior, there seem to have been multiple phases of wall construction, with three concentric wall systems radiating out from the river's edge. Later phases of occupation from the Pre-Angkor and Angkor Periods consisting of a scattering of temples, ponds, and mounds lay further inland from the river and seem to reflect growing confidence in the construction of settlements further away from major water sources, in tandem with the development of more sophisticated techniques for water management (Lorrillard 2010).

Urbanism at Angkor

As detailed by Chevance and Pottier (2023, this volume), urban development in the early centuries of the Angkor Period also experimented—perhaps not always successfully—with major centres located in highland areas further away from the flooded lowland areas that were traditionally the locus of Khmer settlements, in a trend that we can also identify in other parts of the Angkorian World (see Heng 2023, this volume). The Angkor plain is dotted with well over a thousand local temple sites from the Pre-Angkor and Angkor Period consisting of moated temple-mounds surrounded by ponds and occupation mounds (Evans et al. 2007), and Pottier (2017) makes a convincing case that one cluster, in particular, centred on the temple-mountain of Ak Yum, emerged as the first major capital of the area during the Pre-Angkor Period (see Chevance and Pottier 2023, this volume). Alongside this, Pottier proposes that this city, named Bhavapura, emerged in the 6th century and was characterised by a cardinally aligned grid system, as well as a prototype of the giant reservoir or *baray* that would come to characterise later stages of Angkor's development. Both of these would represent major innovations in urban planning, predating by centuries the development of analogous infrastructure on Phnom Kulen in the 8th to 9th centuries (Chevance et al. 2019). This view directly challenges the conventional view that large-scale urbanism and 'capital cities' developed in areas distant from Angkor and instead traces the origins of Angkorian urbanism back several centuries within Angkor itself. However, the precise structure of Bhavapura is partly obscured and confused by subsequent urban developments, and further work will be required to fully disentangle the palimpsest in this area.

With the establishment of Mahendraparvata as capital on the Phnom Kulen massif at the turn of the 8th to 9th centuries CE, we see the earliest and clearest example of the disengagement of Khmer habitation from flooded lowlands, as part of a project of city-building that seems to have been planned and executed by the Angkorian state within a relatively brief period of time (Chevance et al. 2019). Apparently drawing on previous elements from Bhavapura, the king, Jayavarman II, unsuccessfully attempted the construction of a baray—which were typically fashioned of earth—by quarrying deep into raw stone atop the plateau. Although there is evidence of residential enclosures and habitation on the plateau, there are few or no occupation mounds, since there is no need to keep residence above the floodwaters; no evidence for flooded rice field systems; and, instead of excavated ponds, usually small earthen dams. Like Bhavapura, it lacks the enclosures that were characteristic of Khmer cities outside of Angkor from the 6th to 8th centuries. Mahendraparvata thus represents a sharp departure from classical forms of Khmer urbanism. The experiment was short lived, with the capital returning within a few decades to the plains of Angkor, where it would stay for most of the next five or six centuries (Chevance et al. 2019).

The capital of Hariharālaya, built atop several thousand years of continuous occupation, marks a return to a more organic urban form that took advantage of the legacy of the previous habitation on mounds at the edge of the floodplain of the great lake, the Tonle Sap. Although partly formalised and structured into a kind of sacred geography in some areas and containing some infrastructural elements that offer axes in the urban space, Hariharālaya has no grid system, and it also has no overall enclosure. It consists of a central nucleus of monuments, comprising a well-organised space out of which radiates a sprawl of ponds, mounds, and community temples. It is, therefore, characteristic of the 'open cities' that we see in Angkor for the first several centuries of its existence as the capital of the Khmer Empire (Pottier 2012). This pattern was repeated in the initial stages of Yaśodharapura at Angkor from the 9th to 11th centuries and also in the city of the East Baray built by king Rajendravarman in the 10th century.

A brief exception to this model of lowland capital cities comes in the form of Koh Ker, some 100 km to the east of Angkor, in which we can identify an attempt to take the defining elements of the open, unstructured urban layouts of the Angkor floodplain and reproduce them in the gently rolling hills of present-day Preah Vihear province (Evans 2010). As with Mahendraparvata, there are few occupation mounds here, most of the monumental remains date from a single period, and ill-conceived infrastructural projects may have contributed to its ephemeral tenure as the capital of the Khmer Empire (Lustig et al. 2018).

Urban Development in the 11th to 13th Centuries

By the 11th century, the open city model at Angkor had developed to the point where densely inhabited nuclei—in particular forming around current and former capital city locations—punctuated a broad, landscape-scale fabric of community temples, ponds, and occupation areas, which began to expand and become tied together with the urban core at Yaśodharapura by significant amounts of infrastructure (Carter et al. 2018; Evans 2016; Evans et al. 2007, 2013; Gaucher 2017; Klassen et al. 2021). By the 11th to 12th centuries, the open cities of Angkor came to be replaced, at least in part, by the development of the colossal walls of Angkor Thom (Gaucher 2017). Angkor Thom had reached more or less its final (and current) form by the 13th century, but it was elaborated in stages over centuries. Around the time of the reign of Jayavarman VII, Angkor achieved more or less the morphology that we see depicted on maps of the Greater Angkor region today. It consisted of a densely inhabited, formally planned urban core of around 40 km^2 with many thousands of ponds organised along an urban grid that extended far into extramural areas beyond Angkor Thom. This civic-ceremonial core was surrounded by a vast, low-density network of mixed residential and agricultural space, punctuated here and there by nodes of high-density occupation such as at Beng Mealea and tied together into a coherent system by a pervasive network of canal and embankment infrastructure (Carter et al. 2021; Klassen et al. 2021).

Meanwhile, at a smaller scale than that of the settlement complex, the development of true 'temple-cities' from the 11th to 13th centuries can be defined using lidar data, as the increasing amount of space between ever-larger monuments and their enclosure walls becomes organised

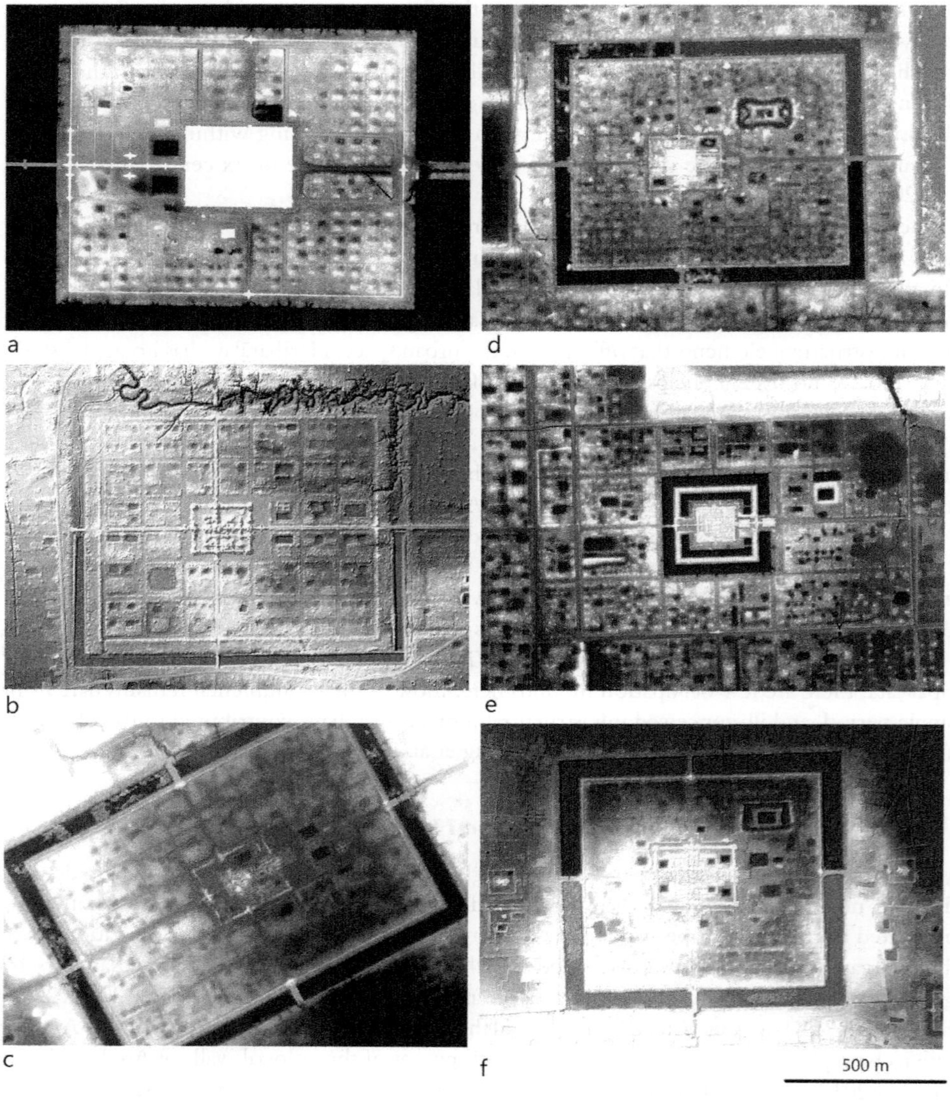

Figure 10.5 Lidar renderings of gridded urban areas of the Angkor Period: a) Angkor Wat; b) Beng Mealea; c) Preah Khan of Kompong Svay; d) Preah Khan of Angkor; e) Ta Prohm; f) Banteay Chhmar. Data from KALC 2012 and CALI 2015. All images are the same scale.

into systematic grid patterns of mounds and ponds (Figure 10.5) (Evans 2016). Sometimes, as with Beng Mealea, these 'temple-cities' form nodes within the extended agro-urban complex; in other cases, as with Ta Prohm, for example, they are firmly embedded in the occupational matrix of the urban core. Recent excavations have provided proof of habitation within these temple precincts, including at Ta Prohm and Angkor Wat (Carter et al. 2018; Stark et al. 2015). Overall, at its height in the 13th century, the region of Greater Angkor was likely home to around 700,000 people (Klassen et al. 2021).

Angkorian Urbanism Beyond Angkor

In 2015, airborne lidar data were acquired over the 11th- to 13th-century temple complex of Preah Khan of Kompong Svay, a provincial industrial centre located 100 km to the east of Angkor, where many years of study using conventional sensors and ground survey had led to the conclusion that the area inside its enclosure wall—at 5 km on each side, the largest in Southeast Asia—was very sparsely inhabited (Hendrickson and Evans 2015), presenting us with something of an anomaly in the history of Khmer urbanism until that point. However, the lidar data clearly revealed an urban layout within the central moat of the site that is analogous to the early 12th-century grids of Angkor Wat and Beng Mealea—complete with the enigmatic 'coiled' embankments. Surrounding the main temple moat is an extended, less-organised urban grid that resembles the late-Angkorian urban centres of Jayavarman VII. Excavations completed at Preah Khan in 2016 led by Mitch Hendrickson and colleagues confirm the accuracy of interpretations of archaeological topography visible within the lidar data. While it remains true that Preah Khan's enclosure seems less densely populated than large enclosures such as Angkor Thom, the evidence for occupation is nonetheless rich and unequivocal, with spatial patterning that fits neatly within schemes of urban development in the Angkorian World.

The same cannot be said of Banteay Chhmar, a provincial centre of the 12th to 13th centuries, located in an arid zone that shows evidence of an extensive water management system (Evans et al. 2011). The new lidar data essentially confirm previous mapping work and do not significantly change the overall interpretation of the archaeological topography. Among all the 11th- to 13th century CE temples of the Khmer, Banteay Chhmar is the only one so far mapped with lidar that shows almost no evidence of a formal urban grid extending throughout any of its successive enclosures and represents a (so far) unique exception to the model of urban development we propose here for the Angkor Period, in which 'open cities' gradually evolve into urban complexes with formally planned urban cores by the 12th to 13th centuries CE. The reasons for this are unclear: was Banteay Chhmar a 'city', or was it a 'garrison-temple' on the fringes of the empire that was inhabited ephemerally or episodically (Sharrock 2015)?

After Angkor

In order to arrive at a relatively complete and consistent view of the development of Khmer urbanism over the course of two millennia or more, airborne lidar data were also acquired over the Post-Angkorian capital regions of Longvek and Oudong, far to the south of Angkor near present-day Phnom Penh (Evans 2016). From the 15th century onwards, this region was the location of the Cambodian capitals of the Early Modern Period. The issue of settlement size and structure in the capitals that came after Angkor is also relevant to the study of the demise of Angkor as the capital of the Khmer Empire and its gradual depopulation up until the 19th century: the tempo of Angkor's decline is a matter of ongoing research interest (Carter et al. 2019; Hall et al. 2021; Lucero et al. 2015; Penny et al. 2019), and understanding Early Modern settlement patterns may offer important insight into patterns of migration from Angkor (Evans 2016). Our understanding of this area has been considerably enhanced by further remote sensing, survey, and excavation work that is described elsewhere in this collection (see Polkinghorne and Sato 2023, this volume), so only a brief summary is warranted here.

Essentially, the mapping work at Middle Period capitals reveals only sparse evidence for occupation in the form of subtle topographic traces within spaces that are either bounded (as in the case of Longvek) or open (as in the case of all other capitals). Traces that we associate with 'classic' Khmer urbanism from the middle of the first millennium CE onward, such as the remains of ponds, occupation mounds, and moated-mound community temples, are poorly represented in this landscape. Polkinghorne et al. (2018) nonetheless argue for substantial populations in these areas, even if the configuration of the built environment differed substantially from that of the Angkor Period and has less visibility in the archaeological record—a conclusion that would be consistent with other important shifts in material culture in the Early Modern Period.

Discussion

Our survey of the literature on Angkorian settlement patterns reveals the extraordinary progress that has been made since the 1990s, when Cambodia began to emerge from decades of conflict, setting the stage for systematic exploration and analysis of archaeological landscapes at scale using aerial photography in concert with innovative and emerging technologies such as GPS, GIS, airborne radar and lidar, and very-high-resolution satellite imagery. Before this work began, maps of Angkorian settlement complexes were largely schematic in nature, consisting of a scatter of points around large infrastructural elements and the major temple complexes. Twenty years ago, arguments that Angkor was an 'orthogenetic' ceremonial centre that was sparsely populated and dedicated largely to ritual and administrative functions (Miksic 2000), or that the walls of Angkor Thom in the 12th to 13th centuries fully enclosed the only 'true' urban context at Angkor (Gaucher 2002, 2003b), were reasonable and tenable positions held by widely respected scholars. Today, it is difficult to see how these perspectives might survive the evidence.

Nonetheless, there are a number of broad lacunae in our understanding of the lived-in spaces of the Angkorian World and some significant issues with definitions and terminology that hinder our ability to draw broad and meaningful conclusions from the data, alongside a range of other methodological and theoretical problems that must be acknowledged to allow a full and fair appraisal of the results and set the stage for future research directions. Some of these issues are by now well known, and researchers have begun to address them in detail. For example, it is relatively difficult to draw chronological information from remotely sensed data, and systematic efforts are being made to link map datasets to related datasets from art history, architecture, and epigraphy that offer finer-grained chronological data and set the stage for mapping the development of urban spaces over space and time (Klassen et al. 2018, 2021). Others are more obscure and are worth discussing here.

Low-Density Urbanism and Cities: Scale and Definitions

Probably the most significant and far-reaching consequence of the last three decades of landscape archaeology in the Angkorian World has been to inspire a broad re-appraisal of lived-in spaces in early Southeast Asia, which in turn has informed emerging perspectives on diverse trajectories of urbanism Worldwide, especially in the tropics (Graham and Isendahl 2018). In particular, we now recognise that the conventional definitions of 'cities' that derive from other archaeological traditions—such as studies of the Classical World and the Near East, in which 'urban' spaces are clearly delineated and differentiated from the 'non-urban' or 'rural' spaces that lay beyond—are entirely inadequate for describing Khmer residential patterning (Fletcher 2020). The survey of the state of the art that we have provided shows that, although enclosures bound parts of Khmer settlements, the formally planned urban spaces in these intra-mural spaces frequently spill beyond the 'enclosing' walls and go on to merge gradually and imperceptibly into low-density residential landscapes incorporating fields and gardens.

Research work produced by the Greater Angkor Project has generally avoided using the term 'cities' to describe this patterning of lived-in space since the word 'city' conjures up images of the walled cities of classical antiquity. Instead, scholarship in recent years typically defines Khmer habitation zones as 'settlement complexes' characterised by 'low-density agrarian-based urbanism,' in which a central, densely populated civic-ceremonial centre is surrounded by an extended hinterland of diffuse urban and agricultural spaces containing occasional nodes of high-density occupation (Fletcher 2009, 2012). In general, a system of infrastructure such as roads and canals radiates out from the centre, permeating the low-density sprawl and lending functional and material coherence to the settlement complex as a whole (Evans et al. 2007).

Although this approach to categorisation neatly elides the problematic category of a 'city', there remains a good deal of confusion and imprecision about the distinction between 'urban' and 'rural' in the archaeological literature, which has given rise to an extensive body of work discussing whether the kind of diffuse residential patterning we see in the homelands of the Maya and Khmer is 'urban' or 'rural' by definition (Michelet and Nondédéo 2019), where and when 'hinterland' (Klassen et al. 2021) or 'peri-urban' (Evans et al. 2013) areas begin, and whether we should describe those in terms of 'low-density urbanism' or 'high-density ruralism' (Scarborough et al. 2012); whether labels such as 'garden cities' or even 'forest gardens' may be more appropriate (Isendahl 2012); whether terms such as 'agro-urban landscapes' should be adopted to accommodate new perspectives on residential patterning in the tropical world (Graham and Isendahl 2018); or whether we may simply settle on 'low-density cities' for some places while divorcing the concept of 'density' from 'urbanism' altogether (Graham and Isendahl 2018).

Notable throughout much of this literature is the absence of precise and uniform criteria against which we may reliably define a given part of the landscape as belonging to one category or another. Michelet and Nondédéo (2019) characterise much of this work as 'fake feuds' about urbanism deriving from confusion and imprecision in the definitions of 'urban' and 'rural', and, as Fletcher (2020) has observed, 'it is now clear that definitions of urbanism are regionally specific and that global definitions have become tenuous and increasingly decoupled from material actuality'. In rare cases, authors have attempted to systematise their classification using quantitative approaches drawn from material culture (e.g. Canuto et al. 2018), but these are based on criteria specific to the local archaeological record (stucco remains in the case of the Maya World) and may not be broadly applicable to other archaeological contexts such as the Angkorian World. Many archaeologists make a compelling case that studies of urbanism from the deep past to the present day are important for understanding the resilience and vulnerability of the sprawling low-density cities which increasingly define present-day urbanism (Hawken and Fletcher 2021; Ortman et al. 2020; Smith et al. 2021), but the categories upon which archaeologists have long relied for classifying lived-in spaces clearly provide us with a poor foundation for this kind of work.

Instead, research on urbanism in the Angkorian World brings into sharp relief some of the challenges and opportunities with this broader comparative project. The first major challenge is that the comparative frameworks proposed by Smith and others still require arbitrary and specific definitions of lived-in spaces at various scales of space and time, in order, for example, to define 'a settlement' or 'a neighbourhood' and its trajectory of growth and decline (Smith et al. 2021; Smith 2020). The 'messy' archaeological landscapes of the Khmer, frequently lacking distinct boundaries between different types of spaces, underscore the need to move beyond these kinds of arbitrary categories and focus instead on continuous fields of density of occupation across the landscape, moving seamlessly through multiple spatial scales without pre-supposing an 'appropriate' or 'natural' scale for the study of lived-in spaces of one category or another (Hawken and Fletcher 2021). This kind of approach offers the possibility of undertaking truly global comparative studies and segues neatly into new perspectives offered by settlement scaling theory (Ortman et al. 2020), which has already begun to make an impact on the study of Khmer urbanism by offering insights into how population densities at different scales contributed to specific kinds of social, political and agricultural organisation (Klassen et al. 2021).

Missing Pieces of the Puzzle

These kinds of quantitative studies of population density across time and space underpin many of the most recent studies of Angkor and inform our latest perspectives on the overall demography and morphology of the agro-urban landscape (Carter et al. 2018, 2019, 2021; Klassen et al. 2018, 2021). The calculation of population density, however, rests on a number of assumptions drawn from household archaeology (see Carter et al. 2023, this volume) and from the study of traces that remain on the surface in the present day. It is important to acknowledge these assumptions here, since it will help us to appraise the precision of the work that has been published and point to a number of useful future directions for research.

One of the core assumptions in this recent work is that the existence of a religious shrine, relatively modest in size in comparison to the better-known temples of Angkor and characterised as 'local temples' or 'community temples' (Carter et al. 2021), lay at the centre of substantial communities of sedentary agriculturalists during the Angkor Period and that the size of those communities can be inferred from the spatial coverage of occupation mounds and ponds associated with that particular temple foundation (Klassen et al. 2018, 2021). For now, this is a working assumption, and although it is a reasonable assumption given the range of epigraphic and archaeological evidence for habitation around *some* of those temples (Bâty 2005; Klassen et al. 2021), it should be acknowledged that we so far have an extremely limited number of excavations to draw from in inferring population densities outside of the urban core of Angkor and that much of our thinking about the role of 'community temples' in the Angkorian World draws from ethnographic analogy with the role of Theravada Buddhist pagodas in contemporary village contexts across mainland Southeast Asia.

Beyond the pioneering work done by Bâty and colleagues, the nature of occupation around community temple sites is a question that will need to be solved by wide-area archaeological excavations across a wide selection of sites, in much the same way as Stark, Carter, and colleagues have pioneered household archaeology in the urban centres of Angkor (Carter et al. 2018, 2019; Stark et al. 2015). The lack of sustained archaeological investigation into the nature of residence alongside roads and canals, and atop other elements of infrastructure in the Angkorian World such as the banks of reservoirs and ponds, is also a matter of concern: by and large, for the time being, habitation in those areas is simply assumed. Moving forward, the study of occupation density based on ceramic material and other durable remains such as macrobotanicals may be complemented by other techniques for estimating population density, such as seeking biochemical markers like faecal stanols, as has been done, for example, in the Maya World (Keenan et al. 2021).

Another major concern derives from our use of durable components of the archaeological record—patterned mounds and depressions that remain inscribed on the landscape—as a proxy for certain kinds of residential and agricultural activity. As pointed out by Hawken in this volume (Hawken and Castillo 2023), based on many years of observations on the ground working alongside rice farmers, a substantial amount of Angkor's population was likely seasonally mobile, living among rice fields during periods of intensive agricultural activity. It is certain that tens of thousands of people would have migrated on a seasonal basis to the urban core for work on infrastructural projects. To what extent, then, may our estimates of Angkor's population be inflated by 'double-counting' residential infrastructure that was used seasonally by the same population? In a similar vein, the lack of obvious surface evidence for certain kinds of rice agriculture (e.g., swidden cultivation and retreating flood rice agriculture) may also be further muddying our perception of the complex mosaic of habitation and agricultural spaces in the Angkorian World. Methods from biogeochemistry—analysing soil chemistry and sampling environmental DNA, for example—may help to elucidate certain patterns of activity that have been obscured by a focus on macro remains (and offer perhaps our only pathway to solving the perennial debate about irrigation and multi-cropping in the 'hydraulic city' of Angkor).

A further issue related to transience and visibility in the archaeological record relates to those living on the margins and peripheries of Angkorian settlement complexes and of the Angkorian World as a whole. Mainland Southeast Asia during the time of Angkor, as today, contains a great deal of ethnolinguistic variation and diverse material cultures, many of which are likely to be poorly represented in the surface archaeological record. The work of Hendrickson et al., for example, shows that the Kuay people played an outsized role in the industry of Angkor, well represented in terms of material remains—and yet their patterns of habitation are poorly understood in the archaeological record, which has likely contributed to some long-standing confusion about the nature of occupation at Preah Khan of Kompong Svay and beyond (Hendrickson and Evans 2015; Pryce et al. 2014). Zhou Daguan mentions highland people on the forested periphery of Angkor who were engaged in the provision of valued goods for the city centre (Zhou 2007[1297]). We know that the 'urban' and 'agricultural' areas of Angkor sprawled into those areas, that increasing contact took place during the Angkor Period (see Heng 2023, this volume), and that major centres such as Mahendraparvata were located in highland regions (Chevance et al. 2019). How might these populations, otherwise largely absent from the discourse on Angkor, be identified and incorporated into our models of socio-ecological dynamics?

Conclusion

Our survey highlights the tremendous progress that has been made in recent years in understanding the diverse trajectories of urbanism in the early Khmer world while underscoring specific areas of work where further research is required. The pattern that emerges is of gradual and continuous development and experimentation with different forms of urbanism over time, for example, as the enclosed cities of the Pre-Angkor Period gave way to the open cities of the early Angkor Period, followed by a time of extremely intense infrastructural development and innovation in the 11th to 13th centuries characterised by rigidly formalised city grids and the imposition of giant walled enclosures in pre-existing urban spaces. Urban agglomerations located in the traditional homeland of the Khmer—seasonally inundated floodplains—persisted for several centuries, supported by elaborate and successful hydraulic works, while urban complexes that emerged in highland areas such as Koh Ker and Mahendraparvata, on the other hand, were short lived and beset by engineering problems. Between and beyond these centres, a vast, diffuse mosaic of community temples and walled rice fields permeated the flooded lowlands of the Angkorian World.

It is difficult, for now, to draw definitive conclusions about the implications for Khmer society from the spatial patterns of these layouts. It is clear that anthropological approaches used in similar contexts Worldwide, such as the use of Gini coefficients to explore wealth inequality, are not applicable in the Angkorian World, since we lack the granular data on residential patterning that are necessary for such approaches. On the other hand, new approaches such as settlement scaling theory offer us promising opportunities for exploring the articulation between urban morphologies and socio-economic developments. These kinds of theoretical approaches provide an overarching rationale for the kind of comparative approaches between 'tropical forest civilisations' proposed by Michael D. Coe more than half a century ago (1957, 1961). Furthermore, the arrival of consistent and comparable datasets in the form of lidar has set the stage for rigorous, systematic, and quantitative studies that move beyond anecdotal observations about the similarities of settlement complexes in different parts of the world and between cities past and present.

Eventually, this work may live up to the promise that the archaeological record of urban environments in the Angkorian World has important insights to offer us in terms of contemporary urbanism and urban futures. So far, efforts to draw relevance have landed on some fairly straightforward observations that reflect core principles in the design of sustainable urban systems: that we ought to have green space and biodiversity, that infrastructural systems should have multiple points of redundancy, and that massive infrastructural works are inertial and impose unforeseen costs and consequences on future generations. What we can see for the time being, therefore, is not so much the study of archaeology informing urban futures but rather contemporary urban studies providing a window through which we can understand the successes and failures of past urban models. However, as the study of urbanism in the Angkorian World moves past old debates about 'hydraulic cities'; better acknowledges its current shortcomings; and adopts more rigorous, systematic, and quantitative approaches to the data now available, we should expect that research on Khmer settlement patterns will be more broadly impactful in terms of understanding trajectories of urbanism from the deep past to the present.

Funding

Funding for this contribution derives in part from the European Research Council (ERC) under the European Union's Horizon 2020 research and innovation programme (grant agreements 639828 and 866454).

References

Barber, M., 2017. *A History of Aerial Photography and Archaeology: Mata Hari's Glass Eye and Other Stories.* London: Historic England Publishing.

Bâty, P., 2005. *Extension de l'aéroport de Siem Reap 2004: Rapport de Fouille Archéologique.* Siem Reap—Paris: APSARA—INRAP.

Bourdonneau, E., 2007. Réhabiliter le Funan. Óc Eo ou la première Angkor. *Bulletin de l'École française d'Extrême-Orient* 94, 111–57.

Canuto, M.A., F. Estrada-Belli, T.G. Garrison, S.D. Houston, M.J. Acuña, M. Kováč, D. Marken, P. Nondédéo, L. Auld-Thomas, C. Castanet, D. Chatelain, C.R. Chiriboga, T. Drápela, T. Lieskovský, A. Tokovinine, A. Velasquez, J.C. Fernández-Díaz & R. Shrestha, 2018. Ancient lowland Maya complexity as revealed by airborne laser scanning of northern Guatemala. *Science* 361(6409), eaau0137.

Carter, A., M.T. Stark, P. Heng & R. Chhay, 2023. The Angkorian house, in *The Angkorian World*, eds. M. Hendrickson, M.T. Stark & D. Evans. New York: Routledge, 494–507.

Carter, A., P. Heng, M. Stark, R. Chhay & D. Evans, 2018. Urbanism and residential patterning in Angkor. *Journal of Field Archaeology* 43(6), 492–506.

Carter, A.K., M.T. Stark, S. Quintus, Y. Zhuang, H. Wang, P. Heng & R. Chhay, 2019. Temple occupation and the tempo of collapse at Angkor Wat, Cambodia. *Proceedings of the National Academy of Sciences* 116(25), 12226–31.

Carter, A.K., S. Klassen, M.T. Stark, M. Polkinghorne, P. Heng, D. Evans & R. Chhay, 2021. The evolution of agro-urbanism: a case study from Angkor, Cambodia. *Journal of Anthropological Archaeology* 63, 101323.

Chevance, J.-B. & C. Pottier, 2023. The early Angkor capitals, in *The Angkorian World*, eds. M. Hendrickson, M.T. Stark & D. Evans. New York: Routledge, 80–96.

Chevance, J.-B., D. Evans, N. Hofer, S. Sakhoeun & R. Chhean, 2019. Mahendraparvata: an early Angkor-period capital defined through airborne laser scanning at Phnom Kulen. *Antiquity* 93(371), 1303–21.

Coe, M., 1957. The Khmer settlement pattern: a possible analogy with that of the Maya. *American Antiquity* 22, 409–10.

Coe, M., 1961. Social typology and the tropical forest civilisations. *Comparative Studies in Society and History* 4, 65–85.

Coe, M. & D. Evans, 2018. *Angkor and the Khmer Civilization*. London: Thames & Hudson.

Cœdès, G., 1906. La stèle de Ta-Prohm. *Bulletin de l'École française d'Extrême-Orient* 6(1), 44–86.

Edwards, P., 2005. Taj Angkor: Enshrining l'Inde in le Cambodge, in *France and 'Indochina': Cultural Representations*, eds. K. Robson & J. Yee. Lanham, MD: Lexington Books, 13–27.

Edwards, P., 2008. *Cambodge: The Cultivation of a Nation, 1860–1945*. Chiang Mai: Silkworm Books.

Evans, D., 2007. Putting Angkor on the map: a new survey of a Khmer 'Hydraulic City' in historical and theoretical context. PhD dissertation. Sydney: The University of Sydney.

Evans, D., 2010. The archaeological landscape of Koh Ker, Northwest Cambodia. *Bulletin de l'École française d'Extrême-Orient* 97–98, 91–150.

Evans, D., 2016. Airborne laser scanning as a method for exploring long-term socio-ecological dynamics in Cambodia. *Journal of Archaeological Science* 74, 164–75.

Evans, D. & A. Traviglia, 2012. Uncovering Angkor: integrated remote sensing applications in the archaeology of early Cambodia, in *Satellite Remote Sensing: A New Tool for Archaeology*, eds. R. Lasaponara & N. Masini. New York: Springer, 197–230.

Evans, D., C. Pottier, R. Fletcher, S. Hensley, I. Tapley, A. Milne & M. Barbetti, 2007. A comprehensive archaeological map of the World's largest preindustrial settlement complex at Angkor, Cambodia. *Proceedings of the National Academy of Sciences* 104(36), 14277–82.

Evans, D. & E. Moylan, 2013. Pixels, ponds and people: mapping cultural and archaeological landscapes in Cambodia using historical aerial imagery, in *Archaeology from Historical Aerial and Satellite Archives*, eds. W. Hanson & I. Oltean. New York: Springer, 291–313.

Evans, D., J. Goodman, J. Sanday & R. Mey, 2011. *The Hydraulic System of Banteay Chhmar*. Siem Reap: Global Heritage Fund.

Evans, D. & R. Fletcher, 2015. The landscape of Angkor Wat redefined. *Antiquity* 89(348), 1402–19.

Evans, D., R.J. Fletcher, C. Pottier, J.-B. Chevance, D. Soutif, B.S. Tan, S. Im, D. Ea, T. Tin, S. Kim, C. Cromarty, S. De Greef, K. Hanus, P. Bâty, R. Kuszinger, I. Shimoda & G. Boornazian, 2013. Uncovering archaeological landscapes at Angkor using lidar. *Proceedings of the National Academy of Sciences of the United States of America* 110(31), 12595–600.

Falser, M., 2019. *Angkor Wat—A Transcultural History of Heritage: volume 1: Angkor in France. From Plaster Casts to Exhibition Pavilions*. New York: Walter de Gruyter GmbH & Co KG.

Fletcher, R. & C. Pottier, 2002. The gossamer city: a new inquiry. *Museum International* 54(1–2), 23–7.

Fletcher, R., 2009. Low-density, agrarian-based urbanism: a comparative view. *Insights* 2(4), 1–19.

Fletcher, R., 2012. Low-density, agrarian-based urbanism: scale, power and ecology, in *The Archaeology of Complex Societies*, ed. M.E. Smith. New York: Cambridge University Press, 285–320.

Fletcher, R., 2020. Urban labels and settlement trajectories. *Journal of Urban Archaeology* 1, 31–48.

Gaucher, J. & P. Husi, 2013. L'archéologie urbaine appliquée à un site archéologique: l'exemple d'Angkor Thom (Cambodge), capitale du royaume khmer angkorien, in *Archéologie de l'espace urbain*, eds. E. Lorans & X. Rodier. Tours: Presses universitaires François-Rabelais, 122–31

Gaucher, J., 2002. The 'city' of Angkor. What is it?, *Museum International* 54(1–2), 28–36.

Gaucher, J., 2003a. New archaeological data on the urban space of the capital city of Angkor Thom, in *Fishbones and Glittering Emblems: Southeast Asian Archaeology* 2002, eds. A. Karlström & A. Källén. Stockholm: Museum of Far Eastern Antiquities, 233–42.

Gaucher, J., 2003b. Premiers Aperçus Sur Des Éleménts De Planification Urbaine À Angkor Thom. *Udaya, Journal of Khmer Studies* 4, 41–52.

Gaucher, J., 2004. Angkor Thom, une utopie réalisée? *Structuration de l'espace et modèle indien d'urbanisme dans le Cambodge ancien, Arts Asiatiques* 59, 58–86.

Gaucher, J., 2017. L'enceinte d'Angkor Thom: Archéologie d'une forme, chronologie d'une ville, in *Deux Décennies de Coopération Archéologique Franco-Cambodgienne à Angkor*, eds. A. Beschaouch, F. Verellen & M. Zink. Paris: Académie des Inscriptions et Belles-Lettres, 27–41.

Goloubew, V., 1941. L'hydraulique urbaine et agricole à l'époque des rois d'Angkor. *Bulletin Économique de l'Indochine* 1, 9–18.

Graham, E. & C. Isendahl, 2018. Neotropical cities as agro-urban landscapes: revisiting 'low-density, agrarian-based urbanism', in *The Resilience of Heritage: Cultivating a Future of the Past*. Essays in Honour of Professor Paul J.J. Sinclair, eds. A. Ekblom, C. Isendahl & K.-J. Lindholm, 165–80.

Groslier, B.-P., 1952. L'avion et l'archéologie indochinoise. *Forces aériennes françaises* 67, 51–83.

Groslier, B.-P., 1956. *Angkor, Hommes et Pierres*. Paris: Arthaud.

Groslier, B.-P., 1958. *Angkor et Le Cambodge Au XVIe Siècle d'après Les Sources Portugaises et Espagnoles*. Paris: Presses universitaires de France.

Groslier, B.-P., 1979. La cité hydraulique angkorienne: exploitation ou surexploitation du sol? *Bulletin de l'École française d'Extrême-Orient* 66, 161–202.

Groslier, B.-P., 1998. *Mélanges Sur l'archéologie du Cambodge (1949–1986); Textes Réunis et Présentés Par Jacques Dumarçay*. Paris: École française d'Extrême-Orient.

Hall, T., D. Penny, B. Vincent & M. Polkinghorne, 2021. An integrated palaeoenvironmental record of Early Modern occupancy and land use within Angkor Thom, Angkor. *Quaternary Science Reviews* 251, 106710.

Hawken, S. & C.C. Castillo, 2023. Angkor's agrarian economy: a socio-ecological mosaic, in *The Angkorian World*, eds. M. Hendrickson, M.T. Stark & D. Evans. New York: Routledge, 195–215.

Hawken, S. & R. Fletcher, 2021. A long-term archaeological reappraisal of low-density urbanism: implications for contemporary cities. *Journal of Urban Archaeology* 3, 29–50.

Hawken, S. & S. Klassen, 2023. Angkor's temple communities and the logic of its urban landscape, in *The Angkorian World*, eds. M. Hendrickson, M.T. Stark & D. Evans. New York: Routledge, 195–215.

Hendrickson, M. & D. Evans, 2015. Reimagining the city of fire and iron: a landscape archaeology of the Angkor-Period industrial complex of Preah Khan of Kompong Svay, Cambodia (ca. 9th to 13th centuries A.D.). *Journal of Field Archaeology* 40(6), 644–64.

Heng, P., 2023. Angkor and the Mekong River: settlement, resources, mobility, and power, in *The Angkorian World*, eds. M. Hendrickson, M.T. Stark & D. Evans. New York: Routledge, 154–72.

Higham, C., 2001. *The Civilisation of Angkor*. London: Weidenfeld & Nicolson.

Higham, C., 2014. *Early Mainland Southeast Asia: From First Humans to Angkor*. Bangkok: River Books.

Isendahl, C., 2012. Agro-urban landscapes: the example of Maya lowland cities. *Antiquity* 86(334), 1112–25.

Keenan, B., A. Imfeld, K. Johnston, A. Breckenridge, Y. Gélinas & P.M.J. Douglas, 2021. Molecular evidence for human population change associated with climate events in the Maya lowlands. *Quaternary Science Reviews* 258, 106904.

Klassen, S., A.K. Carter, D.H. Evans, S. Ortman, M.T. Stark, A.A. Loyless, M. Polkinghorne, P. Heng, M. Hill & P. Wijker, 2021. Diachronic modeling of the population within the medieval Greater Angkor region settlement complex. *Science Advances* 7(19), eabf8441.

Klassen, S., J. Weed & D. Evans, 2018. Semi-supervised machine learning approaches for predicting the chronology of archaeological sites: a case study of temples from medieval Angkor, Cambodia, (ed.) Petraglia, M.D. *PLoS One* 13(11), e0205649.

Lewitz, S., 1967. La toponymie khmère. *Bulletin de l'École française d'Extrême-Orient* 53(2), 375–451.

Lorrillard, M., 2010. Par-delà Vat Phu. Données nouvelles sur l'expansion des espaces khmer et môn anciens au Laos. *Bulletin de l'École française d'Extrême-Orient* 97(1), 205–70.

Lucero, L.J., R. Fletcher & R. Coningham, 2015. From 'collapse' to urban diaspora: the transformation of low-density, dispersed agrarian urbanism. *Antiquity* 89(347), 1139–54.

Lustig, T., J.-B. Chevance & W. Johnson, 2023. Angkor as a "cité hydraulique"?, in *The Angkorian World*, eds. M. Hendrickson, M.T. Stark & D. Evans. New York: Routledge.

Lustig, T., S. Klassen, D. Evans, R. French & I. Moffat, 2018. Evidence for the breakdown of an Angkorian hydraulic system, and its historical implications for understanding the Khmer Empire. *Journal of Archaeological Science: Reports* 17, 195–211.

Mabbett, I., 1978. Kingship in Angkor. *Journal of the Siam Society* 66(2), 1–58.

Malleret, L., 1959. *L'Archéologie Du Delta Du Mékong. Tome Premier: L'Exploration Archéologique et Les Fouilles d'Óc-Èo*. Paris: École française d' Extrême-Orient.

Manguin, P.-Y. & M. Vallerin, 1997. La mission "Archéologie du delta du Mékong". *Bulletin de l'École française d'Extrême-Orient* 84, 408–14.

Manguin, P.-Y. & N. Tingley, 2009. The archaeology of Funan in the Mekong River Delta: the Óc Eo culture of Vietnam, in *Arts of Ancient Vietnam: From River Plain to Open Sea*. New Haven: Yale University Press, 100–18.

Manguin, P.-Y. & V.S. Khải, 2000. Excavations at the Ba Thê/Óc Eo complex (Viet Nam): a preliminary report on the 1998 campaign, in *Southeast Asian Archaeology 1998: Proceedings of the 7th International*

Conference of the European Association of Southeast Asian Archaeologists, Berlin, 31 August-4 September 1998, 107–22.

Maxwell, T.S., 2007. The Stele Inscription of Preah Khan, Angkor with Translation and Commentary. *Udaya, Journal of Khmer Studies* 8, 1–114.

Michelet, D. & P. Nondédéo, 2019. Ancient Maya lowlands: from fake feuds about "urbanism" to renewed studies of settlement patterns. *Origini* 41(2), 249–68.

Miksic, J.N., 2000. Heterogenetic cities in Premodern Southeast Asia. *World Archaeology* 32(1), 106–20.

Moore, E.H., 2009. The Williams-Hunt collection: aerial photographs and cultural landscapes in Malaysia and Southeast Asia. *Sari—International Journal of the Malay World and Civilisation* 27(2), 265–84.

Ortman, S.G., M.E. Smith, J. Lobo & L.M.A. Bettencourt, 2020. Why archaeology is necessary for a theory of urbanization. *Journal of Urban Archaeology* 1, 151–67.

Penny, D., T. Hall, D. Evans & M. Polkinghorne, 2019. Geoarchaeological evidence from Angkor, Cambodia, reveals a gradual decline rather than a catastrophic 15th-century collapse. *Proceedings of the National Academy of Sciences* 116(11), 4871–76.

Polkinghorne, M. & Y. Sato, 2023. Early Modern Cambodia and archaeology at Longvek, in *The Angkorian World*, eds. M. Hendrickson, M.T. Stark & D. Evans. New York: Routledge, 592–613.

Polkinghorne, M., 2018. Reconfiguring kingdoms: the end of Angkor and the emergence of early modern period Cambodia, in *Angkor: Exploring Cambodia's Sacred City*, eds. T. McCullough, S.A. Murphy, P. Baptiste & T. Zéphir. Singapore: Asian Civilisations Museum, 255–69.

Pottier, C. & A. Bolle, 2009. Le Prasat Trapeang Phong à Hariharâlaya: histoire d'un temple et archéologie d'un site. *Aséanie* 24, 61–90.

Pottier, C. & J. Dumarçay, 1993. *Documents Topographiques de La Conservation Des Monuments d'Angkor*. Paris: École française d'Extrême-Orient.

Pottier, C., 1993. *Préparation d'une Carte Archéologique de La Région d'Angkor*. Paris: Université Paris III—Sorbonne Nouvelle.

Pottier, C., 1999. *Carte Archéologique de La Région d'Angkor. Zone Sud*. PhD dissertation. Paris: Université Paris III—Sorbonne Nouvelle.

Pottier, C., 2000a. À la recherche de Goloupura. *Bulletin de l'École française d'Extrême-Orient* 87, 79–107.

Pottier, C., 2000b. Some evidence of an inter-relationship between hydraulic features and rice field patterns at Angkor during ancient times. *Journal of Sophia Asian Studies* 18, 99–120.

Pottier, C., 2006. Angkor et ses cartes, in *Anamorphoses. Hommage à Jacques Dumarçay*, eds. B. Dagens & H. Chambert-Loir. Paris: Les Indes Savantes, 427–42.

Pottier, C., 2012. Beyond the temples: Angkor and its territory, in *Old Myths and New Approaches: Interpreting Ancient Religious Sites in Southeast Asia*, ed. A. Haendel. Clayton: Monash University Publishing, 12–27.

Pottier, C., 2017. Nouvelles données sur les premières cités angkoriennes, in *Deux décennies de coopération archéologique franco-cambodgienne à Angkor*, eds. A. Beschaouch, F. Verellen & M. Zink. Paris: Académie des inscriptions et belles-lettres, 43–79.

Pryce, T.O., M. Hendrickson, K. Phon, C. Sovichetra, M.F. Charlton, S. Leroy, P. Dillmann & Q. Hua, 2014. The Iron Kuay of Cambodia: tracing the role of peripheral populations in Angkorian to colonial Cambodia via a 1200 year old industrial landscape. *Journal of Archaeological Science* 47, 142–63.

Santoni, M. & C. Hawixbrock, 1998. Laos. Fouilles et prospections dans la région de Vat Phu (province de Champassak, sud du Laos). *Bulletin de l'École française d'Extrême-Orient* 85(1), 387–405.

Santoni, M. & V. Souksavatdy, 1996. Fouilles sur le Site de Vat Phou-Champassak, in *Laos: Restaurer et préserver le patrimoine national*. Vientiane: Éditions des Cahiers de France, 167–200.

Santoni, M., V. Souksavatdy, D. Defente, C. Hawixbrock & J.-C. Liger, 1997. Excavations at Champassak and Wat Phu (Southern Laos), in *South-East Asian Archaeology 1992: Proceedings of the Fourth International Conference of the European Association of South-East Asian Archaeologists. Rome, 28*th *September–4*th *October 1992*, eds. R Ciarla & F. Rispoli. Rome: L'Istituto Italiano per l'Africa e l'Oriente, 234–63.

Scarborough, V.L., A.F. Chase & D.Z. Chase, 2012. Low density urbanism, sustainability, and IHOPE-Maya: can the past provide more than history?, *UGEC Viewpoints* 8, 20.

Sharrock, P., 2015. *Banteay Chhmar: Garrison-Temple of the Khmer Empire*. London: River Books.

Shimoda, I., 2010. *Study on the Ancient Khmer city Isanapura*. PhD dissertation. Tokyo: Waseda University.

Shimoda, I., Y. Sugasawa, H. Yonenobu & T. Yukitsigu, 2015. Research on the active habitation period of the ancient Khmer city Isanapura. *Journal of Southeast Asian Archaeology* 35, 1–14.

Smith, M.E., 2020. Definitions and comparisons in urban archaeology. *Journal of Urban Archaeology* 1, 15–30.

Smith, M.E., J. Lobo, M.A. Peeples, A.M. York, B.W. Stanley, K.A. Crawford, N. Gauthier & A.C. Huster, 2021. The persistence of ancient settlements and urban sustainability. *Proceedings of the National Academy of Sciences of the United States of America* 118(20), e2018155118.

Srinivasan, D.M., 1993. Introduction: Multiple Meanings of Space and Place, in *Urban Form and Meaning in South Asia: The Shaping of Cities from Prehistoric to Precolonial Times*, eds. H. Spodek & D.M. Srinivasan. Washington: National Gallery of Art, 11–22.

Stark, M.T., 2006. Pre-Angkorian settlement trends in Cambodia's Mekong Delta and the lower Mekong Archaeological Project. *Bulletin of the Indo-Pacific Prehistory Association* 26, 98–109.

Stark, M.T., D. Evans, R. Chhay, P. Heng & A. Carter, 2015. Residential patterning at Angkor Wat. *Antiquity* 89(348), 1439–55.

Wheatley, P., 1983. *Nagara and Commandery. Origins of the Southeast Asian Urban Traditions*. Chicago: University of Chicago Press.

Zhou, D., 2007[1297]. *A Record of Cambodia: The Land and Its People*, trans. P. Harris. Chiang Mai: Silkworm Books.

11

ANGKOR'S TEMPLE COMMUNITIES AND THE LOGIC OF ITS URBAN LANDSCAPE

Scott Hawken and Sarah Klassen

The Search for Angkorian Communities

Until late in the 20th century, archaeological research on Angkor primarily focused on its greatest temples and associated monuments, art, and inscriptions. As a result, much of what was known of Angkor revolved around these elite monuments and their immediate environs (Clémentin-Ojha et al. 2007; Pottier 2000a). Early researchers of Angkor (Aymonier 1904; Briggs 1999; Cœdès 1963) devoted much less attention to the everyday landscape of consequence to the majority of its population, which is thought to have numbered around 700,000 people (Fletcher et al. 2003, 116; Klassen et al. 2021). This bias is not unique to Angkor, since archaeologists everywhere, until relatively recently, have typically focused on monumental remains in civic-ceremonial centres rather than on the full panoply of occupational sites (Sabloff 2019, 1; Smith 2010, 2013). As low-density agrarian urbanism has developed as a global comparative project (Graham et al. 2018; Smith et al. 2021; Scarborough et al. 2020; Isendahl et al. 2012, 2013, 2021; Hawken et al. 2021), Angkor's low-density settlement pattern, consisting of dispersed populations surrounding a more compact core, has been recognised as deserving of study in its own right (Fletcher 2009, 2011, 2020; Hawken 2012, 2013, 30; Klassen et al. 2021).

As with all cities and complex societies, Angkor was made up of diverse communities. Within Angkor some communities were associated with major state institutions and districts such as the temple of Angkor Wat and the walled district of Angkor Thom. But there were also communities associated primarily with rice fields and agricultural production. Our primary aim in this chapter is to define and identify this second type of rice-growing community throughout Greater Angkor's low-density landscape.

Hundreds of small, local temples and their associated infrastructure, such as ponds and reservoirs, are interspersed among ricefields and dispersed in a patchy halo around Greater Angkor's civic-ceremonial centres (Figure 11.1). Until recently, these communities have featured at the margins of research (Coe et al. 2018, 20–21). These ritual institutions served as anchors for low-density agrarian villages and were central to the life of much of the populace of Greater Angkor (Ang 1990, 151; Pottier 1999, 9; Klassen et al. 2020, 1). Such local temples are the primary marker of community across the Khmer World. Surveys have revealed that there were

DOI: 10.4324/9781351128940-14

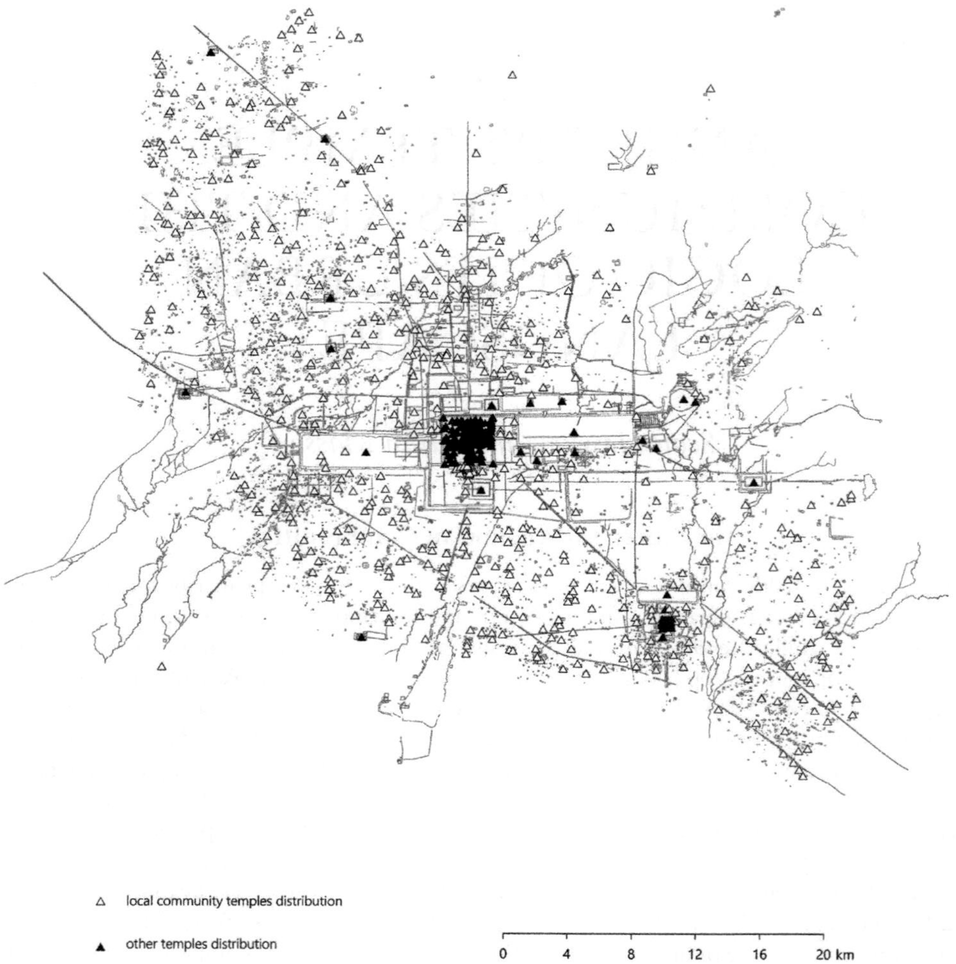

Figure 11.1 Comparison of local community temples versus state and other temples within the civic ceremonial centre and suburban centres of Greater Angkor. For the colour version of this figure and legend, the reader is referred to the web version of this chapter.

GIS Source: C. Pottier 1999, D. Evans 2007 & S. Hawken 2012.

many smaller temples of modest dimensions that operated as centres of worship, politics, and daily ritual for peripheral agricultural communities (Pottier 1999; Evans 2007; Evans et al. 2007, 2013; Chevance et al. 2019). We seek to foreground Angkor's agricultural communities as a subject of study in their own right and consider them distinctive units within the expansive low-density landscape. Temples are useful diagnostic elements in negotiating chronological 'palimpsests' (defined in the following section) as they have greater potential for determining more exacting dates than, for example, rice fields (Hawken 2012; Klassen et al. 2018; Evans et al. 2007). We argue, as others do, that agricultural settlement units are of critical importance when it comes to the study of past communities and landscapes (Canuto and Yaeger 2000; Yaeger et al. 2000, 9; Gerritsen 2006; Canuto et al. 2018).

Finding Angkorian Communities: The Palimpsest Problem

Angkor is a well-known palimpsest that consists of many different phases of development and remains of human activity integrated into one continuous landscape surface. The comprehensive map of Greater Angkor (Pottier 1999; Evans 2007; Evans et al. 2013; Hawken 2012; Chevance et al. 2019) is made up of an 'urban core' that consists of more specialist 'civic-ceremonial' districts and a periphery of more 'agrarian' settlements constructed over hundreds of years. Phases of development include prehistoric, Pre-Angkorian, Angkorian, and Post-Angkorian, along with expanding contemporary urban settlements. Such horizontal integration of sites into a continuous surface is known as a 'spatial palimpsest' as opposed to a 'cumulative palimpsest,' which indicates vertical deposition processes (Bailey 2007, 207).

Although Greater Angkor's palimpsest is singular in terms of its scale and complexity, it shares similarities with settlement landscapes throughout the territories of the former Khmer empire in mainland Southeast Asia. For example, archaeologists working elsewhere in Cambodia have documented the same transition from 'prehistoric' to 'proto-historic' to 'Pre-Angkorian' to 'Angkorian' settlement patterning. At Thala Borivat, on the Mekong in the northeast of Cambodia, Heng (2016) suggests smaller proto-historic settlements from c. 300–500 CE were incorporated into larger Pre-Angkorian centres in what can be called a 'cumulative' palimpsest. In her work at Angkor Borei, Stark's (1999) excavations have demonstrated that the site was linked to the site of Óc Eo as part of a network of sites that form a 'spatial palimpsest' that has been continuously occupied from the first millennium CE to the present. Within the upper Mun Valley, in present-day Thailand, the work of Caitlin Evans et al. suggests prehistoric to proto-historic settlement transitions were gradual and took place through a process of modification rather than through 'the sudden adoption of external ideas' (2016, 438). Similar examples are also noted in Thailand (Murphy 2016) and in the dry zone of Myanmar (Stargardt 2016). This regional-scale palimpsest reflects a complicated mixture of both 'indigenous and exogenous inspiration' (Murphy and Stark 2016, 340). The resulting settlement palimpsest is unique to mainland Southeast Asia (see Stark 2006).

Because newer settlements sometimes erased, overlapped, or evolved adjacent to previous ones, palimpsests often require the application of complex urban and landscape morphological analyses necessary to understand how the landscape developed over time. The complexity of settlement features within Greater Angkor has resulted in a range of misunderstandings and debates around the provenances and association of various archaeological features. An example of this is the confusion around Yaśodharapura I, the first capital of Angkor. Victor Goloubew (1933) incorrectly associated a range of embankment and moat features with the planning of the complex of Phnom Bakheng and the initial Yaśodharapura. It took almost seven decades for this palimpsest to be more accurately deciphered by the archaeologist Pottier (2000c).

However, despite the potential confusion and difficulty in deciphering such palimpsests, they also provide an opportunity: Palimpsests allow us to examine a greater scale of material behaviour and to observe long-term trends and relationships beyond the more limited histories of individual sites (Bailey 2007, 205; Holdaway and Wandsnider 2008; Binford 1987, 1983, 119). They are particularly important when considering the agrarian and low-density settlements, which lack precise chronological information, are expansive, and have been reused over long periods (Erikson 2006, 348; Peterson et al. 2005; Fletcher 2009).

Angkor's spatial palimpsest is the end product of many centuries of landscape engineering and management fused into a single snapshot of surface archaeology. Today, we appraise the remains of these past activities as one extended layer across the landscape (Hawken 2012). Such complex palimpsests may be evident through the spatial relations of a range of archaeological features from different periods, diachronic ceramic scatters on habitation mounds (Evans et al. 2016), the alignment or interface between embankments and temple sanctuaries (Pottier 2000c), or the integration of rice fields from multiple periods (Hawken 2013). To decipher and better understand Angkor's palimpsest, we use the small local temples as indicators of the communities that spread out around them. This archaeological category has also been recorded in southern Cambodia's Mekong Delta (Stark 2006, 106; Stark et al. 1999, 21; 2015, 142–44), where they are described as 'moated mounds'. Excavations by Pottier et al. (2009) have also revealed evidence of residential occupation on such temple mounds, complicating conventional divisions between sacred and profane spaces. By studying the distribution and clustering of local temples across space, we gain insights into the likely scale of operation of local community groups within Angkor and the practical routines and patterns of movement as they grew rice, visited temples, and undertook domestic daily activities within Greater Angkor.

Defining Communities Across Greater Angkor

Angkor's local agrarian communities included a range of features, including ricefields, one or more local temples, one or more ponds, and usually a scattering of habitation mounds. They are consistent with definitions by archaeologists such as Kolb and Snead (1997, 611), who define community as a 'minimal, spatially defined locus of human activity that incorporates social reproduction, subsistence production, and self-identification'.

Our definition is limited to elements identified within Greater Angkor's settlement pattern as discerned through remote sensing, and lacks the richness of information from the 'vertical' dimension that might emerge from extensive excavation. Although archaeological excavation should be an important contributor to the diachronic study of such communities within Angkor, this has generally not been the case due to the sheer number of these temple communities and the practical impossibility of excavating any significant proportion of them. Over 1000 local temples have been identified and mapped using remote sensing, and excavating each temple complex would be prohibitively expensive and time consuming. This challenge is not unique to Angkor and is also relevant within archaeological research beyond Southeast Asia, such as in Mesoamerica (Kolb and Snead 1997, 609). This chapter explains how we recognise local temples in the low-density urban landscape, and how historical and ethnographic data correspond to what we find in the archaeological record of the few local temples that have been excavated. The need to tackle these kinds of issues—arising from very sparse excavation data over a vast archaeological landscape—is a central problem in contemporary archaeology and is a particularly prominent issue in the settlement archaeology of the tropics. Locating concepts of 'community' within low-density tropical urbanism has been recognised as a challenge since it first became the subject of study in the 1950s and 60s for the Maya, Sinhalese, and Khmer (Coe 1957, 1961, 2005; Bronson 1979; Fletcher 2009; Hawken et al. 2021).

To understand the evolution of community landscapes, the patterning of the various phases must be distinguished or filtered through analytic processes involving morphological, typological, and topographic analysis (Pottier 1999; Evans 2007; Klassen, 2018, 2020; Hawken 2012, 2013). Systematic approaches involving orientation, feature type, size, and scale can effectively relate temples, ponds, and rice fields at the scale of the district and city. Topographic morphologies and associated attributes of temples and hydraulic infrastructure (including (1) the presence or absence of the temple moat, (2) presence or lack of a primary reservoir, (3) presence of temple building materials, (4) orientation of temples and associated features, (5) size of the temples and sites, and (6) the morphology of the temple mound) can together help define dates for local communities.

In urban systems, elements of the built environment are typically standardised according to generic or archetypal forms (Dumarçay et al. 2003). This standardisation can be used to both define communities and their associated structures such as temples and rice fields in time (Hawken 2012, 234–251; Klassen et al. 2018). These approaches allow researchers to examine the temporal and functional dimensions related to the horizontal arrangement of the landscape, which we can read and interpret as a series of 'community patches', each with its own 'local temple'. We use the term 'patch' as a generic and malleable unit that approximates the community extent and encompasses the local temple, its surrounding rice fields, and the clusters of ponds and mounds that coalesce in varying configurations.

Archaeological Evidence of Communities

The settlements of Angkor are often grouped into either (1) residential settlements within the Civic-Ceremonial Centres or (2) residential clusters dispersed within the rice field landscape of the Angkor Metropolitan Area (Klassen et al. 2021). The Greater Angkor project has completed excavations of residential communities within significant temples sanctuaries such as Angkor Wat, Ta Prohm, Chau Srei Vibol, Kok Phnov, Wat Athvea, and Wat Prei Einkosei in the civic-ceremonial centre (Stark et al. 2015; Carter et al. 2018). These excavations, guided since 2012 by the occupation mound and house pond patterns revealed by the lidar data (Evans 2013), indicate that the temple sanctuaries in the civic-ceremonial centres were relatively densely occupied residential spaces within the more sparsely occupied agrarian territory of Greater Angkor (Carter et al. 2018).

While much work has been done in the civic-ceremonial centres, a handful of projects have also focused on the dispersed agrarian communities that comprise the Greater Angkor area (which has also been termed the Angkor Metropolitan Area). Pottier et al. (2009) surveyed ten habitation mounds surrounding Trapeang Phong as part of the *Mission archéologique franco-khmère sur l'aménagement du territoire d'Angkor* (Mafkata) project. Bâty's exhaustive excavations (2010), completed in advance of the expansion of Siem Reap International Airport, covered more than 26 ha and involved the study of a complete settlement surrounding the 10th- and 11th-century temples of Prasat Trapeang Ropou and Trapeang Thlok. Excavations of 'commoner' settlement at Angkor at Trapeang Tlok and Prasat Ropou complex (Bâty 2005, 2007, 2010; Bâty et al. 2016) demonstrated that such local temples were stratigraphically related to the many settlement features, including pounds, mounds, and rice fields, that surrounded the temples. Habitation sites were identified upon the mounds and the banks of ponds, known as *trapeang* in Khmer. For example, at Trapeang Roupou, the settlement cluster consisted of a temple of three towers surrounded by a moat. To the east, a causeway connected it to a large pond of 320 × 180 m. A total of 12 such habitation mounds surrounded the community temple. Typically, the habitation mounds were rectangular platforms of 1,500 to 3,000 m^2 and supported timber houses raised above the landscape on timber posts or pilots (Huyen 1934). Such a construction technique is still common throughout Cambodia and Southeast Asia (Dumarçay 1987; Tainturier 2006). Raised houses are helpful for ventilation both during the heat of the summer and to prevent flooding during heavy monsoon rains. Remains of such houses were not found, although the presence of post holes indicates their placement along with a range of fences and smaller structures. The settlement's excavation by Bâty (2010, Bâty et al. 2016) also demonstrated a spatial relationship between the mounded features and adjacent rice fields, which were arranged in a formal gridded pattern.

Ethnographic and Epigraphic Evidence of Communities

In an epigraphic and ethnographic study spanning both contemporary and Angkorian temples, Ang (1990) argues that the local temples are the institution that best integrates the multiple essential functions of the Khmer community. Ang (1990, 151) goes so far as to say that the Buddhist temple 'constitutes the most brilliant expression of the [agrarian khmer] community', noting various continuities between Angkorian and modern times and expanding on Delvert's definition by noting the richness of the various religious and cultural dimensions of the community temple. Ang (1990, 138–42) suggests that temples were critical nodes in space, around which a range of social and historical developments took place during Angkorian times. For example, a temple foundation might be established to revive an abandoned settlement, or it might be established to anchor a new settlement within a new forest clearing. Alternatively, it could provide the authority for annexing landscapes of ambiguous or disputed ownership. Various other scholars subscribe to this view, arguing that temples were the focus of Khmer religious and administrative life and the economy (Sedov 1963; Hall 1975, 2004; Lustig 2009; Wolters 1982; Welch 1997, 70). There is no complete consensus on the relationship between community and temple in past and present Khmer society. Nevertheless, there is sufficient agreement to make the small temples that dotted Angkor's low-density urban landscape a logical starting point when it comes to studying and defining communities.

The epigraphic corpus from the Angkor Period seems to confirm that local temples were centres of social and economic integration (Vickery 1998; Hall 2004). The inscriptions, inscribed on the walls and doors of temples or free-standing stelae, were written by elites with specific agendas and, as such, should be interpreted with care (Jacques 1986, 328). However, they do shed some light on the function of local temples, including how temples were founded (Ricklefs 1967); how land ownership was determined, regulated, and disputed (Sahai 1977); and how the temples were incorporated into the hierarchical economic system of the Khmer Empire (Sahai 1978; Hall 2004). We have relatively little information about the internal organisation of these temples and their associated villages. However, Lustig and Lustig (2019) have traced the relative status of officials mentioned in the Khmer corpus and found that, over time, there was a shift of land ownership and power from mid-level officials to elites.

Beyond the political and economic importance of the temples, the inscriptions paint a picture of daily life for the residents of these local temple communities. Important families would be granted, or request, land from the king and then set forth to clear the forest and found a temple and associated village (Mabbett 1978). The most notable residences of these villages are referred to as *kñum*. These laborers were bought and sold and have often been described as unfree or slaves (Lustig, E. et al. 2013; Lustig, T. et al. 2015). The *kñum* worked in the ricefields, but some engaged in other agricultural activities like tending to the livestock and fruit trees for two weeks of the month (Sahai 2012; Stark 2015). The inscriptions also reference the construction of reservoirs as well as fruit trees (mango, coconut palms, betel nuts, etc.) and livestock (water buffalo, cows, and goats) that were free to forage in the ricefields (Jacob 1978).

Contemporary Khmer settlements also offer a useful analogue for defining the features and organisation of communities in Greater Angkor. A similar situation occurs with modern monasteries or modern pagodas providing a focus for communities (Ang 1990, 152, Hansen 2004). Delvert notes that 'the temple is the centre of rural life' within Cambodia (Delvert 1994, 218–20), acting as a moral, social, and educational institution and gathering point. Local temples are the focus of many holidays and festivals and are sites of formal and informal learning and guidance, both for the institution's immediate inhabitants and the wider community. They are, therefore, significant gathering spaces for communities. Condominas (1968) has emphasised the temple's multi-functional role within Southeast Asia and notes the deep community ties between temple and community.

The best-known anthropological study of a Khmer agrarian community is by Ebihara (Marston 2011). Ebihara (2018) describes a typical lowland rice-growing village that extended over a kilometre in size with 168 houses and 790 inhabitants dispersed amongst rice fields. Ebihara notes that this settlement can be recognised as a community for physical, social, and political reasons. First, it is separated from other villages by swathes of uncleared land or clear topographic features such as a dry streambed. Second, it is a political entity in the government's eyes under the 'jurisdiction of a village chief'. Delvert (1994, 218) suggests that Khmer 'communities' lack a sense of 'communitarianism' and, strictly speaking, have no communal house or communal property. However, Ebihara contests this based on her long study of the village she calls the common Khmer name of 'Svay' (Ebihara 2018, 92–3). Instead, she argues that Svay residents had 'a sense of community, and . . . are bound together by diverse social, economic, political, and religious ties that form a loosely knit but nonetheless true community'.

Interestingly, Ebihara notes that loyalties are divided between several Buddhist temples within Svay. Ebihara adds that in a community that supports only one temple, the residents constitute a congregation and cooperate on 'various religious endeavours' (2018, 93). In such instances, the temples were 'a place of retreat, a place of gathering, a place of assembly: it is a true communal house' (Delvert 1994, 220). Kalab also notes the primary importance of monasteries for communities and that '[although] in theory any person may support any pagoda, the houses giving support to particular monasteries form distinct contiguous areas' (1968, 526, 529). A significant anthropological description of Khmer village life has also been recorded by Martel (1975). Martel's descriptions present a wealth of detail on the institutions of Khmer people living close to Siem Reap prior to the 1970s. Religion is a strong theme throughout the work, and it is clear that both Buddhist temples and indigenous ancestral cults bound the village community, both culturally and spatially, through regular rituals and festivities.

However, more recently such views on contemporary Khmer villages have been contested. Certain scholars argue that early ethnographic and anthropological work on Southeast Asia presents an overly simplistic portrayal of unified, stable communities and the 'one-to-one correspondence' between temple, village, and community (Kobayashi 2005, 514). Ledgerwood has investigated both contemporary and past communities as well as revisiting the communities studied in Ebihara's original work. Consequently, Ledgerwood argues that such recent critiques of Ebihara's study are overstated and reflect that 'anthropological research today is more focused on disjunctures, shifting perceptions and imagined identities, as opposed to stable communities or reified notions of cultural models' (2011, 122).

These insights into Khmer communities in the context of Angkor's extensive territory are taken from archaeological, anthropological, epigraphic, and ethnographic sources (see Table 11.1). However, the most detailed and vivid historical record we have of everyday life in Angkor is from the Chinese emissary, Zhou Daguan (2007[1297], 76–7, 80), to Angkor in the 13th century. Zhou Daguan notes, 'In every village, there is a Buddhist temple or a pagoda' (2007[1297], 79) and describes various scenes from everyday life in the 13th century that remain familiar in Khmer communities today, from personal habits to residential architecture. These similarities suggest a significant continuing heritage within Southeast Asia's urban agrarian life (Hawken 2017; Hawken et al. 2021b). This tableau of Angkorian houses with their community orchards, ponds, and everyday life has been brought to life in the carefully crafted visualisations of Chandler et al. (Figure 11.2) (2012).

While there is a clear correlation between what Zhou Daguan describes and the ethnographic record, there is a problem with locating material correlates in the archaeological record.

Table 11.1 Epigraphic territorial terms and their definitions.

Various territorial terms in the epigraphic corpus	*Interpretation of epigraphic territorial terms by historians, geographers, and linguists*
Praman	Claude Jacques (1972) defines the term 'praman' as a large geographical unit referring to an extensive 'territory'. Wolters (1974, 357–58) and Sahai (1977, 36) emphasise that there is much uncertainty around interpretations of this term.
Visaya	Claude Jacques (1972) defines 'visaya' as an administrative term, for which 'province' may be cautiously used. Scholars such as Sahai (1977, 37) and Vickery (1998, 327) emphasise the ambiguity of the term.
Sruk	The term 'sruk' is frequently mentioned in the inscriptions and most commonly interpreted as 'village' (Lewitz 1967). 'Sruk' are often mentioned in association with rice fields and land grants (Mabbett 1977). Families who established religious foundations on land purchased or given by rulers where described as being given 'sruk' villages. Lewitz presents the three terms, praman, visaya and sruk, as the hierarchy of territory, district, and village (1967). Both Mabbett (1977, 23) and Lewitz (1967, 406) suggests that 'sruk' is 'the division of territory where a religious foundation is set up and a community grows'.
Grama	Sahai (1977, 37) notes that the term 'grama' is used as a synonym for 'sruk' in various inscriptions. The term 'grama' is much less common in the inscriptions than 'sruk'.
Bhumi	'Bhumi', another synonym for 'sruk' found within the inscriptions, is also the term most frequently used to describe khmer villages today (Delvert 1994). Again, the term is much less common in the inscriptions than 'sruk'.

Figure 11.2 Reconstruction of a mediaeval settlement and village shrine in the south of Angkor.

Source: (Image courtesy T. Chandler and M. Lim.

The perishable materials of everyday Angkorian life have left few archaeological traces, and Bâty's excavations are some of the few that have been able to make explicit material links between the archaeological record and with what we can read about in Zhou's record (Bâty 2005; Bâty et al. 2016). As such, we argue that Bâty's excavations and the patterning from ethnographic temple distributions provide the foundation to create models where local temples, often the only remaining evidence of Angkorian occupation on the landscape, can be used to document the spaces of communities. In the following section, we investigate the spatial parameters of this sphere of activity, noting the geometric principles which emerge from a study of the community temples and what we can call their 'patches'.

Local Temples and Their Landscapes

Over 1000 local temples have been identified in Greater Angkor, the great majority of which are associated with the rice-growing communities that extend between and far beyond the city's civic-ceremonial centres and which were the focus of everyday life for the great majority of Angkor's population (Figure 11.1).

The morphologies of these local temples are strikingly similar. Most temples were built upon an earthen mound. They typically had a surrounding moat with a causeway, creating a distinctive horseshoe shape (a name first adopted by Evans 2007) when viewed using remotely sensed imagery. Horseshoe-type (50%) village temples are the most common type, followed by those with irregular morphologies, including rectangular morphologies, two causeways, and four causeways (Hawken 2012, 222–25). The distinctive moat-and-mound configuration makes them relatively straightforward to identify within remote sensing imagery, even if the actual temple structure of brick or perishable materials is no longer visible or destroyed. Each local temple was typically oriented according to the cardinal directions, with a general preference for the east (Pottier 1999, 59–64, Dagens 2003, 166–67, Dumarçay and Smithies 2003; Mabbett 1978). Of the temples mapped by Pottier (1999) and Evans (2007), around half have an accompanying pond to the east at the end of the causeway. With their associated moats and causeways, the dimensions of local temples were modest and, while varied, are typically 40 to 80 m across. This contrasts with the immense dimensions of Angkor Wat, which measures more than 1 km long on each side.

Local temples demonstrate a range of four different configurations or 'topographic classes' that characterise Greater Angkor's low-density settlement pattern beyond the urban core: a single-temple community, a multi-temple community, a colonising temple community grafted onto a pre-existing settlement, and a hydraulic temple community closely associated with state infrastructure (see Figure 11.3).

A single temple community (illustrated in Figure 11.3b) is exemplified by the lone religious structure framed by settlement features and rice fields in the eastern periphery of Angkor Metropolitan Area. One large habitation mound is located in the near west of the community temple, suggesting this community was relatively centralised—and thus quite different from the dispersed contemporary Cambodian community described by Ebihara (1968). Although this assemblage is composed of a relatively modest and uncomplicated spatial arrangement of ponds and mounds, we know from inscriptional evidence that such kinds of temples were nonetheless critical nodes in the extended mosaic of Greater Angkor and that beyond their obvious religious function, they played an important role in the social, political, and economic life of a given area, with various specialised attending officials dedicated to the administration of villages and some specialising in the registration of rice fields and land cadastre, for example (Sahai 1977, 50).

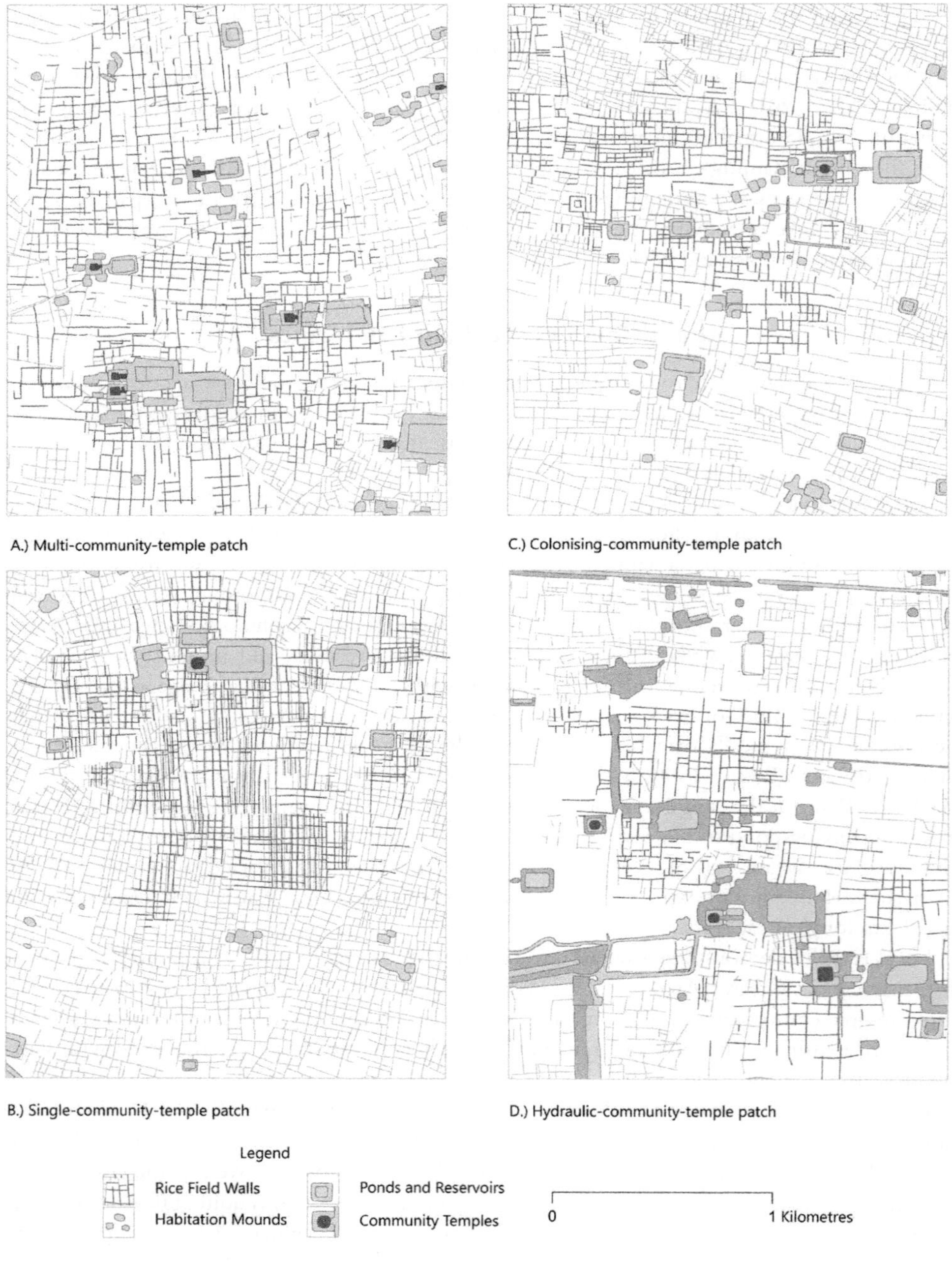

Figure 11.3 Range of variations in local temple sites and their associated community settlements: a) a multi-temple community; b) a single-temple community; c) a colonising temple community grafted onto a pre-existing settlement; d) a hydraulic temple community closely associated with state infrastructure. For the colour version of this figure and legend, the reader is referred to the web version of this chapter. GIS source: C. Pottier 1999, D. Evans 2007 & S. Hawken 2012.

Source: (GIS data C. Pottier 1999 & D. Evans 2007).

In the next example, of a multi-temple community (Figure 11.3a), five community temples are tightly clustered within 1 km of the other. Each temple and associated community pond is aligned along an eastern axis with a grid of rice fields that integrates the features. A distinctive twin temple complex within the patch incorporates two adjacent community temples which are aligned on a north–south axis. Each of the local temples is a good example of the horseshoe-moat temple archetype. This community temple patch is located south of the West Baray. Although no clear channel runs through this area, it may have benefited from the water security presented after the construction of the West Baray. The multi-temple patch suggests intensive management and/or a strong ritual or religious significance to this specific area. Distinguishing patches within dense clusters of the landscape are not always clear or simple. In such cases, how these temples cooperate or are networked, and how to distinguish their roles, are important questions. Again the inscriptions offer some clues. Sahai writes of an instance of two religious foundations seeking to combine their staff—and presumably their land holdings—although the purpose of the union is not clear (Sahai 1978; Ricklefs 1967).

A colonising temple community (Figure 11.3c) is defined by the weak association between the temple and the surrounding rice field grid. Both the complicated topographic assemblage integrating the horseshoe archetype and the relative complexity of the rice field patch suggests time depth and that this temple has been inserted into an older landscape. From the types of foundation frequently described in the Angkorian inscriptions, we may suppose that this foundation may have been either a symbolic or pragmatic move to recolonise or annex the rice fields in this area. Such rice field landscapes may have been previously abandoned or the subject of the kind of land dispute that we see frequently enough in inscriptions (Ricklefs 1967, 40).

The final type is the hydraulic community patch. Three community temples are carefully orchestrated in a remarkable staggered pattern. Significantly, the temples are physically linked to a nearby component of the large-scale hydraulic infrastructure. The community patch demonstrates three east–west temple-pond archetypes. The northernmost temple lacks a clear causeway despite its good alignment with the pond located to its east. Each temple is located at a relatively close distance from the next. The fact that this patch is directly associated with state-level hydraulic engineering via several water channels suggests that this patch may have been either a benefactor of state hydraulic control or potentially had a role in administering or supervising the hydraulic network.

These topographic classes are not exclusive and could co-exist or overlap. For example, multi-community–temple-hydraulic clusters (Figure 11.3d) or a multi-temple colonising clusters (Figures 11.3a and 11.3d) are possible and reasonably common due to the integration of the hydraulic superstructure with Greater Angkor's low density settlement (Klassen and Evans 2020) and due to the fact that Angkor appropriated and adapted much earlier prehistoric landscapes through spatial colonisation (Higham 2014, 196–97, 234; McColl et al. 2018; O'Reilly and Shewan 2016). Such topographic classes suggest a range of possible functional and ritual narratives that might be developed through closer study of community temples and their landscape patches. Each of these classes suggests that the communities associated with local temples were flexible. The institutions were able to adapt to different contexts and pressures within the expansive low-density landscape of Angkor. However, all such configurations integrate common features, namely rice fields, habitation mounds, and ponds. The examples depicted in Figure 11.3 elaborate this variation and repetition within the 'horseshoe' temple archetype that Pottier (1993, 1999, 59–64) has described.

Patterns of Local Temples and Communities in Greater Angkor

Surface archaeological features within Greater Angkor have been systematically mapped over decades (Evans 2007; Pottier 1999; Hawken 2012). With these maps it is possible to consider the implications of the patterning of local temples to for how temples and communities are positioned

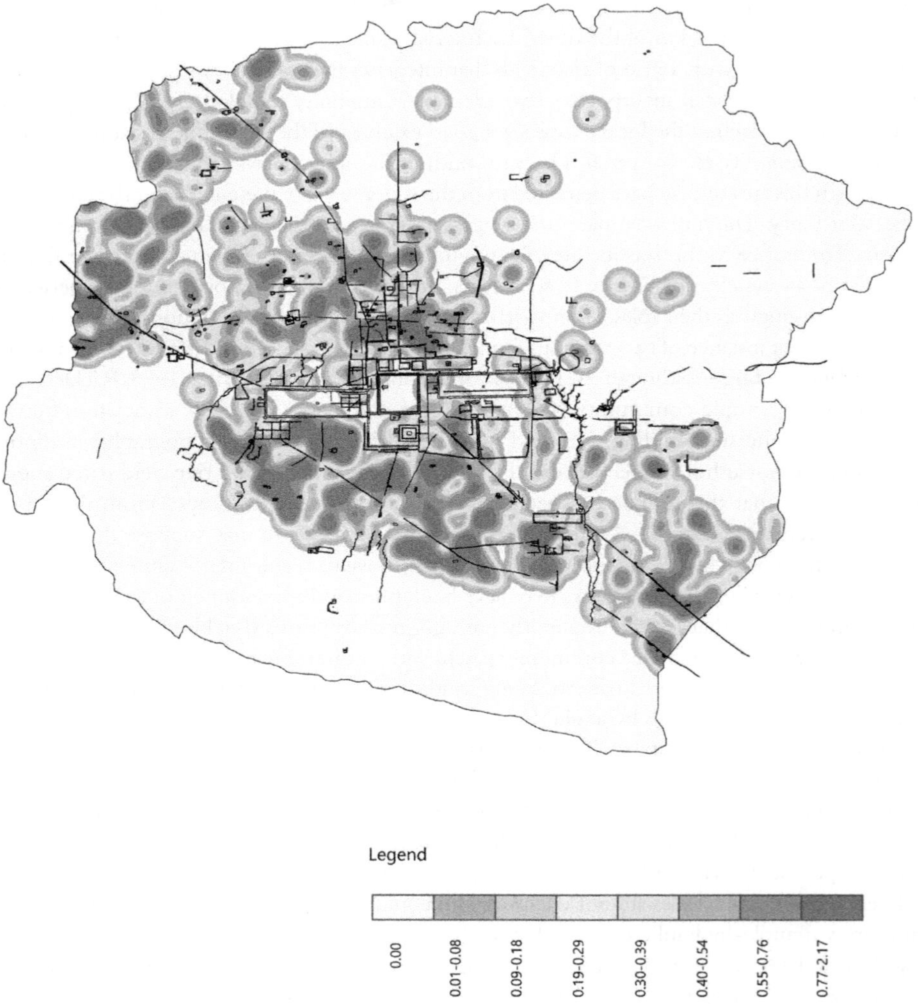

Figure 11.4 Density of local community temples per square kilometre in Greater Angkor. Note that community temples are typically located within a 1 km or so walk, making them easily accessible within the dispersed urban landscape of Greater Angkor. For the colour version of this figure and legend, the reader is referred to the web version of this chapter. GIS source: C. Pottier 1999, D. Evans 2007 & S. Hawken 2012.

Source: (GIS data, C. Pottier 1999, D. Evans 2007 & S. Hawken 2012).

in relationship to the broader hydraulic systems and civic-ceremonial centres. To understand these spatial relationships, we created a density map (Figure 11.4) that shows that local temples form a halo around Angkor's urban core and are clustered south/downstream of the East and West Baray and north and northwest of Angkor and along the massive, state-sponsored linear hydraulic infrastructures. Both clusters of local temples correlate with areas served by hydraulic infrastructure. The southern clusters were positioned below the reservoir systems of the Baray, date from the Pre-Angkor Period (see Chevance and Pottier 2023, this volume), and, therefore, potentially inspired or benefited from the water security such hydraulic infrastructure could offer. The northern cluster could also have inspired or benefited from additional water security through increased storage and distribution capacity made available through the various embankments and channels in the district (see, for example, Groslier 1974, 1979; Pottier 2000c). We may observe that there are few, if any, clusters that are *not* downstream of major water management infrastructure.

Subsequent research by Fletcher et al. (2008a, 2000b) and Klassen et al. (2020) has focused on the expansion of the hydraulic system over time. The co-location of these clusters of temple communities with state-sponsored infrastructure suggests three potential relationships between local temples and the construction of state-sponsored hydraulic and road infrastructure systems.

An initial possibility is that political pressure exerted by the local temple communities may have stimulated state-level infrastructure. In other words, the state developed infrastructure to service pre-existing clustering of temples in the rain-fed zones found in the analysis. These zones are productive rice-growing areas beyond the flood level of the lake, which supports this possibility.

A second is that new communities formed around the pre-existing state-level infrastructure. Intensification of land use and local temple communities followed the development of state-level hydraulic infrastructure within a landscape that was previously sparsely settled. The increase in water resources could have opened opportunities for establishing more temple foundations and for communities to exploit and manage these water resources.

The final possibility is a combination of the previous two: the greater density of community temples results from pre-existing conditions and partly due to an increase in density from the more stable and reliable conditions created by the state infrastructure. This last possibility is convincing, as the centralisation of resources and their administration by local temples could have economically supported continuing hydraulic construction and maintenance through positive feedback, which is characteristic of various societies throughout tropical Asia (Lansing 2006; Scarborough et al. 2010; also Heng and Sahai 2023, this volume). The state requires a tax base and political support from a successful agrarian population to secure its agendas and ultimately success. Thus, it could benefit from ensuring the sustainability, stability, and intensification of its agrarian community base. Analyses of inscriptions indicate that the king granted land, and sometimes multiple foundations were combined into one (Sahai 1977, 1978). There was, of course, always at least some degree of state-level political control over the foundation locations of temple communities.

An equally important issue is the voids within the map, which we may interpret to be extended areas without communities. Two significant voids exist at the periphery of the patchy halo of agrarian temple communities that surround the civic ceremonial zone of Angkor. These voids correlate with fragmented hydraulic works extending north from Banteay Srah in the west and the main channels of the Roluos River system in the east and northeast. Beyond these voids, local temples appear to continue in a similar pattern. Whether this absence of local temples, and by implication the absence of communities, is due to a lack of the resources required to sustain a community, state-level planning or taphonomic processes that have obscured archaeological features is not possible to say without further study.

The presence of significant hydraulic infrastructure within these voids complicates this picture of correspondence between agrarian communities and hydraulic infrastructure. Areas with major state hydraulic infrastructure and without evidence of local community infrastructure may have been primarily or exclusively state controlled. Some areas, such as the district of Phnom Bok, almost completely lack horseshoe temples and contain major state-planned hydraulic infrastructure (see Hawken and Castillo 2023, this volume). Such contrasting patterns of community and state constructions suggest that administration of some of the peripheral areas of Angkor was complex and that perhaps simple elite-commoner and centre-periphery political correlations do not neatly fit in a patchy or polycentric distribution of power.

Significantly, this figure also shows the continuation of Angkor's community temples to the edge and (presumably) beyond the limits of the study area by the region's watershed. Extended patterns of Angkorian occupation that reach beyond the civic-ceremonial centres are known to continue along the road systems of the Empire (Hendrickson 2007, 2010), with such roads often integrating existing ponds and other agrarian features (Hawken 2012, 197) into a greater regional multi-city urban system (Jacques et al. 2007; Evans 2016) continuing along the shores of the Tonle Sap (Groslier 1973).

Change and Dynamic Temple Communities

As previously mentioned, the Angkorian landscape was a palimpsest, and temple communities were founded, abandoned, and potentially re-founded over time. Dating these temples is crucial to understanding how these areas developed over time, especially in response to or anticipation of the construction of large hydraulic features. With statistical approaches, dates for temples can be estimated using an average absolute error of approximately 49–66 years (Klassen et al. 2018). Based upon such methods we can visualise the development of local temples and their associated communities across Greater Angkor. Figure 11.5 shows that construction of local temples in the Angkor Metropolitan Area occurred from the 8th to the 13th centuries, with the largest number of new foundations during the late 10th century. A paucity of new local temple construction on the local level during the period of Jayavarman VII suggests a pattern of urban adaptation and reuse during this time that contrasts with the ruler's reputation as a prolific monument builder (Jacques et al. 1997, 205; Coe et al. 2018, 151).

Evidence from inscriptions (Lustig et al. 2019) suggests that land transactions increased, and competition for land was more intense during the 12th century, which suggests reappropriation of resources rather than expanding new landscapes and the foundation of new temples. A recent study (Klassen et al. 2021) has tried to account for this reappropriation of resources based on statistical patterns of the location of temple construction over time. For example, 10% of new temples constructed each year were within 250 m of the nearest temple. Since most temples are typically 40–80 m in width, this implies a gap between community temples of less than 150 m. Such a small distance or 'gap' between local temples was too small to reflect independent communities. Rather, it is more likely that the newer foundation represented either a reappropriation of land or the aggregation of larger populations of people in these areas that were served by multiple temples (Klassen et al. preprint). The resulting clustering therefore concentrates around anthropogenic hydraulic infrastructure rather than the natural hydrological systems as occurred during the prehistoric period (Hawken 2012, 115). This indicates that during the iconoclastic reign of Jayavarman VII, in which the major state religion was transformed to Buddhism (Dagens 2003, 171–72), emphasis may have been on defending, sustaining, and maintaining the city of Angkor and its many communities rather than prolific expansion, as was evident in the 10th century and to a lesser extent during the 11th century.

Concluding Remarks: Narratives on Community

Local temples were the centre of community life in the Angkorian World. The repetitive yet complex relationships between such temples and their landscapes provide a range of opportunities to address research questions. In this chapter, we have presented current thinking on the role of local temples and their communities in Greater Angkor. In particular, we presented three key ideas.

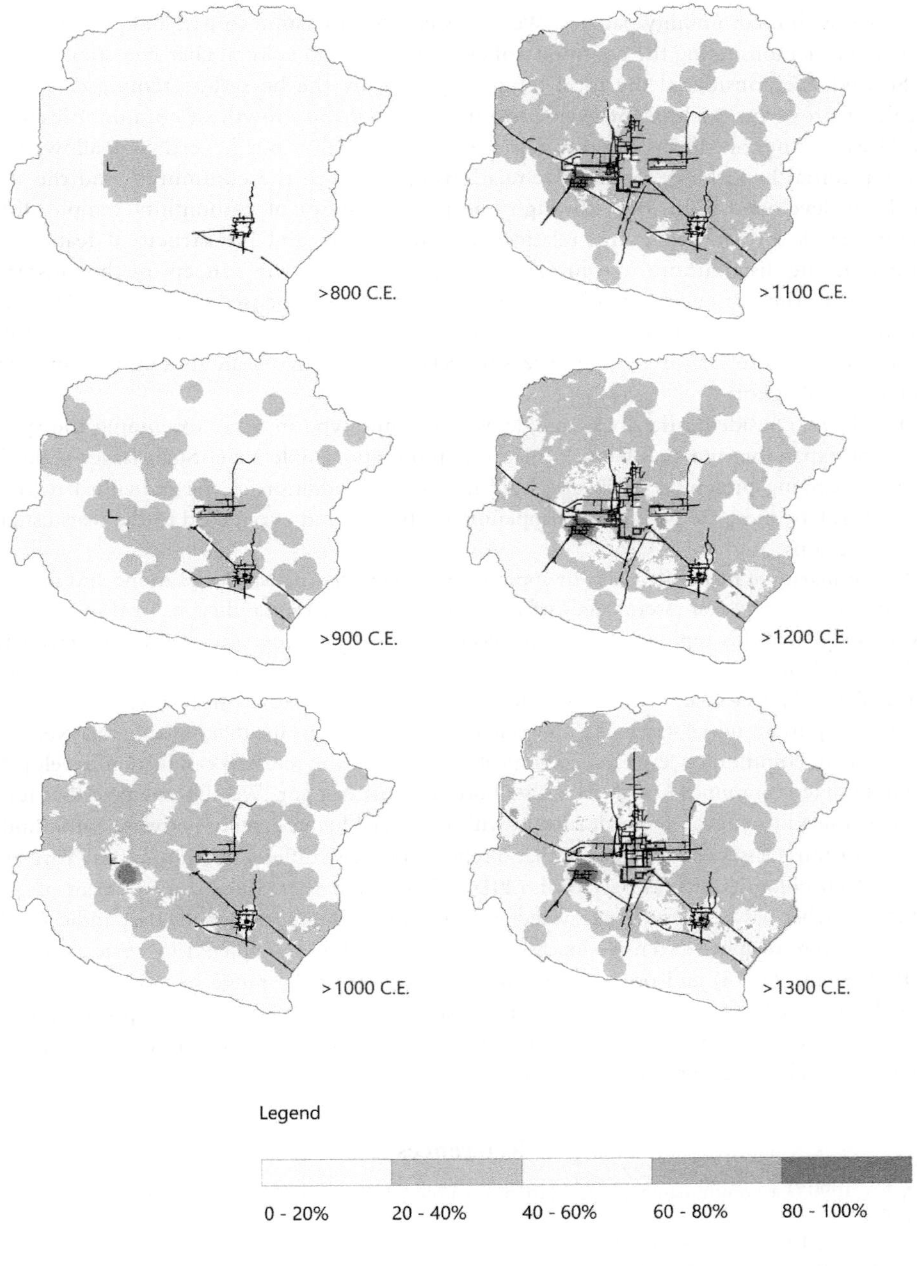

Figure 11.5 Shift in community temple construction within Greater Angkor between the 8th and 13th centuries. For the colour version of this figure and legend, the reader is referred to the web version of this chapter. GIS source: C. Pottier 1999, D. Evans 2007 & S. Klassen et al 2020.

First, we considered the local temple, within its immediate environment, as an ordering influence within community patches. We discussed this in relation to past and present Khmer settlements demonstrating the continuity of certain spatial and cultural characteristics.

Second, we considered the local temple, specifically the horseshoe temple class, as an excellent proxy or 'anchor' for evaluating the location and growth of communities across the Greater Angkor. This simplifies a more complex reality but nevertheless allows us to develop initial hypotheses around the relationship between the community and the state. We have developed such ideas through geospatial analyses of community temple distribution across the landscape and relation to major urban and infrastructural features. In describing the distribution of community temples in space, the concept of the cluster, in turn, reveals the presence of voids, which lack community-focused occupation. We argue that these areas of the landscape are as significant to investigate as the community clusters and patches themselves for a range of reasons related to the hydraulic functioning and management of Angkor.

Third, we considered the local temple as a dynamic type in time, examining the spatio-temporal expansion and proliferation of the community temple type. Such larger-scale diachronic mapping presents a landscape-scale narrative, in addition to the individual reigns of different rulers, indicating what was happening on the ground as opposed to the feats listed in the inscriptions.

In summary, we recognise that our approach is principally spatial. We examine and interpret communities as physical assemblages of material remains in the landscape. In doing this, we acknowledge that this approach to defining community as a homogenous social unit, characterised by 'residential proximity, a shared normative culture, and the daily experiences common to its members' (Yaeger et al. 2000, 3; Murdock 1949) is a conservative one. However, we suggest this is an important initial step and a new one in a research landscape that has seen relatively little in the way of community-level archaeological research. Future research can further develop and define temple communities and their distribution across Angkor. We also envisage that future work will need to engage more decisively with the social heterogeneity between communities and the various classes and livelihoods that might characterise different communities (York et al. 2011). Archaeologists such as Bâty et al. (2016, 331) have hesitated to ascribe notions of community to what has been so far excavated and surveyed at Angkor. Instead, Bâty indicates that we must aspire to more extensive excavations similar to those completed in western contexts by Peytremann (2014) and others. Nevertheless, we suggest the range of work completed is enough to shape future research agendas. To do this, we require working concepts and theories of community and their patterning and interactions across space and time for researchers to engage with, challenge, and develop further.

References

Ang, C., 1990, La communauté rurale khmère du point de vue du sacré. *Journal Asiatique* 278 (1–2), 135–54.

Aymonier, E., 1904. *Le Cambodge: Le Groupe d'Angkor et l'histoire*. Paris: Ernest Leroux.

Bailey, G., 2007. Time perspectives, palimpsests and the archaeology of time. *Journal of Anthropological Archaeology* 26, 198–223.

Bâty, P., 2010. "Les fouilles de l'aéroport de Siem Reap à Angkor." Archéopages. *Archéologie et société, no. Hors-série* 2, 86–93.

Bâty, P., 2005. *Extension de l'aéroport de Siem Reap 2004: Rapport de fouille archéologique*. Siem Reap—Paris: APSARA—INRAP.

Bâty, P., 2007. Les couteaux angkoriens de Trapeang Thlok et de Prasat Trapeang Ropou. *Bulletin de l'École française d'Extrême-Orient* 94(1), 95–110.

Bâty, P., A. Desbat, F. Sellami & S. Marquié, 2016. Le tertre E à Trapeang Ropou: Approche archéologique et géomorphologique d'un habitat angkorien. *Aséanie, Sciences humaines en Asie du Sud-Est* 33, 331–87.

Binford, L.R., 1987. *Bones: Ancient Men and Modern Myths*. San Diego: Academic Pess.

Binford, L.R., 2002 [1983]. *In Pursuit of the Past: Decoding the Archaeological Record*. Los Angeles: University of California Press.

Briggs, L.P., (1999 [1951]). *The Ancient Khmer Empire (American Philosophical Society, Philad. Transactions. New ser. ; v.41, pt. 1.)*. Bangkok: White Lotus.

Bronson, B., 1979. Angkor, Anuradhapura, Prambanan, Tikal: Maya subsistence in an Asian perspective, in *Pre-Hispanic Maya Agriculture, 255–300. Pre-Hispanic Maya Agriculture*. Albuquerque: University of New Mexico Press.

Canuto, M.-A. & J. Yaeger, 2000. *Archaeology of Communities: A New World Perspective*. Abingdon: Taylor & Francis Group.

Canuto, M.A., F. Estrada-Belli, T.G. Garrison, S.D. Houston, M.J. Acuña, M. Kováč, D. Marken, P. Nondédéo, L. Auld-Thomas & C. Castanet, 2018. Ancient lowland Maya complexity as revealed by airborne laser scanning of northern Guatemala. *Science* 361(6409), eaau0137.

Carter, A., P. Heng, M. Stark, R. Chhay & D. Evans, 2018. Urbanism and residential patterning in Angkor. *Journal of Field Archaeology* 43(6), 492–506.

Chandler, T., Polkinghorne, M., 2012. Through the visualisation lens: temple models and simulated context in a virtual Angkor, in *Old Myths and New Approaches: Interpreting Ancient Religious Sites in Southeast Asia*. Melbourne: Monash University Publishing, 218–36.

Chevance, J.-B. & C. Pottier, 2023. The early Angkor capitals, in *The Angkorian World*, eds. M. Hendrickson, M.T. Stark & D. Evans. New York: Routledge, 80–96.

Chevance, J.-B., D. Evans, N. Hofer, S. Sakhoeun & R. Chhean, 2019. Mahendraparvata: an early Angkor-period capital defined through airborne laser scanning at Phnom Kulen. *Antiquity* 93(371), 1303–21.

Clémentin-Ojha, C., École française d'Extrême-Orient., 2007. *A Century in Asia: The History of the École française d'Extrême-Orient, 1898–2006. Éditions Didier Millet*. Paris: École française d'Extrême-Orient.

Coe, M., 1957. The Khmer settlement pattern: a possible analogy with that of the Maya. *American Antiquity* 22, 409–10.

Coe, M., 1961. Social typology and the tropical forest civilizations. *Comparative Studies in Society and History* 4(1), 65–85.

Coe, M., 2005. *The Maya*. London: Thames and Hudson.

Coe, M.D. & D. Evans, 2018. *Angkor and the Khmer Civilization* (2nd ed.). London: Thames & Hudson.

Cœdès, G., 1963. *Angkor. An Introduction. Oxford in Asia*. Hong Kong: Oxford University Press.

Condominas, G., 1968. Notes sur le bouddhisme populaire en milieu rural lao. *Archives de sociologie des religions*, 26, 111–50.

Dagens, B., 2003. *Les Khmers. Guide Belles Lettres des civilisations*. Paris: Les Belles Lettres.

Delvert, J., 1994 [1961]. *Paysan Cambodgien*. Paris: Mouton.

Dumarçay, J., 1987. *The House in Southeast Asia (Images of Asia)*. Singapore: Oxford University Press.

Dumarçay, J. & M. Smithies, 2003. *Architecture and Its Models in South-East Asia*. Bangkok: Orchid Press.

Ebihara, M., 2018 [1968]. *Svay: A Khmer Village in Cambodia*. Ithaca, New York: Cornell University Press.

Erikson, C.L., 2006. Intensification, political economy, and the farming community: defense of a bottom-up perspective of the past, in *Agricultural Strategies*. Los Angeles: Cotsen Institute, 233–65.

Evans, C., N. Chang & N. Shimizu, 2016. Sites, survey, and ceramics: settlement patterns of the first to ninth centuries C.E. in the upper mun river valley, Northeast Thailand. *Journal of Southeast Asian Studies* 47(3), 438–67.

Evans, D., 2007. *Putting Angkor on the map: a new survey of a Khmer 'Hydraulic City' in historical and theoretical context*. PhD dissertation. Sydney: The University of Sydney.

Evans, D., 2016. Airborne laser scanning as a method for exploring long-term socio-ecological dynamics in Cambodia. *Journal of Archaeological Science* 74, 164–75.

Evans, D., C. Pottier, R. Fletcher, S. Hensley, I. Tapley, A. Milne & M. Barbetti, 2007. A comprehensive archaeological map of the World's largest preindustrial settlement complex at Angkor, Cambodia. *Proceedings of the National Academy of Sciences* 104(36), 14277–82.

Evans, D.H., R.J. Fletcher, C. Pottier, J.-B. Chevance, D. Soutif, B.S. Tan, S. Im, D. Ea, T. Tin, S. Kim, C. Cromarty, S.D. Greef, K. Hanus, P. Baty, R. Kuszinger, I. Shimoda & G. Boornazian, 2013. Uncovering archaeological landscapes at Angkor using lidar. *Proceedings of the National Academy of Sciences* 201306539.

Fletcher, R., 2009. Low density, agrarian-based urbanism: a comparative view. *Insights* 2, 1–19.

Fletcher, R., 2011. Low-density, agrarian-based urbanism, in *The Comparative Archaeology of Complex Societies*, ed. M.E. Smith. Cambridge: Cambridge University Press, 285–320.
Fletcher, R., 2020. Urban labels and settlement trajectories. *Journal of Urban Archaeology* 1, 31–48.
Fletcher, R., D. Evans, M. Barbetti, D. Penny, T. Heng, S. Im, K. Chan, S. Tous & C. Pottier, 2003. Redefining Angkor: structure and environment in the largest, low density urban complex of the pre-industrial World. *Udaya, Journal of Khmer Studies* 4, 107–21.
Fletcher, R., Penny, D., Evans, D., Pottier, C., Barbetti, M., Kummu, M., Authority for the Protection and Management of Angkor and the Region of Siem Reap (APSARA) Department of Monuments and Archaeology Team, 2008a. The water management network of Angkor, Cambodia. *Antiquity* 82 (317), 658–70.
Gerritsen, F., 2006. Archaeological perspectives on local communities, in *A Companion to Archaeology*, ed. J. Bintliff. New York: John Wiley & Sons, 141–54.
Goloubew, V., 1933. IV. Le Phnom Bâkhèn et la ville de Yaçovarman. *Bulletin de l'École française d'Extrême-Orient* 33(1), 319–44.
Graham, E. & C. Isendahl, 2018. Neotropical cities as agro-urban landscapes: Revisiting 'low-density, agrarian-based urbanism', in *The Resilience of Heritage. Cultivating a Future of the Past.* Essays in Honour of Professor Paul J.J. Sinclair, eds. A. Ekblom, C. Isendahl & K.-J. Lindholm. Uppsala, Sweden: Uppsala University Press, 165–80.
Groslier, B.-P., 1974. Agriculture et religion dans l'Empire angkorien. *Études Rurales* 53–56, 95–117.
Groslier, B.-P., 1979. La cité hydraulique angkorienne: exploitation ou surexploitation du sol? *Bulletin de l'École française d'Extrême-Orient* 66, 161–202.
Groslier, B.-P., 1973. Pour une géographie historique du Cambodge. *Les Cahiers d'Outre-Mer* 26(104), 337–79.
Hall, K., 2004. Temple networks and royal power in Southeast Asia, in *The World in the Year 1000*, ed. J. Heitzman & W. Schenkluhn Lanham, New York: University Press of America, 183–213.
Hall, K.R., 1975. Khmer commercial development and foreign contacts under Suryavarman I. *Journal of the Economic and Social History of the Orient* 18(1), 318–36.
Hansen, A., 2004. *Khmer Identity and Theravāda Buddhism*, ed. J. Marston. University of Hawai'i Press, 40–62.Hawken, S., 2012. Metropolis of rice fields: a topographic classification of a dispersed urban complex. PhD, University of Sydney.
Hawken, S., 2013. Designs of kings and farmers: landscape systems of the greater Angkor urban complex. *Asian Perspectives*, 52, 347–67.
Hawken, S., 2017. The urban village and the megaproject: linking vernacular urban heritage and human rights based development in the emerging megacities of Southeast Asia, in *Heritage, Culture and Rights: Challenging Legal Discourses*, ed. A. Durbach & L. Lixinski. Hart Publishing, Oxford.
Hawken, S. & C.C. Castillo, 2023. Angkor's agrarian economy: a socio-ecological mosaic, in *The Angkorian World*, eds. M. Hendrickson, M.T. Stark & D. Evans. New York: Routledge, 338–59.
Hawken, S. & R. Fletcher, 2021. A long-term archaeological reappraisal of low-density urbanism: implications for contemporary cities. *Journal of Urban Archaeology* 3, 29–50.
Hawken, S., B. Avazpour, M.S. Harris, A. Marzban & P.G. Munro, 2021b. Urban megaprojects and water justice in Southeast Asia: Between global economies and community transitions, *Cities* 113, 103068.
Hendrickson, M., 2010. Historic routes to Angkor: development of the Khmer road system (ninth to thirteenth centuries A.D.) in mainland Southeast Asia. *Antiquity* 84(324), 480–96.
Hendrickson, M.J., 2007. *Arteries of Empire: An Operational Study of Transport and Communication in Angkorian Southeast Asia (9th to 15th Centuries C.E.).* PhD, Department of Archaeology, University of Sydney.
Heng, P. & S. Sahai, 2023. The temple economy of Angkor, in *The Angkorian World*, eds. M. Hendrickson, M.T. Stark & D. Evans. New York: Routledge, 327–37.
Heng, P., 2016. Transition to the Pre-Angkorian period (300–500 CE): Thala Borivat and a regional perspective. *Journal of Southeast Asian Studies* 47(3), 484.
Higham, C.F. W., 2014. *Early Mainland Southeast Asia: From First Humans to Angkor.* Bangkok: River Books.
Holdaway, S. & L. Wandsnider, 2008. *Time in Archaeology: Time Perspectivism Revisited.* Salt Lake City: University of Utah Press.
Huyen, N. van, 1934. *Introduction à l'étude de l'habitation sur pilotis dans l'Asie du sud-est.* Paris: Geuthner.
Isendahl, C., 2012. Agro-urban landscapes: the example of Maya lowland cities. *Antiquity* 86(334), 1112–25.
Isendahl, C. & M.E. Smith, 2013. Sustainable agrarian urbanism: the low-density cities of the Mayas and Aztecs. *Cities* 31, 132–43.
Isendahl, C., M.L. Smith, F. Sulas, M. Stark & S. Barthel, 2021. Urban ecology in the ancient tropics: foodways and urban forms, in *The Routledge Handbook of Urban Ecology*, eds. I. Douglas, P.M.L. Anderson, D. Goode, M.C. Houck, D. Maddox, H. Nagendra & P.Y. Tan, 13–23.

Jacob, J.M., 1978. The ecology of Angkor: evidence from the Khmer inscriptions, in *Nature and Man in South East Asia,* ed. P.A. Stott. London: Schoolf of African and Oriental Studies, University of London, 109–27.

Jacques, C., 1972, Etudes d'epigraphie cambodgienne: VII. *Bulletin de l'École française d'Extrême-Orient* LIX, 198–99.

Jacques, C., 1986. Sources on economic activities in Khmer and Cham Lands, in *Southeast Asia in the 9th to 14th Centuries*, eds. A. Crothers & D. Marr. Singapore: Institute of Southeast Asian Studies, 327–34.

Jacques, C. & P. Lafond, 2007. *The Khmer Empire: Cities and Sanctuaries, Fifth to the Thirteenth centuries.* Bangkok: River Books.

Jacques, C. & M. Freeman, 1997. *Angkor: Cities and Temples*. London: Thames & Hudson.

Kalab, M., 1968. Study of a Cambodian village. *The Geographical Journal* 134(4), 521–37.

Klassen, S., 2018. *Adaptive capacity of the water management systems of two Medieval Khmer Cities, Angkor and Koh Ker*. PhD, Arizona State University.

Klassen, S., A.K. Carter, D.H. Evans, S. Ortman, M.T. Stark, A.A. Loyless, M. Polkinghorne, P. Heng, M. Hill & P. Wijker, 2021. Diachronic modeling of the population within the medieval greater Angkor region settlement complex. *Science Advances* 7(19): 1–9.

Klassen, S. & D. Evans, 2020. Top-down and bottom-up water management: a diachronic model of changing water management strategies at Angkor, Cambodia. *Journal of Anthropological Archaeology* 58, 101166.1–8.

Klassen, S., J. Weed & D. Evans, 2018. Semi-supervised machine learning approaches for predicting the chronology of archaeological sites: a case study of temples from medieval Angkor, Cambodia. *PLoS One* 13(11), e0205649.

Klassen, S., S.G. Ortman, J. Lobo & D. Evans, 2021. Provisioning an early city: spatial equilibrium in the agricultural economy at Angkor, Cambodia. *Journal of Archaeological Method and Theory* 1657, https://doi.org/10.1007/s10816-021-09535-5

Kobayashi, S., 2005. An ethnographic study on the reconstruction of Buddhist practice in two Cambodian temples: with the special reference to Buddhist Samay and Boran. *Japanese Journal of Southeast Asian Studies* 42(4), 489–518.

Kolb, M.J. & J.E. Snead, 1997. It's a small World after all: comparative analyses of community organization in archaeology. *American Antiquity* 62(4), 609–28.

Lansing, J., 2006. *Perfect Order : Recognizing Complexity in Bali*. Princeton, NJ: Princeton University Press.

Ledgerwood, J., 2011. A tale of two temples: communities and their wats, in *Anthropology and Community in Cambodia: Reflections on the Work of May Ebihara*, ed. J. Marston. Caulfield. Monash: Monash University Press, 105–30.

Lewitz, S., 1967. La toponymie khmère. *Bulletin de l'École française d'Extrême-Orient* 53(2), 375–451.

Lustig, E., 2009. *Power and pragmatism in the political economy of Angkor*. PhD, Department of Archaeology, University of Sydney.

Lustig, E. & T. Lustig, 2013. New insights into "les interminables listes nominatives des esclaves" from numerical analyses of the personnel in Angkorian inscriptions, *Aséanie* 31, 55–83.

Lustig, E. & T. Lustig, 2019. Losing ground: decline of Angkor's middle-level officials. *Journal of Southeast Asian Studies* 50(3), 409–30.

Lustig, T.L. & E.J. Lustig, 2015. Following the Non-Money Trail: Reconciling some Angkorian Temple Accounts, *Journal of Indo-Pacific Archaeology* 39, 26–37.

Mabbett, I., 1977. The 'Indianization' of Southeast Asia: Reflections on the historical sources, *Journal of Southeast Asian Studies* 8(2), 143–61.

Mabbett, I., 1978. Kingship at Angkor. *Journal of the Siam Society* 66 (2), 1–58.

Marston, J.A. & M. Ebihara, 2011. *Anthropology and Community in Cambodia: Reflections on the Work of May Ebihara* (Monash papers on Southeast Asia no. 70). Caulfield, Monash: Monash University Press.

Martel, G., 1975. *Lovea, Village Des Environs d'Angkor: Aspects Démographiques, Économiques et Sociologiques Du Monde Rural Combodgien Dans La Province de Siem-Réap*. Paris: École française d'Extrême-Orient.

McColl, H., F. Racimo, L. Vinner, F. Demeter, T. Gakuhari, J.V. Moreno-Mayar, G. van Driem, U.G. Wilken, A. Seguin-Orlando, C. de la F. Castro, S. Wasef, R. Shoocongdej, V. Souksavatdy, T. Sayavongkhamdy, M.M. Saidin, M.E. Allentoft, T. Sato, A.-S. Malaspinas, F.A. Aghakhanian, T. Korneliussen, A. Prohaska, A. Margaryan, P. de B. Damgaard, S. Kaewsutthi, P. Lertrit, T.M.H. Nguyen, H. Hung, T.M. Tran, H.N. Truong, G.H. Nguyen, S. Shahidan, K. Wiradnyana, H. Matsumae, N. Shigehara, M. Yoneda, H. Ishida, T. Masuyama, Y. Yamada, A. Tajima, H. Shibata, A. Toyoda, T. Hanihara, S. Nakagome, T. Deviese, A.-M. Bacon, P. Duringer, J.-L. Ponche, L. Shackelford, E. Patole-Edoumba,

A.T. Nguyen, B. Bellina-Pryce, J.-C. Galipaud, R. Kinaston, H. Buckley, C. Pottier, S. Rasmussen, T. Higham, R.A. Foley, M.M. Lahr, L. Orlando, M. Sikora, M.E. Phipps, H. Oota, C. Higham, D.M. Lambert & E. Willerslev, 2018. The prehistoric peopling of Southeast Asia. *Science* 361(6397), 88–92.

Murdock, G.P., 1949. *Social Structure*. New York: Macmillan.

Murphy, S.A. & M.T. Stark, 2016. Introduction: transitions from late prehistory to early historic periods in mainland Southeast Asia, c. Early to mid-first millennium C.E. *Journal of Southeast Asian Studies* 47(3), 333–40.

Murphy, S.A., 2016. The case for proto-dvaravati: a review of the art historical and archaeological evidence. *Journal of Southeast Asian Studies* 47(3), 366–92.

O'Reilly, D. & L. Shewan, 2016. Phum Lovea: a moated precursor to the pura of Cambodia? Sociopolitical transformation from Iron Age settlements to early state society. *Journal of Southeast Asian Studies* 47(3), 468–83.

Peterson, C.E. & R.D. Drennan, 2005. Communities, settlements, sites, and surveys: regional-scale analysis of prehistoric human interaction. *American Antiquity* 5–30.

Peytremann, E., 2014, La notion de village en France au premier Moyen age. *Archeopages*, 40, 84–91.

Pottier, C., 1993. Préparation d'une Carte Archéologique de La Région d'Angkor, Thèse, Mémoire de DEA, Sorbonne Nouvelle, Paris III.

Pottier, C., 1999. *Carte archéologique de la Région d'Angkor, Zone Sud*. PhD dissertation. Paris: Université Paris III—Sorbonne nouvelle.

Pottier, C. & A. Bolle, 2009. Le Prasat Trapeang Phong à Hariharâlaya: histoire d'un temple et archéologie d'un site. *Aséanie* 24, 61–90.Pottier, C., 2000a. The contribution of the École française d'Extrême-Orient with respect to the cultural heritage of Angkor during the past 100 years. *The Journal of Sophia Asian Studies* 18, 253–62.

Pottier, C., 2000c. Some evidence of an inter-relationship between hydraulic features and rice field patterns at Angkor during ancient times. *Journal of Sophia Asian Studies* 18, 99–120.

Pottier, C., 2000b. À la Recherche de Goloupura. *Bulletin de l'École française d'Extrême-Orient* 1(87), 79–107.

Pottier, C., 2003. Yasovarman's Buddhist asrama in Angkor, in *The Buddhist Monastery: A Cross Cultural Survey*. Paris: École française d'Extrême-Orient.

Ricklefs, M., 1967. Land and law in the epigraphy of tenth-century Cambodia. *Journal of Asian Studies* 26(3), 411–20.

Sabloff, J.A., 2019. How Maya archaeologists discovered the 99% through the study of settlement patterns. *Annual Review of Anthropology* 48, 1–16.

Sahai, S., 1977. Territorial administration in ancient Cambodia. *The South East Asian Review* 1(2), 35–50.

Sahai, S., 1978. Fiscal administration in ancient Cambodia. *The South East Asian Review* 1(2), 23–137.

Sahai, S., 2012. *The Hindu Temples in Southeast Asia: Their Role in Social, Economic and Political Formations*. Shimla; New Delhi: Indian Institute of Advanced Study ; Aryan Books International.

Scarborough, V.L. & C. Isendahl, 2020. Distributed urban network systems in the tropical archaeological record: toward a model for urban sustainability in the era of climate change. *The Anthropocene Review* 7(3), 208–30.

Scarborough, V.L. & L.J. Lucero, 2010. The non-hierarchical development of complexity in the semitropics: water and cooperation. *Water History* 2(2), 185–205.

Sedov, L., 1963. On the problem of the economic system in Angkor, Cambodia in the IX–XII centuries (translated by Antonia Glasse for O. W. Wolters). *Narody Asii I Afriki, Istoria, Ekonomika, Kul'tura, Akademija Nauk SSR* (6), 73–81.

Smith, M.L., 2010. *A Prehistory of Ordinary People*. Tucson: University of Arizona Press.

Smith, M.L., 2013. *The Social Construction of Ancient Cities*. Washington, DC: Smithsonian Institution.

Smith, M.E., S.G. Ortman, J. Lobo, C.E. Ebert, A.E. Thompson, K.M. Prufer, R.L. Stuardo & R.M. Rosenswig, 2021. The low-density urban systems of the classic period Maya and Izapa: insights from settlement scaling theory. *Latin American Antiquity* 32(1), 120–37.

Stargardt, J., 2016. From the Iron Age to early cities at Sri Ksetra and Beikthano, Myanmar. *Journal of Southeast Asian Studies* 47(3), 341–65.

Stark, M.T., 2006. Pre-Angkorian settlement trends in Cambodia's Mekong Delta and the lower Mekong Archaeological Project. *Bulletin of the Indo-Pacific Prehistory Association* 26, 98–109.

Stark, M.T., 2015. Southeast Asian urbanism: from early city to Classical state, in *The Cambridge World History: volume 3: Early Cities in Comparative Perspective, 4000 BCE–1200 CE*, ed. N. Yoffee. Cambridge: Cambridge University Press, 74–93.

Stark, M.T., Evans, D., Rachna, C., Piphal, H., Carter, A., 2015. Residential patterning at Angkor Wat. *Antiquity* 89, 1439–55.

Stark, M.T., P.B. Griffin, C. Phoeurn, J. Ledgerwood, M. Dega, C. Mortland, N. Dowling, J.M. Bayman, B. Sovath & T. Van, 1999. Results of the 1995–1996 archaeological field investigations at Angkor Borei, Cambodia. *Asian Perspectives* 38(1), 7–36.

Tainturier, F., M. Rethy Antelme & C. Lalonde, 2006. *Wooden Architecture of Cambodia: A Disappearing Heritage = Saṃn'aṅ Qaṃbi Jhoe Nao Prates Kambujā : Kerṭaṃṇael Ṭael KaṃBuṅ Sāp Sūny*. Phnom Penh: Centre for Khmer Studies.

Vickery, M., 1998. *Society, Economics, and Politics in Pre-Angkor Cambodia: The 7th–8th Centuries*. Tokyo: Centre for East Asian Cultural Studies for UNESCO, The Tokyo Bunko.

Welch, D.J., 1997. Archaeological evidence of Khmer state political and economic organisation. *Bulletin of the Indo-Pacific Prehistory Association* 16, 69–78.

Wolters, O.W., 1974. North-western Cambodia in the seventh century. *Bulletin of the School of Oriental and African Studies, University of London* 37(2), 355–84.

Wolters, O.W., 1982. *History, Culture, and Region in Southeast Asian Perspectives*. Ithaca, NY : Southeast Asia Program Publications, Southeast Asia Program, Cornell University.

Yaeger, J. & M.-A. Canuto, 2000. The social construction of communities in the classic Maya countryside: strategies of affiliation in western Belize, in *The Archaeology of Communities: A New World Perspective*, eds. M.-A. Canuto & J. Yaeger. London and New York: Routledge, 1–15.

York, A.M., M.E. Smith, B.W. Stanley, B.L. Stark, J. Novic, S.L. Harlan, G.L. Cowgill & C.G. Boone, 2011. Ethnic and class clustering through the ages: a transdisciplinary approach to urban neighbourhood social patterns. *Urban Studies* 48 (11), 2399–415.

Zhou, D., 2007[1297]. *A Record of Cambodia: The Land and Its People*, trans. P. Harris. Chiang Mai: Silkworm Books.

12
ANGKOR AS A 'CITÉ HYDRAULIQUE'?

Terry Lustig, Jean-Baptiste Chevance and Wayne Johnson

For a century and a half, people have held that a basis for Angkor's six centuries as a major polity in Southeast Asia was its water-management infrastructure (Delaporte 1880, 39; G. Groslier 1924; Goloubew 1941; B.-P. Groslier 1979; Pottier 1999; Fletcher et al. 2008; Penny et al. 2018). This consisted of a network of channels and embankments collecting water from the catchments upstream, flowing to rivers traversing the Angkor plain, and directing it to storages around central Angkor in ponds, moats, and *baray*—above-ground rectilinear tanks measuring up to 16 km^2 in area—and from there to more channels dispersing water and draining to the Tonle Sap (Kummu 2009) (Figure 12.1). This network became increasingly complex as it evolved as part of Angkor's ritualistic and symbolic landscape. It has been frequently described as a system of irrigation that helped to secure Angkor's agricultural production by compensating for fluctuations in rainfall (Groslier 1924; Groslier 1974; Garami and Kertai 1993; Peou, 2013; Peou et al. 2016; Fletcher et al. 2017) or by enabling crop production in the dry season (Dumarcay 1994). Bernard-Philippe Groslier (1974, 1979) used the term '*cité hydraulique*' (hydraulic city) to refer to the large urban area, which, together with its hinterland, utilised this irrigation network, which he viewed as providing for a significant increase in population compared to what might be supported by rain-fed rice cultivation alone (Pottier 2000). Groslier famously theorised that the failure of this irrigation network contributed to Angkor's decline. Others also attribute Angkor's decline to deficiencies in its water management but focus on different aspects. Dumarçay (1994), for example, argues that storage in the baray was replaced by reservoirs created by bridges whose spans were blocked to repurpose them as barrages and that these probably contributed to Angkor's decline by promoting a dispersal of central authority. Penny et al. (2018) put forward an abstract model of a cascading breakdown of Angkor's water network under intense climatic variation through erosion and sedimentation in the channels. They assert that the 'network served several functions, most critically flood regulation and irrigation for agriculture'.

Robert Acker (1998) has contended that Groslier's thesis failed on two counts. The first was that whereas Groslier (1979) had suggested that irrigated rice agriculture could support something in the order of 1,900,000 people at Angkor, the potential population increase was only a small fraction of this number, according to Acker's calculations. Indeed, Groslier's figure was roughly double more recent estimates (e.g. Klassen et al. 2021). Nevertheless, Groslier had already cautioned that this figure was a rough one. Acker's second critique was that the areas available for irrigation downslope from the baray were too small to take up all the water stored.

DOI: 10.4324/9781351128940-15

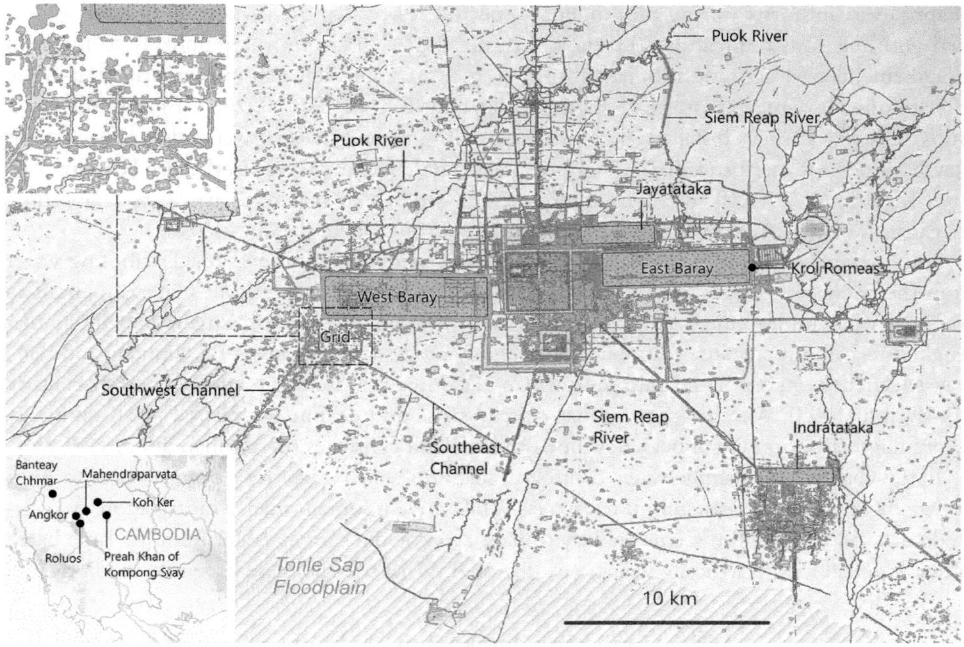

Figure 12.1 Angkor's complex hydraulic network. Upper inset shows channel grid downslope from West Baray. Lower inset shows sites in central Angkor and regional capitals with major water infrastructure.

Source: (GIS data Pottier 1999 and Evans et al. 2007).

Acker estimated the area available for irrigation to be too small by a factor of roughly five. He used Groslier's (1979) suggested irrigation areas, yet even a cursory examination of the topography reveals that Groslier's assumed areas were indicative rather than precise, particularly for the East Baray. Had he used more realistic (i.e. lower) depths of water, his calculated volumes would also have been much smaller.[1] Nor did Acker allow for the possibility of other uses, such as for supplementary water during periods of low or delayed rainfall.

Pillot (2007, 73) argued from an agronomic perspective that it would have been physically impossible to provide supplementary irrigation to individual blocks of land using water that cascades from field to field, as Groslier (1979) proposed. According to Pillot, the variability in soil, evapotranspiration, area, and stage of crop growth between individual fields would require different volumes of supplementing water for each of them at any given time. Yet coordinated irrigation by gravity is demonstrably feasible, particularly if irrigation water supplies are managed by self-governing groups (Lansing et al. 2017; Pillot 2007, 274) rather than by a central authority as Groslier (1974) suggested for Angkor. Even so, the channels south of the West Baray are so large that they are in fact quite likely to have developed in the context of a centrally controlled water-management network (Pottier 1999, 112–23; 2000).

It has also been pointed out that there is no mention of irrigation in the entire corpus of Pre-Angkorian and Angkorian inscriptions. (See, for example, Phillip Stott 1992 and Elizabeth Moore 1995.) Some have regarded the absence of disputes over irrigation in the inscriptions as telling, since these are notorious in even the best-run irrigation systems (Stott 1992), particularly given the need to coordinate multiple varying demands (Pillot 2007, 241). However, as most records of appeals to authority during the Angkorian period concerned the ownership of lands associated with religious foundations (Lustig and Lustig 2019), inscriptions are unlikely to mention disagreements over allocations of irrigation waters. As it is, possible allusions to irrigation in the inscriptions are vague at best. In a Pre-Angkorian text (K. 341, N7–10, 700 CE) from the Neak Buos Temple, channels installed in conjunction with lowlands, rivers, wetlands, and rice fields may have been for irrigation (Cœdès 1937–66, v1, 26), while a stanza in the Pre Rup inscription, K. 806, CCLXXIII, has been interpreted as alluding to Rājendravarman re-establishing irrigation works at Angkor following the capital returning there (Jacques 1978).

A more germane objection was that there was no evidence of systems for distributing water from the baray (van Liere 1980).[2] If irrigation did not provide a significant material benefit to Angkor, what underpinned Angkor's historical importance? One assessment concludes that Angkor's economic surpluses came from the highly productive regions of Battambang and Banteay Meanchey, incorporated into Jayavarman II's domain around the end of the 8th century (de Bernon 1997). Another view is that Angkor's rise and decline are related to an unusually severe fluctuation in rainfall between the 10th and 13th centuries (Lieberman 2003, 224–26).

In this chapter, we examine water-control mechanisms which might have been available to Angkorian engineers for irrigating from reservoirs. While there is some evidence of irrigation, we conclude that, on balance, this seems unlikely to have been by discharging water from the large baray. A question that follows logically will also be discussed: What role did these large reservoirs play?

Irrigation Using Angkorian Technology

Irrigation by gravity from a reservoir requires a means of storing water during periods of rainfall and releasing it later in a controlled manner when it is dry. Farmers must receive enough water, perhaps in a limited time, to maximise the growth of their crops without the risk of damage by flooding. Consequently, the volume of water must be regulated both at the outlet of the storage and at the offtakes from the distributary channels.

It is important to appreciate that outlets at or near the crest of reservoir embankments such as the one at Krol Romeas, which discharged through the eastern dyke of the East Baray (Figure 12.1), could not have been for irrigation. They simply discharged excess water from the tops of the storages when it was raining to prevent water from overtopping the embankments. Where an outlet was located at the top of the embankment, the water in the reservoir below the level of the outlet's crest could not be released. Figure 12.2 shows how uncontrolled discharges through the outlet cannot be used for irrigation. For the full storage capacity of a reservoir to be used, the outlet must take water from the lowest point of the storage, 'to squeeze out the last drop' (Groslier 1979). This would have required a mechanism such as a stoplog sluice gate, a tunnel through the embankment sealed against the pressure of the water, or a pipe capable of operating under high pressure.

Lidar imagery of the Kulen plateau near the early capital of Mahendraparvata shows dams built across river valleys (Figure 12.3a), usually with single outlets (see, for example, Figure 12.3b). Since each outlet had to be able to both pass the peak annual streamflow and to hold water back during periods of low rainfall, they needed to have controlled outlets. These reservoirs, built mostly in the late 8th and early 9th centuries CE (Chevance et al. 2019), may have used stoplog sluice gates to regulate flow. The flow could be controlled by placing or removing timber beams, one on top of the other, across the channel (Figure 12.4 inset). The slots would probably be cut into solid rock or rock pillars embedded in soil.

Erik Hansen (1969, 10) found slots cut into the sides of a sandstone channel, the O Tuk Lich on Phnom Kulen (Figure 12.3), suitable for a small stoplog sluice gate. Although this particular

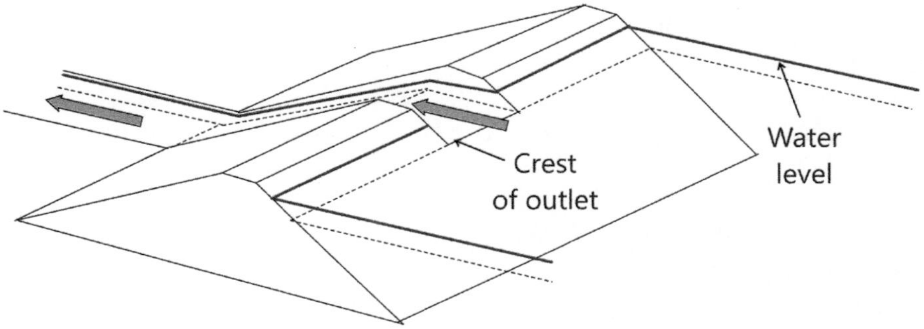

Figure 12.2 Water flowing out from a reservoir during rainfall, when irrigation not needed. Water below crest of outlet cannot be released.

control mechanism was not for flows from a reservoir, Hansen (1969, 16) postulated that there would also be sluice gates at the Thnal Thom, a dam seven kilometres away. The authors have now identified such slots along the zig-zag outlet channel of this dam. These would have been suitable for a series of gates for allowing water to discharge as a cascade without eroding the embankment (Figure 12.4). The channel runs alternately north–south and east–west, respectively perpendicular and parallel to the reservoir embankment.

While such gates could have been used for flow control on many of the dams on Phnom Kulen (Hansen 1969, 17), no channel or other mechanism has been found for distributing the discharging water to fields downstream, indicating that the water from these dams was not used for irrigation by gravity. Two of the dams, Thnal Dac and Spean Pring, were around 6 to 7 metres high, so their gates were likely around this height. It is therefore feasible that gates of similar size could have been installed to control discharges from the large baray on the Angkor plain, as their waters had about the same depth, had this been needed as part of the barays' operation.

In the East Baray at Angkor, there are many cuts in the earthen wall which are now passageways, and these have been postulated as originally being water-control outlets (Pottier 1999, 107). Yet there are no such cuts near the lowest point of the West Baray, in its southwest corner, where an outlet would have been located, had the baray's waters been used for irrigation downstream. This part of the baray has been permanently under water, and there is little foot traffic there, in contrast to other sections which have such cuts but are inundated less often (Figure 12.5). So it is reasonable to suppose that the cuts in the East Baray through the south and west banks result largely from erosion by human and animal traffic, from a time when the East Baray was no longer full—possibly from the 14th century onwards (Fletcher et al. 2017).

On the other hand, the outlet of the Rahal, a baray at the short-lived 10th-century capital at Koh Ker, may have controlled the water flow using stoplog sluice gates. The outlet channel has a zig-zag pattern parallel to the sides of the Rahal (Figure 12.6), similar to that observed at Thnal Thom. It is possible that this water was used for irrigation, but it is difficult to investigate this, since the area downstream was excavated, seemingly to form a reservoir for Prasat Thom.

The feasibility of a method other than that of using stoplog sluice gates was demonstrated in an experiment by George Trouvé at the southwestern corner of the West Baray at Angkor (Figure 12.5) (RCA 1934, Mar–Apr, 1935, Feb–Jun, Pottier 1999, 105–7, 2000). The

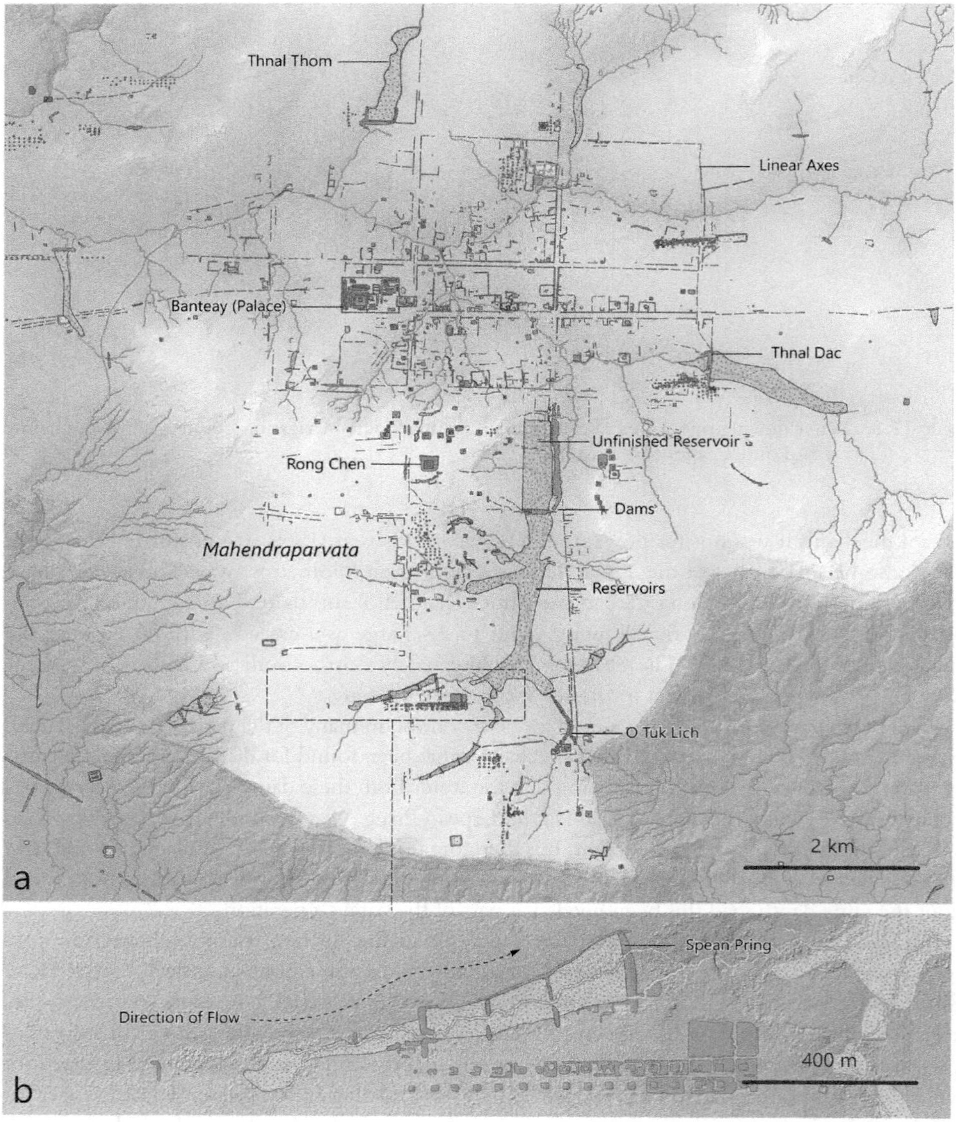

Figure 12.3 Water infrastructure associated with Mahendraparvata: a) the palace, major reservoirs, terrestrial grid and unfinished baray; b) multiple dams with single outlets through their embankments. Note Spean Pring (far right) possibly had one outlet and now shows two outlets.

Source: (Lidar data CALI 2015 and Evans 2016).

experiment was conducted twice by excavating the embankment at the southwestern corner of the baray, down to the level of the stored water. A pipe with a flap gate was set into the base of the excavation to allow water to drain out. The flap could be closed to stop the flow. At the end of each irrigation season, the excavation was filled in again. While the experiments were stopped early because farmers complained about flooding, Trouvé did demonstrate that water sufficient for irrigation could be discharged downstream with quite modest works.

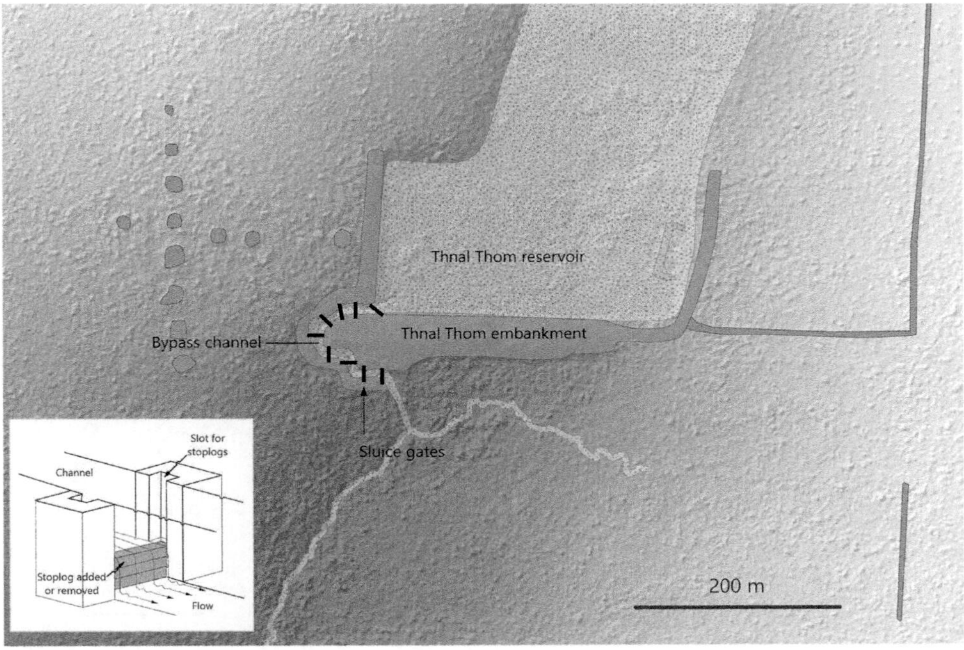

Figure 12.4 Inferred layout of stoplog sluice gates along the outlet from Thnal Thom reservoir at Mahendraparvata.

Source: (Lidar CALI 2015).

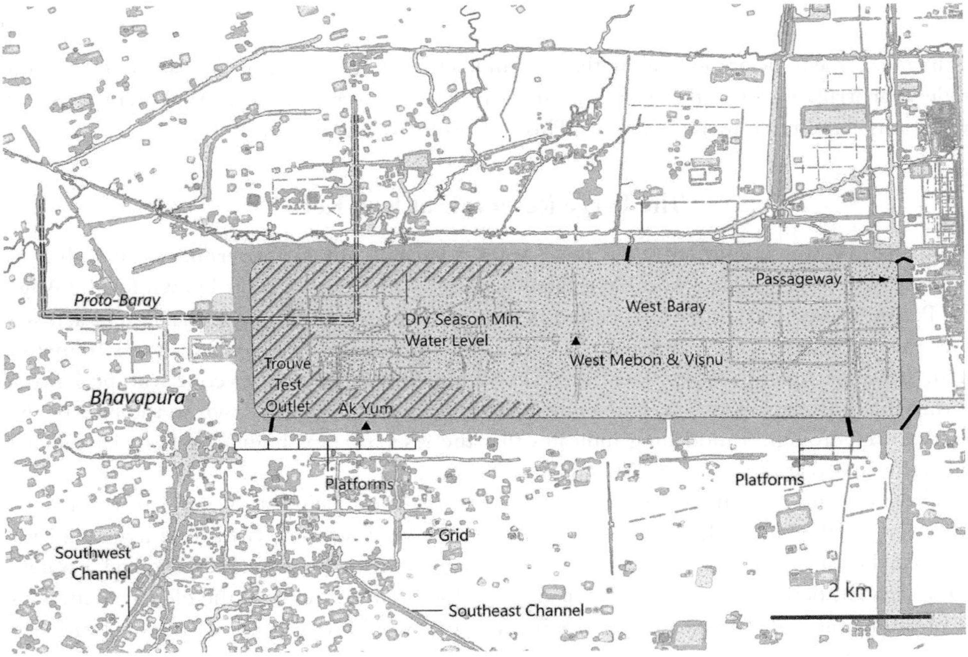

Figure 12.5 West Baray and surrounding water infrastructures and possible proto-baray.

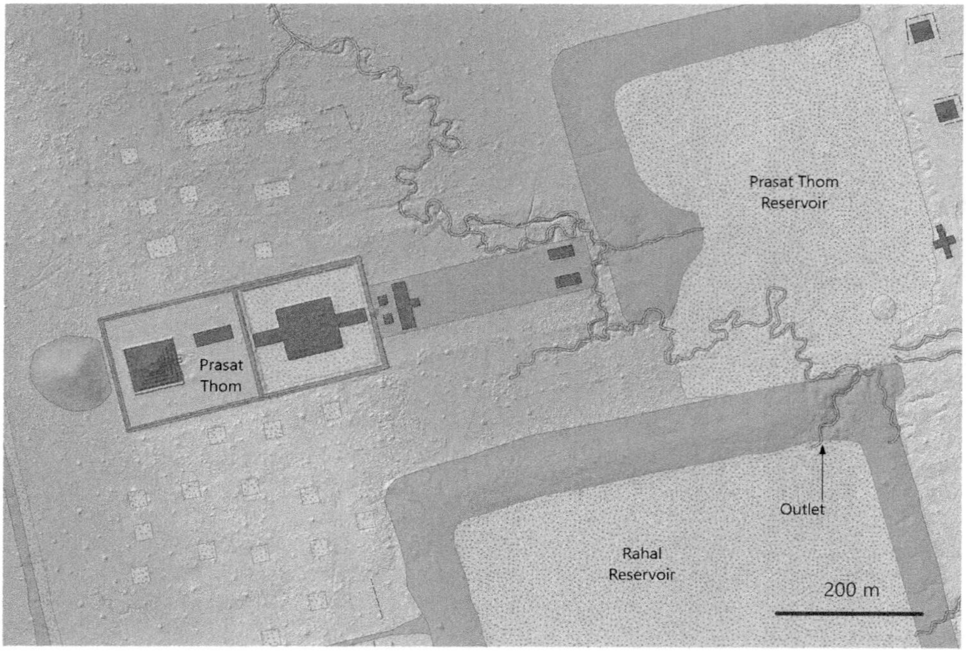

Figure 12.6 Zig-zag outlet of the Rahal (*baray*) at Koh Ker.
Source: (Lidar KALC 2012 and Evans et al. 2013).

Even so, it will be argued below that it is unlikely that Angkorian baray had water-control outlets for irrigation. But first it will be shown that there was one large Angkorian reservoir where it is certain that there was none. This was also constructed at Koh Ker.

The Large Reservoir at Koh Ker

Jayavarman IV was acknowledged as the Khmer ruler by 928 CE,[3] governing from Koh Ker, 80 km east-northeast of Angkor. He created the largest artificial reservoir known for the Angkor Period (Lustig et al. 2018). Its design incorporated a seven-km long embankment across a river valley (Figure 12.7). Where it crossed the bed of the original watercourse, it was 10 metres high. However, the capacity of the reservoir's two outlets was too small to cope with peak flows during the rainy season, and its embankment overtopped and eroded down to the base of the reservoir. Hydrological modelling indicates that the reservoir was highly likely to have failed during its first year of operation (Moffat et al. 2019).

The reservoir's two outlets were not suitable for irrigation, being at the top of the embankment and overflowing only during and soon after the rainy season, when little irrigation was required. Had this reservoir been built for irrigation downstream, it would have had a water-control outlet, perhaps a sluice gate, at its deepest point where it crossed the old riverbed. This had to function regardless of water level. Its operators would have needed to have always had access to it, even when the reservoir water was at full storage. Therefore, the controls of such a mechanism had to be above ground.

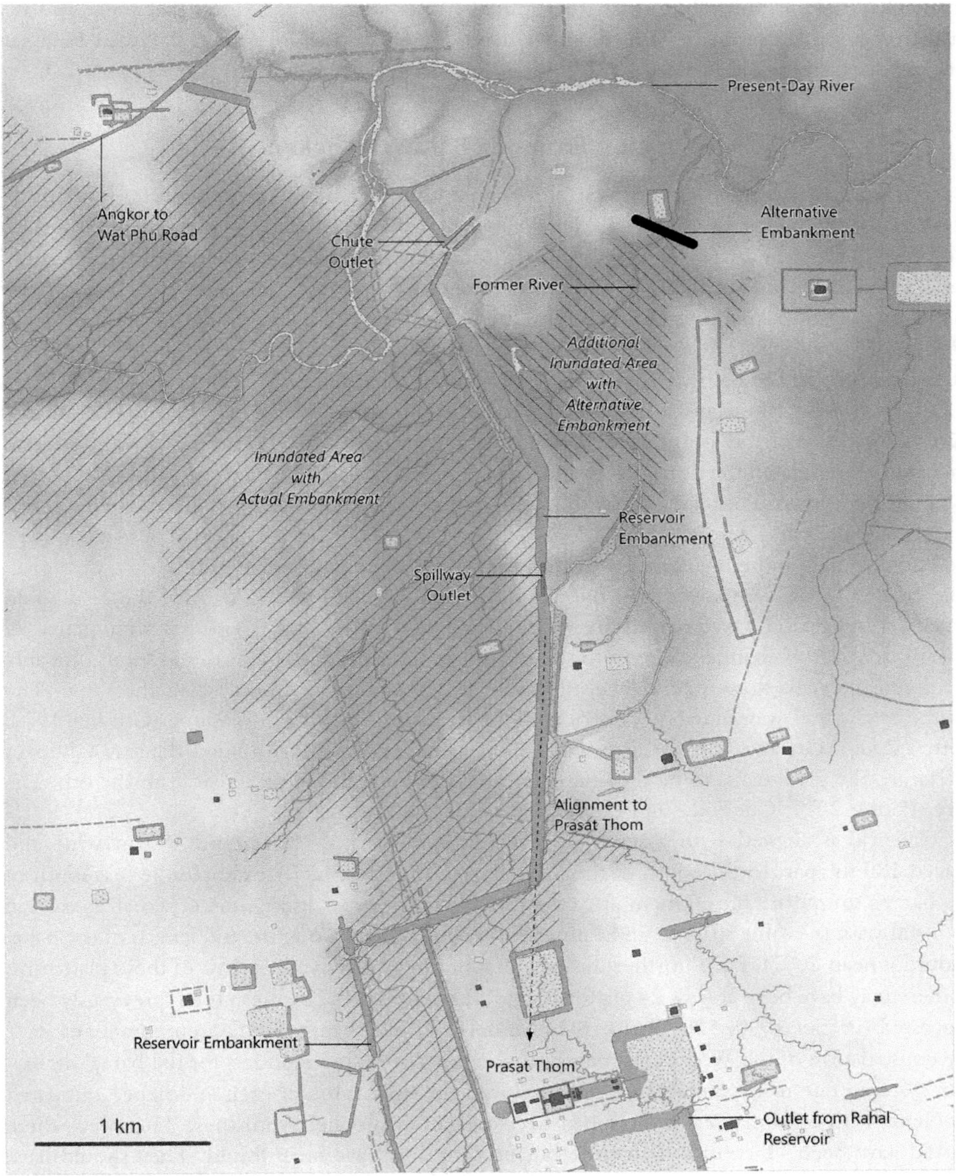

Figure 12.7 Main reservoir at Koh Ker showing existing and former rivers. Alternative embankment across former river downstream of main embankment.

Source: (Lidar KALC 2012 and Evans et al. 2013).

Yet the upstream face of the main embankment is still covered with carefully placed rock, likely put there to protect against erosion by waves. The rock face has no holes or gaps—except where trees are growing through it or there is minor erosion—nor any remains of an outlet-control appliance. It is not feasible that there was a control mechanism which was washed away during the failure, since the embankment overtopped about a kilometre away. There was thus no mechanism for controlling discharge from the reservoir, and it follows that there was no irrigation from this reservoir. On the other hand, the area downslope from the West Baray at Angkor does appear to have had irrigation at some stage.

Irrigation From the Baray at Angkor?

During Trouvé's irrigation experiment, submerged walls were revealed as the water level inside the West Baray dropped (RCA 1935, Feb–May). A year later in the course of an aerial survey, Goloubew (1936) and Lagisquet (RCA 1935, Mar) noted embankments both inside the baray and extending beyond it to the north, west, and south (Figure 12.5). The outside embankments to the south, marking channels lying between them, have since been mapped in detail (Pottier 1999, Maps 2, 3, 8). A possible 'proto-baray' has also been hypothesised, based on structures observed to be partly under the waters of the West Baray (Pottier 1999, 145; Fletcher 2020). This would indicate that there was water storage here before the baray was built by Sūryavarman I, probably in the second quarter of the 11th century (Pottier 2017). The baray is said to have inundated the northern portion of a Pre-Angkorian city, Banteay Chhoeu (Groslier 1979) or Bhavapura (Pottier 2017), with much of its infrastructure likely removed when soil was dug out for the baray's embankments.

The channels and embankments to the south were built on a north–south/east–west grid. The channel beds were lower than the natural ground, so that the fields inside the grid could have been irrigated by water lifted from them (Pillot 2007, 241, 463).[4] The water ran generally southwards to two channels, one to the southwest following the slope of the ground, probably for draining excess flows to the lake, the other to the southeast almost across the slope. The southeast channel was arguably a distributor for irrigating the area downslope (Groslier 1979; Pottier 2000). Groslier (1979) suggested that the same grid also surrounded Banteay Chhoeu. Certainly, the grid seems to be distributed around Ak Yum, a temple active from the 6th century (Pottier 2017; Chevance and Pottier 2023, this volume).

The grid is aligned with a series of rectangular platforms, each about 180 m wide and spaced 180 m apart to the south of the West Baray. The most intact examples lie just south of the baray's southern embankment at its western end. They can also be discerned at its eastern end, still with the same spacing, indicating that they extended along the full length of the baray (Bourdonneau 2007). Each north–south channel of the grid is between two of these platforms, so there may have been at least 24 platforms and 11 north–south channels. It has previously been suggested (Pottier 1999, 120–2) that the channels and platforms were contemporaneous with the construction of the West Baray, being components of multiple outlets for the baray's irrigation system. The many outlets may have reduced the flow through each and hence mitigated problems with erosion. Yet, if there had been irrigation supplied from these 11 outlets, there should have been 11 control structures, but no remnants have been found. They should have been accessible by operators and would therefore have been visible at the time. As it is, these channels have now been recognised as consistent with the development of the earlier capital of Banteay Chhoeu (Chevance and Pottier 2023, this volume).

Even so, it might still be hypothesised that there were such flow regulators operating with the embankments built to a level lower than now, then buried, together with Ak Yum, when the walls of the baray were built to their current height. Radiocarbon dating indicates that Ak Yum was built in the second half of the 6th century (Pottier 2017), and inscriptions K. 749 (674 CE) and K. 753 (704 CE) at this temple would then date to a time possibly one or two centuries after the temple's founding. Another text, K. 752, records an offering by a *steṅ' añ* in 1001 CE, indicating that the temple was functioning undisturbed as late as the beginning of the

11th century, while a short time later, in the second quarter of the 11th century, the embankments of the West Baray were built to the height we see today, burying much of Ak Yum. It is possible that Sūryavarman built the embankments to some lower level, together with irrigation control structures, in the short period between the beginning and the second quarter of the 11th century, and then he buried these large outlets with the higher embankment so that there was no trace, but it seems more likely that the baray was built in one operation.

Alternatively, there could have been Trouvé-style excavations and fills along the southern embankment as outlined previously. Yet, while one break might not be so distinguishable from the rest of the embankment once it was filled in (Pottier 1999, 107), traces of annual excavations and backfillings over centuries should still be visible.[5]

Another possibility is that the distributary channels downstream from the West Baray were part of an irrigation network installed some time after the West Baray was built. On this hypothesis, a flow-control structure may have been installed in the baray's southwest embankment and then buried after irrigation ceased. However, such a structure would again have been large to be able to control high pressures and sizable flows. Consequently, the effort to conceal it such that there was no trace would have been great, and it is reasonable to suppose that this would not have been a high priority.

No flow controls have been found on the other three large baray on the Angkor plain, nor have any been discerned on baray at other Angkorian centres, such as at Banteay Chhmar (Evans et al. 2011) and Preah Khan of Kompong Svay (Hendrickson and Evans 2015). Had there been such mechanisms, it follows that they must have been subsequently buried or removed without leaving any artefact or disturbance. This is unlikely, particularly given that there is now lidar imagery—capable of detecting previously imperceptible anomalies—for all these baray (Evans 2016). As well, there should also have been channels for distributing the water discharging from these control outlets to fields for irrigation, as van Liere (1980) had already pointed out, and there are no indications of these.

A feature of all the structures which display artefacts of outlet controls like those at Mahendraparvata and the Rahal at Koh Ker (discussed above) is that each of them is in the valley of a watercourse. Because the area of the catchment of a valley is many times larger than the area of the reservoir, the storage could fill up and overtop quickly during extended periods of heavy rain. A stoplog sluice gate built as a control outlet for such reservoirs could have been left open in the rainy season and closed off before its end. A fundamental problem with the large reservoir at Koh Ker was the absence of an outlet designed to pass peak flows in the river at the height of the rainy season. By contrast, no stoplog sluice gates were necessary for the various baray, where water was supplied artificially, since such supplies could be stopped as needed.

Other Roles of the Reservoirs

Given the lack of substantiation of irrigation by discharge from the large reservoir at Koh Ker or from the baray at Angkor and elsewhere, it is likely that these fulfilled other roles. One proposition is that rice was grown within their walls as in the West Baray today (Pillot 2007, 222). Water may have been allowed into that baray during the rainy season until the whole of the floor was inundated, at a level of about 20–21 m ASL. With the inflow stopped, water could evaporate or percolate into the sandy clay floor. As the rain eased towards the end of the rainy season, the water level could fall, and rice might then have been planted progressively down the slope (Nesbitt 1997, 36). It is feasible that the water level could have fallen to, say, 18–19 m ASL by the end of the dry season, so that perhaps a third of the area of the West Baray could have come under crop. The average yield today for dry-season rice is 2.6 t/ha (Nesbitt 1997, 64). With roughly 500 ha planted with flood-recession rice in the West Baray, and an annual consumption of 150 kg per person (Nesbitt 1997, 10), this might have fed only about 9000 people. Thus the economic value of any such production would have been small and limited to a sector of the population.

A clue to another, though intangible, role might be found in the placement of the embankment, which held back the waters of the large reservoir at Koh Ker (Figure 12.6). The main route into the capital from the Angkor-Wat Phu Road ran along the embankment's crest and would have offered visitors extensive water views to their right, with the shoreline close by, as they approached the city. Looming directly ahead of them, they would have seen the pyramid of Prasat Thom (Shimoda and Sato 2009)—the earthly symbol of Mount Meru, the abode of the gods—and at that time the tallest structure ever built in the Angkorian kingdom (Cœdès 1937a, 70). Mount Meru was traditionally envisaged as surrounded by the Cosmic Ocean (Cœdès 1973b; Groslier 1974; Roveda 2003, 19, 142). The importance of the Cosmic Ocean in Angkorian symbolism is made plain in a massive bas-relief inside Angkor Wat and the entrances to Angkor Thom. They refer to the legend of demi-gods and demons pulling a *nāga*—wrapped around Mount Mandara—back and forth for a thousand years to churn the Cosmic Ocean or Sea of Milk in order to produce *amṛta*, the elixir of immortality. With bodies of water on each side, the temple-mountain at Koh Ker could have been envisaged as surrounded by the Cosmic Ocean. Few would have failed to be impressed.

The 7-kilometre-long embankment was substantially more costly to build in terms of labour than, say, at a site 1.5 km downstream, which would have required an embankment just 300 m long (Figure 12.7). But then the access road would have been up to 200 m from the water, with Prasat Thom no longer directly ahead. A comparison of the visual impacts anticipated for the different layouts may have contributed to a decision to choose the more costly one.

Likewise with the West Baray, it is difficult to envisage how building the embankments to a height of at least 8 metres above the maximum water level could have produced a material benefit (Garami and Kertai 1993, 28, 30). Yet the intangible benefit would have been substantial, with the visual effect of the baray's high walls and wide water views affirming considerable royal power (Figure 12.8). Such massive works can be perceived as monuments not only by virtue of their bulk, prominence, and the effort in their construction but also for implicit messages about the accomplishments of their creators (Morrison 2012).

These messages could be enhanced by the symbolism built into the waters of the baray. At Angkor, for example, these came largely from catchments on Phnom Kulen, the 45-km-long sandstone massif to the north and northeast, where they were sanctified by flowing over or past representations of Viṣṇu Anantaśayin at many locations (Chevance 2011, 334), symbolising rebirth (Feneley et al. 2016). In the *anantaśayin* mode, Viṣṇu wakes up from a deep sleep at the instant of the recreation of the universe. He has been sleeping on Ananta, a *nāga*—traditionally linked with abundance of water (Roveda 2005, 212)—or a *reachisey*—a Khmer dragon with a lion's head (Boisselier 1966, 320; Roveda 2005, 209), which is floating on the Sea of Milk (Rajan 1967). Brahma appears, sitting on a lotus emerging from Viṣṇu's navel. He becomes aware of Viṣṇu and utters the sound OM, and the world is born again (Feneley 2017). A recurrent scene on rock carvings on Phnom Kulen (Figure 12.9) has Viṣṇu Anantaśayin associated with numerous *liṅga* (Chevance 2011, 203, 334, see also Figure 10). Viṣṇu is concerned with regeneration and fertility, particularly in his anantaśāyin mode (Gutman 2013), while the liṅga symbolise the creative power of Śiva (Chevance 2011, 91). The import of the baray—and other water storages such as moats (Jacques 2008)—was also clear, with inscriptions depicting the large baray as the cosmic Sea of Milk.[6] This seems also to have been made explicit at the West Baray, where the Mebon was apparently centred around a bronze sculpture of Viṣṇu Anantaśayin in the 12th century, perhaps replacing a large liṅga of the 11th century (Feneley et al. 2016).

Figure 12.8 West Mebon inside West Baray. Embankment surrounding baray rises eight metres above water level.

Source: (Photo S. Sharick Photography).

We might note in passing that a water level of roughly 20–21 m ASL, which would be just sufficient to submerge the inside of the West Baray, was possibly close to the level of the nāga, or reachisey, on which the large Visṇu at the West Mebon must have been reclining (Feneley et al. 2016). The platform today is about 19 m ASL, and the nāga or reachisey could have been of the order of a metre thick (cf. Figure 12.9), bringing the base of the Viṣṇu to roughly 20 m ASL. The Viṣṇu could thereby be symbolically floating on the Sea of Milk which fully covered the base of the baray. Thus, had there been flood-recession rice planting inside the West Baray, it may have commenced with Viṣṇu in the state of anantaśayin and the world being reborn.

The construction programs of most of the great kings have appeared to scholars as part of a regular sequence (Stern 1951; Chevance and Pottier 2023, this volume). Chevance and Pottier list the components of this sequence as a reservoir, a temple to ancestors, a royal palace, and a temple-mountain signifying Mount Meru. Perhaps these monarchs, in somewhat comparable circumstances, were consolidating their positions with similar construction programs. Work commenced on three of the six largest reservoirs of the Angkorian capitals following a shift to a new centre. Moving the capital is a strategy often associated with efforts to control or undermine rivals and to consolidate loyalty (Joffe 1998, Schatz 2004). Indeed, five of these six storages were constructed by rulers whose predecessors appear to have had their reigns cut short. As Groslier (1974) remarked, 'most of the grand kings of Angkor were newcomers'.

The earliest baray is the unfinished one at Mahendraparvata, the capital Jayavarman II established after decades of campaigns to amalgamate several small kingdoms (Jacques 1972). Indravarman II

Figure 12.9 Two rock carvings of Viṣṇu in Anantaśayin mode, Kbal Spean River, Phnom Kulen. In rainy season, water flows over *liṅga* in foreground.

Source: (Photo T. Lustig).

built the Indrataṭāka immediately after succeeding Jayavarman III, whose reign may have ceased abruptly (Jacques 1972). Yaśovarman I built the East Baray after moving the capital from Roluos to Angkor. The largest Angkorian reservoir was at Koh Ker, which Jayavarman IV made his capital after Īśānavarman II had reigned for three years (Jacques 2014, 31–4). Sūryavarman I, who defeated Jayavīravarman after a five-year civil war (Vickery 1985), is considered to have built the West Baray (Pottier 2017). The Jayataṭāka was built by Jayavarman VII, who was enthroned after taking Angkor with an army from Champa (Vickery 2005). To some degree, Rājendravarman came close to conforming to this sequence. He moved the capital back to Angkor from Koh Ker following Harśovarman II's reign of only three years. A long passage, K. 806, LXXVI–XCIX, elaborates on Rājendravarman's victory over his enemy, which Cœdès (1937a, 75) interprets as his accession to the throne 'seemingly not without contest'. While he did not build a new reservoir, he apparently restored the East Baray,[7] Angkor (Yaśodharapura) itself,[8] the temple mountain of Pre Rup,[9] and other works that would have included the abandoned palace and temples.

It could have been prudent for a new ruler, conscious of the need to promote his legitimacy, to build monuments, such as a large reservoir symbolising the Sea of Milk and a temple representing Mount Meru. It is perhaps pertinent that while Jayavarman IV boasted that he had built his temple higher than those of his predecessors (K. 675, XXVIII, 928–41 CE), no known inscription mentions him also building the largest known—but doomed—Angkorian reservoir, a feat which remained unappreciated until about a decade ago (Evans 2010–2011).

With each new baray that was built at Angkor, there had to be new offtake structures to divert water from an existing watercourse and new channels to bring the water to the new storage. This increased the complexity of the water network, with new components almost inevitably blocking off or redirecting existing ones, at times even depriving older storages of supplies. For example, there appears to have been a marked fall in the water level of the West Baray from the late 12th century (Penny et al. 2005). This is approximately when Jayavarman VII installed the moats of Angkor Thom, which could have cut off the West Baray—the baray of Sūryavarman I and Sūryavarman II—from a supply coming from the Siem Reap channel. The result of successive additions of hydraulic features was not so much an integrated network but a palimpsest of water-management infrastructure, with some parts adapted to new functions or simply abandoned.

Discussion

With their works on Phnom Kulen in the late 8th and early 9th centuries, and perhaps also with the Rahal at Koh Ker in the 10th century, Khmer engineers demonstrated that they could control the flows discharging from their reservoirs. Apart from stocking a large amount of water for a large population, it is not yet clear what purpose those storages served, and no evidence that they were for irrigation has yet been found. The same technology could have been used for irrigating fields downstream of the baray at Angkor and other centres, as well as the reservoir at Koh Ker, but relics from very large mechanisms should then be apparent, and they are not. As well, there should have been channels for distributing irrigation water from the outlets to fields, and no such remnants have been identified except downslope from the West Baray. At the West Baray, it is possible that there were once control outlets such as stoplog sluice gates along its southern side and that these were buried subsequently. However, it seems that the baray's embankments were built to their current height in a single period of construction and that there was no state-sponsored irrigation from it subsequently. We are conscious of the archaeologist's maxim that absence of evidence is not evidence of absence, and we therefore cannot claim to have disproved the hypothesis that the baray were used for irrigating fields downstream. Nevertheless, we suggest that the likelihood is small.

Angkor's large reservoirs were each constructed following a period of political disturbance or relocation of the capital. These monumental storages, with their symbolic, religious, and aesthetic qualities, may have been intended to convey a message that the ruler was not only powerful but that his Mount Meru was 'intimately associated with the hydraulic system' (Groslier 1974). Each new baray required its own water supply, increasing the extent and complexity of Angkor's water system, with kings sometimes giving priority to their new works at the expense of earlier royal construction. Yaśovarman, at least, was well aware that even a king's works were liable to have a limited life (K. 281 and 282, D22–27). While the economic benefits of the baray must have been limited, their importance to the ruler, particularly those who sought to secure and display their power, must have been great.

Bernard-Philippe Groslier (1974) argued that Angkor's royal hydraulics allegorically recreated components of the water cycle. The rains, from monsoon clouds sourced figuratively from the cosmic ocean, fall on Phnom Kulen, the Angkorian Himalayas. They flow down to the Angkorian Ganga (the Siem Reap River),[10] which drains to Angkor's baray, representing the Sea of Milk. Perhaps this water cycle, through its emblematic hydraulics, was not for the hydraulic city envisaged by Groslier, but it was still one which

> *bore witness, as much through its technology as through its ritual, to a human endeavour sanctioned by the gods, the edification of Angkor.*
>
> (Groslier 1974)

Inscription references

K.	*Reference*	*K.*	*Reference*	*K.*	*Reference*
183	IC vol. I, 52	287	IC vol. IV, 235	752	IC vol. V, 59
186	IC vol. I, 48	341	IC vol. VI, 22	753	IC vol. V, 58
187	IC vol. I, 49	597	IC vol. IV, 231	806	IC vol. I, 73
263	IC vol. IV, 118	675	IC vol. I, 61	1012	Jacques 1999
281	Bergaigne 1893, 272	713	IC vol. I, 17		
282	Bergaigne 1893, 294	749	IC vol. V, 57		

IC = Inscriptions du Cambodge; Cœdès 1937–66.

Notes

1 Acker had assumed that the water levels inside the baray were about a metre below the crest. In the case of the West Baray, for example, this would represent a level of about 29 m ASL (above sea level). Yet the maximum level could not have been higher than the level of the inlet, about 22 m ASL. We have recalculated the storage volumes of the four largest baray—Indrataṭāka, East Baray, West Baray, and Jayataṭāka—using the available lidar-based digital elevation models and have found that overall, Acker overestimated them by a factor of about 2½.

2 Unfortunately, Van Liere wrote further that the Khmer lacked both 'the technique of constructing weir foundations' and of building 'sizeable reservoirs in the hills to store water throughout the dry season', assertions so at variance with the evidence that his judgement on the feasibility of irrigation was also questioned.

3 Inscriptions K. 183, K. 186, K. 187, 928 CE.

4 Had these channels predated the West Baray, the water in the channels would logically have come from an offtake from the Puok River.

5 The geomechanical properties of soil make it almost inevitable that repeated cuts and fills would become evident. The very process of these operations would weaken the soil, making it increasingly prone to dispersion with spillage and erosion by wind and rain. Over centuries of these annual works, this loss of material should become apparent.

6 Inscriptions which liken the baray to the Sea of Milk for the Indrataṭāka: K. 713A, VII, 880–93 CE; for East Baray: K. 281D, XXII; K. 282, XXIII–XXVII, 889–910 CE; K. 263C, XXVIII; and for Jayataṭāka: K. 287, XXVII, LII; K. 597B, S, late 13th–early 14th century CE.

7 Restoration of the East Baray is strongly alluded to in K. 806, CCLXIX and again in CCLXXIV–V, which refers to satisfying the entreaty of Yaśovarman to preserve his baray (K. 281 & 282, D22–27).

8 Re-establishment of Angkor is asserted in K. 806, XVIII, XXXI, and CCLXXIV.

9 K. 806, CCLXXVII.

10 K. 1012.1.

References

Acker, R., 1998. New geographical tests of the hydraulic thesis at Angkor. *South East Asia Research* 6, 5–47.

Bergaigne, A., 1893. *Inscriptions sanscrites de Cāmpa et du Cambodge.* Paris: Imprimerie Nationale.

Boisselier, J., 1966. *Le Cambodge.* Paris: A. et J. Picard et Cie.

Bourdonneau, É., 2007. Réhabiliter le Funan. Óc Eo ou la première Angkor. *Bulletin de l'École française d'Extrême-Orient* 94, 111–58.

Chevance, J.-B., 2011. *Le Phnom Kulen à la source d'Angkor, nouvelles données archéologiques.* PhD dissertation. Paris: Université Paris III—Sorbonne nouvelle.

Chevance, J.-B. & C. Pottier, 2023. The early capitals of Angkor. in *The Angkorian World*, eds. M. Hendrickson, M.T. Stark & D. Evans. New York: Routledge, 80–96.

Chevance, J.-B., D. Evans, N. Hofer, S. Sakhoeun & R. Chhean, 2019. Mahendraparvata: an early Angkor-period capital defined through airborne laser scanning at Phnom Kulen. *Antiquity* 93, 1303–21.

Cœdès, G., 1937–66. *Inscriptions du Cambodge. Collection de Textes et Documents sur l'Indochine*. Vol. I (1937); Vol. II (1942); Vol. III (1951); Vol. IV (1952); Vol. V (1953); Vol. VI (1954); Vol. VII (1964); Vol. VIII (1966). Paris: École française d'Extrême-Orient.

Cœdès, G., 1937a. *Inscriptions du Cambodge. Collection de textes et documents sur l'Indochine (Vol. I)*. Paris: École française d'Extrême-Orient.

Cœdès, G., 1937b. A new inscription from Fu-Nan. *Journal of the Greater Indian Society* 4, 117–21.

De Bernon, O., 1997. Note sur l'hydraulique théocratique angkorienne. *Bulletin de l'École française d'Extrême-Orient* 84, 340–48.

Delaporte, L., 1880. *Voyage au Cambodge: l'architecture khmer*. Paris: Librairie Ch. Delagrave.

Dumarçay, J., 1994. Histoire des retenues d'eau khmères. *Journal Asiatique* 282, 371–89.

Evans, D., 2010–2011. The archaeological landscape of Koh Ker, Northwest Cambodia. *Bulletin de l'École française d'Extrême-Orient* 97–98, 91–150.

Evans, D., 2016. Airborne laser scanning as a method for exploring long-term socio-ecological dynamics in Cambodia. *Journal of Archaeological Science* 74, 164–75.

Evans, D., J. Goodman, J. Sanday & M. Ra, 2011. The hydraulic system of Banteay Chhmar. Available: www.researchgate.net/profile/Damian_Evans2/publications [accessed 25/1/2020].

Evans, D.H., R.J. Fletcher, C. Pottier, J.-B. Chevance, D. Soutif, B.S. Tan, S. Im, D. Ea, T. Tin, S. Kim, C. Cromathy, S. De Greef, K. Hanus, P. Bâty, R. Kuszinger, S. Ichita & G. Boornazian, 2013. Uncovering archaeological landscapes at Angkor using lidar. *Proceedings of the National Academy of Sciences of the U.S.A.* 110(31), 12595–600.

Evans, D., C. Pottier, R. Fletcher, S. Hensley, I. Tapley, A. Milne & M. Barbetti, 2007. A comprehensive archaeological map of the World's largest preindustrial settlement complex at Angkor, Cambodia. *Proceedings of the National Academy of Sciences* 104(36), 14277–82.

Feneley, M., 2017. Reconstructing God: proposing a new date for the West Mebon Viṣṇu, using digital reconstruction and artefactual analysis. *Australian and New Zealand Journal of Art* 17, 195–220.

Feneley, M., D. Penny & R. Fletcher, 2016. Claiming the hydraulic network of Angkor with Viṣṇu: a multidisciplinary approach including the analysis of archaeological remains, digital modelling and radiocarbon dating: with evidence for a 12th century renovation of the West Mebon. *Journal of Archaeological Science: Reports* 9, 275–92.

Fletcher, R., 2020. An opinion on issues for future investigation of the water management of Greater Angkor. *WIREs Water*, 7.

Fletcher, R., B.M. Buckley, C. Pottier & S.-Y.S. Wang, 2017. Fourteenth to sixteenth centuries AD: the case of Angkor and monsoon extremes in mainland Southeast Asia, in *Megadrought and Collapse: From Early Agriculture to Angkor*, ed. H. Weiss. Oxford: Oxford University Press [Accessed 26/7/2018].

Fletcher, R., D. Penny, D. Evans, C. Pottier, M. Barbetti, M. Kummu, T. Lustig & APSARA, 2008. The water management network of Angkor, Cambodia. *Antiquity* 82, 658–70.

Garami, F. & I. Kertai, 1993. *Water Management in the Angkor Area*. Budapest: Angkor Foundation.

Goloubew, V., 1936. Reconnaissances aériennes au Cambodge. *Bulletin de l'École française d'Extrême-Orient* 36, 465–77.

Goloubew, V., 1941. L'hydraulique urbaine et agricole à l'époque des rois d'Angkor. *Bulletin économique de L'Indochine* 1–19.

Groslier, B.-P., 1974. Agriculture et religion dans l'Empire angkorien. Études rurales 53–6, 95–117.

Groslier, B.-P., 1979. Le cité hydraulique angkorienne: exploitation ou surexploitation du sol? *Bulletin de l'École Française d'Extrême Orient* 66, 161–202.

Groslier, G., 1924. *La région d'Angkor: Arts et archéologie khmers: Revue des recherches sur les arts, les monuments et l'ethnographie du Cambodge, depuis les origines jusqu'à nos jours*. Paris: Société d'Editions Géographiques, Maritimes et Coloniales Ancienne, maison Challamel.

Gutman, P., 2013. Relgious syncretism in 11th-century Thaton: a Southeast Asian transformation of Viṣṇu, in *Materializing Southeast Asia's Past: Selected Papers from the 12th International Conference of the European Association of Southeast Asian Archaeologists*, eds. M.J. Klokke & V. Degroot. Singapore: NUS Press Pte Ltd. Available: https://muse.jhu.edu/book/23985 [accessed 29/2/2020].

Hansen, E., 1969. *Cambodge: aménagement du Phnom Kulen*. Paris: UNESCO.

Hendrickson, M. & D. Evans, 2015. Reimagining the city of fire and iron: a landscape archaeology of the Angkor-Period industrial complex of Preah Khan of Kompong Svay, Cambodia (ca. 9th to 13th centuries A.D.). *Journal of Field Archaeology* 40, 644–64.

Jacques, C., 1972. La carrière de Jayavarman II. *Bulletin de l'École Française d'Extrême Orient* 59, 205–20.

Jacques, C., 1978. VI. Études d'épigraphie cambodgienne. XL Autour de quelques toponymes de l'inscription du Prasat Trapan Run K.598: La capitale angkorienne de Yaśovarman Ier à Sûryavarman Ier. *Bulletin de l'École française d'Extrême-Orient* 65, 281–332.

Jacques, C., 1999. Les inscriptions du Phnom Kbal Spãn (K 1011; 1012, 1015 et 1016). *Bulletin de l'École française d'Extrême-Orient* 86, 357–74.

Jacques, C., 2008. Moats and enclosure walls of the Khmer temples, in *Interpreting Southeast Asia's Past: Monument, Image and Text: Selected Papers from the 10th International Conference of the European Association of Southeast Asian Archaeologists*, eds. E.A. Bacus, I Glover & P.D. Sharrock. Singapore: NUS Press, 3–8.

Jacques, C., 2014. *Koh Ker: Temples et inscriptions, avec une étude sur le roi Jayavarman IV et un essai sur l'<<esclavage>> dans l'ancien pays khmer.* Budapest: Hungarian Southeast Asian Research Institute.

Joffe, A., 1998. Disembedded capitals in Western Asian perspective. *Society for Comparative Studies in Society and History* 40, 549–80.

Klassen, S., A.K. Carter, D. Evans, S. Ortman, M.T. Stark, A.A. Loyless, M. Polkinghorne, P. Heng, M. Hill, P. Wijker, J. Weed, G. Marriner & R.J. Fletcher, 2021. Diachronic modeling of the population within the medieval greater Angkor settlement complex. *Science Advances* 7(19), DOI: 10.1126/sciadv.abf8441.

Kummu, M., 2009. Water management in Angkor: human impacts on hydrology and sediment transportation. *Journal of Environmental Management* 90, 1413–21.

Lansing, J.S., S. Thurner, N.N. Chung, A. Coudurier-Curveur, C. Karakas, K.A. Fesenmyer & L.Y. Chew, 2017. Adaptive self-organization of Bali's ancient rice terraces. *Proceedings of the National Academy of Sciences of the United States of America* 114, 6504–09.

Lieberman, V.B., 2003. *Strange Parallels: Southeast Asia in Global Context, c.800–1830.* Cambridge; New York: Cambridge University Press.

Lustig, E. & T. Lustig, 2019. Losing ground: decline of Angkor's middle-level officials. *Journal of Southeast Asian Studies* 50, 409–30.

Lustig, T., S. Klassen, D. Evans, R. French & I. Moffat, 2018. Evidence for the breakdown of an Angkorian hydraulic system, and its historical implications for understanding the Khmer Empire. *Journal of Archaeological Science: Reports* 17, 195–211.

Moffat, I., S. Klassen, T. Attore, D. Evans, T. Lustig & L. Kong, 2019. Using ground penetrating radar to understand the failure of the Koh Ker Reservoir. *Northern Cambodia. Geoarchaeology* 35(1), 63–71.

Moore, E., 1995. The waters of Angkor. *Asian Art and Culture* 8(2), 37–52.

Morrison, K.D., 2012. Doorways to the divine: Vijayanagara reservoirs and rural devotional landscapes. *South Asian Studies* 28, 157–69.

Nesbitt, H.J., 1997. Topography, climate, and rice production, in *Rice Production in Cambodia*, ed. H.J. Nesbitt. Manila: International Rice Research Institute, 15–9. Available at: http://books.irri.org/9712201007_content.pdf [accessed 28/1/19].

Penny, D., C. Pottier, M. Kummu, R. Fletcher, U. Zoppi, M. Barbetti & T. Somaneath, 2005. Hydrological history of the West Baray, Angkor, revealed through palynological analysis of sediments from the West Mebon. *Bulletin de l'École Française d'Extrême Orient* 92, 497–521.

Penny, D., C. Zachreson, R. Fletcher, D. Lau, J.T. Lizier, J.N. Fischer, D. Evans, C. Pottier & M. Prokopenko, 2018. The demise of Angkor: systemic vulnerability of urban infrastructure to climatic variations. *Science Advances* 4, 1–8.

Peou, H., 2013. The Angkorean hydraulic system. *World Heritage* 68, 24–27.

Peou, H., I. Natarajan, T. Hong, & D. Philippe, 2016. From conservation to sustainable development—a case study of Angkor World Heritage Site, Cambodia. *Journal of Environmental Science and Engineering*, A, 141–55.

Pillot, D., 2007. *Jardins et rizières du Cambodge. Les enjeux du développement agricole.* Paris: Karthala/Gret.

Pottier, C., 1999. *Carte Archéologique de la Région d'Angkor. Zone Sud.* PhD dissertation. Paris: Université Paris III—Sorbonne nouvelle.

Pottier, C., 2000. Some evidence of an inter-relationship between hydraulic and rice field patterns at Angkor during ancient times. *Journal of Sophia Asian Studies* 18, 99–119.

Pottier, C., 2017. Nouvelles données sur les premieères cités angkoriennes, in *Deux décennies de coopération archéologique franco-cambodgienne à Angkor*, eds. A. Beschhaouch, F. Verellen & M. Zink. Paris: Académie des Inscriptions et Belles-Lettres, 43–79.

Rajan, K.V.S., 1967. The typology of the Anantaśayī icon. *Artibus Asiae* 29, 67–84.

RCA, 1934. *Rapports de la Conservation d'Angkor.* Paris: École française d'Extrême-Orient.

RCA, 1935. *Rapports de la Conservation d'Angkor.* Paris: École française d'Extrême-Orient.

Roveda, V., 2003. *Khmer mythology: Secrets of Angkor*. Bangkok: River Books.

Roveda, V., 2005. *Images of the Gods: Khmer Mythology in Cambodia, Thailand and Laos*. Bangkok: River Books.

Schatz, E.A.D., 2004. What capital cities say about state and nation building. *Nationalism and Ethnic Politics* 9, 111–40.

Shimoda, I. & K. Sato, 2009. Religious concept in the layout of the ancient Khmer city of Koh Ker. *Udaya, Journal of Khmer Studies* 10, 25–55.

Stern, P., 1951. Diversité et rythme des fondations royales khmères. *Bulletin de l'École française d'Extrême-Orient* 44, 649–87.

Stott, P., 1992. Angkor: Shifting the hydraulic paradigm, in *The Gift of Water*, ed. J. Rigg. London: School of African and Oriental Studies, 47–58.

van Liere, W.J., 1980. Traditional water management in the lower Mekong Basin. *World Archaeology* 11, 265–80.

Vickery, M., 1985. The Reign of Sūryavarman I and royal factionalism at Angkor. *Journal of Southeast Asian Studies* 16, 226–44.

Vickery, M., 2005. Champa revised. Working Paper Series No. 37. Singapore: Asia Research Institute, National University of Singapore.

PART III

State Institutions

13

ANGKORIAN LAW AND LAND

Tess Davis and Eileen Lustig

US v. 10th-Century Cambodian Sandstone Sculpture

On February 29, 2012, the *New York Times* featured a small headline that would lead to big litigation: 'Mythic Warrior Is Captive in Global Art Conflict' (Mashberg 2012). The accompanying story revealed that the Royal Government of Cambodia was fighting Sotheby's auction house to recover a stone figure of Duryodhana (Figure 13.1), the feared antagonist of the Hindu epic the *Mahābhārata*. This thousand-year-old masterpiece had been on the block in Manhattan for $2–3 million USD. However, in the hours before the sale, Cambodia presented evidence that thieves had hacked the statue off at the ankles from a small sanctuary within the massive ruins of Koh Ker, the 10th-century royal capital of the Angkorian Empire. The Duryodhana's feet and pedestal remained behind at the site alongside countless others that had suffered the same fate—reminders of both Angkor's past glory, as well as Cambodia's more recent tragedies, including the long and bloody period of the Khmer Rouge regime.

US attorneys made the case that the Duryodhana and the archaeological remains at Koh Ker more broadly were, and had always been, Cambodian state property. Prosecutors traced the law back a millennium, arguing that 'In ancient Cambodia, all land belonged exclusively to the crown and was inalienable, including the kingdom's archaeological sites and antiquities'. They contended that this ownership system survived into the French protectorate period for archaeological sites and antiquities—citing, among other laws, a decree (GGI 1900) recognising that such material found 'above and below ground' was part of the 'national domain'—and likewise continued into modern times (Complaint 2012, 19–21).

Sotheby's fought back that the US government was relying not on the law but what it dismissed as the 'inherent right of kings' (Claimant's reply 2013, 4). The auction house said, 'there is neither precedent nor justification' for 'a claim that anything built by a king a thousand years ago belongs to the state today'. Nor was there any law,

> much less a clear and unambiguous one, declaring either that the ancient Cambodian king owned everything [at Koh Ker] when it was built one thousand years ago, or that the modern state of Cambodia now owns everything [from Koh Ker] that was abandoned to the jungle fifty generations ago.
>
> (Claimant's memorandum of law 2012, 1)

DOI: 10.4324/9781351128940-17

Figure 13.1 The statue of Duryodhana now returned to Cambodia, June 3, 2014.

Source: (Photo courtesy Department of Homeland Security, www.ice.gov/sites/default/files/images/news/2014/140604phnompenh2_lg.jpg).

However, in November 2012, in light of new evidence that the statue had been stolen in 1972, prosecutors only had to prove the Cambodian state legally owned the statue then and no longer needed to trace the law back to Angkorian times (Verified amended complaint 2012, 7–8). In December 2013, having failed to dismiss the case, the auction house settled (Stipulation and order of settlement 2013). In summer 2014, the Duryodhana finally returned home to Cambodia, where it was later reunited with its feet and pedestal to great fanfare.

This litigation may have divulged the Duryodhana's story, but it left some legal questions unanswered. The court never had the opportunity to rule on whether such a statue was the state property of the Cambodian kingdom when it was created or whether that chain of title continued to the present day. So it is a worthwhile exercise to travel back in time and revisit the law of medieval Cambodia and examine the 'inherent rights' of its kings. What do we know about the law and legal institutions in the Angkorian era? Who owned land, temples, and the treasures within them or below the ground? Who decided judgments in case of disputes?

Our chapter seeks to begin answering these questions by synthesising what is known of Angkorian law, with a focus on ownership and property. It will summarise ancient Cambodia's legal system, including the role of the king, the judicial system, court proceedings, the laws enforced, and punishments. This overview demonstrates that the law, encompassing both rights and obligations, was complex and dynamic.

What Is Law? Sources of Khmer Law

Before going further, it is necessary to acknowledge the largest of this chapter's many limitations: in surveying what is known of Angkorian law, it is applying modern (and primarily Western) concepts, as expressed in the English language, to a Southeast Asian kingdom a thousand years ago. Scholars have debated whether the various texts commonly considered to embody 'ancient Southeast Asian law' can even be called such in today's sense of the word (Hooker 1978, 97). After all, there is no one meaning of 'law' that cuts across cultures, languages, and time. The same is true of 'ownership' and 'property'—the meanings of which, even now, vary widely.

Hooker (1978, 98) warns that in the region's earlier civilisations, it is difficult to separate 'law' from 'religion, dynastic history, the organisation of a bureaucracy, and so on'. Likewise, Lingat (1949) has argued that the royal edicts, *śāsana*, are more indicative of regulatory than legislative power. In his view, the texts do not have the character of laws today, as they lack the permanent sanctions that normally define legislation. Indeed, in this regard, only very few bear any resemblance to legislative texts in a Western sense.[1]

However, despite these qualifications, Hooker convincingly maintains that Southeast Asia's ancient texts (including those from Cambodia) are indeed 'texts of law'. True, they played a very different role in society than their contemporaneous counterparts in the West, let alone the traditions that underlie most legal systems today. But they still dictate 'the relationship between ruler and ruled' (Lingat 1949). This chapter is written on the same basis: there is much in the Cambodian inscriptions that meets the spirit of our modern concept of the 'law', and they may thus be treated as such—with care.

Contemporary lawyers and scholars may find it difficult to pinpoint where morality ends and the law begins in the historical texts of Cambodia and the wider region. Put another way,

> Individual responsibility was as much a moral, ethical, or religious matter as it was a 'legal' one. Moreover, an individual's obligations varied widely according to status. All legal duties were not shared by all, but were rather dependent on race, sex, caste, and religion.
>
> (Lingat 1949)

Rewards, including payments for goods and services, at least insofar as they related to temple matters, were allocated in order of status. This is often seen where more than one person received a share of the payment for a tract of land (Lustig 2009).

Other key differences will stand out, reminding us that many of the legal tenets and practices now considered intrinsic parts of the law are really just products of our place and time. For example, unlike most jurisdictions today, there is no evidence that Angkorian courts differentiated between 'civil' and 'criminal' wrongs, those committed against private entities as opposed to the public at large or the state (Ishizawa 1984)—seen in the respective examples of the 'Case of the Fugitive Slave' (K. 233, 10th c. CE) and the 'Case of the Removal of Boundary Posts for Swindling' (K. 181, 962 CE). Hooker also notes that the texts are largely silent with regard to what we would now call civil law altogether, suggesting it was governed by custom.

Certainly, oral law was (and remains) important throughout the region and was no less legally binding because it was not written down. For these reasons, again, one must be cautious in viewing ancient Cambodian law through the lens of our modern legal language. Similarity between terms and concepts—such as duties and rights, or ownership and property—should not be taken for equivalence (Hooker 1978, 2–7).

This is especially true since a number of terms and concepts in ancient Cambodian law did not originate there. The written record for the Indian legal system, which would so influence the Khmer and many others, began in the Vedic period, approximately 1500–500 BCE, although its origins may have been even earlier. It is centred around the concept of *dharma,* which is often translated as 'law' but is even more difficult to define. In general, 'dharma' signifies the 'totality of duties which bears upon the individual according to his status (*varṇa*) and the stage of life (*āśrama*) at which he stands, the totality of rules to which he must conform' (Lingat 1973, 4; see also Jenner 2009, 2009a; Monier-Williams 2022).

Dharma is so complicated that lengthy Sanskrit texts, the Dharmasūtras, were devoted to explaining it. Starting in around 500 BCE, these were followed by even more complex works, the Dharmaśāstras (Lingat 1973, 28–9). Davis has described the latter in modern terms 'not as codes of black-letter law' but rather textbooks of materials, hypotheticals, and systematisations which were both practical and theoretical (Davis 2006). Of these, the Mānava-Dharmaśāstra, also known as the Manusmṛiti or 'Code of Manu', was arguably the most influential not only in India but wherever its influence reached (including Cambodia). Its 12 books lay out detailed rules for society—for religious practices and rites, personal relationships, politics, war, and, of most relevance to this chapter, the administration of justice and resolution of disputes. This 'legal' section addresses what we would today consider civil (private), contract, criminal, property, and family law, as well as a court system, with no distinction between the religious and the secular (Lingat 1949, 1973, 77–87). It is likely that Manu used an even older treatise, Kauṭilya's Arthaśastra, which covered a broader scope of statecraft, when dealing with the king, governance, and legal procedure (Olivelle 2013, 29).

All of these rich religious and legal traditions were well developed in the early centuries of the Common Era by the time Indian travellers carried them to Southeast Asia, where they would have a lasting impact. These texts were known to the Khmers by the mid-6th century, when the ruler Bhavavarman I was said to have had two ministers versed in the Dharmaśāstra and the Arthaśastra (K. 53, 589 CE). The latter was later cited by Khmer rulers to show their erudition and was quoted directly in an inscription at Prei Prasat (K. 279, ca. 900 CE), a monastery of the reign of king Yaśovarman I. A text found at Preah Khan of Kompong Svay, K. 161, dating to Sūryavarman I's reign (1002–49 CE), likened the king's intelligence to a human body with the Dharmaśāstra for a head (Lingat 1949, 1973, 77–87; Sahai 1970, 9–38).

Khmer temple inscriptions, our main sources for the legal system, reference both local and Hindu gods. This wrongly led early legal scholars to dismiss mediaeval Cambodian law as completely derivative of India, in much the same way as early archaeologists viewed Cambodian culture of that time as derivative of Indian cultural traditions (Hooker 1978, 95). A more accurate interpretation is that rulers consciously gave local concepts and deities an exotic Indian 'veneer'—cultural symbols—to help legitimise their political status and stratify the society (van Leur 1955, 104; Wheatley 1961, 186, Wolters 1982, 9–10, Mabbett 1997), much as today Western legal languages pull from Latin and other Classical traditions. Wheatley (1983, 295) has described Śaivite devotionalism as 'a powerful means of intensifying chiefly charisma without necessarily effecting radical change in the religious and ethical conceptions of early Khmer society'. Likewise, the presence of Indian Brahmins in courts, as well as the possession of inscriptions, helped to enhance the prestige of elites (van Leur 1955, 98).

There are over 1300 Pre-Angkorian and Angkorian temple inscriptions in Old Khmer and Sanskrit, dating from the 6th to 15th centuries. The Sanskrit texts, in verse, primarily eulogise kings and officials and evoke gods, while Khmer language texts generally contain political, bureaucratic, or economic information—setting out donations of working personnel, land, animals, and material goods to endow religious establishments. In the Angkor Period, these often provided detailed histories of land acquisition, including judicial cases, and cited royal edicts. Legal terminology was in Sanskrit, while Khmer recorded the facts of the dispute itself (Ricklefs 1967).

While valuable, these texts nevertheless have their limits. For one, they were unevenly distributed over time and geography. By their very nature, they were most reflective of the elite, and even when the general population is referred to, it is from the elite's perspective. These factors, along with their poor preservation, the narrow scope of their content, our incomplete knowledge of the Old Khmer language, and ambiguities in meaning, have limited their effectiveness as historical documents (Ishizawa 1984, Lustig et al. 2007).

From Communal to Private Possession of Land

Michael Vickery has observed that the corpus of Pre-Angkorian inscriptions contains no information to indicate private individual ownership of land and that, at least in the 7th century, 'this was vested in the local communities, or local chiefly lineages' that were able to carry out land transfers and donations of land and slaves to temples without reference to higher authority. Vickery concluded this meant 'that if, in principle, a superior royal establishment existed, its kings did not have effective ownership of the land, nor did they claim such in theory' (1998, 299).

Over time, however, local control was weakened. In the 7th century, king Jayavarman I appears to have had greater territorial authority than earlier rulers and enough power to have had a say in matters concerning religious foundations (Wolters 1974; Vickery 1998, 294–95, 367–69). Succeeding rulers continued to attract supporters and amalgamate territories, culminating, during the reign of Jayavarman II at the turn of the 8th and 9th centuries CE, in what today is regarded as an empire (see Lowman et al. 2023, this volume). By the beginning of the Angkor Period in the 9th century there must have been some version of private property rights, because we are told in several examples that Jayavarman II and his successors rewarded some of their supporters with land grants.[2] The recipients and their descendants often acquired additional lands in order to provide the means of support for their religious foundations: temples and āśrama.

From the 9th century, religious foundations were being established not only by royalty but also by associates of the rulers, elite families, on lands they were acquiring (Briggs 1999[1951]);

Hall 1985; Pou 2002; see also Chea et al. 2023, this volume). Land was the source of wealth and power, since its possession by royalty and other elites allowed control over agricultural production and most likely the labour of the people who were attached to it (Ricklefs 1967). We read of donations, purchases, sales, and inheritance of land (and its produce), slaves, and precious goods and the delegation of authority to manage these assets—ostensibly to support a temple deity and to acquire merit—though other benefits in the form of immunities and royal protection were often granted (Mabbett 1978).

As the Indian hereditary barrier between priests and nobles did not apply in Cambodia, there was less (if any) division between the modern concepts of 'church and state', and many judicial officials had overlapping responsibilities across religious and secular domains (Mabbett 1978). Hence, a great many titled officials can be seen as members of courts, as well as temple founders and donors of land and slaves. Many authors of inscriptions are high-ranking officials and associates of kings and sometimes hold ecclesiastic positions. In recording their purchases of lands to endow foundations, a key concern, not infrequently, was to ensure the prosperity of their families:

> and I ask, I who have been initiated into holy orders, to look after them [the lands, 'āśrama and slaves], that they may not come under the authority of the *kaṃloñ* and the *kaṃhas*, that none come under any authority other than those of my line, and that it will be my relatives who look after them.
>
> Phnom Chisor (K. 33, 939 CE, lls. 31–4)[3]

Ricklefs (1978) has inferred that the right to 'own' land and the protection of tenure by law in 10th-century Cambodia applied to all free people in the society—not only elite officials—on the grounds that many landowners were categorised in inscriptions as *vāp* or *loñ*, who seemed not always of very high rank. However, we should note that the concept of freedom as being distinct from servitude is not applicable in mediaeval Khmer society. For example, Mabbett (1983) describes a 'complexity of the institution of slavery, the variety of sources from which slaves came and the variety of statuses they could have'. (See also Jacques 1973; Mabbett 1978.) Moreover, we know little about the property rights of people, such as those who could be sold or given to temples.

By the 10th century, a definite system of land and property rights had evolved, and much land was held by private individuals. Numerous texts from this time record royal grants which include a guarantee giving the owner and his descendants 'exclusive right' to the property. Moreover, royal courts enforced these rights, and indeed they 'were essential to guaranteeing the integrity of landholdings and the settling of boundary disputes' (Ricklefs 1967). From the century between 950 and 1050, these disputes were a focus of many inscriptions written by officials with the purpose of validating title to lands (Vickery 1985).

Royal Power and Land

The traditional conception of land ownership in Khmer society, still widely held in rural communities in recent times, has been that the king owned all the land. However, people could claim rights to land if they occupied and cultivated it for a certain period. Collective use of land including forests, grazing land, and fisheries was also organised on the basis of 'customary norms'. Based on 19th-century Cambodian law and practice, the French colonial administration likewise accepted that the kingdom's 'soil' was the exclusive and inalienable property of the crown, until an 1884 treaty instilled a private property regime (Convention entre la France et le Cambodge 1884, Art. 9). Other reforms likewise distinguished between possession in the sense of occupation (*paukeas*) and possession in the sense of ownership (*kamaset*) (Diepart 2015; Scurrah and Hirsch 2015).

While even today, the exact meaning of 'ownership' differs across legal traditions, it is commonly considered 'the bundle of rights allowing one to use, manage, or enjoy property, including the right to convey it to others' (Garner 2004). As several authors have pointed out, this is not an easy notion to apply to Asian institutions of the past (Mabbett 1978). Yvonne Bongert (n.d., cited Mabbett 1978) notes that the concept of absolute and exclusive property rights is a product of the mediaeval Romanists, not necessarily applicable to other societies. For example, bequests mentioned in various (Indian) Sanskrit texts limit authority over property. In most of these texts concerning land, a key element is a king's right to share in its produce in exchange for royal protection (Mabbett 1978). Donations of land were, according to Bongert, of interest to the rulers not for the land itself but rather for the tax revenue that the land would deliver.

The frequency of the Angkorian king's involvement in land matters has suggested he was seen as a 'spiritual overlord' (Battacharya 1955). Indeed, this interpretation far outlasted the Angkorian Empire, with 19th- and early 20th-century laws likewise referring to the king as 'master of the earth' (Kleinpeter 1937, 105). Inscriptions do refer to the ruler as 'master of the surface and below' (*kamrateṅ pdai ta karom*), with the crown domains called *rājadravya* at his disposal.[4] Such characterisations led Georges Cœdès (1965) to ask whether buyers actually owned their land outright or whether the king remained the overall owner. More than half a century later, in *US v. Cambodian Sandstone Sculpture*, prosecutors and expert witnesses made the case for the latter (Complaint, 19). Yet while the king's permission was needed for the amalgamation of foundations—perhaps because taxation revenue might be affected—it does not appear to have been required each time land was given, purchased, or sold (Ricklefs 1967; Mabbett 1978). Moreover, the epigraphy does not paint the medieval ruler as the absolute owner of all land in today's sense of the word (Sahai 1970, 146–47).

Both Sahai (1970) and Ishizawa (1985, 28–30) have argued that an individual's 'ownership' of land was more a right to exclusive use, including the right to buy, sell, or bequeath it. The court cases that are described in the inscriptions dealt with these co-called 'practical rights' (Ishizawa 1985, 30), while what we might call a 'residual right' remained with the Khmer king—although the distinction likely matters far more to 21st-century lawyers and scholars than to Angkorian kings or their subjects. Texts demonstrate that rulers could grant lands which were without inheritors or had lain unoccupied; rulers could also requisition land, replacing it with an equivalent tract (as in the case of the vāp in K. 598 below). They also had the right to confiscate land outright, but as observed by Mabbett (1978), they rarely exercised it, other than in cases of insurrection:

> Śaka 933: when Trakval Vau in league with Tā Pāṅ sought to rise up against His Majesty in the maternal line, [the latter] had [them] convicted, seized [their] land and the temple at Sukhāvāsa—which had belonged to the *tāñ* Tritatī, known to Trakval Vau as [his] ancestress and graciously gave [them] as a gift to the *vraḥ kaṃsteṅ 'añ śri* Lakṣmīpativarman.
>
> O Smach (K. 1198B, 1014 CE, lls. 23–4)

Many texts mention land parcels acquired as *karuṇāprasāda* (royal grace), a royally sanctioned purchase, or a royal gift. Endowments sanctioned by the king were often declared royal foundations (*rājadharma*), and the religious merit for the pious deed was transferred to or shared by the king. The ruler, in return, issued edicts to safeguard the sustainability of the founder's endowments and exemptions from the authority of various officials, such as the district chiefs (*khloñ viṣaya*) and inspectors of the royal service (*rājakāryya*) (Mabbett 1978, Sahai 1970, 123, 147).

Some royal allocations warrant further scrutiny. A tract of land given to Prasat Trapeang Rung (K. 598B, 1006 CE) was said initially to be without an owner and was reallocated by the king to a *mratāṅ khloñ* śri Kavīndrapaṅḍita, despite it already being under the 'sole' authority of a *vāp jnvāl*. Yet the vāp had sold part of it, and when the buyers complained, they had to be compensated with other land of equal quality. While it seems clear that the vāp had some claim to the land from the outset, its transfer from his sole authority, seemingly with little in the way of compensation, appears to have been viewed at the time, in 1006 CE, as unremarkable. The three texts referring to Jayavarman V's (968–1001) newly created varṅa (elite castes), mention that the villages, fields, slaves, and livestock given to these could not be reclaimed by their previous chiefs—suggesting the chiefs may not have been unequivocally satisfied with the arrangement.

It is not clear to what extent the Angkorian endowments and land transfers constitute transfer of ownership, since the rights of all participants were embedded within a variety of relationships linking donors to the land that they sold or donated (Mabbett 1978). Certainly, the ambiguity extends to other kinds of property. The late 10th-century inscription K. 233 from Tuol Rolom Tim records that an official gave a slave to a temple after receiving her as surety against a buffalo he had loaned out. After she ran away, the borrower was obliged to replace her with another slave, and then another when that one absconded. The lender could give the slaves to the temple, yet the borrower remained responsible for keeping them there.

Mabbett (1978) distinguishes between relinquishing land totally and relinquishing the rights to its produce. A temple could benefit from the produce of donated land and slaves; the rights might include part or total authority over the land, or this might be given to the temple, the donor's family, or others. Granting a village to a temple foundation might amount in practice to giving that foundation the right to receive revenue that would otherwise have gone to the state (Chakravarti 1980, 203). The fine line between the property of a god and that of donors or temple officials and their families, which is perceived in some inscriptions, underscores the complexity of ownership. For example, in a text from Phnom Preah Net Preah (K. 216N, 1005 CE), an official's estate included the slaves, *sruk* (villages) and rice fields of his two foundations.

Inscriptions typically specified those given authority to manage a foundation and its resources and frequently set out any immunities granted by the king:

> [This foundation] shall not come under the authority of the *vrīha* (rice officers). [It] shall not come under the authority of the *kandvār cralo*. [It] shall not come under the authority of the *bhūtāśa* of *cañcūli*. [It] shall not be under the jurisdiction of members of [his] family. Only [the founder's] children and grandchildren who are in holy orders in order to know the dharma [and] guard this foundation are ones who are authorised to possess [it].
>
> Pràsàt Ó Roṃduol (K. 659, 968 CE, lls. 10–14)

Some texts indicate that a donor gave full control to the recipient, others that he retained management of the property for his family. Inscription K. 205 (CE 1036), from Wat Baset, records five officials purchasing lands which together they donated to a *vraḥ kaṃmrateṅ 'añ* (*VKA*) Guṇapativarman for his religious foundation. The founder offered up the land to the god and subsequently gave it to his three daughters. In this case, it is not certain if the property remained in the family with the temple receiving the right of use or, Cœdès' preference, that the family were to manage the land for the temple (Cœdès 1951, 4). In another text from Wat Baset (K. 207, 1043 CE), 14 members of a family sold some parcels of land to a *VKA* Kaṇṭhpaṇḍita for his foundation. The family had been providing the foundation's milk and were thereafter entrusted to maintain and protect the god. In a text, ascribed to the Sūryavarman I reign, from Wat Damnak (K. 420), tracts of land were 'given' to a *VKA* Vīrendravarman by a *teṅ tvan*. When she died, a certain *VKA* of Vrac 'bought' the land again from her grandson—suggesting that the original owner had retained some rights, despite the earlier transaction. Indeed, property rights appear to have varied in many ways but were certainly far from outright.

The Courts, Legal Institutions, and Investigations

Texts of the Angkorian era depict the king as the highest judicial authority. According to the Tep Pranam inscription (K. 290, CIII) of Yaśovarman I (889–910), 'the immortal duty of the king is to maintain the standard of law, to abide by the systems of caste and āśrama, to perform the rites for gods, and to punish criminals in accordance with the graveness of the crime'. However, if only out of logistical necessity, authority to create and enforce the law was mostly delegated to the king's courts and judicial officials. While texts do reference the king presiding over cases directly, many of the references are likely to be examples of this kind of delegation, especially where they concern minor legal actions taking place far from the capital (Sahai 1970, 99; Ishizawa 1984).

There was a court in the capital (*vraḥ sabhā nagara*) and territorial courts at the level of district (*vraḥ sabhā viṣaya*) and village (*vraḥ sabhā sruk*), as well as separate courts based at temples, empowered to deal with the affairs of temples and their villages.[5] A 'Chief of Court'—the equivalent of a chief judge—presided over the higher court and each territorial court. Below this position were officials holding the position of associate or deputy judges. There was also an 'Inspector of Merits and Demerits,' attached to both lower courts and temple courts, although much of his role is still poorly understood. Some of these officials were attached to villages and others to temples, and they tried cases in court together with the assistant judges. Other senior officials included the Reciters of Dharmaśāstra, apparently experts in jurisprudence, who helped to determine laws applicable to the different cases. There were also investigators who collected and presented evidence, perhaps senior officials themselves, judging by other titles held by the same individuals. Members of the court, who may have been of lower status, were called upon to interrogate witnesses, in addition to witnessing transfers of land and assisting in their demarcation. (Ishizawa 1984; Sahai 1970, 99–104):

> The leading men, being under oath, identified the limits of the land at Vraḥ 'Aṃvil, took members of the royal court out to set up the boundary-markers □□□□ [and] to give [it] to VKA Śrī Vāgindrapaṇḍita, following the royal instruction.
>
> Stele of Wat Sla Ku (K. 736D, early 12th c. CE, lls. 8–10)

Cases would work their way through this system of courts and officials—from a complaint to the response, the examination of the matter by the Court, and the decision. Many additional details will be familiar to modern readers. Proceedings begin with an 'appeal to the king', either through a petition to him directly or other high officials. Then the king would either hear the case himself or delegate it to a court. If needed, preliminary investigations would be conducted and testimony and other evidence examined. Witnesses were presented and oaths taken. Then the court would deliberate and rule (Sahai 1970, 104–11; Ishizawa 1984; Hooker 1978, 34–5).

> A royal directive bade *VKA* śrī Rājendrapaṇḍita, *sabhāpati* (chief justice) of the sruk of Ya □□□ and *VKA* śrī Rājendropakalpa, member of the royal court of the sruk of

> Varadā, order □□□□□□□□ to delimit [it], [and] interrogate 16 witnesses under oath. [These] declared unanimously that □□□□ the *teṅ hyaṅ* Vasanta and the loñ Ney of the royal gardens were really without family [and] that the land in question had been received as a gift by royal favour to *VKA* the royal servant.
>
> Wat Baset, (K. 208, 11th c., lls. 51–6)

In land disputes, a person could only be considered the legitimate owner of acquired land when the tribunal had assigned him the exclusive right (*siddhi*) to the land and the old owner had formally given over this exclusive right. Exclusive right over a domain could not be granted to an individual or to a religious foundation until the old owner had withdrawn his objection (Sahai 1970, 110–11). Of 25 such disputes resolved by the courts, 18 were over land, with at least 10 involving the minor officials vāp and loñ. The greatest number of disputes, testimony to tensions among these landowners, were recorded in the late 10th century. The greatest number of land sales by the same officials was recorded in the same period (Lustig and Lustig 2019).

A few texts suggest that there were avenues for those with influence to sway or circumvent the decisions of the court. There are at least two accounts of disputes in which witnesses had been paid by the ultimate winner of a court case to corroborate evidence (Lustig and Lustig 2019).[6] The late 10th-century inscription, K. 353S from Prasat Kantop, contains a complex history of a rice field which was bought by a certain preceptor (*'adhyāpaka*) from a *steṅ* Nan who had acquired it from a vāp Gas, who himself was not the owner. The preceptor cultivated the field for 13 years, when steṅ Nan died. It was only then that the true owner, the steṅ 'añ, the *ācārya* Īśānavyāpi, sought compensation, raising the question why he hadn't done this while steṅ Nan was alive. The court upheld his claim, awarding him the rice field. The preceptor, who had acquired the rice field in good faith, received no compensation. Both the ācārya and the preceptor performed a ceremony (*brahmayajña*), presumably over this rice field. The preceptor then apparently asked for the same rice field as an honorarium for his part in the ritual. This raises another question: why did the ācārya submit to the preceptor's request?

Only a few land transactions and grants are known to have been officially registered. The previously mentioned Wat Baset inscription K. 205 refers to a register which recorded the lands providing the revenues for certain officials and likely used for assessing taxes. A text from Thvar Kdei (K. 165S, 957 CE) mentions a record of the original calculations (*caṃlāk gmvar tem*) for a rice field. In the case detailed in K. 598, outlined previously, title to the land granted by the king was to be set out on different materials, placed in three separate locations. It's not certain how common such registration was, because records, many on perishable materials, have long since vanished:

> The [mratāñ khlo]ñ also humbly solicited His Majesty to let [this compensation] be set down on a royal plaque at the royal court; to let [this compensation] be inscribed on the leaves of judgement of the tribunal, on a stele at the holy *brāhmaśālā*; to allow [it] to be inscribed on a palm-leaf manuscript in the royal chamber of ablutions; to let [it] be committed to a proclamation *ta* . . . sruk Vrai Karaṅ; and to not let members of the mratāñ khloñ's family take this land to sell [or] assign [it] to others.
>
> Prasat Trapan Run (K. 598, 1006 CE, lls. 46–8)

Many temple inscriptions, however, perhaps a majority, would have been intended to serve as legal documents, as they set out the author's declaration, if not proof, of land ownership (Ricklefs 1967). Some contain accounts of a family's acquisitions, royal grants, purchases, and gifts, at times going back hundreds of years. These texts often include such details as the names of donors and vendors, witnesses to transactions, and prices paid for individual rice fields. Some report on favourable outcomes of disputes over land ownership. The boundaries of land parcels were also commonly set out in the inscriptions, though with varying degrees of precision, and only very rarely indicating distances between boundary markers. Only one inscription on a door jamb of Prasat Khlan (K. 542N, 1006 CE) illustrates such a text with maps marking the lands attributed to specific sanctuaries. The markers were typically set up at the four or eight principal points of the compass:

> To the east [the domain] extends to the road at the foot of the mountain; to the southeast to the sea of the *viṅvneṅ*; to the south to the boundary-marker; to the southwest [it] touches the land belonging to VKA of Ratipura; to the west [it extends] up to the banyan tree(s), and touches the Kac Syāṅ road; on the northwest [it] extends to Chok Dik Toḥ Chau, meeting land belonging to Tanmar; to the north [it is limited by] all of the hills; on the northeast [it] extends to the boundary-markers east of the *mratāñ kuruṅ* Vagvāl's dam, turning at the southeast corner of the holy reservoir; running east northeast, [it] touches the Krīḍāparvata [and] extends to Khnar Grāṅ.
>
> Banteay Srei (K. 570, 969 CE, lls. 34–40)

But land held on the strength of continuous occupation—likely by traditional owners or people with limited resources—was less likely to have been recorded in inscriptions or administrative registers. Potentially, such lands could have been subject to various claims. In the vāp jnvāl incident above (K. 598B) and in the dispute outlined in K. 262 below, village elders (*grāmavṛddha*) were sometimes called upon to certify land ownership.

Several disputes stem from claims of incorrect boundary marking, which were sometimes upheld, sometimes not. An inscription at Wat Preah Einkosei (K. 262, 982 CE) reports that a woman removed some boundary markers of a rice field. The court investigated the complaint of the owner, a VKA of Dvijendrapura, and found this field had been wrongly included in a parcel of land purchased for a temple and ordered that the markers be placed correctly. It is notable that this judgement required two enquiries by different officials and that some witnesses were not independent. It was only in the second investigation that the vendor acknowledged that the land he sold did not include that owned by the woman. At Nak Ta Carek (K. 181, 962 CE), a mratāñ kuruṅ Vīrabhaktigarjjita was accused of removing the boundary markers of a field and harvesting its rice. Despite his explanation that he had been wrongly informed by a vāp Amṛta that it was another tract, the kuruṅ was found guilty by the court and fined ten *liṅ* of gold, while two of his accomplices received 102 lashes to the back; the field was restored to its owner. The law's perception of a person's obligations, which varied according to their status, is reflected in the imposition of penalties listed in a royal decree at the 9th-century temple of Lolei at Angkor (Table 13.1). The practice appears in a sense not to have favoured the higher classes, as usually the higher their rank, the greater their punishment. However, those of high rank were fined and weren't subject to corporal punishment. The same text states that transgressors who were Brahmins were to be banished from the precinct, as they couldn't be punished otherwise. The chaplain, however, had to pay a fine in silver (Ishizawa 1985, 22; Sahai 1970, 93–100).

The penalties imposed by court officials were seemingly not decided arbitrarily. Court decisions would have been made within a framework of rules, even if those rules have been lost to history. Punishments for offences shared similarities with those in classical Indian law, specifically the Code of Manu (Sahai 1970, 93–9; Hooker 1978, 34; Ishizawa 1985, 21–27; Jacobsen

Table 13.1 Social status and associated fines from K. 323 (889 CE, sts. 78–82).

Social status of the guilty	*Amount of fine in pala of gold*
Royal princes	20
Relatives and counsellors of the king	10
Dignitaries having right to parasol with gold handle	5
Principal merchants	2 ½
Members of the sects of Viṣṇu, Śiva, etc.	1 ¼
Common people	5/8 or 100 bamboo cuts on the back

Source: (Adapted from Sahai 1970, 95).

2005). They include those punishments meted out in the 32 hells, often threatened in imprecations at the end of inscriptions (Jacobsen 2005).

While fines were usually paid in weights of gold or silver, there are also instances where payment in kind was recommended[7]—and in certain situations it was possible for a person found guilty to mitigate the sentence by paying goods to the court:

> The royal court ordered the vāp Jū to be seized, in order to be sentenced. The vāp Jū presented goods [to the king] for his release [and] assigned full title to the said land to the holy kaṃsteṅ añ śrī Lakṣmīpativarman.
>
> O Smach (K. 1198B: 35–6)

For serious crimes, including the theft of land, referred to in the previous citation, the possibilities were detention, imprisonment, corporal punishment, amputation, or death (resulting perhaps from the punishment). In the following text the offence has been omitted or is no longer discerned:

> A royal missive [addressed to] *kaṃsteṅ* Kavīśvaravarman together with the mratāñ khloñ, inspector of qualities and defects, [and] members of the royal court, ordering [them] to condemn vāp Sa, the younger brother of □□āja, to having his feet and hands cut off, [and] ordering [his] family to make allowances as before.
>
> Wat Phu (K. 720C, 1006 CE, lls. 6–13)

Somewhat more brutal, divine trials, or ordeals—judgement and punishment in one—are described by Chinese sources (cited by Sahai 1970, 107–8; Ishizawa 1984) in *Funan* during the early centuries of the Common Era. More than half a millennium later, Zhou Daguan (2007[1297], ch. 14) refers to several of these, one of which entails plunging a suspect's hand into boiling oil. According to Zhou, the victims of crime sometimes instigated the trials themselves. There is no direct mention of such trials in the inscriptions of Pre-Angkor or Angkor, although Cœdès suggests (n. 1) the term *pranidhāna* in inscription K. 566A of the 10th–11th century could be a reference to submission to an ordeal.

Shift in Land Ownership

Much of the discussion about Angkor's legal system is based on texts whose topics of interest were to elites and mostly concerned endowments to religious foundations. The majority were written from the mid-10th to early 11th century—and, in the main, suggest continuity. Yet, as has often been pointed out, Angkor, in common with every other enduring society, was not a static entity. Stern (1951), Mabbett (1978), and Lustig (2011) have each observed structural and economic shifts and cycles over the course of the Angkorian Empire's six centuries. With regard to land, the development of the state of Angkor altered an existing system of ownership, to the extent that prime communal and family-held lands were broken up and transferred to elites.

From the 9th century onward, Angkorian inscriptions contain growing numbers of titles and bureaucratic positions, indicating an increasingly hierarchical society. The 10th and early 11th centuries saw progressively more inscriptions produced by officials than by kings. Enhanced wealth among the elite is evident in the vocabulary for luxury goods which were used for payments and given to the temples (Lustig 2009).

By contrast, not only were middle-level vāp and loñ in litigation and selling land, as mentioned, they seem also to have had social limitations imposed upon them (Lustig and Lustig 2019). Vāp may have been traditional landholders, living in kinship or other communal groups, whose ancestors were granted title to lands at the time of Jayavarman II. Loñ were socially superior to vāp, sometimes claiming descent from royalty or cohorts of Jayavarman II. At least up to the late 10th century, texts show vāp and loñ having foundations, land, and slaves (Mabbett 1977, 431). In land sales, exchanges were never from higher- to lower-status individuals (e.g. loñ to vāp). In common with other hierarchical practices, while seemingly not enforced explicitly by authorities, such a constraint on land transactions could be understood as customary law. Such restrictions on sales contributed to the downgrading of this middle-ranking section of the society (Lustig and Lustig 2019). By the middle of the 11th century, vāp had disappeared from the inscriptions, and in the early 12th century, loñ appeared only as temple servants (Vickery 2002, 100).

A factor behind the high volume of land sales was the way taxes were paid to the centre. Because Angkor didn't have a currency, it would have been more practical for these to be paid in high-value goods if the transport was over a significant distance. Lacking these goods, many less affluent people, such as the previously mentioned middle-ranking officials, were obliged to borrow them. Repayment on such borrowings was always at 100% premium. This requirement, coupled with hierarchical constraints on buying land, meant they could have become net vendors of land within a short period. Both loñ and vāp were affected.

Indeed, most founders from Sūryavarman's reign (1002–1049) are of the elite. After this king, fewer texts were produced, there were far fewer disputes and only four texts referring to land transactions. The concentration of land holdings and the revenues these delivered into the hands of fewer families would have been instrumental in increasing the power they wielded (Lustig and Lustig 2019).

Concluding Remarks

As our discussion shows, ancient Cambodian inscriptions have begun to uncover the outlines of the Angkorian legal system, which governed one of Southeast Asia's most powerful empires between the 9th and 15th centuries. While we may never have a clear picture—and must use care when viewing this historical record through our modern lens—we can see that the law was complex and adaptable to the needs of the changing Angkorian society, in which rulers were assuming increasing powers and the population was increasingly stratified. There are admittedly vast divides between this framework and contemporary judicial systems, from the entanglement of 'church and state' to the lack of codified legislation or the significance of an individual's status. However, much is likely still familiar to today's lawyers and legal scholars, including those in the royal government of Cambodia.

If it is true that a justice system reflects what matters most to a culture, our knowledge of Angkorian law tells us that land was critically important to both rulers and their subjects, as it was the source of power. Many Angkorian texts refer to royal grants of land to supporters (though in practice kings were not able to dispose of land freely). But there are also increasing records of individual purchases, with elites acquiring wealth at the expense of others, who were thus under pressure—evidenced by the disputes. The complex concept of ownership, based on obligations and on the relationships between donor or seller and receiver, is highlighted by the accounts of these disputes.

Both with and beyond the subject of land, the texts reveal a system of rights and obligations that, while fragmented to us, would probably have been well defined to those at its place and time. A hierarchy of courts and officials sought to enforce these rules across the kingdom, seeming to strive for (at least what they considered) consistency and fairness, even if it was not always achieved. Cases were not brought, or decided, arbitrarily. Free people appear to have had access to the law and the courts, although, like today, there are signs that those with influence were at an advantage. Rulers adapted concepts, terminology, language, and practices from India to local traditions, building something that was—like Angkor itself—Khmer. The ruler sat at the head of this framework and loomed large over every aspect of it, at least in name, if not in practice. Yet that did not mean the king was necessarily above the system or above the law. To the contrary, inscriptions demonstrate that he and those he appointed either followed the law or at least prioritised the appearance of doing so, even as they helped to shape and enforce it. The 'inherent rights of kings', in the words of Sotheby's, were strong indeed, but so, it seems, was ancient Cambodia's system of justice.

List of Inscriptions in Text

K.	*Reference*	*K.*	*Reference*	*K.*	*Reference*
33	IC III, 148	233	Cœdès 1954, 49	449	Cœdès 1913, 27
53	Barth 1885, 64	247	IC III, 94	521	IC IV, 167
71	IC II, 54	257	IC IV, 140	542	IC III, 221
85	IC VII, 28	262	IC IV, 108	566	IC V, 182
161	Finot 1904, 672	279	Bergaigne 1893, 238	570	IC I, 144
165	IC VI, 132	290	Cœdès 1908, 203	598	NIC II–III, 230
175	IC VI, 173	323	Bergaigne 1893, 211	659	IC V, 143
181	IC VI, 140	342	IC VI, 236	720	IC V, 212
205	IC III, 3	353	IC V, 133	736	IC V, 306
207	IC III, 16	374	IC VI, 251	868	IC VI, 170
208	IC VI, 287	420	IC IV, 161	1198	NIC II–III, 240
216	IC III, 37	444	IC II, 62		

IC = Inscriptions du Cambodge; Cœdès 1937–66.

NIC = Nouvelles inscriptions du Cambodge; tome II-III: Pou 2001.

Notes

1 Three inscriptions that may be considered akin to legislative texts concern the creation of new elite castes (*varṇa*) by Jayavarman V in CE 974: K. 175; K. 444; K. 868.

2 For example, the stele of Palhal (K. 449, CE 1069) details royal gifts of land to several generations of a family.

3 Quotations from inscriptions are adapted from the original French translations and unpublished English translations by the late Philip Jenner.

4 See K. 85 (CE 981) for an example of *kamrateṇ pdai ta karom*, and K. 521 (CE 11th century) for the term *rājadravya*.

5 Courts functioning at various levels are mentioned as follows: at the capital (K. 342, 1015 CE), district court (K. 247, CE 1060), village court (K. 208, 11th c. CE), temple court (K. 374, 1042 CE).

6 See K. 257N (994 CE); K. 1198B (1014 CE).

7 The mid-10th-century stele of Basak (K. 71) recommends the extraction of a yoke of cows from people wrongfully taking 'cleansing oils' destined for a god. The text concerns a temple facility having cows to produce these oils.

References

Barth, A., 1885. *Inscriptions sanscrites du Cambodge*. Paris: Imprimerie Nationale.

Battacharya, K., 1955. Some aspects of temple administration in the ancient Khmer Kingdom. *Calcutta Review* 134(2), 193–99.

Bergaigne, A., 1893. *Inscriptions sanscrites de Campā et du Cambodge*. Paris: Imprimerie Nationale.

Bongert, Y., n.d. Le notion de proprieté dans l'Inde. *Travaux et recherches de l'institute de droit comparé de l'Université de Paris,* XXIII, 149–62

Briggs, L.P., 1999[1951]. *The Ancient Khmer Empire*. Bangkok: White Lotus.

Chakravarti, A., 1980. *The Sdok Kak Thom Inscription, Part I: A Study in Indo-Khmer Civilization*. Calcutta: Sanskrit College.

Chea, S., J. Estève, D. Soutif & E. Swenson, 2023. Āśramas, shrines and royal power, in *The Angkorian World*, eds. M. Hendrickson, M.T. Stark & D. Evans. New York: Routledge.

Cœdès, G., 1908. La stèle de Tép Praṇaṃ(Cambodge). *Paris, Journal Asiatique* 12, 203–24.

Cœdès, G., 1913. La stèle de Pàlhal. *Bulletin de l'École française d'Extrême-Orient* 13, 27–36.

Cœdès, G., 1937–66. *Inscriptions du Cambodge. Collection de Textes et Documents sur l'Indochine.* Vol. I (1937); Vol. II (1942); Vol. III (1951); Vol. IV (1952); Vol. V (1953); Vol. VI (1954); Vol. VII (1964); Vol. VIII (1966). Paris: École française d'Extrême-Orient.

Cœdès, G., 1954. La stèle de Tuol Rolom Tim. Essai d'interprétation par la langue Bahnar d'un texte juridique Khmèr du Xe siècle. *Journal Asiatique* 242(1), 49–67.

Cœdès, G., 1965. L'Avenir des Études Khmeres. *Bulletin de la Sociétè des Études Indochinoises*, XL (New Series) (3). Originally published by Academie des Inscriptions et Belles Lettres, 1960, 367 ff.

Davis, D.R., 2006. A realist view of Hindu law. *Ratio Juris* 19(3), 287–313.

Diepart, J.-C., 2015. The fragmentation of land tenure systems in Cambodia: peasants and the formalization of land rights. Country profile No. 6, Cambodia. Working paper for The Technical Committee on "Land Tenure and Development", France. www.researchgate.net/publication/279206247_The_fragmentation_of_land_tenure_system_in_Cambodia_Peasants_and_the_formalisation_of_land_rights

Finot, M. L., 1904. L'inscription de Praḥ Khan. *Bulletin de l'École française d'Extrême-Orient,* IV, 672–75.

Garner, B.A. (ed), 2004. *Black's Law Dictionary* (8th ed.). New York, NY: Thomson West.

Hall, K.R., 1985. *Maritime Trade and State Development in Early Southeast Asia*. Sydney: George Allen & Unwin.

Hooker, M.B., 1978. *A Concise Legal History of South-East Asia*. Oxford: Clarendon Press.

Ishizawa, Y., 1984. The preservation of law and order in Angkorian Cambodia. *The Journal of Sophia Asian Studie* 2, 11–32.

Ishizawa, Y., 1985. *The Juridicial System in Angkorian Cambodia*. Tokyo: Sophia University. Departmental bulletin paper.

Jacobsen, T., 2005. Paying through the nose. Punishment in the Cambodian past and lessons for the present. *South East Asia Research* 13(2), 235–56.

Jacques, C., 1973. A propos de l'esclavage dans l'ancien Cambodge. Actes du 29e Congrès international des Orientalistes. Asie du Sud-Est continentale. *L'Asiathèque* 1, 71–6.

Jenner, P.N., 2009a. *A Dictionary of Pre-Angkorian Khmer*. Canberra: Pacific Linguistics, Research School of Pacific and Asian Studies, Australian National University.

Jenner, P.N., 2009b. *A Dictionary of Angkorian Khmer*. Canberra: Pacific Linguistics, Research School of Pacific and Asian Studies, Australian National University.

Kleinpeter, R., 1937. *Le problème foncier au Cambodge*. Paris: F. Loviton.

Lingat, R., 1949. L'influence juridique de l'Inde au Champa et au Cambodge d'après l'épigraphie. *Journal Asiatique* 137, 273–90.

Lingat, R., 1973. *The Classical Law of India. Berkeley Center for South and Southeast Asia Studies.* California: University of California Press.

Lowman, I., K., Chhom & M. Hendrickson, 2023. An Angkor nation? Identifying the core of the Khmer empire, in *The Angkorian World*, eds. M. Hendrickson, M.T. Stark & D. Evans. New York: Routledge.

Lustig, E. & T. Lustig, 2019. Losing ground: decline of Angkor's middle-level officials. *Journal of Southeast Asian Studies* 50(3), 409–30.

Lustig, E. J., 2009. Money doesn't make the World go round: Angkor's non-monetisation, in *Research in Economic Anthropology*, ed. D. Wood, Bingley, UK: Emerald Group Publishing Ltd., 165–99.

Lustig, E., 2011. Using inscription data to investigate power in Angkor's empire. *Aséanie* 27, 35–66.

Lustig, E., D. Evans & N. Richards, 2007. Words across space and time: an analysis of lexical items in Khmer inscriptions, 6th–14th centuries CE. *Journal of Southeast Asian Archaeology*, 1–26.

Mabbett, I. W., 1977. Varṇas in Angkor and the Indian caste system. *Journal of Asian Studies* XXXVI (No. 3), 429–42.

Mabbett, I.W., 1978. Kingship in Angkor. *Journal of the Siam Society* 66 Part 2, 1–51.

Mabbett, I., 1983. Some remarks on the present state of knowledge about slavery, in *Angkor. Slavery, Bondage, and Dependency in Southeast Asia*, eds. A. Reid & J. Brewster. New York: St. Martin's Press, 44–63.

Mabbett, I.W., 1997. The "Indianization" of Mainland Southeast Asia: a reappraisal, in *Living a Life in Accord with Dhamma: Papers in honor of Professor Jean Boisselier on his eightieth birthday*, eds. N. Eilenberg, M. C. Subhadradis Diskul and R. L. Brown. Bangkok: Silpakorn University, 342–55.

Mashberg, T. & R.B lumenthal, 28 February 2012. Mythic warrior is captive in global art conflict. *The New York Times*. https://nyti.ms/2onwgRQ (accessed 2 December 2022).

Monier-Williams 2022. *Cologne digital Sanskrit lexicon* (from Monier-Williams 'Sanskrit-English). Cologne: Institute of Indology and Tamil Studies, University of Cologne. http://webapps.uni-koeln.de/tamil/, [accessed 2 December 2022.]

Olivelle, P., 2013. *King, Governance and Law in Ancient India: Kauṭilya's Arthaśāstra: A New Annotated Translation*. New York: Oxford University Press.

Pou, S., 2001. *Nouvelles inscriptions du Cambodge II & III, traduites et éditées par Saveros Pou*. Paris: École française d'Extrême-Orient.

Pou, S., 2002. Aśrama dans l'ancien Cambodge. *Journal Asiatique* 290–1, 315–39.

Ricklefs, M.C., 1967. Land and law in the epigraphy of tenth-century Cambodia. *Journal of the Asiatic Society* 26 (3), 411–20.

Sahai, S., 1970. *Les Institutions Politiques et L'Organisation Administritive du Cambodge Ancien (VI e-XIIIe Siecles). Publication volume* LXXV. Paris: École française d'Extrême-Orient.

Scurrah, N. & P. Hirsch, 2015. *The Political Economy of Land Governance in Cambodia. University of Sydney, Mekong region land governance*. https://mrlg.org/wp-content/uploads/2015/12/Political_Economy_of_Land_Governance_in_Cambodia.pdf (accessed 2 December 2022).

Stern, P., 1951. Diversité et rythme des fondations royales khmères. *Bulletin de l'École française d'Extrême-Orient* 44(2), 649–85.

Van Leur, J.C., 1955. *Indonesian Trade and Society: Essays in Asian Social and Economic History. Selected Studies on Indonesia by Dutch Scholars, Vol. I.* The Hague: W. van Hoeve.

Vickery, M., 1985. The reign of Sūryavarman I and royal factionalism at Angkor. *Journal of Southeast Asian Studies* 16(2), 226–44.

Vickery, M., 1998. *Society, Economics, and Politics in Pre-Angkor Cambodia: The 7th–8th Centuries*. Tokyo: Centre for East Asian Cultural Studies for UNESCO, The Tokyo Bunko.

Vickery, M., 2002. *A History of Cambodia. Summary of Lectures Given at the Faculty of Archaeology*. Phnom Penh, Royal University of Fine Arts, 2001–2002, Pre-Angkor Studies Society.

Wheatley, P., 1961. *The Golden Khersonese: Studies in the Historical Geography of the Malay Peninsula before A.D, 1500*. Kuala Lumpur: University of Malaya Press.

Wheatley, P., 1983. *Nāgara and Commandery: Origins of the Southeast Asian Urban Traditions*. Chicago, IL: University of Chicago, Dept. of Geography.

Wolters, O.W., 1974. North-western Cambodia in the seventh century. *Bulletin of the School of Oriental and African Studies. University of London* XXXVII, 355–84.

Wolters, O.W., 1982. *History, Culture, and Region in Southeast Asian Perspectives*. Singapore: Institute of Southeast Asian Studies.

Zhou, D., 2007[1297]. *A Record of Cambodia: The Land and Its People*, trans. P. Harris. Chiang Mai: Silkworm Books.

National and International Law

Convention entre la France et le Cambodge pour régler les rapports respectifs des deux pays, le 17 juin 1884, available at https://gallica.bnf.fr/ark:/12148/bpt6k5790647n.texteimage. (accessed 13 January 2022).

GGI (1900). Arrêté du Gouverneur Général de l'Indochine sur la conservation des monuments et objets ayant un intérêt historique ou artistique, le 9 mars 1900, available at https://en.unesco.org/sites/default/files/cambodia_arreteconservation_1900_frorof.pdf. (accessed 13 January 2022).

Court Filings

Complaint in *United States of America v. A 10th Century Cambodian Sandstone Sculpture*, Currently Located at Sotheby's in New York, New York, 4 April 2012.12 CIV 2600.

Verified amended complaint in *United States of America v. A 10th Century Cambodian Sandstone Sculpture*, Currently Located at Sotheby's in New York, New York, 9 November 2012.12 Civ, 2600.

Claimant's memorandum of law in opposition to government's motion for leave to file an amended complaint in *United States of America v. A 10th Century Cambodian Sandstone Sculpture*, Currently Located at Sotheby's in New York, New York, 3 December 2012.12 CIV 2600.

Claimant's reply in support of their letter dated May 10, 2013 requesting a pretrial conference pursuant to F.R.C.P 16 in *United States of America v. A 10th Century Cambodian Sandstone Sculpture*, Currently Located at Sotheby's in New York, New York, 28 May 2013.12 CIV 2600.

Stipulation and order of settlement in *United States of America v. A 10th Century Cambodian Sandstone Sculpture*, Currently Located at Sotheby's in New York, New York, 12 December 2013.12 CIV 2600.

14

WARFARE AND DEFENSIVE ARCHITECTURE IN THE ANGKORIAN WORLD

David Brotherson

Sūryavarman II was crowned in 1113 CE after a bloody civil war. An inscribed stele (K. 364) at Ban That (the 'village of the towers'), a modest-sized temple in southern Laos, records his exploits:

> Releasing the ocean of his armies . . . he gave terrible battle, leaping on the head of the elephant of his enemy he slew him, just as Garuda swooping down from a mountain kills a serpent. . . . He saw the kings of other countries that he desired to subjugate come to bring him tribute. He went into the countries of his enemies and eclipsed the glory of the victorious Raghu.
>
> (Cœdès 1968[1944], 159; Finot 1912, 27)

Taking the throne by force was not unusual for Angkorian kings, nor were military campaigns of conquest. Two millennia of Chinese historical records suggest Southeast Asian polities were repeatedly at war. The Sui dynasty (581–618) frames the Pre-Angkorian transition from *Funan* to *Chenla* as one of conquest (Briggs 1951, 40). The founding of Angkor, inland and removed from preceding political centres in the Mekong Delta, may have been motivated by bellicose relations with emerging Cham polities along coastal Vietnam (Vickery 2009, 49). Rajendravarman II (r. 944–968) was said to have 'cut off the heads of a crowd of kings' (K. 528, Finot 1925, 337). Documentary sources suggest warfare played a significant role in the long-term trajectory of the Angkorian Empire, which would go on to dominate mainland Southeast Asia. Angkor's demise has long been associated with conflict with Ayutthaya, which, in turn, was sacked by Burmese forces in 1767. Given this evident propensity for warfare, this chapter asks: What is the archaeological evidence for militarism and defence in the Angkorian World?

Specific details are lacking for many aspects of the armies of Angkor, yet the available evidence suggests military prowess was instrumental in the expansion of the empire, in the legitimisation of the ruling class, and, eventually, for the defence of the capital itself. Conventionally, the primary forms of evidence have been textual and visual. Inscriptions and histories record wars and rebellions and use terminology related to military structure and hierarchy. Visual evidence consists of the bas-relief carvings at Angkor Wat, the Bayon, and Banteay Chhmar, which present the largest canvases for interpretation (Figure 14.1). However, in recent years, archaeological survey of the built environment and engineered landscape of Angkor has revealed

DOI: 10.4324/9781351128940-18

Figure 14.1 Narrative scenes of warfare from bas-reliefs on Angkor Period temples: a) Angkor Wat; b) Banteay Chhmar; c) Bayon.

Source: (Photos D. Brotherson).

additional evidence for military activity, especially throughout Angkor's demise. These phenomena will be discussed in four parts: military culture, armed forces, expansion and consolidation, and defence mechanisms.

Military Culture

Across Southeast Asia in the early first millennium CE, deep-rooted animist ideas that connected the physical and martial prowess of political leaders to the spiritual world of the ancestors were reimagined, drawing extensively on Indic cultural motifs. Thus the notion of divine kingship, the Sanskrit language, Indian writing systems, and Hindu and Buddhist religions all emerged in Khmer society (Cœdès 1968[1944]). Likewise, Indian mythology and literature, including architectural treatises and epic poetry, became central to the design and inspiration for the decoration of shrines. During the Angkor Period the most popular epics were the *Mahābhārata* and the *Rāmāyana*, which inspired scenes carved in lintels and pediments from the mid-10th century (e.g. Banteay Srei, East Mebon). As Angkorian architecture developed into larger monuments in the 11th and 12th centuries, artisans had larger canvases to decorate and made use of these stories. Sūryavarman II, the builder of Angkor Wat, seems to have especially favoured the depiction of battles, as five of the eight bas-reliefs of the third gallery are battle scenes. Along the west gallery, facing the main entrance, are the Battles of Kurukshetra (Mahābhārata) and the Battle of Lanka (Rāmāyana). The other battles depicted are the Battles of Devas and Asuras, Victory of Viṣṇu over the Asuras, and the Victory of Kṛṣṇa (Krishna) over Bana (all sourced from various *Purānas*) (Roveda 2002). Note that these latter two were not carved until the 16th century, and while the style and craftsmanship are noticeably different, some argue that the preliminary sketch was likely made in the 12th century (see Roveda 2002, 66). The numerous mentions of war and rebellion in 11th- to 12th century inscriptions and historical texts (Table 14.1) suggest that Sūryavarman II's propensity for glorifying military might—honouring

Table 14.1 Epigraphic sources for warfare in the Angkor Period.

Year (CE)	*Source*	*Reference*	*Context*
early 9th C	K. 449	(Cœdès 1913, 33)	rebellion
950	C. 38; K. 528	(Barth and Bergaigne 1885–1893, XXVI, 248; Finot 1925, 346)	attack
1002–04	K. 235; K. 944	(Cœdès and Dupont 1943, 72; Cœdès 1937–1966, Vol. V, 210)	rebellion
1051; 1066	K. 289	(Barth and Bergaigne 1885–1893, XVIII, 140, 4)	rebellion ×3
1069	DVA[1]	(Maspero 1928, 141–2)	defence
1074	C. 95	(Finot 1904, XV, 943)	defence
1076	DVA	(Maspero 1918, 33)	attack
early 12th C	K. 364; K. 288	(Finot 1912, 27; Cœdès 1937–1966, Vol. IV, 230)	rebellion
1128; 1132, 1136; 1138, 1145	DVA	(Maspero 1918, 34; Maspero 1928, 155–6)	attack ×5
1148	C. 101	(Finot 1904, XXI, 965)	attack
1150	DVA	(Maspero 1918, 34)	attack
1170s	K. 485	(Cœdès 1929, 324)	defence
1177	Chinese annals	(Wade 2011, 154)	defence
1177–1181	K. 485	(Finot 1925, 386)	rebellion
c.1182	C. 92	(Finot 1904, XXIV, 974)	rebellion
1190; 1193–94	C. 30; C. 4	(Aymonier 1891, 48, 50–2)	attack ×2
1203	C. 90	(Finot 1904, XII, 940)	attack
1216–18	DVA	(Maspero 1918, 35)	attack
1220	C. 4	(Aymonier 1891, 51)	defence
1268	DVA	(Cœdès 1968[1944], 192)	attack
1283	DVA	(Maspero 1918, 35)	defence

the gods with scenes of victorious battle—may be related to the military expansion of the empire (see subsequently).

The bas-relief in the south gallery of Angkor Wat also depicts a royal procession ('Historical Procession') that includes the army. It shows Sūryavarman II himself, his generals, priests, and officials, as well as hundreds of soldiers, on parade. Short, caption-like inscriptions identify the king and his ministers, who are depicted 'larger than life', riding on the backs of elephants and sheltered with many parasols. It shows a range of handheld and projectile weaponry and cavalry, as well as heraldry, banners, and bands (Jacq-Hergoualc'h 2007[1979]). The Historical Procession is perhaps the first depiction of a non-mythical subject in a Khmer narrative relief, even if it is probably done through an idealising lens.

Angkorian kings were considered both *cakravartin* and *devaraja*, notions which connected kingship to divine authority and are indicative of absolute power. In reality, the exigencies of ruling an empire meant that royal authority would sometimes need to be imposed by force. The loyalty of regional governors was maintained through favours and rewards from the king, and force was applied when persuasion would not suffice (Mabbett 1978). The preoccupation with battle, fanfare, and regalia depicted in the bas-reliefs suggests that military prowess and the ability to maintain order through coercion were fundamental elements of Khmer kingship. The rules of royal succession are unclear, as at times the throne would pass to a brother or a cousin, while at others it would pass to the ruler's son. Angkorian kings were polygamous and typically had many male progeny around which court factions with access to the throne would develop. Rival factions would draw additional support from their provincial connections. If there was no clear, dominant faction when the king passed, a bloody struggle for succession would sometimes follow. Taking the throne by force, therefore, appears to have been commonplace in the Angkorian World.

Armed Forces

The account of Zhou Daguan is the only detailed eyewitness description of classical Angkor that has survived (2007[1297]). He saw soldiers going naked and barefoot, carrying a lance and shield. Zhou also relates, second-hand, that when Angkor was attacked, presumably by Ayutthaya, many of the common people without training or preparation were made to fight. According to him, the Khmers had no bows and arrows, trebuchets, body armour, or helmets (Zhou 2007[1297], 82). However, the bas-reliefs indicate that these weapons and armour did exist at Angkor. Are the reliefs an idealised depiction of the military from the Indian epics reimagined in a Khmer setting? Or had Angkor's military resources declined since its heyday, as Zhou Daguan saw Angkor a century or more after the bas-reliefs were made? A plausible scenario is that the army of Angkor was depleted of resources from repeated conflicts in the late 13th century and was therefore short of supplies and weaponry.

Although bladed weaponry such as knives have been found in domestic contexts at several excavations across Angkor (Bâty 2007), preservation conditions in the tropics do not normally allow for their recovery, especially iron, which typically corrodes to the point of being unrecognisable. Metals such as copper can be easily recycled and reworked, so they are rarely discarded and hence do not enter the archaeological record. Thus, the bas-reliefs are essentially the only evidence we have for the weaponry that may have been used by the army.

Forces and Weaponry

The Indian treatise Kautilya's *Arthaśastra* defines the ideal army consisting of standard units centred on an elephant or chariot, surrounded by five cavalry and 30 foot soldiers (Jacq-Hergoualc'h 2007[1979], 118). Southeast Asian chronicles conventionally applied this ideal to describe their own armies as the 'four war arms'. The Historical Procession bas-relief at Angkor Wat is probably an idealised depiction of Angkorian forces in the early 12th century. The formations depicted feature corps in similar proportions, in which an elephant is preceded and followed by a group of foot soldiers, along with three or four cavalry.

The infantry greatly outnumbers the other corps in the bas-reliefs, and there is great variety in their clothing, weaponry, and accoutrements. The Angkor Wat carvings show two types: soldiers with lance and shield and archers. The lance soldiers have a variety of breastplates, shields, sarongs, and headdresses. The archers have different headdresses and sarongs, carry no shields, and wear a tunic instead of armour. The headdresses are all some form of diadem, and some are decorated with animal headpieces, either real (horse, bull, owl, rabbit, or deer) or imaginary (*garuda* or *makara*). Such ornamentation evokes the ornate headdresses of the *apsara* dancers but also perhaps the protective power of an animal's spirit (see subsequently). Angkor Wat is a Vaiṣṇavite temple and features numerous depictions of garuda, the vehicle of Viṣṇu and enemy of snakes, so perhaps divine protection was also being invoked (Jacq-Hergoualc'h 2007[1979], 87). Additionally or alternatively, these symbols may simply relate to the organisation of the army.

Curiously, the *phka'k*, an axe-like weapon with a curved wooden handle, is shown being handled by high-ranking officers riding on elephants or horseback. Today it is a farmer's implement for general use. Perhaps a farmer's tool being wielded as a general's weapon—even if only symbolically—may be a reflection of the agrarian-based society of Angkor, where the peasantry made up the majority of the rank and file. Recall Zhou Daguan's observation (2007[1297], 82) that Angkor had no standing army.

The army was composed not only of Khmers but also included Cham and Chinese (or Vietnamese) soldiers, as depicted at the Bayon (Jacq-Hergoualc'h 2007[1979], 98–108). The conventional interpretation of these reliefs is that they depict a war waged by Jayavarman VII to retake Angkor from a rebellious faction of Khmers who, with the help of Cham allies, had held the city since 1177 (Jacques and Lafond 2007, 238–9). Ethnic diversity within the ranks is also shown at Angkor Wat: the Historical Procession shows soldiers at the front of the column, referred to as *Syāṃ Kuk* in a small accompanying inscription, who are noticeably different in their hairstyles, headdresses, clothing, and facial structure, which leads to the assumption that they are a different ethnicity. One theory is that they were the Suei, also known as the Suai or Kuy, from the Mun River basin (Groslier 1981).

Unfortunately, we have only one estimate of the army's size in the historical record, appearing in the context of a conflict between Sūryavarman II and the Dai-Viet in the 12th century. Dai-Viet documents claim that Angkor sent 20,000 soldiers in 1128 to attack them via the mountain passes, but they were driven back (Maspero 1928, 155–56).

Strategies

Overwhelming the enemy with superior force and numbers seems the primary tactic employed by the Khmer. Elephants, an unmistakable symbol of power, are used to decorate temples and feature prominently in narrative bas-reliefs depicting violence, armies, and conflict. In front of the Royal Palace of Angkor Thom is the Elephant Terrace, where the eponymous bas-relief shows an elephant hunt in which they overpower other animals—including buffalo and lions—by picking them up with their trunks and throwing them to the ground. Narratives of royal accession often feature an elephant hunt episode (Lowman 2013).

Adding to the cacophony of an elephant charge, the sound of horns, drums, and cymbals of the martial band must also have had a demoralising effect on the enemies of the Khmer. An inscription from Prasat Kumphus (K. 669, 973 CE) (Cœdès 1937–1966, Vol. I, 159) describes the psychological effect of the army's band:

> With the noisy drums, the coarse copper cymbals . . . the lutes, the flutes, the bells and the tambourines . . . and the multitude of conches, he continually inspired the enemy with terror by the multitude of his musical instruments.
>
> (Kersalé 2021)

Other, more indirect strategies were also employed, for example, in the domain of intelligence-gathering. Knowledge of an opponent's size, strength, and movements would have been invaluable, a role which the Kautilya's *Arthaśastra* assigns to the cavalry (Jacq-Hergoualc'h 2007[1979], 118). Regionally, the network of vassal states on the periphery of the empire, especially to the north and east, were well positioned to provide advance notice of an invading army. The extensive road network, along with its associated infrastructure, facilitated such communication (Hendrickson 2010). Finally, covert operatives also gathered intelligence, as inscriptions mention *chara* ('spies') who were deployed to report on the enemy's movements (Jacques and Lafond 2007, 34).

While the Khmer were never a sea power during the Angkor Period, their subsistence depended on seasonal flooding of lakes and rivers. Thus, canoes and other, larger shallow-water craft were an integral part of their lives and were also deployed in the military (Walker Vadillo 2016). Various kinds of riverine craft are depicted at the Bayon. Military craft are decorated with a *makara* at the prow and manned with oarsmen and marines on deck at the ready. Situated on a floodplain adjacent to the Tonle Sap Lake, the ability to manoeuvre troops and engage the enemy in the shallows was crucial to Angkor's defence. Boats were also used in offensive campaigns, for example, in 1129 when an Angkorian fleet of more than 700 vessels assaulted the coastline of Dai Viet (Briggs 1951, 190).

Psychological Factors

The bas-reliefs also indicate non-combat roles within the army. According to Indian treatises, war was considered a sacrifice to the gods, and at the head of the martial band we can identify the 'Royal Sacrificer' who oversaw the necessary rituals. These rituals centred on the Sacred Fire, which is carried on a sheltered palanquin. Offerings would be made to the Fire on the eve of battle to ensure victory (Jacq-Hergoualc'h 2007[1979], 141). Bearers of flags, standards, and parasols are also present. A standard-bearer in the Historical Procession holds aloft an image of Viṣṇu atop garuda at the front of the monarch's party. No doubt these standards played an important psychological role, inspiring confidence and keeping soldiers in formation. It would have been deeply demoralising when they were fallen, lost, or captured, similar to the regimental colours and standards found in other military contexts throughout history.

Superstition also held sway during times of conflict. For instance, one belief held that magical power could be contained within an amulet. The 13th-century king Srindravarman was said to have 'a sacred piece of iron embedded in his body, so that if anything like a knife or an arrow touched him he could not be injured' (Zhou 2007[1297], 82). The Khmers, in common with the other ethnic groups of Southeast Asia, have deeply rooted animist beliefs and practices embedded in their culture. Even today, everyday life involves navigating and negotiating a complex hierarchy of spirits—both ancestral and spirits of place—who range from the benevolent to the malevolent. The belief that tattoos of sacred diagrams can protect the bearer is an important component of indigenous animist beliefs across mainland Southeast Asia (Scheinfeld 2007) and is still a common practice among Cambodian soldiers. Likewise, the magical protection of amulets still has widespread currency and legitimacy in Cambodia. Quaritch-Wales noted them, in the form of a seated, decapitated figure whose head was resting in their lap, as a form of protection against head-hunters (cited in Charney 2004, 16).

Military Expansion and Consolidation

Historical records are the primary source for details concerning Angkor's military expansion, with royal inscriptions (or those of their rivals) recounting their success on the battlefield. However, the various textual sources available—Khmer, Cham, Dai Viet, Ayutthaya, Chinese, and later, European—are generally brief and fragmentary. A survey of texts dating from the eighth to the 13th century identified 14 offensive campaigns, six of defence against invaders, and eight instances of rebellion or civil war (Table 14.1).

The expansion of Khmer dominion took place over several centuries as the frontier advanced primarily to the north of Angkor. In the 10th and 11th centuries, the empire expanded into the Lopburi region, as well as Tambralinga in central and peninsular Thailand. In the first half of the 12th century, Sūryavarman II repeatedly attacked the east coasts of the Cham and Dai Viet and extended his dominion further down the Thai peninsula and towards the Burmese to the west. In the late 12th century Jayavarman VII also attacked the Cham and Dai Viet and further strengthened the Khmer presence on the Thai peninsula (Hall 1975; Mabbett 1978).

Politically, the Angkorian Empire was a *mandala* in which regional rulers acknowledged the monarch's glory by offering tribute instead of being completely absorbed into the central authority (Mabbett 1978, 37). Regional power bases emerged in the provinces, and these were called in to support rival factions at the capital in the (not uncommon) event of a succession dispute. Thus the empire's stability was in fact quite precarious, depending on the character or charisma of the reigning monarch. The army would be called to deal with any problem that could not be resolved peacefully.

Rebellion

One might expect the considerable distance between the capital and periphery to pose problems for the central authority, but even relatively close territories were rebellious. The region known as Malyang, probably located on the south side of the Tonle Sap Lake between Battambang and Pursat (Cœdès 1932, 80, n.1), seems to have been particularly restless: inscriptions indicate its rulers rose in revolt on multiple occasions over the course of 400 years. According to the Palhal inscription (K. 449, 1069 CE), for example, the Malyang region rebelled against Jayavarman II (r. 802–835), who sent forces led by the great mandarin Prithivinarendra to subdue the revolt by 'burning like fire the enemy troops' (Briggs 1951, 83). Centuries later, during the first year of the reign of Jayavarman VII (1182), another revolt arose in Malyang, and the king ordered his Cham ally prince Sri Vidyanandana to deal with the uprising (Briggs 1951, 210).

Maintaining the loyalty of provincial lords was an issue, especially in areas too remote to keep under strict control. Allegiances were fostered through patron-client relationships, which were strategically developed with a view to placating members of the aristocracy as well as enfranchising commoners. A folktale from Sangkha district[2] relates how the king befriended a humble lumberjack and declared him lord of the region (Lowman 2013, 34). Likewise, when Sri Vidyanandana put down the Malyang uprising, the king rewarded him with 'all the pleasures and good things which could be found in the kingdom' (Briggs 1951, 210). An inscription at Phanom Rung (K. 384) tells of a great battle between a rebellious army and the local lord (Cœdès 1937–1966, Vol V, 297–305) who successfully subdued them and was rewarded by the king. The inscription is undated, but the king was most likely Sūryavarman II, who embellished the temple with gold foundation deposits and commissioned the elements of the building that date stylistically to the period of Angkor Wat (Woodward 2003, 157–58).

Defence Mechanisms

Over the long term Angkor's dominance was seldom challenged. Military conquest progressively advanced the frontier of the empire and, despite the persistent possibility of succession disputes, for almost four centuries Angkor had no permanent defensive fixtures. Even casual visitors to Angkor will note the grand enclosure walls that are a typical component of temple architecture, but these were not built for defence. Rather, the enclosures, galleries, and moats served to define and delimit the sacred space of a temple, while the entrance pavilions (*gopura*) and causeways regulated everyday access to it. Concentric arrangements of enclosure walls and moats first appeared during the Pre-Angkor Period at sites such as Sambor Prei Kuk in the 7th century (Table 14.2). The areas enclosed increased significantly in the 11th century (for example, the vast earthwork enclosing Chau Srei Vibol), and by the 12th century, enclosure walls

Table 14.2 Dimensions of temple enclosure walls in the Pre-Angkor and Angkor Periods.

Temple	*Date*	*Enclosure #/total*	*Area (ha)*	*Height (m)*	*Reference*
Sambor Prei Kuk (South group)	7th	2/2	6	3.5	(Dumarçay and Royère 2001, 41)
Bakong	9th	2/3	3.7	1.8	(Lunet de Lajonquière 1902–11, Vol. III, 268)
Royal Palace, Angkor Thom	early 11th	1/2	14	5	(Nafilyan 1967, 64)
Chau Srei Vibol	11th–12th	2/3	7.6	3	
Angkor Wat	early 12th	4/4	83.5	4.5	(Nafilyan 1969, Pl. LXXXIII)
Ta Prohm	late 12th	5/5	68	2.3	(Cunin 2004, 68)
Preah Khan	late 12th	4/4	53	4	(World Monuments Fund 1997, 43)
Banteay Kdei	late 12th	4/4	34	3.2	(Dumarçay and Courbin 1988, Pl. LXXIII)
Krol Ko	late 12th	2/2	1.3	2	(Dumarçay and Courbin 1988, Pl. LXXXIII)

also contained residential space. First at Angkor Wat, and later at the great Buddhist temples of Jayavarman VII, the enclosure wall served to delimit an occupation area in close proximity to the shrine. Again, however, these were not defensive installations.

This situation prevailed until the latter part of the 12th century, after which the kings of Angkor began to fortify the capital. The following section discusses the various mechanisms employed for defence of the region, the capital, and the king himself. Finally, it examines a range of evidence which illustrates how the built landscape of Angkor was engineered to improve its defensibility throughout the late Angkor Period. This includes the construction of a great citadel, Angkor Thom, subsequent efforts to improve and expand its defensibility, and the reconfiguration of the Angkor Wat enclosure wall for defence.

Regional Defence

The vast territory of the Khmer Empire covered the catchments of three main river systems: the Tonle Sap/Lower Mekong, the Mun/Chi of the Khorat Plateau, and the lower Chao Praya as far north as Lopburi. These perennial waterways provided the most cost-effective means to transport bulky commodities, as well as military personnel and supplies. In addition to the river systems, the Khmer utilised a road network which, centred on Angkor, extended from the capital to the provinces in the west, north, and east. The structure of the road network appears designed to complement and improve the spatial coverage and access provided by the river system (Hendrickson 2010, fig. 1). This combined road/riverine network facilitated trade throughout the empire, as well as movement and logistical support for the armed forces. The roads cross the rivers with laterite bridges, spanning the gap by means of corbel vaulted arches. The physical nature of corbel vaults restricts their maximum span, under which only a relatively narrow gap of 2–3 m is formed for water and vessels to flow through. This limits the size of vessels that could pass through unhindered, forming a choke point on the river. Bridges could also be utilised for administering tolls and taxes, as well as conducting general surveillance along the waterway (Walker Vadillo 2019, 19).

Defence of the Capital

Enclosure walls isolated certain spaces from their extramural surrounds and were a passive enforcement of social organisation. The earliest enclosure walls were made of brick, while later most walls were of laterite, with sandstone used on occasion. In early periods, the monumental size of these walls served mainly to restrict everyday access, and they were not intended to defend against a military assault. For most of its history, the layout of Angkor suggests the Khmer were not particularly defensively minded when planning their capital. Consequently, for much of the Angkor Period, defence of the capital relied primarily on guards and soldiers rather than permanent structures. In 1177, however, the capital was overrun by an army of Cham invaders. They were later expelled by Jayavarman VII, but the geopolitical landscape had clearly changed, and Angkor was in need of durable defence measures.

Central Angkor features numerous examples of defensive installations, improvements, and reconfigurations, dating primarily to the 12th century or later. During this time, the core area of Angkor underwent its final major reconfigurations during the reigns of Sūryavarman II and in particular Jayavarman VII, who gave it the layout it bears today. The centrepiece of Jayavarman VII's defence measures was Angkor Thom (a modern Khmer name meaning 'big city'), an immense citadel enclosure measuring 3 km square and surrounded by a massive, near-vertical wall almost 8 metres in height. Unlike previous enclosures, which had all delimited a single major temple, the 9-km^2 area of Angkor Thom encompassed numerous state temples, extended residential areas, and the Royal Palace. In another departure from precedent, the Angkor Thom enclosure was not a freestanding wall; instead, its masonry facade retained a broad earthen embankment, which provided ample space for soldiers to be stationed along the precipice.

In addition to these durable elements, it is possible that temporary defence mechanisms were employed along Angkor's canals. Although no specific evidence survives from the Angkor Period, the Khmer used bamboo pontoon bridges to blockade a flotilla of VOC warships in the 17th century (Van der Kraan 2009, 53–60). Secured to the riverbanks by heavy wooden anchors, these structures spanned the Mekong River at Phnom Penh. While this battle involved artillery, the blockading of waterways would certainly have been a useful strategy in the defensive repertoire of Angkor, where canals are a recurring feature across the landscape.

Defence of the Monarch

The king was therefore protected by several successive layers of security and resided within a palace enclosure which itself was inside a fortified citadel. The Royal Palace of Angkor Thom features the tallest free-standing wall built during the Angkor Period, at almost 5 m in height, which is surrounded by a moat with a second smaller wall outside it. Attributed to Sūryavarman I (r. 1002–1050), it predates the construction of Angkor Thom by almost two centuries. As the king's safety was paramount, it is perhaps expected that permanent defences are first identifiable at the palace. Notably, none of the earlier palace sites, such as Prei Monti or near Pre Rup, feature high walls of durable materials.

An elite squad of guards and soldiers formed a multi-tiered royal bodyguard. Zhou Daguan's description of the royal procession (2007[1297], 82–4) is our primary source for these details. In addition to the numerous wives, concubines, servants, musicians, and other members of his entourage, the king was accompanied by a contingent of female soldiers armed with lances and shields making up the palace guard. The king himself rode atop an elephant and was surrounded on all sides by elephants and soldiers in great numbers, forming another line of defence. This procession took place within the royal plaza, to the east of the Royal Palace of Angkor Thom, and therefore within the citadel, whose five entrances were also protected by guards. In spite of these measures, some kings would not venture outside of the palace due to the potential danger from rival factions and plots against the throne (Zhou 2007[1297], 82).

Angkor in Decline—Defensive Modifications

Beyond the monuments, earthworks define the landscape of Angkor. Keeley et al., in a global comparative study of excavated earthworks examine how their form, especially the cross-section, is related to function. They argue that only a V-shaped ditch is purpose built exclusively for defence (Keeley et al. 2007). Nevertheless, even though the canals of Angkor were broad and shallow and built primarily for drainage, irrigation, and transport, they could still be used defensively as required. Several enclosure walls in central Angkor also show signs of modification to improve their defensibility. These alterations were made in the changing geopolitical landscape of mainland Southeast Asia in the 13th and 14th centuries, when Angkor had to face the threat imposed by rising powers to the west, in particular the kingdom of Ayutthaya in what is now Thailand.

The Gates of Angkor Thom

The original form of the Angkor Thom citadel certainly gives the *impression* of formidable defence, which was no doubt the architect's intent. However, a technical analysis of the lines-of-sight between the defender's positions and would-be attackers reveals significant blind spots, including directly in front of the main outer gate (or *gopura*) (Figure 14.2). In the original design, the exterior gate is recessed between two flanking walls, creating a blind spot of around 7 m^2 in which attackers could work unhindered on breaching the outer gateway. Furthermore, once the attackers had breached the outer gate, only limited resistance could be made to defend the inner gate because the interior of the gopura was a closed system. Only a finite number of guards could be stationed inside the gopura, and they could not be relieved without opening the inner gate. If the outer gate was breached, the only way to reinforce the guards inside the gopura would be to open the inner gate and risk granting attackers access to the citadel proper.

These defensive shortcomings were addressed by structural modifications and additions. Bastions, made of laterite blocks, were installed on both sides of the gate, flanking the access route and significantly reducing the size of the blind spot. Additionally, portals were cut into the interior walls of the gopura pavilion, allowing reinforcements to access the gopura without having to breach the inner gateway. The original gopura dates to the construction of the citadel in the 1180s, but when the modifications occurred is less clear. While Diogo Do Couto's account of Angkor Thom (c. 1585) mentions 'superb bastions' at the city gates (Groslier 2006[1958], 53), it is entirely likely the shortcomings were noticed and dealt with much sooner. How these improvements relate to an apparent attempt to expand defensive space outside Angkor Thom is also unclear.

Angkor Thom Embankment Extensions

Four double-embankments extend from each corner of Angkor Thom (Figure 14.3), and the broad moats which they delimit indicate a hydraulic function. However, the characteristics of those at the northeast and southeast corners also suggest a defensive purpose. They will be referred to, respectively, as the North Bank-Wall and South Bank. The North Bank-Wall connects to the East Baray. The South Bank extends east and then turns north until it reaches the

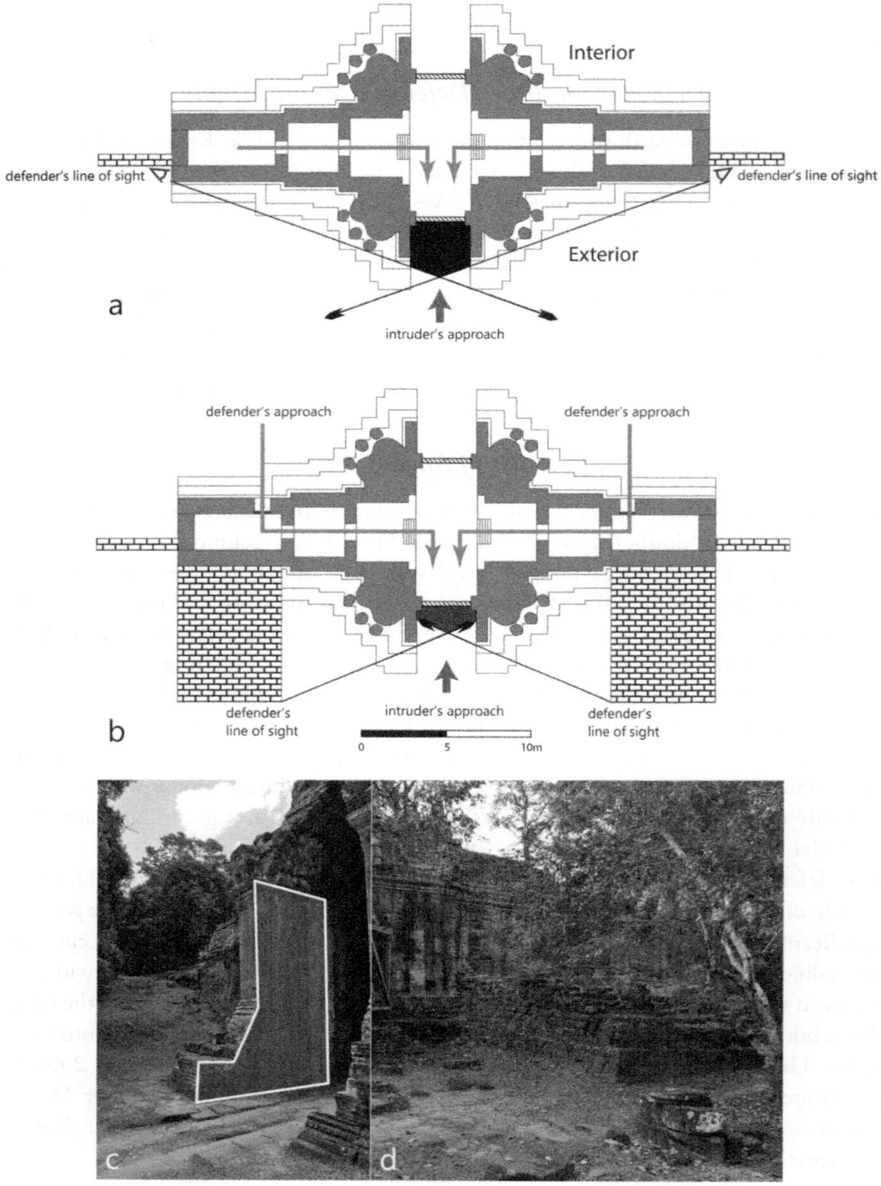

Figure 14.2 Defensive features of the Angkor Thom gopura. Annotated floor plan of the Angkor Thom gopura showing original a) and modified b) designs. Sandstone structure (med. grey), wooden gates and doorways (vertical line fill), defenders' vantage point and line of site (black arrow), blind spot (black area), laterite walls and bastions (brick pattern), approach vectors of intruders and defenders (adapted from Dumarcay 1988: Pl. L); c) entranceway highlighting internal blind spot; and d) laterite wall and bastion on the exterior.

Source: (Photos D. Brotherson).

southwest corner of Ta Prohm. Both were first described by Georges Trouvé (1933, fig. 52, fig. 5). Together with the Ta Prohm enclosure and the west bank of the East Baray, the North Bank-Wall and the South Bank combine to form another enclosed space (Klassen et al. 2021).

Among these Angkor Thom extensions, the North Bank-Wall is morphologically the most similar to the walls of the citadel proper and is considered to be in a 'finished' state: The embankment has a laterite retaining wall on its north side, and the moat running along its north side is the same width as the Angkor Thom moat. In comparison, the South Bank is noticeably incomplete. The lidar shows that the west end is in a finished state, as the moat has been excavated to its full width and the displaced soil heaped to form the inner embankment—but further to the east, the moat is only partially excavated, and the embankments are not as high. Moreover, at the southeast corner the moat is not excavated at all, while the outer embankment is non-existent.

The structural inadequacy of the South Bank presents a conundrum because, arguably, it is likely that an army would approach Angkor from the south, as a maritime attack launched from the Tonle Sap is a plausible scenario. Why then is the South-Bank less finished than its north counterpart? Since neither is effective defensively without the other, it seems that the original ambition of the engineers—to enclose an additional 450 ha of residential space to the east of Angkor Thom—was, for unknown reasons, never fulfilled.

Excavations completed by the Greater Angkor Project in 2013 revealed that the North Bank-Wall is built on top of the bank on the east edge of the Angkor Thom moat (Klassen et al. 2021, 6), postdating it. The North Bank-Wall therefore likely dates to the 13th century and not earlier as previously thought (cf. Jacques 1978, 312). The date for the South Bank is also unclear, but it presumably slightly postdates the North Bank-Wall because if it were exactly contemporary, it should also be finished.

At the eastern edge of this extended eastern perimeter is Ta Prohm, a temple which is contemporary with the original walls of Angkor Thom. Ta Prohm is only 40 m south of the East Baray (Figure 14.3), a gap which could be readily defended or even walled in. Excavations of the residential space within the Ta Prohm enclosure—outside the intended perimeter extension—recovered no material later than the 14th century. The northeast quadrant of Ta Prohm features no residential activity post-dating the 13th century (Carter et al. 2018, 500).

This evidence suggests a scenario in which the outer areas of the urban centre were strategically vacated in the 13th and 14th centuries in an attempt to consolidate a more advantageous defensive line immediately to the rear. While parts of these defensive enhancements were never completed, the moat along the North Bank-Wall also served a hydraulic function, irrigating Angkor Thom, and as an artery for transport and communication.

Another defensive installation, and perhaps the final example from the Angkor Period, requires discussion. The modification and reuse of the Angkor Wat enclosure speaks directly to Angkor's struggle to endure in a period of shifting regional power and is indicative of a diminished army's attempt to effectively secure and defend the capital.

The Fortification of Angkor Wat

Angkor Wat, the jewel in the crown of the Khmer Empire, has always been important to the Khmer people since its construction in the early to mid-12th century. Over the centuries the temple has undergone changes to its design, decoration, function, and spiritual significance; even its name has changed. Conventionally, the historical framework of Angkor is based on inscriptions, but tracing changes in material culture at places like Angkor Wat can reveal phenomena that have been overlooked in, or are missing from, textual sources. The presence of several thousand postholes in the Angkor Wat enclosure wall, which allowed a wooden structure

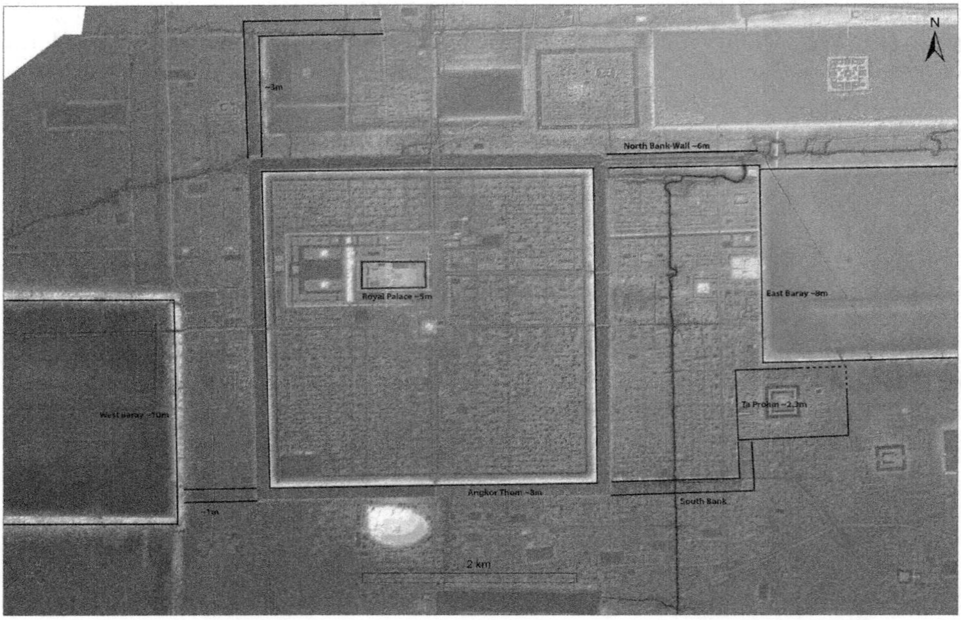

Figure 14.3 Lidar elevation model of central Angkor with highlights of landscape features and embankment extensions in the 12th century. Dashed line shows extent of Ta Prohm enclosure absent.

Source: (GIS data KALC).

to be built onto it, is one such example. The wooden structure has entirely rotted away long ago but would have consisted of an elevated platform as well as a palisade that was built to fortify the temple enclosure. The platform gave the defenders a higher ground advantage over intruders, while the palisade prevented those who did manage to scale the wall from entering the enclosure unhindered.

Disentangling the construction phases of the wall is crucial to understanding its function and how that changed over time. First, we note the parts of the wall referred to as 'gateway gaps'. These are characterised by noticeably different masonry patterns, the use of sandstone, and the use of recycled blocks. There are six of these 'gateway gaps' around the enclosure, symmetrically placed in alignment with staircases within the temple (Brotherson 2015, fig. 3). The carvings on the recycled blocks are consistent with the Bayon style of the late 12th to early 13th centuries, which postdates the main construction period of Angkor Wat by at least half a century; the infill of the gateway gaps is thus a later, subsequent phase of construction.

The postholes were systematically mapped as part of the Greater Angkor Project, with a view to producing a detailed plan of the wall lodgings, attempting a reconstruction of the long-decayed wooden structure, and determining its function. Two main types of hole are found: horizontal holes cut into the upper part of the inside face of the wall and vertical holes cut into the top of the wall (Figure 14.4).

All horizontal holes are located on the inner face, approximately 3.5–4 m above the ground, but not along the corresponding parts of the gopura. Significantly, these holes are highly consistent in size and shape, suggesting they were installed in a single construction phase. Their distribution around the enclosure is also consistent, grouped together in evenly spaced sets, which are also separated by a consistent gap.

Figure 14.4 Horizontal and vertical holes in upper masonry blocks of the external enclosure wall of Angkor Wat.

Source: (Photos D. Brotherson).

The vertical holes can be considered one of two types, large or small, a typology which also exhibits a highly consistent distribution. The vast majority are small, but a clear pattern is evident in which the larger holes are consistently found in sets of three. Significantly, the small holes are only found in between the sets of large ones.

A systematic relationship exists between the sets of horizontal holes and the sets of large vertical holes, whereby a substantial proportion of the vertical sets (79%) coincide with horizontal sets, suggesting that their functions are related. However, the most crucial relationship identified is that between the postholes and the infill of the gateway gaps. Both the horizontal and vertical sets are found in this later construction phase (Figure 14.5). The installation of the wooden structure therefore postdates the blocking up of the gateway gaps.

The defensive hypothesis for the structure's function is as follows: First, the horizontal holes are substantial enough to support a platform for people to stand and walk upon. Second, the horizontal holes are at the same height and only located on the inner face of the wall. The structure they supported was therefore situated on the inside of a sizable boundary and created an elevated, horizontal surface. The defence hypothesis holds that this platform gave the defenders the 'higher ground' over would-be attackers outside the enclosure. The third point is that the consistent relationship between the vertical and horizontal holes makes it reasonable to suppose they are associated and therefore contemporary. The implication is that these regularities are intentional—they are consistent over a considerable distance—and that their purpose is interrelated. If the defence hypothesis is correct, the wide spaces between the platforms provided room for stairs to access them, while a palisade provided a physical barrier on top of the wall (Figure 14.6) (Brotherson 2015). Another hypothesis has been proposed: that the structure formed a shelter. However, this does not stand to reason. First, this theory ignores the evidence on top of the wall—how does the multitude of vertical postholes serve the shelter? Also, why would a shelter built against the wall have recurring gaps of 9 metres in length? If so much shelter was required that it had to extend around the entire enclosure, then why not make use of this additional space? Allowing that the platforms could *also* have provided shelter underneath them, it is nonetheless clear that the impetus for such an extensive structure and embedding it into the enclosure wall itself was surely defence.

Figure 14.5 'Gateway gap' masonry fill in the external enclosure wall of Angkor Wat: a) exterior (north wall, east end); b, c): interior (left—north wall, east end, right—east wall, north end), showing postholes in original (green) and later (red) construction phases.

Source: (Photos D. Brotherson).

Figure 14.6 Hypothetical reconstruction of defensive structure built along the external enclosure walls of Angkor Wat.

The absence of mortar in Angkorian masonry structures has prompted the suggestion that the enclosure wall of Angkor Wat would not make a suitable defensive platform, since the laterite blocks could be pulled apart by a sufficient amount of force. Indeed, this is a problem that all Angkorian fortifications faced. However, the defence hypothesis does not suggest the rampart-palisade installation at Angkor Wat was ideal but rather the simplest and quickest way to downsize the numbers required to defend the perimeter, as Angkor Wat's (3.8 km) is less than one third the length of Angkor Thom's (12 km). Instead of investing the time and energy into acquiring new materials to build an additional, smaller fortress, military engineers modified a suitable, pre-existing structure, even if the solution was less than ideal.

The date of this defensive structure is not yet clear, and additional research is needed to determine how it was supported in the ground. As yet only three small (2 × 1-m) test pits have been excavated to address this issue and have so far proved inconclusive. However, we know that the form of the enclosure wall would render it ineffective against artillery, which is known to have been in use in Cambodia by the mid-17th century (Volker 1954; Kersten 2006; Mikaelian 2009). The vertical facade and uniform, orthogonal plan of the Angkor Wat enclosure wall presented a surface perpendicular to incoming projectiles which would not withstand a sustained bombardment. Thus the circumstances prompting the fortification of Angkor Wat most likely occurred sometime in the late Angkor Period but prior to the 1630s (Brotherson 2015).

Conclusions

Angkorian epigraphy, temple decoration, and landscape engineering offer us an important case study in the use of military power to maintain order and control across the medieval Khmer Empire. Angkor's ascendency as the central power of mainland Southeast Asian was achieved in large part through the might of its armies. While very few intact examples of Angkorian weaponry survive today, we are fortunate that their designs were depicted in the decoration of its great temples, which served both as abodes of the gods and as celebrations of the military prowess and divine mandate that allowed the kings to prosper.

In contrast, defensive installations become prominent in the latter part of the capital's occupation history, reflecting the growing seriousness of military threats from neighbouring states in mainland Southeast Asia and speaking to the reasons for the eventual demise of Angkor at the hands of one of those rival powers, the kingdom of Ayutthaya. The construction of a fortified central citadel at Angkor Thom, the subsequent attempts to extend those fortifications with defensive embankments, and the *ad hoc* retrofitting of their greatest temple enclosure as a defensive structure illustrate a protracted period of weakening regional power for Angkor, extending over centuries, prior to its eventual demise as the capital of the Khmer Empire in the 15th century.

Notes

1 Dai-Viet Annals.
2 Surin province, Thailand.

References

Aymonier, É., 1891. *Première étude sur les inscriptions tchames*. Paris: Imprimerie Nationale.
Barth, A. & A. Bergaigne, 1885–1893. *Inscriptions sanscrites du Cambodge*. Paris: Imprimerie Nationale.
Bâty, P., 2007. Les couteaux angkoriens de Trapeang Thlok et de Prasat Trapeang Ropou. *Bulletin de l'École française d'Extrême-Orient* 94(1), 95–110.
Briggs, L.P., 1951. *The Ancient Khmer Empire*. Philadelphia: The American Philosophical Society.

Brotherson, D., 2015. The fortification of Angkor Wat. *Antiquity* 89(348), 1456–72.
Carter, A., P. Heng, M. Stark, R. Chhay & D. Evans, 2018. Urbanism and residential patterning in Angkor. *Journal of Field Archaeology* 43(6), 492–506. DOI: 10.1080/00934690.2018.1503034
Charney, M.W., 2004. *Southeast Asian Warfare, 1300–1900*. Leiden: Brill.
Cœdès, G., 1913. Etudes cambodgiennes—XI La stèle de Pàlhàl (province de Mon Rusei). *Bulletin de l'École française d'Extrême-Orient* 13(6), 1–36.
Cœdès, G., 1929. Etudes cambodgiennes. XXIV—Nouvelles données chronologiques et généalogiques sur la dynastie de Mahidharapura. *Bulletin de l'École française d'Extrême-Orient* 29, 289–330.
Cœdès, G., 1932. Etudes cambodgiennes. XXVIII—Quelques suggestions sur la méthode à suivre pour interpréter les bas-reliefs de Bantây Chmàr et de la galerie extérieure du Bàyon. *Bulletin de l'École française d'Extrême-Orient* 32(1), 71–81.
Cœdès, G., 1937–1966. *Inscriptions du Cambodge (Vol. 1–8)*. Paris: EFEO.
Cœdès, G., 1968[1944]. *The Indianized States of Southeast Asia*. Honolulu: University of Hawai'i Press.
Cœdès, G. & P. Dupont, 1943. Les stèles de Sdok Kak Thom, Phnom Sandak et Prah Vihar. *Bulletin de l'École française d'Extrême-Orient* 43, 56–154.
Cunin, O., 2004. *De Ta Prohm au Bayon. Analyse comparative de l'histoire architecturale des principaux monuments du style du Bayon*. PhD. L'Institut National Polytechnique de Lorraine.
Dumarçay, J. & P. Courbin, 1988. *Documents graphiques de la conservation d'Angkor: 1963–1973; La fouille du Sras-Srang*. Paris: EFEO.
Dumarçay, J. & P. Royère, 2001. *Cambodian Architecture Eighth to Thirteenth Centuries*. Boston: Brill.
Finot, L., 1904. Notes d'épigraphie: XI. Les inscriptions de Mi-Sơn. *Bulletin de l'École française d'Extrême-Orient* 4(4), 897–977.
Finot, L., 1912. Notes d'épigraphie: XIII. L'inscription de Ban That. *Bulletin de l'École française d'Extrême-Orient* 12(2), 1–28.
Finot, L., 1925. Inscriptions d'Aṅkor. *Bulletin de l'École française d'Extrême-Orient* 25(3/4), 289–409.
Groslier, B.-P., 1981. Les Syam Kuk des bas-reliefs d'Angkor Vat, in *Orients pour Georges Condominas*. Toulouse & Paris: Editions Privat & Sudestasie, 107–26.
Groslier, B.-P., 2006[1958]. *Angkor and Cambodia in the Sixteenth Century. According to the Portuguese and Spanish Sources*. Bangkok: Orchid Press.
Hall, K.R., 1975. Khmer commercial development and foreign contacts under Sūryavarman I. *Journal of the Economic and Social History of the Orient* 18(3), 318–36.
Hendrickson, M., 2010. Historic routes to Angkor: development of the Khmer road system (ninth to thirteenth centuries AD) in mainland Southeast Asia. *Antiquity* 84(324), 480–96.
Jacq-Hergoualc'h, M., 2007[1979]. *The Armies of Angkor: Military structure and weaponry of the Khmers*. Bangkok: Orchid Press.
Jacques, C., 1978. VI. Études d'épigraphie cambodgienne. XL Autour de quelques toponymes de l'inscription du Prasat Trapan Run K.598: La capitale angkorienne de Yaśovarman Ier à Sûryavarman Ier. *Bulletin de l'École française d'Extrême-Orient* 65(1), 281–332.
Jacques, C. & P. Lafond, 2007. *The Khmer Empire: Cities and Sanctuaries, Fifth to Thirteenth Century*. Bangkok: River Books.
Keeley, L.H., M. Fontana & R. Quick, 2007. Baffles and bastions: the universal features of fortifications. *Journal of Archaeological Research* 15(1), 55–95.
Kersalé, P., 2021. Orchestras from the 7th to the 12th century: martial orchestras through epigraphy, www.soundsofangkor.org/english/orchestras/old-orchestras-7-16th-c/ [accessed March 4 2022].
Kersten, C., 2006. Cambodia's Muslim king: Khmer and Dutch sources on the conversion of reameathipadei I, 1642–1658. *Journal of Southeast Asian Studies* 37(1), 1–22.
Klassen, S., T. Attorre, D. Brotherson, R. Chhay, W. Johnson, I. Moffat & R. Fletcher, 2021. Deciphering a timeline of demise at medieval Angkor, Cambodia using remote sensing. *Remote Sensing* 13(11), 2094.
Lowman, I., 2013. The elephant hunt of Jayavarman III: A political myth of Angkorian Cambodia. *Udaya, Journal of Khmer Studies* 11, 29–57.
Lunet de Lajonquière, É., 1902–11. *Inventaire Descriptif des Monuments du Cambodge*. 3 vols. Paris: EFEO.
Mabbett, I., 1978. Kingship in Angkor. *Journal of the Siam Society* 66(2), 1–58.
Maspero, G., 1928. *La royaume de Champa*. Paris: Libr. nationale d'Art et d'Histoire.
Maspero, H., 1918. Etudes d'histoire d'Annam. *Bulletin de l'École française d'Extrême-Orient* 18(1), 1–36.
Mikaelian, G., 2009. Une "révolution militaire" au pays khmer? Note sur l'artillerie post-angkorienne (XVI-XIXe siècles). *Udaya, Journal of Khmer Studies* 10, 57–134.

Nafilyan, G., 1967. *Le mur dans l'architecture khmere, in Annales de l'universite royale des beaux arts: Annee 1967*. Phnom Penh: Faculte d'archeologie institut de reserches et de documentation Vithei Samdech Ouk, 63–78.

Nafilyan, G., 1969. *Angkor Vat, description graphique du temple*. Paris: EFEO A. Maisonneuve.

Roveda, V., 2002. *Sacred Angkor: The Carved Reliefs of Angkor Wat*. Bangkok: River Books.

Scheinfeld, N., 2007. Tattoos and religion. *Clinics in Dermatology* 25(4), 362–6.

Trouvé, G.A., 1933. Chaussées et canaux autour d'Angkor Thom. *Bulletin de l'École française d'Extrême-Orient* 33(2), 1120–8.

Van der Kraan, A., 2009. *Murder and Mayhem in Seventeenth-Century Cambodia: Anthony Van Diemen vs. King Ramadhipati I*. Chiang Mai: Silkworm Books.

Vickery, M., 2009. A short history of Champa, in *Champa and the Archaeology of Mỹ Sơn (Vietnam)*, eds. A. Hardy, M. Cucarzi & P. Zolese. Singapore: NUS Press, 45–60.

Volker, T., 1954. *Porcelain and the Dutch East India Company as Recorded in the Dagh-Registers of Batavia Castle, Those of Hirado and Deshima and Other Contemporary Papers; 1602–1682*. Leiden: Brill Archive.

Wade, G., 2011. The 'Account of Champa' in the song huiyao jigao, in *The Cham of Vietnam, History, Society and Art*, eds. K.P. Tran & B.M. Lockhart. Singapore: NUS Press, 138–67.

Walker Vadillo, V., 2016. *The fluvial cultural landscape of Angkor: an integrated study*. PhD. University of Oxford.

Walker Vadillo, V., 2019. A historiography of Angkor's river network: shifting the research paradigm to Westerdahl's maritime cultural landscape. *SPAFA Journal* 3, 1–30.

Woodward, H., 2003. *The Art and Architecture of Thailand. From Prehistoric Times through to the Thirteenth Century*. Leiden: Brill.

World Monuments Fund, 1997. Preah Khan conservation project: historic city of Angkor—Report VII, Field Campaign IV.

Zhou, D., 2007[1297]. *A Record of Cambodia: The Land and Its People*, trans. P. Harris. Chiang Mai: Silkworm Books.

15

ĀŚRAMAS, SHRINES, AND ROYAL POWER

Chea Socheat, Julia Estève, Dominique Soutif and Edward Swenson

In his article '*Diversité et Rythme des Fondations Royales*' (1951), Philippe Stern argued that the reigns of Angkorian rulers were legitimated by the sponsorship of three types of 'major royal projects', always implemented in the same chronological order: The first included 'foundations of public interest', followed by a temple dedicated to the king's ancestors and then by the construction of a state mountain temple (Stern 1951, 651–54). Archaeological and ethnographic evidence strongly supports this sequence of foundation, especially for a number of the most important reigns in Angkorian history. For instance, this sequence of foundation characterises the reign of Indravarman I at Hariharālaya (Roluos). At the time of his coronation in 877 CE, he founded the Indrataṭāka, a reservoir measuring 3800 m long and 800 m wide, known today as the Lolei Baray. Subsequently, in 879, he dedicated the Preah Ko (Parameśvara) temple to his parents and grandparents. Finally, he founded his mountain temple, the Bakong, where he actually undertook a redevelopment of a pre-existing temple and installed the divine liṅga, Indreśvara, in 881 (Stern 1951, 662–63; see also Pottier et al. 2008; Chea 2018, 27–28). We will focus in this chapter on the first of Stern's categories, the 'foundations of public interest'.

In the Khmer context, 'foundations of public interest' immediately bring to mind the massive hydraulic works essential to the religious and economic lifeways of the great Khmer 'cities', including irrigation agriculture critical to sustain a tropical polity dependent on rice farming, especially in densely populated areas such as Angkor. In addition, the hydraulic infrastructure was integrated with a system of roads and bridges that formed a communication network, as already noticed by Lunet de Lajonquière (1911, XXI–XXVIII and map; Bruguier 2000; Hendrickson 2010). The sophisticated transportation system enabled the movement of administrators, soldiers, and goods across far-flung regions at any season. Indeed, the extent of the territory ruled by Khmer kings in the Pre-Angkor and Angkor Periods necessitated investments in infrastructure and novel institutional mechanisms to administer political control in the most remote regions of the empire (see Lowman et al. 2023, this volume).

Other more subtle but no less powerful measures were adopted by the Khmer kings to impress their seal on the whole of the territory. Certain distinctive classes of temples that were built repeatedly under royal patronage (which we refer to hereafter as 'repetitive royal foundations') encapsulated such strategies by inextricably merging the social, educational, religious, and the infrastructural, and they thus served as effective vehicles of acculturation.

DOI: 10.4324/9781351128940-19

Khmer rulers have often resorted to 'repetitive royal foundations' of various kinds to exert their authority. This tactic was not an Angkorian invention: as early as the 7th century, Citrasena, who ruled in Cambodia under the name of Mahendravarman between 598 and 610, installed about 20 Śivaliṅgas or representations of Śiva's mount, the bull Vṛṣabha. The commemoration of both kinds of sacred objects, as found in K. 116 (Cœdès 1937–66, *IC* II, 134) and K. 377 (Cœdès 1937–66, *IC* V, 3), relied on very similar wording and they occurred both before and after the coronation of the king. These inscriptions have been found in Laos, Thailand, and the Kratie region of central Cambodia, and it is obvious that behind the solemn testament of the king's piety lay a clear intention to signal his control over regions far from his capital of Sambor Prei Kuk.

This commissioning of repetitive foundations on a large scale was subsequently instituted many times over the course of Khmer history (Figure 15.1). The most famous examples are the fire shrines, which were evenly distributed along the 'royal roads' and probably associated with rest houses, and the hospital chapels founded by the king Jayavarman VII at the end of the 12th century. The stelae of Preah Khan of Angkor and Ta Prohm report respectively the foundation of 121 fire shrines and 102 hospitals throughout the empire (Cœdès 1906, 48; Cœdès 1941, 266; Hendrickson 2008). In both cases, these buildings followed a consistent architectural template (Figure 15.2) that facilitated their identification (Dagens 2005; Pottier and Chhem 2010; Swenson 2013). Although not all such establishments have been located, a number of these buildings, made of laterite and/or sandstone, have already been identified. Along the same lines, archaeologists have analysed numerous '*temples d'étape*', once again following a standardised plan, founded at the beginning of the 12th century along the principal roads. Although the epigraphy provides little detail about their purpose, they clearly conformed to the institution of the repetitive foundation (Hendrickson 2011, fig. 1, 447).

Yaśodharāśrama

Since 2010, the Yaśodharāśrama archaeological project has conducted investigations on the first of the Angkorian repetitive royal foundations to extend across Cambodian territory beginning as early as the end of the 9th century: the āśramas or 'monasteries' of the king Yaśovarman I. The foundation of these hermitages is commemorated in inscriptions that provide valuable information on the religious and lay functioning of these institutions. Taking into account the geographical distribution of the hermitages, we may divide them into two categories: the first comprises the four monasteries founded at Angkor, while the second includes the 'provincial monasteries' distributed across the rest of mainland Southeast Asia, including in northeast Thailand, Laos, Cambodia, and potentially southern Vietnam (Figure 15.1).

The epigraphic evidence indicates that they served as rest houses for religious pilgrims as well as dedicated spaces for spiritual retreat and education (see Bergaigne 1893, 355, 413; Cœdès 1908, 1932). The inscriptions also reveal that, far from serving as simple monasteries dedicated to hermits, the āśramas were richly endowed and played an important role in consolidating and disseminating state authority. In Angkor itself, they were dedicated to different religious denominations (Śaiva, Vaiṣṇava, and Buddhist), and they were placed in charge of protecting and sacralising the first great artificial reservoir of the new capital, the East Baray. According to the inscriptions, the heads of the āśramas were responsible for celebrating ceremonies on the banks of the Eastern Baray. However, the irregular layout of the four Angkor āśramas: three along the southern bank and one near the northeastern corner, where the main water supply originates, seems to have been a strategic choice. Thus, their role may not have been only spiritual but actually to ensure the upkeep or at least monitoring of this hydraulic structure (Cœdès 1932, 99, 104; Chea 2018, 179). In the provinces, the inscriptions describe the foundation of 100 monasteries attached to the

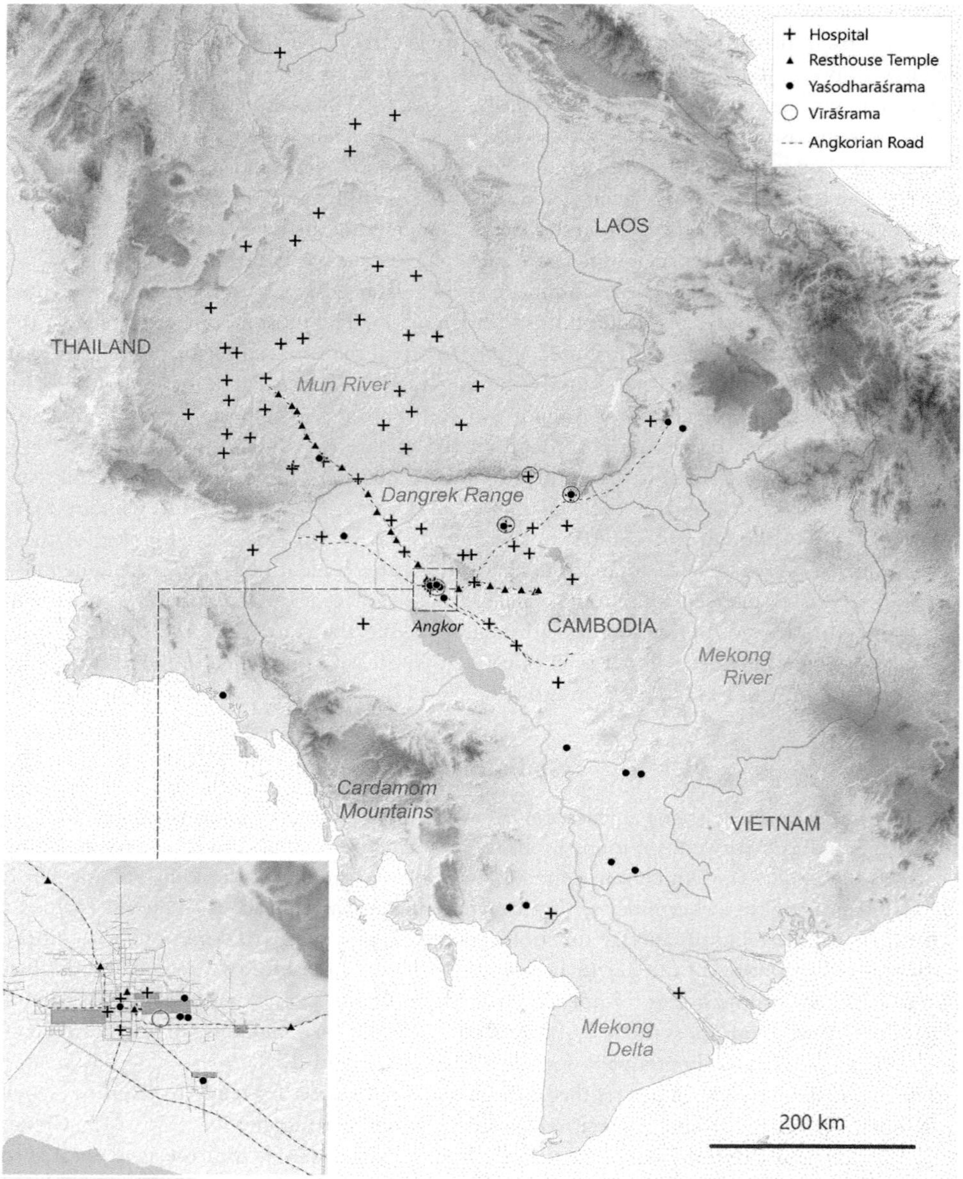

Figure 15.1 Location of known Yaśodharāśramas, Vīrāśramas, resthouses, and hospitals of Jayavarman VII.
Source: (GIS data of Angkorian roads, M. Hendrickson).

most venerable sanctuaries of the kingdom that most likely functioned as effective instruments of acculturation and dissemination of royal power (Estève and Soutif 2010–11).

Yaśovarman I followed the custom of welcoming and patronising all religions, a pattern of political tolerance of religious diversity that is recorded repeatedly in the epigraphic corpus of Cambodia from the 8th to the 14th centuries. But each monastery in the capital constituted an independent religious foundation dedicated to a specific religion: Vaiṣṇavaism, Buddhism, and

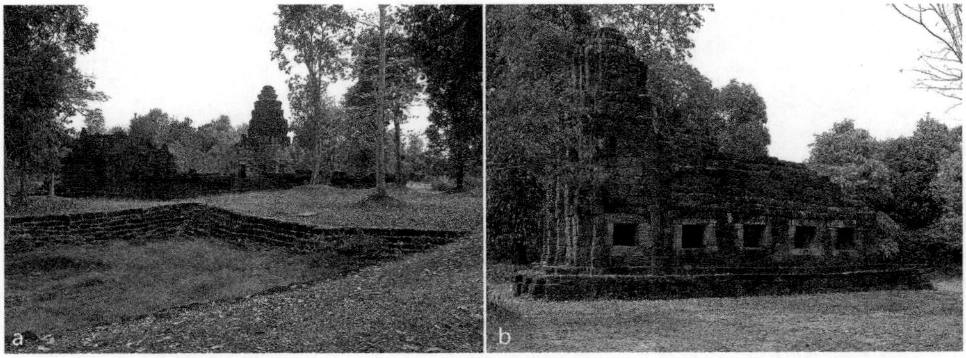

Figure 15.2 Examples of a typical hospital chapel and fire shrine resthouse: a) Ta Muean hospital chapel; and b) Ta Muean Toch fire shrine, both built by Jayavarman VII in northeast Thailand at the end of the 12th century.

Source: (Photo D. Soutif).

likely two distinct streams of Śaivaism, whereas each provincial monastery was affixed to a pre-existing sanctuary. Although dedicated to one deity, the provincial āśramas would welcome followers from any religious denomination, affirming a strong commitment to religious diversity and collaborative, inter-faith ritual practice (Estève and Soutif 2010–11, 331).

Only 20 foundation inscriptions have been found, and it has proven difficult to identify many of the 100 monasteries commissioned in the provinces. Compounding the issue is that some of these stelae were not discovered *in situ* and that many of these structures were likely made of perishable materials. The case of Jayavarman VII's hospitals provides a particularly illuminating comparison that allows us to better understand the āśramas as royal political and religious institutions. The chapels of Bhaiṣajyaguru (the healing Buddha) associated with the hospital complexes share a near-identical plan (Multzer o'Naghten 2011, 196), and the standardised inscriptions commemorating the foundations only varied in specific details relating to the size of the hospital and the location of the installation. The hospitals were generally located near a temple and a major town (Barth 1903). Twenty-five stelae and 61 chapels have been identified to date (Pottier, pers. comm.).

Prior to the excavations we conducted in Angkor, little was known about the physical layout and architectural configuration of Yaśovarman I's monasteries. Therefore, it became particularly important to determine whether the complexes were defined by buildings with common plans, as is the case with hospitals. If such a standardised architectural template could be ascertained, we could improve the likelihood of their archaeological discovery in the future as well as elucidating their function and social constitution.

The Yaśodharāśramas of Angkor

We will first examine the four āśramas in Angkor that have been identified with certainty and are the most studied to date: Prasat Ong Mong, dedicated to the Buddha; the Śiva hermitages of Prei Prasat and Prasat Komnap North; and the Vaiṣṇava monastery at Prasat Komnap South (see also Estève J. and D. Soutif 2010–2018; Chea 2018). The combined results of Pottier's remote sensing studies (2003) and of the archaeological campaigns conducted over the last eight years (Soutif et al. 2010–2018 and Chea 2018) reveal that each āśrama was installed in a large rectangular enclosure oriented east–west (375 × 150 m; Figure 15.3). Each of the four complexes was divided into two or three zones. A basin located to the east of the complex and slightly to the

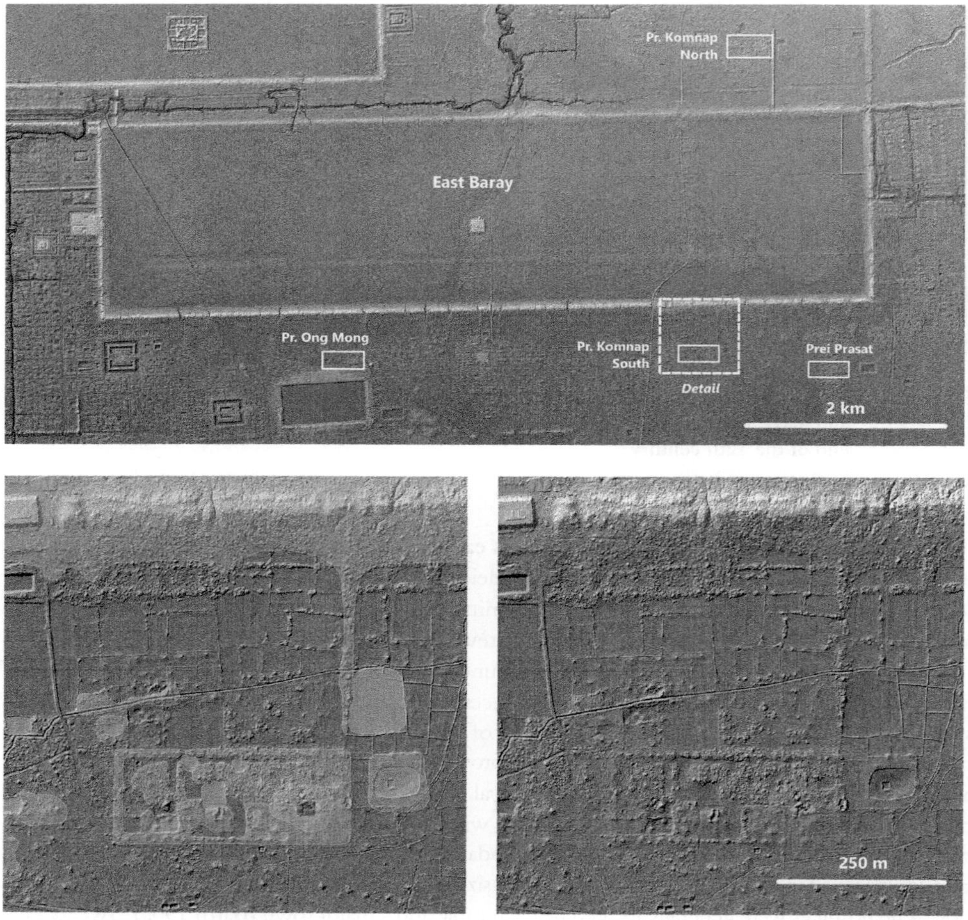

Figure 15.3 Lidar image of Prasat Komnap South.

Source: (Lidar data KALC 2015).

north of the western access road completed the architectural ensemble. An elevated roadway situated at the northeast corner of the rectilinear compound walls established a physical link between the āśrama and the East Baray, thus facilitating movement by religious celebrants to perform ceremonies specifically prescribed in the inscriptions. In fact, Prasat Komnap North, which is situated near the northeast corner of the Baray, was connected to the Baray's northern dike by a causeway extending from the southeast corner of its enclosure.

The western and central parts of the monasteries were respectively dedicated to gardening and to domestic activities. The low mounds in the central zone constitute the remains of housing for āśrama residents and attendants, and in all likelihood workshops, as evidenced by the discovery of tools and slags. These sectors of the āśrama—sometimes gathered in a single and contiguous area as at Ong Mong—lacked permanent buildings in stone or bricks and lacked standardised architectural signatures that would permit easy identification as parts of an āśrama.

The eastern zone of the monastery is distinguished by two major buildings that clearly delineate the sacred space of the āśramas where worship, teaching, and manuscript conservation took place (Chea 2018, 166). The first of the two buildings consists of a laterite shelter with a square

Figure 15.4 Examples of stela shelters: a) Pre Rup; b) Prasat Ong Mong; and c) Kuk Ta Prohm.

Source: (Photos Yaśodharāśrama Research Program).

plan (about 3 × 3 m) open to the four cardinal directions (Figure 15.4). As Dumarçay pointed out (2003, 25), their shape may vary from one shelter to another and some adopt a slightly rectangular plan, as at Ong Mong, where it measures 3.70 m east–west and 3.20 m north–south (for the complete study of this shelter, see 2018, 287–95). Its structure is composed of four groups of three laterite pillars placed at each corner supporting a so-called *voûte en bonnet de prêtre* or 'priest's cap' roof (see Trouvé 1932, 125). The shelter contained the inscription of the foundation, inscribed on a high, square-based stela. Such buildings have been identified in three of Angkor's āśramas, the best example being Ong Mong, where it was intact at the time of its discovery by Marchal in 1920 (*JFCA* 2, 05/1920, 169–70). A stela has been found near Prasat Komnap Nord, but the ruins of the shelter are not visible (*RCA* 1932, 77–78). A contemporary place of worship established on the site prevents verification of the presence of the vestiges of a stela shelter. The same type of building has been found in Pre Rup, as well as at the four corners of the East Baray, the latter also housing a stela by Yaśovarman I (Bergaigne 1893, 432–525).

The second permanent structure, partially visible only at Prei Prasat, is a rectangular laterite building nearly 30 m long located southwest of the stela shelter. The building has access points on its east and west ends and a central room framed on each side by a lateral vestibule and an entrance porch of decreasing width. The entire structure is founded on a high pediment surrounded by a laterite paving (1932, pl. IV, 114; Chea 2018, 295–306). Discovery of a number of roof tiles in the vicinity of the building and evenly spaced concavities in the masonry indicate that it was covered by a tiled roof supported by a wooden superstructure. Although few remains are preserved at Prasat Komnap Nord, Trouvé reported similarities in the moulding of the preserved blocks from this site with the worked stones of the Prei Prasat building (*RCA* 06/1932, 77–78). In Prasat Ong Mong and Prasat Komnap South, GPR studies in 2010 revealed the presence of permanent constructions buried southwest of the stela shelter. The excavation campaigns conducted since then have shown that in both cases the preserved remains corresponded perfectly, in plan and construction technique, with the known layout of the Prei Prasat building (Figure 15.5a; Chea 2018, 300; Yaśodharāśrama Reports 2010–2015). Moreover, in Ong Mong and Komnap South, we proved that these buildings were contemporaneous and that their foundation took place during the first phase of occupation of the āśramas (Chea 2018, 202; Yaśodharāśrama reports 2010).

In sum, the stela shelter and the principal and elongated religious edifice occupied an important place both spatially and symbolically in the Angkor āśramas. Excavations carried out in the three āśramas located south of the Baray have also demonstrated that the sacred area included

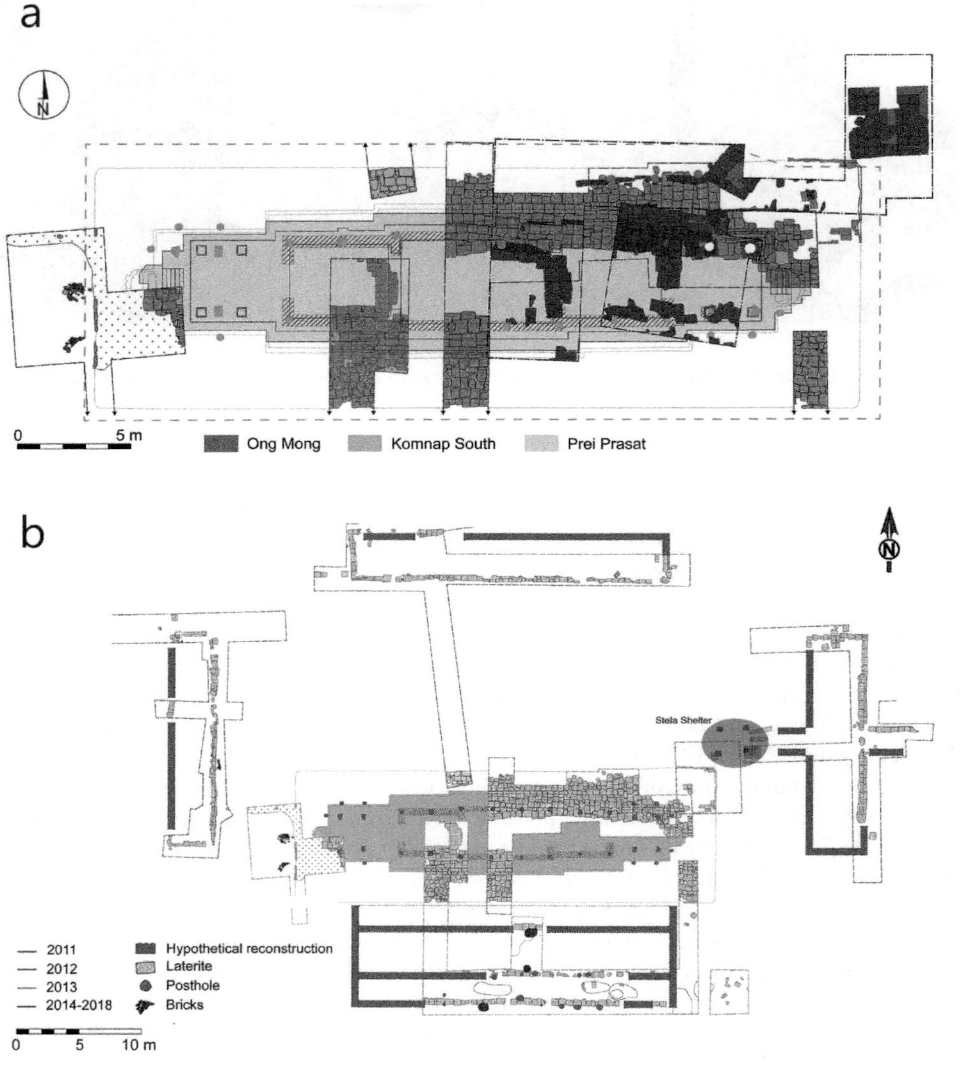

Figure 15.5 Reconstruction of the 'Long Building': a) the principal Long Building of Angkor's āśramas based on an overlay of the excavation plans of Prasat Komnap South and Prasat Ong Mong with Trouvé's plan of Prei Prasat (Image Yaśodharāśrama Research Program; CAD by Chea S.); b) Prasat Komnap South, simplified plan of the Western Part of the monastery.

Source: (Image Yaśodharāśrama Research Program; CAD by Y. Prouin & Chea S.).

several very long rectangular annex buildings built of wood and covered with tiles. These buildings are easily identifiable because their foundations are delineated by an alignment of laterite blocks (of one or two courses) in which post holes were cut to accommodate the posts supporting the floor and the wooden superstructure. Blocks were placed on their sides to mask the subfloor space below the elevated wooden planks forming the actual floor of the edifice. Given the laterite foundations, we refer to these structures as 'semi-permanent buildings' (Chea 2018, 321–22 and Yaśodharāśrama reports 2012–2018). They formed a kind of enclosure interrupted at the corners around the two more prominent masonry buildings (Figure 15.5b). These structures are reminiscent of the proto-galleries of temples built in the middle of the 10th century at Pre Rup; the overall plan of the sacred area is clearly centred on the stela shelter since the main door of the 'enclosure' surrounding the shelter—in the centre of the eastern annex building—provides direct access to the stela shrine. This particular configuration appears to have defined the aesthetic and architectural style of Yaśovarman I's monasteries.

The Āśramas of the Provinces

We now consider the provincial āśramas identified by the discovery of foundation inscriptions. An important objective of our research is to ascertain whether they were defined by comparable layouts, similar infrastructures, and parallel occupation histories, as has been documented at the four principal āśramas in Angkor.

The provincial foundation inscriptions are less precise than the Angkor commemorations and suggest that they served mainly as resthouses and possibly as places of religious instruction. Another important difference from Angkor's āśramas is that the provincial examples are directly connected to a temple and therefore did not operate independently. Furthermore, the combined epigraphic evidence from the provincial āśramas indicates that they were not as richly endowed or as tightly integrated with the centralised political apparatus.

Most of the sites where the provincial inscriptions have been discovered served as important sanctuaries that were founded long before the reign of Yaśovarman I, often during the Pre-Angkor Period. The āśrama dedicated to Bhadreśvara, the god of Wat Phu, provides an especially famous example (Estève and Soutif 2010–11, 351). An important exception is the Preah Ko temple at Hariharālaya (Roluos) where Yaśovarman I settled a monastery according to inscription K. 323 (Bergaigne 1893, 376). This can be explained by the fact that he maintained a special relationship to this temple dedicated to his grandparents, which likely explains this particular foundation (see list in Chea 2018, 101).

Placement of provincial āśramas near pre-existing and especially sacred temples reveals Yaśovarman I's policy to impose his authority over the most venerable places of his kingdom (Estève and Soutif 2010–11; see Figure 15.1). Identifying the locations of the provincial monasteries would therefore prove valuable in creating both a map of Yaśovarman I's territory and a map of the principal religious centres of 9th-century Cambodia. Thus, in the absence of inscriptions, the detection of replicated architectural units, similar to the standardised layout of the monasteries in the capital, would provide the only means to identify provincial āśramas.

Currently, no large rectangular enclosures similar to those discovered in Angkor are known near any of the Yaśodharāśrama sites. Similarly, as no excavations have taken place, it remains unclear whether semi-permanent annex buildings surrounded the main religious edifices of the provincial āśramas. Of course, the presence of a stela shelter would serve as a good indicator of the presence of such monasteries, but comparable shelters are quite rare. Kuk Ta Prohm, an isolated site in Kampong Cham province, is the only well-preserved shelter identified in the provinces (see Figure 15.4). This structure is indeed comparable to the stela shrines of the capital, even if the corner pillars are fitted together differently and not in one piece. However, nothing comparable to Angkor's āśramas is visible around Kuk Ta Prohm's stela shelter. Moreover, the shape and dimensions of the stone of the foundation inscriptions outside Angkor are so different that it would be unsurprising if they were housed in a different kind of structure entirely. In other words, the shelters in the capital were designed to house the tall, narrow, four-sided inscriptions of Angkor, and they would have poorly accommodated the two-sided stelae of the provincial asramas. While the Angkor inscriptions are engraved on high square-based pillars and

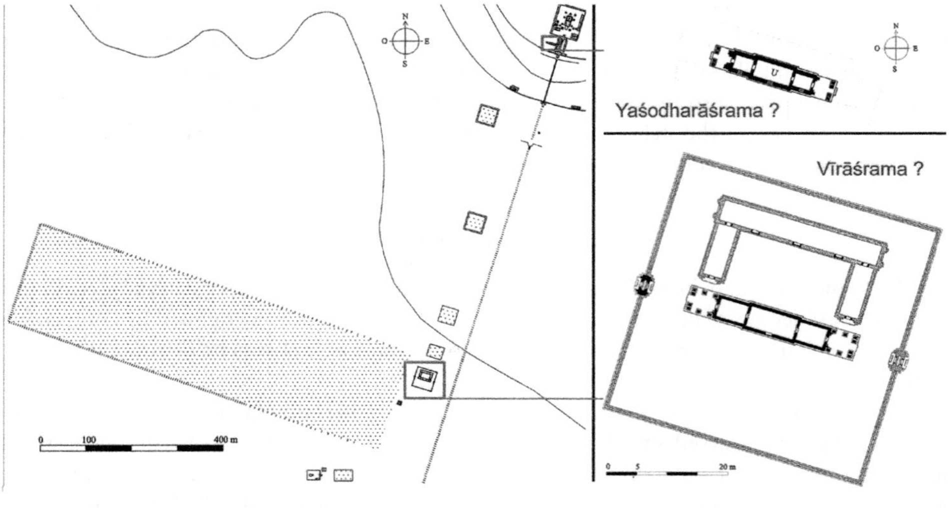

Figure 15.6 Plan of Prasat Neak Buos illustrating the location of the potential Yaśodharāśrama and Vīrāśrama.

Source: (Based on Parmentier 1939, pl. XVII & Bruguier and Lacroix 2013, 456, 459, 462, pl. 80, 82, 83).

use only characters newly imposed by the king, the 'digraphic' inscriptions commemorating the foundation of the āśrama in the provinces are inscribed on flat rectangular stelae decorated with a truncated bracing apex. On the flat provincial stelae, the text is repeated on both sides, one in the new alphabet—which was to fall into disuse—and the other using the 'classical' alphabet, which is still in use today. The dual alphabets likely served a didactic purpose to transmit a new writing system to the most remote provinces of the empire (Estève and Soutif 2010–11, 342).

A number of buildings similar to the 30-m-long Long Building identified in the Angkor āśramas have been reported in direct proximity to venerable sanctuaries in the provinces. The provincial monastery of Prasat Neak Buos, the 'western foot of Śiva' founded during the Pre-Angkor Period, provides one excellent example. The āśrama foundation inscription K. 346 (Bergaigne 1893, 378) was recovered near the building designated 'U' by Parmentier (1927, 172; Figure 15.6). This structure dates between the 9th and 10th centuries and is similar in shape and size to the Long Buildings of the Angkor āśramas. A similarly shaped building is also found at Houay Tomo, an important temple located near Wat Phu on the east bank of the Mekong in Laos. Houay Tomo is a Pre-Angkorian sanctuary that also remained in operation throughout the Angkor Period. The Long Building is extremely ruined, but the slab with a mortise that contained the inscription K. 362 (Bergaigne 1893, 389) is still visible (Nalesini 2000, fig. 1, building C). Finally, we find the same structure—but in sandstone—at Wat Phu, one of the oldest and most venerated temples in ancient Cambodia. The origin of the āśrama foundation stela associated with Wat Phu remains unknown, but the presence of an āśrama of Yaśovarman at this temple has been substantiated by the discovery of the two sets of inscriptions found a few kilometres from this important site. They both mention Bhadreśvara, the tutelary divinity of Wat Phu (K. 1005; Estève and Soutif 2010–11). It is especially noteworthy that each of these three buildings occupies a singular place: to the south of, and perpendicular to, the eastern access road that runs outside the temple.

These spatial and architectural commonalities suggest that Yaśodharāśramas of the provinces included buildings with common characteristics. It is interesting to note that the Long Building finds parallels with the later repetitive foundation of Jayavaman VII, and the latter clearly followed an ancient tradition. Although the Long Buildings are not all made of the same material, they conform to a specific configuration, thus supporting our general hypothesis. Indeed, Jayavarman VII's hospital chapels and fire shrines exemplify how different building materials could be used in construction, as long as the general plan remained identical. Furthermore, it is possible that not all of the 100 āśramas in the provinces and celebrated in the inscriptions were built or that many were simply constructed of perishable materials, as may have been the case with some of Jayavarman VII's foundations. It should be noted that a temporary building made of perishable material seems to have been initially installed at Prasat Ong Mong during the initial construction phase of the monastery (Chea 2018, 208). Of course, as with the architectural remains of masonry buildings excavated at Komnap South and Ong Mong, it is possible that the remains of largely destroyed provincial monasteries remain buried and out of sight. Future excavations are clearly needed to test our hypothesis, but epigraphic analysis provides some additional clues on the location and function of these important buildings.

Long Buildings as Rājakuṭi

The discovery of several statue pedestals in the immediate vicinity of the Long Building at the Prei Prasat āśrama in Angkor strongly suggests that these elongated structures served as the monastery's principal cult compounds, similar to the majority of masonry buildings in the Pre-Angkor and Angkor Periods. The inscriptions support this hypothesis. The foundation stelae of Angkor's āśramas provide a precise list of the personnel assigned to the monasteries, including the guardians of the 'royal cell' (*rājakuṭi*). Cœdès and Barth assumed that this building corresponded to a pavilion intended to welcome the king for 'a kind of spiritual retreat' (Bergaigne 1893, 375, n. 2), but our archaeological investigations and epigraphic analysis cast doubt on this argument.

The inscriptions indicate that the *rājakuṭi* required two guardians, the only such positions mentioned among the monastery staff. Therefore, this structure must have constituted the most sacred place in the monastery. According to Louis Renou's dictionary, *Kuṭi* refers to 'a hut, a shed', and thus a small place of residence. These texts also reference this term to designate the cells of the religious community (Cœdès 1932, 92, 103). In fact, this word is still used today in Cambodia to refer to the housing of monks in pagodas. However, it can also refer to a 'chapel' in the inscriptions and therefore to a sanctuary or residence of a god (Chea 2018, 144; Pou 2001a, 39, n. 2).

The Khmer section of the inscription K. 349 reports that in 954, the king Rājendravarman commissioned a high dignitary to make 'the brick foundations' in the *vraḥ kuṭi* of the Yaśodharāśrama at Śivapāda, the monastery founded by Yaśovarman at Prasat Neak Buos (*IC* V, 108, 110–111). The text is somewhat vague but most likely refers to a dedication ritual indicating that the designated building served as a sanctuary and not as a simple cell (Chea 2018, 144, n. 136).

In Cambodia, the term *vraḥ* refers to a sacred being or object and is employed indiscriminately to designate the king, a divinity, a sanctuary, or a statue (Pou 2004, *s.v.*). Therefore, it seems likely that the compound *rāja-kuṭi* represents only a transposition of the Khmer expression *vraḥ kuṭi* and referred to a 'sacred' or 'royal' 'chapel' founded by the king rather than an actual 'royal cell'. In the end, we hypothesise that this 'royal chapel' corresponds to none other than the elongated cult building of the monasteries of Yaśodharāśrama, the only permanent building common to Angkor's āśramas and to at least three of the provincial monasteries described previously.

Thus, beginning at the end of the 9th century, the repetitive royal foundations of Yaśovarman included structures built on the same plan, easily recognisable to travellers and signalling both the piety of the king and his dominion over the region. This conclusion raises an important point: Yaśovarman was not the only king to order the construction of āśramas, even if no other ruler commissioned as many, at least according to the sources at our disposal. In the following section, we evaluate the epigraphic evidence to determine whether the āśramas founded in other reigns were also marked by specific and specialised buildings.

Vīrāśrama

The foundation stela of Saugatāśrama (K. 290), the Buddhist āśrama of Angkor, now known as Prasat Ong Mong, proves especially valuable in identifying later royal monasteries postdating Yaśovarman's reign. It is unusual because it bears not only the original Sanskrit text commemorating its foundation and establishing its rule but also two later Khmer texts inscribed on its base. In fact, these texts confirm that this monastery was still in operation during the 11th century under the reign of Sūryavarman I and that it was still prestigious enough for a sovereign to make a generous donation. An excerpt from this inscription reads as follows:

> 927 *śaka* [1005 CE], second day of the waxing moon of Vaiśākha, Saturday, New Year's Day, H.M. Śrī Sūryavarmadeva orders the building of the saint Vīrāśrama, . . . This holy Vīrāśrama and all the supplies, H. M. Sūryavarmadeva assigns to the holy Saugatāśrama.
>
> (*IC* III, 231)

The mention of a Vīrāśrama, 'the āśrama of heroes', conferred upon the Saugatāśrama is clearly significant and prompted a search of other occurrences of this particular compound. Excavations carried out at Prasat Ong Mong corroborate the fact that the monastery was occupied for several centuries (Chea 2018, 324).

The inscription K. 381 of Preah Vihear also reports the foundation of a *virāśrama* by Sūryavarman I in 1002. Cœdès notes: '[this *vīrāśrama* corresponds] probably to the so-called "palace" on which the inscription is engraved' (*IC* VI, 255), since it is inscribed on the south pedestal of the west gate of 'Palace H' in the third enclosure. Whatever the function of this building, it was engraved on a particular edifice that was U-shaped in plan (Bruguier 2013, 545, pl. 99). It is significant that several such U-shaped structures, enclosed by a Long Building and incorrectly identified as 'palaces', have been documented in several sanctuaries of the Angkor Period (Bruguier and Lacroix 2017).

Two other occurrences of *vīrāśrama* are found in the inscription K. 342 of Prasat Neak Buos, again attributable to Sūryavarman I (l. 11–14; 1008 CE; *IC* VI, 236). It commemorates a royal donation, including rice provisions, expected to 'go down to the Vraḥ Vīrāśrama' (*cuḥ ta vraḥ vīrāśrama*) in order to 'feed religious saints studying in Vraḥ Vīrāśrama'. The expression *cuḥ ta vraḥ* provides a valuable clue on the location of this complex, since Prasat Neak Buos is located on the lower slopes of the Dangrek. In fact, a U-shaped monument similar to that of Preah Vihear is located directly below the main temple, corroborating the downslope location indicated in the inscription (Figure 15.6). Therefore, it is particularly tempting to identify the U-shaped building at Prasat Neak Buos as our Vīrāśrama. This inscription also sheds light on the responsibilities and function of these institutions that received offerings from Sūryavarman. In the case of Prasat Neak Buos, it indeed served as a monastery that welcomed students, religious experts, and scientists. Similar to the āśramas of Yaśovarman I in Angkor, they thus formed places of study and religious retreat. An 'inspector of the Vīrāśrama' is also mentioned in the inscription K. 353 of Prasat Kantop. However, given the proximity of this sanctuary and Prasat Neak Buos, Cœdès rightly considered that it was the hermitage located at the foot of the hill of Prasat Neak Buos discussed previously (*IC* V, 134, n. 1).

Another *vīrāśrama* is mentioned in a list of toponyms in the inscription K. 194 of Phnom Sandak (face B, col. IV, l. 22; Cœdès and Dupont 1943, 152). Given the proximity of Preah Vihear and Phnom Sandak and the similarity of their inscriptions (Cœdès and Dupont 1943, 134–135), it would first seem that these two *vīrāśrama* refer to the same site. However, a site called Prasat Kon Chen containing the same U-shaped and elongated buildings as Prasat Neak Buos and Preah Vihear is located just at the base of the hill that hosts the sanctuary of Phnom Sandak (Bruguier 2013, 422–423, pl. 72; Chea 2018, ill. 78–81, p. XXXVIII–XXXIX). In light of the joint topographic and architectural evidence, we argue that this site is none other than the *vīrāśrama* of inscription K. 194 and that it also served as a monastery allocated by Sūryavarman I to Phnom Sandak. With these monasteries: the Prasat Kon Chen and the buildings located in Prasat Neak Buos and Preah Vihear, all with a U-shaped plan, we can identify a more recent repetitive foundation of āśramas attributable to Sūryavarman I (Figure 15.1), one that was also based on the construction of standardised permanent buildings designed to accommodate devotees dedicated to study and worship.

If this hypothesis is right, it is surprising that unlike Yaśovarman, Sūryavarman did not wish to associate his name with these royal foundations. However, as Saveros Pou explains in her discussion of the *vīrāśrama* of K. 290 (Ong Mong), 'the first queen [of Sūryavarman] was named Vīralakṣmī', and it deserves consideration that the monasteries were named in her honour (Pou 2001b, 323). The name of this repetitive royal foundation would thus have been formed to pay homage to this first queen.

Similar to Yaśovarman's āśramas, Sūryavarman's monasteries were apparently assigned to large pre-existing temples or monasteries and sometimes to the same institutions that Yaśovarman had already endowed, as in the case of the Prasat Neak Buos. It is impossible to determine whether these foundations were intended to replace or supplement those of Yaśovarman I in the provinces. At Angkor, on the other hand, it seems that the *vīrāśrama* was in one way or another associated with the *Saugatāśrama*, which clearly shows that at least one of Angkor's āśramas had joined the list of major Khmer religious foundations that successive sovereigns were committed to maintain. The inscription K. 277 mentions a donation made by Yogīśvarapaṇḍita, guru of Sūryavarman I, to the 'Royal Foundations of the neighbourhood and to the four āśrama' (l. 31–34; *IC* IV, 160). The four āśrama' most likely refer to Yaśodharāśrama's original monasteries built around the Eastern Baray.

It should be noted that the diagnostic U-shaped edifice also characterises several large shrines, especially Prasat Khna, located in the province of Preah Vihear, which housed a Long Building of the same type as the āśramas of Yaśovarman (Figure 15.7; Bruguier 2013, 135). No inscription can confirm that these were the actual monasteries, but future excavations are designed to test this hypothesis. The epigraphic record proves that Prasat Khna was an important sanctuary, and if confirmed archaeologically, it would highlight the long-lasting prestige that this particular temple enjoyed.

Concluding Thoughts

Our hypothesis is that the Vīrāśramas were built where the provincial āśramas of Yaśovarman were settled. The construction of these repetitive foundations required a considerable investment of labour and resources, especially as they were built in accordance with a standard imposed by the royal authorities. In any event, the āśramas clearly differ from simple and reclusive 'hermitages', as the term 'āśrama' has often been translated and understood. The monasteries of Yaśovarman and later rulers were not intended to simply accommodate world-renouncing hermits. While it seems that these monasteries welcomed renouncers into their community (Chea 2018, 137), their vocation was much more extensive, including the preservation and transmission of knowledge, as indicated by the rules specified in the inscriptions and the considerable resources owed to the different monasteries.

The inscriptions reveal names of other kings who were also associated with āśrama foundations (Indravarman/Indrāśrama, Rājendravarman/Rājendrāśrama), but they are too few and isolated to determine whether they formed part of large-scale building programs with similarly standardised structures. We are confident that future research on these repetitive royal foundations will make it possible to identify further examples of specialised buildings annexed to the most sacred sanctuaries of ancient Cambodia.

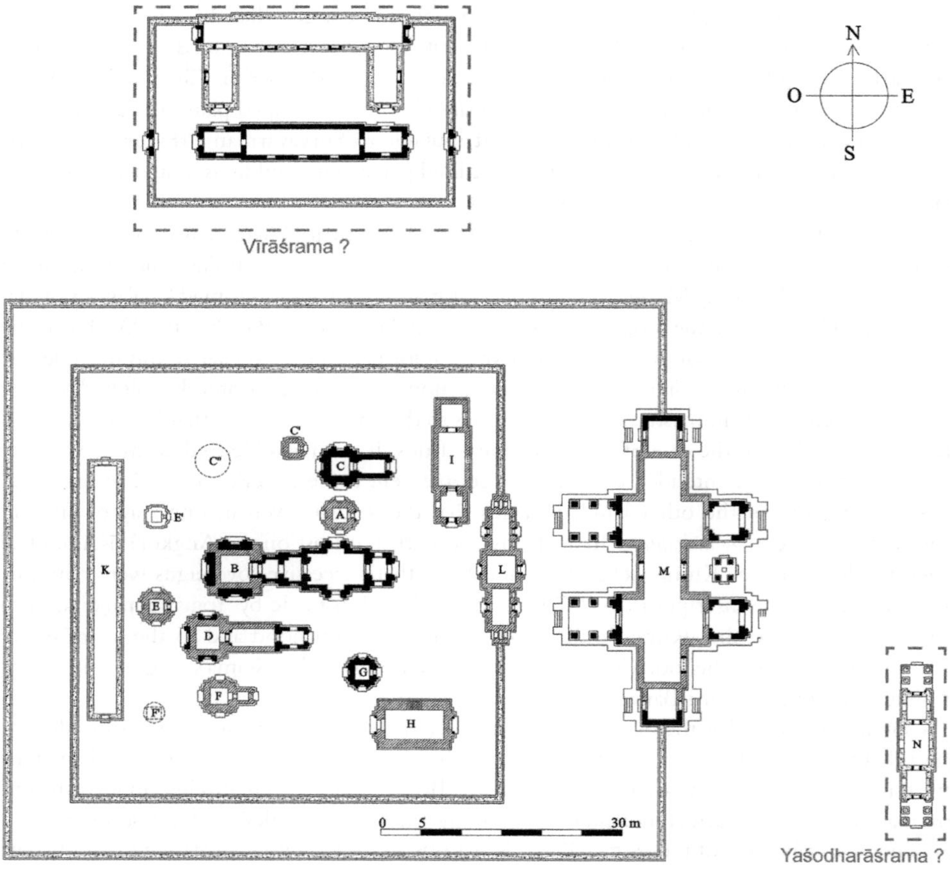

Figure 15.7 Plan of Prasat Khna illustrating the location of the potential Yaśodharāśrama and Vīrāśrama. *Source*: (Based on Parmentier 1939, pl. XXVII & Bruguier and Lacroix 2013, 135, pl. 19).

An analysis of the two traditions of royal repetitive foundations considered in this chapter has significantly improved our understanding of how Angkorian regimes attempted to centralise power in the provinces through the foundation of religious institutions. In addition, the epigraphic and archaeological study of such institutions will shed valuable new light on how macroscale political and religious policies shaped daily life and material culture in ancient Angkor.

List of Inscriptions in the Text

K.	*Reference*
116	*IC* II, 134
194	Cœdès and Dupont 1943, 134
277	*ISC*, 97; *IC* IV, 155
290	Cœdès 1908, 203; *IC* III, 231
323	*ISCC*, 391
342	*IC* VI, 236

K.	Reference
346	*ISCC*, 378
349	*IC* V, 108
353	*IC* V, 133
362	*ISCC*, 389
377	*IC* V, 3
381	*IC* VI, 255
1005	Estève and Soutif 2010–11

IC = Inscriptions du Cambodge; Cœdès 1937–66.

ISC = Inscriptions sanscrites du Cambodge; Barth 1885.

ISCC = Inscriptions sanscrites de Campā et du Cambodge; Bergaigne 1893.

References

Barth, A., 1885. *Inscriptions sanscrites du Cambodge* (extraits des notices et extraits des manuscrits de la Bibliothèque nationale 27, 1re partie, 1er fascicule), Paris, Imprimerie nationale, pp. 1–180.

Barth, A., 1903. Les doublets de la stèle de Say-Fong. *Bulletin de l'École française d'Extrême Orient* 3(3), 460–66.

Bergaigne, A., 1893. *Inscriptions sanscrites de Campā et du Cambodge (extraits des notices et extraits des manuscrits de la Bibliothèque nationale 27, 2e partie, 2e fascicule).* Paris: Imprimerie Nationale, 181–632.

Bruguier, B. & J. Lacroix, 2013. *Guide archéologique du Cambodge, tome V.* Phnom Penh: Japan Printing House Co.

Bruguier, B. & J. Lacroix, 2017. *Guide archéologique du Cambodge, tome IV.* Phnom Penh: Japan Printing House Co.

Bruguier, B., 2000. Les ponts en pierre du Cambodge ancien. Aménagement ou contrôle du territoire? *Bulletin de l'École française d'Extrême-Orient* 87–2, 529–51.

Chea, Socheat, 2018. *Saugatāśrama: Un āśrama bouddhique à Angkor (Ong Mong).* PhD dissertation. Paris: University Paris IV—Paris-Sorbonne.

Cœdès, G. & P. Dupont, 1943. Les inscriptions de Sdok Kak Thom, Phnom Sandak et Prah Vihar. *Bulletin de l'École française d'Extrême Orient* 43, 56–134.

Cœdès, G., 1906. La stèle de Ta Prohm. *Bulletin de l'École française d'Extrême Orient* 6(1–2), 44–82.

Cœdès, G., 1908. La stèle de Tép Pranam (Cambodge). *Journal Asiatique* 10/11, 203–25.

Cœdès, G., 1932. Études Cambodgiennes: 30. À la recherche du Yaçodharāçrama. *Bulletin de l'École française d'Extrême-Orient* 32(1), 84–112.

Cœdès, G., 1937–66. *Inscriptions du Cambodge. Collection de Textes et Documents sur l'Indochine.* Vol. I (1937); Vol. II (1942); Vol. III (1951); Vol. IV (1952); Vol. V (1953); Vol. VI (1954); Vol. VII (1964); Vol. VIII (1966). Paris: École française d'Extrême-Orient.

Cœdès, G., 1941. La stèle du Práḥ Khằn d'Aṅkor. *Bulletin de l'École française d'Extrême Orient* 41(2), 255–302.

Dagens, B., 2005. Centralisme et architecture. Les hôpitaux de Jayavarman VII dans laThailande du Nord-Est. In *Traités, temples et images du monde indien*, eds. B. Dagens, M.L. Barazer-Billoret & V. Lefèvre. Paris: Presses Sorbonne Nouvelle, 253–63.

Dumarçay, J., 2003. Architecture and its models in South-East Asia [1st French ed, 1998, L'architecture et ses modèles en Asie du Sud-est]. Paris: Oriens, Bangkok: Orchid Press.

Estève, J. & D. Soutif, 2010–11. Les Yaśodharāśrama, marqueurs d'empire et bornes sacrées—Conformité et spécificité des stèles digraphiques khmères de la région de Vat Phu. *Bulletin de l'École française d'Extrême-Orient* 97–98, 331–55.

Estève, J. & D. Soutif, 2010–2018. Rapports annuels de la mission Yaśodharāśrama. Unpublished reports. Siem Reap: APSARA-MEAE-EFEO.

Hendrickson, M., 2008. People around the houses with fire: archaeological investigation of settlement around the Jayavarman VII 'resthouse' temples. *Udaya, Journal of Khmer Studies* 9, 63–79.

Hendrickson, M., 2010. Historic routes to Angkor: development of the Khmer road system (ninth to thirteenth centuries AD) in mainland Southeast Asia. *Antiquity* 84, 480–96.

Hendrickson, M., 2011. A transport geographic perspective on travel and communication in Angkorian Southeast Asia (ninth to fifteenth centuries AD). *World Archaeology* 43(3), 444–57.

JFCA: Journaux de fouilles de la conservation d'Angkor, Siem Reap (1909–1955) handwritten documents, unpublished, EFEO archives, Paris.

Lowman, I., K., Chhom & M. Hendrickson, 2023. An Angkor nation? Identifying the core of the Khmer empire, in *The Angkorian World*, eds. M. Hendrickson, M.T. Stark & D. Evans. New York: Routledge, 479–93.

Lunet de Lajonquière, E., 1902–11. *Inventaire descriptif des monuments du Cambodge* (3 vol. and map). Paris: Ernest Leroux.

Multzer o'Naghten, H., 2011. *Les fondations de Jayavarman VII: l'aménagement d'un territoire et son interprétation historique et religieuse.* PhD dissertation. Paris: University Paris III—Sorbonne nouvelle.

Nalesini, O., 2000. The sanctuary of Huei Thamo, and the historical problems raised by its survey. In *Proceedings of the 7th Conference of the European Association of Southeast Asian Archaeologists*, eds. W. Lobo & S. Reinemann. Southeast Asian Archaeology 1998. Hull: Centre for Southeast Asian Studies and Staatliche Museen zu Berlin, 123–38.

Parmentier, H., 1927. *L'Art khmer primitif (2 vol.).* Paris: École française d'Extrême Orient.

Parmentier, H., 1939. *L'Art khmèr classique.* Monuments du quadrant Nord-Est. Paris: EFEO.

Pottier, Ch. & R. K. Chhem, 2010. À la découverte d'un hôpital angkorien. Résultats préliminaire d'une campagne archéologique au Prasat Ta Muong. *Udaya, Journal of Khmer Studies* 6, 169–82.

Pottier, Ch., 2003. About Yaśovarman I's Buddhist açrama in Angkor, in *The Buddhist Monastery: A cross-cultural survey*, eds P. Pichard & F. Lagirarde. Paris: École française d'Extrême Orient, 199–208.

Pottier, C., A. Bolle, E. Llopis, D. Soutif, C. Socheat, S. Sang, H. Komsan & P. Dara, 2008. Bakong, soixante ans après. In *Proceedings of the 11th International Conference of the European Association of Southeast Asian Archaeologists, Gougon September 2006,* Bougon september 2006 (eds. J.-P. Pautreau, A.-S. Coupey, V. Zeytoun and E. Rambault. Chiang Mai: Siam Ratana Ltd, 245–50).

Pou, S., 2001a. *Nouvelles inscriptions du Cambodge, tomes II et III.* Paris: École française d'Extrême Orient.

Pou, S., 2001b. Āśrama dans l'ancien Cambodge. *Journal Asiatique* 290(1), 315–39.

Pou, S., 2004. *Dictionnaire vieux khmer-français-anglais. An Old Khmer-French-English Dictionary. Vacanānukram khmaer cas'-paramn-angles.* Paris: L'Harmattan.

RCA: Rapports de la Conservation d'Angkor. Siem Reap (1908–1972), handwritten and typed documents, unpublished, EFEO archives, Paris.

Stern, Ph., 1951. Diversité et rythme des fondations royales khmères. *Bulletin de l'École française d'Extrême-Orient* 44(2), 649–87.

Swenson, E.R., 2013. Interpreting the political landscape of early state religions, in *A Companion to the Anthropology of Religion*, eds. M. Lambek & J. Boddy, 471–88. London: Wiley-Blackwell.

Trouvé, G., 1932. Étude sur le Prei Prasat, le Prasat Komnap et l'édicule qui abritait la cinquième stèle inscrite du Baray Oriental. *Bulletin de l'École française d'Extrême Orient* 32(1), 113–26.

16

EDUCATION AND MEDICINE AT ANGKOR

Chhem Rethy, Damian Evans, Chhom Kunthea, Phlong Pisith and Peter D. Sharrock

This chapter reviews the evidence of Angkorian educational and medical institutions between the 10th and 13th centuries. Particular emphasis is given to the transformational changes enacted by Jayavarman VII, the king responsible for switching the state religion to Mahāyāna Buddhism and expanding the empire to its territorial zenith between the 12th to 13th centuries. Using epigraphic as well as archaeological and iconographic evidence (e.g., statues and bas-reliefs), this paper evaluates the role of royal patronage in the transfer of knowledge, the structure and functions of universities and hospitals, and the training of physicians. Given the limited amount of Angkorian data—and the desire to locate the subject within a broader context—ethnographic sources from Cambodia and other contemporary Buddhist kingdoms are compared to elucidate Angkor's specific medical practices and the ways in which these were taught and learned. Overall, our treatment of the material endeavours to summarise existing knowledge on these topics while offering new insights on the religious and medical strategies adopted by Angkorian kings to fight the diseases and epidemics that would have continually ravaged the realm.

Angkorian inscriptions and iconography suggest that educational content and teaching methods were based on Brahmanical and Buddhist schools (Mookerji 1951; Chhem 2008). At the capital of Angkor, the education of the king was based on Brahmanical traditions, which played an essential role in confirming the legitimacy of the sovereign and buttressing his ability to consolidate power. Kings were assisted by ministers and learned advisers, who were mostly priests and monks. These individuals would be selected from among local people with high levels of ability as well as migrants originating from the Indian subcontinent (Chhom 2018). This dynamic relationship between South and Southeast Asia is important for understanding the ways in which medical knowledge was encoded and transmitted. The Angkorian World was located within a broader sphere of cultural exchange and interaction that Sheldon Pollock (2001) has termed the 'Sanskrit cosmopolis', in which mastering Sanskrit conferred power because the language was the repository of science and knowledge. Pollock wrote that Sanskrit became the premier vehicle for the expression of royal will, displacing all other codes (see also Bronkhorst 2011; Wolters 1999, 109 *et passim*).

Education was primarily the purview of Angkorian royalty and elites, and the royal court itself was an important venue for teaching and learning. In this context, Angkorian scholars were an elite class that can be divided into four main categories: kings and queens, royal family members, priests (*pandita, acarya, guru, hotar,* or *purohita*), and court officials. In the Khmer Brahmanical and

DOI: 10.4324/9781351128940-20

Buddhist traditions, each had a role to play in the system of teaching and practising medicine and in developing and sustaining the required infrastructure: a priest would conduct rites and rituals for the king, an astrologer/astronomer would calculate auspicious times for specific practices, an architect would build temples such as hospitals by decree of the king, a teacher would instruct in royal institutions, and doctors would care for patients in royal hospitals. In this chapter, we review the ways in which this system functioned at court, in specialised colleges, and at universities as part of a centralised educational system that tutored royals and their elite associates to administer the political, ritual, and economic aspects of the Angkorian World.

Our approach necessarily suffers from an over-reliance on a relatively small number of contemporaneous Sanskrit texts, in particular the 'hospital inscriptions', which are sufficiently numerous to have allowed epigraphers to undertake a broad comparison and arrive at a relatively reliable and widely accepted translation (Finot 1903, 1915). In light of several working hypotheses, this chapter seeks to reassess the content of the hospital inscriptions to place front and centre the issues of medical training and practice and other related questions that have thus far remained mostly overlooked by the Angkorian specialists (Finot 1915; Cœdès 1941a; Jacques 1968). We do this by considering a range of sources beyond just medical texts and religious texts with medical references, drawing from archaeological, architectural, or iconographic evidence, specifically the imagery depicted on the 'universities' of Preah Khan and Ta Prohm and hospital chapels located at the gates of Angkor Thom. Combined, this study provides a provisional interpretation of the role of education and medicine within the social history of Angkor.

The Angkorian World in Its Broader Context

Advanced education was foundational to the establishment of the elite in the Angkorian World. Teaching took place at the royal court, at specialised colleges, and at full-fledged universities. Inscriptions from the 10th to 14th centuries CE indicate a diverse range of curricula such as engineering, construction, architecture, and law, as well as medicine. Together, the teaching of these disciplines built an educational platform for a civic, ceremonial, and social base that allowed the growth of Angkor's elite and made the Khmer Empire one of the most advanced states in Asia. The burgeoning inscriptional record in Sanskrit and Old Khmer languages repeat the terms *paryyan*, 'to teach' or *ryan*, 'to study'. Sanskrit, the sacred language from India, was adopted by the Khmers as a rich medium for new ideas in many fields and was mastered with the help of Khmer translations and explanations. Thus, although the surviving texts use Sanskrit as the formalised language, the material itself was probably taught in vernacular Old Khmer, just as Khmer-language translations of canonical Buddhist texts in Pali aided in the dissemination of such knowledge in Middle Period Cambodia from the 15th to 18th centuries.

The evolution and growth of Angkorian educational institutions through time were probably modelled, at least in part, on the famous 6th- to 8th-century Nalanda and Vikramaśila universities of the Ganges valley (Dutt 1962; Sankalia 1972, 265), which served as nodes for networks of propagation of Buddhism from India to Tibet, China, Japan, Maritime Asia, Burma, Champa, and Angkor (Huber 1911; Cœdès 1989). Early Buddhist educational systems, like the 5th- to 12th-century Buddhist Nalanda University and monastic centre in northeastern India (Mookerji 1951, 564–65), educated the lay public as well as monks (Mookerji 1951, 394). These monasteries were also homes for the Buddhist *sangha*, or monastic order, which performed rites and ceremonies according to Buddhist doctrine (Dutt 1962, 73–76). More broadly, beyond just the Buddhist context, documents from South Asia dating from the 13th to 15th centuries CE suggest that formal schools existed where both Brahmin teachers and their students lived and worked (Dutt 1962, 322).

At the same time, we should underscore that beliefs and practices brought to the Angkorian World by Brahmins and Buddhist monks from South Asia were undoubtedly transformed, adapted, and integrated by the royals and other elites to meet local needs (Sarka 1968, 3; Majumdar 1985, 23–24). In addition, influences from cultural contexts other than South Asia may have had a role to play in shaping local forms of higher education: Chinese influence on Angkorian culture, for example, has not been sufficiently studied, and some recent works tend to suggest that its impact was not negligible, in particular in the medical field (Chhem and Antelme 2004). Be that as it may, it is clear that Sanskrit scholarly culture was profoundly influential across essentially all the literary, religious, philosophical, technological, and medical domains, which drew substantially from the sacred scriptures of the subcontinent (Vedas, Smṛti, Vedaṅga, Upaveda, of which Ayurveda is a part) and were inspired by Hindu philosophies (Saṃkhya, Yoga, Nyāya, Vaiśeṣika, Mīmāṃsā, and Vedanta) (Sarka 1968, 33–45).

Even after more than a century of dedicated scientific research on Angkorian culture, it remains a challenge to link these broader currents in religious doctrine and practice, which draw substantially from literary sources, to material remains and other forms of evidence from research on the ground. Few physical remains of Angkorian educational institutions have been very clearly identified. Nonetheless, recent archaeological investigations by Cambodian and international teams (see Chea et al. 2023, this volume) has reinforced the longstanding notion that *āśrama* were important educational centres of the Angkorian World, appearing in early Angkorian epigraphy as collegial institutions (Pou 2002, 331). These centres of knowledge were founded by Angkorian elites, the grand Brahmins who served the kings. The infrastructure and regulations shaping the *āśrama* of king Yaśovarman I (hereafter Yaśodharāśrama) in the 10th century CE approached those of a small university (Cœdès 1989; Pottier 2003) and had roots that extended back at least three centuries. These *āśrama* will be a core focus of this chapter, since they are characteristic of the early centuries of the Angkor Period. With the gradual decline of Brahmanism as the state religion from the 12th to 13th centuries, medical education and practice become more closely associated with the famous hospital network and monastic centres of teaching and learning established by king Jayavarman VII, such as Ta Prohm and Preah Khan temples at Angkor; this Buddhist system will be the second major focus of our chapter.

Teaching and Learning in the Angkorian World: An Overview

Āśrama (Religious Hermitages)

Although it is difficult to establish a direct lineage or transition from the 10th-century religious hermitages to the great Buddhist monastic universities of the 12th to 13th centuries, we may nonetheless observe that by the 10th century, Yaśovarman I (r. 889–910) had established an enduring tradition of educating students from a broad social base within a well-defined and clearly demarcated campus space (Pottier 2003). The inscriptions of Yaśovarman's new capital at Angkor introduce the creation of Yaśodharāśrama: *āśrama* for different stages of learning attended by members and children of the Angkorian elite. Some served as finishing schools to meet increasing needs for specialised personnel for the Angkorian court and its expanding realm, while others—which Pou (2002, 326–27) suggests qualified as *vidyaṣrama*, centres of scientific learning of wide renown—trained a broader range of students, including master scribes. Somewhat incongruously, many technical subjects like engineering, architecture, or temple construction were missing, even though the construction of the new capital was being undertaken with vigour.

In contrast to the schools at the royal court (see subsequently), *āśrama* accepted students from beyond the court elite. The geographic origins of students are not specified, nor are the criteria according to which they were selected, but these institutions may have admitted students from far beyond the elite circle of princes and high Brahmins. A meritocratic academic system was used to reward and promote outstanding students, using material incentives such as chalk, ink, and other stationery (Cœdès 1989). The rules and regulations of the colleges indicate that students and teachers were surprisingly large in number (Cœdès 1989; Estève and Soutif 2010; Pou 2002). The colleges were run and managed by a rector (*kuladhyaksa*), most likely appointed by the king.[1] Residents—teachers and students alike—were fed and housed and received medical treatment when needed. Secular students and teachers lived side by side with novices and monks on these campuses, although all followed the rules of the Buddhist Sangha (Mookerji 1951; Cœdès 1989). Angkorian Yaśodharāśrama were not simply religious shrines but also educational centres that forged community.

Although inaugurated by a king devoted to Siva, the Yaśodharāśrama reflected the pluralistic character of Angkorian religious devotion, and different *āśrama* were devoted to Śaiva, Vaiṣṇava, and Buddhist disciplines. The inscriptions of Prasat Komnap (K. 701), Prasat Prei (K. 209), and Tep Pranam (K. 290) offer details[2] on the specific content of the teachings, mainly religious, dispensed in the enclosure of these university spaces (Cœdès 1932). The curriculum included the three Vedas, Sanskrit, grammar, and religious studies. The religious doctrines and philosophy taught included the Vaiṣṇava theory of Pancharatra as well as the doctrines of the *Śaivas* and *Pasupatas*—the latter being the oldest Śaivite sect, committed to asceticism. These sources also describe the means of subsistence of the teachers,[3] or payment from the students.

In a way, these early Angkorian colleges resembled small liberal colleges in the modern Western world. Given the number of Yaśodharāśrama that have been so far identified and their footprint on the ground, the quantity of students and teachers were no doubt limited; furthermore, as we have noted, the curriculum was also somewhat limited in scope. Nonetheless, these small colleges in Angkor, and especially the Buddhist one, may have served as a model for subsequent systems of higher education. By the time of King Jayavarman VII, three centuries later, these small institutions of teaching and learning had been replaced by genuine universities (Cœdès 1944; Chhem 2008).

The Monastic Universities of Jayavarman VII

The reign of Jayavarman VII (r. 1181 to 1220) represented the peak of Angkorian power and also a time of profound transition in the state religion from Brahmanism to Mahāyāna Buddhism (Cœdès, 1963). The two religions may have coexisted after that time, but the reign ushered in Tantric Mahāyāna Buddhism as a tool of the monarchy (Sharrock 2009). While Jayavarman VII became known for his contributions to the arts and sciences, he also valued medicine, which was taught and practised in large state temple complexes (Cœdès 1941b). Thousands of students and teachers were housed at their respective campuses in the late 12th-century temples of Ta Prohm and Preah Khan (e.g., Cœdès 1906, 1941a). The transfer of knowledge across the Empire was facilitated by the vast Angkorian Khmer road system, which was fitted with resting stops and temples at regular intervals and served to interconnect the elites in the capital to those ruling over its regional ceremonial centres (Hendrickson 2010, 2012). These temple complexes required a huge investment in sophisticated technical education in multiple trades and basic craftwork presumably taught in artisanal and technological workshops organised by the Cambodian equivalent of guilds (Cœdès 1940, 1941a; Polkinghorne 2013).

In the existing scholarship on Angkor we find several important studies on the monasteries and Buddhist temples of Jayavarman VII, most focusing on architectural characteristics of these structures: their location, their dimensions, and their iconography, which confirm their primarily Buddhist character while offering evidence for the continued cultivation of a pluralistic religious environment at Angkor and beyond (Stern 1965; Boisselier 1966; Glaize 1993, see also Estève 2023, this volume). Several important studies have focused on two inscriptions, the Preah Khan and Ta Prohm foundation stelae, whose extremely rich and detailed texts allow us to identify them as monastic universities and to better understand the administration of hospitals under Jayavarman VII. Yet these same foundation stelae remain silent on the functioning of community life within the royal monasteries, a silence that contrasts markedly with information from these same localities on, for example, foodstuffs and ritual offerings that are painstakingly described in inventories (Cœdès 1906, 1941a). No names of scholarly Brahmins or Buddhist monks who taught in these institutions are listed, nor are names of scholars of the Khmer royal court (Barth 1885, 64–72).

Despite these limitations, texts produced during the reign of Jayavarman VII reign are rich sources of information on the higher education system during this time, including data on medical training and practices specifically, even if few previous scholars have taken a great interest in the subject. Valuable insights can still be gleaned from them on different aspects of Angkorian society. For example, we think it likely that educational institutions were segregated by gender, since Jayavarman VII's first wife, Queen Indradevī, was appointed 'Professor-in-Chief' at a college that opened its campus only to women (Cœdès 1942). The foundation stela of Phimeanakas temple at Angkor indicates that Indradevi taught at places named Narendrāśrama and Tilakottara. Her teaching catered to a 'crowd' comprising women connected with the court. Many other questions remain to be addressed: Were the teachers all women? How were they selected? What were their academic qualifications? Did female students follow the same curricula as their male peers? These intriguing issues remain unanswered but present us with a compelling rationale for a deeper, multidisciplinary study of epigraphic data alongside archaeological evidence and other sources of evidence.

The Royal Court

In addition to the specialised institutions of teaching and learning, all of which were linked in some way or another to religious foundations, there were undoubtedly a wide range of formal and informal training and education taking place in secular contexts across the Angkorian World. Due to the ephemeral nature of Khmer material culture, especially in non-religious contexts, we lack direct evidence for the beliefs and practices of commoners. However, the inscriptions do provide some information in relation to education in the royal court.

The elite 'school' of tutorial classes organised within the Royal Palace provided Brahmanical education in religion, philosophy, governance, art, and architecture to selected members of the royal household and the children of high dignitaries, the majority of students being males. The pre-eminent Rajaguru served both as teacher and as advisor to the ruler (Chhem 2008). Inscription K. 842 from Banteay Srei is instructive about the educational system at the court of King Jayavarman V, showing that Yajñavaraha, the guru of the king, taught his younger brother Viṣṇu Kumara using knowledge that the guru had learned in turn from his father, the high priest Damodara of Angkor (Cœdès 1937, 153).

Sanskrit inscriptions from the Pre-Angkor and Angkor Periods provide considerable information about the content of this high-level curriculum. The Angkorian canon included textbooks or *śāstra* from various sources, including the Vedic literature, epics that provided religious and political ideologies (i.e., *Rāmāyana, Mahābhārata, Purānas*), and scientific literature that guided conduct and in some instances offered specific protocols (*Dharmaśāstra, Arthaśastra, Vyakarana, Brahmana, Nyaya, Vaisesika,* and *Saṃkhya*) (Sarkar 1968). K. 842 also states that the previously mentioned Yajñavaraha, an eminent 'savant' and physician, had a good command of the Mahabhasya (*yoga*) of Patañjali, the Vaisesika of Kanada, the Saṃkhya of Kapila, the Nyaya of Akṣapada or Gautama, Buddhism, medicine, music, and astrology (Cœdès 1937, 153; Chhem 2007b).

Although this inscription from Banteay Srei informs us that Yajñavaraha took care to attend to 'the poor, the disinherited, the blind, the weak, children, the elders, the sick or other unfortunate people crossing the ocean of suffering who flocked in his house everyday' (Cœdès 1937, 154; Chhem 2007a), we should underscore that the Angkorian system of higher education was geared primarily towards the education of elites. This fact is exemplified from the biography of Yajñavaraha, who describes 'a pattern of teaching [that] reflects the typical elite Brahmin education, where the teaching is reserved to a few: mainly the King himself, members of the royal house, or members of his own family' (Chhem 2007b).

As in India, therefore, the curriculum was utilitarian in that one of its ultimate goals was the grooming of young princes to succeed to the throne. Royal succession in Angkor was complex and not based on strict rules (Cœdès 1951); hence competition between many eligible princes in court in which the King had multiple wives and concubines was fierce. Because the Angkorian monarchy was theocratic, education required that a king be versed in religious and spiritual as well as administrative skills to provide him with both real and magical powers to effectively rule the kingdom. In sum, this closed-circuit elite education system offered a sustained and continuing power to kings, princes, Brahmins, and sometimes princesses to maintain supreme dynastic interests. The epigraphy mentions a few highly educated princesses who later became queens, such as Indradevi, a queen of Jayavarman VII, who, as we noted previously, is named in inscriptions as a 'professor' (Cœdès 1925).

Curriculum and Medium of Instruction

Having provided an overview of the three main areas where, according to the remaining evidence, medical instruction took place in the Angkorian World—*āśrama* in the early centuries of the Angkor Period, monastic universities from the 12th to 13th centuries onward, and Royal Palaces presumably throughout Angkor's history—it is worthwhile canvassing the evidence, primarily again drawn from inscriptions, for the curricular and pedagogical aspects of this system.

Traditions Derived From South Asia and the Buddhist World

Angkorian medical practice always took place in a pluralistic context, and epigraphic evidence from the public health system of Jayavarman VII (Finot 1903; Cœdès 1940) demonstrates that the curriculum reflected a mixture of Buddhist and Ayurvedic medicine (Chhem 2008). Fundamental texts of Sanskrit literature that were used by Angkorian scholars encompassed a rich tradition of scientific, technical, philosophical, and religious teaching that include the *vyakarana* 'grammar', *sabdasastra* or *sabdavidya* 'science of sound' or *sabda* 'sound', the judicial treatise Dharmaśāstra, the four vedas (*ṛigveda, yajurveda, samaveda,* and *atharvaveda*), the epics Mahābhārata and Rāmāyana, the Śaiva scriptures, and the texts of *Purāna*. Common textbooks were also mentioned in the Khmer epigraphy such as the *guhya, dharmmasastra, nayottara, vinasikha, viṣṇudharmma, vyakarana, siksa, sirascheda, sammoha,* and *siddhanta* (Chhom 2018). Three of them, *dharmmasastra, vyakarana,* and *siksa*, are generic names of scientific topics, while the rest are composed of religious texts. The expression *svat vrah dharmasastra*, 'to recite the sacred judicial text', was common in practice in the legal system of the kingdom. The expression *vraḥ dharmasastra* could be a Khmer version of the original *dharmasastra* in Sanskrit. It is possible that some Sanskrit manuscripts were translated into vernacular Khmer language to reach out to beginners and novices. Non-Sanskrit manuscripts may also have been used in schools, but they were not recorded as inscriptions (Chhom 2016, 124). Taken together, this body of work, in both Sanskrit and Khmer languages, represents the corpus of scientific knowledge in the Angkorian World, within which medical knowledge was encoded and reproduced.

Medical education emphasised medical diagnosis, specifically the classification of diseases, using physical and magico-religious methods. Contemporary texts from across the Buddhist world written in Sanskrit and other languages (Birnbaum 1989, 244) underscore the universality of the theory of four elements—earth, water, fire, and wind—that may be found in most Buddhist countries today, including in Cambodia (Beyer 1907, 3; Halpern 1963, 196; Mulholland 1979; Chhem 2001). A total of 404 illnesses may therefore be diagnosed, with each element acting as the source of 101 individual ailments (Demiéville, 1985, 7; Chhem, 2001, 13).

Examination of the pulse was further introduced through the *Bhaiṣajyaguru* sūtra and served to enrich the Ayurvedic treatises taught within Buddhist monasteries (Renou and Filliozat, 2001, 158–59). Urine analysis would have been another important diagnostic tool, with practitioners basing their treatments on traits such as taste and colour (Leclère 1894, 397; Benazet 1932, 34; Huard 1963, 3275). In addition to these two types of clinical examination, Khmer doctors of the time would have learned to examine the skin to make a qualitative assessment of body temperature.

Even if documentary evidence for the medical curriculum at Angkor is sparse, there are other useful cultural analogues, particularly from South Asia. If we subscribe to the notion that the Nalanda and Vikramaśila universities in India may have provided an archetype for higher education at the time (Chhem 2006), we may assume that medical science was taught according to the classification of the Āyurveda across eight disciplines: *śalya* (the treatment of wounds), *śalyaka* (the art of acupuncture), *kāyacikitsā* (the treatment of diseases of the body), *bhūta-vidyā* (treatment of demonic illnesses), *kaumāra-bṛhtya* (the treatment of children), *agada* (antidotes), *rasāyana* (treatments to prolong life, or alchemy), and *Vagikarana* (methods to strengthen the limbs and the body) (I-Tsing 1998, 222). A comparative review of medical texts from Tibetan, Indian, Chinese, and Cambodian sources confirms at least the practice of alchemy, of paediatrics, and of the treatment of demonic illnesses and physical illness (Filliozat 1937; Ang 1992; Chhem 2005).

The Blending of South Asian, East Asian, and Indigenous Elements

Angkorian inscriptions derive from formal contexts such as *āśrama* and monasteries and therefore remain silent on the question of vernacular, magico-religious methods rooted in the supernatural, although one can assume that they also had a role to play in diagnosis and treatment, just as they did in Buddhist contexts across East Asia (Demiéville 1985, 87), where Buddhist medicine classifies illnesses according to six principal causes: those caused by disturbances in the four elements, dietary imbalances, deficiencies in the practise of meditation, diseases caused by demonic spirits (comprising diseases of the body), diseases of the demon-lord Māra specifically (comprising diseases of the spirit), and finally diseases of karmic order caused by bad actions in either past lives or the present life.

This overarching Buddhist aetiology would have been interpreted within the framework of traditional Khmer medicine and taught above all using that specific cultural context (Finot 1903, 31; Filliozat 1964, 28; Mulholland 1979; Chhem 2001, 12). In that context, climate and seasonal variability is seen as the origin of other diseases: In stanza XV of the Say-Fong stele, the king Jayavarman VII directly attributes illness to harmful effects caused by the passage of time (Finot 1903, 31).

Chinese sources also describe deep roots for Khmer medical knowledge (Lin 1935). Tang dynastic sources tell of a 7th-century CE Indian Tantric Buddhist monk named Punyodaya, who was sent by the Chinese emperor to collect rare herbs at Angkor and to learn from local monks in the monasteries. Punyodaya found the Khmers so congenial that he stayed for four years. After returning to Chang'an to complete his mission for the emperor, a Khmer delegation travelled to the Chinese capital to plead for his return, and he spent his remaining years in Cambodia. Punyodaya likely had close contact with Khmer court physicians, monks, and local healers engaged in the hospital network (Lin 1935). During his stay, it was likely that active exchange of *materia medica* (knowledge of the therapeutic properties of particular substances) may have operated between the institutionalised medical education system at the royal court and monasteries, alongside knowledge brought in by local healers from cities and villages across the Empire.

Pedagogy

Finally, we know little about pedagogical methods at these institutions. Perhaps, once again, an analogy can be made to Buddhist educational institutions in ancient India, so long as we proceed with caution. In that context, Guruge (1983, 115–25) argues that the pedagogy was focused on individual training. Dialogue and debate were an integral part of teaching methods, and the use of visual aids would have been routine. Formal methods of learning also revolved around rote learning of words and texts, as well as mastering calligraphy and elocution. Analysis of each of these elements may have a useful role to play in future research on teaching methods of the universities of Angkor; for the time being, however, we have no particular evidence—either written or iconographic—of how medical knowledge was transferred, with the sole exception of a panel in the bas-reliefs of the Bayon temple at Angkor, which shows a group of medical students gathering around a master who is in the process of examining a patient.

Medical Treatments in the Angkorian World

Having established in broad terms where medical training took place; the content of the instruction; and how medical knowledge was stored, reproduced, and transferred from teachers to students, it is worth considering what medical treatment and health care in general actually consisted of in the Angkorian World. How was the medical expertise detailed previously operationalised in practice for the benefit and well-being of Angkorian society—and for whom exactly?

A first point to note is that medical knowledge was deployed not only for the practice of medicine with a view to healing patients but also for identifying certain diseases which would make candidates unfit to be ordained as monks. Thus, medical examinations were held for candidates for ordination in order to exclude those affected by disorders such as leprosy, abscesses, skin diseases, tuberculosis, or convulsions (Davids and Oldenberg 1990, 230; Traipiṭaka 1994, 306). Monks charged with undertaking such kinds of examinations would have needed a certain amount of training, equipment, and skill to successfully carry them out. However, we do not know if these examinations were universally performed or how effective they may have been.

By and large, however, Angkorian therapeutic techniques used three primary methods: pharmaceuticals, surgery, and magical treatments associated with alchemy. Two particular medical practices, pulse-taking and alchemy through the use of sulphur mercury or cinnabar, are the signature of the broader Asian *Bhaiṣajyaguru* medical tradition (Chhem 2005, 2017) which as we have noted was also prominent in the Angkorian context. Unfortunately, we once again face here a dearth of historical and archaeological evidence, with only some clues from the inscriptional record. At the very least, it is likely that the practical methods described in the following, such as pulse-taking and the preparation of medicinal unguents, were very specialised tasks that required a long apprenticeship at the teacher's house, *āśrama*, or a specific compound in the monastic universities that we described in the previous section.

Alchemy and Pulse-Taking

Although Ayurveda was the principal medical tradition from Pre-Angkorian times, alchemy using sulphur mercury and pulse-taking was the dominant diagnostic and therapeutic method employed by physicians at Angkorian hospitals (Chhem 2005). Alchemy was also recognised through its religious dimension as a method of lengthening life. At least some Angkorian Khmers by the time of Jayavarman VII viewed alchemy as the key to immortality. The Sanskrit inscription from Say-Fong (Laos) notes, in stanza X: 'Seeing that the earth, which his wisdom had transformed to a heaven, was oppressed by death, he indicated ambrosia remedies for the immortality of mortals' (Finot 1903, 30).

Pharmaceuticals

Within the *Mahāvagga*, a group of texts making up a part of the Buddhist canon, the *Bhaiṣajyaguru khaṇḍaka* ('section on remedies') describes pharmaceutical treatments used in Buddhist monasteries (Davids and Oldenberg 1990, 41–145; Traipiṭaka 1994, 221–331). It evokes five classical remedies (butter, butter clarified, oil, honey, and molasses), all five of which are also evoked repeatedly in Angkorian inscriptions, including those from the universities of Preah Khan and Ta Prohm (Chhem 2005, 9) and the foundation stelae of several hospitals (Finot 1903). Indeed, the *materia medica* of plants and minerals are dominant in the long list of medicinal provisions specified on the Ta Prohm inscription indicating that this vast pharmacopoeia, and its associated uses, was likely also part of the curriculum taught at monastic universities. Furthermore, at least three foundation inscriptions from *āśrama* in the Angkor region (Cœdès 1989, 255) mention 'medical services' involving food and medicines being provided to inhabitants of the *āśrama* and to doctors.[4]

During a visit to Angkor in 1296–7, the Mongol Chinese envoy Zhou Daguan reported that cinnabar—red mercury sulfide, likely from China—was available at markets in Angkor (Pelliot 1951). Through analysis of a large bas-relief on the Western Gallery of Banteay Chhmar temple complex, in which we can see filled sacks similar to those still used today for medicinal herbs blessing in Tibet, Sharrock also demonstrated that this temple served as a venue for a 'medicine blessing ceremony' under the direct patronage of King Jayavarman VII (Sharrock and Jacques 2017). In Angkorian Cambodia, as in Tibet today, a dense mixture of herbs was probably used to treat a variety of illnesses. Studies of plants listed in foundation stones, combined with palaeobotanical analysis from recent archaeological excavations at Angkorian hospitals, may eventually offer further insight into the Angkorian pharmacopoeia.

Surgery

Minor surgery may also have been practised, as the *Vinaya Piṭaka* mentions the use of lancets and scalpels (Davids and Oldenberg, 1990, 41–145; Traipiṭaka 1994, 221–380). Such instruments have not yet been identified in the archaeological record or in medical manuscripts (Chhem

2007a, 120). More recent research on traditional Khmer medicine suggests that Angkorian doctors may have been trained in certain surgical techniques, like abdominal surgery for penetrating wounds and removing gallbladder stones (Norodom 1929; Huard 1963, 3441). Immobilising fractured and broken limbs could also have been part of Angkorian medical treatment. Certainly surgical texts like the *Suśruta* were known since the 10th century (Barth 1885), and advanced surgical techniques were practised by this time in contemporary South Asia (Sharma 1999, 259–66).

Geography, Structure, and Functioning of Medical Institutions

Having established the texts and intellectual traditions of Angkorian medicine, and following our brief survey of how that knowledge was reproduced, transferred, and operationalised in practise, it is worth turning our attention to the broader architectural, geographic, social, legal, and political implications of medical infrastructure across the Khmer Empire. In the discussion that follows, we deal with the two major categories of public health systems for which we have the most evidence: the great temple-monasteries at the urban core of Angkor that may be described as 'universities', and the *āśrama* and hospitals that we find not only at Angkor but also scattered around the Empire.

Epigraphic data inform us about the names of the founders of these temples: the monarch, and sometimes his family and his entourage; the surnames of priests and ministers are also sometimes given. In terms of their internal functioning, ethnographic analogy from contemporary Buddhist monasteries, alongside data from inscriptions, offers insights on the educational system that operated in these establishments, as we have detailed (Cœdès 1989). They also provide insight on the functioning of these spaces beyond their purely educational roles, although only to a limited extent for the temple-monasteries of Jayavarman VII (Chhem 2007a). Earlier inscriptions from the āśramas, however, are particularly informative concerning internal regulations of Angkorian religious institutions, the hierarchy of academic and spiritual values and that of the disciplines taught, the protocol for welcoming the king and of his family, the disciplinary rules that governed students and professors alike, the methods of promotion of the professors, and their academic and religious power.

Temple-Monasteries

Even if the style of pre-modern Buddhist monasteries varies considerably across time and space (Pichard and Lagirarde 2003), the basic organisation of these spaces remains relatively uniform, since common religious, educational, and residential functions shape their design and construction. In most cases, including in the Angkorian World, the monastery consists of a central sanctuary (in our case of stone), annex sanctuaries, certain halls for ceremonies and others for education, a room for copies of manuscripts, a library, a basin for water, a residential structure for monks with annexes such as the kitchen and the dining hall, and sanitary facilities.

We focus our study of the monasteries of Ta Prohm and Preah Khan, the two largest and most important centres of the Angkorian capital, each covering between 50 to 60 hectares; the Bayon is excluded from our discussion for lack of information, although it is possible that it, too, was a monastic university. One may suggest that the sheer size of the monasteries at Angkor—unusual for monasteries of this period elsewhere—is indicative of the broader influence of Ta Prohm and Preah Khan in the teaching of Mahāyāna Buddhism across Southeast Asia in the 12th century. Each of these monasteries was developed according to an identical plan, surrounded by three concentric enclosures offering open space in between.

Recent lidar survey and excavation have confirmed that these monasteries were embedded within the urban fabric of the central Angkor area (Evans et al. 2013). The discovery of structured residential areas within the outer enclosure walls (Carter et al. 2018) confirmed earlier notions (based on discoveries of wooden remains and roof tiles) that open spaces within temple enclosures were occupied and populated by huts, chapels, and other ephemeral infrastructure (Groslier 1921, 321; Glaize 1993, 219). Not only did each of these monastic universities host Buddhist monks (some of whom were also teachers) but also thousands of students and members of laity and yogis, practitioners of Tantric Buddhism who engaged in deep and protracted meditation (Keown 2004). Carter et al. describe the state of the art of our knowledge of Ta Prohm in a recent paper as follows:

> The inscription [K. 273, of Ta Prohm] notes a total of 79,365 people who serviced the temple, including people of Khmer, Burmese, and Cham ethnicities (some of whom may have been prisoners of war), as well as 18 high priests, 2740 officials, 2232 assistants, and 615 dancers. Overall, 12,640 individuals were directly associated with the functions of the temple. Notably, the inscription describes 1409 students and their lecturers as residents . . . it is not clear if others affiliated with the temple also lived within the enclosure. Items associated with life at the temple are also mentioned, including bedspreads, cushions, mosquito nets, and 'Chinese beds of grass'. . . . Additionally, large quantities of perishable goods are itemized, some of which were supplied by the state and surrounding villages, which have thus far been invisible in the archaeological record. These include sesame, rice, black pepper, honey, wax and wax candles, kidney beans, clarified butter, yogurt, and milk. These details provide tantalizing clues to aspects of life that are not readily visible and require careful sub-surface archaeological investigations.
>
> (2018, 4)

In addition to providing extensive information about the internal organisation of the temple-monastery, the epigraphic record from Ta Prohm also offers insight into the role of the temple at the centre of a vast network of infrastructure in which roads connected far-flung parts of the Empire—populated with *āśrama*, hospitals, rest houses, and other specialised installations—to the geographic, religious, and educational centre at Angkor.

Hospitals

The dedicatory inscription K. 273 of Ta Prohm temple in Angkor states that 102 hospitals were constructed by 1186. A recent survey across modern Cambodia, Thailand, and Laos has documented this large network of hospitals built during the reign of King Jayavarman VII (Figure 16.1), with hospitals situated approximately 40 km from each other (Multzer o'Naghten 2014). A study of the standard layout of hospital compounds (Figure 16.2) shows that there were two central Buddhist shrines of stone. Wooden buildings and roof tiles have also been found around the masonry shrines, but the precise nature of other structures associated with this masonry infrastructure is unclear at this point.

As we can see in the plan, the gate of the largest shrine opened to the east, while the gate of the smaller one faced west. The shrines are surrounded by an enclosure wall, with the main entrance facing toward the east. A pond was always present within the walled shrines. The stelae of the hospital foundations states that the king 'erected a Buddha of healing, accompanied by the two sons of the Buddha, to permanently assuage the suffering of his subjects'. This is the

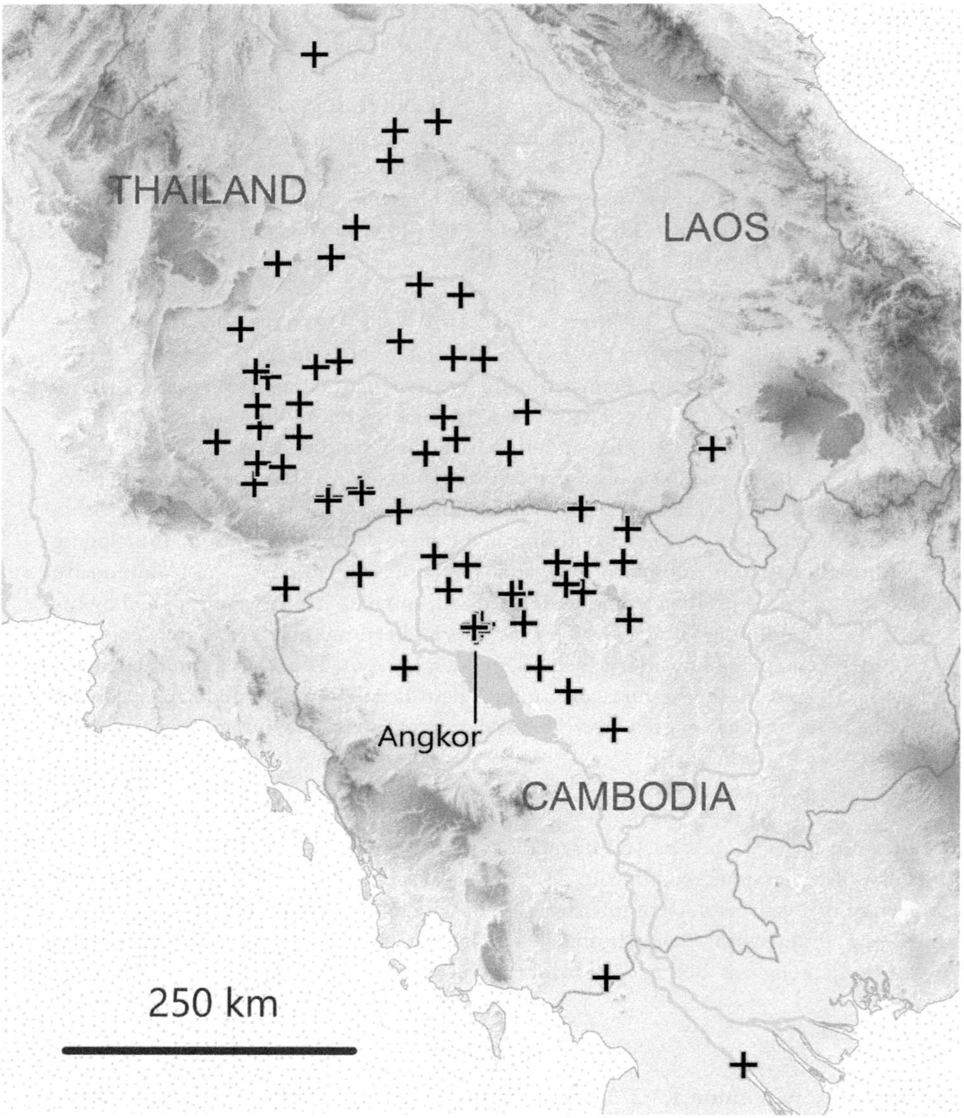

Figure 16.1 Distribution of Jayavarman VII hospital chapels.

Medicine Buddha (Bhaiṣajyaguru) flanked by two Bodhisattvas, *Candravairocana* and *Suryavairocana*, 'two destroyers of illness' (Sharrock and Jacques 2017). This triad (see example in Lavy and Polkinghorne 2022, figure 4) shows that the practice of medicine during that period was placed under the religious patronage of the Bhaiṣajyaguru, the Buddhist 'Master of Remedies' whose cult originated in ancient Central Asia then spread across ancient China to ancient Korea, Japan, Vietnam, Champa, Bagan, and Angkor (Birnbaum 1989; Chhem 2005). Pedestals for the emplacement of three stone statues representing this religious triad have been located near the hospital shrines, and numerous examples of stone triads from excavation and survey of these sites are found in the provincial museums of northeast Thailand. The iconography of the

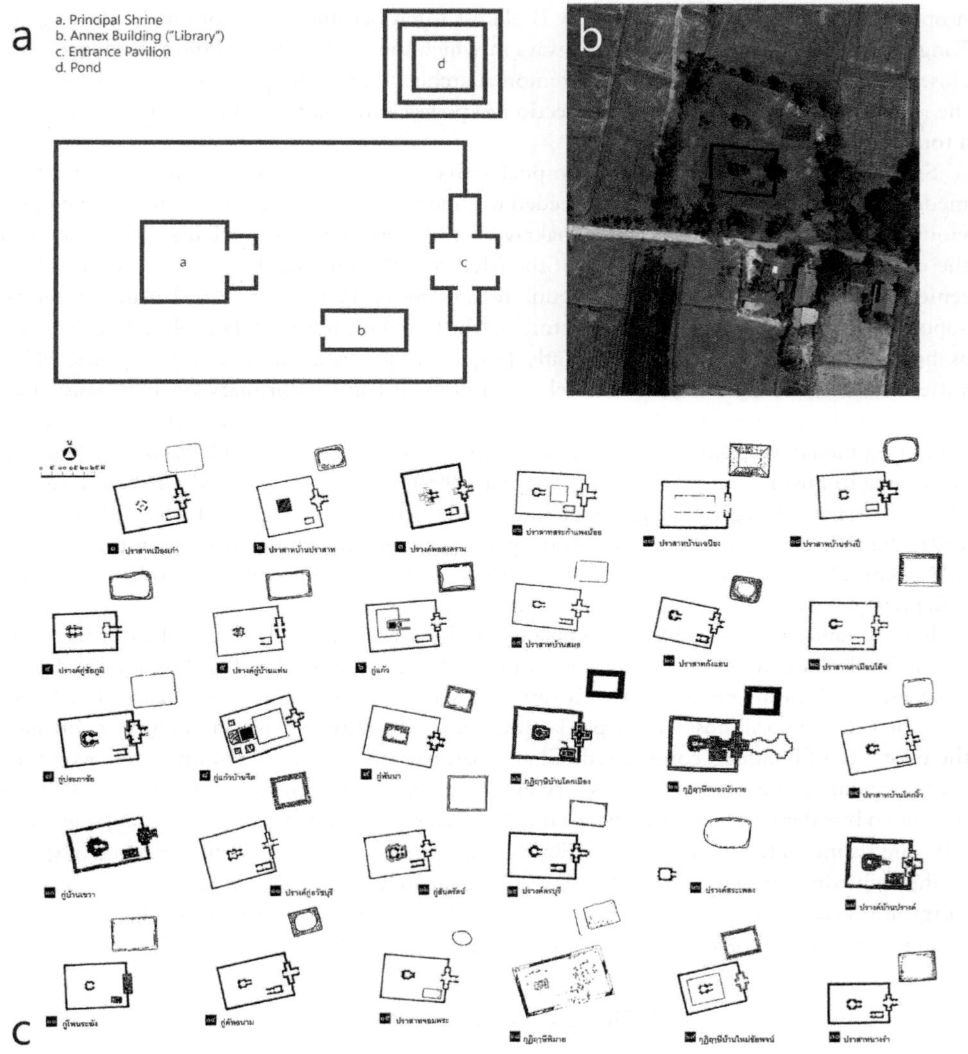

Figure 16.2 Organisation of Jayavarman VII hospital chapels: a) schematic hospital chapel plan (based on Dagens (2003, 282); b) aerial view of the hospital chapel Prasat Ku Phanna, in Sakon Nakhon Province, Thailand (Image courtesy of Maxar Technologies and Google Earth); c) architectural footprints of hospital chapels in Northeast Thailand.

Source: (Based on Luealamai 2004, 72–73).

Cambodian Bhaiṣajyaguru has been further explored by Woodward (2011) and Sharrock (2017) based on a bronze triad located in New York and on similar artefacts found in provincial Thai museums. These images each show Bhaiṣajyaguru with *vajra* (thunderbolt) and *gantha* (bell) crossed at the chest and the two Bodhisattvas holding cylinders (presumably for herbs or minerals). These postures and instruments of the Cambodian medical triad are unique in the Buddhist world. The presumed presence of Bhaiṣajyaguru holding vajra and gantha at the shrines of the hospitals is more evidence of an Esoteric Buddhist Vajrayana cult at Angkor during the reign of King Jayavarman VII and illustrates the ways in which the symbolism of Tantric Buddhism was closely intertwined with public and ceremonial architecture in the provision of health care in the reign of Jayavarman VII. This intersection of power, symbolism, and public infrastructure is a topic that we shall return to later.

Some details of Jayavarman VII's hospital system, particularly its inventory of personnel, medicinal plants, and other resources needed to support the facilities, have been described previously (Cœdès 1941a; Jacques 1968; Chakravarti 1979). More recent work has concentrated on the number of hospitals, iconography of the Medicine Buddha (Bhaiṣajyaguru) and his master remedies (*sūtra*), and diagnostic/therapeutic techniques (Chhem 2005, 2017). Administrators, appointed by the monastic university rector, ran the hospitals, at least at Ta Prohm. Hospital size, as measured by staff size, varied significantly. Jacques (1968) distinguishes four categories, which varied in size from 50 to 200 personnel. Each hospital had two primary doctors, assisted by nurses, 'warehouse' personnel (who supervised sorting and storage), and 'pickers' responsible for harvesting medicinal plants that were likely cultivated on hospital grounds (Jacques 1968, 20). According to Suśruta's surgical treatise (Sharma, 1999), nurses were selected for their kindness, physical strength, caregiving skills, endurance, and obedience to doctors (Leslie and Wujastyk 1991, 28). We do not know the names of specific doctors, but those working in the hospitals of Angkor Thom bore the title of *rĪjyavaidyaka*, with a royal suffix, while the others are called *bhisaj* (Jacques 1968, 17).

Recent (and as yet unpublished) archaeological excavations at the sites of Jayavarman VII's hospitals offer new insights. We can now confirm the structure of the chapel hospital and of its annexes, which in the end corresponds very well with previous architectural analyses that have described the 'typical' hospital chapel layout. These excavations have in addition confirmed the existence of buildings constructed of light materials, such as wood, around and beyond the central sanctuary. The remaining masonry buildings appear to be the religious 'chapel' elements of a much broader complex made of less durable materials, in much the same way as Jayavarman VII's fire shrines (Hendrickson 2008). Finally, excavations have revealed the existence of graves in the immediate vicinity of the hospital. Unfortunately, they did not uncover any artefacts (surgical instruments or materials intended for alchemy, for example) that may have informed us about the medical practices of the time (Pottier et al. 2006; 2008).

Medicine in Service of the State

In addition to the explicit function of the public health system of the Angkorian era, there were also important symbolic and political dimensions to the construction of such infrastructure networks in the Angkorian World. Investments in *āśramas*, universities that taught medical theory and practice, and an extensive hospital system were surely not motivated solely by the benevolence of a ruler and his concern for the health and well-being of his subjects. This leads us to ask: How was this system used by the kings of Angkor to enhance their legitimacy and prestige and to project and consolidate power over their subjects across an Empire that spanned much of the Southeast Asian mainland? In what ways do major milestones in the development of the public health system correspond with major social, cultural, and political changes in the Angkorian World?

Before the reign of Jayavarman VII, court Brahmins held a virtual monopoly on esoteric knowledge such as medicine, alchemy, and the like, and this was a source of tremendous religious, political, and economic power (Sarka 1968). This knowledge and its transmission were acutely restricted and circulated through a system of privileges established at the royal court. The 12th century, however, was a period of profound change and upheaval in the Angkorian World, which included shifts in the 'state religion' promoted by kings and incredibly ambitious programs of urban renewal and expansion and in its final decades saw the capital overrun and held by an enemy for the first time in the Empire's history before it was retaken by forces led by Jayavarman VII in 1181. Undoubtedly this was accompanied by challenges to longstanding structures of elite power and afforded opportunities for restructuring Angkorian society according to new and quite different power dynamics.

Out of this tumultuous context, Jayavarman VII ascended to the leadership of a newly resurgent Khmer Empire. In contrast to most of the previous kings of Angkor, who were devoted to Śiva or Viṣṇu—and whose legitimacy drew substantially on centering themselves as keepers of the royal cult and as the point of articulation between the sacred and profane—the adoption of a more personal, reflexive, inwardly focused religion such as Buddhism presented both challenges and opportunities for Jayavarman VII.

Inspired by Mahāyāna Buddhism, this monarch used two complementary strategies. The first was to promote the worship of Buddha and the Bodhisattvas, particularly those which recognise medicine like Avalokiteşvara (Finot 1925) and the Bhaiṣajyaguru (Birnbaum 1989; Chhem 2005). Supplementing the spread of the cult of these two compassionate deities was the promotion of *Prajñāpārāmita sūtra*, the 'perfection in wisdom' blessing, which granted rulers supernatural powers that protected their kingdoms against calamities (especially diseases and epidemics). Monarchs—not the monks or commoners—were obliged to conserve, protect, read, listen to, and explain the Prajñāpārāmita sūtra because only monarchs were invested with celestial power that established the Dharma (Conze 1974, 176–78). Monks and doctors, in turn, learned the Prajñāpārāmita sūtra to complement their medical expertise in treating the sick. But royal strength, derived from the Dharma, was needed to care for the populace when epidemics arrived. Medical knowledge transmitted to Angkorian 'doctors' thus reinforced the sovereign's power, and he in turn supported these doctors in health interventions across his kingdom. Health, power, and religion were in this way artfully interwoven on political and cultural levels in the 12th–13th-century Angkorian World.

At first glance, this political strategy seems to contrast singularly with the spread of the Buddhist faith. Jayavarman VII would have made a change of paradigm in upsetting the very foundations of Angkorian monarchy, offering a transition from an official and somewhat brutal model of Devarāja ('god-king') to one of Buddharāja (Buddha-king) and establishing by then even the Buddhism Mahāyāna as religion of state In fact, this upheaval sought to minimise the power of the Brahmins established at the royal court, Brahmins whose offices were hereditary and who had probably played a major role in the illegitimate successions of the beginning of the tumultuous 12th century.

Emerging from that context, Jayavarman VII's universities reflect a period of expansion radiating an intellectual and religious transformation that was unmatched in the history of Angkor. The large size and accessibility of his monastic universities located in the heart of Angkor, for example, contrasted sharply with small āśrama founded three centuries earlier that accommodated a small elite of the kingdom's capital and key provinces. The advanced health system of Jayavarman VII in the 12th to 13th centuries CE may also be seen, in one sense, as an inspired gift to win the support of his subjects. His philosophy, as inscribed in foundation stones outside each of hospitals read: *'The suffering of men's bodies became for him the suffering of the soul, which is much more; for the grief of kings is the suffering of their subjects, and not their own'* (Sharrock and Jacques 2017, 227). As a Buddhist king, and in contrast to his largely Hindu predecessors, Jayavarman

VII drew legitimacy from his benevolence, compassion, and degree of care for his subjects, all of which were conspicuously on display in the historical and iconographic records of his reign:

> He suffered from the illnesses of his subjects more than his own: for it is public pain which causes the pain of kings, and not their own pain.
>
> (Finot 1903, 30, St XIII)

This stanza, taken from the stele of the hospital of Say-Fong, founded by Jayavarman VII, evokes the spirit of 'compassionate' Buddhism, which inspired Buddhist monarchs to open hospitals (Filliozat 1934, 303; Cœdès 1941a; Thapar 1997, 231) in populated areas, along trade routes, and in the centre of royal cities (Liu 1988, 107). The foundation of these charitable institutions, however, was ideally achieved when political and economic conditions were sufficiently stable and in a religious environment in which the prevailing faith recognised the spiritual value of the act, which in turn provided not only spiritual but also material benefits to the population. And in this context, 'if religion served to advance medicine by multiplying the number of hospitals, then [religion] gained in return a powerful instrument of proselytism' (Filliozat 1934, 305). We should therefore think of this program as, at the same time, both an instrument of proselytism and also as an instrument for political, religious, and cultural unification deployed by Jayavarman VII, who:

> by the warriors—the doctors—versed in the science of arms—of medicine . . . destroyed the enemies that infested his kingdom—the disease—by means of these weapons: the cures.
>
> (Finot 1903, St XIII)

In a more global context, we should note that what Jayavarman VII achieved here was not without precedent. We note the example of the Emperor Asoka of India (Thapar 1997, 144), who also drew his legitimacy from Buddhism and thus established a politico-religious alliance featuring prominent members of the Buddhist monastic order. It was equally possible for Jayavarman VII to spread Buddhism among the people by sponsoring in particular a system of open monastic universities, democratising access not only to the spiritual domain but also to scientific knowledge.

This agenda, a defining characteristic of the reign of Jayavarman VII, led to the dissemination of knowledge and technical skills, with monasteries functioning as official centres of higher education and also places for organising labour to complete the massive projects of public infrastructure within the capital. Providing work to the temple also served to generate merit for the individual and thus benefitted lay and elite within the Angkorian World. It was in these monasteries that religious and secular education was provided to train monks, doctors, engineers, artisans, architects, and artists, thus providing the human resources required for the expansion and consolidation of an ascendant Khmer Empire. In this way, the links established and maintained between the monarch and the Buddhist clergy helped to articulate a new system of values and knowledge in the form of Mahāyāna Buddhism even as they helped to build and reinforce a particular social and economic order.

Jayavarman VII was able to leverage Buddhism to propagate political and religious beliefs through an elaborate network of temples, monasteries, universities, and hospitals with a relatively consistent and uniform identity, through which the population of the kingdom could be brought into the fold (Chhem, 2007a). Whenever undertaking this consolidation of power over the terrestrial realm, Jayavarman VII took great care to infuse the notion of his cosmic power, as we can clearly see in the symbolism of his many architectural works (Stern 1965, 185–89).

Conclusion

As we learn from the chapters in this volume, Angkor and its Empire reached its political, economic, and geographic zenith in the 12th century CE. The statecraft that enabled this depended on education and literacy across a range of fields that included religious treatises and medical treatments. Education in these subjects was not strictly limited for elites in the Angkorian court; rather, scholarship was widely shared through educational institutions. The foundations for this system were in place by the 10th century CE with the formalisation of a network of *āśrama*, which, although limited in number and capacity, set the stage for the emergence of the vast system of public health and education developed by Jayavarman VII three centuries later.

In conclusion, studying the Angkorian university system under Jayavarman VII offers a valuable window for understanding Angkor's rise or resurgence to regional dominance in the 12th to 13th centuries CE, and also to measure the impact—both religious and socio-political—of Mahāyāna Buddhism on societies across the Angkorian World. Medical training was deeply interwoven into the Mahāyāna Buddhist monastic codes, and our analysis of this material illustrates the myriad ways in which education was embedded in, and of great importance to, state religious centres and to the successful functioning of the Angkorian state. Work on this material is ongoing, and for the moment, inscriptional and archaeological evidence for medical practice in the Angkorian World can be frustratingly sparse; nonetheless, we have shown here that, even by drawing on the limited sources available, we are able to cast some light into the everyday structure and functioning of the Buddhist monasteries of Jayavarman VII and explore the specific ways in which religion and the state articulated in early Cambodia.

Notes

1 See inscriptions Prasat Komnap K. 701 St LII; Prasat Prei K. 209 St LI; Tep Pranam K. 290 St XLVII.
2 See inscriptions Prasat Komnap K. 701 St LXI–LXII; Prasat Prei K. 209 St LX–LXI; Tep Pranam K. 290 St LVII–LVIII 10.
3 See inscriptions Prasat Komnap K. 701 St LXXV–LXXXVIII; Prasat Prei K. 209 St LXXIII–LXXIII–LXXXVIII; Tep Pranam K. 290 St LXII–LXXXVII.
4 See inscriptions Prasat Komnap K. 701 St St LXV; Prasat Prei K. 209 St LXIV; Tep Pranam K. 290 St LXI.

References

Ang, C., 1992. Apports indiens à la médecine traditionnelle khmère: considérations préliminaires. *Journal of European Ayurvedic Society* 2, 101–13.

Barth, A., 1885. *Inscriptions sanscrites du cambodge.* Paris: Imprimerie nationale.

Benazet, A., 1932. *De quelques pratiques de la médecine indigène chez les Cambodgiens.* Paris: Société d'ethnographie de Paris.

Beyer, C., 1907. About Siamese medicine. *Journal of the Siam Society* 4, 1–9.

Birnbaum, R., 1989. *The Healing Buddha.* Boston: Shambala.

Boisselier, J., 1966. *Asie du Sud-Est: 1. Le Cambodge.* Paris: Picard.

Bronkhorst, J., 2011. The spread of Sanskrit in Southeast Asia, in *Early Interactions between South and Southeast Asia: Reflections on Cross-Cultural Exchange*, eds. P.-Y. Manguin, A. Mani, and G. Wade, Singapore: ISEAS-Yusof Ishak Institute, 264–75.

Carter, A., P. Heng, M. Stark, R. Chhay & D. Evans, 2018. Urbanism and residential patterning in Angkor. *Journal of Field Archaeology* 43(6), 492–506.

Chakravarti, A., 1979. Traditional medicine and health services of ancient Cambodia with special references to the time of Jayavarman VII (A.D. 1181–1220*). The South Asian Review* 3(2), 39–52.

Chhem R.K., 2001. Les doctrines médicales khmères: nosologie et méthodes diagnostiques. *Siksacakr* 3, 12–15.

Chhem, R.K., 2005. Bhaiṣajyaguru and tantric medicine in Jayavarman VII hospitals. *Siksācakr* 7, 8–18.
Chhem, R.K., 2006. La médecine angkorienne sous Jayavarman VII (1180–1220 A.D.). Académie des Inscriptions et Belles-Lettres, *Société Asiatique*, Institut de France, Paris (France), 11 Novembre.
Chhem, R.K., 2007a. La médecine au service du pouvoir angkorien: Universités monastiques, transmission du savoir et formation médicale sous le règne de Jayavarman VII (1181–1220 A.D.). *Canadian Journal of Buddhist Studies* 3, 95–124.
Chhem, R.K., 2007b. *Yajñavaraha in Dictionary of Medical Biography, volume 5*, eds. W. F. Bynum and Helen Bynum. Westport: Greenwood Press, 1331–32.
Chhem, R.K., 2008. *Médecine et santé à Angkor: pouvoir royal, compassion et offre médicale sous le règne de Jayavarman VII (1181–1220).* PhD dissertation. Montréal: University of Montréal.
Chhem, R.K., 2017. In quest of Angkorian medicine Buddha and bodhisattva: new archaeological evidence. *Journal of Southeast Asian Studies* 22(1), 128–38.
Chhem, R.K, & M. Antelme, 2004. A Khmer medical text, 'The treatment of the four diseases' manuscript. *Siksâcakr* 6, 33–42 (version khmère, 107–122).
Chhom, K., 2016. *Le rôle du sanskrit dans le développement de la langue khmère: une étude épigraphique du VIe au XIVe siècle.* PhD dissertation. Paris: École Pratique des Hautes Études.
Chhom, K., 2018. *Le Rôle Du Sanskrit Dans Le Développement De La Langue Khmère: Une Étude Épigraphique Du Vie Au Xive Siècle.* Phnom Penh: Sastra Publishing House.
Cœdès, G., 1906. La stèle de Ta-Prohm, *Bulletin de l'École française d'Extrême-Orient Tome* 6, 33–42.
Cœdès, G., 1925. Phimeanakas, Inscriptions d'angkor. *Bulletin de l'École française d'Extrême-Orient* 25, 372–92.
Cœdès, G., 1932. Études Cambodgiennes: 30. À la recherche du Yaśodharāśrama. *Bulletin de l'École française d'Extrême-Orient* 32, 84–112.
Cœdès, G., 1937. Stèles de prasat khna et mlu prey, in *Inscriptions du Cambodge, volume I.* Hanoi: École française d'Extrême-Orient, 195–219.
Cœdès, G., 1940. Les hôpitaux de jayavarman VII. *Bulletin de l'École française d'Extrême-Orient* 344–47.
Cœdès, G., 1941a. IV. La stèle du práḥ khan d'aṅkor. *Bulletin de l'École française d'Extrême-Orient* 41(1), 255–302.
Cœdès, G., 1941b. L'assistance médicale au Cambodge ancien a la fin du XIIème siècle. *Revue médicale française d'Extrême-Orient* 405–15.
Cœdès, G., 1942. Inscriptions du Cambodge, volume II. *Hanoi: École française d'Extrême-Orient*, 195–219.
Cœdès, G., 1944. *Histoire ancienne des États hindouisés d'Extrême-Orient.* Hanoi: Imprimerie d'Extrême-Orient.
Cœdès, G., 1951. Les règles de la succession royale danse l'ancien Cambodge. *Bulletin de la Société d'Études Indochinoises* 26(2), 117–30.
Cœdès, G., 1963. *Angkor: An Introduction.* [Trad. En anglaise de: Pour mieux comprendre Angkor, par Emily Floyd; Rééd. 1984, Oxford University.] Singapore: Oxford University.
Cœdès, G., 1989. A la recherche de yasodhasrama, in *Articles sur le pays Khmer, volume I*, Paris: École française d'Extrême-Orient, 241–64.
Conze, E., 1974. *The Short Prajnaparamita Texts.* London: Luzac & Company LTD.
Dagens, B., 2003. *Les Khmers,* Paris: Les Belles Lettres.
Davids, R., & H. Oldenberg, 1990. *Motilal Banarsidass 13.* Delhi: Vinaya Texts.
Demiéville P. *Buddhism and Healing: Demiéville's Article 'Byō' from Hōbōgirin.* Lanham, MD., and London: University Press of America.
Dutt, S., 1962. *Buddhist Monks and Monasteries of India: Their History and Their Contribution to Indian Culture.* Delhi: Motilal Banarsidass.Estève, J., 2023. Gods and temples: the nature(s) of Angkorian religion, in *The Angkorian World*, eds. M. Hendrickson, M.T. Stark & D. Evans. New York: Routledge.
Estève, J., & D. Soutif, 2010. *Rapport annuel de la mission Yaśodharāśrama,* Siem Reap, APSARA/MAE/EFEO.
Evans, D., R.J. Fletcher, C. Pottier, J.-B. Chevance, D. Soutif, B.S. Tan, S. Im, D. Ea, T. Tin, S. Kim, C. Cromarty, S. De Greef, K. Hanus, P. Bâty, R. Kuszinger, I. Shimoda & G. Boornazian, 2013. Uncovering archaeological landscapes at Angkor using lidar. *Proceedings of the National Academy of Sciences of the United States of America* 110(31), 12595–600.
Finot, L., 1903. L'inscription Sanskrite de Say Fong. Notes d'épigraphie, in *Bulletin de l'École française d'Extrême-Orient* 3, 18–83.
Finot, L., 1915. Notes d'épigraphie: 16. L'inscription de Sdok Kak Thom, 17. Piédroit de Vat Phu, 18. Note additionelle sur l'édit des hôpitaux, 20. L'épigraphie indochinoise. Bibliographie. Supplément à l'inventaire des inscriptions de G. Cœdès. Listes dynastiques. Index. Tables. *Bulletin de l'École française d'Extrême-Orient* 15(2), 53–213.

Finot, L., 1925. Lokeśvāra en Indochine. *Etudes Asiatiques* 19, 227–56.

Filliozat, J., 1934. La médecine indienne et l'expansion bouddhique en Extrême-Orient. *Journal Asiatique* 224, 301–07.

Filliozat, J., 1937. *Le Kumāratantra de Rāva a et les textes parallèles indien, tibétain, chinois, cambodgien et arabe.* Paris: Les Cahiers de la Société Asiatique IV

Filliozat, J., 1964. *The classical doctrine of Indian medicine.* Delhi: M Munshiram and Culture, Atlantic Highlands: Humanities Press.

Glaize, M., 1993. *Angkor.* Paris: J. Maisonneuve.

Groslier, G., 1921. *Recherches sur les Cambodgiens d'après les textes et les monuments depuis les premiers siècles de notre ère.* Paris: Challamel Editeur.

Guruge, A. W. P., 1983. Contribution of Buddhism to education, in *Contribution of Buddhism to World Civilization and Culture*, ed. P.N. Chopra. Atlantic Highlands: Humanities Press.

Halpern, J. M., 1963. Traditional medicine and the role of the phi in Laos. *The Eastern Anthropologist*, 16(3), 191–200.

Huard, P., 1963. La médecine khmère Populaire. *Le Concours Médical* 18(5), 3269–75, 3437–44.

Hendrickson, M., 2008. People around the houses with fire: Archaeological investigation of settlement around the Jayavarman VII 'resthouse' temples. *Udaya, Journal of Khmer Studies* 9, 63–79.

Hendrickson, M., 2010. Historic routes to Angkor: development of the Khmer road system (ninth to thirteenth centuries AD) in Mainland Southeast Asia. *Antiquity* 84(324), 480–96.

Hendrickson, M., 2012. Connecting the Dots: investigating transportation between the temple complexes of the medieval Khmer (9th to 14th centuries CE), in *Old Myths and New Approaches: Interpreting Ancient Religious Sites in Southeast Asia*, ed. A. Haendel. Clayton: Monash University Publishing, 84–102.

Huber, E., 1911. Etudes Indochinoises: l'inscription bouddhique de Ron (Quan-Binh). *Bulletin de l'École française d'Extrême-Orient* 11, 267–69.

I-Tsing. 1998. *A Record of the Buddhist Religion as Practised in India and the Malay Archipelago A.D. 671–95.* New Delhi: Munshiram Manoharlal.

Jacques, C., 1968. Les édits des hôpitaux de Jayavarman VII. *Études cambodgiennes* 13, 14–17.

Keown, D., 2004. *Oxford Dictionary of Buddhism.* Oxford: Oxford University Press.

Leclère, A., 1894. L'anatomie chez les Cambodgiens. *La Revue Scientifique* 4(1), 392–98.

Leslie, J., & D. Wujastyk, 1991. The doctor's assistant: Nursing in ancient Indian medical texts, in *Anthropology and Nursing*, eds. P. Holden & J. Littlewood. London: Routledge.

Ling, L.K., 1935. Punodaya (Na-Ti), un propagateur du tantrisme en Chine et au Cambodge à l'époque de Hiuan-Tsang. *Journal Asiatique* 227, 83–97.

Liu, X., 1988. *Ancient India and Ancient China: trade and religious exchanges (A.D. 1–600).* Oxford: Oxford University Press.

Luealamai, K., 2004. The Arogayāśāla in Isan. *Muang Boran* 30(3), 68–74.

Majumdar, R.C., 1985. *Champa: history and culture of an Indian colonial kingdom in the far east (2nd–16th century A.D.).* New Delhi: Gian Publishing House.

Mookerji, R.K., 1951. *Ancient Indian Education. Brahmanical and Buddhist (2nd ed).* New Delhi: Motilal.

Mulholland, J., 1979. Thai traditional medicine: the treatment of diseases caused by the Tridosa. *The South East Asian Review* 3(2), 29–38.

Multzer o'Naghten, H., 2014. The organisation of space in pre-modern Thailand under Jayavarman VII in *Before Siam: Essays in Art and Archaeology*, eds. N. Revire & S.A. Murphy. Bangkok: The Siam Society and The James HW Thompson Foundation, 396–419.

Norodom, R., 1929. *L'évolution de la médecine au Cambodge.* Paris: L. Arnette.

Pelliot, P., 1951. *Mémoires sur Les Coutumes Du Cambodge de Tcheou Ta-Kouan.* Paris: Adrien-Maisonneuve.

Pichard, P., and F. Lagirarde, 2003. *The Buddhist Monasteries: A Cross-cultural Survey.* Paris: École française d'Extrême-Orient.

Polkinghorne, M., 2013. Decorative lintels and ateliers at Mahendraparvata and Hariharālaya. In *Materializing Southeast Asia's Past*, eds. Marijke J. Klokke and Veronqiue Degroot, Singapore: NUS Press Pte Ltd, 205–17.

Pollock, S., 2001. The death of Sanskrit. *Comparative Studies in Society and History* 43(2), 392–426.

Pottier, C. 2003. Yasovarman's Buddhist asrama in *The Buddhist Monastery: A Cross Cultural Survey*: 199–208, ed. Pierre Pichard and François Lagirarde. Paris: École française d'Extrême-Orient.

Pottier, C. & Chhem, R.C., 2008. A la découverte d'un hôpital angkorien: résultats préliminaires d'une campagne archéologique au prasat tromuong. *Udaya* 9, 169–82.

Pottier, C., Chhem, R.K., and Kolata A., 2006. *Angkor Medieval Hospitals*. Archaeological Project Report. EFEO/APSARA, Siemreap, Cambodge.

Pou, S., 2002. Āśrama dans l'ancien Cambodge. *Journal Asiatique* 20(1), 315–39.

Renou, L., and Filliozat, J., 2001. *Inde classique: manuel des études indiennes, tome II, réimpression (1re édition: 1953)*. Paris: École française d'Extrême-Orient.

Sarka K.K., 1968. *Early Indo-Cambodian Contacts (Literary and Linguistic)*. Santiniketan: Visva-Bharati

Sankalia, H.D., 1972. *The University of Nalanda*. New Delhi: Oriental Publishers.

Sarkar, K.K., 1968. Early Indo-Cambodian contacts (literary and linguistic) Santiniketan. *Visva-Bharati* 76.

Sharma, P. V., 1999. *Susruta Samhita*, (3 vol.), Varanasi: Oriental Publishers & Distributors

Sharrock, P.D., 2009. Garuda, Vajrapāṇni and religious change in Jayavarman VII's Angkor. *Journal of Southeast Asian Studies* 40(1), 111–51.

Sharrock, P.D. & Jacques, C., 2017. The grief of kings is the suffering of their subjects: Cambodian king's 12th century network of hospitals in buddhism and medicine: an anthology of pre-modern sources, in *Buddhism and Medicine: An Anthology of Premodern Sources*, ed. C.P. Salguero. Columbia University Press, New York, 226–32.

Stern, P., 1965. *Les Monuments khmers du style du Bayon et Jayavarman VII*. Paris: Publications du Musée Guimet.

Thapar, R., 1997. *Aśoka and the Decline of the Mauryas*. Oxford: Oxford University Press.

Traipiṭaka. 1994. *Tripiṭaka in Khmer*. Phnom Penh: Buddhist Institute

Wolters, O.W., 1999. *History, Culture, and Region in Southeast Asian Perspectives. Revised Edition. Southeast Asia Program*. Ithaca: Cornell University.

Woodward, H., 2011. Cambodian Images of Bhaisajyaguru, in *Khmer Bronzes: New Interpretations of the Past*, eds. E. Bunker E. & D. Latchford. Chicago: Art Media Resources, 497–502.

PART IV

Economies

17

ANGKOR'S ECONOMY

Implications of the Transfer of Wealth

Eileen Lustig, Aedeen Cremin and Terry Lustig

This chapter examines aspects of Angkor's economy to provide some insights into how it was sustained as an empire and the shortcomings that led to its ultimate decline. The range of sources available to assess these issues—temple inscriptions, foreign records, royal chronicles, and material culture—is broad but patchy. The most immediate historical records are some 1300 inscriptions written by rulers and officials, informing us more about their priorities of power, patronage, and control over land, labour, and other resources than about the wider society, consisting largely of people we might today consider unfree (Vickery 1998, 225–31; Mabbett 1983). Nevertheless, these inscriptions provide insights into the absence of money and its implications for the mode of taxation, the allocation of resources, and the transfer of wealth as land. We look at some essential and high-value resources and consider the role of the state in acquiring them. We suggest that the high concentration of wealth among elites and their demand for luxuries contributed to the transfer of Angkor's capital to the Quatre Bras region, where the modern political centre of Cambodia is located.

Rice and Location of the Capital

From the 6th century CE, with the centres of Khmer population moving inland, rice production became increasingly important in the economy. Central Cambodian inscriptions from early in the Pre-Angkor Period (6th to 9th centuries) indicate that rice was not only the principal resource grown, consumed, and traded, but also the pre-eminent taxation commodity, as underscored by the numerous references to rice officers from whose demands the temples were frequently exempted (Lustig 2009a, 59–60)—and texts such as the 11th century K. 420[1] from Wat Damnak mentioning rice for the royal service.

A key to Angkor's six-century (9th to 15th centuries CE) resilience was the location of its capital by the Great Lake, the Tonle Sap. Not only did the site offer access to routes for trade and transport by land and water, but it also provided an assurance of reliable and substantial rice and fish production. The Mekong River rises and falls about 9 metres each year during the annual monsoon. Where it meets the Tonle Sap River at Phnom Penh, the rising water flows back up into the Lake, which increases more than fourfold in area to more than 10,000 ha between May and November, flooding forests and providing a large juvenile habitat for fish, which makes the Tonle Sap one of the world's most productive freshwater ecosystems (Lamberts 2006). The lake and its

DOI: 10.4324/9781351128940-22

surrounds have provided a diet rich in rice and fish since at least the Bronze Age (Frelat and Souday 2015). The Pre-Angkorian capital Bhavapura may have been located just to the north of the Lake (Pottier 2017).

The great reservoirs and water networks established around Angkor have led many to argue that they were integral to producing the quantities of rice needed to support a large population (Groslier 1979), while others consider these waterworks were not a significant factor (Acker 1998, Van Liere 1980, Lustig et al. 2023, this volume). Evidence of irrigation from channels around Angkor has been confirmed in a few areas, and it is possible that, as today, it was carried out on a small scale. In recent times, 90% of Cambodia's rice cultivation area has been rainfed (Nesbitt 1997). Most production is in areas where Cambodia's population is concentrated, toward the southeast of the country and around the Tonle Sap. The flat alluvial plains around the lake with their high water tables are most suitable for rainfed cultivation, while some deep-water rice is grown along the edges of the lake and large rivers in the rainy season. In the dry season, flood-recession rice is also planted around the lake in bunded fields.

The rise in prosperity of Angkor and other Southeast Asian mainland polities in the mid-10th century and their decline in the late 13th century have been linked to changes in rice production as a response to a widespread increase and subsequent reduction in rainfall (Lieberman 2003, 224–26). While not discounting the benefits of favourable climate, we would stress other elements in decline, in particular a growing concentration of wealth and the dependence on Angkor's trading capability, the seeds for both having been sown centuries earlier with the intensification of Angkor's hierarchical structure and the development of the modes of taxation for its expanded territories.

Taxation, Wealth, and Land

As the Angkorian state grew, tax collection and administrative control became largely decentralised. Autonomous regions were restructured to form provinces, *viṣaya*, or *pramān* (Kulke 1986, Sahai 1970, 71–81), and there was an expansion of the bureaucracy, observed most clearly from the reign of Rājendravarman (944–68). Inscriptions show that district chiefs (*khloñ viṣaya*) were concerned with fiscal and property matters. References to courts indicate that judicial issues could be dealt with at village, district, and central levels. Local elites were given official responsibilities and sanctioned to levy sections of the society, likely passing little on to the centre (Kulke 1986). Taxation appears to have been an essential function of officials of the *vraḥ rājakāryya* (royal service), the *vrīha* (paddy, rice), *paryyaṅ* (oil, ghee), and various other agencies mentioned in inscriptions throughout Khmer territories. The extent of this activity is indicated by the variety of officials involved and the kinds of tax and other immunities that were granted to temple communities (Sahai 1970, 113–25; see also Jenner 2009, 2009a; Monier-Williams 2022).

> The rice chief, the grain (or paddy) chief, the oil chief and the district chief are not to exact rājakāryya from the temple or the temple personnel.
>
> K. 831: 21–3 (968 CE)[2]

From Jayavarman II (802–34), rulers granted or sanctioned the purchase of land by their supporters, many in order to establish religious foundations. Through surplus production, they and their descendants could acquire still more land, provide workforces to grow rice for the deities housed there, and purchase precious gifts for the temple treasuries. Land that was not a god's was subject to levies, and a significant proportion of local and state income would have come from non-elites living in non-temple villages. Agricultural production would have generated a large proportion of the taxation revenue, perhaps based on the area of land under cultivation. In an 11th-century text from Wat Baset, K. 205, five officials, having sold several parcels of land destined for a temple foundation, requested a reduction of 50%, presumably in the amount of tax they had to pay on their lands.

Angkor's economy was moneyless (Wicks 1992, 183–218; Lustig 2009). While coinages are known from several early Indianised urban centres in Southeast Asia, including Angkor Borei in Cambodia, Cambodia did not mint coins until the 16th century (Gutman 1978; Cribb 2013; Epinal 2013). Under Angkor, levies would have been paid mainly in agricultural produce, particularly rice, or as *corvée*. The mode of revenue collection may have depended on the location and population density.

Figure 17.1a shows the combined Pre-Angkorian and Angkorian densities of temple inscriptions, generally indicating zones of economic, religious, and political activity (Lustig 2011). The extent of influence of the sites within each zone was taken to be a circle of radius 25 km, or one day's journey from its centroid. The distribution and density of inscriptions within the zone and hence of populations correspond well with today's rice growing areas (Figure 17.1b)—predominantly located around the communication corridors, the major rivers and roads. The majority of Angkorian sites are to the north of the Tonle Sap. Productive areas around the capital and in the vicinity of the annually flooding lake must have been major sources of Angkor's taxation revenue.

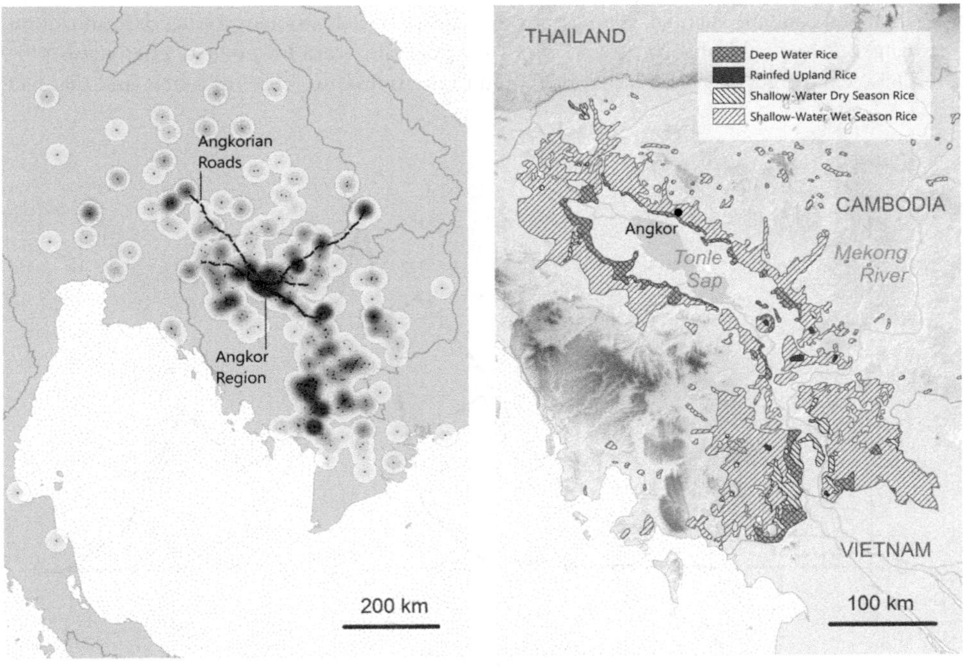

Figure 17.1 Distribution of inscriptions and rice land in Cambodia: a) concentrations of Pre-Angkorian and Angkorian inscriptions. Darker shading indicates a denser assemblage of inscriptions. (GIS data of Angkorian roads M. Hendrickson 2010); b) rice ecosystems map for Cambodia.

Source: (Based on IRRI, https://data.opendevelopmentmekong.net/dataset?extras_taxonomy=Agriculture&type=dataset).

Much of the taxation rice could be allocated locally, perhaps to pay specialist craftspeople and to maintain corvée workers. However, a proportion from each district must have been transferred to the centre. To avoid the costs of transporting bulky rice over long distances, it would have made sense for such payments to be in high-value goods (HVG), such as precious metals; manufactured metal objects, including utensils and jewellery; and quality textiles. The inscriptions record middle-ranking officials exchanging their lands for HVG, at rates of double the value of the goods, to fulfil their tax obligations. Inscription K. 1198 (1014 CE), on the O Smach stele from northwest Cambodia, records that a middle-ranking official required 2 *liṅ* (~12 grams) of gold as payment for the rājakāryya. This amount was obtained from a very senior temple official in exchange for a tract of land valued at 4 liṅ of gold. In another instance, several village entertainers, 'pugilists', were compelled to give up their land to pay their huge debt.

> Not having the goods, the *vāp* Vit then [with] the vāp Dan, head of the *sruk* of Gaṃryāṅ, the vāp In, *khloñ jnvāl* of the boxers, the vāp Go, mūla, the vāp Gāp, *mūla*, the vāp Dan, mūla, [and] the vāp 'Yak, mūla of the boxers of the sruk of Gaṃryāṅ (used) the land of Gaṃryāṅ [belonging to the boxers] to give the *mratāñ khloñ śrī* Narapativīravarman the equivalent of the silver, the precious objects and garments, representing [100 percent] surcharge (*guṇa*) [on the loan].
>
> K. 257N: 7–10 (994 CE)

Because the extra charge was often added immediately and was always 100 percent, we interpret guṅa as '[100 percent] surcharge', replacing Cœdès' 'interest' (Lustig and Lustig 2019). Perhaps such a high rate could be charged, as the goods were obtained only from local elites or foundations.

In Angkor's hierarchical society, land sales were generally from lower- to higher-status officials. These exchanges (Figure 17.2) contributed to the transfer to elites of much land that had

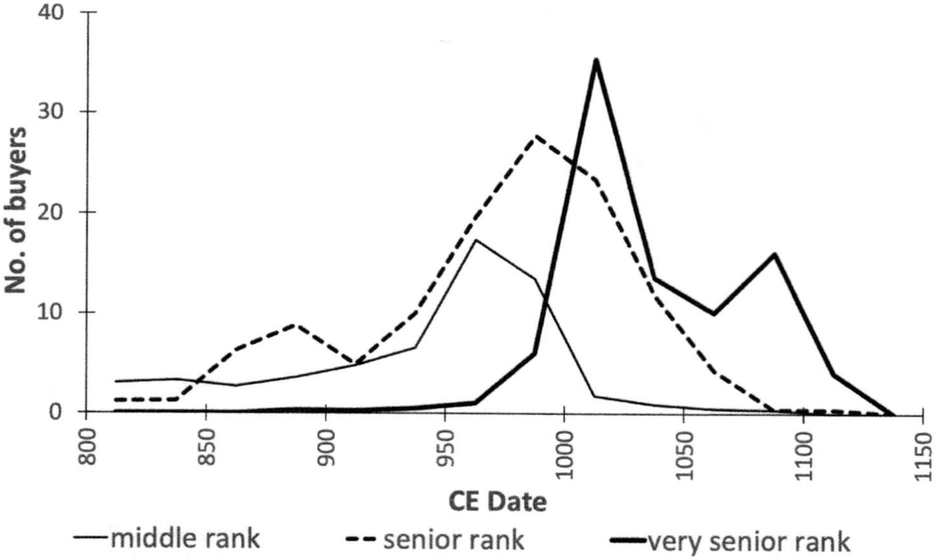

Figure 17.2 Purchase of land by increasingly high-ranking officials.

Source: (Adapted from Lustig and Lustig 2019).

been worked by the families of minor officials and often held communally by kinship, village, or occupational groups. See, for example K. 1238 (1036 CE) where a *varṇāśrama* community sold two parcels of land to a high-ranking official.

By the late 10th century, such transfers must have led to loss of wealth and influence of a section of the society and thus an increased concentration in the hands of fewer high-ranking officials whose temple lands also benefited from fiscal immunities (Lustig and Lustig 2019).

High-value goods could also be levied from the rulers of more remote areas as tribute. An inscription from Wat Phu, K. 1320 (928 CE), specifies the precise quantities of a great variety of HVG, which were levied as tribute from a nearby city of Liṅgapura in the first year of the reign of Īśānavarman II (925–28). These goods were precious metals, livestock, animal and plant products, textiles, and weapons of war and were declared gifts to the temple—and not removed to the capital. The forest products supplied to the state by minorities living in remote, often upland, areas may also have been tribute payments, such as observed by Aymonier (1900, 26) in the French Colonial Period.

Expression of Value and Wealth in Temple Inscriptions

Land was a prime source of wealth and power, since its possession allowed control over agricultural production and most likely the people called *k̃ñum/khñum* attached to it (Ricklefs 1967). Many of the inscriptions record donations of land, and other property to religious foundations, the temples and hermitages (*āśrama*) endowed as acts of piety. Often the barter prices paid for these gifts were recorded, providing evidence of the donor's generosity and proof of ownership, especially if possession was disputed.

Transactions after the start of the Angkor Period differ markedly from those recorded earlier (Lustig 2009). The Pre-Angkorian (6th to 9th centuries) inscriptions contain details of transactions for transferring rice fields and other property to temples. Sometimes donors received goods from the temple in return, indicating the temple was engaged in economic activities. But even where its size or production is stated, there is little sense of how land was valued (Vickery 1998, 281–92). A limited range of items was exchanged, commonly paddy, textiles, and silver, but others, including kñum or their labour, were sometimes included. The Pre-Angkorian texts contain expressions which denoted 'value'. The 7th-century K. 726 refers to rice fields acquired in exchange for paddy equivalent in value (*mūlya*) to amounts of silver and cloth. In K. 1214, from the 8th century, the price of one or several female personnel with children was equivalent to (*'argha*) 15 liṅ of silver.

Organisational and linguistic changes become evident in the early Angkorian epigraphy (Vickery 1998, 87). Inscriptions record a greater volume and diversity of material items, indicating increased wealth and exposure to foreign goods. The greatest number of transactions, mostly land sales, were recorded between the mid-10th and mid-11th centuries, when many officials were seeking 'legal' confirmation of title to lands they or their ancestors had acquired, sometimes two centuries previously.

The enhanced wealth of the elite was exhibited with status symbols in what was now a more stratified society. The inventories of temple treasuries are replete with luxury textiles (Green 2023, this volume), valuable metal objects, and jewellery. The extravagant gifts and insignia bestowed by rulers on their supporters are further indicators of this prosperity. Lists of items given in payments for land or slaves tend to be longer, containing also livestock, metal pieces, paddy and sometimes elephants, khñum, or spices. Despite referring to a variety of monetary concepts, the Angkorian corpus of inscriptions (9th to 15th centuries) has no references to a common currency or unit of account (Wicks 1992 183–218; Lustig 2009).

Yet the lists suggest that gold was more commonly given to temples than was silver, while silver objects were preferred to gold in transactions. In addition, exchange items were much more likely to have their weight recorded, while the object's material was emphasised when the item had been a gift to a temple. Value was therefore not irrelevant. In fact, the focus on the high-value precious metal in donations and temple lists reveals a concern for what was of paramount importance—the display of a donor's status, wealth, and generosity and for the concomitant merit that would be accrued.

> [Goods of] *vraḥ kaṃrateṅ 'añ* (VKA) Bhagavatī: one crown; 1 mace; 2 pikes with 2 gemstones on them; 2 pendant ear-rings; 1 necklace; 1 *śrīvatsa*; 1 waistband; 2 armbands; 2 bracelets; 2 finger-rings [with] 2 gemstones on them; 2 anklets; 1 holy seal [with] 1 gemstone on it; 3 *mās paṃneḥ* with 1 gemstone. One palanquin [with] 4 Garuḍa on it; 2 white [parasols]; 2 screens; 4 [parasols with] gold handles; 29 boxes; 2 silver pikes; 2 brooches; 1 silver *vaudi*; 1 water-jar of *hanira*.
>
> K. 262N: 6–9 (968 CE)

Status and social hierarchy, evident throughout the corpus, influenced relationships between individuals. Material rewards could be determined by status, as we see in payments to officials bearing the higher status title, VKA, who received more for their share of a land parcel than those titled *kaṃsteṅ* and *khloñ* in the 11th century K. 374 from Kampeng Nai, or to members of the court for boundary marking, explained in the Wat Baset inscription, K. 206:

> *Thlās* given to members of the royal court who set up the boundary-markers:
> VKA the superior (?) of the Pūrvāśrama: 2 [pieces of] *thnap*, 10 *yo* of garment cloth;
> VKA of the Vidyāśrama: 1 [piece] of thnap, 5 yo of garments
> VKA of □□□: 1 [piece of] thnap, 2 yo of *ullāra*.
> Kaṃsteṅ Ya Nap, member of the royal court: 1 [piece of] thnap, 1 yo of ullāra.
> Mratāñ khloñ Mat Chlaṅ, *khloñ vala* of the Pūrvāśrama: 1 [piece of] thnap.
>
> K. 206: 40–43 (1042 CE)

It should be stressed that the transactions outlined in the inscriptions depict an elite milieu of rulers, officials, religious institutions, and their gods. They should not be seen as representative of the wider or secular economy, where barter with commonly accepted measures of value must have been used.

Redistribution

Several pre-modern economies have been described as 'redistributive' (after Polanyi et al. 1957). This concept has been applied specifically to the states of Pagan (Aung Thwin 1985, 108) and Angkor (Wheatley 1975; Miksic 2001) in Southeast Asia, where significant portions of the economies were based on and around the monasteries and temples. Resources which flowed into centres were 'redistributed' in accordance with the recipient's status, with limited subsequent return to producers (Wheatley 1975). Further, some cities, such as Angkor, have been characterised as 'orthogenetic', being centrally administered and functioning without the use of money. They were seen as typically stable, ritualised, and monumental, producing surplus staple crops around the city. Most production was controlled through taxation or tribute and redistributed as gifts or payments. The city's inhabitants, small in number (but see Klassen et al. 2021), were predominantly elites and bureaucrats. Their desire for high-status goods was met through foreign trade, which was administered at state level (Miksic 2001).

Rice grown around Angkor, together with fish from the Tonle Sap, must have supported large numbers of corvée workers, craftspeople, and others in the state's employ – this being contrary to the orthogenetic model. The commodities reportedly provided by many thousands of villages to the royal temples of Ta Prohm and Preah Khan in 1186 are an indication of Angkor's capacity to command the movement of substantial quantities of resources to its ritual centre.

> [Here] is what come from the payments from the villages:
> Paddy: 146 891 *khārī*
> Rice supplied during the *śrāddha*, in the month of Māgha, at the time of the markets, etc: 7,848 khārī
> Sesames: 433 khārī
> Peas: the same quantity, reduced by 10 khārī, 1 *droṇa* (=422 khārī, 3 droṇa)
> Melted butter: 545 *ghāṭi*, 7 ½ *prastha* [. . .]
> 22,682 pairs of clothing for the gods, and other clothing.
>
> K. 908: LXL—LXIX (1186 CE)

Recent studies have shown areas of quite dense occupation around fishponds within and extending from the compounds of the Ta Prohm and Angkor Wat temples and across the Angkor Thom compound (Gaucher 2004; Stark et al. 2015; Klassen et al. 2021; Carter et al. 2018, 2023, this volume) and indicate that people were not growing rice but were supplementing their diets from land they were occupying.

Support within religious institutions was allocated in line with the status of the recipients, based on the positions they held and their ages. Texts from three of king Yaśovarman's hermitages of ca. 900 (K. 701; K. 279; K. 290) detail the quantity of rice supplied each day to different members of the community from the master down to young boys, ranging from about 850 to 450 grams per day (Lustig and Lustig 2015). As the average daily consumption by an adult today is 660 grams, one might infer that several among the community were receiving more rice than they could consume.

The mode of dietary support for temple personnel was far from uniform. In an 11th-century text, K. 702 from Wat Preah That of Tuk Cha, yields from rice fields were reserved for certain temple personnel (cooks, thatchers, musicians, dancers, singers, doorkeepers) though apparently not for a number of lower-status khñuṃ. Indeed, many temple personnel appear not to have been supported fully by redistributed temple rice. At Trapeang Don Ong, K. 254, the estimated allocations to both the *khñuṃ vraḥ* (sanctuary slaves) and the clerics from reserved fields were inadequate, implying that their support was supplemented from other sources (Sedov 1963; Lustig and Lustig 2015).

> Riceland reserved for the officiants, number of measures: 3 *thlvaṅ*, 2 *je*, fourteen *liḥ*, 1 *'var*; reserved for the chaplain, number of measures: 3 thlvaṅ, 5 liḥ, 1 'var. Riceland for the subsistence of the khñuṃ vraḥ: fortnight of the waxing moon [9 khñuṃ]: total number of measures: 4 thlvaṅ, 1 je, 10 liḥ, 3 'var. Fortnight of the waning moon [10 khñuṃ]: total number of measures: 4 thlvaṅ, 1 je, 10 liḥ, 3 'var. Total number of measures: 8 thlvaṅ, 3 je, 6 liḥ, 2 'var.
>
> K. 254B: 33–38 (1129 CE)

This quotation illustrates an unusual institution, arguably peculiar to the Khmer, the working fortnight, where teams of workers and goods were assigned to the temple only on alternate fortnights. Mabbett (1983) suggested that temple personnel worked to support themselves on their fortnight off or, alternatively, that working for the temple was a form of usufruct for some, who may have continued to work for their donors during alternate fortnights.

In some instances, the distribution appears to have relied on ceremonial food. At Phnom Bakheng (K. 684, ca. CE 10th–11th c.), the deity received an offering of one *je* at the celebration of *saṅkranta*. The food was subsequently allocated as *yajñaśeṣa* (the leftovers from the sacrifice) to the inspector of the rājakāryya and five temple officials, in accordance with their status. At Prasat Beng (K. 989, 1008 CE) and Trapeang Don Ong (K. 254, 1129 CE), the inscriptions indicate that the gods were offered roughly double the amount allocated to temple personnel, and we infer that this was not wasted

Temples and Elite Families

The Angkor Period saw a growing number of officials acquiring lands where they established religious foundations. In the 10th to 12th centuries, the majority of inscriptions produced were non-royal, an indication of the wealth and influence exercised by some elite families. The temple foundations effectively served as links between the centre and regional elites and between elites and commoners living in villages surrounding the temples. Many of these villages were owned by the foundations, with their inhabitants assigned to the temples in various capacities from 'slaves of the god' (khñuṃ vraḥ) to field labourers. Religious symbolism transmitted through the temples helped to legitimise the hierarchical social structure. Inscriptions report the storage of precious goods in temple treasuries and occasionally refer to transactions made in the name of foundation deities, indicating commercial activities within temples. As well, they seem to have been centres for local administration (Mabbett, 1978) and may well have been stores for taxation commodities. The theory that taxed resources were channelled from villages to state temples at the capital through a hierarchy of temples (Sedov 1967, 183–95) is discussed in Heng and Sahai (2023).

The Angkorian texts are explicit about the mutually beneficial associations between rulers, temples, and elite families. Family members and associates of the founders were appointed to roles which may have been religious, administrative, or both. As in the inscription K. 258 from Samron, we often see court, local, and state officials involved in temple affairs:

> In 1011 *śaka*, [members of the sanctuary at] Travāṅ Gol and the royal court, the khloñ vala ('chief of the population') of Candanagiri [who is] the khloñ viṣaya ('district chief') and the khloñ vala of Travāṅ Gol [who is] *khloñ bhutasa*, went with the head of sruk Daśagrāma, village elders [and] notables, in order that the Khloñ Kanmyaṅ and all his family take [them to] lay out the land of Vraḥ Kapila which had been sold to me.
>
> K. 258B: 12–15 (1107 CE)

Rulers appointed elites to administer new territories and to levy the population. They granted or sanctioned the acquisition of lands by supporters. Some religious foundations established on these lands received royal endowments and immunities, and in return, rulers were often accorded merit for the foundations. Surplus production from temple lands could be converted into personal wealth and more land. As discussed, with the hierarchical impediments to land acquisition and the need for many taxes to be paid in HVG, much land seems to have been transferred to influential families by the late 11th century—at the expense of vendors, who were losing status within the society. It may not be surprising that after the 10th century, non-sanctuary workers came to be regarded increasingly as instruments of agricultural output (Lustig and Lustig 2013).

Markets and Merchants

Marketing in medieval Southeast Asia is the mode of exchange recorded least in archaeology, epigraphy and other literary accounts (Wheatley 1975). These tend to emphasise activities or artifacts concerned with status, merit-gaining, patronage, and display. In Angkor, markets are first mentioned only at the end of the 12th century, in the Ta Prohm inscription (K. 273) of Jayavarman VII (1182-ca.1218), where clothing and other commodities were to be taken 'from the weaver's shop, from the villages, from the market, etc'—presumably as taxation. These local markets appear to have been run predominantly by women (Zhou 2007 [1297], ch. 20), exchanging goods through barter. Coins were not in common usage, even by the late 12th century (Wade 2009). In the 1220s, Zhao Rugua, a superintendent of trade in Quanzhou, reported that lead could be used to buy rice in Kamboja and that foreigners acquired Cambodian forest products with gold, silver, porcelain, and other valuables (Hirth and Rockhill 1911, 53). Objects of small denominations were in use later, as the Chinese envoy Zhou Daguan, living at Angkor in 1296–7, wrote that rice, grain, and Chinese copper coins were for small transactions; fabrics for larger ones; and for the largest transactions, gold and silver. Strong 'slaves' could be worth up to 100 copper coins. Gold and silver, which he said were not found locally, were brought to Cambodia by Chinese merchants and were much in demand (Zhou 2007 [1297], Chs. 9, 20, 21). Market infrastructure is difficult to identify but would likely be located in areas of high traffic such as around temples and at crossroads. While lidar imagery appears to show the remains of formal markets around Mayan settlements (Ruhl et al. 2018), no such infrastructure has yet been identified in the now-extensive lidar for the major Angkorian settlements.

Everyday commodities would not have been exchanged over significant distances. However, we know from the inscriptions and from sherds of imported ceramics that there were trade networks for distribution of valuable goods. Even so, a large proportion of the Chinese ceramics of high quality in Khmer territories are found at the capital in elite contexts (see Stark and Cremin 2023, this volume). From this we may infer that wealth was concentrated there and that the volume of traffic in valuable goods to regional centres was small and thus readily controlled. In Angkor's moneyless society, it would have benefited the dominant class to monopolise the handling of HVG and inhibit the influence of merchants. Wicks (1992, 218) posits that this was why money was abandoned. The lack of money would have reduced the scale of interaction between people (Miksic 2006), limiting access to a range of markets and allowing prices to be controlled by powerful elites. Yet people can be induced to exchange their resources for items of high value in monetised societies as well. In mediaeval Java, for instance, some growers exchanged their rice for the cash of merchant tax-farmers to pay their taxes (Wisseman Christie 1998). So imposing restrictions on markets may not have been a strong motive for abandoning the use of money.

We have no epigraphic evidence for merchants in prominent or entrepreneurial roles at Angkor, as is known for more trade-oriented and monetised societies such as Song and Yuan China (Wade 2009), Mataram Java (Wisseman Christie 1998), or Chola India (Karashima 2009). In both Java and India, traders could operate through merchant guilds under charter granted by the local ruler, for both domestic and foreign trade. Medieval states in the broader region tended not to administer trade directly, opting to gain revenue through taxation, with officials or merchants often acting as tax farmers (Hall 1980, 171; Wisseman Christie 1998).

A Sanskrit text from Wat Khnat (K. 259, 8th century CE), referring to a 'chief of merchants' (*vaṇijam adhipa*), suggests that there was some control of trade quite early on (Vickery 1998, 313). Among the many landowners and officials who feature in Angkorian Period inscriptions, only six traders (*vanik*) are mentioned (in K. 220 and K. 221N,S from Banteay Prav; and K.

843 from Trapeang Don Mas, each dated to the early 11th century). Two of these were chiefs (khloñ), and another, a kaṃsteṅ, was titled 'chief of traders' (*khloñ vanik ni vanik*). The titles of the traders suggest a hierarchy such as might be found in administered agencies. Certainly, the kaṃsteṅ was a confidant of the king (see K. 782, 1071 CE) and he was influential in attracting many donations of slaves to his foundation.

> *Tai* Thṅe, khñuṃ of a trader of Ga'āṅ Laṃpoḥ: the kaṃsteṅ being chief merchant, this trader gave tai Thṅe to the kaṃsteṅ to offer to the divinity.
>
> K. 221N: 13 (1009 CE)

Angkor's Involvement in Trade

Yet, we have little information on how Angkor's foreign exchanges were administered and taxed. As elsewhere, the rulers would have had a strong interest in acquiring prestige goods and taxing their flow, likely involving themselves only with selected commodities through appointed officials. In contemporary states, administrations generally focused on vital and readily controlled areas, such as ports. For example, under South India's Vijayanagara (1336–1646), port customs and highway tolls were the only state-administered taxes, while the state monopolised the trade in the strategically important horses and artillery (Morrison and Sinopoli 1992). In China, trade in imported goods shifted from control by the Song court in the late 10th century to private traders in the ports by the late 11th century. At Guangzhou, the authorities regulated maritime trade, imposing customs duties and purchasing portions of the incoming goods compulsorily—then the official market and merchants had access to the rest. During the Northern Song Period, foreign shipping carried much of the trade, with foreign merchants resident in ports as agents for China's trading partners. These grew in number and influence over time (Heng 2008).

Khmer merchants were resident in Java (Wisseman Christie 1998), and some were likely also living in the enclaves of resident foreign merchants in, for example, South India (Hall 1980, 173) and Pagan (Aung Thwin 1985, 114). Muslim merchants, some representing Southeast Asian polities, made tribute missions to the Song court (Heng 2008; Wade 2009). An Arab merchant claimed to have spent two years at the Cambodian capital some time prior to 903 (Ferrand 1913, 69–70), so we may infer that he had found some commercial potential. There seems also to have been a sizable Chinese community in Angkor, given the appreciable number of Chinese depicted on Jayavarman VII temple bas-reliefs. The large variety of fine Chinese manufactured goods present in the archaeological record indicate that a high proportion of Chinese residents were involved in trade (Zhou 2007[1297], chs. 20; 21; 38; Coe and Evans 2018, 188).

As discussed in Stark and Cremin (2023), Southeast Asian polities became part of a greater world during the first millennium CE, through the ever-expanding maritime trade. Tamsen Sen (2018) has even identified a 'Buddhist cosmopolis of the 7th century' which links both China and India and is intimately involved with the activities of merchants carrying ideas, objects, and practical knowledge, such as literacy. A good instance of this is a 7th–8th century Buddhist inscription in Sanskrit, but in Khmer script (K. 407 from Wat Maheyong on the Isthmus of Kra). The ceremony it describes is Indian, but the accessories include a *cīnadhv(aj)*, a banner of Chinese fabric (Aymonier 1901, 77–8). While the inscription's find spot would suggest the banner came by sea, it could just as well have come overland because, tellingly, the Khmer script is very close to that of central Cambodia, which had by then become the centre of power. The area had connections to southern China via Wat Phu from at least the 7th century (Yang 2004, 25–8, Pelliot 1904, 377–8), while other routes linked the Middle and Lower Mekong to Champa, which already had strong relations with China (Tran 2013).

Maritime Silk Road merchants from the Persian Gulf sailed to China in stages, often using the Isthmus of Kra for transhipment, then calling into Southeast Asian ports to pick up specific local goods, such as the Vietnamese star anise found in the 9th-century Tang wreck from Beilitung (Murphy 2017). Although Cambodia was known to Arab traders from at least the 840s, it was not considered important for trade, writers noting only that *kimari*, the Arabic word for aloes (Aquilaria, or eaglewood), derived from the name of the country (Qmar = Khmer) (Ferrand 1913, 30). Ships generally bypassed the Mekong Delta, making landfall only at one of the Cham ports.

Angkor's interests were still clearly land based, relying on the agrarian sector and overland exchange (Vickery 1998, 20). More land meant more resources, and there seems to have been a steady increase in territory from the 11th century. Sūryavarman I (1002–49) extended Angkor's sphere of influence across the Dangrek into the Khorat Plateau and west into Lopburi and the Chao Phraya basin, providing access to more varied resources, such as rock salt, discussed in the following section.

China's overall trade with Southeast Asian polities increased substantially under the Song (Heng 2008; Wade 2009), yet while Angkor sent only two trade missions during the period up to 1087, Champa sent 44. Chinese copper coins are found throughout most of Southeast Asia but are only known in Cambodia from the early 13th century, even though Chinese coins had been accumulating elsewhere in Southeast Asia since the early 10th century (Wade 2009). Chinese or foreign (*deśa*, perhaps Indian) metal objects and textiles are mentioned in Angkorian texts from only eight sites, dated from the late 9th to late 12th century. Seven are royal or prominent temples in and around Angkor (Lustig 2009); another is from the northwest of Cambodia (K. 1198). These indicators may reflect Angkor's relative isolation or its low status as a trading partner rather than its lack of interest in trade or in becoming monetised.

Although there were restrictions on trade under the Southern Song (1127–1276), these were circumvented, at least in part, by state or port officials or by the increasingly powerful merchant class (Wade 2009). Certainly, by the 12th century, Khmer kings were aware of the advantages of maritime trade to complement the existing land trade. Both Sūryavarman II (1113–49) and Jayavarman VII expanded to the east, each taking control of the central Cham port of Vijaya. Conflicts between the Khmer and Champa and Khmer attacks on Đại Việt up to the mid-13th century were most likely over access to resources and trade routes that developed with Chinese maritime activities (Vickery 2010).

While Angkor's trade may have been hindered by restrictions imposed by the Yuan (1276–1368), the mission of Zhou Daguan to Cambodia and his references to Chinese residents and trade with China suggest otherwise. Certainly, the economies of much of Southeast Asia were markedly transformed by the expanding trade networks between China and the Indian Ocean in the period of the 10th to the 13th centuries, Wade's 'Early Age of Commerce'. New trading ports developed to handle the markets for exotic goods, monetisation increased, and technologies spread in conjunction with the rise of the merchant class (Wade 2009). While the Khmer benefited at least from Chinese ceramic technologies, there is little evidence of broad changes to its economy up to the mid-14th century.

In the early Ming Period, envoys from several Southeast Asian polities, including Cambodia, visited China frequently to trade under the nominal guise of submitting tribute. Between 1371 and 1419 there were more missions between Cambodia and China than during the previous five centuries (Vickery 2010). For a period prior to 1394, only Ryukyu, Cambodia, and Siam were allowed to come and offer tribute (Wade 2004). Two missions seem to have been by a delegate from the Quatre Bras area in 1371 and 1373 (Polkinghorne and Sato 2023). These accelerating contacts are indicative of the development of all-year ports in the Quatre Bras region where Angkor would be better placed to compete against other Southeast Asian polities (Reid 1993, 206–07).

Role of the State in Obtaining High-Value Goods

We have seen that large quantities of domestic resources were delivered to state temples as taxation or tribute (see previously K. 1320; K. 273; K. 908). We examine the relatively few epigraphic clues to how Angkor acquired important commodities, some of which were valuable exports. In the main, these commodities appear not to have been produced or acquired through state monopolies.

Forest Products

Chinese sources record a trade in plant and animal forest products, some of which, from upland areas, would have been supplied by minority communities. Reports refer to rhinoceros horns, elephant tusks, kingfisher feathers, beeswax, cardamom, fragrant timbers, and resins used in perfumes and incense (Hirth and Rockhill 1911, 53, Zhou 2007[1297], ch.19). Several were also consumed domestically and mentioned frequently as items for religious rituals. Beeswax and cardamom are recorded as barter items, while honey and wax, fragrant timbers, and resins are among allocations for the deities in Jayavarman VII's hospitals and temples and were to be taken annually from the royal stores. Evidence of wax, a requirement for bronze casting, has been found at the artisanal workshop at Angkor's Royal Palace (Polkinghorne et al. 2014).

According to Sedov (1967, 201–02), there were specialised industries managed by religious foundations to supply the state with commodities. In fact, three incomplete inscriptions from today's southern Vietnam could imply a state enterprise. In the 8th-century K. 421 and K. 654 from the Plain of Reeds (modern Đồng Tháp Mười), what appear to be significant quantities of honey, wax, and grain are requested by an unknown authority. In an 11th-century edict (K. 913), King Udayādityavarman II asks that rice lands belonging to certain communities furnishing honey and wax be marked out and granted immunities from some levies. However, it is also conceivable, as Sahai (1970, 117) held, that the forest products, honey and wax, were important, normally taxed resources—and the protection provided to the communities was to help ensure their delivery to royal stores.

Iron

Most of Angkor's iron appears to have come from Phnom Dek, the 'Iron Mountain', where Angkorian authority was represented by the massive temple complex of the Preah Khan of Kompong Svay, 30 km away (Hendrickson and Evans 2015). Iron was used for agricultural implements, as crampons in the construction of stone buildings, and for weaponry. By the 13th century, Phnom Dek supplied most of Angkor's needs for temple construction (Hendrickson and Leroy 2020). The scarcity of Angkorian infrastructure around Phnom Dek indicates that the Khmer did not control production directly and were likely reliant on the ethnic Kuay people, a minority group known to have occupied the region and smelted iron since at least the 16th century (Hendrickson et al. 2019; Hendrickson et al. 2023, this volume).

A clue to how the state acquired the metal may be found in the early 11th-century inscription K. 158 from Tuol Prasat, equidistant from both Preah Khan of Kompong Svay and Phnom

Dek. It mentions two land sales during the reign of Jayavarman V (CE 968–1001), where the exchange prices include hundreds of iron implements, crowbars, and axes. In the same text, 100 axes and 100 crowbars are given to the people of the vrīha (grain authority?) to be used as payment for the rājakāryya. This indicates that there was smithing to produce objects of standard design near the iron source, that local officials could obtain iron products, and that these could be traded and accepted as tax. The implication is that the state could acquire its iron through taxation or purchase rather than as a monopoly. The French ethnographer Harmand (1876), who recorded the manufacture of iron, noted that the Kuay of Phnom Dek were in his time required to pay their taxes in iron bars.

Salt

Salt is a basic mineral, recorded even in Pre-Angkorian times. The 7th-century K. 940 from just south of Phnom Penh, a royal order, probably by Jayavarman I, lists a total of 52,000 [measures] of salt to be picked up by six temple boats—and perhaps indicates a royal monopoly on the production and distribution of a 'prestige' item (Vickery 1998, 295–96).

> Those who levy duties on them, those who hinder their passage—those who transgress [this] order will be punished.
>
> K. 940: 10–11 (578–677 CE)

Angkor would have obtained some salt from evaporation pans in the Mekong Delta. Zhou Daguan mentions works along the coast of today's south Vietnam but also describes a 'kind of rock' from the mountains (Zhou 2007 [1297], ch.28). He was likely referring to the rock salt from the Khorat Plateau, which was exploited on a scale well beyond local needs (Higham and Thosarat 2012, 201–6). McNeill and Welch (1991) found that it was brought into Cambodia and traded for fish until the 1950s. Salt is still used as a currency by minority communities and is traded among neighbouring groups in Laos and Vietnam (Tran 2013). It is mentioned in seven Angkorian texts as a tradeable commodity, found among items exchanged for parcels of land or services. It is also listed among allocations for deities. The presence of a salt inspector, *trvāc 'aṃpyal* in the 11th century K. 206 from Wat Baset, indicates that, rather than being a state monopoly, salt was taxed.

Relocating the Imperial Capital: An Economic Perspective

By the 15th century, the capital of the Khmer Empire was no longer at Angkor but in the Quatre Bras region of the Mekong River. The reasons for the move have been variously attributed to climate change, drought, war with Ayutthaya and an increase in maritime trade (summarised in Evans et al. 2023). Concerning trade, Vickery (1978, 522) proposed that Angkor might have continued much as before, unless it was already weakened, and suggested that an explanation 'must be sought in more detailed study of the Angkorian inscriptions in order to discover patterns of social and economic change throughout the Angkor Period itself.' We concur and suggest from an economic perspective that there were three drivers of change. First, the growing wealth of the elite, whose desire for luxury goods would have expanded the volume of international trade. Second, the savings to international shipping of a Quatre Bras port for accessing international trade: according to Zhou Daguan (2007[1297], 45–6), the area could be reached in 15 days from the mouth of the Mekong River, while another 10 days were required to reach Angkor via the Tonle Sap. Third, if high-value forest products were traded for imports, the Quatre Bras would have been a more convenient point of collection, being downstream from much of Angkor's forested catchments.

There is some evidence that elites may have moved to the Quatre Bras region during the 14th century, perhaps while maintaining their landed wealth at Angkor. Brotherson (2019, 285) has shown that Chinese ceramics—imported predominantly by the elite—were discarded around Greater Angkor in significantly greater quantities in the first half of this century than in the second half. Sedimentological and palynological evidence indicates a decline in occupation density in the administrative centre of Angkor from the first decades of this century (Penny et al. 2019). Other paleoenvironmental indicators in the same area suggest that the intensity of agricultural production decreased in the same period (Hall et al. 2021). It was not a steady decline: in the 13th century, there was a break in the occupation of Angkor Wat, followed by re-occupation from the 14th century, but less intense than in the 12th century (Carter et al. 2023, this volume). These indicators are not inconsistent with the idea that members of the elite moved from Angkor to the Quatre Bras region, with Angkor retaining its spiritual centrality.

Our study of the inscriptions has brought to light an additional factor contributing to the shift of the capital: mounting inequality feeding the demand for international trade, in turn making such a move more attractive to the court and other elites.

Summary

Angkor's success over six centuries had depended on a relatively unchanging economy, based on an assured supply of rice and fish, together with elite control of HVG in a moneyless society. This may have disposed the ruling class to suppress the development of an inherently enterprising merchant class.

Temples were centres of economic life, creating much employment and linking the population to central authority. This was referred to frequently in royal edicts, sanctioning land purchases and temple construction. The numerous officials whose individual roles spanned religious and secular duties owed their positions directly or indirectly to royal favour. Temples and their founding families were enriched by the lands and the labour of increasingly commodified workers. Allocation of resources within religious establishments was typically on the basis of status.

Given the extent of its territories, Angkor's tax collection was decentralised, with local officials authorised to collect levies, some of which were directed to the centre. The state likely acquired key commodities such as iron and forest products through taxation or tribute. The extent to which rulers were directly involved in foreign trade is not clear, nor can an entrepreneurial merchant class be discerned from Angkorian texts. However, there are records of foreign merchants, including Khmer, working abroad and of foreign traders active at Angkor. Even so, epigraphic and archaeological evidence points to a limited and readily administered distribution of HVG.

While remaining essentially agrarian, Angkor was moving to augment its participation in international trade from the 10th century. Yet the volumes were smaller than some other parts of Southeast Asia. The absence of money, together with limited circulation of HVG among elites likely meant markets functioned mainly for domestic goods, and traders could not flourish as a class. The surge in maritime trade in the Song Period had little impact on Angkor, although the transfer of wealth to an already advantaged elite helped incline the economy towards international trade. With the advent of the Ming, Angkor's participation could grow substantially, increasing the relative importance of the river ports on the Mekong, now under increasing Ayutthayan influence. Over time, in conjunction with other influences, it would have made sense to enough elites to move the capital.

List of Inscriptions in the Text

K.	Reference	K.	Reference	K.	Reference
158	IC II, 97	279	Cœdès 1932, 84	831	IC V, 147
205	IC III, 3	290	Cœdès 1932, 84	843	IC VII, 109
206	IC III, 11	374	IC VI, 251	908	Cœdès 1941, 255
220	IC VI, 225	407	Cœdès 1929, 51	913	IC V, 270
221	IC III, 54	420	IC IV, 161	940	IC V, 73
245	IC III, 90	421	IC V, 272	989	IC VII, 164
254	IC III, 180	654	IC V, 274	1198	Pou 2001, 240
257	IC IV, 140	684	IC IV, 106	1214	Griffiths 2005
258	IC IV, 175	701	Cœdès 1932, 84	1238	Griffiths and Soutif 2008
259	IC VII, 50	702	IC V, 222	1320	Goodall and Jacques 2014
262	IC IV, 108	726	IC V, 75		
273	Cœdès 1906, 44	782	IC I, 221		

IC = Inscriptions du Cambodge; Cœdès 1937–66.

Notes

1 Khmer inscriptions are referred to by their K. number and are listed in the table at the end of this chapter and in the References.
2 Quotations from inscriptions are adapted from the original French translations and unpublished English translations by the late Philip Jenner.

References

Acker, R., 1998. New geographical tests of the hydraulic thesis at Angkor. *South East Asia Research* 6(1) 5–47.

Aung Thwin, M., 1985. *Pagan: The Origins of Modern Burma*. Honolulu: University of Hawai'i Press.

Aymonier, É., 1900–04. *Le Cambodge: 1.1900, Le royaume actuel; 2.1901, Les provinces siamoises; 3.1904, Le groupe d' Angkor et l' histoire*. Paris: Ernest Leroux.

Brotherson, D., 2019. *Commerce, the capital & community: trade ceramics, settlement patterns & continuity throughout the demise of Angkor*. PhD dissertation. Sydney: The University of Sydney.

Carter, A., P. Heng, M. Stark, R. Chhay & D. Evans, 2018. Urbanism and residential patterning in Angkor. *Journal of Field Archaeology*. https://doi.org/10.1080/00934690.2018.1503034, accessed 13 February 2019.

Carter, A., M.T. Stark, P. Heng & R. Chhay, 2023. The Angkorian house, in *The Angkorian World*, eds. M. Hendrickson, M.T. Stark & D. Evans. New York: Routledge, 494–507.

Coe, M.D. & D. Evans, 2018. *Angkor and the Khmer Civilization*. London: Thames & Hudson Ltd.

Cœdès, G., 1906. La stèle de Ta-Prohm. *Bulletin de l'École française d'Extrême-Orient* 6, 44–86.

Cœdès, G., 1929. *Recueil des inscriptions du Siam. Deuxième partie: inscriptions de Dvāravatī, de Śrivijaya et de Lăvo*. Bangkok: Institut Royal de Siam, Service Archéologique.

Cœdès, G., 1932. Études cambodgiennes. XXX, A la recherche du Yaçodharaçrama. *Bulletin de l'École française d'Extrême-Orient* 32, 84–112.

Cœdès, G., 1937–66. *Inscriptions du Cambodge. Collection de Textes et Documents sur l'Indochine*. (Vol. I (1937); Vol. II (1942); Vol. III (1951); Vol. IV (1952); Vol. V (1953); Vol. VI (1954); Vol. VII (1964); Vol. VIII (1966)). Paris: École française d'Extrême-Orient.

Cœdès, G., 1941. La stèle du praḥ khan d'Ankor. *Bulletin de l'École française d'Extrême-Orient* 41, 255–302.

Cribb, J., 2013. First coin of ancient Khmer kingdom discovered. *Numismatique Asiatique* 6, 9–16.

Epinal, G., 2013. Quelques remarques relatives aux découvertes monétaires d'Angkor Borei. *Numismatique Asiatique* 8, 31–43.

Evans, D., M. Polkinghorne, R. Fletcher, D. Brotherson, T. Hall, S. Klassen & P. Wijker, 2023. Perspectives on the 'collapse' of Angkor and the Khmer Empire, in *The Angkorian World*, eds. M. Hendrickson, M.T. Stark & D. Evans. New York: Routledge.

Ferrand, G., 1913. *Relations de voyages et textes géographiques arabes, persans et turks relatifs a l'Extrême-Orient du VIIIe au XVIIIe siècles.* Paris: Ernest Leroux. https://archive.org/details/relationsdevoyag1a2ferruoft, [accessed 20 March 2020].

Frelat, M. & C. Souday, 2015. The Bronze Age necropolis of Koh Ta Meas: insights into the health of the earliest inhabitants of the Angkor region. *Bulletins et Mémoires de la Société d'Anthropologie de Paris* 27(3–4).

Gaucher, J., 2004. Angkor Thom, une utopie réalisée? Structuration de l'espace et modèle d'urbanisme ancien dans le Cambodge ancien. *Arts Asiatiques* 59, 58–86.

Goodall, D. & C. Jacques, 2014. Stèle inscrite d'Īśānavarman II à Vat Phu: K. 1320. *Aséanie* 33(1) 395–442.

Green, G., 2023. Vogue at Angkor: dress, décor and narrative drama, in *The Angkorian World*, eds. M. Hendrickson, M.T. Stark & D. Evans. New York: Routledge, 508–24.

Griffiths, A. & D. Soutif, 2008. Autour des terres du loñ Śrīviṣṇu et de sa famille: un document administratif du Cambodge angkorien, l'inscription K. 1238. *Bulletin de l'École française d'Extrême-Orient* 95–6, 29–72.

Griffiths, A., 2005. La stèle d'Installation de Śrī Tribhuvaneśvara: une nouvelle inscription préangkorienne du musée national de phnom penh (K. 1214). *Journal Asiatique* 293, 1, 11–43.

Groslier, B.P., 1979. La cité hydraulique angkorienne. *Bulletin de l'École française d'Extrême-Orient* 66, 161–202.

Gutman, P., 1978. The ancient coinage of Southeast Asia. *Journal of the Siam Society* 66(1), 8–21.

Hall, K. R., 1980. *Trade and Statecraft in the Age of Colas.* New Delhi: Abhinav Publications.

Hall, T., D. Penny, B. Vincent & M. Polkinghorne, 2021. An integrated palaeoenvironmental record of early modern occupancy and land use within Angkor Thom, Angkor. *Quaternary Science Reviews* 251, 106710.

Harmand, D., 1876. Voyage au Cambodge. *Bulletin de la Societé de géographie de Paris* (octobre) 337–67.

Hendrickson, M., 2010. Historic routes to Angkor: development of the Khmer road system (ninth to thirteenth centuries AD) in mainland Southeast Asia. *Antiquity* 84, 480–96.

Hendrickson, M. & D. Evans, 2015. Reimagining the city of fire and iron: a landscape archaeology of the Angkor-Period industrial complex of Preah Khan of Kompong Svay, Cambodia (ca. 9th to 13th centuries A.D.). *Journal of Field Archaeology* 40(6), 644–64.

Hendrickson, M. & S. Leroy, 2020. Sparks and needles: seeking catalysts of state expansions, a case study of technological interaction at Angkor, Cambodia (9th to 13th centuries CE). *Journal of Anthropological Archaeology* 57, 101141.

Hendrickson, M., D. Ea, R. Chhay, Y. Tabata, K. Phon, S. Leroy, Y. Sato & A. Desbat, 2023. Crafting with fire: stoneware and iron pyrotechnologies in the Angkorian World, in *The Angkorian World*, eds. M. Hendrickson, M.T. Stark & D. Evans. New York: Routledge, 385–400.

Hendrickson, M., S. Leroy, C. Castillo, Q. Hua, E. Vega & P. Kaseka, 2019. Forging empire: Angkorian iron smelting, community and ritual practice at Tonle Bak. *Antiquity* 93, 1586–606.

Heng, D., 2008. Shipping, customs procedures, and the foreign community: the 'Pingzhou ketan' on aspects of Guangzhou's maritime economy in the late eleventh century. *Journal of Song-Yuan Studies* 38, 1–38.

Heng, P. & S. Sahai, 2023. The temple economy of Angkor, in *The Angkorian World*, eds. M. Hendrickson, M.T. Stark & D. Evans. New York: Routledge, 327–37.

Higham, C. & R. Thosarat, 2012. *Early Thailand: From prehistory to Sukhotai.* Bangkok: River Books.

Hirth, F. & W.W. Rockhill, 1911. (trans. and ed.) *Chau Ju-Kua: His work on the Chinese and Arab trade in the twelfth and thirteenth centuries, entitled Chu-fan-chi. St.* Petersburg: Imperial Academy of Sciences.

Jenner, P.N., 2009. *A Dictionary of Pre-Angkorian Khmer.* Canberra: Pacific Linguistics, Research School of Pacific and Asian Studies, Australian National University.

Jenner, P.N., 2009a. *A Dictionary of Angkorian Khmer.* Canberra: Pacific Linguistics, Research School of Pacific and Asian Studies, Australian National University.

Karashima, N., 2009. South Indian merchant guilds in the Indian Ocean and Southeast Asia, in *Nagapattinam to Suvarnadwipa: Reflections on the Chola Naval expeditions to Southeast Asia*, eds. H. Kulke, K. Kesavapany & V. Sakhuja. Singapore: ISEAS—Yusof Ishak Institute, 135–57.

Klassen, S., A.K. Carter, D. Evans, S. Ortman, M.T. Stark, A.A. Loyless, M. Polkinghorne, P. Heng, M. Hill, P. Wijker, J. Weed, G. Marriner & R.J. Fletcher, 2021. Diachronic modeling of the population within the medieval greater Angkor settlement complex. *Science Advances* 7(19), DOI: 10.1126/sciadv.abf8441.

Kulke, H., 1986. The early and imperial kingdom in Southeast Asian history, in *Southeast Asia in the 9th to 14th Centuries*, eds. D.G. Hall & A.C. Milner. Singapore: Institute of Southeast Asian Studies, 1–22.

Lamberts, D., 2006. The Tonle Sap Lake as a productive ecosystem. *International Journal of Water Resources Development* 22(3), 481–95.

Lieberman, V.B., 2003. *Strange Parallels: Southeast Asia in Global Context, c.800–1830.* Cambridge: Cambridge University Press.

Lustig, E.J., 2009. Money doesn't make the world go round: Angkor's non-monetisation, in *Research in Economic Anthropology*, ed. D. Wood. Bingley, UK: Emerald Group Publishing Ltd., 165–99.

Lustig, E.J., 2009a. Power and Pragmatism in the Political Economy of Angkor. Unpublished PhD thesis, University of Sydney, Sydney.

Lustig, E.J., 2011. Using inscription data to investigate power in Angkor's empire. *Aséanie* 27, 35–66.

Lustig, T., J.-B. Chevance & W. Johnson, 2023. Angkor as a "cité hydraulique"?, in *The Angkorian World*, eds. M. Hendrickson, M.T. Stark & D. Evans. New York: Routledge.

Lustig, E. & T. Lustig, 2013. New insights into 'les interminables listes nominatives d' esclaves' from numerical analyses of the personnel in Angkorian inscriptions. *Aséanie* 31, 55–83.

Lustig, E.J. & T.L. Lustig, 2019. Losing ground: decline of Angkor's middle-level officials. *Journal of Southeast Asian Studies* 50(3), 409–30.

Lustig, T. & E. Lustig, 2015. Following the non-money trail: reconciling some Angkorian temple accounts. *Journal of Indo-Pacific Archaeology* 39, 26–37.

Mabbett, I.W. 1978. Kingship in Angkor. *Journal of the Siam Society* 66, 1–51.

Mabbett, I.W., 1983. Some remarks on the present state of knowledge about slavery in Angkor, in *Slavery, Bondage and Dependency in Southeast Asia*, ed. A. Reid. St Lucia, Queensland: University of Queensland Press, 44–63.

McNeill, J.R. & D.J. Welch, D., 1991. Regional and interregional interaction on the Khorat Plateau. *IPPA Bulletin* 10(1), 327–40.

Miksic, J.N., 2001. Early Burmese urbanisation: research and conservation. *Asian Perspectives: The Journal of Archaeology for Asia and the Pacific*, 40(1), 88–107.

Miksic, J.N., 2006. The city misunderstood: orthogenetic cities in Southeast Asia, in *TAASA Review: The Journal of of the Asian Arts Society of Australia* 15(3), 8–9.

Monier-Williams 2022. Cologne digital Sanskrit lexicon (from Monier-Williams 'Sanskrit-English). Cologne: Institute of Indology and Tamil Studies, University of Cologne. http://webapps.uni-koeln.de/tamil/, [accessed 2 December 2022].

Morrison, K.D. & C.M. Sinopoli, 1992. Economic diversity and integration in a pre-colonial Indian Empire. *World Archaeology* 23(3), 335–52.

Murphy, S.A., 2017. Ports of call in ninth-century Southeast Asia: the route of the Tang shipwreck, in *The Tang Shipwreck. Art and Exchange in the Ninth-Century*, eds. A. Chong & S.A. Murphy. Singapore: Asian Civilisations Museum, 234–49.

Nesbitt, H.J., 1997. Topography, climate, and rice production, in *Rice Production in Cambodia* ed. H.J. Nesbitt. Manila: International Rice Research Institute, 15–9.

Pelliot, P., 1904. Deux itinéraires de Chine en Inde à la fin du VIIIe siècle. *Bulletin de l'École française d'Extrême-Orient* 4, 131–413.

Penny, D., T. Hall, D. Evans & M. Polkinghorne, 2019. Geoarchaeological evidence from Angkor, Cambodia, reveals a gradual decline rather than a catastrophic 15th-century collapse. *Proceedings of the National Academy of Sciences* 116(11), 4871–76.

Polanyi, K., C.M. Arensberg & H.W. Pearson (eds.), 1957. *Trade and Market in the Early Empires. Economics in History and Theory.* New York: The Free Press.

Polkinghorne, M. & Y. Sato, 2023. Early Modern Cambodia and archaeology at Longvek, in *The Angkorian World*, eds. M. Hendrickson, M.T. Stark & D. Evans. New York: Routledge, 592–613.

Polkinghorne, M., B. Vincent, N. Thomas & D. Bourgarit, 2014. Casting for the king: the Royal Palace bronze workshop of Angkor Thom. *Bulletin de l'École française d'Extrême-Orient* 100(1), 327–58.

Pottier, C., 2017. Nouvelles données sur les premières cités angkoriennes, in *Deux décennies de coopération archéologique franco-cambodgienne à Angkor. Actes de la journée d'études organisée à la mémoire de Pascal Royère*, eds. A. Beschaouch, F. Verellen & M. Zink. Paris: Académie des Inscriptions et Belles-Lettres, 43–79.

Pou, S., 2001. *Nouvelles inscriptions du Cambodge, II & III, traduites et éditées par Saveros Pou.* Paris: École française d'Extrême-Orient.

Reid, A., 1993. *Southeast Asia in the Age of Commerce, 1450–1680, volume 2, Expansion and Crisis.* New Haven: Yale University Press.

Ricklefs, M.C., 1967. Land and law in the epigraphy of tenth-century Cambodia. *Journal of the Asiatic Society* 26(3), 411–20.

Ruhl, T., N.P. d'Unning & C. Carr, 2018. Lidar reveals possible network of ancient Maya marketplaces in Southwestern Campeche, Mexico. *Mexicon* 40, 83–91.
Sahai, S., 1970. *Les Institutions Politiques et l'Organisation Administrative du Cambodge Ancien (vie-xiiie siècles).* Paris: École française d'Extrême-Orient.
Sedov, L.A., 1963. On the problem of the economic system in Angkor Cambodia in the IX–XII centuries (translated by Antonia Glasse for O. W. Wolters). *Narody Asii I Afriki, Istoria, Ekonomika, Kul'tura* 6, 73–81.
Sedov, L.A., 1967. *Angkorskaiia Imperiia (The Angkor Empire).* Moscow: Izdatel'sto Nauka.
Sen, T., 2018. Yijing and the Buddhist cosmopolis of the seventh century, in *Texts and Transformations: Essays in Honor of the 75th Birthday of Victor H. Mair*, ed. H. Saussy. Amherst: Cambria Press.
Stark, M.T., D. Evans, R. Chhay, P. Heng & A. Carter, 2015. Residential patterning at Angkor Wat. *Antiquity* 89, 1439–55.
Stark, M.T. & A. Cremin, 2023. Angkor and China: 9th–15th centuries, in *The Angkorian World,* eds. M. Hendrickson, M.T. Stark & D. Evans. New York: Routledge, 112–32.
Tran, K.P., 2013. *Crossing Boundaries—Learning from the Past to Build the Future: An Archaeological Collaboration between Cambodia, Laos and Vietnam. (Research Paper 8) Regional Centre for Social Sciences and Sustainable Development.* Chiang Mai: Chiang Mai University.
van Liere, W.J., 1980. Traditional water management in the Lower Mekong Basin. *World Archaeology* 11(3), 265–80.
Vickery, M., 1978. *Cambodia after Angkor:The Chronicular Evidence for the Fourteenth to Sixteenth Centuries.* Unpublished PhD thesis, Yale University, New York.
Vickery, M., 1998. *Society, Economics, and Politics in Pre-Angkor Cambodia: The 7th–8th Centuries.* Tokyo: Centre for East Asian Cultural Studies for UNESCO, The Tokyo Bunko.
Vickery, M., 2010. Cambodia and its neighbours in the 15th century, in *Southeast Asia in the Fifteenth Century. The China Factor,* eds. G. Wade & L. Sun. Singapore: NUS Press, 271–303.
Wade, G., 2004. Ming China and Southeast Asia in the 15th century: a reappraisal. Working Paper Series, No. 28, Asia Research Institute, *National University of Singapore.* www.google.com/search?client=firefox-b-d&q=Ming+China+and+Southeast+Asia+in+the+15th+Century, [accessed 10 December 2018].
Wade, G., 2009. An early age of commerce in Southeast Asia, 900–1300 CE. *Journal of Southeast Asian Studies* 40(2), 221–65.
Wheatley, P., 1975. Satyānṛta in Suvarṇadvīpa: from reciprocity to redistribution in ancient Southeast Asia, in *Ancient Civilization and Trade*, eds. J.A. Sabloff & C.C. Lamberg-Karlovsky. Albuquerque: University of New Mexico Press, 227–83.
Wicks, R.S., 1992. *Money, Markets, and Trade in Early Southeast Asia: The Development of Indigenous Monetary Systems to AD 1400.* Ithaca: Southeast Asia Program, Cornell University.
Wisseman Christie, J., 1998. Javanese markets and the Asian sea trade boom of the tenth to the thirteenth centuries A.D. *Journal of the Economic and Social History of the Orient* 40(4), 344–81.
Yang, B., 2004. *Between Winds and Clouds. The Making of Yunnan (Second Century BCE to Twentieth Century CE).* New York: Columbia University Press and gutenburg-e.
Zhou Daguan, 2007 [1297]. *A Record of Cambodia, the Land and Its People. Translated with introduction and notes by Peter Harris.* Chiang Mai: Silkworm Books.

18
THE TEMPLE ECONOMY OF ANGKOR

Heng Piphal and Sachchidanand Sahai

Introduction

Angkorian civilisation is best known for its large Brahmanical and Buddhist monuments that dominate the landscape in modern Cambodia, Thailand, and Laos. Most scholarly knowledge regarding Angkorian politics, religious practices, and economics derives from inscriptions and carvings associated with these temples. Patrons and labourers, draft animals, rice fields, land conflicts, and court rulings all emerge from the epigraphy; so do a network of temples and perhaps also the cult of god-king. This chapter examines relationships between the temple economy and Angkorian society over a period of six centuries. Selected epigraphic evidence, other documentary sources, and recent archaeological data all offer insights on such relationships.

This chapter makes three points. First, temples were social and economic anchors of communities in which conspicuous displays of wealth, loyalty, and conflict resolution took place. Second, some Angkorian elites depended on their temple economy for property rights: land, labourers, and agricultural produce. Finally, the Angkorian temple and its associated economy was separated from the state economy. Far from being simply a theocratic symbol, viewing Angkorian political economy through its temple sheds light on Angkorian organisation and political centralisation through time.

Angkorian Temples and Inscribed Landscape

Angkorian temples of various shapes and sizes dot the landscapes of present-day Cambodia, Thailand, and Laos. Their epigraphic records indicate that temples were centres of communities, of learning, performance, refuge, pilgrimage, and shelter, and that they had close relationships with the Angkorian elite, kingship, and power. Angkorian temples transformed the surrounding landscape through their cosmic inspirations and provided legitimacy to rulers through their sacred rituals.

Angkorian gods, ancestors, and their temples bestowed legitimacy to the Angkorian monarchs, who dedicated temples to their royal ancestors with images of Brahmanical gods and goddesses in a practice known as *yaśaḥśarīra* or 'body of glory' in the Pre Rup inscription (Cœdès 1911, 1940, 325; 1958). Aligning royal temples with ancestral gods provided these monarchs with a microcosmic or sacred geographic representation of rightful inheritance

DOI: 10.4324/9781351128940-23

proclaimed in their genealogy inscriptions (Stern 1951). Indravarman I (r. 877–889) placed his royal temple of Bakong to the south of his ancestral Preah Ko temple. Yaśovarman I (r. 889–910) then commissioned the ancestral Lolei temple, in the middle of Indravarman I's great reservoir, or *baray*, the Indrataṭāka, which stands on the same axis north of the Bakong. The third ruler to be based at Angkor, Rajendravarman (r. 944–968), built his royal temple of Pre Rup just south of the East Baray and on the same axis as the ancestral East Mebon temple. The Royal Palace in Angkor Thom built during ca. 10th–11th centuries was also placed on the same axis west of the East Mebon and north of Phnom Bakheng (Gaucher 2013). The same principles inspired the 12th-century CE urbanisation program of the king Jayavarman VII (r. 1181–1218). He dedicated Preah Khan temple to his father as Lokeśvara and Ta Prohm temple to his mother as *Prajñāparamita*. His Bayon royal temple housed provincial deities from across the empire and was dedicated to the king himself, represented as a Buddha, completing the Mahāyāna Buddhist triad of the period (Maxwell 2007a; Woodward 1981, 198).

Angkorian temples marked Angkorian cultural and political space and functioned as pilgrimage centres, rest houses, and healing centres, allowing interactions and flows of information as well as material goods from different regions. The records of endowments suggest that there were central statistics of religious foundations and their resources (re)allocated from the central government. Yaśovarman I commissioned 100 royal shrines (*āśrama*) across the empire (see Chea *et al.* 2023, this volume). Sūryavarman I (r. 1006–1050) established four royal *liṅga, Sūryavarmeśvara*, at four important territories successively at Wat Ek in Battambang, Preah Vihear, *Īśānatirtha*, and Phnom Chisor in Takeo (K. 380, 1018 CE from Preah Vihear: Sanderson 2003, 419). Īśānatirtha was possibly located along the Mekong River (Jacques and Lafond 2007, 141) or perhaps in Kampong Cham, where a variation of the name *Īśānatirtheśvara* was cited in an inscription K. 92 (1028 CE). This latter possibility places this royal *liṅga* in another important territory of Indrapura, a power base of Jayavarman II (r. c. 790–835) prior to his coronation (see Vickery 1998, 414–15), and symbolises the rulers' control over the four directions from Angkor. Sovereigns used temple and statuary to demarcate the extent of their influence and control as well, as we see, for example, in the Preah Khan inscription (K. 908) written in 1191 that Jayavarman VII funded 20,400 provincial gods/temples across the empire (Maxwell 2007b: 85). The king and landowners endowed 208,532 people from 8,176 villages (grama), approximately 25.5 persons/village to service these gods. The Ta Prohm inscription counts 81,640 people from 839 villages assigned to support 102 hospitals and 798 gods (Cœdès 1906, 86; see Chhem et al. 2023, this volume). Ta Prohm was also a centre of Buddhist teaching and learning, hosting 1,409 students and their lecturers, all of whom were supported by the state. Rest houses and shrines were positioned along the Angkorian roadways by Jayavarman VII (Hendrickson 2008; see Lowman et al. 2023, this volume). The ruler supplied food, cloth, ritual articles, medicines, and so on to these temples.

Angkorian temples served as anchors for communities, centres of learning, nodes of interaction, and markers of cultural and political space. Their role in networks of capital and of provincial power enforced citizenship and specified penalties. Temples' axial configurations transformed Angkorian landscapes through their axial orientations, embankments, moats, and reservoirs and structured the residential communities around them (e.g., Hawken 2013). Surrounding residents supported temples and their gods, worked their land, and provisioned their personnel. Smaller temples founded by local elites also required resources and personnel. Generating and channelling such resources required social relations that structured the Angkorian temple economy.

Temple Economy

The following sections provide a survey of the nature of the temple economy (ca. 9th to 15th c.) and its relationships with Angkorian society. Temples were agricultural and craft corporations capable of producing surplus and engaging in economic transactions and were centres of interactions between people of various classes. The 'temple economy' is thus broadly defined as a temple's economic resources and socio-political relations with communities, elites, and the state.

Until recently, epigraphic studies by and large revolved around royal genealogies and political and religious histories of Cambodia (e.g., Cœdès 1960, 1966; Jacques 1986). Yet the same data sources yield important but overlooked information on temple economies (Sahai 2012; Vickery 1998). To sustain their daily rituals and staff, temples were endowed with means such as rice, land, land revenues (*bhūmyākara*), and villages. Temples owned wealth, *devadravya* (god's wealth), manufactured goods (e.g., textiles and metal utensils), workforces, and animals (cows, buffalos, elephants, horses, etc.). Diverse categories of social division appear in the context of temple endowments: middle- and high-ranking individuals were often depicted as landowners and donors, while the lower class, *khñum*, were workforce assigned to the temples (e.g., Sahai 1970' Jacob 1993; Lustig and Lustig 2019). These workforces were composed of many categories, including musicians, dancers, cooks, various categories of guards, weavers, field labourers, herders, and so on (see Sahai 2012, 222–42). Beyond the donors and structured lists of personnel, less is known about the organisation of the temple itself. The donations were presented directly to gods/temples or, rarely, via a temple manager, whose titles include *kulapati* (head of religious community) and *khloñ vnaṃ* (head of a sanctuary). The inscriptional corpus implies that Angkorian temples were agrarian corporations equipped with the necessary means to generate agricultural surpluses.

In earlier scholarship on Angkor, the temple economy has been explored through direct comparison with Indian treatises, for example, those of the Chola of southern India (Bhattacharya 1953; Sahai 1970), through the lens of the Asiatic mode of production (Sedov 1963, 1967, 1978). Angkorian temples were landholders and had associated legal aspects: a major theme of the temple economy and its social relations (Ricklefs 1967). Subsequent scholarship has expanded the scope of this work on the temple economy to explore the nature and evolution of the Pre-Angkorian and Angkorian communities and state (Hall 1985; Vickery 1998; Sahai 2012). Political and economic data found within the inscriptional corpus are often explored using two main themes: (1) the temple economy as the source of state and elite economic and political power (Sedov 1978; Hall 2011) or (2) a much narrower focus on temples, local communities, and stakeholders (Jacques 1986; Vickery 1998).

Angkorian Temples in the Economy

This chapter argues that Angkorian temples can be classified into three broad classes: state or provincial temples, private foundations, and community temples. In addition to those classes, the inscription corpus records two categories of Angkorian religious foundations: the royal foundation (vrah *puṇya, rāja puṇya,* or *rājadharma*) and the commoner foundation (*puṇya rāṣṭra*) for the rest of the population (e.g., K. 444, 974 CE, and K. 171, 969 CE). In the last category we find both private or family/lineage temples, commissioned by middle- and high-ranking elites, and community temples. The existence of the latter, often featured in the Pre-Angkorian inscriptions, is rather obscured in later texts, in all likelihood because they focus much more on elites than on other levels of society. Nonetheless, an account by a Chinese visitor who spent time at Angkor in 1296–1297 recounts that princes and high-ranking officials had family temples and that each village had a temple (Zhou 1992[1297], 5, 65).

Both royalty and provincial governors founded temples in the provinces that housed principal state deities that represented their provinces. A local ruler, *Vīrendrādhipativarman*, who was later depicted in Sūryavarman II's (r. 1113–1050) military procession on the wall of Angkor Wat, consecrated Phimai (in contemporary NE Thailand) in 1109 CE, for example (Cœdès 1924, 345–52). The second category, the private or family temple, is a common theme within Angkorian inscriptions. High- and middle-ranking elite families were sponsors of both temple construction and daily rituals to the images, many of whom were ancestors or founders of the family lineage. Despite the relative obscurity of the third category, the community temple, the existence of these foundations can be inferred via endowments made by different but contemporary donors to the same temple. One rare example is Wat Baset or *Jayakṣetra*, in Battambang. An inscription from Prasat Ta Ngen (K. 212/1027 CE) stipulated that its god's resources be joined (or jointly used with; see discussion in Estève 2009: 411–432) with the god of Baset. *Guṇapativarman* of *Sruk Ga-āñ Laṃpoḥ* endowed this god on June 09, 1036 CE (K. 205), and on June 21, 1042 CE (K. 206). On February 09, 1043 CE (K. 207), another individual named *Kanthapaṇḍita* of *Sruk Phalapriya* endowed the same god and listed Guṇapativarman as one of the witnesses. These multiple endowments suggest that Wat Baset was a community temple that attracted a range of different worshippers.

Some arbitrariness is found in distinctions between the three categories of temples, however. The Angkorian epigraphic corpus suggests that all categories owned the same economic resources, land, and workforces—some of whom were living in the vicinity of the temple. Thus, the differences between the second and third categories can be blurred as a private or lineage temple could become a community temple if it possessed a large population, sanctioned and endowed by a royal decree, and/or attracted more worshippers. For instance, the temples of corporate groups like *varṇa* or *varga* (see discussion in Mabbett 1977), which were essentially community in nature, are family/lineage temples.

Nature of the Angkorian Temple Economy

Since the beginning of the epigraphic record in ca. 6th–7th centuries, temples and their endowments were primarily associated with the royalties and the elites. Four characteristics distinguish the Angkorian from Pre-Angkorian temple economy: (1) individual endowments, (2) large-scale agricultural land expansion, (3) private temples, and (4) complex stipulations about joining some temple foundations with others. Pre-Angkorian temples were endowed with rice fields, fruits, animals, workforces, textiles, utilitarian goods, and other items; most endowments were collective efforts made by groups of local elites, often bearing the titles *poñ* and *mratāñ*. Temples and gods were implied as pre-existing in a given locale, rarely being made or founded in new land.[1] These characteristics tend to suggest that many Pre-Angkorian temples were centres of local communities, the community temples (Vickery 1998, 309).

The Angkorian temple economy contrasts markedly with Pre-Angkorian patterns, particularly in its scale and social relations. The Angkorian endowments were predominantly made by rulers, individual elites, and their families. While the Pre-Angkorian exchange was based primarily on land and animals, manufactured objects became common during the Angkor Period, suggesting an increase in the manufacturing economy (Lustig et al. 2007, 18–19). Angkorian temples and their images were frequently presented as being established in a new land, often with royal consent; some were founded in reclaimed wasteland or forest.[2] The old Khmer terminology *cat sruk*, to create a new village, or *caṃnat* (village), refers to these new lands. Workforces were a common endowment to these new temple establishments. In two instances, the authors stated that their families or lineages were relocated to the new lands (K. 353, 9th–10th c. from Preah Vihear province and K. 229, 10th–11th c. from Preah Net Preah). New temples and gods accompanied and sanctioned the rights to these new properties. They are examples of Angkorian private temples in which the gods were often the deified ancestors of the founders.

Temple, Ancestor, Property, and Inheritance

Like the Angkorian rulers, the elites also practised *yaśaḥśarīra*, the ancestral worship of deified ancestors, and derived their subsistence and power through management of temple economies, particularly of private temples. Property belonged to gods/temples whose images were of, or were associated with, ancestors in the temple founders' lineage. The descendants inherited both the properties and the temples, and through this relationship, they owned or had legitimate claims over the properties. In an early 10th-century inscription (K. 697) from Ubon Ratchathani in northeast Thailand, *Loñ Myaṅ* made an image of his mother alongside other gods and stipulated that the temple property be inherited by his daughter as well as his in-laws and that the image of his mother continue to be worshipped alongside other gods.[3] Via *yaśaḥśarīra*, the worship of and endowment to gods, was equally dedicated to the ancestors. Both entities—god and ancestor—sanctioned the family wealth and legitimised the inheritance through the family line for continued worship. Thus, to seize or transfer a property, the god governing it must be overthrown and replaced, and the practice of destroying gods was common during pillaging raids into the neighbouring kingdoms. A Cham inscription from Po Nagar (C30B, CE 1201) describes the destruction of Śiva liṅgas in Champa by Jayavarman VII's conquering troops (Griffiths and Lepoutre 2012). For example, Sūryavarman I seized the property and temple of the *Trakval Vau* lineage who staged a rebellion in 1011 CE and transferred them to another official, *Lakṣmīpativarman*. This transfer was ritually completed by replacing the original Buddha image of the Trakval Vau with that of a Śivaliṅga. In another instance, during a rebellion against Udayādityavarman II (r. 1050–1066), *Kaṃvau* seized many territories, including the property of the inscription K. 237 (1067 CE from Samrong), whose god image was overthrown.

This system of inheritance mediated through the temple economy began as early as the mid-7th century. An inscription from Prei Veng (K. 49, 664 CE) records an edict from Jayavarman I (r. 652–680) decreeing that the rights over a Buddhist temple and its property be inherited by a nephew—the son of the sister of the two founding brothers. This matrilineal inheritance system, which was commonly practised by Angkorian priestly families (including the family in the famous Sdok Kak Thom inscription), may have root in protohistoric ancestral worship associated with burials and with agricultural land ownership (Heng 2016). Another common characteristic of private temples was their specified inheritance (Cœdès 1951, 3, 181). Unless specified by the patrons that their families or different officials were forbidden from managing the donated land and resources, the management rights were often retained and inherited by the donor's families. How this arrangement worked is unclear. The temple may hold land rights, but the revenues belonged to the families for their service to the god (Sahai 2012, 207), or vice-versa (Hall 2011, 163), or the family may have shared a portion of the revenues with the temples.

Agricultural Land Expansion and Elite Economy

A spate of land donations that took place in northern Cambodia throughout the 9th century indicates that central power clearly shifted north during that period. Inscriptions documenting *caṃnat*, or expansion into new territory, although dated primarily between the 10th and 11th centuries, frequently identified the 9th-century kings Jayavarman II or Jayavarman III (r. c. 835–877) as donors of land to the ancestors of various families in the first half of the 9th century (Ricklefs 1967). These inscriptions are located in the northern territories and only three instances appear to the south in

Svay Rieng (K. 425, 968 CE), Kampong Cham (K. 90, 1080–1107 CE and K. 702, 1025 CE), and Udong (K. 736/Sūryavarman II). In fact, in contrast to Pre-Angkorian inscriptions, which are concentrated in the south, Angkorian inscriptions tend to cluster in the north (see Lustig et al. 2023, this volume). The spatial distribution corresponds to the movement implied by Jayavarman II's conquest of Angkor and the northern territories from his base in southern Cambodia (Heng and Lavy 2018). The newly conquered lands of the north, most of which had sparse evidence of Pre-Angkorian communities, were awarded to his followers for their services in the uprising.

Rights to land and management of temple properties were claimed and validated through land histories, or *śākha*, and accounts by village elders. The claimants laid out their genealogy of when and how their families, with past and present royal approvals, were legitimate owners of that land. Through this śākha, claimants not only established their legitimacy but also their family prestige by highlighting relationships with past and present rulers. One recurrent example is the elephant capture motif, in which a lineage ancestor/ancestress was awarded status and land by participating in elephant capture for the king; the Jayavarman III iteration has been described in some detail (Lowman 2013). The intended audiences were probably the witnesses of the endowments and land transactions, many of whom were governors, royal inspectors, generals, and local officials. For example, the Baset inscription (K. 207, 1043 CE) lists over 45 witnesses of different ranks and localities being assembled during an endowment. The presence of these witnesses of various ranks suggests that the event was a conspicuous display of power and wealth through largesse and merit-making.

Angkorian elite power derived from the management of both private and state temple economies. An inscription from Wat Baset (K. 205, 1036 CE) specified that lands were donated to the temple, then given to three daughters of the donors, most likely to manage the lands. The rulers monitored income and confiscated property outright to suppress and punish rebellion. A damaged inscription from Roluos (K. 886, 902 CE) states that Yaśovarman I ordered the property of the *Kanras* lineage be seized, and members of that lineage appeared to be assigned as temple workforce. An inscription from Preah Vihear (K. 380, 1018 CE) records Sūryavarman I's reassurance to the local population that the management of the temple will not be entrusted to the *Pās Khmau* people, who often rebelled against the central power. Although their properties were not seized, their resources were closely monitored to ensure that their revenues increased at the same rate as that of the temple. Other examples include the seizures of the land and temple of the Trakval Vau (K. 1198; 1014 CE from O Smach/Samrong) and of properties from another rebel named *Arjuna* (K. 92, 1028 CE from Kampong Cham). The practice of reassigning uninherited land as royal/public properties was reported during the Pre-Angkor Period in the 7th century by the History of Sui (Cœdès 1975, 75).

Joint Temple Foundation and State Economy

The Pre-Angkorian temple economy involved symbolic religious practice with possible political and economic significance (Vickery 1998, 155–56), but the Angkorian temple economy was a pragmatic strategy to consolidate political and economic power (Sedov 1978; Hall 1985; Sahai 2012; cf. Jacques 1986, 332). One model suggests that joining resources and personnel from multiple temple foundations helped rulers and elites create a hierarchical network of local, regional, and central temples, through which the state channelled its resource redistribution (Sedov 1978, 114; Hall 1985, 153–67). This practice of joint temple foundation is called *psam* or *sam* (Khmer) *miśraboga* or *paribhoga* (Sanskrit) and is variously translated as joint foundation, joint revenues, and pooling of resources (see discussions in Jacques 1986, 331–32; Vickery 1998, 155–58; Estève 2009, 413–32; Lustig 2009, 201; and Sahai 2012).

Joint temple foundation practices accomplished both symbolic and pragmatic functions, at least at the local level, yet how this operated at state level (or whether it was redistributive) remains unclear. Symbolically, the Angkorian supernatural world was hierarchical. The principal tower contained a royal statue and small chambers of the Bayon housed provincial gods (Maxwell 2007c); however, evidence demonstrating the state system's hierarchical temple network is limited. Among all of the instances where joint foundations can be found documented in the inscriptions, there is only one instance where a three-tier temple hierarchy can be demonstrated, at Liṅgapura—the site of Wat Phu in present-day Laos (Lustig 2009, 209). Some joint foundations were made by the same donors joining personal foundations. For instance, the individual named *Yajñavarāha* who founded Banteay Srei, Sek Ta Tuy (K. 620), and Trapeang Khyang (K. 660) stipulated that the last two foundations be joined. *Divākarbhaṭṭa* founded and joined Preah Einkosei (K. 262) and Kamphus (K. 669) foundations. While joining personal foundations does imply a sacred hierarchical relationship between them, it does not necessarily translate into a state hierarchy but simply means that both establishments could share the same resources.

Of the known 28 Angkorian joint foundation inscriptions, 9 of them, exactly one third, were joint with god *Bhadreśvara* of Liṅgapura (Estève 2009, 424–27; Lustig 2009, 210). The inscriptions suggest that the joint foundation, both properties and personnel, did not physically travel to Liṅgapura; rather, they were symbolically offered to the god who miraculously manifested at the location of the joint temple on a set schedule. For example, the Prasat Kok Chak inscription (Siem Reap, K. 958, 947 CE) prescribed the endowment to Bhadreśvara, who was 'set up at' (*sthāpnā anau*) *Rudramahālaya* (Prasat Kok Chak). A similar concept was recorded in Preah Vihear inscription (K. 380, 1018 CE), where the god Bhadreśvara was miraculously united with the god *Śīkhareśvara* of Preah Vihear through the austerity (*tapah*) of King Sūryavarman I (Sanderson 2003, 412, 418). In another example, the Samrong inscription (Siem Reap, K. 258) stipulated the offering for the seat and the god of Liṅgapura, when the 'god arrives' (*velā kaṃmrateṅ jagat liṅgapura stāc mok*) in the lunar month of *Phalguna* (February–March). This statement implies either that the god was scheduled to miraculously appear at this site on a set date to receive offerings or that the god (or a mobile replica) was carried from Wat Phu to Angkor on a set schedule. The same practice continued through the late 12th–early 13th centuries through which the Buddha of Wat Nokor in Kampong Cham was carried to Angkor and Banteay Chhmar (Maxwell 2009, 181–85). The multiple joint foundations with Bhadreśvara of Liṅgapura at Wat Phu indicate that a double/replica, a fragment or token of this Angkorian national god, was worshipped alongside other gods across the polity (Cœdès 1975, 116; Sanderson 2003, 412).

One tenet of the temple hierarchy model was that property, revenues, and personnel could move between joint temple foundations (e.g., Sedov 1978; Hall 1985). This is possible for temples located in proximity to each other (see discussion in Lustig 2009, 206–07); however, examples of joint foundations with long-distant temples like with the Bhadreśvara deity, which was closely associated with the Angkorian state, were rather symbolic. Enterprising elites throughout the polity consecrated their temples by making symbolic donations to Bhadreśvara in them, thereby exempting their donations from state taxes. A second tenet of the temple hierarchy model was that rulers granted immunities to the joint foundations, thereby sanctioning the resources flowing from smaller temples to central temples (Sedov 1978, 122). The ruler's involvement in these examples only reclassified portions of properties and resources by joining them with Bhadreśvara, which made them tax exempt. Their overall management, however, remained with the owners who only shared their revenues with the gods (Sahai 1977, 133). The evidence suggests a hierarchy of sacredness between the joint temples; on the other hand, it is unclear whether the resources provided by smaller temples to a central temple were economically significant (Sedov 1978, 22; Lustig 2009, 218). The temple-centred state economy model is plausible, but it is quite possible that the joint foundation and temple economy operated independently of the state and used parallel economic strategies to support religious rituals. This is apparent in a new inscription (K. 1320/926 CE), which records that Īśānavarman II (925–928) converted the state tax from Liṅgapura as an endowment the god Bhadreśvara of Wat Phu (Jacques and Goodall 2014). The temple of Wat Phu, thus, was not a state redistributive centre, since its management was separated from the secular administration of Liṅgapura.

Since the prestige and livelihood of elites depended upon the temple economy, the properties of private temples were subject to taxation by various state offices. Exactly how temples, patrons, state officials, and rulers all articulated within the temple economy is not clear, but inscriptions list many officials involved in taxation (see Lustig et al. 2023, this volume). One of these officials was *kloñ vnaṃ*, which is translated as head of a temple or a sanctuary; yet, in an inscription from northeast Thailand (K. 232/1006 CE), they appeared together with other state offices prohibited from levying tax from the specified foundation. Whether kloñ vnaṃwas a superior temple or a state office in charge of temple affairs remains unclear. Land grants and exemptions associated with religious foundations were a feature of royal initiatives for agricultural expansion (du Bourg 1970; Cœdès 1962, 249). A surge of conversion from personal endowments into royal foundations (*Rājapuṇya* or *Rājadravya*) during the 10th to 11th centuries helped Angkorian elites gain trust, prestige, and royal favours as encoded in the śākha, or history of the land.

Discussion and Conclusions

Angkorian temples played a crucial role in sustaining and transforming the Khmer Empire. They were centres of education, healing, art, performance, and social interaction that brought various regions into an Angkorian cultural sphere. Economically, temples were corporate institutions capable of producing agricultural surpluses as well as maintaining and expanding cultivated lands. They were consumers of craft products, including textiles, metal ware, ceramics, and trade goods, driving their distribution across the empire. Politically, temples provided Angkorian rulers with access to various local communities and helped to ensure loyalty by awarding control of temple economies to local communities and elites. Aspiring elites sponsored lavish ceremonies and largesse to temples in order to recruit allies and impress local populations. Royal approval of individuals' endowments to temples elevated the social and political status of the donor, as well as bolstering their claims over land rights and securing inheritance among their lineage (e.g., Lowman 2013). These relationships included marriage alliances through which the parents could earn royal favours to hold state offices by gifting daughters to the rulers (Zhou 1992[1297], 9). Furthermore, the rulers awarded loyal followers with the management of tax-immune temple properties and with validation of private temple properties generating revenues for the communities, elites, and/or the state.

Scholarship on Angkorian temple economies often focuses on the redistributive dimensions of the temple hierarchy network. Yet the Angkorian temple economy, particularly that of the state and elite temples, was intrinsically a state apparatus for agricultural expansion and for political and economic centralisation. Angkorian rulers controlled temples as they validated joint foundations and donated, confiscated, and reassigned lands. Rulers benefited from merit generated through religious rites in temples and, in some cases, through public loyalty oaths. Symbolically, the Angkorian rulers were entitled to a part of merit generated from religious foundations, with estimated rates ranging from a half, a fourth, or a sixth depending on their role in supporting the foundation (e.g., K. 842, 968 CE). An inscription from Lopburi, Thailand (K. 410, 1022 CE), specifies that those in Brahmanical religious sects as well as the Buddhist orders of Mahāyāna and Sthavira must present their merit to Sūryavarman I (as a form of loyalty). Nonetheless, whether this rate of symbolic capital was equally applied to the revenues of a temple is unknown.

Royal power over the temple, however, did not go uncontested by either courts or succeeding rulers. For instance, the Lolei inscription (K. 323, 893 CE) stipulates that personnel assigned to the temples could not be used for services other than war; a later inscription from Koh Ker (K. 682, 1001 CE) specifies that they could be summoned for other royal services. Another inscription (K. 207, 1043 CE) suggests that land reassignment by future rulers may be subject to contestation. Some Angkorian rulers, including Yaśovarman, Rājendravarman, and Jayavarman VII, appealed to future rulers to maintain their foundations, most probably because rulers have the authority over temple management. The Angkorian inscription corpus suggests that the temple economy was institutionalised and that there were varying forms of legal codes or social norms governing and separating temple, elite, and state properties.

While it is clear that Angkorian temples played a crucial role in the state political economy, the role of joint foundation and temple network in a model of state redistributive economy is less clear. The Angkorian state economy was likely separated from the temple economy, even though the latter was institutionalised. The state economy, by contrast, operated via a secular tributary/tax system whereby a portion of provincial or territorial revenues were destined for the state and its local offices (see Tambiah 1977).

List of Inscriptions in the Text

K.	*Reference*	*K.*	*Reference*	*K.*	*Reference*
5	Cœdès 1931, 1–7	257	IC VI, 140	669	IC I, 159
49	IC VI, 6	258	IC IV, 175	682	IC I, 50
90	IC V, 25	262	IC IV, 111	697	IC VII, 94
92	IC V, 229	323	Bergaigne 1893, LV, 391	702	IC V, 222
171	IC VI, 165	341	IC VI, 23	736	IC V, 306
205	IC III, 3	353	IC V, 133	842	IC I, 147
206	IC III, 11	380	IC VI, 257	886	IC V, 151
207	IC III, 16	410	Cœdès, 1929, XIX, 10–12	958	IC VII, 141
212	IC III, 29	425	IC II, 142	908	Cœdès 1941; Maxwell 2007b
229	IC VI, 273	444	IC II, 62	939	IC V, 56
232	IC VI, 228	620	Finot 1928, 51	1198	NIC II-III, 240
237	IC VI, 293	660	IC I, 195	1320	Goodall and Jacques 2014

IC = Inscriptions du Cambodge; Cœdès 1937–66.

NIC = Nouvelles inscriptions du Cambodge; tome II-III: Pou 2001.

Notes

1 K. 939 from Angkor Borei and K. 341/674 CE from Neak Buos refer to the construction of new brick temples.

2 K. 229/978–987 CE (Phnom Sruk) written during Suryarvarman I includes a phrase '*kap panlā chkā vrai cat sruk*' to cut down the brambles, clear the forest, lay out a *sruk*. Only one comparable Pre-Angkorian example, K. 5 in South Vietnam, mentions a land 'conquered on the mud'.

3 Other images of defied ancestors were recorded in the inscriptions of Prasat Char (K. 257/979 CE) and Phnom Sangke Kong (northeast Thailand near Banteay Chhmar, K. 232/1016 CE). These images were often of Brahmanical deities, but in one example, a Buddha image was set up by a female lineage founder, *Tāñ Tritatī*, to govern the property (K. 1198/1014 CE from O Smach/Samrong).

References

Bergaigne, A. M., 1893. *Inscriptions sanscrites de Campā et du Cambodge*. Paris: Imprimerie Nationale.

Bhattacharya, K., 1953. Some aspects of temple administration in the ancient Khmer empire. *Proceedings of the Indian History Congress* 16(1–3), 153–62.

Chea, S., J. Estève, D. Soutif & E. Swenson, 2023. *Āśramas*, shrines and royal power, in *The Angkorian World*, eds. M. Hendrickson, M.T. Stark & D. Evans. New York: Routledge, 272–86.

Chhem, R. D. Evans, K. Chhom, P. Phlong & P.D. Sharrock, 2023. Education and medicine at Angkor, in *The Angkorian World*, eds. M. Hendrickson, M.T. Stark & D. Evans. New York: Routledge, 287–306.

Cœdès, G., 1906. La stèle de Ta-Prohm. *Bulletin de l'École française d'Extrême-Orient* 6(1), 44–86.

Cœdès, G., 1911. *Note sur l'apothéose au Cambodge*. Paris: Ernest Leroux.

Cœdès, G., 1924. XVII. L'épigraphie du temple de Phimai. *Bulletin de l'École française d'Extrême-Orient* 24(1), 345–52.

Cœdès, G., 1929. *Recueil des Inscriptions du Siam, 2e partie. Inscriptions de Dvāravatī, de Çrīvijaya et de Lăvo*. Bangkok: Bangkok Times Press.

Cœdès, G., 1931. Deux inscriptions sanskrites du Fou-Nan. *Bulletin de l'École française d'Extrême-Orient* 31(1–2), 1–12.

Cœdès, G., 1937–66. *Inscriptions du Cambodge. Collection de Textes et Documents sur l'Indochine*. vol. I (1937); vol. II (1942); vol. III (1951); vol. IV (1952); vol. V (1953); vol. VI (1954); vol. VII (1964); vol. VIII (1966). Paris: École française d'Extrême-Orient.

Cœdès, G., 1940. La destination funéraire des grands monuments khmèrs. *Bulletin de l'École française d'Extrême-Orient* 40(2), 315–43.

Cœdès, G., 1941. IV. La stèle du Práh Khằn d'Ankor. *Bulletin de l'École française d'Extrême-Orient* 41(1), 255–302.

Cœdès, G., 1958. Les statues du roi khmèr Jayavarman VII. *Comptes rendus des séances de l'Académie des Inscriptions et Belles-Lettres* 102(3), 218–26.

Cœdès, G., 1960. L'avenir des études khmères. *Comptes-rendus des séances de l'Académie des Inscriptions et Belles-Lettres* 104(1), 367–74.

Cœdès, G., 1962. *Les Peuples de la Péninsule Indochinoise: Histoire-Civilisation*. Paris: Dunod.

Cœdès, G., 1966. *The Making of Southeast Asia. Translated by H.H. Wright. Berkeley, Los Angeles*. London: University of California Press.

Cœdès, G., 1975. *The Indianized States of Southeast Asia,* eds. Walter F. Vella. Translated by Susan Brown Cowing. Canberra: Australian National University Press.

de Bourg, H.M., 1970. La première moitié du XIe siècle au Cambodge: Suryavarman Ier, sa vie et quelques aspects des institutions à son époque. *Journal Asiatique* 258, 281–314.

Estève, J., 2009. *Étude critique des phénomènes de syncrétisme religieux dans le Cambodge Angkorien*. PhD dissertation. Paris: École pratique des hautes études.

Finot, L., 1928. Nouvelles inscriptions du Cambodge. *Bulletin de l'École française d'Extrême-Orient* 28(1), 43–80.

Gaucher, J., 2013. Considérations nouvelles sur la fondation d'angkor thom. In *Angkor, Naissance d'un Mythe: Louis Delaporte et Le Cambodge*, eds. Thierry Zéphir, 215–19. Paris: Gallimard.

Griffiths, A. & A. Lepoutre., 2012. *C. 30 B4 Southern Doorjamb of the Main Shrine of Po Nagar. École française d'Extrême-Orient and Institute for the Study of the Ancient World*. New York: New York University (Corpus of the Inscriptions of Campā, 2012).

Hall, K.R., 1985. *Maritime Trade and State Development in Early Southeast Asia*. Hawai'i: University of Hawai'i Press.

Hall, K.R., 2011. The temple-based mainland political economies of Angkor Cambodia and Pagan Burma, ca. 889–1300. In *A History of Early Southeast Asia: Maritime Trade and Societal Development*. Lanham: Rowman & Littlefield Publishers.100–1500, 159–210.

Hawken, S., 2013. Designs of kings and farmers: landscape systems of the greater Angkor urban complex. *Asian Perspectives* 52(2), 347–67.

Hendrickson, M., 2008. People around the houses with fire: archaeological investigation of settlement around the Jayavarman VII 'resthouse' temples. *Udaya, Journal of Khmer Studies* 9, 63–79.

Heng, P. & P.A. Lavy., 2018. Pre-Angkorian cities: Ishanapura and Mahendraparvata. In *Angkor: Exploring Cambodia's Sacred City*, eds. T. McCullough, S.A. Murphy, P. Baptiste & T. Zéphir. Singapore: Asian Civilisations Museum, 134–55.

Heng, P., 2016. Transition to the Pre-Angkorian period (300–500 CE): Thala Borivat and a regional perspective. *Journal of Southeast Asian Studies* 47(3), 484–505.

Jacob, J.M., 1993. Pre-Angkor Cambodia: Evidence from the inscriptions in Khmer concerning the common people and their environment, in *Early South East Asia: Essays in Archaeology, History, and Historical Geography*, eds. R.B. Smith and William Watson. New York: Oxford University Press, 299–318.

Jacques, C. & D. Goodall., 2014. Stèle inscrite d'Īśānavarman II à Vat Phu (K, 1320). *Aséanie* 33, 405–54.

Jacques, C. & P. Lafond., *2007. The Khmer Empire: Cities and Sanctuaries from the 5th to the 13th Centuries.* Bangkok: River Books.

Jacques, C., 1986. Sources on economic activities in Khmer and Cham lands, in *Southeast Asia in the Ninth to Fourteenth Centuries*, eds. David G. Marr and A. C. Milner. Canberra: Research School of Pacific Studies, Australian National University, 327–34.

Lowman, I., 2013. The elephant hunt of Jayavarman III: a political myth of Angkorian Cambodia. *Udaya, Journal of Khmer Studies* 11, 29–57.

Lowman, I., K., Chhom & M. Hendrickson, 2023. An Angkor nation? Identifying the core of the Khmer empire, in *The Angkorian World*, eds. M. Hendrickson, M.T. Stark & D. Evans. New York: Routledge, 479–93.

Lustig, E., 2009. *Power and pragmatism in the political economy of Angkor.* PhD dissertation. Sydney: The University of Sydney.

Lustig, E., A. Cremin & T. Lustig, 2023. Angkor's economy: implications of the transfer of wealth, in *The Angkorian World*, eds. M. Hendrickson, M.T. Stark & D. Evans. New York: Routledge, 309–26.

Lustig, E., D. Evans & N. Richards, 2007. Words across space and time: an analysis of lexical items in Khmer inscriptions, sixth–fourteenth centuries CE. *Journal of Southeast Asian Studies* 38(1), 1–26.

Lustig, E. & T. Lustig., 2019. Losing ground: decline of Angkor's middle-level officials. *Journal of Southeast Asian Studies* 50(3), 409–30.

Mabbett, I.W., 1977. Varnas in Angkor and the Indian caste system. *The Journal of Asian Studies* 36(3), 429.

Maxwell, T.S., 2007a. Religion at the time of Jayavarman VII. In *Bayon: New Perspectives*, ed. Joyce Clark, 74–121. Bangkok: River Books Press.

Maxwell, T.S., 2007b. The stele inscription Of Preah Khan, Angkor. *Udaya, Journal of Khmer Studies* 8, 1–114.

Maxwell, T.S., 2007c. The short inscriptions of the Bayon and contemporary temples. In *Bayon: New Perspectives*, ed. Joyce Clark, 122–35. Bangkok: River Books Press.

Maxwell, T.S., 2009. A new Khmer and Sanskrit inscription at Banteay Chmar. *Udaya, Journal of Khmer Studies* 10, 135–201.

Pou, S., 2001. *Nouvelles inscriptions du cambodge. Vol. 2 & 3.* Paris: École française d'Extrême-Orient.

Ricklefs, M.C., 1967. Land and the law in the epigraphy of tenth-century Cambodia. *The Journal of Asian Studies* 26(3), 411.

Sahai, S., 1970. *Les Institutions politiques et l'organisation administrative du Cambodge ancien, VIe-XIIIe siècles.* Paris: École française d'Extrême-Orient.

Sahai, S., 1977. Fiscal administration in ancient Cambodia. *South East Asian Review* 1(2), 123–38.

Sahai, S., 2012. *The Hindu Temples in Southeast Asia: Their Role in Social, Economic and Political Formations.* Shimla: New Delhi: Indian Institute of Advanced Study; Aryan Books International.

Sanderson, A., 2003. The Saiva religion among the Khmers Part I. *Bulletin de l'École française d'Extrême-Orient* 90–91, 349–462.

Sedov, L.A., 1963. On the problem of the economic system in Angkor Cambodia in the IX–XII centuries (Translated from Russian by Antonia Glasse for O. W. Wolters). Narody Asii I Afriki, Istoria, Ekonomika, Kul'tura, Akademija Nauk SSR. 6, 73–81.

Sedov, L.A., 1967. *Angkorskaīa︡ imperiīa︡: sotsial'no-ėkonomicheskiĭ i gosudarstvennyĭ stroĭ Kambodzhi v IX-XIV vv. (Angkor Empire: Socio-economic and Political System of Cambodia in the IX-XIV Centuries).* Moskva: Nauka, Glav. red. vostochnoĭ lit-ry.

Sedov, L.A., 1978. Angkor: society and state, in *The Early State*, eds. H.J.M. Claessen & P. Skalnik. The Hague: Mouton, 111–30.

Stern, P., 1951. Diversité et rythme des fondations royales khmères. *Bulletin de l'École française d'Extrême-Orient* 44(2), 649–87.

Tambiah, S.J., 1977. The galactic polity: the structure of traditional kingdoms in Southeast Asia. *Annals of the New York Academy of Sciences* 293(1), 69–97.

Vickery, M., 1998. *Society, Economics, and Politics in Pre-Angkor Cambodia: The 7th–8th Centuries.* Tokyo: Centre for East Asian Cultural Studies for Unesco, Toyo Bunko.

Woodward, H.W., 1981. Tantric Buddhism at Angkor Thom. *Ars Orientalis* 12, 57–67.

Zhou, D., 1992[1297]. *The Customs of Cambodia.* Translated by ed. P. Pelliot & J. Gilman D'Archy Paul. 2. Bangkok: Siam Society.

19

ANGKOR'S AGRARIAN ECONOMY

A Socio-Ecological Mosaic

Scott Hawken and Cristina Cobo Castillo

Introduction

Over the past three decades a dedicated program of survey and settlement mapping has resulted in a remarkable new map of Angkor, in which the city's vast urban form and dispersed settlement structure is now evident (Evans et al. 2007; Klassen et al. 2021). The survey program, named the Greater Angkor Project to emphasise the scale of the city (Pottier 1999; Fletcher et al. 2003, 2006, 2007), has been developed using the theoretical lens of low-density urbanism (Hawken et al. 2021), which challenges the conventional characterisation of agrarian cities as consisting of a dense urban settlement and an agrarian productive rural hinterland. Within low-density agrarian cities, urban communities are distributed throughout a landscape in which open space dominates. The vast urban complex of Greater Angkor is regarded as the most extensive known example of a low-density city, covering 1500 sq km or more at its peak during the 12th to 13th centuries (Carter et al. 2021; Chevance et al. 2019). The structure of Angkor's low-density form consists of a central urban core or specialist ceremonial-civic districts within a landscape of much lower-density residential clusters and community temples (Hawken et al. 2023, this volume), integrated by a hydraulic superstructure that doubled as a local transport system (Fletcher 2009; Hendrickson 2010; Graham and Isendahl 2018; Isendahl 2012; Isendahl and Smith 2013). Within Greater Angkor's periphery are open spaces predominantly used for the cultivation of rice, gardens, managed forests, and orchards.

This chapter is above all about prioritising such agrarian open spaces to present Angkor as a continuous productive landscape rather than a cluster of archaeological sites within a 'void'. Through closer examination of the agrarian landscape and its subdivision, demarcation of boundaries, and patterning we can better understand the social, political, and ecological dimensions of Angkor. Agrarian rice fields, arboriculture, and garden systems provide insight on the positioning of temples and other urban features and also offer rich insights on environmental modifications of the landscape. What follows is first a theoretical framing to contextualise the botanical and agrarian diversity within Greater Angkor. Two separate sections then synthesise the rice field landscapes and the community forests within Angkor's urban landscape. Finally, we present three vignettes of different environmental patches, each providing specific insights into the planning and management of Angkor's agrarian landscape.

DOI: 10.4324/9781351128940-24

The Environment, Hydraulic System, and the Agrarian Economy

Southeast Asia's monsoon and climate is fundamental to agrarian society in Cambodia. High temperatures and a high annual rainfall, usually upwards of 1000 mm and 1358 mm within Siem Reap, characterise the region within the seasonal variation characteristic of monsoon environments. Every year across mainland southeast Asia over four fifths of rainfall falls between May and September in an uneven monsoonal pattern that stimulates great natural abundance and biodiversity while inspiring imaginative and innovative socio-technical systems to manage this variability to best effect. For example the Tonle Sap, the lake that lies at the heart of Cambodia, swells to more than quadruple its size in the wet season to create a nutrient-rich lake that sustains one of the World's richest sources of fish (Halls and Hortle 2021). The dramatic monsoonal pulse was the foundation of the region's ecological richness but also presented challenges for developing agriculture in a successful way. Scholars ranging from Nesbitt to Delvert to B.-P. Groslier suggest that seasonal variability and unpredictability presented the single greatest challenge for Khmer agrarian practice. For example, if the rhythm of the annual monsoon was broken by either a dry spell or an unusually heavy deluge, farmers faced the potential for crop failure (Delvert 1994[1961]). Therefore, since prehistoric times, the management of this monsoonal variability and risk has been at the centre of Khmer agrarian production (Kealhoffer 2002).

Angkor's renowned hydraulic superstructure, consisting of major reservoirs and canal systems, was most likely implemented to manage this variability rather than to directly intensify production per se (Fletcher et al. 2008a, 2008b). Following decades of argument, in recent research, the creation of the hydraulic system is generally seen as a mechanism to help ensure stability in rice production rather than a deterministic strategy to increase yields (Fletcher et al. 2008a). This hydraulic debate is one of the most important in Angkorian scholarship (Groslier 1974, 1979; Acker 1998, 2006; Van Liere 1982; Pottier 2000b; Stott 1992); however, here it is sufficient to say that the scale of the hydraulic superstructure has attracted the greater amount of research and attention and has not always explicitly been linked to rice field cultivation in a detailed and granular way.

Granular studies that have addressed this linkage range from those that tend to support the hydraulic city model (Pottier 2000b; Hawken 2013) to those who question its efficiency (Pillot 2008; Bourdonneau 2010). However, we suggest that while recent scholarship has effectively discredited an exclusive view of hydraulic infrastructure as 'ritual' rather than strictly 'functional', future work may benefit from greater synthesis of ritual, political, and engineering theories. We focus on the idea that no single model will serve to explain or support the hydraulic city concept in relation to Angkor's socio-ecological agrarian mosaic (Fedick 1996). Rather, the emphasis should be on how different parts of the landscape might have been managed to create a diversity of strategies. Thus here we challenge the monolithic view of Angkor and vast rice field estates to suggest a patchwork of systems—some large, some small, and of varying efficiencies managed according to different ritual and political-economic relationships.

Rice and Rice Fields in Angkor

Rice has been a central theme of Khmer life and development since before the time of Angkor (Fox and Ledgerwood 1999; Fuller et al. 2016). Rice was a ubiquitous and dominant economic good within Angkor; this heritage is evident throughout the archaeological and historical record and carries through to many aspects of life, including everyday language. For instance, in Khmer it is common to greet a fellow Khmer with the question,

'Have you eaten rice yet?' Although several excellent treatises on contemporary agrarian Khmer culture exist (Delvert 1994[1961]; Ebihara 2018), systematic and fine-grained analyses of Angkor's agrarian landscape are a more recent development (Hawken 2012, 2013). Khmer temple inscriptions contain many texts describing the establishment of rice fields, as well as transactions relating to agricultural land, the exchange of rice, and also plantations and garden crops (Dagens 2003, 116–24; see also Ricklefs 1967; Jacob 1978; Lustig 2009a). Although mentions of rice and rice fields are ubiquitous in Angkor's inscriptions, spatial relationships and associations must be inferred. For example, while rice fields were described by their dimensions, either in lineal or areal units, or by the quantity of seed needed to cultivate them, such measurements remain opaque (Chakravarti 1978, 213–14). Equally, local toponyms and landmarks are often mentioned, but the vast majority of these spatial markers are unknown or unidentifiable today. Thus, when it comes to understanding the spatial dimensions and qualities of Angkor's urban landscape, archaeological and ethnographic evidence is our most helpful lead. We are also now learning more about the diversity of Angkor's agrarian economy through disciplines such as archaeobotany (Castillo et al. 2018b, 2020; Castillo 2023, this volume) and palynology (Penny et al. 2006; Penny and Hall 2023, this volume).

Angkor's setting can best be visualised as a series of distinctive geographic zones (Rollet 1972; Delvert 1994[1961]) that stretch along the northern edge of the Tonle Sap, the large lake that sits at the centre of Cambodia. Dense evergreen and mixed deciduous forests, with better ability to collect or hold water, cover the Kulen Hills, forming the watershed for Angkor. Foothills and drier plains with mature lateritic and sandy soils with low water holding capacity sit below this watershed, cut through with rivers and streams. Surrounding Angkor is a patchwork of grassy flooded, savannah vegetation and rice fields across expansive alluvial terraces. And at the very edge of the lake at the lowest elevation, there are a mix of seasonally inundated rice fields and mangrove forests.

These geographic zones were profoundly transformed through a range of agricultural systems. *Sre prang*, or dry season, receding flood agriculture utilised the shores and receding waters of the Tonle Sap. In contrast, *sre vea*, deepwater rice, or floating rice, occupied the same zone but relied on the rising waters. *Sre vossa*, or rainfed lowland rice, was situated upon the lacustrine terraces above the lakeside flood zone and relied predominantly on direct rainfall and overland runoff. Finally *chamkar*, or rainfed upland rice, and gardens were practiced upon elevated, drier sandier soils with low water (Delvert 1994[1961], 324–332). Each of these systems presents various advantages and risks—and challenges of interest to both the agronomist and the archaeologist. We examine such risks and opportunities in the following, but suffice it to say here that each rice cultivation system integrated diverse rice varieties and spatial cultivation strategies for ensuring a productive season.

Various scholars including Ng (1979), Van Liere (1980, 1989) and Fox and Ledgerwood (1999) have hypothesised on the diversity and spatial configuration of past cultivation techniques using a mix of mapping of rice environments, documentation of ethnographic practice and the location of past habitation sites, and observation of present-day cultivation practices. For instance, Fox and Ledgerwood (1999) have emphasised the importance of receding rice (*sre prang*) cultivation around the shores of the Tonle Sap and within the Delta region of Cambodia. Fox and Ledgerwood (1999) suggest that the prehistoric and early historic sites of the lower Mekong would have prioritised the cultivation of recession rice. Van Liere has also noted the importance of this 'sophisticated' system suggesting that the system comes into its own in the dry season when the inundated lands around the Tonle Sap and other water bodies begin to recede. Storage is achieved in wedge shaped dams called 'thamnup' (Van Liere's transliteration is tnub) that trap the receding waters. Van Liere suggests that in Siem Reap, water stored by such dams is not enough for irrigation, but we find this is not accurate. The dams hold water to irrigate throughout the dry season, with the water distributed through different types of gates and sluices.

Sre vossa, or rainfed lowland rice, is the most important archaeologically for the study of Angkor, due to the extensive coverage of such systems, their archaeological provenance, their remarkable state of preservation, and the location of Greater Angkor in the midst of this band of rice system surrounding the Tonle Sap. The Khmer systems occur on the almost imperceptibly flat lacustrine terraces, largely above the reach of the flood waters of the Tonle Sap, and today occupy 85.7% of the total area of cultivated rice in Cambodia (Javier 1997, 40). This rice field system represents one of the largest extents of medieval field systems within Asia (Hawken 2012), characterising the lowland plains that surround the floodplains of the Tonle Sap, the Bassac River, and the Mekong River and is easily recognisable by the small dividing walls that define the fields, known as 'bunding'. Such divisions are clearly visible in remote sensed imagery (Van Liere 1980; Pottier 2000b; Hawken 2013).

Bunding serves to improve the hydraulic performance and ecology of the landscape, creating a suspended water table and transforming the biophysical properties of the landscape (Moormann and Breemen 1978, 41), creating an enormous ephemeral wetland that provides improved conditions for growing rice during the wet season. The antiquity of the fields has been a subject of speculation for many decades. As far back as the 19th century, Leclère, an early administrator of Cambodia, suggested that 'The ancient rice fields are ten times more numerous than the currently cultivated land . . . and the land suitable for farming that has never been sown is fifty times larger still' (Pillot 2008, 88). Van Liere (1980, 272) suggested that bunded fields were established from the 8th century on, but this seems far too late based on analysis completed of Angkor's large-scale systems (Hawken 2012). The exact origins and timing of bunded fields are unknown, although Higham (2014, 828–29, Higham 2017) has suggested bunded rainfed lowland rice field systems were already present during the late Iron Age from, 400 to 600 CE, laying a foundation for the 'seamless' transition to protohistoric *Chenla* in the Pre-Angkor Period (Higham 2014, 823; Vickery 1998). Higham bases such assertions on ecological indicators such as the gastropod shellfish species *Pila ampullacea*, a coloniser and indicator species for fixed rice fields (2014, 828).

Cambodian bunded field farmers are fully aware of the challenges they face in the cultivation of rice within a lowland, rainfed landscape using bunded rice fields. Their experience of the variation within this landscape has led to the development of a detailed classification system that they use to describe it. Three interrelated factors are used in farmers' broad classification of their rainfed lowland rice fields: topography, water depth in the field, and type of rice variety. These three variables are factored into decisions regarding the timing and type of cultivation practices used; these include nursery bed establishment, ploughing, transplanting or broadcasting, crop protection, fertilising, harvesting, and winnowing. The timing of these activities is based on experience of past monsoons and local shared knowledge (Hawken 2012). Such rainfed lowland rice fields are described as high (*srai leu*), middle (*srai kandal*), and low (*srai kraom*), and often farmers will have distributed landholdings across this gradient to help distribute risk and also temporal bottlenecks in labour demands. Depending on landscape morphology, fields may be distributed in various configurations. For example, a low field may be adjacent to a high field, or high and middle fields may be adjacent. The varied elevation of fields can either exacerbate or ameliorate climatic conditions—low fields being susceptible to flooding and high fields being susceptible to drought conditions. This means that different fields can fail in different years depending on climatic variation. The resulting diversity of conditions of different moisture and water levels thus creates a mosaic (Rosenswig 2015) of different topographic levels, observable from remotely sensed imagery and aerial reconnaissance. Therefore, whilst Angkor's economy was based on a reliable return from its primary crop, this crop was managed and cultivated through a diverse and sophisticated range of strategies. Further, there is an increasing appreciation that rice agriculture was supported by a diversity of other crops such as millet and mung beans (*Vigna radiata*) (Dagens 2003, 122; Castillo et al. 2020).

While many contemporary rice farmers grow rice primarily for their own consumption, it is also necessary for a range of other purposes (Ebihara 2018, 31). Beyond what is consumed, Khmer farmers use rice for seed, with around 66–110 kg needed to seed 1 hectare of land—about a third to a half of what is consumed by a person annually. Rice is also used for religious ceremonies and contributions and as currency in lieu of money. Finally, after all these other uses have been satisfied, rice may be taken to market (Ebihara 2018, 117–18). These mid-20th-century observations by Ebihara are not so different from what we might have expected during the Angkor Period. In agrarian states, one or two primary grains provide the main food and staple, function as a unit for taxation, and also form the basis for hegemonic relations within an agrarian calendar. Rice, like other grains, is an ideal unit for taxation. Rice also has a particularly good return on investments in energy when compared to other grains (Bray 1986, 15). Such considerations were of importance within Angkor, which went without currency and therefore relied on rice for a range of transactional and financial functions (Lustig 2009b).

All these systems were in use when the French arrived in the 19th and 20th centuries (Delvert 1994[1961]; Gourou 1940). Further sophisticated rice-cultivation technologies were most likely in use in the Mekong Delta during the initial centuries of the first millennium CE, although the archaeological evidence for this is sometimes circumstantial. Polities in the Delta were in contact with societies such as China and India, both of which had been using sophisticated, intensive cultivation techniques involving bunded fields for at least several thousand years by that time (Fuller and Qin 2009).

Gardens, Orchards, Arboriculture, and Angkor

Up until the late 20th century, Khmer people turned to the plants around them for essentially all materials, including those necessary for building, tools, clothing, food, medicine, and religious and spiritual paraphernalia (Martin 1971). And while rice fields were the principal agricultural crop that sustained Khmer society, their productive gardens provided for the diverse uses that Khmer culture required. Delvert (1994[1961]) has suggested that there are two types of Cambodian, the rice farmer and the gardener, but strictly speaking, all Cambodians in settlements such as Siem Reap had gardens of some form or another. For example, farmers' wooden houses were built upon mounds raised above the expanses of surrounding rice fields. These mounds were surrounded by a range of gardens and anthropogenic, community forests used for food, construction, and medicinal purposes. The anthropologist Kalab has said that Khmer

> habitations are one vast garden with houses scattered between the trees, the only prominent buildings elevated well above the rest are temples in pagoda compounds. Residential houses are built mostly of wood, bamboo and palm leaf, with thatch or shingles for roof, the better ones on piles, temporary ones on the ground.
>
> (1968, 522)

This almost complete fusion of settlement, orchards, and community forest means that to study such forests is to study the settlement patterns of the Khmer.

Delvert suggests there were various types of gardens or agriculture, or *chamkar*, which supported the farmers of Cambodia. These include small productive gardens integrated with the settlements in the midst of the rice fields, gardens and orchards and community forests along the riverbanks, and more extensive gardens at the edge of the forested hills (1994[1961], 365–70). Ebihara calls this first type the 'kitchen' garden and orchard and notes that all but five of the many hundreds of houses maintained these community gardens. In contrast to the strenuous labour devoted to rice cultivation, Ebihara suggests that relatively minimal demands are placed by such gardens since the fruit trees are all mature and take little care, even if the vegetables require a little more effort, such as weeding. While there is a great diversity of edible species, other plants were grown for medicinal purposes (areca nuts chewed as betel) or building or tools (bamboo) (2018, 120–21).

Of the second type, gardens along river banks, Delvert (1994[1961]) notes that in mid-20th century Siem Reap, the inhabitants of Phum Treang village, which then consisted of about 200 dwellings, specialised in the cultivation of orchards of lush coconut trees; areca trees; mango trees; mangosteen trees; and vegetable gardens of cabbage, potatoes, and beans. They also had rice fields which they rented to inhabitants of nearby villages and exchanged fruit and vegetables for paddy and fish. Typically, communities that stretch along the banks of the rivers have such mixed activities, dividing their time between rice and such village orchards. Only in exceptional circumstances do they dedicate themselves to the cultivation of productive orchards and gardens alone.

Finally, the extensive forest gardens at the foot of the hills come into their own during the rainy season where, nurtured by the nutrients, humidity, and organic matter of the forest edge, they produce a variety of fruits at a distance from the community settlement. These consist mostly of fruit tree plantations such as coconut trees, areca palm trees, and banana plants which form thick forest gardens at the very foot of the hills. These are complemented by a community of productive but low-maintenance species that include potatoes, peanuts, mulberry trees, and pepper plants (Ebihara 2018, 121).

A profusion of wild flora also grows unattended within Khmer settlements, as Ebihara has noted (2018, 121). These include bushy thickets of grasses, vines, cacti, ferns, shrubs, and trees that also have uses such as informal fences or hedges and may also provide resources for crafts or as fodder for cattle. These untamed species nevertheless form part of this domestic botanical food forest and botanical assemblage. The richness of such botanical assemblages is listed in ethnographic studies of the local vegetation by scholars such as Lewitz and Rollet (1973) and Martin (1971, 1974). Such ethnographic descriptions of garden settlements resonate with what we know about Angkorian settlement from the historic and epigraphic sources. Zhou Daguan, writing in the mid-13th century, is careful to express the diversity of the Khmer botanical World, listing the many fruits, vegetables, and flowers he is familiar with and suggesting a greater diversity by noting the limits of his own knowledge (Zhou 2007[1297], 22, 25).

Angkorian settlement and temple landscapes would have appeared as distinctive forested patches or an arboreal cityscape as Lentz (Lentz et al. 2014, 2021) might say in relation to similarly forested cities of the Maya) within the open, extensive rice field landscapes that dominated the low-density landscapes (Hawken 2013). State temple sanctuaries and specialist urban districts such as Angkor Thom have now been revealed to be highly ordered in layout and structure, consisting of gridded causeways and arrays of small ponds (Gaucher 2003a, 2003b; Evans et al. 2013; Evans 2016;). Furthermore, following excavations at Angkor Wat, Ta Prohm, and Ankgor Thom, we can increasingly appreciate that the major temple landscapes hosted permanent populations along with large numbers of long- and short-term inhabitants. Such temples sourced resources from thousands of communities within Greater Angkor and beyond, thereby serving as anchors for communities living in nearby villages. For example, the inscription of the state temple of Ta Prohm, K. 273 (Cœdès 1951, 1906), states that donations were gathered from a total of 3140 communities. The inscription also lists the dedication of 79,365 personnel to service the temple, and these were made up of diverse backgrounds, including Khmer, Burman, and Cham. The inscription also lists that 12,640 people had right to lodgings, notes the dedication of 615 dancers, and states that 66,652 personnel were dedicated to pious duties in 'service of the Gods'. A program of excavation has revealed that such populations were often inhabitants of such temple sanctuaries and engaged in a range of domestic activities (Stark et al. 2015; Carter et al. 2018). Such epigraphic numbers and archaeological finds indicate that temples and Angkor's various urban centres were thriving centres of activity.

Defining Angkor's Agrarian Patches

The components of Angkor's agrarian system allow us to model the organisation of spaces within the low-density area. We use the terms 'patch' and 'mosaic' to describe the rice landscape (Hawken 2012, 2013), but here we also use it to describe the various productive forests and gardens closely integrated with settlement landscapes. Rice fields made up over 80% of the cultivated land within Cambodia, with the rest consisting of gardens and plantations. Within Angkor, and in fact within all landscapes (Forman and Godron 1981; Riitters 2019; McKey et al. 2010), we can understand and classify such agrarian landscapes as a series of 'patches' across the landscape.

Such patches can be defined through a number of approaches including land cover or land use. In landscape ecology such patches are typically classified through spectral analysis of remotely sensed imagery. In archaeology they are more frequently defined through specific material assemblages which in Angkor consists of Angkorian temples (*prasat*), Angkorian ponds (*trapeang*), and Angkorian rice fields (*sre*). Around Angkor, rice fields and forest patches were established during different periods to take advantage of the variable environmental conditions and satisfy the developmental needs of Angkorian society (Hawken 2012). Further, such agrarian patches are a manifestation of Angkor's political economy, with temples exercising influence over different patches within the landscape.

The regular geometric characteristics of Angkorian rice field systems make it possible to map their distribution across the landscape using approaches borrowed from landscape ecologists (Forman 1996; Turner et al. 2001) and landscape archaeologists working in the Mediterranean and the Fertile Crescent contexts, most notably on Roman centuriation and its endurance and transformation over the centuries (Chouquer 1996a, 1996b, 1997; Wilkinson 2003). In Roman contexts, multiphase field systems can cover as much as 3500 sq km (Hilali 2013), and Angkor's systems rival these in size (Hawken 2012). Rice fields, which share common morphological and contextual characteristics such as size, orientation, and proximity (Hawken 2012), are able to be filtered out from a noisy background and studied as coherent systems or 'patches'. These patches take on a mosaic-like pattern when observed at the scale of Greater Angkor. Patches can be sorted into different classes based on common characteristics such as orientation, scale, and proximity. The most common class of patch forms a contextual 'matrix' in which other less common patch classes are embedded. For example, in some parts of the landscape, prehistoric rice field patches dominate and form a matrix, whilst in others, Angkorian patch classes dominate and form a matrix. Classification techniques revolving around the principal characteristic of orientation, have been found to reliably and powerfully distinguish Angkorian rice field patches from one another. Angkor's rice fields are typically aligned according to the cardinal directions and share common size and spatial relationships with other archaeological features such as temples, many of which can be dated. Using these techniques, Angkorian rice field systems have been distinguished from other rice field systems established prior to or following the Angkor Period.

Mapping of rice fields across Greater Angkor reveals a variety of distinct rice field patch systems that produce a broader matrix of agricultural activity. Each matrix ranges from around 2000 to over 6000 ha in size. While not completely homogeneous, a matrix contains enough patches of the same or similar type to provide the context to more fragmented and diverse patch distributions within it. Such large matrices are an interesting and significant subject of study because they provide insight into engineering and planning principles that link the Khmer rice field farmer and the overarching Khmer state. We can then generate certain hypotheses about how such principles relate to the concentration or devolution of agrarian control in the low-density urban systems of the mediaeval Khmer world.

By examining the variety of agricultural fields or *sre* and household gardens or *chamkar* within Angkor's dispersed urban footprint, we can piece together different socio-ecological relationships within Greater Angkor. In this chapter we consider the vast gridded field systems that transformed whole river systems, move through a discussion of small patchworks of fields laid out ceremoniously around clusters of local community temples, and finish at the scale of the patterning of household activities within Angkor's community gardens and forests. From these three linked discussions, we characterise the scales and types of agrarian activity that make up the socio-ecological mosaic of Angkor.

Three Vignettes of Angkor's Agrarian Patches

We present three different vignettes of Angkor's agrarian patches which demonstrate the diversity of practices at different times and places within the capital in order to emphasise the diversity, and central place, of agrarian landscapes in Khmer society (Figure 19.1). These patches include the forested temple patches of Angkor Wat, Angkor Thom, and Ta Prohm and the rice field patches of Phnom Bok and Pre Rup. Of importance is our contribution to thinking about how such agrarian patches might have been managed. First, we present a complex rice field matrix, composed of many diverse patches and managed by a multitude of community temples. Second, we examine a much more homogenous large-scale rice field matrix consisting of a single patch managed by a large state temple. Last, we grapple with the idea of the productive arboreal cityscape of the Khmer associated with the major temple sanctuaries of the civic-ceremonial central zone of Angkor.

The Pre Rup Complex: A Multi-Patch Rice Field Matrix

The multi-patch type (Figure 19.2) is exemplified in the landscapes that surround and extend south from Pre Rup Temple. Rajendravarman II (944–968) is credited with the restoration of the old capital of Yaśovarman, or what has been called the foundation of the 'Second Yasodharapura' (Briggs 1999, 124). The 10th-century CE urban complex surrounding Pre Rup is without any enclosing walls typical of the dispersed open urban structure that characterises the various urban centres that make up the polycentric networked form of Greater Angkor. The planning of the complex and its rice field patches is closely related to the vast 1800 × 700 m dikes of the East Baray, which align and structure the rice fields, temples, and shrines (Pottier 1999, 176–182).

The different patches share spatial characteristics but can be discerned from each other through subtle variations in gauge, alignment, and proximity to archaeological elements such as community temples and embankments. These patches that make up the matrix range from

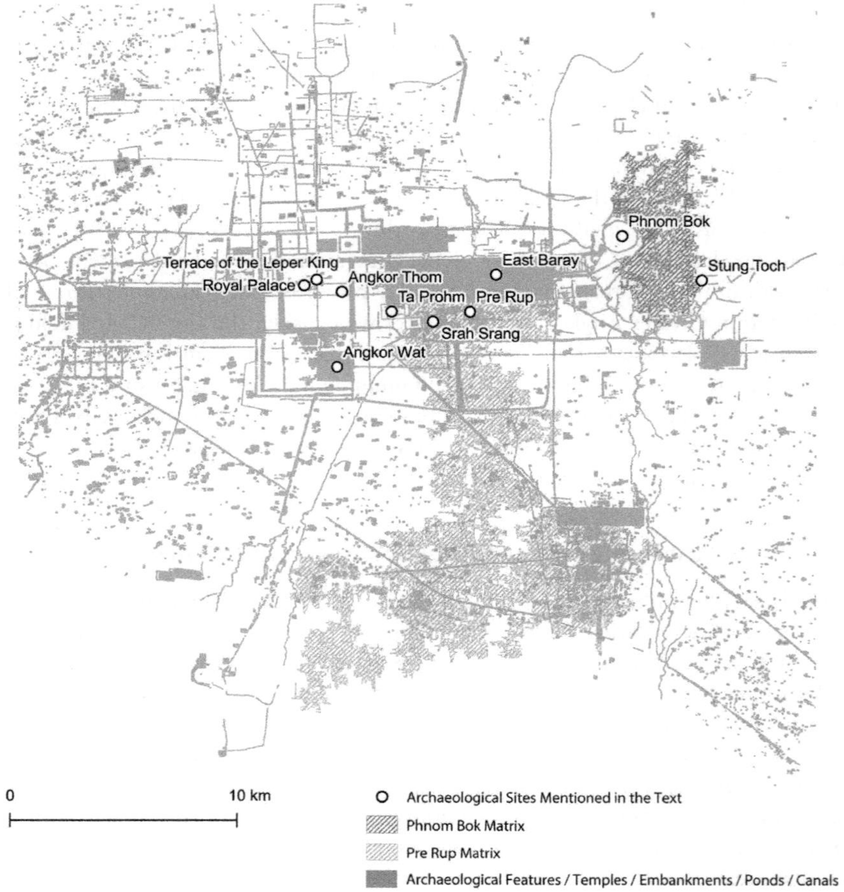

Figure 19.1 Agrarian patches identified within Greater Angkor. For the colour version of this figure and legend, the reader is referred to the web version of this chapter.

GIS Source: C. Pottier 1999, D. Evans 2007 & S. Hawken 2012.

larger-sized patches associated with state temples such as Pre Rup to smaller patches associated with local or village temples (see Hawken and Klassen 2023, this volume) such as Prasat Chuk. The 10th-century temple is an organising element that orders a large coherent rice field patch.

This multi-patch assemblage integrates various significant temples and infrastructure from the reign of Yaśovarman I, such as the East Baray, but also a range of other temples from as early as the 9th century to those from the 12th century. Patches of adjoining cardinal rice fields extend south from the East Baray to form an extensive cardinally oriented matrix that stretches all the way to the floodplain of the Tonle Sap. The matrix has an area of about 6500 ha, making

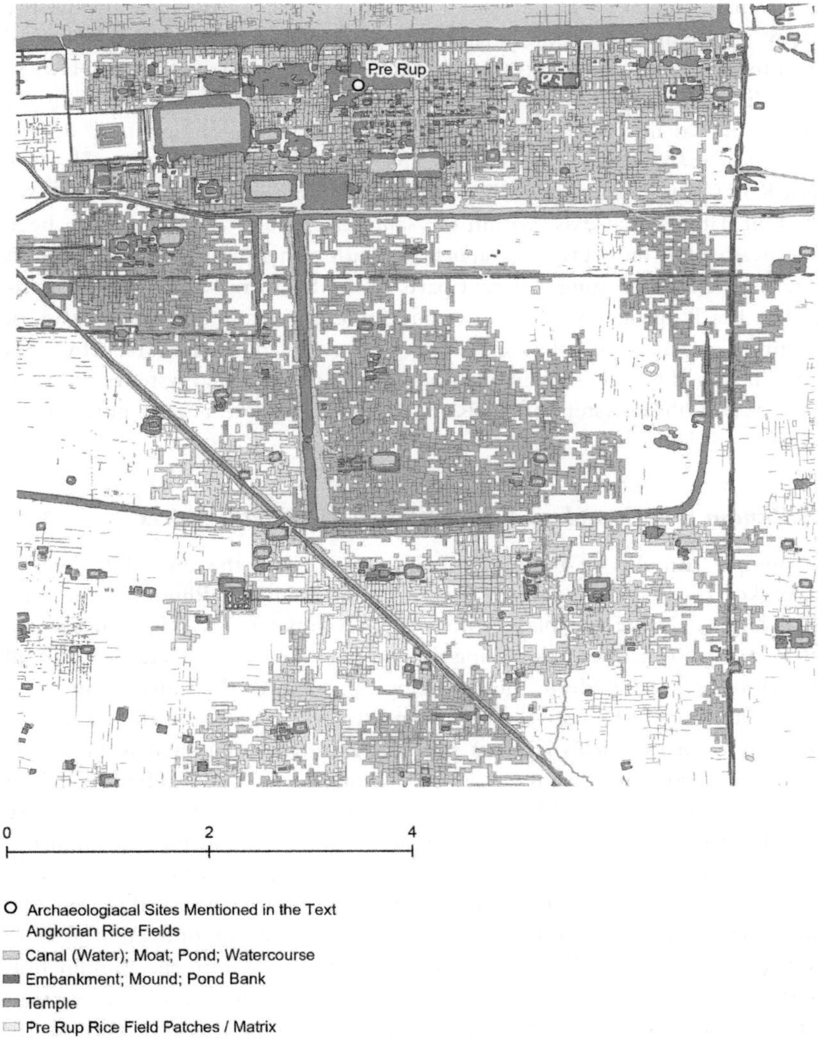

Figure 19.2 The Pre Rup matrix. Note the many smaller patches of rice field systems, here coloured in various shades of green. For interpretation of the references to colour in this figure and legend, the reader is referred to the web version of this chapter.

GIS Source: C. Pottier 1999, D. Evans 2007 & S. Hawken 2012.

it the largest cardinal matrix in Greater Angkor. It is significant for a variety of reasons. For instance, it demonstrates significant time depth through its integration of diverse rice field patches and links the large state temple rice field patches with many smaller rice field patches and their local temples (see Hawken and Klassen 2023, this volume). These rice fields were connected, and water moved through them to the south, although various embankments and hydraulic infrastructure complicate this southerly overland flow. In this way it presents a scalable model for the management of the agrarian landscape and a basis for which to develop various theories on Angkor's political economy.

A consistent cardinal orientation characterises the many patches that make up the Pre Rup Matrix. Many, if not most, of these small patches are organised around smaller and more modest local temples and settlements that have diverse foundation dates (see Hawken and Klassen 2023, this volume). The diversity of temples and patches associated with the matrix indicates that it was developed according to local initiatives, indicating a decentralised or heterarchical management of the landscape. For example, we can see that the sites of Prasat Wat Kok Chan Reangsei and Trapeang Boeng Phlou are associated with two adjacent but different patches that exist within the same catchment. Each may have been responsible for cultivation of the fields and water flows within their ambit, much as occurs today with different farmers managing different parts of the landscape within a single village settlement. The Pre Rup matrix is extensive and integrates many different patches of both local community and state temples, suggesting a complex network driven by both centralised and decentralised forces. This contrast between the centralised system of Phnom Bok and the partly decentralised system of Pre Rup provokes questions of distributed water management across patch landscapes.

The Phnom Bok Complex: A Single Patch Rice Field Matrix

The three-tower temple complex of Phnom Bok sits atop one of the three hills located within Greater Angkor (Figure 19.3). These hills—Phnom Bakheng, Phnom Krom, and Phnom Bok—had a special value and place within the development of Yaśovarman's city, serving as a central locus to organise surrounding development and infrastructure. While all temples aspire to represent Mount Meru, the mythological centre of the universe, in a few rare cases the idea is not merely figurative, and we find temples situated on the summit of natural hills with systems of rice fields laid out around them. These representations of the celestial mountain were surrounded by a moat which represented the ocean (Heine-Geldern 1942, 16–18). We see this in relation to Phnom Bakheng and Goulobews theories on the city of Yaśodharapura, the first capital in the core of Angkor centred around Phnom Bakheng. Phnom Bakheng and Yaśodharapura have been the subject of a number of controversies on the layout and features associated with Phnom Bakheng, with Pottier eventually clarifying the various features associated with Phnom Bakheng through a process of topographical morphological analysis (2000a). As with Phnom Bakheng and Phnom Krom, the Phnom Bok complex was constructed between the 9th and 10th centuries during the reign of Yaśovarman I (889–910) after he moved his capital from Hariharalaya (close to the lake near present-day Rolous) to Yaśodharapura (Briggs 1999, 110) and is the first formalised construction in this area. Phnom Bok is surrounded by a much more extensive rice field system that extends east and north of the *phnom* (hill) in an extensive, regular, gridded pattern. Whether these fields are definitely associated with Phnom Bok is a fair question and one addressed in the following. As is typical of Angkor's major temples, Phnom Bok's three sandstone shrines, dedicated to Śaiva, Brahma, and Viṣṇu, are supported on a sandstone terrace that faces east with false doors facing the other cardinal directions (Briggs 1999, 110). Directly east of the hill and in alignment with Prasat Phnom Bok sits another temple, Prasat Trapeang Chambak, that itself faces east and is associated with a large trapeang. It seems these various structures and Phnom Bok have been conceived as one ensemble.

The rice fields extend from this ensemble rather than any single archaeological element. The ordered rice field system integrates the Stung Toch river system by way of east–west aligned feeder channels (Hawken 2012). Both the small and large topographic features relate in a coherent way, suggesting that the landscape belongs to a single phase of development designed to distribute

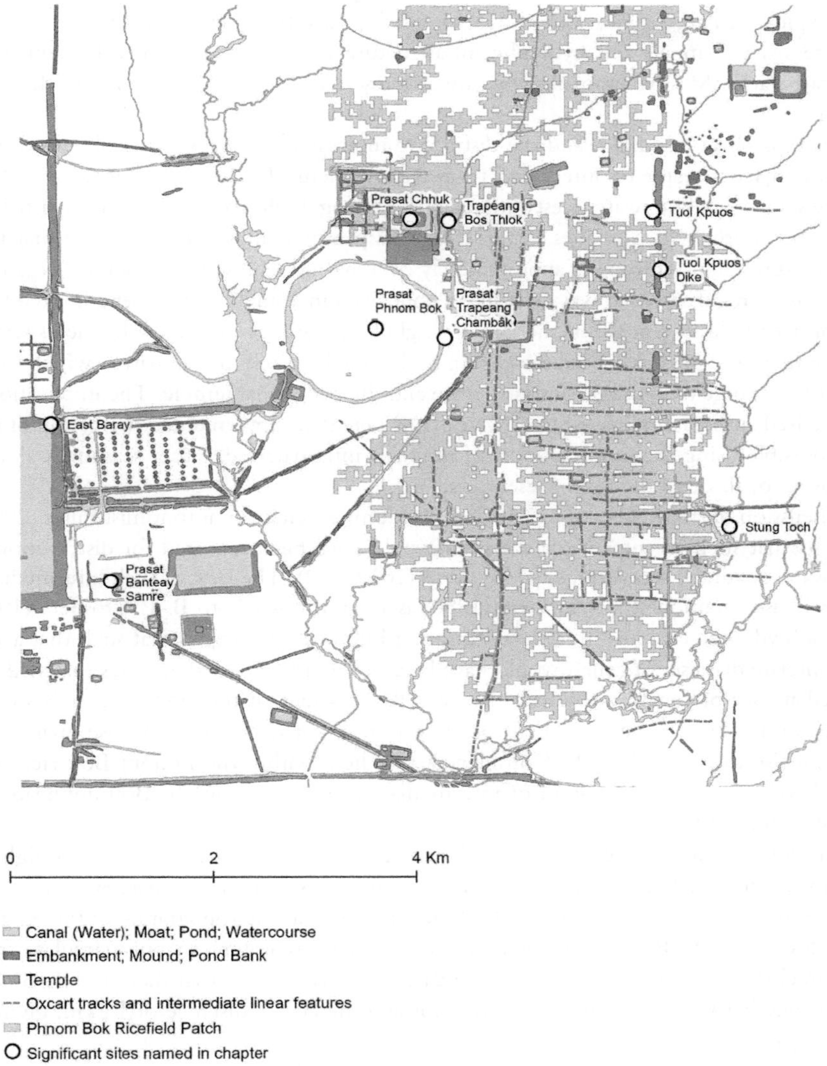

Figure 19.3 The Phnom Bok matrix. Note the large, ordered rice field system, characterised by small channels that could distribute water evenly across the landscape. For the colour version of this figure and legend, the reader is referred to the web version of this chapter.

GIS Source: C. Pottier 1999, D. Evans 2007 & S. Hawken 2012.

water evenly during the wet season. The remnant Angkorian rice field system is still farmed today, allowing us to observe water being distributed from the east to the west via the rice fields.

While not originally considered a hydraulic zone within B.-P. Groslier's (1979) categorisation of the landscape, it is clear that this landscape, with its hydraulic infrastructure and rice fields, could be considered part of the hydraulic city. The channels are relatively straight, with slight variation that is most probably due to degradation over time by weathering and continued use of the landscape as a productive agricultural zone. This is an ordered system, approximately

4 km across and more than twice that in length. It is organised according to a regular cardinal geometry typical of Angkorian features. The rice fields have been set out within a system of intermediate sized channels and hydraulic infrastructure that functioned into the 20th century as oxcart tracks. Massive embankments are also inserted into this system in a north–south orientation.

The single patch of rice fields and the distinctive intermediate canals are so placed to both benefit from adjacent water resources and to distribute them. The structure of the rice field system allows it to distribute water westwards from the Stung Toch river system and to distribute excessive water south, which it does to this day. This planned landscape indicates a managed hydraulic rice-growing landscape of approximately 2000 ha and represents a coherent, organised grid of surprising regularity that was most likely conceived in a single phase over a limited time period. This rice field system forms the largest single homogenous 'patch' of rice fields within Angkor. It is therefore possible to call the system both a single 'patch' and a 'matrix' which forms the context for a range of hydraulic infrastructure and the occasional temple. The implication is that a centralised authority managed this. We can envisage that supplementary irrigation of rice fields was possible using the configuration of remnant infrastructure, either seasonally during the wet season, or through the use of reservoirs.

In his discussion of rice fields and irrigation, Bourdonneau cites the agronomist Pillot (2007), who suggests that such an intermediate system would have been required for distribution of irrigation water accurately to various field systems (2010, 412). The lack of such intermediate-sized canals is also mentioned by van Liere (1980) as a major obstacle to B.-P. Groslier's (1979) concept of a 'hydraulic city'. Bourdonneau, quoting Pillot (2008), argues that such that a secondary or intermediate set of canals would have been necessary and further notes that without an intermediate set of canals, and given the very flat gradient of the landscape, it is strictly 'impossible' for a farmer to be dependent on irrigation, as farmers need a precise quantity of water at a precise time (2010, 412). Considering that here within the Phnom Bok rice field system we have exactly such a system of intermediate canals, we may put Bourdonneau and Pillot's objection to rest.

But then how do we then reconcile Pillot's critique of the irrigation hypothesis in light of the Pre Rup rice field systems previously discussed, which present no immediate evidence of an intermediate set of canals? Bourdonneau and Pillot suggest that the topography of the Angkor plain militates against B.-P. Groslier's hydraulic city theory, as water can only circulate from parcel to parcel if the slope is sufficient and regular; they further note that there is only 8 m of elevation change between the reservoirs of Angkor and the lake, a distance of 10 km, giving a fall of 0.08% (Bourdonneau 2010, 413).

Nonetheless, standing in the rice fields today, even in the absence of a functioning reservoir and canal system, one observes that the water flows from rice field parcel to rice field parcel quite effectively. During a flood, the water can flow rapidly and over top the rice field bunds, causing some damage. However, usually this is managed through a distributed system that is not supremely flat but exhibits a myriad variation in level, all of which the farmer understands and adapts from year to year. In some years some fields are more successful than others, and in different periods of the season different rice fields, either high, mid, or low, are put into action within each patch to distribute, contain, or drain water. Such a system is not of a single engineer's design but, to borrow the words of Dumarçay (1998), 'a work of collective genius'. The difficulty with the critique put forward by Bourdonneau and Pillot is that, being a technocratic one, it is not made with due consideration of farmers and their sophisticated strategies for management and lacks sufficient understanding of the simultaneous failures and successes of their collective and diverse patchwork on a seasonal and annual basis.

Temple Complexes of the Civic Ceremonial Centre: Water Gardens and Food Forest Patches

The final vignette of Angkorian socio-ecological patches is associated with elite state temples and complexes that are delineated by the presence of massive walls and moats and which together make up the densely inhabited urban core of the Greater Angkor complex. Such settlements are distinct from the dispersed urban villages with their rice field patches that surround the civic ceremonial centre of Angkor.

The temple gardens and forests are difficult to find archaeologically, and we therefore rely on ethnographic analogies and archaeobotanical remains to link mapped topographic elements with the precise and spatially focused archaeobotanical studies that we have. The combination of lidar and archaeobotanical evidence provides us with insight into the physical location of arboriculture and gardening plots and the types of plants that were being consumed or grown in them. These approaches allow us to reconstruct day-to-day economic transactions and specific people–plant relationships within Angkor (Castillo et al. 2018b, 2018a; Fuller et al. 2016).

Recent surveys and excavations of Angkor Wat (Carter et al. 2019; Evans and Fletcher 2015; Stark et al. 2015) have reinforced the idea that the temple sanctuary was a lively ritual landscape and also demonstrated evidence of occupation and continued residential activity (Figure 19.4). Topographic surveys of the temple complex have revealed a grid interspersed with an intricate pattern of mounds and a multitude of regularly sized and spaced ponds. If we use contemporary ethnographic sources to generalise, the complex topographic grid of ponds, causeways, and mounds may have been an immense 'arboreal cityscape'. Outside, to the south of the complex, a series of 12th-century earthen rectilinear coils and embankments within what was probably four major sections complete what is a water landscape that may have been a water garden for lotus and other plants (Evans and Fletcher 2015; Evans 2016) and which also had ritual and symbolic dimensions (Feneley et al. 2016).

Evans has remarked that such enigmatic landscapes were possibly 'gardens', though they have revealed little through excavations to suggest as much but are in close proximity to large standing bodies of water such as monumental moats and reservoirs (Evans 2016, 166), making them suitable for cultivation or even possibly fish ponds. Fish and water plants still make up a considerable part of the Khmer diet today. Likewise, the 13th century Chinese emissary Zhou Daguan makes a point of mentioning the diversity of unknown but apparently useful water plants not once but twice in his economical record of everyday life, pausing to note the lotus, for which he does know the name (Zhou 2007[1297], 22, 25).

Inside Angkor Wat, the evidence of gardening and plants has been enhanced by the excavation of mounds and the recovery of archaeobotanical macroremains (Figure 19.4a). Species identified as a result of the excavations are diverse and include many economic species typically grown in gardens in Southeast Asia, such as fruits and spices, and it is hypothesised that these plants were growing in the house gardens of the people living within the temple walls. Edible plants, such as rice and traces of citrus fruit, were found at Angkor Wat, but most of the recovered botanical fragments are from plants, such as long pepper and crêpe ginger, used in condiments and medicines. The samples from Angkor Wat show less diversity following the 13th century, perhaps due to a decline in the ritual activities at the temple. Species identified include rice (*Oryza sativa*), mung bean (*Vigna radiata*), cotton (*Gossypium* sp.), scarlet banana (*Musa coccinea*), crêpe ginger (*Cheilocostus speciosus*), black pepper (*Piper nigrum*), and long pepper (*Piper longum*).

Within Ta Prohm, the spatial organisation of the temple sanctuary—and for what may have been a temple-forest-garden—is more heterogeneous than the rigidly repetitive pattern of ponds

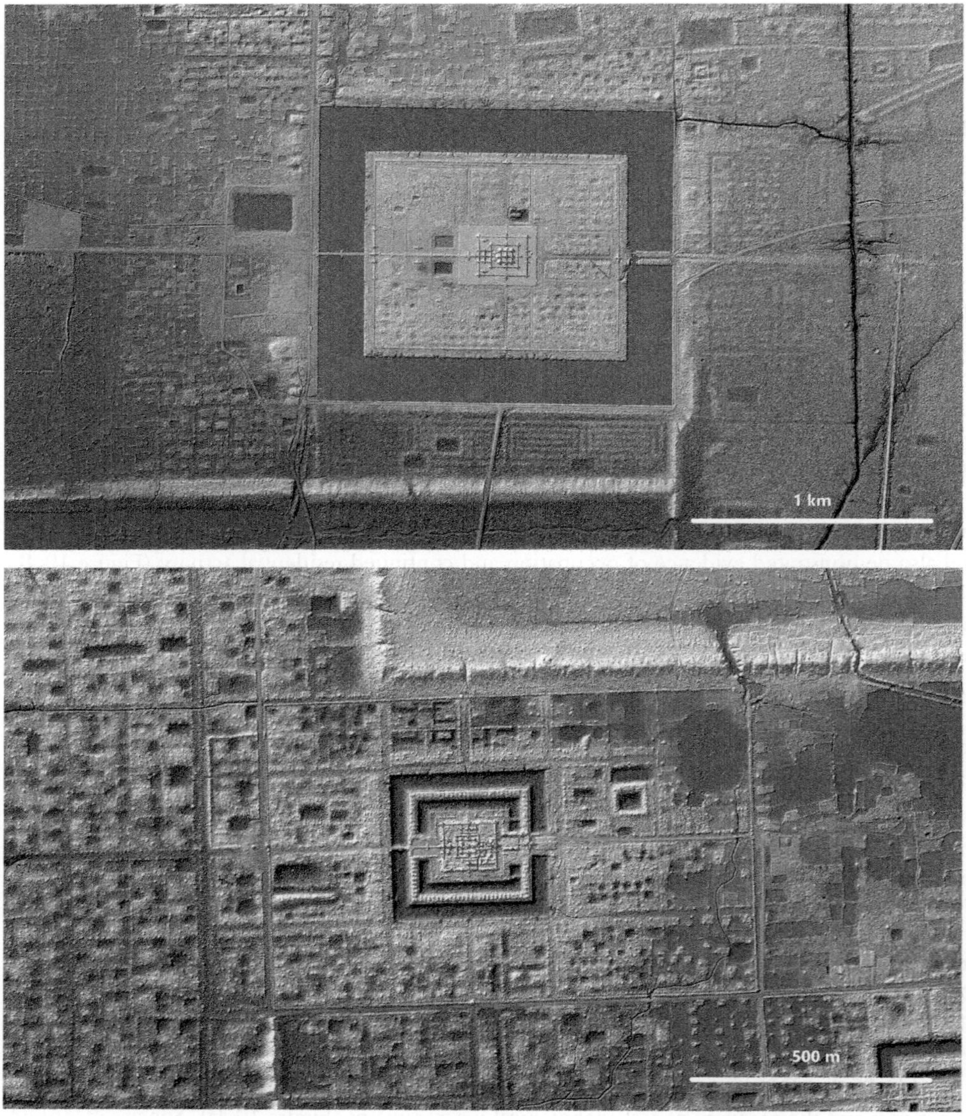

Figure 19.4 Lidar relief maps of Angkor Wat and Ta Prohm. The lidar reveals the highly structured grid pattern of ponds, canals, and mounds. This topography supported an arboreal cityscape with a rich diversity of useful and often edible aquatic and terrestrial plants.

Source: (Data KALC 2016).

and mounds within Angkor Wat (Figure 19.4b). Ponds and mounds in Ta Prohm are of various configurations and may correspond to a variety of uses and practices. Similar to Angkor Wat, the archaeobotanical evidence from Ta Prohm (Castillo et al. 2020) shows the significant relationships between people and plants within the temple enclosure—a population that, according to the famous inscription found at the temple, numbered in the thousands. The interior of Ta Prohm would have featured an abundance of trees based on the large quantities of dicotyledon phytoliths recovered. Palm tree phytoliths were also common in the assemblage, and although these were not identified to species for the three archaeobotanical analyses completed (Castillo et al. 2018b, 2020), we know from previous palynological (Penny et al. 2005, 2006) as well as ethnographic studies (Martin 1969, 1971; Delvert 1994[1961]) that Angkorian temple precincts likely hosted coconut (*Cocos nucifera*), areca palm (*Areca catechu*), sugar palm (*Borassus flabellifer*), and a mix of other useful trees (see Penny and Hall 2023, this volume).

A third urban complex, the giant, walled civic-ceremonial complex of Angkor Thom (Figure 19.5), has also revealed significant macrobotanical assemblages (Table 19.1). Taken from an excavation adjacent to the Royal Palace dating from the 14th and 15th centuries (Polkinghorne et al. 2014), archaeobotanical analysis demonstrates that Angkor Thom continued to be an active urban centre where people cultivated crops, cooked meals, performed rituals, and lived long after its apogee in the 12th to 13th centuries (Castillo et al. 2018b). Economic crops identified include sesame (*Sesamum indicum*), mung bean (*Vigna radiata*), yardlong bean (*Vigna unguiculata* subsp. *sesquipedalis*), hyacinth bean (*Lablab purpureus*), pigeon pea (*Cajanus cajan*), cotton (*Gossypium* sp.), and kapok or silk cotton tree (*Bombax ceiba*). These crops form a distinctive Southeast Asian ethno-botanical assemblage shared with South Asia.

While a diverse array of plants was recovered in all three of the great civic-ceremonial locales discussed in this section—Angkor Wat, Ta Prohm, and Angkor Thom—rice represented the largest proportion of economic crops. Furthermore, it is evident that rice was processed routinely within these areas, as demonstrated by the presence of rice processing waste which includes husk and spikelet bases. At Angkor Thom, desiccated rice was found alongside mung bean and sesame seeds in a lead vessel deposited probably for ritual purposes (Castillo et al. 2018b, 934). The Ta Prohm inscription lists desiccated rice, mung bean, and sesame seeds as ritual offerings (Cœdès 1906).

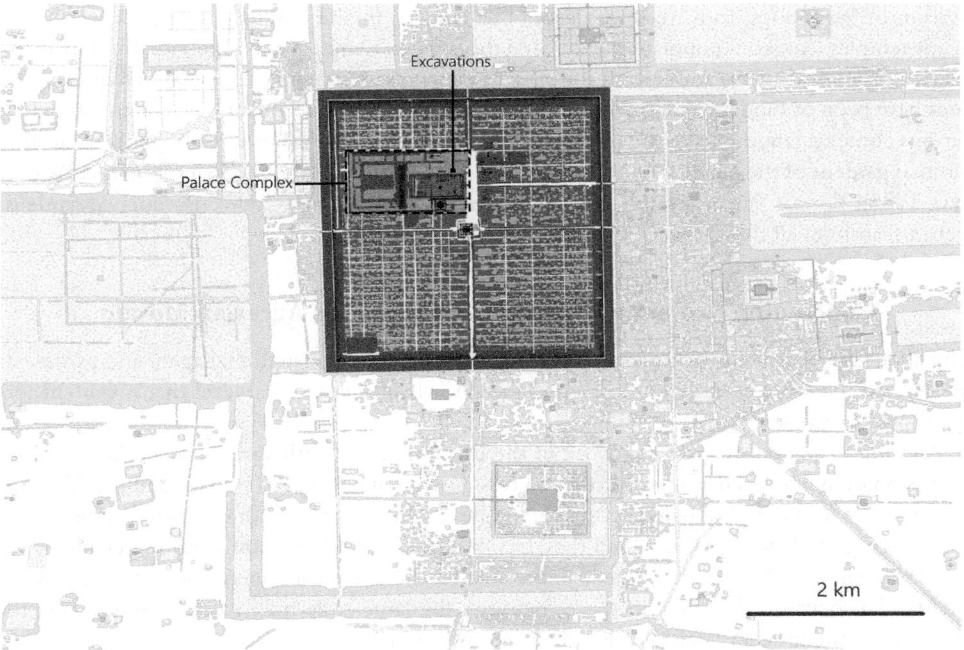

Figure 19.5 Lidar map of Angkor Thom.

Source: (Data KALC 2016).

Table 19.1 Distribution of recovered plants across the three study sites.

Taxon	*Angkor Wat*	*Ta Prohm*	*Angkor Thom*
Abelmoschus sp.	X		
Alpinia sp.		X	
Artocarpus sp.	X		
Bombax ceiba (Indian kapok/silk cotton tree)			X
Cajanus cajan (Pigeon pea)			X
Cheilocostus speciosus (Crêpe ginger)	X		
Citrus sp. (Citrus)	X		
Dracontomelon sp.	X		
Gossypium sp. (Cotton)	X	X	X
Lablab purpureus (Hyacinth bean)			X
cf. *Lithocarpus* (Nut shell)		X	
Musa coccinea (Scarlet banana)	X		
Oryza sativa L. (Rice)	X	X	X
Panicum miliaceum (Broomcorn millet)			X
Phyllanthus emblica (Indian gooseberry)	X		X
Piper nigrum (Black pepper)	X		
Sesamum indicum L. (Sesame)			X
Setaria italica (Foxtail millet)			X
Vigna radiata (Mung bean)	X		X
Vigna unguiculata subsp. *sesquipedalis* (Yardlong bean)			X

The plant diversity represented in archaeobotanical remains (Figure 19.6) indicates the cultivation of food crops, fruit trees, and economic gardens in and around the urban centres and major temples. Angkor's population cultivated these green temple patches for ritual and medicinal use, for nourishment, and to craft the various materials used in their everyday activities. Gardens have been of fundamental importance to societies everywhere and are well documented in various contexts ranging from the productive gardens of the Maya (Ford and Nigh 2016) to the Roman gardens of the Mediterranean (Jashemski et al. 2017) and those of Mesopotamia (Wiseman 1983), China, Japan (Carroll 2003), and the Amazon (Mann 2008). Productive gardens were a feature of all these societies, just as they were at Angkor.

Concluding Remarks: Working With Angkor's Agrarian Mosaic

The landscape of Angkor consists of a diverse patchwork of cultivated, managed, and gardened spaces, and there is a continuity of practice and knowledge at the local level that is evident for any visitor to Angkor today.

Although an extensive body of work in the literature deals with agriculture at Angkor, the discussion of hydraulics has often focused on top-down, state-managed systems and has failed to fully account for the richness and complexity either of the topography or of farmers' approaches to managing the landscapes in which they live. We have considered how both the elements of the urban fabric of Angkor structured, and related to, the botanical dimensions of the city, with a particular focus on the agrarian spaces between the large-scale infrastructure and a view to reappraising the broader landscape as a socio-ecological mosaic.

To appreciate the arboreal and agrarian context of Greater Angkor, approaches linking landscape archaeology with archaeobotany show promise but have only just begun. We emphasise

Figure 19.6 Archaeobotanical remains from some of Angkor's major temples: a) scanning electron microscope image of sesame seed from Angkor Thom; b) fragment of scarlet banana seed showing micropylar plug from Angkor Wat; c) crepe ginger seed from Angkor Wat; d) mung bean cotyledon fragment showing plumule from Angkor Wat; e) a cotton funicular cap from Ta Prohm.

Source: (Photos C. Cobo Castillo).

the need for further research to link current mapping of the agrarian spaces with archaeobotanical data that provide insight into human–plant relationships. There is also a need for archaeobotanical investigations to help reconstruct the ecology of the rice fields in order to better understand how they were managed and what water regimes were present. One way of addressing this is through archaeobotanical weed flora, which can provide a proxy for the ecology of ancient fields and the identification of prehistoric rice-cultivation systems (Fuller and Qin 2009; Castillo et al. 2018b; Castillo 2023). For now, however, we have insufficient archaeobotanical evidence to generate further insights about the hydraulic regimes of rice fields mapped, even those that have been excavated.

Greater Angkor is viewed as a series of patches that provide insights across a number of scales from the scale of large urban districts to the local garden. Through approaching Angkor as a socio-ecological mosaic, we can therefore see a different side of Angkor, distinct from the typical image of archaeological sites, monuments, and megastructures. Rather than seeing the city as clusters of dispersed sites across the low-density landscape, our adopted landscape-ecological perspective evokes an appreciation of the city as a continuous mosaic of diverse management practices and economies that shaped the experience and function of the city.

References

Acker, R., 1998. New geographical tests of the hydraulic thesis at Angkor. *South East Asia Research* 6(1), 5–47.

Acker, R., 2006. Hydrology and the siting of Yasodharapura, in *Phnom Bakheng Workshop on Public Interpretation, Angkor Park, Siem Reap, Cambodia, December 4–6, 2005: Conference Proceedings*. Siem Reap: Center for Khmer Studies, 73–86.

Bourdonneau, É., 2010. Pour en finir avec la "cité hydraulique" ? Note de lecture de l'ouvrage de didier pillot, Jardins et rizières du Cambodge. Les enjeux du développement agricole, 2007, *Bulletin de l'École française d'Extrême-Orient* 97(1), 409–37.

Bray, F., 1986. *The Rice Economies: Technology and Development in Asian Societies*. Berkeley: University of California Press.

Briggs, L.P., 1999. *The Ancient Khmer Empire*. Bangkok: White Lotus.

Carroll, M., 2003. *Earthly Paradises: Ancient Gardens in History and Archaeology, 1st ed.* Los Angeles: Oxford University Press.

Carter, A., P. Heng, M. Stark, R. Chhay & D. Evans, 2018. Urbanism and residential patterning in Angkor, *Journal of Field Archaeology* 43(6), 492–506.

Carter, A.K., M.T. Stark, S. Quintus, Y. Zhuang, H. Wang, P. Heng & R. Chhay, 2019. Temple occupation and the tempo of collapse at Angkor Wat, Cambodia. *Proceedings of the National Academy of Sciences* 116(25), 12226–31.

Carter, A.K., S. Klassen, M.T. Stark, M. Polkinghorne, P. Heng, D. Evans & R. Chhay, 2021. The evolution of agro-urbanism: A case study from Angkor, Cambodia. *Journal of Anthropological Archaeology* 63, 101323.

Castillo, C.C., 2023. Food, craft and ritual: plants from the Angkorian World, in *The Angkorian World*, eds. M. Hendrickson, M.T. Stark & D. Evans. New York: Routledge, 401–20.

Castillo, C.C., A. Carter, E. Kingwell-Banham, Y. Zhuang, A. Weisskopf, R. Chhay, P. Heng, D.Q. Fuller & M. Stark, 2020. The Khmer did not live by rice alone: archaeobotanical investigations at Angkor Wat and Ta Prohm. *Archaeological Research in Asia* 24, 100213.

Castillo, C.C., C.F. Higham, K. Miller, N. Chang, K. Douka, T.F. Higham & D.Q. Fuller, 2018a. Social responses to climate change in Iron Age north-east Thailand: new archaeobotanical evidence. *Antiquity* 92(365), 1274–91.

Castillo, C.C., M. Polkinghorne, B. Vincent, T.B. Suy & D.Q. Fuller, 2018b. Life goes on: archaeobotanical investigations of diet and ritual at Angkor Thom, Cambodia (14th–15th centuries CE). *The Holocene* 28(6), 930–44.

Chakravarti, A., 1978. *The Sdok Kak Thom Inscription (Calcutta Sanskrit College research series ; Studies no. 111–112. no. 74)*. Calcutta: Sanskrit College.

Chevance, J.-B., D. Evans, N. Hofer, S. Sakhoeun & R. Chhean, 2019. Mahendraparvata: an early Angkor-period capital defined through airborne laser scanning at Phnom Kulen. *Antiquity* 93(371), 1303–21.

Chouquer, G., 1996a. *Les Formes Du Paysage Tome 1—Etudes Sur Les Parcellaires*. Paris: Errance.

Chouquer, G., 1996b. *Les Formes Du Paysage Tome 2—Archéologie Des Parcellaires*. Paris: Errance.

Chouquer, G., 1997. *Les Formes Du Paysage Tome 3—L'analyse Des Systèmes Spatiaux*. Paris: Errance.

Cœdès, G., 1906. La stèle de ta-prohm, *Bulletin de l'École française d'Extrême-Orient* 6(1), 44–86.

Cœdès, G., 1951. VII. Études cambodgiennes XXXIX. L'épigraphie des monuments de Jayavarman VII. *Bulletin de l'École française d'Extrême-Orient* 44(1), 97–120.

Dagens, B., 2003. *Les Khmers (Guide belles lettres des civilisations)*. Paris: Les Belles Lettres.

Delvert, J., 1994[1961]. *Paysan Cambodgien*. Paris: Mouton.

Dumarçay, J., 1998. Intelligence collective et architecture en Asie du Sud-Est, Annales. *Histoire, Sciences Sociales* 53(3), 505–35.

Ebihara, M., 2018. *Svay: A Khmer Village in Cambodia*. Ithaca and London: Cornell University Press.

Evans, D., 2016. Airborne laser scanning as a method for exploring long-term socio-ecological dynamics in Cambodia. *Journal of Archaeological Science* 74, 164–75.

Evans, D. & R. Fletcher, 2015. The landscape of Angkor Wat redefined, *Antiquity* 89(348), 1402–19.

Evans, D.H., R.J. Fletcher, C. Pottier, J.-B. Chevance, D. Soutif, B.S. Tan, S. Im, D. Ea, T. Tin, S. Kim, C. Cromarty, S.D. Greef, K. Hanus, P. Baty, R. Kuszinger, I. Shimoda & G. Boornazian, 2013. Uncovering archaeological landscapes at Angkor using lidar, *Proceedings of the National Academy of Sciences* 201306539.

Evans, D., C. Pottier, R. Fletcher, S. Hensley, I. Tapley, A. Milne & M. Barbetti, 2007. A comprehensive archaeological map of the World's largest preindustrial settlement complex at Angkor, Cambodia. *Proceedings of the National Academy of Sciences* 104(36), 14277–82.

Fedick, S., 1996. *The Managed Mosaic: Ancient Maya Agriculture and Resource Use*. Salt Lake City: University of Utah Press.

Feneley, M., D. Penny & R. Fletcher, 2016. Claiming the hydraulic network of Angkor with Viṣṇu: a multidisciplinary approach including the analysis of archaeological remains, digital modelling and radiocarbon dating: with evidence for a 12th century renovation of the West Mebon, *Journal of Archaeological Science: Reports* 9, 275–92.

Fletcher, R., 2009. Low density, agrarian-based urbanism: a comparative view. *Insights* 2(4), 1–19.

Fletcher, R., D. Evans, M. Barbetti, D. Penny, T. Heng, S. Im, K. Chan, S. Tous & C. Pottier, 2003. Redefining Angkor: structure and environment in the largest, low density urban complex of the pre-industrial World, *Udaya* 4, 107–21.

Fletcher, R., D. Penny, D. Evans, C. Pottier, M. Barbetti, M. Kummu & T. Lustig, 2008a. The water management network of Angkor, Cambodia. *Antiquity* 82(317), 658–70.

Fletcher, R., I. Johnson, E. Bruce & K. Khun-Neay, 2007. Living with heritage: site monitoring and heritage values in greater Angkor and the Angkor World heritage site, Cambodia. *World Archaeology* 39(3), 385–405.

Fletcher, R., C. Pottier, D. Evans & M. Kummu, 2008b. The development of the water management system of Angkor: a provisional model. *Bulletin of the Indo-Pacific Prehistory Association* 28, 57–66.

Fletcher, R., D. Penny, M. Barbetti, C. Pottier, T. Heng, C. Khieu & S. Tous, 2006. The Greater Angkor Project 2005–2009: issues and program, in uncovering Southeast Asia's Past: selected papers from the 10th International Conference of the European Association of Southeast Asian Archaeologists. Singapore: NUS Press, 347–54.

Ford, A. & R. Nigh, 2016. *The Maya Forest Garden: Eight Millennia of Sustainable Cultivation of the Tropical Woodlands*. New York: Routledge.

Forman, R., 1996. *Landscape Mosaics: The Ecology of Landscapes and Regions*. Cambridge: Cambridge University Press.

Forman, R.T. & M. Godron, 1981. Patches and structural components for a landscape ecology, *BioScience* 31(10), 733–40.

Fox, J. & J. Ledgerwood, 1999. Dry-season flood-recession rice in the Mekong Delta: two thousand years of sustainable agriculture? *Asian Perspectives* 38(1), 37–50.

Fuller, D.Q. & L. Qin, 2009. Water management and labour in the origins and dispersal of Asian rice, *World Archaeology* 41(1), 88–111.

Fuller, D.Q., A.R. Weisskopf & C. Castillo, 2016. Pathways of rice diversification across Asia. Archaeology International 19, 84–96.

Gaucher, J., 2003a. New archaeological data on the urban space of the capital city of Angkor Thom, in fishbones and glittering emblems: Southeast Asian Archaeology 2002. *Stockholm: Museum of Far Eastern Antiquities*, 233–42.

Gaucher, J., 2003b. Premiers aperçus sur des éléments de planification urbaine à angkor thom. *Udaya* 4, 41–52.

Gourou, P., 1940. *L'utilisation Du Sol En Indochine Française*. Paris: Hartmann.

Graham, E. & C. Isendahl, 2018. Neotropical cities as agro-urban landscapes: revisiting 'low-density, agrarian-based urbanism', in *The Resilience of Heritage. Cultivating a Future of the Past. Essays in Honour of Professor Paul J.J. Sinclair*, eds. A. Ekblom, C. Isendahl & K.-J. Lindholm. Uppsala, Sweden: Uppsala University Press, 165–80.

Groslier, B.-P., 1974. Agriculture et religion dans l'empire angkorien. *Études Rurales* 53–56, 95–117.

Groslier, B.-P., 1979. La cité hydraulique angkorienne: exploitation ou surexploitation du sol? *Bulletin De l' École Française d' Extrême-Orient* 66, 161–202.

Halls, A.S. & K.G. Hortle, 2021. Flooding is a key driver of the Tonle Sap Dai fishery in Cambodia. Scientific Reports 11(1), 3806.

Hawken, S., 2012. *Metropolis of ricefields: A topographic classification of a dispersed urban complex*. PhD dissertation. Sydney: The University of Sydney.

Hawken, S., 2013. Designs of kings and farmers: landscape systems of the Greater Angkor urban complex. *Asian Perspectives* 52(2), 347–67.

Hawken, S. & R. Fletcher, 2021. A long-term archaeological reappraisal of low-density urbanism: implications for contemporary cities, *Journal of Urban Archaeology* 3, 29–50.

Hawken, S. & S. Klassen, 2023. Angkor's temple communities and the logic of its urban landscape, in *The Angkorian World*, eds. M. Hendrickson, M.T. Stark & D. Evans. New York: Routledge, 195–215.

Heine-Geldern, R., 1942. Conceptions of state and kingship in Southeast Asia. *The Far Eastern Quarterly* 2(1), 15–30.

Hendrickson, M., 2010. Historic routes to Angkor: Development of the Khmer road system (9th to 13th centuries CE) in mainland Southeast Asia. *Antiquity* 84(324), 480–96.

Higham, C., 2014. From the Iron Age to Angkor: new light on the origins of a state, *Antiquity* 88(341), 822–35.

Higham, C.F., 2017. Farming, social change, and state formation in Southeast Asia, *The Oxford Handbook of Zooarchaeology* 351.

Hilali, A., 2013. Rome and agriculture in Africa Proconsularis: land and hydraulic development, *Revue belge de Philologie et d'Histoire* 91(1), 113–25.

Isendahl, C. & M.E. Smith, 2013. Sustainable agrarian urbanism: the low-density cities of the Mayas and Aztecs, *Cities* 31, 132–43.

Isendahl, C., 2012. Agro-urban landscapes: the example of Maya lowland cities, *Antiquity* 86(334), 1112–25.

Jacob, J.M., 1978. The ecology of Angkor: evidence from the Khmer inscriptions, in *Nature and Man in South East Asia*. London: School of African and Oriental Studies, University of London, 109–27.

Jashemski, W.F., K.L. Gleason, K.J. Hartswick & A.-A. Malek, (eds.) 2017. *Gardens of the Roman Empire*. Cambridge: Cambridge University Press.

Javier, E.L., 1997. Rice ecosystems and varieties, in *Rice Production in Cambodia*, ed. H.J. Nesbitt. Manila: International Rice Research Institute, 39–81.

Kealhoffer, L., 2002. Changing Perceptions of Risk: the development of agroecosystems in Southeast Asia. *American Anthropologist* 104(1), 178–94.

Klassen, S., A.K. Carter, D.H. Evans, S. Ortman, M.T. Stark, A.A. Loyless, M. Polkinghorne, P. Heng, M. Hill & P. Wijker, 2021. Diachronic modeling of the population within the medieval greater Angkor region settlement complex, *Science Advances* 7(19), 1–9.

Lentz, D., T. Hamilton, N. Dunning, E. Tepe, V. Scarborough, S. Meyers, L. Grazioso & A. Weiss, 2021. *Environmental DNA Reveals Arboreal Cityscapes at the Ancient Maya Center of Tikal, Scientific Reports* 11(1), 1–10.

Lentz, D.L., N.P. Dunning, V.L. Scarborough, K.S. Magee, K.M. Thompson, E. Weaver, C. Carr, R.E. Terry, G. Islebe, K.B. Tankersley, L.G. Sierra, J.G. Jones, P. Buttles, F. Valdez & C.E.R. Hernandez, 2014. Forests, fields, and the edge of sustainability at the ancient Maya city of Tikal *Proceedings of the National Academy of Sciences* 111(52), 18513–18.

Lewitz, S. & B. Rollet, 1973. Lexique des noms d'arbres et d'arbustes du Cambodge. *Bulletin de l'École française d'Extrême-Orient* 60, 117–62.

Lustig, E., 2009a. *Power and pragmatism in the political economy of Angkor*. PhD dissertation. Sydney: The University of Sydney.

Lustig, E., 2009b. Money doesn't make the World go round: Angkor's non-monetisation, in *Economic Development, Integration, and Morality in Asia and the Americas,* ed. D. Wood. Bingley: Emerald, 165–99.

Mann, C.C., 2008. The western Amazon's 'garden cities'. *Science* 321(5893), 1151.

Martin, M.A., 1969. Notes sur quelques végétaux utilisés au Cambodge, *Journal d'agriculture traditionnelle et de botanique appliquée* 16(2), 112–57.

Martin, M.A. 1971. *Introduction a l'ethnobotanique du Cambodge (Atlas ethno-linguistique, recherche coopérative sur programme n° 61).* Paris: Editions du Centre national de la recherche scientifique.

Martin, M.A., 1974. Essai d'ethnophytogéographie khmère, *Journal d'Agriculture Traditionnelle et de Botanique Appliquée* 21(7), 219–38.

McKey, D., S. Rostain, J. Iriarte, B. Glaser, J.J. Birk, I. Holst & D. Renard, 2010. Pre-Columbian agricultural landscapes, ecosystem engineers, and self-organized patchiness in Amazonia. *Proceedings of the National Academy of Sciences* 107(17), 7823–28.

Moormann, F. & N. Breemen, 1978. *Rice: Soil, Water, Land.* Los Baños, Philippines: International Rice Research Institute.

Ng, R.C., 1979. The geographical habitat of historical settlement in mainland South East Asia, in *Early South East Asia: Essays in Archaeology, History, and Historical Geography*. New York: Oxford University Press.

Penny, D. & T. Hall, 2023. An environmental history of Angkor: beginning to end, in *The Angkorian World*, eds. M. Hendrickson, M.T. Stark & D. Evans. New York: Routledge, 17–24.

Penny, D., C. Pottier, M. Kummu, R. Fletcher, U. Zoppi, M. Barbetti & S. Tous, 2005. Hydrological history of the West Baray, Angkor, revealed through palynological analysis of sediments from the West Mebon. *Bulletin de l'École française d'Extrême-Orient* 92(1), 497–521.

Penny, D., C. Pottier, R. Fletcher, M. Barbetti, D. Fink & Q. Hua, 2006. Vegetation and land-use at Angkor, Cambodia: a dated pollen sequence from the Bakong temple moat, *Antiquity* 80, 599–614.

Pillot, D., 2008. *Jardins et Rizières Du Cambodge: Les Enjeux Du Développement Agricole.* Paris: Karthala.

Polkinghorne, M., B. Vincent, N. Thomas & D. Bourgarit, 2014. Casting for the king: the royal palace bronze workshop of Angkor Thom. *Bulletin de l'École française d'Extrême-Orient* 327–58.

Pottier, C., 1999. *Carte archéologique de la région d'angkor, Zone Sud*. PhD dissertation. Paris: Université Paris III—Sorbonne nouvelle.

Pottier, C., 2000a. À la recherche de Goloupura. *Bulletin de l'École française d' Extrême-Orient* 1(87), 79–107.

Pottier, C., 2000b. Some evidence of an inter-relationship between hydraulic features and rice field patterns at Angkor during ancient times, *The Journal of Sophia Asian Studies* 18, 99–120.

Ricklefs, M.C., 1967. Land and the law in the epigraphy of tenth-century Cambodia, *The Journal of Asian Studies* 26(3), 411–20.

Riitters, K., 2019. Pattern metrics for a transdisciplinary landscape ecology, *Landscape Ecology* 34(9), 2057–63.

Rollet, B., 1972. La végétation du Cambodge: 3e partie. *Bois & Forets Des Tropiques* 146, 3–20.

Rosenswig, R.M., 2015. A mosaic of adaptation: the archaeological record for Mesoamerica's archaic period. *Journal of Archaeological Research* 23(2), 115–62.

Stark, M.T., D. Evans, C. Rachna, H. Piphal & A. Carter, 2015. Residential patterning at Angkor Wat, *Antiquity* 89(348), 1439–55.

Stott, P., 1992. Angkor: shifting the hydraulic paradigm, in *The Gift of Water: Water Management, Cosmology and the State in South East Asia*. London: School of Oriental and African Studies, 47–58.

Turner, M., R. Gardner & R. O'Neill, 2001. *Landscape Ecology in Theory and Practice: Pattern and Process*. New York: Springer.

Van Liere, W., 1980. Traditional water management in the lower Mekong Basin. *World Archaeology* 11(3), 265–80.

Van Liere, W., 1982. Was Angkor a hydraulic society? *Ruam Botkhwam Prawat Sat* 4, 36–48.

Van Liere, W., 1989. Mon-Khmer approaches to the environment, in *Culture and Environment in Thailand: A Symposium of the Siam Society*, ed. Siam Society. Bangkok: The Society, 142–60.

Vickery, M., 1998. *Society, Economics, and Politics in Pre-Angkor Cambodia: The 7th–8th Centuries*. Tokyo: Centre for East Asian Cultural Studies for UNESCO, The Tokyo Bunko.

Wilkinson, T.J., 2003. *Archaeological Landscapes of the Near East*. Tucson: University of Arizona Press.

Wiseman, D.J., 1983. Mesopotamian gardens, *Anatolian studies* 33, 137–44.

Zhou, D., 2007[1297]. *A Record of Cambodia: The Land and Its People*, trans. P. Harris. Chiang Mai: Silkworm Books.

20

FROM QUARRIES TO TEMPLES

Stone Procurement, Materiality, and Spirituality in the Angkorian World

Christian Fischer, Federico Carò and Martin Polkinghorne

Introduction

Inspired by the seminal work of Georges Groslier, 'Recherches sur les Cambodgiens' (1921), the objectives here are to explore various aspects of stone material culture in an attempt to establish spatial and temporal connections between sandstone typology, sourcing, and procurement on one hand and the creation of sculptures and Angkorian architecture on the other. The ancient Cambodian culture is best known through its splendid and unique monumental architecture at Angkor, a major cultural centre and home to various capitals which flourished during the Angkor Period, from the beginning of the 9th to the 15th centuries CE. In Pre-Angkorian times (c. 550 to 800), shrines and sanctuaries were built with wood, bricks, and laterite,[1] while stone usage was restricted to inscribed stelae, statuary, and their supporting pedestals, as well as some specific architectural and decorative elements such as door jambs, doorsteps, small columns, and lintels.[2] At the dawn of the Angkor Period, this tradition persisted, but sandstone gradually replaced brick and became the builders' material of choice for the temples erected between the 11th and 13th century. Laterite, widely available and easily processed, was still extensively employed, particularly for basement courses, causeways, and enclosure walls, and sometimes as the primary material for entire sanctuaries (Figure 20.1).

The tradition of sandstone building and carving tradition persisted until the decline of Angkor and as French geologist Edmond Saurin (1954, 620) aptly wrote, (translated):[3] 'Khmer art in its golden age has been the art of sandstone'. Interestingly, stone deities were carved from very similar sandstone types—or lithotypes—and ostensibly different from those used for architectural elements and sculptures. This raises a series of important questions related to material properties and availability, economic constraints, beliefs, and rituals, as well as agency, choice, and the traditions of artists and guilds. This chapter focuses on recent investigations into this vital material and evaluates some of these issues to understand how sandstone was harnessed and contributed to Angkor's imperial development.

Sandstone Lithology and Spatial Distribution

Sandstone is a sedimentary rock composed of an assemblage of mineral grains originating from the disaggregation of preexisting rocks whose fragments were transported, deposited, compacted, and cemented through geological processes. Following some early petrographic

DOI: 10.4324/9781351128940-25

Figure 20.1 Range of materials used in Khmer temple constructions ?: a) Bakong, Prasat 4, brick and sandstone (late 9th c., Polkinghorne 2008, 28); b) Pre Rup: brick, laterite, and sandstone (mid-10th c.); c) Koh Ker, Prasat Chen, laterite and sandstone (2nd quarter of 10th c.); Preah Khan of Kompong Svay (11th–13th c.), sandstone and laterite; d) 3rd enclosure wall, eastern gate; (e) Monument of the Inscription (K.161), Bayon Period (late 12th–early 13th c.); f) Prasat Phnom Banan, Battambang, re-built tower, laterite and sandstone; g) ancient laterite quarry, south of Banteay Chhmar; h) Prasat Hin Phimai, Thailand, Prang Brahmadatta, laterite and sandstone.

Source: (Photos C. Fischer).

analysis (Fromaget and Bonelli 1932),[4] the first insights into the typology of sandstone used for the building of monuments at Angkor were given by Saurin (1954) and about a decade later by Jean Delvert (1963), who extended the research to their weathering and provenance. At the end of the 60s, an extensive survey of Cambodia's geology was carried out by the BRGM,[5] adding significantly to what was known from earlier geological research (Gubler 1935; Saurin 1935; Fromaget 1941). All together, this body of work remains to date the basis for anyone who wants to study and understand stone material culture in ancient Cambodia.

More recently, scholars began to expand this work through further investigations of typologies and potential sources of sandstone combining field surveys with an array of scientific approaches. These include various techniques ranging from non-invasive spectroscopy and magnetic susceptibility (MS) to petrography, electron microscopy, and geochemical analysis on samples from natural outcrops, ancient quarries, temple superstructures, and architectural decorative elements as well as free-standing sculptures and other carved objects still *in situ* or located in the repository of the Conservation d'Angkor (DCA) and various museums (Uchida et al. 1995; Uchida et al. 1996; Uchida et al. 1998; Uchida et al. 1999; Baptiste et al. 2001; Uchida and Ando 2001; Moriai, et al. 2002; Douglas 2004; Reucher et al. 2007; Douglas and Sorensen 2008; Kučera et al. 2008; Carò et al. 2010; Douglas et al. 2010; Carò and Im 2012; Carò and Douglas 2013; Polkinghorne et al. 2013; Carò et al. 2014; Polkinghorne et al. 2015).

Three major sandstone lithotypes were identified and linked to the sedimentary formations of the Triassic (c. 252 to 201 mya), the middle-upper Jurassic (c. 174 to 145 mya) 'Terrain Rouge', and the lower Cretaceous (c. 145 to 100 mya) 'Grès Supérieurs' series. While significant variations occur within each group, particularly for the 'Terrain Rouge' and Triassic sandstones, some sub-lithotypes show specificities that on the other hand make identification easier. Ubiquitous in the Cambodian landscape (Figure 20.2), these sandstones form the Dangrek scarp in the north and the Cardamom mountain range in the west ('Grès Supérieurs') as well as the bedrock on either side of the Mekong north of Kratié (Triassic and 'Terrain Rouge'). They are also found as isolated hills and small mountains scattered in the central basin extending from the northwest along the Tonle Sap to the Mekong delta in the south (Delvert 1963, 526–29; Dottin 1972, 8; Workman 1977, 16).

Triassic Sandstones

Sandstones in this group are compact, often very hard, fine- to coarse-grained, sometimes with a micro-conglomeratic fabric, and show colours that vary from grey to greyish-green to blueish-grey. The sandstones have a 'graywacke'[6] typology (Pettijohn et al. 1987) and are usually classified under the feldspatho-lithic and litho-feldspathic arenites (Table 20.1; Douglas et al. 2010). While their chemical compositions and textures are rather homogeneous, variations in the mineralogical assemblage are frequent and often associated with changes induced by hydrothermal and low-grade metamorphism events. Rocks of Triassic age were deformed to various degrees during the last phase of the Indosinian orogeny (Fromaget 1941; Workman 1977), and both signatures are most likely related to the folding as well as the formation of syn- and post-tectonic felsic intrusions. Triassic sandstone was the material par excellence for the statuary during the Pre-Angkor Period and continued to be employed in Angkorian times, primarily for the representation of gods and deities placed inside temples and sanctuaries as well as for the inscribed stelae. By contrast, the only known architectural use is for the five towers on top of the Ta Keo pyramid, which will be discussed in detail subsequently.

Sandstones From the 'Terrain Rouge' Series

Contrary to the 'red' colour suggested by the name 'Terrain Rouge', the sandstones belonging to this series in northwest Cambodia are rather grey, greenish-grey, or occasionally yellowish-brown. The series represents a transitional facies between marine and continental environments of deposition and the sandstone beds are sub-horizontal. In the eastern regions, the facies becomes more marine, and near Kratié, Terrain Rouge sandstones are often calcareous, a

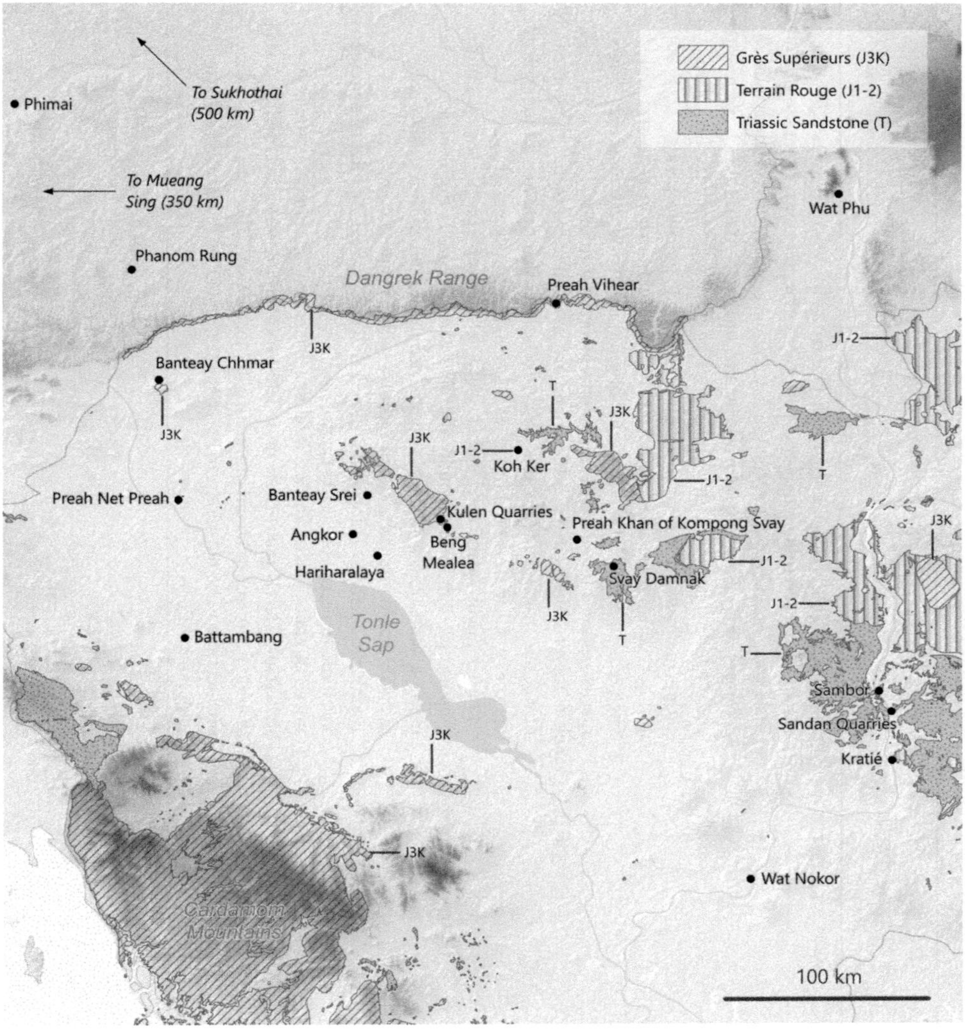

Figure 20.2 Distribution of sandstone formations and location of major archaeological sites and ancient quarries.

Source: (Google Earth topographic map with overlaid geological data in color from https://data.opendevelopmentcambodia.net/dataset/geology-of-cambodia-2006). Last accessed December 2022.

peculiarity already noted by Fleuriot de Langle (1973). Very fine- to fine-grained and primarily composed of quartz and feldspars in similar proportions, they are classified under the feldspathic arenites (Table 20.1). This lithotype was used for the construction of nearly all temples dated to the Angkor Period as well as for some of the associated statuary, the most notable example being the corpus of monumental sculptures found at Koh Ker (Parmentier 1939, 15–117). Decorative lintels, as objects of particular significance (Polkinghorne 2007, 2008), were also carved with Terrain Rouge sandstone, even during the early Angkor Period when brick and laterite were still the prime building materials. Terrain Rouge sandstone is therefore a major—and the most visible—element of Angkor's stone material culture (Figure 20.3).

Table 20.1 Main characteristics of the different sandstone lithotypes used during the Angkor Period.

Geological formation	*Sandstone Lithotypes*	*Hardness (Mohs)*	*Porosity (%)*	*Mean Particle size (mm)*	*QFL Average (%)*	*Mineralogical composition and distinctive features*
Triassic sandstone	Feldspathic-lithic arenite	~5.5	<2	~0.15 to 0.3	$Q_{30}F_{41}L_{29}$	Framework grains: variable proportions of quartz (20–39%), feldspars (26–50%, mainly sodic) and lithic fragments (16–43%). Lithic fragments are predominantly from volcanic and metamorphic sources. Presence of few micas and various accessory minerals (epidote, garnet, titanite, opaques). Matrix is rich in chlorite and secondary calcite is common. Graywacke typology. Some levels contain authigenic prehnite, a mineral marker of low-grade metamorphism.
					$Q_{39}F_{29}L_{32}$	Sub-lithotype 1: Fine grained with a relatively high proportion of quartz. Lithic fragments are largely of metamorphic origin (phyllite, micaceous schist). Slightly metamorphosed (presence of authigenic epidote and chlorite).
					$Q_{12}F_{40}L_{48}$	Sub-lithotype 2: Less quartz and high proportion of lithic fragments, predominantly of volcanic origin (andesite, rhyolite). Presence of calcic amphiboles (hornblende, up to 8%). Characteristic mottled texture visible with the naked eye.
Terrain Rouge	Feldspathic arenite	~3.5 to 4.5	~8 to 19	~0.08 to 0.20	$Q_{52}F_{41}L_7$	Framework grains: quartz and feldspars (alkali feldspars and plagioclase) in similar proportions, with lesser amounts of lithic fragments mostly from volcanic and metamorphic sources. Micas (~2 to 5%, mainly biotite) and various accessory minerals (epidote, garnet, titanite, apatite, rutile, opaques) complete the assemblage. Cement: chlorite and smectite. Secondary calcite might be present and some levels can be clearly calcareous.
Grès Supérieurs	Quartz arenite	~3.5	~7 to 15	~0.06 to 0.50	$Q_{91}F_6L_3$	Framework grains: quartz and a few feldspars. Cement: kaolinite, quartz. Some stratigraphic levels also include more feldspars and rare micas (muscovite) as well as lithic fragments of metamorphic origin (micaschist); others show secondary silicifications. The red-pink variety contains iron oxides (hematite) associated with the kaolinite.

Figure 20.3 Examples of Terrain Rouge sandstone usage in the Angkor Period: a) Baphuon temple, Angkor (mid-11th c.); b) Ta Prohm temple, Angkor (late 12th c.); c) face-tower, Bayon temple, Angkor (late 12th–early 13th c.); d) Prang pyramid, Koh Ker (2nd quarter 10th c.); e) Hanuman, Prasat Chen, Koh Ker; f) Apsaras, Angkor Wat (12th c.); g) Lintel, Lolei, Roluos (late 9th c.).

Source: (Photos a, M. Baufeist; b,c,d,f, C. Fischer; e, Chea Socheat; g, M. Polkinghorne).

Sandstones from the 'Grès Supérieurs' Series

The 'Grès Supérieurs' series overlays the Terrain Rouge and is predominantly composed of fine- to coarse-grained quartz-rich sandstones cemented with kaolinite. They are classified under the quartz arenites (Table 20.1), and their colour varies from red to beige-ochre and grey-white. A fine red-pink type was used during the last quarter of the 10th century almost

Figure 20.4 Examples of 'Grès Supérieurs' series sandstone usage in the Angkor Period: a) Banteay Srei with carving detail; b) Wat Ek, Battambang, and detail of a sandstone block showing Liesegang banding cutting across the natural stratification; c) Preah Vihear, Cambodia; d) Prasat Hin Phimai, Thailand, with the use of a white variety for window frames and pillars g); f) Upper temple, Wat Phu, Laos; and e) carving detail.

Source: (Photos C. Fischer).

exclusively for the construction of the temple of Banteay Srei and for sculptures and carved elements in the eponymous style (Figure 20.4a).[7] A coarser yellowish to light grey variety with some levels containing pebble-size conglomeratic beds or showing iron-rich Liesegang banding (Figure 20.4b) was used for the Wat Ek temple, near Battambang, attributed to Sūryavarman I (Cœdès 1951; Dagens 1968; Jacques and Lafond 2007, 144). The temple of Preah Vihear (11th c.) was also built with sandstone from this series, while in northeastern Thailand and southern Laos, sandstone from corresponding formations in the Khorat group were used for Angkorian constructions such as the temples of Phimai and Wat Phu[8] (Gaucher 1992; Uchida Ito and Shimizu 2010; Figure 20.4).

Sandstone in Context: Tradition and Significance

Knowledge of sandstone typology, distribution, and general use is a prerequisite to better understand stone material culture of the Angkor Period. In this part, with four selected examples, we explore in further detail the relationships between sandstone types and usage and the implications on Khmer technical and cultural choices.

Hariharālaya: Sandstone Usage and Diversity

Hariharālaya was a major political centre of the early Angkor Kingdom (8th–9th century) centred around the Bakong, Preah Ko, and Lolei temple complexes. During the renovation of an 'earlier' Bakong by Indravarman I (r. 877–889), the temple was entirely cladded with sandstone blocks, the first example of large-scale stone usage by Khmer builders (Glaize 1936–44; Dumarçay and Royère 2001, 50; Figure 20.5a, c). The six brick towers of Preah Ko are built with a sandstone base on a common platform also in sandstone (Figure 20.5g), the latter possibly constructed with stone surplus from the nearby much grander Bakong (Pottier and Luján-Lunsford 2005). At both sites, these structures include massive stone architectural elements, such as lintels, false doors, and bas-relief ornamentations as well as sandstone sculptures inserted into the brick framework (Figure 20.5b, h, i).

Recent archaeological and scientific studies have focused on stone materials used at the temples of Bakong and Preah Ko to understand early Angkorian material culture and construction practices (Polkinghorne et al. 2015). Terrain Rouge sandstone was used for the cladding and architectural elements (e.g., lintels and pillars) as well as bas-reliefs, architectural sculptures (e.g., *dvārapāla* and *devatā*), and standing figures installed outside the many shrines (e.g., bulls, lions, and elephants). Conversely, primary deities are all carved from at least two Triassic sandstone sub-lithotypes. The first is commonly found on 9th- and 10th-century sculptures from the Angkor area (Figure 20.5d). The second, a greenish quartz-poor sandstone rich in volcanic fragments with an easily recognisable mottled texture and abundantly used for royal and sacred sculptures during Jayavarman VII's reign (1181/1183–c.1220), is associated with images produced at Hariharālaya during the early to mid-12th century that imitate the past 9th-century style (Polkinghorne et al. 2015, Figure 20.5f).

These results point to a marked difference between stones used for architectural elements and those for divinatory sculptures which might reveal deliberate material choices made by builders and artisans. Adding to this pattern, we also discovered in Hariharālaya that most, if not all, *yoni*, the squared or round spouted bases into which the sculptures were inserted, are carved from the same sub-lithotypes reserved to the primary deities. On the other hand, the supporting decorated pedestals underneath, and part of the architectural elements of the temples, are carved with Terrain Rouge sandstone (Figure 20.5e).[10] Similar observations were made by the authors for *yoni* and pedestals still *in situ* in other Pre-Angkorian and Angkorian temples in Cambodia, indicating that this peculiarity (i.e., difference in sandstone type) is indeed widespread. The choice of a specific lithotype for deities and *yoni* was most likely determined by cultural factors and spiritual motives, although technical reasons might have played a significant role in the selection as well.

A Continuity of Stone: Inscribed Stelae

Among the vast corpus of inscribed stelae (̴900) from the Angkor Period, the 9th- and 10th-century stelae are of particular importance, as they relate to the Pre-Angkor to Angkor transition and the first attempts at establishing the ancient kingdom (Dupont 1943, 1952; Vickery 1999, 2001; Estève and Soutif 2010–11; Lustig 2011). A total of 20 inscribed stelae[11] were selected in order to identify the type of stone and infer potential sources. The group is composed of stelae[12]

Figure 20.5 Examples of Terrain Rouge (a, b, c, e, g, h, i) and Triassic (d, e, f) sandstone usage at Hariharālaya: a) general view of the Bakong temple; b) Prasat 2, Bakong; c) cladding with sandstone blocks over laterite inner structure, Bakong; d) Umāgaṅgāpatīśvara[9] sculpture found at Bakong (DCA, #927); e) yoni and supporting pedestal, Bakong; f) Harihara (NMC, Ka.925), Trapeang Phong, Roluos; g) Preah Ko temple; h) Dvārapāla; and i) Devatā sculptures, Preah Ko.

Source: (Photos b,c,e,h, F. Carò; a,d,f,g,i, C. Fischer).

commissioned during the reign of Yaśovarman I (r. 889–910) as well as others recording the foundation of various temples and/or deities' installation.[13] The stelae were analysed with non-invasive FORS and pXRF[14] as well as petrography for a few that could be sampled.[15]

Despite limitations inherent to non-invasive technologies, results have shown that all stelae were cut from a compact sandstone with a graywacke typology consistent with the general lithology of sandstone from the Triassic series. Moreover, besides the known variability of these sandstones in terms of texture, granulometry, and mineralogical assemblage, two subtypes could be distinguished based on the presence or absence of the mineral prehnite, an indicator of low-grade metamorphism, a result which could possibly reflect two different sources. The occurrence of the prehnite subtype does not follow a particular trend, as among the stelae from

Figure 20.6 Texture and petrography of the Triassic sandstone: a, b, c) Pre Rup stele (K. 806, 961 CE); d, e, f) upper towers of Ta Keo. For the thin section scan, white scale bar is 6 mm. Photomicrographs in XPL (Bt: biotite, Cal: calcite, Chl: chlorite, Ep: epidote, Kfs: potassic feldspar, Prh: prehnite, Pl: plagioclase, Qtz: quartz).

Source: (Photos C. Fischer).

the eastern baray and the Angkor and provincial āśrama, only five contain prehnite (K.283, K.290, K.42, K.95, and K.309), while the others show a more classic Triassic signature. Moving along the timeline, prehnite is absent in the foundation stele of the East Mebon temple (K.528, 952 CE) but present in the ones of Pre Rup (K.806, 961 CE, Figure 20.6) and Preah Ko (K.713, 879 CE). This suggests a sort of continuity[16] in the use of both subtypes over more than 100 years that becomes important when considering the stone used in the Ta Keo towers.

Stone Singularity: The Five Towers of Ta Keo

The usage of Triassic sandstone reached its apex with the construction of the Ta Keo temple, the only example in the Angkor World where this lithotype was employed for large architectural structures. After the initial description by Francis Garnier (1873, 73), a subsequent report by Jean Moura noted that the darker and denser sandstone of the five towers on the top platform was different from the pyramid beneath build with 'Terrain Rouge' (1883, 361; Figure 20.6d). Most blocks were left unfinished, just rough-cut without any decorations, a fact attributed to the hardness[17] of the sandstone that made fine carving a challenging task (Marchal 1928, 145; Saurin 1954). Dumarçay (1971) described it as graywacke and added that inside the towers, blocks were just finished with a point chisel though with such a high density of impacts that the surface looks as if it were bush hammered. Recent analysis of a few samples of this Triassic sandstone has shown that some also contain the mineral prehnite suggesting the same source as certain stelae from the 9th and 10th centuries. The amount of sandstone required for the five towers was precisely evaluated at 2,300 m^3, which represents an impressive weight of about 6000 metric tons (Dumarçay 1971). Why this sandstone was used and where it was sourced from remain open questions. While inscription K. 277[18] mentions that one of the towers was hit by lightning before it was completed and the subsequent need to purchase additional stone, supposedly Triassic sandstone, to finish the construction (Cœdès 1952, 159), it does not provide clues about sourcing. Saurin (1954, 624) conjectured that reasons for its use could be rushed construction, trial, negligence, or provisional necessity. Claude Jacques (1978, 310–11) singled out the latter, arguing that builders knew about the quality of materials and there was plenty of time to complete the temple. As for negligence, it is simply antithetical to the procurement process of large volumes of stone. Jacques justifies the provisional necessity by royal power struggles at the beginning of the 11th century, and whoever built the towers—whether it be Jayavīravarman (r. 1002–1006?) or Jayavarman V (r. 968–1000)—had to use stone available to him even if it was not the ideal quality. Furthermore, this could imply access restrictions to Terrain Rouge sandstone or even a temporary disruption of quarrying activities. The choice of Triassic sandstone for the Ta Keo towers could also be deliberate and directed by spiritual reasons to reflect the sacrality of the whole platform with the five towers by the same token this lithotype was used for deities. As suggested by other scholars, the blocks of the towers were maybe intended to be polished, but this final painstaking work was never completed (Dumarçay and Royère 2001, 22).

Stone Crafting: Carving Workshops of Greater Angkor

Despite the thousands of stone images produced as representations and emanations of gods, spirits, the elite, and ancestors for installation into the temple (e.g., see K. 908, D, st. CXXVII; Cœdès 1941, 280, 297), only two sculpture workshops[19] have been confirmed by archaeological excavations: one adjacent to the Royal Palace of Angkor Thom (Marchal 1924–26, 310, Polkinghorne et al. 2014, 331–32) and another near Bakong (Polkinghorne et al. 2015). In Angkor Thom, 14 unfinished sandstone sculptures and sub-surface deposits containing sandstone chip debitage, the waste of the carving process, are indicative of production in the 12th century. The form and diagnostic decoration of these sculptures may be associated with the stylistic category of Angkor Wat (end of the 11th–mid-12th century), and unfinished Viṣṇu images (Figure 20.7a) are consistent with a preference for the Vaiṣṇava cult during the reign of Sūryavarman II (r. 1113/1114–ca. 1150). At Bakong, two large unfinished sculptures of Umāgaṅgāpatīśvara and a roughly cut *yoni* (Figure 20.7b) as well as sandstone debitage were identified east of the outer enclosure of the temple and recognised together as the location of a possible production centre. Excavation and material characterisation revealed a production site that participated in sculpture manufacture at Hariharālaya from the early to mid-12th century by producing replicas or replacements of earlier 9th century models.

Quarries and Temples: Provenance and Procurement

A key advance in our understanding of stone material culture in the Angkorian World has been made through the identification and investigation of ancient quarries. Owing to extensive field work and further archaeometric analysis, critical correlations could be established with the sandstone types used for temples and sculptures.

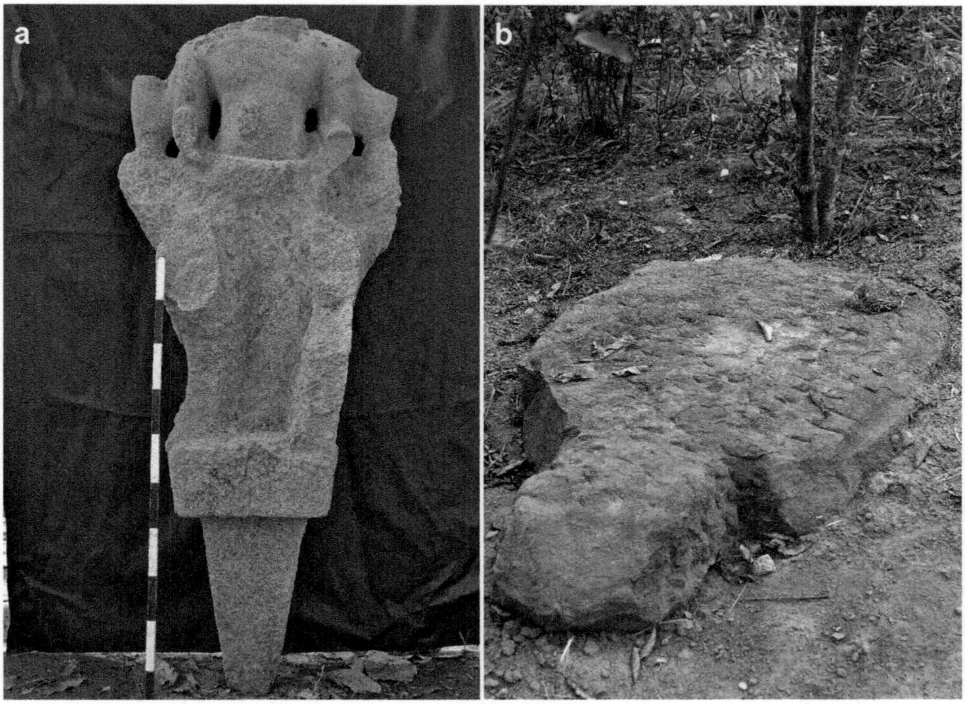

Figure 20.7 Incomplete sculptures from stone workshops in Greater Angkor: a) unfinished Viṣṇu statue, Angkor Thom workshop; b) rough outline of a yoni, Bakong workshop.

Source: (Photos M. Polkinghorne).

'Terrain Rouge' Sandstone

Most temples in the Angkor area were built with Terrain Rouge sandstone that is readily available and extracted from the quarries located in the southeastern foothills of Kulen Mountain,[20] about 40 km east of Angkor near Beng Mealea. The earliest known written account (end of the 16th century) was given by Portuguese chronicler Diogo do Couto, who mentions the usage of a same stone, only found at a significant distance from Angkor, thus wondering about cost, labour, organisation, and servitude the whole process must have entailed (Groslier 1958, 66–74). Explorer Henri Mouhot also writes about the quarries, though he did not see them (1868, 299).[21] In 1866, Doudart de Lagrée visited the Angkor region and gave the first detailed description of the quarries, highlighting the massive sandstone outcrops and the vast spread of the exploitations (Garnier 1873, 26–30). Later, Parmentier and Groslier made additional observations and suggested ideas about extraction and transport methods (Parmentier 1913, 36; Groslier 1921, 159–65).

The quarries provide us with direct evidence of the extraction process. Blocks of sandstone were removed by making three or four right-angled notches (5 to 15 cm wide) from the top with straight crowbars and then detached from the bedrock along the natural bedding plane with wedges or maybe a fire on the surface which induced the split at the base through differential thermal dilation (Groslier 1921, 160). The technique is still employed nowadays in the Trapeang Thmo Dap quarry, which has been exploited for conservation purposes since the 1990s (Carò and Im 2012) and where sandstone is currently quarried for the restoration of the West Mebon temple (Figure 20.8d, e).

Stone slabs were transported from the Kulen quarries to Angkor using natural and artificial waterways, a solution already envisioned by Groslier (1921, 161) and later confirmed by the existence of canals (Boulbet 1979; Evans et al. 2007; Uchida and Shimoda 2013). Despite several surveys of individual quarries (Bruneau 2009; Rocks 2009; Carò and Im 2012) and the identification of more than 50 of them (Uchida and Shimoda 2013), their true spatial extent has come to light only recently owing to a lidar campaign which has revealed the area to be a gigantic quarry field covering ~500 ha (Evans 2016, Figure 20.8a). Given such a surficial spread across elevations ranging from ~80 to ~130 metres, and because sandstones are sedimentary rocks forming here sub-horizontal beds, both lateral and vertical—along the stratigraphy—variations in the mineralogical composition are expected, even within blocks drawn from the same quarry.

This, in turn, can complicate studies of stone provenance by introducing spatial heterogeneity and intra-site variation to physical properties of stone from a single quarry site—such as magnetic susceptibility, for example. Indeed, this particular technique has been frequently used to identify the different stages of the construction process of specific temples and to relate that periodisation to sandstone procurement from specific quarries (Uchida and Shimoda 2013). The magnetic susceptibility technique has so far been applied to several important temples built in the Angkor area and beyond (Uchida et al. 1998; Uchida et al. 2003; Uchida et al. 2007), and while the approach shows clear potential, we suggest here that more fundamental research is needed before its systematic use for interpretative purposes. Nevertheless, in cases where there is a good correlation between magnetic susceptibility data and relative dating based on architectonics and style, inferences are certainly strengthened (Vickery 2006, 163).

Terrain Rouge sandstone was also used for several major temple complexes outside of Angkor, like the short-lived capital of Koh Ker (928–944), Preah Khan of Kompong Svay (PKKS, 11th–13th centuries), and Banteay Chhmar (early 13th c.) (Figure 20.1). In the Koh Ker area, this sandstone forms the bedrock, which is widely exposed, and several quarries were identified on and nearby the site (Parmentier 1939, 77; Evans 2010, 103–106; Carò and Im 2012; Figure 20.8f, g). The easy availability of this resource doubtless facilitated the realisation of Jayavarman IV's (r. 921–941) ambitious architectural and sculptural projects. The latter is represented by a unique corpus of monumental statuary (Parmentier 1939, 15–117; Bourdonneau 2011, 95–141) and the only example where this lithology was used at such a scale to render gods and deities. Remarkably, the sandstone was taken in a peculiar stratigraphic level revealed by a specific mineralogical signature[22] found in all sculptures of this corpus (Fischer, unpublished data). Field surveys combined with scientific analysis have indicated that this level is exposed in the eastern and southern parts of the site, and despite some traces of exploitation, the extraction location of the large monoliths has yet to be discovered. At PKKS, two Terrain Rouge sandstone varieties with a grey and yellowish-brown colour, similar mineralogy, and different magnetic susceptibilities were identified amongst the numerous temple structures. Traces of ancient quarries have not been found, though some evidence indicates that the yellowish-brown type was possibly extracted from the baray (Hendrickson and Fischer 2016). Initial research suggested that the grey type (high MS) used for the first building stages (11th–early 12th c.) was procured from the Kulen quarries (Uchida et al. 2013), but this thought-provoking hypothesis needs to consider the implications of transporting large quantities of massive stone blocks solely via a terrestrial route from the Beng Mealea area to PKKS. Finally, Banteay Chhmar uniquely shows the use of sandstone from both the Terrain Rouge and Grès Supérieurs series (Figure 20.9). This feature is perhaps not surprising given that the latter is exposed next to the temple, while quarries of the former are found further to the west.

Figure 20.8 Evidence of quarries: a) lidar map of the Terrain Rouge sandstone quarries northwest of Beng Mealea; b) Toek Lick quarry; c) O Thmo Dap quarry; d & e) present-day extraction of sandstone for restoration purposes at the Trapeang Thmo Dap quarry. Terrain Rouge sandstone quarries: f) Trapeang Russei; and g) Ang Kna in Koh Ker.

Source: (Photos a, D. Evans; b,f, F. Carò; c,d,e,g, C. Fischer).

'Grès Supérieurs' Sandstone

The only major temple in the capital region built with Grès Supérieurs sandstone is Banteay Srei. The sandstone of this unique temple, located 20 km north of Angkor, was likely quarried from the nearby Kulen Mountain. Delvert (1963) reports quarry pits of limited extension and about 10 metres deep, 3 km from the temple, at the foot of Phnom Dei. However, in a recent survey these pits could not be recognised (Bruneau 2009), and the quarries that supplied the fine-grained

Figure 20.9 Various types of sandstone used in a decorative wall at Banteay Chhmar. Pink to red (Grès Supérieurs) and yellow to beige (Terrain Rouge) sandstone blocks, grey sandstone repair fragments also from the Terrain Rouge series.

Source: (Photo C. Fischer).

red-pink sandstone have yet to be found. Between Kralang and Sisophon, some extraction traces in the red sandstone of the Preah Net Preah hill indicate quarrying at a more local scale to provide the building material of small temples in the area (Aymonier 1901, 320). In a nearby village, known for stone carving activities, there are modern quarries, and it is conceivable that this area was already exploited for stone in ancient times. Based on similarities in the lithology, the sandstone employed for the construction of Wat Ek was possibly procured from this location.[23] Finally, the Preah Vihear temple, erected on the edge of the Dangrek cliff overlooking the Cambodian plain, is also built with Grès Supérieurs sandstone that crops out abundantly at this Angkorian site (Parmentier 1939, Vol.1, 321; Uchida et al. 2010; Uchida et al. 2017).

Triassic Sandstone

Triassic sandstone is not exposed in the Greater Angkor area, and its provenance has been puzzling scholars considering the many sculptures carved with this lithology and the large volumes used for the Ta Keo towers. Delvert (1963, 480) initially inferred without direct evidence that it could come from the Phnom Pours region about 93 km east of Angkor. Recent surveys in the vicinity of Svay Damnak, a village located about 16 km southeast of PKKS, have identified sandstone with a mottled texture that crops out in riverbeds with traces of extraction and also forms boulders (Contri 1972, 12–13; Carò and Douglas 2013, 2014; Figure 20.10a, b). Although Triassic sandstone formations are scattered across several provinces in Cambodia, this specific lithology has so far only been found in the previously mentioned area, and most likely, the sandstone of deities produced during the early to mid-12th century in Hariharālaya and later

Figure 20.10 Triassic sandstone quarries: a, b) Triassic sandstone quarrying evidence in the Svay Damnak area; c) general view of quarries near Sandan between Kratié and Sambor; d, e, f) detail of large and numerous rough-cut blocks scattered over a few square kilometres in the same region.

Source: (Photos a,b,c, F. Carò; d,e,f, C. Fischer).

in the Bayon style under the reign of Jayavarman VII originates from there. In the area around PKKS, outcrops with traces of quarrying of 'standard' Triassic sandstone were also identified and possibly used for sculptural work (Carò and Douglas 2013, 725).

Farther east, Triassic sandstone forms part of the bedrock and is widely exposed on either side of the Mekong, north of Kratié. Along its left bank, the ancient quarries of Sandan and Trâpeang Tuol Kros were discovered by Adhémard Leclère (1904, 743), who described the stone as a fine-grained blue granite, but it is actually a sandstone (Bruguier and Lacroix 2017, 103, 131; Carò and Douglas 2013) from the Triassic series. Two short surveys of the Sandan area in 2013 and 2017 revealed that the quarrying activities covered several square kilometres, and more than 30 rough-cut sandstone blocks of various sizes were spotted during a few hours' walk (Figure 20.10c–f). Scientific analysis of collected samples showed substantial textural and mineralogical variations, notably the occurrence of the subtypes with and without prehnite mentioned previously. Based on sandstone lithology correlations and site features, we argued that the large quarry field east of Sandan (and possibly other extraction sites in the Kratié–Sambor area) provided the stone for the Angkor foundation stelae of the 9th- and 10th-century built structures and *āśrama* commissioned during the reign of Yaśovarman I and possibly some sculptures of deities. Furthermore, comparable results were obtained for the analysis of the Ta Keo graywacke, providing compelling evidence for procurement from the very same area. Although the detailed recording of block dimensions in the central tower shows large variations due to on-site cutting, Dumarçay (1971, 49) suggested that most blocks were delivered, and possibly quarried, in only two standard squaring sizes (140 × 45 × 55 and 80 × 45 × 55 cm), consistent with the dimensions of some blocks left in the Sandan quarry field. The fact that Pre-Angkorian stelae found in the Kratié–Sambor region such as K. 127, K. 129, and K. 132 (6th–7th c. CE) also share similar typologies indicates that this area was already an active stone production centre before the rise of Angkor.

Multiple interconnected reasons could explain why the Triassic sandstone used for stelae, deity images, and the Ta Keo towers was procured from as far as the Kratié–Sambor region when similar rock formations outcrop closer to the capital. An explanation may be inferred from the royal lineages of 9th- and 10th-century Angkor rulers. Specifically, we can point to the connections between Jayavarman II (r. 770–830) and the polity of Śambhupura over which he took sovereignty through marriage, thus acquiring power and control of the land (Dupont 1943, 29–33; Jacques 1972, 219; Vickery 2001; Jacobsen 2003, 371–73) that gave him *de facto* access to an already established stone production region. This assumption would also make sense from an economic standpoint, as the creation of such activity anew implies a significant investment, complex logistics, and levels of organisation. Moreover, despite the distance, transport on water offered many advantages in monsoon Cambodia, where ancient roads and paths became almost impracticable during the rainy season, not to mention that floating stone is easier than hauling it overland. It might even be conjectured that Khmer engineers and traders preferred to transport large volumes of stone from May to September, when the water flow is inverted and goes from the Mekong towards the Tonle Sap (Kummu and Sarkkula 2008). Benefiting from these favourable conditions to reach the lake and further the rivers and canals connected to the Angkor area, the voyage would have only taken about four days with a travelled distance of ~100 to ~120 km per day (Deloche and Walker 1993, V.2, 171).

Timeline of Stone Usage: During and After Angkor

This comprehensive review of stone materials used by Angkorian Khmers reveals how sandstones selected for the representation of gods and inscribed stelae were—with a few exceptions—consistently different from sandstones used for the construction of temples and decorative elements. In continuity with Pre-Angkorian practices, Triassic sandstones with a graywacke typology were used to sculpt deities and engrave foundation texts and allegories during the Angkor Period. However, around the 9th century, in concomitance with the emergence of a more centralised Angkorian state, the supply of stone reserved for the deities might have changed. Most 9th–10th-century statuary is in fact carved from a graywacke-type sandstone that is generally coarser and better sorted than Pre-Angkorian stone materials and richer in metamorphic rock fragments. With possible sources in the PKKS area and along the Mekong or somewhere else, stone provenance for deities' sculptures is still hypothetical (Carò and Douglas 2013; Polkinghorne et al. 2015), while for inscribed stelae and the Ta Keo towers, the Kratié–Sambor Triassic sandstone, already exploited for sculptural work during Pre-Angkorian times, emerges as a likely source. At the end of the 9th century, stone facing at Bakong and Preah Ko, a technological paradigm attributed to Indravarman I (r. 877–889), marks the first extensive use of Terrain Rouge sandstone for construction purposes that intensified quarrying activities in the Kulen foothills (see Polkinghorne et al. 2015; Lithotype 1: 60–62). It also heralds a material culture transition period which extended well into the 10th century (Pottier 1996, 2005). Beside the selective use of Grès Supérieurs sandstone and idiosyncratic choice of a Triassic graywacke for the Ta Keo towers, Terrain Rouge sandstone became for the next three centuries the prime material to build temples and carve architectural elements, decorations, and free-standing figures such as *nandi*, lions, *dvārapāla*, and other guardians.

By mid-11th century, a new source of stone material appeared, as most deities in the Baphuon style were carved from a distinctive, very fine-grained feldspathic arenite that was not used before and whose provenance is unknown (Carò and Fischer, unpublished data).[24] In the early 12th century, the Triassic sandstone sub-lithotype sourced to the Svay Damnak area with a characteristic mottled texture was first documented in the sacred statuary from Hariharālaya (Polkinghorne et al. 2015) and later became Jayavarman VII's iconic stone material (Douglas and Sorensen 2008; Carò and Douglas 2013; Figure 20.11). In relation to this specific sub-lithotype,

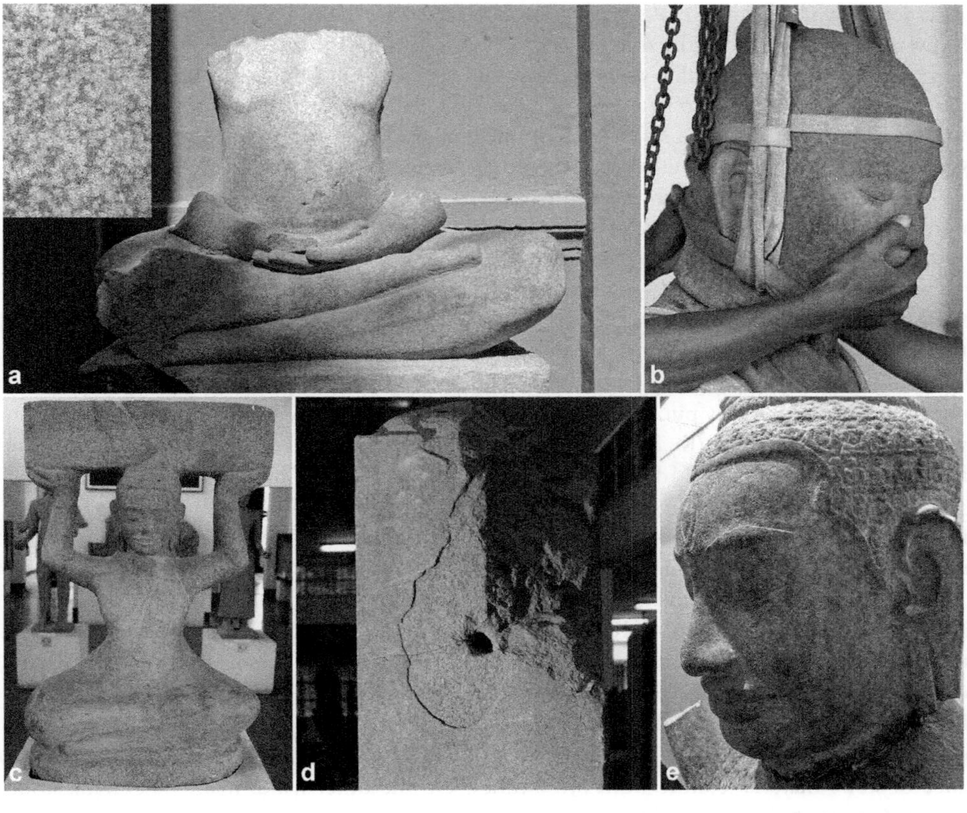

Figure 20.11 Triassic sandstone with the characteristic mottled texture: a) statue body presumably representing Jayavarman VII with a detail of the mottled texture (PKKS); b) Jayavarman VII's head reunited with its torso (both fragments also found at PKKS); c) seated figure with inscription K. 888, Preah Chatumukh (PKKS); d) inscribed stele K. 754; e) Radiating Avalokiteçvara, Prasat Mueang Sing, Thailand.

Source: (Photos a,c,d, C. Fischer; b, B. Porte; e, C. Pottier).

it should be noted that neither the foundation stele of Ta Prohm (K. 273, 1186 CE) nor Preah Khan (K. 908, 1192/3 CE) were cut from this sandstone. On the other hand, it was widely used for later Bayon-style sculptures such as the monumental Buddha on *nāga* from the Bayon and the statues portraying a meditative Jayavarman VII discovered in Angkor and Preah Khan of Kompong Svay (Figure 20.11a, b). Interestingly, the 'portrait' statue of Jayavarman VII found at Prasat Hin Phimai (Multzer o'Naghten 2014) is not carved with the mottled sandstone.

The mottled sandstone sandstone was also used in sculptures found as far from Angkor as Wat Nokor in Kompong Cham, and much farther away towards the west, in Sukhothai and Mueang Sing (Figure 20.11e) near the border with Myanmar (C. Pottier, pers. comm.). These sculptures of the gods were carved in 'royal' workshops and represent only a small fraction of the statuary production during Jayavarman VII's reign. According to the Preah Khan inscription (K. 908), an impressive number of 20,400 deities in gold, silver, bronze, and stone, as well as 23 'Jayabuddhamahānāta' sculptures, were sent to the provinces of the empire (Cœdès 1941, 266, 296). Considering this broad distribution, the absence of this stone in Angkor during the first years of Jayavarman VII's reign creates a sort of anomaly contradicting a 12th-century continuity, as this very same sandstone was already used during the early to mid-12th century. Jayavarman VII may have been unaware of the existence of this source while building Ta Prohm and Preah Khan toward the end of the 12th century and only discovered it during the construction projects at PKKS with the modifications of Prasat Stoeng and erection of Preah Tkohl. Further strengthening this hypothesis, the Phimeanakas and Prasat Chrung stelae, undated but thought to be early 13th century (Cœdès 1942, 1952), as well as the ones from Banteay Chhmar (K. 1206, K. 1208) found in the third enclosure built in the second Bayon Period (Cunin 2004, T1, 296), were all cut in the same sandstone.

The turn of the 13th century could therefore represent a *terminus post quem* for usage of the mottled sandstone by Jayavarman VII. This probably represented a deliberate choice that carried a profound symbolic meaning in relation to the expansion of the Khmer empire, as well as the vast religious reform associated with his evolving spiritual beliefs—in particular the preeminent worship of Mahāyāna Buddhism (Cœdès 1942; Vickery 2006; Maxwell 2007; Estève 2009). It also provides additional support for Pottier's (2000) argument against the idea of a 'much younger' Jayavarman VII for the head and bust found at PKKS. Finally, a *terminus ante quem* for its use might be tentatively put at the beginning of the 14th century based on a stele inscription written in Pāli and Khmer (K. 754, 1308 CE; Jacques 2007, 42, Vickery 2006, 23–24) cut in the same sandstone (Figure 20.11d). A second example from Preah Chatumukh (PKKS, Mauger 1939), now on display at the National Museum of Cambodia (NMC 1697) featuring a seated figure holding a cartouche over his head inscribed in Sanskrit (K. 888), is also carved with the mottled Triassic sandstone and dates most likely to the same period (Figure 20.11c).

Stone seems to have become less important when the Angkorian Khmer turned to Theravāda Buddhism in the late 13th and early 14th centuries. Although it had been known and practised in the Angkorian World, Theravāda Buddhism emerged as among the most significant characteristics of Cambodia's material and artistic culture from this time period. Some writers imply that Theravāda Buddhism's philosophy of impermanence favoured perishable images and architecture in wood (Finot 1908, 224; Cœdès 1943, 206–07), which could explain the lesser importance of stone material culture from those times. On the other hand, many Theravāda stone images (Giteau 1975; Tun 2015) and the reconfiguration of existing Brahmanical stone structures (Marchal 1918; Thompson 1998) suggest the emergence of Theravāda and the diminution of stone use was coincident rather than causal. Already in the 13th century (after Jayavarman VII's death), there was a steep decline in construction activities and the number of inscriptions (Lustig 2011; Vickery 2006, 82), pointing to economic and other stone procurement–related issues. It equally affected sacred sculptures, and data about the lithotypes used to render deities in this period are rather scarce, and further research is required. However, it seems that the distinction between stone for sacred sculptures and architecture became less established, as shown by a 13th-c. Ganeśa (Baptiste and Zéphir 2008, 315) carved with 'Terrain Rouge' sandstone (Fischer, unpublished data). The convergence was confirmed in the early 15th century when artists used the same lithotype for seated Buddha sculptures, some still visible in the galleries of Angkor Wat, thus ending a six-century-long tradition (Polkinghorne et al. 2013).[25]

Concluding Thoughts

This research on Angkor stone material culture has elucidated some of the intricate processes behind the choice, procurement, and usage of specific stone resources. The results highlight the differences between sandstone types used for architectural and decorative elements on the one hand and on the other hand the representation of deities and other sculptures that were sacred or of outstanding royal significance. From the evidence collected thus far, we can reasonably state that Angkor's monarchs and Khmer builders, craftsmen, and artists had multiple interrelated motives that guided these choices. For monumental constructions, stone availability and quality defined by the surrounding geology played a fundamental role in the decision process. When sandstone is present on or near the site, it was indeed exploited, as we see at Koh Ker, Preah Vihear, and Phimai. Similar patterns are observed in other cultures like the Incas, who built Machu Picchu with granite quarried on site and Sacsayhuaman with gigantic limestone blocks from nearby outcrops (Ogburn 2004, 419; Ogburn 2013, 48–52). This geological determinism, often overshadowed by spiritual considerations, was inevitably constrained by technical and economic factors, notably those related to labour agency and transportation when a sizable distance separated potential sources and building sites. Although an elaborated road system was developed in Angkorian times for the movement of commodities (Hendrickson 2011), stone was preferentially and logically transported on waterways in Cambodia, as it was in pharaonic Egypt on the Nile (Klemm and Klemm 2008) or the pre-Inca Andes on Lake Titicaca (Janusek et al. 2013, 81–82). Also, for Angkorian rulers and engineers, the use of waterways was certainly the only sustainable option—from both an environmental and economical viewpoint—to solve the problem of moving vast quantities of stone, as exemplified by the evidence of connected waterways for the transportation of Terrain Rouge sandstone from the Kulen quarries to the Angkor area. However, there is also a historical reason which explains why sandstone was sourced from there. At the turn of the 8th and 9th centuries, when Angkor's landscape was only sparsely built with wood, brick, and laterite structures with modest sandstone elements, and monumental stone projects started with the Bakong temple, calling for the earliest order of large volumes of sandstone, the closest source was actually the 'Terrain Rouge' outcropping northwest of Beng Mealea. Subsequently, and because of the massive and extended exposure of this sandstone, the quarrying activities could be developed along with the necessary infrastructure and logistics to deliver the colossal amounts needed from the 10th century onwards.

Stone physical properties were also of prime importance, and Terrain Rouge sandstone, even if not ideal, is particularly well suited for architecture and decoration, as its extraction and further cutting and carving were relatively easy—at least much easier than its Triassic equivalent. This workability fulfilled the needs of both engineers and artisans when they had to execute the architectural and artistic projects commissioned by Angkor rulers. Taken together, these aspects help us to better understand the close spatial and temporal relationships between Angkor's imperial expansion and the occurrences of Terrain Rouge sandstone as well as Grès Supérieurs that offered important raw material.

For the representation of deities, foundation stelae, and other revered sculptures, the motives behind the choice of a specific sandstone type were closer to the realm of beliefs and rituals. In this context, stone durability may be the one property that bridges the physical and spiritual spheres in a similar way this notion was valued in Egyptian beliefs, making stone an ideal, almost 'eternal', material for construction (Wright 2009, 56–57). This symbolism of longevity associated with other physical attributes was probably a key factor behind the choice of Triassic sandstone. Its compacity, hardness, and peculiar colour, combined with its ability to be smoothed to a high-grade polish, offered a sense of uniqueness and higher aesthetics that was perfectly suited for the representation of deities. Moreover, the Bakong foundation stele (K.826) mentions that the central liṅga was carved with stone extracted from a riverbed, while inscription K. 245 describes the careful search of an appropriate stone for a sculpture (Polkinghorne et al. 2015), underscoring the ritualistic dimensions of procuring stone for the creation of divine figures. Finally, the choice by Jayavarman VII of a distinctive, easily recognisable Triassic sandstone for sculptures designed to assert his authority and promote his religious beliefs throughout the Angkorian World provides us with a perfect example of the entanglements between materiality, power, and spirituality. However, despite the knowledge gained through the study of Angkor's stone material culture, assumptions still outnumber certainties. Many questions remain unanswered, and further research is necessary for the completion of this challenging puzzle whose pieces were shaped by both nature and human hands.

Notes

1 Laterite is a residual soil material rich in iron and aluminum. It forms in hot and humid climates from the weathering of the underlying bedrock and becomes hard when dry.

2 Notable exceptions are the Asram Maha Rosei and Kuk Prah That small sanctuaries built with basalt.

3 Original quote: 'L'art khmèr a été à sa grande époque un art du grès'.

4 A few samples from monuments in Angkor were provided by H. Parmentier and analysed by J. Fromaget and F. Bonelli, who distinguished two lithotypes, a greenish arkosic sandstone and a reddish quartz rich. Unfortunately, the analysed samples were poorly documented, and these results remained of limited interest.

5 Bureau de Recherches Géologiques et Minières (French geological survey). The survey led to the creation of a set of 1:200,000 maps with detailed field notes.

6 Although the definition and use of the term has engendered much controversy among sedimentary petrologists, graywacke is a kind of immature sandstone and corresponds to a fairly homogeneous group of rocks. Their essential characteristics are a dark, fine-grained, often chloritic matrix in which the quartz grains, rock fragments, and other minerals are set; a continuum in the particle size distribution from coarse to fine; the dominance of sodic plagioclase over K-feldspars; and a marked induration.

7 Aside from a few exceptions, the same sandstone type was used for sanctuaries and decorative lintels, and those in the Banteay Srei style are indeed carved with 'Grès Supérieurs' sandstone.

8 The small temple of Nang Sida, located in the valley about 1 km south of the Wat Phu's middle Baray, is however built with 'Terrain Rouge' sandstone.

9 Triad representing Śiva flanked by his consorts Umā and Gaṅgā.

10 Sandstone analysis of the *yoni* and upper pedestal base (currently stored at the DCA) of the Pre-Angkor Durga sculpture from Sambor Prei Kuk (NMC 1593) show the same difference (C. Fischer, unpublished results).

11 The 'Corpus of Khmer Inscriptions' program run by the EFEO and currently directed by Dominique Soutif has provided an opportunity to study a number of stelae from a materials perspective.

12 This group included the stelae from the Eastern Baray (K. 280, K. 281, K. 282, K. 283), the Angkor āśrama (K. 290, K. 701, K. 279, K. 1228), and digraphic stelae from provincial āśrama (K. 42, K. 95, K. 223, K. 309, K. 362, K. 1005, K. 1223).

13 Preah Kô: K. 713 (879 CE), Lolei: K. 323 (889 CE), East Mebon: K. 528 (952 CE), Pre Rup: K. 806 (961 CE).

14 FORS: Fiber Optics Reflectance Spectroscopy; pXRF: portable X-ray fluorescence spectrometry.

15 K. 42, K. 279, K. 528, K. 806.

16 Without considering the Koh Ker episode (Jayavarman IV, r. 921–941) as most inscriptions from this period, if not all, were carved on pillars and door jambs still *in situ* and have not been analysed yet.

17 Hardness measurements showed it to be about 5.5 (Mohs scale), implying that even with a hardened steel (hardness ~6) chisel, carving would have been difficult.

18 Located on the north jamb of the eastern door of the Ta Keo's temple interior gate.

19 An additional potential workshop complex has been postulated on the mounds of Phnom Dei and Phnom Bei directly north of Angkor Thom; however, further survey and excavation are required to confirm this assumption.

20 In this area, 'Terrain Rouge' sandstone crops out in sub-horizontal beds and is overlaid by the 'Grès Supérieurs' series which forms the main part of the Kulen mountain.

21 Henri Mouhot reports, looking at the surrounding scenery from the top of Phnom Bakheng, that the [Kulen] mountains (so he had been told) have supplied the sandstone to build Angkor.

22 Presence of zeolites which reflect rock transformations of metasomatic origin (hydrothermal and other fluid circulation).

23 Sandstone outcrops from the same series located ~20 km southwest of Battambang near Ompel could also be a potential source and have yet to be surveyed.

24 Petrographic analysis of Baphuon-style sculptures are relatively few, but visual inspection of figures in the National Museum of Phnom Penh, as well as from the Angkor National Museum in Siem Reap, seems to corroborate this hypothesis.

25 With the notable exception of Koh Ker.

References

Aymonier, E., 1901. *Le Cambodge II. Les Provinces Siamoises*. Paris: Ernest Leroux.

Baptiste, P. & T. Zéphir, 2008. *L'art khmer dans les collections du musée Guimet*. Paris: Reunion des Musees Nationaux

Baptiste, P., C. Chevillot, C. Raynaud, A. Bouquillon, S. Pagès, A. Leclaire & P. Recourt, 2001. La restauration des sculptures khmères du musée Guimet. *Technè* 13–14, 131–40.

Boulbet, J., 1979. Le Phnom Kulen et sa région, Paris, École Française d'Extrême-Orient.

Bourdonneau, É., 2011. Nouvelles recherches sur Koh Ker (Chok Gargyar). Jayavarman IV et la maîtrise des mondes. *Monuments et mémoires de la Fondation Eugène Piot* 90, 95–141.

Bruguier, B. & J. Lacroix, 2017. *Guide archéologique du Cambodge, Tome IV. De Thalat Borivat à Srei Santhor: Le bassin du Mékong*. Phnom Penh: JSRC Printing House.

Bruneau, E., 2009. *Contribution à l'étude des carrières de grès dans la région d'Angkor. Master 1 Archéologie, Université*. Paris: Panthéon Sorbonne.

Carò, F. & J.G. Douglas, 2013. Nature and provenance of the sandstone used for Bayon style sculptures produced during the reign of Jayavarman VII. *Journal of Archaeological Science* 40, 723–34.

Carò, F. & J.G. Douglas, 2014. Stone types and sculptural practices in Pre-Angkor Southeast Asia, in *Lost Kingdoms: Hindu-Buddhist Sculpture of Early Southeast Asia*, ed. J. Guy. New York: The Metropolitan Museum of Art, 265–66.

Carò, F. & S. Im, 2012. Khmer sandstone quarries of Kulen mountain and Koh Ker: a petrographic and geochemical study. *Journal of Archaeological Science* 39, 1455–66.

Carò, F., J.G. Douglas & S. Im, 2010. Towards a quantitative petrographic database of Khmer stone materials—Koh Ker style sculpture. *Archaeometry* 52, 191–208.

Carò, F., M. Polkinghorne & J.G. Douglas, 2014. Stone materials used for lintels and decorative elements of Khmer temples. *Metropolitan Museum Studies in Art, Science, and Technology* 2, 51–68.

Cœdès, G., 1941. IV. La stèle du Práh Khằn d'Ankor. *Bulletin de l'École française d'Extrême-Orient* 41, 255–302.

Cœdès, G., 1942. *Inscriptions du Cambodge, vol. II*. Hanoi: École Française d'Extrême-Orient.

Cœdès, G., 1943. *Pour mieux comprendre Angkor*. Hanoi: Imprimerie d'Extrême-Orient.

Cœdès, G., 1952. *Inscriptions du Cambodge, vol. IV*. Paris: École Française d'Extrême-Orient.

Cœdès, G., 1951. *Inscriptions du Cambodge, vol. III*. Hanoi: École Française d'Extrême-Orient.

Contri, J., 1972. *Carte Géologique de Reconnaissance 1/200000, Tbeng-Meanchey. Service National des Mines, de la Géologie et du Pétrole*. Paris: Editions du Bureau de Recherches Géologiques et Minières.

Cunin, O. 2004. *De Ta Prohm au Bayon, Analyse comparative de l'histoire architecturale des principaux monuments du style du Bayon, T1*. PhD, Institut National Polytechnique de Lorraine-INPL.

Dagens, B., 1968. Étude iconographique de quelques fondations de l'époque de Sūryavarman Ier. *Arts Asiatiques* 17, 173–208.

Deloche, J. & T. Walker, 1993. *Transport and communications in India prior to steam locomotion, V.2*. Delhi: Oxford University Press.

Delvert, J., 1963. Recherches sur l'érosion des grès des monuments d'Angkor. *Bulletin de l'École française d'Extrême-Orient* 51(2), 453–534.

Dottin, O., 1972. *Carte Géologique de Reconnaissance 1/200000, Phnom Penh, Service National des Mines de la Géologie et du Pétrole.* Paris: Editions du Bureau de Recherches Géologiques et Minières.

Douglas, J. G. & S.S. Sorensen, 2008. Mineralogical characteristics of Khmer stone sculpture in the Bayon style, in *Scientific Research on the Sculptural Arts of Asia: Proceedings of the 3rd Forbes Symposium at the Freer Gallery of Art*, eds. J.G. Douglas, P. Jett & J. Winter. Washington D.C.: Smithsonian Institution, 115–24.

Douglas, J. G., F. Carò & C. Fischer, 2010. Evidence of sandstone usage for sculpture during the Khmer Empire in Cambodia through petrographic analysis. *UDAYA: Journal of Khmer Studies* 9, 1–17.

Douglas, J.G., 2004. Stone materials used in Khmer sculpture from the national museum of Cambodia. *UDAYA: Journal of Khmer Studies* 5, 5–18.

Dumarçay, J. & P. Royère, 2001. Cambodian Architecture, Eighth to Thirteenth Centuries. Leiden: Brill.

Dumarçay, J., 1971. *Tā Kèv: Etude architecturale du temple.* Paris: École française d'Extrême-Orient.

Dupont, P., 1943. I. La dislocation du Tchen-la et la formation du Cambodge angkorien (VIIe-IXe siècle). *Bulletin de l'École française d'Extrême-Orien*, 43, 17–55.

Dupont, P., 1952. Études sur l'Indochine ancienne: II Les débuts de la royauté angkorienne. *Bulletin de l'École française d'Extrême-Orient* 46, 119–76.

Estève, J. & D. Soutif, 2010–11. Les Yaśodharāśrama, marqueurs d'empire et bornes sacrées: Conformité et spécificité des stèles digraphiques khmères de la région de Vat Phu. *Bulletin de l'École française d'Extrême-Orient* 97–98, 331–55.

Estève, J., 2009. *Étude critique des phénomènes de syncrétisme religieux dans le Cambodge angkorien.* PhD dissertation. Paris: École Pratique des Hautes Études.

Evans, D., 2010–11. The archaeological landscape of Koh Ker, northwest Cambodia. *Bulletin de l'École française d'Extrême-Orient* 97–98, 91–150.

Evans, D., 2016. Airborne laser scanning as a method for exploring long-term socio-ecological dynamics in Cambodia. *Journal of Archaeological Science* 74, 164–75.

Evans, D., C. Pottier, R. Fletcher, S. Hensley, I. Tapley, A. Milne & M. Barbetti, 2007. A comprehensive archaeological map of the World's largest preindustrial settlement complex at Angkor, Cambodia. *Proceedings of the National Academy of Sciences* 104, 14277–82.

Finot, L., 1908. Les études indochinoises. *Bulletin de l'Ecole française d'Extrême-Orient* 8, 221–33.

Fleuriot De Langle, P., 1973. *Carte Géologique de Reconnaissance 1/200000, Mondulkiri, Service National des Mines, de la Géologie et du Pétrole.* Paris: Editions du Bureau de Recherches Géologiques et Minières.

Fromaget, J. & F. Bonelli, 1932. A propos des matériaux d'Angkor et sur quelques points de la stratigraphie et de la structure géologique du Cambodge septentrional et oriental. *Comptes rendus de l'Académie des Sciences* 195, 538–43.

Fromaget, J., 1941. L'Indochine Française: sa structure géologique, ses roches. *Ses Mines Et Leurs Relations Possibles Avec La Tectonique Bulletin Du Service Géologique De L'indochine Xxvi.* 1–133.

Garnier, F., 1873. *Voyage d'exploration en Indo-Chine effectué pendant les années 1866; 1867 et 1868 par une Commission Française présidée par M. le capitaine de frégate Doudart de Lagrée. Tome I.* Paris: Hachette.

Gaucher, J. 1992. A propos d'une visite des sites khmers de Thaïlande. *Bulletin de l'École française d'Extrême-Orient* 249–56.

Giteau, M., 1975. *Iconographie du Cambodge Post-Angkorien. Publications de l'École française d'Extrême-Orient 100.* Paris: École française d'Extrême-Orient.

Glaize, M., 1936–44. *Rapports de la Conservation d'Angkor.* Siem Reap: École française d'Extrême-Orient.

Groslier, B.P., 1958. *Angkor et le Cambodge au XVIe Siècle d'après les Sources Portugaises et Espagnoles.* Paris: Presses Universitaires de France.

Groslier, G., 1921. *Recherches sur les Cambodgiens.* Paris: A. Challamel.

Gubler, J., 1935. *Études géologiques au Cambodge occidental.* Saigon: Service géologique de l'Indochine.

Hendrickson, M. & C. Fischer, 2016. *Industries of Angkor Project. The Two Buddhist Towers: Preliminary Report for the Field Campaign at Preah Khan of Kompong Svay* (Report submitted to the Ministry of Culture and Fine Arts). University of Illinois at Chicago.

Hendrickson, M., 2011. A transport geographic perspective on travel and communication in Angkor Southeast Asia (ninth to fifteenth centuries AD). *World Archaeology* 43, 444–57.

Jacobsen, T., 2003. Autonomous queenship in Cambodia, 1st–9th centuries AD. *Journal of the Royal Asiatic Society*, 13, 357–75.

Jacques, C. & P. Lafond, 2007. *The Khmer Empire: Cities and Sanctuaries from the 5th to the 13th Century, translated by Tom White.* Bangkok: River Books.

Jacques, C., 1972. VI. Études d'épigraphie cambodgienne. *Bulletin de l'École française d'Extrême-Orient* 59, 193–220.

Jacques, C., 1978. VI. Études d'épigraphie cambodgienne. XL Autour de quelques toponymes de l'inscription du Prasat Trapan Run K. 598: La capitale angkorienne de Yašovarman Ier à Sûryavarman Ier. *Bulletin de l'École française d'Extrême-Orient* 65, 281–332.

Jacques, C., 2007. The historical development of Khmer culture from the death of Suryavarman II to the 16th century, in *Bayon: New Perspectives*, eds. V. Roveda & J. Clark. Bangkok: River Books, 28–50.

Janusek, J. W., P.R. Williams, M. Golitko & C.L. Aguirre, 2013. Building taypikala: Telluric transformations in the lithic production of Tiwanaku, in *Mining and Quarrying in the Ancient Andes*, eds. N. Tripcevich & K.J. Vaughn. New York: Springer, 65–97.

Klemm, R. & D.D. Klemm, 2008. *Stone and Stone Quarries in Ancient Egypt*. London: British Museum Press.

Kučera, J., J. Novák, K. Kranda, J. Poncar, I. Krausová, L. Soukal, O. Cunin & M Lang, 2008. INAA and petrological study of sandstones from the Angkor monuments. *Journal of Radioanalytical and Nuclear Chemistry* 278, 299–306.

Kummu, M. & J. Sarkkula, 2008. Impact of the Mekong River flow alteration on the Tonle Sap flood pulse. AMBIO: *A Journal of the Human Environment* 37, 185–93.

Leclère, A., 1904. Une campagne archéologique au Cambodge. *Bulletin de l'École française d'Extrême-Orient* 4, 737–49.

Lustig, E., 2011. Using inscription data to investigate power in Angkor's empire. *Aséanie, Sciences humaines en Asie du Sud-Est* 27, 35–66.

Marchal, H., 1918. "Monuments secondaires et terrasses bouddhiques d'Aṅkor Thom". *Bulletin de l'École française d'Extrême-Orient* 19, 1–40.

Marchal, H., 1924–26. Notes sur le palais royal d'angkor thom. *Arts et Archaeologie Khmers* 2, 303–28.

Marchal, H., 1928. *Guide archéologique aux temples d'Angkor: Angkor Vat, Angkor Thom et les monuments du petit et du grand circuit*. Paris: Van Oest.

Mauger, H. 1939. Prah Khan de Kompong Svay. *Bulletin de l'École française d'Extrême-Orient* 39(2), 197–220.

Maxwell, T., 2007. Religion at the time of Jayavarman VII, in *Bayon: New Perspectives*, eds. V. Roveda & J. Clark. Bangkok: River Books, 72–135.

Moriai, T., Y. Matsumura & Y. Akama, 2002. Geological study on Angkor monuments, part 3. Memoirs of the Tohoku Institute of Rechnology. Series 1. *Science and Engineering* 22, 23–39.

Mouhot, H., 1868. *Voyage dans les Royaumes de Siam, de Cambodge, de Laos et autres parties centrales de l'Indo-Chine*. Paris: Hachette.

Moura, J., 1883. *Le Royaume du Cambodge*. Paris: E. Leroux.

Multzer o'Naghten, H., 2014. The organisation of space in pre-modern Thailand under Jayavarman VII, in *Before Siam: Essays in Art and Archaeology*, eds. N. Revire & S. Murphy. River Books & The Siam Society Production 397–419.

Ogburn, D., 2004. Evidence for long-distance transportation of building stones in the Inka Empire, from Cuzco, Peru to Saraguro, Ecuador. *Latin American Antiquity* 15, 419–39.

Ogburn, D., 2013. Variation in Inca building stone quarry operations in Peru and Ecuador, in *Mining and Quarrying in the Ancient Andes,* eds. N. Tripcevich & K. Vaughn. New York: Springer, 45–64.

Parmentier, H., 1913. Complément à l'inventaire descriptif des monuments du Cambodge. *Bulletin de l'École française d'Extrême-Orient* 13, 1–64.

Parmentier, H., 1939. *L'art khmèr classique: monuments du quadrant nord-est*. Paris: Les Éditions d'Art et d'Histoire.

Pettijohn, F. J., P.E. Potter & R. Siever, 1987. *Sand and Sandstone*. New York: Springer-Verlag.

Polkinghorne, M., 2007. Artists and Ateliers: Khmer decorative lintels of the ninth and tenth centuries. *UDAYA: The Journal of Khmer Studies* 8, 219–41.

Polkinghorne, M., 2008. Khmer decorative lintels and the allocation of artistic labour. *Arts Asiatiques* 63, 21–35.

Polkinghorne, M., J.G. Douglas & F. Carò, 2015. Carving at the capital: a stone workshop at Hariharālaya, Angkor. *Bulletin de l'École française d'Extrême-Orient* 101, 55–90.

Polkinghorne, M., C. Pottier & C. Fischer, 2013. One Buddha can hide another. *Journal Asiatique* 301, 575–624.

Polkinghorne, M., B. Vincent, N. Thomas & D. Bourgarit, 2014. Casting for the king: the royal palace bronze workshop of Angkor Thom. *Bulletin de l'École française d'Extrême-Orient* 100, 327–58.

Pottier, C. & R. Luján-Lunsford, 2005. De brique et de grès: précisions sur les tours de Prah Kô. *Bulletin de l'École française d'Extrême-Orient* 92, 457–95.

Pottier, C., 1996. Notes sur le Bakong et son implantation. *Bulletin de l'École française d'Extrême-Orient* 83, 318–26.

Pottier, C., 2000. A propos de la statue portrait du roi Jayavarman VII au temple de Préah Khan de Kompong Svay. *Arts Asiatiques* 55, 171–72.

Reucher, R., H. Leisen, E. von Plehwe-Leisen & R. Kleinschrodt, 2007. Petrographical and geochemical investigations on the building stones of the Khmer temples in the Angkor Park/Cambodia. *Zeitschrift der Deutschen Gesellschaft für Geowissenschaften*, 617–29.

Rocks, D.F., 2009. *Ancient Khmer Quarrying of Arkose Sandstone for Monumental Architecture and Sculpture*. Cottbus, Germany: Brandenburg University of Technology. (Third International Congress on Construction History, 20th-24th May 2009.1235–42).

Saurin, E., 1935. Etudes Géologiques sur l'Indochine du Sud-Est (Sud-Annam—Cochinchine—Cambodge Oriental). *Bulletin du Service Géologique de l'Indochine* 22, 1–417.

Saurin, E., 1954. Quelques remarques sur les grès d'Angkor. *Bulletin de l'École française d'Extrême-Orient* 46, 619–34.

Thompson, A., 1998. The ancestral cult in transition: reflections on spatial organization of Cambodia's early Theravada Complex, in *Southeast Asian Archaeology: Proceedings of the 6th International Conference of the European Association of Southeast Asian Archaeologists, 2–6 September, Leiden*, eds. M.J. Klokke & T. de Brujin. Hull: Centre for Southeast Asian Studies, 273–95.

Tun, P., 2015. *Bouddhisme Theravāda et production artistique en pays khmer: Étude d'un corpus d'images en ronde-bosse du buddha (xiiie-xvie siècles)*. PhD dissertation. Paris: Université Paris IV—Paris-Sorbonne.

Uchida, E., Y. Ogawa & H. Tsumagari, 1996. Petrology, in *Annual Report on the Technical Survey of Angkor Monuments*, ed. T. Nakagawa. Tokyo: Japan International Cooperation Center, 385–96.

Uchida, E. & D. Ando, 2001. Petrological survey, in *Annual Report on the Technical Survey of Angkor Monuments*, ed. T. Nakagawa. Tokyo: Japan International Cooperation Center, 225–36.

Uchida, E. & I. Shimoda, 2013. Quarries and transportation routes of Angkor monument sandstone blocks. *Journal of Archaeological Science* 40, 1158–64.

Uchida, E., A. Mizoguchi, H. Sato, I. Shimoda & R. Watanabe, 2017. Determining the construction sequence of the Preah Vihear monument in Cambodia from its sandstone block characteristics. *Heritage Science* 5, 42.

Uchida, E., I. Shimoda & M. Shimoda, 2013. Consideration of the construction period of the Khmer temples along the east royal road to Preah Khan of Kompong Svay and the provenance of sandstone blocks based on their magnetic susceptibility. *Archaeological Discovery* 1, 37–48.

Uchida, E., K. Ito & N. Shimizu, 2010. Provenance of the sandstone used in the construction of the Khmer monuments in Thailand. *Archaeometry* 52, 550–74.

Uchida, E., O. Cunin, C. Suda, A. Ueno & T. Nakagawa, 2007. Consideration on the construction process and the sandstone quarries during the Angkor period based on the magnetic susceptibility. *Journal of Archaeological Science* 34, 924–35.

Uchida, E., O. Cunin, I. Shimoda, C. Suda & T. Nakagawa, 2003. The construction process of the Angkor monuments elucidated by magnetic susceptibility of sandstone. *Archaeometry* 45, 221–32.

Uchida, E., Ogawa, Y., Maeda, N. & Nakagawa, T., 1999. Deterioration of stone materials in the Angkor monuments, Cambodia. *Engineering Geology* 55, 101–12.

Uchida, E., Y. Ogawa & H. Tsumagari, 1996. Petrology, in *Annual Report on the Technical Survey of Angkor Monuments*, ed. T. Nakagawa. Tokyo: Japan International Cooperation Center, 385-96.

Uchida, E., Y. Ogawa & T. Nakagawa, 1998. The stone materials of the Angkor monuments, Cambodia. The magnetic susceptibility and the orientation of the bedding plane of the sandstone. *Min. Petr. Econ. Geol.* 93, 411–26.

Uchida, E., Y. Ogawa & K. Hirai, 1995. Petrology, in *Annual Report on the Technical Survey of Angkor Monuments*, ed. T. Nakagawa. Tokyo: Japan International Coorperation Center, 353–62.

Vickery, M., 1999. The Khmer inscriptions of Roluos (Preah Ko and Lolei): documents from a transitional period in Cambodian history. *Seksa Khmer* 1, 48–88.

Vickery, M., 2001. Resolving the chronology and history of 9th century Cambodia. *Siksācakr* 3, 17–23.

Vickery, M., 2006. Bayon: new perspectives reconsidered. *UDAYA: Journal of Khmer Studies* 7, 101–76.

Workman, D.R., 1977. Geology of Laos, Cambodia, South Vietnam and the eastern part of Thailand. *Overseas Geol. & Miner. Resources* 50, 1–33.

Wright, G.R., 2009. *Ancient Building Technology, volume 3: Construction*. Leiden: Brill.

21

CRAFTING WITH FIRE

Stoneware and Iron Pyrotechnologies in the Angkorian World

Mitch Hendrickson, Ea Darith, Chhay Rachna, Yukitsugu Tabata, Phon Kaseka, Stéphanie Leroy, Yuni Sato and Armand Desbat

Fire was integral to the Angkorian Empire's rise and resilience. In Khmer ritual, the sacred fire, or *yajna*, was a galvanising mechanism of Brahmanical power and kingship dating back to at least the Pre-Angkor Period. Fire was also essential in the daily lives of households and to help clear fields and lands for new settlements (see Carter et al. 2023 and Hawken and Castillo 2023, this volume). The ability to control fire at high temperatures requires considerable skill and was essential for the production of objects—ceramics, iron, bronzes—that facilitated the economic growth of the empire. These objects also served as important hallmarks of Angkorian identity and imperialism (see Lowman et al. 2023, this volume). Recent discoveries of ceramic kilns and iron smelting sites across Angkor's former territories have enabled researchers to finally move beyond object-based typological inquiries. We are now beginning to understand the nature and scale of Angkor's pyrotechnologies, how they developed, and how objects were moved around the empire. Considering these crafts together, rather than individually, allows us to identify developmental synergies and how these relate to events within the Angkor Period. This chapter reviews evidence and intersections between ceramic and iron traditions in the Angkorian World. Bronze, which was equally important in the manufacture of ritual statuary and objects, is not considered in detail here because production evidence is currently limited to secondary casting. The following provides a summary of Angkorian stoneware and iron production sites and their spatio-temporal development, and then addresses questions of mass production, elite control, and the origins of each pyrotechnology.

Products of Fire: Ceramics and Iron

Our understanding of Angkorian ceramics and iron is based on—and somewhat biased by—the relative visibility of each material in the archaeological record. Earthenwares and distinctive glazed (green, brown, '*lie-de-vin*') and unglazed stonewares collected from excavations and museum collections have enabled researchers to document the enormous diversity within the Khmer ceramic tradition (Brown 1981; Rooney 1984; Groslier 1995; Guy 1997; Cort 2000). Unlike Thai, Vietnamese, Burmese, and Chinese wares, the Khmer types are virtually unknown in the larger maritime exchange systems. In Khmer territories, earthenwares are the most commonly found ceramic

DOI: 10.4324/9781351128940-26

material, but stoneware ceramics are consistently found at every site. Characteristic Angkorian vessels include small covered boxes, *kendis*, large baluster jars, zoomorphic containers presumably used for ritual purposes, and large architectural roof tiles placed on elite houses (Figure 21.1). B.-P. Groslier argued that stonewares were an essential part of religious practice at temples, and some vessel forms appear to be skeuomorphs of ritual metal vessels commonly used in Indian temple contexts (1995, 38, 56). In an effort to understand the functionality of locally made shapes and move beyond western jar/bowl/plate terminologies, the APSARA National Authority developed a local typology comprising dozens of forms based on Khmer ethnographic associations (Chhay et al. 2020). Vessel manufacture in the Angkor Period typically involved wheel-throwing as well as coiling and hand-moulding (Franiatte 2000). Surface decoration is used very sparsely and is commonly limited to incision or rouletting around vessel necks on earthenwares. Arguably the most important decorative indicator is the use of glazes. Colour (e.g., green, green/brown,

Figure 21.1 Angkorian stonewares types and vessel forms. a) Green glaze; b) 'lie de vin'; c) brown glaze; d) various vessel forms; e) architectural roof tiles.

Source: (Photos R. Chhay and A. Desbat; elephant effigy vessel courtesy National Museum of Cambodia).

brown) and thickness are useful indicators of temporal and spatial associations. The first model of ceramic change between the 9th to 13th centuries by B.-P. Groslier (1995) and Brown (1981) used stratigraphic correlations of Khmer glazed types with temple inscriptions and well-dated Chinese imports: green glaze was produced between the 9th and late 12th century; 'lie de vin' between the late 10th and early 11th century; brown glaze from the late 10th to early 13th century. This chronology was slightly refined and expanded with the addition of initial evidence of ceramics from kilns (Tabata 2005; Ea 2010; Desbat 2011a). The most obvious and significant events within the ceramic chronology are the transition from green to brown glazes and the actual appearance of the enigmatic 'lie de vin' type.

Iron objects are rarely recovered from Angkorian sites because iron corrodes (and sometimes disintegrates) quickly in moist environments like Monsoon Asia. Few well-preserved iron artefacts are therefore recovered from excavations, but depictions of iron tools and weapons on bas-reliefs, as well as lists of iron objects in temple inventories, indicate that Angkorian Khmers used iron quite extensively. A rare record of iron quantities from the Preah Khan inscription (K. 292, 1181 CE) shows that the Khmer elite required 300 *bhara*, or approximately 1 tonne, to build one of Jayavarman VII temple projects (Cœdès 1992[1941]). Twentieth-century restoration of Angkor's numerous temples confirmed iron's role in temple construction through the recovery of hundreds of *in situ* crampons, or architectural ties, placed into slots of individual blocks to stabilise the walls (Nafilyan 1967). The crampons recovered from 11th-to-13th century temples in Angkor (Figure 21.2) show a clear increase in size and quantity as well as a transition from high-carbon to low-carbon steel (Leroy et al. 2017). Such shifts in metal quality suggest a desire

Figure 21.2 Iron objects produced during the Angkor Period: a) tools, including nails and a blade; b) crampons from the Royal Palace in Angkor (late 10th c.) (upper), the Baphuon (early 11th c.) (middle), and Preah Khan, Angkor (late 12th c.) (lower).

Source: (Photos M. Hendrickson and S. Leroy).

for more malleable steel and/or a decrease in the quality of metal production due to the huge demand for building materials generated by expansionist kings like Jayavarman VII in the 12th and 13th centuries.

A Historical Geography of Angkor's Pyrotechnologies

Cambodia's reopening to archaeologists in the 1990s began a surge of research by Khmer and international teams that focused predominantly on the urban and hydraulic characteristics of Greater Angkor (see Chevance and Pottier 2023; Evans et al. 2023; Lustig et al. 2023a, this volume). While a few kiln sites were discovered inside the capital region (Nara National Cultural Properties Institute & APSARA 2001; Tabata 2006; Tabata and Chhay 2007; Tabata 2008; Ea et al. 2008; Miksic 2009; Miksic and Chhay 2010; Chhay et al. 2013), the true

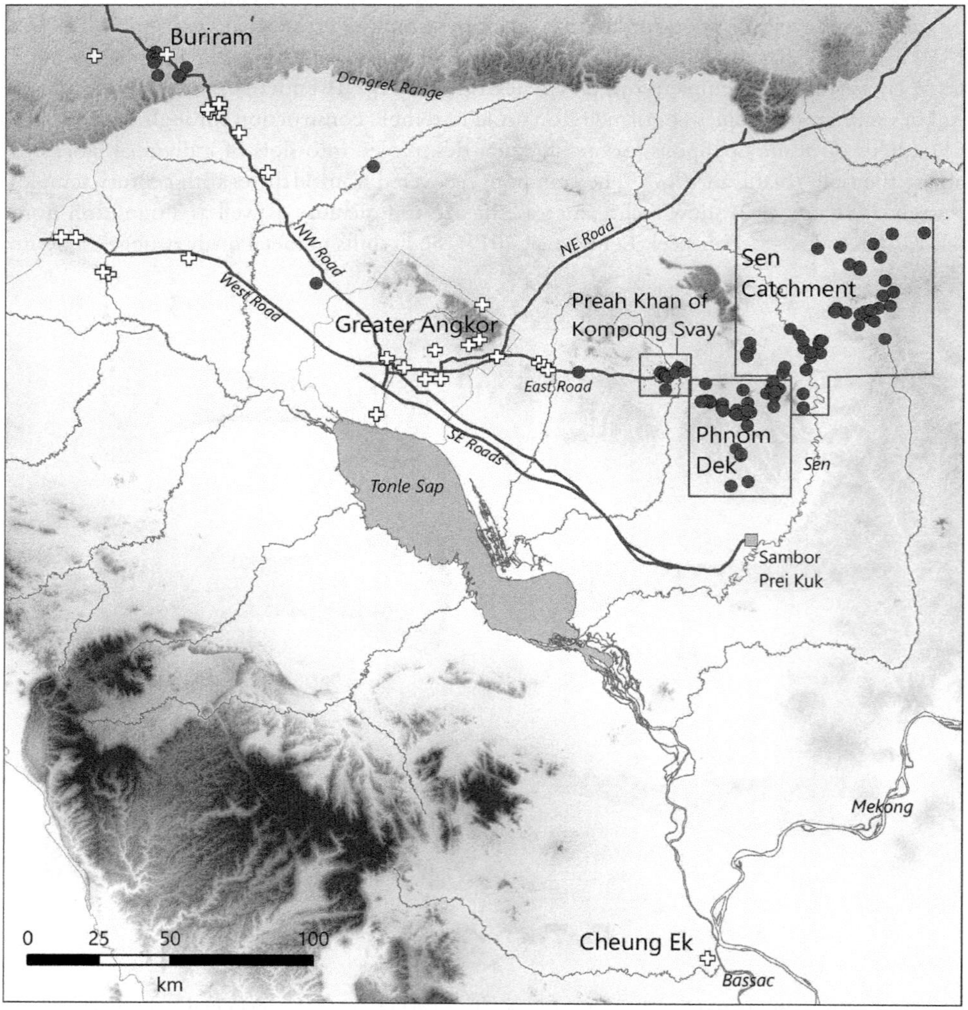

Figure 21.3 Pryotechnological production sites in Cambodia and northeast Thailand, stoneware (crosses) and iron (circles).

scale of Angkorian ceramic and iron production only became apparent with increased access to more remote areas of the Cambodian landscape. Khmer stoneware sites typically have 15–30 mounds visible in the contemporary land surface; some sites like Cheung Ek may have 60 or more. Iron production sites are similarly marked by multiple slag concentrations; the site of Bangkaun Phal, for example, has at least 50 unique smelting emplacements. For both types of pyrotechnological sites, it is unclear how many of these individual mounds were in operation concurrently. Over 150 stoneware and iron production sites are currently known from five primary regional contexts: Greater Angkor; Cheung Ek; along Angkor's road system; around Phnom Dek; and across the middle Sen River catchment (Figure 21.3) (Tabata 2008; Hendrickson 2008; Ea 2013; Phon et al. 2013; Thuy 2014; Pryce et al. 2014; APSARA National Authority and Nalanda-Sriwijaya Centre 2016; Hendrickson et al. 2017; Tabata 2021a).

Kilns

Excavation and dating of numerous kilns have identified two primary phases of stoneware production in the Angkor Period (Ea et al. 2008; APSARA National Authority and Nalanda-Sriwijaya Centre 2016; Marriner et al. 2018; Desbat 2020; Chhay et al. 2020). In the first phase (late 9th to 11th c.), relatively small, oval kilns (6–9 m long by 1.5–3.6 m wide) with a single fire box, firing chamber, and vent were built on earthen embankments and produced green glaze, unglazed, and the 'lie de vin' type (Figure 21.4). Subtle transitions are visible at specific kiln sites in this initial phase. For instance, production at Thnal Mrech, formerly known as Anlong Thom, switches from green to brown glaze wares and is the only kiln in Greater Angkor known to produce this type (Miksic et al. 2009). The craftspeople north of the Dangrek Range at the Buriram kilns employed slightly different kiln forms than in Greater Angkor but also produced green, green-brown, and brown and unglazed types.

The second phase (11th to 15th c.) sees an increase in the size of kilns (15–20 m long by 3–3.5 m wide), the number of firing trenches, and new technical additions (e.g., side-stoking). These kilns mainly produce brown glaze and unglazed wares. The largest example from Torp Chey on the East Road, extending over 21.5 m long with four firing chambers and three firing trenches, is sometimes referred to as a Khmer 'dragon kiln' due to its relatively large size (not because it is a direct copy of the famous Chinese 'dragon kilns' from Dehua). These kilns are found on artificial mounds formed partly from the rebuilding of successive kiln floors. They produced brown glaze wares in a new repertoire of forms, including zoomorphs and large baluster jars. In contrast to the earlier phase, kiln shapes between sites along the East Road, including Chong Samrong and Veal Kok Treas, are much more heterogeneous and could indicate an internal shift in technological practice (Tabata 2021b; Hein et al. 2013).

The two phases of Angkorian kiln construction show distinct shifts in morphology and respective ceramic outputs but are part of a continuous stoneware tradition (Hein 2008; Ea et al. 2008; Miksic 2009; APSARA National Authority and Nalanda-Sriwijaya Centre 2016). The Khmer constructed oval or rectilinear cross-draft kilns using clay over a bamboo or wooden frame located on an artificial mound near a source of water. The internal structure incorporates one or more fire boxes, a chamber, and a vent, with clay pillars arranged in the middle to support roof structures that are sloped at an angle to facilitate a partial up-draft effect. Individual kilns were reused multiple times and often fixed between firings. New kilns were built on top of earlier structures, up to three times at any given site. It is unclear how long each structure was used, but based on ethnographic estimates, it is likely to be less than a decade (Marriner et al. 2018).

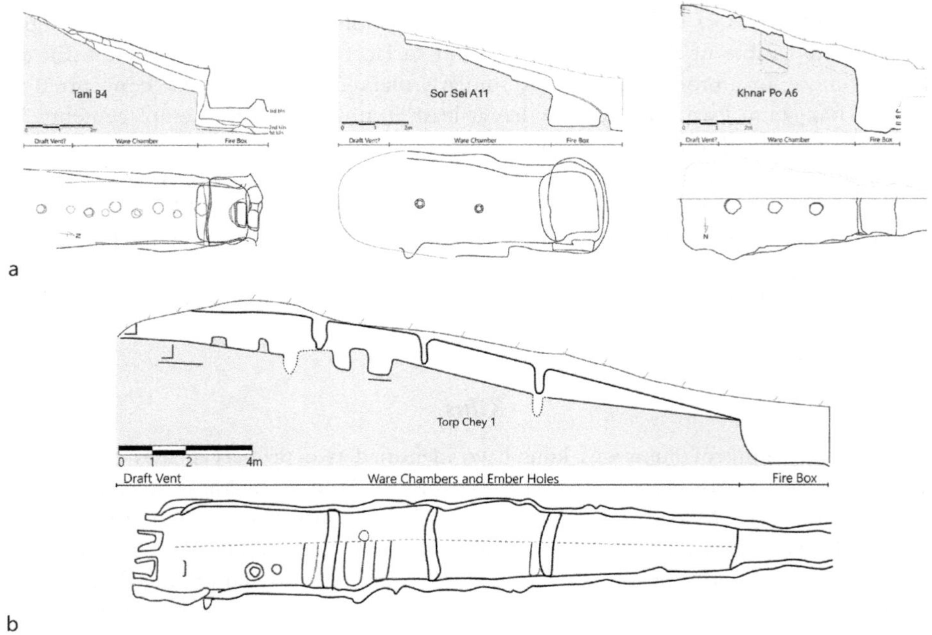

Figure 21.4 Kiln morphologies in the Angkor Period: a) Phase 1; and b) Phase 2.
Source: (Images R. Chhay).

Slag Concentrations and Furnaces

Discussions of iron-working in Cambodia initially focused on the Kuay ethnic minority who smelted bloomery iron around Phnom Dek (the 'Iron Mountain') from at least the 16th century until the early 20th century (Dupaigne 2016). The Kuay used 2-m-long rectilinear furnaces pierced with up to 40 tuyères on either side. Air delivery was achieved through a bellows made of deer and operated using a bamboo lever. Until the discovery of furnace bases at Tonle Bak (Hendrickson et al. 2019), smelting sites were defined solely by the morphology and composition of slag concentrations (Figure 21.5). Like stoneware sites, a typical iron smelting site contains one or more mounds of metallurgical debris composed of layers of slags, tuyères, broken furnace wall, unused ores, and charcoal. Individual slag concentrations vary in size from low scatters to massive ovate or linear features rising up to 5 m above the ground surface. This formation process represents a uniquely Khmer trait within the metallurgical traditions in mainland Southeast Asia. Surveys have currently identified 100 sites with over 400 individual mounds around Phnom Dek, inside Preah Khan of Kompong Svay, in association with the Angkorian road system, and across the Sen River Catchment.

The metallurgical landscape around Phnom Dek, Cambodia's single largest source of mineral ore, spans 200 km^2 and contains evidence of production from at least the 8th to 20th centuries. Three distinct smelting traditions are identifiable from the different types of tap slags, tuyère gauges, and mound morphology (Thuy 2014; Hendrickson et al. 2017). The earliest sites (8th to 11th c.) are concentrated to the northeast and east of Phnom Dek and characterised by small, fragmented tap slags, infrequent pairs of broad gauge tuyéres and linear mounds measuring up

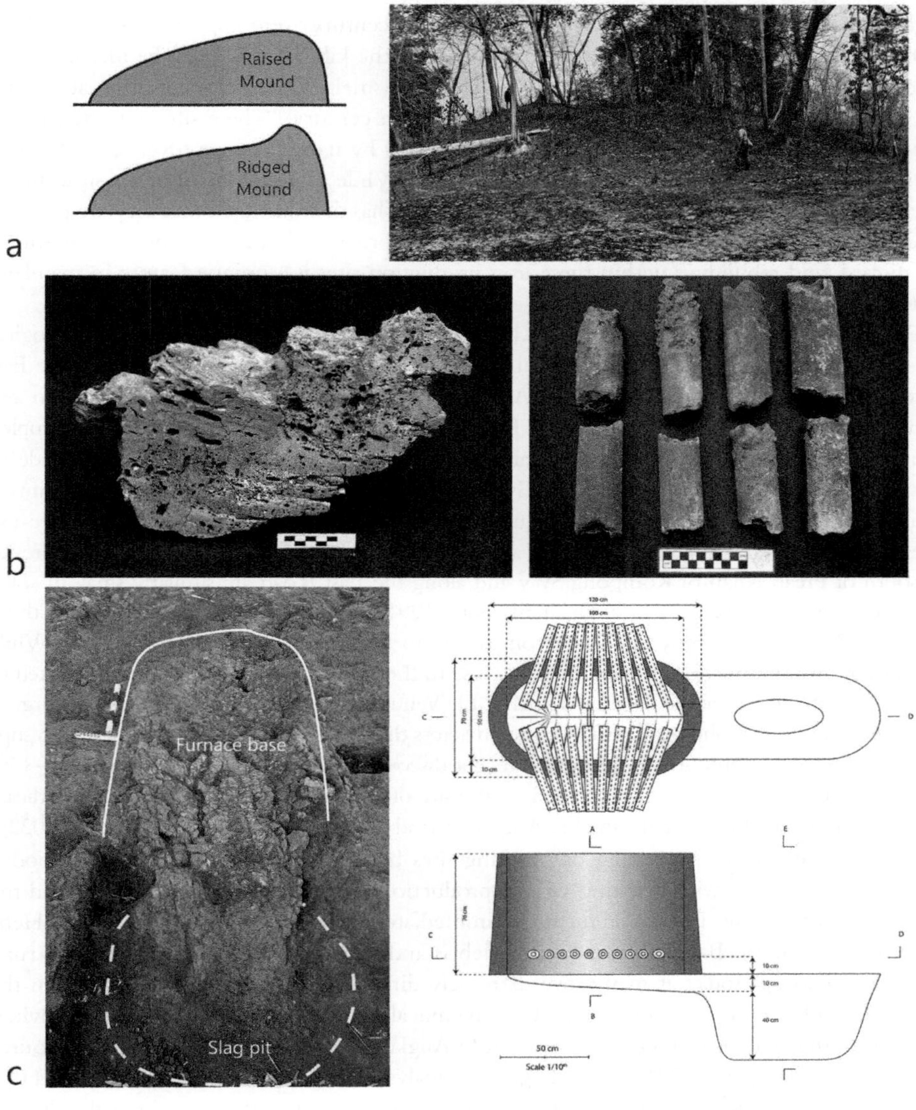

Figure 21.5 Characteristics of Angkorian iron smelting sites: a) typical slag concentration profiles; b) cross-section of tap slag 'cake' and examples of medium-gauge tuyères; c) furnace base and schematic reconstruction of Angkorian furnace.

Source: (Photos M. Hendrickson; adapted from S. Leroy et al. 2020, fig. 5).

to 100 × 20 m in the horizontal and up to 5 m in height. The second technology (11th to 16th c.) is broadly distributed around Phnom Dek and is identifiable by the increased presence of medium gauge tuyéres and the formation of large tap slag 'cascade' cakes weighing up to 80 kg (see Figure 21.5a–b). Mounds during this phase tend to be ovate and slope upward toward the west, reaching a maximum height of 5 m. Cross-sections of a mound at Tonle Bak, located 2 km south of Phnom Dek, showed at least seven different smelting phases that took between

20–50 years to form (Hendrickson et al. 2019). Tonle Bak also revealed the first details about Angkorian furnace morphologies, which in the 13th century were approximately 2 m long by 0.5 m wide with a slag pit at the western end. Like the kilns, the base of the furnaces were reused multiple times, with walls being re-built for each smelt. The third technology at Phnom Dek is associated with the Kuay tradition (18th to 20th century). These sites are often found near the Angkorian slag concentrations but are typified by narrow-gauge tuyères, smaller slag cakes, and lower mounds in a ring or crescent shape. While there are obvious physical differences between these two later systems, chemical analysis has demonstrated that they are part of a shared smelting lineage (Pryce et al. 2014). Overall, the process of repeated construction, smelting, discard, and rebuilding within these iron production sites is a unique feature in mainland Southeast Asian metallurgy.

The smelting sites in other parts of the Khmer Empire show similarities with the technological styles at Phnom Dek. Concentrations found at Preah Khan of Kompong Svay and along the East Road align, not surprisingly, with typical Angkor Period production systems (Hendrickson and Evans 2015). Located at the end of the East Road, it is both the single largest Angkorian complex outside the capital and the only known Khmer settlement with traces of iron smelting inside its walls. Smelting at Preah Khan of Kompong Svay was conducted on a small scale during the primary occupation between the 11th and 13th centuries and again as part of a 15th to 17th century re-use of reservoir embankments after the site was abandoned as an urban centre. Other smelting sites to the south of Preah Khan of Kompong Svay and along the East Road are similarly small in scale. Sites along the Northwest Road in Buriram (Nitta 1991; Nitta 1997) and the majority of those in the Sen Catchment (Thuy 2014) are comparable to the earlier phase at Phnom Dek. While the Buriram iron production sites are situated close to the kiln groups, they have been re-dated to the late Prehistoric period (first half of 1st M. CE) (Venunan 2016). Similar types of metallurgical debris and mound morphology broadly scattered across the central Sen River Catchment also support earlier phases of production. However, recent discovery of ceramics dating to the 11th–13th centuries around the 54 slag concentrations at the site of Sanlong Russei Trep in Chhep indicate that this region was also active during the Angkor Period (K. Phon, pers. comm., June 28, 2022).

Definitive secondary processing or smithing sites have yet to be identified in Cambodia. Smithing slags present with smelting slags at production sites and slag prills found around the furnaces indicate some level of refinement immediately after removal of the bloom (Hendrickson et al. 2019). Based on the limited debris and perishable infrastructure used in rural smithing workshops today, it may prove extremely difficult to identify an analogue from the Angkor Period. The clearest evidence of the technical choices behind the smithing activities comes from the analysis of metal crampons from Angkor's temples, which shows broad source heterogeneity (Leroy et al. 2017). Metallographic analysis and provenance analysis revealed that crampons manufactured during the 13th century were welded together using metal collected from different smelting locations and possibly suggests the presence of intermediate iron redistribution workshops. Decreasing efforts to remove the impurities from iron in this later phase indicates that smiths were also less concerned with metal quality and more focused on meeting the increased demands of the Khmer state.

Shifts in Pyrotechnological Production: Scale and Control

The scalar transition of Angkor's pyrotechnologies toward mass production between the 11th and 13th centuries coincides with the Khmer state's most intense period of urbanism (Klassen et al. 2021). Increases in the footprint of kilns and slag concentrations is matched by the quantity and size of individual objects and a shift in 'quality' from fine, white paste green glaze and homogenous high-carbon steels to coarse, dark paste brown glaze wares and heterogeneous, low-carbon steel. Changes in geographic placement and scale of Angkorian pyrotechnological production also provide insights into economic requirements and the nature of political control (Tabata 2021a). For stonewares, green glaze and unglazed ceramic kilns found on artificial embankments near the early capitals of Mahendraparvata and Hariharālaya support a model of elite oversight between the 9th and 11th centuries. Potters exploited local deposits of light kaolin clays—perhaps mimicking popular Chinese porcelain imports—and had access to abundant fuels from the vast forested regions between the Tonle Sap floodplain and the Kulen massif. The stability of stoneware production may have been impacted by recurring episodes of monumental 're-capitalisation' across Greater Angkor (see Chevance and Pottier 2023, this volume) that required acquisition of new lands, an act recorded in the epigraphy as kings 'clearing the forest' (see Lowman 2013). Increasing land for agriculture will attract new populations who in turn require wood fuel and goods. Direct competition between kiln workers and Angkor's growing population could therefore generate an unsustainable situation in the capital and necessitate relocation of stoneware production. A comparable example of an empire actively moving production away from the capital can be seen in the Roman World, in which glass and metal manufacture transitioned to the forested regions of Europe (Wertime 1983, 451–52).

Movement of kilns out along Angkor's roads, initially the Northwest and then East, arguably solved any issues of fuel and space and appears to have decreased the direct control by elites over production. The Buriram kilns began producing ceramics while the green glaze kilns were in operation at Angkor and continued to evolve their repertoire over time. Though located over 130 km from the capital, the kilns were still connected with the regional economy via the Northwest Road through the Dangrek and northwards to the state temples of Phnom Rung and Phimai, both of which flourished between the 11th and 12th centuries. The variations in kiln number and form at different sites on the East Road in 13th to 14th centuries suggests a lack of standardisation and perhaps local autonomy. The Chong Samrong and Veal Kok Treas sites have small kiln mounds and are interpreted as a family managed with relatively low levels of production (Hein et al. 2013; Tabata 2021b). Torp Chey has 12 large kilns clustered around two 'resthouse' temples, but their dates indicate activity decades after the establishment of the monuments (APSARA National Authority and Nalanda-Sriwijaya Centre 2016). On the other hand, regardless of the technological heterogeneity and temporal gap, the fact remains that these 'provincial' kiln sites were placed along well-established terrestrial arteries; thus, they were probably at least monitored by the Khmer elites, if not directly managed by them.

Beyond economic necessity, the geographic shift in kiln locations is also linked to the increasing political significance of Khmer stonewares in the Angkorian World. Suitable clays for making stonewares are broadly available in Cambodia, but some specific types—such as the light kaolins used to imitate Chinese porcelains—are much more limited. The switch to the darker pastes found in brown glaze wares could be viewed as a passive response to local resource availability. Another interpretation is that the shift towards brown glaze wares—along with the broad distribution of kilns beyond the capital—represents a conscious decision to establish a distinctly Khmer tradition across the Angkorian World. As a variation of green ash-glaze, thin and dark-brownish transparent glazed wares appear initially at kilns in the north of Angkor. The transition to thick, translucent, or opaque iron blown glaze type is more clearly evident in the Buriram kilns along the Northwest Road, which produced green, green-brown, and brown glaze vessels and developed many new, uniquely Khmer forms (Brown 1988, 44–48). The initial experimentation in glaze colours ultimately became the preferred marker of stonewares disseminated across Angkor's lands.

Increased ceramic activity in Buriram may be linked to a major geopolitical shift in the 11th century: the rise of powerful elite families, known as the Mahidharapura Dynasty, who ruled lands above the Dangrek Range (Briggs 1951, 178; see also Jacques and Lafond 2004, 301). Meanwhile, the permanent switch to darker paste products in the 13th- to 14th-century brown glaze kilns along the East Road represents the culmination of techno-cultural experimentation and major political events beginning in the late 12th century, including the territorial expansions of Jayavarman VII (1181–1219) and decreased politico-economic interaction with the late Song and Yuan Dynasties (see Stark and Cremin 2023, this volume). In this period, Angkorian kiln technology became uniquely Khmer, and the brown glaze wares are a portable symbol of belonging within Angkor's empire distributed through its network of roads. The decision to place these later kilns along the East road is also linked to the importance of that route in facilitating the movement of iron between Phnom Dek and Angkor through the vast entrêpot of Preah Khan of Kompong Svay (Hendrickson and Leroy 2020).

The relationship between Cheung Ek and Angkor is less clear. The majority of the documented kiln mounds remain undated, but Angkorian production between the 11th and 14th centuries included unglazed and each of the glazed wares, including the enigmatic 'lie de vin' type known for its distinctive purplish paste (Phon et al. 2013; Grave et al. 2021). In contrast to the broad distribution of green and brown glaze wares across Angkor's territories, 'lie de vin' is commonly found only in southern Cambodia (M. Stark, pers. comm. June 20, 2022). Cheung Ek's remote position from Angkor, along with the lack of any considerable state or repeated royal foundations (e.g. hospitals, *āśrama*) in the immediate vicinity, suggests that it was an independent potting community whose longevity was directly linked to its proximity to abundant resources (e.g. mangrove forest, clays) and a transportation network via the Bassac River into the Mekong's vast riverine network (see Heng 2023, this volume).

The dispersal and changes within iron production present a slightly different picture of Angkorian control. Iron can be produced from laterites and iron sands, but large-scale, pre-modern bloomery smelting is typically associated with the exploitation of substantial hematite/magnetite outcrops. In contrast to clays, viable mineral ore sources in Cambodia are restricted to the central Sen Catchment and Phnom Dek (Dottin 1971; United Nations 1993). A further constraint on smelting is the increased demand for wood fuel. Ironworkers require considerable amounts of charcoal, which is reduced from raw wood, to sustain the temperatures necessary to transform a load of ore to metal (>1200 °C). In the Sen Catchment, the absence of roads, major state temples and typical settlement infrastructure (e.g., *trapeang* reservoirs) near Pre-Angkor and early Angkor Period slag concentrations indicates that the Khmer elites had little direct control over iron smelting communities. Production may have focused on riverine transport to Sambor Prei Kuk; however, no iron from this period has been identified at this Pre-Angkorian capital. Imperial interest is more clearly visible during the 11th century with the general shift of iron production toward the south and west of Phnom Dek and the corresponding establishment of Preah Khan of Kompong Svay by king Sūryavarman I (Hendrickson et al. 2017). A rare and early indicator of Angkor's interest in iron is provided from the inscription at Tuol Prasat (K. 158, early 11th c. CE), whose text describes quantities of iron objects used to pay for land exchanges and state taxes (see Lustig et al. 2023b, this volume). Tuol Prasat, known locally as Prasat Svay Damnak, is one of a few temples within the vast metallurgical landscape around Phnom Dek and is positioned a mere 400 m from the smelting site of Russei Prei. The implication is that the iron payment was derived from locally made metal.

There are indications that the Khmer state was directly implicated in iron production in the 12th to 13th centuries: the repeated architectural investments at Preah Khan of Kompong Svay; the increased size of slag mounds around Phnom Dek; and the co-occurrence of iron production sites, albeit infrequently, with rectilinear *trapeang*. Furthermore, the ratios of glazed ceramics and diverse plant remains found at Tonle Bak indicate that its iron smelting community was directly connected to the Angkorian economy by the mid- to late 13th century. Advances in metallurgical analysis also demonstrated Angkor's increasing reliance on Phnom Dek metal to construct its sandstone temples. Iron from this source first appeared in limited amounts in the 11th-century Baphuon temple, and by the 13th century, Phnom Dek was the predominant source of iron used in Preah Khan at Angkor, one of the major temples of Jayavarman VII (Leroy et al. 2017).

Pryotechnological Origins and Transformations

The ability to craft at high-firing temperatures (1000 °C+) requires a specific set of skills gained through processes of local experimentation and/or dissemination of knowledge. Before the rise of Angkor, only the potters in northern Vietnam were capable of making high-quality ceramics. Cort (2000) notes that stoneware production is a completely different technical process from earthenware production, and it is not necessary to see one developing directly from the other. Furthermore, as stoneware represents a specialist industry, the ability to adopt and support the technology on a large scale is linked to the political and economic stability of Angkor's inland agrarian polity and the demand that this generated (Desbat 2011b). B.-P. Groslier (1995, 57) argued that the very sudden transition to stonewares in Cambodia could not be the result of an internal evolution and must have relied on external ideas, specifically from China. Cambodia's long history of interactions with Chinese dynasties dates back to nearly the start of the first millennium CE (see Stark and Cremin 2023, this volume). The small pale-paste, green glaze Khmer wares made in large quantities in the initial phase of stoneware production were clearly local imitations of Chinese celadons (Wong 2010). Comparison of production sites across mainland Southeast Asia demonstrates clearly that Khmer cross-draft kilns are part of a broader transmission along the coast from China and share general similarities in kiln form at Binh Dinh in central Vietnam (Hein 2008).

The foundations of cross-draft kilns are definitively Chinese in origin, but their layout and size, and the later modifications to kiln form and ware production, are clearly the product of local or perhaps regional inspiration. The lack of Chinese occupational evidence around these kilns (e.g., coins, burials, etc.) supports a model of Chinese interaction with Khmer potters rather than a migration of specialised communities of foreign potters into Cambodia (Hein 2008). For the Torp Chey kilns, Hein argues for a scenario where someone who was aware of dragon kilns in southern China, perhaps to the point of watching them work, but not familiar with the kiln's internal design. Chinese traders or merchants, on visiting a working Angkorian kiln, could have informed the local potters of details such as the side-stoke method and of the possibility of extending the length of the kiln. Regardless of how these changes arrived into the Angkorian World, we now have consumption data (Desbat 2020) and production data (Marriner et al. 2018, Table 2) that indicate continuous stoneware ceramic production through the 14th century.

Insights into the development of Angkorian iron technology are complicated by both the general dearth of bloomery production evidence in Southeast Asia and by the uniqueness and particularity of local smelting practices, especially when compared to well-studied traditions in China and India. The historic-period sites identified in Laos (Pryce et al. 2011), Malaysia (Mokhtar et al. 2011), and Myanmar (Hudson 2006) bear little resemblance to the rectilinear, multi-tuyère furnace structures in the Angkor Period. Chinese iron metallurgy was heavily focused from the late first millennium BCE on cast iron production, a technology not found in mainland Southeast Asia (Wagner 2008). Bloomery iron production sites dating from the Han to Qing periods in southern and central China currently do not show any obvious technological similarities with those in the Angkor Period (Larreina-Garcia et al. 2018; Zhang et al. 2020; Qian and Huang 2021). This does not rule out Chinese influence but requires consideration of other sources. The Gupta and other Indic polities provided the intellectual basis for Angkor's political and religious infrastructures (see Stark and Manguin 2023, this volume), but these two regions had limited economic contact or exchange of non-ritual material culture (Smith 1999). Another model emphasising a South Asian origin by Juleff (2009) tracked the transmission of multi-tuyère, linear furnaces from Sri Lanka (4th c. BCE to 1st c. CE) through Southeast Asia and finally to Japan (6th c.). While the 20th-century Kuay example used in her model contradicts the proposed unidirectional trajectory, the shared lineage between Kuay and Angkor furnace structures (see Pryce et al. 2014) supports some level of interaction with this early knowledge system. Defining the differences between Angkorian and earlier smelting traditions will be essential to understanding whether the transition is a new, externally derived technology or innovation within local practices.

The technical similarities between the Angkorian and Kuay smelting systems ultimately raise the question of whether this minority group made the iron for the Khmer Empire. The Kuay currently occupy the lands around Phnom Dek and have likely done so for many centuries. Historic records also indicate that the Kuay were brought by a Khmer king to smelt iron in the Phnom Penh region during the 16th century (Khin 1988, 151). The argument that the Phnom Dek is the long-term homeland for the Kuay is supported by the fact that it is situated in the middle of Angkorian territory and yet lacks the typical settlement infrastructure (temples, *trapeang*, etc.) found across Cambodia, northeast Thailand, and southern Laos. The site of Tonle Bak complicates this simple correlation both in the comparability of its economic assemblage and the fact that the iron production is scattered around a 245-m-long trapeang with a low mound positioned in the middle of its western side (Hendrickson et al. 2019). Excavation near the mound revealed the presence of roof tiles and nails from a wooden shelter likely used to house a statue of an Indic god. Furthermore, other ethnic groups including the Samre and Cham are known historically to have come to Phnom Dek to take advantage of its high-grade ores. While not denying the Kuay hypothesis, it is not yet possible to directly attribute this group as being the sole smelters of Angkor's iron.

Crafting With Fire: Reflecting on the Future

The Khmer had metallurgical and ceramic traditions for centuries before the rise of the Angkor, but the Angkor Period represents a marked shift in pyrotechnological capabilities and knowledge. Control of high-fire pyrotechnology coincided with the emergence of the state and was a prerequisite for many of its 'building blocks', from temples to stoneware ceramics. The ubiquity of stonewares in temple and occupation sites, the massive consumption of iron in temples, and the large quantities of bronze and copper-alloy statues of Indic gods in museums around the world all attest to a productive capacity and technological prowess unmatched by regional contemporaries in Bagan, Dvaravati, and Champa. The Angkorian pyrotechnological traditions described here also reflect multiple influences rather than a single source. These technical relationships offer further evidence that the Angkorian Khmers were not an isolated inland kingdom but regularly engaged with their neighbours and operated in a broader global context. As with the transformation of Khmer politico-religious structures from Indic influence, Angkorian people harnessed ideas from external groups to develop unique forms of technological expressions in stoneware and iron.

Ongoing archaeological investigations into pyrotechnological traditions are providing key insights into the mechanics of empire. For example, an analysis of taxa of the carbonised woods from stoneware kilns shows utilisation of miscellaneous broadleaf trees. It does not seem to have been a strictly controlled resource (Tabata 2021a, 71). Angkorian potters probably employed a resource strategy of collecting many species of locally available wood rather than preparing specific tree plantings for fuel, as we sometimes observe in East Asian pyrotechnology. If we designate the latter type of resource strategy as a highly controlled resource strategy, the strategy used for Angkorian kilns would be a kind of *bricolage*. The spatial and temporal characteristics of ceramic and iron metallurgical traditions also offer insights into the broader historical trajectory of the Angkorian World. Did the 9th-century florescence of stoneware technology facilitate the transformation in iron production witnessed in the late 10th or early 11th century? As we have seen in the previous examples, changes in Angkorian pyrotechnologies reflect broader transformations in politics, society and material culture that are perhaps most visible in temple construction, where we see a shift in the use of brick to sandstone in the 11th century alongside a dramatic increase in the number and size of temple projects in the reigns of kings such as Jayavarman VII (1181–1219) (Hendrickson and Leroy 2020).

Angkor's mastery of fire at an imperial scale was central to its success and collectively ended sometime in the 14th century. This decline in the production and consumption of stoneware and iron needs to be understood in the context of regional demographic and political developments such as the rise of Thai and Vietnamese neighbours and is also clearly linked to the environmental, political, and economic stressors that led to Angkor's gradual denouement. Perhaps the most significant factor behind the attenuation of these pyrotechnologies is the transition of the Khmer state religion from Brahmanical-Mahāyāna Buddhism to Theravāda Buddhism in the late 13th to early 14th century (Tabata 2016, 47). Stoneware products (e.g., roof tiles and vessels) and iron implements (e.g., crampons tools), once essential for ritual practices and the construction of stone temples, lost their value within this new politico-religious milieu. Like the farming populations around Angkor, the craftspeople responsible for making stoneware and iron did not 'disappear'. Rather, they likely adapted their skills and industries to meet the new demands of the early Post-Angkor or Early Modern period (see Polkinghorne and Sato 2023, and Krajaejun 2023, this volume). For pottery, the tradition moved its focus toward Kompong Chhnang and the production of pottery. For iron, the Kuay continued to make iron for the Khmer kings, but on a much more limited scale. Overall, the future of pyrotechnological research is extremely promising. Surveys and dating will continue to add nuance to the movement of stoneware and iron production in the Angkorian landscape and its politico-economic implications. Crucial work in the coming years will focus on dating and analysis of kiln sites in Buriram and slag concentrations in the Sen Catchment as well as the location of copper smelting sites. Equally important is the intensive study of anthracology or wood fuel use. As modern development expands rapidly across Cambodia, it is urgently important to record the range of tree species that were available to the craftspeople who transformed the Angkorian World through fire.

References

APSARA National Authority. & Nalanda-Sriwijaya Centre, 2016. *Torp Chey. Analysis of an Angkorian Kiln*. Singapore: Nalanda Sriwijaya Centre.

Briggs, L.P., 1951. *The Ancient Khmer Empire*. Philadelphia: The American Philosophical Society.

Brown, R.M., 1981. Khmer ceramics of the Korat Plateau: unravelling the mysteries, in *Khmer Ceramics 9th–14th Century*, ed. D. Stock. Singapore: Southeast Asian Ceramic Society, 41–50.

Brown, R.M., 1988. *The Ceramics of South-East Asia: Their Dating and Identification*. Singapore: Oxford University Press.

Carter, A., M.T. Stark, P. Heng. & R. Chhay, 2023. The Angkorian house, in *The Angkorian World*, eds. M. Hendrickson, M.T. Stark. & D. Evans. New York: Routledge, 494–507.

Chevance, J-B. & C. Pottier, 2023. The early Angkor capitals, in *The Angkorian World*, eds. M. Hendrickson, M.T. Stark. & D. Evans. New York: Routledge, 80–96.

Chhay, R., P. Heng. & V. Chhay, 2013. Khmer ceramic technology: a case study from Thnal Mrech kiln site, Phnom Kulen, in *Materializing Southeast Asia's Past: Selected papers from the 12th International Conference of the European Association of Southeast Asian Archaeologists*, volume 2, eds. M.J. Klokke. & V. Degroot. Singapore: NUS Press, 179–95.

Chhay, R., T. Tho. & S. Em, 2020. Guide to understanding Khmer stoneware characteristics, Angkor, Cambodia, in *Material culture and Heritage. Papers from the Fourteenth International Conference of the European Association of Southeast Asian Archaeologists,* volume 2, ed. H. Lewis. Oxford: Archaeopress, 53–62.

Cœdès, G., 1992[1941]. La stele du Prah Khan d'Ankor, in *Articles Sur Le Pays Khmer.* Paris: École française D'Extrême Orient, 119–66.

Cort, L.A., 2000. Khmer Stoneware Ceramics, in *Asian Traditions in Clay: The Hauge Gifts,* ed. L. Cort. Washington, D.C: Freer Gallery of Art and Arthur M. Sackler Gallery, Smithsonian Institution, 91–149.

Desbat, A., 2011a. Pour une révision de la chronologie des grès Khmers. *Aséanie* 27, 11–34.

Desbat, A., 2011b. *Programme Cerangkor: Recherches sur les Ateliers de Potiers Angkoriens.* Siem Reap: École française d'Extrême-Orient.

Desbat, A., 2020. New data on the chronology of Khmer stonewares, in *Material Culture and Heritage. Papers from the Fourteenth International Conference of the European Association of Southeast Asian Archaeologists*, ed. H. Lewis. Oxford: Archaeopress, 63–75.

Dottin, O., 1971. *Geologie et mines du Cambodge.* Phnom Penh: Service National des Mines, de la Geologie et du Petrole.

Dupaigne, B., 2016. *Les Maîtres du Fer et du Feu dans le Royaume d'Angkor.* Paris: CNRS Editions.

Ea, D., 2010. *Angkorian Stoneware Ceramics: The Evolution of Kiln Structure and Ceramic Typology.* Unpublished PhD thesis. Osaka: Osaka Ohtani University, 235.

Ea, D., 2013. Angkorian stoneware ceramics along the east road from Angkor to Bakan at Torp Chey village. *Udaya, Journal of Khmer Studies* 11, 59–98.

Ea, D., V. Chhay, S. Chap, S. Lam, R. Loeung, S. Sok Keo. & S. Em, 2008. New data on Khmer kiln sites, in *Interpreting Southeast Asia's Past, volume 2: Monument, Image and Text,* eds. E.A. Bacus, I. Glover. & P.D. Sharrock. Singapore: NUS Press, 275–84.

Evans, D., R. Fletcher, S. Klassen, C. Pottier. & P. Wijker, 2023. Trajectories of urbanism in the Angkorian World, in *The Angkorian World*, eds. M. Hendrickson, M.T. Stark. & D. Evans. New York: Routledge, 173–94.

Franiatte, M., 2000. Nouvelles analyses de la céramique khmère du Palais royal d'Angkor Thom: Étude préliminaire. *Udaya, Journal of Khmer Studies* 1, 91–124.

Grave, P., L. Kealhofer, K. Phon, P. Heng, M.T. Stark, B. Marsh, D. Ea, R. Chhay. & G.P. Marriner, 2021. Centralized power/decentralized production? Angkorian stoneware and the southern production complex of Cheung Ek, Cambodia. *Journal of Archaeological Science* 125, 105–270.

Groslier, B-P., 1995. Introduction à la céramique Angkorienne (fin IXe-début XVe. s). *Péninsule 2*, 5–60.

Guy, J., 1997. A reassessment of Khmer ceramics. *Oriental Ceramic Society* 61, 39–63.

Hawken, S. & C.C. Castillo, 2023. Angkor's agrarian economy: a socio-ecological mosaic, in *The Angkorian World*, eds. M. Hendrickson, M.T. Stark. & D. Evans. New York: Routledge, 338–59.

Hein, D., 2008. Ceramic kiln lineages in Mainland Southeast Asia, in *Ceramics in Mainland Southeast Asia. Collections in the Freer Gallery of Art and Arthur M. Sackler Gallery*, eds. L.A. Cort, G.A. Williams IV. & D.P. Rehfuss. Washington, D.C: Smithsonian Institution, 1–38.

Hein, D., L.A. Cort, D. Ea. & Course Members, 2013. *The Chong Samrong Kiln Site in Cambodia: Report on a Training Excavation,* ed. L.A. Cort. Washington, DC: Freer Gallery of Art and Arthur M. Sackler Gallery, Smithsonian Institution, 70.

Hendrickson, M., 2008. New evidence of brown glaze stoneware kilns along the east road from Angkor. *Bulletin of the Indo-Pacific Prehistory Association* 28, 52–6.

Hendrickson, M. & D. Evans, 2015. Reimagining the city of fire and iron: a landscape archaeology of the Angkor-Period industrial complex of Preah Khan of Kompong Svay, Cambodia (ca. 9th to 13th centuries A.D.). *Journal of Field Archaeology* 40(6), 644–64.

Hendrickson, M. & S. Leroy, 2020. Sparks and needles: seeking catalysts of state expansions, a case study of technological interaction at Angkor, Cambodia (9th to 13th centuries CE). *Journal of Anthropological Archaeology* 57, 101141.

Hendrickson, M., S. Leroy, C. Castillo, Q. Hua, E. Vega. & K. Phon, 2019. Forging empire: Angkorian iron smelting, community and ritual practice at Tonle Bak. *Antiquity* 93(372), 1586–606.

Hendrickson, M., S. Leroy, Q. Hua, K. Phon. & V. Voeun, 2017. Smelting in the shadow of the iron mountain: preliminary field investigation of the industrial landscape around Phnom Dek, Cambodia (ninth to twentieth centuries A.D.). *Asian Perspectives* 56(1), 55–91.

Heng, P., 2023. Angkor and the Mekong River: settlement, resources, mobility, and power, in *The Angkorian World*, eds. M. Hendrickson, M.T. Stark. & D. Evans. New York: Routledge, 154–72.

Hudson, B., 2006. Iron in Myanmar. *Enchanting Myanmar* 5, 6–9.

Jacques, C. & P. Lafond, 2004. *L'Empire Khmer. Cités et Sanctuaires Vth-XIIIth siècles*. Paris: Fayard.

Juleff, G., 2009. Technology and evolution: a root and branch view of Asian iron from first-millennium BC Sri Lanka to Japanese steel. *World Archaeology* 4, 557–77.

Khin, S., 1988. *Les Chroniques royales du Cambodge: II*. Paris: EFEO.

Klassen, S., A.K. Carter, D.H. Evans, S. Ortman, M.T. Stark, A.A. Loyless, M. Polkinghorne, P. Heng, M. Hill, P. Wijker, J. Niles-Weed, G.P. Marriner, C. Pottier. & R.J. Fletcher, 2021. Diachronic modeling of the population within the medieval greater Angkor region settlement complex. *Science Advances* 7, eabf8441.

Krajaejun, P., 2023. Uthong and Angkor: material legacies in the Chao Phraya Basin, Thailand, in *The Angkorian World*, eds. M. Hendrickson, M.T. Stark. & D. Evans. New York: Routledge.

Larreina-Garcia, D., Y. Li, Y. Liuc. & M. Martinón-Torres, 2018. Bloomery iron smelting in the Daye County (Hubei): technological traditions in Qing China. *Archaeological Research in Asia* 16, 148–65.

Leroy, S., M. Hendrickson, S. Bauvais, T. Blanchet, A. Disser, E. Vega. & E. Delqué-Kolic, 2017. The ties that bind: archaeometallurgical typology of architectural crampons as a method for reconstructing the iron economy of Angkor, Cambodia (10th to 13th c.). *Archaeological and Anthropological Science* 10(8), 2137–57.

Leroy, S., S. Bauvais, E. Delqué-Kolic, M. Hendrickson, N. Josso, J-P. Dumoulin. & D. Soutif, 2020. First experimental reconstruction of an Angkorian iron furnace (13th–14th centuries CE): archaeological and archaeometric implications. *Journal of Archaeological Science Reports* 34, 102592.

Lowman, I., 2013. The elephant hunt of Jayavarman II: a political myth of Angkorian Cambodia. *Udaya, Journal of Khmer Studies* 11, 29–57.

Lowman, I., K., Chhom. & M. Hendrickson, 2023. An Angkor nation? Identifying the core of the Khmer empire, in *The Angkorian World*, eds. M. Hendrickson, M.T. Stark. & D. Evans. New York: Routledge, 479–93.

Lustig, T., J-B. Chevance. & W. Johnson, 2023a. Angkor as a "cité hydraulique"?, in *The Angkorian World*, eds. M. Hendrickson, M.T. Stark. & D. Evans. New York: Routledge, 216–34.

Lustig, E., A. Cremin. & T. Lustig, 2023b. Angkor's economy: implications of the transfer of wealth, in *The Angkorian World*, eds. M. Hendrickson, M.T. Stark & D. Evans. New York: Routledge, 309–26.

Marriner, G.P., P. Grave, L. Kealhofer, M.T. Stark, D. Ea, R. Chhay, K. Phon. & B.S. Tan, 2018. New dates for old kilns: a revised radiocarbon chronology of stoneware production for Angkorian Cambodia. *Radiocarbon* 60(3), 901–24.

Miksic, J., 2009. Kilns of Southeast Asia, in *Southeast Asian Ceramics. New Light on Old Pottery*, ed. J.N. Miksic. Singapore: Southeast Asian Ceramic Society, 48–69.

Miksic, J., R. Chhay, P. Heng. & V. Chhay, 2009. *Archaeological report on the Thnal Mrech Kiln Site (TMK 02), Anlong Thom, Phnom Kulen, Cambodia in Asia research institute* (Working Paper Series No. 126 ed. M.B. Mohamad. Singapore: Asia Research Institute). Singapore: National University of Singapore, 43.

Miksic, J.N. & R. Chhay, 2010. Khmer potters emerge from the shadows: Thnal Mrech and Bangkong kiln sites. *SPAFA Journal* 20(2), 5–16.

Mokhtar, N.A., M. Saidin. & J. Abdullah, 2011. The ancient iron smelting in SG. Batu, Bujang Valley, Kedah, in *Postgraduate Student Forum 2011*. Hong Kong: Chinese University of Hong Kong.

Nafilyan, G., 1967. Les mur dan l'architecture khmere. *Annales de la Universite Royale des Beaux-Arts*, 62–77.

Nara National Cultural Properties Institute (Japan) & APSARA, 2001. Investigations of the Tani kiln site: geophysical prospections, excavations and site presentation proposal. *Udaya, Journal of Khmer Studies* 2, 133–39.

Nitta, E., 1991. Archaeological study on the ancient iron-smelting and salt-making industries in the north-east of Thailand. Preliminary report on the excavations of Non Yang and Ban Don Phlong. *Journal of Southeast Asian Archaeology* 11, 1–46.

Nitta, E., 1997. Iron-smelting and salt-making industries in Northeast Thailand. *Bulletin of the Indo-Pacific Prehistory Association* 16, 153–60.

Phon, K., C. Rachna, V. Vuthy, C. Vicheata, K. Savon. & M. Dega, 2013. *The Ceramic Production Center of Cheung Ek Report*. Phnom Penh: Royal Academy of Cambodia, Ministry of Culture and Fine Arts.
Polkinghorne, M. & Y. Sato, 2023. Early modern Cambodia and archaeology at Longvek, in *The Angkorian World*, eds. M. Hendrickson, M.T. Stark & D. Evans. New York: Routledge, 592–613.
Pryce, T.O., C. Chiemsisouraj, V. Zeitoun. & H. Forestier, 2011. An 8th–9th century AD iron smelting workshop near Saphim village, NW Lao PDR. *Historical Metallurgy* 45(2), 81–9.
Pryce, T.O., M. Hendrickson, K. Phon, C. Sovichetra, M.F. Charlton, S. Leroy, P. Dillmann. & Q. Hua, 2014. The Iron Kuay of Cambodia: tracing the role of peripheral populations in Angkorian to colonial Cambodia via a 1200 year old industrial landscape. *Journal of Archaeological Science* 47, 142–63.
Qian, W. & X. Huang, 2021. Invention of cast iron smelting in early China: archaeological survey and numerical simulation. *Advances in Archaeomaterials* 2(1), 4–14.
Rooney, D., 1984. *Khmer Ceramics*. Singapore: Oxford University Press.
Smith, M.L., 1999. "Indianization" from the Indian point of view: trade and cultural contacts with Southeast Asia in the early first millennium C.E. *Journal of the Economic and Social History of the Orient* 42(1), 1–26.
Stark, M.T. & A. Cremin, 2023. Angkor and China: 9th–15th centuries, in *The Angkorian World*, eds. M. Hendrickson, M.T. Stark. & D. Evans. New York: Routledge, 112–32.
Stark, M.T. & P-Y. Manguin, 2023. The Mekong Delta before the Angkorian World. In *The Angkorian World*, eds. M. Hendrickson, M.T. Stark & D. Evans. New York: Routledge, 64–79.
Tabata, Y., 2005. Stoneware ceramic production in the Angkor area in Cambodia—A comparative study of artifacts from Tani, Anglong Thom and Sar Sai kilns. *The Journal of Sophia Asian Studies* 23, 7–35.
Tabata, Y., 2006. Technical aspects on Khmer stoneware ceramics from the Tani kiln site. *La Renaissance Culturelle du Cambodge* 22, 171–82.
Tabata, Y., 2008. Some aspects of the Anglong Thom Kiln, Cambodia. *Journal of Southeast Asian Archaeology* 28, 61–74.
Tabata, Y., 2016. Chronological framework of ceramic trading in Angkorian Cambodia, in *Multidisciplinary Research in the Ancient History of Southeast Asia*, ed. S. Fukami. Osaka: Research Institute of St. Andrew's University, 37–49.
Tabata, Y., 2021a. A resource management strategy in the Angkorian stoneware industry. *Preah Nokor* 2, 71–81.
Tabata, Y., 2021b. *The Veal Kok Treas Kilns 1. An Archaeological Investigation at a Brown-Glazed Stoneware Production Center in Cambodia*. Tokyo: APSARA National Authority, Institute for Cultural Heritage, Waseda University.
Tabata, Y. & V. Chhay, 2007. Preliminary report of the excavation of the Anlong Thom kiln site, Cambodia. *Journal of Southeast Asian Archaeology* 27, 63–9.
Thuy, C., 2014. *Iron and Stone. Ancient Khmer. Result of Research into the Ancient Khmer Iron Smelters*. Phnom Penh: Cambodia Research.
United Nations, 1993. *Atlas of Mineral Resources of the ESCAP Region volume 10: Cambodia*. New York: United Nations Economic and Social Commission for Asia and the Pacific.
Venunan, P., 2016. *An Archaeometallurgical Study of Iron Production in Ban Kruat, Lower Northeast Thailand: Technology and Social Development from the Iron Age to the Imperial Angkorian Khmer Period (fifth century BC–fifteenth century AD)* PhD Thesis. London: University College London.
Wagner, D.B., 2008. *Science and Civilization in China. volume 5. Chemistry and Chemical Technology. Part II: Ferrous Metallurgy*. Cambridge: Cambridge University Press.
Wertime, T.A., 1983. The furnace versus the goat: the pyrotechnologic industries and Mediterranean deforestation in antiquity. *Journal of Field Archaeology* 10(4), 445–52.
Wong, W.Y.S., 2010. *A Preliminary Study of Some Economic Activities of Khmer Empire: Examining the Relationship between the Khmer and Guangdong Ceramic Industries during the 9th to 14th centuries in Southeast Asian Studies Programme*. Singapore: National University of Singapore.
Zhang, M., Y. Li, Z. Xiong, S. Li. & Y. Li, 2020. Iron production and trading in lingnan during the qin and han dynasties. *Antiquity* 94(373), e4.

22

FOOD, CRAFT, AND RITUAL

Plants from the Angkorian World

Cristina Cobo Castillo

The study of the Khmer Empire has benefitted from multidisciplinary studies, including archaeological research. Lagging behind the work done by scholars on the architecture, religious, and symbolic nature of the temples and epigraphy of Angkor has been the archaeological sub-discipline of archaeobotany, or the study of archaeological plant remains. Although archaeological fieldwork has been expansive in the Angkor region, very few archaeobotanical studies have been conducted, particularly looking at macroremains. Macroremains analyses are useful in fine resolution studies, including the identification of diets, farming practices, trade and exchange networks, human activities such as crop-processing, and plants used in craft or ritual (Bowdery 1999; Fuller 2005; Paz 2001; Smart and Hoffman 1988). Of all the archaeobotanical sub-disciplines, palynology has been the most widely applied in Angkor, with results providing a broad understanding of past environments (Penny et al. 2005, 2006, 2014).

However, since 2015, several large collaborative projects, such as the Greater Angkor Project (GAP) and the Industries of Angkor Project (INDAP), have included flotation as part of their field practices (Table 22.1). To date, three macrobotanical studies from the Greater Angkor Project have been published from the site Terrace of the Leper King at Angkor Thom, Angkor Wat and Ta Prohm (Castillo et al. 2018, 2020). The investigations in the Terrace of the Leper King focus on a ritual consecration deposit and Post-Angkorian habitation areas within the Royal Palace at Angkor Thom dating to the 14th and 15th centuries CE. 'The Industries of Angkor Project' and 'The Iron and Angkor Project' incorporated archaeobotany in their fieldwork and include the results of the macroremains analysis in Hendrickson et al. (2019). That paper focuses on the community of producers and the ritual aspects at the smelting site Tonle Bak but also the plant remains identified.

Even fewer phytolith studies have been conducted than macroremains studies, with two studies published and the rest still awaiting publication (Castillo et al. 2020). Although phytoliths can overcome some preservation issues encountered with macroremains sampling, these, like palynological studies, provide mostly a general overview. Finally, wood charcoal analysis has only begun recently in the Kulen site, and results are forthcoming.

This chapter presents a summary of the macroremains results from five sites where the non-elite inhabitants of the area dwelt or worked. The samples are derived from three sites located in the Angkorian capital, Angkor Wat, Ta Prohm and the Terrace of the Leper King, Angkor Thom (henceforth AW, TP, and TRL, respectively), and two peripheral sites, Preah Khan of Kompong Svay and Tonle Bak (henceforth PKKS and TB, respectively). All the sites discussed,

DOI: 10.4324/9781351128940-27

with the exception of TRL, have a long chronological sequence, including the 'Classic' Angkor Period (11th to 13th c.), whereas TRL dates to the Post-Angkor Period (14th–15th c.).

A variety of plants used by the Khmer for food were identified in the samples, such as rice and mung bean, but also plants used in ritual and craft production, such as sesame, cotton and kapok. Many of the crops used for fibre, food, and ritual do not originate in Southeast Asia but from South Asia. Although the early translocation histories of some of these crops have been pieced together archaeologically, such as for rice, cotton, and mung bean, the exact timing of the introduction of other crops to mainland Southeast Asia remains elusive. The archaeobotanical studies also reveal plants native to mainland Southeast Asia, some of which were probably cultivated in gardens near households, such as gingers and fruit trees. Just like the bas-reliefs at the Bayon temple with images portraying market and hunting scenes, the study of plant remains provides a representation of everyday life for Angkorian Khmers.

The role of plants as ritual deposits or donations in the Angkorian World is also examined in this chapter. Some plant products and crops are featured in the inscriptions at Ta Prohm (K. 273) and Preah Khan (K. 908), such as rice, mung bean, sesame, cloth, fruits, and spices. Some of these are also mentioned in South Indian ritual texts as forming part of consecration deposits (Slaczka 2007).

Last, I will examine the rice evidence from Angkorian sites, including the mode of cultivation and the variety of rice present (see Hawken and Castillo 2023, this volume). A previous study noted that by at least the 14th century, rice was of the *indica* subspecies, which is originally from South Asia. However, like many of the crops that come from South Asia, the trajectory of the introduction of *indica* rice to mainland Southeast Asia is not fully understood.

Methodology and Sites

Macroremains from five sites in Cambodia have been analysed, and the following section summarises some of the key finds. Some of the sites have chronological sequences that belong to the Pre-Angkor, Angkor, and Post-Angkor Period or one of these. Some sites are situated in the political centre where the Angkorian elite were based, such as AW, TP, and TRL, whereas others are peripheral, such as PKKS and TB. However, the results from the archaeological investigations suggest that all the contexts studied belonged to either habitation or craft areas of the non-elite (Carter et al. 2019; Castillo et al. 2018, 2020; Hendrickson et al. 2019).

Methodology

The same archaeobotanical sampling and processing methodology was applied in all five sites. Soil samples were collected and processed using the wash-over flotation method to retrieve macrobotanical remains. The water used in flotation was filtered through a 250-*μm* mesh to get rid of contaminants, and the mesh size of the bags used for flotation was 250 *μm*. The heavy fraction that remained after flotation was wet-sieved to collect botanical macroremains that did not float, faunal and human remains, and artefacts such as shards and metal fragments. The botanical samples were then dried, bagged, and sent off to London for sorting, identification, and analysis. Samples were sorted and identified to 0.25 mm using low-powered microscopes including a Zeiss Axiolab stereomicroscope and the Leica S6-D stereomicroscope to take images. Some samples were subsampled using a riffle box.

The average amount of soil collected in each site ranged from as little as 4.85 litres at TRL to 11 litres at TP. There was a large amount of variation in the number of samples analysed per site (Table 22.1) and likewise in the average number of plant remains per site, with Angkor Wat having the fewest plant remains per litre of soil (66) and TB having the most (3262),

Table 22.1 Summary statistics of the five sites.

Site	*Ave. soil collected (l)/context*	*No. of samples studied*	*Number of identified specimens (NISP)*	*Ave. plant parts*
Angkor Wat	7.9	28	1857	~66
Preah Khan of Kompong Svay (PKKS)	9	11	1666	~151
Ta Prohm	11	12	1120	~93
Terrace of the Leper King*	4.85	5	2495	~624
Tonle Bak	9	1	3262	3262

* One sample is from the ritual deposit, and the frequencies are not included; therefore NISP and ave. plant parts are from four contexts.

although this is derived entirely from only one sample studied. The difference in the number of plant remains per site may be due to a number of reasons; better preservation would increase the number of plant remains, whereas good household management practices such as cleaning living spaces would generally decrease the number of plant remains found. It is possible that at AW, the inhabitants kept their living quarters clean and fewer plant remains survived. On the other hand, the high density of plant remains at TB is probably due to the nature of the site being both an industrial and settlement site. Excavations unearthed hearths, iron tools, and trade ceramics, and alternating layers of metallurgical activities and habitation layers were identified. It is possible that at TB the workers did not clean their floors as frequently as at AW, but also, the large number of husked rice remains found signifies a conflagration event took place and a rice storage unit probably burnt down (Hendrickson et al. 2019).

Angkor Wat

The temple of Angkor Wat dates to the 12th century during the reign of Suryavarman II (1113–1145). However, three layers and a period of hiatus were identified from the excavations and confirmed with radiocarbon dating (Stark et al. 2015; Carter et al. 2019). Botanical remains were analysed from these three layers. The initial phase, also known as Layer 3, belongs to the 11–12th centuries; Layer 2 dated to the 12–13th centuries is the habitation layer; and Layer 1 belongs to the period of re-occupation in the Post-Angkor Period dating to the late 14th to early 18th centuries. Four AMS radiocarbon dates were also obtained from archaeological plant remains. A directly dated rice grain and a mung bean corresponded to Layer 2, a cotton fragment yielded a later date than expected and probably represents intrusive material to Layer 3, and finally, the boddhichitta seed was modern (Castillo et al. 2020). One of the main issues working in Angkor Wat is the high level of bioturbation caused by tree roots and the constant movement of soil by the inhabitants, a process observed in the geoarchaeological analysis of mound and pond features from this site (Castillo et al. 2020).

A total of 85 soil samples were collected for archaeobotanical research in 2013 and 2015. The summary results of 28 of these contexts are presented here.

Several economic species were identified in AW. These include rice (*Oryza sativa*), cotton (*Gossypium* sp.), mung bean (*Vigna radiata*), nut and fruit fragments including *Citrus* sp. rind, scarlet banana (*Musa coccinea*) belonging to the banana family Musaceae, crêpe ginger (*Cheilo-costus speciosus*), black pepper (*Piper nigrum*), long pepper (*Piper longum*), *Abelmoschus* sp., and *Dracontomelon* sp. (Figures 22.1d, 1h, 1i, 1q, and 1r).

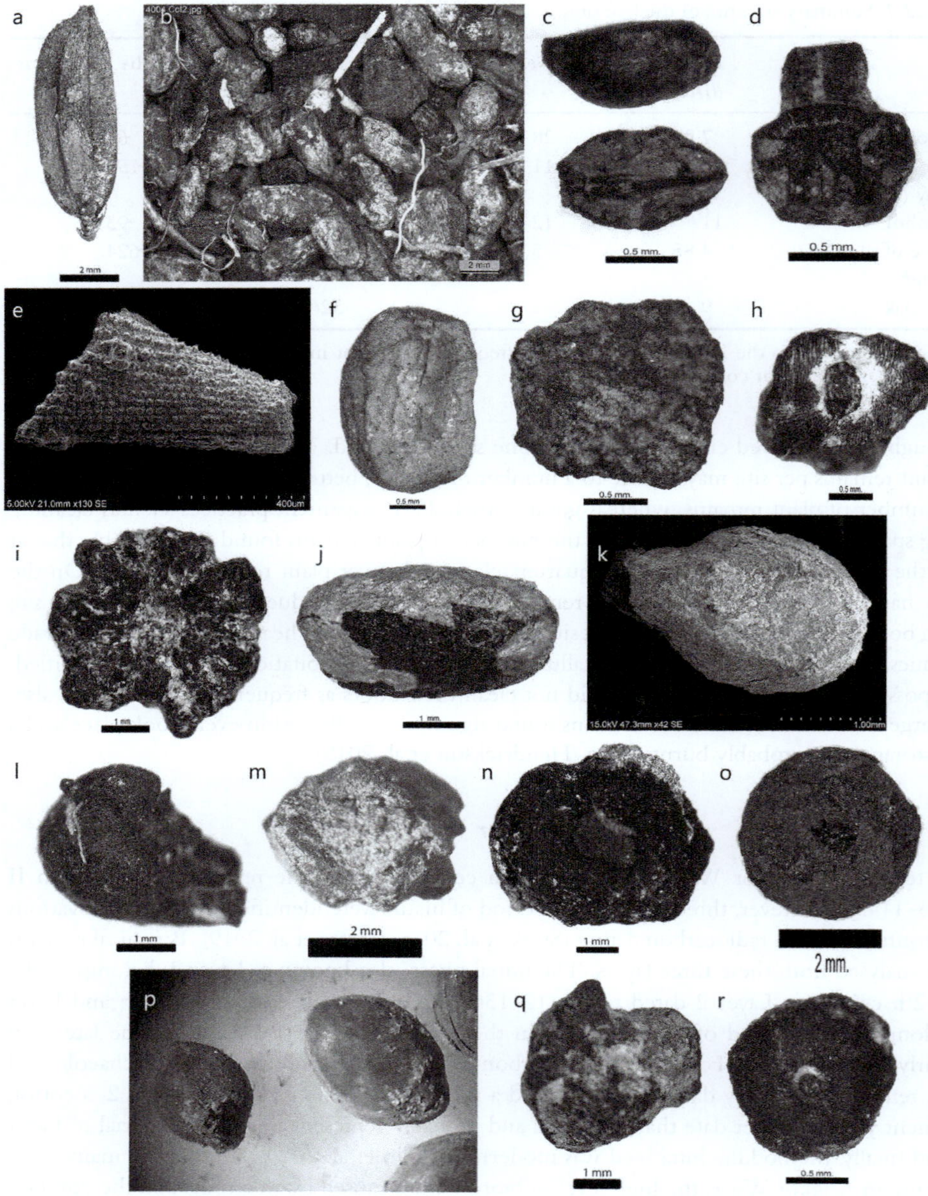

Figure 22.1 Examples of archaeobotanical remains recovered from five Angkorian sites: a) rice grain from TRL ritual deposit; b) an unsorted sample from TB 4004 Col2 showing a high proportion of rice.; c) charred rice embryos from PKKS 3002; d) rice spikelet base domesticated-type from AW53004; e) charred lemma apex from PKKS 3003; f) mung bean from TRL ritual deposit; g) cf. *Lithocarpus* nut shell from PKKS 3007; h) *Abelmoschus* fragment from AW48016; i) *Dracontomelon* fragment from AW49021; j) Indian gooseberry from PKKS 3003; k) sesame from TRL ritual deposit; l) a seed identified as *Moraceae* from AW49021; m) *Ziziphus* sp. fragment from TB 4004; n) pigeon pea cotyledon from TRL T4 27; o) black pepper seed from TB 4004; p) on the left a foxtail millet and on the right a broomcorn millet seed from TRL ritual deposit; q) scarlet banana fragment from AW36003; r) cotton funicular cap from AW57005.

The ubiquity index for rice at AW is 85.7%. Rice grains, grain fragments, spikelet bases, embryos, and husk were retrieved at AW. The embryos and husk were identified in the 0.25 to 0.5 mm fraction and are excluded from Figure 22.2. The proportion of rice is 18% of the total plant assemblage (excluding unidentified plant remains), which is the largest proportion of any of the economic crops identified in AW (Figure 22.2) However, rice spikelet bases dominate the rice assemblage.

Ta Prohm

The Ta Prohm temple dates to 1186 and was built during the reign of Jayavarman VII (1181–1218). Four phases were identified at Ta Prohm and confirmed with ten radiocarbon dates from wood charcoal and from one plant remain (Castillo et al. 2020; Carter et al. 2018). Phase I represents the period before the temple was constructed dating to the 8th–10th centuries. An AMS radiocarbon date of 800–970 cal. was taken from an *Alpinia* seed belonging to Phase I (Castillo et al. 2020). Phase II belongs to the early 11th–13th centuries and is defined by a grid system constituting mounds and depressions. Post-temple construction habitation dates to the 12th–14th centuries and is designated as Phase III. The radiocarbon dates representing Phase IV date to the 13th–14th centuries, and it is posited the mounds were inhabited until the 14th century. Some of the phases in TP overlap, and these are described in Carter et al. (2018).

The TP assemblage is composed mainly of two economic crops, rice and cotton. The representation of rice increases over time and is 64% of the economic crop assemblage in the final Phase III (Figure 22.3). On the other hand, the proportion of cotton decreases over time, with 74% cotton remains in Phase I falling to 30% in Phase III. The other plant remains found in the assemblage are *Alpinia* belonging to the ginger family Zingiberaceae and fruit mesocarp and nut fragments. A large proportion of the plant remains consists of weedy plants, in particular *Acmella paniculata*. The rice finds consisted of fragmented rice grains, husk, spikelet bases, embryos, and lemma apices. The lemma apices were broken off at the apex, suggesting these would have been awned.

Preah Khan of Kompong Svay

PKKS is an important Angkorian provincial centre with a role in the production and distribution of iron to the rest of the Khmer Empire. Conventional radiocarbon dates place the three trenches between the early 10th and late 12th centuries. A total of 67 soil samples were collected for archaeobotanical research. However, the summary results from 11 contexts from PKKS trenches 1, 2, and 3 are presented here.

Eight economic crops have been identified at PKKS, of which rice (*Oryza sativa*) is the most abundant (Figures 22.1c and 22.1e). The other economic crops identified are mung bean (*Vigna radiata*), cotton (*Gossypium* sp.), kapok (*Bombax ceiba*), Indian gooseberry (*Phyllanthus emblica*), leaf flower (*Phyllanthus urinaria*), *Terminalia*, and *Lithocarpus* (Figures 22.1g and 22.1j). Unidentified mesocarp fragments, possibly of fruit, have also been identified and are included under the heading 'fruits and nuts' (Figure 22.2).

The ubiquity index for rice at PKKS is 72.7%. Rice plant parts consisted of rice grains, grain fragments, spikelet bases, embryos, lemma apices, and husk. The proportion of rice at PKKS is 31% of the total botanical assemblage (excluding unidentified plant remains; Figure 22.2), making this the most important economic crop at the site. What we can infer is that rice was consumed as a staple, a trend similarly examined in all the other sites.

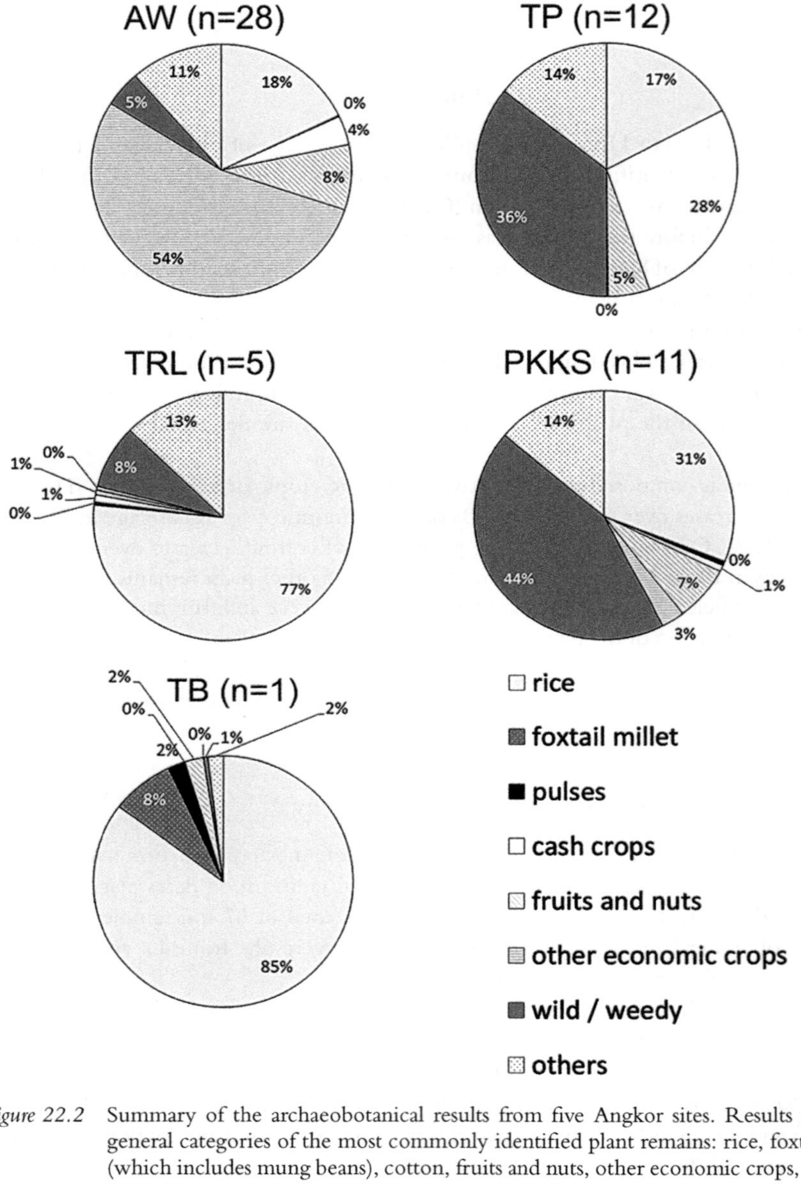

Figure 22.2 Summary of the archaeobotanical results from five Angkor sites. Results are divided into general categories of the most commonly identified plant remains: rice, foxtail millet, pulses (which includes mung beans), cotton, fruits and nuts, other economic crops, wild and weedy, and others, excluding unidentified plant parts. The number of contexts for each of the sites is in parenthesis. AW—Angkor Wat; TP—Ta Prohm; TRL—Terrace of the Leper King, Angkor Thom; PKKS—Preah Khan of Kompong Svay; TB—Tonle Bak.

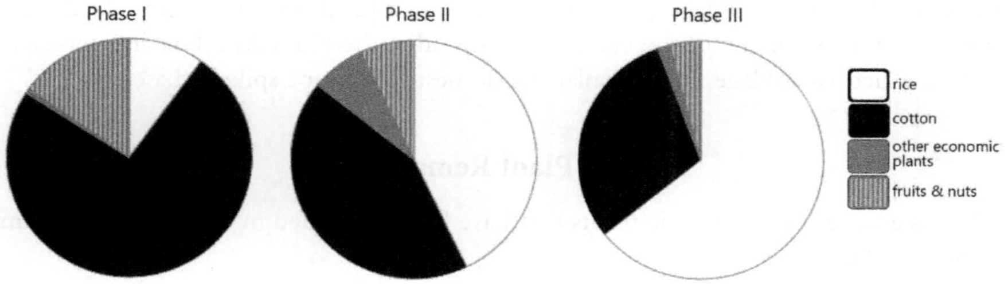

Figure 22.3 Proportions of economic crops found in Ta Prohm over time.

Tonle Bak

TB is a metallurgical working site situated approximately 25 km southeast of PKKS. Although plant remains from four trenches were collected, plant remains from only one context from Trench 4 have been analysed, and the results are presented here. Trench 4 belongs to the 12th–mid-13th centuries per eight radiocarbon dates, two of which were from charred rice grains (Hendrickson et al. 2019). Whilst the soil samples were being processed, a large amount of charcoal was observed in some of the samples. Furthermore, examination of some samples with the naked eye showed the presence of rice in abundant quantities.

Only one sample (4004) has been sorted and identified so far. It contained four economic crops, unidentified, modern, and non-botanical remains. When viewed under a low-powered microscope, the sample had abundant remains of rice, foxtail millet, and mung beans but also contained some black pepper (*Piper nigrum*) (Figures 22.1b and 22.1o). Rice represents more than 79% of the sample, but there is also a large proportion of unidentified botanical fragments. The rice plant parts included complete husked spikelets, rice spikelet bases mostly of the domestic type, lemma apices, husk, and embryos. Rice embryos were found in the 0.25–0.5 mm fraction.

Terrace of the Leper King, Angkor Thom

The excavations conducted north of the Royal Palace within the Angkor Thom complex are known as the site of the Terrace of the Leper King. Soil samples for archaeobotanical investigations were collected from an in-filled pond and from a ritual deposit (Castillo et al. 2018). The in-filled pond corresponded to five phases dating to the 14th century based on the ceramic assemblage and two AMS radiocarbon dates from charred rice grains. The ritual deposit, on the other hand, yielded an AMS radiocarbon date of early 15th century from a desiccated mung bean with the testa still attached (Castillo et al. 2018; erratum: reported as rice husk).

A total of 11 soil samples were processed for archaeobotanical research, but five of these are presented here, including from the ritual deposit. The economic crops identified in TRL are rice (*Oryza sativa*), mung bean (*Vigna radiata*), cotton (*Gossypium* sp.), kapok (*Bombax ceiba*), pigeon pea (*Cajanus cajan*), hyancinth bean (*Lablab*), foxtail millet (*Setaria italica*), broomcorn millet (*Panicum miliaceum*), sesame (*Sesamum indicum*), and yardlong bean (*Vigna unguiculata* subsp. *sesquipedalis*) (Figures 22.1a, 1f, 1k, 1n, and 1p). The economic crop with the largest proportion is rice (Figure 22.2).

The ubiquity index for rice at TRL is 100%. The rice plant parts present include grains, grain fragments, spikelet bases, embryos, husk, and silicified awns. The proportion of rice is 30% of the total plant assemblage (77% of total identified plant remains; Figure 22.2), which is the largest proportion of any of the economic crops identified in TRL. The rice spikelet bases dominate the rice assemblage, in particular the domesticated-type spikelet bases.

The Plant Remains

Table 22.2 is a list of the economic plants that have been identified in the five Cambodian sites (see Appendix A).

Table 22.2 Presence and absence of economic crops in the five study sites.

Taxon/Site	*Angkor Wat*	*Ta Prohm*	*Preah Khan of Kompong Svay*	*Tonle Bak*	*Terrace of the Leper King*
Abelmoschus sp.	X				
cf. *Adansonia*					?
Alpinia sp.		X			
Artocarpus sp.	X				
Bombax ceiba (Indian kapok/silk cotton tree)			X		X
Cajanus cajan (pigeon pea)					X
cf. *Canarium*					?
cf. *Castanopsis*	X				
Cheilocostus speciosus (crêpe ginger)	X				
Citrus spp.	X				
Dracontomelon sp.	X				
Fagaceae/Betulaceae					X
Gossypium sp. (cotton)	X	X	X		X
Lablab purpureus (hyacinth bean)					X
Lithocarpus sp.	X	X	X		
Moraceae	X				
Musa coccinea (scarlet banana)	X				
Oryza sativa (rice)	X	X	X	X	X
Panicum miliaceum (broomcorn millet)					X
Phyllanthus emblica (Indian gooseberry)	X		X		?
Phyllanthus urinaria (leaf flower)			X		?
Piper nigrum (black pepper)	X			X	
Piper longum (long pepper)	X				
Sesamum indicum (sesame)					X
Setaria italica (foxtail millet)				X	X
Terminalia sp.			X		
Vigna radiata (mung bean)	X		X	X	X
Vigna spp.			X		
Vigna unguiculata subsp. *sesquipedalis* (yardlong bean)					X
Ziziphus sp.				X	

Abelmoschus sp.

A seed fragment from AW containing several features, including the chalaza and a linear testa pattern surrounding it, was identified as *Abelmoschus* sp. in the Malvaceae family (Figure 22.1h). There are at least 11 species that belong to the *Abelmoschus* genus, including the economically important *A. esculentus*, or okra, eaten as a vegetable and *A. manihot*, which provides fibre used for cordage (Patil et al. 2015). Narrowing the identification to species is difficult based on one fragmentary seed, but initial examination of the salient features using scanning electron microscopy imagery matched modern *Abelmoschus manihot* seeds from the Institute of Archaeology reference collection. It is generally accepted that Southeast Asia is the centre of diversity of the *Abelmoschus* genus (van Borssum Waalkes 1966; Patil et al. 2015)

Alpinia sp.

One seed of *Alpinia* sp., in the cardamom/ginger family (Zingiberaceae), was found in TP. The seed resembles modern specimens from the Institute of Archaeology reference collection but also those from the archaeological site Kirinda, Sri Lanka (Murphy et al. 2018). *Alpinia* seeds are ovate or slightly trigonous with a conical end. *Alpinia* is the largest genus in the Zingiberaceae family, comprising approximately 230 species distributed in tropical and subtropical Asia, New Guinea, Australia, and the Pacific Islands (Rahayu and Ibrahim 1999). The *Alpinia* genus contains many economic species used for ornamental, medicinal, and culinary purposes. Many species are planted in gardens and sought after for their distinctive flowers. Others, such as *A. galangal* and *A. malaccensis*, are cultivated for their essential oils and as a spice.

Artocarpus sp.

There are 47 species of *Artocarpus* in the fig family Moraceae (Heywood et al. 2007). One important economic species widely cultivated in Southeast Asia today and known for its edible fruits is the jackfruit (*Artocarpus heterophyllus*). Jackfruit was probably introduced from the Western Ghats, India (Burkill 1936; Soepadmo 1991), although some scholars propose two separate domestications, one in India and another in Southeast Asia (Blench 2008). The archaeological remains from AW are fragments of the rind tentatively classified as cf. *Artocarpus*. Fragments of rind with attached mesocarp and a small seed were also found in AW and identified as Moraceae (Figure 22.1l).

Bombax ceiba (Indian kapok/silk cotton tree)

Kapok seeds were identified in PKKS. There are two species of kapok, *Ceiba pentandra*, attributed to the New World (Blench and Dendo 2007; Vaughan 1970), and *Bombax ceiba* (syn = *B. malabaricum*), a regional species originating from South Asia (Burkill 1936). PKKS predates any possible introduction of plants from the Americas ca. 1500; therefore, the specimens are probably of *Bombax*, such as *Bombax ceiba* (Indian kapok). Comparison of the testa pattern between the two species using modern collections and the archaeological sample will be carried out in the future.

The tree grows to a height of 10 to 20 metres, and it can often be seen growing along streets in Siem Reap today. Zhou Daguan mentions silk cotton trees growing higher than a room (Zhou 2007[1297]). Zhou Daguan also mentions groups of people living close to towns who use the kapok or cotton tree lint to weave textiles, although coarse and thick and therefore of inferior quality. The tree is an important economic resource which yields soft and light wood, oil from the seed, and floss used for stuffing and padding (Burkill 1936). In Cambodia, the flowers, seeds, bark, and roots are used medicinally (Burkill 1936; Dy Phon 2000).

Cajanus cajan (Pigeon pea)

Pigeon pea was found in TRL and is an important pulse originating in Odisha and the southern peninsula of India (Fuller et al. 2019; Figure 22.1n). The earliest documented pigeon peas in Southeast Asia are from the sites of Khao Sam Kaeo and Phu Khao Thong, Thailand, dating to the last centuries BCE (Castillo et al. 2016a; Castillo 2013). It has been hypothesised that the Indian craftsmen that traveled to peninsular Thailand more than 2000 years ago brought with them a whole suite of Indian crops which included pulses such as the pigeon pea, mung bean, black gram, and horsegram (Bellina et al. 2014; Castillo et al. 2016a). The length width ratios of the pigeon peas from all of the Southeast Asian sites fall within the domesticated range (Fuller et al. 2019).

The pigeon pea shrub can reach 4 metres in height and is planted in house gardens to form fences in Cambodia (Dy Phon 2000). The culinary tradition of pigeon pea in India differs from that of Southeast Asia, where the seeds are eaten fresh and the young pods are eaten as a vegetable compared to Indian preparations as dhal (van der Maesen 1989).

Cheilocostus speciosus (Crêpe ginger)

A crêpe ginger seed or *Cheilocostus speciosus* (formerly *Costus speciosus*) in the pantropical Costaceaeceae family was identified in AW. The dimensions and surface pattern of the archaeological specimen match those from the UCL Institute of Arachaeology reference collection. Most species are located in humid areas and, *C. speciosus* in particular is found in moist and evergreen parts of India, Sri Lanka, and Southeast Asia.

Crêpe ginger is an herb that grows up to a metre in height and is normally found in the forest undergrowth. In Cambodia, rhizomes are used medicinally and the young shoots are prepared in liquid dishes called 'samla' (Dy Phon 2000).

Citrus Spp.

Small charred fragments of *Citrus* fruit rind were identified only in AW. The author conducted charring experiments of modern *Citrus* rind, and the results show it is possible to make tentative species identifications, such as for pomelo, papeda, or citron (Castillo 2013; Fuller et al. 2017). However, the *Citrus* rind found in AW cannot be identified to species.

The difficulty in identifying archaeological fragmentary *Citrus* to species is the high phenotypic and genetic diversity due to natural outcrossing and hybridisation. The distribution range of *Citrus* trees covers a vast area in Asia including northeast India, south China, and Southeast Asia (Fuller et al. 2017).

Dracontomelon sp.

A nut fragment of *Dracontomelon* sp. was identified in AW (Figure 22.1i). *Dracontomelon* is a small genus of trees in the Anacardiaceae family distributed from India to Southeast Asia and extending into the Pacific (Burkill 1936). The fragment found in AW closely resembles *Drocontomelon dao* in size and general morphological features. The fruit of *Drocontomelon dao*, or the Argus pheasant tree, is edible, as well as the flowers and the leaves, which are eaten as vegetables in Southeast Asia (Jansen et al. 1991). Other economic uses are wood for timber and furniture and bark for medicinal purposes (Burkill 1936; Jansen et al. 1991).

An Argus pheasant tree nut was identified in Sabah in the site of Madai-1 dating to 2200–1500 BP, making this the earliest find in Southeast Asia, although it has not been directly dated (Paz 2005).

Gossypium sp. (Cotton)

Charred testa fragments and funicular caps of cotton were identified in all sites except in TB (Figure 22.1r). Cotton has been found in archaeological contexts dating to as early as the 4th–2nd c. BCE in Khao Sam Kaeo and Ban Don Ta Phet, Thailand (Cameron 2010; Castillo 2013; Castillo et al. 2016a).

There are four types of cultivated cotton, although the Metal Age and Angkorian cotton in Southeast Asia probably originated from India. The cotton from India is *Gossypium arboreum* or tree cotton (not to be confused with cotton tree or kapok), which can grow to a height of 3 metres (Brink 2011). Clovis Thorel (2001 [1873]) observed in the 19th century that *Gossypium arboreum* or tree cotton was grown in the Mekong Basin.

The fibres are unicellular and are attached to the cotton bolls. Depending on the species of cotton, the long fibres or lint measure between 10 and 64 mm. The length of the lint affects the quality of the thread derived from these. *G. arboreum* produces short (<25 mm long), coarse, and thick cell-walled fibres which would be considered of lower quality than those of *G. hirsutum* or *G. barbadense* (Brink 2011). The process of spinning short fibres into thread using a wheel is more difficult than by hand, and it was noted by Zhou Daguan that the Khmer did not know how to use the spinning wheel (Zhou 2007[1297]).

Lablab purpureus (Hyacinth bean)

The hyacinth bean has been identified in TRL. The hyacinth bean is native to tropical east Africa, although India and Southeast Asia have often been proposed as alternative areas of origin (Shivashankar and Kulkarni 1989). There may be scant evidence for early archaeobotanical remains in Africa, but genetic studies confirm the hyacinth bean to have been domesticated in Africa (Fuller and Harvey 2006).

Hyacinth bean has been identified in peninsular Thailand dating to the end of the first millennium BCE (Castillo 2013; Castillo et al. 2016a). It is hypothesised that the hyacinth bean formed part of the Indian package of crops brought across the Bay of Bengal in this early period.

The immature pods of the hyacinth bean are a popular vegetable in Cambodia and other Southeast Asian countries. Other parts that are eaten as vegetables are the leaves, young shoots, and inflorescences (Shivashankar and Kulkarni 1989).

Lithocarpus sp.

Fragments of *Lithocarpus* sp. in the Fagaceae family were identified in TP and PKKS (Figure 22.1g). Several species from the *Lithocarpus* genus found in mainland Southeast Asia have important economic uses, such as edible nuts. Today in Cambodia the *Lithocarpus* trees are valued mostly for wood (Dy Phon 2000).

Musa coccinea (Scarlet banana)

One charred seed in the banana or Musaceae family was identified in AW (Figure 22.1q). The shape and size of the seed as well as the seed coat matched those of scarlet banana or *Musa coccinea. M. coccinea* is an ornamental plant, although its leaves can be used as wrappers for cakes, rice, or other products (Castillo and Fuller 2015). Many species of bananas grow in Cambodia, and besides using the leaves for packaging, the so-called apparent trunk, which are rolled-up leaves growing out of an underground stem, is edible, and so are the young inflorescences, which are eaten as a vegetable (Dy Phon 2000).

Oryza sativa (Rice)

Rice is the only economic plant found in all the sites studied. The rice plant parts identified included grains, spikelet bases, husk, lemma apices, awns, and embryos. Rice caryopses or grains are easily recognisable from their distinctive grooves and husk from the chequerboard pattern. The rice spikelet base scars are examined in order to classify the rice as either domesticated or wild-type. The rice spikelet bases found in the five sites were predominantly of the domesticated type.

Panicum miliaceum (Broomcorn millet)

Broomcorn millet was identified in the ritual deposit from TRL together with rice, mung bean, sesame, and foxtail millet (Figure 22.1p). Whole broomcorn millet spikelets with their husk intact are preserved desiccated at TRL. Although Weber et al. (2010) reported *Panicum* in the Khao Wong Prachan Valley, the *Panicum miliaceum* from TRL is the first to be positively identified in a Southeast Asian archaeological site.

Broomcorn millet was domesticated in northern China prior to 6000 BCE and therefore preceded both foxtail millet and rice domestication (Lu et al. 2009). This cereal has also been found in west Eurasian archaeological contexts as early as 3000 BCE (Liu et al. 2019). Broomcorn millet is a short-maturing and drought-tolerant crop and is important in areas where other crops do not do well (Grubben and Partohardjono 1996).

Phyllanthus emblica (Indian gooseberry)

Whole and fragmented seeds of Indian gooseberry were found in PKKS and AW (Figure 22.1j). Indian gooseberry is widely distributed in tropical Asia, from India, Indo-China, and south China to Malesia. All plant parts are used for medicinal purposes (van Holthoon 1999), and the fruits are also eaten, although these are mostly cooked or pickled. Indian gooseberry is known to be cultivated in home gardens (Blench 2008). The carbonised remains at PKKS include a whole fruit, a seed, and fragments of the fruit.

Today, the immature fruits are used in India and Thailand for tanning, sometimes in combination of either of two species of *Terminalia*, *T. chebula* and *T. bellirica*, which belong to the Combretaceae family (van Schaik-van Banning 1991). Interestingly, a fragment of a seed belonging to the genus *Terminalia* is also present in the same trench although belonging to a different context (PKKS 3015). The wood of *Phyllanthus emblica* is used for building material and is also considered good-quality firewood or charcoal (van Schaik-van Banning 1991).

Piper (Pepper)

There are approximately 1000 species in the genus *Piper*, and most are found in the tropics. The *Piper* family consists of several economic species, and two of these were identified in AW; black pepper (*Piper nigrum*) and long pepper (*Piper longum* or *Piper retrofractum*). The origin of *P. nigrum* is the western Ghats. *P. longum* is from Assam, northeast Himalayas, and the Indo-Burmese hills extending westward to the middle Himalayas (Burkill 1936; Cappers 2006; Jaramillo and Manos 2001). The local Southeast Asian long peppers are *P. retrofractum* and *P. cubeba* (Dalby 2000). The long pepper fragments found in AW could be either *P. longum* or *retrofractum*. The infructescence of long pepper is made up of a composite of drupes. Fragments of long pepper have been noted in other Southeast Asian archaeological contexts, such as in Khao Sam Kaeo and Phu Khao Thong (Castillo 2013, 2017a).

As well as long pepper fragments, a black pepper seed fragment with its epicarp preserved was identified in AW. Five black pepper seeds without their epicarp preserved were also found in TB (Figure 22.1o).

Both black and long pepper are important spices used mainly as food flavouring but also for medicinal purposes. The earliest written record mentioning black and long pepper is the *'Periplus of the Erythraean Sea,'* a 1st-century travel journal that documents some traded items from the Indian Ocean to the Red Sea (Schoff 1974).

Sesamum indicum (Sesame)

Desiccated sesame seeds were identified in a ritual deposit found at TRL (Castillo et al. 2018; Figure 22.1k). The remains were very well preserved and sometimes found in clusters with the testa intact. Examination of the testa shows that the sesame from TRL is domesticated (Castillo et al. 2018).

Although sesame is a South Asian domesticate, it reached the Near East in the third millennium BCE (Bedigian 2003; van der Veen 2011). The 1st-century travelogue, Periplus of the Erythraean Sea, mentions sesame oil as an import from the Gulf of Cambay to Arabia and Africa (Schoff 1974). In mainland Southeast Asia, the first evidence of sesame occurs in the last centuries BCE at Phu Khao Thong, Thailand, and it is hypothesised that it was during this period that sesame was brought in from South Asia to Southeast Asia (Castillo et al. 2016a).

Setaria italica (Foxtail millet)

Foxtail millet has been identified in TB and TRL. At TRL, this cereal was found together with rice, mung beans, sesame, and some broomcorn millet in a lead vessel identified as a ritual deposit, and all were desiccated (Castillo et al. 2018; Figure 22.1p). Due to good preservation, distinctive morphological features of foxtail millet can be observed such as the finely rugose or beaded sculpturing of the lemma. At TB, the grains were all charred, and identification was based on criteria set by Fuller (1999). Foxtail millet seeds are small, measure ~2 mm in diameter, and are plump and oval with an embryo that spans 2/3 to 3/4 of the length of the grain.

Foxtail millet (*Setaria italica*) was domesticated in northern China ca. 6000 BCE. It spread into mainland Southeast Asia in the third millennium BCE. One foxtail millet grain from Non Pa Wai in the Khao Wong Prachan Valley, Thailand, yielded an AMS radiocarbon date of 2300 BCE (Weber et al. 2010). Non Mak La and Nil Kham Haeng, also in the Khao Wong Prachan Valley, show evidence that foxtail millet was introduced before rice in this particular area (idem).

A few more sites in mainland Southeast Asia have evidence of foxtail millet such as Khao Sam Kaeo and Rach Nui, although these are not found in the same quantities as the rice remains (Castillo 2017b). It has been hypothesised that the larger proportion of rice in archaeological contexts compared to foxtail millet may be due to a charring preservation bias resulting in underrepresentation of foxtail millet in the archaeological record (Castillo 2019). In Cambodia, millets are mentioned in Khmer inscriptions and could refer to foxtail and/or broomcorn millet (Cœdès 1906).

Terminalia sp.

A seed fragment of *Terminalia* sp. was identified in PKKS. *Terminalia* in the Combretaceae family comprise 150 to 200 species of which at least six are important economic trees (Heywood et al. 2007). In Cambodia, three species are of importance, *T. bellirica*, *T. cattapa*, and *T. chebula*. These are all used for tanning purposes, for timber, and in local medicine (Lemmens and Wulijarni-Soetjipto 1991). Out of the three, *T. cattapa* yields edible fruits with delicious kernels.

Vigna radiata (Mung bean)

Carbonised whole seeds and fragments of mung bean were identified in contexts from AW, PKKS, TB, and TRL (Figure 22.1f). The mung bean is an Indian domesticate that has been found in Southeast Asian archaeological contexts from as early as the 2nd century BCE in peninsular Thailand and the 1st century CE in Bali (Bellina et al. 2014; Calo et al. 2015; Castillo 2013). It is one of the crops introduced via the early Maritime Silk Route to peninsular Thailand that has persisted until modern times. Evidence of this cultivar in PKKS adds to the hypothesis that once introduced into mainland Southeast Asia, it was continuously cultivated and consumed by Southeast Asians.

The mung bean is an important crop in both India and Southeast Asia, and although brought over from India, the culinary tradition for the mung bean in Southeast Asia is very different from the Indian dhal tradition (Castillo et al. 2016a). In Southeast Asia, the mung bean is eaten mainly as a germinated seedling or bean sprout, as vermicelli, and as a confectionary ingredient.

Vigna unguiculata subsp. *sesquipedalis* (Yardlong bean)

Two complete immature seeds of yardlong bean were identified in TRL. Although *Vigna unguiculata* is of African origin, it has been posited that *V. unguiculata* subsp. *sesquipedalis* had a separate domestication trajectory in East or Southeast Asia (Pandey and Westphal 1989). The TRL finds are the first evidence of the yardlong bean at an archaeological site in Southeast Asia.

The immature pods of yardlong bean are eaten as a vegetable in Southeast Asia. Immature pods will yield small seeds not dissimilar to those found at TRL (see Castillo et al. 2018, Figs. 7b, 7c).

Ziziphus sp.

Fragments of *Ziziphus* sp. were identified in TB. *Ziziphus* belongs in the Rhamnaceae family, which is distributed in tropical and subtropical regions. There are three species of economic importance used in Cambodia: *Z. cambodiana* (unresolved name, also *Z. cambodianus*), *Z. mauritiana*, and *Z. oenopolia* (Dy Phon 2000). The fruits of *Z. mauritiana* (Indian jujube) and *Z. oenopolia* (jackal jujube) are edible, and the bark of *Z. cambodiana* and *oenopolia* is used in traditional medicine (Dy Phon 2000). Indian jujube is often classified as Chinese jujube (*Z. jujuba*), and more work needs to be done to differentiate the two.

Chinese jujubes have acute tips compared to Indian jujubes, which have more rounded ends. The TB fragments conform more to Indian jujube (Figure 22.1m).

Discussion and Conclusion

The plant remains from the five sites show some similarities in the suite of plants found, such as the prevalence of rice, mung beans, and cotton. Rice is consistently found across all sites, whereas mung bean is found in all sites except TP, indicating that these crops form the basis of the Khmer diet. Furthermore, rice and mung beans are frequently mentioned in inscriptions, indicating these would have also been used for ritual (Cœdès 1906, 1941; Maxwell 2008).

Rice is found in all sites (Figure 22.2; Table 22.3). There is a large proportion of rice represented in all sites. The lowest proportion of rice is 17% at TP, and the largest is 85% at TB. This is indicative of the important role rice had in Khmer society. As discussed in Castillo et al. (2020), rice was the staple cereal but was also prescribed in the inscriptions for the proper functioning of the temples.

TB had the largest number of rice plant parts, with a high grain to spikelet base ratio of 2.9:1. The rice as well as the foxtail millet in TB had adhering husk, signifying these cereals were unprocessed and their preservation was a result of stored food items catching fire. A similar event has been documented in Ban Non Wat, a northeastern Thai site dating to the Iron Age (Castillo 2019). One context at Ban Non Wat with a high percentage of rice remains (40%) suggests a burnt-down rice store.

A high proportion of rice spikelet bases and in some cases husk and lemma apices suggests rice processing was taking place. For example, at AW, the rice grain to spikelet base ratio is 1:6.9, at TP it is 1:12.5, and at TRL it is 1:20.7. The rice was probably stored as spikelets and dehusked on-site due to the high percentage of rice spikelet bases, lemma apices, and husk found in most contexts. Table 22.3 excludes rice husk since these were counted as percentages in the fractions and were mostly found in the 0.25–0.5 mm fraction.

Table 22.3 Charred rice plant parts found in the five sites excluding rice husk.

	AW	*TP*	*TRL**	*PKKS*	*TB*
Oryza sativa	2		3	8	590
Oryza sativa fragment	22	4	24	86	879
Oryza sativa spikelet base domesticated-type	129	37	329	101	362
Oryza spikelet base wild-type	1	3	14	15	48
Oryza spikelet base immature-type		1		1	
Oryza spikelet base indeterminate	36	8	217	26	96
Oryza lemma apex			98	5	566
Oryza lemma apex—awned		24		8	
Oryza lemma apex—awnless				34	
Oryza—immature and fragment	1				
Oryza charred embryo		3	55	6	48
Oryza carbonised frag with husk	4				
Oryza awn			8		
Total rice	195	80	748	290	2589

Excludes the desiccated remains from the ritual deposit

There are two subspecies of domesticated rice, *Oryza sativa* spp. *japonica* and *O. sativa* spp. *indica*. The former originated from the Lower and Middle Yangtze, whereas the latter was from India. *Japonica* rice was present in mainland Southeast Asia since the Neolithic Period, and it is hypothesised that *indica* rice arrived in mainland Southeast Asia in the Historic Period (Castillo 2011; Castillo 2017b; Fuller et al. 2010). Recently, aDNA and morphometric analyses have been conducted on Southeast Asian and Indian rice samples to determine the subspecies of ancient rice grains found in six archaeological sites (Castillo et al. 2016b). The aDNA study concurred with the morphometric analysis, showing that morphometric analysis is a useful guide in determining rice subspecies with a certain degree of confidence. Only two sites, TRL and TB, had enough whole rice grains to measure, and the results are found in Figure 22.4. At TRL, the L/W of rice falls within the indica-type measurements, whereas at TB, a large percentage of the L/W measurements fall in an area which corresponds to both *indica* and *japonica* rice measurements. These results suggest that several species of rice were cultivated in TB in the 12th to mid 13th centuries.

Cotton macroremains are absent only in TB, the metal working site. The presence of cotton seeds illustrates cotton bolls were brought and processed into fibres on a household level. The fibres could have been woven into textiles in a domestic setting or passed on to weavers in a workshop, although it is hard to tell them apart from the archaeobotanical evidence. Citrus rind fragments identified in AW suggest *Citrus* fruit consumption. Citrus trees would have been planted in gardens, as these are easy to manage and are readily found in modern gardens across Southeast Asia. There is evidence from bas-reliefs and written sources that other trees were cultivated in Angkor, such as the jackfruit (*Artocarpus heterophyllus*), identified in the Bayon bas-reliefs (Blench 2008), and the silk cotton tree (Zhou 2007[1297]). Finally, there is a large proportion across all sites of unidentified plant remains, mainly due to their fragmented and badly preserved state but also the lack of modern reference material to compare with the archaeological samples.

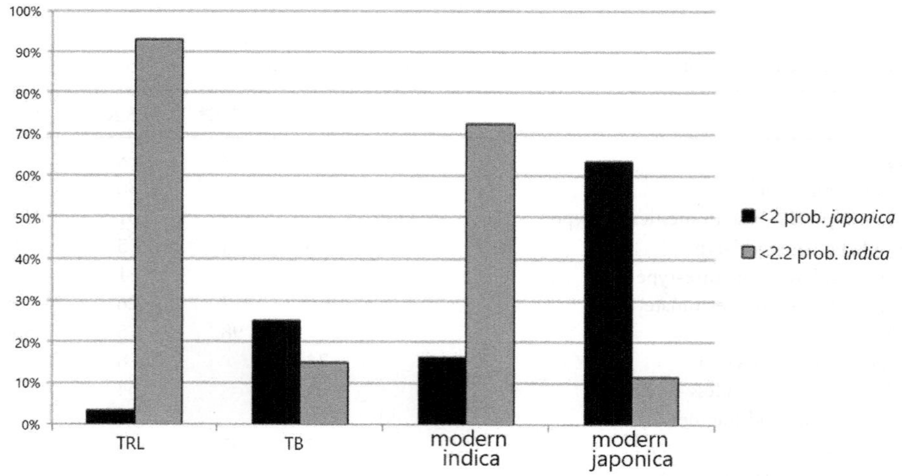

Figure 22.4 Proportion of *indica* and *japonica* rice. Designation is based on the L/W ratio of archaeological rice grains from the Terrace of the Leper King (TRL) and Tonle Bak (TB).

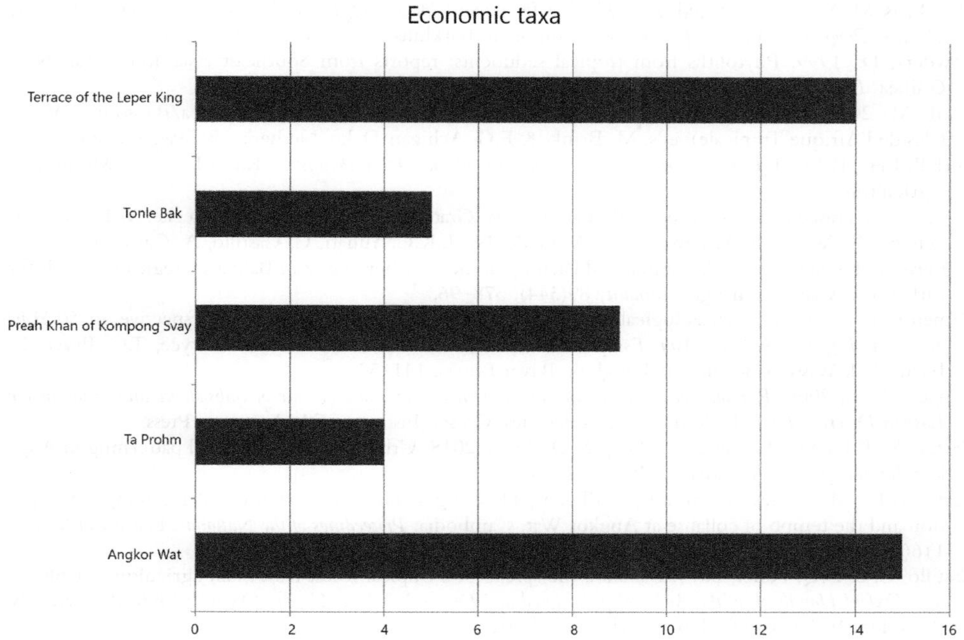

Figure 22.5 Number of economic taxa identified in each of the sites.

From the archaeobotanical studies, it is evident that the Khmer cultivated and consumed a wide range of plants. Houses located in the Angkorian capital would have tapped into plant resources grown in their gardens. Many of the plants identified in the samples are found in today's tropical gardens of Southeast Asia such as citruses, long pepper, black pepper, bananas, pigeon pea, and gingers. Rice was most probably brought in from further afield and together with mung bean was a staple in the Khmer diet. Away from the centre, such as at TB, the plant remains indicate food items were brought into the site to feed the craftsmen working nearby. It is also evident from the number of plant taxa found in the five sites that there was more diversity in sites located in the centre, such as at AW and TRL, than those found in the periphery, such as PKKS and TB (Figure 22.5). There are 15 and 14 economic taxon in AW and TRL, respectively, compared to 9 and 5 in PKKS and TB (Appendix A). This may represent a concentration of wealth in the Angkorian capital but also the availability of more products which would be brought in from different parts of the empire, including those sourced locally.

References

Bedigian, D., 2003. Evolution of sesame revisited: domestication, diversity and prospects. *Genetic Resources and Crop Evolution* 50(7), 779–87.

Bellina, B., P. Silapanth, B. Chaisuwan, J. Allen, V. Bernard, B. Borell, P. Bouvet, C. Castillo, L. Dussubieux, J. Malakie, S. Perronnet. & T.O. Pryce, 2014. The development of coastal polities in the Upper Thai-Malay Peninsula of the late first millennium BCE and the inception of the long lasting economic and cultural exchange between the East of the Indian Ocean and the South China sea, in *Before Siam: Essays in Art and Archaeology*, eds. N. Revire. & S. Murphy. Bangkok: River Books, 68–89.

Blench, R., 2008. A history of fruits on the Southeast Asian Mainland. *Occasional Paper* 4, 115–37.

Blench, R.M. & M. Dendo (eds.), 2007. *The Intertwined History of The Silk-Cotton and Baobab. Fields of Change; Progress in African Ethnobotany*. Gröningen: Barkhuis and Gröningen University, 1–20.

Bowdery, D., 1999. Phytoliths from tropical sediments: reports from Southeast Asia and Papua New Guinea. *Indo-Pacific Prehistory Association Bulletin* 18, 159–68.

Brink, M., 2011. *Gossypium arboreum* L, in *PROTA* (Plant Resources of Tropical Africa/Ressources Végétales de l'Afrique Tropicale), eds. M. Brink. & E.G. Achigan-Dako. Netherlands: Wageningen.

Burkill, I.H., 1936. *A dictionary of the economic products of the Malay Peninsula*. Kuala Lumpur: Ministry of Agriculture.

Calo, A., B. Prasetyo, P. Bellwood, J.W. Lankton, B. Gratuze, T.O. Pryce, A. Reinecke, V. Leusch, H. Schenk, R. Wood, R.A. Bawono, I.D.K. Gede, Ni, L.K.C. Yuliati, C. Castillo, A. Carter, C. Reepmeyer & J. Fenner, 2015. Sembiran and Pacung on the Northern coast of Bali: a strategic crossroads for early trans-Asiatic exchange. *Antiquity* 89(344), 378–96.

Cameron, J., 2010. The archaeological textiles from Ban Don Ta Phet in broader perspective, in *50 Years of Archaeology in Southeast Asia: Essays in Honour of Ian Glover*, eds B. Bellina-Pryce, T.O. Pryce, E. Bacus. & J. Wisseman-Christie. Bangkok: River Books, 141–52.

Cappers, R.T., 2006. *Roman Foodprints at Berenike: Archaeobotanical Evidence of Subsistence and Trade in the Eastern Desert of Egypt* (volume 55). Los Angeles: Cotsen Institute of Archaeology Press.

Carter, A., P. Heng, M. Stark, R. Chhay. & D. Evans, 2018. Urbanism and residential patterning in Angkor. *Journal of Field Archaeology* 43(6), 492–506.

Carter, A.K., M.T. Stark, S. Quintus, Y. Zhuang, H. Wang, P. Heng. & R. Chhay, 2019. Temple occupation and the tempo of collapse at Angkor Wat, Cambodia. *Proceedings of the National Academy of Sciences* 116(25), 12226–31.

Castillo, C. & D.Q. Fuller, 2015. Bananas: the spread of a tropical forest fruit as an agricultural staple, in *The Oxford Handbook of the Archaeology of Food and Diet*, ed. J. Lee-Thorp. Oxford: Oxford University Press. Doi:10.1093/oxfordhb/9780199694013.013.7

Castillo, C., 2011. Rice in Thailand: the archaeobotanical contribution. *Rice* 4(3–4), 114–20.

Castillo, C., 2013. *The archaeobotany of Khao Sam Kaeo and Phu Khao Thong: the agriculture of late prehistoric Southern Thailand*. PhD dissertation. London: Institute of Archaeology, University College London.

Castillo, C., 2017a. Archaeobotany: evidence of exchange networks and agricultural practices, in *Khao Sam Kaeo: An Early Port-City between the Indian Ocean and the South China Sea*, ed. B. Bellina. Paris: École française d'Extrême-Orient, 71–123.

Castillo, C.C., 2017b. Development of cereal agriculture in prehistoric mainland Southeast Asia. *Man in India* 97(1), 335–52.

Castillo, C., 2019. Preservation bias: is rice over represented in the archaeological record? Open fire charring experiments of Asian crops illuminate. *Archaeological and Anthropological Sciences* 11(12), 6451–71.

Castillo, C., K. Tanaka, Y. Sato, M. Kajale, B. Bellina, C. Higham, N. Chang. & D.Q. Fuller, 2016b. Archaeogenetic study of prehistoric rice remains from Thailand and India: evidence of early *japonica* dispersal to South and Southeast Asia. *Archaeological and Anthropological Sciences* 8(3), 523–43.

Castillo, C.C., A. Carter, E. Kingwell-Banham, Y. Zhuang, A. Weisskopf, R. Chhay, R., Heng, P., Fuller, D.Q. & M. Stark, 2020. The Khmer did not live by rice alone: archaeobotanical investigations at Angkor Wat and Ta Prohm. *Archaeological Research in Asia* 24(100213), 2352–67.

Castillo, C.C., B. Bellina. & D.Q. Fuller, 2016a. Rice, beans and trade crops on the Early Maritime Silk Route in Southeast Asia. *Antiquity* 90(353), 1255–69.

Castillo, C.C., M. Polkinghorne, B. Vincent, Tan Boun-Suy. & D.Q. Fuller, 2018. Life goes on: archaeobotanical investigations of diet and ritual at Angkor Thom, Cambodia (fourteenth to fifteenth centuries CE). *Holocene* 28(6), 930–44.

Cœdès, G., 1906. La Stèle De Ta-Prohm. *Bulletin de l'École française d'Extrême-Orient* 6(1–2), 44–85.

Cœdès. G., 1941. La Stèle De Práh Khan D'Angkor. *Bulletin de l'École française d'Extrême-Orient* 41, 255–302.

Dalby, A., 2000. *Dangerous Tastes: The Story of Spices*. California: University of California Press.

Dy Phon, P., 2000. *Plants Used in Cambodia*. Phnom Penh: Imprimerie Olympic.

Fuller, D.Q. & E.L. Harvey, 2006. The archaeobotany of Indian pulses: identification, processing and evidence for cultivation. *Environmental Archaeology* 11(2), 219–46.

Fuller, D.Q., 1999. *The emergence of agricultural societies in South India: botanical and archaeological perspectives*. PhD dissertation. Cambridge: Cambridge University.

Fuller, D.Q., 2005. Ceramics, seeds and culinary change in prehistoric India. *Antiquity* 79, 761–77.

Fuller, D.Q., C. Castillo, E. Kingwell-Banham, L. Qin. & A. Weisskopf, 2017. Charred pomelo peel, historical linguistics and other tree crops: approaches to framing the historical context of early Citrus cultivation in East, South and Southeast Asia, in *The History and Archaeology of the Citrus Fruit from the Far East to the Mediterranean: Introductions, Diversifications, Uses*, eds. V. Zech-Matterne. & G. Fiorentino. Naples: Publications du Centre Jean Bérard, 29–50.

Fuller, D.Q., C. Murphy, E. Kingwell-Banham, C.C. Castillo. & S. Naik, 2019. *Cajanus cajan* (L) Millsp. Origins and domestication: the South and Southeast Asian archaeobotanical evidence. *Genetic Resources and Crop Evolution* 66(6), 1175–88.

Fuller, D.Q., Y-I. Sato, C. Castillo, L. Qin, A.R. Weisskopf, E.J. Kingwell-Banham, J. Song, S-M. Ahn. & J. Van Etten, 2010. Consilience of genetics and archaeobotany in the entangled history of rice. *Archaeological and Anthropological Sciences* 2(2), 115–31.

Grubben, G.J.H. & S. Partohardjono (eds.), 1996. *Plant Resources of South-East Asia No. 10: Cereals*. Leiden: Backhuys Publishers.

Hawken, S. & C.C. Castillo, 2023. Angkor's agrarian economy: a socio-ecological mosaic, in *The Angkorian World*, eds. M. Hendrickson, M.T. Stark. & D. Evans. New York: Routledge.

Hendrickson, M., S. Leroy, C. Castillo, Q. Hua, E. Vega. & K. Phon, 2019. Forging empire: Angkorian iron smelting, community and ritual practice at Tonle Bak. *Antiquity* 93(372), 1586–606.

Heywood, V.H., R.K. Brummitt, A. Culham. & O. Seberg (eds.), 2007. *Flowering Plant Families of the World*. Surrey: Royal Botanic Gardens, Kew.

Jansen, P.C.M., J. Jukema, L.P.A. Oyen. & T.G. Van Lingen, 1991. *Dracontomelon* dao (Blanco) Merr. & Rolfe, in *Plant Resources of South-East Asia No. 2: Edible Fruits and Nuts*, eds. E.W.M. Verheij. & R.E. Coronel. Wageningen: Pudoc, 329–30.

Jaramillo, M.A. & P.S. Manos, 2001. Phylogeny and patterns of floral diversity in the genus *Piper* (Piperaceae). *American Journal of Botany* 88(4), 706–16.

Lemmens, R.H.M.J. & N. Wulijarni-Soetjipto (eds.), 1991. *Plant Resources of South-East Asia No. 3: Dye and Tannin-Producing Plants*. Wageningen: Pudoc, 120–22.

Liu, X., P.J. Jones, G.M. Matuzeviciute, H.V. Hunt, D.L. Lister, T. An, N. Przelomska, C.J. Kneale, Z. Zhao. & M.K. Jones, 2019. From ecological opportunism to multi-cropping: mapping food globalisation in prehistory. *Quaternary Science Reviews* 206, 21–8.

Lu, H., J. Zhang, K.B. Liu, N. Wu, Y. Li, K. Zhou, M. Ye, T. Zhang, H. Zhang, X. Yang. & L. Shen, 2009. Earliest domestication of common millet (*Panicum miliaceum*) in East Asia extended to 10,000 years ago. Proceedings of the National Academy of Sciences 106(18), 7367–72.

Maxwell, T.S., 2008. The stele inscription of Preah Khan, Angkor. *Udaya, Journal of Khmer Studies* (8), 1–114.

Murphy, C., A. Weisskopf, W. Bohingamuwa, G. Adikari, N. Perera, J. Blinkhorn, M. Horton, D.Q. Fuller. & N. Boivin, 2018. Early agriculture in Sri Lanka: new archaeobotanical analyses and radiocarbon dates from the early historic sites of Kirinda and Kantharodai (Kandarodai). *Archaeological Research in Asia* 16, 88–102.

Pandey, R.K. & E. Westphal, 1989. Vigna unguiculata (L.) Walp, in *Plant Resources of South-East Asia No. 1: Pulses*, eds L.J.G. van der Maesen & S. Somaatmadja. Wageningen: Pudoc, 77–81.

Patil, P., S. Sutar, J.K. Joseph, S. Malik, S. Rao, S. Yadav. & K.V. Bhat, 2015. A systematic review of the genus *Abelmoschus* (Malvaceae). *Rheedea* 25(1), 14–30.

Paz, V., 2001. *Archaeobotany and cultural transformation: patterns of early plant utilisation in Northern Wallacea*. PhD dissertation. Cambridge: University of Cambridge.

Paz, V., 2005. Rock shelters, caves, and archaeobotany in island Southeast Asia. *Asian Perspectives* 44(1), 107–18.

Penny, D., C. Pottier, M. Kummu, R. Fletcher, U. Zoppi, M. Barbetti. & T.O.U.S. Somaneath, 2005. Hydrological history of the West Baray, Angkor, revealed through palynological analysis of sediments from the West Mebon. *Bulletin de l' École française d'Extrême-Orient* 92, 497–521.

Penny, D., C. Pottier, R. Fletcher, M. Barbetti, D. Fink. & Q. Hua, 2006. Vegetation and land-use at Angkor, Cambodia: a dated pollen sequence from the Bakong temple moat. *Antiquity* 80, 559–614.

Penny, D., J-B. Chevance, D. Tang. & S. De Greef, 2014. The environmental impact of Cambodia's ancient city of Mahendraparvata (Phnom Kulen). *PLoS One* 9(1), e84252.

Rahayu, M. & H. Ibrahim, 1999. Alpinia Roxburgh, in *Record from Proseabase*, eds. Oyen L.P.A. & Nguyen Xuan Dung. Bogor: PROSEA (Plant Resources of South-East Asia) Foundation. www.proseanet.org.

Schoff, W.H., 1974. *The Periplus of the Erythraean Sea: Travel and Trade in the Indian Ocean by a Merchant of the First Century*. New Delhi: Munshiram Manoharlal Publishers.

Shivashankar, G. & R.S. Kulkarni, 1989. *Lablab purpureus* L. (Sweet), in *Plant Resources of South-East Asia No. 1: Pulses*, eds. L.J.G. Van der Maesen. & S. Somaatmadja. Wageningen: Pudoc, 48–50.

Ślączka, A.A., 2007. *Temple Consecration Rituals in Ancient India: Text and Archaeology*. Leiden: E.J. Brill.

Smart, T.L. & E. Hoffman, 1988. Environmental interpretation of archaeological charcoal, in *Current Paleoethnobotany*, eds. C.A. Hastorf. & V.S. Popper. Chicago: The University of Chicago Press, 167–205.

Soepadmo, E., 1991. Artocarpus heterophyllu Lamk, in *Record from Proseabase*, eds. Verheij, E.W.M. & Coronel, R.E. Bogor: PROSEA (Plant Resources of South-East Asia) Foundation. www.proseanet.org.

Stark, M.T., D. Evans, R. Chhay, P. Heng. & A. Carter, 2015. Residential patterning at Angkor Wat. *Antiquity* 89(348), 1439–455.

Thorel, C., 2001 [1873]. *Agriculture and Ethnobotany of the Mekong Basin,* translated from French by. W. Tips. Bangkok: White Lotus Press.

Van Borssum Waalkes, J., 1966. Malesian malvaceae revised. *Blumea* 14, 89–105.

Van Der Maesen, L.J.G., 1989. Cajanus cajan (L) Millsp, in *Plant Resources of South-East Asia No. 1: Pulses*, eds L.J.G. van der Maesen. & S. Somaatmadja. Wageningen: Pudoc, 39–42.

Van der Veen, M., 2011. Consumption, trade and innovation: exploring the botanical remains from the Roman and Islamic ports at quseir al-qadim, Egypt. *Journal of African Archaeology Monograph Series* 6 (Africa Magna Verlag).

Van Holthoon, F.L., 1999. Phyllanthus emblica L, in *Plant Resources of South-East Asia No. 12(1): Medicinal and Poisonous Plants 1*, eds L.S. de Padua, N. Bunyapraphatsara. & R.H.M.J. Lemmens. Leiden: Backhuys Publisher, 388–89.

Van Schaik-Van Banning, A.J.J., 1991. Phyllanthus emblica L, in *Plant Resources of South-East Asia No. 3: Dye and Tannin-producing Plants*, eds. R.H.M.J. Lemmens. & N. Wulijarni-Soetjipto. Wageningen: Pudoc, 105–08.

Vaughan, J.G., 1970. *The Structure and Utilization of Oil Seeds*. London: Chapman & Hall.

Weber, S., H. Lehman, T. Barela, S. Hawks. & D. Harriman, 2010. Rice or millets: early farming strategies in prehistoric central Thailand. *Archaeological and Anthropological Sciences* 2(2), 79–88.

Zhou, D., 2007[1297]. *A Record of Cambodia: The Land and Its People*, trans. P. Harris. Chiang Mai: Silkworm Books.

PART V

Ideologies and Realities

23

GODS AND TEMPLES

The Nature(s) of Angkorian Religion

Julia Estève

The Problem

Our understanding of religion in the Angkorian World was initiated by Indianists and Khmerologists more than one century ago. The standard academic narrative developed from this work focused on the Khmer kingdom's adoption of Indian religions (Hinduism, Buddhism) around the beginning of the Common Era (Chatterjee 1964[1927]; Bareau 1976). At this time, the long-standing maritime exchanges between South and Southeast Asia germinated and created the hypothesis of a 'natural' impregnation of peninsular and insular Southeast Asian cultures by Indian models (Pollock 1996, 239). A first wave of Indianisation swept over the peninsula into Cambodia, then known as *Funan*, spreading South Asian habits and customs and thereby ensuring a particularly strong diffusion of their religion(s) (Cœdès 1989[1948]). Śaivism and Vaiṣṇavism became deeply integrated within the local milieu, with Buddhism also being adopted, though to a lesser degree (Briggs 1951; Cœdès 1953). An important part of this religious package, the Khmer temple, first appeared around the 5th–6th centuries CE and would eventually become the apex symbol of Angkor's political, religious, and economic power.

Scholars recognising these obvious connections to India soon came to consider Angkorian religion as a classic example of syncretism, a label originating in mid-19th-century Indian scholarship (Burnouf 1876[1845]; Senart 1883; Lévi 1896). Hinduism and Buddhism were seen as being intertwined throughout their histories, most dramatically in the formation of Buddhist Tantra. Given the intellectual influence of this research in Cambodia, it is perhaps unsurprising that syncretism was also discovered within multiple domains of Angkorian religion within Hinduism (Śaivism and Vaiṣṇavism), between Śaivism and Buddhism, and also between the Indian religions and local chthonic belief systems (Barth 1889; Finot 1901; Briggs 1951). How well these interpretations reflect local realities of Angkorian religious organisation is not yet clear, especially since Indic gods were absorbed into the Khmer cultural substrate with its own collection of landscape-based tutelary spirits (Mus 1933). This chapter suggests that viewing Angkorian religion as pluralistic, not syncretic, more accurately represents the diversity of faiths—exogenous and local—that Angkorian kings, brahmins, and commoners practised than does syncretism. Key to this view is the recognition that Angkorian religion stems from inherently indigenous manifestations linked to a particular Cambodian landscape. This discussion also evaluates the nature of religious practice and seeks to explain how and why Śaivism was selected as the primary focus of Angkor's Brahmins and elites.

DOI: 10.4324/9781351128940-29

Deconstructing Syncretism

The concept of Angkorian syncretism was largely imposed by colonial (i.e., non-Khmer) scholars, most of whom were trained Indologists (Burnouf 1845; Senart 1883; Lévi 1896). These arguments generally rest on the premise that elite temples were home to Indic gods and assume that local people preferred Indic religious ideals over extant animist beliefs. The fact that Angkor Period Indic evidence (Śaivism and Vaiṣṇavism, Buddhism, both Theravāda and Mahāyāna) are more visible than animist expressions exacerbates the problem (Sanderson 2003–2004). Close reading of the religious contexts in the epigraphic record offers alternate views to the conventional 'syncretism' model. To demonstrate this point, this discussion examines three increasingly problematic examples of the Angkorian texts: discrepancies between the invocative and recording parts of inscriptions and between donations, resource-sharing between gods of different denominations, and foundations of statues and holy places of various faiths.

Discrepancy Between Invocative and Recording

Among the 1400-plus Khmer inscriptions at our disposal, the richest texts are generally divided into one text versified in Sanskrit focusing on the historical data, starting with the eulogies of the gods, sovereigns, and dignitaries and showcasing their good deeds and another text written in ancient Khmer providing administrative information such as donation lists, trial reports, and so on.

Differences between the dedications and deities listed in the introductory and body of an inscription provide initial evidence to doubt the syncretic nature of Khmer religion (Estève 2009). Inscriptions K. 161 (1002/1003 CE) and K. 953 (1041/1042 CE), for example, begin with a *maṅgala* (the stanzas of auspicious invocation opening any inscription) worshipping both Śaiva and Buddhist divinities but in separate stanzas (K. 161, Finot 1904, 672; K. 953, *IC* VII, 124; *RS* III, n. 59, 125). During the reign of Dharaṇīndravarman I (r. 1107–1113), inscription K. 258 draws a link between the king and the Buddha, but the rest of the inscription is generally Śaivite in content (K. 258 C22–23, *IC* IV, 175). The text of K. 290.1 (9th c. CE) shows inconsistencies, as its foundation is a hermitage for Buddhist monks and its invocative part uses terminology found in Śaivite and Vaiṣṇava inscriptions (K. 1228; K. 279) of the hermitages founded by king Yaśovarman I (Cœdès 1908[a], 203; *IC* III, 23; Estève 2009, 338). A further example is noted in the Buddhist invocation opening K. 432, while the remaining parts of this text record only Śaivite foundations (10th c. CE, *IC* II, 119). These patterns are combined in K. 158 (1003/1004 CE), where the maṅgala is divided between a tribute to Śiva and a tribute to the Buddha, and the donations are for both Śaivite and Buddhist deities (*IC* II, 97). These inscriptions reflect a diversity of denominational settings and also reveal co-residence of practitioners of different faiths.

Donations and Sharing of Resources Between Gods of Various Denominations

The Khmer language parts of the inscriptions most often record the donations of goods, land, or personnel made to the temples in order to ensure their functioning (Soutif 2009). Several Angkorian elite donations to various denominations inscribed in stelae also do not reflect religious syncretism. Inscription K. 180 (948 CE) from Prasat Pram tells us that Śivasoma, *ācārya* [master, teacher] of king Rājendravarman (944–c. 968), gave workers at the same time to the Devī of Maruktalapura, the *liṅga* of Śivapurālaya, and the Buddha of Amarendrapura (Cœdès 1913, 17). Meanwhile, in K. 198 (966 CE), an individual named Upendra gave land and workers both to the gods Parameśvara (Śiva) and Āryamaitri (Maitreya) (*IC* VI, 147). Pooled resources to deities of different denominations, much more frequent, have been recorded elsewhere, such as the Viṣṇu from Preah Enkosei temple who had to share his resources (*miśrabhoga*, 'co-using') with the deity of Prasat Komphus temple, a Śiva Bhadreśvara during the reign of Jayavarman V (Bhattacharya 1961, 33). The inscriptions show either an elaborate system of resource pooling or exclusivity of use and or ownership and specify which individuals have the use or the property of the offerings and more specifically the property of lands given to deities. As such individuals can be lay or religious people, this raises questions about who owns the land and who can use it and why these texts deal with the juridical and commercial aspects (see Estève 2009, 425–32).

Our record of elite donations to Angkorian temples reflects the diverse religious Cambodian landscape, structured by an implicit hierarchy of deities who exercised varying levels of power. Specific Śaivite representations, for example, were highly ranked and so powerful that other lower-ranked deities and temples sought to associate with them. The fact that certain temples wanted to be codependent with a more sacred and typically larger temple (K. 165; *IC* VI, 132) suggests that they did so to be granted some kind of financial independence or immunity towards taxes. The connection between temples also explains why these associations had to be vetted by the king. Since the king was the lord of the land, all matters concerning the income from the land had to be submitted to his approval, but he was inferior to the god from the point of view of property, since the god's property automatically fell under the authority of the deity. These exemptions were probably made to reward some elite servants and dignitaries.

Foundations of Statues and Temples of Various Denominations

Inscriptions on statue and temple foundations also challenge the notion that Angkorian religion was syncretic, since donors often supported multiple denominations at one location rather than a single denomination. Some inscriptions report that Śaiva, Vaiṣṇava, and Buddhist statues were founded in a single location (K. 1155, K. 1141, K. 173, K. 174, and K. 1198; Estève 2009, 2016), and we know therefore that these diverse religious foundations can be made successively or jointly in the same holy place on the same date. According to inscriptions K. 1155 and K. 1141 (839/840 CE; 972/973 CE), the holy place named Damraṅ hosted a succession of heterogeneous foundations, during which statues of Buddhist and Śaiva religions repeatedly replaced one other (Chaem 1986, 1987; Estève 2009; NIC II—III, 115–118). A holy place can therefore welcome multiple religions, not combinations of faiths. This practice is illustrated in inscription K. 1198 (beg. 11th c. CE) in which a Śrī Lakṣmīpativarman founds a *liṅga* in a temple, replacing the Buddha who until then had occupied that sacred place (Pou 2001, 240–60; Griffiths 2006, 2009). What is significant here is that the temple is linked to a familial lineage, and thus the religious identity of the deities it hosted may be linked to the diverse beliefs of these ancestors. That holy places welcomed multiple religious faiths is demonstrated in K. 158 (beg. 11th c. CE; *IC* II, 97), which tells us that the Śaiva divinity is surpassed in number by the Buddhist divinities, who are also allocated greater quantities of supplies. Thus, we cannot state that gods were shared or combined in a syncretic way but replaced each other to suit the reverence of elite families.

Local Cults, Sacred Places, and the Web of Power

The traditional view of Angkorian religion emphasises the model that Indic deities were overlain onto a passive indigenous Khmer animism. This, however, is far from accurate, as the local faith provided its own unique system, with chthonic gods and sacredness more generally being deeply intertwined with specific places in the landscape. The chthonic principles of the local Khmer religion, and the inherent connection to earthly places, were central to the success of Angkor. It is difficult to talk about the local beliefs of the Angkor Period because the inscriptions say almost nothing about them, and that is why they appear rarely in academic discussions. Today *neak ta* or village spirits occupy a central place in popular religion, and this presence naturally leads us to consider that they existed in ancient times (Forest 1992, 24). This cult of terrain and place gathers the community around it through a stone or a tree, which comes to symbolise and materialise the local god. Its essential quality lies in its location, and those who venerate it belong to this community. Each community therefore has at its disposal a limited area demarcated by the space where the god of the terrain is recognised. If someone doesn't recognise it, he or she therefore belongs to another village (Forest 1992, 24). This mosaic landscape remains an integral part of modern Cambodia, which is home to hundreds or even thousands of local gods (Ang 1986).

Similar models of sacred spatial organisation appear in the Angkorian epigraphy, with deities and shrines associated with a territory and the community responsible for their protection. These were places of great power, and pilgrimages to deities of all backgrounds thus created a wide range of religious diversity in the landscape. The heterogeneity and reverence of local gods is clearly illustrated through the work of Yaśovarman I, who at the end of the 9th century claims to have built 100 *āśramas* on sites where powerful and renowned gods had already existed for a long time (Estève and Soutif 2011). The later Pre Rup inscription tells us that under king Rājendravarman in the 10th century, there was a pre-existing cult of '30 self-created gods (*svayambhū*)' (K. 806, *IC* I, st. CCLXX). The considerable number of gods mentioned in these two texts helps us to understand the religious cadastral organisation and paints a picture of ancient Cambodia as a territory filled with gods, some of whom were more important than the others.

As the patron of all religions, kings present themselves as the protectors of all denominations and essentially of sacredness itself. The king also stands at the apex of the religious hierarchy of temples, which requires redistribution of economic goods upward to serve the greater elites. Though required to share resources, a temple aims to be exempt from any authority other than that of a temple whose sacredness is superior and therefore other than divine authority. The inscriptions provide clear examples for this web of temples and the diverse gradations of power between them. Angkorian gods had powers of protection—and destruction—in the Khmer world. Their deities were imbued with magical powers, and it is reasonable to believe that, from the perspective of the insider and outsider enemies of the kingdom, it was necessary either to divest them of these powers or to monopolise them to take possession of territories and subjugate the local population. According to the inscription K. 235 (1004 CE), people under Sūryavarman I 'threw down the statues from Bhadrapattana and Stuk Ransi' (D, l. 40–42), leaving these *sruks* 'totally devastated' (D, l. 46). Given that places retain power, the act of destruction is often followed by the founding once again of the statues, expressed by '*phoṅ viṅ unmīlita*' re-opening of their eyes (D, l. 46–47; see Jenner 2009 s.v.). This process was recorded in K. 258 (1069 CE; A, l. 65–70) by King Harṣavarman III, who ordered the new foundation of the gods Vraḥ Śivaliṅga, Vraḥ Nārāyaṇa, and Vraḥ Bhagavatī because 'the enemies had taken them off Stuk Sramo' (*IC* IV, 198). The act of corruption or destruction occurs precisely because these deities were Kaṃrateṅ Jagat or 'the High Lord of the World'. During the Pre-Angkor Period and until the early Angkor Period, the gods bore the same title as the king, princes, and high dignitaries, namely Vraḥ Kaṃrateṅ 'Añ, but starting in the 10th century, the Kaṃrateṅ Jagat gods multiplied to the point of overtaking them. The majority of these gods have names formed from the terrain (mountain, city, garden, forest, etc.), which shows that their power was linked to this very terrain and they held control of a sacred domain (Estève 2014, 182–86). These deities come from an indigenous conception of religion linked to an essential animism for the Khmer population which considers sacredness deeply linked to the locus or terrain.

A further example of conquering gods in the landscape comes from K. 237 (1066 CE), where one sees Kaṃvau, a *senāpati* or general of the army of King Udayādityavarman II, who had a desire to conquer power: he took possession of the 'domains' (*kaṃvau khmāṅ ni ter cāp viṣaya phoṅ*), in that he captured not only the land but also the temples erected on them and the arable land and workers who were associated with them. In inscription K. 289 (C. st. XXI), it is said that Kaṃvau has 'wish[ed] to conquer all the gods', while according to inscription K. 237, he hit these religious images and has somehow denatured them (st. II, the *liṅga* was 'altered' and l. 6–7, the images were 'torn'). Barth had noted this insistence on the destruction of statues, and he wondered about the religious intentionality of the practice (1885, 174). The high-ranking army chief named Saṃgrāma who was sent by King Udayādityavarman II to stop Kaṃvau's rebellion visited temples before battle in order to invoke the assistance of various representations of the god Śiva (K. 289, 1066 CE), suggesting that he engaged in rituals intended to confer, through magic, a phenomenal power as well as a practical means to overcome his enemies. This was not his first battle, as he stopped other rebellions before: a first led by a certain Aravindahrada in 1051 in the south of the country (st. X); a second led by the Kaṃvau with whom we are concerned, presumably in the northwest of the country (in the region of Phnoṃ Ruṅ); and a third, led by an enemy chief named Slvat, also in 1061, in a region named Praśānvrairmmyat (st. XIV). Each time Saṃgrāma defeated his enemies, he made pious donations: to the Śiva of Rājatīrtha for his victory in the south, then to the Śiva of Pṛthuśaila for his victory over Kaṃvau, and finally to the deities of Mādhava for his last victory. The fact that the deity worshipped by Saṃgrāma changes according to his enemy, or more likely the place where the critical battle will take place, confirms the sacredness of territory.

Certain deities of various religious backgrounds also frequently appear side by side in the epigraphy, such as Śiva of Liṅgapura and Buddha of Chpār Ransī (see Estève 2009, 453–54, for tables of these deities and references and Estève and Vincent 2010, 149). Throughout the 10th and early 12th century, six inscriptions (K. 158, K. 276, K. 277, K. 237, K. 249, and K. 254) notably recall the allocation of resources for the Buddhist temple but also to other Kaṃrateṅ Jagat gods: the Kaṃrateṅ Jagat Liṅgapura (Śiva), the Kaṃrateṅ Jagat Śrī Campeśvara (Viṣṇu), and the Kanloṅ Kaṃrateṅ 'Añ Aṅve Danle (the defunct queen). Offerings in these inscriptions are made without consideration of religious denomination, suggesting that it did not matter at this level precisely because they concern deities named Kaṃrateṅ Jagat who stand above such religious divisions. When one of these Kaṃrateṅ Jagats is associated with a deity whose title is only 'Vrah Kaṃrateṅ 'Añ', donations are shared with the Kaṃrateṅ Jagat, as if it needed to pay tribute to the higher deity. Thus, these deities seem to have possessed completely independent temples and were independently managed by the religious personnel directly attached to them. The existence of this recurring group of deities named Kaṃrateṅ Jagat—their shared donations and relationship to terrain notwithstanding the apparent religious heterogeneity—again supports the idea of religious pluralism.

Temples must be kept prosperous and flourishing because they match the openness advocated by the Khmer rulers in religious affairs and because the political control of the territories directly depends on their existence as linked to the sacredness of the terrain. This variety of Kaṃrateṅ Jagat deities forms the sacred landscape and parallels the administrative landscape. In this sense, the religious sphere and the political sphere were so intertwined in Angkorian Cambodia that it was necessary to wage war against the reigning king's gods for whoever wished to overcome and monopolise his political power. The conception of sacredness is so much linked to the terrain that it affects the relationship to power, and it is the source of the adoption of Śaivism as the primary state religion in the early Angkor Period. Śaivism provided the most appropriate framework for the organisation and expression of power, but it also provided political power with a very powerful magic. The power belongs to whoever controls these religious topographical centres, and this power had chosen to take the clothes of Śaivism. Owing to this link, multiple deities are welcomed in the same place since the crucial component is the terrain, and, along with it, animism prevails.

The indigenous religion welcomed new deities without embracing their exclusivity. For example, the Śaiva impregnation of the territory that has been highlighted (Sanderson 2003–2004, 421) reveals, in our opinion, a fundamental aspect of the religion of ancient Cambodia in that it is the names of great Indian pilgrimage sites that have been adopted by the Khmers. If we relate this practice to the designation of the deity by his place of residence for the first rank deities named Kamrateṅ jagat (Estève 2014, 182–192) and second to the theme of duplicates that appears as a filigree in epigraphy (Estève 2009, 365 *sqq.* and 437 *sqq.*), we find a space of religiosity that is inherently indigenous.

Khmer Religion in Action: Brahmins, Śaivism, and Royal Patronage

Angkor's pluralistic religion(s) had its most obvious impact on the world of Khmer elites. Brahmanism in India started to evolve from the Vedic priesthood after the Mauryan Period (322–185 BCE), and its socio-political status enabled it to spread widely and diversely. Francis (2013) shows for example that early states in Southern India had no priests, and therefore the king was responsible for necessary magic-religious functions. It is only with the Pallava dynasty (ca. 300–ca. 900 CE) that the Brahmanical culture started spreading and slowly began divesting magical power from the hands of the rulers. The Brahmin ultimately came to represent both a social order and orthodoxy in Indic culture (Bronkhorst 2011). This new formula of Brahmanism also convinced rulers of 'Indianised' Southeast Asia to adopt it as an essential politico-religious mechanism to shift from local chiefdoms to unified kingdoms. Brahmins were the holders of ancestral and timeless knowledge (coming from the Vedic India) and as such were seen as the most eminent members of society because they were the depositories of a magic, ritualistic power that was valuable to the kings. They could predict the future, create protection spells, and, of course, serve as political advisers, and the Bakus still present in the palace claim to be Brahmins of foreign origin. Cambodian inscriptions praise the Brahmins for their textual knowledge, particularly the Veda. For example, Inscription K. 267 (10th c. CE) from Bat Cum (*JA* 1908 [2], 213) registers the Buddhist foundations made by Kavīndrārimathana, minister (*apabhṛtya*) of Rājendravarman, and nonetheless specifies the injunction: 'Let no one, except the Brahmin who knows the Veda, bathe here, in this pure water, in the great moat dug according to the rites' (st. XXXVIII, ibid., 247). But their own religious flavour did not really matter, for, as Bronkhorst claims, Brahmanism could not be assigned to the category 'religion' but was instead primarily linked to ensuring the social order (2011, 54–55). This explains numerous references where we see coexisting vocabularies or individuals possessing textual or theoretical training that seems to belong to various religious affiliations such as Śaivism, Vaiṣṇavism, and Buddhism. Knowledge of Indian Sanskrit texts and rituals was conceived as a sign of great intelligence, while the connection to India guaranteed authenticity and enhanced local prestige (see Pollock 1996, 2006). Brahmins coming from India, such as Hiraṇyadāma from K. 235 (1053 CE), were so highly revered that kings often offered them a daughter or sister to marry to become part of the familial lineage and provide politico-religious clout.

Angkor's priests were thus living sources of esoteric and powerful knowledge in Cambodia by the 7th century. For example, inscription K. 604 (627 CE) from Sambor Prei Kuk records the erection of a *liṅga* by the high official Vidyāviśeṣa, a Pāśupata brahman, who was versed in grammar (*śabda*), the brahmanical systems of Vaiśeṣika, Nyāya, and Sāṃkhya, and 'the doctrine of the Sugata' (*IC* IV, 17–18). Brahmins' central role is visible in the plurality of attributions of the *purohita* ('brahmanic priest of the king's house') in the Buddhist inscription of Wat Sithor (K. 111, 968/969 CE; 1883, 190) who is said to be 'versed in the knowledge of Buddhist letters and rites'. This centrality explains that king Yaśovarman I built four hermitages for the important communities at the end of the 9th century, one for the Brahmins, one for the Śaivas, one for the Vaiṣṇavas, and one for the Buddhists. The superiority of Brahmins is clearly seen in these very foundation inscriptions of the monasteries of Yaśovarman I: one joint stanza to the four monasteries explains that Brahmins should be honoured first (st. LVIII in K. 701, LVII in K. 279, LIV in K. 290 and LIII in K. 1228, all from 9th to 10th c.) and only then the religious scholars belonging to each monastery: 'Immediately after the brahman (*vipra*), the master Śaiva and the master Pāśupata (*śaivapāśupatācāryyau*) shall be honoured, and if one of them is learned in grammar, he shall be honoured more than the other.' An example here is the Śaiva monastery stanza LXI from K. 279, the equivalent stanzas being LXII in K. 701, LVIII in K. 290, and LVII in K. 1228, 9th–10th c. CE. Clearly, therefore, these were the communities with a key socio-political and religious role. While Khmer society ignored some aspects of Indic religious organisation such as the caste system or *varnas*, Angkorian power and kingship were undeniably defined in Brahmanical terms that remained unchanged for centuries (Sanderson 2003–2004, 389). However, these examples demonstrate that, within this Brahmanical framework, religious pluralism was encouraged or at least tolerated. The creation of separate spaces for each faith in the āśrama is perhaps the clearest evidence for pluralism.

The Strength of Śaivism

Brahmanism's success in the Angkorian World lay in its religious neutrality, serving to anchor the social order and legitimise Angkorian kingship. However, this lack of partisanship led to struggles between sects for religious supremacy, and Śaivism eventually solidified itself at the head of early historic states in India and most of early historic Southeast Asia (Bronkhorst 2011). Together, Brahmanism and Śaivism formed a two-tiered hierarchy that became rooted in this socio-political milieu (Sanderson 2018, 22). Śaivism succeeded because of its ability to provide a body of rituals and theories that legitimised the key elements of the social, political, and economic process at work at that time. This included the spread of the monarchical model of government, the movement of political and economic power of the capital into the peripheral territories, and the progress of rural territories through infrastructural development and the growth of new urban centres (Sanderson 2009, 253).

As noted, temples were primarily the dwellings of gods, fulfilling functions as ritual and scholarly centres, but they also served significant political and economic roles as landowners, employers, consumers, recipients of gifts, and mediators of political legitimation (Morrison 1995, 214). During these early centuries Śaivism was itself evolving and offered different paths for salvation that managed to seduce kingship in two ways: (1) the Siddhānta path via the legitimation and sacralisation of royal authority and (2) the Śākta Śaiva path offering rituals of state protection, particularly in times of danger (the introduction of Śaiva Tantric path known as Mantramārga in Cambodia can be spotted in K. 1236 (CE 763) according to Goodall 2013, 354–55). As such, Śaiva ascetics knowledgeable in Tantrism grew to great fame in Cambodia and often occupied the office of Royal Preceptor (*rājaguru*) and priest of the elite. Perhaps the strongest illustration of this fact is the founding of the *devarāja* cult that happened, according to the Sdok Kak Thom inscription (K. 235), in the 9th century. Most authors agree that this Devarāja was a Śaiva entity, as union of the king and Śiva (see Finot 1915; Bagchi 1930; Cœdès and Dupont 1943; Filliozat 1960; Cœdès 1961; Jacques 1994; Bourdonneau 2016). Śaivism became the cornerstone of the Angkorian Empire and was propelled to the status of state religion through the support of Śaiva tantric texts called 'The Four Faces of Tumburu' coming from the main *Tantra* of the Vidyāpīṭha Vāmā branch (Sanderson 2001, 7, n. 5; 2003–2004, 355), which achieved a supernatural authority greater than that of any previous texts (see Einoo 2009, 31–32 for these rituals).

Royal Patronage

Angkorian kings respected state Śaivism but also supported other religions. Although some instances of royal patronage have been offered as evidence for 'syncretism' (see Cœdès 1908b, 206–208 about Yaśovarman's *āśramas* and 1908b, 213 about Bat Cum inscriptions), these are better viewed as being politically rather than ideationally motivated. Royal patronage—kings subsidising great temples of all religious denominations present on their lands—during Angkorian times is more often cited as evidence of pluralism (Salomon 1998, 238), and many examples of this process are visible in the epigraphic record. The inscriptions indicate that religious obedience was dependent on family lines and also the idea of a personal religiosity (as *iṣṭadevata*). Thus, the discrepancies identified in the inscriptions, whether between the invocative and descriptive parts or even within them, often derive from the point of view adopted by a given passage in the inscription. In K. 485 (12th–13th c. CE), for example, the differences in the religious obedience of the characters involved in the story shifts depending on whether it is about Indradevī, a Buddhist, or her sister, who was successively Hindu and Buddhist (Finot 1925, 372; *IC* II, 161). Even if the protagonist of the inscription K. 237 (1066 CE) bore a name with a strong Vaiṣṇava sound, the text shows that he also respected state Śaivism, paid homage to the great Buddhist temple of the kingdom, and followed the Khmer idea of sacrality of the terrain (Estève 2014).

In K. 528 (953 CE) stanza CIII, Rājendravarman is said to be devoted to Śaivism, while in stanza CLXXII, we learn that he was also versed in Buddhism (Finot 1925, 309; 953 CE). In K. 834 (10th–11th c. CE), Śrī Sūryavarman I's *praśasti* (r. ca. 1002–1050) is typically built around comparisons with deities (Indra, Brahmā) and mythological episodes (Rāvaṇa) and is said to be united with or embodying Śiva. But by stanza XXV we see an element of Buddhist religion appearing as the king is compared to Śrīghana, a name of the Buddha (Skilling 2004). The Bat Cum inscriptions (K. 266, 960 CE; K. 267 and K. 268, 10th c. CE) relate the foundations of the king Rājendravarman (944–ca. 968) and his minister Kavīndrārimathana (Cœdès 1908b, 213). Instead of highlighting the kind of religious unity we might expect from the king and his minister, the text instead tells us that the king's foundations belonged to the Hindu faith, while those of his minister were Buddhist. This is corroborated by another text (K. 157, 953 CE), independent of Bat Cum, which also notes the fundamentally Buddhist character of Kavīndrārimathana, who was nevertheless respectful of royal Śaivism.

Angkor's kings generally patronised all religions in a political strategy used to ensure the contentment of all faith communities and maintain social order. It is also a mechanism that provided power through the propitiation of all the divinities and the magical powers belonging to them. Ultimately, it was the surest way to achieve success in all their endeavours.

Conclusion

The Khmer adopted a practice of patronising many religious faiths and a structure of power and society based on the Indian texts. While this politically clever approach served to please the respective religious communities it does not mean the religions were amalgamated into a single system or single collective thought. Looking over the specific cases used to support the qualification of 'syncretic', we see a diversity of situations and instead must recognise that the Angkorian World is more accurately seen as pluralistic. More practically, the term does not in itself explain much (Augé 1993; Baird 2004; Kitiarsa 2005) and is actually insufficient in explaining the myriad of cases and forms that religious phenomena took throughout the five centuries of political history that constitute the Angkor Period.

Based on this review of Cambodian inscriptions, the most useful tool to think about moving towards pluralism or eclecticism is the notion of magic, efficiency, or power of the landscape. Khmer animism began to use Indian religious tools in their own manner. Another way of conceptualising this is from the human point of view: the person from ancient Cambodia was taking in everything to ensure his or her health, happiness, and prosperity, to protect him- or herself from evil. The place was of utmost importance and sacredness. Statues of Śiva or Buddha added to a place reinforced its effectiveness, and perhaps each had a special power, a specific function. The most surprising cases can therefore be explained by adopting a logical systemic thinking of religion in context. The foundations of the monasteries were built by the king Yaśovarman I at the end of the 9th century in Angkor to represent separate religious communities in our Western conception of religion (see Chea et al. 2023, this volume). But for the provincial monasteries, planted in places where a local deity already existed, they all lived under the same roof. This does not mean that Buddhist monks, once outside the capital, followed the Śaiva rites. This means that all religions lived side by side, and this is what we understand by pluralism. What was important in the end was the chthonian divinity to whom the monastery was dedicated and the magical force that these religions participated in to increase their power.

List of Inscriptions in the Text

K.	*Reference*	*K.*	*Reference*
89	IC III, 164	289	ISC, 140
111	Cœdès 1942; IC VI, 195	290	Cœdès 1908a, 203; IC III, 231
136	ISC, 122; IC VI, 284	342	IC VI, 236
143	IC VI, 218	366	IC V, 288
157	IC VI, 123	432	IC II, 119
158	IC II, 97	468	IC III, 225
161	Finot 1904, 672	485	IC II, 161
165	IC VI, 132	528	Finot 1925, 309
173	Roeské 1914, 638	604	IC IV, 17; Goodall 2019
174	Roeské 1914, 644	659	IC V, 143
180	Cœdès 1913, 17	701	Cœdès 1932
194	Cœdès & Dupont 1943, 134	706	IC V, 217
198	IC VI, 147	818	IC VI, 65
235	Finot 1915, 53; Cœdès & Dupont 1943, 56	834	IC V, 244
237	ISC, 173; IC VI, 293; Estève 2014	842	IC I, 147
249	IC I, 267; IC III, 97	933	IC IV, 47
254	IC III, 180	953	IC VII, 124

(Continued)

(*Continued*)

K.	Reference	K.	Reference
257	IC IV, 140	957	IC VII, 137
258	IC IV, 175	958	IC VII, 141
263	ISC, 77; IC IV, 118	1141	NIC II-III; 115-118; Estève 2009
266	Cœdès 1908b	1155	Estève 2009
267	Cœdès 1908b	1171	-
268	Cœdès 1908b	1198	NIC II-III, 240-260 (Ka. 18)
276	ISC, 97; IC IV, 153	1228	-
277	ISC, 97; IC IV, 155	1236	Goodall 2012
279	ISCC, 418		

IC = Inscriptions du Cambodge; Cœdès 1937–66.

ISC = Inscriptions sanscrites du Cambodge; Barth 1885.

ISCC = Inscriptions sanscrites de Campā et du Cambodge; Bergaigne 1893.

NIC = Nouvelles inscriptions du Cambodge; tome I: Pou 1989; tome II-III: Pou 2001; tome IV: Pou 2011.

References

Ang, C., 1986. *Les êtres surnaturels dans la religion populaire khmère*. Paris: Centre de Documentation et de Recherche sur la Civilisation Khmère.

Augé, M., 1993. Une anthropologie résolument surmoderne, Entretien de Yves Goudineau avec Marc Augé, in *Cahiers des Sciences Humaines: Trente Ans (1963–1992)*, eds. J-L. Boutillier. & Y. Goudineau. Paris: Éditions de l'ORSTOM, 25–31.

Bagchi, P., 1930. Further notes on tantrik texts studied in Cambodia. *Indian Historical Quarterly* 1, 97–107.

Baird, R.D., 2004. Syncretism and the history of religions, in *Syncretism in Religion*, eds. A.M. Leopold & J.S. Jensen. London: Equinox Publishing Ltd., 48–59.

Bareau, A., 1976. Le Bouddhisme à Ceylan et dans l'Asie du Sud-Est, in *Histoire des religions, III*. Paris: Encyclopédie de la Pléiade, 330–52.

Barth, A., 1885. *Inscriptions sanscrites du Cambodge*. Paris: Imprimerie nationale.

Barth, A., 1889. Bulletin des religions de l'Inde: IIe partie: bouddhisme, jainisme, hindouisme. *Revue de l'histoire des religions* 19, 259–311.

Bergaigne, A., 1884. Chronologie de l'ancien royaume khmer d'après les inscriptions. *Journal Asiatique* 8(3), 51–76.

Bergaigne, A., 1893. *Inscriptions sanscrites de Campā et du Cambodge*. Paris: Imprimerie nationale.

Bhattacharya, K., 1961. *Les religions brahmaniques dans l'ancien Cambodge d'après l'épigraphie et l'iconographie*. Paris: École française d'Extrême-Orient.

Bourdonneau, É., 2016. La stèle de Sdok Kak Thom et le Devarāja. Récits et acteurs d'une "naissance", in *Le passé des Khmers: langues, textes, rites*, eds. N. Abdoul-Carime, J. Thach & G. Mikaelian. Berne, Peter Lang, 115–66.

Briggs, L.P., 1951. The syncretism of religions in Southeast Asia, particularly in the Khmer empire. *Journal of the American Oriental Society* 71(4), 230–49.

Bronkhorst, J., 2011. *Buddhism in the Shadow of Brahmanism*. Leiden: Brill.

Burnouf, E., 1876[1845]. *Histoire du bouddhisme*. Paris: Maisonneuve.

Chaem, K., 1986. [Édition et traduction de l'inscription K. 1141]. *Charuek Nai Prathet Thai* 3, 105–17.

Chaem, K., 1987. Charuek phra siwatsa sang thwa rup [Inscription de Srivatsa] [K. 1155]. *The Silpakorn Journal* 31(5), 91–96.

Chatterjee, B.R., 1964[1927]. *Indian Cultural Influence in Cambodia*. Calcutta: University of Calcutta.

Chea, S., J. Estève, D. Soutif. & E. Swenson, 2023. Āśramas, shrines and royal power, in *The Angkorian World*, eds. M. Hendrickson, M.T. Stark & D. Evans. New York: Routledge.

Cœdès, G. & Dupont, P., 1943. Les stèles de Sdŏk Kăk Thoṃ, Phnoṃ Sandak et Práḥ Vihār. *Bulletin de l'École française d'Extrême Orient*, 56–154.

Cœdès, G., 1908a. La stèle de Tép Pranam (Cambodge). *Journal Asiatique* 10(11), 203–25.

Cœdès, G., 1908b. Les inscriptions de Bàt Čuṃ (Cambodge). *Journal Asiatique* 10(12), 226–52.

Cœdès, G., 1913. Études cambodgiennes 9. Le serment des fonctionnaires de Sûryavarman Ier. *Bulletin de l'École française d'Extrême Orient* 13(6), 11–17.

Cœdès, G., 1932. Études cambodgiennes 30. A la recherche du Yaçodharāçrama. *Bulletin de l'École française d'Extrême Orient* 32(1), 84–112.

Cœdès, G., 1937–66. *Inscriptions du Cambodge. Collection de Textes et Documents sur l'Indochine*. Vol. I (1937); Vol. II (1942); Vol. III (1951); Vol. IV (1952); Vol. V (1953); Vol. VI (1954); Vol. VII (1964); Vol. VIII (1966). Paris: École française d'Extrême-Orient.

Cœdès, G., 1942. Un document capital sur le bouddhisme en Indochine: la stèle de Vat Sithor. *Studies on Buddhism in Japan* 4, 110.

Cœdès, G., 1989[1948]. Histoire ancienne des états hindouisés d'Extrême-Orient. Paris: de Boccard.

Cœdès, G., 1953. Le substrat autochtone et la superstructure indienne au Cambodge et à Java. *Cahiers d'Histoire Mondiale* 1/2, 368–77.

Cœdès, G., 1961. Les expressions vraḥ kamrateṅ añ et kamrateṅ jagat en vieux-khmèr. *The Adyar Library Bulletin* 25(1–4), 447–60.

Einoo, S., 2009. From kāmas to siddhis — Tendencies in the Development of Ritual towards Tantrism, in *Genesis and Development of Tantrism*, ed. S. Einoo. Japan: Institute of Oriental Culture, University of Tokyo, 17–40.

Estève, J. & B. Vincent, 2010. L'about inscrit du musée national du Cambodge (K. 943). Nouveaux éléments sur le bouddhisme tantrique à l'époque angkorienne. *Arts Asiatiques* 69, 133–58.

Estève, J. & D, Soutif, 2011. Les Yaśodharāśrama, marqueurs d'empire et bornes sacrées—Conformité et spécificité des stèles digraphiques khmères de la région de Vat Phu. *Bulletin de l'École française d'Extrême-Orient* (97–98), 331–55.

Estève, J., 2009. *Étude critique des phénomènes de syncrétisme religieux dans le Cambodge ancient*. PhD dissertation. Paris: École Pratique des Hautes Études.

Estève, J., 2014. L'inscription K. 237 de Prāsāt Preaḥ Khsaet. Une caturmūrti insolite? *Bulletin de l'École française d'Extrême-Orient* 100, 167–200.

Filliozat, J., 1960. Sur l'esprit de la civilisation khmère. *Cambodge d'aujourd'hui*, 21–27.

Finot, L., 1901. La religion chame d'après les monuments. *Bulletin de l'École française d'Extrême-Orient* 1(1), 12–26.

Finot, L., 1904. Notes d'épigraphie. VII. L'inscription de Práḥ Khan. *Bulletin de l'École française d'Extrême Orient* 4(3), 672–79.

Finot, L., 1915. Notes d'épigraphie. XIV. Les inscriptions du Musée de Hanoi. *Bulletin de l'École française d'Extrême Orient* 15(2), 1–38.

Finot, L., 1915. Notes d'épigraphie. XVI. L'inscription de Sdok Kak Thom. *Bulletin de l'École française d'Extrême Orient* 15(2), 53–106.

Finot, L., 1925. Inscriptions d'Angkor. *Bulletin de l'École française d'Extrême Orient* 25, 289–410.

Forest, A., 1992. *Le culte des génies protecteurs au Cambodge. Analyse et traduction d'un corpus de textes sur les neak ta*. Paris: L'Harmattan.

Francis, E., 2013. *Le discours royal dans l'Inde du Sud ancienne. Inscriptions et monuments pallava* (IVème-IXème siècles). Louvain: Peeters Publishers.

Goodall, D., 2012. Les influences littéraires indiennes dans les inscriptions du Cambodge: l'exemple d'un chef-d'œuvre inédit du VIIIe siècle (K. 1236). *CRAI 2012* I, 345–57.

Goodall, D., 2019. Nobles, Bureaucrats or Strongmen? On the "Vassal Kings" or "Hereditary Governors" of Pre-Angkorian City-States: Two Sanskrit inscriptions of Vidyāviśeṣa, Seventh-century Governor of Tamandarapura (K. 1235 and K. 604), and an Inscription of Śivadatta (K. 1150), Previously Considered a Son of Īśānavarman I. *Udaya, Journal of Khmer Studies* 14, 23–86.

Griffiths, A., 2006. *Zolang als Zon en Maan nog Schijnen*. Leiden: Leiden University.

Griffiths, A., 2009. Sūrya's Nāgas, Candra's square seat and the mounted bull with two guardians—iconographical notes on two Khmer illustrated stela inscriptions, in *Prajñādhara. Essays on Asian Art, History, Epigraphy and Culture* (in Honour of Gouriswar Bhattacharya), eds. G. Bhattacharya, Gerd J.R. Mevissen & Arundhati Banerji. Dehli: Kaveri Books, 466–79.

Jacques, C., 1994. Les kamrateṅ jagat dans l'ancien Cambodge, in *Recherches nouvelles sur le Cambodge*, ed. F. Bizot. Paris: École française d'Extrême-Orient, 213–25.

Jenner, P.N., 2009. *A Dictionary of Angkorian Khmer*. Canberra: Pacific Linguistics.

Kitiarsa, P., 2005. Beyond syncretism: hybridization of popular religion in contemporary Thailand. *Journal of Southeast Asian Studies* 36(3), 461–87.

Lévi, S., 1896. Notes sur les Indo-Scythes. *Journal Asiatique* 8, 444–84.

Morrison, K.D., 1995. Trade, urbanism, and agricultural expansion: Buddhist monastic institutions and the state in the Early Historic western Deccan. *World Archaeology* 27(2), 203–21.

Mus, P., 1933. Cultes indiens et indigènes au Champa. L'Inde pré-âryenne et l'Asie des Moussons. La religion védique et le brâhmanisme. La synthèse hindouiste. Formes actuelles des cultes chams. Les kuṭ. Le culte cham des linga. Survivances et profondeur de l'influence indienne au Champa. *Bulletin de l'École française d'Extrême Orient* 33, 367–411.

Pollock, S., 1996. The Sanskrit cosmopolis, 300–1300: Transculturation, vernacularization, and the question of ideology, in *Ideology and Status of Sanskrit, Contributions to the History of the Sanskrit Language*, ed. J.E.M. Houben. Leiden: E.J. Brill, 197–247.

Pollock, S., 2006. *The Language of the Gods in the World of Men: Sanskrit, Culture and Power in Premodern India*. Berkeley and Los Angeles: University of California Press.

Pou, S., 1989. *Nouvelles inscriptions du Cambodge I*. Paris: École française d'Extrême-Orient.

Pou, S., 2001. *Nouvelles inscriptions du Cambodge II et III*. Paris: École française d'Extrême-Orient.

Pou, S., 2011. *Nouvelles inscriptions du Cambodge IV*. Paris: L'Harmattan.

Roeské, J., 1914. Les inscriptions bouddhiques du Mont Koulen, Po'n Prâh Put Lo'. *Journal Asiatique* 11(3), 637–44.

Salomon, R., 1998. *Indian Epigraphy. A Guide to the Study of Inscriptions in Sanskrit, Prakrit, and the other Indo-Aryan Languages*. New York: Oxford University Press.

Sanderson, A., 2001. History through textual criticism in the study of Śaivism, the Pañcarātra and the Buddhist Yoginītantras, in *Les Sources et le Temps. Sources and Time*, ed. F. Grimal (A colloquium, Pondicherry, 11–13 January 1997). Paris: Institut Français de Pondichéry, 1–48.

Sanderson, A., 2003–2004. The Śaiva religion among the Khmers. Part 1. *Bulletin de l'École française d'Extrême Orient* 90–91, 349–462.

Sanderson, A., 2009. The Śaiva age: an explanation of the rise and dominance of Śaivism during the early medieval period, in *Genesis and Development of Tantrism*, ed. S. Einoo. Tokyo: Institute of Oriental Culture, University of Tokyo, 41–349.

Sanderson, A., 2018. How public was Śaivism? in *Tantric Communities in Context: Sacred Secrets and Public Rituals*, eds. N. Mirnig, M. Rastelli. & V. Eltschinger. Vienna: Austrian Academy of Sciences Press, 1–48.

Senart, É., 1883. Une inscription buddhique du Cambodge. *Revue archéologique Mars-Avril*, 182–92.

Skilling, P., 2004. *Random Jottings on Śrīghana: An Epithet of the Buddha* (Annual Report of the International Research Institute for Advanced Buddhology at Soka University for the Academic Year 2003, Vol. VII). Tokyo: The International Research Institute for Advanced Buddhology, Soka University, 147–58.

Soutif, D., 2009. *Organisation religieuse et profane du temple khmer du viie au xiiie siècle*. PhD dissertation. Paris: Université Paris III—Sorbonne Nouvelle.

24
BODIES OF GLORY
The Statuary of Angkor

Paul A. Lavy and Martin Polkinghorne

Statuary has long been a centrepiece of Khmer religious and artistic expression. Since the late 19th century, Angkorian sculpture has also attracted much outside interest from the scholarly community, including art historians, archaeologists, and curators, as well as from colonial and post-colonial politicians, art dealers, auction houses, collectors, looters, and tourists (Edwards 2007; Baptiste and Zéphir 2013; Falser 2020). It is prominently displayed in many major museums in Cambodia, Thailand, Laos, Vietnam, Singapore, Australia, Europe, Japan, and the United States, most notably the National Museum of Cambodia, Phnom Penh (Dalsheimer 2001; Jessup 2006; Khun 2008), and the Musée National des Arts Asiatiques—Guimet in Paris, France (Baptiste and Zéphir 2008). It has also been featured in numerous international exhibitions and their accompanying catalogues (e.g., Beijing Capital Museum 2015; Brand and Chuch 1992; Jessup and Zéphir 1997; Lobo and Jessup 2006; Ishizawa 2009; McCullough et al. 2018). Much of this global attention has stemmed from the singular aesthetic qualities that Khmer sculpture exhibits (Giteau 1955; Jessup 1998; Brown 2011a). Until the late 20th century, scholars tended to focus on matters of iconography, chronology, and style. Throughout the course of this work, pioneering French scholars developed a method for the study of sculpture and architecture which continues to provide the framework for much of what we know about Khmer art history (key monographs include Boisselier 1955, 1966; Coral-Rémusat 1940; Dupont 1955; Giteau 1975; Stern 1927, 1965). While new evidence and new ways of thinking have led some scholars to question many of these conventional assumptions and offer adjustments to the framework, the overall model of stylistic development developed in early French scholarship has nonetheless held up reasonably well and continues to serve as an important foundation for Khmer Studies.

At the same time, ongoing and recent research by both international and Khmer scholars—and particularly by archaeologists, epigraphers, religion specialists, and cultural historians working alongside art historians—has offered an expanded set of tools and approaches for the study of Khmer statuary. Rather than approaching through the conceptual lens of the 'artwork', we seek to integrate some of these diverse perspectives to provide an interdisciplinary, state-of-the-field assessment of the religious, political, cultural, and technological contexts of Angkorian statuary as embodiments of divinity and what, based on Angkorian inscriptions, can be called 'bodies of glory'.

DOI: 10.4324/9781351128940-30

The Religious and Temple Context of Statuary

The religious milieu of Angkorian statuary incorporated diverse elements of Brahmanism (or Hinduism), Buddhism, and autochthonous forms of spirit worship. Brahmanism and Buddhism initially spread more or less simultaneously into Southeast Asia and the Khmer cultural region during the early to-mid first millennium CE. The earliest surviving Brahmanical and Buddhist stone sculptures in Southeast Asia have been found in peninsular Thailand and probably date to ca. late 5th–early 6th centuries, with Khmer stone sculpture following shortly thereafter (Brown 2011b, 325–29; Lavy 2014). In all likelihood, wood had already served as a medium for sculpting in mainland Southeast Asia, but the earliest surviving examples in this medium seem to be Buddha images found in the Mekong Delta region that probably date to approximately the same period (Lê 2006, 33–33, 42–48). By this time, bronze technology in Southeast Asia was at least 1500 years old (e.g., Higham 2020; cf. White and Hamilton 2009), but the production of Brahmanical and Buddhist icons was also probably first applied within the region by around the 6th century (Brown 2014; Lavy 2020).

Upon arriving in Khmer lands, these Indic religions encountered what must have been well-established local and regional traditions, typically oriented around the veneration of ancestor and nature spirits (Khmer: *neak tā* or *anak tā*) associated with particular places, trees, and natural features such as mountains, hills, rocks, termite mounds, caves, and springs (Ang 1986; Forest 1992). The merging of Indic and local (i.e., pre-Indic) Khmer divinities is a defining feature of the Pre-Angkor and Angkor Periods (Jacques 1985; Vickery 1998, 139–74; Sanderson 2003/4, 377–79), and localised traditions of Vaiṣṇavism, Śaivism, and Buddhism coexisted and at times commingled (Bhattacharya 1961, 11–42; Estève 2009; Estève 2023, this volume). Each religion enjoyed particular phases of favour, but, by the 7th century, Śaivism increasingly became the predominant 'state' religion with Pāśupata Śaivism, or Atimārga, prevalent during the Pre-Angkor Period and Tantric Śaivism, or Mantramārga, characterising the Angkor Period (Sanderson 2003/4, 435). Relative to Brahmanism, both Śrāvakayāna and Mahāyāna Buddhism (Harris 2005, 6–28) enjoyed more limited support among Khmer elites until the state religion became a Śaiva-infused form of Vajrayāna (Tantric) Buddhism during the mid- to late 12th century (Sharrock 2009). After a brief Śaiva resurgence in the 13th century, Theravāda Buddhism, with continued incorporation of diverse elements of spirit worship and Brahmanism, expanded to become the central religion, both at the popular and state level (Harris 2005, 26–48; Woodward 2022).

All of these traditions involved the veneration of deity-images that were installed in temples (Figure 24.1a) and that today we view as statuary (see Figures 24.2–6). Sometimes conceived as celestial palaces, Khmer temples were the abodes of the resident deities (Dumarçay and Royère 2001 Dagens 2016, 58–104;). Like statuary, temples can also be interpreted as divine bodies (Dagens 2005[1996], 125–49). They were furthermore intentionally invested with a commemorative and funerary role in which kings and royal family members achieved a form of apotheosis through their fusion with the principal divinities residing within the shrines (Cœdès 1911a, 1951b). While the funerary associations of temples may or may not have been literally achieved through the interment of physical remains, they nevertheless functioned as 'funerary temples' (Cœdès 1940, 1963, 34–38). To serve as an appropriate home for the gods and destination for ancestral spirits, temples were extravagantly carved and decorated; while much does not survive, this could include stucco, plaster, paint, gilding, metallic casing, and carved wooden elements (Plehwe-Leisen and Leisen 2008; Cunin 2013). Together with statuary, relief sculpture of figural mythological scenes manifested divine presence, while intricate vegetal patterns emanated blessings of abundance and fertility, and motifs derived from imported Chinese silk and Indian cotton textiles further contributed to the adornment and delineation of sacred space (Green 2007).

Figure 24.1 Relief sculptures depicting deity-images in worship. a) Veneration of sculpture (Bayon, late 12th–early 13th century); b) ritual procession of sculpture (Banteay Chhmar, late 12th–early 13th century).

Source: (Photos M. Polkinghorne).

The temples that housed these statues comprised a wide range of sizes, configurations, and layouts, all of which corresponded with spatial, divine, and socio-political hierarchies. The links between Khmer architecture and sovereignty were typically expressed through mountain symbolism, which is articulated most clearly in the famed temple-mountains of Angkor (Multzer o'Naghten 2000). The ultimate origins of these stepped-pyramidal structures may be sought in prehistoric megaliths and terraces, but their distinctive form and symbolism was the result of the incorporation of Indian cosmological principles and the concept of Mt. Meru (or Mt. Sumeru) (Filliozat 1954). In both Hindu and Buddhist traditions, Mt. Meru is the centre of the universe (*axis mundi*), abode of the gods, and a cosmic pivot linking heavens, earth, and under worlds (Mabbett 1983, 66–68). Although the specific details of this cosmography vary, Mt. Meru is typically understood to be surrounded by a concentric series of ring-shaped mountains and seas. Angkor Period temples recreated this sacred geography through vertical layering, an axial and symmetrical plan, and the concentric arrangement of enclosures, tanks, and moats surrounding the central pyramidal structure with the main shrine(s) on the top housing the god(s) and ancestor(s) to whom the temple was dedicated (Dagens 2016, 105–50). By replicating the structure of the cosmos in miniature and by bridging heaven and earth, kings, as patrons of temples and statuary, sought to generate and consolidate power and to assure their kingdom's blessedness and prosperity.

Image Production

The production of Angkorian statuary was truly prodigious. In addition to the thousands of sculptures that survive to the present day, the foundation stele from the sprawling temple of Preah Khan (*nagarī* Jayaśrī), dedicated in 1191/92 CE, provides a remarkable indication of the scale of fabrication during the reign of Jayavarman VII (r. ca. 1182/83–1219/20 CE). It declares that 20,400 statues rendered in precious metals and stone were distributed across the kingdom (K. 908, D, st. CXXVII, Cœdès 1941, 280, 297). This one temple complex alone housed 430 deities surrounding the central image, with another 85 deities residing in nearby shrines (B, st. XLIII, Cœdès 1941, 275, 290). Other temples of the same reign further indicate the immense scale of production. Ta Prohm (Rājavihāra), dedicated in 1186/87 CE, housed 260 deities surrounding the principal icons (K. 273, B, st. XXXVII; Cœdès 1906, 55, 75) and hosted an annual festival with offerings to 619 deities who were present there (C, st. LXXXVIII; Cœdès 1906, 63, 78). At the nearby temple of Banteay Kdei, Japanese archaeologists excavated a cache of 274 Buddhist sculpture fragments mostly dating to ca. late 12th to early 13th centuries (Marui 2002, 411–28).

Although there were likely numerous centres and workshops of statuary manufacture, to date only three workshops have been verified through archaeological excavation (Polkinghorne et al. 2014; Polkinghorne Douglas and Carò 2015a). A stone and bronze workshop northeast of the Royal Palace in Angkor Thom and another stone workshop north of the Hariharālaya Royal Palace at Prei Monti preserve unfinished sculptures and the archaeological waste of stone and copper-base alloy production. There is some evidence that metallurgical activity also took place within the Angkor Thom Royal Palace complex (Groslier 1957), and another stone workshop may have existed at Phnom Dei north of Angkor Thom (Polkinghorne et al. 2015b).

The close proximity of the known workshops to Royal Palaces and the physical and ceremonial centres of the kingdom imply that the royal court directly commissioned their products. Specialised artisans, including sculpture stonemasons and bronze casters, were of great significance to the political administration, who employed their outputs to confer and maintain political legitimacy and spiritual authority. Additionally, the specific position of ateliers north or northeast of the Royal Palace may reproduce a tradition of urban planning observed throughout Cambodian history. For example, a representation of the Royal Palace of Oudong in the early 1860s denotes gold ateliers in the northern-eastern quadrant of the enclosure (Spooner 1864). Furthermore, royal ateliers were situated close to the northeast corner/quadrant of the Royal Palace of Phnom Penh in the early 20th century (Groslier 1921, fig. 168).

Specific materials of sculpture production were likely favoured for their supernatural properties. Research dedicated to characterising sandstone use in the Angkorian World has commonly, but not exclusively, observed two broad sandstone lithotypes for architecture and its ornamentation (Terrain Rouge and Grès Supérieur) and another two for sculptures of deities (highly specific Terrain Rouge [feldspathic arenite] and Triassic) (Carò and Douglas 2013; Carò, Polkinghorne and Douglas 2014; Douglas, Carò and Fischer 2010; Douglas and Sorensen 2007; Polkinghorne, Douglas and Carò 2015a; Fischer, Carò and Polkinghorne 2023, this volume). From at least the 12th century, the selection of sandstone for images of deities does not appear to correspond with the geological proximity or technical specifications of the material. Further research on this point is required, but specific sandstone was likely selected for its esoteric and transmundane qualities. For example, the Bakong foundation stele indicates that the central *liṅga* was made of stone procured from a riverbed (K. 826, st. XXXV; Cœdès 1937, 33, 35), and another inscription advocates the deliberate search for appropriate stone to create a sculpture (K. 245, line 17; Ang n.d.; Cœdès 1951a, 91–92).

Similarly, there is evidence of a preferred hierarchy of metals for image production based on value, magical qualities, and availability. Numerous inscriptions declare that statuary was made in precious metals (see Vincent 2012, 118–21). The Preah Khan stele lists images of 'gold, silver, bronze' (K. 908, D, st. CXXVII; Cœdès 1941, 280, 297). While inventories of metals likely relate to the extravagance of donors rather than specific donations, Soutif (2009, 355) and Vincent (2012, 207–17) argue that their order was not left to chance. For example, the Ta Prohm stele lists eight metals beginning with gold and silver, followed by copper and copper-based alloys (K. 273, B, st. LXVIII–LXXII; C, st. LXXIII–LXXV; see Cœdès 1906, 59–61, 77). Bronze composed of varying combinations of copper, tin, and lead was undoubtedly the most widely used material for metal sculptures. Use of the Old Khmer word *saṃrit* suggests sculptures were made from an esoteric copper-base or copper alloy with magical properties. Colonial observations made in the 19th and 20th centuries note that *saṃṛiddh*, the homophonic and etymological descendent of *saṃrit*, possessed supernatural virtues of success, prosperity, and abundance (Vincent 2012, 297–311), and it is probable that these associations had their origins during the Angkor Period.

Despite the application of contemporary analytical methods that can distinguish the elemental signatures of bronze sculptures, discovery of precise alloying recipes has thus far eluded researchers because images were in many cases likely composed of recycled materials (cf. Griswold 1954, 637; Malleret 1954; Strahan 1997). Nevertheless, there are some notable temporal and geographic assemblages that can be identified by alloy composition. For example, Angkor Wat style sculptures are high in tin, lead, and nickel, while Bayon style sculptures contain less lead and both high and low percentages of tin (Vincent 2012, 317–21). Likewise, workshops active in the region of Angkor have small quantities of lead and tin, while those located around Phimai produced bronzes high in both tin and lead (Drayman-Weisser Lauffenburger and Strahan 1997, 279; Vincent 2012, 317–19; Woodward 1997, 79). Other sculptures may provide clues to the rituals of casting. A Buddha found in the north library of Angkor Wat, dating to ca. second half of the 12th century, has a higher content of zinc in its head than in its body (Phnom Penh Nat Mus., Ka. 2081; Jessup and Zéphir 1997, 270–72; Vincent 2012, 330–31), while an approximately contemporary Angkor Wat style Buddha, found at the Cham site of Tháp Bánh Ít in Vietnam, has a higher gold content than its *nāga* seat (Phnom Penh Nat. Mus., Ka. 3296; Bourgarit et al. 2003, 112–18; Jessup and Zéphir 1997, 272–73). Although more research is required, one explanation is that the metals of higher value were ritually reserved for the most auspicious components of the sculptures during the manufacturing process.

Image Concepts, Consecration, and Veneration

Whether made of metal, stone, or wood, inscriptions refer to temple statuary, or what can be called 'deity-images' (Colas 2009, 100), using a range of Sanskrit and Old Khmer terms adapted from Indian traditions, in which we find a wealth of image-related terminology and concepts with complex histories, permutations, contestations, and various doctrinal specificities (e.g., Banerjea 1985, 36–40; Padoux 1990; Colas 2004, 2012). To what extent the meanings of these terms shifted in the Khmer context—and they almost certainly did—is not always evident, and meaning cannot be assumed on the basis of Indian analogies alone (Maxwell 2007, 121). An example of a distinctive use of statuary in Khmer culture, apparently unique in early South and Southeast Asian art, was the dramatic arrangement of large-scale three-dimensional stone sculpture to portray narratives from the *Rāmāyana* and *Mahābhārata* at Prasat Chen, one of the temples in the 10th-century royal complex of Koh Ker (Bourdonneau 2011, 116–118).

As in South Asia, a commonly employed designation for a statue, image, or icon is *pratimā*, which in the Khmer context occurs in both Sanskrit and Old Khmer inscriptions (Jenner 2009b, 361; Pou 1992, 305). In Sanskrit (from *prati* + root *mā*-, "to copy" or "to imitate"), it carries connotations of symbol, likeness, and effigy. Another translation is 'reflected image', with a possible dual sense, in India at least, of a 'reflection' of the likeness of divinity as well as the reception and 'reflection' of worship from image to deity (Liebert 1986, 227). Numerous instances of the erection of *pratimā* of various Hindu deities and Buddha statues occur in the corpus of surviving inscriptions, with some examples illustrated in Table 24.1. An Old Khmer term *vuddhapratimā* (Skt.: *buddhapratimā*) is also used to occasionally reference Buddha images (e.g., K. 453/1206; Cœdès 1951a, 117).

Another general term for deity-images, sometimes used interchangeably with *pratimā*, is *arcā* (Old Khmer: *'arccā*), which literally means 'worshipping' or 'worship' (Jenner 2009b, 728; Pou 1992, 24), and typically referred to material images as embodiments of deities that were intended for devotional rituals. One inscription (K. 230/1026 CE, line 16), for example, records the casting of an *'arccā* of the Bodhisattva Lokeśvara (Cœdès 1954, 240–46). A second inscription (K. 277N, line 29) mentions an offering of regalia to an *'arccā* and to dancers (Cœdès 1952, 155–59).

Table 24.1 Epigraphic references for the emplacement of *pratimā* (likenesses) of Hindu deities and Buddha statues.

Inscription number/date	*Stanza*	*Contextual information*	*Example*	*References*
K. 713/880	28	foundation stele of Preah Ko	three *pratimā* of Īśa (Śiva) and three of the goddess	Cœdès 1937, 21
K. 324/893	B1	Lolei Northeast Tower, door jamb	*pratimā* of Śiva and Gaurī (Pārvatī)	Bergaigne 1893, 327
K. 323/893	59	foundation stele of Lolei	four *pratimā* of Śiva and Śarvāṇī (Pārvatī)	Bergaigne 1893, 399, 408
K. 235/1052 or 1053	LVIII (58)	Sdok Kak Thom stele	*pratimā* of Hara (Śiva), Viṣṇu, and Sarasvatī	Cœdès and Dupont 1943–6, 81, 98;
K. 504/1183 (Th. 25)	Lines 2–3	'Buddha of Grahi' in the National Museum, Bangkok	*pratimā* of the Buddha	Cœdès 1918, 34–5; Cœdès 1961[1929], XXV, 29–31

Other related terminology includes the term *rūpa* (also Old Khmer: *rūpa, rūppa,* and *rupa*), meaning form, shape, representation, image, figure, and so on (Jenner 2009b, 481; Pou 1992, 406); *mūrti* (Old Khmer: *mūrtti*), meaning manifestation, incarnation, embodiment, representation, and so on (Jenner 2009b, 442); *deva*, meaning deity or god (Jenner 2009b, 258); *devatā*, or deity (Jenner 2009b, 259); and, particularly for Śiva images, *liṅga*, meaning mark, sign, or emblem (Jenner 2009a, 427; Jenner 2009b, 505; Pou 1992, 419). Most commonly, *liṅga* (Figure 24.2a) were phallic pillars of carved stone; however, the term could also apply to naturally occurring or *svayambhū* (self-existing) *liṅga*, anthropomorphic images, and hybrid *liṅga* with Śiva's face(s). Moreover, due to the strong influence of Śaivism at Angkor, the term *liṅga* could also designate other deities, for example, the Bodhisattva Lokeśvara (Sanderson 2003/4, 424–25).

While Brahmanical beliefs and practices varied widely across South and Southeast Asia, cult images were often brought into worship through installation rituals that animated the image as a dwelling for the deity and, in some contexts, led to the identification of the material image as the body of god (Clementin-Ojha 1990; Colas 2012; Davis 1997; Eck 1998). Beginning during the Pre-Angkor Period and with greater frequency during the Angkor Period, the terms *pratiṣṭhā* and *supratiṣṭhā* are encountered in inscriptions to designate the ritual establishment, installation, consecration, or dedication of images, temples, steles, and so on (Jenner 2009a, 330, 525; 2009b, 362, 655). As described in South Asian Hindu, Buddhist, and Jain texts, pratiṣṭhā ceremonies varied according to place, time, and context and could involve not just initial consecration but also reinstallation and rehabilitation (Colas 2010; Einoo and Takashima 2005; Gonda 1975; Keul 2017). In general, however, they were concerned with the endowment of the material image with life, knowledge, divine presence, and supernatural powers so that it became 'an effectual means of contact between the divinity and the worshipper' (Hikita 2005, 143).

Figure 24.2 Brahmanical (Hindu) deities. a) Śiva *liṅga* (Ka. 034, N. 560, Angkor National Museum; Image courtesy Angkor National Museum]; b) Viṣṇu (Angkor Wat, 12th century, Ka. 37, Angkor National Museum; Image courtesy Angkor National Museum); c) goddess (Samrong Tong, late 7th–early 8th century, Ka. 1609, Angkor National Museum; Image courtesy Angkor National Museum).

Angkorian inscriptions do not provide descriptions of *pratiṣṭhā* ceremonies, but several refer to the awakening of divinities through an eye-opening ceremony (*unmīlita*) (Bizot 1994, 105, 123; Jenner 2009b, 769), also known in Indian Sanskrit texts as *nayanonmīlana* and by other names (Hikita 2005, 191–94). For example, the Preah Khan stele declares that King Jayavarman 'opened the eyes of [the Boddhisattva] Lokeśa [Avalokiteśvara] under the name Lord Jayavarmeśvara' (K. 908, A, st. XXXIV, in Cœdès 1941, 274–75, 288). Other instances of *unmīlita* are recorded in various inscriptions: K. 908, C, st. CXII (Cœdès 1941, 279, 295); K. 235D, lines 46, 48, 49, 60 (Cœdès and Dupont 1943–46, 90–91, 123, 125); K. 412, line 6 (Cœdès 1961, 16–18); and K. 1141, st. 13 (Pou 2001, 115–18). This ceremony, still practised to consecrate contemporary Buddha images, entailed ritually inscribing, painting, or affixing semi-precious or precious stones to open the statue's eyes (Bizot 1994, 105–59; Swearer 2004, 94–107, 189, 215).

Consecration ceremonies probably also included, at least in certain contexts, a sprinkling of water upon the deity-image (*abhiṣeka*). Like the eye-opening ceremony, *abhiṣeka* rituals have a long history of development and variability in Hinduism and Buddhism (Colas 2010, 332; Davidson 2012; Orzech 2011; Swearer 2004). They originated in South Asia as part of the coronation of kings (*rājasūya, rājyābhiṣeka*, etc.) before being adapted into pratiṣṭhā ceremonies and *pūjā* (worship) practices (Geslani 2017; Tsuchiyama 2005). That some version of these ceremonies was known to Khmer elites is indicated by references in inscriptions (Jenner 2009b, 724; Pou 1992, 17) and by the 7th-century lintel of Wat Eng Khna, which portrays a royal *abhiṣeka* scene (Southworth 2012). Unlike the eye-opening ceremony, however, Angkorian inscriptions do not explicitly mention anointment with water as part of image consecration ceremonies. In any case, epigraphic evidence and the presence of ablution basins (*snānadroṇī*) with drainage spouts on *liṅga* bases and on many image pedestals (*bhadrāsana*) indicate that ritual bathing of images must have been a regular practice (K. 908, D, st. CLXVI, Cœdès 1941, 282, 299; Jenner 2009b, 687; Soutif 2009, 221–25). Such baths and lustrations (Skt.: *snāna*, *snāpana*; Old Khmer: *sroṅ*) would have involved not only water but, depending on circumstances, might also have included milk, clarified butter (Skt.: *ghṛta*), honey, molasses, and sesame oil, among other liquids (K. 908, B, st. LVII–LX; Cœdès 1941, 276, 291; Soutif 2009, 250).

Also depending on the circumstances, worship of deity-images (Figure 24.1a) might occur daily, at regular calendrical or seasonal intervals, or on the occasions of particular festivals and holy days and were often undertaken on a colossal scale (e.g., K. 713, Cœdès 1937, 17–31; K. 273, Cœdès 1906; K. 908, Cœdès 1941). Offerings were varied and included such things as food, spices, flowers, perfumes and fragrant resins, incense, beeswax, vessels and utensils made of precious metals, palanquins, furniture, lamps, mirrors, umbrellas, fans, cushions, textiles, mosquito nets, clothing, jewellery, and mobile iconographic accessories (Soutif 2009). Deity-images were also honoured in processions (Figure 24.1b), with music and dance and, at least in certain specific cases, through clockwise circumambulation (*pradakṣiṇa*) (K. 273, C, st. LXXXV, Cœdès 1906, 62, 78).

Rites dedicated to other supernatural beings were also likely to have occurred during the production of Brahmanical and Buddhist images. The most featured deity on architectural decorative lintels and also known in freestanding sculpture was the divine architect, Viśvakarman. Although there is no material or epigraphic evidence linking Viśvakarman to sculpture production, there are indications that reverence of him played some role. All Cambodian artists venerate his contemporary descendent, Braḥ Biṣnukār in the production of creative arts (Ang 1986, 145; Dolias 1990; Dupaigne 2016, 171–76). Similarly, some acknowledgement of ancient animist spirits like Kruṅ Bālī was logically crucial to guarantee successful sculptures and the ritual and physical safety of the artists and community (cf. Ang 1986, 18–19, note 31; Porée-Maspero 1961).

Statues, Spirits, and Ancestors

The original (first millennium CE) diffusion of Śaiva forms of Hinduism may have had a particular resonance with pre-Indic Southeast Asian belief-systems. At times in both India and Southeast Asia, Śiva, a deity intimately tied to agriculture and fecundity, became assimilated with local spirits dwelling under or within the earth (chthonic) (e.g., Chaudhuri 1939; Chakravarti 1994, 94–97, 106–42). In particular, the liṅga (Figure 24.2a) may have been readily identified with ancestral spirits, territorial divinities, and pre-Indic earth gods that had been represented in the form of rough stones or megaliths (Ang 1995). Thus, the Śiva-liṅga became an expression of 'old territorial rituals in which the materialisation of the god of the soil, in the person of a dynastic ancestor, expressed the contract, defined in time and space, of the group with its territory' (Mus 2011, 62). Moreover, because many of these liṅga were named after the forms of Śiva associated with pilgrimage sites in India, the sacred Śaiva landscape of India was replicated in, or relocated to, the lands of the Khmer (Sanderson 2003/4, 403–21).

The close association of Śiva and chthonic cults is particularly evident in the preference for situating Śiva temples on hills or mountaintops or in close proximity to prominent geological features like caves and springs, as can be seen, for example, at the small cave temples of Kampot, Cambodia (some dating as early as the 7th c.), which consist of brick shrines situated so that the natural and growing vertical axes of stalagmites and stalactites constitute dynamic liṅga-like foci for devotion (Bruguier 1998). However, it is perhaps Wat Phu in southern Laos (ca. 7th–12th c. with earlier origins) that provides the premier example. It was built on the slopes of a mountain, today known as Mt. Phu Kao, with a liṅga-like crowning rock formation. Pre-Angkor and Angkor Period inscriptions refer to the mountain as *liṅgaparvataḥ* and *liṅgādriḥ* ('mountain of the liṅga') and the nearby town as *liṅgapura* ('city of the liṅga'). The mountain was furthermore venerated as a liṅga named Niṣkala, probably to be understood as a natural, undifferentiated, and self-existing (Skt.: *svayambhū*) form of Śiva manifested permanently and unconditionally in the landscape (Sanderson 2003/4, 410–11). Among the particular features of the Wat Phu sanctuary was a seemingly unique system of water management for ritual purposes. Behind the temple, there is a cave at the foot of a cliff which perpetually seeps water. This spring water was apparently channelled along a small stone aqueduct to the temple, where it perpetually lustrated the main cult image, probably a liṅga, before being channelled out of the temple to consecrate the surrounding land (Santoni et al. 1997).

Similar divine sanctification of water through carved imagery occurred on an even larger scale at the famous site of Kbal Spean, a hill in the Kul'en massif in Siem Reap province. The Kulen plateau is the likely location of Mahendraparvata (Chevance et al. 2019) where, according to the Sdok Kak Thom inscription, Jayavarman II initiated the Devarāja rituals in 802 CE that made him a sovereign *cakravartin* (Skt.: universal monarch), an act sometimes associated with the Prasat Rong Chen on the Kulen plateau and conventionally seen as defining the start of the Angkor Period (Mabbett 1969; Kulke 1978; Chevance et al. 2013; Bourdonneau 2016). At nearby Kbal Spean, a ca. 200-metre stretch of a river's bed and banks was carved during the 11th–12th century with hundreds of liṅga and numerous images of Viṣṇu Anantāśāyana (Viṣṇu reclining upon the serpent Ananta) (Boulbet and Dagens 1973). The Kbal Spean River is a tributary of the Siem Reap River, which delivered water from the Kulen massif to the temples of Angkor about 40 km to the southwest (Fletcher et al. 2008). Thus, the Kbal Spean River of 'a thousand lingas' (Skt./Old Khmer: *sahasraliṅga*; K. 1011; Jacques 1999, 3–4) was a potent conduit for the delivery of holy water and divine blessings from the abode of gods on sacred Mahendraparvata downstream to the temples and divine images of Angkor.

Most, if not all, Angkorian deity-images (Figure 24.2), liṅga included, also doubled as images of kings, royal family members, royal gurus, heroes, and so on (Cœdès 1911a, 1951b, 1963, 22–33; Maxwell 2007, 119–20; Maxwell 2009). Equivalences between ancestor spirits and deities were established in the poetry of inscriptions in which the composite names given to deity-images combined a personal name—either the person who commissioned the image or that of a designated recipient of honour—and a term referencing the chosen deity, such as *-iśvara* for Śiva, *-nārāyaṇa* for Viṣṇu, *Surya-* or *-āditya* for the sun god Surya, and *-devī* or *-īśvarī* for the Goddess. Further personalisation may have occurred through the investment of corporeal remains or personal items into the statue, although the clearest evidence for such practices dates to later periods. An inscription of 1577/8 CE, for example, records the pious resolve of Queen Mother Mahākalyāṇavattī Srī Sujātā, who cut off her hair—perhaps shaving her head—so that it could be burned and the ashes added to a resinous varnish (*kmuk, kmuka,* or *khmuk*) for coating Buddha images at Angkor Wat (IMA 2 in Lewitz 1970, 103–4; Jenner 2009b, 70; 2011, 25; Khin 1980, 134, n. 7; Pou 1989, 30–31).

Personalisation of images was applied to Buddhist divinities, most notably during the reign of Jayavarman VII (Figure 24.3). In 1186/87 CE he dedicated an image of the Buddhist goddess Prajñāpāramitā ('perfection of wisdom') named Jayarājacūḍāmaṇī and embodying his mother (K. 273, A, st. XXXVI; Cœdès 1906, 55, 75). And in 1191/92 he dedicated the aforementioned image of the Bodhisattva Lokeśa named Jayavarmeśvara as an 'image of [his] father' (K. 908, A, st. XXXIV; Cœdès 1941, 274–75, 288). Similarly, a form of apotheosis was sought for kings through the bestowal of posthumous names that indicated the union of king and god, the attainment of heaven, and/or the fulfilment of religious objectives. Examples of this include king Suryavarman II's posthumous name Paramaviṣṇuloka ('He who has gone to the highest world of Viṣṇu'; K. 298; Cœdès 1911b, 201; Maxwell 2006, 7) and Jayavarman VII's posthumous name, Mahāparamasaugatapada, meaning he who 'has attained the domain reached by those who are supremely devoted to the Buddha' (K. 569/1303 CE, line 9; Finot, Parmentier

Figure 24.3 Personalisation of images during the reign of Jayavarman VII. a) Presumed portrait of King Jayavarman VII (Ta Prohm [?], late 12th–early 13th century, P 430, Musée national des arts asiatiques—Guimet; Image RMN-Grand Palais/Art Resource, NY); b) presumed portrait of Queen Jayarājadevī (Preah Khan, late 12th–early 13th century, MG 18043, Musée national des arts asiatiques—Guimet; Image RMN-Grand Palais/Art Resource, NY); c) Buddha–Lokeśvara–Prajñāpāramitā triad (Dang Run, late 12th–early 13th century, Ga. 4417, National Museum of Cambodia; Image courtesy the National Museum of Cambodia).

and Goloubew 1926, 79, 81; Pou 2001, 166–71; Sanderson 2003/4, 429). In South Asian Hindu contexts this practice of identifying royalty with deities is well-attested (Nilakanta Sastri 1957–8; Sengupta 2005), but, unlike Southeast Asia, its application to Buddhist divinities was perhaps unknown there (Sanderson 2003/4, 426–7).

The ancestral component of deity-images is also evoked through the Sanskrit term *yaśaḥśarīra*, literally meaning 'body in the form of fame' (Apte 1959, 1307) or 'body of glory' (Jenner 2009b, 452, 587). In an inscription from the temple of Lolei in the early Angkorian capital of Hariharālaya, King Yaśovarman addresses his successors as, 'You, who have a permanent body of glory' (*yaśaśśarīrā*) while urging them to protect his various religious dedications, which are a 'bridge of merit' (*dharma*) (K. 324/893 CE, st. III; Bergaigne 1893, 325–6). Because these dedications at Lolei included four images of Śiva and his consort installed in honour of the king's ancestors, the 'body of glory' amounted to an enduring fusion of the royal ancestors, the reigning king, and his successors (see K. 323, st. 59; Bergaigne 1893, 399, 408). Similarly, the term *yaśaśśarīre* appears in the Pre Rup foundation inscription, in which King Rajendravarman exhorts his descendants, through funeral rites and the consecration of an image, 'to give life to the *dharma* in my body of glory' or, in other words, to animate the king's *dharma* in an image that will perpetuate his fame (K. 806/961 CE, st. CCXCIII; Cœdès 1937, 104, 142; 1940, 325–28). Thus *yaśaḥśarīra* statues can be said to represent 'the concentration of past and future, of ancestors and successors' (Thompson 2008, 187–88), to function as 'bridges' between generations, and to embody a form of immortality through perpetuation of *dharma* (Cœdès 1963, 27–28; Mabbett 1969, 216).

Can we label Angkorian statuary 'portraiture'? If so, it seems that some individuals, both posthumously and while still living, were portrayed according to various degrees of idealisation and physiognomic likeness in the guise of divinities (cf. Klokke 1994). Particular Pre-Angkorian statues, like the eight-armed Viṣṇu from Phnom Da (ca. late 6th or 7th c.) and the Harihara of Prasat Andet (ca. late 7th–early 8th c.), have been interpreted as idealised portraits of specific Pre-Angkorian kings, depicting traces of ageing and even physical aberrations (Cooler 1978, 33–34). More convincing arguments regarding physical likeness have been made about a remarkable series of late 12th–early 13th century sculptures believed to depict King Jayavarman VII (Figure 24.3a) and his family (Figure 24.3b–c) as Mahāyāna Buddhist devotees and divinities (Cœdès 1958, 1960, 1963, 92; Jessup and Zéphir 1997, 300–7, 324–25; Pottier 2000, 2015; Thompson 2008). These or similar statues are likely referenced in the Phimeanakas inscription which states that Jayavarman's first queen, Jayarājadevī, 'everywhere erected her mother, her father, her brothers, friends, and relatives, known to her or whom she had heard about' (K. 485, st. XCIII; Cœdès 1942, 180) and that, after her death, her older sister and Jayavarman's second queen, Indradevī, 'erected many images of Jayarājadevī, along with images of herself, and the king in every city' (st. XCVI) (Figure 24.3b). Irrespective of when the portrait-as-physical-likeness was introduced, it is probably not possible to draw a strong distinction between idealistic and realistic representations in Khmer art (Thompson 2008, 183). Ambiguity in visual language, like punning and double-entendres in Angkorian inscriptions, was probably intentional, with the objective being to bring about a total fusion of individuals, ancestors, and gods, or, as stated by Mabbett, 'to fit the world of men to the shape of the world of the gods according to sacred ritual, and thus make possible the transmission of favours and salvation from one world to the other' (1969, 214–19).

Distribution of Statuary and Political Consolidation

In addition to representations of divinities, spirits, and ancestors, the embodiment of elite individuals within images can also be understood as an imperial strategy for expressing, maintaining, and extending political power (cf. Morrison 2001; Sinopoli 2003). Through the distribution of sculptures, embodiments of divinities, and artistic styles from the centre, the Angkorian elite articulated their power via symbolic means without necessarily resorting to coercion; the foundation for such practices were probably laid during the Pre-Angkor Period (Bhattacharya 1964; Lavy 2003). Statues were symbols of incontrovertible supernatural legitimacy and mutually intelligible symbols of power that transmitted the radiating ideology of the state (cf. Tambiah 1976).

In the aforementioned inscription of Lolei, King Yaśovarman describes the installation of four statues as 'works of his own art' (*sva śilpa racita*), ostensibly connecting himself to the style of the sculpture (K. 323, st. 58–59, Bergaigne 1893, 399, 408). Accordingly, Thompson (2008, 181–83, 200) argues that each period's style was in some way a recognised representation of the reigning king. Thus when sculptures of a particular style were distributed throughout the kingdom, or manufactured on its periphery, they were understood as agents of Angkor's imperial cosmology. During the time of Jayavarman VII, 25 radiating Lokeśvara (Figure 24.4a), named Jayabuddhamahānātha, were distributed throughout the kingdom as objects of esoteric or Tantric worship (K. 908, D, st. CLIX; Cœdès 1941, 281, 298; 1963, 99–100; Woodward 1994/5, 105–11). Previously in the same inscription (K. 908, C–D, st. CXV–CXXI; Cœdès 1941, 279, 295–96), 23, rather than 25, Jayabuddhamahānātha images are mentioned in association with the locations where they were installed. Maxwell (2007, 80–82, 95) supposes that two more images had been added as work on the inscription progressed. At the same time, the so-called portrait images of Jayavarman VII were transported from a single point of creation to the farthest reaches of the king's influence. Similarly, the large number of Buddha–Lokeśvara–Prajñāpāramitā triads (Figure 24.3c) may be interpreted as ambassadors of Jayavarman VII's state ideology in

Figure 24.4 Sculptural innovation, archaism, and transformation. a) Radiant Lokeśvara (Jayabuddhamahānātha [?]) (Don Tei, late 12th–early 13th century, DCA. 5739); b) Rājendradevī in the form of Gaurī (Lolei, 12th century, Ka. 1645, National Museum of Cambodia; Image courtesy the National Museum of Cambodia); c) Lokeśvara transformed into Śiva (Bakong, late 12th–early 13th century, DCA. 4690; Image courtesy EFEO, EFEO_CAM07988).

which the king, his mother, and his father are embodied as Buddhahood, wisdom, and compassion, respectively (cf. Woodward 1994/95, 106).

Conversely, mutual obligation, and allegiance to Angkor was also assured by the representation of regional deities in the central state temples of the capital. Inscriptions at the Bayon and Preah Khan indicate statuary from the provinces were sheltered in subsidiary shrines. For example, K. 908 states that in the month of Phālguna each year, several important regional deities were brought to the Preah Khan temple, including the 25 images of the Jayabuddhamahānātha, Śrī Vīraśakti from Wat Nokor in Kampong Cham, Vimāya from Phimai in northeast Thailand, Bhadreśvara from Wat Phu in Laos, Cāmpeśvara whose residence is unknown, Pṛthuśaileśvara from Phanom Rung in northeast Thailand, and their attendant deities numbering 122 images (K. 908, D, st. CLVIII—CLX; Cœdès 1941, 281–82, 298–99).

Possession of statuary was invested with sacred and royal potency, and the fragmentation of Cambodian polities has at times been explained by the theft or destruction of images. Versions of the Ayutthayan chronicles report that during the invasion of Angkor, images, including those of animals, were brought to Ayutthaya (Cushman 2000, 15). In Early Modern Cambodia the disappearance and demolition of the named Buddha images Braḥ Buddh Tralaeṅ Kaeṅ (installed at Wat Trâleng Kèng) and the Braḥ Buddh Kāyasiddhi (installed at Wat Preah In Tép), contrived by two imposter monks, is said to have presaged the fall of Longvek (Laṅvaek) (Khin 1988, 191–93, 347–54). During the same period, the capture of two spirits, possibly embodied in images—the brothers Preah Kô (Braḥ Go) and Preah Keo (Braḥ Kaev)—is thought to explain an enduring Cambodian cultural rupture at the hands of rival foreign powers (Ang 1997; Khing 1991; Mak 1984, 79–80, 83–85, 114–15, 152).

Archaising and Iconoclasm

Angkorian artisans and religious devotees were aware of their own art history, and we know of numerous instances of 'archaism', in which images are deliberately produced in older styles (e.g. Coral Rémusat 1940, 47; Polkinghorne 2007, 157–59). This suggests that specific deities were bound to particular representations of dress and iconography. For example, a 12th-century archaising sculpture of Rājendradevī in the form of Gaurī (Figure 24.4b), identified by an inscription in the southwest sanctuary tower of Lolei temple, reproduces the original 9th-century sculpture of Indravarman I's maternal grandmother, evidently in an act of piety and deference to a specific style (Ka. 1645; K. 331, in Aymonier 1883, 470; 1901, 456–57). At the same time, combining stylistic and petrographic analysis has shown that numerous 12th-century images produced at Hariharālaya imitated styles of the 8th–9th centuries (Polkinghorne, Douglas and Carò 2015). Even though the political administration had relocated from Hariharālaya to Yaśodharapura many centuries before this 12th-century production of archaised statuary, it is clear that investing resources in maintaining and restoring statuary and deities of their predecessors remained politically and religiously expedient.

When Angkorian religious or political institutions did not align with the belief systems of previous elites, there is some evidence of this conflict rendered on statuary. Although we may never recognise the perpetrators or fully understand their motivations, the most-cited example is the immense destruction of Buddhist temple reliefs supposedly carved during the reign of Jayavarman VII. Nearly all early Mahāyāna Buddhist iconography on the Angkorian temples was defaced. At the Bayon temple a second phase of vandalism is evidenced by reworking of the first iconoclasm, possibly to re-establish Buddhist pre-eminence (see Cœdès 1968, 212). While sectarian rivalries were not unknown in Khmer history (e.g., Goodall et al. 2021), the obliteration of Buddhist images as a result of devout fundamentalism is anomalous (cf. Estève 2009), and some writers have suggested that the reaction was not primarily religious but instead political and focused on statuary linked to officials and dignitaries (Maxwell 2007, 121). Brahmanism and Buddhism continued to coexist and, in contrast to temple reliefs, comparatively few sculptures from this period show evidence of desecration, including the central Buddhist image of the Bayon (Polkinghorne et al. 2013). Nevertheless, a small group of sculptures was transformed from Buddhist to Brahmanical deities, possibly during this time. One example is a Lokeśvara (Figure 24.4c) from Bakong whose defining emblem of a chignon-adorned Adi-Buddha was replaced with a crescent moon and the addition of a third eye which modified the image into Śiva (see EFEO_CAM07987–EFEO_CAM07989).

The Emergence of Theravada, 'Disposal', and Continuity

The most significant influence on Cambodia's statuary from the late 13th century through the Early Modern Period was the ascendancy of Theravāda Buddhism (Thompson 2022). Theravāda was recognised and practised in the Angkorian World, but it was not until the end of the 1200s that this form of Buddhism, probably inspired by members of the *saṅgha* travelling from what are now central and northeastern Thailand, gained importance at Angkor (Woodward 2022). Like Brahmanism before it, Theravāda followed a longstanding pattern of coalescence with local and animist spirits in sites and in sculptures (Assavavirulhakarn 2010; Mus 2011; Thompson 1998). Cambodian Theravāda images of the Buddha are embodiments of the living Buddha, *dharma*, deceased ancestors, tutelary genies, and local spirits (Ang 1986, 134, 220; 1995, 215–18, 228–29; Bizot 1994). From this period several iconic representations of the so-called historical Buddha existed side by side: in *parinirvāṇa* (Figure 24.5a), seated and protected by a *nāga* in *dhyānamudrā*, seated in *māravijaya* (Figure 24.5b), standing with two hands raised in *vitarkamudrā*, one or two hands raised in *abhayamudrā* (Figure 24.5c), or standing with one hand at the side and the other in a hand-on-chest gesture (Figure 24.5d) (Lavy 2012; Woodward 1997, 113–24). Theravāda architectural ensembles often required monumental images of the Buddha to be placed atop ritually interred images. Colossal images of seated Buddha in *māravijaya* at Tep Pranam (Marchal 1950) and Phnom Bakheng (Dumarçay 1971, 15–16) above caches of 'disposed' images explain the large cache of Buddha fragments at Banteay Kdei, mentioned previously, which was likely a ritual deposit rather than a collection of discarded images (Marui 2002, 411–28). New iconographic models emerged as Angkor declined and other Cambodian capitals achieved pre-eminence. In the 16th century at the capital of Longvek, King Ang Chan commissioned four Buddha images positioned back to back facing the cardinal directions in *abhayamudrā*. Also associated with a *stūpa*, this template was a metaphorical representation of Maitreya, the future Buddha (Khin 1988, 149–50; Thompson 2004).

Although the seat of Post-Angkorian (or Middle Period) Cambodian political authority moved south to capitals along the Mekong and Tonle Sap rivers, Angkor nevertheless remained a spiritual centre. In Theravāda Buddhism, commissioning, making, and donating images accumulates merit (Pali: *puñña*), resulting in favourable rebirth (Bizot 1994; Swearer 2004). Correspondingly from around the early to mid-16th century, Angkor, and specifically Angkor Wat, was the focus of pilgrimage, donation, and restoration within Cambodian and other Southeast Asian Theravāda belief systems (Thompson 2004, Polkinghorne 2022). Inscriptions dating between the 16th and 18th centuries establish Angkor Wat as the destination for devotees who attained Buddhist merit by reciting a 'vow of truth' (Middle Khmer: *sādhupraṇidhāna* or *sātapraṇīdhāna*; Skt.: *satyapraṇidhāna*) (Jenner 2011, 200, 358; Thompson

Figure 24.5 Types of Buddha images from the late Angkor and Middle Periods. a) Buddha in *parinirvāṇa* (Wat Preah Ngok [Angkor Thom], late 13th century, DCA. 763, N. 308; Image courtesy Angkor National Museum); b) Buddha seated in *māravijaya* (Tep Pranam, late 14th century) (Photo M. Polkinghorne); c) standing Buddha with left hand raised in *abhayamudrā* (Angkor Wat, 16th century [?], DCA. Ka. 157; N. 1322; Image courtesy Angkor National Museum); d) standing Buddha with one hand at the side and the other in a hand-on-chest gesture (Phnom Bakheng, late 13th–early 14th century [?], DCA. Ka. 274, N. 1000; Image courtesy Angkor National Museum).

2004). The epigraphy additionally attests to the endowment of statuary, materials for their manufacture, and dutiful maintenance as habitual acts of honouring deities, ancestors, and royalty (e.g. IMA 4 in Lewitz 1971, 112). The specific focus of donations at Angkor Wat was Preah Pean, or the Hall of a Thousand Buddhas, known by that toponym from the 1600s (IMA 11 in Lewitz 1972). Many inscriptions tell of the command, gift, and repair of Buddhist statuary. One example declares that six pious commoners installed 19 new or restored statues of the Buddha (IMA 16b in Lewitz 1972). The proliferation of images also continued at the Bakan, the third and highest terrace of Angkor Wat, and it is estimated that more than 500 images of the Buddha were cared for at Angkor Wat until rearrangement of the galleries by École française d'Extrême-Orient conservators in the early 20th century (Polkinghorne 2022).

Concluding Remarks: Towards the Present

In spite of changing religious and historical contexts, the statuary of the Pre-Angkor, Angkor, and Post-Angkor Periods has continued to play vital spiritual and political roles in Khmer culture up to the present. While precise meanings have changed, old sculptures are often subject to continued and/or renewed veneration, usually in connection with various forms of Khmer animism (e.g., Ang 1997). In addition to their centrality in Buddhist devotional practices discussed previously, Buddha images and their pedestals may host spirits (*boramei* or *bray preah pāramī*) which act as temple guardians (Ang 1988, 37–38; Bizot 1994, 110–19; Harris 2005, 52–59). The aforementioned tutelary spirits, *neak tā*—associated with localities, territories, and often with heroes and ancestors—can be materialised in ancient Hindu and sometimes Buddhist statuary, contemporary sculpture, and sculpted images that blend the old and the new (Guillou 2017; Miura 2004, 51–81). Veneration of *boramei* or *neak tā* embodied in statues can often be seen at Cambodian temples, museums, and even storage facilities and, in some cases, may involve recent replicas or restorations of particularly potent ancient images (Miura 2015).

Among the most well-known examples are the various sculptures in Siem Reap and Phnom Penh associated with the legend of the Leper King (Stec Gaṃlaṅ or Sdach Komlong) (Miura 2015, 272–80). Perhaps dating as early as the late 12th or early 13th century, the 'original' sandstone statue of the Leper King (Figure 24.6a), which probably represents Yama ('the god

Figure 24.6 Angkorian statuary venerated in the present: a) Leper King (Yama, 13th century [?], Ga. 1860, National Museum of Cambodia) [Image courtesy the National Museum of Cambodia]; b) Ta Reach (Standing Avalokiteśvara/Neak Ta, Angkor Wat, late 12th–early 13th century).

Source: (Photo M. Polkinghorne).

of law who is the god of death'), is intimately associated with Angkorian sovereignty, narratives of Angkor's decline, and the reestablishment of cosmic and political order (Chandler 1979). Today it is housed in the National Museum, Phnom Penh, while a cement replica occupies a prominent shrine in the museum's courtyard and receives regular veneration. A counterpart is nearly identical to ca. 12th–13th-century sandstone image (save for the head, which is a cement replacement) enshrined on a traffic island in Siem Reap Town, where it is venerated as Yiey Tep ('divine female ancestor'). Numerous replicas of these images have been made in stone and cement (or concrete), but, irrespective of material, alterations, or questions of originality, they, together with their *boramei*, are routinely worshipped for protection, health, prosperity, and 'political integrity' (Hang 2004). With a similar role, there is the 3.5-meter-tall statue of the Ta Reach (Figure 24.6b) enshrined near the western gateway of Angkor Wat's third enclosure. Probably originally a late 12th- or early 13th-century sculpture of the Bodhisattva Avalokiteśvara, it has been much restored, and today it is venerated as the 'King of Spirits' and the embodiment of Angkor's royal ancestors (Warrack 2013).

Angkorian statuary has also acquired new functions and expanded significance: designation as artwork and archaeological artefact; political symbol; local/national/global heritage; commodity; and vehicle for cultural renewal, historic preservation, and economic opportunity (Abbe 2014, Biddulph 2018; Edwards 2007; Eggert 2011; Falser 2020; Grant Ross 2015; Hauser-Schäublin 2011). Changing forms of valuation have also led to calamitous levels of looting, destruction, and forgery (Davis and Mackenzie 2015; Hauser-Schäublin and Kim 2016; Lafont 2004; Mackenzie and Davis 2014; Miura 2016) but also to occasional repatriation (Hauser-Schäublin 2016; Chea, Moung and Tythacott 2021) and collaboration (Warrack 2013). Through all of these diverse 'lives' (Davis 1997) and their ever-growing fame (*yaśas*), Angkorian 'bodies of glory' persist in their capacity to inspire as they bind together past, present, and future generations.

References

Abbe, G., 2014. Le développement des arts au Cambodge à l'époque coloniale: George Groslier et l'école des arts cambodgiens (1917–1945). *Udaya, Journal of Khmer Studies* 12, 7–39.

Ang, C., 1986. *Les êtres surnaturels dans la religion populaire khmère*. Paris: Centre de documentation et de recherche sur la civilisation khmère.

Ang, C., 1988. The place of Animism within popular Buddhism in Cambodia: the example of the monastery. *Asian Folklore Studies* 47(1), 35–41.

Ang, C., 1995. Le sol et l'ancêtre, l'amorphe et l'anthropomorphe. *Journal Asiatique* 283(1), 213–38.

Ang, C., 1997. Nandin and his avatars, in *Sculpture of Angkor and Ancient Cambodia: Millennium of Glory*, eds. H.I. Jessup & T. Zéphir. Washington, D.C.: National Gallery of Art, 62–9.

Ang, C., n.d. Bikarana—Consider, at *Khmerenaissance*. www.yosothor.org/publications/khmer-renaissance/chapter-six/picharana.html, accessed 05/09/19.

Apte, V.S., 1959. *Revised and Enlarged Edition of Prin. V.S. Apte's The Practical Sanskrit-English Dictionary*, volume 3. Poona: Prasad Prakashan.

Assavavirulhakarn, P., 2010. *The Ascendancy of Theravāda Buddhism in Southeast Asia*. Chiang Mai: Silkworm Books.

Aymonier, É., 1883. Quelques notions sur les inscriptions en vieux khmèr. *Journal Asiatique* 8(1), 441–505.

Banerjea, J.N., 1985. *The Development of Hindu Iconography*, 4th ed. New Delhi: Munshiram Manoharlal.

Baptiste, P. & T. Zéphir, 2008. *L'art khmer dans les collections du Musée Guimet*. Paris: Réunion des musées nationaux.

Baptiste, P. & T. Zéphir, 2013. *Angkor, naissance d'un mythe—Louis Delaporte et le Cambodge*. Paris: Gallimard & Musée national des art asiatiques Guimet.

Beijing Capital Museum, 2015. *Gao mian de wei xiao: Jian pu zhai wu ge wen wu yu yi shu= Smile of Khmer: Cambodian Ancient Cultural Relics and Arts*. Beijing: Bei jing mei shu she ying chu ban she.

Bergaigne, A., 1893. *Inscriptions sanscrites de Campā et du Cambodge* (Académie des Inscriptions et Belles-Lettres. *Notices et extraits des manuscrits de la Bibliothèque nationale et autres bibliothèques* 27(2), 181–632.

Bhattacharya, K., 1961. *Les religions brahmaniques dans l'ancien Cambodge: d'après l'épigraphie et l'iconographie. Publications de l'École française d'Extrême-Orient 49*. Paris: École française d'Extrême-Orient.

Bhattacharya, K., 1964. Hari Kambujendra. *Artibus Asiae* 27(1–2), 72–8.

Biddulph, R., 2018. Social enterprise and inclusive tourism. Five cases in Siem Reap, Cambodia. *Tourism Geographies* 20(4), 610–29.

Bizot, F., 1994. *La consécration des statues et le culte des morts, in Recherches nouvelles sur le Cambodge* (Études thématiques, volume 1). Paris: École française d'Extrême-Orient, 101–40.

Boisselier, J., 1955. *La statuaire khmère et son evolution*. Saigon: École française d'Extrême-Orient.

Boisselier, J., 1966. *Asie du Sud-Est: I. Le Cambodge* (Manuel d'archéologie d'Extrême-Orient, vol. 1). Paris: Picard.

Boulbet, J. & B. Dagens, 1973. Les sites archéologiques de la Région du Bhnaṃ Gūlen (Phnom Kulen). *Arts Asiatiques* 27, 3–130.

Bourdonneau, E., 2011. Nouvelles recherches sur Koh Ker (Chok Gargyar). Jayavarman IV et la maîtrise des mondes. *Monuments et mémoires de la Fondation Eugène Piot* 90, 95–141.

Bourdonneau, E., 2016. La stele de Sdok Kak Thom et le *Devarāja*. Récits et acteurs d'une "naissance", in *Le passé des Khmers. Langues, textes, rites*, eds. A.C. Nasir, G. Mikaelian & J. Thach. Berne: Peter Lang, 167–212.

Bourgarit, D., B. Mille, T. Borel, P. Baptiste & T. Zéphir, 2003. A millennium of Khmer bronze metallurgy: analytical studies of bronze artifacts from the Musée Guimet and the Phnom Penh National Museum, in *Scientific Research in the Field of Asian Art: Proceedings of the First Forbes Symposium at the Freer Gallery of Art, London*, ed. P. Jett. Washington, D.C.: Archetype Publications, 103–26.

Brand, M. & Chuch Phoeurn (eds.), 1992. T*he Age of Angkor: Treasures from the National Museum of Cambodia*. Canberra: The Australian National Gallery.

Brown, R.L., 2011a. An aesthetic encounter: Khmer art from Thailand, Cambodia and Vietnam. *Orientations* 42(3), 50–56.

Brown, R.L., 2011b. The importance of Gupta-period sculpture in Southeast Asian art history, in *Early Interactions between South and Southeast Asia: Reflections on Cross-Cultural Exchange*, eds. P.Y. Manguin, A. Mani & G. Wade. Singapore: Institute of Southeast Asian Studies, 317–31.

Brown, R.L., 2014. *Carrying Buddhism: The Role of Metal Icons in the Spread and Development of Buddhism*. Amsterdam: J. Gonda Fund Foundation of the KNAW.

Bruguier, B., 1998. The cave temples of Kampot: a comparative study, in *Southeast Asian Archaeology 1996: Proceedings of the 6th International Conference of the European Association of Southeast Asian Archaeologists, Leiden, 2–6 September 1996*, eds. M.J. Klokke & T. de Bruijn. Hull: Centre for South-East Asian Studies, University of Hull, 193–200.

Carò, F. & J.G. Douglas, 2013. Nature and provenance of sandstone used for Bayon style sculptures produced during the reign of Jayavarman VII. *Journal of Archaeological Science* 40, 723–34.

Carò, F., M. Polkinghorne & J.D. Douglas, 2014. *Stone materials used for lintels and decorative elements of Khmer temples, in Metropolitan Museum Studies in Art, Science, and Technology 2*. New York: Metropolitan Museum, 51–68.

Chakravarti, M., 1994. *The Concept of Rudra-Śiva through the Ages,* 2nd Revised ed. Delhi: Motilal Banarsidass Publishers.

Chandler, D.P., 1979. Folk memories of the decline of Angkor in nineteenth century Cambodia: the legend of the Leper King. *Journal of the Siam Society* 67(1), 54–62.

Chaudhuri, N., 1939. Rudra-Śiva—As an agricultural deity. *The Indian Historical Quarterly* XV(2), 183–96.

Chea, S., C. Muon & L. Tythacott, 2021. The Looting of Koh Ker and the return of the Prasat Chen Statues, in *Returning Southeast Asia's Past: Objects, Museums, and Restitution*, eds. L. Tythacott & P. Ardiyansyah. Singapore: NUS Press, 62–86.

Chevance, J-B., P. Bâti & C. Seng, 2013. The sources of the Khmer Empire, in *Unearthing Southeast Asia's Past: Selected Papers from the 12th International Conference of the European Association of Southeast Asian Archaeologists,* volume 1, eds. M.J. Klokke & V. Degroot. Singapore: National University of Singapore, 257–74.

Chevance, J-B., D. Evans, N. Hofer, S. Sakhoeun & R. Chhean, 2019. Mahendraparvata: an early Angkor-period capital defined through airborne laser scanning at Phnom Kulen. *Antiquity* 93(371): 1303–21.

Clementin-Ojha, C., 1990. Image animée, image vivante: l'image du culte hindou, in *L'Image divine: culte et méditation dans l'hindouisme*, ed. A. Padoux. Paris: Éditions du Centre national de la recherche scientifique, 115–32.

Cœdès, G., 1906. La stèle de Tà-prohm. *Bulletin de l'École française d'Extrême-Orient* 6 (1–2), 44–85.

Cœdès, G., 1911a. Note sur l'apothéose au Cambodge. *Bulletin de la Commission archéologique de l'Indochine*, 38–49.
Cœdès, G., 1911b. Les bas-reliefs d'Angkor-Vat. *Bulletin de la Commission archéologique de l'Indochine*, 170–220.
Cœdès, G., 1918. Le royaume de Çrīvijaya. *Bulletin de l'École française d'Extrême-Orient* 18(6), 1–36.
Cœdès, G., 1937. *Inscriptions du Cambodge*, volume 1 (Collection de textes et documents sur l'Indochine III). Paris: École française d'Extrême-Orient.
Cœdès, G., 1940. Études cambodgiennes XXXIII—La destination funéraire des grands monuments khmèrs. *Bulletin de l'École française d'Extrême-Orient* 40(2), 315–43.
Cœdès, G., 1941. La stèle du Práḥ Khằn d'Aṅkor. *Bulletin de l'École française d'Extrême-Orient* 41(2), 255–301.
Cœdès, G., 1942. *Inscriptions du Cambodge,* volume 2 (Collection de textes et documents sur l'Indochine III). Hanoi & Paris: École française d'Extrême-Orient.
Cœdès, G., 1951a. *Inscriptions du Cambodge,* volume 3 (Collection de textes et documents sur l'Indochine III). Paris: École française d'Extrême-Orient.
Cœdès, G., 1951b. *Le culte de la royauté divinisée, source d'inspiration des grands monuments du Cambodge ancien,* in *Conferenze,* volume 1. (Serie Orientale Roma, vol. 5). Rome: Istituto Italiano per il Medio ed Estremo Oriente, 1–23.
Cœdès, G., 1952. *Inscriptions du Cambodge,* volume 4 (Collection de textes et documents sur l'Indochine III). Paris: École française d'Extrême-Orient.
Cœdès, G., 1954. *Inscriptions du Cambodge,* volume 6 (Collection de textes et documents sur l'Indochine III). Paris: École française d'Extrême-Orient.
Cœdès, G., 1958. Les Statues du roi khmèr Jayavarman VII. *Comptes rendues de l'Académie des Inscriptions et Belles-Lettres*, 218–26.
Cœdès, G., 1960. Le Portrait dans l'art khmèr. *Arts Asiatiques* 7(3), 179–98.
Cœdès, G., (ed. & trans.), 1961[1929]. *Recueil des inscriptions du Siam. Deuxième partie: inscriptions de Dvāravatī, de Çrīvijaya et de Lăvo,* 2nd ed. Bangkok: Momchao Piyarangsit Rangsit.
Cœdès, G., 1963. *Angkor: An Introduction*, translated by E.F. Gardiner. London: Oxford University Press.
Cœdès, G., 1968. *The Indianized States of Southeast Asia*, 3rd ed., W.F. Vella, translated by S.B. Cowing. Honolulu: University of Hawai'i Press.
Cœdès, G. & P. Dupont, 1943–1946. Les stèles de Sdŏk Kăk Thoṃ, Phnoṃ Sandak et Práḥ Vihăr. *Bulletin de l'École française d'Extrême-Orient* 43, 56–154.
Colas, G., 2004. The competing hermeneutics of image worship in Hinduism (fifth to eleventh century AD), in *Images in Asian Religions: Texts and Contexts*, eds. P. Granoff & K. Shinohara (Asian Religions and Society Series). Vancouver: UBC Press, 149–79.
Colas, G., 2009. Images and territory of gods: from precepts to epigraphs, in *Territory, Soil and Society in South Asia*, eds. D. Berti & G. Tarabout. New Delhi: Manohar, 99–139.
Colas, G., 2010. Pratiṣṭhā: ritual, reproduction, accretion, in *Hindu and Buddhist Initiations in India and Nepal*, eds. A. Zotter & C. Zotter. Wiesbaden: Harrassowitz, 319–39.
Colas, G., 2012. Iconography and images (*Murtī*): Ancient Concepts, in *Brill's Encyclopedia of Hinduism*, eds. K.A. Jacobsen, H. Basu, A. Malinar & V. Narayanan (Consulted online 16 June 2014). http://dx.doi.org/10.1163/2212-5019_beh_COM_000380, first appeared online: 2012.
Cooler, R.M., 1978. Sculpture, kingship, and the triad of Phnom Da. *Artibus Asiae* 40(1), 29–40.
Coral-Rémusat, G. de, 1940. *L'art khmer. Les grandes étapes de son évolution.* Paris: Les éditions d'art et d'histoire.
Cunin, O., 2013. A study of wooden structures: a contribution to the architectural history of the Bayon style monuments, in *Materializing Southeast Asia's Past: Selected Papers from the 12th International Conference of the European Association of Southeast Asian Archaeologists,* volume 2, eds. M.J. Klokke & V. Degroot. Singapore: National University of Singapore, 82–107.
Cushman, R.D., 2000. *The Royal chronicles of Ayutthaya: A synoptic translation*, ed. D. Wyatt. Bangkok: The Siam Society.
Dagens, B., 2005[1996]. Le temple comme corps du dieu, in *Traités, temples et images du monde indien: études d'histoire et d'archéologie*, eds. M-L. Barazer-Billoret & V. Lefèvre. Pondichéry: Institut français de Pondichéry.
Dagens, B., 2016. *The Indian Temple: Mirror of the World.* New Delhi: Indira Gandhi National Centre for the Arts and New Age Books.

Dalsheimer, N., 2001. *Les collections du Musée national de Phnom Penh: l'art du Cambodge ancien.* Paris: École française d'Extrême-Orient, Magellan & Cie.

Davidson, R.M., 2012. Some observations on an Uṣṇīṣa Abhiṣeka Rite in Atikūṭa's Dhāraṇīsaṃgraha, in *Transformations and Transfer of Tantra in Asia and Beyond*, ed. I. Keul. Berlin: De Gruyter, 77–98.

Davis, R.H., 1997. *Lives of Indian Images.* Princeton: Princeton University Press.

Davis, T. & S. Mackenzie, 2015. Crime and conflict: temple looting in Cambodia, in *Cultural Property Crime: An Analysis of Contemporary Perspectives and Trends*, eds. J.D. Kila & M. Balcells. Leiden: Brill, 292–306.

Dolias, J., 1990. Viśvakarman: un exemple d'adaptation des mythes indiens en pays khmer. *Cahiers de l'Asie du Sud-Est* 28, 109–46.

Douglas, J.G. & S.S. Sorensen, 2007. Mineralogical characteristics of Khmer stone sculpture in the Bayon style, in *Scientific Research on the Sculptural Arts of Asia, Proceedings of the Third Forbes Symposium at the Freer Gallery of Art*, eds. J.G. Douglas, P. Jett & J. Winter. Washington, D.C.: Archetype Publications in association with the Freer Gallery of Art, Smithsonian Institution, 115–24.

Douglas, J.G., F. Carò & C. Fischer, 2010. Evidence of sandstone usage for sculpture during the Khmer empire in Cambodia through petrographic analysis. *Udaya, Journal of Khmer Studies* 9, 1–18.

Drayman-Weisser, T., J.A. Lauffenburger & D.K. Strahan, 1997. Appendix C: metal analyses, in *The Sacred Sculpture of Thailand*, ed. H.W. Woodward, Jr. Baltimore: Walters Art Gallery, 278–87.

Dumarçay, J., 1971. *Phnom Bakheng. Étude architecturale du temple.* Paris: École française d'Extrême-Orient.

Dumarçay, J & P. Royère, 2001. *Cambodian Architecture: Eighth to Thirteenth Centuries.* Leiden: Brill.

Dupaigne, B., 2016. *Les maîtres du fer et du feu dans le royaume d'Angkor.* Paris: CNRS Éditions.

Dupont, P., 1955. *La statuaire préangkorienne* (Artibus Asiae Supplementum, no. 15). Ascona: Imprimerie Artibus Asiae.

Eck, D.L., 1998. *Darśan: Seeing the Divine Image in India*, 3rd ed. New York: Columbia University Press.

Edwards, P., 2007. *Cambodge: The Cultivation of a Nation 1860–1945.* Honolulu: University of Hawai'i Press.

Eggert, A.A., 2011. Cambodian "Leitkultur"? Cambodian concepts of art and culture, in *World Heritage: Angkor and Beyond: Circumstances and Implications of UNESCO Listings in Cambodia*, ed. B. Hauser-Schäublin. Göttingen: Göttingen University Press, 69–93.

Einoo, S & J. Takashima (eds.), 2005. *From Material to Deity: Indian Rituals of Consecration.* New Delhi: Manohar.

Estève, J., 2009. *Etude critique des phénomènes de syncrétisme religieux dans le Cambodge angkorien.* PhD dissertation. Paris: École Pratique des Hautes Études.

Estève, J., 2023. Gods and temples: the nature(s) of Angkorian religion, in *The Angkorian World*, eds. M. Hendrickson, M.T. Stark & D. Evans. New York: Routledge, 423–34.

Falser, M., 2020. *Angkor Wat: A Transcultural History of Heritage,* 2 vols. Berlin: De Gruyter.

Filliozat, J., 1954. Le symbolisme du monument du Phnom Bakheng. *Bulletin de l'École française d'Extrême-Orient* 44(2), 527–44.

Finot, L., H. Parmentier & V. Goloubew, 1926. *Le temple d'Içvarapura* (Bantãy Srĕi, Cambodge). (Mémoires archéologiques I). Paris: G. Vanoest.

Fischer, C.F. Carò & M. Polkinghorne, 2023. From quarries to temples: stone procurement, materiality and spirituality in the Angkorian World, in *The Angkorian World*, eds. M. Hendrickson, M.T. Stark & D. Evans. New York: Routledge.

Fletcher, R., C. Pottier, D. Evans & M. Kummu, 2008. The development of the water management system of Angkor: a provisional model. *IPPA Bulletin* 28, 57–66.

Forest, A., 1992. *Le culte des génies protecteurs au Cambodge: analyse et traduction d'un corpus de textes sur les neak ta.* Paris: L'Harmattan.

Geslani, M., 2017. Vedic astrology and the prehistory of Varāhamihira's Pratiṣṭhāpanādhyāya: image installation as apotropaic consecration, in *Consecration Rituals in South Asia*, ed. I. Keul. Leien: Brill, 17–44.

Giteau, M., 1955. L'expression de la sensibilité dans l'art khmer. *Arts Asiatiques* 2(3), 209–28.

Giteau, M., 1975. *Iconographie du Cambodge post-angkorien.* Paris: École française d'Extrême-Orient.

Gonda, J., 1975. *Pratiṣṭhā, in Selected Studies,* volume 2, *Sanskrit Word Studies.* Leiden: E.J. Brill, 338–74.

Goodall, D., C. Hun, D. Acharya, K. Chhom, C. Chollet & N. Mirnig, 2021. Sectarian rivalry in ninth-century Cambodia. A Posthumous Inscription Narrating the Religious Tergiversations of Jayavarman III (K, 1457). *Medieval Worlds* 13, 266–95.

Grant Ross, H., 2015. The civilizing vision of an enlightened dictator: Norodom Sihanouk and the Cambodian post-independence experiment (1953–1970), in *Cultural Heritage as Civilizing Mission: From Decay to Recovery. Proceedings of the 2nd International Workshop on Cultural Heritage and the Temples of Angkor* (Chair of Global Art History, Heidelberg University, 8–10 May 2011), ed. M. Falser. Heidelberg: Springer, 149–78.

Green, G., 2007. Angkor vogue: sculpted evidence of imported luxury textiles in the courts of kings and temples. *Journal of the Economic and Social History of the Orient* 50(4), 424–51.

Griswold, A.B., 1954. Bronze-casting in Siam. *Bulletin de l'École française d'Extrême-Orient* 46(2), 635–40.

Groslier, B-P., 1957. *Excavations at the Royal Palace of Angkor Thom, Preliminary Report, in Proceedings of the XXIIIrd Congress of Orientalists, Cambridge, 21st–28th August 1954.* London: Royal Asiatic Society.

Groslier, G., 1921. *Recherches sur les Cambodgiens, d'après les textes et les monuments depuis les premiers siècles de notre ère.* Paris: Augustin Challamel.

Guillou, A.Y., 2017. Khmer potent places: Pāramī and the localisation of Buddhism and monarchy in Cambodia. *The Asia Pacific Journal of Anthropology* 18(5), 421–43.

Hang, C.S., 2004. Stec Gaṃlaṅ' and Yāy Deb: Worshipping kings and queens in Cambodia today, in *History, Buddhism, and New Religious Movements in Cambodia*, eds. J. Marston & E. Guthrie. Honolulu: University of Hawai'i Press, 113–26.

Harris, I., 2005. *Cambodian Buddhism: History and Practice.* Honolulu: University of Hawai'i Press.

Hauser-Schäublin, B., 2011. New chances for local farmers and artisans? Efforts and strategies to change the existing structures of tourism supply in Siem Reap, in *World Heritage Angkor and Beyond Circumstances and Implications of UNESCO Listings in Cambodia*, ed. B. Hauser-Schäublin. Göttingen: Göttingen University Press, 177–202.

Hauser-Schäublin, B. & S. Kim, 2016. Faked biographies: the remake of antiquities and their sale on the art market, in *Cultural Property and Contested Ownership: The Trafficking of Artefacts and the Quest for Restitution*, eds. B. Hauser-Schäublin & L.V. Prott. London: Routledge, 108–29.

Hauser-Schäublin, B., 2016. Looted, trafficked, donated and returned: the twisted tracks of Cambodian antiquities, in *Cultural Property and Contested Ownership: The Trafficking of Artefacts and the Quest for Restitution*, eds. B. Hauser-Schäublin & L.V. Prott. London: Routledge, 64–81.

Higham, C.F.W., 2020. Ban Chiang: the metal remains in regional context. A review essay. *Journal of the Siam Society* 108(1), 161–94.

Hikita, H., 2005. Consecration of divine images in a temple, in *From Material to Deity: Indian Rituals of Consecration*, eds. S. Einoo & J. Takashima. New Delhi: Manohar, 143–97.

Ishizawa, Y., 2009. *Sekai isan Ankōru Watto ten: Ajia no daichi ni saita kamigami no uchū: Punonpen Kokuritsu Hakubutsukan/Shihanūku Ion Hakubutsukan shozō = Angkor Wat: collection of National Museum of Cambodia, Phnom Penh, collection of Preah Norodom Sihanouk-Angkor Museum, Siem Reap.* Komono: Okada Bunka Zaidan.

Jacques, C., 1985. The kamrateṅjagat in ancient Cambodia, in *Indus Valley to Mekong Delta: Explorations in Epigraphy*, ed. Noboru Karashima. Madras: New Era Publications, 269–86.

Jacques, C., 1999. Études d'épigraphie cambodgienne—XI: Les inscriptions du Phnoṃ Kbal Spān (K 1011; 1012, 1015 et 1016). *Bulletin de l'École française d'Extrême-Orient* 86, 357–74.

Jenner, P.N., 2009a. *A Dictionary of Pre-Angkorian Khmer.* Canberra: Pacific Linguistics, Research School of Pacific and Asian Studies, The Australian National University.

Jenner, P.N., 2009b. *A Dictionary of Angkorian Khmer.* Canberra: Pacific Linguistics, Research School of Pacific and Asian Studies, The Australian National University.

Jenner, P.N., 2011. *A Dictionary of Middle Khmer.* Canberra: Pacific Linguistics, Research School of Pacific and Asian Studies, The Australian National University.

Jessup, H.I. & T. Zéphir (eds.), 1997. *Sculpture of Angkor and Ancient Cambodia: Millennium of Glory.* Washington, D.C.: National Gallery of Art.

Jessup, H.I., 1998. The Khmer aesthetic: a chance for new insights. *Orientations* 29(1), 46–55.

Jessup, H.I., 2006. *Masterpieces of the National Museum of Cambodia: An Introduction to the Collection.* Norfolk: Friends of Khmer Culture.

Keul, I., 2017. *Consecration Rituals in South Asia.* Leiden: Brill.

Khin, S., 1980. L'inscription de Praḥ Thom du Kulên K 715. *Bulletin de l'École française d'Extrême-Orient* 67, 133–34.

Khin, S., 1988. *Chroniques royales du Cambodge* (de Bañā Yāt jusqu'à la prise de Lanvaek: de 1417 à 1595). *Traduction française avec comparaison des différentes versions et introduction.* Paris: École française d'Extrême-Orient.

Khing, H.D., 1991. La légende de Braḥ Go Braḥ Kaev. *Cahiers de l'Asie du Sud-Est* 29–30, 169–90.

Khun, S., 2008. *The New Guide to the National Museum-Phnom Penh*, 3rd ed. Phnom Penh: Ministry of Culture and Fine Arts.

Klokke, M.J., 1994. The iconography of the so-called portrait statues in late east Javanese art, in *Ancient Indonesian Sculpture*, eds. M.J. Klokke & P. Lunsingh Scheurleer. Leiden: KITLV Press, 178–201.

Kulke, H., 1978. *The Devarāja Cult*, translated by I.W. Mabbett (Cornell University Data Paper no. 108). Cornell: Cornell University.

Lafont, M., 2004. *Pillaging Cambodia: The Illicit Traffic in Khmer Art*. Jefferson: McFarland & Co.

Lavy, P.A., 2003. As in Heaven, so on earth: the role of Vishnu, Harihara, and Shiva images in the politics of Preangkorian Southeast Asia. *Journal of Southeast Asian Studies* 34(1), 21–39.

Lavy, P.A., 2012. A Lopburi Buddha at the Honolulu Museum of Art. *Orientations* 43(5), 53–9.

Lavy, P.A., 2014. Conch-on-hip images in peninsular Thailand and early Vaiṣṇava sculpture in Southeast Asia, in *Before Siam: Essays in Art and Archaeology*, eds. N. Revire & S.A. Murphy. Bangkok: River Books, 152–73.

Lavy, P.A., 2020. Early Vaiṣṇava sculpture in Southeast Asia and the question of Pallava influence, in *Across the South of Asia: A Volume in Honor of Robert L. Brown*, eds. R. DeCaroli & P.A. Lavy. New Delhi: DK Print world, 213–50.

Lê Thị Liên, 2006. *Nghệ thuật Phật giáo và Hindu giáo ở Đồng bằng sông Cửu Long trước thế kỷ X* (Buddhist and Hindu Art of the Mekong Delta before the Tenth Century). Hanoi: Thế Giới.

Lewitz, S., 1970. Textes en khmer moyen. Inscriptions modernes d'Angkor 2 et 3. *Bulletin de l'École française d'Extrême-Orient* 57, 99–126

Lewitz, S., 1971. Inscriptions modernes d'Angkor 4, 5, 6 et 7. *Bulletin de l'École française d'Extrême-Orient* 58, 105–23.

Lewitz, S., 1972. Inscriptions modernes d'Angkor 10, 11, 12, 13, 14, 15, 16a, 16b, et 16c. *Bulletin de l'École française d'Extrême-Orient* 59, 221–49.

Liebert, G., 1986. *Iconographic Dictionary of the Indian Religions*. Delhi: Sri Satguru Publications.

Lobo, W. & H.I. Jessup (eds.), 2006. *Angkor. Göttliches Erbe Kambodschas*. Bonn: Kunst- und Ausstellungshalle der Bundesrepublik Deutschland GmbH/München: Prestel.

Mabbett, I.W., 1969. Devarāja. *Journal of Southeast Asian History* 10(2), 202–23.

Mabbett, I.W., 1983. The symbolism of Mt. Meru. *History of Religions* 23(1), 64–83.

Mackenzie, S. & T. Davis, 2014. Temple looting in Cambodia: anatomy of a statue trafficking network. *The British Journal of Criminology* 54(5), 722–40.

Mak, P., 1984. *Chroniques royales du Cambodge* (des origines légendaires jusqu'à Paramarājā 1er). Paris: École française d'Extrême-Orient.

Malleret, L., 1954. À propos d'analyses de bronzes archéologiques, *Bulletin de la Société des études indochinoises* 29(4), 297–307.

Marchal, H., 1950. *Julliet 1950: Tep Pranam. in Rapports de la Conservation d'Angkor* (Unpublished Archives). Paris: École française d'Extrême-Orient.

Marui, M., 2002. The Banteay Kdei temple re-examined: some evidence to interpret the history through and after Angkor periods. *The Journal of the Sophia Asian Studies* 20, 411–28.

Maxwell, T.S., 2006. *Of Gods, Kings, and Men: The Reliefs of Angkor Wat*. Chiang Mai: Silkworm Books.

Maxwell, T.S., 2007. Religion at the time of Jayavarman VII, in *Bayon: New Perspectives*, ed. Joyce Clark. Bangkok: River Books, 74–121.

Maxwell, T.S., 2009. A new Khmer and Sanskrit inscription at Banteay Chhmar. *Udaya, Journal of Khmer Studies* 10, 135–201.

McCullough, T., S.A. Murphy, P. Baptiste & T. Zéphir (eds.), 2018. *Angkor: Exploring Cambodia's Sacred City*. Singapore: Asian Civilisations Museum.

Miura, K., 2004. *Contested heritage: people of Angkor*. PhD dissertation. London: School of Oriental and African Studies, University of London.

Miura, K., 2015. From "originals" to replicas: diverse significance of Khmer statues, in *Kultur als Eigentum: Instrumente, Querschnitte und Fallstudien*, eds. S. Groth, R. F. Bendix & A. Spiller. Göttingen: Göttingen University Press, 269–93.

Miura, K., 2016. Destruction and plunder of Cambodian cultural heritage and their consequences, in *Cultural Property and Contested Ownership: The Trafficking of Artefacts and the Quest for Restitution*, eds. B. Hauser-Schäublin & L.V. Prott. London: Routledge, 23–44.

Morrison, K.D., 2001. Coercion, resistance, and hierarchy: local processes and imperial strategies in the Vijayanagara empire, in *Empires: Perspectives from Archaeology and History*, eds. S.E. Alcock, T.N. D'Altroy, K.D. Morrison & C.M. Sinopoli. Cambridge: Cambridge University Press, 252–78.

Multzer o'Naghten, H., 2000. *Les temples du Cambodge: Architecture et espace sacré*. Paris: Librairie orientaliste Paul Geuthner.

Mus, P., 2011. *India Seen from the East: Indian and Indigenous Cults in Champa* (Revised ed), translated by I.W. Mabbett and edited by I.W. Mabbett & D.P. Chandler (Monash Papers on Southeast Asia, vol. 72). Caulfield: Monash University Press.

Nilakanta Sastri, A., 1957–1958. The cult of the Devaraja in Kambuja. *Transactions of the Archaeological Society of South India*, 1–23.

Orzech, C.D., 2011. On the subject of Abhiṣeka. *Pacific World: Journal of the Institute of Buddhist Studies* 3rd series 13, 113–28.

Padoux, A., 1990. *L'Image divine: culte et méditation dans l'hindouisme*. Paris: Éditions du Centre national de la recherche scientifique.

Plehwe-Leisen, E. von & H. Leisen, 2008. *Paint, Plaster, and Stucco—Decorative Features of Khmer Temples in Cambodia, in Interpreting Southeast Asia's Past: Monument, Image and Text (*Selected Papers from the 10th International Conference of the European Association of Southeast Asian Archaeologists, volume 2). Singapore: National University of Singapore.

Polkinghorne, M., 2007. *Makers and models: decorative lintels of Khmer temples, 7th to 11th centuries*. PhD dissertation. Sydney: The University of Sydney.

Polkinghorne, M., 2022. 17th and 18th century images of the Buddha from Ayutthaya and Lan Xang at Angkor Wat, in *Early Theravādin Cambodia: Perspectives from Art and Archaeology*, ed. A. Thompson. Singapore: National University of Singapore Press, 269–305.

Polkinghorne, M., J.G. Douglas. & F. Carò, 2015a. Carving at the capital: a stone workshop at Hariharālaya, Angkor. *Bulletin de l'École française d'Extrême-Orient* 101, 55–90.

Polkinghorne, M., C. Pottier & C. Fischer, 2013. One Buddha can hide another. *Journal Asiatique* 301(2), 575–624.

Polkinghorne, M., B. Vincent, N. Thomas & D. Bourgarit, 2014. Casting for the king: the Royal Palace bronze workshop of Angkor Thom. *Bulletin de l'École française d'Extrême-Orient* 100, 327–58.

Polkinghorne, M., B. Vincent, D. Thomas, D. Bourgarit, J.G. Douglas & F. Carò, 2015b. *Sculpture Workshops of Angkor—Report (2011–2015)* (Unpublished Report). Siem Reap: The University of Sydney, The APSARA National Authority.

Porée-Maspero, É., 1961. Krŏṅ Pāli et rites de la maison, (Suite), VI. Krŏṅ Pāli, Práḥ Phum, Práḥ Thorni et la Mnāṅ Phtăḥ (Suite et fin). *Anthropos* 56(1–2, 3–4, 5–6), 179–251, 548–628, 883–929.

Pottier, C., 2000. À propos de la statue portrait du Roi Jayavarman VII au temple de Préah Khan de Kompong Svay. *Arts Asiatiques* 55, 171–72.

Pottier, C., 2015. Le Roi dans le temple: le cas de Jayavarman VII, de Phimai à Angkor. *Bulletin d'études indiennes* 33, 419–61.

Pou, S., 1989. *Nouvelles inscriptions du Cambodge*. Paris: École française d'Extrême-Orient.

Pou, S., 1992. *Dictionnaire vieux khmer-français-anglais/An Old Khmer-French-English Dictionary*. Paris: Cedoreck.

Pou, S., 2001. *Nouvelles inscriptions du Cambodge II & III*. Paris: École française d'Extrême-Orient.

Sanderson, A., 2003–2004. The Śaiva religion among the Khmers, Part 1. *Bulletin de l'École française d'Extrême-Orient* 90–91, 349–462.

Santoni, M., V. Souksavatdy, D. Defente, C. Hawixbrock & J-C. Liger, 1997. Excavations at Champassak and Wat Phu (Southern Laos), in *South-East Asian archaeology, 1992: proceedings of the fourth international conference of the European Association of South-East Asian Archaeologists, Rome, 28th September–4th October 1992*, eds. R. Ciarla & F. Rispoli. Rome: Istituto italiano per l'Africa e l'Orient, 233–63.

Sengupta, A.R., 2005. *God and King: The Devarāja Cult in South Asian Art and Architecture*. New Delhi: Regency Publications.

Sharrock, P.D., 2009. Garuḍa, Vajrapāṇi and religious change in Jayavarman VII's Angkor. *Journal of Southeast Asian Studies* 40(1), 111–51.

Sinopoli, C.M., 2003. *The Political Economy of Craft Production: Crafting Empire in South India, c., 1350–1650*. Cambridge: Cambridge University Press.

Southworth, K., 2012. The lintel of Vat Eng Khna, Cambodia: image, text and precedent, in *Connecting Empires and States: Selected Papers from the 13th International Conference of the European Association of Southeast Asian Archaeologists,* volume 2, eds. M.L. Tjoa-Bonatz, A. Reinecke & D. Bonatz. Singapore: National University of Singapore Press.

Soutif, D., 2009. *Organisation religieuse et profane du temple khmer du VIIe au XIIIe siècle*. PhD dissertation. Paris: Université Paris III—Sorbonne nouvelle.

Spooner, A., 1864. Correspondance de Cochinchine. 30 janvier 1864. *L'Illustration, Journal Universel* 43(1092) (in Les Grands Dossiers de L'Illustration, L'Indochine, Histoire d'un siècle: 1843–1944. Bagneux: Le livre de Paris, 34–37).

Stern, P., 1927. *Le Bayon d'Angkor et l'évolution de l'art khmer* (Annales du Musée Guimet, Bibliothèque de vulgarisation, volume 47). Paris: Librairie orientaliste Paul Geuthner.

Stern, P., 1965. *Les monuments khmers du style du Bàyon et Jayavarman VII* (Publications du Musée Guimet. Recherches et documents d'art et d'archéologie, volume 9). Paris: Presses universitaires de France.

Strahan, D., 1997. Bronze casting in Thailand, in *The Sacred Sculpture of Thailand*, ed. H.W. Woodward, Jr. Baltimore: Walters Art Gallery, 27–41.

Swearer, D., 2004. *Becoming the Buddha. The Ritual of Image Consecration in Thailand.* Oxford: Princeton University Press.

Tambiah, S.J., 1976. *World Conqueror and World Renouncer: A Study of Buddhism and Polity in Thailand against a Historical Background.* Cambridge: Cambridge University Press.

Thompson, A., 1998. The ancestral cult in transition: reflections on spatial organization of Cambodia's early Theravada complex, in *Southeast Asian Archaeology: Proceedings of the 6th International Conference of the European Association of Southeast Asian Archaeologists, 2–6 September, Leiden*, eds. M. J. Klokke & T. de Bruijn. Hull: Centre for Southeast Asian Studies, 273–95.

Thompson, A., 2004. The future of Cambodia's past: a messianic middle-period Cambodian royal cult, in *History, Buddhism, and New Religious Movements in Cambodia*, eds. J. Marston & E. Guthrie. Honolulu: University of Hawai'i Press, 13–39.

Thompson, A., 2008. Angkor revisited: the state of statuary, in *What's the Use of Art?: Asian Visual and Material Culture in Context*, eds. Jan Mrázek & Morgan Pitelka. Honolulu: University of Hawai'i Press, 179–213.

Thompson, A., 2022. Introduction, in *Early Theravādin Cambodia: Perspectives from Art and Archaeology*, ed. A. Thompson. Singapore: National University of Singapore Press, 1–57.

Tsuchiyama, Y., 2005. Abhiṣeka in the Vedic and post-Vedic rituals, in *From Material to Deity: Indian Rituals of Consecration*, eds. S. Einoo & J. Takashima. New Delhi: Manohar, 51–93.

Vickery, M., 1998. *Society, Economics, and Politics in Pre-Angkor Cambodia: The 7th–8th Centuries.* Tokyo: The Centre for East Asian Cultural Studies for UNESCO, The Toyo Bunko.

Vincent, B., 2012. Saṃrit. Étude de la métallurgie du bronze dans le Cambodge angkorien (fin du xie—début du xiiie siècle). PhD dissertation. Paris: Université Paris III—Sorbonne nouvelle.

Warrack, S., 2013. Developing conservation approaches to living heritage at Angkor: the conservation of the statue of Ta Reach, in *'Archaeologizing' Heritage? Transcultural Entanglements between Local Social Practices and Global Virtual Realities. Proceedings of the 1st International Workshop on Cultural Heritage and the Temples of Angkor* (Chair of Global Art History, Heidelberg University, 2–5 May 2010), eds. M. Falser & M. Juneja. Heidelberg: Springer, 217–32.

White, J.C. & E.G. Hamilton, 2009. The transmission of early bronze technology to Thailand: new perspectives. *Journal of World Prehistory* 22, 357–97.

Woodward, H. W., Jr., 1994–1995. The Jayabuddhamahānātha images of Cambodia. *Journal of the Walters Art Gallery* 52–53, 105–11.

Woodward, H.W., Jr., 1997. *The Sacred Sculpture of Thailand.* Baltimore: Walters Art Gallery.

Woodward, H.W., Jr., 2022. Angkor and Theravada Buddhism: some considerations, in *Early Theravādin Cambodia: Perspectives from Art and Archaeology*, ed. A. Thompson. Singapore: National University of Singapore Press, 58–106.

25

'OF CATTLE AND KINGS'

Bovines in the Angkorian World

Mitch Hendrickson, Eileen Lustig and Siyonn Sophearith

Bovines have played an integral part in societies across monsoonal Asia. In Southeast Asia, remains and representations of water buffalo and cattle appear in agricultural and burial contexts from the Bronze Age. To date there has been limited discussion of these animals during the Early Historic Period (5th to 15th centuries) and more specifically of their religious, political, and economic significance in the development of Angkor. In his study of milking consumption in Southeast Asia, Wheatley (1965) presents evidence from Pre-Angkor and Angkor Period inscriptions documenting the adoption of Indian practices of using and consuming milk and milk products in their rituals. Historic records, such as those of Zhou Daguan, a Chinese visitor to Angkor in the late 13th century, also indicate a ban on eating meat or using hides (2007[1297], 73), which was likely an enduring legacy of Indic traditions. However, the widespread adoption of Indic cattle veneration by the Khmer is somewhat paradoxical, in that Cambodians today are among the many in Southeast Asia with cultures of consuming bovine meat while being averse to dairy. The apparent inconsistency here immediately raises questions about the extent to which Indic reverence for cattle was limited, perhaps to the world of elites, and about the broader and more pragmatic practical roles that cattle and buffalo played in the Angkorian World.

This chapter examines the epigraphic, art historical, and archaeological evidence of the roles of bovines (both cattle and water buffalo) in the early Khmer states. We begin by highlighting some religious ideas and depictions of bovines drawn by the Khmer from Indic traditions and discuss their significance in enhancing the status of rulers and elites. We then assess references to cattle and buffalo in the written records of temple endowments, transactions, and ritual prescriptions and explore some issues of bovine management, including where they might have been raised and their roles in the broader economy.

Bovines in Indic Traditions: Myth, Ritual, and Elite Power

Khmer interaction with India from the early centuries CE brought a range of sophisticated cosmological concepts, language (Sanskrit and written text), and models for religious architecture and sculptural representation (Cœdès 1968; Stark 2021). Accompanying these cultural and ideological frameworks were new forms of socio-political organisation based on texts such as the Arthaśastra, a treatise on statecraft, economics, and military strategy dating from the

DOI: 10.4324/9781351128940-31

2nd century BCE to the 3rd century CE and attributed to Kautilya (Olivelle 2013). These ideas were likely brought into Southeast Asia by traders (Wolters 1967, 64; 246; Wheatley 1975, 238–42; de Casparis 1961), Southeast Asian pilgrims travelling to India (Assavavirulhakarn 2010), and, importantly, educated Brahmin priests invited by local rulers (van Leur 1955). The significance of Indic priests is highlighted in one mythological origin story of Cambodia, of Indian derivation, that tells of the Brahmin prince Kaundinya arriving by sea and marrying a local Naga princess to establish the country Kambuja-deśa (Gaudes 1993). By the 5th or 6th centuries, Khmer people were among the most 'Indianised' groups in Southeast Asia, having established several small kingdoms, set in motion a program of masonry temple construction, and begun to author a corpus of refined poetic verse in classical Sanskrit (Pollock 1966). The myths and imagery dominant in Khmer art and writing are clearly rooted in episodes from the great Indian literary epics, including the *Mahābhārata* the *Rāmāyana* and *Harivamsha*, and the sacred Hindu texts of the *Purānas* (Roveda 2005, 17–19). As with the introduction of any cultural package, some ideas, such as the Indian caste system, were not adopted by the local Khmer peoples (Mabbett 1977). Other concepts were adapted to fit local traditions. Mus (1975[1934]) and others (Groslier 1958; Groslier 1998[1974]; Maxwell 2007) have argued that the Brahman and Buddhist deities of Indian religions were attractive to Southeast Asians because they corresponded neatly with pre-existing, indigenous spiritual concepts—typically, animistic beliefs in agrarian divinities and water spirits associated with specific locations—that could be expressed by way of Indian religious and linguistic constructs. An elegant example of this correlation is seen in the similarity of the Khmer belief that indigenous divinities inhabit natural stone objects to the Indian notion of natural *liṅga* as focal points for manifestations of Śiva. Although Wheatley (1965) has reasoned that the habits of thought and ways of life of the Indianised elite of Kambuja influenced those of the peasant communities to a certain degree, he has offered little in the way of evidence. Cœdès, on the other hand, in his extensive study of the Indianisation of the states of Southeast Asia, has viewed this process more as one of adopting a veneer of Indic culture while maintaining and developing the essentials of the local cultures (Van Leur 1955; Cœdès 1968, 33–35). The extent to which even the elite understood the texts may well have been limited (Pollock 1966).

The veneration of cattle, first seen in India in texts of the Vedic Period (ca. 1500–500 BCE), appears to have become ubiquitous there towards the end of the first millennium CE (Harris 1978). Cattle and buffalo both featured in Hindu mythology, while cow products were essential for conducting Brahmanic rituals (Biardeau 1984; Freed et al. 1981; Ganguli 1931). The Khmer adoption of bovine veneration (Siyonn 2017; Wheatley 1965) therefore provides a further opportunity to evaluate the incorporation of Indic concepts, particularly as water buffalo were already a feature of prehistoric Southeast Asian rituals. Expanding on this earlier work, we now highlight some of the ways that cattle (bulls, cows) and buffaloes were depicted and assess how these choices enhanced the politico-religious authority of Khmer elites.

The Bull

Bulls are frequently mentioned in Sanskrit textual sources and depicted in Khmer art. Sandstone bulls, commonly found in front of temples dedicated to Śiva (Porte and Chea 2010), speak to the animal's role as Nandin, the *vāhana*, who serves as the god's vehicle (Figure 25.1). In Indic mythology, the bull and this supreme deity are further associated through an avatar of Śiva known by the name Vṛṣadhvaja, the god who has a bull as its attribute (Ang 1997). Their shared status is similarly witnessed in Khmer epigraphy, where stone impressions of Śiva's footprints (*śivapada*) and bull hoofprints (*nandipada*) were equally revered (Bhattacharya 1961). Bulls in

Figure 25.1 Sandstone Nandin statues: a) Preah Ko, Angkor; b) Prasat Preah Ko, Thalaborivat; c) Kampong Cham.

Source: (Photos S. Siyonn).

Sanskrit-language texts are also known by the word *vṛṣabha*, a term associated with traits such as being vigorous, strong, and eminent (Monier-Williams 2005[1899]). Imagery of bulls is deployed as a metaphor for the king's enduring power in inscriptions of the Pre-Angkor Period:

> Having conquered all the lands, he (King Mahendravarman) erected a bull (vṛṣabha) of stone in this land.
>
> K. 377 (600–615 CE), II

The animal's symbolic importance to the Khmer is further underscored by reference to the *Dharma*-bull, a concept that symbolises the social order in Indic philosophy. *Dharma* is a complex term variously used to describe the moral and religious laws governing the universe and individual action (Lingat 1973, 4). In this context, the societal pillars of austerity, cleanliness, kindness, and truthfulness are symbolised by the legs of the Dharma-bull. In the Hindu tradition, the concept of dharma is bound up with the four cyclical ages (*yuga*): *Kṛta, Treta, Dvapara,* and *Kali*, the final and current era (Dimmitt and van Buitenen 1978). The idea of an 'intact' Dharma-bull in the Kṛta yuga refers to the belief that, during the first era, he stands on his four feet and thus represents the perfect stability and social order of the world. Human action here is motivated by goodness, devotion, and intent on self-discipline rather than self-interest. The gradual decay of mankind over time is reflected in the fact that the Dharma-bull stands on three feet in the Treta yuga, on two in the Dvapara yuga, and balances precariously on one foot in the Kali yuga. This final era—a time of disease, ritual impropriety, and political upheaval—witnesses numerous Brahmanical errors in prayer recitation, few ritual sacrifices, improper association between members of different castes and all manner of social taboos such as killing of Brahmins, abortion, and hero-murder. The desire to move beyond the Kali yuga and return to the first era is invoked in inscription K. 440 of King Iśānavarman I:

> He (King Iśānavarman) erected this image of (the bull) Vṛṣabha in silver, just like the intact image of Dharma in the age of Kṛta.
>
> K. 440 (615–635 CE), XXXIV

The Dharma-bull concept appears in numerous Khmer inscriptions praising kings for presiding righteously over their kingdoms and for trying to restore dharma to its pristine form. A stanza from the 10th-century inscription of Pre Rup, K. 806, states that,

> The Dharma with only one foot . . . mutilated by Kali, was provided somehow with eighteen feet by this (king) who knows the verse with eighteen feet.
>
> K. 806 (944–968 CE), CXLIII

Here, the mutilation of the Dharma-bull by the wrathful goddess Kali signifies the continued decline of the social order and prosperity that will ultimately lead to the end of the cycle and to the beginning of a new *Kṛta* age (Dimmitt and van Buitenen 1978). The poet of this inscription praises King Rājendravarman II (944–968) by using the metaphor of his re-establishing the Dharma-bull, not only by restoring its four feet but also by increasing their number to 18.

Another example from an inscription at Banteay Srei alludes metaphorically to the king's maintenance of order through adverse times,

> Even old, even deprived of (three) feet in the Kali yuga, the royal dharma (*rājadharma*), relying on his political wisdom (*daṇḍanīti*), pursues his road without tottering.
>
> K. 842 (967 CE), XI

Here, while the Dharma-bull rests in a precarious position in the Age of Kali, the social order can be stabilised with well-established royal rule and the strong administration of justice. It is likely that the poet was referring to Rājendravarman II, who successfully returned the Khmer capital to Angkor following a brief interlude at Koh Ker, and also, metaphorically, to the Dharma-bull in the age of Kali. By the time the inscription was written in 967, the king was very old and probably weak, like the Dharma-bull in the Kali yuga. The ability of a monarch to transform the Kali yuga into the Krta yuga is also asserted in the Sai Fong inscription of Jayavarman VII (K. 368 [CE 1186]: XI). This Buddhist king is poetically said to have fixed the three wounded legs of the Dharma-bull, despite the failure of his kingdom's spiritual and physical efforts. The recurring use of this metaphor demonstrates both understanding of the precarious nature of politics and an inherent linkage between the prosperity of the kingdom and the actions of its sovereign.

The Cow

Khmer texts and bas-reliefs refer less frequently to cows than to bulls but do incorporate some Indic traditions including that of the divine wish-granting cows known variously as Kāmadhenu, Surabhi, or Sabala. Stanza CCLVII of the 10th-century Pre Rup inscription (K. 806) recalls a story drawn from the Viṣṇu Purāna regarding the mythical King Pṛthu who, during a famine, attempted to force the Goddess Earth to yield the edible plants she was withholding. She assumed the form of a cow and fled but, unable to escape, promised to restore all the plants if she was given a calf so that she would be able to secrete milk. Pṛthu was eventually able to milk her, and the Goddess Earth yielded all kinds of fruits, vegetables, and grains on which her people could subsist. Cows are traditionally associated with bounties supporting the kingdom.

Cows appear as important elements in the consecration rituals of Angkorian kings. A stanza of the 12th-century stele of Trapeang Don Ong (K. 254) suggests that cows might ensure the prosperity and stability of the reign:

> Then, during the coronations of King Śri Harṣavarman (1066–1080) and other kings, he (an unnamed dignitary) led the sacred cow (*dhenu*) at the head of the procession around the royal palace.
>
> K. 254 (1126 CE), IX

Cows also played a role in facilitating the deceased's journey to the world of Yama (see Ang 2023, this volume). Hindu tradition holds that a dying person should give away eight items to a Brahmin: cotton-pods, iron vessels, salt, earth, grain, clarified butter, *laddu* (a round sweet), and a cow with her calf. The offering of a cow with her calf was to help the person cross the Vaitaraṇi River, the last barrier before entering into the realm of Yama, (Stevenson 1920, 140-2). This ritual is depicted in three consecutive scenes from an 11th-century bas-relief on the Baphuon temple (Figure 25.2a).

The gifting of cows and calves to Brahmins, *go danam*, is a recurring theme in Angkorian art and literature, which points to the importance of milking for ritual purposes. The eulogy to the royal preceptor, Yajñavarāha, in the Banteay Srei inscription K. 842 (XVII) mentions his generosity in giving gold, clothes, and 'cows with puffed-up udders' to the Brahmins each month at the four phases of the moon. The act of presenting cows with their calves is illustrated in two bas-reliefs from Banteay Chhmar and Bayon (Figure 25.2b–c).

The Water Buffalo

Water buffalo symbolism is deeply rooted in mainland Southeast Asian culture. Small clay buffalo statues have been found interred with burials at the Bronze Age site of Ban Na Di in northeast Thailand (Higham and Kijngam 1984), while numerous horn-shaped bronze rings and other objects suggests the presence of a local buffalo cult in Iron Age Cambodia (Reinecke et al. 2009). With the arrival of Indic ideology came a decline in the prominence of water buffalo in Khmer art, now featured primarily on bas-reliefs as either the vāhana of Yama, god of death and justice (see Ang 2023, this volume), or more commonly as the demon Mahiṣāsura being defeated by the goddess Durga (Roveda 2005). Two examples offer insights into the animal's role in the synthesis of Indic and local religious ideas: a Pre-Angkorian buffalo head-shaped ablution cistern found near the early capital, Angkor Borei and the sacred mountain of Phnom Da, and a scene of a buffalo sacrifice in a late 12th-century bas-relief at the Bayon temple at Angkor (Figure 25.3).

The Khmer worshipped a range of Indic and local deities in the early Pre-Angkor Period. During the 7th to 8th centuries, increased references to Durga in the Khmer inscriptions are associated with a general acceptance of goddess worship (Jacobsen 2008). Ashley Thompson has hypothesised that the large, finely carved buffalo cistern served as the base for a Durga statue and can be seen as an important marker of her cult before the rise of Angkor and the widespread adoption of Śaivism (2019, 102–03). Vickery (1998, 142) has also argued that early Khmer depictions of Durga slaying the buffalo demon should be interpreted in terms of an indigenous cult rather than a simple borrowing from India, while Sanderson considered that ethnographic accounts of buffalo sacrifices in Cambodia were not ritually linked to Durga (2003, 379). Regardless, this large cistern shows the important role of buffalo symbolism in the conceptual development of the early Khmer state.

Figure 25.2 Depiction of cows in Angkorian bas-relief. a) Baphuon: the *go danam* ritual, dying Brahmin gifting a cow with her calf; b) Banteay Chhmar: Brahmins and cow with calf; c) Bayon: Brahmins and cow with calf.

Source: (Photos S. Siyonn).

The Bayon scene shows a buffalo tied to a post in front of a tree, surrounded by soldiers, ascetics, and elites, and presents an intriguing example of animal sacrifice that may reflect the integration of ideas and shifting religious practices during Angkor's imperial zenith. This striking but relatively minor panel has been interpreted variously as a sacrifice to ensure military victory for king Jayavarman VII (Im, pers. comm, July 2013), as part of a cremation ceremony

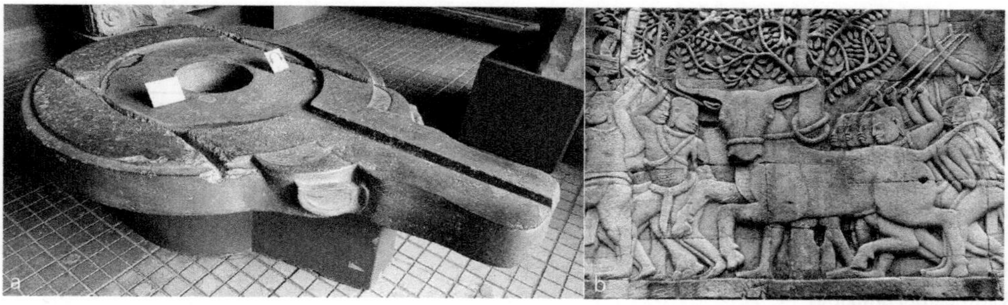

Figure 25.3 Buffalo images from the Pre-Angkor and Angkor Period: a) buffalo-shaped ablution cistern from Phnom Da region. (Photo P. Lavy, image reproduced courtesy of the National Museum of Cambodia); b) buffalo sacrifice scene from the Bayon. (Photo M. Hendrickson).

depicted in a connected panel (Roveda 2005, 288) or a rare example of indigenous practices co-existing with Brahmanical and Buddhist ideas (Groslier 1973, 168). Groslier's view has certain merit, given the widespread evidence and ethnographic persistence of buffalo sacrifice in mainland Southeast Asia (Sprenger 2005; Cort and Lefferts 2013). In Cambodia, the practice of buffalo sacrifice by minority upland groups is associated with possession ceremonies to propitiate local spirits (*neak ta*) that protect villages (Ang 1986). An account of the act among the Lamet in northern Laos describes the animal being tied to a post at the village centre (Sprenger 2005, 299–301). After the ceremony, this post, anointed with its blood, is the place from which the flesh is divided amongst the villagers.

While the Bayon scene may be derived from indigenous practice, it is important to note that this act and its meaning are woven into Indian mythologies, both Brahmanical and animist. Buffalo sacrifices are described in the Mahābhārata and Rāmāyana and accounts of Vedic ritual refer to tying the animal to a wooden post known as a *yūpa*. The sacrifice in India was also co-opted from animist practices and came to be used to celebrate Durga's victory over the buffalo demon and in ethnographic contexts is typically conducted to protect a village. On a larger scale, the ritual signifies the unity of the kingdom and is one of the few rituals designed to bring all castes together. A further indication of the Bayon relief's Indic roots is the presence of the tree behind the post. The Indian buffalo sacrifice is associated with the *śami* tree (*Prosopis cineraria*, a variety of mesquite) which, in addition to its many medicinal properties, is associated with sacrificial fire rituals in Brahmanical veneration and specifically with the goddess Durga (Hiltebeitel 1980; Biardeau 1984). The morphological similarity between a living śami tree and the one in the Bayon image, combined with the fact that the species was likely introduced to Cambodia from India (European and Mediterranean Plant Protection Organization 2019, 290–91), again suggests that the scene derives from or at least shares ideals with Brahmanical or perhaps older Vedic sources. Since the Bayon was constructed by Jayavarman VII after reclaiming Angkor in 1181, the inclusion of this scene on his central temple-mountain could represent a ritual enacted to Durga either before his victory over Cham-Khmer forces who were controlling Angkor or a prayer for unification of the kingdom after the fact. Given that goddess worship was largely abandoned in the Angkor Period (Thompson 2019, 103), this scene could represent an attempt by Jayavarman VII—who converted the state religion to Mahāyāna Buddhism—to turn away from Śaivite worship. While representations of buffalo are rare, these two examples, the cistern and the bas-relief, nonetheless demonstrate that the animal retained ritual significance during the Angkor Period.

Table 25.1 Pre-Angkorian and Angkorian inscription data on bovines.

	Pre-Angkorian	*Angkorian*
Inscriptions referring to bovines in endowments	55	57
Inscriptions referring to bovines in exchanges	3	33
Inscriptions with cattle	55	69
Inscription with buffalo	31	64
Cattle in inscriptions	1955	2173
Buffalo in inscriptions	588	393
Ratio cattle/buffaloes	3.3	5.5
Cattle in endowments	1953	1942
Buffalo in endowments	587	293
Ratio cattle/buffaloes in endowments	3.3	6.5
Cattle in exchanges	2	231
Buffalo in exchanges	1	95
Ratio cattle/buffaloes in exchanges	Not meaningful	2.4

Bovines in the Temple Economy

We know from the corpus of inscriptions that cattle and water buffalo were among the most prominent donations to temples, and herds of more than 100 were 'not uncommon' (Wheatley 1965). Cows in particular were valued for their milk products which were essential components in temple rituals. In the Old Khmer corpus of around 850 published inscriptions (200 Pre-Angkorian and 650 Angkorian), about 150 refer to cattle, buffalo, or both (Table 25.1). Most mentions are found in endowments to temples, although in 36 (mostly Angkorian) texts bovines constitute all or part of an exchange (or barter) price, generally for land. Cattle and buffalo are well represented in both the Pre-Angkor and Angkor Periods, but the cattle-to-buffalo ratio is significantly higher in Angkorian (5.5) than in Pre-Angkorian texts (3.3). The most striking contrast is between Angkor Period exchanges (2.4) and Angkor Period temple endowments (6.5). The endowments were elite religious donations, while the exchanges were of goods and services not necessarily related to temples. Thus, cattle appear more important to temple operations than to the general economy. Buffaloes would have been used for agriculture and transport in both temples and the wider economy: the milk of buffaloes was not used for temple ritual.

The increasing proportion of cattle in the Angkor Period corresponds with the rising population in the Tonle Sap Basin and the expanding wealth of elites as more land became settled. This provided the resources to build temples (Lustig and Lustig 2019), leading to an increase in demand for cow by-products. As it is, cattle are better suited to areas beyond the wet delta and the Tonle Sap fringes, where most farming land is characterised by (seasonally) dry soils (Delvert 1961, 236–39).

Terms for Bovines

Many of the terms for animals and farming in the Khmer texts were already in use in the Pre-Angkor Period (Vickery 1998, 87; Lustig et al. 2007), but increased communications and foreign trade, in particular with India, led to the introduction of new words early in the Angkor era. Many of these were Sanskrit, but the majority of agricultural terms continued to be expressed in the vernacular. While buffalo were almost always referred to as *krapi*, within a century there were many more terms for cattle, including *poṅ* (pregnant), *thpvac* (calf), *jmol* (male), *canmat* (bulls), and *kryav* (oxen) (Jenner 2009; Jenner 2009a), pointing to their increasing prominence. But the clearest evidence of their rising status is that the general term for cattle (*tmur* in the Pre-Angkor Period and *thmur* in the Angkor Period) was used until the late 10th century, when it was replaced by the expression *vraḥ go* (sacred cattle) in temple contexts. The last known date for thmur is 982 CE (K. 214), with the earliest known vraḥgo appearing a short time earlier (K. 425, 968 CE). The period of this linguistic transition perhaps corresponds with the period when reverence for cattle became widespread in India towards the end of the first millennium CE (Harris 1978).

Cow Products

There are numerous inscription references to products derived from cows used in Hindu and Buddhist rituals as well as for consumption by Brahmins and ascetics (Table 25.2). The most important were those that made up the *pañcagavya*, the five products of the cow: clarified butter (ghee), coagulated milk, thickened milk, dung, and urine—typically offered daily to the gods in addition to prepared rice. In Cambodia, only the first four of these feature in Angkorian texts.

> These are the terms of the donor's endowment: 1 *je* daily of milled rice for offerings; daily requisites for ablutions; pañcagavya: ghee; honey; coagulated milk; thickened milk; molasses; coconuts; perfumes and incense; lamps; candles; betel-leaf [and] areca nuts; [. . .].
>
> K. 659 (968 CE), 14–17

Khmer iconography and epigraphy frequently refer to the churning of butter, an act symbolically linked with the creation of the elixir of immortality (*amṛta*) in the Hindu Purānas and famously depicted on the walls of Angkor Wat. Bas-reliefs at several temples in Angkor also show the more prosaic undertaking of Brahmins churning milk to make butter using tools and techniques similar to those found in contemporary times (Figure 25.4).

Oil or semi-fluid butter (*paryyaṅ*) was the main product of the churning process and is mentioned in close to 40 inscriptions. This fluid was used as a combustible fuel for cult lamps but more importantly to perform the daily ritual of feeding and anointing the gods (Soutif 2009, 221–70). The 10th-century inscription K. 71 from Svay Rieng, a royal edict concerning the foundation of a minister of Rājendravarman II, deals with the fortnightly provision of oil from the 'sacred herd' for anointing a divinity to be taken from the 'sacred herd'. The inscription records how tasks were

Table 25.2 Cow products in the Khmer inscriptions. Terms in Sanskrit or Khmer (Kh).

Cow product	*Gloss (Monier-Williams 2005[1899]; Jenner (2009, 2009a)*
pañcagavya	The five products of the cow: milk, curds, ghee, urine, dung
kṣīra	Milk, thickened milk
dadhi	Coagulated milk
pareṅ, paryyaṅ (Kh)	Oil, clarified semi-fluid butter
ghṛta	Clarified butter; ghee
'ājya~'āja, 'ājyaśeṣa	Melted or clarified butter
gomayā, gomaya	Cow dung
madhuparkka	Honey-milk oblation
caru	Oblation of rice, barley and pulse boiled with butter and milk

Figure 25.4 Milk churning imagery: a) the Baphuon; and b) Angkor Wat.

Source: (Photos S. Siyonn).

allocated, indicating that many aspects of temple life such as the scheduling of the labour force and the ritual activities were organised according to the lunar half-month:

> [several dignitaries] receive the order to give the oil for anointing the god, but to not give it to those who . . . in the sacred Islet. We hereby appoint four requisitioners of oil for each fortnight, responsible for collecting the oil. This oil and the four requisitioners shall be under the authority of *mrateñ* Rājadvāra of the clear fortnight who allocates the oil for each fortnight for anointing the divinities.
>
> K. 71 (878–977 CE), 6–11

Production and distribution of oil were strictly regulated. The same edict specifies that a penalty of two cows be paid by anyone found giving out oil rightfully belonging to the god, which, Wheatley (1965) points out, would have helped sustain herd numbers. He further argues that mentions of 'collectors of paryyaṅ' in K. 71 suggest a general levy imposed on the whole district or perhaps on the 'beneficed' lands of the foundation. Both the term *paryyaṅ viṣaya* (melted butter of the district), found in other texts and the frequent mentions of tax immunities with regard to paryyaṅ, support this view.

An 8th-century text from Kampong Cham points to the high value placed on clarified butter after use in the anointing ceremony and indicates how it could be traded within local communities,

> Paddy fields acquired in exchange for the residues of the *ghṛta* of the god, which are to be burnt by [? other] people and whose price is rice to the value of 5 *tamlin* of silver.
>
> K. 726A, 12–15

Milk products were important in the rituals of the Hindu and Mahāyāna Buddhist religions, whose other commonalities were acknowledged by Yaśovarman (889–910 CE), when he established *āśrama* for the Śaiva, Vaiṣṇava and Mahāyāna Buddhist sects with almost identical inscriptions (K. 701, K. 279, K. 290). The ritual use of dairy seems to have continued into the reign of the Buddhist king Jayavarman VII (1181–1218 CE). Milk products were advocated as remedies in his monasteries and hospitals (Chhem et al. 2023, this volume). The Ta Prohm (K. 273) and Preah Khan (K. 208) inscriptions list butter, milk, and curd for oblations, while clarified butter, herbs, spices, and curative applications were prescribed for the 102 hospitals scattered across the provinces (see, for example, K. 368). These practices ceased when Mahāyāna Buddhism was replaced by Theravada Buddhism in the 13th century (Wheatley 1965).

Although milk products are known to have been widely used in religious contexts (Wheatley 1965) the issue of who in Angkorian society consumed them seemingly presents certain contradictions. While milk drinking was associated with Brahmins, it also appears to have been practised by some elites. Milking and milk drinking are depicted in a 12th-century lintel at Ta Prohm temple (see Figure 25.5), while epigraphic evidence from a cave inscription in Battambang (K. 1049) refers to 'a prince of ascetics who consumed only milk' (Goodall 2015). A line from the 10th-century inscription K. 156 from Wat Moha also refers to Kambu, an agent of the king, as a 'drinker of milk'. Perhaps, as Wheatley (1965) suggests, water buffalo milk was also consumed. A stanza from the Preah Ko inscription K. 713 (893 CE) refers to enemies of Indravarman I as 'subsisting on forest fruits when they could have been drinking the milk of buffalo cows'.

The Lower Mekong basin is today located beyond the so-called 'milking line'. It is presumed that much of its pre-modern population may not have consumed this product either through lack of access, preference, or perhaps lactose intolerance (Simoons 1970). Indeed, scholars of the French Colonial Period rarely or never observed milk being consumed (e.g., Groslier 1921; Delvert 1961, 154–55). Wheatley (1965) argues that since Angkorian milk production was primarily for ritual purposes under Hinduism and Mahāyāna Buddhism, the demand for milk would have declined significantly as these beliefs were replaced by Theravāda Buddhism in the 13th and 14th centuries.

A further question about Angkor's bovines is whether the people, elite or otherwise, consumed their meat. As mentioned, Zhou Daguan's late 13th-century account of Angkor indicates that cattle were not eaten and that their hides were never used (Zhou 2007[1297], 53). Zhou later comments that Buddhist monks ate meat, without noting what kind of animal. This may reflect differences between religious groups or Zhou's exposure to dietary practices of non-elite groups. Regardless, if there was a society-wide ban, it has not persisted into the present.

Figure 25.5 Scene depicting Brahmins milking a cow and drinking milk from Ta Prohm.

Source: (Photo S. Siyonn).

Management

Cows would have been maintained wherever there were temples (Wheatley 1965). Kautilya's Arthaśastra, the Indian treatise well known to Angkor's temple and court Brahmins, describes a cattle management system in which livestock were protected, often in stables, and outlines optimal grazing conditions, healthcare, and ways of standardising purity of milk products (Olivelle 2013). In the Khmer texts, there are a few references to the terms *gośāla* (stable) and *karol* (pen; stable) and occasional mentions of the individuals employed in care of the animals. For instance, in inscription K. 258 from Samron in northern Angkor, a chief (*khloñ*) of the royal stables (*vraḥ gośāla*) is recorded as one of several land vendors. K. 71 highlights the importance of stables in maintaining dairy cattle at the temple of the 'Sacred Islet' at Bassac in Svay Rieng province:

> It shall be the Custodian of the Court of Justice who shall manage the said herd. It devolves on the lord Keeper of the Palace Gate for the first fortnight, the sanctuary head, the *āśrama* Superior, directors of public works, servants of the deity, village guards, [and] inspectors to build cow stables, one for the second fortnight, one for the first fortnight [as] places to keep the sacred herd.
>
> K. 71 (878–977 CE), 16–19

Another text from Prah Non in Kampong Cham mentions a stable and cow products prescribed for a single deity, the Sacred Fire. We can see that the providers of these ritual products were kept at or in close proximity to the temple:

> [They] next built a cow stable, assigned a herd to it, and made a garden. Allowance of holy articles of food: □ *mās* of coagulated milk; 1 *mās* of milk; 3 *'var* of clarified butter. These are for the Sacred Fire.
>
> K. 88 (1003 CE), 6–8

The importance of stables is inferred from a line in K. 299 from Angkor Wat, which enumerates the 33 hells and the people who go to them:

> The Aṅgāranicaya (one of the hells—Heap of Coals): those who burn down a village or city or the stable of sacred cows (*karol vraḥ go*); those who urinate [or] defecate on the grounds of a sanctuary.
>
> K. 299 (1078–1177 CE), 20

In modern Cambodia, where there is no ritual demand for cow products, bovines tend to be kept in small numbers in the vicinity of houses and pasture during the day up to 5–6 km away. These animals are often shepherded for longer periods over greater distances during the dry season (Delvert 1961, 245–51), since maintaining cattle and buffalo requires year-round adequate grazing land and, more importantly, access to reliable sources of water. A strategy widely employed by Pre-Angkorian times to ensure water supplies in areas beyond the flood zone was to construct *trapeang*, earthen-banked, rectilinear reservoirs excavated to below the water table (Figure 25.6a). The Angkorian Khmer dramatically expanded the use of trapeang, constructing thousands of these reservoirs in association with temple complexes and villages across their territories (Pottier 1999; Evans et al. 2007). These hydraulic structures served symbolic and economic purposes and provided water for people and their animals. Away from settlements,

Figure 25.6 Trapeang in the Angkorian World: a) trapeang integrated with temple complex and settlement mounds; b) perishable hut located next to a remote trapeang.

Source: (Photos M. Hendrickson).

trapeang were surrounded by matrices of bunded rice fields. Today, these premodern reservoirs often have perishable raised shelters used by farmers and herders (Figure 25.6b). This practice likely has roots in the Angkorian past.

The highest concentrations of cattle in modern Cambodia are in the rice-growing areas of the Mekong Delta and the lowlands around the Quatre Bras confluence (Figure 25.7a). Large numbers also appear around the peripheries of Greater Angkor, and the area to the northwest is recognised by locals as being ideal for raising cattle. This landscape is covered with bunded premodern rice fields and dozens of Pre-Angkorian and Angkorian temples as well as hundreds of trapeang (Figure 25.7b). Declining numbers of temples in the western part of this area, together with the continued presence of trapeang, many of which appear to lack any associated settlement infrastructure (e.g., mounds, canals, etc.), indicate a decrease in population density, while water sources exploitable for pasturing cattle remained. Thus, larger numbers of cattle could be raised or shepherded there than in the areas to the east, and used primarily for agriculture and transportation. However, while the number of bovines mentioned in the temple inscriptions as goods for barter point to economic activities, they do not indicate numbers present in the landscape.

Ploughing

The intensification of early agricultural systems and rise of complex societies is often associated with the input of beasts of burden and, specifically, the introduction of animal ploughing (Sherratt 1983; Pryor 1985; Isaakidou 2006). Prehistoric archaeologists have offered various lines of evidence to demonstrate the increased role of this technology across mainland Southeast Asia during its 'Iron Age' (late 1st millenium BCE to early 1st millenium CE). These include the appearance of metal ploughshares (metal tips attached to wooden ploughs), the increased size of animal phalanges, and bovine hoofprints interpreted as the location of a corral for a moated site in northeast Thailand (Higham et al. 1981; Higham and Kijngam 1984; Higham and Rispoli 2014; Castillo et al. 2018). Modern Cambodian ploughing is taken to be similar to past practices, that is, rice field preparation entails pairs of animals yoked to a wooden plough with an iron tip (Delvert 1961, 221). The annual royal ploughing ceremony, in which the king guides a

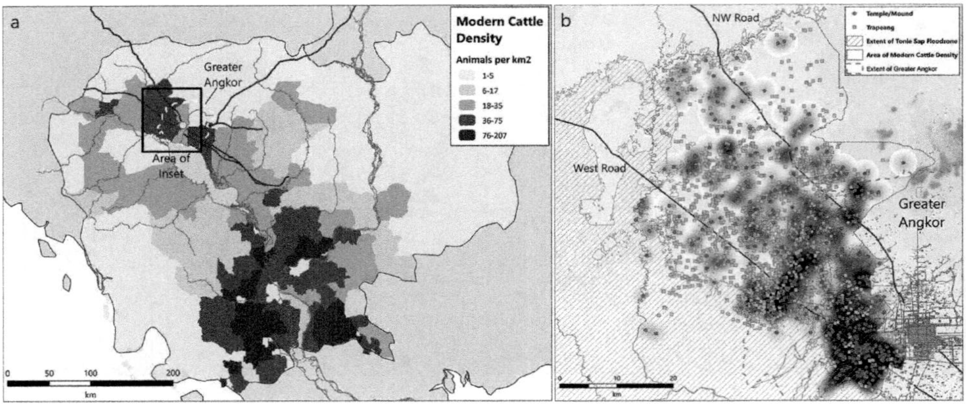

Figure 25.7 Comparison of modern cattle densities, Angkorian trapeang and temples: a) current distribution of cattle in Cambodia (based on Pham et al. 2015, fig. 2); b) premodern temples and trapeang to the north west of Greater Angkor.

Source: (GIS data D. Evans and M. Kummu).

pair of oxen to initiate the agricultural season, is an important ritual dating back some centuries in Cambodia. Like many ritual practices, the origins of the ceremony may lie in an episode of the Indian epic Rāmāyana which was well known in Cambodia as the Ramakerti or Reamker (Jacob and Kuoch 2006, 2).

Whether ploughing played a significant role in agricultural practices in the Khmer Empire is not clear. Zhou Daguan's 13th-century eyewitness account indicated that local ploughs were known, but neither buffalo nor cattle were used with them to prepare fields (2007[1297], 67). Epigraphic examples of ploughs (*'aṅgāla*) are rare and mostly occur as toponyms, perhaps indicating areas where they were manufactured or employed. An unusual instance of a temple donation of 'real' ploughs is found in the inscription of Prei Yan, from Siem Reap province:

> Four pairs of sacred cows: two (are) offered up to the central tower, two (are) offered up to the south tower. One pair of bulls: one to the central tower, one to the south tower. Four ploughs: two (are) offered up to the central tower, two (are) offered up to the south tower.
>
> K. 845 (878–1077 CE), 14–16

Reference to cattle and ploughs together in this text might imply they were used together, though this raises some questions about Zhou's account. Given the focus of Khmer temple inscriptions, highlighting the wealth and generosity of the founders and donors, the fact that ploughs are referred to infrequently suggest that agricultural tools were of little intrinsic value in this context. The absence of metal ploughshares in excavations may also be explained by the focus of archaeologists on temple sites or by taphonomic processes: metal ploughshares would be used until broken, reworked, or reused, while any remains would have difficulty surviving in Cambodia's acidic soils and monsoonal climate. Regardless, many Asian ploughs even today do not have metal tips (Pryor 1985). With regard to the number of epigraphic mentions of buffalo, which do not produce ritual products but are well suited to wet conditions, they would have been used in agriculture. Today buffaloes are the major source of power for ploughing and harrowing in wet rice agricultural lands (Helmers 1997).

Regardless of Angkor's contact with contemporary states that made use of intensive animal ploughing (specifically China and India), one cannot be certain that this technique played a major role in Angkorian wet-rice agriculture. Francesca Bray's treatise on rice production in Asia argues that intensification of rice paddy production was enhanced less by technological advances than by increased access to labour and organisation into communal work units (1986, 27). In fact, for a great many Khmer temples and the many more deities, the activities of food provision and the multitude of rituals for maintaining the gods were scheduled according to half months, of either the waxing or the waning moon. The citations from K. 71, above, illustrate this scheduling in the production of paryyaṅ for a temple. However, we don't know how widespread this system of organising temple workforces was or if it was applied in the general population. Nevertheless, organised labour, in various degrees of servitude (Mabbett 1983; Vickery 1999), and *corvée* conscription (Sahai 1970, 117–19; Lustig 2009, 93) would have provided much of the workforce for producing the state's rice, as well as its building and infrastructure projects. The large numbers of indentured labourers referred to in the inscriptions appear to have become increasingly commodified over time (Lustig and Lustig 2013). Instead of subscribing to the Eurocentric model of agricultural intensification via technological enhancement, we might better view Angkor's increased agricultural output as resulting from 'extensification', the bringing of increasing areas of land into rice production.

Transportation

Bovines definitely played a major role in facilitating the movement of Angkorian people and goods, including the vital rice taxes and ritual products required by the state. Zhou Daguan noted that cattle were used to pull carts (2007[1297], 73), and many examples of ox-driven carts are found on temple bas-reliefs in military processions and in scenes of daily life. While buffalo are not depicted as beasts of burden, early colonial records highlight their ability to haul heavy loads (Thorel 2001, 32), and they would certainly have been valuable for moving stone or iron ore during Angkorian times. There are a few mentions of vehicular (cart) roads (*phlu rddeḥ*) in inscriptions (Lustig and Hendrickson 2012), and ethnographic accounts show that ox carts of different types were used to move produce and facilitate trade and communication (Ebihara 1968, 554–56). The trapeang placed at 1–2-km intervals along each of Angkor's raised earthen roads, radiating out over 1000 km from the capital, would have served to provide drinking water for animals used in transportation and for water buffalo to bathe in.

Herd Composition

Cambodia is home to both endemic and introduced species of cattle and water buffalo that have interbred over the centuries to produce its modern livestock. In the past, this region contained at least two known species of cattle: gaur (*Bos gaurus*) and kouprey (*Bos sauvelis*) as well as the swamp and river water buffalo (*Bos bubalis*) (Yue et al. 2013, 12; Hassanin et al. 2006), which were exploited in wild or domesticated form (Beavan et al. 2012; Groves 2006). Two other types of cattle introduced to Southeast Asia, the banteng (*Bos javanicus*) from Indonesia and the zebu (*Bos indicus*) from India, likely appeared in domesticated form during the late Prehistoric Period (0–500 CE) (Lenstra and Bradley 1999; Chen et al. 2009). The sacred status of the humped zebu in Hindu tradition is presumed to be part of the package that facilitated the political transformations from small chiefdoms to centralised states in Southeast Asia during the early first millennium CE (Pigott et al. 2006, 159–61). The Khmer epigraphic corpus does not refer to a particular variety of cattle. However, given Angkor's association with India, zebu might be considered to have been the predominant or even preferred breed. One possible mention in a Sanskrit text of 1052 CE (K. 235, CXI) appears to indicate the zebu breed, referring to '500 humped cows with their calves'. Another type of cow mentioned in texts is the *kapila*. In the Indian Purānas, the kapila or red cow was held to yield an endless supply of milk, as in the tale of Surhabi mentioned previously. The high regard in which the kapila was held in Cambodia is evidenced in this imprecation from the Stele of Palhal:

> Should there chance to be anyone so wilful as to disregard the provisions of this foundation, his guilt shall be that of one who betrays his king or harms his spiritual preceptor, or of one who kills a *brāhmaṇa*, a parent, or a sacred reddish cow (kapila), and he shall end in one of the hells such as the Avīci or Atiraurava for all eternity.
>
> K. 449 (1069 CE): B26–28 [Free translation by Philip Jenner]

The 12th-century Ta Prohm temple inscription, K. 273 (CXVI), lists a kapila cow decorated in gold with its calf among the stored treasure. It might be pointed out here that the preference for reddish-brown cows may have been more allusion to Indic mythology than indicative of species.

Determining the types of animals from physical remains is complicated by the dearth of bones, in part due to poor preservation. Ingalls' (2010) examination of bovine remains from Angkor Borei has demonstrated the potential for species identification based on tooth morphology but ultimately indicated the need for DNA testing. Analyses of cattle and buffalo species in other parts of Asia have proven useful for studies of domestication and for tracking movement and crossbreeding (Hassanin et al. 2006; Chen et al. 2009; Yue et al. 2013). As more samples are identified, the hope is that future genetic research in Cambodia will be able to determine the stock they were derived from, when their Indian ancestors arrived (see Savalia et al. 2019), which could indicate if the zebu breed played a significant part in Angkor's politico-religious transformations.

Concluding Remarks

The veneration of cattle in India, first seen in texts of the Vedic Period (ca. 1500–ca. 500 BCE), appears to have become ubiquitous in Cambodia towards the end of the first millennium CE. It was around this time that the Khmer turned to the expression vraḥ go for cows offered to their temples to provide products to anoint their gods. The rituals, and cow maintenance in general, became an important aspect of the temple economy, persisting until the adoption of Theravada Buddhism in the 13th–14th century. Reverence for cattle is evidenced in Sanskrit verses alluding to the bounties derived from wish-granting cows; statues of the bull Nandin, Śiva's mount; images of Brahmins receiving and milking cows; and eulogies in which the rule of the king is likened to the Golden Age of the Dharma-bull. Yet it seems unlikely that there would have been high spiritual regard for cattle among those of lower socio-economic status. Perhaps the high incidence of lactose intolerance within modern Khmer populations could provide insight into the restricted use of cattle products in the past. Arguably, cattle reverence associated with milk-drinking may have developed as a mechanism for elites to display their elevated status. Buffalo, which played an important role in prehistoric ritual contexts, were less prominent in religious practice in the Angkor Period. Rare representations of buffalo in Khmer art demonstrate some fusion of Indic beliefs with local earth cults and highlight the continuation of goddess worship within a religious system largely focused on Śiva and Viṣṇu.

The Khmer's reliance on cattle was facilitated by the relatively dry conditions across the northern Tonle Sap Basin. Both water buffalo—better suited to Cambodia's wetter regions—and oxen were used to facilitate transportation and to enhance agricultural production. The extent to which ploughs using animal traction aided economic development is unclear, yet the ubiquity of trapeang demonstrates the potential to employ bovines in areas far from permanent water sources. Rice produced from Angkor's territories is viewed as the critical factor in enabling Khmer kings to fund the labour forces that built their imperial powerbase and was used to 'feed' the gods housed in masonry temples. Bovine power was essential for moving rice into the capital, while cow products ritually brought the gods to life every day. From this perspective, cattle and water buffalo literally and figuratively provided the 'wheels' and 'oil' for Angkor's massive imperial machine.

List of Inscriptions in the Text

K.	*Reference*	*K.*	*Reference*	*K.*	*Reference*
71	IC II, 54	299	Pou 2001, 156	726	IC V, 75
88	IC VII, 30	368	Finot 1903, 18	806	IC I, 73
156	IC V, 178	377	IC V, 3	842	IC I, 147
208	IC VI, 287	425	IC II, 142	845	IC V, 186
214	IC II, 202	440	IC IV, 5	947	Soutif 2009, 533
235	Finot 1915, 53	449	Cœdès 1913, 27	1049	Goodall 2015, 3
254	IC III, 180	659	IC V, 143		
273	Cœdei€s 1906, 44	713	IC I, 18		

IC = Inscriptions du Cambodge. Cœdès 1937–66.

References

Ang, C., 1986. *Les êtres surnaturels. dans la religion populaire khmère*. Montrouge: Cedoreck.

Ang, C., 1997. Nandin and his avatars, in *Sculpture of Angkor and Ancient Cambodia: Millennium of Glory*, eds. H.I. Jessup. & T. Zephir. Washington, DC: National Gallery of Art, 62–9.

Ang, C., 2023. Yama, the god closest to the Khmers, in *The Angkorian World*, eds. M. Hendrickson, M.T. Stark. & D. Evans. New York: Routledge.

Assavavirulhakarn, P., 2010. *The Ascendancy of Theravada Buddhism in Southeast Asia*. Chiang Mai: Silkworm Books.

Beavan, N., S. Halcrow, B. McFadgen, D. Hamilton, B.M. Buckley, L. Shewan, O. Sokha, S. Fallon, J. Miksic, R. Armstrong, D. O'Reilly, K. Domett. & K.R. Chhem, 2012. Radiocarbon dates from jar and coffin burials of the Cardamom mountains reveal a previously unrecorded mortuary ritual in Cambodia's late- to Post-Angkor Period (15th–17th centuries AD). *Radiocarbon* 54, 1–22.

Bhattacharya, K., 1961. *Les Religions Brahmaniques Dans L'Ancien Cambodge. D'Après l'Épigraphie et l'Iconographie*. Paris: École française d'Extrême-Orient.

Biardeau, M., 1984. The śami tree and the sacrificial buffalo. *Contributions to Indian Sociology* 18(1), 1–23.

Bray, F., 1986. *The Rice Economies. Technology and Development in Asian Societies*. Los Angeles: University of California Press.

Castillo, C.C., C.F.W. Higham, K. Miller, N. Chang, K. Douka, T.F.G. Higham. & D.Q. Fuller, 2018. Social responses to climate change in iron age North-East Thailand: new archaeobotanical evidence. *Antiquity* 92(365), 1274–91.

Chen, S., B-Z. Lin, M. Baig, B. Mitra, R.J. Lopes, A.M. Santos, D.A. Magee, M. Azevedo, P. Tarroso, S. Sasazaki, S. Ostrowski, O. Mahgoub, T.K. Chaudhuri, Y-P. Zhang, V. Costa, L.J. Royo, F. Goyache, G. Luikart, N. Boivin, D.Q. Fuller, H. Mannen, D.G. Bradley. & A. Beja-Pereira, 2009. Zebu cattle are an exclusive legacy of the South Asia Neolithic. *Molecular Biology and Evolution* 27(1), 1–6.

Chhem, R., D. Evans, K. Chhom, P. Phlong. & P.D. Sharrock, 2023. Education and medicine at Angkor, in *The Angkorian World*, eds. M. Hendrickson, M.T. Stark. & D. Evans. New York: Routledge, 287–306.

Cœdès, G., 1906. La stèle de Ta-Prohm. *Bulletin de l'École française d'Extrême-Orient* 6(1), 44–86.
Cœdès, G., 1913. La stèle de Pàlhal. *Bulletin de l'École française d'Extrême-Orient* 13, 27–36
Cœdès, G., 1937–66. *Inscriptions du Cambodge. Collection de Textes et Documents sur l'Indochine* (Vol. I (1937); Vol. II (1942); Vol. III (1951); Vol. IV (1952); Vol. V (1953); Vol. VI (1954); Vol. VII (1964); Vol. VIII (1966)). Paris: École française d'Extrême-Orient.
Cœdès, G., 1968. *The Indianized states of Southeast Asia*. Honolulu: University of Hawai'i Press.
Cort, L.A. & L. Lefferts, 2013. Jars in the central highlands of mainland Southeast Asia, in *Materializing Southeast Asia's Past. Selected Papers from the 12th International Conference of the European Association of Southeast Asian Archaeologists*, eds. M.J. Klokke. & V. Degroot. Singapore: NUS Press, 233–41.
de Casparis, J.G., 1961. New evidence on cultural relations between Java and Ceylon in ancient times. *Artibus Asiae* 24(3–4), 241–8.
Delvert, J., 1961. *Le Paysan Cambodgien*. Paris: Mouton et Co.
Dimmitt, C. & J.A.B. van Buitenen, 1978. *Classic Hindu Mythology. A Reader in the Sanskrit Puranas*. Philadelphia: Temple University Press.
Ebihara, M.M., 1968. *Svay, a Khmer Village in Cambodia*. PhD dissertation. New York: Columbia University.
European and Mediterranean Plant Protection Organization, 2019. *Prosopis juliflora* (Sw) DC. *Bulletin OEPP/EPPO Bulletin* 49(2), 290–97.
Evans, D., C. Pottier, R. Fletcher, S. Hensley, I. Tapley, A. Milne. & M. Barbetti, 2007. A comprehensive archaeological map of the World's largest preindustrial settlement complex at Angkor, Cambodia. *Proceedings of the National Academy of Sciences of North America* 104(36), 14277–82.
Finot, L., 1903. L'inscription sanskrite de Say-fong. *Bulletin de l'École française d'Extrême- Orient* 3, 18–33.
Finot, L., 1915. L'inscription de Sdok Kak Thom. *Bulletin de l'École française d'Extrême-Orient* 15, 53–106.
Freed, S.A., R.S. Freed, R. Ballard, K. Chattopadhyay, P. Diener, L. Dumont, J.V. Ferreira, C.J. Fuller, M. Harris, D.O. Lodrick, S.L. Malik, S.N. Mishra, W.H. Newell, D.M. Nonini, S. Odend'hal, A.R. Rajapurohit, E.E. Robkin, U.M. Sharma, M. Suryanarayana. & H.S. Verma, 1981. Sacred cows and water buffalo in India: the uses of ethnography [and comments and reply]. *Current Anthropology* 22(5), 483–502.
Ganguli, R., 1931. Cattle and cattle-rearing in ancient India. *Annals of the Bhandarkar Oriential Research Institute* 12(3), 216–30.
Gaudes, R., 1993. Kauṇḍinya, Preah Thaong, and the "Nāgī Somā": some aspects of a Cambodian legend. *Asian Folklore Studies* 52(2), 333–58.
Goodall, D., 2015. On K, 1049, a tenth-century cave-inscription from Battambang, and on the sectarian obedience of the Śaiva ascetics of non-royal cave-inscriptions in Cambodia. *Udaya, Journal of Khmer Studies* 13, 3–34.
Groslier, B-P., 1958. Angkor et le Cambodge au XVIe siècle d'après les sources portugaises et espagnoles. Paris: Presses Universitaires de France.
Groslier, B-P., 1973. *Les Inscriptions du Bayon, in Le Bayon*. Paris: École française d'Extrême-Orient.
Groslier, B-P., 1998[1974]. *Agriculture et religion dans l'empire angkorien, in Mélanges sur l'archéologie du Cambodge* (1949–1986) (Réimpressions de l'école française d'extrême-orient. Jan-Dec.) Paris: Presses de l'école française d'extrême-orient, 105–29.
Groslier, G., 1921. *Recherches sur les Cambodgiens*. Paris: Augustin Challamel.
Groves, C.P., 2006. Domesticated and commensal mammals of Austronesia and their histories, in *The Austronesians. Historical and Comparative Perspectives*. Canberra: ANU E Press, 161–73.
Harris, M., 1978. India's sacred cow. *Human Nature* 1(2), 28–36.
Hassanin, A., A. Ropiquet, R. Cornette, M. Tranier, P. Pfeffer, P. Candegabe. & M. Lemaire, 2006. Has the kouprey (*Bos sauveli*) been domesticated in Cambodia? *Comptes Rendus Biologies* 329(2), 124–35.
Helmers, K., 1997. *Rice in the Cambodian Economy: Past and Present, in H. J. Nesbitt Rice Production in Cambodia*. Manila: International Rice Research Institute.
Higham, C.F. & F. Rispoli, 2014. The Mun Valley and Central Thailand in prehistory: integrating two cultural sequences. *Open Archaeology* 1, 2–28.
Higham, C.F.W. & A. Kijngam, 1984. *Prehistoric Investigations in Northeast Thailand. Part II*. Oxford: British Archaeological Reports.
Higham, C.F.W., A. Kijngam, B.F.J. Manly. & S.J.E. Moore, 1981. The bovid third phalanx and prehistoric ploughing. *Journal of Archaeological Science* 8(4), 353–65.
Hiltebeitel, A., 1980. Rama and Gilgamesh: the sacrifices of the water buffalo and the bull of heaven. *History of Religions* 19(3), 187–223.

Ingalls, T., 2010. *Variation in dental morphology in four species of bovids: applications for Southeast Asian archaeology and the Angkor Borei Site, Cambodia.* MA dissertation. Honolulu: University of Hawai'i, Manoa.

Isaakidou, V., 2006. Ploughing with cows: Knossos and the secondary products revolution, in *Animals in the Neolithic of Britain and Europe*, eds. D. Serjeantson & D. Field. (Neolithic Studies Group Seminar Papers 7). Oxford: Oxbow Books, 95–112.

Jacob, J.M. & H. Kuoch, 2006. *Reamker (Ramakerti). The Cambodian Version of the Ramayana.* London: Routledge Curzon.

Jacobsen, T., 2008. *Lost Goddesses. The Denial of Female Power in Cambodian History*. Copenhagen: NIAS Press.

Jenner, P.N., 2009. *A Dictionary of Pre-Angkorian Khmer, Canberra: Research School of Pacific and Asian Studies, Australian National University.* CanberraPacific Linguistics.

Jenner, P.N., 2009a. *A Dictionary of Angkorian Khmer, Canberra: Research School of Pacific and Asian Studies, Australian National University*. Canberra: Pacific Linguistics.

Lenstra, J.A. & D.G. Bradley, 1999. Systematics and phylogeny of cattle, in *The Genetics of Cattle*, eds. R. Fries. & A. Ruvinsky. Wallingford: CAB International, 1–14.

Lingat, R., 1973. *The Classical Law of India.* Berkeley: Unversity of California Press: Berkeley Center for South and Southeast Asia Studies.

Lustig, E., 2009. *Power and pragmatism in the political economy of Angkor.* PhD dissertation. Sydney: The University of Sydney.

Lustig, E., D. Evans. & N. Richards, 2007. Words across space and time: an analysis of lexical items in Khmer Inscriptions, sixth–fourteenth centuries CE. *Journal of Southeast Asian Studies* 38, 1–26.

Lustig, E. & M. Hendrickson, 2012. Angkor's roads: an archaeo-lexical approach, in *Connecting Empires: Selected Papers from the 13th International Conference of the European Association of Southeast Asian Archaeologists*, eds. D. Bonatz, A. Reinecke. & M.L. Tioa-Bonatz. Singapore: NUS Press, 191–208.

Lustig, E. & Lustig, T., 2013. New insights into 'les interminables listes nominatives d' esclaves' from numerical analyses of the personnel in Angkorian inscriptions. *Aséanie* 31, 55–83.

Lustig, E. & T. Lustig, 2019. Losing ground: decline of Angkor's middle-level officials. *Journal of Southeast Asian Studies* 50(3), 409–30.

Mabbett, I.W., 1977. Varnas in Angkor and the Indian caste system. *The Journal of Asian Studies* 36(3), 429–42.

Mabbett, I.W., 1983. Some remarks on the present state of knowledge about slavery in Angkor, in *Slavery, Bondage and Dependency in Southeast Asia*, ed. A. Reid. Brisbane: University of Queensland Press, 44–66.

Maxwell, T.S., 2007. The stele inscription of Preah Khan, Angkor. Text with translation and commentary. *Udaya, Journal of Khmer Studies* 8, 4–114.

Monier-Williams, M., 2005[1899]. *A Sanskrit-English Dictionary: Etymologically and Philologically Arranged with Special Reference to Cognate Indo-European Languages*. Cologne: Cologne institute of Indology and Tamil Studies.

Mus, P., 1975[1934]. *Inde vu de l'Est: cultes indiens et indigènes au Champa* (India seen from the East: Indian and indigenous cults in Champa). Melbourne: Clayton Centre of Southeast Asian Studies, Monash University.

Olivelle, P., 2013. *King, Governance, and Law in Ancient India. Kautilya's Arthasastra.* Oxford: Oxford University Press.

Pham, L., D. Smith, S. Soun. & V. Sau, 2015. *Cambodia Beef Cattle Industry*. Ben Tre, Vietnam. Online Report.

Pigott, V.C., K.M. Mudar, A. Agelarakis, L. Kealhofer, S.A. Weber. & J.C. Voelker, 2006. A program of analysis of organic remains from prehistoric copper-producing settlements in the Khao Wong Prachan Valley, Central Thailand: a progress report, in *Uncovering Southeast Asia's Past: Selected Papers from the 10th International Conference of the European Association of Southeast Asian Archaeologists*, eds. E.A. Bacus, I.C. Glover. & V.C. Pigott. Singapore: NUS Press, 154–67.

Pollock, S., 1966. The Sanskrit cosmopolis, 300–1300: Transculturation, vernacularization, and the question of ideology, in *Ideology and Status of Sanskrit: Contributions to the History of the Sanskrit Language*, ed. J.E.M. Houben. Leiden: E.J. Brill, 197–247.

Porte, B. & S. Chea, 2010. Sur les chemins de Tuol Kuhea: note sur un site préangkorien. *Udaya, Journal of Khmer Studies* 9, 151–68.

Pottier, C., 1999. *Carte archéologique de la Région d'Angkor. Zone Sud, in Sorbonne Nouvelle* (UFR Orient et Monde Arabe) Paris: UFR Orient et Monde Arabe, Universite Paris III—Sorbonne Nouvelle, 3 Vols.

Pou, S., 2001. *Nouvelles inscriptions du Cambodge II & III, traduites et éditées par Saveros Pou*. Paris: École française d'Extrême-Orient.

Pryor, F.L., 1985. The invention of the plow. *Comparative Studies in Society and History* 27(4), 727–43.

Reinecke, A., L. Vin. & S. Seng, 2009. *The First Golden Age of Cambodia: Excavation at Prohear*. Phnom Penh: Bad Langensalza Embassy of the Federal Republic of Germany.

Roveda, V., 2005. *Images of the Gods. Khmer mythology in Cambodia, Thailand and Laos*. Bangkok: River Books.

Sahai, S., 1970. *Les Institutions Politiques et L'Organisation Administritive du Cambodge Ancien (VI e-XIIIe Siecles)*. Publication volume LXXV. Paris, École française d'Extrême-Orient.

Sanderson, A., 2003. The Śaiva religion among the Khmers (Part I). *Bulletin de l'École française d'Extrême-Orient* 90–91, 349–462.

Savalia, K.B., A.R. Ahlawat, V.V. Gamit, S.S. Parikh. & A.D. Verma, 2019. Recently recognized indigenous cattle breeds of India: a review. *International Journal of Current Microbiology and Applied Sciences* 8(12), 161–8.

Sherratt, A., 1983. The secondary exploitation of animals in the old World. *World Archaeology* 15(1), 90–104.

Simoons, F.J., 1970. The traditional limits of milking and milk use in Southern Asia. *Anthropos* 65(3–4), 547–93.

Siyonn, S., 2017. Cows in Ancient Cambodia: a reflection on Indians and Indian tradition in Khmer Society, in *India and Southeast Asia: Cultural Discourses*, eds. A. Dallapiccola. & A. Verghese. Mumbai: K.R. Cama Oriental Institute, 83–97.

Soutif, D., 2009. *Organisation religieuse et profane de temple du VIIe au XIIIe siècle*. PhD dissertation. Paris: Université Paris III—Sorbonne nouvelle.

Sprenger, G., 2005. The way of the buffaloes: trade and sacrifice in northern Laos. *Ethnology* 44(4), 291–312.

Stark, M.T., 2021. Landscapes, linkages, and luminescence: first-millennium CE environmental and social change in Mainland Southeast Asia, in *Primary Sources and Asian Pasts*, eds. C.B. Peter. & A.C. Elizabeth. Leiden: De Gruyter, 184–219.

Stevenson, S., 1920. *The Rites of the Twice-Born*. London: Humphrey Milford Oxford University Press.

Thompson, A., 2019. *Engendering the Buddhist State: Territory, Sovereignty and Sexual Difference in the Inventions of Angkor*. New York: Routledge.

Thorel, C., 2001. *Agriculture and Ethnobotany of the Mekong Basin. The Mekong Exploration Commission Report (1866–1868)—volume 4*. Bangkok: White Lotus Press.

van Leur, J.C., 1955. *Indonesian Trade and Society: Essays in Asian Social and Economic History*. The Hague: van Hoeve.

Vickery, M., 1998. Society, Economics, and Politics in Pre-Angkor Cambodia: the 7th to 8th centuries. Tokyo: The Toyo Bunko.

Vickery, M., 1999. The Khmer inscriptions of Roluos (Preah Ko and Lolei): documents from a transition period in Cambodian History. *Seksa Khmer Nouvelle Série* 1.

Wheatley, P., 1965. A note on the extension of milking practices in Southeast Asia during the first millennium A.D. *Anthropos* 60, 577–90.

Wheatley, P., 1975. *Nagara and Commandery: Origins of the Southeast Asian Urban Traditions*. Chicago: University of Chicago Press.

Wolters, O.W., 1967. *Early Indonesian Commerce: A Study of the Origins of Srivijaya*. Ithaca: Cornell University Press.

Yue, X-P., R. Li, W-M. Xie, P. Xu, T-C. Chang, L. Liu, F. Cheng, R-F. Zhang, X-Y. Lan, H. Chen. & C-Z. Lei, 2013. Phylogeography and domestication of Chinese swamp buffalo. *PLOS ONE* 8(2), e56552.

Zhou, D., 2007[1297]. *A Record of Cambodia: The Land and Its People*, trans. P. Harris. Chiang Mai: Silkworm Books.

26

AN ANGKOR NATION? IDENTIFYING THE CORE OF THE KHMER EMPIRE

Ian Lowman, Chhom Kunthea and Mitch Hendrickson

One of the defining features of politics in pre-modern South and Southeast Asia was the royal claim to universal authority. Universality was ingrained in the language of Sanskrit, through which a culture of cosmocratic kingship was transmitted throughout the region in the first millennium (Pollock 2006). Kings aspired to the role of *cakravartin*, the world ruler, or to the title of *mahārāja*, the 'great king' above all other kings. Universalist empire, characterised by the ambition to continually expand a polity's circle of power by subjugating its surrounding competitors, was not so much a regional tendency as it was the cultural standard (Wolters 1999, 27). Angkor in many ways set the imperial standard in Southeast Asia. The size and symbolism of Angkor's state temples envisioned royal sovereignty on a cosmic scale. The expansion of Angkor's power and influence into Cham and Mon realms at the height of its empire suggests that royal success was measured by how far the king's armies could push outward and how many vassals and clients he could bring within his orbit.

The reputation of early Southeast Asia and of Angkor in particular for the empire would appear to preclude any discussion of Angkor in relation to the nation. A nation, to use a spare definition, is the social relation of a people conflated with the image of an extensive, though bounded, political territory (Grosby 2018, 2). For most historians, the global ascendance of the system of independent nation-states in the 19th and 20th centuries marks a way of thinking about politics in terms of popular community and territorial sovereignty that was largely non-existent in pre-modern contexts, particularly in regions like Southeast Asia that were immersed in an Indic culture of hieratic kingship and universalism (Lieberman 2003, 39–40).

There is certainly a risk of anachronism in evoking the nation in the study of Angkor. Even so, excluding the nation as a broadly salient interpretive framework can be analytically limiting. As the historian of pre-Meiji Japan, Mary Elizabeth Berry (2006, 212) has argued, 'labels [like 'nation'] are heuristic devices . . . that help organise inquiry rather than hallowing absolutes' (2006, 212). While recognising in Angkor the features of an expansionist empire, we can also acknowledge that certain qualities consistent with the nation, such as a system of governance and distribution consistent with a circumscribed heartland, and the association of the polity's people with a bounded, autonomous political space, contributed to Angkor's unique character and legacy. Surveying the epigraphic and archaeological evidence, this chapter evaluates the heuristic value of 'empire' and 'nation' for understanding Angkorian political space and identity.

DOI: 10.4324/9781351128940-32

The Khmer Empire

Angkor's polity was in an important sense cosmocratic or 'proleptically universal' (Lieberman 2009, 40). The kings of Angkor celebrated and pursued an ideal of power extending infinitely outward from a charismatic centre 'to the horizons'. The field of command of the 9th-century king Indravarman (ca. 877–889/890), which was confined approximately to the area of present-day lowland Cambodia, was compared (K. 809, verse XX) to a crown resting above the heads of the kings of China (*cīna*), Champa, and the island of Java (*yavadvīpa*). Three centuries later Jayavarman VII (1181–ca. 1220), a king who largely realised Angkor's imperial ambitions, was said to have received tribute in person from two kings of Champa and the king of Đại Việt (*yavana*) but also incredibly from the king of 'Javā' (K. 908, verse CLXVI). These claims, however hyperbolic, were consistent with an image of imperial politics inherited ultimately from the Indian subcontinent: the *maṇḍala* or circle of vassal kings orbiting a self-styled king of kings.

Maṇḍala politics at Angkor was the art of claiming progressively distant others as royal subjects. Royal culture therefore embraced the realm's extensiveness and diversity as tokens of royal power. The inscription memorialising Jayavarman VII's temple constructions at Angkor and throughout his empire (K. 908, verse CLXXVII) stressed that the 306,372 workers in these temples included subjected Chams (*cāmpa*), Viets (*yavana*), Burmans (*pukāṃ*), and Mons (*rvvañ*, likely for rmmañ). In frontier regions, such diversity was likely the norm. According to the inscription K. 1198, in the 11th century Sūryavarman I (1002–1050) sent a general, Śrī Lakṣmīpativarman (verse XXII), to govern 'the Mons (*rāmanya*) who occupy (*avakāśin*) the western region/direction (*āśā*)', with responsibility for 'subduing' them and collecting taxes (verses XXIII–IV). At the same time, Lakṣmīpativarman was assigned to rescue the far-western city of Lopburi (*Lavapur*) from neglect and an encroaching jungle (verse XXXVII). It is tempting to interpret the official's campaign against the Mons as a case of Khmer aggrandisement and his restoration of Angkor's western marches as Khmer irredentism. More likely, however, these actions reflected a political culture in which the heterogeneity of a king's subjects was a sign of his strength and a king's efforts to civilise his polity's frontiers signalled the universality of his benevolence. The imperial ideal of governing diverse peoples likely accounts for the depiction of a ragtag band labelled 'Syāṃ Kuk' (Figure 26.1), referring to an ethnic other, perhaps Tai or even Suei, at the head of a royal procession in the famous bas-relief panel at Angkor Wat (Groslier 1981, 115).

Viewed from its peripheries, Angkor appears to fit O.W. Wolters' influential definition of a maṇḍala as a kingdom in pursuit of quasi-universal authority which in practice presided over an 'often unstable political situation in a vaguely definable geographical area without fixed boundaries' (1999, 28). However, Wolters insists that Angkor was 'the single exception' to the overall pattern in early Southeast Asia. 'The Khmer elite', Wolters asserts, 'had a vested interest in the territorial integrity of metropolitan Cambodia' (1999, 36). By 'metropolitan Cambodia', Wolters implies the existence of a territorial state and identity that was differentiated from 'the otherwise ephemeral' political situation of Angkor's more remote imperial claims (ibid.).

Angkor was in fact conceived as a territorially limited state in spite of exaggerated assertions of regional supremacy. The late 9th- or early 10th-century Lolei inscription states that the Angkorian king Yaśovarman I (889–ca. 910) governed a space extending 'from the border of China (Cīna) to the sea' (K. 323, verse LVI), while a later 10th-century Baksei Chamkrong inscription specifies that the boundaries of Yaśovarman's realm were China, the sea, Champa (*campā*), and an unidentified place called Sūkṣmakāmrāta (K. 286, verse XXVII). On the one hand, these political boundaries contradict facile assumptions about Angkorian universalism, while

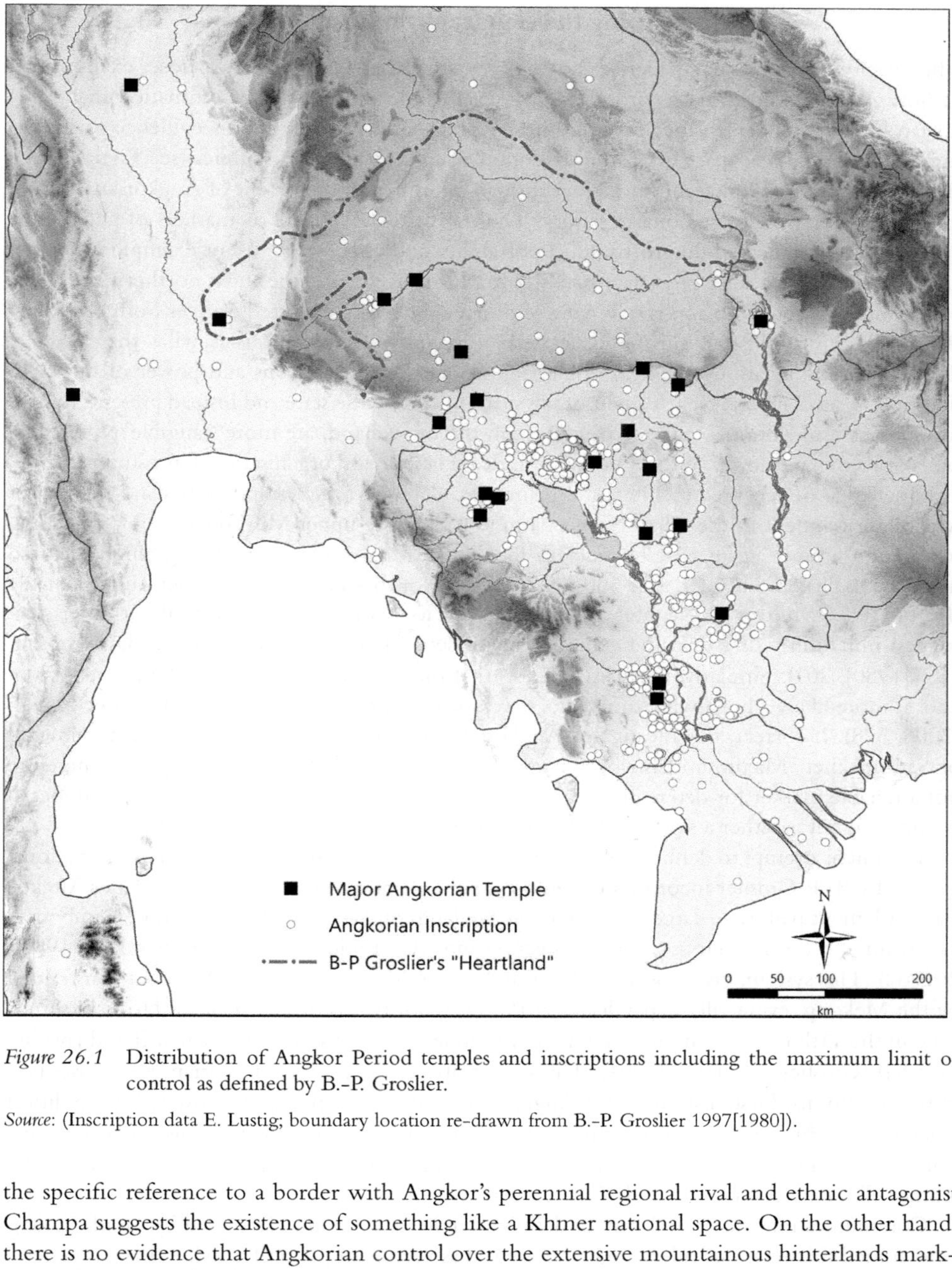

Figure 26.1 Distribution of Angkor Period temples and inscriptions including the maximum limit of control as defined by B.-P. Groslier.

Source: (Inscription data E. Lustig; boundary location re-drawn from B.-P. Groslier 1997[1980]).

the specific reference to a border with Angkor's perennial regional rival and ethnic antagonist Champa suggests the existence of something like a Khmer national space. On the other hand, there is no evidence that Angkorian control over the extensive mountainous hinterlands marking its frontiers with Champa and China (northern Vietnam in the 10th century) was ever anything more than ephemeral. In other words, it is unclear whether the space within these borders was meant to represent something like a national territory—a political space of actual Khmer governance and imagined Khmer belonging—or if it merely indicated the extreme limits of 10th-century Angkor's imperial ambitions far beyond its existing realm.

Defining the Geography of Angkor

The opacity of this textual evidence for Angkor's territorial extent invites a closer examination of how Angkor marked its territory in practice. Beyond the likely over-estimation that Angkorian lands 'extended to the seas', the most visible—and typically used—evidence for tracking Angkor's political space are the distribution of inscriptions and temples (see Figure 26.1). Both, however, have inherent limitations in helping us define the extent of Angkorian control, especially in terms of a national territory. The use of text locations as markers of geographic authority is complicated due to issues of portability and context. A recent example in central Laos revealed that a stele of Jayavarman VII found in Vientiane, the most northern discovery of an Angkorian state object, is now viewed as having been transported upriver from elsewhere (Lorrillard 2006, 398). A further issue with using *in situ* inscriptions is what they actually demarcate. The location of a text, while rich in detailing the actions and power of the king, does not necessarily represent a point of physical control by the state and instead presents temple inventories or devotional content. Temples, on the other hand, are more 'tangible' representations of Khmer authority, as they require significant labour and organisational investment as well as knowledge of accepted architectural principles. 'Khmer' temples appear beyond the Lower Mekong catchment in the Chao Phraya basin as well as the upper Mun River valley, but using maximum distance again poses a problem for demarcating the nation. Muang Singh, situated in western Thailand border over 500 km from Angkor, has been viewed as an outpost of the 'Bayon' style (Multzer O'Naghten 2014, 414), but its layout shows significant variations that suggest imitation rather than the centre of major settlement occupied by Angkorian (Groslier 1997[1980], 201). Similarly, Lorillard suggests that the presence of laterite buildings in parts of Laos is more likely a borrowing of Angkor's architectural practices rather than direct occupation (2006, 398). If correct, this means that Angkor's direct influence in Laos did not extend north of Savannakhet. Maximum distribution of 'Angkorian' inscriptions and temples is therefore not a reliable marker for determining the extent of a national space or even a zone of imperial occupation but is rather a sign of attenuated influence on the political periphery.

The initial attempt to define an Angkorian 'heartland'—or something more akin to a national space—by B.-P. Groslier incorporated temples and inscriptions but emphasised broader Angkorian settlement patterns—largely following viable land for rice agriculture—within Cambodia's vast plain and the numerous rivers connecting into the Tonle Sap lake (Groslier 1997[1986], 261–62). This system, visible from earlier Pre-Angkorian contexts in the Delta and constrained by the Mekong, eventually expanded over the Dangrek Range into northeast Thailand sometime in the 11th century and reached its zenith under the reigns of Sūryavarman II and Jayavarman VII (Groslier 1997[1980], 201). This demarcation of a specific Angkorian space raises two important points. First, assuming that Angkorian territory was not static, how did this political space evolve? And second, how homogeneous was Angkorian control? To answer these questions we consider the different mechanisms of communication and integration used by the Khmer elite between the 9th and 13th centuries.

Communication is a critical part of defining territories, a point elaborated by Smith (2005), who argued that reigns of rulers are better viewed as vectors of political activities than as generic blobs of spatial 'control'. The Angkorian road system (Figure 26.2) represents the best example of shifting elite interests, each arm radiating out to major state-level temples that often have their origins in the Pre-Angkor Period (Hendrickson 2010). Of greater geographic consequence here is that the roads terminate at the natural waterways and watersheds of the Mun, Mekong, and the Tonle Sap catchment (Hendrickson 2017). Together this network creates a zone of communication that more accurately represents the 'heartland' space controlled by Angkor.

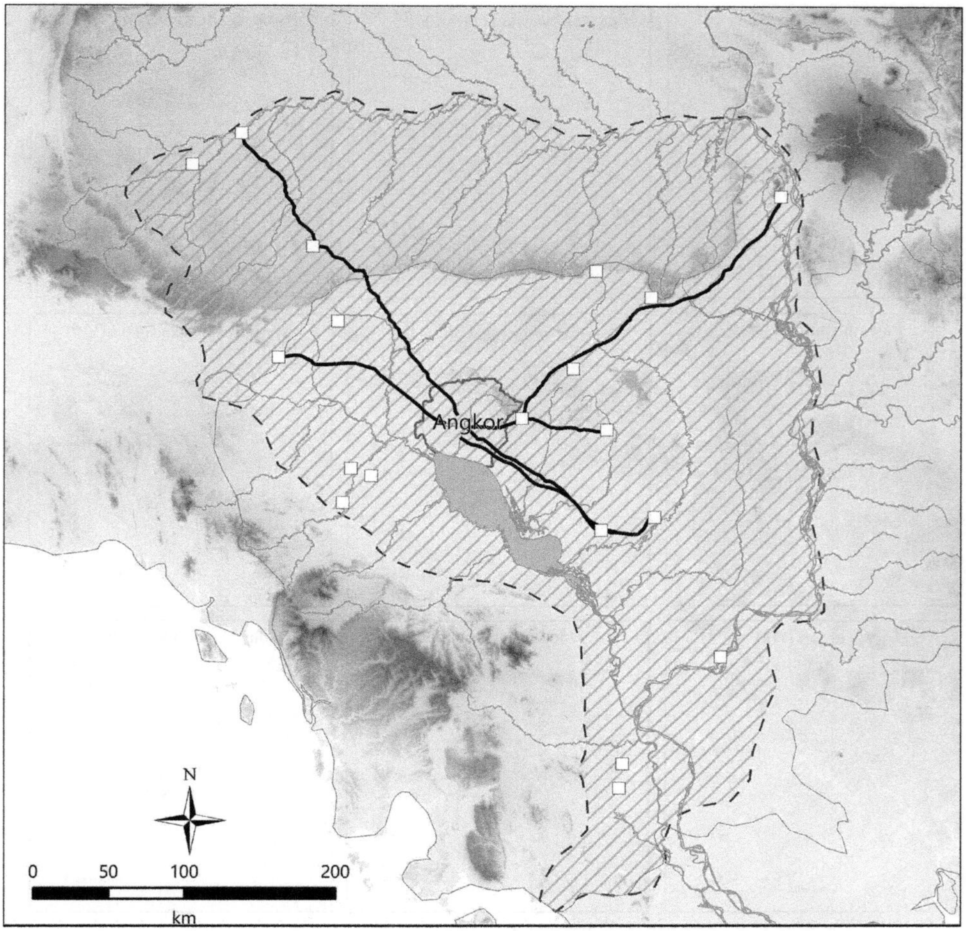

Figure 26.2 Proposed extent of the Angkorian heartland.

Based on their records and the scale of Angkor's feats, the Khmers could have extended past this point but chose not to, or, more realistically, the lands beyond were occupied by the Mon Dvāravatī on the west and northwest (Groslier 1997[1980]) and various groups occupying the hills east of the Mekong (see Heng 2023, this volume). This more constrained spatial extent of Angkor can now be examined in relation to how the polity grew over time, beginning with a reconsideration of inscription density and state temples as forms of boundary marking. Lustig et al. (2007) showed that the majority of stelae are predominantly found inside Cambodia and, as suggested by Groslier, spread north of the Dangrek in more considerable numbers between the 10th and 12th centuries. The areas between major state temples built or modified by successive Angkorian kings show a similar northward progression (Figure 26.3) but also highlight an accordion-like spatial dynamic. By viewing these areas as communication corridors within which the 'state' maintained direct geographic sovereignty, the continual shifts in size correspond with the fractious nature of Angkorian kingship and the numerous internal conflicts over succession that took place throughout its history (Cœdès 1968).

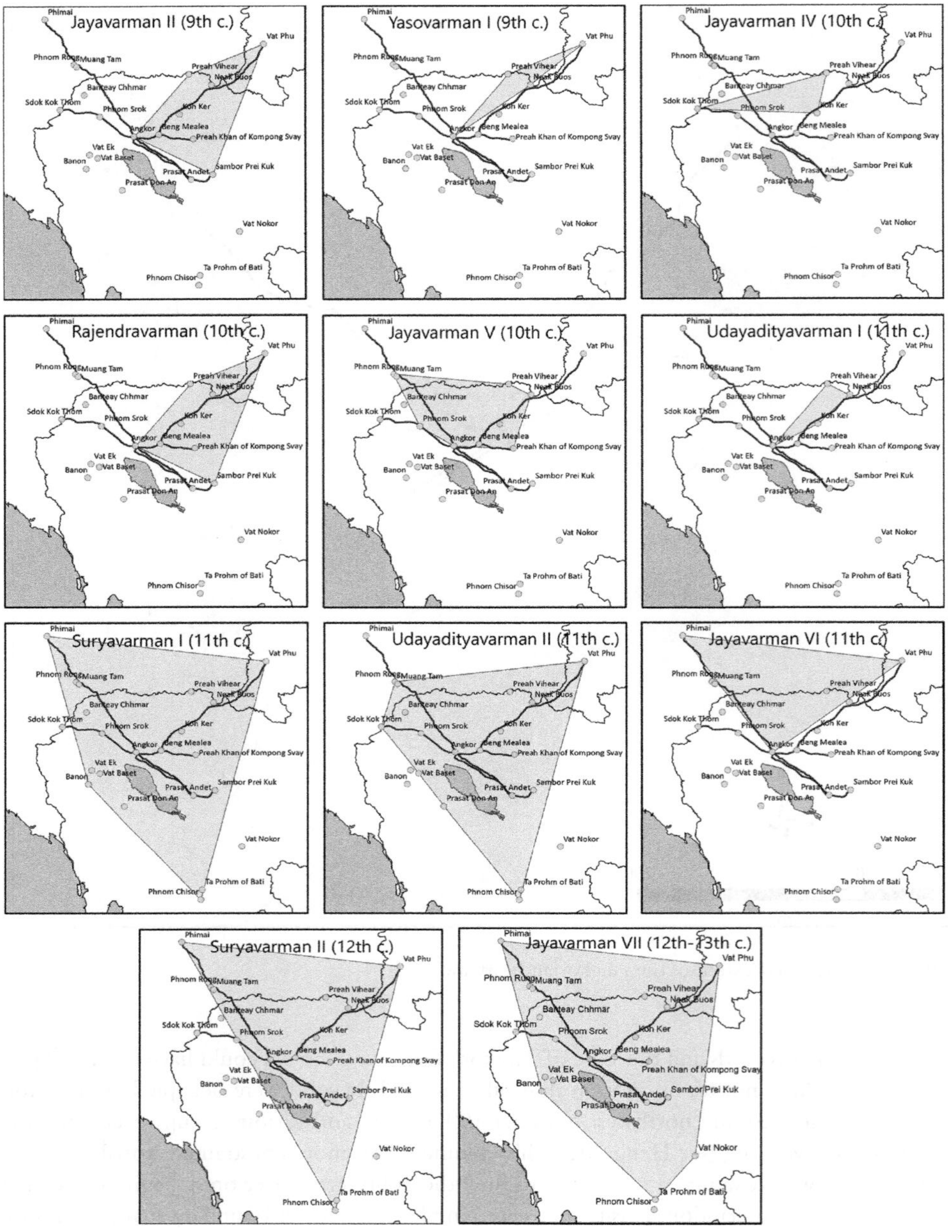

Figure 26.3 Communication corridors of the major Angkorian kings. Each corridor connects the furthest distant temples built or modified or the location of inscriptions.

Within these shifting 'nation boundaries' various kings used unique strategies in the form of repeated architectural types and sacred images to integrate specific spaces (Figure 26.4). Yaśovarman I's construction of *āśramas* (see Chea et al. 2023, this volume) is the earliest example of a repeated set of temples used to integrate communities by providing education, religious guidance, and likely health services. A century later, Sūryavarman I enacted multiple

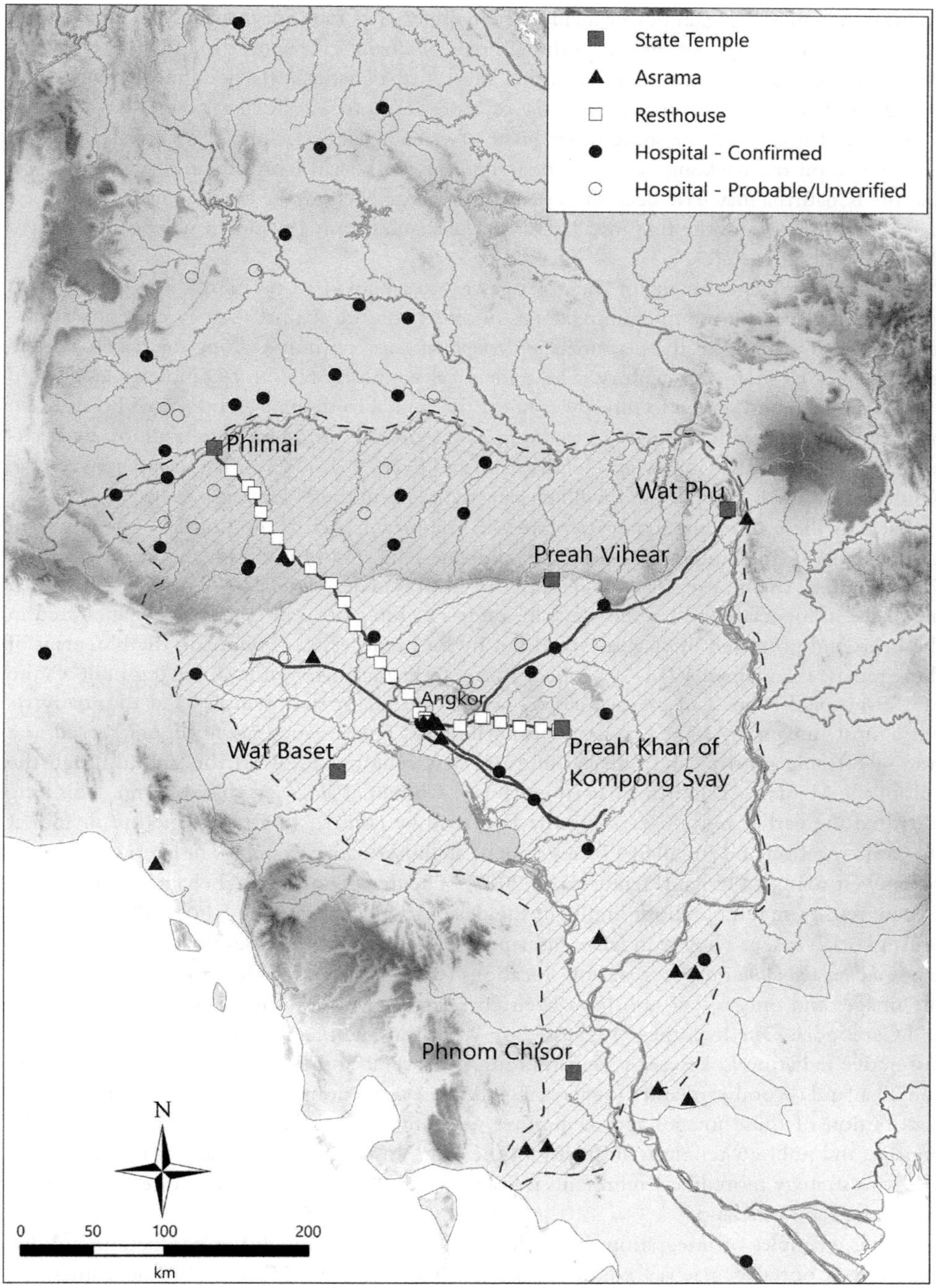

Figure 26.4 State-level infrastructures used by Khmer kings to assert influence within the Angkorian heartland.

Source: (GIS āśrama data D. Soutif; hospital data C. Pottier).

political strategies to regain power including the dispersal of four Sūryavarmeśvara *liṅgas* to key sites identified through toponyms to the temples of Preah Vihear (north), Wat Baset (west), Phnom Chisor (south), and an unidentified site called Īśānatīrtha (Jacques and Lafond 2004, 203–204). The name Īśānatīrtha, or '*tīrtha* of Śiva', refers to a sacred site, typically associated with a riverbank, pond, or some other body of water. Claude Jacques places this Īśānatīrtha somewhere on the Mekong but offers no candidate Angkorian temple. Another possibility is that the Īśānatīrtha may have been the 11th-century West Mebon, the island temple of the West Baray reservoir, where the first installation on the island's central platform was possibly a *liṅga* (Feneley et al. 2016, 276).

Regardless, the placement of these images at sites known to be within Angkorian lands strongly suggests their use in defining zones of direct control. A final strategy currently attributed to Sūryavarman II is the placement of '*temples d'étape*' resthouses along the East road during the early to mid-12th century. These identical sandstone masonry complexes are spaced 12–13 km apart and served to directly connect the capital to the important site of Preah Khan of Kompong Svay, which had access to the iron and forest resources in lands traditionally occupied by the ethnic Kuay minority (Hendrickson and Evans 2015). The relationship between the Khmer and Kuay is complex and will be evaluated more in the following.

Each of these different strategies played an important part in the political operations of Jayavarman VII, the king who transformed the state religion to Buddhism and was responsible for extending Angkor's reach to its territorial zenith (Cœdès 1968, 167–76). While his reach may have influenced lands to the west, his efforts to integrate and control were anchored in the heartland governed by spaces carved out by his predecessors. Following the blueprint of the āśramas, Jayavarman VII is described in the Ta Prohm inscription as having built a suite of 102 hospital chapels in regions largely away from major state temples and the roadways but almost universally linked to a river or tributary. These structures no doubt served as a way of offering services and proselytising the new religious ideals of the state through the cult of the Medicine Buddha, Bhaiṣajyaguru (see Chhem et al. 2023, this volume). This king mirrored the earlier resthouses along the East road by constructing sandstone fire shrines at the same location and installed a series of new, slightly smaller examples in laterite along the Northwest road to Phimai (Hendrickson 2008). The density of hospital chapels and creation of new resthouse temples both highlight the desire to incorporate the Khorat Plateau as part of Angkorian space. The Preah Khan inscription (K. 908) also describes the distribution of 23 *Jayabuddhamahānātha* images to various locations (Cœdès 1941), but the text does not identify the image, and only a few sites have been correlated with the listed toponyms in Thailand and Cambodia. One hypothesis suggested by Woodward connects these images to a group of distinctive radiating Lokeśvara sculptures found at several of this king's temples in Cambodia and Thailand (Woodward and Douglas 1994–95; see also Thompson 2023, this volume). The distribution of these images acts as another measure of symbolically linking sites with the prestige and politico-religious authority of the king. In contrast to the sets of repeated temples, this strategy more likely represents influence and prestige rather than a direct measure of an Angkorian homeland.

Other examples of integration at a local level are visible through the production and distribution of portable material culture associated with the state. Metal and stone statues and inscriptions are perhaps the most sacred and important artifacts of 'belonging' within the Khmer world, but from a decidedly elite perspective. A more populist tool of belonging is the presence of glazed stoneware ceramics, one of the hallmarks of occupation sites between the 9th to the 14th centuries in archaeological surveys (see Hendrickson et al. 2023, this volume). While their specific functions are unknown, these ceramics were limited to Angkorian sites and were never used as a major trade item beyond their territories. Guy (1989) and Wong (2010) both posited that green and later brown glazed stonewares represent important markers of affiliation, a situation seen in the limited distribution of Aztec ceramics (Umberger and Klein 1993) and the association of Hamrin polychromes in Mesopotamia (Emberling 1997, 323).

The question of ceramics as a symbol of Angkorian incorporation leads us to an interesting case around Phnom Dek, the 'Iron Mountain', located 30 km east of Preah Khan of Kompong Svay. The Phnom Dek region has few traces of temples or settlements typical of Khmer sites even though it is so close to this massive Angkorian centre and the East Road that connects directly to the capital. Instead, it is dominated by hundreds of mounds of iron production waste, peaking in scale and quantity between the 11th and 13th centuries, and is the home for the Kuay ethnic minority who have smelted iron here since at least the 16th century (Hendrickson et al. 2017). Situated in the middle of Angkorian territory, the implication is that these sites were independent actors to Khmer authority. Recent work at Tonle Bak, situated 2 km south of Phnom Dek, shows extensive iron production along with a typical Angkorian water reservoir and remains of a perishable shrine on its western side (Hendrickson et al. 2019). Overlapping layers with metallurgical and glazed ceramics shows that the occupants were incorporated into the Khmer economy between the 11th and 13th centuries. While it is extremely difficult and problematic to attribute ethnicity in the past (Emberling 1997), the presence of glazed stoneware sherds around Phnom Dek suggests at least two options: Kuay smelters being included, but not incorporated, within the Angkorian World or a Khmer enclave among lands traditionally held by the Kuay.

All these signs of integration—road infrastructure, temples, sacred images, and 'common objects' like ceramics—point to Angkor as a political hub with multiple strategies at its disposal to correlate its various territorial claims. At one level, these strategies served to mark the polity's 'boundaries', incorporating multiple groups and lands into a heartland, or 'national' space, that was capable of meeting the state's specific economic demands (e.g., rice agriculture). Meanwhile, the projection of power and influence outside this heartland served to maintain effective buffer zones, Angkor's 'empire', between Angkor and its regional rivals.

The Idea of Kambuja

The problem of characterising Angkor as either an empire or a nation is at heart a question of how the polity defined itself. Any attempt to understand how the Angkorian polity did this must underscore the significance of its political name. The common use of the term 'Angkor', the modern Khmer name for the polity's capital, Yaśodharapura, to designate the polity in its entirety reflects the polity's reputation as a city-based empire, like a Southeast Asian Rome. However, unlike imperial Rome, the name of the polity in the so-called 'Angkor Period' was distinct from the name of its capital. According to the inscriptions, the consistent name for the polity was the land of Kambuja or Kambu.

Kambuja as a geographic term first appears in an inscription of Po Nagar (C 31) in the neighbouring region of Champa dated 817 CE. In the greater Khmer political realm the name is first found in an inscription from western Khorat in northeast Thailand dated 868 CE (K. 400), which refers to an individual's acquisition of land in *kamvudeśāntara*, a phrase which could be translated as 'a foreign land (*deśāntara*) of Kambu', perhaps a foreign dependency, or 'within the land of Kambu'. Despite this text's ambiguity, Kambu clearly denoted an extensive political space incorporating various territories. This sense is confirmed by another 9th-century inscription from the Bakong, the state temple of Indravarman (877–889) at Hariharālaya, which states that a priest 'came here' (*ihāgataḥ*), or to the capital, 'for the purification of the eminent countries (*deśa*) of Kambu' (K. 923, st. XIV), no doubt alluding to the various provinces, literally 'countries' (*viṣaya*), that characterised the geography of the polity's internal administration throughout the Angkor Period.

The origin of this term for the greater space of the Khmer realm remains a mystery. The name Kambuja or Kambu is conspicuously absent in Cambodia's rich pre-9th-century epigraphic record, which is proof of either its relative insignificance in the Pre-Angkorian polity or the lack of such an idea altogether. The resemblance of Kambuja to Kamboja, the name of an important tribe in Indian epic tradition, has often been noted, though the form Kamboja is unknown in the Angkorian inscriptions (Mabbett and Chandler 1995, 9–10). Kambu, whether as a place or personal name, is unknown in Sanskrit literature, apart from being mentioned once in the *Skandapurāṇa* in reference to a demon (Chhom 2016, 111). We can speculate whether Kambu, Sanskrit for 'conch shell', was not simply a back formation of Kambuja, which in turn may have been a pseudo-etymology of a word of possibly non-Indian origin such as **kaṃvuc~ *kambuc.*

By the 10th century, however, the term Kambuja unambiguously designated a polity ruled by a certain royal lineage: 'those born of (or descended from) Kambu'. Kambu was understood to be the name of an ancient great sage (*maharṣi*) and the ultimate progenitor of Angkor's kings. Inscription K. 958 from Prasat Kok Chak states that Kambu was the father of the polity's first king, Śrī Śrutavarman (verse II). In the most important text for our understanding of this legendary figure, K. 286 from Prasat Baksei Chamkrong emphasises Kambu's 'self-created' (*svāyambhuva*), divine origin while also uniquely mentioning Kambu's union, arranged by the god Hara or Śiva, to a celestial woman (*suranārī*) Merā (verses XI–XII).

The myth of Kambu was consistent with political myths of semi-divine sage-ancestors found elsewhere in the Sanskrit cultural world of South and Southeast Asia at that time. In neighbouring Campā, the kings were believed to be descended from the famous sage Bhṛgu, while the Pallavas of southern India identified their primordial ancestor as the sage Aṅgiras, a son of Brahmā. The account of the union of the couple Kambu and Merā, for its part, resembles the myth recounted in Kālidāsa's *Abhijñānaśākuntalam (Recognition of Śakuntalā)* about the sage Viśvāmitra and the celestial nymph Menakā, parents of Śakuntalā and grandparents of Bharata, who became the first cakravartin or universal monarch in Indic tradition and the progenitor of the two warring princely lineages dramatised in the epic *Mahābhārata*. The central purpose of such myths was to bathe certain political lineages in the aura of divinity and universal imperial power. Seen within this Indic context, the polity of Kambu or the descendants of Kambu would appear to be a straight-forward manifestation of the universalist cakravartin tradition.

This view conflicts, however, with a long-standing scholarly consensus that the name Kambuja connoted not merely a dynastic line but a people of perceived common descent—an ethnic group. This is why George Cœdès (1966, 24), in his inventory of Cambodia's Sanskrit and Old Khmer inscriptions, categorised the term Kambuja as an ethnonym. Cœdès' interpretation of the most detailed account of the Kambu origin myth, K. 286 from Prasat Baksei Chamkrong, reflects this choice of categorisation. He proposed that the names of the mythical ancestors Kambu and Merā formed an etymology of the ethnonym *kmer* or *khmer*: *kambu* + *merā* = *kmer ~ khmer*. This kind of semantic interpretation is called *nirvacana* in Sanskrit literary tradition. To cite one example from the Mahābhārata (*Karṇa Parva*, chapter 30, verse XL), the name of a *janapada* or tribal realm Bāhlīka is said to be derived from the names of two demons, Bahi and Hlīka, whose coupling is the basis of a concise (derogatory) origin story:

bahiś ca nāma hlīkaś ca vipāśāyāṃ piśācakau
tayor apatyaṃ bāhlīkā naiṣā sṛṣṭiḥ prajāpateḥ

> There were two *piśāca* (demons) named Bahi and Hlīka. Their descendants, who were not the creation of Prajāpati, [were called] Bāhlīka.

In Cœdès' compelling interpretation of the Kambu and Merā myth, Merā may have been invented to provide, alongside Kambu, a creative etymology of the word *khmer* and to place the progenitor Kambu at the centre of the story of Khmer ethnic origins.

Admittedly, interpreting the Kambu-Merā myth as a Khmer origin story in this way requires a leap of scholarly imagination which the text of K. 286, lacking the word *khmer*, does not adequately justify. Nonetheless, relating the two identities Kambuja and Khmer is not mere wishful thinking. The late-12th or early 13th century inscription K. 227 from Banteay Chhmar records how a royal figure, campaigning in 'the land of the Chams (*dvīpa cāmpa*)' (line 15), 'led the Khmers (*qnak khmer*)' in battle before returning to 'the land of Kambuja (*kamvujadeśa*)' (lines 27–28). The text appears to differentiate between two peoples, Khmers and Chams, and their respective lands, and draws an implicit connection in identity if not meaning between the word *khmer* and the political name *kambuja*. The almost banal takeaway from the passage is that the polity of Kambuja was understood to have *its own* land and (Khmer) people, distinguished from the land and people of the Chams against whom Angkor's sovereigns waged war.

What if, one might ask, the Khmer people were an important or even the core population at Angkor's military disposal, but were not central to the polity's self-definition? The appearance of the ethnonym *khmer* in foreign inscriptions (*kmir* in Old Javanese, *kvir* in Old Cham) during the Angkor Period suggests that outsiders at the very least attached a Khmer identity to Angkor. One Angkorian inscription dispels any ambiguity. The 11th-century Sab Bak inscription (K. 1158) from present-day northeast Thailand describes how at an unspecified time in the past an official named Śrī Satyavarman installed nine Buddhist images on a mountain called Abhayagiri 'to prevent Javā from attacking Khmer Country (*sruk khmer*)' (lines 31–32). The phrasing echoes a similar account in K. 956 from Prei Veng in southern Cambodia concerning the late eighth and early 9th century king Jayavarman II who is said to have commanded one of his ministers, Śrī Pr̥thivīnarendra, to perform a ritual in a place called Rdvāl 'to make it impossible for the venerable land of Kambuja (*vraḥ kamvujadeśa*) to be seized by Javā' (lines 15–17). Setting aside the long-debated question of this Javā's identity (Griffiths 2013), these two accounts of a historical threat from an imperial aggressor confirm that Kambuja and Khmer were, if not necessarily synonymous, mutually coherent and practically interchangeable terms in Angkor's political imagination. Kambuja was understood to be an autonomous political territory associated with a specific people, the Khmers—by our definition a national state.

If we choose to characterise Angkor as a nation state by virtue of its identity with a specific territory and people, we must still confront the seeming contradiction of Angkor's imperial ambitions. The most well-known account of Kambuja's independence from Java, from the 11th-century Sdok Kak Thom stela (K. 235), may offer insight into the seeming ambiguity of Angkorian sovereignty. King Jayavarman II, the text informs us, invited a brahmin in 802 CE to perform a ritual at the king's capital of Mahendraparvata 'to prevent this land of Kambuja (*kambujadeśa*) from being dependent on Javā, and so that there would only be one king, who would be cakravartin' (lines 72–73). The text succinctly discloses three desired outcomes of the brahmin's ritual: the birth or renewal of Kambuja's territorial autonomy—its status as a nation—serving as a rebuke of imperial aggression; the realisation of national unity under 'one king'; and the rise of a Kambuja-based cakravartin staking his own claim to quasi-universal authority. Nation and empire, we might conclude, were not contradictory modes of sovereignty in the Angkorian imagination. Nation and empire were believed to have emerged at the same moment, manifestations of a single though multifaceted political project of Khmer self-determination, unification, and expansion.

National Legacy

This assessment of Angkorian geography and political identity raises inevitable questions about Angkor's legacy. In the study of Cambodian history, the Angkorian Period is often treated as an isolated florescence of statecraft and culture, traces of which survived Angkor's precipitous decline in degenerate courtly institutions and in shadowy remembrances of former glory. The territorial spoils of Angkor's crumbling empire in central mainland Southeast Asia largely went to Siamese Ayutthaya. This narrative of decline tends to obscure significant stretches of Khmer assertiveness in the 16th and 17th centuries, but when judged by an imperial standard, Post-Angkorian elites cultivated a more distinctly defensive, rather than expansionist, political mentality in response to the country's vulnerable position at the margins of empire.

One consequence of this defensiveness in the Post-Angkor Period was a seemingly more explicit articulation of national identity, expressed in terms of territorial sovereignty and the well-being of the polity's people, than anything we find in the Angkorian epigraphic corpus. Hence a member of the Khmer elite, in an inscription at Angkor Wat (IMA 6) dated to the turbulent late 16th century, ends his record of pious donations with a petition to the gods assembled at Angkor Wat to inspire the enemies of the kingdom 'to not invade the land of Kambuja (*kaṃpioy pyet pyen kaṃmbujades*)' and to ensure that 'all the people of this land of Kambuja (*rāstr phoṅ Aṃpāl kaṃluṅ kambujades neḥ*) [would] enjoy peace and be free from turmoil' (Pou 1971, 111). Along similar lines, we encounter in 19th-century literary accounts of the 1830s Vietnamese annexation of Cambodia the themes of a territorially imperilled Kambujā and Khmer Country (*sruk khmer*) and a Khmer population menaced by foreign overlords (Khin 2002). In truth, the Post-Angkorian sources elicit a far more nuanced picture of political loyalties than a selectively nation-centric survey of the evidence conveys, with Khmer kings and claimants mobilising polyethnic armies across porous borders and celebrating the internal diversity of their subject populations. Likewise, Angkorian accounts of royal and religious figures supernaturally safeguarding the land of Kambuja or Khmer Country from a threatening Javā belie assumptions about Angkor's exclusively imperial character. Both Angkor and Post-Angkorian Cambodia presented a complicated mix of maṇḍala and national politics, a sign of continuity across the supposed Angkor/Post-Angkor divide.

No doubt for some historians, the European origin of modern Khmer nationalism excludes the possibility that an Angkorian national tradition survives in the present-day nation-state of Cambodia. Following a global trend, a European-educated Khmer literati in the early to mid-20th century reoriented loyalties away from royal and religious authority and towards a narrow conception of the nation as the political embodiment of the people, couched in a neologism for race (*jāti*) (Edwards 2007, 13–15). For those who insist on this secular understanding of the nation with its implicit basis in the European enlightenment and the populism of the post-French revolution, neither Angkor nor its Post-Angkorian Khmer successor state before the 20th century qualifies as a nation.

There are two useful ways to address the undeniable persistence of the political identity expressed in the terms Kambuja and Khmer Country (*sruk khmer*) while remaining sensitive to the currently conventional academic definition of the nation as a form of secular mass politics. The first is to offer a substitute term for pre-modern political identities, divested of secular and populist connotations. In his comparative study of precolonial Southeast Asia and early modern France and Russia, Victor Lieberman (2009, 41) proposes 'politicized ethnicity', a term which encompasses for Lieberman various 'forms of cultural loyalty focused on the state'. Such a broad formulation may enable the historian to circumvent charges of nationalist teleology, though it does not adequately capture the specifically territorial implications of the nation as a category of analysis. A second approach, promoted by Anthony Smith (2008), is to recognise different forms of the nation specific to time period and tradition: the hierarchical nation of Capetian France, characterised by mutual fidelity between the people and the person of the king and a territorial loyalty inspired by a royally sanctioned cult of the saints (98–102); or the republican nation of revolutionary France with its ideals of popular liberty and secularism (153–55). In this at once subtler and more intuitive view of the nation, contemporary Cambodia can be said to exhibit both hierarchical and republican strains, the former inherited ultimately from Angkor and the latter originating in the ideological innovations of the Colonial Period.

Though the vast Khmer Empire has ceased to exist, Angkor's political identity has remarkably survived the vicissitudes of time for at least 1200 years—one of the World's longest unbroken traditions. This is undoubtedly a testament to the stubbornness of ethnic identity, in this case Khmer identity, with its common inheritance of language, culture, and perceived kinship undergirding unity in spite of political incursion and fracture. But many other identities, such as the Mon and the Cham, have politically floundered or expired in similar conditions. The longevity of Kambuja, if not a mere accident of history, can best be attributed to the territorial cohesion of the polity's once imperial core. Angkor's empire, though shedding its outer layers during centuries of decline, preserved a thick tradition of nationality—of territory and community—that continues to define the polity in the present. Perhaps the empire can be said to live on through this national legacy.

List of Inscription in the Text

K.	*Reference*
227	Cœdès 1929, 309; Cœdès 1951, 117
235	Finot 1915, 53; Cœdès and Dupont 1943, 56; Bhattacharya 2009, 123; Sak-Humphry 2005
286	Cœdès 1909, 467; IC IV, 88
323	ISCC, 391; Bhattacharya 2009, 82
400	IC VI, 83; Cœdès 1958, 127
809	IC I, 37
908	Cœdès 1941, 255
923	IC IV, 39
956	IC VII 128
958	IC VII, 141
1158	Prapandvidya 1990, 11
1198	NIC II-III, 240-260 (Ka. 18)

IC = Inscriptions du Cambodge; Cœdès 1937–66.

NIC = Nouvelles inscriptions du Cambodge; tome II–III: Pou 2001.

References

Berry, M.E., 2006. *Japan in Print: Information and Nation in the Early Modern Period.* Berkeley: University of California Press.

Bhattacharya, K., 2009. *A Selection of Sanskrit Inscriptions from Cambodia.* Phnom Penh: Center for Khmer Studies.

Chea, S., J. Estève, D. Soutif. & E. Swenson, 2023. Āśramas, shrines and royal power, in *The Angkorian World*, eds. M. Hendrickson, M.T. Stark. & D. Evans. New York: Routledge.

Chhem, R., D. Evans, K. Chhom, P. Phlong. & P.D. Sharrock, 2023. Education and medicine at Angkor, in *The Angkorian World*, eds. M. Hendrickson, M.T. Stark. & D. Evans. New York: Routledge, 287–306.

Chhom, K., 2016. *Le rôle du sanskrit dans le développement de la langue khmère: une étude épigraphique du VIe au XIVe siècle.* PhD dissertation. Paris: École Pratique des Hautes Études.

Cœdès, G. 1909. L'inscription de Baksei Camkron. *Journal Asiatique* 10(13), 467–510.

Cœdès, G., 1937–66. *Inscriptions du Cambodge. Collection de Textes et Documents sur l'Indochine.* Vol. I (1937); Vol. II (1942); Vol. III (1951); Vol. IV (1952); Vol. V (1953); Vol. VI (1954); Vol. VII (1964); Vol. VIII (1966). Paris: École française d'Extrême-Orient.

Cœdès, G., 1941. La stèle du Práh Khằn d'Ankor. *Bulletin de l'École française d'Extrême-Orient* 41(1), 255–302.

Cœdès, G., 1951. Études cambodgiennes XXXIX: L'épigraphie des monuments de Jayavarman VII. *Bulletin de l'École française d'Extrême-Orient* 44, 97–120.

Cœdès, G., 1958. Nouvelles données épigraphiques sur l'histoire de l'Indochine centrale. *Journal Asiatique* 246, 125–42.

Cœdès, G., 1968. *The Indianized States of Southeast Asia.* Honolulu: University of Hawai'i Press.

Cœdès, G. & P. Dupont. 1943. Les inscriptions de Sdŏk Kăk Thoṃ, Phnoṃ Sandak et Práḥ Vihār. *Bulletin de l'École française d'Extrême-Orient* 43, 56–154.

Edwards, P., 2007. *Cambodge: The Cultivation of a Nation, 1860–1945.* Honolulu: University of Hawai'i Press.

Emberling, G., 1997. Ethnicity in complex societies: archaeological perspectives. *Journal of Archaeological Research* 5(4), 295–344.

Feneley, M., D. Penny. & R.J. Fletcher, 2016. Claiming the hydraulic network of Angkor with Viṣṇu: a multidisciplinary approach including the analysis of archaeological remains, digital modelling and radiocarbon dating. *Journal of Archaeological Science Reports* 9, 275–292.

Finot, L., 1915. Notes d'épigraphie, XVI : L'inscription de Sdok Kak Thom. *Bulletin de l'École française d'Extrême-Orient* 15(2), 53–106.

Griffiths, A., 2013. The problem of the ancient name Java and the role of Satyavarman in Southeast Asian international relations around the turn of the ninth century CE. *Archipel* 85, 43–81.

Grosby, S.E., 2018. Time, kinship, and the nation. *Genealogy* 2(2), 17.

Groslier, B-P., 1981. Les Syam Kuk des bas-relief d'Angkor Vat. Melanges G. Condominas. *École Pratique des Hautes Etudes*, 107–26.

Groslier, B-P., 1997[1980]. Prospection des sites Khmers du Siam, in *Mélanges sur l'archéologie* du Cambodge (1949–1986), ed. J. Dumarçay. (Réimpressions de l'École française d'Extrême-Orient 10) Paris: Presses de l'École française d'Extrême-Orient, 189–220.

Groslier, B.-P., 1997[1986]. For a geographic history of Cambodia, in *Mélanges sur l'archéologie du Cambodge* (1949–1986), ed. J. Dumarçay. (Réimpressions de l'École française d'Extrême-Orient 10) Paris: Presses de l'École française d'Extrême-Orient, 255–92.

Guy, J., 1989. *Ceramic Traditions of South-East Asia.* Singapore: Oxford University Press.

Hendrickson, M., 2008. People around the houses with fire: archaeological investigation of settlement around the Jayavarman VII 'resthouse' temples. *Udaya, Journal of Khmer Studies* 9, 63–79.

Hendrickson, M., 2010. Historic routes to Angkor: development of the Khmer road system (9th to 13th centuries CE) in mainland Southeast Asia. *Antiquity* 84, 480–96.

Hendrickson, M., 2017. Transportation and the anomaly of road systems in medieval mainland Southeast Asia, in *Handbook of East and Southeast Asian Archaeology*, eds. J. Habu, P.V. Lape. & J.W. Olsen. New York, NY: Springer, 535–45.

Hendrickson, M. & D. Evans, 2015. Reimagining the city of fire and iron: a landscape archaeology of the Angkor-Period industrial complex of Preah Khan of Kompong Svay, Cambodia (ca. 9th to 13th centuries A.D.). *Journal of Field Archaeology* 5, 1–21.

Hendrickson, M., D. Ea, R. Chhay, Y. Tabata, K. Phon, S. Leroy, Y. Sato & A. Desbat, 2023. Crafting with fire: stoneware and iron pyrotechnologies in the Angkorian World, in *The Angkorian World*, eds. M. Hendrickson, M.T. Stark & D. Evans. New York: Routledge, 385–400.

Hendrickson, M., S. Leroy, C. Castillo, Q. Hua, E. Vega & K. Phon., 2019. Forging empire: first evidence of Angkorian iron smelting, community and ritual practice at Tonle Bak, Cambodia. *Antiquity* 93(372), 1586–606.

Hendrickson, M., S. Leroy, Q. Hua, K. Phon, K., V. Voeun, 2017. Smelting in the shadow of the iron mountain: Preliminary field investigation of the industrial landscape around Phnom Dek, Cambodia (ninth to twentieth centuries A.D.). *Asian Perspectives* 56, 55–91.

Heng, P., 2023. Angkor and the Mekong River: settlement, resources, mobility, and power, in *The Angkorian World*, eds. M. Hendrickson, M.T. Stark & D. Evans. New York: Routledge, 154–72.

Jacques, C. & P. Lafond, 2004. *L'Empire Khmer. Cités et sanctuaires Vth–XIIIth siècles.* Paris: Fayard.

Khin, S., 2002. *L'annexion du Cambodge par les Vietnamiens au XIXe siècle, d'après les deux poèmes du vénérable Bâtum Baramey Pich*. Paris: You Feng.
Lieberman, V., 2003. *Strange Parallels: Southeast Asia in Global Context, c. 800–1830, volume 1: Integration on the Mainland*. Cambridge: Cambridge University Press.
Lieberman, V., 2009. *Strange Parallels: Southeast Asia in Global Context, c. 800–1830, volume 2: Mainland Mirrors: Europe, Japan, China, South Asia, and the Islands*. Cambridge: Cambridge University Press.
Lorrillard, M., 2006. Lao history revisited. Paradoxes and problems in current research. *South East Asia Research* 14(3), 387–401.
Lustig, E., D.E.H. Evans & N. Richards, 2007. Words across space and time: an analysis of lexical items in Khmer inscriptions, sixth–fourteenth centuries CE. *Journal of Southeast Asian Studies* 38(1), 1–26.
Mabbett, I. & D. Chandler, 1995. *The Khmers*. Oxford: Blackwell Publishers.
Multzer O'Naghten, H., 2014. The organisation of space in pre-modern Thailand under Jayavarman VI, in *Before Siam: Essays in Art and Archaeology*, eds. N. Revire & S.A. Murphy. Bangkok: River Books, 396–419.
Pollock, S., 2006. *The Language of the Gods in the World of Men: Sanskrit, Culture, and Power in Premodern India*. Berkeley, CA: University of California Press.
Pou, S., 1971. Inscriptions modernes d'Angkor 4, 5, 6, et 7. *Bulletin de l'École française d'Extrême-Orient* 58, 105–23.
Pou, S., 2001. *Nouvelles inscriptions du Cambodge II et III*. Paris: École française d'Extrême-Orient.
Prapandvidya, C., 1990. The Sab Bak Inscription : evidence of an early vajrayana Buddhist presence in Thailand. *The Journal of the Siam Society* 78(2), 11–14.
Sak-Humphry, C., 2005. *The Sdok Kak Thom Inscription (K. 235): With a Grammatical Analysis of the Old Khmer Text*. Phnom Penh: Buddhist Institute.
Smith, A., 2008. *The Cultural Foundations of Nations*. Oxford: Blackwell Publishing.
Smith, M.L., 2005. Networks, territories, and the cartography of ancient states. *Annals of the Association of American Geographers* 95(4), 832–849.
Thompson, A., 2023. Mainland Southeast Asia after Angkor: on the legacies of Jayavarman VII, in *The Angkorian World*, eds. M. Hendrickson, M.T. Stark & D. Evans. New York: Routledge.
Umberger, E. & C.F. Klein., 1993. Aztec art and imperial expansion, in *Latin American Horizons. A Symposium at Dumbarton Oaks. 11th and 12th October 1986*, ed. D. S. Rice. Washington, DC: Dumbarton Oaks Research Library and Collection, 295–336.
Wolters, O.W., 1999. *History, Culture, and Region in Southeast Asian Perspectives: Revised Edition*. Ithaca, NY: Cornell Southeast Asia Program Publications.
Wong, W.Y.(S)., 2010. *A Preliminary study of some economic activities of Khmer Empire: examining the relationship between the Khmer and Guangdong ceramic industries during the 9th to 14th centuries*. PhD dissertation. Singapore: National University of Singapore.
Woodward, H.W. & J. G. Douglas, 1994–5. The Jayabuddhamahānātha images of Cambodia. *The Journal of the Walters Art Gallery* 52/53, 105–11.

27

THE ANGKORIAN HOUSE

Alison K. Carter, Miriam T. Stark, Heng Piphal and Chhay Rachna

Introduction

Households form the basic social unit in every culture yet have been long ignored within studies of Angkorian society (Bâty et al. 2014; Wilk and Rathje 1982). In contrast to the monumental stone temples for which Angkor is well known, domestic residences were built from perishable materials that are difficult to see in the archaeological record. Recent technological advances such as lidar and increased field-based research have begun to expand our knowledge of the locations for Angkorian houses and with it the daily lives of Angkorian people, including non-elites. In this chapter we examine the archaeological, historic, art historic, and ethnographic data to 'reconstruct' what we know about the Angkorian house.

The study of past households and their activities is an important avenue for understanding daily practices of people in the past (e.g., Allison 1999; Flannery 1976; Robin 2013; Webster and Gonlin 1988; Wilk and Rathje 1982). Household archaeology can be especially informative for understanding the socio-political and economic variations within communities and between communities or settlements, as well as between elites and non-elites (Flannery 1976; Robin 2003). In this chapter, we take a broad view of 'the Angkorian house' to include documenting the structure itself, the range of occupants, and the quotidian activities that took place in and around it. This examination of life at a local or village level complements earlier research on Angkor that has focused on ritual and elite contexts like temples or landscape scale research on broader settlement patterns and water management networks. Viewing Angkorian society from the household offers new perspectives on the daily lives of the majority of the Empire's inhabitants.

Sources of Information

A variety of sources including historic documents and inscriptions, archaeology, and bas-reliefs can help scholars reconstruct the Angkorian house. One of the most informative accounts on Angkorian life was written by Zhou Daguan (2007[1297]), a Chinese visitor to Angkor, who lived in the city for 11 months between 1296 and 1297 CE. Sanskrit and Khmer inscriptions, written by the Cambodians themselves, also provide information on elite activities and the functions of the temples as well as the non-elite community members who may have worked

DOI: 10.4324/9781351128940-33

and perhaps lived in the temple grounds and nearby region. Glimpses of daily life and wooden buildings can also be seen in the bas-reliefs of Jayavarman VII's Bayon and Banteay Chhmar temples (Figure 27.1a-b). Archaeological evidence is also proving to be increasingly important for understanding the daily lives of the Khmer. Excavations on occupation mounds within the temple enclosures of Angkor Wat (Stark et al. 2015) and Ta Prohm (Carter et al. 2018), as well as the site of Prasat Trapeang Ropou (Bâty et al. 2014; Bâty 2005), have produced post-holes from now-decomposed structures and the material remains of the activities that took place around the house. Although the Khmer people are certainly not timeless, ethnographic and ethnohistoric data also provide useful information about household activities, both tangible and intangible, as well as clues to the organisation of households during the Angkor Period (e.g., Delvert 1961; Ebihara 2018). Drawing on these sources we will address several questions related to the Angkorian house and household: Where did Angkor's population live? Who were the people who lived in Angkorian houses? What did their houses look like? What kinds of activities took place around Angkorian houses? Last, we consider phases of occupation at different Angkorian household sites.

Where Did Angkorian People Live?

The Khmer Empire expanded its influence over large portions of what is now mainland Southeast Asia, but most Angkorian sites are concentrated in the lowlands of the Mekong Basin in Cambodia. The majority of the population likely lived within the area around Angkor's capital known as Greater Angkor (Evans et al. 2007; Pottier 1999). Within this 1000-square-kilometre region there were portions of the landscape that were more rural or agrarian in focus, as well as the central monumental zone that was more densely populated (Carter et al. 2021; Klassen et al. 2021; Gaucher 2002; Gaucher 2003; Groslier 1979).

Angkorian Khmers lived on occupation mounds raised above the landscape often interspersed with small ponds, a habitation pattern that persists in Cambodia today (Delvert 1961; Prak 2006; Stark et al. 2015). Occupation mounds are frequently clustered together, often near a moated mound that may have housed a small village temple (Evans 2007; Pottier et al. 2001a; Pottier et al. 2001b; Stark 2006). Archaeologists have interpreted these as small hamlets or villages (similar to Khmer *phum*) (Delvert 1961, 180–198; Evans 2007, 24–26; Stark et al. 2015; Stark 2006). These patterns, as well as more dispersed moat-mound configurations, have also been identified at Pre-Angkorian sites in southern Cambodia (Stark 2006).

As urban centres coalesced and grew during the Angkor Period, Khmer settlement patterns transformed and a linear settlement pattern emerged along canals, dikes, rivers, and roads (Pottier 2012). In addition, ground survey and remote sensing of the Greater Angkor region identified the development of an orthogonal grid system, in which habitation was concentrated on mounds oriented according to the cardinal directions and sub-divided into city-blocks or neighbourhoods (see Evans et al. 2007; Pottier 2012; Evans et al. 2013; Evans 2016; Evans et al. 2023, this volume). This grid system appears within temple enclosures, such as Angkor Wat or the walls of Angkor Thom and also extends into the zones around these enclosed areas (e.g., Stark et al. 2015, 1444–45). As with the rural settlement configuration, these mounded habitation areas were also associated with small ponds or depressions for water storage (Pottier 2000; Acker 2012; Hanus and Evans 2016).

An inscription from Ta Prohm notes people living on the temple grounds (Cœdès 1906), and excavations at Ta Prohm and Angkor Wat have demonstrated evidence for occupation within these enclosures (Stark et al. 2015; Carter et al. 2018). Smaller religious structures, known as asramas, were also loci of religious practice, instruction, and habitation (see Pottier

2003 Estève and Soutif 2010–2011; Chea et al. 2023, this volume). Outside of Greater Angkor, regional capitals were connected to Angkor through road and transportation networks, and habitation areas have also been identified along Angkorian roads near rest houses or 'fire shrines' (Hendrickson 2008; Hendrickson 2010; Hendrickson 2011; Hendrickson 2012; Hendrickson and Evans 2015). In summary, people lived in diverse contexts but were united in that habitation areas were constructed on top of mounds.

Who Lived in the Angkorian Houses?

Angkorian society was made up of people of different classes and social status. Pre-Angkorian inscriptions describe a variety of terms for local elites of different ranks as well as commoners (Jacob 1979; Vickery 1998). This social organisation continued and likely expanded in the Angkor Period with inscriptions describing the king and ruling family, elites, middle-ranking officials, and commoners, including a large number of 'slave' categories (Zhou 2007[1297]; Mabbett 1977; Sedov 1978; Mabbett 1983; Lustig and Lustig 2013; Lustig and Lustig 2019). Little is known about these slaves, but inscriptional evidence suggests that a large part of the population may have worked as servants in some capacity (see discussion in Coe and Evans 2018, 167–168; Lustig and Lustig 2013).

Much like in Cambodia today, we expect that most Angkorian residences were organised around family groups. French scholars in the 19th and 20th centuries observed that many Khmers followed a matrilineal residential pattern, in which newlywed couples would frequently live with or near the wife's family; however, it is not clear if this practice extended back to the Angkor Period (Aymonier et al. 2016; Delvert 1961; Kaleb 1968; Ebihara 1977; cf. Ledgerwood 1995). Angkorian inscriptions do provide indirect evidence of family organisation. A study of over 100 inscriptions identified over 17,000 personnel affiliated with temples in some format (Lustig and Lustig 2009). Some of these personnel appear to have been family groups and communities who largely worked in rice fields. Angkorian bas-reliefs also depicted families, including scenes with children.

Rural households would have included farmers and their families, and many small villages contained people who were related to one another through blood or marriage (Ebihara 1977). Ethnographic evidence suggests that small rural hamlets would slowly expand as children get married and construct their own dwellings near their parents' house (Delvert 1961, 207; Ebihara 2018, 39–40). Family households were also common in the urban centre, and Zhou Daguan noted that the unit often included unrelated individuals such as slaves working and living with them (Zhou 2007[1297], 58–59).

Temples and religious communities might have also housed groups of individuals who were not related to one another but shared a common occupation. Inscriptional data from Ta Prohm (K. 273) note that the temples were inhabited by students and teachers undergoing religious study at the temple (Cœdès 1906; Bhadri 2007). Smaller religious institutions, such as *asramas*, would also likely house a small resident population of religious practitioners and students (Pottier 2003; Estève and Soutif 2010–2011). Other scholars have observed that inscriptions document the presence of specifically female temple staff (Lustig 2009; see also Vickery 1998 for the Pre-Angkor Period).

It is possible, then, that some of the occupants within the temple enclosure spaces of Angkor Wat and Ta Prohm were servants or temple labourers, but it is not clear if these residents would have also included family groups or people who were unrelated to one another. For example, would groups of temple dancers (who are depicted on bas-reliefs and mentioned in several inscriptions as serving the gods; see Pou 1997) have lived in houses surrounding the temple enclosures? Or did temple residences include occupants and their families? Archaeological excavations of residential areas both within and outside of temple zones are so far inconclusive about the specific make-up of these households.

What Did Angkorian Houses Look Like?

Angkorian residential architecture, including the Royal Palace, was constructed out of perishable materials, such as wood, bamboo, and thatch. A Chinese visitor to Cambodia in the 5th century described people living in houses on piles (Pelliot 1903; Briggs 1951). Evidence of what these structures looked like in the Angkor Period is illustrated on temple bas-reliefs, specifically along the walls of the Bayon (Figure 27.1b). These depictions show dwellings on piles with daily activities taking place in the raised area above as well as the space below. This house form is consistently replicated across Cambodia and many parts of Southeast Asia today (Figure 27.1c).

Zhou Daguan discussed the houses of different classes of society in his writings. He observed that the Royal Palace was constructed of massive beams and pillars, a roof made of ceramic roof tiles, 'soaring structures', and 'complicated walkways' (Zhou 2007[1297], 49). Other elite members of society had spacious homes with some portions of the house being covered in thatch and the main bedroom and family shrine having a roof covered with rooftiles. Common people's homes were more modest in size with only a thatch roof.

Ethnographic accounts of Cambodian house construction indicate that one of the first activities involved the demarcating of the living space was the construction of a fence (Népote 2004, 17–20; Tainturier 2006, 16). Possible fence post or palisades have been identified around occupation mounds at Prasat Trapeang Ropou (Bâty et al. 2014, 356, 378, 383). Possible fence posts have also been identified along the southern edge of an occupation mound at Angkor Wat. Although not conclusive, one trench contained two small holes aligned with one another running east–west that could be the remains of fence posts (Figure 27.2).

Figure 27.1 Everyday life in Cambodia, past and present: a–b) details from bas-reliefs on the Bayon temple depicting scenes from everyday life and Angkorian residential architecture; c) examples of contemporary Cambodian houses on piles.

Source: (Photos A. Carter).

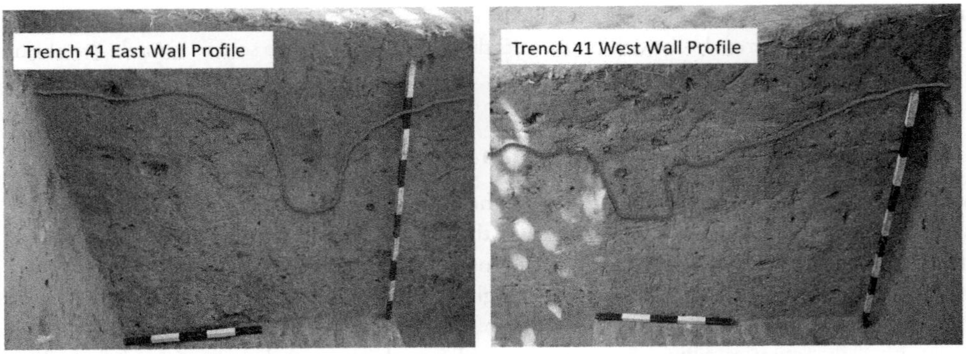

Figure 27.2 Possible fence posts identified in an excavated wall profile at Angkor Wat.

Source: (Photo A. Carter).

These same ethnographic accounts describe intangible aspects to house construction, such as the great care taken in selecting wood, which took into consideration the availability of different wood resources and the spiritual and physical power of the trees (Tainturier 2006). House construction is also frequently accompanied by ceremonies and rituals to bless the construction and ensure a good relationship with the spirits (Luco 2006; Népote 2006). Excavations around Angkor have provided possible evidence for ritual deposits, including a Chinese coin found at the base of a posthole at the Trapeang Ropou site (Bâty et al. 2014) and a complete stoneware vessel buried underneath an occupation surface within the Angkor Wat temple enclosure.

Areas underneath and around the house structure were also important. A house garden was identified at the agrarian Prasat Trapeang Ropou homestead (Bâty et al. 2014). Within the Angkor Wat enclosure, we have identified numerous flat-lying sandstone pieces, which in many cases appear to be cast-offs from the construction of the temple (Stark et al. 2015; Carter et al. 2018) (Figure 27.3). The exact function of these stones is still unclear, but they may have been placed underneath or around the houses as floors or walkways. Houses were also associated with small ponds or water storage features, called *trapeang* in Khmer. Trapeang have also been found in association with occupation mounds extending back into the Pre-Angkor Period (Stark et al., 2015, 1443–44); (Stark 2006). Zhou Daguan observed that Cambodian families each had their own pond or pool, or shared one with two or three families, and it may have served as a bath (Zhou 2007[1297], 80). Families also likely shared a toilet, digging a hole that was covered in grass and then using the pond to wash themselves afterward (Zhou 2007[1297], 68).

The Angkorian Royal Palace was a particular kind of residential structure that differed from those of the majority of Angkor's inhabitants. As noted, Zhou Daguan described the palace and other residences of officials and elites in the late 13th century (Zhou 2007[1297], 49–50). He observed that structures faced east, with lead roof tiles on the main building and others of 'yellow clay', likely ceramic. The palace was constructed of wood, with large beams and pillars that were carved and decorated, including with mirrors. Zhou was unable to see the inner palace area, but he notes that 'there were many wonderful places' (Zhou 2007[1297], 49). The outline of the Royal Palace area has been identified in Angkor Thom and consisted of a 15-hectare enclosure, surrounded by a double-wall separated by a moat. Inside the enclosure were a series of five courtyards, which were used by different members of the royal court including the King, the royal household, and the king's consorts or the women of the court (Dumarçay 1991, 41). The palace was likely modified multiple times, and although the wooden remains of the structure are gone, more public-facing stone additions built during the reign of Jayavarman VII can

Figure 27.3 Overhead view of excavation trenches at Angkor Wat showing flat-lying sandstone pieces.
Source: (Photo P. Vitou).

still be found, including the Elephant Terrace and the Terrace of the Leper King. Depictions of the palace on the walls of the Bayon display a series of open pavilions with textile curtains and wall hangings. From Zhou Daguan's writings and depictions on the Bayon bas-reliefs, the Royal Palace compound was a bustling place full of activity.

Activities in and Around Angkorian Houses

Household activities during the Angkor Period took place within the house structure itself, as well as in the areas around, under or near the houses. Ethnographic data demonstrate that Khmer houses are sub-divided into public areas, such as those where people received guests, and private spaces like sleeping quarters (Népote 2006). However, we cannot be sure that Angkorians held similar beliefs and ideas about house construction and the use of space. The space underneath houses was frequently used to keep animals, conduct various activities of daily life, or in some cases, as Zhou Daguan (2007[1297], 58–59) describes, where slaves lived.

Household activities within agriculturally focused homesteads likely varied from those in the more densely occupied city centre. People living in these zones participated in agricultural activities, and indeed excavations at Prasat Trapeang Ropou have identified locations for grain storage, the raising and tending of animals, cooking, and other activities (Bâty et al. 2014). The more urban households within the central ceremonial zone of Angkor likely did not have a major focus on such agricultural activities; however, the presence of house gardens seems important in both locations. Bâty and colleagues (2014, 383) have suggested based on ethnohistoric documents and the presence of possible holes from windfallen trees that house or kitchen gardens with fruit-bearing trees may have been present in the occupation mound they excavated at Prasat Trapeang Ropou, but microbotanical analysis confirming the presence of these gardens has not yet been undertaken due to preservation conditions. Microbotanical and macrobotanical plant remains at Ta Prohm and Angkor Wat suggest that within the civic-ceremonial centre people were growing bananas, palm trees, and spice plants like long pepper and crepe ginger (Castillo et al. 2020). Additionally, Zhou Daguan lists a wide variety of fruits and vegetables grown by the Angkorians, including lotus flowers, bananas, gourds, onions, and watermelons (Zhou 2007[1297], 71–73). House and herb gardens continue to be important components of contemporary Cambodian homes (Népote 2004; Népote 2006, 114).

Preparation and eating of food was an important daily activity and, based on ethnographic evidence, likely took place in a separate structure or area near the main house (Delvert 1961, 186; Ebihara 2018, 41; Népote 2006, 114). Zhou Daguan describes how poor families cooked food using earthenware pots over three stones in the ground and ate from organic containers, including leaf bowls and used coconut husk spoons (Zhou 2007[1297], 76–77). In contrast, wealthier families might use metal objects (Zhou 2007[1297], 76–77). Bas-reliefs also depict the use of clay stoves similar to the clay stoves used by Cambodian people today, and numerous earthenware stove fragments have been identified in the archaeological record (Cremin 2009). A small circular group of stones and brick, likely a hearth, was identified at Angkor Wat. On top of this feature was a group of broken ceramics and burnt plant remains (Figure 27.4). Excavations in an occupation mound surrounding the Ta Prohm temple uncovered a trash pit that contained a broken cooking stove, a spice mortar, and other ceramics (Figure 27.5) (Carter et al. 2018).

Figure 27.4 Trash pit from excavations within the Ta Prohm enclosure. Artefacts include ceramics and a sandstone spice mortar on the right.

Source: (Photo P. Heng).

Figure 27.5 Possible hearth from excavations within the Angkor Wat enclosure.

Source: (Photo A. Carter).

In addition to the locally produced earthenware and stoneware ceramics (Groslier 1995), Angkorians also procured foreign trade wares, primarily from China, that had both ritual functions and may have served as status symbols (Miksic 2000; Cremin 2009; Wong 2010). These items make up a small proportion, less than 10%, of the ceramic assemblages at Angkor Wat and Ta Prohm (Carter et al. 2018). Covered boxes may have had ritual functions, been used to store cremated remains, or been containers for products like beeswax or perfume (Dupoizat 1999; Wong 2010, 256–257). One notable find from an occupation mound at Angkor Wat was a small chicken-shaped water dropper (Figure 27.6). In China, these objects were used in calligraphy in order to drop water on an inkstone. Other objects typical of Chinese calligraphy, such as an inkstone or brush, have not been found at Angkor, so it is unclear if this vessel performed a similar function (for further discussion on writing in Angkor, see Sullivan 1957, 41). However, the presence of this unique object in the occupation mound at Angkor Wat suggests that the residents in the temple enclosure had access to a variety of ceramic objects.

Archaeological work has also shed light on other possible craft production taking place in residential contexts. Cotton seed fragments and funicular caps were found in excavations at Ta Prohm and Angkor Wat suggesting cotton processing was taking place at both sites, perhaps at the household level (Castillo et al. 2020). Cotton fragments and a seed have also been found near the Terrace of the Leper King in Angkor Thom in contexts that date from the 14th–15th centuries CE (Castillo et al. 2018). Cloth and garments are an important item mentioned in temple inscriptions, and Zhou Daguan specifically mentions that Angkorians wove cotton (Zhou 2007[1297], 75–76). The presence of cotton in occupation mounds within temple enclosures may be related to the production of the high quantity of cloth and garments

Figure 27.6 Chinese water dropper in the shape of a chicken found in an excavation at Angkor Wat.
Source: (Photo P. Vitou).

mentioned in temple inscriptions that were used to decorate statues of the gods and in elite contexts (Green 2003; Maxwell 2007; see Green 2023, this volume).

Decorative carving was often done *in situ* on temples by specialised artisans (Polkinghorne 2008), and reused or cast-off sandstone pieces have been found within our excavations within the Angkor Wat enclosure. An initial phase of occupation on the mounds at Angkor Wat might have included the people who assisted with the construction of the temple. Once the temples were constructed, inscriptional evidence describes a variety of occupations associated with the functions of the temple, including religious specialists, teachers, students, temple dancers, singers, musicians, guards, umbrella bearers, cooks, and others (Sahai 2012; Lustig and Lustig 2013). While it is probable that many of the people who lived on the mounds around the temple performed some of these activities, it is impossible to confirm based on the current archaeological evidence.

An even wider variety of activities took place within the Royal Palace compound and elite houses in this area. Archaeological investigations in the early 20th century by Henri Marchal identified different activity areas, including those associated with cooking and food preparation, residential zones, and areas with evidence for make-up and medicine (Marchal 1926; Chandler and Polkinghorne 2016;) Zhou Daguan (2007[1297], 54–55) describes a large number of servant women associated with the Royal Palace who would come and go from the compound conducting business. He also describes how the King himself would conduct state affairs from a 'gold window' in the palace. The palace was also a locus for the performance and pageantry of state power (Stark et al. 2018). Zhou (2007[1297], 62–64) describes numerous state festivities that would take place in front of the palace, including celebrations with fireworks and elephant fights.

Phases of Occupation

Excavations at Angkorian residential sites show phases of occupation whose intensity shifted over time. At Prasat Trapeang Ropou, the initial Angkorian occupation, dated to the 10th–11th centuries, includes post-holes but no clear structure. The second occupation phase was more intensive, with greater quantities of artifacts, and is associated with the use of the nearby village temple in the 12th–14th centuries. After a brief period of abandonment, the final Post-Angkorian occupation is associated with two small buildings, perhaps more temporary structures related to agricultural activities and an area where people may have been making palm sugar (Bâty et al. 2014).

Excavations within the civic-ceremonial centre show similar shifts in occupation over time. At Angkor Wat, we have identified three phases of occupation between the 11th and 18th centuries (Stark et al. 2015; Carter et al. 2019). An initial phase, dating to the 11th century, is associated with the construction of the mound-depression grid system inside the temple enclosure. A second phase of occupation is associated with increased habitation during the 11th–12th centuries. This phase has the highest density of ceramics and is associated with the flat-lying stones and hearth feature described previously. After this phase is a brief gap and then a reoccupation in the 14th–15th centuries until the 17th or 18th centuries. However, this final phase does not show the same intensity of occupation as during the Angkor Period and might suggest more temporary habitation associated with pilgrimage to the Angkor Wat temple (Thompson 2004).

Excavations within the Ta Prohm enclosure importantly show evidence for occupation in this landscape prior to the construction of the temple, in the 8th–10th centuries. This was followed by a transformation of the landscape, development of a mound-depression grid system, and increased ceramic frequencies sometime between the 11th and 13th centuries (Carter et al.

2018). A third phase of additional habitation and building up of mounds continued in the 12th–14th centuries. In contrast to Angkor Wat and Prasat Trapeang Ropou, there is no strong evidence for occupation or re-occupation of this space post-14th century, and the site seems to have been abandoned. Based on this limited sample of archaeological data, as well as recent diachronic population estimates for Angkor (Carter et al. 2021; Klassen et al. 2021), occupation in both Angkor's civic-ceremonial centre and more rural areas grew from the 11th–13th centuries CE, reaching a peak in the 13th century. As Angkor declined, some portions of the landscape appear to have been abandoned, while others show reoccupation, although less intensely.

Conclusion

Angkorians lived in a wide variety of contexts, from more rural and agriculturally oriented to those situated in an 'urban' or grid system linked to temple enclosures. Archaeological, ethnographic, and historic evidence can help us envision what an Angkorian house looked like and some of the activities that took place within and around them. What is still missing, however, is a clear understanding of who lived in Angkorian houses. We hope that future work might address questions such as how elite houses differed from those of commoners. Slaves have been frequently discussed in inscriptions but have not yet been identified archaeologically. Examination of residential spaces could help us further investigate this key component of the Angkorian community. We also know little of how Angkor's domestic economy was organised, and further work could explore the diversity of household organisation both within the capital as well as Angkor's agrarian metropolitan area. As we continue to excavate and study Angkorian occupation sites, we hope to understand Angkorian society more fully through the lens of its residential spaces.

References

Acker, B., 2012. Mysteries of Angkor revealed: hydrology and the siting of Angkor, in *Old Myths and New Approaches. Interpreting Ancient Religious Sites in Southeast Asia*, ed. A. Haendel. Clayton, Victoria: Monash University Publishing, 28–41.

Allison, P. (ed.) 1999. *The Archaeology of Household Activities*. London: Routledge.

Aymonier, E., E. Gsell, J.G. Montague, M.-H. Arnauld & J. Mizerski, 2016. *Cambodia Past: Explaining the Present: A Translation of Notice sur le Cambodge (Notes on Cambodia), 1875*. Holmes Beach, FL: DatAsia.

Bâty, P., 2005. *Extension de l'Aéroport de Siem Reap. Rapport de diagnostic archéologique*. Trapeang Thlok-Prasat Trapeang Ropou: Base INRAP de Poitiers.

Bâty, P., A. Desbat, F. Sellami & S. Marquié, 2014. Le tertre E à Trapeang Ropou Approche archéologique et géomorphologique d'un habitat angkorien. *Aséanie* 33, 331–87.

Bhadri, K.M., 2007. Ta Prohm inscription of Jayavarman VII, AD 1186, in *Ta Prohm: A Glorious Era in Angkor Civilization*, eds. P.K. Kapur & S. Sahai. Bangkok: White Lotus Press, 49–56.

Briggs, L.P., 1951. *The Ancient Khmer Empire*. Philadelphia: American Philosophical Society.

Carter, A.K., P. Heng, M.T. Stark, R. Chhay & D.H. Evans, 2018. Urbanism and residential patterning in Angkor. *Journal of Field Archaeology* 43(6), 492–506.

Carter, A.K., S. Klassen, M.T. Stark, P. Heng, D. Evans, and R. Chhay, 2021. The evolution of agro-urbanism: a case-study from Angkor, Cambodia. *Journal of Anthropological Archaeology* 63, 101323.

Carter, A.K., M.T. Stark, S. Quintus, Y. Zhuang, H. Wang, P. Heng & R. Chhay, 2019. Temple occupation and the tempo of collapse at Angkor Wat, Cambodia. *Proceedings of the National Academy of Sciences* 116(25), 12226–31.

Castillo, C., A.K. Carter, E. Kingwell-Banham, Y. Zhuang, A. Weisskopf, R. Chhay, P. Heng, D.Q. Fuller & M.T. Stark, 2020. The Khmer did not live by rice alone. *Archaeological Research in Asia* 24, 100213.

Castillo, C.C., M. Polkinghorne, B. Vincent, B. Suy Tan & D.Q. Fuller, 2018. Life goes on: archaeobotanical investigations of diet and ritual at Angkor Thom, Cambodia (14th–15th centuries CE). *Holocene* 28(6), 930–44.

Chandler, T. & M. Polkinghorne, 2016. A review of sources for visualising the royal palace of Angkor, Cambodia, in *Virtual Palaces, Part II. Lost Palaces and their Afterlife*, eds. S. Hoppe & S. Breitling & H. Messemer. Munchen: Palatium, 149–70.

Chea, S., J. Estève, D. Soutif & E. Swenson, 2023. Āśramas, shrines and royal power, in *The Angkorian World*, eds. M. Hendrickson, M.T. Stark & D. Evans. New York: Routledge.

Coe, M.D. & D. Evans, 2018. *Angkor and the Khmer Civilization*. (2nd ed.) New York: Thames & Hudson.

Cœdès, G., 1906. La stèle de Ta-Prohm. *Bulletin de l'École française d'Extrême-Orient* 6(1), 44–86.

Cremin, A., 2009. Image and reality: ceramics on Angkorian temple reliefs in Cambodia. *Australasian Historical Archaeology* 79–86.

Delvert, J., 1961. *Le paysan cambodgien*. Paris: Mouton & Co.

Dumarçay, J., 1991. The palaces of Cambodia, in *The Palaces of South-East Asia: Architecture and Customs*, ed. M. Smithies. Oxford: Oxford University Press, 40–54.

Dupoizat, M-F., 1999. La céramique importée à Angkor: étude préliminaire. *Arts Asiatiques* 54(1), 103–16.10.3406/arasi.1999.1435

Ebihara, M., 1977. Residence patterns in a Khmer peasant village. *Annals of the New York Academy of Sciences* 293(1), 51–68.

Ebihara, M., 2018. Svay. *A Khmer Village in Cambodia*. Ithaca, NY: Southeast Asia Program Publications.

Estève, J. & D. Soutif, 2010–2011. Les Yaśodharāśrama, marqueurs d'empire et bornes sacrées: Conformité et spécificité des stèles digraphiques khmères de la région de Vat Phu. *Bulletin de l'École française d'Extrême-Orient* 97–98, 331–55.

Evans, D.H., 2007. *Putting Angkor on the map: a new survey of a Khmer hydraulic city in historical and theoretical context*. PhD dissertation. Sydney: The University of Sydney.

Evans, D.H., 2016. Airborne laser scanning as a method for exploring long-term socio-ecological dynamics in Cambodia. *Journal of Archaeological Science* 74, 164–75.

Evans, D.H., R.J. Fletcher, C. Pottier, J.-B. Chevance, D. Soutif, B.S. Tan, S. Im, D. Ea, T. Tin, S. Kim, C. Cromarty, S. De Greef, K. Hanus, P. Baty, R. Kuszinger, I. Shimoda & G. Boornazian, 2013. Uncovering archaeological landscapes at Angkor using lidar. *Proceedings of the National Academy of Sciences* 110(31), 12595–600.

Evans, D.H., C. Pottier, R. Fletcher, S. Hensley, I. Tapley, A. Milne & M. Barbetti, 2007. A comprehensive archaeological map of the World's largest preindustrial settlement complex at Angkor, Cambodia. *Proceedings of the National Academy of Sciences of the United States of America* 104(36), 14277–82.

Evans, D., R. Fletcher, S. Klassen, C. Pottier & P. Wijker, 2023. Trajectories of urbanism in the Angkorian World, in *The Angkorian World*, eds. M. Hendrickson, M.T. Stark & D. Evans. New York: Routledge.

Flannery, K.V. (ed.) 1976. *The Early Mesoamerican Village*. New York: Academic Press, 173–94.

Gaucher, J., 2002. The City of Angkor. What is it? *Museum International* 54(1–2), 28–36.

Gaucher, J., 2003. New archaeological data on the urban space of the capital city of Angkor Thom, in *Fishbones and Glittering Emblems: Southeast Asian Archaeology 2002*, eds. A. Karlstrom & A. Kallen. Stockholm: Museum of Far Eastern Antiquities, 233–42.

Green, G., 2003. Khmer costume and textile history, in *Traditional Textiles of Cambodia: Cultural Threads and Material Heritage*. Bangkok: River Books, 27–41.

Green, G., 2023. Vogue at Angkor: dress, décor and narrative drama, in *The Angkorian World*, eds. M. Hendrickson, M.T. Stark & D. Evans. New York: Routledge, 508–24.

Groslier, B.P., 1979. VII. La cité hydraulique angkorienne: exploitation ou surexploitation du sol? *Bulletin de l'École française d'Extrême-Orient* 66(1), 161–202.

Groslier, B.P., 1995. Introduction à la céramique Angkorienne (fin IXe–début XVe s.). *Péninsule* 31(2), 5–60.

Hanus, K. & D. Evans, 2016. Imaging the waters of Angkor: A method for semi-automated pond extraction from LiDAR data. *Archaeological Prospection* 23, 87–94.

Hendrickson, M., 2008. People around the houses with fire: archaeological investigation of settlement around the Jayavarman VII 'Resthouse' Temples. *Udaya, Journal of Khmer Studies* 9, 63–79.

Hendrickson, M., 2010. Historic routes to Angkor: development of the Khmer road system (ninth to thirteenth centuries AD) in Mainland Southeast Asia. *Antiquity* 84, 480–96.

Hendrickson, M., 2011. A transport geographic perspective on travel and communication in Angkorian Southeast Asia (ninth to fifteenth centuries AD). *World Archaeology* 43(3), 444–57.

Hendrickson, M., 2012. Connecting the dots: investigating transportation between the temple complexes of the medieval Khmer (9th–14th centuries CE), in *Old Myths and New Approaches. Interpreting Ancient Religious Sites in Southeast Asia,* ed. A. Haendel. Clayton, Victoria: Monash University Publishing, 84–102.

Hendrickson, M. & D. Evans, 2015. Reimagining the city of fire and iron: A landscape archaeology of the Angkor-Period industrial complex of Preah Khan of Kompong Svay, Cambodia (ca. 9th to 13th centuries A.D.). *Journal of Field Archaeology* 40(6), 1–21.

Jacob, J.M., 1979. Pre-Angkor Cambodia: evidence from the inscriptions concerning the common people and their environment, in *Early South East Asia: Essays in Archaeology, History, and Historical Geography*, eds. R.B. Smith & W. Watson. New York: Oxford University Press, 406–24.

Kaleb, M., 1968. Study of a Cambodian village. *The Geographical Journal* 134(4), 521–37.

Klassen, S., A.K. Carter, D. Evans, S.G. Ortman, M.T. Stark, A.A. Loyless, M. Polkinghorne, P. Heng, M. Hill, P. Wijker, J. Niles-Weed, G. P. Marriner, C. Pottier & R. Fletcher., 2021. Diachronic modelling of the population within the medieval Greater Angkor region settlement complex. *Science Advances* 7(19), eabf8441.

Ledgerwood, J.L., 1995. Khmer kinship: the matriliny/matriarchy myth. *Journal of Anthropological Research* 51(3), 247–61.

Luco, F., 2006. House-building rituals and ceremonies in a village of the Angkor Complex, in *Cambodian Wooden Architecture: A Disappearing Heritage*, ed. F. Tainturier. Siem Reap: Center for Khmer Studies, 90–107.

Lustig, E., 2009. *Power and Pragmatism in the political economy of Angkor*. PhD dissertation. Sydney: The University of Sydney.

Lustig, E. & T. Lustig, 2013. New Insights into "les Interminables Listes Nominatives d'Esclaves" from Numerical Analyses of the Personnel in Angkorian Inscriptions. *Aseanie* 31, 55–83.

Lustig, E. & T. Lustig, 2019. Losing ground: decline of Angkor's middle-level officials. *Journal of Southeast Asian Studies* 1–22.

Mabbett, I.W., 1977. Varnas in Angkor and the Indian caste system. *The Journal of Asian Studies* 36, 429–42.

Mabbett, I.W., 1983. Some remarks on the present state of knowledge about slavery in Angkor, in *Slavery, Bondage and Dependency in Southeast Asia,* ed. A. Reid. Queensland: University of Queensland Press, 44–63.

Marchal, H., 1926. Notes sur le Palais Royal d'Angkor Thom. *Arts et archéologie khmers; revue des recherches sur les arts, les monuments et l'ethnographie du Cambodge, depuis les origines jusqu'à nos jours*, 2(3), 303–28.

Maxwell, T.S., 2007. The Stele inscription of Preah Khan, Angkor. *Udaya, Journal of Khmer Studies* (8), 1–114.

Miksic, J., 2000. Chinese ceramics and local cultural statements in fourteenth-century Southeast Asia, in *Studies in Southeast Asian Art: Essays in Honor of Stanley J. O'Connor*, ed. N.A. Taylor. Ithaca: Cornell University Southeast Asia Program, 194–216.

Népote, J., 2004. Comprendre la maison cambodgienne (II)—Troisième et dernière partie: à la recherche du sens. *Péninsule* 48, 5–95.

Népote, J., 2006. Understanding the Cambodian dwelling: space and gender in traditional homes, in *Wooden Architecture of Cambodia: A Disappearing Heritage,* eds. F. Tainturier, C. Lalonde & M. Rethy. Siem Reap: Center for Khmer Studies, 90–107.

Pelliot, P., 1903. *Le Fou-Nan*, Paris: École Française d'Extrême Orient.

Polkinghorne, M., 2008. Artists and ateliers: Khmer decorative lintels of the ninth and tenth centuries. *Udaya, Journal of Khmer Studies* 8, 219–42.

Pottier, C., 2000. Some evidence of an inter-relationship between hydraulic features and rice field patterns at Angkor during ancient times. *The Journal of Sophia Asian Studies* 18, 99–119.

Pottier, C., 2003. Yasovarman's Buddhist asrama in Angkor, in *The Buddhist Monastery: A Cross Cultural Survey*, eds. P. Pichard & F. Lagirarde. Paris: École Française d'Extrême-Orient, 199–208.

Pottier, C., 1999. *Carte archéologique de la region d'Angkor Zone Sud*. PhD dissertation. Paris: Université Paris III—Sorbonne nouvelle.

Pottier, C., 2012. Beyond the temples: Angkor and its temple, in *Old Myths and New Approaches. Interpreting Ancient Religious Sites in Southeast Asia,* ed. A. Haendel. Clayton, Victoria: Monash University Publishing, 12–27.

Pottier, C., A. Guerin, T. Heng, S. Im, C. Khieu & E. Llopis, 2001a. Mission Archéologique Franco-Khmère sur l'Aménagement du Territoire Angkorien (MAFKATA). Rapport sur la campagne de fouilles 2001, Siem Reap: APSARA—MAE-École française d'Extrême-Orient.

Pottier, C., A. Guerin, T. Heng, S. Im, T. Koy & E. Llopis, 2001b. Mission Archéologique Franco-Khmère sur l'Aménagement du Territoire Angkorien (MAFKATA). Rapport sur la campagne de fouilles 2000, Siem Reap: APSARA—MAE-École française d'Extrême-Orient.

Pou, S., 1997. Music and dance in ancient Cambodia as evidenced by old Khmer epigraphy. *East and West* 47(1–4), 229–48.

Prak, V., 2006. Wooden houses of the early twentieth century: settlement patterns, social distinction and ethnicity, in *Wooden Architecture of Cambodia: A Disappearing Heritage*, eds. F. Tainturier, C. Lalonde & M. Rethy. Siem Reap: Center for Khmer Studies, 66–89.

Robin, C., 2003. New directions in classic Maya household archaeology. *Journal of Archaeological Research* 11(4), 307–56.

Robin, C., 2013. *Everyday Life Matters: Maya Farmers at Chan*. Gainesville: University Press of Florida.

Sahai, S., 2012. *The Hindu Temples in South East Asia: Their Role in Social Economic and Political Formations*, New Delhi: Aryan Books.

Sedov, L.A., 1978. Angkor: society and state, in *The Early State*, eds. H.J.M. Claessen & P. Skalnik. The Hague: Mouton, 111–30.

Stark, M.T., 2006. Pre-Angkorian settlement trends in Cambodia's Mekong Delta and the Lower Mekong Archaeological Project. *Bulletin of the Indo-Pacific Prehistory Association*, 26, 98–109.

Stark, M.T., A.K. Carter, P. Heng, R. Chhay & D. Evans, 2018. The Angkorian city: from Hariharalaya to Yashodharapura, in *Angkor. Exploring Cambodia's Sacred City*, eds. T. McCullough, S.A. Murphy, P. Baptiste & T. Zephir. Singapore: Asian Civilizations Museum, 156–77.

Stark, M.T., D. Evans, C. Rachna, H. Piphal & A. Carter, 2015. Residential patterning at Angkor Wat. *Antiquity* 89(348), 1439–55.

Sullivan, M., 1957. Kendi. *Archives of the Chinese Art Society of America*, 11, 40–58.

Tainturier, F., 2006. Building in wood: notes on a vanishing age-old tradition, in *Wooden Architecture of Cambodia: A Disappearing Heritage*, ed. F. Tainturier. Siem Reap: Center for Khmer Studies, 12–37.

Thompson, A., 2004. Pilgrims to Angkor: A Buddhist "cosmopolis" in Southeast Asia? *Bulletin of the Students of the Department of Archaeology* 3, 88–119.

Vickery, M., 1998. *Society, Economics, and Politics in Pre-Angkor Cambodia. The 7th and 8th Centuries*. Tokyo: The Centre for East Asian Cultural Studies for Unesco.

Webster, D. & N. Gonlin, 1988. Household remains of the humblest Maya. *Journal of Field Archaeology* 15(2), 169.

Wilk, R.R. & W.L. Rathje, 1982. Household archaeology. *American Behavioral Scientist* 25(6), 617–39.

Wong, W.Y., 2010. A preliminary study of some economic activities of the Khmer Empire: examining the relationship between the Khmer and Guangdong ceramic industries during the 9th to 14th centuries, in *Southeast Asian Studies Programme*. Singapore: National University Singapore.

Zhou, D., 2007[1297]. *A Record of Cambodia: The Land and Its People*, trans. P. Harris. Chiang Mai: Silkworm Books.

28

VOGUE AT ANGKOR

Dress, Décor, and Narrative Drama

Gillian Green

No textiles have been recovered from Angkor Period excavations, a situation by no means unusual in tropical environments, as textiles by their very nature are fragile unless preserved by favourable natural circumstances. In their stead, a survey of 8th- to 13th-century Angkor Period stone and bronze sculptures, both bas-relief and in the round, clearly reveals a lavish use of textiles for dress, accessories, and décor. These celebrated works of art thus become an invaluable resource with which to elucidate societal, cultural, economic, and even political issues via the medium of textiles.

A number of strategies have been adopted here to address these issues. Dress on sculpted images of deities, royalty, soldiers, and the general populace has been analysed to establish stylistic changes through the Angkor Period. This specific approach, initiated by scholars George Cœdès (1913), George Groslier (1921), and Jean Boisselier (1966), in itself becomes an aid to establishing a sculptural typology. Comparisons are made with dress and textiles from neighbouring regions as well as those from the Indian sub-continent during the Angkor Period. Dress items, however, are not the only textiles depicted at Angkor. There is plentiful sculpted evidence that accessories and décor items fashioned from textiles graced the environs of the royal court. Textiles adorned palaces' wooden walls, used for upholstery, draped as canopies, curtains and altar surrounds, litters for personal transport, and fashioned into parasols and fans emblematic of royalty. Textiles were also fashioned into banners and animal trappings used in a military context. This visual analysis is enhanced by epigraphic and literary sources, archaeological finds, technical specifics concerning spinning and weaving, and insights into trading relationships with other polities in the region. Collating results from these resources reveals a much broader context in which these textiles functioned.

Textiles for Dress

Trends in dress over the Angkor Period are depicted in precise detail on statues and bas-reliefs of deities both male and female and demonstrate, over time, increasing levels of complexity (Green 2000, 2003). Accoutrements such as jewellery and belts embellish dress of deities, higher ranks of society, and the military, while the clothing needs of the general population are practical and unadorned. The ubiquitous form of dress is the hipwrapper, *sampot* in Khmer language. The word 'sampot' means a 'length of cloth' but in this context specifically refers to a hipwrapper. In

DOI: 10.4324/9781351128940-34

the 7th to 8th centuries, male deities are depicted with a length of plain cloth simply wrapped round the waist and, extending halfway down the thigh, secured by knotting or by a thin belt. A century later the sampot is depicted with one end passing through the legs to be tucked under the belt at the back, while the other remains folded into a looped 'pocket' in front (Figure 28.1a). This style with cloth passing between the legs is known as *sampot chong kbun*, where *chong* means 'to tie, to bundle', and *kbun* has the functional meaning of a strip of cloth that covers the private parts. Male sampot may feature additional decorative lengths of narrow cloth tucked into the belt draping down in front either centrally or to the sides.

Sampot depicted on female deities are wrapped then knotted and tucked in at the front waist edge and extend to the ankles (Figure 28.1b). From the late 10th century, they are embellished with a lavish jewelled belt. Around this time finely pleated sampot appear on both male and female deities, thigh length for men and ankle length for women. These pleated sampot are associated with a number of typologies characterised as Bakheng, Koh Ker, Angkor Wat, and Banteay Srei. By the late 11th century a modification characterised as the Baphuon style appears (Figure 28.2). As worn by a male deity, this sampot chong kben of pleated cloth features a characteristically high waist edge at the back which dips down in front. Both ends of the cloth are then drawn between the legs to the back, fanning out from under the belt at the back. Females wear similarly high-waisted sampot of pleated fabric, wrapped and knotted round the waist, extending to the ankle. Both styles have elaborate jewelled belts, as in earlier forms. The late

Figure 28.1 Examples of Angkorian individuals wearing sampot: a) male wearing a sampot chong kben with pocket fold and additional decorative panel at the waist. Banteay Srei, 10th century; b) devata wearing a sampot knotted at the waist, secured with an elaborate belt. Banteay Srei, 10th century.

Source: (Photos G. Green).

Figure 28.2 Śiva wearing a pleated sampot worn high at the waist, Baphuon style, 11th–12th century. Bronze, silver, and black glass, amalgam gilding.

Source: (Photo courtesy National Gallery of Australia, Canberra 80.874).

12th- to 13th-century Bayon style for male deities changes to a much shorter, mid-thigh sampot chong kben with prominent additional panels draped front and back, while females retain the longer wrapped sampot.

A more complex dress form appears on some of the 1800 images of *devata* portrayed on 12th century bas-reliefs at Angkor Wat. Devata were 'dancers and women attached to the service of the temple . . . their costumes, their jewels were those worn by the women of the period' (Marchal 2005, 1). Their ensembles quite clearly show two long end pieces emerging upwards and outwards from underneath the side waist edges of their ankle-length sampot (Figure 28.3). Two lengths of cloth are needed to fashion this style. One is a narrow sampot chong kben style undergarment just covering the hips being worn beneath the upper, ankle-length wrap-round sampot. The end pieces of the undergarment emerging from beneath the upper sampot then clearly account for the two arched panels as depicted. Marchal's detailed sketches illustrate some devata wearing just such a sampot chong kben style undergarment but simply worn on its own (2005, 45, 53). Both upper and under sampot may be patterned. The use of two lengths of patterned cloth with its implied level of extravagance would be deemed appropriate for women attending the deity.

The Khmer warrior king Suryavarman II and his soldiers, as depicted on early 12th-century Angkor Wat reliefs, wear a particular style of sampot chong kben (Figure 28.4a). A narrow length of patterned or pleated cloth is wrapped round the hips then knotted at the waist, the ends then passed between the legs and tucked under the belt at the back, allowing the long end

Figure 28.3 Devatas wearing double-layer sampot ensembles, Angkor Wat, 12th century.

Source: (Photo G. Green).

Figure 28.4 Examples of short sampot chong kben: a) Khmer warrior with short sampot chong kben with flower-in-square pattern and bodice with flower-in-trellis pattern. Angkor Wat, 12th century; b) minimal sampot chong kben worn by figures on right lower tier, Bayon, late 12th to early 13th century; c) Siamese soldiers in historical procession.

Source: (Photos G. Green).

panels to flare out to the sides. Other individuals pictured in these reliefs wear what may be termed minimal sampot chong kben where a narrow length of cloth wrapped around the waist passes between the legs, being just sufficient to function as a cache-sexe. The ends drape down the front (Figure 28.4b). This is the style worn by *rishis* (Hindu sages), slaves, prisoners, and sinners, as well as both the Khmer and Cham soldiers as depicted on Bayon bas-reliefs.

Upper body garments are apparently worn specifically in a military context, as neither males nor females in day-to-day Khmer life are depicted wearing such garments. This exception is in the form of a tight-fitting, short-sleeved bodice worn by soldiers as pictured on the Angkor Wat historical procession relief (see Figure 28.4a). A variation appears on Bayon bas-reliefs depicting a conflict between the Khmer and the Cham. Soldiers, both Khmer and their Cham adversaries, wear looser, waist-length tunics or knee-length jackets and sometimes both these two styles together, one overlaying the other (Green 2003, 35).

Jewellery in the form of diadems, earrings, neckpieces, pendants, armbands, bangles, and anklets adorns males and females. Extant archaeologically recovered examples are made of beaten gold with moulded floral, vegetal, and mythic decorative imagery, often enhanced with precious stones and pearls. Elements from nature such as jasmine flowers become decorative additions to devatas' elaborate headpieces.

Comparisons of Angkor Period Khmer dress with Indian dress within a similar time frame are significant. Chandra (1973) has published his extensive investigation of Indian dress dating from the beginning of the Common Era to the 16th century. His survey of sculpted and painted representations demonstrates many commonalities when compared with those of the Khmer. These include sampot chong kben, popular for male images in the Khmer domain, recorded on Indian images as early as the Kushan Period in the first four centuries CE. This practical hipwrapper form may have been an indigenous form in the Khmer domain or it might have been adopted due to Indian influence during the period of their developing interaction. Pleated cloth, so popular for Khmer sampot of the early 10th century, is also seen used for Indian sampot. The short-sleeved bodices worn by Khmer soldiers closely resemble those of Gupta Period (320–550) Indian images (Chandra 1973, figs. 29, 61). They presumably afford a level of protection to the wearer. These particular garments, cut and stitched as they would have been, are very unlikely to be indigenous to the Khmer, who neither wore upper body garments nor had a tradition of stitched garments. These criteria indicate the Khmers' adoption of this Indian form.

The kingdom of Champa was a powerful Hinduised state contemporary with Angkor situated in what is present-day central and south Vietnam. In regional terms it is interesting to note that dress forms and their components seen on Cham sculpted deities bear close resemblance to many of the Khmer in the Pre-Angkor and Angkor Periods (Phuong et al. 2018). Cham deities, like their Khmer counterparts, are not depicted wearing upper body garments, though Cham soldiers did wear jackets in a military context, as previously noted. Interestingly, while pleated cloth was popular at Angkor through the 10th to 12th centuries, it is not evident in Cham dress at the time. These broad similarities between Khmer and Cham dress traditions in this period point to their close cultural relationship.

Availability of Textiles at Angkor

Surveying dress on the diversity of participants in Angkorian life has demonstrated a variety of sampot lengths—hip, thigh, and ankle—and patterns. These features raise a number of interesting questions about the supply of textiles in the Khmer domain. Did the Khmer produce and prepare their own thread for weaving? If they did weave, was that supply adequate for all their textile needs? Were their weavers proficient in patterning techniques? What kinds of cloth were available—cotton, bast fibre, silk, other? Did they acquire textiles from outside sources? Details derived from epigraphy, historical sources, archaeological discoveries, and weaving technology contribute significantly to answering these questions.

Inscriptions at Angkorian temples provide useful insights into textiles and their production technology. A dictionary compiled from old Khmer and Sanskrit words appearing on 9th to 15th century temples lists 14 words relating to types of cloth, 20 to dress or dress components, 17 to non-dress textile items, and 13 to techniques related to spinning and weaving (Pou 1992). There are also words for colours, including red, indigo blue, and black. While these inscriptions itemise tributes to temples, they do reflect the types of cloth and dress generally available in the region at the time.

Zhou Daguan, Chinese envoy to Angkor in the late 13th century, published his observations of life there, and these afford a unique window into that world at that time. He commented, as much as he was witness to, not only on local dress and types of textiles but also on their method of manufacture. He observed that the Khmer did not spin thread on a spinning wheel but used the simpler hand spindle (2007[1297], 79). This tool, which could be made from a short length of wood, bone, or bamboo, operates together with a spindle whorl to spin fibres into thread ready for weaving. While spindles themselves have not survived, those spindle whorls made with durable materials often have and as such are significant indicators of hand spinning activity. Archaeological excavations at prehistoric sites Mlu Prei, Samrong Sen, and Krek in the eastern region of Cambodia have unearthed clay spindle whorls (Cameron 2002). Examples have also been excavated in Óc Eo (*Funan*), the 2nd to 6th century maritime entrepôt on the Mekong delta (Cameron 2002, 122). None have been found in the Greater Angkor Region (see Castillo 2023, this volume).

Zhou observed Khmer weaving on looms corresponding to the foot-braced, backstrap category on which relatively narrow lengths of cloth are woven. This type of elementary loom was, and still is, used by minority peoples living in regions distant from urban centres in many parts of the world. The product is a length of plain cloth which could serve many purposes, including dress, wrapping, and bedding. Evidence of the type of thread used comes from recent archaeological excavations adjacent to the Royal Palace at Angkor Thom. Archaeologists unearthed a single cotton seed (*Gossypium arboreum*) in one trench and fragments of cotton in three others (Castillo 2018, 7). Also cotton seed fragments have been reported from the site of Angkor Wat and Ta Prohm (Castillo et al. 2020). These finds, minimal as they are, constitute evidence of the possibility of textile manufacture because the fibres surrounding a cotton seed may be spun into thread ready for weaving. Collating the archaeological evidence of excavated spindle whorls, cotton seed, and fragments, together with backstrap loom weaving, argues for domestic production of plain cotton cloth during the Angkor Period.

Plain cloth was not, however, the only kind in use at Angkor. Much more sophisticated 'luxury' varieties such as brocade and taffeta are indicated. Brocade is a silk weave with a raised pattern, usually woven with gold or silver thread, while taffeta is a fine, plain weave or self-patterned silk fabric. There were reportedly several sources of such luxury cloth at Angkor: India, China, Siam, and Champa. Zhou observed that the Khmer king wore cloth 'worth more than three or four ounces of gold; . . . extremely fine and costly . . . some come from Siam and Champa, but the most esteemed are in general those which come from India, for their fine and delicate texture' (2007[1297], 25). He noted that the 'multi-coloured' silk fabric used for litters and gold-speckled mosquito nets in the king's court were gifts from overseas merchants (2007[1297], 81). He described silk woven with gold used for food covers, red silk taffeta for parasols, and oiled green taffeta for umbrellas (2007[1297], 27). Inscriptions mention other specific textile items which can be classified as 'luxurious'.

> Inscription K. 618 (1026 CE) at Sek Ta Tuy refers to a garment and a hanging sourced in India; the Ta Prohm inscription. K. 273 (CE 1186) refers to superior quality silk, a mattress and voiles from China; K. 908 (1186–91) CE at Preah Khan mentions Chinese silk mosquito nets; and inscription K. 485 (1200 CE) at Phimeanakas, cloth for a banner and silk fabric, both of Chinese origin.
>
> (Lustig 2009)

Zhou Daguan (2007[1297], 79) noted that the Khmer did not weave silk themselves, this skill actually being the expertise of the 'Siamese' in the kingdom. They acquired the silkworms and mulberry leaves needed to produce the silk for spinning and weaving cloth for themselves as well as for the Khmer. The designation 'Siamese' may refer to one of a number of minority groups such as the *Kui* (a.k.a. *Gui, Suei*) who lived in the further reaches of the Angkorian domain corresponding to the area around the current Thai/Cambodian border. They are represented by a group of male figures wearing calf-length sampot, some patterned, and all with jewelled belts with beaded hanging elements, as seen in the historical procession bas-relief at Angkor Wat (Figure 28.4c). Their sampot form is distinctly different to the sampot chong kbun style worn by the Khmer warriors. The width of the cloth points to its being woven on a frame loom which, more complex than a backstrap loom, is suitable for silk weaving. Patterned bodices similar to those worn by their fellow Khmer soldiers complete the outfit.

Luxury is not restricted to silk. Fine cotton cloth also fits this description. Seen on sculptures dated to the later years of the Angkor Period, cotton cloth is recognised and characterised by its printed patterns produced not by weaving but by surface patterning techniques applied directly onto cotton cloth. The technique utilises block and resist printing, hand painting, and mordant application, either individually or in combination, the motifs enhanced with natural dyes such as indigo blue and madder red. Patterns distinctive of printed cotton cloth are depicted on both Khmer male and female dress, on accessories, and on décor items (Green 2003, 34). A pattern frequently depicted is one of flowers bounded by narrow bands at the weft ends filled with a variety of geometric designs. Other patterns described as 'meandering flowers on trellises' and 'solar symbols' appear in free-form on soldiers' bodices (Green 2003, 34). This printing and dyeing technology has long been a specialty of Gujarat, northwest India. Fragments of Gujarati export cotton cloth with patterns such as these, one C14 dated to the 13th century, have been found in Egypt, evidence that such cloth was at least in circulation (Guy 1998, 186). Patterns on sampot of painted Indian images dated to between the 11th and 15th centuries have counterparts both in the patterns on 12th-century Angkorian sampot and on soldiers' bodices (Chandra 1973, 176–77). These pattern similarities support the likely Indian provenance of the majority of patterned Angkorian textiles.

Textiles for Décor

Patterns sculpted on particular temple structural elements replicate those seen on dress items, asserting both their textile identity and their function as an item of interior decor. There are two particularly interesting types of decor items. One is a window covering and the other a wall hanging. The form of window covering depicted corresponds to what in contemporary terms is termed a pull-down blind (Figure 28.5). Stone window frames with their blinds sculpted in bas-relief are incorporated in the outer walls of widely dispersed 12th-century temples associated with Jayavarman V11. These include Bayon and Preah Khan temples in Angkor; Ta Prohm at Tonle Bati, Takeo Province; Preah Khan of Kompong Svay; Wat Nokor in Kampong Cham Province; and Wat Banon in Battambang, completed slightly later in the 12th to 13th century. The window frames are typically rectangular in shape with the longer side vertical. The blind is indicated by the pattern incised on the outer face of the stone block or blocks that infill the upper section of the frame. Below the blind but still within the frame are stone balusters, imitating their turned wood prototypes, carved in deep relief. Another interesting feature depicted on some of these blinds is a raised V-shape, about pencil size in cross section, sculpted across the patterned surface of the blind. This deliberately sculpted element, most likely representing strings used for raising and lowering the blind, features at Wat Banon, Preah Khan, Preah Khan of Kompong Svay, and the Bayon.

A number of different patterns appear on the blinds. Those at Preah Khan and the Bayon are patterned with 'cash' medallions. This motif description is derived from its resemblance to Chinese 'cash' coinage which is disc shaped with a square hole cut out of the centre. In this pattern the four points of the disc's square hole contact its outer rim, thus introducing an intriguing visual effect. The medallions in the symmetrical array can be read as either contacting each other at the medallion's cardinal points or as a seemingly overlapping series of four-petal flowers, depending on the viewer's interpretation. Textile equivalents displaying this pattern and dating to this period exist. One is a set of silk garments with a Chinese provenance dated to the 10th to 11th centuries (Vainker 1996, 168). The fabric's yellow silk ground is patterned with woven cash medallions with green and blue floral elements in the interstices. This pattern appears on cotton cloth as well. Two cotton fragments recovered from a site in Egypt (now in the Newberry Collection, Ashmolean Museum, Oxford) feature cash patterns in blue and red, block-printed in the manner typical of Gujarat, northwest India. The aesthetic appeal of this cash pattern, be it woven as in Chinese sourced silk or printed as in Indian origin cotton, is thus attested to over a wide region within the Angkor Period.

Different patterns appear at the other locations. The blind at Wat Banon has a four-petal flower pattern in its central field bordered by three bands, one infilled with small raised dots, one with coiled spirals, and one with bands of diamond shapes. This design combination features on sampot of 12th- to 13th-century female deities as well as of a number of devatas at Angkor Wat (see

Figure 28.5 Variations in window blind decorations: a) cash medallion pattern. V-shaped detail, Bayon, late 12th to early 13th century; b) four-petal flower in grid matrix, Ta Prohm at Tonle Bati, Takeo, late 12th century; c) floral medallion pattern. V-shaped detail. Preah Khan of Kompong Svay, late 12th century (Photo M. Hendrickson); d) four-petal flower pattern and geometric patterned borders. V-shaped detail. Wat Banon, late 12th to early 13th century.

Source: (Remaining photos G. Green).

Figure 28.3). Combinations of these same particular elements are seen on the designs of patterned sampot on mid-12th-century Indian painted images (Chandra 1973, I, figs.1, 2, 9, 16, 21). At Ta Prohm of Tonle Bati, Takeo province, there are two window spaces covered with textile patterns. One is a blind with four petal flowers symmetrically positioned within a square lattice framework. An identical pattern is seen on a sampot on a 12th- to 13th-century dvarapala figure at Preah Khan (Jessup 1997, 289) and on a sampot on a painted Indian figure (Chandra 1973, i. fig. 26). The second window has a simple curtain with the same four-petal flower pattern depicted loosely knotted and hanging free to just above the sill. These patterns exemplify Indian-sourced printed cloth. The remaining examples of medallion patterned blinds, those at Preah Khan of Kampong Svay and at Wat Nokor, feature medallions with identical floral motifs. This style of medallion pattern is more typical of Chinese-sourced fabrics with their identical repeat medallions woven, not printed.

The second interior decor item is represented by panels consisting of medallions enclosing figurative motifs, arranged so as to contact each other. These have been designated by the term 'tapestry reliefs', with the clear implication that they represent textiles (Roveda 2005, 306). This scholar further divides these tapestry relief panels into two groups, each defined by its distinct motifs: the first group by its 'heraldic' medallions and the second its 'narrative' medallions. Particular attributes differentiate heraldic from narrative medallions. These include their size, the heraldic form generally being 30 to 35 cm in diameter, over twice as large as the 12-cm-diameter narrative form; the style, that is, whether the medallion's circumference is continuous as in the heraldic or discontinuous as in the narrative forms; and the identity of the motif itself contained within the medallion.

Heraldic medallions are sculpted on vertical structural surfaces: door and window jambs, pilasters, and occasionally window sills at Angkor Wat and the Bayon. Their motifs include paired birds, either two confronted phoenix or parrots, depicted with their wings and tails curved to fit the medallion (Figure 28.6). Examples of silk textiles of a similar period with medallion patterns originating from China exist for comparison. One example of paired parrots woven on a late 9th-century silk fragment (Feng 1999, 148). Another is a mid-Yuan Dynasty (1279–1368) embroidered silk canopy textile featuring a paired phoenix (Watt 1997, 197). Other heraldic medallion patterns appear at Angkor Wat, Banteay Kdei, Banteay Samre, Preah Khan, Ta Prohm, and the Bayon. They feature repeated motifs of a dancing figure or a single bird, flower, or animal (Roveda 2005, 319). As with the parrot and phoenix examples, actual textile examples with these other medallion patterns have been archaeologically recovered, presenting a source of woven examples with which to compare these sculpted versions (Green 2007).

Narrative tapestry medallion patterned bas-relief panels mainly appear at Angkor Wat. These were first described by Cœdès (1913) who published a paper featuring ink rubbings of these particular wall panels, noting that there were no associated inscriptions. A representative selection of Cœdès' original ink rubbings has been published (Roveda 2003, 228–37). The completed panel comprises a lattice of medallions with each individual medallion created by a leaf curving round in arabesque form. These medallions linked together project alternately to the left and the right side, forming a connected column. Each medallion encloses a single iconic figurative motif. Cœdès identified these distinctive motifs with elements and themes of Hindu narratives such as the *Rāmāyana* and concluded that the purpose of the panel was to 'show us the main legendary scenes treated with a minimum of detail and characters, but permit[ting] us to identify the essential elements, their essential characteristics' (1913, 3). Roveda further classified the narrative medallion figures into Vaiṣṇavite and Śaivite, characters in the Rāmāyana and *Mahābhārata* as well as rishis, commoners, 'flowermen', hunters, and mundane animals (2005, 306–08). If these medallion bas-reliefs do indeed represent textile wall panels patterned with shorthand forms of mythical narratives, these could be functionally termed 'story cloths'.

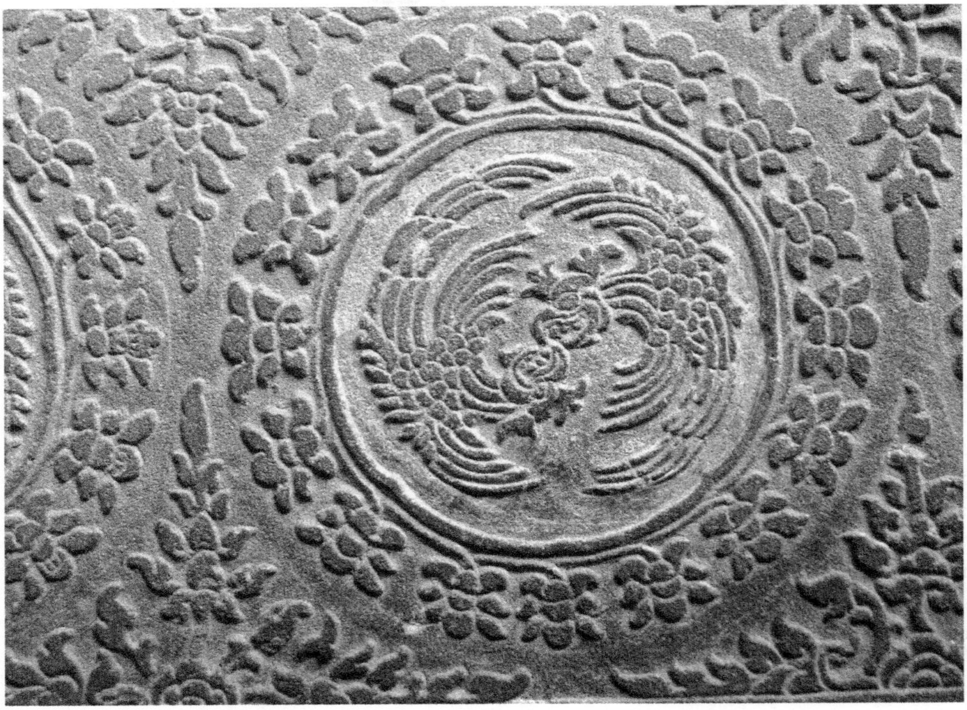

Figure 28.6 Tapestry medallion with paired phoenix, Angkor Wat, 12th century.
Source: (Photo G. Green).

For textile scholars, two particular motifs from this narrative tapestry category allude to an additional level of significance. One is the so-called 'flowerman' (Figure 28.7a). Roveda describes the image from the wall of Angkor Wat as 'combin[ing] the torso and arms of a man . . . shown on the corolla of a flower as if . . . blossoming or growing like a fruit' (2005, 308). A number are illustrated (Roveda 2005, figs. 8.48–61). The other, described as a 'mythological warrior', appears both in the form of a crowned human figure in a combative stance (see Figure 28.7b) as well as a garuda figure in the same stance (Figure 28.7c) (Roveda 2005, 319 figs. 8.121–6). The significance of these motifs in textile terms lies in their re-appearance on 17th- to 18th-century textiles found in Siam. From at least the 17th century the Siamese royal court imported cotton textiles from India with printed patterns specifically ordered and reserved for its exclusive use. Amongst the cotton textiles in the collection of the National Museum in Bangkok are a number of textiles with medallion patterns featuring crowned figures called *thepanom* (Natthapatra 2002). These fit the description of the flowermen of the Angkor panels. A monkey in the guise of a warrior figure avatar is depicted on the border of an 18th-century Siamese sampot sourced from India (Guy 1998, 60). Its stance closely resembles that of the bas-relief mythological human and garuda warriors. These observations are highly significant in textile terms because they connect the subjects of Khmer sculpted images—flowermen, human, and garuda warrior figures—with textile motifs seen printed on prestige cotton cloth made in India destined for Siam. These particular icons illustrate that Hindu mythical characters were equally significant in both Khmer and Siamese art.

Figure 28.7 Specific motifs found in narrative tapestries: a) modern example of flowerman, modelled detail on Thai temple (Photo J. Puranananda). b) crowned human figure in a combative stance; c) medallion enclosing garuda in warrior stance, Angkor Wat, 12th century.

Source: (Photos G. Green).

Sources of Imported Textiles at Angkor

Maritime traders, both southeast Asian and Indian, plied the Indian Ocean and Southeast Asian seas long before, and continuing long after, the Angkor Period. Early first-millennium Óc Eo (Funan) south of Angkor Borei 'was a fully fledged trading city-state, regularly sending and receiving embassies to and from India and China' (Manguin 2004, 291–96 as cited in Polkinghorne 2007, 102).

In textile terms this maritime activity resulted in Indian cloth being traded to Southeast Asia. Inscriptions on Javanese *sima* (tax transfer charters inscribed on stone and metal) indicate the presence of Indian cloth there as early as the 9th and 10th centuries (Wisseman Christie 1993, 11). The Sanskrit word *yau*, with the meaning of a measurement of a textile length, appears both in the sima and in Old Khmer inscriptions (Pou 1992, 387). Wisseman Christie concludes

> This may reflect the impact of Indian fashion or Indian trade cloth . . . upon local male dress styles. Adult men depicted on reliefs on Central Javanese temples dating to the late 8th or 9th century . . . [wear] either a knee-length wrapped lower garment or one of thigh length, the end of which is drawn up between the legs.
>
> (1993, 11)

This Sanskrit word, appearing in both Javanese and Khmer inscriptions, when taken together with the particular method of wearing the hipwrapper attested to in both regions, is strong evidence of their common Indian origin.

Regions to the north and northwest of Angkor were prolific sources of luxury silk cloth. As early as the late Han Dynasty (25–225), southwest China's Sichuan province, in particular its capital Chengdu, was renowned for 'luxury brocades and other fabrics [which were] as famous as its lacquers' (Rudolf 1987, 43). Fragments of silk textiles with woven medallion patterns dating to the Song and Yuan Periods, recovered from archaeological excavations in China and central Asia, demonstrate those weavers' expertise in producing these luxury textiles (Feng 1999; Watt 1997). These capabilities strongly suggest that heraldic medallion patterned cloth used for décor at Angkor originated from its north. Lee Chor Lin describes one mode by which these luxury textiles from China found their way to Southeast Asia during the period from the Song to the end of the Ming Dynasty.

According to Lee Chor Lin,

> The ritual traditions of the Chinese and South East Asians involved extensive use of textiles. In both societies, the exchange of textiles was integral to the process of reinforcing ties between different groups of people, particularly in the relationship between superior and the subordinate. . . . If the Chinese thought that the South East Asians were vassals paying appropriate respect to the Imperial order of China, then the act of giving textiles to the South East Asians may also have followed the same philosophy of gift and reward [as to Chinese officials].
>
> (1995, 171–86)

While Angkor's neighbouring kingdoms in Vietnam, Champa, and Srivijaya sent numerous tributary missions to China, it is recorded that the Khmer only sent two missions, in 1116 and 1120, probably in the reign of Sūryavarman II (Miksic 2006). Even though this contact was comparatively slight, as Chinese textiles were, however, circulating in the region, they could well have found their way indirectly to the Khmer court through trade with its neighbours. In addition, the document *Zhu Fan Zhi*, compiled by a Chinese trade agent Zhua Ru Kua around 1225, noted that Chinese textiles were bartered for 'Kambuja's' forest products such as yellow dye, incense resins, ginger peel, and animal products (1911, 53).

This broad-reaching overview confirms the extensive use of luxury textiles for both personal and for interior decor needs by the Khmer royal court during the Angkor Period. It also makes plain that Angkorian kings had, from the 9th century onwards, access to the 'next level' of silk and cotton textile sophistication in terms of fineness and patterning. What motivation other than sheer ostentatious display of luxury could there have been for the acquisition and display of these textiles at Angkor? Political ambitions have been mooted. Polkinghorne posits that 'local authorities of early Southeast Asia imported luxury goods, and commissioned inscriptions and sculptures possessed with the authoritative power of the "long-distant" to bolster their state control and sacred powers' (2007, 88). Therefore 'By the early first millennium CE, trade networks now included regional and international maritime routes, and command of foreign prestige goods became essential to the political economies of Southeast Asian polities' (Polkinghorne 2007, 96). Patterned textiles, whether block printed cotton from India or woven silk brocade from China, would qualify for this category of foreign prestige goods, thus bolstering the notion of royal political motivation driving acquisition of foreign textiles.

Textiles as 'Story Cloths'—The Locus of Narrative Drama

The narrative tapestry bas-relief patterns seen at Angkor argued to represent textile wall panels patterned with shorthand forms of mythical narratives suggests their functional designation as 'story cloths'. Several thousand km to Angkor's northwest is another location of narrative panels which, although painted, closely correspond to those at Angkor. They are situated in the mid-10th to 11th-century Sum Tsek temple at Alchi in the Ladakh region of the Himalayas. Perhaps the most visually striking artistic constructions in this temple are the images of three Bodhisattvas—Maitreya, Manjusri, and Avalokiteshvara—modelled in clay over a wooden frame and 4 to 4.5 metres high (Goepper 1996). Maitreya's and Manjusri's brightly painted ankle-length sampot features medallions containing images similar to the panels at Angkor. Maitreya's sampot features medallions, each one enclosing a motif depicting an episode in the life of the historical Buddha, Shakyamuni (Figure 28.8). There are 48 episodes in total. The first sequence of 41 commences with the sojourn in the Tavatimsa heaven and ends with the First Sermon at Deer

Figure 28.8 Clay model of Maitreya from Sum Tsek temple, Alchi, Ladakh, mid-10th to 11th century.
Source: (Photo J. Poncar).

Park. This is followed by five scenes of the Buddha preaching, then two depicting the Buddha's parinirvana. Manjusri's sampot is slightly different in that it has a framework of interlocked stepped diamond-shaped spaces, each accommodating one of the 84 mahasiddhas. Unlike the other two clay statues, the images painted on the Avalokiteshvara sampot are dispersed in free form over its surface (Green 2014, 85–94).

The sampot with painted medallions arguably have the same intent as the narrative tapestry panels at Angkor Wat but with one major thematic difference: the iconic images at Angkor Wat are derived from Hindu themes, while those at the Sum Tsek are derived from Buddhist narratives. Goepper, a renowned researcher of the Sum Tsek temple, notes that

> Whereas narrative scenes from [other nearby temples] are usually arranged in horizontal friezes as if from scenes in a comic book, the version on the dhoti [sampot] of the Maitreya sculpture . . . presents the scenes as transpositions into decorative context, isolating them into separate units, the sequence of which is not obvious at first sight. This striking phenomenon may perhaps be seen in context with the general interest in textiles to be observed throughout the Sum Tsek murals.
>
> (1996, 26)

Could the depiction of these themes on the Bodhisattvas' sampot portray patterned textiles available at that time, the 11th century? If so, are they in the same category of textile panel as the narrative medallion tapestries serving as wall hangings identified at Angkor? Can one conclude that narrative medallion patterned surfaces, sculpted at Angkor and painted at Sum Tsek, portray textiles with a specific purpose, beyond simply decor or dress, that of a story cloth? Their Hindu and Buddhist themes imply that India would be the source of their narratives. Further indication of their Indian origin can be inferred by the technique by which these textiles would have been patterned. Their designs could only have been realised by the block printing and painting technique in the manner perfected by Indian craftsmen.

Conclusion

Textiles are visualised as dress, accessories, and interior decor in Khmer sculpted art. Close attention to the dress form detail allows appreciation of progress from simple forms to the more complex through the Angkor Period. These details are meticulously depicted in the draping, pleating, knotting, and patterning of dress styles, implying that the sculptors portrayed what they observed in real life. Dress forms and their patterns have been shown to closely relate to Indian forms of the period. Items of interior decor such as window blinds sculpted on 12th-century temples display many of the same patterns, implying that not only were textiles used in this context but that they also originated from the same source. The majority of patterns could only have been achieved by block printing, a speciality of Gujarat, northwest India. A number of other wall hangings, however, used solely as interior decor items have patterns composed of repeats of identical 'heraldic' medallions. This characteristic is consistent with the product of a frame loom. This weaving technology, a speciality of China and central Asia weavers at the time, reveals another source of luxury patterned textiles.

Medallion patterns painted on hipwrapper (sampot) textiles on Buddhist images several thousand km to Angkor's northwest in the Himalayas are intriguing in this context. Their similarity in format to the 'narrative' medallion patterned wall hangings at Angkor at the very least indicates the widespread use of block-printed patterned textiles produced in India at this time. Despite the difficulties of research into ancient textiles, this wide-ranging exploration has demonstrated that it is possible to make a contribution to the research into material culture and thus animate the participants within their society and their culture.

References

Boisselier, J., 1966. *Asie du Sud-Est, Tome 1, Le Cambodge.* Paris: A&J Picard.

Cameron, J., 2002. *Textile technology in the prehistory of Southeast Asia.* PhD dissertation. Canberra: Australian National University.

Castillo, C.C., 2023. Food, craft and ritual: plants from the Angkorian World, in *The Angkorian World*, eds. M. Hendrickson, M.T. Stark & D. Evans. New York: Routledge, 401–20.

Castillo, C., A. Carter, E. Kingwell-Banham, Y. Zhuang, A. Weisskopf, R. Chhay, P. Heng, D.Q. Fuller & M. Stark, 2020. The Khmer did not live by rice alone: archaeobotanical investigations at Angkor Wat and Ta Prohm. *Archaeological Research in Asia* 24, 100213.

Castillo, C., M. Polkinghorne, B. Vincent, S. Tan Boun & D. Fuller, 2018. Life goes on: archaeobotanical investigations of diet and ritual at Angkor Thom, Cambodia (14th–15th centuries CE). *The Holocene* 28(6), 930–44.

Chandra, M., 1973. *Costumes, Textiles, Cosmetics and Coiffure in Ancient and Mediaeval India.* Delhi: Oriental Publishers.

Cœdès, G., 1913. Etudes Cambodgiennes, V11, Second Etude sur les Bas-reliefs d'Angkor Vat. *Bulletin de l'École française d'Extrême-Orient* V111–6, 13–36.

Feng Zhao, 1999. *Treasures in Silk.* Hong Kong: ISAT Costume Squad Ltd.

Goepper, R., 1996. *Alchi. Ladak's Hidden Buddhist Sanctuary.* Boston: Shambhala [New York].

Green, G., 2000. Indic impetus? Innovations in textile usage in Angkorian period Cambodia. *Journal of the Economic and Social History of the Orient* 43(3), 277–96.

Green, G., 2003. *Traditional Textiles of Cambodia.* Bangkok: River Books.

Green, G., 2007. Angkor vogue: sculpted evidence of imported luxury textiles in the courts of kings and temples. *Journal of the Economic and Social History of the Orient* 50(4), 424–51.

Green, G., 2014. Medallion patterns at Angkor Wat and Sumstek (Ladakh). *Arts of Asia* 44(3), 85–94.

Groslier, G., 1921. *Recherches sur les Cambodgiens.* Paris: Augustin Challamel, 39–56.

Guy, J., 1998. *Woven Cargoes.* London: Thames & Hudson.

Jessup, H., 1997. *Sculpture of Angkor and Ancient Cambodia.* Washington DC: National Gallery of Art.

Lee Chor Lin., 1995. Textiles in Sino-South East Asian trade: Song, Yuan and Ming Dynasties, in *South East Asia & China, Interaction and Commerce*, eds. R. Scott & J. Guy. London: Percival David Foundation of Chinese Art, 171–86.

Lustig, E., 2009. Money doesn't make the World go round: Angkor's non-monetisation, In *Research in Economic Anthropology,* ed. D. Wood. Bingley, UK: Emerald Group Publishing Ltd., 165–99.

Manguin, P., 2004. The archaeology of early maritime polities of Southeast Asia, in *Southeast Asia. From Prehistory to History,* eds. I. Glover & P. Bellwood. London: Routledge Curzon, 282–313.

Marchal, S., 2005. *Khmer Costumes and Ornaments.* Bangkok: Orchid Press.

Miksic, J., 2006. Angkor's contacts with China. Paper delivered at the conference Angkor- Landscape, City and Temple, University of Sydney, Australia.

Natthapatra, C., 2002. *Phaa Phim laay booraan nay phiphithaphan thasathaan heng chaat, Krungtheep, Krom Silpaakon PS 2545 [Ancient Chintz Fabrics in the National Museums].* Bangkok: National Museum.

Phuong, T.K., V.V. Tang & P. Sharrock, 2018. *Vibrancy in Stone.* Bangkok: River Books.

Polkinghorne, M., 2007. *Makers and models: Decorative lintels of Khmer temples, 7th to 11th centuries*. PhD dissertation. Sydney: The University of Sydney.

Pou, S.1992. *An Old Khmer-French-English Dictionary.* Paris: Centre de Documentation et de Recherche sur la Civilisation Khmere.

Roveda, V., 2003. *Sacred Angkor.* Bangkok: River Books.

Roveda, V., 2005. *Images of the Gods.* Bangkok: River Books.

Rudolf, R., 1987. *Stories from China's Past,* ed. L. Lim. San Francisco: The Chinese Culture Foundation of San Francisco, 41–45.

Vainker, S., 1996. Silk of the Northern Song: reconstructing the evidence, in *Silk and Stone: The Art of Asia,* ed. J. Tilden. London: Hali Publications, 160–75.

Watt, J. & A. Wardwell, 1997. *When Silk Was Gold*. New York: The Metropolitan Museum of Art.

Wisseman Christie, J., 1993. Ikat to Batik? Epigraphic data on textiles in Java from the ninth to the fifteenth centuries, in *Weaving Patterns of Life*, Nabholz-Kartaschoff, eds. M.-L. Barnes, R. & J. Stuart-Fox. Basel: Museum of Ethnography, 11–29.

Zhou, D., 2007[1297]. *A Record of Cambodia: The Land and Its People*, trans. P. Harris. Chiang Mai: Silkworm Books.

29

GENDER, STATUS, AND HIERARCHY IN THE AGE OF ANGKOR

Trude Jacobsen Gidaszewski

Surprisingly little has been written on the nuances of social hierarchy in the Angkorian Empire. Scholars have traced the chronologies of the kings whose names appear in the inscriptions (Briggs 1951; Majumdar 1944); their faces are known to us from the statues commemorating their apotheosis. But what of the rest of the population? It hardly seems possible that all women of the Angkor Period resembled the apsara or devata that grace the temple walls. Did ordinary women have agency? Were they completely dependent upon the good will of their fathers and husbands? Despite references in the inscriptions to a mysterious *kanlong kamraten an*—a cult of female deities that existed for some 400 years on the banks of the Tonle Sap—the prevailing opinion has been that elite women were pawns in a game of thrones.

Yet it was through marriage with Angkorian princesses that most kings were able to secure support for their reigns. We know that 'women of the palace', who moved freely between palace and town, were accorded special fabrics and entitled to certain perquisites denied to their male counterparts. Others made donations to religious establishments, indicating that personal property remained theirs regardless of marital status. Remarriage following the death of a husband or divorce was not only possible, it was encouraged, contrary to prevailing custom in South and East Asian societies at the time. Similarly, although the institution of slavery at Angkor has been studied at length, a clear understanding of the fluidity of bondage structures has been absent in the scholarship until recently. Slaves did not always remain slaves—and those who thought themselves beyond the reach of the ties of obligation sometimes found themselves and their families firmly enmeshed. It is this fluidity of status that distinguishes Angkorian society. Using sources drawn from epigraphy, Chinese records, and material culture, this chapter will elucidate the concept of the individual at Angkor—their legal, social, and religious status—and how this understanding was mutable, never fixed. In doing so, it challenges existing notions of gender and status in the Angkorian World (see Figure 29.1).

Once silent and still, Angkor has been given life through advances in animation technologies that permit us to colour, populate, and hear interpretations of what might have been (Chandler and Polkinghorne 2012). While we may be able to conceptualise an Angkor full of life and movement, however, we have understood little of how its society functioned. The institutions of kingship and slavery have been studied almost detached from any other considerations, leaving the roles of gender and status as abstract concepts (Kulke 1978; Mabbett 1969, 1977, 1983;

DOI: 10.4324/9781351128940-35

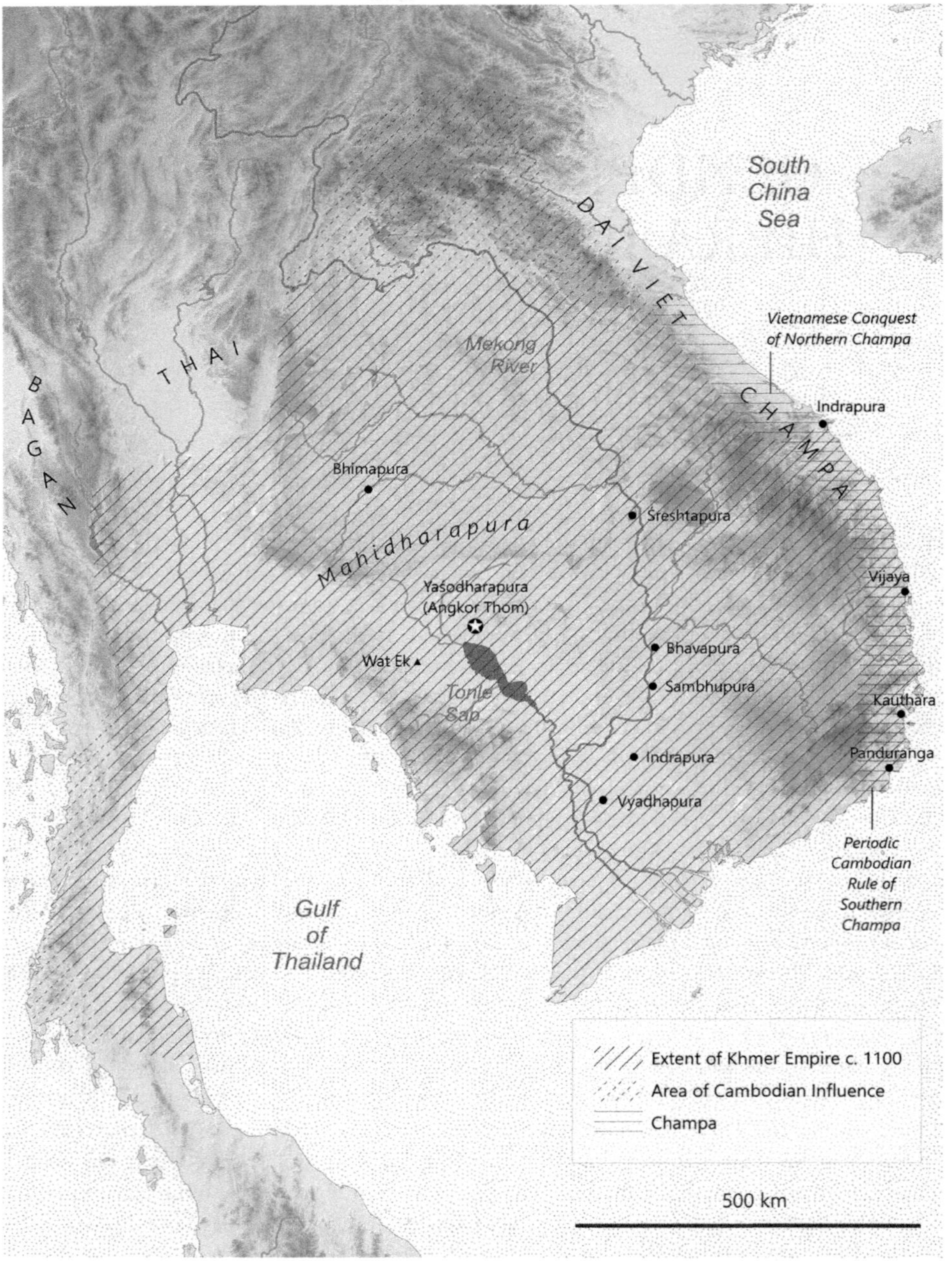

Figure 29.1 Key sites discussed in the text.

Wolters 1973). Anthropologists have spilled considerable ink questioning whether kinship at Angkor was cognatic or matrilineal while not addressing what this may mean for notions of power and political culture (Ebihara 1984; O'Sullivan 1962; Kirsch 1976; Ledgerwood 1995). This chapter seeks to redress this omission by interrogating epigraphic and literary texts from new angles. The evidence indicates that social status was mutable, not fixed, in the Angkorian

World; there were avenues for climbing high as well as for swift descent due to sudden reversals of fortune. Gender had little impact on political power, albeit men and women exercised agency in different ways. Slavery was endemic, but could be either permanent or temporary.[1] Regardless of status, privilege, or gender, no-one was free of obligation to others (Jacobsen and Stuart-Fox 2013; Stark 2019). A provincial official might be ordered to repair a road in the name of the king. A wealthy widow might be asked to provide new robes for priests at a certain temple by her uncle, a court advisor. Farmers might be commanded by the local intermediary between their village and the provincial court to clear a forest so as to make room for a new shrine. Slaves, even those bonded temporarily, could be ordered to do anything by their masters and mistresses at any time—including relocating hundreds of miles away, as we shall see.

Beyond **Apsara** *and* **Devata**

Pre-Angkorian society (ca. 3rd–9th c.) has undergone substantial reimagining in the last century. A handful of scholars (Jacques 1986; Vickery 1994, 1998; Jacobsen 2003, 2008) have reinterpreted the inscriptions without the gender biases of earlier historians, who could not conceive of women holding politically significant roles (Briggs 1951). Even George Cœdès, when confronted with incontrovertible evidence in the K. 904 inscription that a queen had occupied the throne in the eighth century, had to qualify his findings by pointing out in his analysis of the epigraphy that this corresponded with 'a period of troubles that were not ended until the accession of Jayavarman II' (*IC* 4, 55)—implying that only in such a time of strife would Cambodians accept such an arrangement. Contrary to common belief, however, Cambodia had not one but several queens before the Angkor Period who appear to have ruled before marriage and after their husbands' deaths.

The creation mythology of this early era, as recorded by the Chinese in the mid-3rd century, states unequivocally that the original ruler of '*Funan*', the name by which southernmost Cambodia and part of the lower Mekong Delta was known, was an unmarried queen named Liu Ye or Ye Ye (Pelliot 1925). The Vo-Canh stela in neighbouring Champa has a similar explanation explaining the establishment of Bhavapura (Jacobsen 2003). The sculptural and epigraphic record of Pre-Angkorian Cambodia attests to a strong association between female agency and supernatural powers; one of the most popular female goddesses was Durga Mahiasuramardani, Devi in her aspect as the slayer of the Demon Buffalo. Other goddesses were depicted independently of their male consorts; in fact, Brahma, the god corresponding to Sarasvati, goddess of wisdom, almost never appears (Jacobsen 2020).

One of the curious features of Cambodian historiography is an apparent lack of interest on the part of historians as to why gender roles shifted abruptly to reflect a new inferior role for women in the Angkor Period. Creation mythology, having once entertained an unmarried warrior queen as the original ruler of the land before the 9th century, devolved to one in which the princess, named Mera in the epigraphy, was dependent upon her father and husband, described as 'most renowned of beautiful deities', but without agency (Jacobsen 2003). Concurrently, graceful *apsara* and stoic *devata* replaced the fierce statues of Durga Mahishasuramardani, standing triumphant atop the vanquished demon buffalo. Goddesses began to be shown only with their male counterparts and in submissive postures (Jacobsen 2008; see discussion in Hendrickson et al. 2023, this volume).

The history of Angkor has been the history of its kings. Primogeniture was believed to have been the prevailing means of transferring power. Kings who did not fit this model were dubbed 'usurpers'; princesses and queens were simply married off to consolidate alliances and bring forth heirs to the throne and more potential marriage partners for more alliances (Briggs 1951;

Cœdès 1968; Hall 1981). New approaches to the historical record, however, show that women and men were integral for the transmission and conservation of power, maintenance of religious institutions, and the wealth of the kingdom. Elsewhere I have written that the early Angkorian custom of representing pairs of ancestors, one male and one female, reflected a devolution in status for royal women, as it began at precisely the moment that autonomous queens disappear from the epigraphic record after the 9th century (Jacobsen 2008, 42). This practice confirms the continued importance of women in the transmission of power from generation to generation and as a source of legitimation for aspiring kings. It also explains the existence of a practice in which collective ancestor worship of specifically *female* royal women were honoured for some 400 years. They may not have ruled alone during the Angkor Period, but their significance was confirmed in another fashion.

Indravarman I (r. 877–889) dedicated the six *prasat* of Preah Ko to three pairs of ancestors: his mother and father, Prthivindradevi and Prthivindravarman; his mother's parents, Rajendradevi and Rudravarman; and his maternal aunt and her husband, Dharanindradevi and Jayavarman II (Jacobsen 2008, 31). Significantly, he did not stress his relationship to Jayavarman II, whom historians have designated the 'creator' of the Khmer Empire (Briggs 1951, 148). Instead, he emphasised that his mother was 'born into a family where sovereigns succeeded each other' (Cœdès 1937, 18–29). Indravarman I also wed two queens that he took the trouble to acknowledge as equals at the Bakong monument, in which he was depicted as Śiva with his consorts Uma and Ganga in the *Uma-ganga-patesvara* sculpture. These two queens, reigning under the names Indradevī and Indralaksmi—'queen of Indra' and 'fortune of Indra', respectively—hailed from two separate semi-autonomous polities to the south of the Tonle Sap (Jacobsen 2008). Indravarman I also honoured Indrani, 'queen of Indraloka', at the Bakong monument. Indrani and Indraloka ruled at Sambhupura in the middle of the 8th century (Jacobsen 2003, 373). The implication is that it was more important for Indravarman I to demonstrate his legitimacy through his female relatives and his queens rather than any relationship to Jayavarman II or Jayavarman III. This effectively upends the argument that Angkorian kingship was based upon primogeniture.

This practice was borne out by the reign of Indravarman I's descendants. Yaśovarman I (r. 889–912), also established pairings of ancestors. The Lolei monument, dedicated in 893, depicts Yaśovarman I's mother and father, Indradevi and Indravarman I, and his mother's parents, Rajendradevi and Mahipatesvara. One of Yaśovarman I's clients, a court official named Jayayudha, erected an image of Yaśovarman I's sister, Jayamahesvari, to commemorate a victory over 'Champa and others' as well as making further donations to Indradevi (*IC* 4, 153–4). Rajendravarman II (r. 944–968), son of Jayamahesvari and her husband Mahendravarman, claimed his right to the throne through his mother, not his uncle Yaśovarman I (Jacobsen 2008, 50). This is not to suggest that women were more important than men but to illustrate that they were as integral in processes of legitimation and therefore in political life. These relationships are shown in Figure 29.2.

We can see further evidence that women were integral to Angkorian rule in the case of Vijayendralakshmi, who was married to three brothers in succession in the late 11th and 12th centuries. The first of these was a *yuvaraja*, or heir to the throne, of the *Mahidharapura* kingdom to the northwest of Angkor. The K. 191 inscription indicates that he was the youngest of three sons born to the rulers of Mahidharapura.[2] Vijayendralakshmi's brother was given the title Nrpendradhipativarman for his services as head of the army at a time when the *yuvaraja*, whose name we never learn, was a 'favourite of Jayavarmadeva', another name for Jayavarman VI (r. ca. 1080–1107). Vijayendralakshmi was promised the territory of Amalakasthala, where she was born, by the yuvaraja, which was later affirmed by Jayavarman VI (*IC* 6, 300–11). We can

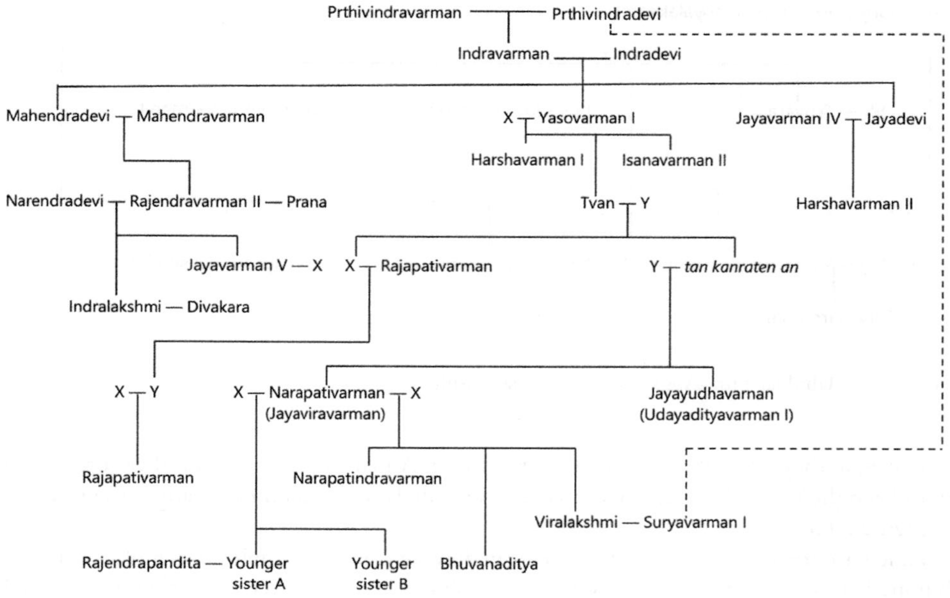

Figure 29.2 Relationships between Pre-Angkorian and Angkorian elite, 7th–11th centuries.

deduce that Vijayendralakshmi was married to the yuvaraja to consolidate an alliance between her family and that of the Mahidharapura clan and that she was bequeathed control of her native land as part of the marriage settlement. Yet when the yuvaraja was on his deathbed, he wished Vijaendralakshmi to marry his brother, the king. Why would this be necessary, unless to fulfil terms of a political alliance that the Mahidharapurans could not afford to lose?

The 11th century was a time of considerable upheaval. Udayādityavarman I (1001?–1002 CE) reigned for barely a year before disappearing in 1002, and his successor Jayaviravarman fought an eight-year battle with Sūryavarman I before the latter prevailed. Significantly, Sūryavarman I (r. 1002–1049) consolidated his reign through marriage to Viralakshmi of Vanapura, offering her jewels, fine clothing, and a gold palanquin (*IC* 7, 164–89). She was the sister of Udayadityavarman II (r. 1050–1066) and Harshavarman III (r. 1066–1080) and therefore a member of an established royal clan (Jacobsen 2008, 55–6). Sūryavarman I was not from Angkor; he hailed from the west and insisted on his officials taking an oath of loyalty upon his accession (Cœdès 1913; Vickery 1985). He needed a marriage alliance with a woman of royal blood who had long-standing ties to the land he wished to rule. After his death, her brothers ruled in turn.

The next king, Jayavarman VI (1080–1107), did not claim descent from previous kings. We know from the inscriptions that Mahidharapura had existed on the periphery between the Khmer and the Mon since at least 921, when Mahidharapura had taken slaves from Phimai and offered them to Angkor as tribute (Cœdès 1929, 169). Both the yuvaraja of Mahidharapura and Narendradhipativarman were engaged in military service for Jayavarman VI. We can surmise that Harshavarman III's reign was not without conflict, since no monuments were commissioned during this time and few donations recorded. One interpretation is that Jayavarman VI enlisted the support of local elites, including Vijayendralakshmi and Narendradhipativarman's family, in routing Harshavarman III. Both men must have been contenders for the throne

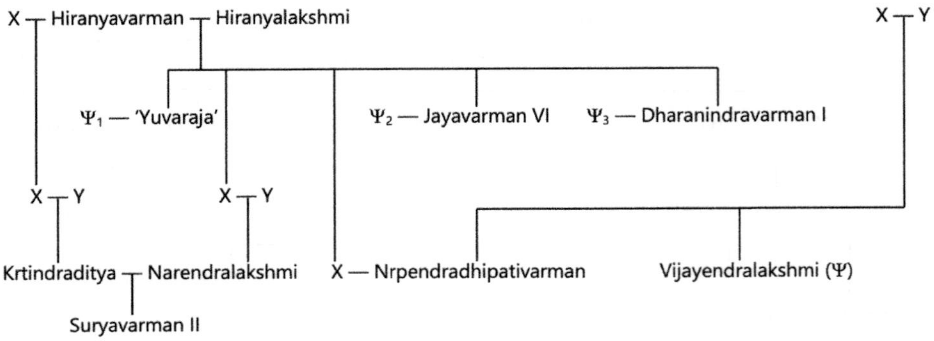

Figure 29.3 Mahidharapura-Angkor marriage relationships.

themselves, as they were likely related to Viralakshmi. A marriage alliance was therefore necessary to keep the peace. Jayavarman VI married Vijendralakshmi upon the death of the yuvaraja (see Figure 29.3).

While remarriage was never prohibited for widows in Cambodia, unlike other places in Asia, it is nonetheless startling to find that Vijayendralakshmi was married yet again to a third husband after Jayavaraman VI died. The inscriptions tell us that as a consequence of 'familial affection, when King Jayavarman [VI] followed his ancestors and the yuvaraja to the heavens, he gave her to Dharanindra[varman I]', the eldest of the Mahidharapura brothers. Her importance in cementing the legitimacy of the Mahidharapura dynasty as rulers at Angkor is simply conveyed in the inscription commemorating her own death: 'Considered the fruit of *Lakshmi* [fortune] and *Vijaya* [Victory], she bore the name Vijayendralakshmi' (*IC* 6, 61–8).

We can find several other examples of royal women, daughters and sisters of kings, providing the genealogical legitimacy for their husbands' reigns. Rajendravarman II (r. 944–968) emphasised his descent from Mahendradevi (the elder sister of Yaśovarman I) and her husband Mahendradevi, not that he was the king's nephew. Sūryavarman I, in addition to marrying Viralakshmi, claimed his right to rule through his mother, a descendant of Prthivindradevi (mother of Indravarman I). Jayavarman VII (r. 1181–ca. 1220) described his mother Chudamani as 'a daughter of King Harshavarman' (*IC* 2, 161–81); he married two sisters, Jayarajadevi and Indradevi, members of a *kshatriya* clan that were 'amongst the elite of the royal family'. The sisters claimed that their father was descended from 'Rudravarman', possibly a reference to the Pre-Angkorian king, and their mother from Rajendradevi, the maternal grandmother of Yaśovarman I (Jacobsen 2008, 58). We also have the observations of Zhou Dagaun in 1297. He recounted that the king ruling at Angkor came to the throne through his wife, a princess, who stole the regalia from her father the king and gave it to her husband. Her brother attempted to take back the throne by rallying his clients, but the king 'cut off his brother-in-law's toes and threw him into a dark dungeon' (Zhou 2007[1297], 72). This had the effect of preventing him from any further pretensions to power, as kings had to be physically perfect.

We may extrapolate from the preceding examples that royal women were crucial in legitimating the kings of Angkor—so important, in fact, that they formed the basis of a funerary cult peculiar to Cambodia: the *kanlong kamraten an*. This title was bestowed on women through whom kings had established their claim to the throne of Angkor. The first of these women to appear in the epigraphic record was *kanlong kamraten an* Jayamahesvari, elder sister of Yaśovarman I, apotheosised as 'the holy queen of the field of victory' in reference to a battle with the Chams (Inscriptions du Cambodge [hereafter *IC*] 4, 153–4). The *kanlong kamraten an* were always associated with a naturally occurring place, such as a field, a cave, a lake, or a forest around Angkor, underscoring the association in the Angkorian World between women and the land. Significantly, most of the women in Figure 29.2—those who conferred legitimacy upon their husbands to rule—were part of the cult of *kanlong kamraten an* anve tonle, or 'queen of the lake', in modern-day Siem Reap province.

These gifts were a reference to the practice of adorning statues of deities, including deceased royalty, with jewels, clothing, flowers, and perfumes, and pressing gold leaf onto them. It was also necessary to repaint their forms and maintain their space with incense and other offerings. Jayavarman V bestowed a sheet of gold leaf upon the *kanlong kamraten an* anve tonle in 974. In 978, a client of Jayavarman V offered her a gold palanquin; the next year, a statue of the goddess Durga Mahishasuramardani was erected in the image of the dead queen. This is one of only two references to Durga in the Angkor Period. In the first decade of the 11th century, Jayaviravarman admonished those nearby for attempting to use a forest that had been donated to the queen's cult in 952. During the tumultuous reign of Harshavarman III, land belonging to *kanlong kamraten an* anve tonle was seized by others and had to be restored to her in 1071 (*IC* 1, 159–86; *IC* 3, 57; *IC* 4, 140–50; *IC* 6, 218–23). Significantly, the name of the place in which the *kanlong kamraten an* anve tonle, Narendradevi, and Indralakshmi resided was Rajaguha, which can mean either 'royal cave' or 'royal womb'—a fitting pun on words for the mothers of kings.

The K. 380 inscription of 1019 refers to Viralakshmi as being from the 'district of the holy place'. Another states that she and her brother were the elite family of *Vrai Kanlong*, or 'forest of the *kanlong*'. As Viralakshmi was most likely the daughter of Jayaviravarman, Narendradevi and Indralakshmi were distant cousins—their nearest common maternal ancestor was Indradevi, wife of Indravarman I, who died some 200 years before Viralakshmi was born. Rajaguha was located in the *sruk* of Jrai Garyyak; a nephew or great-nephew of Viralakshmi bearing the title Narapatindravarman was known as the '*vap* of the holy Jrai' in 1071 (Jacobsen 2008, 54–5). He recorded that his family had been entrusted with the official records of administration, history, and the lists of goods that had been donated to two gods and 'at the *kanlong*' since the reign of king Śrutavarman, a possible 5th-century king of the Kambuja (Aymonier 1908, 13). The latest reference to the Rajaguha sanctuary was in 1109, when a large group of elite men and women donated goods to 'the god of Lingapura and the *kanlong kamraten an*' (IC 3, 97–9). Most women through whom sovereignty was reckoned were worshipped posthumously as k *anlong kamraten an* for centuries.

It is clear, therefore, that women *did* play an important part in providing would-be kings of Angkor with sufficient legitimation to rule. They continued to be associated with true possession over the land, in a throwback to the same Pre-Angkorian notion that women were the ones who had stewardship of it. Inscriptions explicitly anthropomorphise places as brides, eager for consummation with the kings who seek to conquer them. Thus 'the land, having obtained that king for a husband, was full of virtue, pleasure, and profit, and fertile' (*IC* 2, 183–5) during the reign of Yaśovarman I. The city of Angkor Thom was 'adorned with powder and jewels, burning with desire, daughter of an elite family' at the time that Jayavarman VII acceded to the throne (*IC* 4, 235–53). It also explains the ritual in which Angkorian kings were required to engage in sexual union with a *nagini* each night.

> Out of the palace rises a golden tower, to the top of which the ruler ascends nightly to sleep. It is a common belief that in the tower dwells a spirit, formed like a serpent with nine heads, which is lord of the entire kingdom. Every night this spirit appears

> in the shape of a woman, with whom the sovereign couples. . . . Should the spirit fail to appear for a single night, it is a sign that the king's death is at hand. If, on the other hand, the king should fail to keep his tryst, disaster is sure to follow.
>
> (Zhou 2007[1297], 5)

Once this critical association between women and the land is understood, other aspects of Angkorian social practice become more clearly elucidated. Women were accorded greater access to the space inhabited by the king in his role as arbiter between the mundane and supernatural Worlds because they themselves had greater proximity to it than men. The palace at Angkor teemed with women. As soon as a new king was enthroned, the various queens, lesser queens, and wives of the palace from the previous reign were reorganised. Kings often married their aunts, sisters, or their wives' mothers in order to ensure that nobody else would attempt to demonstrate a claim to the throne through them (*IC* 7, 128–35). Officials rushed to offer their daughters in marriage to the new king in the hopes of securing royal favour. Thus Zhou Daguan observed that in 1296 'when a beautiful girl is born into a family, no time is lost in sending her to the palace' (2007[1297], 13). Even kings from neighbouring polities carried out this practice. In one example, a princess sent from the king of Lanka to the king of Cambodia as a bride was intercepted by the Mons and kidnapped in the 12th century (*Culavamsa*, 67).

Hierarchy, Gender, and Signalling at Angkor

The space to which people were assigned; their ability to move between spaces; and the encoded meanings of their hairstyles, dress, and tasks provided a detailed context for determining hierarchy in Angkorian society. The principal queen would live in the central palace with four queens, one for each cardinal direction. There were lesser queens and other wives, their relatives and retainers, and other women of the palace, numbering in their hundreds. The latter were a group who were permitted to leave the palace and return to their homes and families at the end of the day. Many women of the palace were entitled *hyan*, a Malay word that refers to the possession of supernatural powers (Gokhale 1971, 326). Designated by a hairstyle in which their hair was shaved at the front and bedaubed with three red marks, women of the palace were entitled to sumptuary considerations not given to their male counterparts. The use of skirt cloths was restricted to women of the palace and apsaras in the Angkorian bas-reliefs (see Green 2002; Green 2023, this volume). Only women of the palace could stain their feet and palms with henna. They were allowed to wear a particular floral patterned cloth otherwise restricted to male court officials; no other people in the kingdom were permitted to do so (*IC* 6, 284–6; Zhou 2007[1297], 72–3). The king would then distribute these gifts to his officials and the women of the palace whom he favoured. Those who particularly pleased him would reap considerable benefits. Indravarman I bestowed upon a *ten hyang*, daughter of a client of Jayavarman II, the title and name of *ten kamraten* an Kshitindradevi. Some years later, she asked the king to order her brothers Satyayudha and Ripunathana to erect an image at Vak Ek. Another woman bearing the same title was given 'the command of the servants gathered in the land of Suvarnapura' by Jayavarman III. With these perquisites came the possibility that the king could command service that one did not necessarily relish, however. One of Rajendravarman II's palace servants, Thun, had already been married for some years when she was ordered to marry a second man of a higher rank (Jacobsen 2008). Cloth was given to the king and his consorts as marks of distinction by neighbouring courts, particularly the Chinese emperors. The *Ming Shilu* relates that in 1387, envoys were sent to the countries of Cambodia and Siam (Hu). A silver seal plated in gold, 28 bolts of fine silks and other silks interwoven with gold thread, and 12 bolts of fine silks and other silks decorated with coloured embroidery were to be conferred upon the king of the country of Cambodia. Fourteen bolts of patterned fine silks were to be conferred upon the king's consort (MSL Hong-wu 20, 8, 13).

Within the palace, women could perform any number of tasks, from arranging flowers in the palace to keeping the royal jewels to overseeing public works (Jacobsen 2008). In the early 14th century, a woman named Maliniratanalakkha rebuilt a *vihara* and excavated a ditch and a pond. In 1309 she erected a statue of the Buddha and donated slaves and goods on behalf of the king. Some had a more militaristic role, acting as the king's personal bodyguards, equipped with lances and shields, carrying his palanquin when he travelled, and lifting the curtain that separated the king from his courtiers during the daily audience (Jacobsen 2008). Those who had been good at their assigned role did not necessarily have to lose it upon the accession of a new king; Prana, a queen of Rajendravarman II, carried out administrative duties for Jayavarman V, his successor. We should not be surprised that women were entrusted with administrative and logistical duties; all children born in the palace, regardless of gender, received instruction from a *guru*. As the Angkor Period drew to a close, the inscriptions relate that elite women became more involved in the nascent transition to Buddhism as state religion. Indradevi and Jayarajadevi, queens of Jayavarman VII, established nunneries and taught Buddhist doctrine (*IC* 2, 161–81).

Outside the Palace Walls

What of life outside the palace? Everyday existence seems to have been less gendered than one might have thought. Men and women both wore bracelets of gold on their arms and scented themselves with perfumes made from sandalwood and musk; both shaved their heads to denote mourning. Both could own and donate land to religious establishments, in tandem with their spouse or alone. Women frequently inherited property. One woman, Konti, who served in the palace of Rajendravarman II, inherited her uncle's 'divine power, his land, his fields and his gardens' (Cœdès 1936, 16). This implies that there were no strictures as to brides giving up their own possessions upon marriage or that women were not seen as capable of administering their own goods.

Women also seem to have some agency in their choice of mates and their sexual lives. A widow, Sok, asked the man of her choice to marry her and had her grandfather give him and his family gifts to sweeten the deal (Jacobsen 2008, 66). Sexual freedom was commonplace, and virginity, at least at the end of the 13th century, seems to have been unnecessary before marriage, as long as a ritual in which girls, aged between 7 and 11 years old, were deflowered by Buddhist and brahmanical priests had taken place. After the ceremony, which lasted all night accompanied by music and feasting, the girl no longer had to sleep in her parents' bedroom and could come and go as she pleased (Zhou 2007[1297], 19). Premarital sex was common, and husbands who did not please their wives were likely to be discarded:

> Everyone with whom I talked said that the Cambodian women are highly sexed. . . . When a husband is called away on matters of business, they endure his absence for a while; but if he is gone as much as ten days, the wife is apt to say, 'I am no ghost; how can I be expected to sleep alone?'
>
> (Zhou 2007[1297], 15)

Infidelity did come with a price for the woman's lover, however; his feet were 'squeezed between two splints of wood till the pain grows unendurable and he surrenders all his property' to the wronged husband (Zhou 2007[1297], 19).

It was the women who were involved in commercial activities, prompting Zhou Daguan to relate that 'for this reason a Chinese, arriving in the country, loses no time in getting himself a mate, for he will find her commercial instincts a great asset' (2007[1297], 43). At least some of them were engaged in the production of commodities alongside their menfolk. Chau Ju-kua recorded that Cambodia's 12th–13th century products were,

> [E]lephants' tusks, the chan and su (varieties of gharu-wood), fine and coarse shou, yellow wax, kingfisher's feathers (Note: Of which this country has great store), dammar resin and gourd dammar, foreign oils, ginger peel, gold coloured incense, sapan-wood, raw silk and cotton fabrics. . . . The foreign traders offer in exchange for these gold, silver, porcelain-ware, satinets, kittysols, skin drums, samshu, sugar, preserves, and vinegar.
> (Chau Ju-kua 1911[13th c.], 530)

Khmers also raised and trained elephants, many of which were presented to the Chinese emperor as tribute. It is important to note that clans, such as Viralakshmi's previously, often were imbued with specific functions by the king that they kept in perpetuity (Day 1996, 393), thus in a sense obligating them to the performance of these tasks. Udayadityavarman II gave a piece of land, along with its produce and tenants, to Jayendrapandita, as the original owners of the land 'had no children nor grandchildren and their line was extinguished'. The king also decreed that the maternal line of Jayendrapandita would possess the land and its produce in the future. A similar inscription from another place stated that 'the *varna* of *vrah kamraten an* Rajendrapandita . . . in maternal lines are designated to guard the foundation of Prasat Khtom' (*IC* 5, 153–55). Ian Mabbett has shown that these hereditary tasks, and the places associated with them, constituted a Cambodian version of the Indian social system of *jati*, albeit without the same connotations of *varna* (1977). Both men and women, therefore, were expected to carry out a range of tasks that were the responsibility of their family clan and ensured the smooth running of society at Angkor.

Patrons, Clients, and Slaves

Adherence to one's place, manifested as obedience to parents, performance of rites appropriate to the stages of life, observance of religious festivals, and labour ascribed to one's status, meant that *dharma*—a concept as familiar to brahmanical religions as to Buddhism—was being followed correctly (Jacobsen 2017, 21; Jacobsen and Stuart-Fox 2013). Everyone, regardless of status, was obligated in some fashion to others. It is helpful to think of the individual in Angkorian society as a single link in a chain, dependent upon the link before and that follows for its place. Removal from the chain, by asserting rights outside of one's place, was to disrupt the harmonious existence of the universe.

The two types of 'slave' in Angkorian society—permanent and temporary—have already been discussed. Within the category of permanent service were two distinct groups who were obliged to perform services for those higher placed within Angkorian society but remained able to marry, work their own land or enterprises, and otherwise live their lives relatively freely. The first consisted of people—often entire villages—known as *neak n'gear*, or 'people of the state', who were obligated to perform labour or make donations of some sort to, or on behalf of, the king and other members of the royal family. Importantly, this group included lesser relatives of the reigning king (Lasker 1950, 62). We have seen that various kings instructed clients to make donations to the Rajaguha. The second group were the *pol*. Within this group were the *komlas*, usually very physically attractive people who were obliged to work at the royal temples and in other ceremonial roles until the age of 25, after which they could marry and live as free persons (Jacobsen 2014,

34–5).[3] The exact nature of their work depended entirely upon the whim of the king. In 1404, a Chinese delegation was sent to the Cambodian court; three Chinese soldiers absconded en route. The Cambodian king ordered three pol to take their place in the entourage; they returned with the delegation to the Ming court with the expectation that they would be serving out the rest of their lives in China. Fortuitously for the Cambodians, the Chinese emperor felt that they 'would be happier at home' and sent them back to Angkor (*MSL*, Yong-le 2, 9, 4).[4]

The slaves who were not accorded the same rights as the neak n'near and pol were called *khnum*, and there were three categories: those who were purchased (*agama*); those who were inherited (*mrtakadhana*); and *vrah*, those who belonged to religious establishments, not other people (Mabbett 1977, 430). Those born to slaves were inevitably slaves themselves. People could become slaves as punishment for crimes or through capture during conflict. We know that the mass movement of captured enemies was a common aspect of warfare in mainland Southeast Asia. In 1384, the king of Angkor marched on Thonburi and Chanthaburi and 'carried captive men and women to the number of more than 6,000'. On another occasion, the Siamese king is said to have taken 'possession of the capital of Cambodia, and leaves but 5,000 souls therein' (Briggs 1948, 6–7, 9). Debt bondage was also common; a free person might pledge his labour or that of his wife or children in order to work off the interest on a loan or the debt itself (Jacobsen 2014). Children were seen not as individuals but as the property of their parents, and the earliest law codes in mainland Southeast Asia, dating to the height of the Angkor Period in the 12th century, were explicit in this regard (Gaung 1934). Parents who wished to raise capital regularly did so by pledging the labour of their children, or the children themselves, either temporarily or in perpetuity.

The *vrah* constituted people attached to religious establishments. They were responsible not only for the maintenance of the temple, its cleanliness and repair, and carrying out rituals, but for ceremonial performances. While it was more usual for men to be involved in officiating, it was not uncommon for women of a certain varna to step in should the male line run out. The varna of Aninditapura received a directive from Jayavarman II that should the male line of *bhagavati* die out, any women in the family, married or not, could take their place in attending the god (Jacobsen 2008, 64). A special category of vrah were women who danced at the temples. Chau Ja-kua claimed that there were 300 women who danced and offered food to the Buddha in Cambodia in the 13th century (1911[13th c.], 53). We know from the inscriptions that these women were given names such as 'Jasmine Blossom'. They also formed part of the king's processions, 'gaily dressed, with flowers in their hair and tapers in their hands . . . other girls carrying gold and silver vessels from the palace and a whole galaxy of ornaments, of very special design' (Zhou 2007[1297], 13, 33).

Aside from the specific role of the temple dancers, male and female slaves seem to have had similar tasks. Some slaves were of foreign extraction. Zhou Daguan (2007[1297], 20) related that slaves could be ethnic minorities from the mountain areas near Angkor or from other kingdoms. All were equally subject to being moved without any say in the matter; in 1388 the king of Cambodia sent as tribute to the Ming court 45 slaves (*MSL* Hong-wu 21, 9, 15). Harsh punishments awaited disobedient slaves and often were extended to the slave's family. Varuna, a slave attached to the Rajaguha, absconded during the night. Local officials caught him, cut off his nose and ears, and returned him, and his parents, who had not been enslaved previously, to the *kanlong kamraten an*'s service (Jacobsen 2005, 238).

Slaves could not object to any labour they were commanded to perform by their master or mistress. It is inevitable that many slaves were expected to provide sexual services, if not for their owner then for his guests or retainers. This is doubtless why some female slaves received names such as 'Born-for-love', 'She-who-laughs-for-penis', and 'She-who-eats-penis', and male slaves called 'Catch-him-if-you-want-him' and 'Mischievous-penis' (Jacobsen 2003, 363).[5] It was in the interest of slave owners that their female slaves bear children, as these would increase his stock of slaves and thus the available labour force or a potential commodity to sell for cash (Jacobsen 2017). At the same time, owners of female slaves did not appreciate people helping themselves. Zhou Daguan confided that 'if by chance a Chinese, arriving in the country after long abstinence, should assuage his appetite with one of the women slaves, and the fact becomes known to her owner', the latter would be extremely piqued (2007[1297], 20).

Conclusions

The Angkorian World was a dynamic one, filled with human joys and sorrows. Life was not restricted to sombre ceremonies in the temples nor the majestic terraces of palace compounds. Angkor was a place of movement, colour, and noise. Throngs of brightly clothed women walked to the palace each day and returned to their simpler homes each evening. On special occasions, the capital must have dazzled with the silver and gold adornments of the king's female entourage. Commodities from the uplands, brought by river to the markets of the capital, were haggled over by quick-tongued traders, usually women, in the market; Chinese and other travellers walked amazed through the piles of feathers, spices, woods, and medicines. The temple dancers, ornamented as living apsaras, enacted their stylised rituals in honour of the gods and goddesses whom they served.

Yet despite the glory of Angkor, none of its inhabitants were free. Slaves performed tasks that others would not, including manual labour. Clients of wealthy patrons sent a portion of their harvest and their children to fulfil the terms of their relationship, knowing that at any time they may be summoned to fight for whichever aspiring prince their patron supported. The elite too knew that their king might insist on a generous donation in their name to a particular deity or that they might be sent far away on court business. Even the daughters of the kings knew that despite their privileged position and their jewels, they may at any time be given in marriage to a man that they had never met and whose good will their father wished to secure. Society in the Angkorian World was much more female than scholars had originally thought; it was also much more egalitarian. Nobody was free of obligation to others; not even the king of Angkor, who climbed the steps of the Baphuon each night to keep his tryst with the nagini.

Notes

1 'Slavery' is a term with many meanings. In my 2017 exploration of social contracts in mainland Southeast Asia, I describe slavery as the permanent or 'fixed' form of an institution that obliges an individual or their families (or, in some cases, entire villages) to provide service, in the form of labour, sexual as well as manual, to another who has the rights to that labour (acquired through capture or birth). Debt bondage is the temporary or 'mutable' form of slavery. Those in debt bondage expect to be released from it after the satisfactory completion of a time period of service, the repayment of a debt, or payment of a fine. Those who are enslaved have no such expectation.

2 At least one sister was also born to the same parents, although we do not know her name; she was the grandmother of Sūryavarman II.

3 This practice continued well into the Colonial Period.

4 His exact words were 'How can we expect them to compensate us for Chinese people who deserted by themselves! We have these three people whose language is different and whose customs are not familiar. How can we use them! Moreover, they all have families and would be happier at home. Ministry of Rites, you are to give them clothing, provide them with travelling expenses and then send them back to Cambodia'.

5 There was also a woman named 'Penis-Hater'.

References

Briggs, L.P., 1951. *The Ancient Khmer Empire*. Philadelphia: The American Philosophical Society.

Briggs, L.P., 1948. Siamese Attacks on Angkor before 1430. *The Journal of Asian Studies* 8(1), 3–33.

Chandler, T. & M. Polkinghorne, 2012. Through the visualisation lens: temple models and simulated context in a virtual Angkor. In *Old Myths and New Approaches: Interpreting Ancient Religious Sites in Southeast Asia*, ed. A. Haendel. Clayton, Vic: Monash University Publishing, 218–236.

Chau Ju-kua, 1911[13th c.]. Chi-fan-chi. St Petersburg, Russia: Printing Office of the Imperial Academy of Sciences.

Cœdès, G., 1913. Études cambodgiennes 9: Le serment des fonctionnaires de Sūryavarman I. *Bulletin de l'École française d'Extrême-Orient* 13, 11–17.

Cœdès, G., 1929. Études cambodgiennes 24: Nouvelles données chronologiques et généalogiques sur la dynestie de Mahidharapura. *Bulletin de l'École française d'Extrême-Orient* 29, 297–330.

Cœdès, G., 1936. Études cambodgiennes 32: La plus ancienne inscription en Pali du Cambodge. *Bulletin de l'École française d'Extrême-Orient* 36, 1–21.

Cœdès, G., 1937–1966. *Inscriptions du Cambodge*, 8 vols. Paris and Hanoi: Imprimerie de l' École française d'Extrême-Orient and Imprimerie Nationale.

Cœdès, G., 1968. *The Indianized States of Southeast Asia*, trans. Susan Brown Cowing. Canberra: Australian National University Press.

Day, T., 1996. Ties that (un)bind: families and states in premodern Southeast Asia. *Journal of Asian Studies* 55(2), 384–409.

Ebihara, M.M., 1984. Societal Organization in Sixteenth and Seventeenth Century Cambodia. *Journal of Southeast Asian Studies* 15(2), 280–295.

Gokhale, J.B., 1971. Tantrism and political ideology: a study of ninth century Angkor. *The Indian Journal of Political Science* 32(3), 319–31.

Green, G., 2002. Indic impetus? Innovations in textile usage in Angkorian period Cambodia. *Journal of the Economic and Social History of the Orient* 43(3), 277–313.

Green, G., 2023. Vogue at Angkor: dress, décor and narrative drama, in *The Angkorian World*, eds. M. Hendrickson, M.T. Stark & D. Evans. New York: Routledge.

Hall, D.G.E., 1981. *A History of South-East Asia*, 4th ed. London: Macmillan.

Hendrickson, M., E. Lustig & S. Siyonn, 2023. 'Of cattle and kings': bovines in the Angkorian World, in *The Angkorian World*, eds. M. Hendrickson, M.T. Stark & D. Evans. New York: Routledge, 459–78.

Jacobsen, T., 2003. Autonomous queenship in pre-classical Cambodia, 1st–9th centuries AD. *Journal of the Royal Asiatic Society* 13(3), 357–75.

Jacobsen, T., 2005. Paying through the nose: punishment in the Cambodian past and lessons for the present. *South East Asia Research* 13(2), 235–56.

Jacobsen, T., 2008. *Lost Goddesses: The Denial of Female Power in Cambodian History*. Copenhagen: NIAS Press, 2008.

Jacobsen, T., 2014. Debt bondage in Cambodia's past—And present. *Studies in Gender and Sexuality* 15(1 February 2014), 32–4.

Jacobsen, T., 2017. *Sex Trafficking in Southeast Asia: A History of Desire, Duty, and Debt*. London: Routledge.

Jacobsen, T., 2020. Querulous queens, bellicose brai: Cambodian perspectives toward female agency. In *Women Warriors in Southeast Asia*, eds. V. Lanzona & F. Rettig. London: Routledge, 48–63.

Jacobsen, T & Stuart-Fox, M., 2013. Power and political culture in Cambodia. Asia Research Institute (ARI) Working Paper Series (Singapore), 200.

Jacques, C., 1986. Le pays khmer avant Angkor. *Journal des savants* 1–3, 59–95.

Kirsch, A.T., 1976. Kinship, genealogical claims and social integration in ancient Khmer society: an interpretation. In *Southeast Asian History and Historiography: Essays Presented to D.G.E. Hall*, eds. C.D. Cowan & O.W. Wolters. Ithaca, NY: Cornell University Press, 190–202.

Kulke, H., 1978. *The Devaraja Cult*, trans. I.W. Mabbett. Ithaca, NY: SEAP, Cornell University.

Lasker, Bruno, 1950. *Human Bondage in Southeast Asia*. Chapel Hill, NC: University of North Carolina Press.

Ledgerwood, J., 1995. Khmer kinship: the matriliny/matriarchy myth. *Journal of Anthropological Research* 51(3), 247–262.

Mabbett, I.W., 1969. Devaraja. *Journal of Southeast Asian History* 10(2), 202–223.

Mabbett, I.W., 1977. Varnas in Angkor and the Indian caste system. *Journal of Asian Studies* 36(3), 429–42.

Mabbett, I.W., 1983. Some remarks on the present state of knowledge about slavery in Angkor. In *Slavery, Bondage and Dependency in Southeast Asia*, ed. Anthony Reid. St Lucia, Queensland; London; New York: University of Queensland Press, 44–63.
Majumdar, R.C., 1944. *Kambuja-deśa: Or, An Ancient Hindu Colony in Cambodia*. Madras: University of Madras.
O'Sullivan, Kevin, 1962. Concentric conformity in ancient Khmer kinship organization. *Bulletin of the Institute of Ethnology, Academia Sinica*, 13, 87–95.
Pelliot, P., 1925. Quelques textes chinois concernant l'Indochine hindouisée, in *Etudes Asiatiques, publiées à l'occasion du 25e anniversaire de l'EFEO*. Paris: École française d'Extrême-Orient, 243–63.
Stark, M., 2019. Universal rule and precarious empire: power and fragility in the Angkorian State, in *The Evolution of Fragility: Setting the Terms*, ed. N. Yoffee. Cambridge: McDonald Institute for Archaeological Research, University of Cambridge, 161–182.
U Gaung, 1934. *The Aṭṭasankhepa Vaṇṇanā Dhammathat: Chapters on Inheritance, Partition, Marriage, and Divorce*. Rangoon: Superintendent of Government Printing and Stationery.
Vickery, M., 1985. The reign of Suryavarman I and royal factionalism at Angkor. *Journal of Southeast Asian History* 16(2), 226–244.
Vickery, M., 1994. What and Where was Chenla?, in *Recherches nouvelles sur le Cambodge*, ed. F. Bizot. Paris: École française d'Extrême-Orient, 197–212.
Vickery, M., 1998. *Society, Economics, and Politics in Pre-Angkor Cambodia: the 7th-8th Centuries*. Tokyo: Centre for East Asian Cultural Studies for UNESCO/The Tokyo Bunko.
Wolters, O.W., 1973. Jayavarman II's military power: the territorial foundation of the Angkor Empire. *The Journal of the Royal Asiatic Society of Great Britain and Ireland* 1, 21–30.
Zhou, D., 2007[1297]. *A Record of Cambodia*. Seattle, WA: University of Washington Press.

PART VI

After Angkor

30

PERSPECTIVES ON THE 'COLLAPSE' OF ANGKOR AND THE KHMER EMPIRE

Damian Evans, Martin Polkinghorne, Roland Fletcher, David Brotherson, Tegan Hall, Sarah Klassen and Pelle Wijker

The decline of Khmer political dominance in mainland Southeast Asia in the mid-second millennium CE has been a topic of enduring fascination for scholars since the 19th century. The phenomenon is conventionally described as a 'collapse' and is usually traced to some combination of social, political, and economic factors including religious change, shifting currents in international trade, invasion and warfare, and overexertion from the immense building works of the 12th to 13th centuries. In the mid-20th century, a growing preoccupation with long-term relationships between humans and their environment set the stage for another hypothesis: that the elaboration of a vast engineered landscape either created or amplified a series of profound challenges to Angkor's long-term sustainability. In this view, processes such as urban and agricultural extensification, infrastructural development and the rise of densely populated urban areas significantly degraded the local environment, increased dependence on an over-extended infrastructural network, and created systemic vulnerabilities to social and environmental change.

These hypotheses were first systematically elaborated from the 1950s to the 1970s, and since then they have been met with widespread resistance and occasional controversy. For example, few researchers these days accept B.-P. Groslier's precise vision of Angkor as a powerhouse of irrigated rice agriculture. Others have questioned his famous 'hydraulic city' theory on theoretical or even ethical grounds, as scholars have sought to come to terms with the colonial legacies that are clearly entangled with classic notions of 'abandonment' and 'collapse'. On the other hand, evidence from recent work makes it difficult to deny that there were profound demographic and cultural shifts in Cambodia toward the end of the Angkor Period, even if the precise nature and tempo of those changes remain to be elucidated. To explain these transformations remains a central challenge in regional history.

Defining the Problem

In recent years, there has been a broad re-evaluation of the notion of 'collapse' in the archaeological literature (see Hall 2017 for a discussion), even as the notion has been brought to the forefront of the popular imagination by the work of Jared Diamond (2011) in particular. Critics (see McAnany and Yoffee 2009 for a representative cross-section) contend that the very concept of collapse is a legacy of racist and colonial approaches to the past that systematically underestimates and ignores evidence for persistence and resilience in the archaeological record;

DOI: 10.4324/9781351128940-37

cherry-picks or misrepresents the evidence; and offers naively deterministic models to explain the supposed failures of early societies, often in ways that have been politically useful for those seeking to justify present-day occupation and subjugation (Edwards 2008) or, conversely, to promote narratives of nostalgia and loss (Mikaelian 2013, 2016).

These critiques should immediately give us reason to pause and reflect on the validity of the notion of 'collapse' as applied to Angkor and the broader Khmer world: fantasies about the 'decline' of the Angkorian civilisation have always been used as a tacit justification for European colonialism in Cambodia (Edwards 2005, 2008; Falser 2020), archaeological practise has been tightly linked with the creation of the modern nation-state since the mapping and survey work of the earliest 'explorers' who 'rediscovered' Angkor and the Khmer Empire (Evans 2007, 31–44), and efforts to restore 'lost' cities and civilisations to their former grandeur have featured prominently in political messaging in Cambodia from as early as the Angkor Period (Evans 2007, 124–25) right through to the Khmer Rouge regime in the 20th century (Evans 2007, 107–15).

It is important therefore to define what we mean when we speak of the 'decline' of Angkor and the Khmer Empire, to get a sense of whether there is a phenomenon here that actually exists and is worth explaining, and to understand what measures may be useful for quantifying it. A detailed treatment is beyond the scope of this chapter, but in summary, recent attempts to redefine or re-orient the notion of 'collapse' have tended to point toward social and political complexity as key considerations in tracing and evaluating the trajectories of past societies (Hall 2017, 1). In this view, following Tainter (1988), the building of societal complexity ostensibly presents as a hugely successful problem-solving tool and in its initial stages encourages population surges; human health improvements; the development of social hierarchy; differentiation and specialisation of economic duties; higher degrees of social, political, and economic integration; and greater information processing and exchange; conversely, 'collapse' or 'transformation' can be defined as a substantial decline in urban and regional populations, a reduction in social complexity and territorial control and the failure or restructuring of economic and ideological systems (Hall 2017, 1–2).

There is significant evidence that the 13th to 15th centuries at Angkor represented a time of profound transformation in the Khmer world across various domains such as religion, politics, economy, trade, engagement with the outside world, spatial organisation, and material culture (see Coe and Evans 2018, 239–80 for a recent summary). In many cases, the details or even the overall nature of these changes are unclear or contested. Still, we may usefully narrow in on demographic change as a key indicator of broader societal transformations, since it has been the focus of intensive archaeological research in recent years and there is abundant evidence for patterns of residence and occupation in the later Angkor Period (Carter et al. 2018, 2019, 2021; Klassen et al. 2021b).

At the height of the Angkor Period in the 12th to 13th centuries CE, the Greater Angkor region of 3000 km^2 was home to something in the order of three-quarters of a million people (Klassen et al. 2021b), with a densely inhabited, formally planned urban core giving way to a diffuse urban and agricultural network marked by nodes of dense habitation around major temple sites (Evans 2016; Evans et al. 2007, 2013). By the 19th century, however, European accounts describe a sparsely populated landscape consisting of a handful of villages, with two reliable sources from the turn of the 19th and 20th centuries giving population estimates of 2000–4000 people for Siem Reap district and 10,000–18,000 people for the entire province spanning around 10,000 km^2 (Brotherson 2019, 374).

Therefore, historical and archaeological evidence indicates a decline in the population of the Angkor area of around two orders of magnitude between the 13th and 19th centuries, concurrent with seismic changes in the social, political, and cultural landscape of the region. At the same time, we should move beyond problematic notions of 'collapse' and the 'rise and fall of civilisations' while recognising that understanding the processes at work here provides us with critical insights into long-term socio-cultural trajectories and the making of modern Southeast Asia.

Perspectives on Collapse

The reasons for the 'collapse' of Angkor have long fascinated observers, who typically infer from the existence of massive temples that Angkor had an extremely large population that was overwhelmed and greatly diminished by external environmental or military pressures, or some combination of the two. For instance, Delaporte (1880, 39) assumed that Angkor was home to 'millions'. Indeed, with only two notable exceptions (Coe 1957, 1961; Miksic 2000), the idea that Angkor was a populous city has been the dominant one in the literature since the mid-1800s. Notwithstanding persistent difficulties in defining exactly where the 'urban' space of Angkor begins and ends (see Evans et al. 2023, this volume), it is now reasonably clear that the Greater Angkor landscape was home to between 700,000 to 900,000 people at its height (Klassen et al. 2021b). It is worthwhile, therefore, to re-assess traditional theories of 'collapse', which since the 1970s have tended to converge around a population estimate of around a million or so inhabitants (Groslier 1979).

Conflict

The first detailed European accounts of Angkor in the 19th century drew on local histories, myths and legends, and evidence from Ayutthayan and Cambodian chronicles to argue that the demise of Angkor and the Khmer Empire was due to military conflict with the neighbouring Ayutthayan civilisation (Briggs 1948; Brotherson 2019, 10–16; Vickery 1977), whose capital was 350 km due west of the Angkorian heartland. The dominant view here was that, from around the 12th century onward, expanding populations in present-day Thailand gave rise to ever more powerful kingdoms which by the 14th century began to pose an existential threat to Angkor, and that after multiple invasions in the Angkorian heartland throughout the 14th and 15th centuries, the capital of the Khmer was finally overrun by Ayutthaya.

Over the course of the 20th century, there was growing scepticism about this conventional narrative. Briggs (1948), for example, rejected the idea that there were multiple invasions by Ayutthaya and pointed to a single, decisive conquest of Angkor by the forces of Ayutthaya in 1431. By the 1970s Michael Vickery, after an exhaustive review of the primary sources (1977), also concluded that a series of 'invasions' by Ayutthaya was unlikely and pointed instead to a single occupation event lasting from 12 to 15 years. The idea of an 'invasion' is difficult to square with other lines of evidence: although signs of fortification and defensive modification of Angkor's urban infrastructure suggest an increased concern for the security of its population from perhaps the 13th century onwards, these alterations are difficult to date with precision, and there is no archaeological evidence at all which suggests a violent collapse or destruction of the capital (Brotherson 2015, 2019; Klassen et al. 2021a). The few scholars who have studied the issue in detail in recent years tend to underscore the remarkable cross-pollination in religious and artistic expression between Ayutthaya and Angkor in the 15th to 16th centuries (Polkinghorne et al. 2013). Nevertheless, the notion of an Ayutthayan 'sacking' of Angkor continues to enjoy widespread currency in the tertiary literature on Angkor (Hall 2018).

Even if we do accept that the Ayutthayan invasion of 1431 was as violent and as final as conventional sources would have us believe, then, as Michael Vickery has noted, this still leaves us with the question of why Angkor, which had been resilient in the face of external military incursions for several centuries, was weak enough to finally fall to Ayutthaya in the mid-1400s (1977, 509–10). Since the 1800s, scholars have therefore sought to identify the ultimate cause of Angkor's decline in addition to the proximal explanation provided by military aggression from Ayutthaya. Typically, these theories have revolved around one or two main ideas: that overbuilding and overextension of the Empire in the 12th to 13th centuries 'exhausted' Angkorian society and that the transition from Brahmanism to Buddhism as the state religion undermined the rigid ideologies and power structures that had traditionally held Angkor together (Brotherson 2019, 10–23; Polkinghorne 2018).

Overextension, Exhaustion, and Religious Transformation

King Jayavarman VII, whose reign spanned around 40 years straddling the turn of the 12th to 13th centuries, was responsible for more monumental construction activity than any of his predecessors. In addition to temples such as the Bayon and Ta Prohm at Angkor, his works included massive and sprawling temple complexes across the Empire at places like Banteay Chhmar and Preah Khan of Kompong Svay and many hundreds of smaller temples dotting the region. His civil engineering works were also unmatched by any monarch before or after: cities and giant reservoirs were built at Angkor and beyond, connected to Angkor by a network of earthen highways (Hendrickson 2010, 2012). The sheer scale and ambition of these works has led many to believe that his reign exhausted the Empire by depleting its resources or demoralising the work force, making it vulnerable to invasion by foreign invaders; in some accounts, a rebellious and overworked populace revolted against Brahmanical rulers by adopting the more democratic or anti-authoritarian faith of Theravāda Buddhism (Briggs 1999[1951], 257–61; Brotherson 2019, 15; Finot 1908; Polkinghorne 2018).

Despite its widespread currency since the 19th century, there is no particular evidence to support this hypothesis, and there are some reasonably compelling counter-arguments. As Vickery (1977, 511) has pointed out, the building spree of Jayavarman VII occurred more than two centuries before the purported sacking of the capital, which would have provided ample opportunity to recover and regroup from the mammoth building efforts of the 12th to 13th centuries. The raw materials from which cities and temples were built—stone, iron, thatch, and earth—remained in abundant supply. Moreover, in many cases—for example, Angkor Thom (Gaucher 2017) and Preah Khan of Kompong Svay (Hendrickson and Evans 2015)—we see that temples and cities typically ascribed to the reign of Jayavarman VII have long and complex life histories and were developed over decades or even centuries leading up to his reign.

Indeed, a new and as-yet unpublished inscription, K. 1297, brings to light the very important career of the Buddhist king Tribhuvanāditya (r. 1149–ca.1180 CE) and underscores that all but one of the major kings for a 200-year period from 1080 to 1270 CE were Buddhist (Sharrock 2018), which tends to undermine the supposed exceptionalism of the reign of Jayavarman VII. This also has far-reaching implications for another recurring explanation for the vulnerability of Angkor in 1431: that the transition from Brahmanism to Buddhism as the state religion—and in particular the rise of Theravāda Buddhism toward the very end of the Angkor Period—undermined the power structures that had held together a fractious Empire over many centuries. In this view, with its inward and personal focus, Theravāda was a subversive force against a state ideology that had for many centuries revolved around religious and personality cults focused on Brahmanical kings (Briggs 1999[1951], 259–60; Brotherson 2019, 18–19; Finot 1908; Polkinghorne 2018, 2022).

First of all, it is important to underscore, after Stark (2019), that the Angkorian state was always inherently fragile under kings of all religious faiths. Second, although we can imagine that the transition to Buddhism as a state religion may have challenged longstanding power structures in the Angkorian World, we must once again recognise that it was a process that unfolded over centuries, that Angkorian religion was always characterised by coexistence and syncretism (see Estève 2023, this volume), and that the high-water mark of the Khmer Empire was under the reign of Buddhist kings (Hendrickson 2010, 2012; Sharrock 2018). There is nothing *necessarily* or inherently 'democratic' or 'anti-authoritarian' about Theravāda Buddhist political ideology *in practise*: one only needs to look across the Indian Ocean to early historic and medieval Sri Lanka to find Theravāda Buddhist monarchies of the 'Classic' Period that were stable, durable, and capable of undertaking and sustaining vast engineering projects while ruling over diverse and cosmopolitan societies (Coningham et al. 2017). Indeed, as Vickery (1977, 511) has pointed out, it is logically incoherent to claim that an ascendant Theravāda Buddhist state—Ayutthaya—was only able to overcome Angkor because the Khmer state was doomed by the embrace of Theravāda Buddhism.

Trade and Globalisation

The historiography of Southeast Asia is characterised by a distinctive model of the growth and decline of early civilisations and their urban centres, revolving around indigenous responses to exogenous cultural currents. In this view, early chiefdoms along the 'Maritime Silk Road' developed into complex societies through exposure to Chinese and Indian socio-cultural systems (see e.g. Hall 1982; Higham 2014; Mabbett 1977). Through the selective appropriation of elements of Indian culture, in particular, indigenous elites were able to fundamentally transform Southeast Asian societies, eventually translating the success of coastal trading centres into vast inland agrarian-based empires largely disengaged from the changing fortunes of international trade. Extending this model some centuries forward in time, the logical corollary has been that a resurgence in maritime trade in the 12th to 15th centuries driven by China (Vickery 1977, 515–22) and in subsequent centuries by Europeans (Reid 1988, 1993) presented a profound challenge to the sustainability of the classic inland agrarian empires of Southeast Asia. By the 15th century, they had collapsed, as local elites increasingly sought to exploit the economic opportunities afforded by globalisation, and coastal, trade-oriented centres of power flourished once again across mainland Southeast Asia (see also Hall 2023, this volume).

Although compelling on some levels, this model is not without its problems. Lieberman (1995), for example, points out the substantial variability between circumstances in particular sub-regions of Southeast Asia and calls into question Reid's notion of an overarching 'Age of Commerce'. Wade (2009) points out that a burgeoning maritime trade existed in the region for several centuries before the 'Age of Commerce', even as the great inland empires of Southeast Asia developed to their apogee. Although an inland agrarian capital, Angkor was always connected to regional and international trading networks, and according to studies of material culture by David Brotherson, it remained so for centuries after its 'collapse' (Brotherson 2019). Reynolds (1995), meanwhile, suggests that the historiographical fascination with trade and external influences is a function of Eurocentric scholarship; still others point to the over-reliance on external records, in particular Chinese texts, which are often trade-centric (Stark 1998; Stark and Allen 1998). Finally, we may reasonably question the degree of relative trading advantage conferred by any relocation to the Phnom Penh region, since it, too, sits at a distance of hundreds of kilometres from the coast by way of (the very same) difficult-to-navigate network of Mekong Delta waterways.

Recent research has undoubtedly highlighted how Post-Angkorian urban centres were very much engaged in, and oriented towards, burgeoning international trading activity in the Early Modern Period (Polkinghorne 2018; Polkinghorne et al. 2019; see also Polkinghorne and Sato 2023, this volume). Once again, however, we are also left with the question of proximate vs. ultimate causes. As Vickery (1977, 522) notes:

> One question which cannot yet be answered is why the Angkorean elite, or part of it, decided sometime in the 13th–14th centuries that it would be worthwhile to shift emphasis from inland agrarian activities to integration in the China-Southeast Asia trading network, or, phrased in another way, why the new Mekong ports were able to accumulate enough wealth to attract people away from Angkor.

The Hydraulic City, Climate, and Infrastructural Breakdown

Since at least Delaporte (1880, 39), many (if not most) observers have believed that the success of Angkor derived at least partly from the ability to manage seasonal monsoon water flows and irrigate rice fields using massive hydraulic infrastructure. It was B.-P. Groslier who, from the 1950s onwards, developed this notion into a coherent theoretical framework (most fully elaborated in Groslier 1979; see Evans 2007 for a broader overview). According to Groslier's famed 'hydraulic city' theory, the immense, state-run network of *baray*, reservoirs, and canals around which the city of Angkor cohered could have enabled the harvest of multiple crops of rice per year and certainly acted as a hydraulic failsafe device, 'smoothing out' disruptive fluctuations in the yearly monsoon by storing water and, when necessary, distributing it across vast stretches of the landscape for irrigation. According to Groslier, however, the system carried within it the seeds of its own downfall, as overexploitation led to erosion, siltation, and soil degradation. A race to the bottom ensued: new channels and reservoirs were dug to replace defunct sections of the network, with ever-decreasing returns, until the system ceased to function entirely. With Angkor's elites no longer able to guarantee the provision of water and rice to their subjects, the polity itself finally fell victim to its enemies.

Groslier's 'hydraulic city' theory was problematic for several reasons (Bourdonneau 2010; Evans 2007) and provoked a fierce debate that has still not been entirely resolved (see Terry Lustig et al. 2023, this volume). For example, recent scholarship has tempered his overly generous estimates of the hydraulic system's capacity to sustain additional population numbers (Acker 1998). Nevertheless, as Pottier (2000), Fletcher et al. (2003, 116) and Evans et al. (2013, 12598) have argued, even a modest increase in rice production through irrigation could have played a key role in stabilising the annual food supply. Crucially, it would have allowed for the support of a large and specialised population of non-rice-producers in the densely inhabited urban cores that developed throughout the 11th to 13th centuries (Evans 2016; Evans et al. 2013); conversely, failure of the system would have disrupted that support and undermined the foundations of Angkor as an urban society (Brotherson 2019, 339).

Moreover, evidence has emerged in recent decades that supports elements of Groslier's narrative, although perhaps in ways that he may not have precisely foreseen. The emergence of long-term, high-resolution paleoclimate data is a case in point. Analysis of tree ring data has shown that the region suffered a series of severe and prolonged droughts, punctuated by episodes of heavy rain, in the mid- to late 14th and early 15th centuries (Buckley et al. 2010). These would have dealt a double blow to Angkor's hydraulic infrastructure: sustained drought overtaxed the capacity of the *baray* to act as a 'failsafe', while rapid floods caused critical damage to key components of the hydraulic network and threatened habitation areas. Indeed, the archaeological record shows several instances of failure and hasty repair of the hydraulic infrastructure (Evans et al. 2007, 2013). Eventually, the damage to the water management system may well have become so severe that repair was either impossible or simply too costly to pursue (Buckley et al. 2014). As shall be seen subsequently, however, although these climatic stresses broadly coincided with the period of Angkor's decline, significant demographic and cultural shifts were already in motion by this time (Brotherson 2019; Penny et al. 2019).

Engineering, Inertia, and Adaptive Capacity

Despite the so-called 'collapse' of Angkorian civilisation, many of its works have proven remarkably durable: most of the great temples remain, of course, and the *baray* still stand, even if not all retain water. The floodplain between the Tonle Sap and the Kulen hills is crisscrossed by the remains of hundreds of kilometres of canals, roads, and causeways constructed during the Angkor Period. Roland Fletcher has argued that it is precisely the scale and durability of these monumental constructions that contributed to Angkor's vulnerability and eventual decline (2009, 2012). In this view, 'The huge scale and interconnectedness of the network would largely have precluded any abrupt and easy alterations to the system. The system, therefore, suffered from severe inertia' (Fletcher and Evans 2012, 53). In essence, Angkor's infrastructure imposed a path dependency effect, as infrastructure became progressively less adaptable to changing circumstances, and society became ever more limited in its range of responses to external challenges. This line of reasoning revives some of the fundamental ideas of the 'hydraulic city' model within a new theoretical framework: note that Groslier, too, commented that 'once they [the Khmer] had adopted their course of action, they found themselves as if dragged down the slope without any power to stop themselves' (Lustig and Pottier 2007, 174).

Lending support to this view is an analysis by Penny et al. (2018) of Angkor's hydraulic network, drawing on systems theory. Penny et al. conclude that because of its immense size and the functional interdependence of its many parts, the system in its final phase of development was highly vulnerable to cascading failure in response to even moderate perturbation. The previously identified climatic stresses of the 14th and 15th centuries (Buckley et al. 2010, 2014) could easily have triggered such a failure, leading to breakdown within the water management network and significant attenuation of the diverse practical and symbolic functions that it served.

A similar lack of adaptive capacity can be seen at other settlement complexes within the Angkorian World. At Koh Ker, a provincial centre that briefly blossomed as the capital of the Empire in the mid-10th century, a single, unprecedentedly large water control structure in the form of a 7-kilometre-long dam was responsible for as much as 85% of the water supply (Klassen 2018). When structural flaws in the dam's construction led to its failure, Lustig et al. (2018) argue that the resulting damage to Koh Ker's subsistence as well as to royal prestige contributed to the subsequent decision to move the seat of power back to Angkor.

Mobility and Diaspora

As we have seen, the long period between the 13th and 19th centuries saw a decline in the population of the Angkor region of up to two orders of magnitude, raising the obvious question of what kind of fate befell such a large population. In the conventional narrative that held sway for much of the 20th century, the answer was straightforward, if extraordinary in its claims: following the devastating Ayutthayan invasion of 1431, the urban population abruptly moved south, along with its kings, to the new capitals established near the confluence of the Mekong and Tonle Sap rivers. Briggs (1999[1951], 261), for instance, described the end of Angkor as 'the sudden and permanent movement of [an] immense mass of people from one side of the kingdom to the other'.

While much of this traditional narrative has been called into question, a more recent perspective, advanced by Lucero et al. (2015), also envisages an episode of significant demographic movement, in which infrastructural breakdown induced by climate change triggered both political reorganisation among the elite and abandonment of the metropolitan heartland by the farming population. In this model, the latter demographic abandoned the agricultural mode dependent on hydraulic infrastructure and reverted to more sustainable practices in the peripheral regions of the former Empire. Suggested parallels to this process can be seen in Sri Lanka and Mesoamerica, where other low-density, agrarian-based urban complexes, under similar circumstances, likewise experienced a rapid decline and a move into an 'urban diaspora' on the fringes of their polities.

Others have pointed to the current lack of evidence for mass migration (Evans 2016; Polkinghorne 2018). Analysis of remote sensing data for the Post-Angkorian capitals of Srei Santhor, Longvek, and Oudong has made it clear that they could not have housed populations at anywhere near the scale of those of Angkor, casting doubt on the notion that urban populations migrated along with the political centre of gravity. Instead of moving away *en masse*, populations may simply have fallen over time in the absence of the food security that the urban water management system had provided. In this view, the 'illusion of pre-modern mobility and urban disjuncture' (Evans 2016, 172) created by the movement of royal centres across the political landscape masks a far slower process of gradual demographic decline.

Resilience, Continuity, and the Scale and Tempo of Decline

In the current literature on Angkor, it is common, and unfortunately still necessary, to emphasise that Angkor was never completely abandoned, in contrast to the popular myth of a 'lost city' in the jungle (see e.g. Polkinghorne 2018). Increasingly, scholars underscore the degree of continuity between the Angkor Period as traditionally defined and the subsequent centuries, and various lines of investigation have converged that point to a complex and protracted period of decline spanning several centuries instead of a sudden and precipitous 'collapse' (Castillo et al. 2018; Hall et al. 2021; Penny et al. 2019).

Stratigraphic and palaeobotanical analysis of the Angkor Thom moat by Penny et al. (2019) indicates that land use patterns in the surrounding area, the very heart of Angkor's urban complex, began to shift in the early 1300s, suggesting a gradual demographic decline that predated the severe droughts of the mid-14th century by a matter of decades and the supposed Ayutthayan invasion by more than a hundred years. By the end of the 14th century, the moat was overgrown and appears no longer to have been maintained. Similarly, inside Angkor Thom geochemistry, palynology, and fire history analysis demonstrate that from the 14th century land use attenuation continued, with the exception of a possible short period of reoccupation in the 16th century (Hall et al. 2021). Ceramics survey of an array of sites in central Angkor likewise shows that a contraction in the range of settled spaces took place over the course of the 14th century (Brotherson 2019, 323–40).

If population numbers and centralised control at Angkor were much reduced thereafter, key parts of the complex nevertheless remained in use. The accounts of early European visitors indicate the continued existence of an urban centre at Angkor in the 15th to 16th centuries (Groslier 2006). Religious and economic activity and even architectural restoration works continued into the 15th and 16th centuries (Castillo et al. 2018). Some of these projects, such as the reconfiguration of Phnom Bakheng and the Baphuon into enormous representations of the Buddha, are of a considerable scale, indicating the presence of a sizeable number of worshipers (Leroy et al. 2015; Polkinghorne 2018; Polkinghorne et al. 2013). At Angkor Wat, similarly converted into a Theravāda sanctuary and pilgrimage site, excavation and radiocarbon dating hint at a complex occupation history extending as late as the 18th century (Carter et al. 2019; Polkinghorne 2022). Continuity is also apparent in the more peripheral agricultural zone of Angkor. While ceramic remains decline there from the 14th century onwards, its dispersed settlement pattern nevertheless persists into the 16th and 17th centuries (Brotherson 2019, 353–64). Overall, the evidence seems to underscore the long-term resilience and durability of rural, agrarian life at Angkor and beyond, especially when compared to the apparent fragility of the Angkorian state and the urban centres populated by elites (Brotherson 2019; Lucero et al. 2015; Stark 2019).

Turning to the other urban complexes in the Angkorian World, the chronology of collapse is complicated further, as a series of palaeobotanical studies led by Tegan Hall (2017) and Dan Penny has shown. Mahendraparvata in the Kulen hills was largely abandoned as an urban centre in the 12th century (Penny et al. 2014). The ephemeral 10th-century capital of Koh Ker, on the other hand, appears to have maintained a relatively intense degree of occupation until the 15th century, when populations at Angkor had already fallen substantially (Hall et al. 2018). Finally, the complex of Preah Khan of Kompong Svay saw a gradual attenuation of land use during the 14th century, but occupation and iron production at the site continued for another two or three centuries (Hall et al. 2019). Overall, it would seem that the 'collapse' of settlement in the Angkorian World was a protracted process, starting as early as the 12th to 13th centuries in some areas, gathering pace in the 14th century in particular at Angkor, with a 'long tail end' and a significant degree of variability in the life histories of individual settlement complexes across the region, depending on localised factors (Hall 2017).

Discussion and Conclusion

Broadly speaking, our view of these processes is complicated by shifts in material culture in the late Angkor Period towards less durable materials, which have much less visibility in the archaeological record (Coe and Evans 2018, Chapter 8; Polkinghorne 2018): inscriptions in stone gave way to manuscripts inscribed on palm leaves and other more perishable media; religious construction began to privilege the reconfiguration of existing masonry structures and the use of wood and brick as architectural materials, instead of raising vast stone monuments from scratch; and the production of stone statuary diminished relative to the production of works in other media such as wood. All of these processes intensified and became well-established in Early Modern Cambodia, as Khmer society transitioned decisively away from re-engineering entire landscapes and from vast, industrial-scale exploitation of stone resources, towards a suite of materials and behaviours that is more recognisably 'modern' in character and that persisted until the 20th century.

As with questions of urbanism (see Evans et al. 2023, this volume), a large part of the difficulty here derives from ill-defined categories, loose definitions, and inadequate consideration of scale (both spatial and temporal). The term 'collapse' implies a loss of social complexity that is sudden and catastrophic, and even the term 'transformation' requires that we define a particular temporal frame of reference in order to identify it or present it as a compelling alternative to 'collapse'. Again, the unique scale of Angkor creates a dilemma, since we may choose to see the Angkor region as a succession of distinct and relatively fragile urban centres spanning a period from the mid-first millennium CE to the mid-second millennium CE, prone to constant transformation and change, or, on the other hand, and on a completely different spatial scale, a uniquely resilient and sustainable urban complex which endured as the capital of the Empire for half a millennium. Seeing 'the end of Angkor' through either of these lenses necessarily changes our perception of the significance and uniqueness of the changes that took place at Angkor in the 14th and 15th centuries CE and also the degree to which the 'shifting capitals' that came after Angkor in the Middle Period (see Polkinghorne and Sato 2023, this volume) represent something different and new.

The lack of archaeological data is also a serious problem. In particular, more spatial and chronological resolution is needed within our data to elucidate demographic change and trajectories of both urbanism and agriculture. This is particularly true of the Early Modern Period, a long-neglected era that is not only deserving of study in its own right (see Polkinghorne and Sato 2023, this volume) but whose story will also have much to tell us about the end of Angkor and its Empire. Again, the sheer scale of what was achieved at Angkor creates a specific set of practical and interpretive problems: the amount of archaeological excavation that has been completed at Angkor is vanishingly small in relation to the spatial extent of the archaeological remains, and this situation is unlikely to ever change. For now, there is a wide zone of archaeological uncertainty between data from excavations focusing on household archaeology, which offer rich chronological detail but are very constrained in spatial scale (see Carter et al. 2023, this volume) and new archaeological maps that provide excellent spatial coverage but relatively coarse chronological resolution (see Evans et al. 2023, this volume). Studies of pollen have already gone some way to filling in this broad lacuna (see Hall and Penny 2023, this volume); in the future, we may hope to complement that work with other approaches, for example, using biomarkers to infer demographic change and using environmental DNA to infer land-use change over wider areas with much higher spatial and temporal resolutions.

In conclusion, what emerges from a quarter-century of intensive archaeological research into the decline of Angkor and the Khmer Empire is a complex set of data that moves us further away from neat explanations such as 'exhaustion', 'sacking', or 'religious transformation'. Instead, recent work tends to suggest that the development of massive, inertial infrastructures of a particular model severely constrained the available responses to specific social and environmental changes, that this lack of adaptive capacity characterised settlement complexes across the Angkorian World, and that transformations were relatively long and drawn-out and thus inconsistent with longstanding theories of 'collapse'. Although significant gaps remain in our knowledge, the causal linkages between climate variability, societal challenges, and large-scale transformations are particularly well articulated in the Angkorian World and compel us to move beyond merely noting the correlation between events like megadroughts and significant societal change. As more data become available, there will also be debate and discussion about the role of exogenous forces such as globalisation in shaping the trajectory of Southeast Asian societies and how to balance that with evidence for indigenous agency, about how we may assign proximal and ultimate causes to transformations at specific scales of time and space, and about the extent to which those transformations may be explained by more generalised social theory (see e.g. Fletcher 2009; Hall 2017; Hawken and Fletcher 2021; Lucero et al. 2015; Penny et al. 2018). In the meantime, one thing that we may conclude with relative certainty is that the evidence is inconsistent with conventional narratives that proposed an abrupt and dramatic ending for Angkor deriving from one or two factors in isolation.

Funding

Funding for this contribution derives in part from the European Research Council (ERC) under the European Union's Horizon 2020 research and innovation programme (grant agreements 639828 and 866454).

References

Acker, R., 1998. New geographical tests of the hydraulic thesis at Angkor. *South East Asia Research* 6(1), 5–47.

Bourdonneau, É., 2010. Pour en finir avec la "cité hydraulique"? *Bulletin de l'École française d'Extrême-Orient* 97–98, 409–37.

Briggs, L.P., 1948. Siamese attacks on Angkor before 1430. *The Journal of Asian Studies* 8(1), 3–33.
Briggs, L.P., 1999[1951]. *The Ancient Khmer Empire* (American Philosophical Society, Philad. Transactions. New ser. ; v.41, pt. 1.). Bangkok: White Lotus.
Brotherson, D., 2015. The fortification of Angkor Wat, *Antiquity* 89(348), 1456–72.
Brotherson, D., 2019. *Commerce, the capital & community: trade ceramics, settlement patterns & continuity throughout the demise of Angkor*. PhD dissertation. Sydney: The University of Sydney.
Buckley, B.M., K.J. Anchukaitis, D. Penny, R. Fletcher, E.R. Cook, M. Sano, L.C. Nam, A. Wichienkeeo, T.T. Minh & T.M. Hong, 2010. Climate as a contributing factor in the demise of Angkor, Cambodia. *Proceedings of the National Academy of Sciences of the United States of America* 107(15), 6748–52.
Buckley, B.M., R. Fletcher, S.-Y.S. Wang, B. Zottoli & C. Pottier, 2014. Monsoon extremes and society over the past millennium on mainland Southeast Asia. *Quaternary Science Reviews* 95, 1–19.
Carter, A., P. Heng, M. Stark, R. Chhay & D. Evans, 2018. Urbanism and residential patterning in Angkor. *Journal of Field Archaeology* 43(6), 492–506.
Carter, A.K., S. Klassen, M.T. Stark, M. Polkinghorne, P. Heng, D. Evans & R. Chhay, 2021. The evolution of agro-urbanism: a case study from Angkor, Cambodia. *Journal of Anthropological Archaeology* 63, 101323.
Carter, A.K., M.T. Stark, S. Quintus, Y. Zhuang, H. Wang, P. Heng & R. Chhay, 2019. Temple occupation and the tempo of collapse at Angkor Wat, Cambodia. *Proceedings of the National Academy of Sciences* 116(25), 12226–31.
Carter, A., M.T. Stark, P. Heng & R. Chhay, 2023. The Angkorian house, in *The Angkorian World*, eds. M. Hendrickson, M.T. Stark & D. Evans. New York: Routledge, 494–507.
Castillo, C.C., M. Polkinghorne, B. Vincent, T.B. Suy & D.Q. Fuller, 2018. Life goes on: archaeobotanical investigations of diet and ritual at Angkor Thom, Cambodia (14th–15th centuries CE). *The Holocene* 28(6), 930–44.
Coe, M., 1957. The Khmer settlement pattern: a possible analogy with that of the Maya. *American Antiquity* 22, 409–10.
Coe, M., 1961. Social typology and the tropical forest civilisations, *Comparative Studies in Society and History* 4, 65–85.
Coe, M. & D. Evans, 2018. *Angkor and the Khmer Civilization*. London: Thames & Hudson.
Coningham, R., M. Manuel, C. Davis & P. Gunawardhana, 2017. Archaeology and cosmopolitanism in early historic and medieval Sri Lanka, in *Sri Lanka at the Crossroads of History*, eds. Z. Biedermann & A. Strathern. London: UCL Press, 19–43.
Delaporte, L., 1880. *Voyage au Cambodge: L'architecture Khmer*. Paris: C. Delagrave.
Diamond, J., 2011. *Collapse: How Societies Choose to Fail or Succeed*. New York: Penguin.
Edwards, P., 2005. Taj Angkor: enshrining l'Inde in le Cambodge, in *France and 'Indochina': Cultural Representations,* eds. K. Robson & J. Yee. Lanham, MD: Lexington Books, 13–27.
Edwards, P., 2008. *Cambodge: The Cultivation of a Nation, 1860–1945*. Chiang Mai: Silkworm Books.
Estève, J., 2023. Gods and temples: the nature(s) of Angkorian religion, in *The Angkorian World*, eds. M. Hendrickson, M.T. Stark & D. Evans. New York: Routledge, 423–34.
Evans, D., 2007. *Putting Angkor on the map: a new survey of a Khmer 'hydraulic city' in historical and theoretical context*. PhD dissertation. Sydney: The University of Sydney.
Evans, D., 2016. Airborne laser scanning as a method for exploring long-term socio-ecological dynamics in Cambodia, *Journal of Archaeological Science* 74, 164–75.
Evans, D., R.J. Fletcher, C. Pottier, J.-B. Chevance, D. Soutif, B.S. Tan, S. Im, D. Ea, T. Tin, S. Kim, C. Cromarty, S. De Greef, K. Hanus, P. Bâty, R. Kuszinger, I. Shimoda & G. Boornazian, 2013. Uncovering archaeological landscapes at Angkor using lidar. *Proceedings of the National Academy of Sciences of the United States of America* 110(31), 12595–600.
Evans, D., C. Pottier, R. Fletcher, S. Hensley, I. Tapley, A. Milne & M. Barbetti, 2007. A comprehensive archaeological map of the World's largest preindustrial settlement complex at Angkor, Cambodia. *Proceedings of the National Academy of Sciences* 104(36), 14277–82.
Evans, D., R. Fletcher, S. Klassen, C. Pottier & P. Wijker, 2023. Trajectories of urbanism in the Angkorian World, in *The Angkorian World*, eds. M. Hendrickson, M.T. Stark & D. Evans. New York: Routledge.
Falser, M., 2020. *Angkor Wat—A Transcultural History of Heritage*. Berlin/Boston: Walter de Gruyter GmbH & Co KG.
Finot, L., 1908. Les études indochinoises. *Bulletin de l'École française d'Extrême-Orient* 8(1), 221–33.
Fletcher, R., 2009. Low-density, agrarian-based urbanism: a comparative view. *Insights* 2(4), 1–19.
Fletcher, R., 2012. Low-density, agrarian-based urbanism: scale, power and ecology, in *The Archaeology of Complex Societies*, ed. M.E. Smith. New York: Cambridge University Press, 285–320.

Fletcher, R., M. Barbetti, D. Evans, H. Than, I. Sokrithy, K. Chan, D. Penny, C. Pottier & T. Somaneath, 2003. Redefining Angkor: structure and environment in the largest, low density urban complex of the pre-industrial World. *Udaya, Journal of Khmer Studies* 4, 107–21.

Fletcher, R.J. & D. Evans, 2012. The dynamics of Angkor and its landscape: issues of scale, non-correspondence and outcome, in *Old Myths and New Approaches: Interpreting Ancient Religious Sites in Southeast Asia*, ed. A. Haendel. Clayton: Monash University Publishing, 42–62.

Gaucher, J., 2017. L'enceinte d'Angkor Thom: Archéologie d'une forme, chronologie d'une ville, in *Deux Décennies de Coopération Archéologique Franco-Cambodgienne à Angkor*, eds. A. Beschaouch, F. Verellen & M. Zink. Paris: Académie des Inscriptions et Belles-Lettres, 27–41.

Groslier, B.-P., 1979. La cité hydraulique angkorienne: exploitation ou surexploitation du sol? *Bulletin de l'École française d'Extrême-Orient* 66, 161–202.

Groslier, B.P., 2006. *Angkor and Cambodia in the Sixteenth Century: According to Portuguese and Spanish Sources*. Bangkok: Orchid Press.

Hall, K.R., 1982. The "Indianization" of Funan: an economic history of Southeast Asia's first state. *Journal of Southeast Asian Studies* 13(1), 81–106.

Hall, K.R., 2018. *Gale Researcher Guide for: The Angkor Khmer Empire*. Farmington Hills, MI: Gale.

Hall, K.R., 2023. Angkor's multiple Southeast Asia overland connections, in *The Angkorian World*, eds. M. Hendrickson, M.T. Stark & D. Evans. New York: Routledge, 91–111.

Hall, T., 2017. *A broader view of collapse: using palaeoecological techniques to reconstruct occupation dynamics across a networked society undergoing transformation*. PhD dissertation. Sydney: The University of Sydney.

Hall, T., D. Penny & R. Hamilton, 2018. Re-evaluating the occupation history of Koh Ker, Cambodia, during the Angkor period: a palaeo-ecological approach. *PLoS ONE*13(10), e0203962.

Hall, T., D. Penny & R. Hamilton, 2019. The environmental context of a city in decline: the vegetation history of a Khmer peripheral settlement during the Angkor period. *Journal of Archaeological Science: Reports* 24, 152–65.

Hall, T., D. Penny, B. Vincent & M. Polkinghorne, 2021. An integrated palaeoenvironmental record of early modern occupancy and land use within Angkor Thom, Angkor. *Quaternary Science Reviews* 251, 106710.

Hall, T. & D. Penny, 2023. Forests, palms and paddy fields: the plant ecology of Angkor, in *The Angkorian World*, eds. M. Hendrickson, M.T. Stark & D. Evans. New York: Routledge, 135–53.

Hawken, S. & R. Fletcher, 2021. A long-term archaeological reappraisal of low-density urbanism: implications for contemporary cities. *Journal of Urban Archaeology* 3, 29–50.

Hendrickson, M., 2010. Historic routes to Angkor: development of the Khmer road system (ninth to thirteenth centuries AD) in mainland Southeast Asia. *Antiquity* 84(324), 480–96.

Hendrickson, M., 2012. Connecting the dots: investigating transportation between the temple complexes of the medieval Khmer (9th to 14th centuries CE), in *Old Myths and New Approaches: Interpreting Ancient Religious Sites in Southeast Asia,* ed. A. Haendel. Clayton: Monash University Publishing, 84–102.

Hendrickson, M. & D. Evans, 2015. Reimagining the city of fire and iron: a landscape archaeology of the Angkor-Period industrial complex of Preah Khan of Kompong Svay, Cambodia (ca. 9th to 13th centuries A.D.). *Journal of Field Archaeology* 40(6), 644–664.

Higham, C., 2014. *Early Mainland Southeast Asia: From First Humans to Angkor*. Bangkok: River Books.

Klassen, S., 2018. *Adaptive capacity of the water management systems of two medieval Khmer cities, Angkor and Koh Ker*. PhD dissertation. Tempe: Arizona State University.

Klassen, S., T. Attorre, D. Brotherson, R. Chhay, W. Johnson, I. Moffat & R. Fletcher, 2021a. Deciphering a timeline of demise at medieval Angkor, Cambodia using remote sensing. *Remote Sensing* 13(11), 2094.

Klassen, S., A.K. Carter, D.H. Evans, S. Ortman, M.T. Stark, A.A. Loyless, M. Polkinghorne, P. Heng, M. Hill & P. Wijker, 2021b. Diachronic modeling of the population within the medieval greater Angkor region settlement complex. *Science Advances* 7(19), eabf8441.

Leroy, S., M. Hendrickson, E. Delqué-Kolic, E. Vega & P. Dillmann, 2015. First direct dating for the construction and modification of the Baphuon temple mountain in Angkor, Cambodia. *PLoS ONE* 10(11), e0141052.

Lieberman, V., 1995. An age of commerce in Southeast Asia? Problems of regional coherence—A review article. *The Journal of Asian Studies* 54(03), 796–807.

Lucero, L.J., R. Fletcher & R. Coningham, 2015. From 'collapse'to urban diaspora: the transformation of low-density, dispersed agrarian urbanism. *Antiquity* 89(347), 1139–54.

Lustig, T., S. Klassen, D. Evans, R. French & I. Moffat, 2018. Evidence for the breakdown of an Angkorian hydraulic system, and its historical implications for understanding the Khmer Empire. *Journal of Archaeological Science: Reports* 17, 195–211.

Lustig, T. & C. Pottier, 2007. Bernard Philippe Groslier. The Angkorian Hydraulic City: Exploitation or Over-Exploitation of the Soil? Translated by Terry Lustig and Christophe Pottier. *Aséanie* 20, 133–40.

Lustig, T., J.-B. Chevance & W. Johnson, 2023. Angkor as a "cité hydraulique"?, in *The Angkorian World*, eds. M. Hendrickson, M.T. Stark & D. Evans. New York: Routledge, 216–34.

Mabbett, I.W., 1977. The 'indianization' of Southeast Asia: reflections on the historical sources. *Journal of Southeast Asian Studies* 8(2), 143–61.

McAnany, P.A. & N. Yoffee, 2009. *Questioning Collapse: Human Resilience, Ecological Vulnerability, and the Aftermath of Empire*. Cambridge: Cambridge University Press.

Mikaelian, G., 2013. Des sources lacunaires de l'histoire à l'histoire complexifiée des sources. Éléments pour une histoire des renaissances khmères (c. XIVe–c. XVIIIe siècles). *Péninsule* 65, 259–304.

Mikaelian, G., 2016. Le passé entre mémoire d'Angkor et déni de Laṅvaek: La conscience de l'histoire dans le royaume khmer du XVIIe siècle, in *Le Passé Des Khmers. Langues, Textes, Rites,* eds. G. Mikaelian, N. Abdoul-Carime & J. Thach. Bern: Peter Lang, 167–212.

Miksic, J.N., 2000. Heterogenetic cities in premodern Southeast Asia. *World Archaeology* 32(1), 106–20.

Penny, D., J.-B. Chevance, D. Tang & S. De Greef, 2014. The environmental impact of Cambodia's ancient city of Mahendraparvata (Phnom Kulen). *PLoS ONE* 9(1), e84252.

Penny, D., T. Hall, D. Evans & M. Polkinghorne, 2019. Geoarchaeological evidence from Angkor, Cambodia, reveals a gradual decline rather than a catastrophic 15th-century collapse. *Proceedings of the National Academy of Sciences* 116(11), 4871–76.

Penny, D., C. Zachreson, R. Fletcher, D. Lau, J.T. Lizier, N. Fischer, D. Evans, C. Pottier & M. Prokopenko, 2018. The demise of Angkor: systemic vulnerability of urban infrastructure to climatic variations. *Science Advances* 4(10), eaau4029.

Polkinghorne, M., 2018. Reconfiguring kingdoms: the end of Angkor and the emergence of early modern period Cambodia, in *Angkor: Exploring Cambodia's Sacred City*, eds. T. McCullough, S.A. Murphy, P. Baptiste & T. Zéphir. Singapore: Asian Civilisations Museum, 255–69.

Polkinghorne, M., 2022. 17th- and 18th-century images of the Buddha from Ayutthaya and Lan Xang at Angkor, in *Early Theravadin Cambodia: Perspectives from Art and Archaeology*, ed. A. Thompson. Singapore: NUS Press, 269–305.

Polkinghorne, M., C.A. Morton, A. Roberts, R.S. Popelka-Filcoff, Y. Sato, V. Vuthy, P. Thammapreechakorn, A. Stopic, P. Grave, D. Hein & L. Vitou, 2019. Consumption and exchange in early modern Cambodia: NAA of brown-glaze stoneware from Longvek, 15th-17th centuries. *PLoS One* 14(5), e0216895.

Polkinghorne, M., C. Pottier & C. Fischer, 2013. One Buddha can hide another. *Journal Asiatique* 301(2), 575–624.

Polkinghorne, M. & Y. Sato, 2023. Early modern Cambodia and archaeology at Longvek, in *The Angkorian World*, eds. M. Hendrickson, M.T. Stark & D. Evans. New York: Routledge.

Pottier, C., 2000. Some Evidence of an inter-relationship between hydraulic features and rice field patterns at Angkor during ancient times. *Journal of Sophia Asian Studies* 18, 99–120.

Reid, A., 1988. *Southeast Asia in the Age of Commerce 1450–1680: volume 1: The Lands Below the Winds.*: New Haven and London.

Reid, A., 1993. *Southeast Asia in the Age of Commerce 1450–1680: volume 2: Expansion and Crisis*. New Haven and London.

Reynolds, C.J., 1995. A new look at old Southeast Asia. *The Journal of Asian Studies* 54(2), 419–46.

Sharrock, P.D., 2018. Cham-Khmer interactions in 1113–1220 CE, in *Vibrancy in Stone: Masterpieces of the Đà Nẵng Museum of Cham Sculpture*, eds. T.K. Phương, V.V. Thắng & P.D. Sharrock. Bangkok, Thailand: River Books, 111–19.

Stark, M.T., 1998. The transition to history in the Mekong delta: a view from Cambodia. *International Journal of Historical Archaeology* 2(3), 175–203.

Stark, M.T., 2019. Universal rule and precarious empire: power and fragility in the Angkorian State, in *The Evolution of Fragility: Setting the Terms*, ed. N. Yoffee. Cambridge: McDonald Institute for Archaeological Research.

Stark, M.T. & S.J. Allen, 1998. The transition to history in Southeast Asia: an introduction. *International Journal of Historical Archaeology* 2(3), 163–74.

Tainter, J., 1988. *The Collapse of Complex Societies*. Cambridge: Cambridge University Press.

Vickery, M.T., 1977. *Cambodia after Angkor: the chronicular evidence for the fourteenth to sixteenth centuries*. PhD dissertation. New Haven: Yale University.

Wade, G., 2009. An early age of commerce in Southeast Asia, 900–1300 CE. *Journal of Southeast Asian Studies* 40(2), 221–65.

31

UTHONG AND ANGKOR

Material Legacies in the Chao Phraya Basin, Thailand

Pipad Krajaejun

The Angkorian World had a broad geographic reach westward into what is now the Maenam Basin in central Thailand. The legacies of Angkor are clearly seen in the many laterite *prasāt* and sandstone statues incorporating classic Khmer style across this region. Some of these places are listed in the 1191 CE Preah Khan inscription, which described Jayavarman VII sending 23 *Jayabuddhamahānātha* images to various cities such as Lavodayapura (Lavo/Lopburi), Suvarnapura (Suphanburi), Çambūkapaṭṭana (Prasat Srakosinarai in Ratchaburi), Jayarājapuri (Ratchaburi), Çri Jayasimhapuri (Prasat Muang Singh), and Çri Jayavajraburi (Phetchaburi) (Cœdès 1941, 295–296; Woodward 1994/1995, 105–111). While this list suggests possible Angkorian control during its imperial peak, Chinese records from the 13th and 14th centuries state that cities such as Xian (Suphanburi) and Lohou (Lavo/Lopburi) sent missions to China, and these were clearly independent following the death of Jayavarman VII c. 1218 (Flood 1969, 245; Pelliot 1904, 240–244; see also Lowman 2011, 51–75). It is during this latter period that the new artistic style, which George Cœdès called the *'École de Ū Thòng'*, or Uthong art school, emerged. Named after a group of Buddha images that Cœdès identified as the last Khmer art production in Lopburi before the rise of Ayutthaya, the Uthong style represents an intermingling of Angkor with various characteristics of 'Siamese art', specifically the styles associated with Sukhothai and Ayutthaya (Cœdès 1928a, 33–34).

Previous scholars have seriated Uthong statuary between the Khmer (Angkor) and Thai periods using stylistic changes in facial and body characteristics to create a simple unilinear narrative in Thai art (Cœdès 1928a, 33–34; Griswold and Buriphan 1952, 30–32). Challenges to this model have come from contemporary art historians like Siripoj Laomanacharoen, who contends that the aim of Uthong art was to create a link between Khmer and Thai art as a kind of racial theory in Thai art historical scholarship (Laomanacharoen 2016, 250–73). Senior art historian Prayoon Uluchata and architectural historian Somkiet Lohphetrat (1996) also critiqued this linear conceptualisation of the Uthong art style. They suggested the operation of two contemporary schools, Lavo (Lopburi) and Suphannabhumi (Suphanburi), which produced stylistically different statuary (Somkiet 1996, 181; Uluchata 1986, 75–97). This interpretation supports a model of political heterogeneity rather than unification in Thailand's central plain during this period.

This chapter explores debates over the creation and nature of the Uthong art style and contends that it reflects Angkor's influences and legacies beyond Angkor proper. It reviews the

DOI: 10.4324/9781351128940-38

historiography of the Uthong art style to identify an underlying nationalist agenda that explains why so little is known about post-Bayon art in Thailand. A definition of Uthong is offered as a first step in trying to understand both the post-Bayon style and the impact of Angkor on the edges of its territorial boundaries. This chapter also reviews competing models of Uthong art—as linear development and as political disunity—through an in-depth analysis of artistic styles, distribution analysis, and archaeometric dating of bronze Uthong statues from various localities across the central plain of Thailand. The discussion moves beyond statuary and assesses potential variabilities in architecture, a source that has to date received little attention (Diskul 1971[1970], 17; Leksukhum 2009, 151–158). This gap is partly explained by the apparent lack of variation in architectural styles in this period and issues in dating construction phases. To examine these problems, it is very important to embed architectural traits within the formation and movement of state polities and Buddhism on the central plain of Thailand and Angkor.

The Origin and Mission of King Uthong in the Thought of the Siamese Elites

The term 'Uthong art' is associated with the process of nation-building resulting from the relationships between Siamese (Thai), Cambodian, and French scholars in the Colonial Period. Following the mid-19th century emergence of the modern Siamese/Thai state (with Thailand officially used since 1939), Siamese elites attempted to create a national history in order to assimilate people, annex territories, and consolidate the nation (Kasetsiri 2015, 33). Writing Ayutthaya's dynastic history became a focal theme of national historiography, since it was both an earlier Siamese kingdom in the Bangkok region and the central plain of Siam, focusing on the Chao Phraya River Basin (hereafter Chao Phraya), which they considered Siam proper (Prakitnoonthakarn 2014, 1–19). As a result, attention has concentrated on King Uthong or Ramathibodi, the first king of Ayutthaya, in order to proclaim the legitimacy of the Siamese elites as rulers of the country and ancestors of the Thai/Tai (Kasetsiri 2015, 220–23).

There were many versions of the origin of King Uthong in the past. In the Ayutthaya Period, for example, Dutch merchant Jeremias Van Vliet (2005[1639], 12–18) recorded that King Uthong came from China, landed at Pattani (in the south of Thailand), and then moved to Phetchaburi and built Ayutthaya, while according to *Testimony of Ayutthaya Captives*, he came from Phetchaburi (in the west of Thailand/Siam) but descended from Angkorian and Sukhothai kings (PKKSA 2010[1767], 57–66). However, from the mid-19th century, his origin as the first king of the Thai nation in modern history became more static. King Mongkut (r. 1851–1868) suggested that King Uthong descended from the northern king Sirichai Chiang Sen (now in Chiang Rai) and then conquered the Malayan Peninsula (Malaysia). He also wrote, '[O]ur ancient capital Ayutthaya before the year A.D. 1350, was but the ruin of an ancient place belonging to Kambuja (now known as Cambodia), formerly called Lawèk' [Longvek] (Mongkut 1851, 345). This story changed the direction from which the ancestors of the Tai king came—from the north, not from the south or west of Siam—but it also linked the country's origins closely to 'Kambuja'. The rationale for claiming Siam's legitimacy over Kambuja was directly motivated by French colonial expansion across Indochina (Keyes 1991, 264–66; Kasetsiri 2015, 220–33).

The true origins of King Uthong remained a mystery to modern history until 1892, when Prince Damrong Rajanubhab, King Chulalongkorn's young brother and the father of Thai history, visited Suphanburi on a royal tour and heard from local people the story that 'a long time ago King Uthong ruled that city, but one day an epidemic disease spread in the city. He and his people had to move out and finally built Ayutthaya city' (Damrong 1974[1944], 363–74). This story also coincided with the events written in the Ayutthaya Chronicle that King Uthong's brother ruled at Suphanburi, and Damrong's archaeological survey of Uthong City revealed evidence of Dvaravati art, a local style contemporary with the Angkorian Khmer, in the form of Buddha images, monuments, and city walls. At that time, he assumed that the Dvaravati evidence related to the story of King Uthong, and he equated Uthong with the former name of Suphanburi because '*thong*' (Thai) and '*suphan*' (Sanskrit) mean gold, while '*U*' (Thai) and '*buri*' (Sanskrit) mean place or city. Damrong concluded that this city must have been the remains of the city created by King Uthong. Damrong's belief in Uthong city would become the source for the coining of the term 'Uthong art' a few decades later.

The verification of the history of King Uthong remained the mission of early 20th-century Siamese elites as they sought to consolidate the origins of the Thai people by documenting the life of their shared ancestor and at the same time to refuse the Khmer influence. On the evening of December 2, 1907, King Chulalongkorn gave a speech to the Antiquarian Society (*Borankhadi Samoson*). This society had a mission to 'study and search for the ancient history of Siam', in particular the pre-Ayutthaya Period and the origin of King Uthong (Peleggi 2017, 78). King Chulalongkorn's speech gave legitimacy to the royal Ayutthaya chronicles' history of Siam and to Uthong as the first Siamese king, and he urged members of the Antiquarian Society to investigate the 'true Thai race' through the history of King Uthong (Baker 2001, 95–96). Eventually, King Uthong was written into the story of Thai history as a great hero. Damrong's interventions—both archaeological and oratorical—effectively embedded the myth of King Uthong in Thailand's national historical narrative and led to the earliest conceptualisation of a Kingdom of Siam whose boundaries coincided with those of the modern nation-state. Damrong's 1924 lecture at Chulalongkorn University proposed that in King Uthong's reign, his city was independent from the Sukhothai kingdom and extended its territory eastwards to Ayutthaya, the Tachin River, and the Chao Phraya River; southwards to Ratchaburi; westwards to the Mon kingdom; and northwards to Muang San (var. Sankhaburi, Sanburi) (Damrong 1924, 46–53). This narrative was sufficient to support the nationalist imaginary of the great kingdom of the Thai located on the central plain of Thailand, and was a way of splitting the Thai kingdom from Angkor and its imperial legacy because he came from the west or the north, not from the east of Thailand (Cambodia).

The Creation of the Term Uthong Art and the Problem of Its Classification and Chronology

In 1927, the Bangkok National Museum carried out a project to reclassify its collections in order to become a modern, 'truly national museum' (Peleggi 2004, 149). During this work, Cœdès and Damrong examined a group of Buddha images that reflected a blend of Ayutthaya, Khmer, and Dvaravati stylistic traits. Soon afterwards, in *Les Collections Archéologiques du Musée National de Bangkok*, Cœdès introduced the new term 'Uthong school', or L'École de U Thòng to describe those Buddha images whose transitional art style straddled Dvaravati, Khmer, and Siamese traditions (Cœdès 1928a, 33–34). The Thai version of Cœdès' textbook established Uthong as both an art tradition (*skul*) and a historical period (*smai*): '*Smai Uthong*' referred to the period before and after King Uthong established Ayutthaya, and the Buddha images from this time were also created by the 'southern Thai' (*Thai fai tai*), meaning the Maenam Basin (Cœdès 1928b, 39). The difference in meaning between school (*skul*) and *smai* is significant, because *smai* creates a space for Uthong art in the linear structure of Thai art history and archaeology. Uthong art was subsequently positioned between non-Thai art (Dvaravati/Mon, Srivijaya, and Khmer) and Thai art (Sukhothai, Chiang Saen, and Ayutthaya) and effectively created the first Thai style as its endpoint. Laomanacharoen suggests that the term 'Uthong style' had nationalist origins and that it was coined to distinguish Thai-originating images from Khmer art while asserting the Thai origins of the sculptors who made these images. From this perspective, the Uthong art tradition emerged from a Thai/Khmer foundation on the central plain or Chao Phraya River basin to become a distinctively Thai tradition (Laomanacharoen 2016, 250–78).

Cœdès identified two principal groups of Uthong images to illustrate the transformation from Khmer into Thai art traditions. Statuary in the first group dates to the 14th to 15th centuries and has Khmer characteristics, with shorter faces, more prominent chins, and sharp-edged legs originating mostly from Lopburi and Sanburi. Images in the second group have elongated oval faces analogous to the Sukhothai style and are most commonly found at Suphanburi and Ayutthaya. This latter group made up the direct ancestors of the Buddha images of the Ayutthaya School and were 'the work of Siamese artists who have tried to copy the Khmer and . . . fear[ed] to fall into the style of Sukhothai' (Cœdès 1928a; cited in Le May 2013[1938], 138). Le May suggested that the Bayon style of Khmer art played an important role in influencing the work of the 'Tai artists' by the end of the 12th century. Uthong art thus represents a natural development from the Khmer to the Tai. Early Tai-Khmer or Tai artists 'fashioned their images in their own localities and entirely independently of one another, until the School of Sukhothai eventually penetrated this region [the Lower-Central Siam] and cast its all-pervading influence over them [Khmer]' (Le May 2013[1938], 138–39). This shows that Sukhothai art, because it represented the first Thai style, had the power to change Khmer into Thai art and also that in this process it met with resistance. Such a narrative is similar to the account of fighting the Khmer at Sukhothai in Thailand's national history.

The standard stylistic classification of Uthong statuary, developed by Griswold and Buriphan (1952) and Thailand's national museums, divided the collections into three groups (Figure 31.1). Facial characteristics and aureole styles became the important criteria for classification. The first group (Style A) reflects a mix of Dvaravati and Khmer traditions. This style is characterised by features such as the cone-shaped aureole and is linked to the 11th-century Khmer occupation of Lopburi, when the official Dvaravati art was dominated by Angkorian. The second group (Style B) also shows Khmer influence in the face, specifically a band between the hair and forehead and a flame aureole. In the third group, Style C, we also see the band and a flame aureole, but the face is an elongated oval similar to that of Sukhothai art. The *Maravijayamudra* posture is common in Buddha statuary seated on a concave pedestal. While the dating is uncertain, it appears that Style A relates to the 12th or 13th centuries during the period of Khmer influence, with Style B developing slightly later and before the penetration of Sukhothai artistic ideals evident from Style C.

The last group started at some point after Ayutthaya was established and continued until the late 15th century (Griswold and Buriphan 1952, 30–32). Subhadradis Diskul, son of Damrong and creator of the Department of Art History at Silpakorn University, dated Uthong Style A to the 12th to 13th centuries and Style B to the 13th to 14th centuries. In this chronology Style C dates to the early Ayutthaya Period and more specifically to between the second half of the 14th and the first half of the 15th centuries (Diskul 1971[1970], 17; see also Leksukhum 2009, 96). Scholars in the 'Silpakorn school' still use this typology and dating, including most recently Saisingha, who (for example) placed Styles B and C in the early Ayutthaya Period and labelled Style A with the term 'Lopburi art' (Saisingha 2021, 124–52). However, these three styles of Uthong statuary have become an established typology used by national museums as a link between non-Thai and Thai arts. It should be noted here that Sakchai Saisingha proposes that Style A Uthong statues should be renamed 'Lopburi art' or the 'Lopburi Period' (*Smai Lopburi*) because they resemble the artistic styles of Angkor and Bayon (Saisingha 2021, 126–27).

Figure 31.1 Sequence of Uthong Art style based on classification by Griswold and Buriphan (1952): a) Style A, found at Wat Mahathat Sanburi (inventory no. อท.2); b) Style B, found at Lopburi (inventory no. อท.1); c) Style C, of unknown provenance (inventory no. อท.12) (1952, figs. 10, 11, 12).

While I agree with the need to generate a new name for this style, his use of Lopburi remains somewhat controversial, as it was coined in accordance with the anti-colonial Siam movement prevalent since the 1920s (Rienravee 2002). If Style A is in fact an off-shoot of Angkor's Bayon phase, and we also consider the lack of modern national borders during that time, it seems appropriate to employ the term 'post-Bayon art'.

Later attempts to define the Uthong art style—and the story of King Uthong itself—were initially complicated by Boisselier's (1966, 161–67) excavations at Uthong city which identified no archaeological evidence relating to this ruler. This excavation changed the term 'Uthong art' and its origin models for many Thai scholars. A few years later, senior archaeologist Manit Vallibhotama (1967, 1–33) proposed that Uthong art possibly originated from 'Ayodhaya city', which was the forerunner of Ayutthaya city located in the east of Ayutthaya. This was because, according to many primary sources, King Uthong ruled as the eighth king of this city, and many Dvaravati, Khmer, and Uthong statuaries were also found in this area. Thus, Manit Vallibhotama proposed the new term 'Ayodhaya art' to replace or be used along with the older term, although 'Uthong art' was also used as an umbrella term. In addition, he also noted that although this art was a consequence of Khmer Bayon art, it was created by the 'Thai ancestors (*Buraphachon khon Thai*)' rather than the Khmer (Vallibhotama 1967, 32–33). His work clearly reflects a strongly nationalistic view and uses this art as a starting point for Thai art.

The term 'Uthong art' is therefore interconnected with nationalistic sentiments. Uluchata's more complex conceptualisation considers Uthong art a product of many *nakhon or rattha*, meaning sovereign cities which served as political centres, each with different historical backgrounds and stylistic details. Stūpas, for example, were popular in Suphanburi city, while *prangs* were popular in Lopburi, but both cities produced Uthong statuary. Thus, both architectural constructions could not be separated into sub-schools or art traditions like Suphannabhumi art and Lavo or Lopburi art (Uluchata 1986, 77; 1997a[1973], 57–70). 'Uthong art' is therefore used as an umbrella term that encompasses stylistic variations within each city on the central plain of Thailand after Angkor (Uluchata 1983, 51–59). Uluchata's model has received little attention from mainstream scholars because it shows a problem of consistency in defining Uthong art—both the Buddha images and monuments—and a longer chronology of statues that he assumed continued from Dvaravati and Pala arts (from the 12th to 15th centuries) (Uluchata 1986, 75–89). While these competing views continue to shape our understanding of the development of, and debate over, Uthong styles, the primary issue remains the lack of direct dates for the statues themselves. The following section presents the first thermoluminescence dating of Uthong statuary and the implications of the standard and alternative hypotheses for the development of the broader styles. While previous work on Post-Angkorian Khmer Buddhas (e.g., Giteau 1975, 1–143; Polkinghorne et al. 2013) offers a basic framework for stylistic comparison, that cannot be used to assess the ages of objects recovered from the central plain of Thailand.

Thermoluminescence Dating and Changing the Sequences of Uthong Buddha Statues

Twelve bronze Uthong statues were selected from a broader collection of 22 museums across Thailand to be dated at the Thermoluminescence Laboratory at Kasetsart University. These samples were selected because there was enough clay core material on the interior surface of the statuary. Unfortunately, no Style A bronze Buddhas were sampled in the study due to insufficient quantities of clay core material within the collections. Analysis of Styles B and C was facilitated by the larger number housed within the national collections. In addition to having sufficient clay core material, eight of the sampled statues had known provenances from different sites in the central plain. The results of thermoluminescence (TL) are shown in Table 31.1.

TL dating was chosen for this project because of its accuracy, the possibility of running in-country analyses, and its affordability, the funds being provided by the Southeast Asian Academic Programme (SAAAP) at SOAS, University of London. TL is used to date the heating or firing of materials containing crystalline minerals such as ceramics, bronze casting cores, and heated soil. Bronze Uthong statues produced by the lost wax method were shaped around clay core materials that were heated to over 600 °C. A remnant of this clay core material, about 1–2 cm thick, is often left on the interior surface of the statue as part of the casting process, and a sample of this was collected for TL dating using the photon counter and thermoluminescence detector (see Won-in 2011, 3–5). When the absolute dating is acquired, it is then easier to place Uthong statues and architecture within the timeframe, which leads us to greater knowledge of the history of the 13th and 14th centuries. The results of the TL dating from Style B and C bronze Uthong Buddha images are shown in Table 31.1.

The TL results suggest that Uthong Style B statues were produced between 1277 ± 19 and 1320 ± 15 CE (Sample Nos. 1, 2, 3 4, 5) and align with previous research (e.g., 1971; Leksukhum 2009) that placed Style B between the pre- and early Ayutthaya Periods. Some uncertainty remains concerning the dating of this style. Saisingha (2021) suggests instead the early Ayutthaya Period. Thermoluminescence dating, however, does not provide a specific date range for Style B, for which relative dating methods must be used. The *Phongsawadan chabab Luang Prasert (the Luang Prasert version of the Ayutthaya Chronicle)*, written in 1680, noted that the giant Buddha image in Style B at Wat Panan Choeng (Figure 31.2a) was created in 1325 (Vachirayan Library 1914[1680], 115). No TL sample was taken from this giant Buddha image, but 2018 excavations of the Ayutthaya's earliest habitation layer yielded Yuan Period Cizao sherds (a small-mouth bottle or mercury jar) at a depth of 150 cm below the surface. This layer also yielded an AMS date of 620 ± 30 BP or 1298–1324 CE (Beta-540155) (Krajaejun 2021). Dates for the giant Buddha in the *Phongsawadan* coincide with documentary data and suggest that

Table 31.1 Thermoluminescence dating results from this study.

No.	*Inventory number*	*Provenance*	*Uthong style*	*TL lab ID.*	*Apparent age (BP)*	*Calendar date (CE)*
1	อท.19	Found in Kamphaeng Phet Province. Displayed at Bangkok National Museum.	B	A1739	743 ± 19	1277 ± 19
2	อท.4	Unknown provenance. Displayed at Bangkok National Museum.	B	A1740	739 ± 20	1281 ± 20
3	99/59/2554	Unknown provenance. Displayed at Bangkok National Museum.	B	A1743	718 ± 16	1302 ± 16
4	อท.1	Found at Wat Sao Tong Thong, Lopburi Province. Displayed at Bangkok National Museum.	B	A1737	707 ± 16	1313 ± 16
5	13/1164/2504	Found at Wat Thammikkarat, Ayutthaya, and made in the pre- or early Ayutthaya period. Displayed at Chao Sam Phraya National Museum.	B	A1735	700 ± 15	1320 ± 15
6	33/140/2544	Found in the main *prang* crypt of Wat Ratchaburana, Ayutthaya, and dated to 1424 CE. Displayed at Suphanburi National Museum.	C	A1734	700 ± 17	1320 ± 17
7	131	Found in the main *prang* crypt of Wat Ratchaburana, Ayutthaya. Displayed at Chao Sam Phraya National Museum.	C	A1736	675 ± 15	1345 ± 15
8	25/194/2526 (596/2526)	Unknown provenance. Displayed at Bangkok National Museum.	C	A1742	675 ± 19	1345 ± 19
9	No	A stupa crypt at Wat Mahathat Sankhaburi, Chai Nat Province.	B-C	A1693	654 ± 17	1366 ± 17
10	อท.18	Found at Nakhon Chaisri, Nakhon Pathom Province. Displayed at Bangkok National Museum.	C	A1738	632 ± 14	1388 ± 14
11	25/205/2524	Unknown provenance. Displayed at Bangkok National Museum.	C	A1741	615 ± 13	1405 ± 13
12	No	A stupa crypt at Wat Mahathat Sankhaburi, Chai Nat Province.	C	A1694	596 ± 17	1424 ± 17

Style B continued until 1325. It should be mentioned that around this period another giant Buddha image was built at Wat Thammikkarat. The senior archaeologist Manit Vallibhotama proposed that this giant head was the crucial evidence for proving the existence of 'Ayothaya city'—the city before the establishment of 'Ayutthaya' in 1351—because it was mentioned in the *Northern Chronicle (Phongsawadan Neu)* that this temple (*wat*) was built during the reign of Thammikkarat (r. 1165–1205) (Vallibhotama 1967, 13–14). This date is too early, however, but luckily a bronze Buddha image of Style B (Figure 31.2b) was found at this temple during its restoration by the Fine Arts Department, and its face is similar to the giant head. This statue (Sample 5, inventory no. 13/1164/2504) was TL dated to 1320 ± 15 CE in this project. It can be argued that in the 1320s Style B was very popular and that this also indicates that Ayutthaya/Ayodhaya had already become a large city by this time. After this date we do not have much evidence for Style B, which appears again in the early Ayutthaya Period. Two small gold Style B Buddha statues were found in the crypt of Wat Mahathat's northeastern corner *prang*, which was built in Ayutthaya between 1374 and 1384 (Vachirayan Library 1914[1680], 116). Given their stylistic coherence to Style B, it seems more likely that these very portable and precious objects were produced before 1374—or between 1374–1384—but Style B was still recognised as an important iconography of this period. It can be concluded that Style B was initially produced at least by 1277 (Sample No. 1), and the tradition possibly continued into the 1370s or 1380s.

Results from TL dating six samples suggest that Style C was produced from the early 14th through early 15th centuries (1320 ± 17–1424 ± 17 CE). This result indicates that Style C may have overlapped with Style B for a long period. The chronology of Style C contrasts with previous research, such as that of Diskul (1971[1970], 17), Leksukhum (2009, 156), and Saisingha (2021, 145–51), as seen from the fact that Style C was not produced after Style B, but rather they overlapped between 1320 and 1384 and then continued into the late 14th century. The new dating of Style C from TL reflects the problem of the unilinear evolution theory in Thai art history, which arranged the different artistic styles within the framework of a national history in which the Lopburi or Angkor Period emerged before the Sukhothai and Ayutthaya Periods. According to this

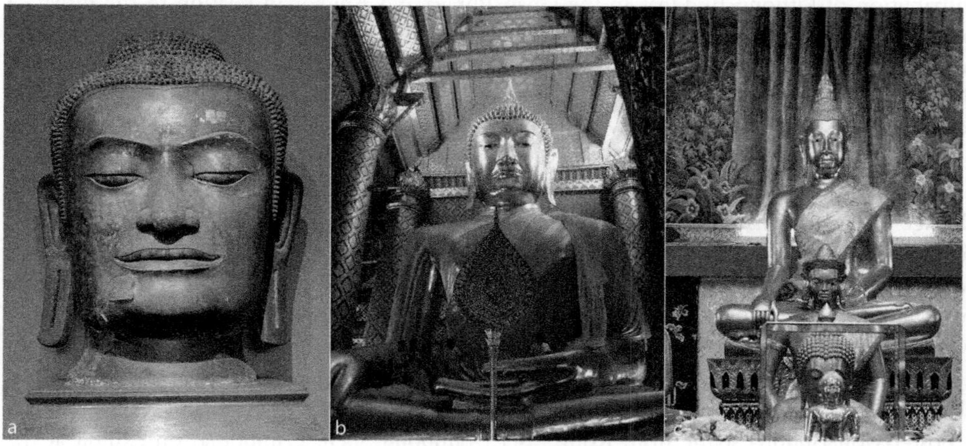

Figure 31.2 Examples of Buddha statues with traits of Style B and C: a) Style B—the main Buddha of Wat Panan Choeng temple, Ayutthaya; b) Style B giant bronze Buddha head, height 2 metres, Wat Thammikkarat, Chao Sam Phraya National Museum (inventory no. 17/05); c) Style C sandstone Buddha statue, Wat Lantakpha, Nakhon Pathom.

Source: (Photos P. Krajajeun).

framework, Style B, which has a Khmer-like face, was automatically presumed to have appeared before Style C. Another factor is that mainstream Thai art history placed the start of Style C in the early Ayutthaya Period, because it was assumed that Sukothai's political influence began during the reign of King Borommarachathirat I (r. 1370–1388), who married a Sukhothai princess (Leksukhum 1999, 16–17). Most art historians then assumed that Sukhothai's art influence began during this reign or during the early Ayutthaya Period, despite documentary and archaeological evidence that indicate the occupation of multiple contemporary polities (e.g., Lavo, Suphanburi, Ayodhaya) in the Lower Chao Phraya at the same time as Sukhothai (before 1351) (Cœdès 1941, 295–96; Phumisak 2004[1983], 31–47; Vallibhotama 1967, 1–33).

In general, Style C sandstone Buddha statues are common in the Lower Chao Phraya at sites such as Ayutthaya, Suphanburi, Nakhon Pathom, Ratchaburi, Phetchaburi, Lopburi, and Bangkok (Uluchata 1997a[1973], 57–70). Most Thai art historians associate Style C sandstone with the early Ayutthaya Period, not the pre-Ayutthaya Period (Chuvichean 2019, 60–88) based on the Khmer-style carving technique that was introduced after the invasion of Ayutthaya, while art historian Sakchai Saisingha suggests that Style C sandstone might have developed from the long-faced Lopburi sandstone Buddha statues which were influenced by Sukhothai, and he dates them all to the early Ayutthaya Period using the comparative method to analyse stucco motifs and styles of monuments (2013, 396–97). However, these statues have no calendar dating, and, as shown in Table 31.1, three samples of Style C, namely Nos. 6, 7, and 8, were produced before the Ayutthaya Period. The TL dates presented here require us to conclude that Style C should not be included within the Ayutthayan artistic tradition. This dating provokes us to reconsider the sandstone Buddha images in temples in the Chao Phraya that we cannot simplify to date them in the Ayutthaya Period. For example, the main Buddha of Wat Lantakpha temple (Nakhon Pathom, Chao Phraya), which itself was made from sandstone and gilded with gold (Figure 31.2c), shows stylistic parallels with sample Nos. 6, 8, and 11 and dates from 1320 ± 17 to 1388 ± 14 CE. Therefore, the timespan of Style C according to TL dating reminds us to carefully consider the variation of ages of Style C in the central plain.

This linear view of the chronology becomes problematic when we examine the geographic distribution of Uthong Buddhas in the Chao Phraya and Angkor in relation to the disparate models of multiple competing polities or a single unified state. Martin Polkinghorne has examined a group of Style C or Uthong sandstone images that were discovered at the Bayon temple dated to the first half of 15th century according to the historical incident when the Ayutthayan King Borommarachathirat II (Chao Sam Phraya, r. 1424–1448) invaded Angkor in 1431/1432 and a group of Uthong statues were deposited in the crypt of Wat Ratchaburana (Polkinghorne et al. 2013). It seems the early Ayutthaya Period has become the point of time for determining the age of the Ayutthayan influence in Angkor, but I propose it must be older than that. Connections between polities on the central plain of Thailand can be seen in the Siamese historical records as well. *The Chronicle of Siam: A Master Copy from the British Museum, London*, written in 1795, notes that Ramesuan ruled Lavo/Lopburi and was assigned by King Uthong to battle Kamboja (Angkor) (FAD 1964[1795], 20–22). Uthong statues reflect both locally distinct traits and a set of shared characteristics of post-Bayon art. For example, the Style B Uthong statue (Figure 31.3a) displayed at Sawanvoranayok National Museum in Sukhothai closely resembles a post-Bayon Buddha statue from Kong Pisei (Kampong Speu, Cambodia) on exhibit at the National Museum of Cambodia (Phnom Penh) (Figure 31.3b). Specific traits include the rectangular facial shape (or 'Khmer face'), flame aureoles on the skull-protuberances, the use of band belt robes, and the depiction of the double *abhaya* mudra. Seated Uthong statues in Styles B and C in the Chao Phraya also resemble many post-Bayon seated images in Angkor Thom, such as a post-Bayon frieze inside Prasat Ta Tuot (Figure 31.4). Jessup and Zephir suggest that

Figure 31.3 Comparison of Style B Uthong and post-Bayon Buddhas: a) Style B Uthong statue found in Sukhothai and now at Sawanvoranayok National Museum; b) post-Bayon Buddha statue found at Kong Pisei (Kampong Speu) and now at the National Museum of Cambodia, Phnom Penh.

Source: (Photo P. Krajaejun).

these post-Bayon statues, which date to between the second half of the 13th and the mid-14th centuries, were rarely made and show the influence of the Style B Uthong School. After the Bayon phase, Khmer Buddhist art clearly played a compelling role in the formation of Uthong art which reflects the establishment and development of the specific Theravāda iconography and aesthetic in the Chao Phraya (Jessup and Zephir 1997, 114–15). Krairiksh (2012, 343) suggests that Buddhist art in Thailand between the 12th and 14th centuries was possibly crafted by a Theravāda sect which emphasised the creation of images of Gautama Buddha seated in the

Figure 31.4 Post-Bayon Buddha frieze inside Prasat Ta Tuot, Angkor. Their faces and flame aureoles are similar to Style B and C Uthong Buddha statues.

Source: (Photo P. Krajaejun).

maravijaya mudra and wearing robes with one shoulder bare, which became characteristic of Theravāda Buddhism on the central plains of Thailand.

The Distribution of Uthong Sites: The Unity and Disunity

Most Uthong style statuary is associated with four major Chao Phraya and Tachin settlements—Lopburi, Ayutthaya, Sankhaburi, and Suphanburi (Cœdès 1928a, 33–35; Vallibhotama 1967, 1–3)—but the broader distribution of statues remains poorly documented. A further issue is that most Uthong Buddha statues from the Chao Phraya lack proper provenance, the majority being transported to temples in Bangkok in the early Rattanakosin Period (Chanprakhone 2004, 43), relocated to the national and provincial museums in the 19th–20th centuries, or stolen from temples in the last century. Nevertheless, my 2018–2019 archaeological survey found that Uthong statues, of sandstone in particular, have also been found concentrated in the Mae Klong and the lower part of the Chao Phraya River basins (Krajaejun 2021, 13–30). A valuable model for understanding the state polity on the central plain of Thailand was proposed by historian Thida Saraya (1989). In the Dvaravati Period, each river basin had its dominant city; for example, Nakhon Pathom was the centre of the Tachin, the Mae Klong had Kua Bua (in Ratchaburi), the Petchaburi had Cha-Um, and the Chao Phraya had Inburi (Singburi). These centres were surrounded by many small cities, like satellite towns, which supplied food and forest products. Saraya called this the 'riverine system'. As a model, it can be applied to the relationship between the distribution of Uthong statuary and state polities.

The number of Style A and Style B Uthong statues in each riverine system is many times less than that of Style C (see Table 31.2 and Figure 31.5). It is difficult to find the reason for this, because there are only a small number of documents that mention this period, but this lower number of statues may reflect the lessening of court patronage with the decline of Angkor in the first half of the 13th century and/or the shift to more perishable materials such as wood rather than stone for images, a technical trait characteristic of Post-Angkorian Cambodia (Giteau 1975, 27–28, 130, 135–137). The samples of Style A and Style B Uthong statues were found across the central plain, including Lopburi, Suphanburi, Sankhaburi, Sukhothai, Petchaburi, and Ayutthaya, and some sites are 12th-century Jayavarman VII temple sites (e.g., Lopburi, Sukhothai, Petchaburi), suggesting that some polities in this region, as with Post-Angkorian temples in the Siem Reap region of Cambodia (Thompson 1997, 28), were founded upon pre-existing Angkorian foundations. Most Style A and Style B Uthong Buddha images were found in Lopburi, but, as mentioned, the number of sites and statues shown here in some locations does not represent the real density of Uthong sites because many statues were removed to Bangkok and so on. For example, according to the historical record, in 1794 King Rama I ordered Phyarachniklom and Phyaraksamontien to collect Buddha statuaries in Lopburi and move them to Wat Phra Chetuphon in Bangkok. Historian Kitiyawadee Chanprakhone has suggested that Uthong Buddha statues may have come from Lopburi, Sanburi, Chainat, and the cities around Ayutthaya (Chanprakhone 2004, 43–45). However, the number of sites that appear in each city may at least indicate the domination of that city.

Table 31.2 Uthong sites identified in each river basin and city in Thailand based on 2018–2019 surveys.

River basin	*Sub-river basin*	*City*	*Number of sites*		
			Style A	*Style B*	*Style C*
Chao Phraya	Yom	Sukhothai	2	1	3
	Yom	Sri Satchalai	–	1	–
	Ping	Kampaeng Phet	–	2	1
	Nan	Phitsanulok	–	–	2
	Yom, Nan	Phichit	–	–	1
	Pasak	Phetchabun	–	1	–
	Pasak	Saraburi	–	1	1
	Loburi	Lopburi	5	4	10
	Mae Nam Noi	Sanburi	1	2	3
	Chao Phraya	Chainat	1	2	8
	Chao Phraya	Singburi	–	1	–
	Chao Phraya	Ang Thong	–	1	–
	Chao Phraya, Pasak, Lopburi	Ayutthaya	–	7	10
	Chao Phraya	Pathum Thani	–	1	2
	Chao Phraya	Nonthaburi	–	1	15
	Chao Phraya	Bangkok	–	–	25
Tachin	–	Suphanburi	2	7	15
	–	Nakhon Pathom	–	2	11
	–	Samut Sakhon	–	–	1
Mae Klong	–	Ratchaburi	1	1	50
	–	Samut Songkram	–	–	4
Phetchaburi	–	Phetchaburi	1	3	6
Total			13	38	168

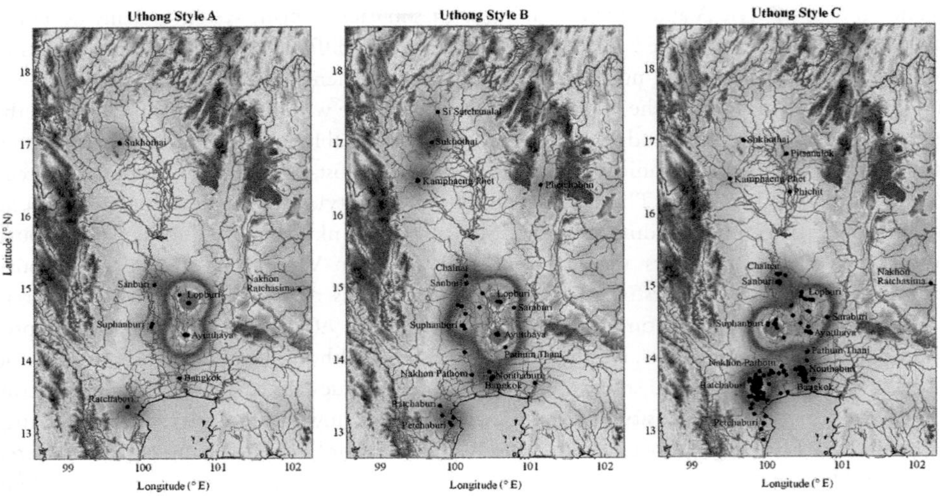

Figure 31.5 Distribution of Uthong Style A, B, and C Buddha statues on the central plain of Thailand.

During the 13th and 14th centuries, Lavo (or Lopburi in the Ayutthaya Period) became the dominant centre of the polity in the western part of the Chao Phraya, as can be seen from the fact that Lavo sent tribute missions to the Chinese court between 1289 and 1339 (Pelliot 1904, 240–44; Sun Lin 2013). Prince Damrong assumed that Ayodhaya was founded by the Khmer who ruled at Lopburi, specifically as it is located at the meeting of the Pa Sak, Lopburi, and Chao Phraya rivers. At that time, Ayodhaya was possibly an outpost and port for Lavo/Lopburi (Damrong 1924, 53–54). Lopburi and Ayodhaya were therefore directly connected through the Lopburi river, itself a tributary of the Chao Phraya. Many Style A and Style B Uthong statues, therefore, were discovered in Ayutthaya; for example, the majority of Style A and Style B bronze statues and numerous amulets came from the Wat Ratchaburana crypt (Chao Sam Phraya Museum 2020; Saisingha 2021, 124–46).

Style B is associated with 38 sites and is more widely spread throughout the central plain. It appears that between the 1270s and the 1380s, the school of Uthong art developed and appropriated a new standardised style, which might have related to the recent movement of Buddhist sects from Sri Lanka and Sukhothai. This latter shift is demonstrated through the flaming aureole found on Style B statues (Thammarungrueng 2020, 115–28). Figure 31.5 clearly shows that Style B can be divided into two clusters. The first cluster is in the Upper Chao Phraya, where one or two Buddha statues were found in each city, namely Si Satchanalai, Sukhothai, and Kampaengphet. These statues may have been brought here from the Lower Chao Phraya to there, because only a small number have been found. The second cluster was discovered in the Lower Chao Phraya, particularly in four major cities, Suphanburi, Lopburi, Petchaburi, and Ayutthaya.

Chinese documentary sources suggest that these four cities played important roles in the pre-Ayutthaya Period. For example, the 'Kan-mu-ting' (*kamrateng* in Khmer means king) of Petchaburi sent tribute to the Yuan court in 1294 (Flood 1969, 223–26), and legends suggest that King Uthong came from this city (Van Vliet 2005[1639], 13–14; La Loubère 2017, 42). Between 1292 and 1322, Xien (Suphanburi) sent envoys and tribute eight times to the Chinese court, while Lavo (Lopburi) did so five times between 1289 and 1298 (Pelliot 1904, 241–43; Promboon 1986). 'Ayodhdya', an early name for Ayutthaya, was mentioned in *The Northern*

Chronicle (*Phongsawadan Neu*) as a leading center with relations with China (Vallibhotama 1967, 13–14). The new TL dating of Style B, creation of the main Buddha statues for Wat Panan Choeng in 1325, and recovery of Cizao small-mouth bottles or mercury jars (noted previously) and Putian and Longquan green-glaze bowls also support the documentary evidence (Krajaejun 2021). In addition, Yuan ceramics were found from excavations by the Fine Arts Department in many sites (Uamthong 1999). The evidence therefore indicates that at this time Ayodhaya was a small port city from the 1320s before rising to be the centre of the Ayutthaya Kingdom. It can be concluded that in the late 13th to early 14th centuries, the increase of the number of Style B Uthong Buddha statues may reflect the increase in polities on Thailand's central plain that were independent from Angkor, and each named polity sent envoys to gain political legitimacy under China's imperial tribute system. However, they shared the same art style because Angkor was still the archetype and ideology, but this style was changed when intensively contacted by Sukhothai.

Uthong Style C paralleled Style B from the 1320s to the 1380s and then grew in frequency into the early 15th century (Figure 31.5). The number of Style C statues increased significantly in this period, appearing at 168 sites throughout the central plain and at every major center. The highest density of Style C appearing in the lower central plain can be divided into two clusters. The first cluster is the inland cities including Ayutthaya, Suphanburi, Lopburi, Chainat, and Sankhaburi, while the second is near the coastal or hinterland cities, such as Ratchaburi, Petchaburi, Nonthaburi, and Bangkok. The second cluster of Style C (see Figure 31.5c) in the hinterland cities of each river basin is interconnected with their roles as port cities, namely Suphanburi, Ayutthaya, and Lopburi. Even though Table 31.2 shows the number of Uthong statue sites is fewer than in some cities such as Bangkok, Nonthaburi, and Ratchaburi, they still acted as satellite cities in historical documents. The majority of Style C statues are the main Buddha image in temples made of sandstone, while those examples recovered from crypt deposits are bronze. Saisingha (2013, 395–400) suggests that the Style C sandstone statue developed from a group of long-faced sandstone Lopburi Buddha statues (post-Bayon or Uthong Style A), and he has found many samples in Lopburi and Ayutthaya which have been influenced by Sukhothai art. Red sandstones, perhaps quarried from Photharam (Rachaburi), are most common in sites in the western Chao Phraya. White sandstone statues, likely quarried from Sikhio (Nakhon Ratchasima), were more common in the eastern Chao Phraya. Therefore, it is possible that the Style C sandstone statue may have developed from these two cities before spreading to other cities.

The sudden prevalence of Style C at both inland and hinterland centers in this period potentially reflects the transformation of Uthong art—and the octagonal stūpa—into emblems of a unified and independent Ayutthaya (see Figure 31.6 and Table 31.1). A Style C sandstone walking statue housed in Ayutthaya's Chantharakasem National Museum has an inscribed date (1375) that falls under the reign of King Borammarachathirat I or Khunluang Pha Ngua, who ruled Ayutthaya from 1370–1388 (Pakdeekam 2017, 44–47). Yet TL samples 6 and 7 (Table 31.1) suggest that Style C emerged before 1351 (or before the Ayutthaya Period). According to the *Jinakalamali* (Lanna chronicle), the wife of King Borammarachathirat I was a Sukhothai princess (Rattanapanyathera 1972[1517; 1528], 295–96). So the relationship between Suphanburi/Suphannabhumi (Tachin River Basin) and Sukhothai predates the reign of King Borammarachathirat I. Ophakul (2004[1985], 75–77) noted that almost all of the many damaged stūpas and Buddha statues from Suphannabhumi were Style C.

Nearly 500 late Uthong (Style C) statues have been recorded from the 30–40 Suphanburi temples, and the crypt of the main *prang* at the city's central Wat Phra Sri Rattana Mahathat contained 200 bronze statues in Style B and Phra Ti Sang Nai Smai Uthong ton pai, or Style C

Figure 31.6 Four bronze miniature stūpas typical of the Pre-Ayutthaya and Ayutthaya Periods: a) unknown provenance, Bangkok National Museum (inventory no. ลบ. 344) (photo courtesy of Rungroj Piromanukul); b) Suphanburi in 1927, Suphanburi National Museum (inventory no. 33/104/2544); c) Wat Phrapai Luang, Sukhothai, Sukhothai National Museum (inventory no. 12/1134/2508); d) Lopburi, Narai Palace National Museum (inventory no.66/2540).

Source: (Photos P. Krajajeun).

(Opakul 2004, 76). Four golden inscriptions found in the crypt stated that Borammarachathirat II (Chao Sam Phraya), King of 'Ayochachaya' (Ayutthaya), ordered the construction of this 'stūpa' or *prang* around 1447 for his father, who had ruled Suphanburi after his father, King Borammarachathirat I (Opakul 2004, 77–86; Pakdeekam and Pakdeekam 2019, 226–30). It was also Borammarachathirat I whose forces, in 1433 or 1434, sacked Angkor Thom. Perhaps, then, the continuity in Style C (and the octagonal-shaped stūpa style) reflects the Suphanburi lineage and a royal patronage style that also appeared at Ayutthaya during the reign of King Borammarachathirat I, ruler of Suphanburi.

'Uthong' Architecture

Debates over 'Uthong' architecture have addressed similar issues: which architectural styles can be defined as 'Uthong', what unifies them, and their construction date range. Two main architectural styles defined within 'Uthong' architecture are the prang (in some contexts called *prasāt*) and octagonal-based stūpas (Uluchata 1986, 75–90; Leksukhum 2009, 157). Ulachata, a pioneer in defining Uthong architecture (1893, 1896), referred to this style as 'Pre-Ayutthaya art'. He pointed out that the Uthong or Lavo dynasty preferred prang, because this dynasty descended from the Khmers and they had close relationships with Angkor. However, the prang differed from the Angkorian prototype *prasāt* in the decoration on the base and the fact that the buildings are quite high. This architectural style came to be called 'Lavo art'. By contrast, the Suphanabhum family preference for octagonal-based stūpas was based on Suphanburi more proximal access to influences from Pala, Pagan, Hariphunchai, and Lanna art. This idea was ultimately rejected because his dating was too old and did not correlate with the pre-Ayutthaya Period (see Leksukhum 1999, 78 and footnote 57).

The main prang of Wat Mahathat Lopburi was constructed no later than the second half of the 13th century, based on a range of mid- to late 13th-century estimates (e.g., Boisselier 1965;

Leksukhum 2009, 157; Saisingha 2016, 18–58; Woodward 1975, 1–15); Longquan and Dehua Chinese ceramics recovered from our 2019 excavations of the main *prang* at Lopburi and a TL date of 1289 ± 18 CE from its brick foundation (Kasetsart University, Lab no. A1730/Monument #003) support this date range. A second prang style at Wat Mahathat Lopburi, *Prang Kleeb Maphueng*, illustrates a local innovation whose top component has devas whose faces resemble Uthong Style B. Uluchata (1997b, 180–83) therefore assumed that this could be classified as Uthong art and dated it to before the foundation of Ayutthaya. In contrast, Saisingha dated the building of this prang to the early Ayutthaya Period based on the presence of triangular moulding on its base (2016, 115–21). TL of a brick from the base recovered from our excavations dated it to 1347 ± 15 CE (A1720) (Krajaejun 2021, 476). This *prang* style is therefore a product of the pre-Ayutthaya Period, which then spread to Sankhaburi city in the north of the central plain (Ulachata 1997b, 180–83; 1999[1972], 14–26). The main *prang* of Wat Mahathat Lopburi became the prototype for subsequent prang constructions at Ayutthaya—such as Wat Phutthai Sawan, Wat Mahathat Ayutthaya, Wat Ratchaburana—to symbolise kingship and the universe. The *Prang Kleeb Maphueng* style gained favour during the pre- and early Ayutthaya Periods following the decline of the Lavo family after the death of King Ramathibodi. These quintessential Lopburi prang styles might also reflect the emergence of new art styles as Chao Phraya populations asserted their new identity after the fall of Angkor.

The pre-Ayutthaya and Ayutthaya high octagonal-based stūpa was the dominant form of architecture in Suphanburi, Sankhaburi, and Ayutthaya. This stūpa style reflects the reach of Angkor's influence to Thailand's central plains. A group of Khmer miniature stūpas were quite popular in Lopburi, Suphanburi, and Sukhothai but also indicate local stylistic developments (Figure 31.6). The art historian Piriya Krairiksh suggested that these miniature stūpas show a mix of earlier styles and the Pala-Sena Indian style which was created under Tantric Buddhism, as seen from the decoration of many Buddha images around the stūpas, and they were produced during the second half of the 13th century (2012, 371–73). Although the exhibition at King Narai National Museum classifies this miniature stūpa style as Bayon art and dates it to the first half of the 13th century, this stūpa style was not used in the Bayon, and it should therefore be classified as a post-Bayon form. Thai art historians such as Uluchata (1986) and Saisingha (2016) have suggested that the Uthong high octagonal-based stūpa was inspired by the Khmer/Lopburi miniature stūpa. Uluchata instead suggested that the pre- and early Ayutthaya high octagonal-based stūpa style initially developed from the Dvaravati stūpa, which was influenced by Pala art, and was then influenced by Bayon art and developed into the Lopburi miniature stūpa, subsequently mixing with Lanna and Sukhothai art. Examples of these Uthong stūpas are found today at Wat Phra Kaew and Wat Mahathat in Sankhaburi, Wat Phra Rup, and Wat Phra In in Suphanburi and Wat Yai Chai Mongkon in Ayutthaya, which range in dates between the 10th and 13th centuries (Uluchata 1986, 76–81). Saisingha suggested another influence from the northern schools, namely the Hariphunchai octagonal stūpa plan at Wat Kukud in Lamphun (near Chiangmai), and the Sukhothai traits like niches known as *krob nanang* and the decorated walking Buddha images. The stūpas at Wat Phra Kaew and Wat Phra Rup, created during the second half of the 14th century or the early Ayutthaya Period, therefore relate to the rise of the power of King Borommarachathirat I (Saisingha 2016, 151–57).

Controversies in the dating of Uthong architecture parallel the situation with Uthong statues. Our excavation at the main stūpa of Wat Mahathat at Sankhaburi employed absolute techniques and stratigraphic sequences to enhance the dating based on art historical sources. Pramet Wichachu's digital reconstruction also provides a useful interpretation of its original form, which was similar to Wat Phra Kaew and Wat Phra Rup and consisted of a stūpa in three main parts: the square lower base decorated with niches; the octagonal plan in the middle with eight niches; and the circular bell at the top, with an octagonal *harmika*. A brick from the collapsed main stūpa of Wat Mahathat Sankhaburi was dated by TL dating to 1344 ± 15 CE (A1804), which links it to the pre-Ayutthaya Period (Krajaejun 2021, 668). Style C Uthong statues are also associated with the high octagonal-based stūpa, as seen in the main Buddha statue of Wat Phra Kaew (Saisingha 2016, 153) and the base of the Wat Phra Rup stūpa, where three sandstone Buddha statues were found (Morradoklok 1994, fig. 89). It can be concluded that the popularity of Style C and the high octagonal-based stūpa arose in conjunction with the domination of the Suphanburi family. After the death of King Ramathibodi in 1369, the Lavo and Suphanburi families fought with each other, but finally, the Suphanburi family gained victory and took the throne of Ayutthaya. This incident was reflected through a mixture of architectural style and influences. The most important example is Wat Ratchaburana, where the main *prang* built at the centre is surrounded by four octagonal, high-based stūpas in brick placed at the four corners. It reflects the succession of the combination of those two families or state polities, where the prang generally represents the identity of Lavo architecture and Mount Sumeru and the stūpa the identity of Suphanburi architecture and the four continents at the same time.

Conclusion

The fluorescence of multiple statuary and stūpa art styles during this Uthong Period reflects the complex politics and religions of the central plain of modern-day Thailand and Angkor. It also challenges conventional models of linear progress in Thai art history. Uthong Buddha statues reflected and projected an Angkorian style in conceptual terms and melded the Khmer Empire's political and aesthetic power to generate cohesion over time and space in the Menam Basin. As Angkor's influence waned, we see the rise of multiple smaller polities in this region and a broader, local artistic evolution between the 13th and early 15th centuries.

Disarticulating art historical from nationalist arguments to understand the Uthong tradition is challenging, particularly in explaining the timing and meaning of Styles A and B and that contentious transition from 'Khmer' to 'Thai'. The innovative application of TL dating to statuary presented here helps us move beyond stylistic conjecture and ground the sequence of artistic development more clearly and connect the sequence of artistic development more clearly to the rise of Ayutthaya. The establishment of an Ayutthayan art style, which drew from but also developed independently from Angkor, was part of the broader economic shift in power from an inwardly focused agricultural state to a thriving trading port within early modern Southeast Asia. Regardless of their final political forms, this chapter has highlighted our ability to track and follow the deep roots of Angkor's legacy within the Post-Angkorian world in the central plain of Thailand.

References

Baker, C., 2001. The Antiquarian society of Siam: speech of King Chulalongkorn. *Journal of the Siam Society* 89(1&2), 95–99.

Boisselier, J., 1965. Récentes recherches archéologiques en Thailande. Rapport préliminaire de mission (25 juillet-28 novembre 1964). *Arts Asiatiques* 12, 125–174.

Boisselier, J., 1966. U-Thong et son importance pour l'histoire de thaïlande et nouvelles données sur l'histoire ancienne de thaïlande, in *Boran Vittaya Rueang Muang Uthong (Archaeology of Uthong City)*, translated by Subhadradis Diskul. Bangkok: Sivaporn Printing.

Chanprakhone, K., 2004. *The Studies of the Buddha Images at the Inner Side Cloister of the Ubosoth Wat Pra Chetuphon Vimolmangklaram Rajchaworamahaviharn*. MA dissertation. Bangkok: Silpakorn University.

Chao Sam Phraya Museum, 2020. *Raikarn Boran Watthu Silpa Uthong, Phiphitthaphanthasathanhaengchat Chao Sam Phraya (Inventory of Uthong Art Objects in Chao Sam Phraya Museum, Fine Arts Department).* Ayutthaya: Fine Arts Department.

Chuvichean, P., 2019. *Ayutthaya Nai Yan Krung Thep: Silpakam Ti Samphan Kab Maenam Lam Klong (Ayutthaya in Bangkok: Work of Arts in the River Systems).* Bangkok: Matichon Publishing House.

Cœdès, G., 1928a. *Les Collections Archéologiques du Musée National de Bangkok.* Ars Asiatica; Paris; Bruxelles: Les Éditions G. van Oest.

Cœdès, G., 1928b. *Boranwatthu Nai Phiphitthasathan Samrab Phra Nakorn (Archaeological Collections in Bangkok National Museum).* Bangkok: Sophon Phiphat Thanakorn Printing House.

Cœdès, G., 1941. La stèle du Práḥ Khằn d'Aṅkor. *Bulletin de l'École française d'Extrême-Orient* 41, 255–302.

Damrong, R. [Prince], 1924. *Sadaeng Banyai Phonsawadan Siam (Lecture on History of Siam).* Bangkok: Prasert Samud Publishing.

Damrong, R. [Prince], 1974[1944]. *Nothan Borankhadi (The Legends and Archaeological Stories).* Bangkok: Khangvittaya.

Diskul, S., 1971[1970]. *Art in Thailand: A Brief History, 2nd ed.* Bangkok: Silpakorn University.

FAD (Fine Arts Department), 1964[1795]. *Phraratcha phongsawadan krung Siam chak ton chabab ti pen khong British Museum Krung London (The Chronicle of Siam: A Master Copy from the British Museum, London),* edited by Montri Amatayakul. Bangkok: Fine Arts Department, and Kawna Printing.

Flood, E.T., 1969. Sukhothai-Mongol relations: a note on relevant Chinese and Thai sources (with translations). *Journal of the Siam Society* 57(2), 203–257.

Giteau, M., 1975. *Iconographie du Cambodge Post-Angkorien. Publications de l'École Française d'Extrême-Orient volume C.* Paris: École française d'Extrême-Orient.

Griswold, A.B. & Boribhan Buriphan, 1952. *Silpawatthu Nai Phiphitthasathan Haeng Chat (Art Objects in Bangkok National Museum).* Bangkok: Phakdī Pradit.

Jessup, H.I. & T. Zephir, 1997. *Sculpture of Angkor and Ancient Cambodia: Millennium of Glory.* Washington and Paris: Thames and Hudson.

Kasetsiri, C., 2015. *Studies in Thai and Southeast Asian Histories.* Bangkok: The Foundation for the Promotion of Social Science and Humanities Textbooks Project and Toyota Thailand Foundation.

Keyes, C.F., 1991. The case of the purloined lintel: the politics of Akhmer shrine as a Thai national treasure, in *National Thai Identity and Its Defenders: Thailand, 1939–1989*, eds. C.J. Reynolds. Monash Papers on Southeast Asia No. 25. Clayton, Victoria, Australia: Monash University Centre for Southeast Asian Studies, 261–292.

Krairiksh, P., 2012. *The Roots of Thai Art.* Bangkok: River Books.

Krajaejun, P., 2021. *Borankadi Nai Yukroitor Nai Chong Phutthasattawat Ti 18–19 (The Archaeology of the Transition Period in the 13th–14th Centuries).* Bangkok: Fine Arts Department.

La Loubère, S. de, 2017. *Chodmaihet La Loubère Ratcha Anachak Siam (The Kingdom of Siam Simon de la Loubère),* translated in Thai by Sant Komonbutra. Bangkok: Sri Panya.

Laomanacharoen, S., 2016. Samai (Silpa) Uthong: Phad luead Khom peinpen luead Thai (Uthong Art: Transforming Khmer Art to Thai Art), in *Yook mued khong prawattisadthai (The Dark Ages of Thai History),* eds. Pipad Krajaejun. Bangkok: Matichon Publishing House.

Le May, R., 2013[1938]. *A Concise History of Buddhist Art in Siam.* Cambridge: Cambridge University Press.

Leksukhum, S., 1999. *Silpa Ayutthaya: Nganchangluang haeng phandin (Ayutthaya Art: The Royal Art of Thailand).* Bangkok: Muang Boran Publishing House.

Leksukhum, S., 2009. *Karn Roemton Lae Karn Sueb Nueang Ngan Chang Nai Sasana: Prawattisat Silpa Thai Chabab Yo (The Beginning and Continuity of Religious Artworks: A Brief History of Art History in Thailand), 4th ed.* Bangkok: Muang Boran Publishing House.

Lohphetrat, S., 1996. *Phraphuttharub Silpa Samai Ayutthaya (Buddha Images in the Ayutthaya Art Period).* Bangkok: Dansutha Printing.

Lowman, I. N., 2011. *The descendants of Kambu: the political imagination of Angkorian Cambodia.* PhD dissertation. Berkeley: University of California, Berkeley.

Mongkut, [King], 1851. Brief history of Siam, with a detail of the leading events in its annals. *The Chinese Repository* 20(7), 345–363.

Morradoklok Company Ltd., 1994. *Rai-Ngan Karn Burana Chedi Wat Phra Rup, Thambon Tha Phi Liang, Amphur Muang, Jangwat Shupanburi (The Restoration Report of Wat Phra Rup, Tha Pi Liang, Amphur Muang, Shupanburi).* Shupanburi: The Second Regional Office of Fine Arts Department Suphanburi.

Ophakul, M., 2004[1985]. *Prawattisat Maung Suphan (A History of Suphanburi).* Bangkok: Matichon Publishing House.

Pakdeekam, S., 2017. Silajaruk lang phaphuttharup pang leela: "Silajaruk" lakrak klong ayutthaya ti konpubmai (The inscription of the walking Buddha statue: the new discovery and the oldest Ayutthaya inscription). *Silpawatthanatham Magazine* 38(7), 44–47.

Pakdeekam, S. & N. Pakdeekam, 2019. *Prawatisat Ayutthaya Chak Juk: Jaruk Smai Ayutthaya (The History of Ayutthaya from Inscriptions: Ayutthaya Inscriptions)*. Bangkok: The Historical Society under the Royal Patronage of H.R.H. Princess Mahachakri Sirindhorn.

Peleggi, M., 2004. Royal antiquarianism: European orientalism and the production of archaeological knowledge in Siam, in *Asia in Europe, Europe in Asia*, eds. S. Ravi, M. Rutten & B. Goh. Leiden: International Institute for Asian Studies. Singapore: Institute of Southeast Asian Studies, 133–161.

Peleggi, M., 2017. *Monastery, Monument, Museum: Sites and Artifacts of Thai Cultural History*. Honolulu: University of Hawai'i Press.

Pelliot, P., 1904. Deux itinéraires chinois de chine en inde à la fin du viiie siècle. *Bulletin de l'École française d'Extrême-Orient* 4, 241–243.

Phumisak, Chit, 2004[1983]. *Sangkom Thai Lum Chao Phraya Kon Smai Krung Sri Ayutthaya (The History of the Pre-Ayutthaya Period in the Chao Phraya River Basin), 3rd ed*. Bangkok: Pha Diao Kan.

(PKKSA) Prachum kamhaikarn Krung Sri Ayutthaya, 2010[1767]. *Kamhaikarn Chao Krung Kao (The Testimony of Ayutthaya Captive), in Prachum kamhaikarn Krung Sri Ayutthaya (The Anthology of Ayutthaya Testimonies)*. Bangkok: Saeng Dow Publishing Company.

Polkinghorne, M., C. Pottier & C. Fischer, 2013. One Buddha can hide another. *Journal Asiatique* 301(2), 575–624.

Prakitnoonthakarn, C., 2014. *Rethinking Tamnan Phutthachedi Siam: The Rise of New Plot within Thai Art History* (Paper presented at the 12th International Conference on Thai Studies, 22nd–24th April 2014). Sydney: University of Sydney.

Promboon, S., 1986. Xian Nai Chodmaihet Chin, (Xian in Chinese Records). *Panha Nai Prawattisat Thai (The Problems in Thai History)* 1(1), 85–90.

Rattanapanyathera, P., 1972[1517; 1528]. *Jinakalamali, trans. Monvitoon, Saeng*. Bangkok: Fine Arts Department.

Rienravee, K., 2002. *Umnat Kong Ong-Kwaam-Ru Nai Ngan Watakarm Tang Prawattisat-Silpa Lae Borankadee Nai Prathes Thai (The Power of the Knowledge in the Discourse of the History of Khmer Art and Archaeology in Thailand)*. MA dissertation. Bangkok: Thammasat University.

Saisingha, S., 2013. *Phraphurtharub Nai Prathes Thai: Rubbab, Phatthanakarn, Lae Kwamchua Khong Khon Thai (Buddha Images in Thailand: Typology, Development and Belief in the Thai)*. Bangkok: Samaphan Printing.

Saisingha, S., 2016. *Lopburi Lang Watthanatham Kamen (Lopburi in the Period of Post Khmer Culture)*. Bangkok: Matichon Publishing House.

Saisingha, S., 2021. *Phraphuttharub Phraphim Chak Kru Phra Prang Wat Ratchaburana (Buddha Statues and Amulets from the Crypt of Wat Ratchaburana, Phra Nakorn Sri Ayutthaya)*. Bangkok: Muang Boran Publishing House.

Saraya, T., 1989. *(Sri) Dvaravati: Prawattisat Yuk Ton Klong Siamprathes ((Sri) Dvaravati: The Initial Phase of Siam's History)*. Bangkok: Muang Boran Publishing House.

Somkiet, L., 1996. *Phraphuttharub Silpa Samai Ayutthaya (Buddha Images in the Ayutthaya Art Period)*. Bangkok: Dansutha Printing.

Thammarungrueng, Rungroj, 2020. *Buddhasilpa Thai Sai Samphan Kab Sri Langka (The Relationship between Thai and Sri Lanka Arts)*. Bangkok: Princess Maha Chakri Sirinhord Anthropology Centre.

Thompson, A., 1997. Changing perspectives: Cambodia after Angkor, in *Sculpture of Angkor and Ancient Cambodia: Millennium of Glory*, eds. H.I. Jessup & T. Zephir. Washington: National Gallery of Art, 22–32.

Uamthong, R., 1999. *Rai-ngan Karn Khud Khon – Khud Tang Lae Ok-bab Phue Karnburana Boransathan Wat Sika Samut Changwat Phra Nakhon Sri Ayutthaya (The Report of Excavation-Restoration and Design for Restoring Wat Sika Samud Ruin, Ayutthaya)*. Ayutthaya: The Conservation and Development of Ayutthaya Historical Park, Fine Arts Department and Surasak Construction Co., Ltd.

Uluchata, P., 1983. Phraphuttharub kon krung sri ayutthaya pre-Ayutthaya Buddha images. *Muang Boran Journal* 9(3), 51–58.

Uluchata, P., 1986. *Kwaam Penma Khong Satup Chedi Nai Siam Prathes (The History of stūpas and Chedi in Siam)*. Bangkok: Maung Boran Publishing House.

Uluchata, P., 1997a[1973]. *Silpakarm haeng Anachak Sri Ayutthaya (The Art of the Ayutthaya Kingdom), 2nd ed*. Bangkok: Thanesavara Publishing.

Uluchata, P., 1997b. *Silpa Kon Krung Sri Ayutthaya (The Art of Pre-Ayutthaya)*. Bangkok: Muang Boran Publishing House.

Uluchata, P., 1999[1972]. *Teaw Muang Silpa Uthong (Travel to Cities of Uthong Art)*. Bangkok: Ton Aoe Publishing House.

Vachirayan Library, 1914[1680]. Phra ratcha phongsawadan chabab luang prasert (Ayutthaya chronicle, Luang phrasert version), in *Prachum Phongsawadan Lemthi Neung (The Anthology of Chronicles volume 1)*. Bangkok: Thai Printing House.

Vallibhotama, M., 1967. *Silpa Samai Uthong (The Uthong Art Period)*. Bangkok: Fine Arts Department.

Van Vliet, J., 2005[1639]. *Phongsawadan Krung Sri Ayutthaya Chabab Van Vlie (The Chronicle of Ayutthaya, van Vliet Version), translated by. Wanasri Samonsen*. Bangkok: Matichon Publishing House.

Won-in, K., 2011. *Karnsuksa Thoraninsanthan Boriwen Langtaoboran Mae Nam noi, Changwat Singburi Lae Karnkamnod Aryu Taoboranduaywithiruengsangkwamron: Rainganvijaichababsomboon (Geomorphologic Study on Maenam Noi Ancient Kiln Changwat Singburi and Thermoluminescence Dating Applied to Bricks from Ancient Kiln)*. Bangkok: Thailand Science Research and Innovation (TSRI).

Woodward, H., 1975. *Studies in the art of Central Siam, 950-1350 A.D.* PhD dissertation. New Haven: Yale University.

Woodward, H.W. & J.G. Douglas, 1994/1995. The Jayabuddhamahānātha Images of Cambodia. *The Journal of the Walters Art Gallery* 52/53, 105–111.

32

MAINLAND SOUTHEAST ASIA AFTER ANGKOR

On the Legacies of Jayavarman VII

Ashley Thompson

> Using sacred knowledge from the past, the king has built this bridge to ultimate happiness for someone else—a bridge which he regards as the continuity, long interrupted, of the Dharma. As the first to safeguard this continuity, he says this to kings yet to come, who will safeguard this continuity in the future:
>
> [. . .]
>
> I have done these good works with the greatest devotion in memory of my parents. . . . For kings who likewise acknowledge their indebtedness to the past, it is enough that they safeguard these good works of mine to obtain the abundant rewards of one who propagates the Dharma.
>
> Kings will in any case put into effect the work of protecting the foundations of their predecessors without being asked, as they are bound by precept to do so. I am aware of this, yet I request you, kings of the future, to be—of your own accord—insatiably zealous in protecting my foundations.'
>
> (K. 908, st. 173–6, from Preah Khan temple, Angkor. Translation by T. Maxwell 2007, 103–05, with minor stylistic modifications)

> A monument does not commemorate or celebrate something that happened but confides to the ear of the future the persistent sensations that embody the event.
>
> *(Deleuze and Guattari 1994, 176)*

Conceptualising Angkorian Legacies

The reach of Angkor will always exceed the territorial and temporal delimitation which scholars and politicians alike seek to give it; indeed, attempts to pin down dates and borders shed light on the very uncontainability of empire which defines empire, so to speak, at its core. While historians continue to debate if Angkor qualified, empirically, as an empire and, if so, when exactly it did so during the five centuries that the capital was centred on Cambodia's Tonle Sap plain (Bourdonneau 2014; Mikaelian 2015; Thompson 2016, esp. 59–65; Lowman

DOI: 10.4324/9781351128940-39

et al. 2023, this volume), the reach of Angkorian constructs beyond Angkor in space and time demonstrates how it finished quite literally in reaching beyond itself, making it, metaphorically and retrospectively, always an empire. As our day and age so vividly and urgently attest, here and there, empires loom large in their own aftermath. We find ourselves stumbling over their ruins—material and immaterial remains alike.

This chapter will look beyond Cambodia as we know it today in geographic terms, and beyond the early 13th century, to highlight legacies of Angkor beyond Angkor on the Southeast Asian mainland (see Figure 32.1). To begin this exploration, allow me to point out the discreetly deceptive premises of this chapter's title: that we all, author and readers alike, share established understandings of what Angkor was as of what a legacy is. Alas, we cannot pretend to stand on such firm ground. Instead, with reference to the opening epigraphs, I propose a working definition of Angkor as legacy. The conceptual assimilation of 'Angkor' and 'legacy' is of course another temporising gloss on empire: where the present, commemorating what has been as a means of heralding what will be, is always already gaining time for itself.

The first epigraph is extracted from the closing stanzas of a Sanskrit *prasasti*, or praise poem, recording the foundation of Preah Khan temple at Angkor in the late 12th century. In its content, the text celebrates the temple and its founder, King Jayavarman VII (r. 1181–1220), as well as the King Father to whom the temple is dedicated and for whom it serves as a posthumous abode. In its form, the text celebrates its own composer, the first-born son of Jayavarman VII's first wife, as he makes himself known at the poem's end—effectively giving himself the last word. The 'bridge' of the text is the temple of Preah Khan conceived as a realisation or embodiment of the Buddhist Dharma, where the deceased father, embodied in a statue of the compassionate bodhisattva Lokeśvara, is to find 'ultimate happiness.' The appearance of the term *sthiti*, translated here as 'continuity', thrice in quick succession performatively conveys the purpose

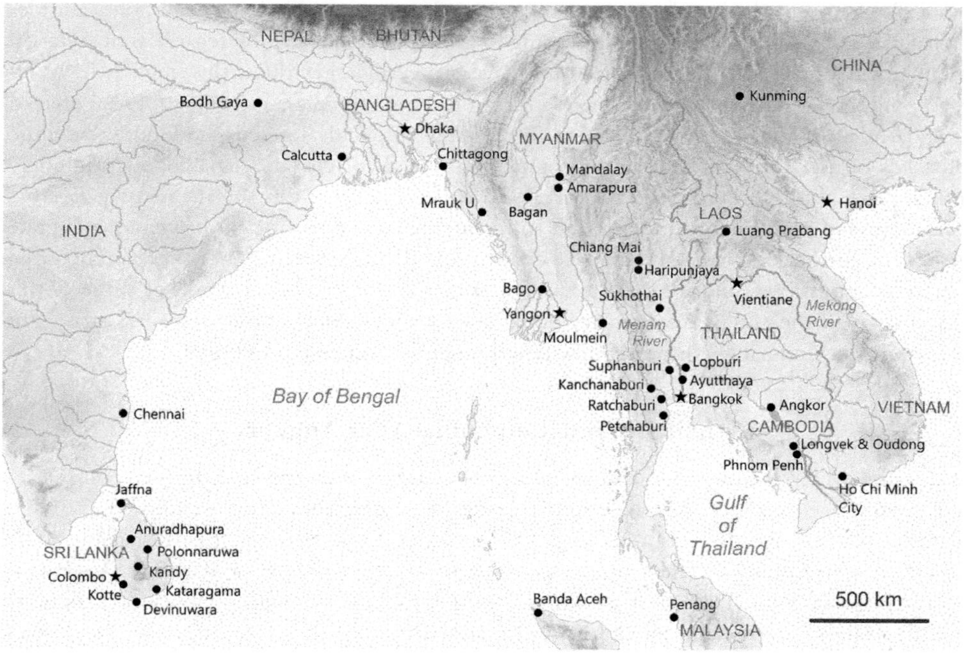

Figure 32.1 12th–18th c. mainland Southeast Asian sites mentioned in the text.

of the highly wrought architectural and poetic constructions. Jayavarman VII makes much of having vanquished Cham occupiers of Angkor and a challenger to the throne and so knowing first-hand the risk of interruption; his abundant works, recorded and thus supplemented by his son, were conceived as the means of ensuring continuity from father—past and present—to son, as from king to king. Apostrophising kings-to-come as protectors of the Dharma, the future is explicitly and officially heralded in these commemorative works. To pursue Éric Bourdonneau's reminder in his work on early Southeast Asian state formation, that the word 'state' derives from the Latin *status* designating 'that which stands' (2005, 419), I note that the 'state' and sthiti both stem from the proto-Indo-European root, *stā, 'to stand firmly'—the 'State' being the outcome, the exemplar, and the insurer of stability as continuity. What sthiti conveys, in and of itself and the more so in its insistent repetition in the voice of Jayavarman VII's eldest son as he prepares to ventriloquise his father, is that though leaders may come and go, if they are meritorious in preserving the Dharma, their State endures.

The way in which the 'Dharma' famously holds together two apparently mutually incompatible modalities is instructive here. The Dharma is at once descriptive and prescriptive; it is Natural Law (a description of the way things are) and moral or juridical law (a prescription of the way things should be). It endures, always; yet, in equal measure, it must always be activated. Dharma is a model of legacy, where the same old enduring unchanging thing reappears, preserved, yet always necessarily transformed in the (re)activation process. Channelling Deleuze and Guattari's terms in the second epigraph (1994, 176) to our purposes here, Dharma embodies the present moment that is the moment of its embodiment as much as—if not more than—the past. Inseparable from its monumentalisation, that moment of reactivation is to be heard, sensed, experienced in its very reactivation by future generations. At the heart of Angkor's legacy will be this model of legacy which by definition confounds any simple understanding of history as linear progression of time.

If the Preah Khan text is exceptionally florid, its closing appeal to the perpetuation of the founder's legacy couched in the promise of perpetually reactivated religious and political order is a hallmark of the Angkorian praśasti serving to gloss a temple's purpose regardless of sectarian orientation. Simply put, Angkor would not have been Angkor without this singular focus on legacy, producing Dharma in the concrete form of statues, temples, and texts in stone erected far and wide. Of course, the very plea to future kings implicitly foresees the founder's demise and feeds on the threat of that of the foundation. Read in retrospect and for its stunningly prolific production, the reign of Jayavarman VII appears to sense this threat intensely. Even as it distinguished itself from its predecessors in manifestly and systematically striving to integrate further and further outlying areas into the centre's fold (Bourdonneau 2014), the reign betrayed Angkor's foundational, motivational fears. Together, the over-abundant works in stone of this period stave off the end of Angkor they nonetheless foretell. And yet they remain—as remains and reminders, enduringly inspiring new developments on their age-old theme.

'Thailand' and 'Cambodia' After Angkor

The region which is now central Thailand can be said to have cultivated the legacy in a particularly sustained manner, contributing ultimately to a significant politico-cultural shift on the mainland placing Ayutthaya as a privileged if contested Angkorian heir (see Krajaejun 2023, Hall 2023, this volume). The region hosted disparate Mon polities well before Angkorian extension this far west. The 'Mon' ethnonym (*rmañ* in Old Khmer, *ramanya* in Sanskrit) appears in 10th–11th-c. Angkorian epigraphs suggest this 'western' region, as seen from Angkorian eyes, to have been understood as inhabited by the Mons but not as a singular entity competing with Angkor. The polity of 'Lavapurā' (today's Lopburi) stands out in this context:

named on 7th-century medals found in the region, Lavapura became an Angkorian outpost, governed by Khmer envoys, from at least the early 11th century (Lowman 2011, 51–75).

Apparent ethno-linguistic differences between this or that Post-Angkorian polity—in Cambodia or in Thailand—can pale in comparison to the shared Angkorian legacies evidenced in monuments, sculpture, ritual, language, and associated political structures, with the ancient politico-aesthetic mould variously underpinning and undermining borders often made to appear natural by colonial and national historiographies. In this regard scholars today are indebted to the œuvre of historian Michael Vickery, whose early work focused on Cambodian and Thai historical chronicles. In the few years before his death in 2017, Vickery revised a series of essays on early Thai history. A note added to one essay originally published in 1979 crystallises the broad interpretive shifts which he in part engendered: 'I have become [nearly forty years on] less convinced that the relations between Angkor and the central Menam basin were relations of conquest and subordination rather than assimilation of two areas of similar ethno-linguistic identity and culture' (Vickery 1979 unpublished revised, 5, n. 29). Vickery is not arguing that Thai and Khmer share ethno-linguistic roots but rather that the Angkorian legacy came to be shared by the two groups to such an extent as to structure politico-cultural developments on what would become two sides of a border. If connectivities between Angkor and Mon polities in the Menam Basin evolved in response to the incursion of Tai peoples from the north, the adoption of Angkorian constructs by Mon and Tai populations participated in diverse ways in the coalescing of political identity in the Menam basin.

As should be apparent by now, contemporary interpretive explorations themselves constitute a legacy of the still-evolving historiographical matrix from which emerge particular sensitivities to the epistemological effects of European colonisation and of those nationalisms to which decolonisation gave way across the Southeast Asian mainland in the 20th century. The consequences for understanding the legacies of Angkor are multiple. First, benefiting from our 21st-century hindsight, we see a certain artificiality in those borders drawn on past places and times in response to the needs of the modern era; this is not to deny in any way another hard reality periodically experienced of those same borders, which have at times meant the difference between life and death. This vision sheds light on relations often obscured by historiographies obeying, wittingly or not, political directives to portray, on the one hand, the collapse of once-glorious Angkor and, on the other, the enduring cultivation of the autonomous modern Thai state from indigenous roots, with the 'indigenous' of the latter historiographical paradigm referencing alternately Tai or Mon (which is to say not Khmer) ethnic groups at the origins of Thailand on the problematic and now outdated premise that ethnicity itself exists short of culture. The narrative of collapse and rise has equally given shape to cross-border appropriations of Angkor as Thai heritage in the modern era, where the Thai state purports to act as conservator-in-chief (Keyes 1991; Denes 2011). What we can see now in between the cracks of the stories viewed as an ensemble is that Angkor reverberated in both 'Cambodia' and 'Siam', with the 12th–13th century Angkorian Buddhist turn constituting a formidably creative moment of transformation with reverberations across the Southeast Asian mainland up to the present day. As the historical materials discussed in some detail in this chapter will demonstrate, the tension between rejection and appropriation is not strictly modern, nor are the two phenomena incompatible, with shades of violence lurking at the heart of both. In fact, rejection and appropriation go hand in hand as Angkor's rather motley crew of descendants establish varying degrees of independence on the back of its legacy and as part of it. Our day has indeed brought to light previously unseen legacies of Angkor, which, at its greatest extent in the mix of this major transformation, likely reached to Vientiane in modern-day Laos in the north, to today's central and southern Vietnam to the east, to the Malay peninsula to the south and west, to the limits of western Thailand.

Religion plays a leading role in the historiographical drama I have just evoked. Angkorian political and social order is generally understood to have been structured by Śaivism and Vaiṣṇavism, with Buddhism playing an increasingly critical role from the late 11th century. Sanskrit, the self-proclaimed 'language of the gods', consistently partnered with Khmer to underpin the evolving Angkorian border (Thompson 2016). Theravada Buddhism associated with the Pali language, on the other hand, is understood to have predominantly shaped political and social order in ancient Burma, Siam, and Laos (Blackburn forthcoming; Berkwitz and Thompson 2022). In this well-established interpretive frame, the Sanskritic Brahmanic/Buddhist and the Pali Buddhist are set in an opposition embedded in and consolidating the other operative oppositions between ethno-linguistic groups and historical periods. Most importantly, perhaps, the binaries convey perceived civilisational hierarchies on the one side and the other. From certain French colonial and Cambodian nationalist points of view, the spread of Theravada Buddhism across the mainland from the 13th century coincided with, or even determined, a decline of politico-cultural prowess with which the Sanskritic religious complexes were identified (Cœdès 1958). From other Thai perspectives, Theravada Buddhism is seen to have enabled a politico-cultural prowess which the Sanskritic religions had proven unable to sustain; Siam, in this vision, would become the source of the spread of Theravada Buddhism into Cambodia itself.

Such categorical sectarian distinctions may have proven expedient in historical political contexts as well as modern academic ones; the extent to which they maintain on the mainland Southeast Asian ground at a given place and time is, however, questionable. Albeit messier, consideration of the permeability of religious and broader politico-cultural affiliations, along with permutations of these in diachronic and synchronic terms, appears, today, more often than not to be in order. To understand the transformations of Angkor from the 13th century—those accomplished by Angkor, along with those made to it—it is crucial to measure the importance of the politico-cultural production of Jayavarman VII's reign with reference to this famous Buddhist monarch's ancestral origins. Jayavarman VII descended from an aristocratic Buddhist family from what is now northeast Thailand, which imposed itself at the capital of Angkor in the late 11th century. The perpetuation of this line through periodic renewal at the helm of Angkor for well over a century effectively integrated an outlying region into the centre while transforming an outlying religion into the very shape of the Angkorian mould. In a give-and-take process, as Jayavarman VII's Angkor further spread its reach into established Buddhist cultures underpinned by Mon, Pali, Sanskrit, and ultimately also Tai usage, so did 'Angkorian' culture continue to evolve within these cultural complexes—continuing even more so as the political power structure long based on the Angkor plain shifted south on the one 'Cambodian' hand and west and north on the other 'Thai' one.

Of note for ongoing conceptual innovation in interpretation of these and other related historical processes is the recent work by Éric Bourdonneau and Grégory Mikaelian on the long history of the Angkorian devaraja. In tracking links between a set of statues known as the *pañcaksetr* housed today in Phnom Penh's Royal Palace grounds and the more famous Angkorian devarāja, the authors draw from historiographic theorisation striving to hold together in dynamic balance the apparently incompatible terms of change and continuity. In their own words:

> *Pañcaksetr* and *devaraja* . . . share a same history, not by virtue of a strict identification of the one with the other over centuries but as related elements within a larger structure whose successive warpings (what could be called 'vibrations' of the structure) ensure at once transformation and continuity over the long term.
>
> (Bourdonneau and Mikaelian 2020, 85, with reference to Lepetit 1999, 295. My translation)

This examination of 'warpings' (*gauchissements*) of a larger structure is explicitly posited as a means of transcending dominant interpretive paradigms 'illustrating [transmission of] "the Angkorian Brahmanic heritage"' to later royal courts or 'bridging the supposed caesura between the 13th and 15th centuries to find on either side the monolithic blocks of historiography's grand narratives' (Bourdonneau and Mikaelian 2020, 85). Note that the story these two authors tell, about the warpings of a foundational Angkorian cult over centuries, has Sukhothai playing a key transformational role. While the authors are concerned with the history of Cambodia 'proper', from ancient Angkor to modern Phnom Penh, their telling seamlessly weaves in this 'Tai' polity which historiography frequently posits to have effectively posited itself as the cradle of the Thai state. The Sukhothai matrix gave birth to Thai writing in support of the melding of Pali Buddhist and Tai politico-cultural structures overcoming Angkorian ones before giving way to Ayutthaya, a new Tai polity in ancient Mon Pali Buddhist heartlands, which ultimately bore modern Bangkok as the beating heart of the modern Thai Buddhist kingdom. Or so one version of the story goes (Wongthes 1996; Thammarungruang 2008; Krairiksh 2012 [2010], 2014); Peleggi 2015, 79–93; Krajaejun 2016).

For those prepared to lend an ear, other stories can be heard resonating as 'vibrations' of the larger structure of Angkor at once on this and that side of today's borders. This is how we might hear K. 489, a fragmentary Post-Angkorian inscription found at Vihear Prampil Laveng inside Angkor Thom (Cœdès 1951, 229–30). The remaining legible text is in Khmer with well-integrated Sanskrit vocabulary along with a smattering of Pali. It contains an optative vow in the first person, an elaborate expression of a Buddhist wish to reach a level of enlightenment enabling knowledge of one's own past lives and ensuring a long, powerful, and prosperous future life. Vihear Prampil Laveng is the most elaborate of the 'Buddhist terraces' inside Angkor Thom. These structures were modest by Angkorian standards and were set within the urban form definitively shaped by Jayavarman VII. Along with select Angkorian temples, they appear to have served as focal points of Theravadin Buddhist expression in the centuries leading up to and then following the move of the Khmer capital from the Angkor plain. That the sculptural remains at Vihear Prampil Laveng have been shown to evince close relations with Ayutthayan art supports Michael Vickery's speculation that the first-person voice of K. 489 belonged to the Ayutthayan royal purported to have taken Angkor in 1431/1432 and that the lost portions of the text recounted that very conquest (Polkinghorne et al. 2018; Vickery 1977, 225–30). The royal title which appears in variants in K. 489, *rajadhiraja*, or 'king of kings', is the same as that used for an early 15th-century monarch of Ayutthaya recorded in Thai-language epigraphs found at both Ayutthaya and Sukhothai as well as in the 17th-century Thai Luang Prasoet Chronicle in its account of the ephemeral yet monumental 15th-century Ayutthayan occupation of Angkor. The Khmer (-speaking) voice of the (presumably Ayutthayan) royal at Vihear Prampil Lavaeng tells us that the remains of Angkor—temples, sculptures, language, and epigraphic practices associating the ones with the other—served indeed as a 'bridge' embodying the continuity of the Dharma on the order of that envisaged in Jayavarman VII's plea recorded by his son at Preah Khan. Of course this Post-Angkorian response would have sounded warped to Jayavarman's ears had he heard it across the centuries—and this despite his own much-vaunted ancestral origins in the Buddhist lands of what is now Thailand.

In probing the Post-Angkorian material heritage of the central Menam basin, Krajaejun's work joins other contemporary scholars in complicating the Sukhothai-to-Ayutthaya story of the Siamese state, as well as the ancillary narrative of Siam as the source of Post-Angkorian Pali Buddhism in Cambodia itself. Insofar as the Buddhist materials of central Thailand are as much Post-Angkorian as they are pre-Ayutthayan, Angkor—writ large as it was from the 12th century—constituted a formidable matrix of Post-Angkorian Theravadin Buddhist Cambodia as well (Thompson 2022). In the following I will highlight a few other specific instances of Jayavarman VII's Dharma (re)activated beyond the Worlds of its most privileged heirs.

With the exception of central and northern Vietnam, as well as in some highland areas, Theravadin Buddhist principalities and kingdoms grew across the mainland in the wake of Angkor. The 12th-century Buddhist institutional reforms in Sri Lanka, along with Mongol pressures on more northerly regions of the subcontinent, contributed to this Theravadin dynamism in mainland Southeast Asia (Gornall 2020). The evolution of maritime trade and associated monastic exchange networks furthered this process (Blackburn 2015a, 2015b). In the process, Sri Lanka became a reference competing with or supplementary to Angkor or other local historical polities such as Bagan (Burma) or Haripunjaya (northern Thailand) in the development of the multiple religiously anchored and interlinked polities of mainland Southeast Asia. By the 19th century and under the further influence of colonialism, these would coalesce into the Theravadin Buddhist nation-states of Laos, Siam, Burma, and Cambodia (Blackburn, forthcoming). Embodying the Angkorian ancestry in its own distinctly cosmopolitan Buddhist political idiom, Jayavarman VII's legacy was embedded in these developments in various ways.

Building on the Dharma of Jayavarman VII: The Reach of Empire

As noted in the opening, the Preah Khan inscription is exemplary of the Angkorian Sanskrit epigraphic model. Like its closing plea cited previously, the inscription's celebratory account of the marvellous prowess of the King, including enumeration of religious foundations and the attribution of land, personnel, and abundant supplies to each temple site, follows in established tradition. Among the ways in which the Preah Khan text does stand out from the standard, however, is its pairing with the inscription of Ta Prohm (K. 273) celebrating the foundation of that temple in honour of Jayavarman VII's mother embodied in a statue of the Goddess of Wisdom, Prajñāpāramitā, and their shared affirmation of Angkorian presence across an exceptionally extensive territorial range (Multzer O'Naghten 2011, 2015). The distribution of 'staging posts with fire' recorded in the Preah Khan text and proven in remains along roads radiating out from the capital at Angkor, along with 'hospitals' scattered across the land and named in both texts, attests to a programme of public works expanding in both territorial and conceptual terms on those known in earlier phases of Angkorian development (Maxwell 2007, 42–45; Lowman et al. 2023, this volume). Much the same can be said for the distribution of images. For their timing, for their tentacular reach not limited to but still emphasising ancestral territorial attachment, and for their particular forms, the works of this period both ensured and inflected Angkor's impact after Angkor. This section takes seriously the import of the latter dimension of the works in question: their forms. A review of the range of scholarly speculation on the identification of a particular image type named in the epigraphic corpus cited previously—the Jayabuddhamahānātha—highlights a group of closely related sculptural forms which embody a spectrum of iterations of the concomitant personalisation and Buddhicisation of power characteristic of late Angkor which came to mingle in the subsequent development of regional Buddhist states.

The Jayabuddhamahānātha is one of many images—or image types—specifically named in the Preah Khan text. To be exact, the text records the distribution of 25 *Jayabuddhamahānātha* across the land. A number of the toponyms of the installation sites can be identified with sites in modern Thailand, including Lopburi, Suphanburi, Ratchaburi, Kanchanaburi, Phetchaburi, and likely Sukhothai (K. 908, st. CXV–CXXI, CLIX; Maxwell 2007, 80–82, 95; Multzer O'Naghten 2015, 412). We find a sort of mirror image of this radiating distribution at the Bayon temple, where the name is inscribed on the door jambs of two cellae; one is of Ratchaburi, the other of Petchaburi. This temple honouring Jayavarman VII at the centre of his capital was a microcosm of the kingdom, with a Buddha image associated with the king surrounded by small sanctuaries housing provincial divinities presumably embodied by replicas of the provincial 'originals'—unless of course it was the other way around, with the 'originals' installed at Angkor and their replicas at provincial sites (Groslier 1973, 86–87; 105–06). The Sanskrit compound Jayabuddhamahānātha can be translated as 'Jaya (after the King's name which means 'victory'), the Great (mahā) Protector (nātha, a divine epithet commonly translated as "Lord") Buddha', or 'Buddha, Great Lord of Victory', or 'The Great Lord Buddha of Jayavarman', with the ambivalence of the genitive in the last formulation rendering the ambivalence of the Sanskrit phrase, which allows for interpretation of the image as representing at once the Buddha venerated by King Jayavarman and the King as the Buddha himself.

Taking into account this distinctive name, as well as the wide geographic distribution claimed in the epigraphy and the implication of replica production, scholars have sought for over a century to identify the Jayabuddhamahānātha with known image types. Hiram Woodward has proposed to identify the named figure with a singular group of the Jayavarman VII era Bayon-style statues known amongst art historians as 'radiating bodhisattvas' (Figure 32.2a). These are standing eight-armed Lokeśvara figures adorned with an effusion of small Buddhas in low relief on the torso as well as, for some, the upper portions of the arms and hair, a larger image of what is thought to be the Prajñāpāramitā goddess emerging at the centre of the chest and a ring of seated figures encircling the waist (Woodward 1994; for a review of the image type with bibliography, see Zéphir 2008, 282–87). The distinct corporeal iconography of this 'radiating Lokeśvara' is unique in the Indic world but has been associated by scholars with Sanskrit texts. Other hypotheses have honed in on images which are seen to more explicitly emphasise, in formal terms, an assimilation of the king and the Buddha (Cœdès 1943, 198–99; 1958b, 1960; Zéphir 2008, 274–75; Lorillard 2014, 70–71). These are all seated, subdued figures; in conception, they are likewise unique to the art of Jayavarman VII.

For some, the Jayabuddhamahānātha can be identified with those Buddhas in the Bayon style which harbour facial traits strongly resembling those featured in the monarch's supposed portraits (Figure 32.2b). Others single out a sub-type of these particular period Buddhas; the sub-type is demarcated by a notably modest treatment of the Buddha's characteristic cranial protuberance or uṣṇīṣa; the slight pointed and smooth rise at the summit of the head of these figures is distinguished from the pronounced and decorated protuberance typical of the common period Buddha, as illustrated in Figure 32.2b, and is seen to enhance the liminal dimensions of this figure as if representing the King (with a hair chignon now replaced by the barely emerging uṣṇīṣa) in the very process of becoming a Buddha (Figure 32.2c). For others still, the Jayabuddhamahānātha can be seen in the supposed statue-portrait itself, an image of a man seated in *virasāna* with hair pulled tautly into a chignon and hands clasped in veneration. Exemplars of this image type have been found from the Angkor plain up to Phimai in modern Thailand (Figure 32.2d). Last, the name has been seen to best designate an intriguing iteration of this statuary complex associating the Buddha with the particular reigning king: an intensely hybrid piece which mimics the 'portrait' of the monarch in body and face but with a number of distinguishing features, including a transformation of the statue-portrait's posture of meditative veneration into a posture of venerable meditation, the *dhyānamudrā*, and of the statue-portrait's hair, normally combed into a chignon atop the head, into the same slight uṣṇīṣa noted previously (see also Pottier 2000). These have been found from the Angkor plain up further north, even to Sukhothai in Thailand and Vientiane in Laos (Figures 32.2e–f).

There is of course a manifest difference between the 'radiating Lokeśvara' and the range of other images noted previously: the first is a bold figure exuding the cosmic power of the divine; the others exude the power of human religiosity even when emphasising that obtained by the

Figure 32.2 Jayavarman VII period imagery: a) 'Radiating Boddhisattva' Lokeśvara sandstone statue of the Jayavarman VII period. Prasat Kosi Narai, Ratchaburi Province, Thailand. Held at the Ratchaburi National Museum. (Photo P. Krajaejun); b) Bayon-period sandstone Buddha head with characteristics resembling those of the presumed portraits of Jayavarman VII. From the Angkor region, Cambodia. Held by the Guimet–Musée national des Arts Asiatiques. Inventory number: MG17482. (Photo RMN-Grand Palais [MNAAG, Paris]/T. Ollivier); c) Jayavarman VII-period sandstone Buddha statue with characteristics recalling those of the presumed portraits of Jayavarman VII. Phimai. Held at the Phimai National Museum, Thailand. (Photo R. Bhiromanukul); d) Jayavarman VII-period sandstone statue presumed to represent Jayavarman VII. Phimai. Held at the Phimai National Museum, Thailand; e) Jayavarman VII-period sandstone statue with variation on elements of the presumed portraits of Jayavarman VII. Wat Phra Phai Luang, Sukhothai. Held at Ramkhamhaeng National Museum, Thailand; f) Jayavarman VII-period sandstone Buddha statue with variations on the presumed traits of Jayavarman VII. Held at That Luang temple, Vientiane, Laos. (Photos P. Krajaejun).

Buddha. Yet each of these forms contributes to a distinct political function. Produced in multiple copies, distributed with apparent precision across a wide territorial range, these image types can all be said to embody the uniquely personalised paradigm of Angkorian reach at this crucial moment in time. To understand the process of replication at work in this period, it is important to note that in and of itself the Bayon style subtly integrates the presumed facial features of the reigning king. In each of the image types we see a different iteration of the king-and-the-Buddha at once—or even as one, be it in the body of the bodhisattva effectively producing Buddhas, a figure associated with Jayavarman's father and consequently the King himself on the path to Buddhahood, or in the quintessentially hybrid figures which explicitly challenge definitive physical distinction between the sovereign and the Buddha.

Each of these image types answers to the name Jayabuddhamahānātha insofar as they share in the productive ambivalence by which the king is made to mingle with the Buddha to render the transformative regal power of Buddhist devotion across the land. As a group anchored in some sense by the famous statue-portraits of the king, they embody a transformative introduction of realism into the Angkorian politico-aesthetic repertoire. Prior to Jayavarman VII's reign, statuary known to conceptually assimilate historical figures with gods largely rendered the god's ideal features in material terms and with posthumous intent; against this backdrop the particular statuary of Jayavarman VII's reign in question evinces, in both conceptual and material terms, a mingling of the living and the posthumous as of the historical figure and the god. In making with these images a vivid and encompassing mark on traditionally Buddhist territories beyond the Angkor plain, Jayavarman VII could be seen to have accomplished his own duties in reactivating the Dharma of past kings to expand distinctly Angkorian reach.

Sukhothai: 'Liberated' From Angkor?

The Jayavarman VII statue-portrait-Buddha featuring in Fig. 32.1e and now in the Ramkamhaeng National Museum at Sukhothai was found at Wat Phra Phai Luang, an Angkorian temple stylistically dated to Jayavarman VII's reign with annex structures suggesting affinity with early 'Buddhist terraces' at Angkor and Pali Buddhist practices (Gosling 1991, 7–19). The long-dominant historical discourse alluded to previously, by which Sukhothai was posited as the cradle of the Thai state, drew from readings of the area's epigraphic and architectural materials to posit 'liberation' from Angkor as a foundational act in the 13th century and to emphasise the polity's subsequent development through exchange with Sri Lanka and other related Pali Buddhist centres to the southwest, to the north, and ultimately in a determining manner with Ayutthaya (Cœdès 1921, 1958; Griswold and Prasert na Nagara 1968, 1972; Gosling 1996). The more recent scholarship largely by Thai scholars cited previously has revisited the complexity of these understandings of relations to Angkor and points to the need for further examination of both the materials and the early scholarship on them. While the Sri Lankan model was explicitly celebrated and instrumentalised in the development of Sukhothai from the 14th century (Skilling 2008; Blackburn forthcoming), the polity was to build on the Angkorian material legacy and its conceptual underpinnings in more discreet yet profound ways. The Buddhist ruler (to come) embodied in the statue-portrait-Buddha was in fact a ready-made prototype for the rulers of Sukhothai.

The late 13th-century Tai prose of Sukhothai's Inscription One, also known as the Ramkamhaeng Inscription, is at first glance a far cry from the formal Sanskrit verse of Jayavarman VII's reign. A first clue to the entanglement of Sukhothai's development on Khmer forms lies nonetheless in the very form of the text. With Inscription One, King Ramkamhaeng famously, self-consciously, and performatively invents Tai writing—for posterity, as part and parcel of his invention of the Tai Buddhist state; yet the novel writing system is based on Khmer script. The gist of the text likewise betrays a family resemblance. Recording the king's right to the throne through a dynamic combination of genealogical descent and proven prowess, promoting his commitment to the public good and his care for the Dharma in building new monuments to house ancient venerated relics and naming the very geographical reaches of his expanding kingdom, Ramkamhaeng can be seen to portray himself in this text as much on the model of Jayavarman VII as on that of any Pali Buddhist monarch past or then present. While Inscription One stands out in the corpus of Sukhothai inscriptions for its celebration of a whole territory rather than of a specific religious foundation, in its grand and proudly Buddhist political-territorial ambitions it speaks to Jayavarman VII's own corpus. Writing in stone, the two monarchs—and their offspring—share an address to posterity. The model is nonetheless transformed in the very process of its reactivation. Inscription One concludes: 'All the people who live in these lands have been reared by him in accordance with the Dharma, every one of them' (Cœdès 1924, 37–48; Griswold and na Nagara 1971; Blackburn forthcoming). If Jayavarman VII entrusted the preservation of the Dharma in kings, Ramkamhaeng took up the torch, preserving the Dharma to entrust it to the people of what are now his lands.

The fabrication and celebration of links with Angkor through marriage, titles, or possession of sacred objects constitute another legacy of Angkor in its extra-Cambodian reach. While in the Preah Khan text we learn of the King's generosity in offering his daughters in marriage to political allies gained through conquest, in later accounts from Sukhothai and the proto-Lao kingdom Lan Xang, we hear local voices re-citing such links as a means of affirming power. Sukhothai's Inscription Two, written in Tai some 50 years after Ramkamhaeng's text, contains an account of the tumultuous establishment of Tai suzerainty at Sukhothai and neighbouring regions leading up to Ramkamhaeng's reign (Inscription Two, Side 1, ll. 20–35, Griswold and Nagara 1972; Blackburn, forthcoming, ch. 2). The original royal ancestor is said to have wedded a daughter of the ruler of Angkor, who bestowed him also with a royal title and sword. A challenger bearing a lower Angkorian title is distinctly identified in the text as a *khom*, or 'Khmer'; this khom, as he is repeatedly called, was defeated by a third man serving the first who subsequently transferred his own Angkor-bestowed title to his victorious ally. It is this man who would become Ramkamhaeng's father. On the one hand this is a story of Tai defeating Khmer; on the other it demonstrates the power of the Angkor name as it were, conferring legitimacy even at a remove and even as the gesture of Angkorian entitlement itself endows a Tai leader with the very authority endowed Angkorian rulers (Wongthes 1996, 152–53; Baker and Pasuk 2017, 35).

The contours of 'extra-territorial' use of the Khmer language are further shaped and demonstrated in a triad of epigraphic texts celebrating the arrival of a Lankan-trained monk and the Buddhist ordination of the reigning King in Sukhothai's 'Mango Grove' (Brai Svāy in Khmer, Pa Mamuang in Tai) in 1361 (Cœdès 1924, 103–16; Griswold and na Nagara 1973; Pou 1978). The first text is in Khmer; the second is a near replica of the former, but in Tai; the third, with different but related content, is in Pali written in Khmer script. The three stelae share also in material form, with a notable difference: They are four-sided with pyramidal tops, though the Khmer stela stands out from the other two for its larger size. The evolving legacy of Angkor is evidenced in intriguing ways in the Khmer-Tai tandem in particular. Mirroring the relatively larger size of its stone support, the Khmer text is the most elaborate, with its Tai replica omitting telling details and filling the gaps with others. The Khmer text opens with an account of the military campaign led by the reigning King to take back the Sukhothai area, presumably following troubles at the death of his father. His victory and royal consecration are sealed with the repair and/or installation of a set of Brahmanic statues whose identity derives from Angkor (Bourdonneau and Mikaelian 2020). The Tai text, on the other hand, opens with a brief history of the Mango Grove, originally planted by Ramkamhaeng; this sets the scene for an abbreviated account of the royal consecration before falling into line with the Khmer text. These slight differences point up simultaneous appeals to two different politico-cultural constructs—militaristic prowess and Angkorian divinity on the one side and peaceful Tai royal descent on the other. In terms of language use, they show how Khmer has taken the place of Sanskrit as the cosmopolitan or prestige language in the bilingual cosmopolitan-vernacular tandem once operative at Angkor. In Post-Angkorian Cambodia 'proper', the Sanskrit composition known at Angkor is effectively replaced not by Pali composition but rather by development of Khmer literary production (Thompson 2016, chapters 1 and 4). In other words, while Khmer can be said to have taken the place of Sanskrit in both contexts even as Pali language usage develops, the ways and means of this transformation are different here and there. In reproducing bilingualism at the heart of Tai state-building, Khmer is transformed from a vernacular to a cosmopolitan language, while Tai takes the place of the Khmer vernacular. Pali accompanies this process but does not simply play the role of Sanskrit at Angkor as the cosmopolitan language. The Mango Grove author's savvy manipulation of bilingual composition to convey slightly different messages mirrors Angkorian textual strategies. In the gaps between languages we can detect sensitivities inherent to the politico-cultural developments at hand. At Sukhothai and when addressing a Tai readership, it would seem somehow best to remain silent on the Angkorian gods underpinning royal power and to trumpet instead another style of territorial delimitation, planting a grove where one's descendants will cultivate Pali Buddhism. Still, perhaps more important than the divergence of the two narratives is the very fact that they were recorded together in 14th-century Sukhothai.

Lan Xang: Born of Angkor?

Angkor, by way it would seem of Jayavarman VII's material legacy, left an otherwise enduring trace in Lao historiography (Tambiah 1970, 29; Holt 2009, 40–53; Lorillard 2001, 2008, 2010, 2014). Legend likely first recorded in early 16th-century chronicles from the north of what is now Laos, and widely known today, effectively recounts how the Lao Buddhist state was born of Angkor. According to this strand of the tradition and its popular interpretation, a mid-14th-century Lao prince exiled in Cambodia was married to an Angkorian princess. Leading an army provided him by his father-in-law the Khmer king, the prince united disparate Lao principalities under the name of 'Lan Xang'. In bringing home from exile a Lankan Buddha image gifted by the Khmer king, the prince and his Khmer wife are credited with bringing Buddhism itself to Laos. This is the famous Phra Bang Buddha statue, whose name, often popularly interpreted today as Khmer meaning 'August Older Brother' or 'Brother Buddha' to emphasise familial relations, has lent itself to the ancient royal city in which the statue is housed, Luang Prabang. Research probing any historicity of this legendary account at once disproves its detail and affirms the strategic importance of yoking Angkorian and Sri Lankan Buddhist constructs in the narrative reconstruction of the birth of the state, whereby an image of the Buddha could be imbued with the personality of a historico-legendary figure as a microcosm of the territory at large. This discursive appeal to Buddhist Angkor in the wake of Angkor at the foundation of Lan Xang has reverberations in the material record beyond the famed Phra Bang image in a diffuse presence of Angkorian Buddhism on the Vientiane plain prior to the development of Lan Xang as a Buddhist state.

Historian Michel Lorillard suggests that Vientiane's monumental stupa, That Luang, which has become, on the order of Angkor Wat for Cambodia, a privileged emblem of the state, appears to have been built on an Angkorian site dating to Jayavarman VII's reign—possibly the chapel of the 'hospital' whose foundation was recorded in a Sanskrit inscription found at nearby Say Fong, one of the 102 'hospitals' enumerated in the Ta Prohm epigraph. It is here, amongst a homogenous collection of Bayon style sculpture at That Luang that we find displayed today the northernmost exemplar of the Jayavarman VII statue-portrait-Buddha (Figure 32.2f). This statue is outshone in the national historical consciousness by the Phra Bang image supposedly brought from Angkor in the 14th century. Neither can be taken as evidence of an Angkorian hand in the foundation of Lan Xang. Nor do they attest to any full-fledged Angkorian 'occupation' of this region. Angkorian statuary, like statuary stylistically influenced by Angkorian forms, is in fact dwarfed in the region by an art associated with that of the neighbouring Lanna region (now northern Thailand) from the 15th century (Giteau 1968–1969, 2001). Yet, read together for their multiple real, strategic, and phantasmatic relations to Angkor, the two statues tell a compelling story of how Angkor lived on well beyond Angkor. Literally or metaphorically stumbling over 12th-century Angkorian remains in the Vientiane plain, 16th-century Lao chroniclers would have taken inspiration in reactivating the Angkorian Dharma to imagine Lan Xang.

Angkor as Dharma: Enduring Claims in Burma

Let me leave readers with one final multidimensional example of this phenomenon of Angkorian legacy tied up as it is in an all-consuming concern for legacy. Contrary to the other examples discussed from Sukhothai to Vientiane, the last lasting trace of Jayavarman VII in Burma does not stand as evidence of the actual physical reach of the Angkorian empire in its day, nor is it a seminal component of the development of this modern Southeast Asian state—be it in the order of the real or the phantasmatic. Reflecting the order of relations between the Angkorian World in its heyday and its immediate aftermath with the multiple polities which will become Burma, it is on a more distant, subtle, and humble order.

First, there is epigraphic evidence of a Khmer, Pali-based monastic presence at highly cosmopolitan Bagan in the wake of Jayavarman VII's death in the early 13th century; a veritable Khmer community seems to have been associated with this, developing most clearly after 1230. This textual evidence has given birth to a remarkable multilingual and multicultural line of textual production culminating, for the moment at least, in historian Tilman Frasch's ongoing arduous attempts to distinguish fact from fiction in this complex narrative where Angkor meets Bagan. One Pali inscription dated 1248 CE records a Khmer monk leading a ceremony to 'purify' the Theravadin monastic order and a Burmese princess according her patronage to his good works, for which she is nicknamed the 'Khmer' princess.

A second recently discovered Pali epigraph likely from the 1270s mentions a monk—perhaps from Sri Lanka—having travelled to Cambodia before settling in Bagan [Frasch 2017, 2018, 2020]. By the late 15th century, this history appears to have become warped as Pali-Mon epigraphs at Bago, the capital of a Mon polity in what is now Burma, identify a certain influential Theravadin monk having ordained in Sri Lanka before settling in Bagan as being a son of the king of 'Kamboja' [Taw Sein Ko 1892, 5 (Pali); 51–52 (English)]. A further warping of the 15th-century records appearing in a 19th-century Burmese chronicle ultimately incites Angkor's most influential modern historian, George Cœdès, to identify the said monk in late 12th-century Bagan as 'undoubtedly' the son of Jayavarman VII himself (Pe Maung Tin and Luce 1923, 143–44; Cœdès 1975 [French original 1944], 178). As Pipad Krajaejun states (see Krajaejun 2023, this volume), it is not known if the 'Kamboja' mentioned in these texts refers to Cambodia proper, as it were, or to Khmer communities in what is now Thailand, namely in the area of modern Lopburi. In short, the call of Jayavarman VII to protect the Dharma is answered beyond the grave but in ever fainter Pali, Mon, Burmese—and even French and English—echoes of the original.

The effects of the 13th-century Angkor-Bagan tandem, with the one Sanskritic Buddhist power waning and the other Pali Buddhist power rising, are otherwise discernible in a group of large Bayon-style bronzes now venerated in the Mahamuni temple of Mandalay, upper Burma. Again, Angkorian territory at its greatest extent, under Jayavarman's reign, certainly did not extend to Mandalay, and the presence of these bronzes here does not attest to any other form of Angkorian reach at that time. It attests instead to another reach from beyond the grave. The sculptures are reputed to have been first taken to Ayutthaya in the wake of the taking of the capital at Angkor by Siamese forces in 1431/1432 CE. Successive wars saw them taken from Ayutthaya to Bago, from Bago to Mrauk-U (capital of the Arakan kingdom in what is now Burma), and then finally to Amarapura, now Mandalay, in the late 18th century. At each of their removes, further and further from Angkor, they constituted empowering war booty (FAD 1964[1795], 29; PKKSA 2010[ca. 1767], 325; Taw Sein Ko 1916, 1917; Rajanubhab 1991[1946], 115–16).

The sculptural group includes seven pieces, an adorned tricephalous elephant, three anthropomorphic guardian figures, and three lions. They have been dated, largely on stylistic grounds, to the reign of Jayavarman VII; for their iconography coupled with interpretation of passages in the Preah Khan and Phimeanakas inscriptions, they have been hypothetically identified as originally commissioned for installation at Preah Khan, Ta Prohm, and the Bayon temples, the architectural triad forming the beating familial heart of Jayavarman VII's reign (Boisselier 1967; Vincent 2015). The gem of the collection, which is understood to have originally been more extensive, is the elephant. An intriguing and convincing if not yet fully developed hypothesis by Angkorian bronze specialist Brice Vincent, building on the work of his predecessor Jean Boisselier, has it that this tricephalous elephant is the posthumous statue-portrait of Jayavarman VII's royal mount assimilated with the God Indra's famous elephant mount named Airavata (Figure 32.3). In its first remove to Ayutthaya, the bronze elephant appears to have been prized for its distinct embodiment of Angkorian royal power; this would be repeated in each successive

Figure 32.3 Bronze tricephalous elephant statue from the Jayavarman VII period. Note the third trunk is broken off. Held at Mahamuni pagoda, Mandalay, Burma.

move, with the palladia effect transferred to a new owner at every turn. The 18th-century Thai records suggest, for example, that when the raiding troops of King Bayinnaung took the Angkorian bronzes from Ayutthaya in 1569, they were understood to be taking the palladia of Ayutthaya's founding King Ramathibodhi I, otherwise known as King Uthong (PKKSA 2010[ca. 1767], 325).

This remarkable iteration of the Angkorian statue-portrait tradition appears to live on in a relatively literal manner in Bangkok's Royal Palace display of the statue-portraits of the elephant mounts of each of the Chakri rulers. If Burma, like the other Southeast Asian Buddhist states, all perpetuate in various ways the cult of the royal white elephant, in the Mahamuni temple of Mandalay today, the Angkorian bronze elephant and its entourage are perceived by local worshippers as possessing healing powers to the touch (Boisselier 1967; Vincent 2015). These bronzes have come a long way from Angkor in space and time. Yet, as objects of worship, they still constitute a bridge to Jayavarman VII's Dharma. The legacy of Angkor as legacy—vividly embodied in the royal statuary distributed far and wide in Jayavarman VII's day—endures, transformed. Those touching them today are not commemorating Jayavarman VII or his elephant mount in historical terms, yet they are reactivating a persistent sensation of history and power exuding from Angkor.

The import of the sculpture and texts discussed here has always exceeded the material realm—the stone of which they are carved, the geographic find spot, the dating derived from the style, or the networks these data reveal. Their aesthetic dimensions imbue them with that power short of force or complementary to it that made Angkor extend beyond itself in space and time and which continues to make it an enduring regional reference.

References

Baker, C. & P. Phongpaichit, 2017. *A History of Ayutthaya: Siam in the Early Modern World.* Cambridge: Cambridge University Press.

Berkwitz, S. & A. Thompson (eds), 2022. *Handbook of Theravāda Buddhism.* London: Routledge.

Blackburn, A., 2015a. Buddhist connections in the Indian Ocean: Changes in monastic mobility, 1000–1500. *Journal of the Economic and Social History of the Orient* 58, 237–66.

Blackburn, A., 2015b. Sīhaḷa saṅgha and Laṅkā in later premodern Southeast Asia, in *Buddhist Dynamics in Premodern and Early Modern Southeast Asia*, ed. C. Lammerts. Singapore: ISEAS Publishing, 307–32.

Blackburn, A., *forthcoming. Making Buddhist Kingdoms across the Indian Ocean, 1200–1500.* Honolulu: University of Hawai'i Press.

Boisselier, J., 1967. Notes sur l'art du bronze dans l'ancien Cambodge, II. Les bronzes khmers de la pagode Arakan de Mandalay, précisions nouvelles sur la statuaire du règne de Jayavarman VII. *Artibus Asiae* 29(4), 312–34, figs. 25–8, 30–2, 34–7.

Bourdonneau, Éric (2005) *Indianisation et formation de l'état en asie du sud-est: Retour sur trente ans d'historiographie. Matériaux pour l'étude du Cambodge ancien.* PhD dissertation. Paris: Université Panthéon-Sorbonne—Paris I.

Bourdonneau, É., 2014. Angkor. Le siècle de la démesure. *Histoire et Civilisations* 1, 62–75.

Bourdonneau, É. & G. Mikaelian, 2020. L'histoire longue du *devarāja*: *Pañcaksetr* et figuier à cinq branches dans l'ombre de la danse de Śiva, in *Rāja-maṇḍala: le Modèle royal en Inde*, eds. E. Francis & R. Rousseleau. Collection Puruṣārtha, École des hautes études en sciences sociales 37, 81–130.

Cœdès, G., 1921. The origins of the Sukhodaya dynasty. *Journal of the Siam Society* 14(1), 1–11.

Cœdès, G. (ed. and transl), 1924. *Recueil des Inscriptions de Siam. Première partie: Inscriptions de Sukhodaya.* Bangkok: Bangkok Times Press.

Cœdès, G., 1943. *Pour mieux comprendre Angkor.* Hanoi: Imprimerie d'Extrême-Orient (2nd ed Paris: Librairie d'Amérique et d'Orient Adrien Maisonneuve, 1947, translated by. as Angkor: An Introduction, Hong Kong, 1963).

Cœdès, G., 1951. *Inscriptions du Cambodge. Tome III.* Paris: Éditions de Boccard.

Cœdès, G., 1958. Une période critique dans l'Asie du Sud-est: le XIIIè siècle. *Bulletin de la Société des Etudes Indochinoises, XXXIII* 4, 387–400.

Cœdès, G., 1958b. Les statues du roi khmer Jayavarman VII. *Comptes Rendus de l'Académie des Inscriptions et Belles-Lettres* 102–3, 218–26.

Cœdès, G., 1960. Le portrait dans l'art khmer. *Arts Asiatiques* 7, 179–98.

Cœdès, G., 1975 [French original 1944]. *The Indianized States of Southeast Asia, 3rd ed,* eds. W. F. Vella, translated by Susan Brown Cowing. Canberra: Australian National University Press.

Deleuze, G. & F. *Guattari, 1994. What Is Philosophy?* translated by. H. Tomlinson & G. Burchell. New York: Columbia University Press.

Denes, A., 2011. The revitalization of Khmer ethnic identity in Thailand: Empowerment or Confinement? in *Routledge Handbook of Heritage in Asia,* eds. P. Daly & T. Winter. London: Routledge, 168–81.

FAD (Fine Arts Department) (1964)[1795] Phraratcha phongsawadan krung Siam chak ton chabab ti pen khong. in *British Museum Krung London (The Chronicle of Siam: A Master Copy from the British Museum, London),* ed. M. Amantayakul. Bangkok: Fine Arts Department, and Kawna Printing.

Frasch, T., 2017. A Pāli cosmopolis? Sri Lanka and the Theravāda Buddhist ecumene, c. 500–1500, in *Sri Lanka at the Crossroads of History,* eds. Z. Biederman & A. Strathern. London: University College London Press, 66–76.

Frasch, T., 2018. Kontakte, Konzile, Kontroversen: Begegnungen in der theravada-kosmopolis, c., 1000–1300 CE in *Religionsbegegnung in der asiatischen Religionsgeschichte: Kritische Reflexionen über ein etabliertes Konzept,* eds. M. Deeg, O. Freiberger & C. Kleine. Göttingen: Vandenhoeck & Ruprecht, 129–52.

Frasch, T., 2020. Pali at Bagan: the lingua franca of Theravada Buddhist ecumene. Talk in the rainy season research seminar series, *Transnational Network of Theravada Studies.* Available at: https://theravadastudies.org/recordings/.

Giteau, M., 1968–1969. *Laos. Étude de collections d'art bouddhique, 17 décembre 1968–17 mars 1969.* Paris: United Nations Educational, Scientific and Cultural Organization.

Giteau, M., 2001. *Art et Archéologie du Laos.* Paris: Picard.

Gornall, A., 2020. *Rewriting Buddhism. Pali Literature and Monastic Reform in Sri Lanka, 1157–1270.* London: University College London Press.

Gosling, B., 1991. *Sukhothai: Its History, Culture and Art.* Singapore: Oxford University Press.

Gosling, B., 1996. *A Chronology of Religious Architecture at Sukhothai: Late Thirteenth to Early Fifteenth Century.* Chiang Mai: Silkworm Books.

Griswold, A.B. & Prasert na Nagara, 1968. A declaration of independence and its consequences. Epigraphic and historical studies no. 1. *Journal of the Siam Society* 56(2), 207–49.

Griswold, A.B. & Prasert na Nagara, 1971. The inscription of King Rām Gaṃhèṅ of Sukhodaya (1292 A.D.). Epigraphic and historical studies no. 9. *Journal of the Siam Society* 59(2), 179–228.

Griswold, A.B. & Prasert na Nagara, 1972. King Lödaiya of Sukhodaya and his contemporaries. Epigraphic and historical studies no. 10. *Journal of the Siam Society* 60(1) 21–152.

Griswold, A.B. & Prasert na Nagara, 1973. The epigraphy of Mahādharmarāja of Sukhodaya and his contemporaries. Epigraphic and Historical studies no. 11, Part 1. *Journal of the Siam Society* 61(1), 71–179.

Groslier, B.-P., 1973. *Inscriptions du Bayon. Publications de l'École française d'Extrême-Orient: Mémoires archéologiques III-2. Paris:* École française d'Extrême-Orient.

Hall, K.R., 2023. Angkor's multiple Southeast Asia overland connections, in *The Angkorian World,* eds. M. Hendrickson, M.T. Stark & D. Evans. New York: Routledge, 97–111.

Holt, J. C., 2009. *Sprits of the Place: Buddhism and Lao Religious Culture.* Honolulu: University of Hawai'i Press.

Keyes, C.F., 1991. The case of the purloined lintel: the politics of a Khmer shrine as a Thai national treasure, in *Thailand: Aspects of Identity, 1939–1989.,* ed. C. J. Reynolds. Melbourne: Monash University, Centre for Southeast Asian Studies, Monash Papers on Southeast Asia 25, 261–92.

Krairiksh, P., 2012 *[Original in Thai 2010]. The Roots of Thai Art.* Bangkok: River Books.

Krairiksh, P., 2014. Revisioning Buddhist art in Thailand. *Journal of Southeast Asian Studies* 45(1), 113–18.

Krajaejun, P., 2016. *Yug meut korng prawatisat thai: lang bayon buddh theravad kan khao ma korng kon thai (A Dark Age of Thai History: Post-Bayon, Theravada Buddhism, and the Coming of the Tai).* Bangkok: Matichon Press.

Krajaejun, P., 2023. Uthong and Angkor: material legacies in the Chao Phraya Basin, Thailand, in *The Angkorian World,* eds. M. Hendrickson, M.T. Stark & D. Evans. New York: Routledge.

Lepetit, B., 1999. La longue durée au présent, *in Carnet de Croquis. Sur la Connaissance Historique.* Paris: Albin Michel, 284–99.

Lorillard, M., 2001. D'Angkor au Lān Xāng: une révision des jugements. *Aséanie* 7, 19–33.

Lorillard, M., 2008. Pour une géographie historique du bouddhisme au laos, in *Nouvelles Recherches Sur Le Laos*, eds. Y. Goudineau & M. Lorillard. Études thématiques no. 18, Vientiane-Paris: École française d'Extrême-Orient, 113–81.

Lorillard, M., 2010. Par-delà Vat Phu. Données nouvelles sur l'expansion des espaces khmer et môn anciens au Laos. *Bulletin de l' École française d'Extrême-Orient* 97–98, 205–70.

Lorillard, M., 2014. La Plaine de Vientiane au tournant du second millénaire. Données nouvelles sur l'expansion des espaces khmer et môn anciens au Laos (II). *Bulletin de l'École française d'Extrême-Orient* 100, 38–107.

Lowman, I., 2011. *The descendants of Kambu: the political imagination of Angkorian Cambodia.* PhD dissertation. Berkeley: University of California, Berkeley.

Lowman, I., K., Chhom & M. Hendrickson, 2023. An Angkor nation? Identifying the core of the Khmer Empire, in *The Angkorian World*, eds. M. Hendrickson, M.T. Stark & D. Evans. New York: Routledge.

Maxwell, T. S., 2007. The stèle inscription of Preah Khan, Angkor. Text with translation and commentary. *Udaya, Journal of Khmer Studies* 8, 1–113.

Mikaelian, G., 2015. Guṃnit thā khmae coh srot aonthay niṅ prịṅ ṅoep ḷoeṅ viñ nūv samai kaṇṭāl (The idea of Khmer decline and renaissance in the middle period) *Udaya, Journal of Khmer Studies* 13, 35–45.

Multzer O'Naughten, H.M., 2011. *Les fondations de jayavarman VII: l'aménagement d'un territoire et son interprétation historique et religieuse.* PhD dissertation. Paris: Université Paris III—Sorbonne nouvelle.

Multzer O'Naughten, H.M., 2015. The organisation of space in pre-modern Thailand under Jayavarman VII, in *Before Siam: Essays in Art and Archaeology*, eds. N. Revire & S. Murphy. Bangkok: Siam Society and River Books, 397–419.

Pe Maung Tin & G.H. Luce, transl., (1923) *The Glass Palace Chronicles of the Kings of Burma.* London: Oxford University Press.

Peleggi, M., 2015. *A Sarong for Chloe: Essays on the Intellectual and Cultural Histories of Thailand.* Ithaca: Cornell University Press.

Prachum kamhaikarn krung sri Ayutthaya (PKKSA), 2010[ca.1767]. Kamhaikarn khun luang hawat (The testimony of Khun Luang Hawat), in *Prachum kamhaikarn Krung Sri Ayutthaya (The Anthology of Ayutthaya Testimonies).* Bangkok: Saeng Dow Publishing Company, 323–408.

Polkinghorne, M., C. Pottier & C. Fischer, 2018. Evidence for the 15th century Ayutthayan occupation of Angkor. The renaissance princess lectures. In *Honour of Her Royal Highness Princess Maha Chakri Sirindhorn.* Bangkok: Siam Society, 98–132.

Pottier, C., 2000. À propos de la statue portrait du roi Jayavarman VII au temple de Preah Khan de Kompong Svay. *Arts Asiatiques* 55, 171–72.

Pou, S., 1978. Inscription dite de Brai Svāy ou "Bois des Manguiers " de Sukhoday [K.413]. *Bulletin de l'École française d'Extrême-Orient* 65(2), 333–59.

Rajanubhab, D., 1991[1946]. *Journey through Burma in 1936: A View of the Culture, History and Institutions,* translated by K. Breazeale. Bangkok: River Books.

Skilling, P., 2008. *Past Lives of the Buddha. Wat Si Chum: Art, Architecture and Inscriptions.* Bangkok: River Books.

Tambiah, S.J., 1970. *Buddhism and the Spirit Cults of Northeast Thailand.* Cambridge: Cambridge University Press.

Taw Sein Ko, 1916. The bronze figures in the Arakan Pagoda, Mandalay. *Journal of the Burma Research Society*, 6(1), 19–20.

Taw Sein Ko, 1917. *Archaeological Notes on Mandalay.* Rangoon: Government Printing.

Taw Sein Ko., (trans). 1892. *The Kalyani Inscriptions Erected by King Dhammaceti at Pegu in 1476 AD.* Rangoon: Government Printing.

Thompson, A., 2016. *Engendering the Buddhist State: Territory, Sovereignty and Sexual Difference in the Inventions of Angkor.* London: Routledge.

Thompson, A., (ed). 2022. *Early Theravādin Cambodia: Perspectives from Art and Archaeology.* Singapore: NUS Press.

Thammarungruang, R., 2008. *Prawat Naeo Khwamkhit Lae Witthikhon Khwa Wicha Silpa Thai (Historical Perspectives and Methodological Approaches Concerning the Discipline of Thai Art History).* Bangkok: Muang Boran Publishing.

Vickery, M., 1977. *Cambodia after Angkor, the chronicular evidence for the fourteenth to sixteenth centuries.* PhD dissertation. New Haven: Yale University.

Vickery, M., 1979. A new Tāmnān about Ayudhya, *Journal of the Siam Society* 67(1), 123–86.

Vincent, B., 2015. *Éléments pour une nouvelle étude des bronzes angkoriens du Mahāmuni Phaya de Mandalay (Birmanie). Bulletin de l'AEFEK 20.* Available at: www.aefek.fr/page79.html.

Wongthes, S., 1996. *Kwan Sukhothai: Rath Nai Udomkathi (Sukhothai: the Ideal State).* Bangkok: Matichon Press.

Woodward, Jr., H. W. & J. G. Douglas, 1994/1995. The Jayabuddhamahānātha images of Cambodia. *The Journal of the Walters Art Gallery* 52(5)3, 105–11.

Zéphir, T., 2008. Catalogue 80: Tête de buddha, in *L'Art khmer dans les collections du musée Guimet*, eds. P. Baptiste & T. Zéphir. Paris: Éditions de la Réunion des musées nationaux, 274–75.

33

EARLY MODERN CAMBODIA AND ARCHAEOLOGY AT LONGVEK

Martin Polkinghorne and Yuni Sato

Cambodia in a Global Early Modern Context

Life in Cambodia remained vibrant after Angkor, yet we know very little about the period. This dearth of information is partially explained by the relative absence of durable monumental architecture and art and by archaeologists' obsession with the Angkor Period. Systematic archaeological investigations of Early Modern Period Cambodia (ca. 1400–ca. 1850 CE) are now beginning. This chapter provides a review of recent investigations into the economic transformations that situated Cambodia in its global Early Modern context and that are often credited with contributing to the decline of Angkor as capital. The pursuit of new economic opportunities was seen as the most plausible early explanation for the demise of Angkor as capital (Vickery 1977a, 515). Angkor's population declined as regional mercantile opportunities emerged further south, but the causal relationship between these transformations remains unclear. Large segments of Angkor's population were theoretically drawn southward in response to intensification of Chinese trading patterns that produced new commercial options at river ports near the junctions of the Tonle Sap, Mekong, and Tonle Touc Rivers. Understanding these economic transitions in the wake of decline at Angkor in the 14th and 15th centuries is largely limited to historical analyses at present, but a growing body of archaeological evidence from the 16th- and 17th-century capital of Longvek (*laṅvaek*) demonstrates that Cambodia was increasingly connected to bourgeoning global trade.

The Post-Angkor Period suffers from the pejorative perception of a 'dark age' (cf. Chandler 1983) despite more nuanced research that offers contrary perspectives (e.g. Moura 1883; Leclère 1914; Groslier 1958; Chandler 1973; Giteau 1975; Pou 1977; Vickery 1977a; Mak 1995; Thompson 1999; Kitagawa 2009; Mikaelian 2009a; Nhim 2014–2016). This conception of Post-Angkorian decline is not purely an invention of modern historiography or colonial suppression. Ashley Thompson (1999, 2000, 2004) reasoned that, during times of political upheaval, Khmer kings continued to justify their authority by looking back at Angkor. From at least the 16th century, rulers promised to restore order by repeatedly remodelling Jayavarman VII's iconographic emblem of the four-faced Buddha according to the Theravāda faith (Thompson 2000). Significantly, Early Modern Cambodian elites drew upon notions of an Angkorian rupture to legitimise royal power. Grégory Mikaelian (2013, 267) observed that the thesis of decline associated with civil wars and foreign invasions is precisely the founding myth deployed

DOI: 10.4324/9781351128940-40

in the corpus of chronicles of Early Modern Cambodia, which represents our most significant body of historical evidence from this period. 'Loss' should therefore be considered a heuristic tool, developed by Cambodian institutions to claim rebirth and to counter challenges to their authority (Mikaelian 2013, 2015, 2016; Thompson 1998, 1999, 2000, 2004). Not surprisingly, however, and in contrast to these perennial themes of absence and retreat, recent investigations of Post-Angkorian Cambodia have begun to reveal the richness and complexity of the period.

Interpreting Cambodian history after Angkor has been aggravated by the complexity of its fundamental written sources, the Royal Cambodian Chronicles (Garnier 1871; Garnier 1872; Khin 1988; Leclère 1914; Mak 1984; Moura 1883). Although translations and syntheses of these documents were prepared as early as the 1870s, scholars have questioned their value for reconstructing historical events (Aymonier 1904, 736; Cœdès 1914, 49, 53; Cœdès 1918 15; Khin 1986, 197; Maspero 1904, 8; Porée-Maspero 1961, 397; see especially Mikaelian 2013; Vickery 1977a). The Chronicles are compilations of history recorded long after the events they report and were, in part, reproduced from oral traditions. No versions can be dated earlier than the year 1800. While seeking to develop a chronology for Cambodia's history, Vickery declared that the Chronicles appear to be totally fictional in relation to events before about 1500 (1977a, 367, 461, 490). He argues that events could only be confirmed when verified against European accounts that began in the mid-16th century (1977a, 3, 19ff). On the other hand, Khin Sok (1986), Mak Phoeun (1995), and Mikaelian (2013) argue that the value of the Chronicles lies not in their reliability in reporting linear dynastic chronologies and conveying cultural continuity but rather in their interpretation of past events (Mikaelian 2013, 2015). Accordingly, this chapter does not contest the minutiae of events or the dates of royal reigns but instead uses a commonly accepted historical framework within recent scholarship (Khin 1988; Mak 1984, 2002). In this schema, after the early 15th-century Ayutthayan invasion of Angkor, Cambodian kings and courts occupied a sequence of settlements south of the Tonle Sap Lake (Figure 33.1) beginning at Srei Santhor, then Phnom Penh (Catumukh), Pursat, and Barbaur. The political administration later relocated to Longvek in the first half of the 16th century and then to nearby Oudong, where they remained intermittently until the mid-19th century.

As archaeology begins to devote more attention to this period, it is useful to interrogate the origins of 'Post-Angkor' as a chronological definition and help us to explain the characteristics of its material culture within a global context (see also Mikaelian 2013, 2015). The exceptionalism of Angkor's massive city and of the Khmer Empire has understandably consumed most research efforts and subordinated the study of other periods, meaning that the period after Angkor was more typically conceived in terms of a 'lost' kingdom. Early research was bound to imperial tropes based on the rediscovery of a 'lost' civilisation, offering both a foundation for 'modernity' and a rationale for colonial 'progress' (Edwards 2007, Mikaelian 2013). The earliest European scholarship on Cambodia's past reflects this general context. For example, at the turn of the 20th century, the savant Étienne Aymonier (1904, 734–807) was already categorising the period after Angkor as 'modern times'. The term 'Post-Angkorian' originates with art historians Jean Boisselier (1965) and Madeleine Giteau (1966), who used it to situate Cambodian wooden sculptures in a chronological framework. Giteau notably made the art of this era the subject of her doctoral thesis, published as *Iconographie du Cambodge Post-Angkorien* (1975). One of the most significant revisions of 'Post-Angkorian' history was catalysed by the scholarship of Pou Saveros. From the late 1960s and into the 1970s, inspired by the recognition of cultural continuity (Au 1962: 585), and in reaction to the disjuncture implied by the term 'Post-Angkor', Pou made convincing arguments for 'l'époque moyenne' or 'Middle Period' (Mikaelian 2013, 272–76; Pou 1977, 2000; Thompson 1997, 2016, 6–7). Pou focused on linguistics and noted the absence of Sanskrit, the adoption of Pāli, and the interaction between Khmer and

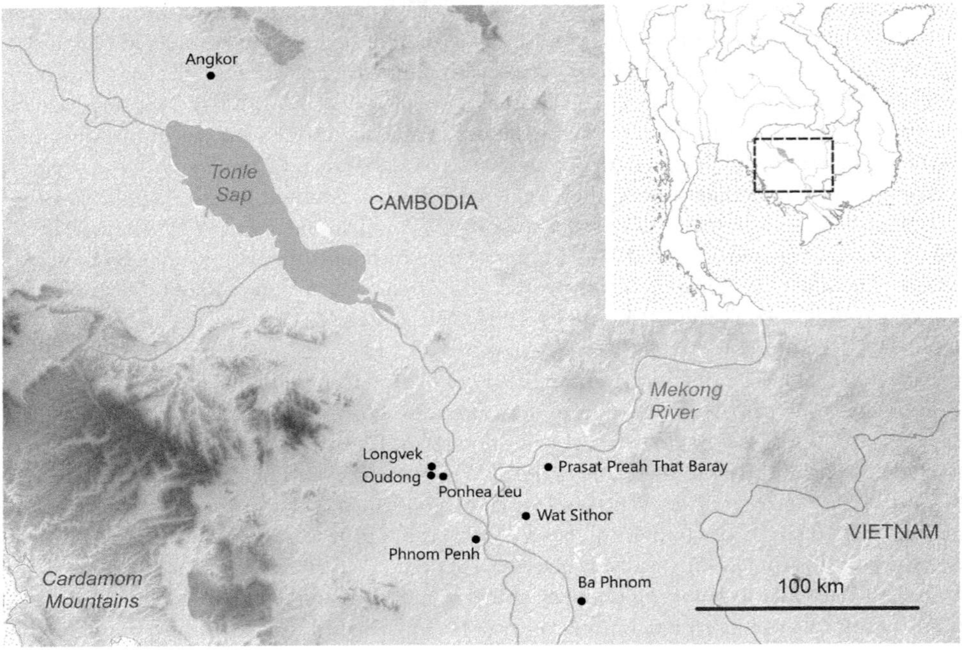

Figure 33.1 Overview map of major Early Modern sites in Cambodia. (Shuttle Radar Topography Mission [SRTM] data has been released and distributed without restrictions).

Siamese loan words. By foregrounding elite support for Theravāda Buddhism, Pou emphasised that transformations rather than terminations were the hallmarks of Middle Period Cambodian culture (Pou 1977, 1981).

Situating Cambodia in the Early Modern world offers an alternative to using 'Post-Angkor' or 'Middle Period' to characterise this important time in its history. Leonard and Barbara Andaya (1995, 93) trace the classification of Early Modern Southeast Asia back more than 50 years in the literature. Inspired by scholarship on Europe, some Southeast Asian historians began to actively use the term 'Early Modern' from the late 1980s and early 1990s to recognise emerging interaction and trade patterns that connected the globe (Andaya and Andaya 1995, 2015; Frank 1998; Lieberman 1993, 1995, 1999, 2003, 2009; Reid 1988, 1990a, 1993a, 1993b; Wade 2010). However, few scholars of the Cambodian past have used this term. Rather, they tend to note economic, political, and social developments that arose alongside the expansion of trade in Southeast Asia, led by foreign Asians and Europeans, between the late 14th and mid-18th centuries. We should underscore that our use of the term 'Early Modern' in this chapter does not require the assumption of inevitability or other suppositions about 'modernity'. The task of describing and understanding the many changes across insular and mainland Southeast Asia from the late-14th century remains a work in progress, and this chapter draws together historical and archaeological understandings to offer a contribution to that collective undertaking.

Comparatively few Southeast Asian archaeologists publish on this period, despite pleas from historians for archaeologically based research on Early Modern Southeast Asia (Stark 2014). While some studies deal with the material culture of Early Modern Cambodia

(Boisselier 1950, 1962; Brotherson 2019; Ewington 2008; Les étudiants de la Faculté Royale d'Archéologie de Phnom Penh 1969; Giteau 1966, 1971, 1975; Hall et al. 2021; Khun 2000; Kitagawa 1998, 2009; Leroy et al. 2015; Men 2007; Mikaelian 2009b; Nhim 2014–2016; Polkinghorne 2018; Polkinghorne et al. 2019; San 1971; Thompson 1997, 1998, 1999, 2000, 2004, 2016), further large-scale archaeological investigations have the potential to reveal novel aspects of indigenous agency and international integration. To that end, we submit that archaeological investigations of material culture at Longvek provide affirmative evidence for the expansion of communication and trade. The primary challenge is to consider evidence for interventionist mercantile and diplomatic exchange, without diminishing internal mechanisms for change (Mikaelian 2013). The 16th- and 17th-century occupation of Longvek connected Cambodia to the globe, but the hallmarks of Early Modern Southeast Asia had emerged by the mid-15th century, when Angkor ceased to function as the capital.

Srei Santhor and New Diplomatic Channels From the 14th Century

Southeast Asia experienced an expansion in trade between the 9th and 14th centuries—coinciding precisely with the period of Angkor's dominance and tenure as capital (Hall 1975, 1979, 1985, 2016; Wade 2009). That Angkor was open to trade is evident from citations to merchants and trade in the corpus of Angkorian inscriptions (Hall 1975), from the account of Chinese sojourner Zhou (2007[1297], 46, 70–71), from well-known evidence of Sino-Khmer diplomatic exchange (Briggs 1999[1951], 91, 189, 223, 242), and from the copious quantities of foreign material culture found at Angkor itself (e.g. Brotherson 2019; Carter et al. 2019; Dupoizat 1999, 2018). Thus, mercantile maritime activities at southern ports must have developed over hundreds of years, and these established conditions that compelled many from Angkor to pursue commercial opportunities there.

We see some evidence for increases in wealth generated by taxing trade at southern commercial centres during the time in which Angkor's urban occupation diminished and on the eve of the Ayutthayan occupation, but the form of the trade networks and political frameworks that exploited this trade remain unclear. First among the proposed beneficiaries of trade is the region of Srei Santhor (*srī sanṭhar*), and in particular the centre of Tuol Basan, which is presumed to have had independent diplomatic relations with the Ming court (Vickery 1977a, 1977b, 2004, Wade 2005, 2011; Wolters 1966). Tuol Basan is named in the Chronicles as the first capital after Angkor (Khin 1988, 66). Forming a kind of 200-square-kilometre island between the parallel Mekong and Tonle Touc Rivers, the region of Srei Santhor comprises a series of settlements, field systems, ponds, embankments, and pagodas running north–south from where the Mekong runs west–east to the village of Sithor. Much of the area is flooded during the rainy season, and water for agriculture is provided by a series of tributary canals (*braek*) dug at angles to the Mekong or Tonle Touc Rivers, as well as semi-circular and linear dams (*daṃnap*) (Nhim 2014–2016, 73–77). Its position east of the Mekong offered a strategic geographical location against rival Cambodian political factions at Longvek and Oudong, protection from Ayutthayan military incursions, and options to negotiate with neighbouring polities in Vietnam.

Srei Santhor was evidently the centre of late 14th-century exchanges with China when Cambodian political centres were opening up diplomatic channels (Vickery 1977a, 223, 515–22, 1977b, 79–80; Vickery 2004, 4; Wolters 1966; Wade 2005, 2011). Thirty-five records of official contact with Cambodia between 1370 and 1419 are listed in the annals of emperors of the Ming dynasty, the *Ming shi-lu* (明實録) (Wade 2005, 2011). The implication is that the Cambodian polities that corresponded with the Ming court were also capitalising on the emerging commercial possibilities of Early Modern Period trade. The precise Cambodian sources of the early Ming exchanges are not altogether clear, but we can say with some certainty that at least two missions emerge from the region of Srei Santhor. The *Ming shi-lu* declares that, in the years 1371 and 1373, an individual named Hu-er-na (忽児那), the Ba-shan (巴山) prince of the country of Cambodia (真臘), Zhen-la, sent an envoy to the Ming court and returned home with various gifts (Wade 2005, 2011). Significantly, Ba-shan was a political centre of comparable status to Angkor and capable of sending its own envoys to China. Most scholars have linked Ba-shan of the *Ming shi-lu* with Tuol Basan of the Royal Cambodian Chronicles, named as the first Cambodian capital after Angkor when King Ponhea Yat (Cau Bañā Yāt) (r. 1373/4–1433/4) and his court fled from the Ayutthayan occupation to establish a new palace (Khin 1988, 66).

The precise location of Ba-shan/Tuol Basan is a matter of some debate. Vickery (1977a, 2004) believed Ba-Shan was present-day Ba Phnom, Prey Veng Province. While there is longstanding occupation at sites around Ba Phnom from a 7th-century inscription (K. 60, trans. Barth 1885, 38–44) to 13th- and 14th-century sculptures and architecture (Lunet de Lajonquière 1902, 58–61), pedestrian survey and preliminary analysis of aerial remote sensing appears to offer little evidence for Early Modern Period occupation in this area. Another location proposed by Takako Kitagawa (2000) correlated the contemporary toponym of Tuol Basan with significant quantities of Early Modern Period surface ceramics on mounds around the temple of Prasat Preah Theat Baray, Baray Commune, Srei Santhor District. Kitagawa suggests these sites might be the political centre that traded with China and accommodated Ponhea Yat (Kitagawa 2000, 57–58). Pedestrian survey, ceramic collection, and excavation reveal occupation in the Early Modern Period up until the 18th century. The most intense occupation, however, is associated with the Angkor Period and the extensive stoneware production evidenced by the discovery of Angkorian kilns adjacent to Prasat Preah Theat Baray. The period of Angkor's decline as capital between the 14th and 15th centuries is barely evident in Baray Commune, and this location appears to hold little prospect as the Tuol Basan of Ponhea Yat.

Other scholarship has led researchers to favour the location of Wat Sithor, Srei Santhor District, approximately 25 kilometres northeast of Phnom Penh. Located adjacent to the Tonle Touc River and close to the sites of Preah Vihear Suor and Wat Yeay Bang, numerous sculptures and large *stūpa* at Wat Sithor suggest the existence of workshops of artists, architects, and builders active under wealthy patronage (Figure 33.2). Drawing upon Cambodian and foreign historical sources and reviewing relevant material culture, several researchers (Giteau 1975; Forest and Ros Chantrabot 2001; Nhim Sotheavin 2014–2016) recognise the Tuol Basan of Sithor Commune, Kandal Province as the temporary seat of Ponhea Yat's authority, Ba-shan of the *Ming shi-lu*, and the core of Early Modern Period settlement at Srei Santhor. Studies of text, architecture, and sculpture have been illuminating, but the scale and chronology of settlement at Srei Santhor remain to be revealed by future archaeological investigations.

Longvek as Mercantile Centre From the 16th Century

Precise links between trade and political authority in the 15th century, immediately after Angkor ceased to be Cambodia's capital, remain unclear, but we know that Longvek had emerged as the country's commercial, political, and religious centre by the 16th to 17th centuries (Khin

Figure 33.2 Stūpa and sculptures from Wat Sithor: a) photometric image of principal stūpa Wat Sithor (Photo T. Haraguchi); b) sculptures of deity (l) and the Buddha (r), Wat Sithor, 15th c. (?).

Source: (Photo M. Polkinghorne).

1988; Mak 1984; Mikaelian 2009a; Vickery 1977a). Sometime in the early 16th century King Ang Chan (Cau Bañā Cand/Aṅg Cand) (r. 1516/17–1566) returned from Ayutthaya, where he had been residing during a civil war, to claim Cambodian royal authority. After vanquishing the usurper Stec Kan, Ang Chan established a new capital about 40 kilometres upriver from Phnom Penh (Khin Sok 1988, 101–50; Kitagawa 1998; Mikaelian 2016; Vickery 1977a). While the Chronicles declare the principal *vihara* and palace of Longvek were constructed around 1530, texts and material culture clearly demonstrate occupation in the area before this date, including epigraphic material, architecture, and sculpture from the Pre-Angkor and Angkor Periods (e.g. see K. 137, trans. Cœdès 1942, 115–18; K. 432, trans. Cœdès 1942, 119–20; K. 136, trans. Cœdès 1954, 284–86; Revire 2016).

Longvek holds a distinctive place in the collective memory of Cambodians as the location of the successful Ayutthayan invasion of 1594 (Khin 1988; Mak 1984; Mikaelian 2009a; Nhim 2020; Vickery 1977a). After serving as capital for more than 60 years, Longvek was captured by Ayutthaya, and the reigning Cambodian king fled to southern Laos (Nhim 2020). The Chronicles recount a period of political instability in this power vacuum, as the recognised Cambodian Crown moved between Srei Santhor, Phnom Penh, and Lovea Aem until installation of an Ayutthayan-sponsored king at Longvek at the turn of the 17th century (Khin 1988; Mak 1984). This 1594 cultural rupture has been conflated with the 1431 Ayutthayan occupation of Angkor and mythologised in the legend of the magical brothers Preah Kô and Preah Keo, whose capture and detention in Siam during the invasion is used to illustrate the subjugation of Cambodian authority and prosperity (Ang 1997; Khing 1991; Leclère 1914; Mak 1984; Mikaelian 2016). Despite these episodes of conflict and political instability, however, both historical sources and archaeological evidence offer unequivocal evidence for extensive, and durable connections to global systems of trade and cultural exchange throughout the Early Modern Period at Longvek.

The visible archaeological features within Longvek (Figure 33.3) include a series of earthen embankments that form a 7-square-kilometre rectilinear citadel. Along its edge are fortified

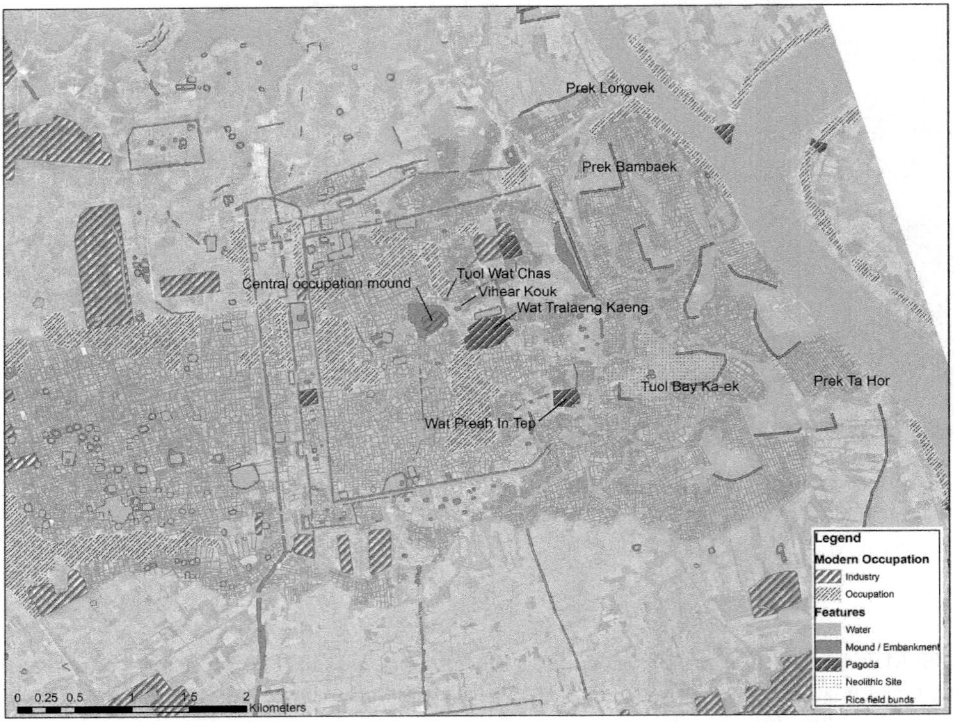

Figure 33.3 Archaeological map of Longvek.

Source: (Lidar data Evans 2016; mapping by CALI; Department of Prehistory and Archaeology–Ministry of Culture and Fine Arts, Flinders University, and The Nara National Research Institute for Cultural Properties; GIS rice field bund data B. Duke 2021).

bastions and wooden palisades that may have surrounded the entire enclosure. Judging from the number of ponds, available occupation space, and other settlement infrastructure, Longvek accommodated a much smaller population compared to Angkor (Evans 2016). Longvek sits at a strategic position on the Tonle Sap River at the first major upriver junction after Phnom Penh. Cambodian rulers could control upstream access to Kompong Cham, the Tonle Sap Lake, and eventually the region of Angkor. The enclosure was defensible from the river behind a barrier of low-lying paddy and accessible to maritime craft via two riverine entry points all year round. At the height of the rainy season, small craft could be moored at any location along the eastern edge or southeastern corner of the citadel and may have had a thoroughfare to Longvek's central occupation mound and religious precinct at Wat Tralaeng Kaeng (Wat Tralaeṅ Kaeṅ). Entry points from the river take the form of *prek*, or excavated canals typically used for diverting water for rice field irrigation. A southern entry point at Prek Ta Hor opened a route to Toul Bay Ka-ek island and the southeast corner of the citadel (Phon et al. 2020).

Foreign sources indicate that mercantile exchange was the primary means of generating wealth at Longvek (Briggs 1950; Cabaton 1911; Groslier 1958; Ishii 1998; Iwao 1966; Kage 2012; Kitagawa and Okamoto 2015; Kersten 2003; Lejosne 1998; Népote 2007; Piat 1973). International communities of numerous ethnicities including Cham, Chinese, Malay, Japanese, Vietnamese, Portuguese, Dutch, and English were established on the banks of the Tonle Sap River at Ponhea Leu and negotiated trade through specific official representatives or *shahbandar*, themselves foreign nationals (Iwao 1966, 90–7; Mak 1995, 176ff.; Sato 2016). European sources are often cited in secondary literature; however, these accounts tend to be descriptive and political in nature with little verifiable data about the scale of exchange (Cabaton 1911; Groslier 1958; Kersten 2003; Lejosne 1998; Népote 2007). Moreover, while these contacts existed, they were likely small in comparison to Asian mercantile traffic in the Kingdom. On the other hand, contemporary foreign Asian sources, and especially those from Japan, provide a unique window into the objects and quantity of trade. The dynamics, magnitude, and beneficiaries of this trade are all the focus of ongoing research.

Archaeological research into goods that Cambodia provided to foreign markets can offer this degree of insight. Japanese folding-screen 'Maps of the World' (世界図屏風) dated to the end of the 16th and beginning of the 17th century were produced to demonstrate elite cosmopolitanism and status. One example in the Kawamori Kōji Collection (four-fold screen, ink, colour, and gold leaf on paper 109.5 × 270 cm, kept in Sakai City Museum) lists rare animal and forest products—deer skin, ivory, lacquer, and wax—as Cambodia's primary exports. The *Tōsen Fusetsu-gaki* (唐船風説書) archives of intelligence gleaned from crewmen of Chinese junks arriving in Nagasaki (Hayashi and Hayashi 1958–1959) reveal coveted sources of sappan wood in Cambodia (Ishii 1998, 155,181). A 16th-century history of the domain of Bungo, the *Houfu-Kimon*, tells of a merchant named Nakatani Sotatsu trading in Cambodian goods from a Ming merchant named Lin Cunxuan (林存選) whom he had known for some time through commercial activities (Kage 2012).

While Japanese trade with Cambodia may have begun as a private enterprise, communication between political authorities soon followed. Letters preserved in the Reiun-in (Tōfuku-ji) temple in Kyoto record unique exchanges between the political leaders of Cambodia and Japan. The first, a letter written by Shimazu Yoshihisa, *daimyō* and the chief of the Shimazu clan, to the 'King of Cambodia' refers to a Cambodian ship that drifted ashore in Satsuma, Kyushu, in 1579, supposedly on its way to the domain of Bungo with official offerings. In reply, the king of Cambodia, probably Saṭṭhā (r. 1579 – 95), returned gifts and requested the opening of trade between Longvek and the Lord of Ōtomo (Kage 2012, 2015). Later, there is correspondence from an individual bearing the Cambodian honorific title of *ukñā* to Tokugawa Ieyasu, founder of the Tokugawa Shogunate of Japan. Written in both Khmer and Chinese, the 1605 letter issues a Cambodian certificate of passage for trade to the Japanese merchant Nagai Shirōemon (Kitagawa and Okamoto 2015, 71–79), and a vermillion seal certificate (朱印状, *shuinjo*) issued by the Tokugawa Shogunate. Beginning from the mid-17th century, sources like the *Tōsen Fusetsu-gaki* (Hayashi and Hayashi 1958–1959; Ishii 1998) offer information on the number of vessels, the products of trade, and their value. Cambodia received 24 ships between 1604 and 1616, and at least 76 Cambodian charted *Tōsen* ships arrived in Nagasaki between 1641 and 1745, carrying products like sappan wood, deer-hide, brown sugar, lacquer, ivory, areca nut, and other natural drugs (Nagazumi 1987, 36–116).

Perhaps the most revealing historical source on the control of trade is a late 17th-century Cambodian royal decree or legal code (khm.: *cpāp*) (Mikaelian 2009a). The *cpāp saṃbauv* was written during the reign of King Chey Chettha III (Jayajeṭṭhā III) (intermittent r. 1677–1709) as part of broad institutional reforms to generate new wealth after the successful Ayutthayan siege of Longvek. References to former reigns, and its use of anachronistic language, suggest that these laws may have been established prior to its writing. The text records the imposition of taxes, establishment of purchasing monopolies, the appointment of a hierarchy of officials and indentured labourers, and the enlistment of foreign nationals and their mixed-Cambodian offspring in service of the Crown. It reveals the complexity of levying wealth from trade and offers insight into royal governance of numerous ethnic Southern Chinese interest groups including

Hokkien, Cantonese, Teochew, and Hainanese, and the *shahbandar* who were responsible for the management of their trading 'guilds'. Mikaelian (2009a, 284, 289–91) proposes the *Cpāp saṃbauv* was enacted so the Crown could make greater use of commercial networks at the expense of, and to protect itself from, rival princes. If so, the *Cpāp saṃbauv* and its forerunners may represent a belated response to address a systemic royal deficiency to tax and generate wealth from trade.

Evidence for Trade at Longvek

While the relationship between historical texts and material culture is complicated and unclear, preliminary archaeological investigations at Longvek have identified significant quantities of trade ceramics and their patterns of distribution, evidence of riverine disembarkation points, and consumption behaviour at central elite sites. These investigations demonstrate that Longvek was both a territorial power and mercantile hub. As objects of exchange and consumption, trade ceramics have a unique value for establishing chronologies, since they can be located in time from a study of their morphology or decoration. Among the most reliable indicators of early modern Southeast Asian trade are blue and white porcelains, which are highly durable and portable (e.g. Cole 1912; Brown 2009; Dupoizat 2003; Gotuaco Tan and Diem 1997; Guy 1986). Chinese ceramics, especially from the Ming Period onwards, can supply valuable chronological information by way of reign marks that denote the presiding emperor at the time when the object was manufactured.

Following the diminution of Angkor's high-fired ceramic industry, increased numbers of trade ceramics were imported from regional and international neighbours. While the ceramic record at Longvek shows evidence of continuity from Angkor, it highlights development in global commerce, as evidenced by trade ceramics from China (Dehua, Jingdezhen, Zhangzhou), Japan (Hizen), Thailand (Bang Rachan), and Northern Vietnam. Pedestrian survey and ceramic collection initiated by the Nara National Research Institute for Cultural Properties (NRICPN) (2011–2015) (Sugiyama and Sato 2015) and expanded by Ministry of Culture and Fine Arts, NRICPN, and Flinders University (2015–2019) reveal flourishing trade and occupation at Longvek from the late 16th and into the 17th centuries.

Our study has registered nearly 35,000 sherds collected from a non-probabilistic surface sample of more than one-quarter Longvek's archaeological landscape. Trade ceramics account for 48% of all ceramics collected, and cataloguing is ongoing. Additional examination may reveal even more brown-glaze trade ceramics from China, Thailand, and Vietnam that may, on first look, be mistaken for Cambodian and Angkorian sherds (cf. Polkinghorne et al. 2019). Figure 33.4 illustrates the highest-density surface ceramic concentrations recorded across Longvek during our fieldwork and the relative proportions of different diagnostic types (top-left inset).

The largest numbers and densities of trade ceramics are found:

1 At Prek Longvek, the main riverine entry point to the settlement;
2 On the island of Tuol Bay Ka-ek;
3 Along the eastern and southern edges of the settlement, which includes several prominent religious foundations; and
4 At the centre of the citadel.

The northern and principal riverine entrance point to Longvek was at Prek Longvek and Prek Bambaek (Nhim 2014–16, 80–81). Densities of trade ceramics in the Prek Longvek, Prek Bambaek, and northeast bastion areas are indicative of the exchange in goods serviced by small craft

Table 33.1 Types of ceramics recovered from surface collection and excavation at Longvek.

Date (CE)	*Country of manufacture*	*Site of manufacture*	*Vessel form*
Pre-1500	Cambodia	Unknown	Jar
	China	Jingdezhen	Bowl
			Dish
		Longquan	Bowl
	Thailand	Bang Rachan (Maenam Noi)	Jar
1500–1599	Cambodia	Unknown	Jar
			Other
	China	Jingdezhen	Bowl
			Dish
			Covered Box
			Other
		Zhangzhou	Bowl
			Dish
		Dehua	Bowl
			Dish
			Other
		Fujian/Guangdong	Bowl
			Dish
			Covered Box
			Jar
			Other
	Thailand	Si Satchanalai	Bottle
			Covered Box
			Other
		Bang Rachan (Maenam Noi)	Jar
	Vietnam	North Vietnam	Bowl
			Dish
			Jar
1600–1699	China	Jingdezhen	Bowl
			Dish
			Covered Box
			Other
		Zhangzhou	Bowl
			Dish
		Fujian/Guangdong	Bowl
			Dish
			Jar
			Other
	Japan	Hizen	Bowl
			Dish
	Thailand	Bang Rachan (Maenam Noi)	Jar
	Vietnam	North Vietnam	Jar
1700–1799	China	Jingdezhen	Bowl
			Dish
		Dehua	Dish
		Fujian/Guangdong	Bowl
			Dish
			Jar
	Vietnam	North Vietnam	Bowl

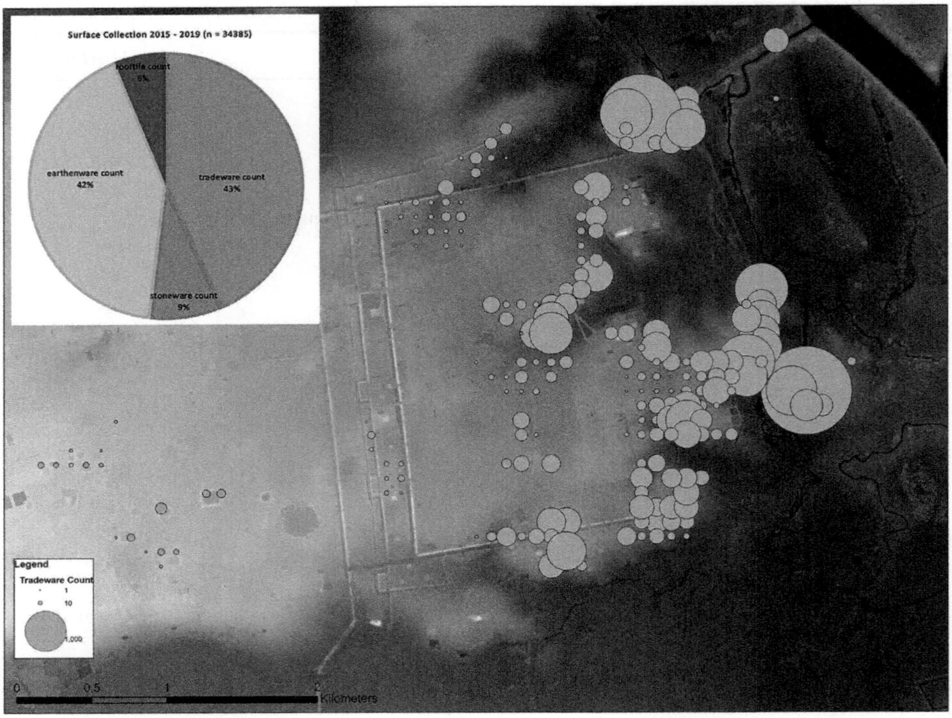

Figure 33.4 Distribution and relative quantities of trade ceramics and types from surface collections (n = 34,385 registered sherds).

Source: (Lidar data CALI 2015; Nara National Research Institute for Cultural Properties Survey, 2018–2019 Department of Prehistory and Archaeology—Ministry of Culture and Fine Arts, NRICPN, and Flinders University Survey).

and between larger vessels moored on the Tonle Sap. Between the river and the citadel is a kind of island or mound with the Wat of Tuol Bay Ka-ek as its focal point (Figure 33.5). During the Early Modern Period, there was a causeway or raised linear embankment between Tuol Bay Ka-ek and the important religious complex of Wat Preah In Tep in the southeast corner of the citadel. This mound and its landscape have undergone intense contemporary modification and, possibly as a result of this disturbance, surveys in this region have the highest sherd density in all of Longvek. However, distribution and organisation of small buildings demonstrated by the dynamic arrangement of post holes may also point to a trading hub such as a wharf or market, where trade ceramics were unloaded and possibly exchanged for other commodities. The island of Tuol Bay Ka-ek was easily accessed by communities who serviced, worshipped at, and lived beside the nearby religious foundations inside the eastern edge of the citadel. Correspondingly, surface collections in the areas around the eastern and southeastern precincts yielded significant quantities of trade ceramics, demonstrating that occupation and trade occurred in and around the religious installations.

Ceramic concentrations from surface collections and excavations on an occupation mound in the geographic centre of the citadel support a hypothesis that 16th- and 17th-century trade in Cambodia was facilitated from Longvek. The centre of the citadel is near Wat Tralaeng Kaeng (the citadel's preeminent temple) and the Buddhist terraces of Vihear Kouk and Tuol Wat

Figure 33.5 Details of infrastructure and excavations at Longvek and the site of Tuol Bay Ka-ek: a) lidar image of Tuol Bay Ka-ek (Image Cambodian Archaeological Lidar Initiative); b) aerial view of Tuol Bay Ka-ek and Wat Tuol Bay Ka-ek looking west towards Wat Preah In Tép (Photo T. Haraguchi); c) archaeological drawing of rescue excavation at Tuol Bay Ka-ek (Trench 41).

Source: (Drawing S. Tsuzuki, M. Shimoda, P. Suy, M. Polkinghorne).

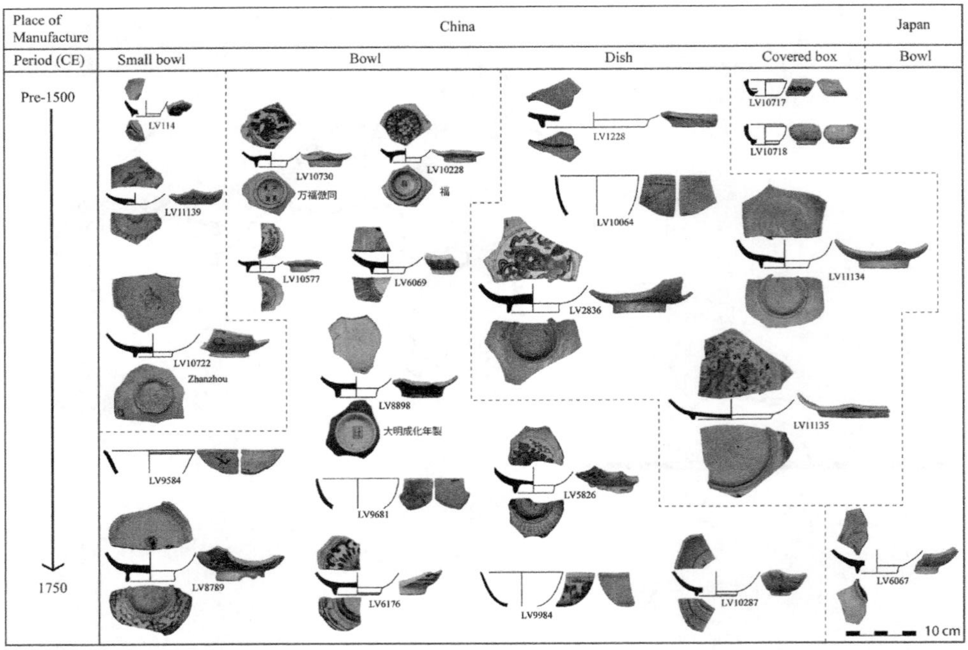

Figure 33.6 Selection of imported ceramic types from Longvek surface collections. Images are ordered by chronology of manufacture and country of manufacture. China: Small bowl: LV114, Unknown Chinese kiln, 15th c.; LV11139, Jingdezhen, early–mid-16th c.; LV10722, Zhangzhou, late 16th–early 17th c.; Bowl: LV10730, Jingdezhen, late 16th c.; LV10228, Jingdezhen, late 16th c.; LV10577, Jingdezhen, late 16th c.; LV6069, Jingdezhen, late 16th–early 17th c.; LV8898, Jingdezhen, late 16th–early 17th c.; LV9584, Fujian/Guangdong, early 17th c.; LV9681, Fujian/Guangdong, late 17th c.; LV5826, Jingdezhen, early 17th c.; LV8789, Jingdezhen, 18th c.; LV6176, Jingdezhen, 18th c.; LV9984, Jingdezhen, 18th c.; LV10287, Jingdezhen, early 17th c.; Dish: LV1228, Jingdezhen, late 15th–early 16th c.; LV10064, Jingdezhen, early–mid-16th c.; LV2836, Jingdezhen, late 16th c.; LV11134, Jingdezhen, late 16th c.; LV11135, Jingdezhen, late 16th c.; Covered box: LV10717, Jingdezhen, late 16th c.; LV10718, Jingdezhen, late 16th c.; Japan: Bowl: LV6067, Hizen, late 17th c.

Source: (Image compiled by S. Nhoem).

Chas, and comprises a raised platform of approximately 2 hectares. Large quantities of surface and excavated trade ceramics (including exceptionally high-value vessels) suggest that the area accommodated elite residents who accessed these prestige objects in the context of burgeoning Early Modern trade.

Figure 33.6 illustrates the range of non-local high-fired (or 'trade') ceramics recovered during surface collection activity, ordered by time. The wealth of the inhabitants is demonstrated by examples of Chinese ceramics associated with the central occupation mound of Longvek. A rare example of this type is a Southern Chinese brown-glaze pottery jar lid, incised with coin-motif and good luck symbols on the exterior surface and characteristic paddle traces on the interior surface (Figure 33.7). This kind of lid is generally only known outside China from excavations of contemporary 16th- to 17th-century sites in Sakai city (Sakai Shiritsu Maizō Bunkazai Sentaa 2004) and Kozen Machi, Nagasaki (Nagasaki-shi Kyōiku Iinkai 2011). Similarly, we found examples of Southern Chinese three-coloured green, yellow, and purple glaze low-fired pottery dishes illustrating a waterfowl on a lotus pond from kilns in Fujian or Guangdong provinces,

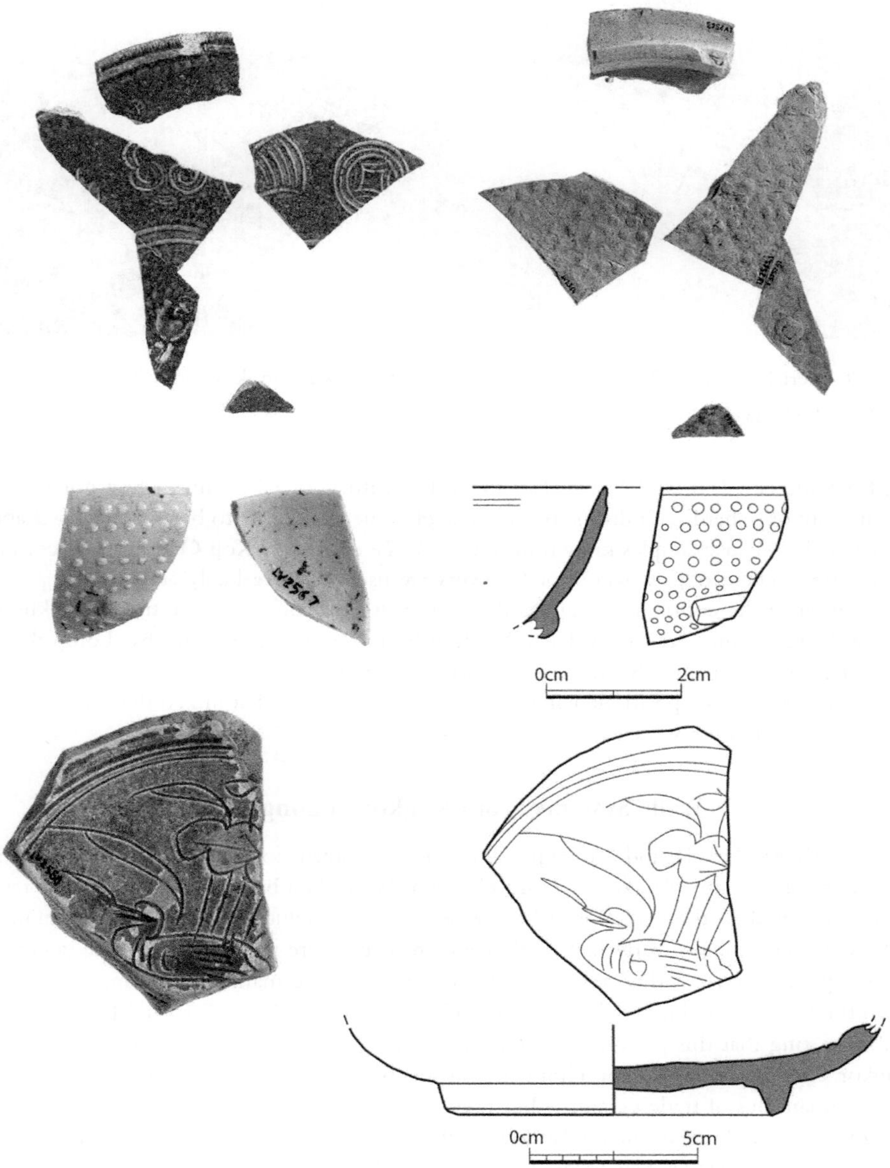

Figure 33.7 High-value trade ceramics from central occupation mound, Trench 28: (top to bottom) southern Chinese brown-glaze pottery jar lid, 16th–17th c.; fragment of frog-shaped container; southern Chinese three-coloured green, yellow, and purple glaze low-fired pottery dish Fujian or Guangdong, late 16th and early 17th c.

Source: (Photos and drawings Y. Sato).

Figure 33.8 Aerial view from Tonle Sap River looking south. Prek Longvek is on the bottom right.
Source: (Photo T. Haraguchi).

dating from the late 16th and first half of the 17th century. Finally, while white porcelain is very common; one shard with distinctive dot-like glaze beads appears to be a small frog-shaped container with similar examples known from the Musée d'Ennery (Koji Ohashi, pers. comm., 23 May 2018). These objects were not for everyday use and were likely acquired by people attached either to the court or by high-ranking bureaucrats. The vessels are unique to known Southeast Asian assemblages of the Early Modern Period and demonstrate that Longvek was connected to the most lucrative trade networks in the region. It is likely for this reason that Longvek was strategically positioned at a key riverine confluence that linked the capital to the Mekong Delta and South China Sea (Figure 33.8).

Trade Systems From Angkor to Longvek

Since the Early Modern Period can be partly defined by international trade, it follows that the economic transition from Angkor to Longvek might be tracked by relative quantities of trade ceramics compared to those produced locally. While fine-resolution cataloguing of ceramics from Longvek continues, nearly half of all sherds recovered are recognised as trade ceramics. Moreover, preliminary scrutiny suggests that the majority were manufactured and exchanged between the late 16th and mid-17th centuries (Figure 33.6; Sato 2016; Sato and Polkinghorne 2017), suggesting that this period was the peak of Cambodia's Early Modern trading activity. At Angkor, excavations in Angkor Thom and outside the Royal Palace enclosure have revealed significant quantities of trade ceramics, but they rarely exceed 5% (Gaucher 2004, 71) or 2% (Polkinghorne et al. 2015) of the total amount exhumed. Conversely, inside the Royal Palace at Angkor, imports are reported to correspond to about 45% of the whole between the late 10th century and the mid-11th, and 50% from the end of the 11th century to the beginning of the 13th (Dupoizat 2018, 133–34). These shifts in concentration are significant in understanding social and economic change.

An increase in proportional quantities of trade ceramics at Longvek may relate to the diminution, and possible termination, of local stoneware production that accompanied the end of Angkor as capital. Stoneware ceramic sherds from a variety of production localities in Cambodia, Thailand, Vietnam, and China were recorded in Longvek as part of the project (Figure 33.9), and a subsample was subjected to compositional study. Instrumental neutron activation analysis of surface and excavated ceramics from Longvek has detected the geochemical signature of the

Angkorian brown-glaze stoneware storage jars in 16th- to 17th-century contexts (Polkinghorne et al. 2019). Large storage jars were used for many purposes during the Angkor Period and throughout the entire kingdom. These vessels might be first associated with an 11th-century occupation at Longvek, and endured there until at least the mid-17th century, as many as 300 years after the Angkorian kilns that produced them ceased to operate (cf. Marriner et al. 2018). Based on the chemical data, the jars found at Longvek were not produced at the industrial sites associated with the capital but possibly from the nearby kilns of Tuol Preah Theat (Eang 2016) or Prasat Preah Theat Baray in the region of Srei Santhor. Although the people of Longvek used and cared for a range of vessels, including storage jars from the Angkor Period, they also sought new functional replacements on the early modern market from China, Thailand, and Vietnam. Significantly, these large utilitarian vessels were used and re-used to transport all kinds of commodities, including foodstuffs, other forest products, and manufactured objects, across Early Modern Asia.

While Angkorian inscriptions demonstrate the capacity of the Cambodian Crown to generate wealth from agricultural surplus, there is little evidence of corresponding frameworks to impose levies on trade. On the royal control of trade, Vickery argued that 'the central government would have increased its interest in maritime trade' (1977a, 520) and links the movement of King Ponhea Yat from Angkor to the region of Phnom Penh as part of that process (1977b, 80). On the other hand, rival elites, like those in the Srei Santhor region, could make commercial gains from emerging Early Modern trade outside state-controlled systems. The envoys of Hu-er-ner, the Ba-shan

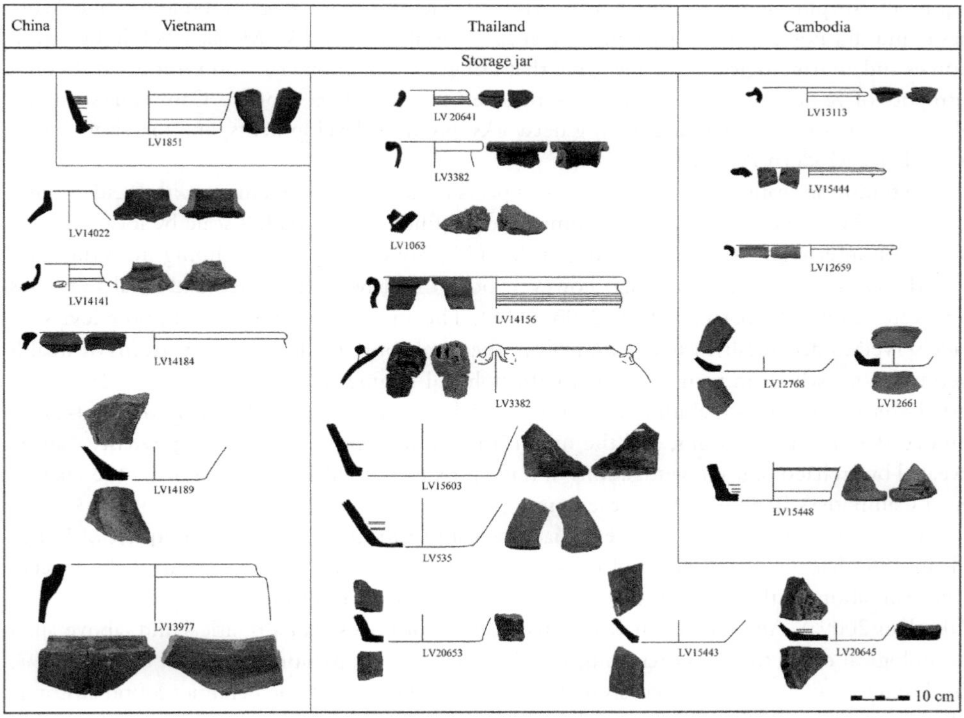

Figure 33.9 Selection of brown-glaze storage jars from Longvek ordered by country of manufacture.

Source: (Image compiled by S. Nhoem).

prince, provide 14th-century evidence that rivals were challenging royal power structures with diplomacy and trade. Claims to royal power did not necessarily provide control over commerce, and Cambodian political instability in the 14th and 15th centuries suggests that competing elites had effectively usurped the long-established agrarian-based wealth-generation strategies.

The *Cpāp saṃbauv* was written approximately 300 years after Angkor ceased to function as capital, as a response to the Ayutthayan invasion of Longvek. It underscores the tardiness of efforts by the Crown to tax trade and control the minority groups who administered it. It is unclear if Cambodians were part of the merchant classes at all. Mikaelian (2009a, 270–74) notes an absence of a merchant class in the institutional codes as late as the 17th century. The only references to people who trade are made alongside mentions of other occupations, or are listed as 'foreigners' (Mikaelian 2009a, 270). Resident merchants, office bearers who mediated trade, and *shahbandar* are noted for their foreign heritage (Iwao 1966, 107; Mikaelian 2009a, 272–73). Equally, in the context of mercantile competition, the Dutch describe mid-17th-century administration of trade in Cambodia as being controlled by Chinese or those of Chinese descent (Kersten 2003; Van Dyk, reported in Winkel 1882, 505).

Conclusions

Longvek rose to prominence more than 200 years after the first signs of the demise of Angkor as capital were evident. According to Vickery, by the end of the 16th century, Cambodia (from Longvek) and Siam (from Ayutthaya) were again military equals (Vickery 1977a, 502). Nevertheless, Longvek did not accommodate a population equivalent to that of Angkor, did not acquire the surplus wealth to source materials to initiate imposing religious buildings like Ayutthaya, and did not occupy a strategic mercantile coastal position like Melaka. While historical sources and archaeological evidence agree that Longvek was among the most important trading entrepots of Southeast Asia, further investigation is required to appraise Cambodia's unique relationship between expanding trading networks, political developments, and material culture of the Early Modern Period.

The transition from Angkor to Longvek appears to have some agreement with Reid's (1988, 1990b, 1993a) homogenous 'Age of Commerce', defined in its broadest scale by local engagement with international trade emerging in the mid-15th century and declining from the early to mid-17th century. In Cambodia, however, both the drivers of change and local responses to it were unique (Lieberman 1995, 2003, 2009). The ability of rival elites to impose levies on trade served to decentralise the economy from the royal court and led to new patterns of wealth accumulation, which in turn coincided with political fragmentation until the early 16th century. External dynamics including the 14th- to 15th-century Ming trading ban, the mid-17th-century Bakufu interventions, and the mid-17th-century demise of the Ming dynasty, can be revealed by archaeological investigations of trade proxies and will help to illuminate the character of Cambodia's Early Modern settlements.

Although it is still invisible in the archaeological record, the Ayutthayan conquest of Longvek in 1594 had profound political consequences that included the relocation of the capital, a reorganisation of the political elite, and the imposition of institutional reforms (Mak 1995; Mikaelian 2009a). Ang Choulean wrote that the 'fall of Lovek had a political and, above all, a psychological effect that was disastrous; Cambodians still talk passionately about it' (Ang 1997, 65). Preliminary quantitative analysis reveals that the majority of trade ceramics found at Longvek were produced and traded between the late 16th and mid-17th centuries (Figure 33.5; Sato 2016; Sato and Polkinghorne 2017). Significantly, trade occurred throughout and across periods of war and political disintegration, and notably despite the capture of Longvek by the army of

Ayutthaya. On the other hand, from the mid-17th century, when historical sources note that Cambodian territories were threatened by Thai and Vietnamese expansion and internal political rivalries (Mak 1995), there is limited evidence for trade or occupation. After initially acquiring a share of customs revenue at the end of the 17th century, the Nguyễn lords of Vietnam finally seized control over sea outlets at Prey Nokor (present-day Ho Chi Minh City) (Mak 1995; Mikaelian 2009a). While the Chronicles centre political and trade activities at Oudong and Ponhea Leu during this period, a sharp decrease in the quantity of diagnostic trade ceramics at Longvek may also relate to the Nguyễn control of commerce from the Mekong Delta.

Further research will be necessary to understand how cycles of international trade articulated with local trajectories of political consolidation and disintegration in Early Modern Period Cambodia. Nonetheless, the proximity of trading activities to the administrative and religious centre of the Cambodian state during this period confirms some degree of control over trade. Future research on Cambodia after Angkor will help to clarify the relationship between endogenous factors on the one hand—such as the capacity of local actors to leverage commerce for political and economic objectives—and exogenous drivers such as variations in regional climate on the other hand. Critically, material histories are not necessarily bound to entrenched historical narratives, and new archaeological studies should therefore continue to reveal the characteristics of an Early Modern Cambodia that is no longer principally defined by looking back at Angkor.

References

Andaya, L.Y. & B.W. Andaya, 1995. Southeast Asia in the Early Modern Period; Twenty-five years on. *Journal of Southeast Asian Studies* 26(1), 92–8.

Andaya, L.Y. & B.W. Andaya, 2015. *A History of Early Modern Southeast Asia, 1400–1830*. Cambridge: Cambridge University Press.

Ang, C., 1997. Nandin and his avatars, in *Sculpture of Angkor and Ancient Cambodia: Millennium of Glory*, eds. H.I. Jessup and T. Zéphir. Washington, DC: National Gallery of Art, 62–9.

Au, C., 1962. Études de Philologie indo-khmère II. *Journal Asiatique* 250(4), 575–91.

Aymonier, É., 1904. *Le Cambodge, III. Le groupe d'Angkor et l'Histoire*. Paris: Ernest Leroux.

Barth, A., 1885. *Inscriptions sanscrites du Cambodge*, Paris: Imprimerie nationale.

Boisselier, J., 1950. Note sur deux Buddha parés des galeries d'angkor Vat. *Bulletin de la Société des Études Indochinoises* 25(3), 299–306.

Boisselier, J., 1962. Note sur les bas-reliefs tardifs d'angkor Vat. *Journal Asiatique* 250(2), 244–8.

Boisselier, J., 1965. Récentes recherches archéologiques en Thaïlande. Rapport préliminaire de mission (25 juillet-28 novembre 1964). *Arts Asiatiques* 12, 125–74.

Briggs, L.P., 1950. Les missionnaires portugais et espagnols au Cambodge (1555–1603). *Bulletin de la Société des Études Indochinoises* 25(1), 5–29.

Briggs, L.P., 1999[1951]. *The ancient Khmer empire*. Bangkok: White Lotus.

Brotherson, D., 2019. *Commerce, the capital, & community, trade ceramics, settlement patterns, & continuity throughout the demise of Angkor*. PhD dissertation. Sydney: The University of Sydney.

Brown, R.M., 2009. *The Ming Gap and Shipwreck Ceramics in Southeast Asia. Towards a Chronology of Thai Trade Ware*. Bangkok: The Siam Society.

Cabaton, A., 1911. Notes sur les sources européennes de l'histoire de l'Indochine. *Bulletin de la Commission archéologique de l'Indochine* 1, 58–84.

Carter, A., L. Dussubieux, M. Polkinghorne & C. Pottier, 2019. Glass artifacts at Angkor: evidence for exchange. *Archaeological and Anthropological Sciences* 11, 1013–27.

Chandler, D.P., 1973. *Cambodia before the French: politics in a Tributary Kingdom, 1794–1848*. PhD dissertation. Ann Arbor: University of Michigan.

Chandler, D.P., 1983. *A History of Cambodia. 1st ed.* Boulder (CO): Westview.

Cœdès, G., 1914. Compte rendu, Histoire du cambodge, A Leclère. *Bulletin de l'École française d'Extrême-Orient* 14:9.

Cœdès, G., 1918. Essai de classification des documents historiques cambodgien conservés à la Bibliothèque de l'École Francaise d'Extrême-Orient. *Bulletin de l'École française d'Extrême-Orient* 18, 15–28.

Cole, F.-C., 1912. *Chinese Pottery in the Philippines*. Chicago: Field Museum of Natural History Publication

Duke, B., 2021. *The hidden landscapes of the Cambodian early modern period (c, 1400–1800). A landscape-scale geophysical exploration*. PhD dissertation. Adelaide: Flinders University.

Dupoizat, M.-F., 1999. La Céramique Importée à Angkor: Étude Préliminaire. *Arts Asiatiques* 54, 103–116.

Dupoizat, M.-F., 2003. Chinese ceramics, in *Histoire de Barus, (Sumatra) Le Site de Lobu Tua. Vol. II: étude archeologique et documents*, ed. C. Guilllot, Paris: Cahiers d'Archipel, 103–70.

Dupoizat, M.-F., 2018. La Céramique Importée à Angkor Thom. *Péninsule* 76, 129–86.

Eang, S., អៀង ស 2016. Tuol komplong ទួលកំផុលង់, BA dissertation. សាកលវិទ្យាល័យភូមិន្ទវិចិត្រសិល្បៈ Phnom Penh: Royal University of Fine Arts.

Edwards, P., 2007. *Cambodge: The Cultivation of a Nation, 1860–1945*. Honolulu (HI): University of Hawai'i Press.

Ewington, G., 2008. *Yaśodharapura to Yaśodharapura. Mobility, rupture and continuity in the Khmer World*. BA(Hons) dissertation. Sydney: The University of Sydney.

Evans, D., 2016. Airborne laser scanning as a method for exploring long-term socio-ecological dynamics in Cambodia. *Journal of Archaeological Science* 74, 164–175.

Forest, A. & C., Ros, 2001. Autour d'une Visite Aux Sites de Srei Santhor. *Péninsule* 42(1), 43–79.

Frank, A.G., 1998. *ReOrient: Global Economy in the Asian Age*. Berkeley: University of California Press.

Garnier, F., 1871. Chronique royale du Cambodge. *Journal Asiatique* 6(18), 336–85.

Garnier, F., 1872. Chronique royale du Cambodge. *Journal Asiatique* 6(20), 112–44.

Gaucher, J., 2004. Angkor Thom, une utopie réalisée? Structuration de l'espace et modèle indien d'urbanisme dans le Cambodge ancien. *Arts Asiatiques* 59, 58–86.

Giteau, M., 1966. Note sur une école cambodgienne de statuaire bouddhique inspirée de l'art d'Angkor Vat, *Arts Asiatiques* 13, 115–26.

Giteau, M., 1971. Note sur quelques pièces en bronze récemment découvertes à vatt deb pranamy d'oudong. *Arts Asiatiques* 24, 149–55.

Giteau, M., 1975. *Iconographie du Cambodge Post-Angkorien*. Paris: École française d'Extrême-Orient.

Gotuaco, L., R.C. Tan & A. Diem, 1997. *Chinese and Vietnamese Blue and White Wares Found in The Philippines*. Makati City: Bookmark.

Groslier, B.-P., 1958. *Angkor Et Le Cambodge Au Xvie Siècle D'après Les Sources Portugaises Et Espagnoles*. Paris: Presses universitaires de France.

Guy, J., 1986. *Oriental Trade Ceramics in South-East Asia: Ninth to Sixteenth Centuries*. Singapore: Oxford University Press.

Hall, K.R., 1975. Khmer commercial development and foreign contacts under Suryavarman I. *The Journal of the Economic and Social History of the Orient* 18(3), 318–36.

Hall, K.R., 1979. Eleventh-century commercial developments in Angkor and Champa. *Journal of Southeast Asian Studies* 10(2), 420–34.

Hall, K.R., 1985. *Maritime Trade and State Development in Early Southeast Asia*. Honolulu (HI): University of Hawaii Press.

Hall, K.R., 2016. Commodity flows, diaspora networking, and contested agency in the Eastern Indian Ocean c, 1000–1500. *Trans Regional and National Studies of Southeast Asia* 4, 387–417.

Hall, T., D. Penny, B. Vincent & M. Polkinghorne, 2021. An integrated palaeoenvironmental record of Early Modern occupancy and land use within Angkor Thom, Angkor. *Quaternary Science Reviews 251*.

Hayashi, S., & Hayashi, N., 1958–1959. 林春勝 林信篤編 *(compiled by). Kaihen'tai* 華夷變態. Tokyo: Toyo Bunko 東洋文庫叢刊.

Ishii, Y. (ed), 1998. *The Junk Trade from Southeast Asia. Translations from the Tôsen Fusetsu-gaki, 1674–1723*. Singapore: Institute of Southeast Asian Studies.

Iwao, S. 岩生成一, 1966. *Nan'yōnihonmachi no kenkyū* 南洋日本町の研究 *(A Study of Japanese Quarters in Southeast Asia in the Sixteenth and Seventeenth Centuries)*. Tokyo: Iwanami Shoten 岩波書店. Tokyo.

Kage, T. 鹿毛敏夫, 2012. 'Sengoku daimyō no kaiyō katsudō to tōnan'ajia kōeki.' 戦国大名の海洋活動と東南アジア交易 (an ocean voyage and trade with the Countries of Southeast Asia by a Daimyo in the warring states period in Japan.), *Bōekitōji kenkyū* 貿易陶磁研究 *(Trade Ceramic Studies)* 32, 23–33.

Kage, T. 鹿毛敏夫, 2015. *Ajia no naka no sengoku daimyō* アジアの中の戦国大名 *(Sengoku Daimyo in Asia)*. Tokyo: Yoshikawa Kobunkan 吉川弘文館.

Kersten, C. (trans., annot., and intro.) 2003. *Strange Events in the Kingdoms of Cambodia and Laos (1635–1644)*. Bangkok: White Lotus.

Khin, S., 1986. Quelques réflexions sur la valeur historique des chroniques royales du Cambodge. *Bulletin de l'École française d'Extrême-Orient* 75, 197–214.

Khin, S., 1988. *Chroniques royales du Cambodge (de 1417 à 1595)*. Paris: École française d'Extrême-Orient.

Khing, H.D., 1991. La légende de braḥ go braḥ kaev. *Cahiers de l'Asie du Sud-Est* 29–30, 169–90.

Khun, S., 2000. *Post Angkorian Buddha*. Phnom Penh: Ministry of Culture and Fine Arts.

Kitagawa, T., 北川香子, 1998. 'Posuto ankōru no ōjō—ron'vuēku oyobi udon chōsa hōkoku' ポスト・アンコールの王城ーロンヴェークおよびウドン調査報告 (Capitals of the Post-Angkor Period Longvek and Oudong). *Tōnan'ajia—rekishi to bunka* 東南アジアー歴史と文化 *(Southeast Asia: History and Culture)* 27, 48–72.

Kitagawa, T., 北川香子, 2000. 'Mizu-ō no keifu' 水王 の系譜 (History of the water kings in Srei Santhor). *Tōnan'ajia kenkyū*東南アジア研究 *(Japanese Journal of Southeast Asian Studies)* 38(1), 50–73.

Kitagawa, T., 北川香子, 2009. Ankōru watto ga nemuru ma ni—Kanbojia rekishi no kioku o tazunete アンコール・ワットが眠る間に-カンボジア 歴史の記憶を訪ねて (While Angkor Wat was sleeping. *A visit to the memories of history in Cambodia)*. Tokyo: Rengōshuppan 連合出版.

Kitagawa, T. & M. Okamoto, 2015. Correspondence between Cambodia and Japan in the seventeenth and eighteenth centuries. *Memoirs of the Research Department of the Toyo Bunko* 73, 65–110.

Leclère, A., 1914. *Histoire du Cambodge depuis le 1er siècle de notre èra, d'après les inscriptions lapidaires, les annales chinoises et annamites et les documents européens des six derniers siècles*. Paris: Paul Geuthner.

Lejosne, J.-C., 1998. Historiographie du cambodge aux 16e et 17e siècles: les sources portugaises et hollandaises, in *Bilan et perspectives des études khmères (langue et culture)*, ed. P.L. Lamant. Paris, L'Harmattan, 179–200.

Leroy, S., M. Hendrickson, E. Delqué-Kolic, E. Vega & P. Dillmann, 2015. First direct dating for the construction and modification of the Baphuon temple mountain in Angkor, Cambodia. *PLoS One* 10(11), doi.org/10.1371/journal.pone.0141052.

Les étudiants de la Faculté royale d'archéologie de phnom penh, 1969. Le monastère bouddhique de tep pranam à Oudong. *Bulletin de l'École française d'Extrême-Orient* 56, 29–57.

Lieberman, V., 1993. Local integration and Eurasian analogies: structuring Southeast Asian history, c. 1350–c. 1830. *Modern Asian Studies* 27(3), 475–572.

Lieberman, V., 1995. An age of commerce in southeast Asia? Problems of regional coherence—A Review article. *The Journal of Asian Studies* 54, 796–807.

Lieberman, V., 1999. *Beyond Binary Histories: Imagining Eurasia to c, 1830*. Ann Arbour: University of Michigan Press.

Lieberman, V., 2003. *Strange Parallels: Southeast Asia in Global Context, c.800–1830. volume 1. Integration on the Mainland*. Cambridge: Cambridge University Press.

Lieberman, V., 2009. *Strange Parallels: Southeast Asia in Global Context, c.800–1830. volume 2. Mainland Mirrors: Europe, Japan, China, South Asia, and the Islands*. Cambridge: Cambridge University Press.

Lunet de Lajonquière, É., 1902. *Inventaire Descriptif des Monuments du Cambodge* (vol. 1). Paris: Ernest Leroux.

Mak, P., 1984. *Chroniques royales du Cambodge (des Origines Legéndaires Jusqu'à Paramarājā Ier Traduction française Avec Comparaison Des Différentes Versions Et Introduction)*. Paris: École française d'Extrême-Orient.

Mak, P., 1995. *Histoire du Cambodge de la fin du XVIe siècle au début du XVIIIe siècle*. Paris: École française d'Extrême-Orient.

Mak, P., 2002. Essai de tableau chronologique des rois du Cambodge de la période post-angkorienne. *Journal Asiatique* 290(1), 101–61.

Maspero, G., 1904. *L'Empire Khmer, Histoire et Documents*. Phnom Penh: Imprimerie du protectorat.

Marriner, G., P. Grave, L. Kealhofer, M. Stark, D. Ea, R. Chhay, K. Phon & B.-S. Tan, 2018. New dates for old kilns: a revised radiocarbon chronology of stoneware production for Angkorian Cambodia. *Radiocarbon* 60(3), 901–24.

Men, R.S., 2007. *Les stoupas et les temples de la colline d'Oudong*. MA dissertation. Paris: Institut National des Langues et Civilisations Orientales.

Mikaelian, G., 2009a. *La royauté d'Oudong. Réformes Des Institutions Et Crise Du Pouvoir Dans Le Royaume Khmer Du Xviie Siècle*. Paris: Presses de l'Université Paris-Sorbonne.

Mikaelian, G., 2009b. Une "révolution militaire " au pays khmer? note sur l'artillerie post-angkorienne (XVI-XIXe siècles). *Udaya, Journal of Khmer Studies* 10, 57–134.

Mikaelian, G., 2013. Des sources lacunaires de l'histoire à l'histoire complexifiée des sources. Éléments pour une histoire des renaissances khmères (c. XIVe-c. XVIIIe s.). *Péninsule*, 65(2), 259–304.

Mikaelian, G., 2015. គំនិតថាប្រទេសខ្មែរចុះស្រុតឱនថយនិងប៉ុនប៉ងងើបឡើងវិញនៅសម័យកណ្តាល(The idea of decline and of attempts at renaissance of middle period Cambodia. *Udaya, Journal of Khmer Studies* 13, 35–45.

Mikaelian, G., 2016. Le passé entre mémoire d'Angkor et déni de Laṅvaek: La conscience de l'histoire dans le royaume khmer du XVIIe siècle, in *Le Passé Des Khmers. Langues, Textes, Rites*, eds. G. Mikaelian, N. Abdoul-Carime & J. Thach. Bern: Peter Lang, 167–212.

Moura, J., 1883. *Le royaume du Cambodge*. Paris: Ernest Leroux.

Nagasaki City Board of Education 長崎市教育委員会, 2011. Kōzenmachi Iseki: Minkan Byouin Ken-setsu ni Tomonau Maizou Bunkazai Hakkutsu Houkousho 興善町遺跡：民間病院建設に伴う埋蔵文化財発掘調査報告書 *(Kouzen-machi Site: Report on the Archaeological Excavation associated with the construction of a private hospital)*. Nagasaki: Nagasaki-shi Kyōiku Iinkai 長崎市教育委員会.

Nagazumi, Y., (ed.), 永積洋子編, 1987. Tôsen Yushutsunyuhin Suryou lchiran 1637–1833 Fukugen Tôsen Kamotu Aratamechô-Kihan Nimotsu Kaiwatashichô 唐船輸出入品数量一覧 1637–1833-復元唐船貨物改帳•帰帆荷物買渡帳-. Tokyo: Sōbunsha 創文社.

Népote, J., 2007. Les Portugais, le Cambodge et la vallée du mékong au xvie siècle, logique d'une découverte. *Péninsule* 54, 7–26.

Nhim, S., 2014–2016. Factors that led to the change of the Khmer capitals from the 15th to 17th century. *Renaissance Culturelle du Cambodge* 29, 33–107.

Nhim, S., 2020. Considerations regarding the fall of Longvek. *Udaya, Journal of Khmer Studies* 15, 39–56.

Piat, M., 1973. Note sur la première apparition du Cambodge dans la cartographie européenne. *Bulletin de la société des études indochinoises* 48(1), 119–20.

Phon, K., V. Leng, S. Taketh & B. Sour, ភុន ក ឡេង វ ស តាកតេ និង សួ ប, 2020. *Pro Pean Tharasas nov Tombon Peak Khang Keut Banteay Longvek, Khum Kampong Luong, Srok Ponhea Leu, Khet Kandal* ប្រព័ន្ធធារាសា;;;តនៅតំបន់ភាគខាងកើតបន្ទាយលង្វែក ក្នុងឃុំកំពង់ហ្លួង ស្រុកពញាឮ ខេត្តកណ្តាល *(The hydraulic system in the eastern area of Banteay Longvek in Kompong Luong Commune, Ponhea Leu District, Kandal Province). Unpublished Report.* Phnom Penh: Royal Academy of Cambodia រាជបណ្ឌិត្យសភាកម្ពុជា។.

Polkinghorne, M., B. Vincent, N. Thomas, D. Bourgarit, J. Douglas & F. Carò, 2015. *Sculpture Workshops of Angkor—Report (2011–2015), APSARA National Authority*. Sydney: The University of Sydney.

Polkinghorne, M., 2018. Reconfiguring kingdoms: the end of Angkor and the emergence of early modern period Cambodia, in *Angkor. Exploring Cambodia's Sacred City*, eds. T. McCullough, S.A. Murphy, P. Baptiste & T. Zéphir. Singapore: Asian Civilisations Museum, 252–71.

Polkinghorne, M., C.A. Morton, A.L. Roberts, R.S. Popelka-Filcoff, Y. Sato, V. Voeun, P. Thammapreechakorn, A. Stopic, P. Grave, D. Hein & V. Leng, 2019. Consumption and exchange in early modern Cambodia: NAA of brown-glaze stoneware from Longvek, 15th–17th centuries. *PLoS One* 14(5), e0216895.

Porée-Maspero, E., 1961. Traditions orales de pursat et de kampot. *Artibus Asiae* 24 (3/4), 394–98.

Pou, S., 1977. *Études sur le Rāmakerti (XVIe-XVIIe siècles)*, Paris: École française d'Extrême-Orient.

Pou, S., 1981. Notes historico-sémantiques khmères. *Asie Du Sud-Est Et Le Monde Insulindien* 12(1–2), 111–24.

Pou, S., 2000. *What Is Khmerology?* Phnom Penh: Ministry of Culture and Fine Arts.

Reid, A., 1988. *Southeast Asia in the Age of Commerce 1450–1680. Vol. 1: The Lands Below the Winds*. New Haven: Yale University Press.

Reid, A., 1990a. The seventeenth-century crisis in Southeast Asia. *Modern Asian Studies* 24(1), 639–59.

Reid, A., 1990b. An 'age of commerce' in Southeast Asian history. *Modern Asian Studies* 24(1), 1–30.

Reid, A., 1993a. *Southeast Asia in the Age of Commerce 1450–1680. Vol. 2: Expansion and Crisis*. New Haven: Yale University Press.

Reid, A., ed, 1993b. *Southeast Asia in the Early Modern Era: Trade, Power, and Belief*. Ithaca and London: Cornell University Press.

Revire, N., 2016. "L'habit ne fait pas le moine ": note sur un Buddha préangkorien sis à Longvek (Cambodge) et accoutré en Neak Ta. *Arts Asiatiques* 71, 159–66.

Sakai City Archaeological Centre, 堺市立埋蔵文化財センター, 2004. *Sakai Kangō Toshi Iseki hakkutsu chōsa gaiyō hōkoku* 堺環濠都市遺跡発掘調査概要報告:*SKT*二六三•甲斐町東二丁 *(Sakaki Walled City Site—SKT263•Kainochō Higashi 2chō)*. Sakai: Sakai Shiritsu Maizō Bunkazai Sentaa 堺市立埋蔵文化財センター.

San, S., 1971. Quelques chedei du phnom preah reach treap. *Bulletin des Étudiants de la Faculté d'Archéologie* 3–4, 52–62.

Sato, Y., 佐藤由似, 2016. Chūkinsei kanbojia ōto shūhen chiiki ni okeru tōjiki no juyō to ryūtsū中近世カンボジア王都周辺地域における陶磁器の需要と流通 (Demand and distribution of ceramics in the middle and early modern period of Cambodia capitals), in *Tōjiki no kōkogaku, daiyonkan, Yūzankaku* 陶磁器の考古学, 第四巻、雄山閣 *(Ceramic Archaeology in the Medieval and Early Modern Period 4)*, ed. T. Sasaki 佐々木達夫. Tokyo: Yuzankaku 雄山閣, 207–28.

Sato, Y. & M. Polkinghorne, 2017. Trade ceramics from Longvek, the 16th and 17th century capital of Cambodia: evidence from the first systematic archaeological investigations. *Journal of Southeast Asian Archaeology* 37, 67–71.

Seng C., 2017. *Conservation of Wooden Buddha. Post-Angkor Period.* Phnom Penh: Unpublished presentation.

Stark, M., 2014. The Archaeology of Early Modern South East Asia, in *The Oxford Handbook of Historical Archaeology*, eds. J. Symonds & V.-P. Herva. Oxford: Oxford University Press, 14pp.

Sugiyama, H. & Y. Sato, 2015. *Research Report on Royal Capital Sites in the Post-Angkor Period.* Nara: Nara National Research Institute for Cultural Properties.

Thompson, A., 1997. Changing perspectives: Cambodia after Angkor, in *Sculpture of Angkor and Ancient Cambodia: Millennium of Glory*, eds. H. I. Jessup & T. Zéphir. Washington (D.C): National Gallery of Art, 22–32.

Thompson, A., 1998. The ancestral cult in transition: reflections on spatial organization of Cambodia's early Theravada complex, in *Southeast Asian Archaeology: Proceedings of the 6th International Conference of the European Association of Southeast Asian Archaeologists, 2–6 September, Leiden*, eds. M.J. Klokke & T. de Brujin. Hull: Centre for Southeast Asian Studies, 273–95.

Thompson, A., 1999. *Mémoires du Cambodge.* PhD dissertation. Paris: Université Paris 8 Vincennes-Saint-Denis.

Thompson, A., 2000. Lost and found: the stupa, the four-faced Buddha and the seat of royal power, in *Middle Cambodia, in Southeast Asian Archaeology: Proceedings of the 7th International Conference of the European Association of Southeast Asian Archaeologists, 1998, Berlin*, eds. W. Lobo & S. Reiman. Hull: Centre for Southeast Asian Studies. Berlin: Ethnologisches Museum, 245–64.

Thompson, A., 2004. The future of Cambodia's past. A messianic middle-period Cambodian royal cult, in *History, Buddhism, and New Religious Movements in Cambodia*, eds. J. Marston, J. & E. Guthrie. Honolulu: University of Hawai'i Press, 13–39.

Thompson, A., 2016. *Engendering the Buddhist State: Territory, Sovereignty and Sexual Difference in the Inventions of Ankgor.* Oxford: Routledge.

Vickery, M., 1977a. *Cambodia after Angkor: the chronicular evidence for the fourteenth to sixteenth centuries [annotated by the author 2012].* PhD dissertation. New Haven: Yale University.

Vickery, M., 1977b. The 2/k.125 Fragment, A lost chronicle of Ayutthaya. *Journal of the Siam Society* 65(1), 1–80.

Vickery, M., 2004. *Cambodia and Its Neighbours in the 15th Century. Asia Research Institute Working Paper No. 27, Asia Research Institute, National University of Singapore, viewed.* https://ari.nus.edu.sg/publications/wps-27-cambodia-and-its-neighbors-in-the-15th-century/.

Wade, G., 2005. *Southeast Asia in the Ming Shi-lu: an open access resource. Asia Research Institute and the Singapore E-Press, National University of Singapore.* Available at: http://epress.nus.edu.sg/msl/

Wade, G., 2009. An early age of commerce in southeast Asia, 900–1300 CE. *Journal of Southeast Asian Studies* 40, 221–65.

Wade, G., 2010. Southeast Asia in the 15th century, in *Southeast Asia in the Fifteenth Century. The China Factor*, eds. G. Wade & S. Laichen. Singapore: National University of Singapore Press, 3–43.

Wade, G., 2011. 'Angkor and its external relations in the 14th–15th centuries as reflected in the Ming Shi-lu', paper presented to the International Conference on Angkor and Its Global Connections, Siem Reap, 10th–11th June 2011.

Winkel, Dr., 1882. Les relations de la Hollande avec le Cambodge et la Cochinchine au xviie siècle. *Excursions et reconnaissances* 12, 492–514.

Wolters, O.W., 1966. The Khmer king at Basan (1371–3) and the restoration of the Cambodian chronology during the fourteenth and fifteenth centuries. *Asia Major* 12(1), 44–89.

Zhou, D., 2007[1297]. *A Record of Cambodia: The Land and Its People*, trans. P. Harris. Chiang Mai: Silkworm Books.

34

YAMA, THE GOD CLOSEST TO THE KHMERS

Ang Choulean

As the god of death and the underWorld in Indian religious traditions, Yama occupies a special place in the pantheon, and he has been the focus of many scholarly works. In the Cambodian context, mentions of Yama appear in some of the earliest inscriptions, and representations of him also feature prominently in the iconography of Khmer monuments. He remains a popular figure in Cambodia even today. In this chapter, we set out to trace the history of Yama in the Khmer cultural milieu from the earliest times to the present day and to explore how traditions surrounding Yama have developed over time and continue to inform beliefs and practises in contemporary Cambodia.

Ancient Cambodia

In Brahmanic religious traditions originating in India, we find elaborate narratives about the journey of the dead into the underWorld, where the dead face Yama's judgement and their form of reincarnation is decided (see, for example, Stevenson 1920). These beliefs were well known in ancient Cambodia.

An inscription dating from the 7th century, K. 22, provides an account of the foundation of a temple dedicated to the divinity Harihara. According to the translation of George Cœdès (1951, 146), its Sanskrit text contains a warning to would-be vandals and thieves: *'may the impious . . . be, in the hells with various tortures, endlessly beaten by (Yama's) servants with mouth grimacing in anger'*. Yama's servants are known, in Sanskrit, as *kiṅkara*.

An 11th-century inscription, K. 277, contains similar warnings to potential vandals in both Sanskrit and Khmer, also featuring *kiṅkara*: line 20 of the Sanskrit text states *'May they be put in the terrible hell, endowed with an awful body beaten with iron sticks by [Yama's] violent servants'*, while lines 14–16 of the Khmer text warn us that vandals *'will undergo all sorts of royal punishments . . . to be reborn at the thirty-two hells of Yama's world without remission'* (Cœdès 1952, 159).

There is a noteworthy and recurring parallel in the inscriptional corpus between the king, on the one hand, inflicting punishment in the earthly realm and Yama, on the other hand, passing judgement in the afterlife. Each, in their own domain, is the preserver and guarantor of *dharma*, or 'order'. The comparison is made explicit in K. 598, dating from 1006 CE, which warns the reader to respect a judgement passed down by a tribunal, and endorsed by the king, in relation to a land dispute: *'If they do [disregard the deed] they will be punished by the kings; in the hereafter,*

DOI: 10.4324/9781351128940-41

they will be punished by Vraḥ Yama through sentence of the hells, starting with a stay in Avīci until the dissolution of the world' (Pou 2001, 237). Indeed, in the Indian tradition, as far back as the Vedic Period (ca. 1500 to ca. 500 BCE), Yama was regarded as somewhat analogous to a human king: Macdonnell (1897, 171), for example, notes that 'Yama is a god. He is, however, not expressly called a god, but only a king who rules the dead'.

Yama appears frequently in the iconography of monuments, sometimes as the central or solitary figure in a given context. To the best of my knowledge, all images of Yama are shown in association with the south, which, in a tradition also dating back to the Vedic Period, is conventionally the direction of his abode. To mention only a few examples, the imposing (but somewhat eroded) pediment of the central tower atop the 10th-century pyramid of Bakheng, at Angkor, has Yama on his buffalo as the main motif above the southern entrance. The southwest tower of the pyramid-temple of Pre Rup, as well as the central and northeastern towers of the East Mebon temple, all have an image of Yama on his buffalo as the centrepiece of their southern lintels. A pediment on the southern tower of Banteay Srei, as well as an associated lintel, both have Yama in their centre. At Angkor Wat, the god majestically occupies a central position in the eastern panel of the southern side of the Gallery of Bas-Reliefs, in a narrative relief showing a scene of judgement with depictions of the heavens and the hells. The upper register of the 60-metre-long relief is devoted to scenes of heaven, while the lower register is occupied with scenes of the 32 individual hells, each with a short inscription in Sanskrit naming the Worldly transgressions that have landed souls there in the afterlife. Towards the centre of the relief, and set high on the panel, the large and imposing figure of Yama presides over this scene, atop his buffalo. He is depicted with multiple hands, each one holding a stick, and the emphasis in this particular scene is on punishment: Yama is consigning souls to hell, assisted by his fearsome servants (cf. K. 22 and K. 277, previously) who brutalise the damned and ignore their pleas for mercy (Cœdès 1911; Pou 2001; Maxwell 2006) (Figure 34.1).

Although Yama is conventionally associated with the direction south, we notice that by the 13th to 14th centuries, the direction northeast rises to prominence in the symbolism of this god and eventually overshadows the southerly aspect. In Khmer culture, the northeast is associated with reincarnation, so we might interpret this as a ritual response to the fear of death and the uncertainties of the afterlife. Rebirth, the related dimension of death, draws attention henceforth. In theory, especially according to Theravāda Buddhism, one's present condition is determined by past actions; nonetheless, we need not simply resign ourselves to this and may actively seek ways to improve conditions in the hereafter. Only a perfect funerary ritual performance allows for such a hope.

In Angkor Thom, the Terrace of the Leper King stands at the northeast angle of the Angkor-era Royal Palace. Its double wall is totally covered by sculptures, arranged in superimposed ranges. Most sections of these ranges repeatedly show, in a seated position, a fierce character, rather demonic, holding a stick or a knife, but flanked on each side by a number of beautiful females. Were there scenes of torture, we could be almost certain that these female figures are *kiṅkara*. As things stand, however, the meaning of the figures is difficult to interpret, although it remains an intriguing hypothesis that they are, in fact, the servants of Yama. They are, in any case, not human. The most significant element is found atop the terrace: a statue of a strikingly handsome male, apparently human, but endowed nevertheless with a slight physical variation: two discreet canines, almost imperceptible, coming out from the upper lips. Another remarkable point is his complete nudity, yet with no genitals depicted. Obviously the sculptor tried to present him in his best light possible. In spite of the canines, he appears without the slightest ferocity. Thanks to George Cœdès (1928, 83), we know that this character is Yama, presented as the 'Supreme Lord of Order' (Figure 34.2). Originally, this figure likely held a stick in its hand,

Figure 34.1 Yama judging souls to hell on the bas-reliefs of Angkor Wat.
Source: (Photo C. Ang).

this being the classic attribute of Yama—but only one, not many as with the Yama depicted in Angkor Wat. This terrace of the so-called 'Leper King'—who we recognise, in reality, as Yama—is widely believed to have functioned as a cremation area and to have inspired the present configuration of Veal Men in Phnom Penh and Sanam Luang in Bangkok, which are both cremation areas situated to the northeast of Royal Palaces in modern-day Cambodia and Thailand (Cœdès 1947, 79–80). To the best of my knowledge, this association between Yama and the northeast direction is not found in India, or at least has not been remarked upon, but from this point forward it became an entrenched tradition in Cambodia.

Modern Cambodia

In modern Cambodia, Yama is systematically called Vraḥ Yamarāja[1] or 'King Yama', which, once again, emphasises his closeness to human beings (Cœdès 1947, 79–80). For many centuries, and up until recently, *yamarāja* was also the title of an office in Cambodia equivalent to the minister of justice. One particular mural found in a modern-day Khmer monastic hall, or *vihāra*, is rather special: here, the abode of Yama is nothing other than the 'Ministry of Justice', inscribed in Khmer text on the upper part of the panel. In the foreground are those who conducted themselves morally in their human life; opposite, on the right, are the authors of bad actions. Because this scene is set in the human world, Yama and his staff are rather benign and relatively natural in appearance; otherwise, scenes of hells shown in monasteries are always frightening.

Figure 34.2 Statue of Yama, Angkor Period.
Source: (Photo C. Ang).

As for directions, the south is no longer privileged in contemporary Cambodia, and one could say that its significance has been neglected or even forgotten. Scenes of hells on the interior walls of a *vihāra* are systematically located on the western side, opposite the entrance to the building, which we typically find on the eastern side. The vihāra of Wat Trach pagoda, in the compound of Chau Srei Vibol temple near Angkor, even presents scenes of heavens and hells on its outer walls: heavens on the east and hells (featuring 'King Yamarāj') once again on the west. In reality, the switch from south to west has no symbolic significance: it is simply because modern *vihāra* do not have four entrances like ancient Khmer temples (even if, in many ancient temples, we might find that three of those entrances are 'false doors'). Symbolically, the axis of a *vihāra* is only east–west, and in terms of symbolism, the west may sometimes have negative connotations, being associated with the sunset and with death. In this respect, the symbolism of Yama in modern monasteries can be compared with the symbolism of Angkor Wat, which also has an unusual orientation toward the west, perhaps because of its role as a funerary temple. A frightening figure, Yama is there to remind us of the principles of law and order.

Appeals to Yama can also be made to allay the consequences of moral transgressions. In some rituals, in particular as they relate to the deceased, an invocation is made to Yamarāj, 'King Yama', or to related figures known as Vraḥ Kālayamarāj and Vraḥ Kiṅkaraṇaṃ. In the figure of Kālayamarāj we see an association, or even a kind of merger, between the identity of *kāla* (a common figure and motif in Khmer art, carrying connotations of 'time', 'time of death', 'death') and *yama*. This fusion is occasionally even translated into iconography (Ang 2004, 96), although this is rare. As for Kiṅkaraṇaṃ, it is simply an altered form of the Sanskrit *kiṅkara*, which we recognise once again from the inscriptional record as servants of Yama.[2] The Khmer word does not specify whether it is singular or plural, but nonetheless a native speaker has no trouble in recognising it as referring to a sole character. Thus we see that the troop of torturers associated with Yama—the kiṅkara of ancient Cambodia—has evolved in the Modern Period to a single, prominent assistant known as *Kiṅkaraṇaṃ*. This figure makes another important appearance in present-day rituals: Tā Kiṅ, literally the 'Grand-father Kiṅ', is invoked in a short prayer that devotees whisper while making rice balls called *piṇḍa* to be offered to the damned souls, or *preta*, during the annual Fortnight of the Dead, thus enabling their reincarnation.

Fortnight of the Dead

I provide a detailed summary of the Fortnight of the Dead, known as Pchum Ben in the Khmer language, elsewhere (Ang 2006), but a brief summary will be useful here. In this most important religious event (which falls in the months of September to October), the same specific rite is performed within Buddhist monasteries during each of its 14 nights:

- People gather in an open building called a *sālā* around 7 or 8 o'clock in the evening, making small rice balls, each one of them symbolising a human body, to be offered to the *preta*, or souls without a body, who need a corporeal form to reincarnate. While shaping the balls, the makers whisper a short incantation, imploring 'Grand-father Kiṅ'—the modern equivalent of the *kiṅkara* of ancient times—to secure the dog(s), so that the rice balls can be safely conveyed to their ancestors (some of whom may still be in a state of wandering souls). As for the reference to dog(s), this can probably be understood as being one sole dog, and as the dog of Tā Kiṅ specifically. We recognise here an altered memory of the classical Indian belief, certainly vivid in ancient Cambodia, of the two fierce dogs of Yama, each of them endowed with four eyes.
- Before dawn, around 4:30 AM, people undertake a procession around the temple (*vihāra*), completing three tours around it. While walking, they throw the rice balls one by one toward different spots: the rice balls are intended for the *preta*. On each tour around the *vihāra*, the procession passes by an altar that has been built specially for the festival, located at the north-east corner of the temple's veranda. Each time the procession reaches this altar, everyone halts and, following the lead of an officiant, declares a short prayer addressing Vraḥ Yamarāj.

We observe that Yama, in this context, is being invoked not so much as an implacable judge but rather as a merciful king who is ready to deliver the *preta*, the disembodied souls of one's ancestors, from their predicament. In this context, the Buddhist doctrine that previous behaviour determines one's fate is transcended by appeals to Yama, who offers the possibility of escape from the consequences of past actions.

Cremation

In the Angkor region today, including in villages that are very rural in character, funerals appear at first glance to be very elaborate and complex. However, by taking the time to analyse the ritual, we can grasp not only its general meaning but also the specific meaning behind each individual sequence. Animism, Brahmanism, and Buddhism are blended in these rituals, but in a perfectly coherent way. The Brahmanic part is still strong, if not particularly prominent. Looking at cremation in particular, we can reasonably hypothesise that ritual legacies of the Angkor Period persist in rural villages in present-day Cambodia. Ang, Preap, and Sun (2014) offer a detailed description of the proceedings, and what follows is an abridged account.

To begin with, the body of the recently deceased is rapidly buried in an area belonging to the whole village community, called *gok khmoc*, or 'forest of the dead'. This first step involves quite a simple ritual, to be undertaken by any officiant that the bereaved family can call upon. From that point, the period of interment in the ground should ideally last three years, although the stay may be shorter or longer depending on the family's means.

The second and final step is cremation. Most of the time, it is a collective ceremony, and it can be very spectacular and costly, especially if—as sometimes happens—it is organised around and alongside the cremation of a monastery's abbot. But even the poorest cremation will follow the main principles. It takes place in a cremation area, featuring a fine architectural ensemble that is nonetheless usually provisional and destined to be dismantled after the event (Figure 34.3).

The cremation area is square, oriented east–west and north–south, and delimited by a fence. The fence is made with thin slats of bamboo; it is low, appears very light, and is almost imperceptible most of the time. Yet it is indispensable since it stands for the limit of the world, here rendered as a microcosm. In the middle of each side stands a gate, made clearly visible to indicate the four main directions.

The cremation pavilion itself sits in the centre of the square. Close to the southwest fence is a light building designed for Buddhist monks and lay people to perform necessary rituals. This building is only partly walled: some or all of the western and southern sides will be enclosed by a wall, and the rest remains totally open. But the southwest corner must always be enclosed, and the meaning of this is clear: the whole building looks towards the northeast, through the pyre at the centre of the square, towards a third construction in the northeastern quadrant of the walled cremation area. This symbolic axis is materialised by a cotton thread which actually links the three constructions.

The construction in the northeast corner of the square consists of three components: an altar called *buddhaguṇ*, a second altar called *yamarāj*, and, directly on the ground, five *bhnaṃ khsāc'* or 'sand-mounds' arranged in a quincunx. The two altars have no images of the divinities implied in their names: there is no Buddha image on the *buddhaguṇ*, and there is no Yama image on the *yamarāj*. One can only see common ritual objects, made of vegetal material (called *pāy sī, slā dharm*, etc.) whose original meaning is lost to us in the present day (Ang 1986, 85–95). The five sand-mounds represent the whole world, reduced to a central mound surrounded by its four satellites; it elaborates a concept of space, or more precisely here the concept of a new (or

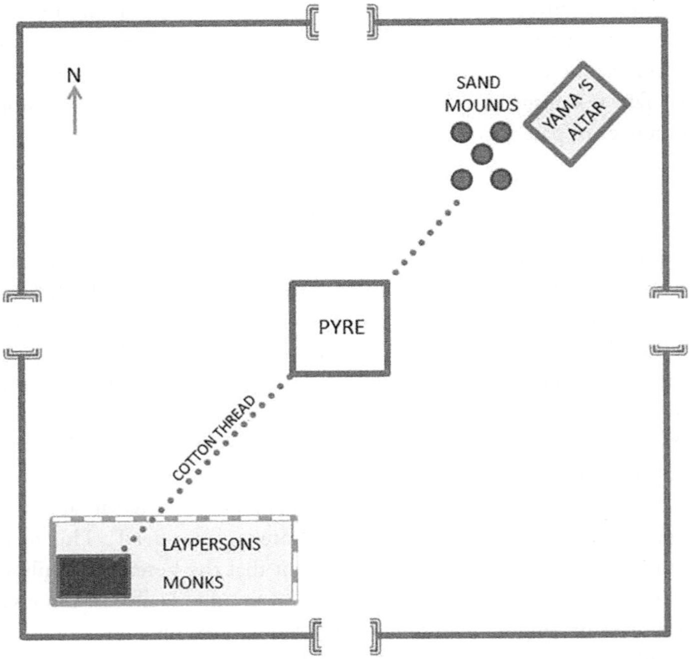

Figure 34.3 Schematic layout of cremation area typical in rural Khmer villages.

renewed) space deriving from a new (or renewed) time. The new time is re-birth, since the aim of any cremation is to ensure (a good) reincarnation.

The buddhaguṇ altar is always built with care and makes for an attractive sight, but what it stands for is somewhat vague. The word itself means 'virtues of the Buddha'. It is true that cremation today is performed in a Buddhist context—if not always a Buddhist monastery, then at least with the systematic presence and religious performance of Buddhist monks. It is also true that the Buddhist moral dimension is ever present, reminding devotees that good or bad actions committed in this life unavoidably engender a good, or bad, reincarnation. But this Buddhist moral order is situated somehow at an upper level of reasoning, as an ideal to which one aspires. The more immediate concern of the living is to ensure a good new life for the actual soul[3] who will shortly be reborn through the final ritual sequence of cremation, called *prae rūp*, or 'reversal of the body (thus the personhood)', which explains the presence of the second altar, that of Yama (see Thompson 2005). Located near the first one, it appears more modest in size, but the presence of the Yama altar is crucial. In the course of the cremation, as the fire quickly grows, the people gather and sit in front of the two altars. Led by an officiant, they repeat after him a series of verses. In these verses, homage is paid first of all to the Buddha, of course—but the homage sounds rather cursory, we might say, with the Buddha merely being given customary due as the highest moral authority. We arrive directly at more practical and immediate concerns as the prayer is turned to Yama. He is begged to keep the souls safe from any punishment and from any kind of bad sojourn in the afterlife.

At this point, it is worth coming back briefly to consider the altars. In the rural areas of the present-day Angkor region, a cremation ceremony may be extravagant and spectacular or, on the contrary, may appear very modest. But even the poorest cremation still follows the main ritual pattern, obviously inherited from Angkorian times. If only one altar appears in the north-east corner, instead of the customary three, it is systematically that of Yama (Figure 34.4). Once again, the emphasis here is on pragmatism: after all, the destiny of the dead, on their journey to rebirth, rests in Yama's hands.

Another key element should be mentioned here, as it relates to Yama: the *daṅ' braliṅ*, or 'banner of the souls' (Ang 2017, 77–79). This is a personalised banner that must be made for each of the dead in a cremation ceremony. It is no more, and no less, than an ID card. The name of the deceased is inscribed upon it. Sometimes the name of the main officiant, called a *yogī*, is also inscribed, since the participation of a prestigious and renowned *yogī* in the ceremony may draw the attention of Yama and his attendants, ease the deceased's passage through the afterlife, and ensure a good rebirth.[4] Here we arrive at a crucial concept: that a funeral ritually conducted in the correct way is the *sine qua non* of a favourable rebirth. If, in addition, the chief officiant is someone whose religious and moral prestige is unanimously recognised, then one can have even higher hopes.

To sum up, and roughly speaking, the buddhaguṇ altar reflects an ideal—a moral one, and a Buddhist one—while dealing with the Yama altar is a pragmatic way of responding to more immediate concerns. Let's recall that in Buddhism, one cannot escape, in the next life, the fruit of a bad action committed in the present one. No devotee of Buddhism would deny it. At the same time, however, everyone is well aware that bad actions and bad thinking are, to some degree or another, an unavoidable part of human life. A solution has to be found, and the dreadful Yama may turn out to be a saviour.

Figure 34.4 Altar dedicated to Yama (far left) placed within the northeast corner of cremation area.
Source: (Photo C. Ang).

A Backwards Rite of Passage

Among the rites marking the different steps of an individual's life, the one called *camroen āyu* or 'age expanding' aims to prolong the duration of an aged person's life (a mother, or a respected person among the family or the village community) from around 65 years old onward. It can be considered a rite of passage, even if the passage in question is a backward one rather than a progression forward (Ang et al. 2014, 67–72). In this rite, the candidate, although living, is considered dead. As new life follows from death, he or she is considered to be symbolically reborn in the course of, or more precisely at the end of, the ritual. As in cremation ceremonies, a microcosm is laid out. In the example shown in Figure 34.3, only the four corners of the sacred area are marked by a fence. The Yama altar, set up in the northeast corner, with five tiny sand-mounds on it, is linked by a thread (invisible on the photo) to the construction sheltering monks and laypersons. In the centre, the elderly candidate will lay like a dead person, entirely covered by a shroud, recalling the positioning of the funeral pyre in cremation ceremonies. The shroud will be slowly withdrawn by a monk, suggesting that the candidate is reborn. Although summarised to the extreme, the ritual of *camroen āyu* is not difficult to understand. It is focused on rebirth—specifically, on appealing to Yama in order to ensure a favourable one.

Rice Cycle

For the reasons stated previously, Yama is intimately associated with the idea of a 'cycle', more precisely the cycle of death and rebirth. In addition to his role in the cycles of human life, Yama's involvement also extends to cycles of rice cultivation. Why rice? To various degrees, the closeness between humans and rice stands out as a common theme among the different cultures in Asia, and one could argue that this is especially so in Cambodia. More than closeness, we can say in a figurative sense that rice is a kind of double, or a twin, of humans. This is particularly true in the Angkor region. And because this area, more so than many others, still keeps many 'Angkorian' traditions, and especially beliefs and ritual practices, we have good reason to believe that what we observe here is as old as the Angkor civilisation itself.

The rice cultivation cycle, stretching approximately from May to December, features two ritual events, the first marking the opening of the cycle and the second its closing. Two 'gods' or spirits are implicated in both events in different ways: the *qnak tā* (neak ta) and Yama. The former, an animist guardian spirit of village communities, is the most prominent of all the animistic pantheon in Cambodia and is too well known to warrant further description here (see Porée-Maspéro 1952, 6–15). We might underline, however, that this spirit is associated with cultivation, and with rice cultivation in particular, and recall that his main dimension is the capacity to ensure an abundant crop. It is natural therefore that the two ritual events of the cultivation cycle implicate the qnak tā, given his status and his function. By contrast, the presence of Yama requires some explanation.

Throughout Cambodia, rituals related to rice cultivation are generally performed right in front of, or very close to, the house of the qnak tā, which is often tiny and visually unattractive. Aside from a basic set of offerings, no large-scale arrangement is needed, because only the qnak tā is implicated. In the Angkor area, on the other hand, a much larger space is usually required for these rituals. Let's consider an example from Thlork village (Banteay Srei district), specifically the ritual opening of the rice cultivation season. Called *chlaṅ cetr*, this is a ritual that would seem odd even to Cambodians who are unfamiliar with this area. The name means 'crossing over [the month of] *cetr*', which implies entering into *bisākh*—the month of the first rains, in a typical year—and therefore the beginning of the new rice cycle. In our example, which comes from the year 2006, that day was the third day of the waxing moon of *bisākh*, corresponding to April 30. The qnak tā, whose name is Daok, is a flat square stone. Built under a tree, his hut is small and rather dilapidated. Inside, one can notice a number of packs of seed-rice that people have placed as offerings, as if to receive some kind of benediction from the qnak tā before rice is sown.

In places other than the Angkor region, villagers would gather directly in front of the hut. However, people convert the surface of a desiccated rice-field, located directly to the south of the hut and left fallow since the previous December's harvest, into a square space of about 15 m on each side in which to perform the ritual (Figure 34.5). If we compare this space to the ones prepared for cremation ceremonies (see, for example, Figure 34.3), we notice that it lacks a cremation pavilion in the centre, since there is no body to be burned; nonetheless, in the northeast corner there is still a Yama altar, associated once again with five sand-mounds on the ground (Figure 34.6). In the southwest of the square space, the monks assemble in a shelter, which is linked to the Yama altar by a cotton thread. The focus of proceedings is on the next cycle of cultivation, which is due to arrive shortly.

The ritual that I have briefly described here (*chlaṅ cetr*) is concerned only with the opening of a new cycle of cultivation. As for its counterpart, the closing of the cycle (around December–January), in general, the event is richer and more solemn. But schematically the spatial layout remains the same. One addition that is very noticeable, even though it has no special symbolic meaning, involves piling up mounds of paddy rice in the shelter for monks and laypersons or outside the shelter as well. For that, each family brings a basket of paddy rice, in general harvested a few weeks before. As the amount brought grows, people shape it into mound(s), usually numbering one to five.

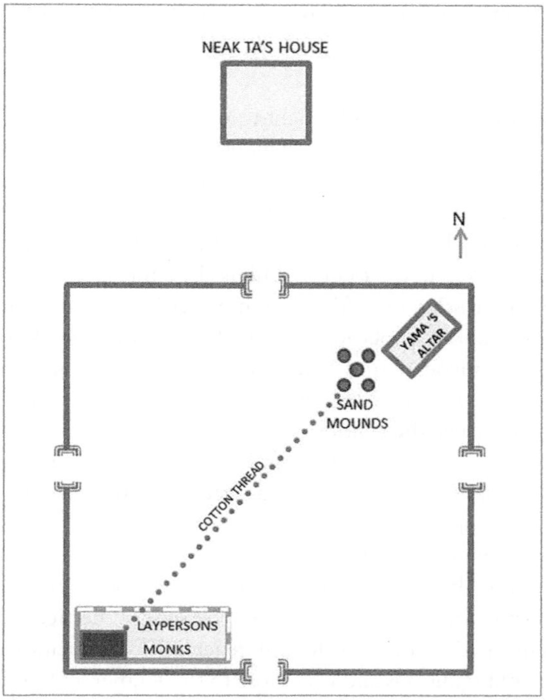

Figure 34.5 Schematic layout of area for rice cultivation ritual at Thlork village.

Figure 34.6 Five sand mounds and Yama altar erected for rice cultivation ritual, Thlork village.
Source: (Photo C. Ang).

After the ceremony, the whole amount is brought to the monastery and offered to its inhabitants. Not only is this visually striking, but its socio-religious dimension is genuine, since the amount of paddy gathered is often significant in terms of sustaining the monastery. Importantly, the event periodically reinforces the links between ancestral Animism and Buddhism and between villagers and the monastery. Indeed, the rituals express a kind of tripartite relationship, since the old Brahmanistic Yama is also present and is linked to the Buddhist monks by a thread.

Now let's think about 'crossing over [the month of] *cetr*' in its pure ritual signification, irrespective of the social or religious implications. Do villagers in the Angkor area believe that the qnak tā alone, without the invocation of Yama, isn't capable of ensuring sufficient rainfall and a good harvest in the season to come? Certainly not, or rather the reasoning is not articulated in these terms. Unquestionably the world of rice cultivation is basically that of the qnak tā. The square space constructed immediately south of his abode is not put in place to 'complete' anything. Nothing is lacking. One might conclude, therefore, that the two constructions—permanent in the case of the qnak tā's house and provisional in the case of the Yama altar—are two independent yet complementary elements.

It will be worthwhile to briefly consider traditional practices among the Kuoy, an ethnic group in present-day Cambodia, as they relate to the closing of the rice cultivation season. The choice of the Kuoy is dictated by the fact that, in general, this population is known to be conservative with regard to old traditions and very close to the Khmer, culturally speaking. We have reasons to believe that since ancient times the Kuoy were 'Indianized', so to speak, by way of cultural exchange with the Khmer. In other words, some traditions now lost among the Khmer may persist among some of the multiple Kuoy groups now scattered across northern Cambodia and northeast Thailand. Relevant here is an unpublished ethnographic survey, conducted in late December 2004 by Preap Chanmara and Siyonn Sophearith, in the village of Veal Vèng, in the northern part of Kompong Thom province. It focuses on the ceremony called /sɒ:y ve:/ which marks the closing of the rice cycle. The ceremony spans two days—the afternoon of the first day and the morning of the second—and is performed in two distinct locations, although these are not far from each other. Thus there is an interesting spatial and chronological separation between the animistic rites performed on the first day and Buddhist rites on the second day.

On the first day, the rituals deal with the qnak tā. The villagers and the spirit communicate with each other through a female medium, who enters into a trance for that purpose. It is notable that before everything, the medium pays her respect to Yama by performing a dance (Figure 34.7). It is only afterwards that she starts serving as a medium, allowing conversation between human and spirit. Therefore, from a pure ritual standpoint, this first day deals with the world of rice cultivation, which is the primary target of the event. The people thank the qnak tā for the recent crop and beg him to ensure a good one in the next season. Yama is there to remind people that rice cultivation obeys cycles: for now, the rice-fields are drying out, but they will be full of life in the next cycle.

In the second location, on the second day, there is a light structure on stilts sheltering monks and laypersons. A few metres to the northeast is an altar for Yama. Between the two structures lies a stack of paddy rice that has been brought from all households, which will be erected in 'paddy-mounds' (Figure 34.8 shows a preparatory step).

Figure 34.7 Female medium performing dance to Yama before rice cultivation ritual.

Source: (Photo C. Ang).

Figure 34.8 Rice stacked between the Yama altar and shelter.

Source: (Photo C. Ang).

What we see among this Kuoy community is essentially the same as what we observe in the Angkor area, as far as this closing rite is concerned, except for the clear separation—both in terms of space and of time—between the animistic and the Buddhist rituals. In all cases, however, the presence of Yama, through his altar, is constant.

A Brief Return to the Early Period of the Religious History of Cambodia

So far we have seen that, in modern times, the idea of endlessly repeating 'cycles' of death and rebirth is inseparable from Yama, to such an extent that important events relating to human life—as well as the source of that life, which is to say rice—are marked by rituals featuring this special god. Unfortunately, ancient Cambodia left no trace of any sacred texts dealing with these questions. But this is unremarkable: no other comparable text reaches us, either. Most surviving texts from the Angkor era are inscriptions in stone, and they typically deal with different matters. However, from studies of Angkor and its cultural legacy, we have no doubt whatsoever that classical Indian religious texts were well known, at least by a certain social class, in this country.

There is abundant scholarship about Indian myths which explain the origin and the status of Yama. All studies point out that Yama's death marks the origin of time, and, since humankind is subject to time, we came to the world subsequent to Yama's death. And since time is cyclical, human existence is involved in an endless loop of time cycles. Malamoud (2002,

55–65) provides a detailed treatment of this subject, and it is worthwhile to summarise one of these Indian myths from his text in order to shed light on contemporary Khmer ritual practices:

> In the beginning there was no night, only day, because there was only light which lasted without interruption. There were only gods, no human. Yama had a twin sister named Yami. Once, Yama died (we don't know either how or why),[5] which put Yami in an inconsolable sorrow. All the other gods came to see her and ask: 'why do you cry?'. She answered 'because my brother dies'. The gods: 'when?'. Yami: 'today'. And she continues crying incessantly. Long after that the gods came back. Same question 'why?', same answer 'today'. The unbearable situation continued like that without an issue. Then the gods discussed between themselves and took the decision to create night, in view to have 'time'. From then on time exists with day and night alternating. One day later the gods come to see Yami who still cries, but in a lesser degree. Question 'why?'. Answer: 'because my brother died'. Question 'When?'. Answer: 'Yesterday'. Days after Yami's pain and sorrow went down and down, because time wears out everything 62.

Adopted in Khmer vocabulary with no alteration, Sanskrit *kāla* means both 'time' and 'death'. Now, let's repeat that Yama was at the origin of time, and, time being engendered following Yama's death, humankind was born from then on. Just like the alternation of day and night, a human is born and eventually dies, then is reborn, then dies again, and so on. The cycle has no end. Yama is then the god of the dead and, at the same time, of the living. He is the god of the human condition. In a manner of speaking, he can be considered the first human, at least the god closest to the human condition, both dead and alive. In addition to this, it seems that the Indian prototype, without changing its basic nature, is subject to a particular emphasis in Cambodia: the dimension of rebirth—or, more exactly, a *good rebirth*[6]—seems to overshadow Yama's role as the judge of past actions.

Conclusion

The lesson drawn from what we see here can be summarised in two main points. The first one is the shift of the direction associated with Yama from south to northeast since ancient Cambodia, visibly from around the 14th century with the Terrace of the Leper King in Angkor Thom. Based on his position as god of the dead, Yama is actively sought as a saviour enabling good reincarnation. In cremation ceremonies, as well as in rituals symbolising birth and rebirth (for example, the 'age expanding' rituals and those of the Fortnight of the Dead) Yama appears more as the god of salvation than a strict and righteous supreme judge. If he keeps inspiring fear, he also represents hope. All known rituals in relation to Yama show that the latter dimension is the most valorised. For that reason, and this is the second point, not only is he close to being human,[7] but he is also the closest thing to humans—which is rice.

Notes

1 Pronounced (/preah yomɔriəc/).

2 In grammatical terms, it can be said that the Sanskrit word is declined in genitive plural; I express my thanks to Dr Chhom Kunthea for this observation.

3 The term 'soul' is not totally accurate but is used here for the sake of convenience. The plural 'souls' is closer to the Khmer notion of *brali*.

4 I have witnessed two cases where *yogi*, both now deceased, strongly believed that they were personally known to Yama and his entourage.

5 By definition a god is immortal. Therefore, Yama is an entirely special god, since he has experienced death.

6 From an Indian or a classical Indo-Khmer standpoint, this would be a rebirth in the group of deceased called *pit┘*, literally 'fathers', who are recognized and venerated ancestors.

7 In inscription K. 277 (previously) we saw a parallel between the human king and Yama who, between them, punish temple vandals.

References

Ang, C., 1986. *Les Êtres Surnaturels dans la Religion Populaire Khmère.* Paris: Cedoreck.

Ang, C., 2004. La mort-renaissance en abstraction iconographique. *Udaya, Journal of Khmer Studies* 5, 84–98.

Ang, C., 2006. Vom Brahmanismus zum buddhismus betrachtungen zum totenfest in kambodscha, in *Angkor*, eds. W. Lobo & Helen Ibbitson Jessup. Bonn: Göttliches Erbe Kambodschas, 238–42.

Ang, C., 2017. Bringing India to Cambodia: two examples of bridges, in *India and Southeast Asia: Cultural Discourse*, eds. A. Dallapiccola & A. Verghese. Mumbai: The K R Cama Oriental Institute, 71–82.

Ang, C., C. Preap & C. Sun, 2014. *The Course of Individual Khmer Life, Seen through Rites of Passage (in Khmer).* Phnom Penh: Yosothor.

Cœdès, G., 1911. Les bas-reliefs d'Angkor Vat. *Bulletin de la Commission Archéologique Indochinoise*: 170–220.

Cœdès, G., 1928. Etudes cambodgiennes. XIX. La date du Bayon. *Bulletin de l'École française d'Extrême-Orient* 28, 81–112.

Cœdès, G., 1947. *Pour Mieux Comprendre Angkor.* Paris: Adrien Maisonneuve.

Cœdès, G., 1951. *Inscriptions du Cambodge, III.* Paris: E. de Boccard.

Cœdès, G., 1952. Id., IV.

MacDonell, A.A., 1897. *Vedic Mythology.* Strassburg: Verlag Von Karl J. Trübner.

Malamoud, C., 2002. *Le Jumeau Solaire.* Paris: Editions du Seuil.

Maxwell, T. & J. Poncar, 2006. *Of Gods, Kings and Men: The Reliefs of Angkor Wat.* Germany: Edition Panorama.

Poree-Maspero, E., 1952. *Etudes sur les rites agraires des Cambodgiens, Tome I.* Paris-La Haye: Mouton & Co.

Pou, S., 2001. *Nouvelles Inscriptions du Cambodge II et III,* Paris: École française d'Extrême-Orient.

Sinclair Stevenson, M., 1920. *The Rites of the Twice-Born.* Oxford: Oxford University Press.

Thompson, A., 2005. *Calling the Souls. A Cambodian Ritual Text.* Phnom Penh: Reyum.

35
INARGUABLY ANGKOR

Penny Edwards

Archaeological research and scientific discovery continue to reveal new layers of Angkor's existence, while epigraphic and philological research drill ever deeper into the temples' inscriptions. The depth and granularity of such scholarship seem at odds with the icon of Angkor Wat, instantly decipherable, whether on the Cambodian flag, a UNESCO website, or tattooed in body ink. But both archaeologist and iconographer share a fascination with Angkor *in situ*. In this chapter I argue that Angkor has only ever existed in relation to elsewhere and explore how the temple derives its meaning from other places and other eras.

There is nothing inherently new in this argument. Sheldon Pollock has emphasised Angkor's linkage to a Sanskrit cosmopolis, Ashley Thompson has established Angkor's meaning as a site of pilgrimage in the mediaeval to early modern era, and Ang Choulean has documented the polylingual inscriptions of the temple over time (Thompson 2004; Pollock 2009; Ang 2013). But where that body of scholarship begins with the runes of Angkor, and works outward from them, this chapter works back to Angkor through poetry and song. Inspired by Angkor Wat and written and circulated off-site, these mobile inscriptions enabled Cambodians to navigate episodes of loss and trauma and created circuits of collective memory in ways that often skirted the national. 'In music and songs there are no borders', reflected drummer Ouk Sam Art, reminiscing about Cambodia's music industry in the 1960s and 1970s (Pirozzi 2014).

Poetry and song conjure the paradox of Angkor's ephemeral endurance, in Cambodia and among its diaspora. As the anthropologist Maurice Bloch famously argued, '*You cannot argue with a song*' (Bloch 1974, 71 his emphasis). Written at significant historical junctures of 20th-century Cambodia, these texts are works in motion. Unlike the inscriptions at the temple, their function is not to record an act but rather to enact a relationship between the writer, the reader/listener, and the temples. These lyrical fragments offer a wide-angle view of Angkor as a site of heritage that is at once national and global, tangible and intangible.

The first text I consider, *Niras Nokor Vat* (Journey to Angkor Wat) was composed at a time of political transition by the polymath intellectual and ethicist Suttantaprija Ind, to commemorate the retrocession of Siem Reap—annexed by Siam in 1794—to Cambodia in 1909 (Ind 1934). Written in the *niras* verse form also popular in Siam, where it is known as *nirat*, the poem was completed between 1909 to 1915, initially circulated in hand-written copies, and broke posthumously into print in a 1934 issue of the Buddhist Institute journal Kambuja Surya.

DOI: 10.4324/9781351128940-42

The second text I consider, written at a time of acute political transition and in the aftermath of genocide, is the song *Oh Phnom Penh Euy*. Composed in 1979 by Keo Chenda, minister of culture and information in the People's Republic of Kampuchea, *Oh Phnom Penh Euy* works as a *niras/nirat* in verso. Replete with longing for what has been lost, it seeks to rally morale against Khmer Rouge guerrilla forces while rousing artists and a deeply traumatised people to return to the country's capital. A eulogy for the victims of the Khmer Rouge genocide, Keo's song touches only tangentially on Angkor: as a symbol on a flag, an icon of a civilisation. But it is precisely this gesture that galvanises Keo's dirge into a call to arms: to protect those same temples whose shade offers protection, a metaphor in turn for the new regime's pledge to protect the people from the Khmer Rouge. The third text I consider is *Sacred Vows*, a full-length poetry collection spanning several regimes written by the Cambodian American poet U Sam Ouer, who was the victim of political persecution by the People's Republic of Kampuchea and sought asylum in the United States in the early 1990s (Oeur 1998). In my analysis of the place and displacement of Angkor in U Sam Oeur's poetry, I pay particular attention to his haunting verse *Niras Wobatoa* (*The Fall of Culture*) and to other poems in the collection that owe to the *niras* genre in title, form, or mood.

Angkor in Verse: *Niras Nokor Vat*

In erudition and literary merit, Suttintaprija Ind's *Niras Nokor Vat* (Journey to Angkor Wat) stands out among the scores of travelogues to Angkor published in the colonial era. It is also the only known published long verse narrative in Khmer by a Cambodian author about Angkor from the early 20th century. Written in a time of linguistic tension and political change, Ind's work provides a transcript of transition and reflects critical shifts in the craft of writing as texts moved from hand to print production.

Composed in 525 stanzas in tetrameter, *Niras Nokor Vat* charts Ind's voyage from Battambang to Siem Reap to Angkor. Ind set sail on the Sangke River on 3 September 1909 to join a ceremony at Angkor Wat, presided over by King Sisowath and the Governor General of Indochina marking the retrocession of Siem Reap, Battambang, and Sisophon to Cambodia from Siam.

Ind's *Niras Nokor Vat* navigates different realms of geography and consciousness, downstream and upriver to Angkor, as the author reflects on loss, longing, and landscape. My analysis of Ind's poem focuses on a few stanzas that convey his sense of place and journey as part of the poem's wider contemplation on the natural world and the Buddhist universe. Unlike the inscriptions at Angkor, Ind's verse is intrinsically mobile. Its allure does not diminish with the passage of time and space from the places that inspired it: Conversely, distance enhances the allure of the spaces it describes.

Oknya Suttantaprija Ind was born in Roka Kaoung, Muk Kampoul district of Kandal Province in 1859. At 19, he moved to Battambang town where he resided and studied at Wat Kaev, ordaining as a Bhikku (monk) at 20. Ind continued his studies in Bangkok for seven years before returning to Battambang city, where he joined Wat Kandal, disrobing in circa 1896. Throughout these formative years of Ind's life, Battambang, along with Siem Reap and Sisophon, were administered by Siam through a system of locally appointed governors (Chhuong 1994: 42–43).

Schooled in Theravada Buddhist ethics, Ind wrote and translated 44 Pali texts and gained local renown for his Khmer poems (Hansen 2007). His inquisitive mind, literary sensibility, and proficiency in Khmer, Pali, and Thai would likely have exposed him to a range of genres. In her study of Buddhism and modernity in colonial Cambodia, Anne Hansen has observed how 'in the midst of the movement toward print, the whole enterprise of Khmer writing itself was undergoing scrutiny and reevaluation' with the lack of a unified system of writing described as 'anarchy' by French scholar official George Cœdès (Hansen 2007, 140–41; 218). From 1901 to 1904, Ind collaborated with Sindulphe Tandart, a Catholic missionary priest in Battambang, to compile *The Tandart Dictionary*. From 1914 to 1924 Ind lived in Phnom Penh, where he worked with the Dictionary Commission and remained a passionate advocate for the Khmer orthography and pronunciation of the Battambang region, earning the illustrious title Oknya Suttantaprija (Buakamsri 2012, iii). Hansen links Ind's textual innovations and his modes of critical and synoptic writing in Gatilok to the emergence of print culture in Phnom Penh (Hansen 2007, 153–54).

Composed and inscribed between 1909 and 1915, *Niras Nokor Vat* was discovered after Ind's death among a number of *kraeng* manuscripts in his possession. Concertina-like manuscripts of stiff paper commonly made from mulberry leaves and inscribed with a reed, *kraeng* were the preferred medium for folktales, medical manuals, or magic formulae. As Trent Walker has shown in his brilliant doctoral dissertation, *kraeng* were also used for liturgical texts and were crucial to the transmission of sonic rites (Walker 2018). Since the development of the Khmer written script in the 6th century, treatises, religious scriptures, and official literature were named after the medium in which they were preserved, as *satra-slik-rit* (literally, stiff-leaf-scripture) (Nath 1967). Long, young leaves were gathered from the *traing* tree and then dried, hardened, and treated for inscription. In scent and feel, these media were textured echoes of the natural environment. Each would have reinforced the writer's, copyist's, and reader's sensory connection to the plants and trees evoked in the script. Ind's *Niras Nokor Vat* was written in an era of transition between such hand-produced texts and machine printing. 'While Cambodia had no printed books, the people of Battambang borrowed [Suttantaprija Ind's] books (*siw-piw*) from each other', writes historian Tauch Chhuong, 'copying them out by hand to keep and distributing them one to the other for reading, and some memorised many pages of his poems' (1994, 99). The Phnom Penh manuscript from which the Buddhist Institute later printed Ind's verse narrative *Nirat Nokor Vat* was, as the work's editor described, 'a copy' found among Ind's possessions.

Most commonly used to refer to printed books today, the Khmer term *siw-piw* as defined in the Chuon Nath dictionary—to which Ind also contributed—also referred to notebooks stitched together from paper and used for writing (1967). People memorised Ind's poems page by page until they tripped off the tongue, indicating the importance of oral recital and transmission alongside transcription (Chhuong 1994, 161).

Memorisation of Ind's *niras* was made easier by the highly complex system of metrification, in the eight-syllable meter *pad baki prambi* (Buakamsri 2012, vii). Textual transmission and transference were often bound up in a personal relationship between mentor and student. In the late 1960s, writes Solange Thierry, the travelling balladeer Ta Krut would narrate the Reamker (a Khmer epic verse that closely draws on Valmiki's *Rāmāyana*) in performances for hours at a time. When he died, the manuscript was cremated with him (Thierry 1985, 20). The anthropologist Fabienne Luco interprets this act as a dual mortality and immortality. The text, attached to the master, dies with him: The story, passed on countless times, lives on (Luco 2016, 569). As Solange Thierry writes, 'this literature was only written down so that it could be recounted, sung, and listened to' (1985, 21).

Ind adopted and advocated a regionally distinct orthography aligned with early Khmer writing and inscriptions (Hansen 2007, 140). In a closing stanza of *Niras Nokor Vat*, Ind reflects on the longevity of his own writings and instructs any copyists to observe specific pronunciation and spellings:

> Don't mock my verse, saying that it's easy to compose . . .

If anyone wants to make a copy
In the proper form of this *niras*
Then be mindful to distinguish words ending in 'r' and 'l'
Should you drop them then it's me, the writer, who will suffer
(Ind 1934, 80–81)

This was not just about spelling. Like Ind's ethical reflections in the Gatilok, *Niras Nokor Vat* was written to be shared aloud and was circulated in a 'partially oral, partially textual fashion' long after his death (Hansen 2007, 194). Ind's instructions were likely designed to ensure that as his *niras* moved ever further from its point of origin, oral recitations would hew to the pronunciation of the Battambang region.

Ind's *Journey to Angkor* at once documents and constitutes a transitional passage in writing culture and identity formation in modern Cambodia. Composed to commemorate King Sisowath's participation in a ceremony to celebrate the retrocession of the provinces of Battambang, Sisophon, and Siem Reap from Siam to the French Protectorate of 'Cambodge' (Edwards 2007), Ind's verse gives insight into the imagining of individuality (that of the author), of community (that of 'enemies', 'Khmers', divinities), of temporality (past glory, troubled present, better future), of space and place. It offers reflections on loss and longing, desire and suffering, temporality and the precarity of human existence. Within the text, transitions are marked by what is fixed—or what is shared. Ind's poem shares strong stylistic elements with Thai *nirat* poetry, a genre that he would have encountered during his years in Bangkok among his cohort of monastic scholars.

The late scholar of Thai literature Gilles Delouche defined *nirat* as 'separation poetry'. A hallmark of the genre is its mood of loss and longing (Maurel 2002, 99–112). Ind's poem takes us on a journey through time and space and through his reflections on life, suffering, love, longing, cycles of birth and rebirth, Buddha and Dharma. Ind's verse pays particular attention to the names and naming histories of places. His verses lend a particular legibility to the landscape, grounded in images and memories. Readers from Battambang would have identified many of the sites described in the poem. Ind's text connects modern innovation with France (*barang*) and the ability to innovate with a particular power and greatness. Ind's *niras* points to the fallibility and inhumanity of a materialist modernity that seeks to renovate and restore the surface while all around, as Ind observes along his journey, inequality persists.

In her insightful analysis of 'Thai literary modernity' Arnika Fuhrman describes Thai *nirat* as 'travelogue poems written in the first person in which the journey itself constitutes the framework and in which the themes of separation, longing, and identity are prominent' (2009, 271). Distinctive features of the *nirat* include the narrator's intense reflections on the landscape of the moment and his inter-related musings about the person or place that he has left behind. 'The tone of *nirat*', writes Fuhrman, 'is one of lamentation, typically, several verses or even whole sections of *nirat* express sadness or melancholy' (2009, 271). Nirats are necessarily poems of absent presence: they are written in lament for the departed, but that separation has been set in motion by the author as he proceeds to his next destination. They are thus, at heart, a reflection on impermanence.

In his analysis of a 1900 *nirat* composed by a Cambodian minister visiting France, Frédéric Maurel describes the genre as 'specifically Thai' (2002, 99–112). Maurel takes the translation and transposition of texts from Thai into Khmer to indicate that 'Thai poetic traditions acted as a model for Khmer poets'. He suggests 1850 as the likely starting date for the entry of the *nirat* form into Cambodia and traces the history of the genre in Thailand to the early 16th century (Maurel 2002, 100, 108).

Like Furhman, Maurel emphasises the centrality of nature to the *nirat* genre (2002, 108). Maurel recognises the role of toponyms as a metronome for emotion and considers the listing and naming of plants and places as a 'highly stylistic' mark of 'aesthetic merit' (2002, 105). The elaborate naming of trees, plants, and fauna is present in other works of vernacular and literary Khmer hailing from the eastern province of Kompong Cham, including the epic romance *Tum Teav*, traceable to the 15th century (Chigas 2005), and the 16th-to-19th-century chronicles of Vat Srolauv and Lboek Robah Khsat (Khin 2002). The lists associated with *nirat* are therefore neither exclusive to the genre nor necessarily Thai in derivation or invention. Indeed, the 'lists' that feature in Khmer *niras* and Thai *nirat* might also share a direct lineage with Angkor. Like Sanskrit inscriptions, writes historian Ian Lowman, the superficially mundane but textually rich genre of property histories inscribed in Khmer on stone in the early Angkor era 'were capable of recording events in historical time'. Such Old Khmer inscriptions, Lowman argues, were 'if not more poetic, then more expressive and imaginative than mere lists' (2011, 22–23, 87).

The settings of Ind's *Niras Nokor Vat* ripple with specificity, universality, and multi-temporality, mapping one stanza on another as the poem navigates time and territory. Marked in time and place by specific sights, the aquatic and sylvan settings on Ind's voyage, like the forests in Vat Srolauv and Tum Teav, reverberate with allusions to Khmer legends and Buddhist Jataka and are hosts at once to their narrator and to the denizens of different realms (Sok 2002, 336; cf. Edwards 2008). Ind lists plants by name rather than describing their appearance, aroma, and texture, presuming a sensory knowledge of this landscape in his audience. This literary device would have stirred recognition, and connection, in people familiar with the terrain and impressed others with Ind's command of both naming and rhyming schemes.

Early in the poem, a decrepit riverside temple fills Ind with melancholy and wonder (1934, 24–25). As he travels closer to Angkor, the crumbling and unattended '*prang*' (towers) and '*prasat*' (temples) lead him to despair at the ignorance of 'wild forest' people who have left such structures to decay but also to ponder on the past glory and piety of their builders (Ind 1934, 42–43). At Angkor, Ind gives stark portraits of Khmer labourers conscripted to the French Protectorate's conservation of Angkor, a project which he otherwise applauds. Against their sweat and toil, he juxtaposes curator Monsieur Commaille's painterly restoration work (Ind 1934, 44–45). The startling image of a broken-necked statue of Buddha, smashed beyond recognition by unknown vandals from an unknown era, fills Ind with deep unease (Edwards 2007, 125–26, 134–36). This dislocation of an ancient statue resonates with a recent relocation, unspoken in Ind's poem. Commaille had recently overseen the removal of several contemporary monastery buildings to the west of the temple to clear the frontal view of Angkor Wat (Edwards 2005, 17).

Evoking a higher authority than the French governor or King Sisowath, Ind despairs that the forest is no place for Indra or Devada Kausi (1934, 75). Perhaps intentionally echoing the setting of stones to build a bridge to Lanka by Hanuman on his bid to rescue the hostage Sita, wife of Rama, Ind pledges to Indra:

> If Your Lordship were to come live in my country
> I would build a temple for you
> And make it glorious in form and style
> Just as it was in the beginning
> It's only that the statue is too heavy to lift
> They are heavy because they are so massive
> But if there were small statues, I could receive these
> And carry them across as an offering.
>
> (Ind 1934, 76)

Pondering the origins of the temples of Angkor, Ind earlier dismisses local legends that cast Indra as their builder, reasoning that the architectural range and diversity of design cannot be the work of any single figure, god or man (1934, 49–51). It is at this juncture in the poem that Ind reflects on Phnom Penh not as a modern or new city, nor as a place of creature comforts, but as the seat of royal authority:

> Now Srok Khmer (Khmer Country) will enjoy future well-being
> For Phnom Penh has been made the royal capital
> Its glory spreads across the country
> The French especially are the father
> As with the Temple of Angkor Wat (Prasat Nokor Vat)
> In antiquity, the King erected it within the boundaries (*seyma*)
> So long ago, we can't tell in which kingdom
> It became wild forests, where monkeys roamed
> No one could repair it
> It was abandoned, deserted, unclean.
>
> (Ind 1934, 50–51)

A lover of words and their proper usage, Ind is particularly critical of local naming practices. Coming across a village named 'Three Sources', a Buddhist formula for the three realms or stages of existence (desire, form, formlessness), Ind despairs at the coarseness of the local fishermen who named it, scolding that they shouldn't have given it a name reserved for Buddhist scripture. He then pleads for mercy and calls upon Buddha to spare his life and divulge its meaning, for however hard he ponders, Ind can find no explanation for the name (1934, 15–16).

Ind invokes Buddha in both these higher realms and within the Worldly landscape, providing records of contemporary monasteries and offering poetry and pledges to monks (Preah Kun) and Buddha (Preah Kaev). Crossing the boundary (*seyma/sima*) of a district at the mouth of the river, Ind reaches the 'beautifully named' Srok Peam:

> They lowered the *seyma* (boundary) from that time
> On the north of the stream there's a creek that opens as wide
> I hear they call this river *Water Rising*
> Oh the water in this river flows from the mountain
> It flows down to the boundary of the estuary until it overflows
> The water flows on and spreads out to Black Wood Temple
> Thinking about it, it's easy for monks to reach the temple by elephant,
> The land is appropriate for a monastery
> And this temple is named 'Wood'
> Whichever monk called it 'Black Wood'?
> Or did the followers of the black lady (Srey Khmau) build this temple?
> Did they name it in her name
> If there was black wood here before
> Then [perhaps that's why] they chose the name it has now
> The name Black Wood resembles my gloomy state
> My heart aches from missing my gorgeous jewel
> Oh august merit (Preah Kun) and jeweled Buddha (Preah Kaev) of Black Wood Temple
> As I depart for Angkor Wat I feel bereft of my loved one

Please august merit (Preah Kun) help the King prosper
And save my life by giving me the rank of Oknya

(Ind 1934, 16–17)

In Cambodia, as elsewhere in Theravada Southeast Asia, *seyma* (Pali sima) can mark the sacred precinct of a monastery, territorial boundaries, and boundaries between earthly and celestial realms (Lowman 2011, 40–41). The *seyma* stone to which Ind refers has the protective properties associated with *seyma* in monasteries and was likely one of the stones described by historian Tauch Chhuong:

> *seyma* were made from sandstone blocks, inscribed with magical letters, and placed on the bottom of Sangke River: one at Wat Kompong Seyma and the other at Peam Seyma, the confluence of the Sreng and Sangke rivers. The *seyma* stones were put in the river to protect people against enemy armies and wild animals.
>
> (Chhuong 1994, 28)

Elders regarded the *seyma* stones as effective deterrents against hidden dangers. The magical formula ensured that from Kompong Seyma to Peam Seyma, 'crocodiles . . . floated on the surface because of the power of these *seyma'* (Chhuong 1994, 28). Ind's audience familiar with the area would have identified these places and protective powers as subtexts in his verse. Further afield and closer to home, readers and listeners of the poem would have related to his more universal bid for Worldly status and material success, although not all might have aspired to the high rank of Oknya. On the cusp of the 21st century, Cambodians inscribed similar wishes for high office in the ephemeral and living manuscripts of leaves growing on a sacred mound in Phnom Penh's Royal Palace (Edwards 2006, 232–33).

In late 18th century Europe, artists treated the ruin as 'the empty space (*Leerstelle*) par excellence', into whose void they inserted 'texts, images and imagination' (Geimer 2002, 8; Ward 2006, 58). To Ind, Angkor was no void. Rather, the monument was replete with meaning, inspiring reflections on existence, eternity, identity, and history. The walls tell the stories of the Reamker. The ancient towers and their builders form a counterpoint to the wild ignorance and neglect of 'forest dwellers'. The *prang*'s antiquity signals a civilised order when the pious raised and maintained such structures. To Ind, this order is manifest in both the external environment and the names of places.

Historian David Chandler recognises two broad categories of Khmer textual corpus: the primarily idealistic and sacred and the profane or secular (Chandler 1996, 97). Ind's text embraces elements of both. As he approaches Angkor, Ind's reflections on his desire for his loved one recede. The temples now loom as the object of Ind's emotional attachment, together with the *seyma* stones and the complex cosmos they invoke: a realm that embraces Indra, Khmer kings, Khmer coolies, destruction and repair; matter broken and healed, spirit revealed and concealed. Ind's visceral descriptions of nature and structure lend vitality to his discursions on the natural world, framing his critical interrogation of Muslim and Christian visions of Allah or God as the master of creation with references to Cham communities and the waters of Tonle Sap (Ind 1934, 20–22). These latter reflections lead Ind to ponder Buddhism and nature but also invite comparison with the *rihla* genre of Arabic, Persian, and Urdu literature. Named for the Arabic term for voyage and travel, this genre includes work by travellers from the Mughal Empire to Southeast Asia and evokes features that became hallmarks of *niras* and *nirat*: a sense of loneliness, of separation, and of journeying through a world of wonders as a means of moving closer to God (Oualdi 2020, 35; Khazeni 2020, 25–45).

As he gains on his destination, Ind is overcome with a strange sensation of bereavement. His journey is nearly over, but his work will live on. Reaching the grounds of Angkor Wat, he maps a scriptural topography. On the initiative of Achar Em (the reformist monk Em Sou), Buddhist manuscripts have been laid out in the open so that people may study in the course of the two-day-long retrocession ceremony.

Historian Tauch Chhuong interprets Ind's prodigious literary career as proof that Siam's administration of Battambang could not penetrate the 'Khmer mind' or interfere with the mentality of Khmers under Thai rule (1994, 99). Literary scholar Khing Hoc Dy describes Ind's particular synthesis of 'preaching and literary' styles in his later work, the *Gatilok*, as representative of a morality that is 'truly Khmer' (1993). Like Angkor Wat, whose walls are decorated or inscribed with Quoc ngu, Burmese, Chinese and Thai graffiti, and Japanese calligraphy (Thompson 2004; Edwards 2006), Ind's world was never singularly Khmer in literary or linguistic range. What moved the polyglot Ind to poetry was not solely an identification with 'race' but the locomotion of place.

Ind's *Niras Nokor Vat* anchors him, and his readers, in a layered history and mythology. Toponyms mark the stages of his journey through time and space and his interior voyage of rumination. Phnom Penh and Angkor function as two clear compass points. Along the way, references to Srey Kmau—a tutelary spirit popular in the Angkor region and associated with the Goddess Kali, Durga, and Parvati, and also commonly called Neang Khmau (Luco 2016)—anchor the journey in both a celestial cosmos and a spiritual topography of Cambodia.

What did the retrocession of Angkor mean to this brilliant poet of elegant wit? His verse leaves us guessing. Ind used a genre closely linked to Siam to narrate his journey to Angkor for a ceremony to mark the temple's return to Khmer sovereignty. This literary framing might have been an ironic riposte to the *ancien regime* of Siam, whose administration in Battambang had shaped the first 45 years of Ind's life. As an ardent devotee of Old Khmer orthography and regional dialect, Ind might also have been seeking to set new boundary markers around the *niras* genre and to gesture to the possibility of the form's Angkorian ancestry.

Angkor in Verso: A Postrevolutionary *Niras*

On 17 April 1975, after five years of civil war between Republican and Communist forces, the Khmer Rouge entered Phnom Penh and began the forced evacuation of the capital, ushering in a genocidal regime that would claim close to a third of Cambodia's population. Phnom Penh soon acquired the status that had secured Angkor its place in late 19th-century imaginations: as a ruin par excellence, an abandoned city.

But the leadership of Democratic Kampuchea never fled Phnom Penh. The Khmer Rouge leaders still did business here. They held Prince Sihanouk and his family hostage in the palace; hosted diplomatic missions from China and North Korea and well-wishers from Europe; staged revolutionary performances, used monasteries as granaries, and equipped schools as murderous interrogation centres, most notoriously at S-21, or Tuol Sleng. Inaugurated with mass executions at the Olympic Stadium, the revolutionary capital became a mass, unmarked burial ground, and a Chinese cemetery on the outskirts of the city grew into a shallow grave for the victims of S-21. In this murderous landscape, Phnom Penh became a microcosm of the regime of Democratic Kampuchea [DK] (1975–1978).

The DK regime condemned all forms of emotion (other than affection for the Communist Party or hatred of its enemies) as bourgeois sentiment and made nostalgia a capital crime. The regime's 'desire to annihilate all art and culture' led to the execution and suppression of performers, musicians, artists, and artisans. Court dance was forbidden (Ly 2019, 116). All non-revolutionary songs, music, and lyrics were banned. The new canon of revolutionary songs (*camrian pativatt*) were 'cheerful in tone, with a strong, quick rhythm' and celebrated the 'golden lineage of rice cultivation' and the pace of production (Marston 2002, 108, 114, 119). Kong Deoum, a Khmer Rouge survivor who had been a DJ in Phnom Penh before the DK took power, would later recall that the Khmer Rouge 'used art to serve politics', but the art was so subordinate to the message and the room for individual expression so ruthlessly crushed that 'when we heard it, it was not art' (Pirozzi 2014)

In his study of Khmer Rouge songs, anthropologist John Marston considers the traumatic effect of being forced to sing of joy and glory in a time of deep suffering under a regime that forbade all expressions of personal emotion. In addition to glorifying revolution, these 'public texts' were used as metronomes of ideological purity and revolutionary fervour. Performances of revolutionary songs were used 'to clean out the enemy' from within: failure to display emotional identification with the message in the song was a sign of dissent. Being a member of the audience thus required a state of vigilance and a constant display of conformity (Marston 2002, 101–103, 105).

For all their revolutionary claims, these songs shared elements of earlier Khmer texts: including long lists of plants, and a curious reference to the 'heritage of our grandparents' (Marston 2002, 119). Their lyrics both confirm and contradict anthropologist Maurice Bloch's thesis about language and authority. In his seminal essay on symbolic and ritual expression, Bloch contends that,

> formalised language, the language of traditional authority, is an impoverished language: a language where many of the options at all levels of language are abandoned so that choice of form, of style, of words and of syntax is less than in ordinary language.
> (Bloch 1974, 60–62)

The Khmer Rouge regime simultaneously impoverished tradition and overturned class hierarchy. The Democratic Kampuchea regime imposed a new formalisation of speech acts that required the rejection of a complex and layered vocabulary for verbs and pronouns preferred by the revolutionary organisation (*Angka Padevat*). Bloch charts song and formalised oratory on a gradual continuum, linking 'say, the language of political party broadcasts, to the language of politicians making public appeals in time of emergencies, to the language of sermons, to the way prayers are spoken in church, to the way psalms are intoned, to full-scale singing'. Songs, particularly those performed at ceremonies, become essentially passive acts: 'so passive that it is as though the singer were experiencing language from outside himself' (Bloch 1974, 70). Emotion is missing from Bloch's analysis. Female survivors of the Khmer Rouge regime later recalled how they risked death to sing while working in the fields in defiance of the Khmer Rouge ban (Chou 2011; Pirozzi 2014).

In December 1978, the United Front for the National Salvation of Kampuchea (FUNSK), led by Chea Sim, Heng Sam Rin, and Hun Sen rolled in to Cambodia from Vietnam and toppled the DK regime, which reassembled in a fledgling resistance on the Thai-Cambodia border. The FUNSK flag was identical to that hoisted by the anti-colonial Khmer Issarak Movement in the 1940s. Its geometric form showed a bright yellow, five-towered Angkor on a red background (Slocomb 2003, 55). Under this flag in December 1978, the FUNSK leadership announced an 11-point program and pledged to create a 'new culture', to 'eliminate illiteracy, develop education at all levels, and preserve and restore historical relics and structures' and to 'develop the Angkor traditions' (Slocomb 2003, 45). Heading up this effort was Minister of Propaganda, Information, and Culture Keo Chenda.

Keo Chenda was among the thousands of Khmer Issarak who, banned by the Geneva Accords of 1953, fled to Vietnam and became known as 'Khmer Viet Minh'. In Hanoi, Keo Chenda worked for the National United Front radio, a broadcast program helmed by future Khmer Rouge leader Ieng Thirith (Kiernan 2004, 359–60). In January 1979, days after the defeat of the Khmer Rouge and the establishment of the People's Republic of Kampuchea, Keo Chenda made a public appeal to artists and performers to return to the liberated capital. His medium was radio, but his genre was a capella song. Composed by Keo Chenda, the lyrics were possibly influenced by his time in Hanoi: *Oh Phnom Penh, Euy*.

'O Phnom Penh,' Keo Chenda's lyrics go, 'I've missed you for three years' . . . 'I'm meeting you again'. The song eulogises the soul of the Khmer nation and lauds the fame of Khmer civilisation. It is a *niras* in reverse: a song of parting and reunification. Phnom Penh has sheltered in the shadow of Angkor, the lyrics tell us. The singer's sorrow and loss as well as joy at her return to Phnom Penh unite both the temple and the new regime as protectors, who offer sanctuary in the shadow (*mlup*) of the Angkor flag. Mlup implies not a sinister shadow but a place of shelter and of transit. The phrase 'entering the shade' (*coul mlup*) refers to the rites of a young woman attaining puberty and evokes the maternal penumbra of a matrilineal society. The DK regime broke with such traditions. Under Khmer Rouge leadership, for the first time in history, writes Boreth Ly, the female body was removed from its central, symbolic role, leaving the nation 'motherless' (2019, 125). In early 1979, Keo Chenda's lyrics were set to music by Morm Bunnary and recorded by her sister Morm Sokha (Duong 2011). Played over loudspeakers and radio, the haunting lyrics and plaintive melody formed a stark contrast to the jubilant revolutionary music of the DK regime. *Oh Pnum Penh Euy* sought to reassure listeners that Phnom Penh was now safe, protected by the flag of Angkor—a symbol of the new regime's authority.

A love song to the capital and its liberators, *Oh Phnom Penh Euy* was also a war song, a rallying cry for the country to unite against the Khmer Rouge, whose remnant troops were regrouping, with international backing, on the Thai border, forming a new united front with Buddhist and Republican factions in that same terrain once crossed by Suttantprija Ind when he journeyed to Siem Reap in 1909. In 1979, recognising the power of music to rally morale at a time of acute trauma, fear, and uncertainty, Keo Chenda put out an appeal to artists to return to Phnom Penh.

One dancer who responded to the call was Om Sovandy. The daughter of a leading light of the royal ballet, Om Sovandy had learned to dance in the palace and in the school of fine arts. On 17 April 1975, the Khmer Rouge evicted her family from Phnom Penh and sent them to Battambang. Her mother took her costume with her and, in a rare instance of Khmer Rouge tolerance of cultural dissent, became known locally as Yay Lakhon (Grandma Dancer). In January 1979, at a ceremony to celebrate the FUNSK victory and the fall of the DK, Om Sovandy performed before Chea Sim, president of the new regime, at Angkor Wat.

Initially broadcast over the radio and in public places through loudspeakers, Keo Chenda's *Oh Pnum Penh Euy* was later set to moving images of the capital in early 1979. The jumpy, grainy noir footage shows evacuees returning to the capital, on foot, or by cart, carrying their possessions on their heads or backs. The camera pans to derelict buildings and streets of rubble. The film was screened by the Ministry of Culture's mobile film unit on its 230 trips from Phnom Penh into the provinces and reached audiences of some 345,000 people in 1979 (Slocomb 2003, 183).

The plaintive notes of *Oh Phnom Penh Euy* might have reminded listeners, especially older women, of the lament of Maddi, Vessantara's wife, as she scours the forest for her children in the final episode of the Cheadok (Vessantara Jataka) both in its tone and sensibility (Walker 2013, 20–23). Maddi's lament is linked to Buddhist notions of suffering (*dukkha*) and giving (*dana*). But the Cheadok is ultimately a redemption narrative: Prince Vessantara, sent into exile, regains a lost kingdom; his wife Maddi, bereft, is reunited with her children. *Oh Pnum Penh Euy* vocalises memories of suffering to invite revenge on the Khmer Rouge enemy. But it is also a eulogy to the People's Republic of Kampuchea as saviours of the nation and revolution, who have liberated the country, regained the capital, and allowed Cambodians to be reunited with family. It is a redemption song.

In his work on Khmer traditions of Dhamma song, Buddhist Studies scholar Trent Walker directs attention to the 'experience of being stirred', described in Khmer as *sangvek*, from the Pali *samvega*. This affective and experiential dimension of Dhamma songs—involving the skill of the singer, the quality of the melody and lyric, and the embodied and engaged listening of the audience—is extremely important to singers such as Sophea, the focus of Walker's study. Sophea belongs to a network of Dhamma practitioners in Cambodia and in diaspora that 'maintains this tradition of expressive melodies, powerful narratives, and healing rituals' (Walker 2011, 528). Where the Khmer Rouge songs studied by Marston were designed to 'clean out' the ranks (2002), the Dhamma songs performed by Sophea 'allow us to contemplate our existence . . . to make our mind calm. We use them to clean our mind, so that we can be free from greed, hatred and delusion. We use them to experience *samvega*' (Walker 2011, 526). The late doyen of Pali studies, Steven Collins defines '*samvega*' as the 'animation' of a 'stronger emotion (from a root meaning to tremble or quiver) . . . used when some shock inspires an increase in the intensity of religious feelings and intentions' (Collins 1998, 593; Scheible 2016, 41). A secular song, *Oh Pnum Penh Euy* was also designed to stir. Scattered across the country, a battle-scarred population wept on hearing it (Pirozzi 2014). Several Cambodians who returned to Phnom Penh in the early 1980s have shared with me their recall of the intensely emotional experience of hearing the song at screenings in 1979. Where sorrow had been banned in communal Khmer Rouge meetings, tears were now shed in collective grief.

Oh Pnum Penh Euy's vocal and emotional range also resonates with Cambodian rock and roll, music outlawed by the Khmer Rouge for its bourgeois sentimentality. Haunting in tone, the song invokes the past and the notion of return while also summoning the ghosts of fallen singers. The solo female vocal of *Oh Pnum Penh Euy* recalled such artists as Ros Soreysothea, the Battambang singer believed to have been tortured to death by the Khmer Rouge. Listeners might also have recalled Sihanouk's composition, *Phnom Penh*, released in the 1960s and played on the airwaves and through loudspeakers.

By 1981, the FUNSK had morphed into the People's Republic of Kampuchea (PRK), and a campaign against 'degenerate, corrupt culture' boasted its success in 'wiping out . . . the playing of songs from the old society and foreign songs of weak quality' and advocated a 'ban of music from the old society in coffee shops' (Gottesman 2002, 179). The PRK also banned royal vocabulary from songs (Um 2015, 239). A decade earlier, Lon Nol's Khmer Republic (1970–75) had banned the National Broadcasting Service from airing songs from the 60s and promoted nationalist songs over love songs (Pirozzi 2014).

After the Paris Peace Accords of 1990, tentative reconciliation of the four armed factions, the repatriation of refugees, and the contestation of elections by multiple political parties, *Oh Pnum Penh Euy* became tainted by association with the Cambodian People's Party. But the song kept its resonance for many survivors of the Khmer Rouge. The popular performer Meng Keo Pich Chenda relaunched the song in the early 2000s. In January 2011, San Putheary, director of the Audiovisual Department of the Ministry, declared Keo Chanda's original song a 'part of Cambodia's national heritage' that must be 'protected forever'. The Ministry of Culture and Information embargoed a new 'pop' cover of *Oh Pnum Penh Euy*, and minister Khieu Kanharith declared any departure from the initial lyrics 'improper' (Kunthear 2011).

By making the 1979 original song an inviolable monument, the government hoped to freeze a new generation's boundaries of invention. Defying the embargo, the new cover was released on various media platforms. Four years later, at a music festival in Long Beach, California, Rumany Long performed a new interpretation of *Oh Phnom Penh Euy*, 'from the perspective of a Khmer Rouge labour camp in the countryside of Cambodia who is longing to return home to Phnom Penh'. Interviewed for a Long Beach newspaper, Long stated: 'It's such an emotional song. I hope people really connect to the song and take a moment . . . to remember what a tragic thing happened to our country' (Guzman 2015).

Niras in Diaspora: Angkor in the Poetry of U Sam Oeur

Oh Phnom Penh! O pagoda where we worship!
O, Angkor Wat, sublime monument to the
Aspirations of our ancient Khmer forefathers.
Ah, I can't see across those three wildernesses.
I'll be nowhere,
I'll have no night,
I'll have no day anymore:
I shall be a man without identity.
(Sam Oeur 1998, 50–53)

Cambodian-American poet U Sam Oeur addresses Angkor as witness, as oracle, as a receptacle of his anguish, and as the antithesis of his 'nowhere' in his poem *Niras Wobatoar*. Translated by Kenneth McCullough as *The Fall of Culture*, the Khmer title evokes desolation, separation, and a sense of journey. We hear a man caught in the jaws of the Khmer Rouge regime (1975–9) who looks away from Phnom Penh, his local monastery, and Angkor Wat to a future where his memory will have vanished. A triple wilderness has dulled the triple gems of Buddhism (Buddha, Dhamma, Sangha), fracturing his identity.

Born into a farming family in the southeastern province of Svay Rieng in 1936, U Sam Oeur studied in the United States in the 1960s, completing a Master of Fine Arts at the University of Iowa before returning to Cambodia in 1968. His boyhood experience with buffaloes and his feigned illiteracy were key to his survival of the Khmer Rouge regime. After the fall of DK, U Sam Oeur returned to Phnom Penh to work for the Ministry of Industry. In the 1980s, he was forced to resign on the discovery of a pro-democracy poem in his desk. In 1992, he migrated to the United States, where he published his first full-length poetry collection, *Sacred Vows*, in 1998.

U Sam Oeur has described his poetry as an attempt to 'nudge Cambodian people out of living in the Angkor era into a present which is tempered by traditions but not encumbered by them' (1998, iii). Combining traditional rhyming schemes, narrative sections, and free verse, his poems offer tribute to 'the myths and prophecies of the Angkor era' (Smith 1998). They confront personal loss and conjure dark traces of that past, giving voice to 'what has so far remained inexpressible' (May 2004, 193). Moving between monotonal chant and 'emotionally charged aria', his poetry ruptures the regimented narratives of Angkor circulated in national anthems and revolutionary propaganda. Through his innovative play with classical form, Oeur rejects the blind reverence of authority, literary or otherwise (1998, iii).

'Culture' is the titular locale of his *Niras Wobatoar*, and this, like others of U Sam Oeur's poems, condemns attempts to ossify and glorify culture as bait for totalitarian violence. Fusing selective elements of *niras* with the agony of loss in a time of revolution, U Sam Oeur's poem addresses Angkor as witness and as a sentient being. In conjuring Angkor not as a site of achievement but as a monument to aspiration, *Niras Wobatoar* breaks step with the nationalisation of Angkor and its mobilisation by regimes of all political hues (Chandler 1983)—including the Khmer Rouge, whose depravity his poem laments.

In *The Loss of My Twins* (*Niras Koun Pleuh*), U Sam Oeur calls forth the Triple Gem of Buddhism (Buddha, Dhamma, Sangha) from the three wildernesses. In the spirit of the *niras* genre, the poem expresses a wrenching longing for loved ones lost, addresses Buddha, and speaks to the souls of his buried babies as he moves away from them. Since it is clear that his twins were his chosen destination in life, the effect is a reverse motion. This is no voluntary separation or tour of duty but the brutish truncation of a nurturing family by a monstrous regime. That regime did not spring from nowhere. U Sam Oeur's *Oath of Allegiance* speaks to past injustice, opening with a reference to French colonisation and closes with a vision of 'Khmers . . . half-nude, shivering like chickens, no money to pay taxes, no land to grow rice' (1998, 13).

In her analysis of cultural transmission in the Cambodian diaspora, political scientist Khatharya Um describes a 'broken chain' of past lives whose 'severed links' are strung, unstrung, and restrung by the 'ghost imprints of past connections' (184). *Swimming in the Sea of Nostalgia* (*Hael knong tonle sronaoh mettephum*, literally: *Swimming in the Lake of Mourning My Motherland*) evokes palm trees, forests, and mountains and closes with the lament 'Tonle Sap Euy, how I long for thee' (U Sam Oeur 1998, 182–183). *Indra's Prophecy* conjures the promise of Angkor's long shadow, asking whether Sihanouk had stayed away from Cambodia for so long due to the absence of shade (*mlup*) in which to shelter (U Sam Oeur 1998, 6–7).

In *The Ruins of Angkor Cry out for National Concord*, U Sam Oeur implores Cambodian poets to listen to the temples' cries (*sdap Angkor sraek*). The second stanza describes the cries of the Bayon, beset with pity for the Khmer people; the third lends an ear to Banteay Srei's lament of lost husbands. Enjambed in this 1990s poem, mirroring the inner chamber of Angkor Wat, is a rhyming prophesy attributed to Kram Ngoy (1865–1936). Written in the colonial era, Kram Ngoy's verse contrasts the façade of Cambodia's prosperity with inner rot and predicts scarcity in cotton, silk, tobacco, and prahok (preserved fish, a staple of the Khmer diet). The final two stanzas of U Sam Oeur's poem give voice to the sobs of Angkor Wat, 'our most sublime monument', who weeps for the integrity of Cambodia's territory (*boranaphiep tuk-dae*) and freedom from tyranny, in the hope that '*koun chiw*' (descendants) will hear the temple's tears (1998, 160–63). Angkor is neither empty metaphor nor fixed script but a living, breathing monument. Inscribed offshore, Oeur's contemporary *niras* pulse with the *samvega* of diaspora.

Conclusion

The poems and songs considered here are stanzas in the life of Angkor. Ind's Angkor is a place of water, plants, and spirits. Keo's Angkor is flat architecture: an icon on a flag, it offers *mlup* (protection and shade), a Khmer term with strong cultural and emotional resonance, and is grounded in its relation to Phnom Penh. U Sam Oeur's Angkor listens, weeps, and cries out. Each of these three Angkors is existentially dependent on people, spirits, and the 'land'—a noun that inadequately renders the Khmer compound *tuk-dae*: water-earth, a term in which water precedes, and thus leads to, land. None of these Angkors stand alone, and none exists solely or wholly in the realm of its courtly creator and ancestral avatar.

Each text is framed by a distinct aesthetic. Ind's verse is burnished by his monastic training, Pali repertoire, and cosmopolitan schooling; Keo Chenda's lyrics are war scarred and charged with socialist realist rhetoric, and U Sam Oeur's poems gyrate between the caged symmetry of traditional Khmer meter and the free form of Walt Whitman. Composed in distinct political eras—from King Chulalongkorn's Siam to the French Protectorate of Cambodge, from 1970s Hanoi to 1990s Iowa—these texts have transcended those historical junctures. Each circulates beyond its site, and story, of origin. At once detached from and attached to the temples, these are mobile inscriptions. More than vehicles of transmission, they are sites of transition. Read together or apart, these texts navigate spaces and places in flux, tethering them to a sensory realm of history and story through the wiring of emotion.

Shimmering between and across these ephemeral inscriptions is the unspoken realisation that Angkor, while holding the artist and audience captive, remains beyond capture. The idea of Angkor as an immutable national essence over time is, I have argued elsewhere, a fiction (Edwards 1996, 2007). But the very fixity of Angkor *in* place anchors the temple to individual imaginings. In that respect, as long as Angkor stands, it functions as a vehicle of remembrance.

Just as Angkor has eluded capture, so, too, scripts inspired by Angkor have gained lives and afterlives. Angkor stands as witness and offers solace. And ultimately, it is Angkor that captivates and captures, in a mesh of memory as tenuous and finely wrought as Khmer goldwork. Probing these links, to return to the metaphor of a broken chain (Um 2015, 184) unchains more questions. Is Angkor a mirror or museum? A vessel or vehicle? Chimera or camera, obscura or lucida? Only time, and memories, will tell. Angkor resists arrest.

References

Ang, C., 2013, *Inscriptions of Angkor Wat: Ancient, Middle and Modern Periods*. Phnom Penh: Apsara Authority.

Bloch, M., 1974. Symbols, song, dance, and features of articulation: is religion an extreme form of traditional authority? *European Journal of Sociology/Archives Européennes de Sociologie/Europäisches Archiv für Soziologie* 15(1), 55–81.

Buakamsri, T., 2012. *Niras Nagar Vat: A Journey to Angkor Wat by Oknya suttantaprechea Oen* (1859–24) u.p. paper

Chandler, D., 1983. Seeing red: perceptions of Cambodian history in Democratic Kampuchea, in *Facing the Cambodian Past: Selected Essays, 1971–1994*. Chiang Mai: Silkworm Books., 233–54

Chandler, D., 1996. Songs at the edge of the forest: perceptions of order in three Cambodian texts, in *Facing the Cambodian Past: Selected Essays, 1971–1994*, Chiang Mai: Silkworm Books. 76–99

Chhuong, T., 1994. *Battambang during the Time of the Lord Governor*, translated by H. Sithan, C. Mortland & J. Ledgerwood. Phnom Penh: CEDORECK.

Chigas, G., 2005. *Tum Teav: A Translation and Analysis of a Khmer Literary Classic*. Phnom Penh: Documentation Center of Cambodia.

Chou, D., 2011. *Golden Slumbers*. Documentary film. Directed by D. Chou. Original Release 9 October 2011. Vycky Films, Bophana Production & Araucania Films.

Collins, S., 1998. *Nirvana and Other Buddhist Felicities: Utopias of the Pali Imaginaire*. Cambridge: Cambridge University Press.

Duong, D., 2011. http://Dara-Duong.blogspot.com/2011/01/oh-phnom-penh-euy.html, accessed 9 July 2020

Edwards, P., 1996. Imaging the other in Cambodian nationalist discourse before and during the UNTAC period, in *Propaganda, Politics, and Violence in Cambodia: Democratic Transition under United Nations Peace-keeping*, eds. S. Heder & J. Ledgerwood. Armonk (NY): M.E. Sharpe, 50–72.

Edwards, P., 2005. Taj Angkor: enshrining l'Inde in le Cambodge, in *France and 'Indochina': Cultural Representations*, eds. K. Robson & J. Yee. Lanham, MD: Lexington Books, 13–27.

Edwards, P., 2006. Subscripts: reading Cambodian pasts, presents and futures through graffiti, in *Expressions of Cambodia: The Politics of Tradition, Identity, and Change*, eds. L. C. P. Ollier & T. Winter. (Routledge Contemporary Southeast Asia Series 12.) New York: Routledge, 223–36.

Edwards, P., 2007. *Cambodge: The Cultivation of A Nation (1860–1945)*. Honolulu: Hawai'i University Press.

Edwards, P., 2008. Between a song and a prei: tracking Cambodian cosmologies and histories through the forest, in *At the Edge of the Forest: Essays on Cambodia, History, and Narrative in Honour of David Chandler*, eds. A. Hansen & J. Ledgerwood. Ithaca (NY): Cornell University Press, 137–62.

Fuhrman, A., 2009. The dream of a contemporary Ayutthaya: Angkhan Kalayanaphong's poetics of dissent, aesthetic nationalism, and Thai literary modernity. *Oriens Extremis* 48, 271–90.

Geimer, P., 2002. *Die Vergangenheit der Kunst: Strategien der Nachträglichkeit im 18.* Jahrhundert, Weimar: Verlag und Datenbank für Geisteswissenschaft.

Gottesman, E.R., 2002. *Cambodia After the Khmer Rouge: Inside the Politics of Nation Building.* New Haven, CT: Yale University Press.

Guzman, R., 2015. Long Beach Cambodians hold genocide remembrance day. Press-Telegram, 13 April. Available at: www.presstelegram.com/2015/04/13/long-beach-cambodians-to-hold-genocide-remembrance-day-on-friday, [accessed 30 July, 2020].

Hansen, A., 2007. *How to Behave: Buddhism and Modernity in Colonial Cambodia, 1860–1930*, Honolulu, HI: University of Hawai'i Press.

Ind, S., 1934. Niras Nokor Vat (un pélerinage à Angkor en 1909). កម្ពុជសុរិយា *[Kambuja Surya/Kampuchéa Suriya]*. Phnom Penh: Buddhist Institute, 5–81.

Khazeni, A., 2020. *The City and the Wilderness: Indo-Persian Encounters in Southeast Asia.* Oakland: University of California Press.

Khin, S., 2002. *L'annexation du Cambodge par les Vietnamiens au XIXeme Siècle d'après les deux poèmes du Vénérable Batum Baramey Pich*, volume III. Paris: Editions You Feng.

Khing, H.D., 1993. *Contribution à l'histoire de la littérature khmère, volume 2: Ecrivains et expressions littéraires du Cambodge au XXe siècle.* Paris: L'Harmattan.

Kiernan, B., 2004. *How Pol Pot Came to Power: Colonialism, Nationalism, and Communism in Cambodia, 1930–1975* (2nd ed.). New Haven: Yale University Press.

Kunthear, M., 2011. Ministry bans remake of classic song. Phnom penh post, 4 January. Available at: www.phnompenhpost.com/national/ministry-bans-remake-classic-song, [accessed 9 July, 2020].

Lowman, I., 2011. *The Descendants of Kambu: the political imagination of Angkorian Cambodia.* PhD dissertation. Berkeley: University of California, Berkeley.

Luco, F., 2016. *Les habitants d'Angkor: une lecture dans l'espace et dans le temps des inscriptions sociales de populations villageoises installées dans un territoire ancien.* PhD dissertation. Paris: École des Hautes Études en Sciences Sociales.

Ly, B., 2019. Traces of Trauma: Cambodian visual culture and identity in the aftermath of genocide. Honolulu (HI): Hawai'i University Press.

Marston, J., 2002. Khmer rouge songs. *Crossroads: An Interdisciplinary Journal of Southeast Asian Studies* 16(1), 100–27.

Maurel, F., 2002. A Khmer Nirat, 'Travel in France during the Paris World exhibition of 1900': influences from the Thai? *South East Asia Research* 10(1), 99–112.

May, S. & U Sam Oeur, 2004. Ambassador of the silent World: an interview with U Sam Oeur. *MĀNOA: A Pacific Journal of International Writing* 16(1), 189–94.

Nath, C. (ed.), 1967. *Vacananukrum Kmae: Dictionnaire Cambodgien.* Phnom Penh: Buddhist Institute.

Oualdi, M., 2020. *A Slave between Empires: A Transimperial History of North Africa.* New York, NY: Columbia University Press.

Pirozzi, J., 2014. *Don't Think I've Forgotten: Cambodia's Lost Rock'n'Roll*, Produced by John Pirozzi and Andrew Pope.

Pollock, S., 2009. *The Language of Gods in the World of Men: Sanskrit, Culture and Power in Premodern India.* Berkeley: University of California Press.

Scheible, K., 2016. *Reading the Mahāvamsa: The Literary Aims of a Theravāda Buddhist History.* New York: Columbia University Press, 41.

Slocomb, M., 2003. *The People's Republic of Kampuchea, 1979–1989: The Revolution after Pol Pot.* Chiang Mai: Silkworm Books.

Smith, D., 1998. From misery to flight: a Cambodian soars through his poems. New York times, May 23. Available at: www.nytimes.com/1998/05/23/books/from-misery-to-flight-a-cambodian-soars-through-his-poetry.html, [accessed July 9, 2020].

Sok, K., 2002. *Satra Voat Kroch, in L'annexion du Cambodge par les Vietnamiens au XIXème siècle d'après les deux poèmes du Vénérable Batum Baramey Pich*, vol. 3. Paris: Editions You-feng.

Thierry, S., 1985. *Le Cambodge des contes.* Paris: L'Harmattan.

Thompson, A., 2004. Pilgrims to Angkor: a Buddhist 'cosmopolis' in Southeast Asia? *Bulletin of the Students of the Department of Archaeology, Department of Archaeology, Royal University of Fine Arts, Phnom Penh* 3, 88–119.

U Sam Oeur, 1998. *Sacred Vows: Poetry by U Sam Oeur, translated by K. McCullough.* Minneapolis: Coffee House Press.

Um, K., 2015. *From the Land of Shadows: War, Revolution and the Making of the Cambodian Diaspora.* New York, NY: New York University Press.

Walker, T., 2011. How Sophea lost her sight. *Peace Review: A Journal of Social Justice* 23(4), 23–4, 522–9.

Walker, T., 2013. *Framing the Sacred: Cambodian Buddhist Paintings.* Berkeley, CA: University of California, Institute of East Asian Studies, 20–3.

Walker, T., 2018. *Liturgical texts in Khmer leporello manuscripts: a preliminary analysis.* PhD dissertation. Berkeley: University of California, Berkeley.

Ward, S., 2006 Ruins and poetics in the works of W. G. Sebald, in *A Critical Companion*, eds. J. J. Long & A. Parry. Edinburgh: Edinburgh University Press.

APPENDIX A

Taxon	*Trench 4 #22*	*Trench 4 #27*	*Trench 4 #30*	*Trench 4 #31*	*Total*
Volume of soil before flotation	2.25	2.5	4	2	10.75
Plant parts / Litre of soil	310.7	217.2	173	281	
No. of taxa	14	13	8	12	
ECONOMIC PLANTS					
Oryza sativa				3	3
Oryza sativa fragment	7	3	3	11	24
Oryza sativa spikelet base domesticated-type	9	113	95	112	329
Oryza spikelet base wild-type		6	8		14
Oryza spikelet base indeterminate	2	34	44	137	217
Oryza lemma apex	2	16	50	30	98
Oryza charred embryo	4	12	26	13	55
Oryza awn - silicified			8		8
Total rice	24	184	234	306	748
Cajanus cajan		1			1
Lablab purpureus	1				1
Vigna radiata				1	1
Vigna unguiculata subsp. *sesquipedalis*	1			1	2
Total pulses	2	0	0	2	4
cf. *Bombax*				3	3
Gossypium sp.	4	1			5
Sesamum indicum	1				1
Total cash crops	5	1	0	3	9
Phyllanthus sp.	1		2		3
endocarp poss. Baobab (cf. *Adansonia*)		1	1		2
Total other economic crops	1	1	3	0	5

Taxon	*Trench 4 #22*	*Trench 4 #27*	*Trench 4 #30*	*Trench 4 #31*	*Total*
FRUIT AND NUT PARTS					
Canarium tip?			2		2
Fagaceae / Betulacreae nut shell frag		1		2	3
mesocarp fragment / fruit flesh			1		1
Total fruit and nut parts		1	3	2	6
WEEDY / WILD					
Acmella paniculata	3	4	8		15
Alternanthera cf. *sessilis*	1				1
Carex sp. peryginium				28	28
Cenchrus sp. involucre				1	1
Cleome viscosa				1	1
Limnophila villosa		2			2
Lindernia crustacea	2				2
Mollugo cf. *pentaphylla*			12		12
Pennisetum sp.		2			2
wild rice (maybe *O. rufipogon*)			1		1
Portulaca oleracea	2				2
cf. *Sagina japonica*				12	12
Sida cf. *rhombifolia*	1				1
Total weedy / wild	9	8	21	42	80
OTHERS					
Amaranthaceae		1			1
Fabaceae		1			1
Cyperaceae	2	22	3	1	28
Nymphaceae fragment				2	2
Poaceae	4	10	14	5	33
Ranunculaceae		2			2
Scrophulariaceae	1				1
pedicel			1		1
base of capsule			1		1
node		1			1
parenchyma - prob. Rice			18	35	53
Total others					124
Total unidentified	651	310	394	163	1518
NISP	699	543	692	561	2495
NON-BOTANICAL / MODERN					
Total non-botanical and modern	21	68	235	316	640
NSP	720	611	927	877	3135

* samples have been interpolated using percentages of amounts sampled. Rice husk was present in all samples but are not included in the Table.

GLOSSARY

The following list provides definitions of Sanskrit and Khmer (Kh) words as they appear in the context of this volume. To find more details or wider meaning about words in either language please refer to the SEALang website (http://sealang.net/khmer/dictionary.htm) or any of Philip Jenner's published dictionaries:

Jenner, P.N., 2009. *A Dictionary of Pre-Angkorian Khmer*. Canberra: Pacific Linguistics, Research School of Pacific and Asian Studies, Australian National University.

Jenner, P.N., 2009. *A Dictionary of Angkorian Khmer*. Canberra: Pacific Linguistics, Research School of Pacific and Asian Studies, Australian National University.

abhayamudrā - gesture of reassurance with the raised right palm held outward and upward
abhiṣeka - anointing, consecrating, inaugurating by a sprinkling of water; bathing of a divine image
ācārya - teacher, instructor; professor, pedagogue, often religious
adhyāpaka - preceptor
agada - freedom from disease, health
āgama - chattel acquired by legal process through purchase
ājya, āja, ājyaśeṣa - melted, clarified butter
***'aṃpyal* (Kh)** - salt
amṛta - elixir of immortality
anantaśayin - Viṣṇu reclining on back of the nāga Ananta
***'aṅgāla* (Kh)** - plough
apsara - supernatural female deity of great beauty
arcā - image, object of worship
argha - equivalence, value
āśrama - monastery; stage of life
asura - evil spirit, demon
baku - Cambodian Brahmins
***baray* (Kh)** - a reservoir, typically very large, rectangular, and bounded by an earthen wall
Bhagavatī - epithet of *Lakṣmī* and *Durgā*
Bhaiṣajyaguru - the Buddhist Master of Remedies, or Medicine Buddha
bhnaṃ khsāc ' (Kh) - sand mounds
bhūmyākara - land revenues

bhūtāśa - clerk or secretary
bhūta-vidyā - treatment of demonic illnesses
***bisākh* (Kh)** - month of the first rains
***boramei* (Kh)** - spirit guardian
***braek* (Kh)** - tributary canal
***brāhmaṇa* (Kh)** - member or priest of sacerdotal caste
brahmaśālā - Brahma's hall
brahmayajña - ceremony
buddhaguṇ - altar
cakravartin - universal sovereign
***caṃlāk* (Kh)** - record (of calculations)
***caṃnat* (Kh)** - village
***camroen āyu* (Kh)** - age expanding rite to prolong duration of an aged person's life
cañcūli - castor oil plant
***canmat* (Kh)** - bull, uncastrated animal
caru - the food offered to Śiva
***chawng* (Kh)** - bundled
***chlaṅ cetr* (Kh)** - ritual opening of the rice cultivation season
cīnadhv(aj) ~ cīnadhvaja - banner of Chinese fabric
***cpāp* (Kh)** - royal decree or legal code
dadhi - coagulated milk
***daṃnap* (Kh)** - dam
***daṅ' braliṅ* (Kh)** - banner of the souls
deva - divine being, god
devadravya - god's wealth
devatā - deity, god
dhenu - a milk cow, offering to Brahmans
dhyānamudrā - mediation gesture typically with both hands placed palm upward in the lap of a seated figure, with the right hand on the left
droṇa - measure of volume (paddy, sesame)
dvāpara-yuga - the third age of the world in Hindu cosmology
ghaṇṭā - bell
Garuda - mythical half bird/half man vehicle of Viṣṇu
ghaṭikā - quantity of melted liquid
ghṛta - clarified butter, ghee
***go, ko* (Kh)** - cattle
go dānam - gifting of a cow at an auspicious occasion, e.g. at death
***gok khmoc* (Kh)** - forest of the dead
gomayā - cow dung
gopura - monumental gateways or entrance pavillions
gośāla - cow stable
grama - smaller-scale settlement, freequently interpreted as a 'village'
grāmavṛddha - village elders
***hanira* (unknown)** - metal; alloy of silver (?)
hyan* or *hyang - Malay term indicating a woman of elite status
***jaṁnvan* (Kh)** - donation
jāti - Subset of class, denoted by particular professions or functions
Javā - *Kambuja*'s original political nemesis, either Java or a Malay polity.

***je* (Kh)** - measure of volume of production (riceland)
***jmol* (Kh)** - male
***jnvāl* (Kh)** - vendor; merchant (?)
kalaśa - ewer
kali-yuga - the fourth age of the world in Hindu cosmology
***kamaset* (Mod Kh)** - possession (ownership [land])
Kambu - a sage, the ultimate progenitor of Angkorian royalty, and the namesake of the Khmer polity
***kaṃhass; kanhas* (Kh)** - people of rank
***kaṃloñ* (Kh)** - people who are khloñ
***Kamrateṅ pdai ta karom* (Kh)** - master of the surface and below
***Kamraten jagat* (Kh)** - divine title
***kaṃsteṅ* (Kh)** - elite title
***kanloṅ kaṃmrateṅ 'an* (Kh)** - cult worshipping deceased royal women between the 10th and 14th centuries
***karol* (Kh)** - stable, pen
karuṇāprasāda - royal grace
kaumāra-bṛhtya - the treatment of children
kāyacikitsā - the treatment of diseases of the body
***kbun* (Kh)** - cache-sexe, modesty garment
khārī - measure of volume of grain
***khloñ* (Kh)** - chief
khloñ* (Kh) *vala - chief of forces
khloñ* (Kh) *viṣaya - district chief
khloñ vnaṃ - head of sanctuary
***khñuṃ vraḥ* (Kh)** - temple slave, servant
***khñuṃ, kñuṃ* (Kh)** - slave, bondsman, servant
***komlas* (Kh)** - a subset of pol who were assigned to religious and administrative offices until age 25
***krapi* (Kh)** - water buffalo
kṛta-yuga - the first age of the world in Hindu cosmology
***kryav* (Kh)** - gelding, ox
kṣatriya - elite class that produced the rulers and leaders of armies
kṣīra - cow's milk, thickened
kulādhyakṣa - rector of college or university
kulapati - head of religious community
kumbha - jar
laḍḍu - a sweet
***liḥ* (Kh)** - unit of volume for rice, other commodities
***liṅ* (Kh)** - metal weight
liṅga - mark, sign, emblem; a representation of Śiva as a phallic symbol
Lokeśvara - Bodhisattva of Compassion
***loñ* (Kh)** - middle ranking male title
madhuparka - oblation of honey and milk
maṅgala - anything auspicious or tending to a lucky issue, by extension, the prayer at the beginning of a text
Mantramārga - 'higher' tantric path of Śaivism
Māravijaya - the Buddha's triumph over Mara

***mās* (Kh)** - gold
Merā - the divine consort of Kambu.
***mratāñ kurun* (Kh)** - title of ruling official
***mratāṅ(ñ) (Khloñ)* (Kh)** - elite title
mṛtakadhana - acquisition through inheritance, including slaves
murti - incarnation, manifestation, embodiment of divinity
nāga - snake deity associated with water, fertility, treasure, and the underworld
nāginī - female supernatural serpent that can manifest in the form of a human woman
nandipāda - hoofprint of a bull; symbol of Nandi, Śiva's humped bull
***neak n'gear* (Kh)** -slaves owned by the state
***neak ta* (qnak tā*)* (Kh)** - ancestral tutelary spirit/deity; genies of territories and rural communities
***paṃneḥ* (Kh)** - small amount (?)
pañcagavya - the five products of the cow
parinirvāṇa - "complete nirvana"; the Buddha's passing away and cessation of rebirth
***paryyan* (Kh)** - to teach
***paryyaṅ, pareṅ* (Kh)** - oil, ghee, clarified semifluid butter
***paukeas* (Mod Kh)** - possession (occupation [land])
peṣaṇī - grinding stone
***phlu rddeḥ* (Kh)** - cart road
***phum* (Kh)** - village
***pol* (Kh)** - free persons obligated to perform specific functions at the behest of the royal family
***poṅ* (Kh)** - pregnant animal
pradakṣiṇa - devotional clockwise circumambulation around an image, object, or shrine
Prajñāpāramitā - Buddhist Goddess of Wisdom
pramāṇa ~ praman - unidentified area of land
praśasti - Sanskrit praise poem
prasat ~ prasāda - stone tower
prastha - unidentified unit of weight or capacity
pratimā - statue, image, icon, figure, reflection, likeness
pratiṣṭhā - ceremonies for installation and consecration of images
***prek* (Kh)** - excavated canal for diverting water
psam paribhoga - joint foundation, joint revenues, pooling of resources
puja - ritual honouring deities
Pukāṃ - the polity and people of Pagan Burma
***puñña* (Pali)** - merit
puṇya - foundation
puṇya raṣṭra - commoner foundation
pura - large-scale urban area, frequently interpreted as a 'city'
rājadharma - royal rule; king's justice or duty
rājadravya - crown domains
rājakārya - royal service; tax
rājakuṭi - royal chamber or cell
Rāmanya/Rmañ - the Mons who inhabited the Menam Basin of present-day central Thailand.
Rasāyana - treatments to prolong life, or alchemy
rūpa - form, shape, representation, image, figure
***ryan* (Kh)** - to study
śābda - sound

śābdaśāstra* or *śābdavidyā - science of sound
sabhāpati - chief justice
śākha - land histories
śalya - the treatment of wounds
śalyaka - the art of acupuncture
***sam miśraboga* (Kh)** - joint foundation, joint revenues, pooling of resources
śamī - a tree, variety of mesquite
***sampot* (Kh)** - hipwrapper, length of cloth
***saṃrit* (Kh)** - copper-based metal alloy believed to have magical properties
saṅkrānta - passage of sun/ planet to new position; new year
śāsana - royal edict
Śāstra - ancient Indian treatises
satyapraṇidhāna - vow of truth
siddhi - exclusive right
śivapāda - Śiva's footprint
śrīvatsa - flower-shaped pectoral ornament, notably of Viśṇu
***sruk* (Kh)** - village, neighborhood, community, or homeland
***steṅ 'añ* (Kh)** - elite title
Sūryavarmeśvara - name of four *liṅgas* erected in important regional shrines by Sūryavarman I
svat vrah dharmasastra - to recite the sacred judicial text
***tai* (Kh)** - appellative for female slave, commoner
***taṃliṅ* (Kh)** - a weight for gold or silver
***tāñ* (Kh)** - female title of rank
***teṅ hyaṅ* (Kh)** - female title of respect
***teṅ tvan* (Kh)** - female title of rank
***thlvaṅ, thloṅ, tloṅ* (Kh)** - unit of volume for paddy, salt
***thnap* (Kh)** - type of textile
***thpvac* (Kh)** - young animal, calf
***tmo/thmo* (Kh)** - stone
***tmo/thmo pi pas* (Kh)** - grinding stone
***tmur, thmur* (Kh)** - cattle (until late 10th c.)
***travāṅ* (Mod. trapeang) (Kh)** - reservoir, tank
***treta-yuga* (Kh)** - the second age of the world in Hindu cosmology
***trvac* (Kh)** - inspector
***ukñā* (Kh)** - Cambodian Honorific title 'lord'
***ullāra* (Kh)** - type of luxurious textile
umā-gaṅgā-patīśvara - triad depicting the god Śiva with two of his female consorts, Uma and Ganga
unmīlita - eye-opening ceremony in the consecration of images
upacāra - the acts of civility
uṣṇīṣa - the Buddha's cranial protuberance - one of the 32 bodily marks signifying Buddhahood
vāhana - god's vehicle
vajra - thunderbolt
vaṇijām adhipaḥ - chief of merchants
vanik - merchant, trader
***vāp* (Kh)** - middle ranking male title
***var* (Kh)** - a weight or capacity
varga - corporate groups

varṇa - status; elite caste; order of officials
***vaudi* (Kh)** - a vessel, pitcher
vidyaṣrama - centres of scientific learning of wide renown
Vīrāśrama - 'the *āśrama* of heroes', royal monasteries funded by Sūryavarman I
viṣaya - district, district chief
vitarkamudrā - gesture of discourse or discussion in which the tips of the index finger and thumb are pressed together to form a circle
***vraḥ* (Kh)** - sacred, royal
***vraḥ go* (Kh)** - sacred cattle
***vraḥ kaṃmrateṅ ('añ)* (Kh)** - title for divinities, royalty, and eminent ecclesiastics
***vraḥ kaṃsteṅ ('añ)* (Kh)** - elite title
vraḥ kuṭi - sacred or royal chapel
vraḥ sabhā - royal, holy court
vṛṣabha - bull; strong, vigorous
vyākaraṇa - grammar
yajñaśeṣa - leftovers from a sacrifice
yaśaḥśarīra - "body in the form of fame" or "body of glory"
Yavadvīpa - "Island of barley," usually associated with Java, though some scholars identify it with Sumatra
yavana- "Greek", in Angkorian inscriptions it refers to Đại Việt (northern Vietnam)
yoni - womb, uterus, female organs of generation; stone pedestal for liṅga image
yūpa - wooden post to which a buffalo is tied during sacrifice
yuvarāja - king-in-waiting (a son, brother, or uncle designated as such by the reigning king)

INDEX

Age of Commerce 319, 545, 608; *see also* Early Modern Period; Post-Angkor

agriculture 98, 135, 138, 143–6, 148, 163, 176, 189, 216, 339, 393, 443, 466, 595; crops 140, 143, 217, 314, 341–2, 351–4, 401–17 (*see also* rice); cultivation 136, 159, 340, 342–4, 471–3, 482 (*see also* rice cultivation); fields 339–42, 345–50; gardens 140, 186, 246, 342–3, 345, 351, 354, 409, 410, 412, 416–17, 499–500; irrigation 189, 216–25, 229, 263, 272, 310, 340–1, 350, 546, 598; *see also baray*

Ak Yum 81, 89–92, 182, 224; *see also* temple-mountains

aloeswood 107, 116

Ang Chan (*Cau Bañā Cand/Aṅg Cand*) 66, 448, 597

Angkor: collapse 28, 46, 64, 120, 128, 148–9, 541–50, 577; establishment of 80–1 (*see also cakravartin*; *devarāja*; political organisation, kingship); expansion 98, 104, 118, 140, 142, 145, 148–9, 231–2, 254–5, 259–60, 301,-02, 310, 330, 331–4, 378, 379, 394, 479, 482–7, 489–90, 595 (*see also* economy, trade; political organisation); population 71, 89, 98, 174, 188–9, 195, 216, 229, 309–10, 352, 466, 471, 542–3, 546–8, 592

Angkor Borei (Vyadhapura) 40, 68, 71, 73, 93, 154, 158, 162, 163, 181, 197, 311, 463, 474, 519; *see also* Funan

Angkor Thom 5, 40, 80, 93, 103, 104, 118, 119, 124, 127, 135, 141, 143, 146, 149, 176, *177*, 183, 229, 258, 261–3, *264*, 265, *266*, 288, 300, 315, 328, 343, 345, *353*, 370, 401, 407, 438, 498, 502, 514, 531, 544, 548, 562, 568, 579, 606, 615, 627; *see also* Baphuon; Bayon; Jayavarman VII; Royal Palace, Angkor Thom (Yaśodharāpura)

Angkor Wat 5, *12*, 42, 43, 104, 121, 125, 135, 184, 199, 203, 226, 230, 254, 255–6, 257–8, 260–1, 265–6, *267*, *268*, 269, 322, 330, 343, 351, 352, 355, 378, 401, 403–5, 439, 444, 448–9, 467, 470, 480, 490, 495, 497–504, 511–21, 514, 517–19, 522, 549, 585, 615–16, 629–30, 634, 636, 640, 641; *see also* Sūryavarman II

animals 4, 241, 258, 327, 329, 330, 447, 459, 466, 473, 474, 499, 517, 635; *see also* cattle; horses; buffalos

animism 425–8, 431, 450, 619, 624; local spirits 114, 116, 259, 293, 370, 423, 442, 448, 498, 622, 641; *neak ta (qnak ta)* 426, 436, 450, 465, 622, *623*

arboriculture 342–4, 351

archaeobotany 340, 354, 401

architecture: defensive 260–8; residential 201, 497–9, 555, 559, 568–70, 592, 596, 641; temple 6, 37, 72, 82, 85, 106, 142, 156, 161, 180, 255, 289, 300, 360, 364–7, 368–70, 371–80, 387, 437, 439, 459

armies 162, 254, 257, 258, 269, 479, 490; *see also* military; warfare

āśramas 158, 159, 161, 162, 241, 272–85, 289–90, 292, 295–6, 300, 301, 328, 368, 375, 394, 426, 429, 430, 468, 484, *485*, 486, 495, 496; *see also* repetitive royal foundations

Aymonier, Étienne 26, 44, 52, 594

Ayutthaya 259, 322, 545, 554, 555–62, 565–70, 576, 579, 587–8, 599; invasion of Angkor 22, 120, 254, 257, 269, 321, 447, 490, 543–4, 547, 548, 586, 593, 595–6, 597, 608

Bagan (Bago/Pagan) 102, 103, 107, 298, 396, 580, 586

Bakheng (Phnom Bakheng) 46, 93, 143, 197, 316, 328, 348, 448, 508, 548, 615; *see also* temple-mountains

Bakong 31, 81, 82, 93, 141–5, 146, 149, 272, 328, 365–7, 370–1, 376, 379–80, 439, 448, 487, 528; *see also* temple-mountains
Banteay 87; *see also* Royal Palace, Banteay (Mahendraparvata)
Banteay Chhmar 121, 127, 162, 179, 185, 225, 254, 295, 333, 373, 374, 378, 463, 489, 544
Banteay Chhoeu 89, 91, 224
Banteay Kdei 141, 145, 438, 448, 517
Banteay Srei 29, 247, 255, 292, 333, 364, 373, 380, 462, 463, 509, 615
Baphuon 377, 381, 395, 463, 509, 548; *see also* temple-mountains
baray 85, 87, 89, 216–18, 219, 224–9, 546–7; proto-baray 5, 90, 91, 182; *see also* East Baray; Indrataṭāka (Lolei Baray); irrigation; Jayataṭāka; West Baray
Barth, Auguste 26, 38, 281, 427
bas-reliefs 120, 127, 163, 226, 254–5, *256*, 257–9, 287, 294, 295, 318, 366, 402, 416, 462–4, 465, 467, 473, 480, 494, 496, *497*, 499–500, 508, 511–12, 514–23, 532, 615, *616*
Bassac River 97, 101, 157, 158, 341, 394
Battambang 100, 218, 260, 328, 330, 364, 381, 469, 539, 630–2, 636, 638, 639
Bay of Bengal 66–7, 97–8, 100–3, 106, 113, 411
Bayon: Period 35–6, 378, *444*; temple 112, 120, 160, 161, 177, 294, 402, 447, 463, 562, 580; *see also* bas-reliefs; Jayavarman VII
bees 164; *see also* forest products
Beng Mealea 183–4, 185, 371, 373, 379
Bergaigne, Abel 26, 38
Bhadreśvara 160, 166, 279, 280, 333–4, 425, 447; *see also Śiva*
Bhaiṣajyaguru 275, 295, 298–300, 486; *see also* Mahāyāna Buddhism
Bhavapura 5, 81, 89–94, 154, 157, 158, 161, 166, 182–3, 224, 310, 527
Bhavavarman I 60, 92, 160, 240
Brahmanism 289, 290, 428–9, 436, *441*, 448; *see also* Śaivaism; Vaiṣṇavaism
brahmins 27, 241, 247, 288–90, 291, 292, 300, 301, 423, 428–9, 460, 461, 463, 467, 480; *see also* priests
brick 68–9, 72, 73, *87*, 156, 203, 262, 281, 335, 360, *361*, 363, 363, 397, 443, 500, 549, 569, 570; *see also* temples
Briggs, Lawrence Palmer 70, 81, 543, 547
bronze 26, 27, 71, 119, 120, 126, 157, 226, 229, 378, 385, 439, 508, 555, 559, 566, 567, 587–8; production 126, 320, 396, 436, 439
Bronze Age 90, 310, 459, 463
Buddha images 331, 559, 436, 440, 442, 444, 447, 448, 450, 554, 556–9, 562–9; *see also* statuary
Buddhism 42–7, 112, 113, 127, 208, 274, 288, 292, 302, 423, 430, 436, 442, 486, 533, 534, 555, 578, 585, 619, 621, 623, 630, 635, 640–1; monks 103, 115, 127, 281, 287, 288–91, 294, 296–7, 301–2, 424, 431, 447, 469, 619–25, 634; transition to 290, 397, 533, 544–5; *see also* Mahāyāna Buddhism; Theravāda Buddhism
Buddhist terraces 579, 583, 604
buffalos 156, 166, 200, 259, 463–5, *465*, **466**, 472, 473–5
bulls 460–2
Buriram 388, 392, 393–4, 397
Burma/Burmese 101–2, 103, 106, 119, 254, 259, 288, 297, 344, 385, 489, 578, 580, 586–8, 636

cakravartin 5, 256, 443, 479, 488–9; *see also* political organisation, kingship
canals 83, 89, 91, 163, 176, 178, 181, 187, 188, 263, 350, 371, 376, 471, 495, 546, 547, 595, 598; *see also* water management
Candravairocana 298
cattle 343, 459–60, 466–7, **466**, 470–4; *see also* bulls; cows
cavalry 121, 256, 257, 258
celadons 124, 395; *see also* China; porcelains
ceramics 385–6, 486–7, 500–1, 548; production 54, 68, 163, 388–9, *389*, *390* (*see also* stonewares); trade ceramics 5, 67, 317, 596, 600–9, **601**, *602*, *604*, *605*, *607* (*see also* China, trade with/goods from); *see also* earthenwares; glazed wares
Cham: inscriptions 103, 106, 162, 331; invasion of Angkor 262; people 99, 107, 122, 480, 498, 531
Champa/Cham civilisation 66, 72, 73, 85, 97, 98, 99, 101, 104–8, 113, 115, 117–20, 127–8, 158–9, 160, 162–3, 228, 254, 258–60, 298, 319, 331, 344, 396, 439, 465, 479–81, 489, 498, 491, 512–14, 527–8, 531, 576, 598, 635
Chao Phraya River 97–104, 118, 319, 482, 555–70; *see also* Menam Basin
chariots 121; *see also* transportation
Chau Srei Vibol 199, 260, 617
Chenla (*Zhenla*) 8, 64, 70, 71, 72, 90, 103, 108, 117, 154, 159, 166, 181, 254, 341; *see also* Pre-Angkor
Cheung Ek 54, 158, 388, 394
China 66, 112–28, 177, 354, 480–1, 519; Chinese in Angkor 120–1; cultural influences in Angkor 64, 69, 124–6, 288, 298, 342, 395–6, 473, 517, 519, 522; trade with/goods from *5*, 66–7, 71, 82, 99, 100–3, 112–24, **115**, 295, 318–19, 410, 412, 413, *502*, 514, 520, 545, 546, 595, 600–3, *604*, *605*, 606 (*see also* economy); tribute/political missions to 70, 112–24, 520, 535, 554, 567, 596, 636; *see also* Ming dynasty; Song dynasty; Tang dynasty; Yuan dynasty
cities *see* settlement forms; urbanism
Citrasena 159, 160, 161, 273, 555
climate 18, 19, 20–2, 136, 148–50, 293, 339, 546–7, 609; *see also* palaoenvironment

cloth 107, 114, 120, 124, 313, 314, 328, 402, 502, 508–20, 532; *see also* China, trade goods; textiles; trade
clothing 165, 257, 258, 315, 317, 342, 442, 508, 509, *510*, *511*, *512*, 529, 531, 536; *see also* textiles
Coe, Michael D. 190
Cœdès, George 26, 29, 44, 47, 64, 66, 243, 488, 489, 554, 556
Colonial Period 52, 55, 69, 313, 469, 491, 536, 555
Corpus des inscriptions Khmères *see* inscriptions, corpus of
cotton 32, 67, 101, 114, 140, 163, 165, 351, 353, 402, 403–5, 407, 410, 416, 436, 463, 502, 513–15, 518, 520, 534, 619; *see also* textiles
courts 240, 241, 245–6, 250, 310, 335; *see also* laws; legal texts
cows 462–3, *464*, 466, 470, 474; *see also* buffalo; bulls; rituals
Cpāp saṃbauv 599–600, 608
craft production *see* iron; statuary; stonewares; textiles
cremation 6, 464, 616, 619–22
crops 137, 163, 218, 314, 340, 342, 353–4, 355, 402–3, *404*, 405–8, **408**, 411, 415, 546; *see also* agriculture; mung beans; rice

dairy products **467**, 467–9; *see also* cows; rituals
Dai Viet 98, 107, 258, 259–60
Dangrek Range 388, 394, 482; *see also* Khorat Plateau
Democratic Kampuchea 636–7; *see also* Khmer Rouge
devarāja 5, 56, 80, 248, 256, 301, 430, 443, 578; *see also cakravartin*; political organisation, kingship
Dharma 240, 244, 301, 445, 448, 461–2, 534, 574, 575–6, 579, 580–8, 614, 632, 639
Dipterocarpaceae 127, 136, 139, 146; *see also* arboriculture
Do Couto, Diogo 371
drought 20–3, 147–50, 321, 341, 412, 546, 548, 550; *see also* Angkor, collapse
Durga 380, 463, 465, 527, 531, 636
Duryodhana 237, *238*, 239
Dvaravati 65, 68, 69, 72, 98, 126, 396, 483, 556–9, 564, 569

Early Modern Period 45, 185–6, 397, 448, 546, 550, 592–3, *594*, 596–600; *see also* Post-Angkor
earthenwares 68, 71, 385, 386, 395, 500, 502; *see also* ceramics
East Baray 145, 183, 217, 218, 219, 228, 230, 263, 265, 273, *276*, 277, 328, 346–7; *see also* baray; water management; West Baray
East Mebon 29, 255, 328, 368, 380, 615
economy 101, 146, 200, 309, 311, 319, 322, 327, 339, 341, 393, 395, 466, 474, 487, 608 (*see also* rice); barter 3, 165, 313, 314, 317, 320, 466, 520; consumption of goods 396, 397, 600; control of trade 100, 104, 128, 161–2, 165, 310, 318, 320, 322, 334, 599, 607–9; debt bondage 312, 535, 536; distribution 124, 162, 164, 165, 166, 321, 322, 334, 405, 445–7, 468, 479, 486–7, 600; donations 3, 30, 34, 159, 174, 241–2, 243, 313–14, 318, 329, 331, 333, 344, 402, 424, 424–5, 427, 439, 449, 466, 490, 525, 528, 534; international trade 98, 101, 104, 107, 321–2, 541, 545, 606, *607*, 608–9; luxury/high-value goods 67, 114, 117, 126, 127, 249, 309, 313, 321, 514, 519, 520, 522; maritime trade 18, 71, 97, 98, 100–4, 106–7, 117–20, 128, 318, 319, 321, 322, 545, 580, 607; production 71, 121, 158, 165, 216, 310, 313, 314, 316, 320, 321, 329, 370, 371, 378, 385, 388, 392, 393–4, 397, 402, 405, 438, 468, 469, 473, 486, 526, 513, 514, 534, 549, 554, 576, 584, 630; redistribution 314–16, 332, 426; taxation 162, 243, 309, 310–13, 314, 316, 317, 320–1, 322, 334, 342; taxes 26, 104, 164, 165, 246, 249, 261, 316–17, 318, 321, 333, 394, 425, 473, 480, 599, 641; temple 329–31, 331–5, 466; transactions 208, 246–7, 249, 313–14, 316, 317, 329, 332, 340; wealth 176, 189, 242, 249, 250, 310–16, 317, 321–2, 327, 329, 331, 332, 417, 466, 472, 546, 595, 598–600, 604, 607–8
education: Angkorian 273, 287–93, 303; medical 113, 115, 116, 140, 164, 292–5, 300–2, 342, 414–15, 503; modern Cambodia 43, 47, 49, 50, 52, 54, 55, 637
elephants 70, 103, 117, 120, 256, 257, 258, 262, 313, 329, 534
environment *see* climate; Monsoon; palaeoenvironment
ethnic groups 159–60, 259, 396, 488, 577; *see also* Kuay; minority groups

Faxian 113; *see also* China
fish 154, 163–4, 351; *see also* Mekong River; Tonle Sap Lake
forest 121, 135–40, 142–6, 149–50, 159, 164, 203, 220, 330, 342, 344, 393, 394, 527, 531, 619, 633, 638
forest products 2, 99, 103, 107, 114, 163, 165, 313, 317, 320, 321, 520, 564, 599, 607; *see also* minority groups
Funan (*Fou-nan*) 8, 64–5, 68–72, 112, 114–15, 127, 140, 154, 157, 158, 163, 180–1, 248, 254, 423, 513, 519, 527; *see also* Pre-Angkor
furnaces *see* iron, production

Ganbozhi 119
Gatilok 631, 632, 636
gharuwood 117, 120, 128
globalisation 545–6, 550; *see* economy, maritime trade

goddess worship 463, 465, 474; *see also* Durga; Kali (Srey Kmau); Parvati
Goloubew, Victor 45, 85, 176, 197, 224
Greater Angkor Project 2, 55, 178, 187, 199, 265, 266, 338, 401
Grès Supérieurs *see* sandstone, types and sources
Groslier, Bernard-Philippe 46, 47, 48, 52, 81–2, 89, 124, 139, 146, 175–6, 216, 217, 227, 229, 339
Groslier, Georges 47, 360, 482, 508, 546
Gulf of Thailand (Siam) 97, 101
Gupta 66, 67, 72, 396, 513

Harihara 83, 445, 61
Hariharālaya (Roluos) *13*, 80–3, *84*, 143, 183, 272, 279, 348, 365–8, 370–1, 374, 377, 393, 438, 445, 447, 487
Haripunjaya 580
Harśovarman II 228
herding 468, 470–1; *see also* cattle
heritage management 42, 43, 50, 51, 54, 56
hermits 273, 283; *see also* Brahmanism; brahmins
Hinduism 46, 423, 436, 442, 443, 469; *see also* Brahmanism; Śaivaism; Vaiṣṇavaism
historiography 81, 527, 545, 555, 576, 592
Holocene 17–20, 135
horses 121, 318, 329
hospital chapels 161, 164, 273, *275*, 288, 297, *298*, *299*, 300–2, 320, 328, 469, *485*, 486, 580, 585; *see also* Bhaiṣajyaguru; Jayavarman VII; Mahāyāna Buddhism; repetitive royal foundations
Houay Tomo 280
Hydraulic city (*Cité hydraulique*) 1, 25, 81–2, 176, 189, 216, 229, 339, 339, 350, 541, 546–7

iconography 72, 287, 291, 298, 300, 435, 447, 467, 561, 563, 581, 587, 614, 615, 618
identity: Angkorian 302, 385, 479–81, 489–90; modern Khmer 43, 45, 47, 56, 490–1, 632, 635; *see also* ethnic groups; Kuay (Kuy)
Ind 46, 630–6
India: cultural influences 26, *28*, 30, 31, 34, 49, 67, 68, 240, 241, 250, 288, 292, 293, 302, 329, 342, 395, 473, 474; trade with/goods from 67, 101, 317, 318, 409–12, 414, 416, 423, 428–9, 440, 443, 459–65, 466–7, 473, 514–15, 518–20, 522, 614
Indianisation 26, 66, 69, 90, 94, 423, 460
Indian law texts: *Dharmaśāstra* 240, 245, 292; *Dharmasūtras* 240; Kautilya's *Arthaśastra* 240, 257, 258, 292, 459, 470
Indra 430, 528, 587, 633–4, 635, 641
Indradevī 291, 292, 430, 445, 528, 530, 531, 533; *see also* political organisation, queens
Indrapura 89, 154, 157, 158, 159, 161, 166
Indrataṭāka (Lolei Baray) 81, 228, 230, 272, 328; *see also baray*
Indravarman I 81, 82, 272, 328, 365, 376, 469, 528, 530, 531, 532
Indravarman II 227
inscriptions: toponyms 30, 165, 174, 282, 340, 472, 486, 580, 633, 636; *see also* Khmer-language texts; Pali-language texts; Sanskrit-language texts
inscriptions, corpus of: topical gaps in 29, 35, 177, 217, 241, 313, 473, 580; trends in 25, 26, 27, 38, 39, 80, 140, 174, 200, 274, 293, 314, 329, 330, 440, 466, 595, 614
iron 6, 257, 259, 320–1, 322, 387, 387–8, 405, 463, 471, 486–7, 544, 614; furnaces 390–2, *391*; production 388, *389*, 390, *391*, 394–7, 473, 549; *see also* Phnom Dek
Iron Age 68, 71, 90, 139, 341, 415, 463, 471; *see also* Prehistoric Period
irrigation 189, 216–25, 229, 263, 272, 310, 341, 350, 546, 598; *see also* baray; water management
Iśānavarman I 158, 461
Īśānavarman II 26, 166, 228, 313, 334
Isthmus of Kra 98, 100, 101, 102, 103, 106, 318–19

Jacques, Claude 26, 38, 48
Java 29, 56, 103, 106, 107, 117, 118, 317, 318, 480, 489, 490
Jayabuddhamahānātha 446–7, 486, 554, 580–2; *see also* statuary
Jayarājadevī 445, 530, 533; *see also* Jayavarman VII; political organisation, queens
Jayarvarman V 160, 250, 291, 321, 369, 425, 531, 533
Jayataṭāka 228, 230; *see also baray*; Jayavarman VII
Jayavarman I 29, 158–9, 241, 321, 331
Jayavarman I bis 29–30
Jayavarman II 29, 56, 65, 69, 81, 82, 85, 89, 90, 154, 157, 160, 161, 182, 241, 249, 260, 310, 328, 331, 376, 467, 489, 527–8, 532, 535
Jayavarman III 81, 228, 331, 332, 528, 532
Jayavarman IV 222, 380
Jayavarman VI 99, 528, 529–30
Jayavarman VII 118, 120, 127, 158–9, 183, 185, 208, 258, 260, 261, 262, 275, 287, 289–91, 293, 295, 297–303, 319, 328, 335, 374, 377, 378, 380, 387, 394, 397, 444, 445, 446, 447, 462, 464–5, 480, 482, 486, 530, 531, 533, 544, 554, 575–6, 578, 579, 580–1, 582, 583, 586, *587*, 588; *see also* Bayon, Period
Jayavīravarman 36–7, 228, 369, 529, 532
Jenner, Philip 26

Kali (*Srey Kmau*) 461–2, 634, 636; *see also* goddess worship
Kambu 73, 469, 487–9
Kambuja (Kambujadesa) 119, 460, 487–91, 531, 555, 629; *see also* Kambu
Kaṃrateṅ Jagat 30, 56, 426–8

Kbal Spean *228*, 443; *see also* Phnom Kulen; Viṣṇu; water management
Kendi 68, 410; *see also* India; rituals
Khao Sam Kaeo 410, 411, 413–14; *see also* Maritime Southeast Asia; Prehistoric Period
Khmer-language texts 25, 26, 64, 282, 288, 462, 466, 468, 470; *see also* inscriptions
Khmer Rouge 46, 49, 54, 56, 70, 237, 542, 630, 636–40
Khmer Studies 2, 42, 43–7, 49–51
Khone Rapids 160; *see also* Mekong River
Khorat Plateau 67, 68, 97, 101, 159, 161–2, 164, 261, 319, 321, 448, 486
kilns *see* stonewares, kilns
Koh Ker 93, 179, 183, 189, 219, 222, *223*, 224, 225–6, 229, 237, 335, 363, 373, 379, 440, 462, 533, 547, 549
Kompong Cham 377, 598, 633
Kompong Chhnang 397
Kuay (Kuy) 189, 320–1, 390–2, 396, 397, 486–7, 624; *see also* ethnicity
Kuk Ta Prohm 279
Kulen *see* Phnom Kulen

labour/labourers 5, 6, 94, 149, 226, 242, 283, 302, 313, 316, 322, 327, 329, 341, 371, 379, 468, 473, 475, 482, 496, 534–6, 599, 633
land ownership 3, 200, 218, 239, 240, 241–50
land use *136*, 137, 207, 344–5, 548, 549; *see also* agriculture
Lanna 567, 568, 569, 585
Lan Xang 584, 585–6
laterite 37, 82, 89, 156, 160, 261, 262, 263–5, 273, 276–8, 360, 363, 379, 380, 482, 486; *see also* sandstone; temples
laws: Angkorian 239–41, 535, 576, 618; modern 237–8, 250
law texts *see* Indian law texts
lidar (LiDAR) 2, 85, 87, 91, 140, 173, 177, 178–9, 181–6, 199, 218, 225, 265, 297, 317, 351, 371, 494
liṅgas/liṅgam 106, 159, 160, 226, 272, 328, 380, 424, 425, 427, 429, 439, 441, 442, 443, 460, 486
lintels 37, 255, 360, 363, 366, 442, 615
Lokeśvara 328, 440, 441, 446, 448, 486, 575, 581
Lolei 247, 328, 335, 365, 440, 446, 447, 480, 528
Longvek (*Laṅvaek*) 4, 179, 185, 447, 448, 548, 555, 596–609, *598*, 603
looms 513–14, 522; *see also* textiles
looting 46, 50, 451
Lopburi (Lavo, Lavapura) 98–104, 554, 558, 562, 566, 568–9, 570
Lower Mekong Basin 6, 64, 66, 68–9, 70, 71–2, 94, 97, 99, 103, 154, *156*, 469
Luang Prasert Chronicle 559

Mahābhārata 121, 237, 255, 292, 440, 460, 465, 517; *see also* myths, Hindu
Mahāyāna Buddhism 46, 100, 103, 104, 115, 287, 290, 296, 301–3, 328, 334, 378, 397, 424, 436, *444*, 447, 465, 469; *see also* Buddhism
Mahendraparvata 80, 84–9, 93–4, 182–3, 189, 218–19, *221*, 225, 227, 393, 443, 489, 54; *see also* Phnom Kulen
Mahendravarman 158, 159, 160, 161, 273, 461, 528
Maitreya 425, 448, 520, *521*, 522; *see also* Mahāyāna Buddhism
Malay Peninsula 67, 68, 71, 97, 98, 100–3, 577
maṇḍala 260, 480, 490; *see also* Mount Meru; sacred geography
Mandalay (Amarapura) 586, 588
Maritime Silk Road 66, 68–9, 72, 120; *see also* economy, maritime trade
Maritime Southeast Asia 112, 319; *see also* economy, maritime trade
markets 5, 118, 315, 317, 319, 322, 536; *see also* economy; merchants
Maya 187, 188, 198, 317, 343, 354; *see also* Mesoamerica
medicine *see* education, medical
Mekong Delta 64, *65*, 69–72, 107, 154, *157*, 158–9, 163, 319, 321, 342, 436, 471, 513
Mekong River 17–21, 66, 69, 72, 99, 108, 119, 154–6, 157, 160–7, 182, 197, 262, 280, 309, 321, 322, 328, 341, 362, 374, 376, 482, 483, 486, 547, 595, 606
Menam Basin 570, 577, 579; *see also* Chao Phraya River
merchants 67, 73, 100, 103, 104, 108, 114, 118, 119, 128, 317–19, 322, 395, 514, 595, 60; *see also* economy; markets
mercury 115, 124, 126, 294, 295, 559, 567
Mesoamerica 1, 198, 548; *see also* Maya
Middle Period *see* Early Modern Period; Post-Angkor
military: campaigns 103–4, 162, 480, 584; depictions of 97, 98, 120, 121, 123, 254–7, 330, 473, 508, 512
milk/milking 245, 297, 442, 459, 462–3, 466–7, *468*, *469*; *see* dairy products; rituals, Hindu
millet 140, 342, 407, 412, 413–15
Ming dynasty 112, 119–20, 519, 596, 608
Ming shi-lu 119, 596
minority groups 320, 321, 390, 396, 465, 486, 487, 513, 514, 608; *see also* ethnic groups; identity; Kuay
Mon civilisation 155, 161, 479, 483, 491, 529, 556, 576–9, 586; *see also* Dvaravati
Monsoon 17, 20–2, 148–9, 154, 229, 309, 339, 546; *see also* drought; palaoenvironment
Mount Meru 226, 227, 228, 230, 348; *see also* maṇḍala; sacred geography

Mrauk-U 586
Muang Singh 482, 554
Mun River 71, 98–9, 101, 482; *see also* Prehistoric Period
mung beans 67, 140, 342, 351, 353, 402, 403, 405, 407, 414, 415
myths: Hindu 430, 460–3, 465, 474, 488, 518, 527, 626; myths Khmer 460, 488–9, 518, 527, 636

Nalanda 288, 293
Nanhai 69, 112
neak ta (*qnak tā*) *see* animism, local spirits

Óc Eo 68–71, 93, 158, *180*, 181, 197, 513, 519
Oh Phnom Penh Euy 630, 638, 640
oil 119, 164, 248, 251, 295, 310, 409, 410, 413, 442, 467–8, 514, 534; *see also* butter; rituals
orchards 140, 338, 342–4; *see also* arboriculture; gardens; settlement forms, houses
Oudong 42, 179, 185, 438, 548, 593, 595, 609

palaces *see* Royal Palaces
palaeoenvironment 17–21, **142**, *144*; *see also* climate; Holocene
Pali: modern Cambodia 47, 52
Pali-language texts 64, 288, 578, 584, 630; *see also* Theravāda Buddhism
Parvati 636; *see also* goddess worship
Pāśupata 426, 429; *see also* Śaivaism/Śaiva
Phanom Rung (Phnom Rung) 260, 393, 447
Phetchaburi 554–5, 580
Phimai 68, 98, 99, 104, 161, 330, 364, 377, 379, 393, 439, 447, 486, 529, 581
Phimeanakas 46, 291, 378, 445, 514, 587; *see also* temple-mountains
Phnom Bakheng 46, 93, 143, 197, 316, 328, 348, 381, 448, 509, 548, 615
Phnom Bok 93, 207, 345, 348, *349*, 350
Phnom Da 93, 158, 443, 445, 463, 465
Phnom Dek 320–1, 388, 390–2, 394–5, 396, 487; *see also* iron
Phnom Krom 348
Phnom Kulen 80–1, 84–9, 93, 136, 140, 182, 218, 219, 226, 229, 340, 371, 373, 376, 379, 381, 393, 401, 443, 547, 549
Phnom Penh (Catumukh) 2, 4, 45, 47, 54, 185, 396, 438, 593, 597, 631, 634, 636–7, 639–40
Phnom Sandak 282–3
Phra Bang Buddha 585
plants 135, **137**, 140–6, 295, 300, 342–3, 351–4, **354**, 401–2, 408–15, 631, 633, 637; *see also* agriculture; mung beans; palaeobotany; rice
Pleistocene 18, 20
ploughing 341, 471–3; *see also* agriculture; buffalos; cattle; rice
political organisation: administration 33, 44, 203, 207, 242, 291, 316, 334, 438, 447, *484*, 488, 531, 593; geneaology 328, 332, *529*, *530*; kingship 98, 255, 256, 385, 429–30, 479, 480–1, 482–7, 525, 528, 569; legitimacy 106, 127, 228, 287, 300, 302, 327, 332, 438; officials 36, 200, 203, 241–2, 244–7, 249–50, 256, 287, 297, 310–11, 312–14, 316–19, 321–2, 329, 331, 332, 334, 448, 496, 498, 529, 532, 535; queens 283, 291, 292, 427, 444, 445, 527–8, 530–1, 532–3 (*see also* Indradevī; Jayarājadevī); succession 106, 127, 192, 256–7, 260, 425, 483, 527–32
Ponhea Leu 598, 609
Ponhea Yat (Cau Baññā Yāt) 596, 607
porcelains 104, 107, 120, 127, 317, 393, 534, 606; *see also* celadons; China
ports 66, 69, 99, 100–1, 107–8, 113, 114, 117–19, 127, 318–20, 592, 595; *see also* Maritime Southeast Asia
Post-Angkor 43, 107, 185–6, 197, 392, 397, 401, 402, 448, *449*, 490, 503, 546, 548, 559, 565, 570, 576–80, 592–5, 596–9; *see also* Early Modern Period
Pottier, Christophe 178, 182
Pou, Saveros (Lewitz, Saveros) 26, 33, 38, 47, 51, 53, 283, 593
Prajñāpāramitā 301, 328, 444, 446, 580, 581
prasat *see* temples
Prasat Khna 283, *284*
Prasat Komnap South 275, 277–8, 281; *see also* āśramas
Prasat Neak Buos 160, 218, *280*, 281, 282–3
Prasat Ong Mong (Saugatāśrama) 275–8, *277*, 278, 281, 282–3; *see also* āśramas
Prasat Preah Theat Baray 596, 607
Prasat Thom 219, 226; *see also* Koh Ker
Prasat Trapeang Ropou 199, 495, 497, 498, 499–500, 503
Preah Keo (Braḥ Kaev) myth 447, 597
Preah Khan (Angkor): inscription 103, 174, 273, 328, 378, 387, 439, 442, 486, 514, 554, 574, 576, 580, 584, 587; temple 162, 288–91, 295, 296, 315, 328, 377, 378, 402, 447, 515, 516, 575, 579
Preah Khan of Kompong Svay 35, *36*, 37, 38, 179, 185, 189, 225, 240, 320, 373, 377, 390, 392, 394, 401, 405, 486, 487, 515, 544, 549
Preah Ko 31, 81, 272, 279, 328, 365–7, 368, 400, 461, 469, 528, 597; *see also* Hariharālaya
Preah Kô (Braḥ Go) 447, 597; *see also* Preah Keo
Preah Vihear 282–3, 328, 332, 333, 364, 373, 379, 486
Prei Prasat 240, 275, 277, 281
priests 67, 242, 256, 287, 296, 428–9, 460, 527, 533; *see also* Brahmins
Pre Rup 29, 218, 228, 262, 277, 279, 327–8, 345–6, *347*, 348, 350, 368, 426, 445, 462, 615

queens *see* political organisation

Rahal (Koh Ker) 219, 222, 225, 229; *see also* irrigation
Rājendravarman II 98, 158, 160, 162, 183, 218, 228, 254, 281, 283, 328, 335, 345, 424, 426, 430, 445, 462, 467, 528, 530, 532, 533
Ramathibodi 555, 569, 570
Rāmāyana 255, 292, 440, 460, 465, 472, 517, 631; Reamker (Khmer) 472, 631; *see also* myths, Hindu
religion *see* animism/local spirits; Brahmanism; Mahāyāna Buddhism; rituals; Śaivaism; Theravāda Buddhism; Vaiṣṇavaism
religious pluralism 4, 72, 427, 429, 430, 431
religious syncretism 423–4, 430
remote sensing 2, 89, 175, 185, 198, 203, 275, 495, 548, 596; *see also* lidar
repetitive royal foundations *see* āśrama; hospital chapels; resthouses
reservoir *see baray; trapeang*
resthouses 275, 393, 485, 486; *see also* repetitive royal foundations
rice 140, 143, 145, 163, 339–40, 342, 351–3, 402, 403–8, 412, **415**, 415–17; production 315, 341, 471–3, 546; use in Angkorian culture 140, 163, 164, 282, 297, 309–12, 315, 317, 329, 417, 467, 468, 473, 546, 618
rice cultivation 622–6, 637; bunded 341, 342, 350, 471; floating 6, 163, 340; flood-recession 6, 140, 163, 226–7, 230, 310, 340; household garden (*chamkar*) 340, 342, 345; irrigated 176, 216, 541, 598; wet-rice 98, 148, 154, 340–1, 472–3
rice fields: organization 340, 344–50, 471; ownership and trade 246–7, 313, 320
rituals: animist 465, 618–26, *619*, *621*, *623*, *624*, *625*, *626*; Brahmanical 428, 429, 459, 460, *464*, 465, 618; objects and materials 28, 32, 26–35, 467; role of 327, 443, 462, 498; sacrifice 259, 316, 461, 463–4, *465*; temple 31–3, 259, 330, 334, 401–2, 427, 440–2, 445, 462–3, 466, 473, 474, 536, 584
roads 99, 101, 156, 160, 162, 176, 187, 208, 226, 247, 258, 261, 272, 273, 276, 280, 290, 297, 311, 376, 379, 388, 389, 392–4, 394, 418, 473, 482, *483*, 486–7, 495, 527, 547, 580; *see also* transportation
Rong Chen 85, *86*, 93, 443; *see also* Phnom Kulen; temple-mountains
Royal Cambodian Chronicles 26, 543, 577, 593, 596, 597, 609
Royal Palace: Angkor Thom (Yaśodharāpura) 118, 121, 124, 258, 262–3, 291, 320, 328, 353, 370, 407–8, 438, 497, 498–9, 503, 514, 532, 606, 615; Banteay (Mahendraparvata) 85–9, 93; Phnom Penh 578, 635, 636, 638; Prei Monti (Hariharālaya) 82–3, 93, 124, 262, 438
royal palaces 33, 81, 83, 93, 227, 228, 282, 428, 438, 463, 470, 525, 531–3, 535, 536, 596–7
Royal University of Fine Arts 42, 47, 48, 50

sacred geography 176, 183, 438; *see also* mandalas; Mount Meru
Śaivaism/Śaiva 33, 65, 81, 89, 273, 290, 292, 331, 424, 425, 428, 429–31, 436, 443, *461*, 489
salt 158, 163–4, 319, 321, 463
Sambhupura (Sambor) 65, 99, 154, 160, 161, 162, 164, 165, 166, 528
Sambor Prei Kuk 65, 92, 93, 115, 158, 160, 162, 179, *181*, 182, 260, 273, 380, 394
sandalwood 34, 117, 120, 140, 533; *see also* forest products
Sanskrit: in Angkorian culture 255, 287, 288, 290, 292, 460, 479, 488, 578, 579, 584–5, 593, 629, 633; *see also* India; Indianisation; Sanskrit-language texts
Sanskrit-language texts 25, 26–7, 33, 64, 107, 174, 240, 241, 243, 255, 288–90, 291, 292–3, 428, 440, 442, 459, 460–1, 474, 488, 494, 578, 579, 580, 581, 584–5, 593, 633; *see also* Khmer-language inscriptions
sandstone 82, 156, 218, 360; quarrying 5, 362, *372*, *375*, 376; types and sources 136, 360–4, 360, 363, **364**, 371–6; uses 262, 266, 280, 360, *361*, 364–9, 370–1, 376–8, 439, 460, *461*, 486, *499*, 554, 564, 567, *582*, 635; *see also* bas-reliefs; lintels; statuary; temples
sculptures *see* statuary
Sdok Kak Thom inscription 65, 80, 81, 89, 331, 430, 443, 489
Sea of Milk 226–30; *see also* myths, Hindu
Sen River 388, 390, 392
settlement forms: cities 5, 6, 30, 64, 80, 81, 93–4, 173, 174–5, 176–7, 182–5, 186–7, 314, 338, 343, 558, 564; houses 140, 174, 199, 201, 273, 342, 386, 417, 470, 494–6, 497, 498–503; occupation mounds 176, 178, 181–3, 186, 188, 495, 497–8; temple-cities/enclosures 146, 173, 175–7, 183, *184*, 189, **261**, 265–6, 269, 352, 496, 498, 502, 503; villages 35, 139, 164, 195, 200–2, 203, 244, 245, 311, 315, 316, 317, 328, 343, 351, 465, 470, 495–6, 534, 536, 542, 619; *see also* urbanism
seyma (*sima*) stones 101, 161, 634–5; *see also* Buddhism; sacred geography
Siem Reap River 229, 443
silk 67, 104, 107, 114–15, 118, 120, 121, 124, 163, 436, 513, 514, 515, 517, 519, 520, 534, 641; *see also* textiles
Sisowath 46, 630, 633
Śiva 27, 31, 160, 226, 275, 280, 292, 331, 427, 441, 444, 445, 448, 460, 468, 474, 528; *see also* Śaivaism
Śivaliṅgas 273; *see also* liṅgas/liṅgam

social hierarchy: elites 4, 80, 124, 127, 128, 162, 200, 241, 242, 248–50, **248**, 287, 289, 292, *312*, 329–32, 393, 426, 436, 442, 459, 466, 474, 490, 498, 592, 608; local/regional elites 162, 163, 166, 310, 312, 316, 328, 330, 334, 496, 529, 545, 555–6; non-elites 6, 311, 494; slaves 27, 99, 200, 241–2, 244, 249, 313, 315, 316, 317, 318, 496, 499, 504, 512, 525, 527, 529, 533, 534–6
social organisation: gender 4, 291, 525–7, 532–3; wives 262, 292, 532, 533; women 34, 291, 317, 498, 503, 509, 511, 525–34, 535–6, 638; *see also* political organisation, queens
Song dynasty 102, 104, 108, 117–19, 121, 126, 128, 317, 318–19, 322, 394, 519
speleothems 22, 148
Srah Srang 141, 145, 148
Srei Santhor (*Srī Santhar*) 548, 593, 595–6, 597, 607, 608
Sri Lanka 68, 103, 106, 396, 409, 410, 545, 548, 566, 580, 583, 585–6
Srindravarman 259
Srivijaya 71, 72, 100, 117, 520, 556
Śrutavarman 531
statuary: distribution 161, 445–7, 564–5, 566, 567–8, 588; function and use 85, 328, 385, 436–8, 443–5, 448–9; impact on later states 553, 556–64, 583, 585; introduction of 69, 70, 72; production 165, 360, 362, 363, *370*, 373, 376–8, 438–9, *446*, 549; veneration 64, *125*, *437*, 440–2, **440**, 450
stelae 367
Stern, Philippe 80–2, 85, 90, 272
stonewares 124, 126, 163, 385–7, 396, 486–7, 498, 502, 596, 606–7; glazed 385, *386*, 387, 393–5, 486–7; kilns 54, 83, 126, 158, 387, *389*, *390*, 397, 596, 607; production 3, 127, 158, 388, 392–4, 395
Straits of Melaka 71, 97, 98, 100, 101, 103, 608; *see also* economy, maritime trade
stupas 448, 567, *568*, 569–70, 585, 596; *see also* Theravāda Buddhism
Sukhothai 377, 554, 556–7, 561–2, 565–7, 569, 579, 583–5
Suphanburi 554, 555–6, 557, 558, 562, 564–70, 580
Sūryavarman I 35–6, 38, 98–100, 102, 104, 118, 158–9, 161, 240, 262, 282–3, 328, 331, 332, 333, 334, 364, 394, 426, 430, 480, 484, 529–30
Sūryavarman II 104, 118, 254, 255–6, 258, 259, 260, 262, 330, 370, 403, 444, 482, 486, 511, 520, 536
Sūryavarmeśvara 159, 328, 486; *see also liṅgas/liṅgam*
Syāṃ Kuk 258, 480; *see also* minority groups

Tai 480, 555, 557, 579, 583–5; *see also* Sukhothai
Ta Keo 5, 362, 368–70, *369*, 374–6
Tambralinga 98, 100, 101, 102–3, 259
Tang dynasty 115, 117, 124, 127, 128, 294, 319
tantra 423, 430
Tantric/Tantrism 31, 34, 103, 290, 294, 297, 300, 436, 446, 569
Ta Prohm (Angkor) 26, 120, 159, 162, 174, 184, 199, 265, 273, 279, 288, 290, 291, 295, 296–7, 300, 315, 317, 328, 343, 345, 351, 352, 353, 377–8, 401, 402, 405, 438, 439, 469, 474, 495, 496, 500–2, 503, 514, 515, 517, 544, 580, 585, 587
Ta Prohm Bati 161, 164
taxes *see* economy
technologies 68, 72, 124–6, 163, 319, 342, 385, 388–92, 395–6, 436, 471–2, 513, 515; *see also* agriculture; architecture; iron; stonewares
temple d'étape 273, 486; *see also* resthouses
temple enclosure *see* settlement forms, temple-cities/enclosures
temple-mountain 80–1, 83, 85, 87, 89–90, 93, 141, 143, 182, 226, 227–8, 345, 437, 465; *see also* Ak Yum; Bakheng; Bakong; Baphuon; Bayon; Rong Chen
temples (*prasat*): building material(s) 365–8, 368–70, 376–80; conservation 1, 2, 44, 45–6, 47, 49, 52, 56, 70, 371, 633; construction 6, 149, 208, 289, 320, 322, 330, 387, 397, 460; decoration 255, 265, 269, 370, 379, 515–18, 516, 568; foundation of 200, 207, 244, 311, 316, 330, 332–3, 425; hierarchy 3, 316, 333, 334, 425, 426; local/village 160, 182, 188, 195, *196*, 198–200, 203–5, *206*, 207–10, 316, 346–8, 348, 495, 503; state 3, 262, 316, 320, 345, 346, 348, 351, 393, 394, 447, 479, 481, 483, 486; *see* sandstone
Terrace of the Leper King 401, 407–8, 416, 499, 502, 615–16
Terrain Rouge *see* sandstone, types
textiles: import/trade 5, 67, 97, 107, 114–15, 120, 121–4, 312–13, 319, 436, 508, 519–20; production 165, 334, 409, 416, 513–14; uses 442, 508–13, 515–19, 520–1
Theravāda Buddhism 424, 615, 635; modern Cambodia 44–6, 188, 630; spread into SE Asia; 103, 106, 563–4; transition to 42, 43, 378, 397, 436, 448, *449*, 469, 474, 544–5, 578, 592, 593; *see also* Angkor, collapse; Buddhism
Tonle Sap Lake 2, 17–20, 22, 72, 81, 83, 99, 135–6, 163–4, 183, 208, 216, 259, 309, 315, 321, 339–41, 362, 376, 482, 506, 525, 593, 598
Tonle Sap River 17, 100, 309, 598
trade *see* economy
transportation 272, 394, 471, 473, 496; *see also* Maritime Southeast Asia; roads
trapeang (ponds) 81, 82, 178, 199, 344, 348, 394, 395, 396, 470–1, *471*, 473, 475, 498; *see also* water management
Trapeang Phong 81, 82, 83, 199, *367*; *see also* Hariharālaya

Triassic *see* sandstone, types
Trouvé, Georges 52, 89, 219–20, 265

Udayādityavarman II 331, 427, 529
universities 287–8, 290–1, 293, 296, 301–2; *see also* education, Angkorian
urbanism 4, 80, 148, 182–8, 392, 549–50; development of 81, 173–6, 179–82; low-density 93, 150, 183, 186–8, 195–6, 197, 198, 203, 338, 344, 548; *see also* Hydraulic City; settlement forms
Uthong 554–9, *557*, *561*, 562–70, **565**

Vaiṣṇavaism/Vaiṣṇava 30, 33, 67, 273, 274, 275, 370, 424, 425, 430; *see also* Brahmanism; Viṣṇu
Vedas/Vedic 289, 290, 292, 428; *see also* rituals
Vickery, Michael 38, 241, 543, 544, 545, 577
Vientiane 155, 161, 165, 482, 577, 581, 585, 586
vihara 45, 533, 597, 616–18; *see also* Buddhism
Vijaya 104, 106–8, 319, 530
Vīralakṣmī 283; *see also* political organisation, queens
Viṣṇu 30, 126, 158, 226–7, 255, 257, 259, 301, 370, 425, 427, 443, 444, 445, 462, 474
Viśvakarman (*Braḥ Biṣnukār*) 442
Vyadhapura 70, 154, 157, 158–9, 161, 162, 164, 165; *see* Angkor Borei

warfare 254–5, **256**, 535, 541
water buffalo *see* buffalo
water management 2, 6, 149, 181, 182, 185, 207, 216, 217, 218, 348, 443, 547–8; *see also* baray; canals; Hydraulic City; irrigation
Wat Mahatat 567, 568–70; *see also* Lopburi
Wat Phra Phai Luang 583
Wat Phu (Liṅgapura) 30, 73, 93, 101, 156, 159–60, 162, 163, 165, 166, 226, 248, 279–80, 313, 318, 333–4, 364, 443, 447
Wat Preah In Tép 447, 602
Wat Tralaeng Kaeng (Wat Tralaeṅ Kaeṅ) 598, 602
weaponry 256–7, 269, 313, 320; *see also* military
West Baray 5, 89–91, *92*, 141, 145, 205–6, 219, *221*, 224–30, 486; *see also* West Mebon
West Mebon 126, 141, 145–6, 149, 227, 371, 486; *see also* West Baray
Wheatley, Paul 241, 459, 460, 469

Xi hanglu 113, 117; *see also* Maritime Southeast Asia

Yama 4, 450, 463, 614–16, *616*, *617*, 618–27
Yaśodharāpura (Angkor) *12*, 30, 80–1, 82, 93, 143, 149, 183, 197, 228, 345, 348
Yaśodharāśrama 273, *274*, 275–83, 289–90; *see also* āśramas
Yaśodharataṭāka *see* East Baray; Yaśovarman I
Yaśovarman I 80, 159–60, 228, 229, 230, 240, 245, 273–4, 275, 277, 279–83, 289, 328, 332, 335, 345–6, 348, 368, 375, 424, 426, 429, 431, 445, 446, 468, 480, 484, 528, 530, 531
Yuan dynasty 119, 317, 319, 394, 517, 519, 559, 566

Zhao Rugua 115, 118, 124, 317
Zhou Daguan 47, 119, 127, 164, 165, 189, 201, 248, 257, 295, 317, 319, 321, 343, 351, 409, 411, 459, 473, 494, 496–500, 502–3, 513, 532, 534, 535–6